Trigonometric Identities

$\sin^2 x + \cos^2 x = 1$

$\sec^2 x = 1 + \tan^2 x$

$\sin(2x) = 2\sin x \cos x$

$\cos(2x) = \cos^2 x - \sin^2 x = 2\cos^2 x - 1 = 1 - 2\sin^2 x$

$\sin^2 x = \dfrac{1}{2}(1 - \cos(2x))$

$\cos^2 x = \dfrac{1}{2}(1 + \cos(2x))$

$\sin(x \pm y) = \sin x \cos y \pm \cos x \sin y$

$\cos(x \pm y) = \cos x \cos y \mp \sin x \sin y$

$\tan(x \pm y) = \dfrac{\tan x \pm \tan y}{1 \mp \tan x \tan y}$

$\sin x \sin y = \dfrac{1}{2}\left(\cos(x - y) - \cos(x + y)\right)$

$\cos x \cos y = \dfrac{1}{2}\left(\cos(x - y) + \cos(x + y)\right)$

$\sin x \cos y = \dfrac{1}{2}\left(\sin(x + y) + \sin(x - y)\right)$

Derivative Formulas

$\dfrac{d}{dx}c = (c)' = 0$

$\dfrac{d}{dx}x = (x)' = 1$

$\dfrac{d}{dx}x^n = (x^n)' = nx^{n-1}$

$\dfrac{d}{dx}e^x = (e^x)' = e^x$

$\dfrac{d}{dx}\ln x = (\ln x)' = \dfrac{1}{x}$

$\dfrac{d}{dx}\sin x = (\sin x)' = \cos x$

$\dfrac{d}{dx}\cos x = (\cos x)' = -\sin x$

$\dfrac{d}{dx}\tan x = (\tan x)' = \sec^2 x$

$\dfrac{d}{dx}\sec x = (\sec x)' = \sec x \tan x$

$\dfrac{d}{dx}\arcsin x = (\arcsin x)' = \dfrac{1}{\sqrt{1 - x^2}}$

$\dfrac{d}{dx}\arctan x = (\arctan x)' = \dfrac{1}{1 + x^2}$

Derivative Rules

$\left(f(x) + g(x)\right)' = f'(x) + g'(x)$ [Sum Rule]

$\left(f(x)g(x)\right)' = f'(x)g(x) + f(x)g'(x)$ [Product Rule]

$\left(\dfrac{f(x)}{g(x)}\right)' = \dfrac{f'(x)g(x) - f(x)g'(x)}{\left(g(x)\right)^2}$ [Quotient Rule]

$\left((f \circ g)(x)\right)' = \left(f(g(x))\right)' = f'(g(x))g'(x)$ [Chain Rule]

Hyperbolic Functions

$\cosh x = \dfrac{e^x + e^{-x}}{2}$

$\sinh x = \dfrac{e^x - e^{-x}}{2}$

$\tanh x = \dfrac{\sinh x}{\cosh x} = \dfrac{e^x - e^{-x}}{e^x + e^{-x}}$

$\cosh^2 x - \sinh^2 x = 1$

$\cosh(x + y) = \cosh x \cosh y + \sinh x \sinh y$

$\sinh(x + y) = \sinh x \cosh y + \cosh x \sinh y$

$\dfrac{d}{dx}\cosh x = (\cosh x)' = \sinh x$

$\dfrac{d}{dx}\sinh x = (\sinh x)' = \cosh x$

$\dfrac{d}{dx}\tanh x = (\tanh x)' = \dfrac{1}{\cosh^2 x}$

$\cosh^{-1} x = \ln\left(x + \sqrt{x^2 + 1}\right)$

$\sinh^{-1} x = \ln\left(x + \sqrt{x^2 - 1}\right)$

$\tanh^{-1} x = \dfrac{1}{2}\ln\left(\dfrac{1 + x}{1 - x}\right),$

$\dfrac{d}{dx}\cosh^{-1} x = (\cosh^{-1} x)' = \dfrac{1}{\sqrt{x^2 - 1}}$

$\dfrac{d}{dx}\sinh^{-1} x = (\sinh^{-1} x)' = \dfrac{1}{\sqrt{1 + x^2}}$

$\dfrac{d}{dx}\tanh^{-1} x = (\tanh^{-1} x)' = \dfrac{1}{1 - x^2}$

Calculus

From Graphical, Numerical, and Symbolic Points of View

SECOND EDITION

Single Variable

Calculus

From Graphical, Numerical, and Symbolic Points of View

SECOND EDITION

Single Variable

Arnold Ostebee
St. Olaf College

Paul Zorn
St. Olaf College

HOUGHTON MIFFLIN COMPANY

Boston • New York

Editor-in-Chief: Jack Shira
Sponsoring Editor: Lauren Schultz
Editorial Associate: Marika Hoe
Senior Project Editor: Nancy Blodget
Senior Production/Design Coordinator: Carol Merrigan
Senior Manufacturing Coordinator: Marie Barnes
Senior Marketing Manager: Michael Busnach

Cover Image: Surf: Maui, Hawaii © Bill

Printed in the U.S.A.

Library of Congress Control Number: 2001090881

ISBN
Student Texts:
Volume 1: 0-618-24750-5
Volume 2: 0-618-24787-4
Single Variable: 0-618-24788-2
Annotated Instructor's Edition:
0-618-24860-9

123456789-DOW-05 04 03 02

To Kay, Kristin, and Paul
To Janet, Anne, and Libby

ABOUT THIS BOOK:
NOTES FOR INSTRUCTORS

This book—like the first edition—aims to do exactly what its title suggests: present calculus from graphical, numerical, and symbolic points of view. In this preface we elaborate briefly on what this goal means, why we chose it, and how we try to achieve it.

For more information More detailed information on many topics related to this book can be found at the following Web sites:

```
www.stolaf.edu/people/zorn/ozcalc/
math.college.hmco.com/instructors
```

Three volumes

We treat single-variable calculus in two volumes, each suitable for a semester-length course; Volume 3 offers a one-semester introduction to multivariable and vector calculus, culminating with Green's theorem and its three-dimensional analogues. Several "combination" volumes are also available; please see the Web sites for details.

Changes from the first edition

Why did we revise the first edition of our textbook? In short, to make the text easier to use, for teachers *and* for students. To this end, building on many suggestions from teachers and students, we've made various changes to narrative, exercises, content, emphasis, and order of presentation. Some of these changes are outlined briefly below. Much more detailed information about the second edition, including a chapter-by-chapter overview of changes and a list of frequently asked questions, can be found at the Web sites.

- **What hasn't changed** The basic principles and strategies underlying the first edition remain unchanged. Conceptual understanding is still our main goal, and combining various viewpoints is still the main strategy for achieving it. This edition and the first share basic assumptions and operating premises: an emphasis on concepts and sense-making, complementing symbolic with graphical and numerical points of view, exercises of varied nature and difficulty, and a narrative aimed at student (rather than faculty) readers.

- **Getting more quickly to derivatives**   We've somewhat compressed and redistributed the "precalculus" material of the first edition to get to the derivative idea faster. (The word *derivative* now appears in Section 1.4.) Chapter 1 now includes essentially complete coverage of the graphical approach, Chapter 2 introduces and interprets the symbolic point of view, and Chapter 3 presents the combinatorial rules for differentiation.

- **Earlier differential equations**   Differential equations (DEs) appear a little earlier and reappear more often. The idea of a DE is introduced in Section 2.5, soon after the ideas of derivative and antiderivative are first met in symbolic form. Mentioning DEs early lets us say early (and economically) that polynomial, exponential, and trigonometric functions have important growth properties that help account for the importance of these function classes. DEs also provide a natural approach to scientific and engineering applications. Once introduced, DEs reappear often in following sections and in exercises.

- **Not a DE course**   Although we give DEs somewhat increased emphasis in this edition, we are not jamming a DE course into an already well-filled calculus syllabus. We want to convey the *idea* of a DE and its solutions, but we make *no* effort to cover or even catalog the huge variety of DEs and solution techniques.

- **A new chapter on function approximation**   Chapter 9 treats approximation of one function by another. Taylor polynomials are the main objects of study; Taylor's theorem is the main theoretical result. Separating these ideas from convergence and divergence of series should aid students' understanding. It also permits teachers who wish to do so to cover Taylor's theorem without requiring a long introduction to infinite series.

- **Helping students read**   We want students to *read* the narrative—not just scan the assigned problems and search for cloned examples. To help students read more successfully, we've added many more examples, rewritten many parts of the narrative, and included more detail and brief commentary on many calculations.

- **Other content changes and reorganization**   Various other changes have been made to content and organization; the following are several:
  - earlier treatment of slope fields and l'Hôpital's rule (now in Chapter 4);
  - a new section on sigma notation and some of its properties (in Chapter 5);
  - earlier treatment of basic antidifferentiation ideas, including the method of substitution (in Chapter 5).

  For more information on changes to content and organization, please see the Web sites.

- **Exercises and answers**   Many new exercises, of various types, have been added. Many users found the first edition short on "routine" exercises; many more have been added (but this edition still contains plenty of nonroutine problems). Other new exercises point to specific issues and examples raised in the narrative. A third new category is end-of-chapter exercises, which provide review and encourage synthesis. We have also included printed answers (not full-fledged solutions) to most of the odd-numbered exercises. (Students *and* teachers requested this change!)

- **End-of-chapter Interludes**   Most chapters end with one or more Interludes—brief, project-oriented expositions designed for independent student work—addressing topics or questions that are "optional" or out of that chapter's main stream of development.

Philosophy

What should a beginning course in calculus be about? What topics and ideas should it contain? What are its most important goals and organizing principles? What level of mathematical rigor is appropriate? How should applications and theory be balanced?

Questions like these have been "live" for a very long time. For instance, debates over how and whether to teach related rates problems, and more generally over the role of applications, sprang up in the 1850s; for a delightful exposition, see "The Lengthening Shadow: The Story of Related Rates," by Bill Austin, Don Barry, and David Berman, *Mathematics Magazine*, February 2000. The relatively recent discussions on "calculus reform" continue an old tradition of questioning and revision, though in a new and different educational and technological environment. Although the phrase *calculus reform* now has little clear meaning, the continuing discussion it denotes has been useful both in directing attention to calculus courses and in identifying a few common threads of widespread (if not universal) agreement. These include calls for leaner, more concept-focused courses and for courses that better reflect modern technology in content and in pedagogy.

Focus on concepts; our strategy Elementary calculus courses can serve various purposes: to introduce analytic mathematics, to support mathematical applications in the sciences, to provide a language for stating physical laws and deducing their consequences, to introduce mathematical ways of thinking. Whatever the goals of any particular course, the conclusion is the same: Concepts are fundamental. Whatever uses they make of the calculus, students need more than a compendium of manipulative techniques; they need conceptual understanding that is deep and flexible enough to accommodate diverse applications.

Our key strategy for improving conceptual understanding is combining, comparing, and moving among graphical, numerical, and algebraic representations of central concepts. By studying, representing, and manipulating ideas and objects in several forms, students gain better perspective on, and deeper understanding of, important concepts.

Audience and prerequisites

Our text is aimed at a broad mathematical audience, including (but not limited to) students majoring in mathematics, science, and engineering. Although we emphasize concepts more than detailed applications to specific disciplines, we regard a more conceptual calculus as also more applicable. To use calculus ideas and techniques effectively in any area, students must know what they are doing and why, not just how.

We expect that students have the "usual" precalculus preparation, including basic algebra and trigonometry and the rudiments of logarithmic and exponential functions. However, the appendices include reviews of these subjects, with routine exercises, written in a style that supports independent reading and self-study.

Distinctive features

Several special features of our treatment deserve brief mention. For many more details and specific examples, see the Instructor's Resource Materials described on page xiv.

- **Early differential equations** Differential equations are mentioned early in Chapter 2, introduced informally (but at some length) in Chapter 4, and then revisited from time to time in later chapters. We believe that DEs are so basic and so important that students should see them early and often. Calculus I emphasizes the *idea* of a DE and its solutions. Several techniques for finding numerical and symbolic solutions are treated in Calculus II.

- **Graphs, then symbols** Derivatives and integrals are introduced in a parallel manner, in which the graphical approach precedes the symbolic viewpoint. Thus, Chapter 1 stresses the *geometry* of the derivative; the *symbolic* approach enters in Chapter 2. Similarly, Chapter 5 begins with a graphical definition of the integral and proceeds later to the Riemann sum definition.

- **The level of rigor** Proving theorems in full generality is less valuable, we think, than helping students understand concretely what theorems say, why they're reasonable, and why they matter. Too often, fully rigorous proofs address questions that students are unprepared to ask.

  Still, we believe that introducing calculus students to the idea of proof—and to some especially important classical proofs—is essential. We prove major results but emphasize only those proofs that we believe contribute significantly to understanding calculus concepts. In examples and problems, too, we pay attention to developing analytic skills and synthesizing mathematical ideas.

- **Foreshadowing** Important concepts and associated vocabulary often appear more than once—first informally and later in more detail. The geometric idea of concavity, for instance, is mentioned in Section 1.1 and then revisited several times. Instructors should know that it is *not* necessary to cover these ideas in full rigor at their first appearance.

The role of technology

Combining graphical, numerical, and symbolic views of important calculus ideas is forbiddingly laborious by hand. Technology makes this useful combination feasible.

We see computers and graphing calculators as valuable and practical tools, but computing is not an end in itself in our course. We want students to focus on key calculus ideas, not on machines, and so we encourage thoughtful and balanced uses of computing. We believe, for instance, that students benefit substantially from frequent, careful study of well-drawn graphs; thus, we often encourage students to generate their own graphs (often by machine but sometimes by hand) to suggest guesses, gain insights, and check answers for plausibility.

Symbolic computing—boon or bane?
Symbolic computing has become widely available to students in the last few years; even inexpensive calculators such as the TI–89 now handle symbolic derivatives and even antiderivatives. What's left to teach when every student has such a machine? Although some may fear that sophisticated technology reduces calculus to mindless button-pushing, we find exactly the opposite effect more common in practice. With machines available to handle some routine calculations, calculus courses can and should become more, not less, focused on concepts and structures. Problems that are posed graphically, for instance, are essentially impervious to technology. More traditional, find-the-derivative-type problems, by contrast, are more likely to need new reasons for being.

We make no assumption either way about students' access to symbolic computing. Given the wide variety of problems and viewpoints we present, we think our text makes sense in almost any technological environment.

Symbol manipulation and hand computation
We take the symbolic point of view in our title just as seriously as the graphical and the numerical, and we cover the "usual" methods of formal differentiation and antidifferentiation. Why do we do so?

The fact that machines can "do" symbolic manipulations does not render by-hand operations obsolete. Nor are skills and ideas truly in opposition, as is sometimes asserted. On the contrary, a reasonable modicum of manipulative practice builds and supports conceptual understanding. Hand computation helps fix ideas, illustrates concepts concretely, builds symbolic intuition, and gives students a sense of mastery. It does not follow, however, that harder, more "baroque" computational problems are always better; we deemphasize convoluted symbolic calculations in order to free time and energy for work on concepts.

About the exercises

However clear its exposition, a textbook's exercises generate most of students' mathematical activity and occupy most of their time. The exercises we assign tell students concretely what we think they should know and do. Both routine drills and challenging theoretical exercises are standard in calculus texts, and our text contains some of each. More distinctive, perhaps, are the exercises that fall between these poles:

- Exercises that combine and compare algebraic, graphical, and numerical viewpoints and techniques.
- Exercises that test and stretch a student's understanding of concepts, definitions, and theorems.
- Exercises that develop students' problem-solving and mathematical reasoning skills.
- Exercises that use calculus as a *language* for interpreting and solving problems. Students "translate" problems into mathematical language, solve the resulting problems using the calculus tools, and reinterpret results in the original context.

''Basic'' and ''Further'' exercises   Each section has exercises of two types: "Basic" and "Further." Typical "Basic" exercises are relatively straightforward and focus on a single important idea. All students should aim to master most of these exercises. "Further" exercises are a little more ambitious; they may require the synthesis of several ideas, deeper or more sophisticated understanding of basic concepts, or better symbol manipulation skills. For more details and advice on assigning exercises, see the Instructor's Resource Materials described on page xiv.

Exercises and technology   Because we view graphing and other technologies as tools for exploring and problem solving, not as ends in themselves, we seldom tag or label "technology exercises." We expect students themselves to decide in context which tools are most appropriate and how and when to employ them.

Annotated Table of Contents

Brief chapter-by-chapter information follows. (See the Web sites for more detailed descriptions and for information about Volume 3.)

Chapter 1: Functions and Derivatives: The Graphical View   We move quickly to the subject of derivatives and rate functions, giving the graphical viewpoint first. Standard elementary functions appear as examples, but we don't—in this chapter—use nontrivial symbolic properties of these functions. The "Field Guide" section briefly reviews the standard elementary functions but concentrates mainly on their graphical properties.

Chapter 2: Functions and Derivatives: The Symbolic View   We review and expand on ideas of Chapter 1, but now in the symbolic setting. The ideas of antiderivative and differential equation appear for the first time—systematic treatments appear later. Sections 2.5, 2.6, and 2.7 describe some classical applications (linear motion, growth, and oscillation) related to finding derivatives and (in the simplest cases) antiderivatives of polynomial, exponential, and trigonometric functions.

Chapter 3: New Derivatives from Old   This chapter treats "combinatorial" ideas: producing new functions and new derivatives from old functions and *their* derivatives. We also cover implicit differentiation and derivatives of inverse functions and then apply these ideas to inverse trigonometric functions.

Chapter 4: Using the Derivative   This chapter is a selection of applications, extensions, and uses of the derivative and other ideas from earlier chapters. Some sections are independent of each other; not all are required for later work. Sections 4.8 and 4.9 (on continuity and differentiability) offer glimpses at some of the theoretical side of calculus. The mean value theorem, for instance, is discussed and proved fairly carefully in Section 4.10.

Chapter 5: The Integral   The first few sections introduce the definite integral *geometrically*, as signed area. Then the integral is linked to antiderivatives via the fundamental theorem. Substitution and use of tables, the most basic methods of finding antiderivatives, are covered here; much more discussion of antidifferentiation is given in Chapter 8. The general treatment of integrals mirrors that of derivatives: We start with geometric intuition and proceed to the limit-based analytic definition.

Chapter 6: Numerical Integration   This chapter treats basic numerical views of the integral. Section 6.1 presents and compares different types of approximating sums. Some error-bound analysis appears in Section 6.2 (which some instructors may omit). Section 6.3, on Euler's method, applies similar numerical ideas to solve differential equations numerically. Interludes treat Simpson's rule and Gaussian quadrature.

Chapter 7: Using the Integral   This chapter treats applications, extensions, and uses of the integral—geometric, physical, mathematical, and economic. (As in Chapter 4, instructors can choose among topics.) Section 7.1 offers a variety of applications, including arc length, chosen partly to show the integral as a general tool for measuring things. Later sections and an Interlude treat volumes, work, separable DEs, present value, mass, and center of mass. Some integrals that arise might be done with the help of numerical methods, tables, or computers.

Chapter 8: Symbolic Antidifferentiation Techniques   The chapter contains a fairly standard menu of techniques. Even though antidifferentiation is readily handled by computer nowadays, we think that some practice of this sort is useful for building symbol-manipulation skills of the sort many students will need in later courses; such practice also requires students to recognize and grapple with the structure of various classes of functions. Interludes treat functions *defined* by integration and methods for solving first-order linear DEs.

Chapter 9: Function Approximation   The chapter itself is entirely new to this edition, although most of its contents appeared (elsewhere) in the first edition. Moreover, the general theme of approximating one function with another runs through both volumes (e.g., in connection with differentiable functions being "almost" linear). Sections 9.1 and 9.2, on Taylor polynomials and Taylor's theorem, are intended to help disentangle these important ideas from questions of series convergence and divergence—topics that are sometimes conflated. Section 9.3 introduces Fourier approximation—an integral-based counterpart to Taylor approximation. An Interlude treats splines.

Chapter 10: Improper Integrals   Improper integrals are both practically useful and closely analogous to infinite series—hence our relatively extended treatment. Many texts cover the subject in only one section, but we hope to use improper integrals to build intuition for the difficult ideas of infinite series, coming in Chapter 11. Section 10.3 applies improper integrals to probability, with emphasis on the normal probability distribution.

Chapter 11: Infinite Series   Unlike some reform texts, we do treat convergence and divergence of numerical series but in a somewhat nontraditional way. We stress (i) the analogy with improper integrals; (ii) concrete (sometimes graphical) treatment of partial sums; and (iii) numerical estimation of limits. We think these strategies help make this difficult subject more concrete and accessible than it often is when the principal concern is the abstract question of convergence or divergence. The chapter ends with power series—but, with the new Chapter 9, students will already have had some exposure to this idea. A brief Interlude explores Fourier series.

Chapter V: Vectors and Polar Coordinates   This chapter is a basic introduction to vectors in the plane, vector notation, vector-valued functions and derivatives, and to the polar coordinate view of the plane and of plane curves. (Students who continue to Calculus III will see this material in more detail later—this treatment is aimed mainly at students who will not continue in calculus.)

Chapter M: Multivariable Calculus: A First Look   This chapter is a basic introduction to rudiments of functions of several variables. Some instructors may choose to cover it as an alternative to (or, if time permits) in addition to infinite series. Some instructors might choose material on partial derivatives but not on multiple integrals. Like Chapter V, this chapter is aimed mainly at students who will not continue in calculus.

Supplements to the text

The following aids for students are available from the publisher:

- **Student Solutions Manual**   In three volumes, these manuals contain solutions, prepared by the authors, to all odd-numbered exercises. (Brief answers to selected exercises are available in the back of the text.)
- **Technology Projects and Lab Manual**   Written by Glen Van Brummelen and Michael Caraco of Bennington College, this manual enables students and instructors to explore a wide range of technology products available to mathematicians and engineers. It offers the foundations for innovative projects and lab activities as well as tutorials and hints for using a variety of graphing calculators and math software packages, such as *Maple* and *Mathematica*. As students complete each lab, they learn basic commands and reinforce key calculus concepts.
- **Navigating Calculus** CD–ROM   The companion CD–ROM, *Navigating Calculus*, authored by Jason Brown of Dalhousie University in Nova Scotia, and by Arnold Ostebee and Paul Zorn, is keyed closely to the book's table of contents and covers both single variable and multivariable material. *Navigating Calculus* contains a variety of useful activities, tools, and resources, including a powerful graphing calculator utility, a glossary with examples, and many interactive activities that deepen students' understanding of calculus fundamentals. This learning aid is accompanied by the *Navigating Calculus Workbook* written by Stephen Kokoska of Bloomsburg University of Pennsylvania. This workbook is designed to help both instructors and students fully utilize *Navigating Calculus* by offering guided instruction through the workings of the CD–ROM and providing examples and exercises that supplement those on the CD–ROM itself.
- **Web-based learning resources**   Additional learning tools can be found at the following Web site:
  `math.college.hmco.com/students`

The following aids for instructors are available from the publisher:

- **Annotated Instructor's Edition**   This special edition includes the full text of the student version together with marginal annotations that offer pedagogical hints and suggestions.

- **Instructor's Resource Materials**   This information, available via the authors' and publisher's web sites, offers a variety of additional teaching resources, including (1) advice on using technology, facilitating group work, assigning homework, and testing; (2) sample lecture plans; (3) section-by-section notes; and (4) writing assignments.
- **Instructor's Solutions Manual**   In three volumes, the manual contains complete solutions, prepared by the authors, for all exercises.
- **Test Bank**   Prepared by Scott Inch of Bloomsburg University of Pennsylvania, this resource contains more than 500 questions covering multiple viewpoints and levels of difficulty. Answers to all questions are included.
- **Computerized Test Bank**   Available in a Windows and Macintosh hybrid CD-ROM, this resource combines the items of the Test Bank with convenient features that allow instructors to prepare quizzes and examinations quickly and easily. Instructors can edit questions, add their own, administer tests over a computer network, and record student grades with the gradebook software.
- **Electronic Overhead Transparencies**   These may be downloaded in PDF format from the instructor's resource section of the Houghton Mifflin Web site. The set includes selected figures from both expository and exercise portions of the text.

For more information   For more information, please see the following Web sites:

www.stolaf.edu/people/zorn/ozcalc/
math.college.hmco.com/instructors

Advice from you

We appreciate hearing instructors' comments, suggestions, and advice on this edition. Our physical and e-mail addresses are below.

Arnold Ostebee and Paul Zorn
Department of Mathematics
St. Olaf College
1520 St. Olaf Avenue
Northfield, Minnesota   55057-1098

e-mail: ostebee@stolaf.edu   zorn@stolaf.edu

Acknowledgments

This text owes its existence to (literally) countless professors, students, publishing company professionals, friends, advisors, critics, "competitors," family, and others. (These categories are not mutually exclusive!) It is a pleasure to acknowledge by name some—but, necessarily, only some—of the people who attended this text through its long gestation, birth, and publication.

Various versions of the manuscript were meticulously reviewed and suggestions made and errors caught by Mary Kay Abbey, Montgomery College – Takoma Park; Roy Alston, Stephen F. Austin State University; David Austin, Grand Valley State University; William Barnier, Sonoma State University; Neil Berger, University of Illinois – Chicago; Kelly Black, University of New Hampshire; Przemyslaw Bogacki, Old Dominion University; Jack Bookman, Duke University; Raouf N. Boules, Towson University; Holly Broesamle, Oakland Community College; Thomas Bullock, Brookdale Community College; Veena Chadha, University of Wisconsin – Eau Claire; Joseph Conrad, Solano Community College; Vittoria Cosentino, Metro Community College – Omaha; Ruth Dover, Illinois Math and Science Academy; Mary Ellen Davis, Georgia Perimeter College; David A. Edwards, University of Georgia; John Emert, Ball State University; Doug Ensley, Shippensburg University; Johanna Halsey, Dutchess Community College; Donald Hartig, California Polytechnic State University; Dorothy Hawkes, Solano Community College; Judy Holdener, Kenyon College; Linda Horner, Broward Community College – North; Henry Hosek, Purdue University Calumet; Alan Jian, Solano Community College; Matthias Kawski, Arizona State University; David Keller, Kirkwood Community College; James W. Lea, Middle Tennessee State University; Glenn Ledder, University of Nebraska; Mickey Levendusky, University of Arizona; Betty Liu, Monmouth University; Richard Maher, Loyola University of Chicago; Augustine Maison, Eastern Kentucky University; David Meredith, San Francisco State University; Edward S. Miller, Lewis–Clark State College; Charles Oelsner, Manlius Pebble Hill School; David Olson, Michigan Technological University; Sergei Ovchinnikov, San Francisco State University; Neville Robbins, San Francisco State University; Doug Shaw, University of Northern Iowa; Murray Siegel, Sam Houston State University; Marlene Sims, Kennesaw State University; Joanne Snow, St. Mary's College; Jerry Stonewater, Miami University of Ohio; K.D. Taylor, Utah Valley State College; Bruce Teague, Santa Fe Community College; and Kenneth Word, Central Texas College.

We are indebted, for many and different reasons, to members of Harcourt College Publishing's staff, including (alphabetically) Lisa Adamitis, Art Director; Carol Bleistine, Manager for Art & Design; Julie Conover, Executive Marketing Strategist; Alexa Epstein,

Manager of Technology; Bianca Huff and Pamela Meyers, Editorial Assistants; Alicia Jackson, Senior Production Manager; Amanda Loch, Technology Editor; Leslie Lahr, Developmental Editor; and Angus McDonald, Executive Editor.

We have learned much from professional colleagues, here at St. Olaf, elsewhere in the United States and around the world. Some are our teachers; some are departmental colleagues; some course-tested preliminary versions of these volumes at their own schools; some reviewed our grant proposals; some reviewed our project; some invited us to review theirs; some invited us to speak on panels or at workshops; some spoke on panels we organized; some helped us run our workshops; some are "calculus reform competitors"; some are advisers; some are critics. We list a small sample below, in alphabetical order. Regardless of category, we thank them all. Janet Andersen, Nazanin Azarnia, Russell Blythe, Mike Bolduan, Judith Cederberg, Caspar Curjel, Tom Dick, Ed Dubinsky, Wade Ellis, Bob Foote, Bonnie Gold, Michael Henle, Beth Hentges, Deborah Hughes Hallett, Allen Holmes, Paul Humke, Zaven Karian, John Kenelly, Dan Kennedy Charley Kerr, Harvey Keynes, Steve Kuhn, John Kurtzke, Reg Laursen, Sergio Loch, Joe May, Mike May, Bill McCallum, Richard Mercer, Eric Muller, Steve Monk, Lang Moore, Steven Olson, Lenore Parens, John Peterson, Tommy Ratliff, Wayne Roberts, Don Small, David Smith, Keith Stroyan, Douglas Swan, Tom Tucker, Jerry Uhl, Ted Vessey, and Roger Woods.

We thank St. Olaf College in general, and our departmental colleagues in particular, for their advice, support, good humor, and (sometimes) forbearance during the many years of this project's development and progress to a second edition. Countless students, here and at other institutions, also offered generous advice, praise, and criticism—all of it useful.

Our families, finally, deserve our deepest thanks. They have coped cheerfully with peculiar hours, extended absences, mental distraction, blizzards of paper, missed meals, and every other vagary that such a project entails. Without their love and sacrifice, we would never have begun—let alone completed—this project.

How to Use This Book: Notes for Students

All authors want their books to be *used*: read, studied, thought about, puzzled over, reread, underlined, disputed, understood, and, ultimately, enjoyed. So do we.

That might go without saying for some books—beach novels, user manuals, field guides, and so on—but it may need repeating for a calculus textbook. We know as teachers (and remember as students) that mathematics textbooks are too often read *backwards*: faced with Exercise 231(b) on page 1638, we've all shuffled backwards through the pages in search of something similar. (Very often, moreover, our searches were rewarded.)

A calculus textbook isn't a novel. It's a peculiar hybrid of encyclopedia, dictionary, atlas, anthology, daily newspaper, shop manual, *and* novel—not exactly light reading, but essential reading nevertheless. Ideally, a calculus book should be read in *all* directions: left to right, top to bottom, back to front, and even front to back. That's a tall order. Here are some suggestions for coping with it.

Read the narrative Each section's narrative is designed to be read—perhaps more than once—from beginning to end. The examples, in particular, are supposed to illustrate ideas and make them concrete—not just to serve as templates for homework exercises.

Read the examples Examples are, if anything, more important than theorems, remarks, and other "talk." *We* use examples both to show already-familiar calculus ideas "in action" and to set the stage for new ideas. *You* should use them to learn new ideas and review old ones.

Read the pictures We're serious about the "graphical points of view" mentioned in our title. The pictures in this book are not "illustrations"or "decorations." Pictures are everywhere in this book—sometimes even in the middle of sentences. That's intentional: Graphs are an important part of the language of calculus. An ability to think "pictorially"—as well as symbolically and numerically—about mathematical ideas may be the most important benefit calculus can offer.

Read with a calculator and pencil This book is full of requests � to check a calculation, sketch a graph, or "convince yourself" that something makes sense. Take these requests

Sometimes they're put in margin notes, like this one.

seriously: Mastering mathematical ideas takes more than reading; it takes doing, drawing, and thinking.

Read the language   Mathematics is not a "natural language" like English or French, but it has its own vocabulary and rules of usage. Calculus, especially, relies on careful use of technical language. Words like rate, amount, stationary point, and root have precise, agreed-upon mathematical meanings. Understanding such words goes a long way toward understanding the mathematics they convey; misunderstanding the words leads inevitably to confusion. When in doubt, consult the index.

Read the Appendices   The human appendix generally lies unnoticed—unless trouble starts, when it's taken out and thrown away. Don't treat this book's appendices that way. Though perhaps slightly enlarged, they're full of healthy matter: reviews of precalculus topics, help with "story problems," proofs of various kinds, and more. Used as directed, the appendices will help appreciably in digesting the material.

Read the Instructors' Preface   Get a jump on your teacher.

In short: *Read the book*.

A last note   Why study calculus at all? There are plenty of good, practical, and "educational" reasons: because it's good for applications, because higher mathematics requires it, because it's good mental training, because other majors require it, because jobs require it. Here's another reason to study calculus: because calculus is among our species' deepest, richest, farthest-reaching, and most beautiful intellectual achievements. We hope this book will help you see it in that spirit.

A last request   Last, a request. We sincerely appreciate—and take very seriously—students' opinions, suggestions, and advice. (Changes to this edition of the text stem partly from students' views of the first edition.) We invite you to offer your advice, either through your teacher or by writing us directly. Our addresses appear below.

Arnold Ostebee and Paul Zorn
Department of Mathematics
St. Olaf College
1520 St. Olaf Avenue
Northfield, Minnesota 55057-1098
e-mail: **ostebee@stolaf.edu   zorn@stolaf.edu**

Contents

1

FUNCTIONS AND DERIVATIVES: THE GRAPHICAL VIEW

1.1 FUNCTIONS, CALCULUS STYLE

Calculus is the mathematics of change. Calculus can describe—and predict—the behavior of changing quantities: falling apples, orbiting spacecraft, growing populations, decaying radioactive materials, rising consumer prices, and many more.

Functions are the basic objects we study in calculus. As an apple falls, for instance, its height above the ground, the speed of its fall, and the time elapsed since the stem broke all vary together. Functions describe relationships among these quantities; calculus helps us discover and quantify such relationships and deduce their consequences.

What kinds of functions are there? What can functions do? Which functions matter most in calculus? What, exactly, *is* a function? To answer these questions we'll start with examples and then proceed to more formal definitions.

In this chapter we move quickly to the subject of derivatives and rate functions, giving the graphical viewpoint first. Standard elementary functions appear as examples, but we don't—in Chapter 1—use non-trivial symbolic properties of these functions. The Field Guide section (1.3) briefly introduces the standard elementary functions, but concentrates (for the moment) mainly on their graphical properties; we revisit these functions in Chapter 2 when we differentiate them.

Students tend to equate "function" with "formula." Examples here show a larger idea of "function." Following the examples we introduce (or review) standard functional concepts: domain, range, and rule.

Functions in calculus: a sampler

The most familiar calculus functions, such as

$$f(x) = x^3 - 4x + 3 \quad \text{and} \quad g(x) = \frac{x^2 - 4}{x + 3}$$

are given by algebraic formulas. Functions like these are easy to plug numbers into, easy to plot, and easy to manipulate symbolically. But not every function comes with, or even has, an algebraic formula. Functions described by graphs, by tables of data, in words, and in other ways are common in practice—and in this book. The following examples illustrate some of the possibilities.

EXAMPLE 1 **(Functions from graphs)** Hot days on the Kansas prairie generate strong updrafts and downdrafts. In the gondola of a hot air balloon, two instruments monitor the balloon's course over an 8-minute period. An altimeter shows the balloon's altitude, and a rate-of-climb meter shows how fast the balloon rises or falls. Figures 1(a) and 1(b) show the results.

1

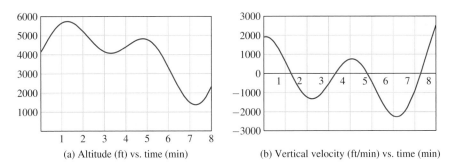

(a) Altitude (ft) vs. time (min)   (b) Vertical velocity (ft/min) vs. time (min)

FIGURE 1
Altitude and vertical velocity graphs of a balloon

The graphs in Figures 1(a) and 1(b) describe two functions we'll call A and V: At time t minutes, $A(t)$ is the balloon's altitude in feet above sea level (east–central Kansas lies about 960 feet above sea level); $V(t)$ is the balloon's vertical velocity in feet per minute. (Velocity is "signed speed": here, *negative* velocity means *downward* movement.)

The two graphs convey a lot of information. They show, for instance, that at time $t = 2$ minutes the altitude was about 5200 feet, and the balloon was falling at about 1200 feet per minute. (These numbers—like *all* data read from graphs—are only approximate.) The graphs also show—in different ways—when the balloon rose and when it fell. For instance, the balloon descended throughout the interval $5 \le t \le 7$. We can see this either from the A-graph, which falls over this interval, or from the V-graph, which is negative over the same interval. Following are some other implications from the graphs:

Compare the two graphs to check this claim.

- **Up or down?**   The *sign* of $V(t)$ tells whether the balloon rises or falls: $V(t) > 0$ when $A(t)$ increases, and $V(t) < 0$ when $A(t)$ decreases. ◄

- **Fast or slow?**   The V-graph is *highest* (so upward velocity is greatest) near $t = 0$, $t = 4$, and $t = 8$. At the same times, the A-graph is *steepest* upward. Around $t = 6$, the passengers might feel nervous: the V-graph is lowest, the A-graph is steepest downward, and the balloon is descending most rapidly.

- **How fast?**   The velocity graph shows that $V(6) \approx -2000$, so at this moment the balloon is descending at about 2000 feet per minute. Can we read the same information from the A-graph?

  As we've seen, the balloon's velocity has to do with the *steepness* of the altitude graph, so we'd like to find the *slope* of the A-graph at $t = 6$. The A-graph is a curve, not a straight line, which means we can only estimate this slope. One approach is to find the rise and run over a small interval containing $t = 6$, say $5.5 \le t \le 6.5$. A close look shows that the altitude falls by about 2000 feet over this 1-minute interval; therefore, the slope is (as expected) about -2000 feet per minute.

We do not assume here that students know about slope involving limits in any rigorous sense. Here, slope is simply a visual property of a graph.

- **Slope of a curve: a big idea**   The idea just illustrated—finding and interpreting the slope of a curve at a point—is one of the most important in calculus, and we'll have much to say about it.

Functions (like V) that describe how *fast* another function (like A) changes, and in what direction, are at the heart of calculus. To the balloon's passengers, How fast? may matter at least as much as How high?   ∎

EXAMPLE 2 (A function from data) The following table gives world population over 20 centuries. Source: Population Division, United Nations Secretariat. ➔

C.E. means Common Era—a synonym for A.D.

Human Population							
Year (C.E.)	0	1000	1600	1750	1800	1850	1900	1930
People (millions)	100	110	500	790	980	1260	1650	2070
Year (C.E.)	1940	1950	1960	1970	1980	1990	2000	
People (millions)	2300	2520	3020	3700	4450	5300	6090	

The table shows what our experience suggests: Population grows faster and faster over time. Plotting the data (one dot per table entry, as in Figure 2) shows this even more clearly:

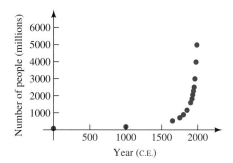

FIGURE 2
Human population

World population is a function of time: for any time t, the population is $g(t)$. Does $g(t)$ have some convenient formula? Not likely—human population is too complex a phenomenon to predict precisely. But we can look for a formula that "models" the known data reasonably well. Figure 3 shows one possibility: the mathematical function

$$p(t) = 906e^{0.008(t-1800)}$$

is plotted along with the data.

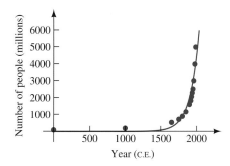

FIGURE 3
Human population: fitting the data

Why we chose this particular function p and the specific constants 906, 0.008, and 1800 doesn't matter for the moment.← What *does* matter is the idea of using mathematical functions to approximate real-world situations.   ■

E X A M P L E 3   **(A tabular function)**   The following table gives values of a function k.

x	−3	−2	−1	0	1	2	3	4
$k(x)$	−4	−9	−1	0	1	8	3	−2

Our knowledge of k is, to say the least, incomplete. What's $k(100)$? For what inputs x is $k(x)$ defined? Is the graph of k a smooth curve? Does k have an algebraic formula?

   We'd need more information to answer these questions. Imagine, for instance, that $k(x)$ is the Celsius temperature x hours after midnight on a winter night in Minnesota. Then quantities like $k(0.3)$ and $k(-\sqrt{2})$ make sense, but we don't expect k to have a simple, exact formula.   ■

E X A M P L E 4   **(A function in pieces)**   Let m be the function shown in Figure 4.

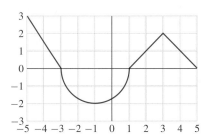

FIGURE 4
A piecewise-defined function

Some values of m, such as $m(-1) = -2$, are clear at a glance. Other values are less clear. For example, the graph gives $m(-2) \approx -1.7$, but the *exact* value isn't immediately clear. In fact, m *can* be represented algebraically, by a **piecewise-defined formula**. The graph consists of three line segments and a semicircle with pieces as follows:

$$m(x) = \begin{cases} -\frac{3x}{2} - \frac{9}{2} & \text{if } -5 \le x \le -3; \\ -\sqrt{4 - (x+1)^2} & \text{if } -3 < x \le 1; \\ x - 1 & \text{if } 1 < x \le 3; \\ -x + 5 & \text{if } 3 < x \le 5. \end{cases}$$

Using this "formula," we can find $m(-2)$ exactly:

$$m(-2) = -\sqrt{4 - (-2+1)^2} = -\sqrt{4 - (-1)^2} = -\sqrt{3} \approx -1.7321.$$

   Functions like m, defined "in pieces," have many practical uses. Computer-drawn graphs, for example, are often made up of many short line segments or curves, each of which can be described algebraically. The process of **splining** (joining properly chosen curves or line segments to form a single smooth curve) is used in computer-assisted design, engineering, and other applications.   ■

EXAMPLE 5 **(A function from words)** To make a flimsy box from an ordinary
$8.5'' \times 11''$ sheet of paper, cut squares from the corners and fold up the sides, as shown in
Figure 5. (Cut on the heavy lines and fold on the dashed lines.) Which such box has the
largest volume? How large can the volume be?

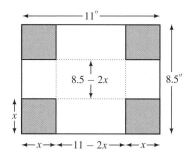

FIGURE 5
Boxmaking

Solution No function is immediately apparent. But we'll distill one from the words of
the example and use it to solve our problem. As Figure 5 suggests, the volume v of the
box depends only on the edge length x of the removed corners:

$$v(x) = \text{length} \times \text{width} \times \text{depth} = (11 - 2x)(8.5 - 2x)x.$$

Notice that, although the formula $(11 - 2x)(8.5 - 2x)x$ makes *algebraic* sense for *any*
real number x, it makes sense for paper folding only if all three factors are nonnegative,
that is, if $0 \le x \le 4.25$. A graph (Figure 6) shows $v(x)$ for these values of x:

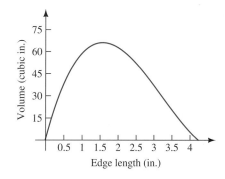

FIGURE 6
$v(x) = (11 - 2x)(8.5 - 2x)x$: **how volume varies**

The graph shows that $v(x)$ is largest if $x \approx 1.6$. Thus, the largest possible volume is
(approximately) $v(1.6) \approx 66$ cubic inches, and the "best" box has approximate
dimensions $7.8'' \times 5.3'' \times 1.6''$. We could improve our accuracy by zooming in on the
graph. But with calculus methods we can—and soon will—do even better. ∎

EXAMPLE 6 **(Building one function from another)** Let ℓ be the straight-line function
$\ell(x) = x + 2$; we'll use ℓ to define a new function D. For any number x, let $D(x)$ be the
distance from the origin $(0, 0)$ to the point $(x, \ell(x))$ on the graph of ℓ. Find a formula
for $D(x)$. Which point P on the line ℓ is *closest* to the origin?

Solution   Points on the line ℓ have the form $(x, x+2)$; the distance from any such point to the origin is

$$D(x) = \sqrt{x^2 + (x+2)^2} = \sqrt{2x^2 + 4x + 4}.$$

The point P corresponds to the smallest possible value of $D(x)$. To find P, we could plot either $\ell(x)$ or $D(x)$ or both and see readily that $P = (-1, 1)$. For variety, however, let's work algebraically with the formula for $D(x)$. Notice first that

$$2x^2 + 4x + 4 = 2(x^2 + 2x + 2) = 2((x+1)^2 + 1).$$

Appendix D has details on completing the square.

(We completed the square in the last step.) ← Now we can write $D(x)$ in the form

$$D(x) = \sqrt{2((x+1)^2 + 1)} = \sqrt{2}\sqrt{(x+1)^2 + 1},$$

and the last form shows that $D(x)$ is as small as possible when $x = -1$. Because P lies on the line $y = x + 2$, it has coordinates $(-1, 1)$, as claimed. ∎

We try often throughout the text to emphasize quadratic functions. They're important in their own right and nicely illustrate connections between symbolic and graphical properties. Completing the square is a simple, powerful, and under-appreciated method.

What is a function? Formal definitions

As we've seen, functions can be given by formulas, by words, by graphs, and by tables of data. But what do *all* functions—however they're defined—have in common? We'll use five examples (two of which we've already seen) to illustrate the general definition:

These apparently repetitive examples aim to show how a concept such as "domain" makes sense for any function, not just for a formula.

- f $f(x) = x^2 + \dfrac{3}{x}$ (an algebraic function)

- g $g(t) = $ the human population t years C.E. (a function described in words)

- h the piecewise-defined function $h(u) = \begin{cases} 1 - u & \text{if } u \leq 0 \\ u^2 & \text{if } 0 < u < 2 \\ 42 & \text{if } u \geq 30 \end{cases}$

- j The function given by the following graph (Figure 7):

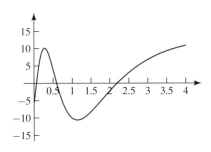

FIGURE 7
A function given graphically

- k The function given by the following table:

s	-3	-2	-1	0	1	2	3	4
$k(s)$	-4	-9	-1	0	1	8	3	-2

These five functions have little in common other than the property of *being* functions. Here is a formal definition:

> **DEFINITION** A function is a **rule** for assigning to each member of one set, called the **domain**, one (and only one) member of another set, called the **range**.

The definition uses three key words: *rule*, *domain*, and *range*. We'll discuss each one.

Rule A function accepts an input and—somehow—assigns one and only one output. The **rule** describes how this assignment is made. For our sample functions:

- *f* The rule is an algebraic "recipe": *Given a real number x, compute $x^2 + 3/x$.* To the input 5, for example, *f* assigns the output $f(5) = 5^2 + 3/5 = 25.6$.

- *g* To a number *t*, *g* assigns the world population at *t* years C.E. The table on page 3 says for instance, that $g(1950) = 2520$. Even though world population is never known exactly, *g* makes good sense as a function, because, at any time *t*, there is one and only one population $g(t)$—whether or not we can compute it.

- *h* The rule for *h* involves "cases": different inputs are treated differently. For instance, $h(-5) = 1 - (-5) = 6$, because the input -5 satisfies the first case of the definition, but $h(175) = 42$ since the input 175 satisfies the third case.

- *j* The rule for *j* is purely graphical: *j(x) is the height of the graph at horizontal position x.* Thus, $j(3) \approx 7$ and $j(1) \approx -10$, whereas $j(10)$ is not defined. (As always with graphs, values of *j* can be read only approximately.)

- *k* The rule for *k* uses the table: *For any input s in the top row, k(s) is the entry below s.* Thus, $k(-2) = -9$, $k(2) = 8$, and $k(42)$ is undefined.

A variable by any other name. For most functions we give names—*x, t, u, s*—to the input variables. This was for convenience; the particular variable names don't matter. For example, all three of the following expressions define exactly the same function:

$$f(x) = x^2 + \frac{3}{x}; \quad f(T) = T^2 + \frac{3}{T}; \quad f() = ()^2 + \frac{3}{()}.$$

The last form looks strange, but it emphasizes that the rule matters, not the variable name.

Domain A function's domain is its set of "acceptable" inputs. For our sample functions:

- *f* The algebraic rule $f(x) = x^2 + 3/x$ makes good sense unless $x = 0$, so the domain of *f* is the set of nonzero real numbers. In interval notation, the domain is $(-\infty, 0) \cup (0, \infty)$. (The $\cup$ symbol means "union.") ➡

- *g* The rule $g(t) =$ "the world human population *t* years C.E." makes logical sense for *any* real number *t*, but the inputs *t* for which $g(t)$ can be known or even estimated are more restricted. Conceding something to reality, we might restrict the domain to a smaller set such as $-5000 \le t \le 2500$.

- *h* The piecewise definition shows that *h* accepts as input any real number *u* except those for which $2 \le u < 30$. Thus, the domain of *h* is the union of two intervals: $(-\infty, 2) \cup [30, \infty)$.

- *j* Acceptable inputs to *j* lie in the interval $[0, 4]$—the set of *x*-values shown on the graph.

- *k* The domain of *k* is an 8-member set: $\{-3, -2, -1, 0, 1, 2, 3, 4\}$.

See Appendix B for more details on sets, set notation, and uses of the ∞ symbol.

The idea of natural domain may deserve emphasis — while in practice it's pedantic always to state domains explicitly, every function does have a domain. Occasionally it's important to say so.

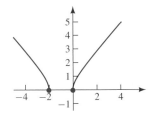

FIGURE 8
$p(x) = \sqrt{x^2 + 2x}$

We don't usually do much with ranges, since they're usually difficult to calculate, and there's often little reason to do so. But the concept is simple and the word should be understood.

"Natural" domains   In calculus, function domains are usually understood from context, not mentioned explicitly. The "default" is the **natural domain**: the set of inputs for which the rule successfully assigns an output. (Unless stated otherwise, "domain" in this book always means "natural domain.") For example, $s(x) = \sqrt{1 - x^2}$ has natural domain $[-1, 1]$ because the formula makes sense for inputs from this interval—and *only* for those inputs. The next example is a little more challenging.

EXAMPLE 7   Find the natural domain of the function $p(x) = \sqrt{x^2 + 2x}$.

Solution   A computer-drawn graph (Figure 8) suggests the answer. Why the gap in the graph from $x = -2$ to $x = 0$? Well, $p(x)$ makes sense (because of the square root) only if $x^2 + 2x = x(x + 2) \geq 0$, and $x(x + 2) = 0$ only where $x = 0$ or $x = -2$. Thus, we see that $x(x + 2) > 0$ everywhere *outside* this interval. The gap is there for a good reason: the natural domain is $(-\infty, -2] \cup [0, \infty)$, which omits the interval in question. ∎

Range   A function's domain is the set of allowable inputs; the range is the corresponding set of *outputs*. For example, 4 is in the range of $f(x) = x^2 + 3/x$ because $f(1) = 4$. But 4 is *not* in the range of $s(x) = \sqrt{1 - x^2}$, since there is no real number x for which $\sqrt{1 - x^2} = 4$.

Calculating a function's range exactly can be difficult. Sometimes a graph can help, as it does in Figure 9, which shows part of the sine function:

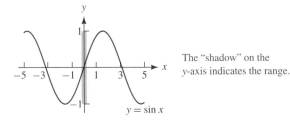

The "shadow" on the y-axis indicates the range.

FIGURE 9
The range of $y = \sin x$ is $[-1, 1]$

The graph shows that $-1 \leq \sin(x) \leq 1$ for all x and that all outputs between -1 and 1 are achieved. Thus, the sine function's range is the interval $[-1, 1]$. In particular, the number 2 is *not* in the range—as the graph shows—because the horizontal line $y = 2$ misses the graph. In general: *The range of a function f is the set of y-values at which a horizontal line hits the graph of f.* Here's a more illuminating way to say the same thing:

Let lights shine horizontally, from both left and right, on the graph of f. The range of f is the "shadow" thrown by the graph on the vertical axis.

BASIC EXERCISES

Exercises 1–4 are based on the situation described in Example 1.

1. **(a)** What (approximately) was the balloon's altitude at time $t = 1$?

   (b) What (approximately) was the balloon's velocity at time $t = 1$?

2. At what times (approximately) was the balloon's altitude at least 3000 feet above sea level?

3. **(a)** Was the balloon ascending at time $t = 1$? At time $t = 6$?

   (b) How does the graph of the balloon's altitude vs. time shown in Figure 1 illustrate the answers to the questions in part (a)?

   (c) How does the graph of the balloon's vertical velocity vs. time shown in Figure 1 illustrate the answers to the questions in part (a)?

4. (a) Was the balloon ascending more rapidly at time $t = 1$ or at time $t = 4$?

(b) How does the graph of the balloon's altitude vs. time shown in Figure 1 illustrate the answer to the question in part (a)?

(c) How can the graph of the balloon's vertical velocity vs. time shown in Figure 1 illustrate the answer to the question in part (a)?

5. (a) What does the approximate population function p given in Example 2 predict for the year 2010?

(b) What does it "predict" for the year 1000?

(c) What does it "predict" for 1000 B.C.E.?

(d) Are the predictions in parts (a)–(c) reasonable? Explain.

6. Let k be the function defined in Example 3. Evaluate $k(-2)$, $k(1)$, and $k(4)$.

Exercises 7–10 refer to the function m in Example 4.

7. Use the algebraic representation of m given in Example 4 to compute the following values *exactly*:

(a) $m(-4)$

(b) $m(0)$

(c) $m(2.3)$

(d) $m(\pi)$

8. (a) What is the slope of the line segment connecting the points $(1, m(1))$ and $(3, m(3))$?

(b) Find an equation, in point–slope form, of the line with slope 1 that passes through the point $(2, 1)$.

(c) How is the result in part (b) related to the piecewise-defined formula for m given in Example 4?

9. (a) Find an equation of the circle with radius $r = 2$ and center at the point $(-1, 0)$.

(b) How is the result in part (a) related to the piecewise-defined formula for m given in Example 4?

10. (a) Is 4 in the natural domain of m? Justify your answer.

(b) Is 4 in the range of m? Justify your answer.

In Exercises 11–12, find a piecewise-defined formula for the function whose graph is shown. [NOTE: Each graph is made up of line segments and circular arcs.]

11.

12.

Exercises 13–14 refer to the function v in Example 5.

13. (a) Explain, in physical terms, why $x = -1$ is not in the domain of v.

(b) Explain, in physical terms, why $x = 5$ is not in the domain of v.

14. (a) Is 75 in the range of v?

(b) What does the answer to part (a) mean in physical terms?

15. An open box is made by cutting squares w inches on a side from the four corners of a sheet of cardboard that is $24'' \times 32''$ and then folding up the sides. [HINT: See Example 5.]

(a) Express the volume of the box as a function of w.

(b) Estimate the value of w that maximizes the volume of the box.

16. Let $\ell(x) = 2x + 1$.

(a) Draw a graph of $\ell(x)$ for $0 \le x \le 5$.

(b) Let $D(x)$ be the distance from the origin to the point $(x, \ell(x))$. Find a formula for $D(x)$. [HINT: See Example 6.]

(c) Plot $D(x)$ for $0 \le x \le 5$.

17. For any $t \ge 0$, let $A(t)$ be the area of the rectangle bounded above by the line $y = 3$, below by the x-axis, on the left by the y-axis, and on the right by the line $x = t$.

(a) Write a formula for $A(t)$.

(b) Graph $A(t)$ for $0 \le t \le 5$.

18. For any $t \ge 0$, let $A(t)$ be the area of the right triangle bounded above by the line $y = x$, below by the x-axis, and on the right by the line $x = t$.

(a) Write a formula for $A(t)$.

(b) Graph $A(t)$ for $0 \le t \le 5$.

19. Let $\ell(x) = 2x + 1$, and let $A(t)$ be the area of the trapezoid bounded by the x-axis, the y-axis, ℓ, and the line $x = t$.

(a) Write a formula for $A(t)$.

(b) Graph $A(t)$ for $0 \le t \le 5$.

20. Is 42 in the range of the function $G(x) = -x^2$? Justify your answer.

21. Let $g(w) = 12 - \sqrt{w}$.

(a) What is the domain of g? (Express your answer using interval notation.)

(b) Is 10 in the range of g? Justify your answer.

22. (a) What is the natural domain of the absolute value function?

(b) What is the range of the absolute value function?

(c) Write the rule for the absolute value function as a piecewise-defined function.

23. Suppose that $f(3) = 7$.

(a) What, if anything, does this statement imply about the natural domain of the function f?

(b) What, if anything, does this statement imply about the range of the function f?

(c) Could the rule for f be $2x + 1$? Justify your answer.

(d) Could the rule for f be $t^2 - 2$? Justify your answer.

(e) Could the rule for f be $z^3 - z^2$? Justify your answer.

24. Explain why the rules $f(x) = x^2 + 3/x$ and $f(z) = z^2 + 3/z$ define the same function.

25. Explain why the graph of the equation $x^2 + y^2 = 1$ is *not* the graph of a function.

26. The **vertical line test** states, "A curve in the xy-plane is the graph of a function only if each vertical line $x = k$ intersects the graph at most once." Explain why this test works.

In Exercises 27 and 28, sketch a graph of the function f and use it to find the natural domain and the range of f.

27. $f(x) = \begin{cases} 0 & \text{if } 0 \leq x < 1 \\ -2 & \text{if } 1 \leq x < 2 \\ x & \text{if } 2 \leq x \end{cases}$

28. $f(x) = \begin{cases} 0 & \text{if } x \leq -1 \\ 3x - 2 & \text{if } 1 < x < 1.5 \\ x^2 & \text{if } 1.5 \leq x < 2 \end{cases}$

In Exercises 29–32, find the natural domain of the function.

29. $f(x) = \sqrt{x^2 - 4}$

30. $j(x) = \sqrt{4 - x^2}$

31. $r(x) = \dfrac{1}{\sqrt{(x+2)(1-x)}}$

32. $t(x) = \sqrt{\dfrac{1-x}{x+2}}$

FURTHER EXERCISES

33. Let f be the function defined by $f(x) = x^2$. Define the function g by this rule: $g(x)$ is the distance from the origin to $(x, f(x))$. For instance, $g(7) = \sqrt{2450}$, the distance from $(0, 0)$ to $(7, 49)$.

(a) Find $g(0), g(-1), g(1), g(2),$ and $g(500)$.

(b) Write a formula for $g(x)$.

(c) Graph $g(x)$ for $-5 \leq x \leq 5$.

34. Let f be the function defined by $f(x) = x^2$. Define the function m as follows: For any $x \neq 0$, $m(x)$ is the slope of the line through $(0, 0)$ and $(x, f(x))$. For instance, $m(10) = 10$, the slope of the line through $(0, 0)$ and $(10, 100)$.

(a) Find $m(-1), m(-2), m(1), m(2),$ and $m(500)$.

(b) Write a formula for $m(x)$.

(c) Graph $m(x)$ for $-5 \leq x \leq 5$.

35. Let f be the function defined by $f(x) = x^2$. Define the function j as follows: For any $x \neq 1$, $j(x)$ is the slope of the line through the points $(1, 1)$ and $(x, f(x))$. For instance, $j(10) = 11$, the slope of the line through $(1, 1)$ and $(10, 100)$.

(a) Find $j(2), j(1.1), j(1.01), j(0.99), j(0.9),$ and $j(0)$.

(b) Why is $x = 1$ not in the domain of j?

(c) Write a formula for $j(x)$.

(d) Graph $j(x)$ for $-2 \leq x \leq 2$.

36. Let f be the function $f(x) = x^2 + 3x - 4$ and ℓ the line that intersects the graph of f at the points where $x = 2$ and $x = 2 + h$.

(a) Find an algebraic expression for the slope of ℓ. [*Note: The answer depends on h.*]

(b) Use your answer to part (a) to find an equation of the line that intersects the graph of f at the points where $x = 2$ and $x = 2.003$.

(c) Use your answer to part (a) to find an equation of the line that intersects the graph of f at the points where $x = 2$ and $x = 1.995$.

37. When you drive an Ace Rental compact car x miles in a day, the company charges $f(x)$ dollars, where

$$f(x) = \begin{cases} 30 & \text{if } 0 \leq x \leq 100; \\ 30 + 0.07(x - 100) & \text{if } x > 100. \end{cases}$$

Describe Ace Rental's pricing policy in plain English. (Be sure to interpret the constants 30, 0.07, and 100 that appear in the pricing formula.)

38. Here's a highly simplified version of the U.S. federal income tax system. A taxpayer pays no federal tax on the first \$15,000 of annual income, 15% on the the next \$25,000 of income, and 28% on all earnings above \$40,000. Let x denote a taxpayer's annual income (in dollars), and let $T(x)$ denote the tax owed (in dollars) at income level x.

(a) The tax function T is piecewise-linear—its graph consists of straight lines. Use this fact to draw the graph of $T(x)$ for $0 \leq x \leq 60,000$. [HINT: First calculate $T(x)$ for some convenient values of x.]

(b) Give a piecewise-defined formula for $T(x)$.

(c) A taxpayer earning, say, \$50,123 yearly would have to pay 28 cents more tax if he or she earned *one more dollar*. A taxpayer earning \$20,123 a year would need to pay only 15 cents tax on the next dollar of income. In tax jargon, the first taxpayer has a **marginal tax rate** of 28%, and the second has a **marginal tax rate** of 15%. Let $MR(x)$ denote the marginal tax rate (as a decimal) at income level x. Give a piecewise-defined formula for $MR(x)$.

(d) Plot MR as a function of x for $0 \le x \le 60{,}000$. Describe in words how the graphs of T and MR are related.

39. Suppose that water is flowing into a cubical tank 10 feet on an edge.

(a) Write a formula for V, the volume of water in the tank, as a function of d, the depth of water in the tank.

(b) What is the natural domain of V?

(c) What is the range of V?

(d) Write a formula for d as a function of V.

40. Suppose that water is flowing into a cylindrical tank that has a diameter of 6 feet and a height of 20 feet.

(a) Write a formula for V, the volume of water in the tank, as a function of d, the depth of water in the tank.

(b) What is the natural domain of V?

(c) What is the range of V?

(d) Write a formula for d as a function of V.

41. Let $f(x) = |x|$ and g be defined by the rule "$g(x)$ is the slope of the graph of f at x."

(a) Find the natural domain and range of f.

(b) Explain why 0 is not in the natural domain of g.

(c) Find the natural domain and range of g.

(d) Find a symbolic expression for g. [HINT: Use a piecewise-defined function.]

42. Let $f(x) = x + |x|$ and g be defined by the rule "$g(x)$ is the slope of the graph of f at x."

(a) Find the natural domain and range of f.

(b) Write f as a piecewise-defined function.

(c) Find the natural domain and range of g.

(d) Find a symbolic expression for g.

1.2 GRAPHS

Every function f has a **graph**:

> **DEFINITION** The graph of a function f is the set of points (x, y) that satisfy the equation $y = f(x)$.

Figure 1 shows three simple examples: graphs of $f(x) = 1 - x$, $g(x) = 2^x$, and $h(x) = x^2$: ➤

Graphs are in a basic sense very familiar to students, so our main objects are to sharpen intuition, remind students of key vocabulary, illustrate some subtleties, and emphasize links between properties of functions (e.g., odd and even functions) and the special shapes of their graphs.

Decide for yourself which is which.

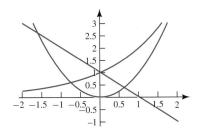

FIGURE 1
Graphs of $f(x) = 1 - x$, $g(x) = 2^x$, and $h(x) = x^2$

Graphs are essential tools for understanding calculus. This book contains hundreds of graphs, and the attentive reader will draw (by hand or by machine) hundreds more. Even the simplest graphs tell a great deal about the functions they represent. For instance, we see in Figure 1 that as x increases from -2 to 2, $f(x) = 1 - x$ always decreases, $g(x) = 2^x$ always increases, and $h(x) = x^2$ first decreases and then increases, taking its smallest value at $x = 0$. Questions like these, about how one quantity varies with respect to another, are at the heart of calculus.

Equations vs. functions   Every calculus function has a graph. Figure 2 shows the "generic" graph of a function f:

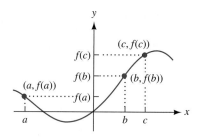

FIGURE 2
A "generic" graph

Functions often have equations, but equations may not correspond naturally to functions. Many students, it seems, do not know the function–equation distinction well.

Every point on the f-graph has the form $(x, f(x))$. Because f is a function, each input x corresponds to just *one* output y, so the f-graph cannot contain two different points with the same x-coordinate. (This humble fact has a pompous name: the **vertical line test**.)

Every function has a graph, but not every graph comes from a function—graphs can also come from *equations*. The graph of any equation in two variables x and y is the set of pairs (x, y) that satisfy the equation.

Appendices B and C have more on circles, lines, and other basic graphs.

Which x-values are exceptional?

An equation may or may not define a function. For example, the equation $y = x^2$ corresponds in an obvious way to the function $h(x) = x^2$ shown in Figure 1. But the graph of an equation of the form $(x - a)^2 + (y - b)^2 = r^2$ is a *circle*, with center (a, b) and radius r. ◄ Circles, although simple and useful, are *not* graphs of functions because most x-values correspond to two y-values. ◄

Most graphs in calculus are of the everyday, $y = f(x)$ style. For variety, Figure 3 shows some slightly stranger examples, graphs of the three equations $x^2 + y^2 = -1$, $x^2 + y^2 = 0$, and $x^2 + y^2 = 1$.

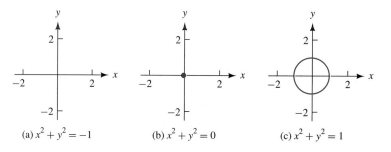

(a) $x^2 + y^2 = -1$ (b) $x^2 + y^2 = 0$ (c) $x^2 + y^2 = 1$

FIGURE 3
Three equation graphs

There's no mistake: *no* pair (x, y) of real numbers satisfies the first equation, and so the first graph is indeed empty. Only the origin $(0, 0)$ satisfies the second equation, so its graph is a single point. The third graph, a circle of radius 1, plays no tricks.

This is one of many places in which we introduce an idea (continuity, in this case) first informally in the graphical sense; we sharpen the idea later.

Continuous functions — graphs without breaks   Most of the graphs we'll see in calculus can be drawn without lifting the "pencil"; they're without "jumps" or "breaks." The functions these graphs represent are called *continuous*. The property called "continuity" plays a crucial role in the formal *theory* of calculus; we'll define continuity precisely in Chapter 2 and return to the matter in Chapter 4. But for now (and also, as a rule, throughout elementary calculus) nearly all of the functions we'll meet are continuous except perhaps at a few obvious points, so an informal understanding of continuity as "unbrokenness" will be adequate.

A sampler of graphs

Not every function has a nice formula—or any formula at all. Real-world functions, especially, are often given *only* graphically or by tables of values. The following examples illustrate some of the possibilities—with or without formulas. Notice especially the bold-faced "vocabulary" words: they'll arise repeatedly in our study of functions.

EXAMPLE 1   (Graph with formula)   In the best cases, functions come with graph *and* formula; combining both types of information tells us a lot. Figure 4 shows part of the graph of $p(x) = x^3 - 2x^2 + x - 2$. (We seldom see *all* of a graph because most graphs are infinitely long.)

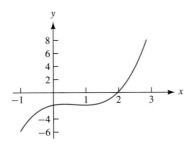

FIGURE 4
Graph of $y = p(x)$

- **Intercepts:**   The graph appears to have a y-**intercept** at $y = -2$ and an x-**intercept** at $x = 2$. The formula shows that these guesses are correct: easy calculations give $p(2) = 0$ and $p(0) = -2$. Could p have any other x-intercepts, perhaps outside the x-interval shown? The graph alone doesn't say, but rewriting the formula in **factored form**,

$$p(x) = x^3 - 2x^2 + x - 2 = (x-2)(x^2+1),$$

gives our answer. The right side can be zero only if one of the two factors is zero, and that occurs only if $x = 2$.

- **Where is p increasing?**   The function p appears to be rising (**increasing**, in calculus language) from $x = 1$ to $x = 3$. What happens for larger values of x? From the graph alone we can't tell, but we can see from the factored formula that $p(x)$ increases for *all* $x > 2$. (Both factors are positive and both increase with x, so their product increases, too.) ➡   ■   *Soon we'll develop calculus methods to show the same thing more conveniently.*

EXAMPLE 2   (Graph, no formula)   Figure 5 shows part of the graph of a function f; no formula is given. Two interesting points are labeled.

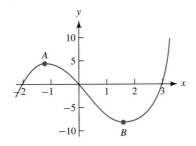

FIGURE 5
$y = f(x)$

What can (and can't) the graph tell us about f? Some samples follow. As with all graphs, only approximate answers are possible.

- **Roots**   The point $(3, 0)$ lies on the graph, and so $f(3) = 0$. Thus, f has a **root** at $x = 3$. Other roots of f lie at $x = -2$ and $x = 0$.

- **Guessing values**   What's $f(10)$? We might *guess* from the graph's general shape that $f(10)$ is some large positive number. But we can't even be sure that $f(10)$ exists; 10 may not be in the domain of f.

- **Special points**   Notice the points A and B; their coordinates show (approximately) that $f(-1.2) = 4$ and $f(1.6) = -8$. "High" and "low" points like A and B are especially important in calculus, so it pays to take special care with language. We say, for instance, that f has a **local maximum** at $x = -1.2$. The input $x = -1.2$ is a **local maximum point** of f, and the output $f(-1.2) = 4$ is a **local maximum value** of f. Similarly, $x = 1.6$ is a **local minimum point**, and $f(1.6) = -8$ is the corresponding **local maximum value** of f. ◄

"Local" means "compared to other points nearby." We'll define these words more formally in later sections.

- **Increasing and decreasing**   The graph falls between A and B and rises elsewhere. This means in calculus language that (allowing for estimation) f is **increasing** for $-2.5 < x < -1.2$, f is **decreasing** for $-1.2 < x < 1.6$, and f is increasing for $1.6 < x < 3.5$.

We'll say more about concavity in the derivative context, of course, but it's already visible in graphs, so we point it out here.

- **Concavity**   Concavity is another geometric property of graphs; we'll study it in detail later in this chapter. The f-graph of Figure 5 is **concave down** (like an open umbrella) at the point A; it's **concave up** (like the bowl of a spoon) at B. Somewhere between A and B, therefore, is an **inflection point**, where the direction of concavity switches. A close look suggests that this occurs somewhere between $x = 0$ and $x = 1$, but it's hard to be more precise. We'll soon see how to use a formula (if one exists) and calculus methods to locate a graph's inflection points precisely. ■

EXAMPLE 3   **(Graphs in context)**   In certain epidemics, the affected population falls naturally into three groups: the *susceptible*, the *infected*, and the *recovered*. An epidemic's progress can be charted by observing how these populations vary. The graphs labeled S, I, and R in Figure 6 show how the respective populations vary over a 25-day period during a fictional measles epidemic in a large school district.

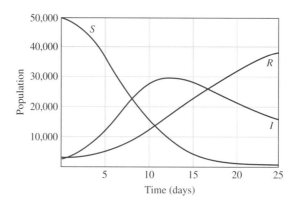

FIGURE 6
An epidemic's course

The graphs tell a lot about the epidemic. They show, for instance, that on day 10, the populations were (allowing for estimation errors)

Susceptible $\approx 15{,}000$;   Infected $\approx 28{,}000$;   Recovered $\approx 12{,}000$.

The "peak" near day 12 on the I-graph means that the infected population was largest on this day.

Other questions about the epidemic require judgment. We might ask, for instance, when the epidemic was at its worst. The answer depends on how we measure "badness." One possible measure is the number of people who fall ill on a given day. To fall ill means to leave the susceptible population, so the "worst" day (from this viewpoint) occurs when the susceptible population drops fastest. This happens around day 7, where the S-graph points most steeply downward. ∎

E X A M P L E 4   (Graphs from tabular data)   Consider the tabular function that follows (we discussed it in Example 3, page 4).

x	-3	-2	-1	0	1	2	3	4
$k(x)$	-4	-9	-1	0	1	8	3	-2

Note that the four graphical possibilities represent different choices of domain.

How should we plot k? One problem is that many different functions "agree" with k (i. e., have the same values) for $x = -3, -2, \ldots, 4$. In graphical language, many different possible graphs pass through the eight data points, as shown in Figure 7.

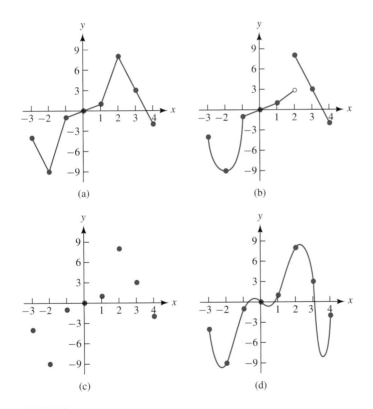

FIGURE 7
Four graphs from tabular data

Is one of these graphs "right"? Without more information, we can't say. If, say, the table represents hourly temperature readings on a winter night, we might prefer one graph to the others.➡ Notice, for instance, the "jump" in the graph in Figure 7(b). Because air temperature varies smoothly, this graph seems an unlikely candidate. ∎

Which would you choose?

New functions from old: operations with constants

Many students seem quite familiar with the graphical effects of constant operations, so the rather long-winded treatment following may go more quickly than it appears.

Creating new functions and new graphs by "operating" on old ones is a recurring theme in calculus. The simplest new-from-old operations involve attaching **constant parameters** in various ways to an original function. From the ordinary sine function, for instance, we can produce mutants such as

$$m(x) = 42 + 31 \sin \left(\frac{2\pi}{52} x \right).$$

Try plotting this function on a calculator. Do traces of the basic sine graph remain?

How do constant parameters affect *any* function and its graph? ◄

Additive constants: vertical and horizontal translations   Given a function f and a constant a, consider the new functions

$$g(x) = f(x) + a \quad \text{and} \quad h(x) = f(x + a),$$

formed by attaching *additive constants*. (If $a = 0$, then $g(x) = f(x) = h(x)$.) The formulas for g and h look similar, but the functions behave quite differently. Figure 8 shows graphs of g for several values of a.

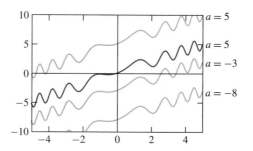

FIGURE 8
Vertical translations: $y = f(x) + a$ for several values of a

The graphs show the effect of the constant a: *The graph of $y = f(x) + a$ is the result of shifting the f-graph a units upward. (If $a < 0$, the shift is downward.)* In math-speak, a's effect is a **vertical translation**.

The effect of a on $h(x) = f(x + a)$ is different, as Figure 9 shows.

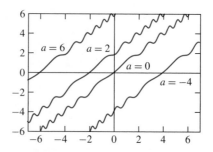

FIGURE 9
Horizontal translations: $y = f(x + a)$ for various values of a

This time a causes a **horizontal translation**: *The graph of $y = f(x + a)$ is the result of shifting the f-graph a units to the left.*

Left, not right?   Is it surprising that a positive a in $f(x + a)$ moves the f-graph left, not right? To see why, consider $h(x) = f(x + 2)$. Then $h(-2) = f(0)$, $h(-1) = f(1)$, $h(0) = f(2)$, and so on. In effect, h has a two-unit head start on f—whatever h does, f does two units later.

Multiplicative constants: stretching, compressing, and reflecting   We can also make new functions from old by attaching *multiplicative* constants. Given a function f and a constant a, let

$$g(x) = af(x) \quad \text{and} \quad h(x) = f(ax).$$

(If $a = 1$ then $g(x) = f(x) = h(x)$.) Notice the difference: g results from multiplying *outputs* by a, while h comes from multiplying *inputs* by a. Figure 10 shows the effect of a on $g(x) = af(x)$:

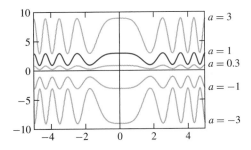

FIGURE 10
Vertical stretching: $y = af(x)$ for various values of a

As the graphs illustrate, multiplying outputs from f by a causes **vertical stretching** by a factor of $|a|$. If $a < 0$, there is also a **reflection** about the x-axis. More precisely:

- **Stretching**   Stretching by a factor $a > 1$ is simplest. The graph of $y = 3f(x)$, for instance, results from *tripling* the y-coordinate of each point on the f-graph.
- **Compressing**   If $0 \le a < 1$ (the case $a = 0.3$ is shown in Figure 10), then "stretching" by a factor of a actually flattens the f-graph toward the x-axis. Such a "stretch" is sometimes called a **compression**.
- **Reflecting**   A negative factor a adds a reflection about the x-axis to the picture. The cases $a = -1$ and $a = -3$, for example, are mirror images of the cases $a = 1$ and $a = 3$ (all are shown in Figure 10).

The function $h(x) = f(ax)$ is formed by multiplying *inputs* to f by a. The effect, this time, is to stretch or compress the f-graph *horizontally*. Figures 11(a)–11(d) show h for several values of a:

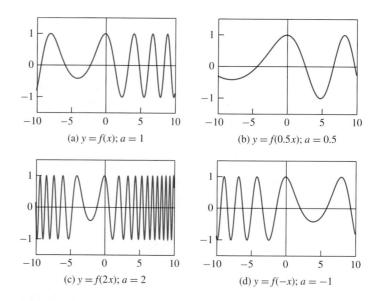

(a) $y = f(x)$; $a = 1$ (b) $y = f(0.5x)$; $a = 0.5$

(c) $y = f(2x)$; $a = 2$ (d) $y = f(-x)$; $a = -1$

FIGURE 11
Horizontal stretching and compression

Notice the similarities to—but also the differences from—vertical stretching:

- The graphs of $f(x)$, $f(2x)$, and $f(0.5x)$ show that if $a > 0$, the graph of $f(ax)$ is the result of compressing the f-graph horizontally by a factor of a (or, alternatively, stretching it by a factor of $1/a$).
- A negative value of a causes a reflection—this time, about the y-axis. The graph of $f(-2x)$, for instance, results from *both* compressing by a factor of 2 *and* reflecting about the y-axis.

Odd and even functions: reflective symmetry

We discuss oddness, evenness, and periodicity here because they illustrate nicely the link between functional and graphical properties of functions. The topics may also appeal to students' graphical intuition, which is often better than their "symbol sense."

Although graphs of functions *can* have quite bizarre shapes, most of the standard calculus functions have simpler, more regular graphs. Some of the simplest graphs are symmetric in some way or other; these symmetries nicely reflect (pun intended) properties of the functions themselves. Odd and even are among the simplest examples.

> **DEFINITION** A function f is **even** if $f(-x) = f(x)$ for all x in its domain; f is **odd** if $f(-x) = -f(x)$.

EXAMPLE 5 **(Detecting oddness and evenness)** Consider the functions $f(x) = x^2$, $g(x) = x^3$, and $h(x) = x + x^2$. Are any of f, g, and h even or odd?

Solution Let's check symbolically:

$$f(-x) = (-x)^2 = x^2 = f(x), \quad \text{while} \quad g(-x) = (-x)^3 = -x^3 = -g(x),$$

so f is even and g is odd. But

$$h(-x) = -x + (-x)^2 = -x + x^2 \neq \pm h(x);$$

therefore, h is *neither* even nor odd.

Functions like these help explain the "even" and "odd" terminology: Functions like x^2, x^4, and x^6 are even, while x, x^3, and x^5 are odd. ∎

Graphical views The symbolic method of Example 5 works well for functions with simple algebraic formulas. But what about, say, the sine and cosine functions, which have no simple algebraic formulas? Let's look at their graphs (Figures 12(a) and 12(b), respectively):

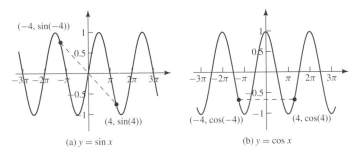

(a) $y = \sin x$ (b) $y = \cos x$

FIGURE 12
Different types of symmetry

The two graphs have different types of symmetry. The sine graph (Figure 12(a)) is **symmetric about the origin**: If any point (x, y) lies on the graph, then so does its reflection through the origin, the point $(-x, -y)$. This means for the sine function that, if $\sin(x) = y$, then $\sin(-x) = -y = -\sin(x)$. (The dotted points and dashed line show the case $x = 4$.) In other words, the sine function is odd.

The cosine graph (Figure 12(b)) is **symmetric about the y-axis**: If a point (x, y) lies on the graph, then so does $(-x, y)$, the first point's reflection across the y-axis. (The case $x = 4$ is shown.) This means that $\cos(-x) = \cos(x)$ for all x, so the cosine function is even.

Here are the rules in general:

A function f is odd if the graph of f is symmetric about the origin. A function is even if its graph is symmetric about the y-axis.

These rules link nicely to our earlier discussion of multiplicative constants. We saw, for example, that if f is any function, then the graph of $y = f(-x)$ is obtained by reflecting the graph of $y = f(x)$ across the y-axis. If f happens to be even, then $f(x) = f(-x)$, so these two graphs are actually *identical*, which is another way of describing symmetry with respect to the y-axis.

Periodic functions: repeating patterns

Figures 12(a) and 12(b) show that the sine and cosine graphs have another type of symmetry: they repeat themselves on horizontal intervals of length 2π. Figure 13 shows graphs of three other functions with repeating graphs:

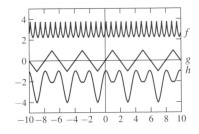

FIGURE 13
Three periodic functions

The functions in Figure 13 are all **periodic**: their graphs repeat themselves on horizontal intervals of some fixed length called the **period**. Here is the formal symbolic definition:

> **DEFINITION** A function f is **periodic** if the equation
>
> $$f(x + P) = f(x)$$
>
> holds for all x in the domain of f and some positive number P. The smallest such number P is the **period** of f.

Graphically speaking, the period is the horizontal length of the most basic repeating shape. It's easy to see in Figure 13, for instance, that both g and h have period 4. To find the period of f (and avoid seasickness) we can count 30 repetitions of f from $x = -10$ to $x = 10$, an interval of length 20. Thus, we estimate that f has period $20/30 = 2/3$.

Here are some comments on the definition:

- **Periods and horizontal shifts** We've seen that if f is any function and P any positive number, then the graph of $y = f(x + P)$ is the result of shifting the graph of $y = f(x)$ to the left by P horizontal units. Therefore, the equation $f(x) = f(x + P)$ means that shifting the f-graph P units to the left leaves the graph unchanged.

- **Repeats on bigger intervals** If a graph repeats itself on intervals of length P, then it also repeats on intervals of length $2P$, $3P$, $4P$, and so on. The period is the length of the *shortest* interval on which a function repeats. The sine and cosine functions, for example, have period 2π.

EXAMPLE 6 **(Periodic functions)** Figure 14 shows graphs of two periodic functions: $f(x) = \sin(2x) + 3$ and $g(x) = (\cos x)^2 + \cos(x) - 1$. Which graph is which? What is each function's period?

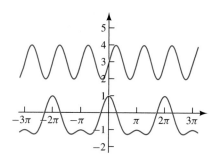

FIGURE 14
Two periodic functions

Solution The upper curve is f (it's formed from $y = \sin(x)$ by a horizontal compression and an upward shift), and the lower curve is g. Figure 14 suggests that f has period π and g has period 2π. We can check these guesses symbolically, using what we know of sines and cosines. Here is the argument for f:

$$f(x + \pi) = \sin(2(x + \pi)) + 3 = \sin(2x + 2\pi) + 3 = \sin(2x) + 3 = f(x).$$

A similar calculation shows that g (like the cosine function itself) has period 2π. ∎

BASIC EXERCISES

1. Let R be the function defined by $R(t) = 1/t^2$.

 (a) What is the natural domain of R?

 (b) What is the range of R?

 (c) Is R continuous on the interval $(-5, 5)$? Justify your answer.

 (d) Is R increasing over the interval $(-5, -1)$? Justify your answer.

 (e) Is R increasing over the interval $(1, 5)$? Justify your answer.

2. Suppose that the graph of a function B crosses the x-axis at $x = -\pi$ and the y-axis at $y = 3$.

(a) Evaluate $B(0)$.

(b) Evaluate $B(-\pi)$.

3. Suppose that the graph of a function B crosses the x-axis at $x = -3$ and the y-axis at $y = \pi$. Where does B have a root?

4. Suppose that $F(0) = -2$ and $F(2) = 0$.

(a) Which of the four points $(0, -2)$, $(-2, 0)$, $(2, 0)$, $(0, 2)$ must be on the graph of F?

(b) Does F have a root at $x = 0$? Justify your answer.

(c) Does F have a root at $x = 2$? Justify your answer.

5. Suppose that $u = \sqrt{2}$ is a root of the function $Y(u)$. Evaluate $Y(\sqrt{2})$.

6. Suppose that the points $(2, 3)$ and $(3, 2)$ are on the graph of a function f. Evaluate $f(2)$.

In Exercises 7–10, $g(t) = (t + 1)(t - 2)^2$.

7. Is g even, odd, or neither?

8. Is g increasing over the interval $[0, 2]$? Justify your answer.

9. Is g concave up over the interval $[-2, 2]$? Justify your answer.

10. How many roots does g have? Where are they located?

11. Suppose that the graph of $y = W(x)$ is concave down for $1 < x < 4$ and concave up for $4 < x < 9$.

(a) Sketch the graph of a continuous function W with these properties.

(b) Explain why $x = 4$ is an inflection point of W.

In Exercises 12–15, let S, I, and R be the functions in Example 3.

12. I is increasing on the interval $(5, 10)$. What does this mean in the context of the example?

13. Where does I have a local maximum? What does this mean in the context of the example?

14. S is decreasing on the interval $(0, 20)$. What does this mean in the context of the example?

15. The graph of $S(t)$ has an inflection point near $t = 7$. What does this imply about the rate of change of the susceptible population?

16. (a) Let $g(x) = f(x + 2)$. How are the graphs of f and g related?

(b) Let $h(x) = f(x) + 2$. How are the graphs of f and h related?

17. (a) Let $j(x) = 2f(x)$. How are the graphs of f and j related?

(b) Let $k(x) = \frac{1}{2}f(x)$. How are the graphs of f and k related?

(c) Let $m(x) = -2f(x)$. How are the graphs of f and m related?

18. (a) Let $n(x) = f(2x)$. How are the graphs of f and n related?

(b) Let $r(x) = f(x/2)$. How are the graphs of f and r related?

19. Suppose that f is an even function, and that $f(1) = 2$. Explain why this implies that $f(-1) = 2$.

20. Suppose that the domain of g includes all real numbers, that g is an odd function, and that $g(1) = 2$. Evaluate $g(-1)$. Justify your answer.

In Exercises 21–25, suppose that the function T has period 7 and that $T(0) = 3$.

21. Evaluate $T(7)$.

22. Evaluate $T(-14)$.

23. Explain why $T(-30) = T(40)$.

24. Let $S(v) = T(v + 21)$. How are the graphs of S and T related?

25. Let $U(r) = T(5r)$.

(a) Explain why $U(1.4) = 3$.

(b) U is periodic. What is its period?

Exercises 26–27 refer to the sketch below.

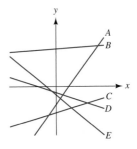

26. Which lines have positive slope?

27. Let m_A be the slope of line **A**, m_B be the slope of line **B**, and so on. Rank the numbers $m_A, \ldots, m_E$ in increasing order.

Exercises 28–31 refer to the function f whose graph is shown below.

28. Use the graph shown above to complete the following table. (Estimate as necessary.)

x	-2	0	1		
$f(x)$				-1	3

29. Estimate the minimum value of f over the interval $[-3, 3]$. What value of x corresponds to this value of $f(x)$?

30. Between which pair(s) of consecutive integers does f have a maximum point?

31. Is f increasing over the interval $(-1, 2)$? Justify your answer.

32. (a) Sketch the graph of a function that is concave up and increasing over the interval $[-3, 5]$.

(b) Sketch the graph of a function that is concave up and decreasing over the interval $[-3, 5]$.

33. Can a function have more than one local maximum value? If not, why not? If so, give a graphical example of a function that does.

34. Can a function have more than one inflection point? If not, why not? If so, give a graphical example of a function that does.

In Exercises 35–40, use the function g shown below to sketch a graph of the function f.

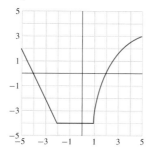

35. $f(x) = g(x) + 1$

36. $f(x) = g(x + 1)$

37. $f(x) = g(2x)$

38. $f(x) = 2g(x)$

39. $f(x) = -g(x)$

40. $f(x) = g(-x)$

41. Suppose that f is an even function and that the point $(-3, -5)$ is on the graph of f. Find another point on the graph of f.

42. Suppose that g is an odd function and that the point $(3, -5)$ is on the graph of g. Find another point on the graph of g.

43. Let $f(x) = x^3$ and $g(x) = f(x) + 2$.
  (a) Give an algebraic formula for $g(x)$.
  (b) Describe how to obtain a graph of g from a graph of f using translation, compression, stretching, and so on.
  (c) Sketch a graph of g over the interval $[-2, 2]$.

44. Repeat Exercise 43 with $g(x) = f(x + 2)$.

45. Repeat Exercise 43 with $g(x) = 2f(x)$.

46. Repeat Exercise 43 with $g(x) = f(2x)$.

In Exercises 47–50, indicate whether the function whose graph is shown is even, odd, or neither. Justify your answers.

47.

48.

49.

50.

FURTHER EXERCISES

In Exercises 51–54, suppose that the graph of the function g lies between a line A, with slope 2, and a line B, with slope −1, for all x, as shown below:

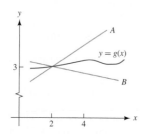

51. Find an equation for line A.

52. What is the height of line B at $x = 3$?

53. Find numbers L and U such that $L < g(4) < U$.

54. Find numbers L and U such that $L < g(-1) < U$.

55. Examine this sketch of a hemispherical water tank.

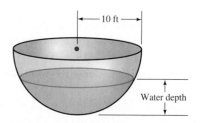

Let the letter D represent the depth of the water in the tank, and let V be the volume of the water in the tank. Regard volume as a function of water depth.

(a) What is $V(0)$?

(b) What is $V(10)$?

(c) Which of the graphs (A)–(D) could be the graph of $V(D)$? Explain your reasoning.

Graph A

Graph B

Graph C

Graph D

56. (a) Sketch a graph of temperature as a function of time that is consistent with the scenario described in the following sentence: "The child's temperature has been rising for the last 2 hours, but not as rapidly since we gave her the antibiotic an hour ago." (Let $t = 0$ correspond to the time when the medicine was given.)

(b) What is the significance of the fact that the graph in part (a) is increasing on the interval $t = -1$ to $t = 1$?

(c) What is the significance of the fact that the graph in part (a) is concave down on the interval $t = 0$ to $t = 1$?

In Exercises 57 and 58, sketch the graph of a function described by the sentence. Then give a brief description of the graph using phrases like "increasing," "concave up," and so forth.

57. Health insurance costs continue to increase at an increasing rate.

58. The world's population is growing more slowly now than it was 5 years ago.

59. Suppose that F is a periodic function with period 7 and that F has a local maximum at the point $(-3, 5)$. Find another point on the graph of F that is also a local maximum.

60. Let $f(x) = x^2$ and $g(x) = x^2 + 4x + 3$.

(a) Show that $g(x) = f(x + 2) - 1$.
[HINT: Complete the square.]

(b) Explain how to obtain the graph of g from the graph of f.

61. Let $f(x) = x^2$ and $g(x) = 2x^2 - 4x + 5$.

(a) Show that $g(x) = 2f(x - 1) + 3$.
[HINT: Complete the square.]

(b) Explain how the graphs of f and g are related.

62. Let $q(x) = ax^2 + bx + c$, where a, b, and c are constants.

(a) Suppose that q is an even function. Show that $b = 0$ must be true.

(b) Suppose that q is an odd function. What can be said about the values of the constants a, b, and c?

63. Suppose that f is a periodic function.

(a) Is it possible that f is an even function? If so, sketch the graph of an even periodic function. If not, explain why not.

(b) Is it possible that f is an odd function? If so, sketch the graph of an odd periodic function. If not, explain why not.

(c) Is it possible that f is neither even nor odd? If so, sketch the graph of a periodic function that is neither even nor odd. If not, explain why not.

64. Suppose that the graph of a function f is symmetric with respect to the y-axis and that $f(3) = 1$. Evaluate $f(-3)$.

65. Suppose that the graph of a function f is symmetric with respect to the origin and that $f(1) = 3$. Evaluate $f(-1)$.

66. Suppose that f is an odd function and that $-12 \le f(x) \le 9$ if $x \ge 0$.

(a) Is it possible that $f(-5) = 10$? Explain.

(b) Is it possible that $f(-5) = -10$? Explain.

67. If a function f is concave up on the interval $[a, b]$, then the line segment joining the points $(a, f(a))$ and $(b, f(b))$ lies above the graph of f over this interval.

(a) Suppose that f is concave up on the interval $[a, b]$. Explain why

$$f(a) + \frac{f(b) - f(a)}{b - a}(x - a) > f(x)$$

for all x such that $a < x < b$.

(b) Show that if f is concave up on the interval $[a, b]$, then

$$\frac{f(x) - f(a)}{x - a} < \frac{f(b) - f(a)}{b - a}$$

for all x such that $a < x < b$. [HINT: Use part (a).]

(c) Suppose that g is concave down on an interval $[a, b]$. What is the relationship between the line segment joining the points $(a, g(a))$ and $(b, g(b))$ and the graph of g? [HINT: If g is concave down on an interval, $-g$ is concave up on that interval.]

68. Suppose that f is concave up on the interval $[0, 10]$, that $f(1) = 4$, and that $f(5) = 2$.

(a) Explain why $f(3) < 3$.
[HINT: Use part (a) of Exercise 67.]

(b) Find a number U such that $f(4) < U$. Justify your answer.

69. Suppose that g is concave down on the interval $[0, 10]$, that $g(1) = 4$, and that $g(5) = 2$.

(a) Explain why $g(3) > 3$.

(b) Find a number L such that $g(4) > L$. Justify your answer.

70. Suppose that f is concave up on the interval $[a, b]$. Show that if $0 < t < 1$, then $f((1 - t)a + tb) < (1 - t)f(a) + tf(b)$. [HINT: Use part (a) of Exercise 67 and let $t = (x - a)/(b - a)$.]

1.3 A FIELD GUIDE TO ELEMENTARY FUNCTIONS

This section briefly reviews the standard elementary function classes. Considerably more practice with and review of these functions appear in the Appendices. We return to each class separately in the next chapter when we find derivatives.

An **elementary function** is one built from certain allowed basic "elements," using certain allowed operations. For example, the function

$$f(x) = \ln\left(\frac{\sin(2x)}{1 + 3x^4}\right)$$

is elementary because it is constructed by combining several standard elements (the sine and natural logarithm functions, powers of x, and constants) in various ways. Just as many different buildings can be built from a few sizes of brick, a huge variety of elementary functions can be constructed from a few basic functions—ones that have proved their value over centuries of use.

Note that "elementary" doesn't mean "easy"—it has to do with "elements" from which other functions are built up.

This "field guide" contains brief descriptions, with pictures, of various elementary function "species." We'll study each one in more detail when we meet it in its natural habitat. (Appendices D, E, and F also contain reviews of each type of function.)

Function families The basic functions of calculus fall naturally into three prominent "families": (i) **algebraic functions** (such as $f(x) = x^2 + 3/x$); (ii) **exponential and logarithm functions** (such as 2^x and $\ln x$); and (iii) **trigonometric functions** (such as sines and cosines).

How functions combine, and how their descendants' traits reflect their own, are important themes of the following chapters. Our concern right now is with the basic functions themselves.

Algebraic functions

Students may not understand that algebraic formulas are "computational recipes," but transcendental expressions (such as sin x) are really just names for functions.

Algebraic functions are defined using only algebraic operations: addition, multiplication, division, raising to powers, and taking roots. Roughly speaking, algebraic functions are those that even the simplest calculator can handle. If, say, $f(x) = x - 3\sqrt{x+1}$, then checking with a calculator that $f(1.7) = 1.7 - 3\sqrt{2.7} \approx -3.229$ requires nothing fancier than the square root and arithmetic keys.

See Appendix D to review basic properties of polynomials.

Polynomials Polynomials are the simplest algebraic functions; their rules require only addition, multiplication, and taking positive integer powers. ◄

> **DEFINITION** A **polynomial** in x is an expression that can be written in the form
> $$p(x) = a_0 + a_1 x + a_2 x^2 + a_3 x^3 + \cdots + a_n x^n,$$
> where the coefficients a_i are constants. The **degree** of $p(x)$ is n, the largest power of x.

EXAMPLE 1 The expressions

$$5x + 2, \quad -x + 5x^{17}, \quad \text{and} \quad (x+3)(\pi x^{17} + 7)$$

are all polynomials in x. The last expression can be expanded to give a standard polynomial form. The expressions

$$3 - \frac{1}{x}, \quad \sqrt{x}, \quad \text{and} \quad \frac{x+3}{\pi x^{17}+7}$$

are not polynomials because all involve negative or fractional powers.   ∎

The polynomial *expression* $2x^3 + 5x$ corresponds naturally to the polynomial *function* $p(x) = 2x^3 + 5x$. The technical difference between polynomial expressions and polynomial functions seldom matters in calculus, so we'll use the terms interchangeably.

Because polynomials involve only multiplication and addition, they accept all real numbers as inputs. Thus, every polynomial has the same natural *domain*: the full set of real numbers. Polynomials' *ranges* vary drastically, as the three graphs in Figure 1 illustrate.

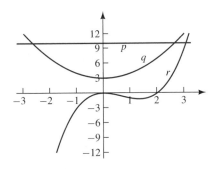

FIGURE 1
Three polynomials: $p(x) = 10$, $q(x) = x^2 + 3$,
$r(x) = x^3 - 2x^2$

- **Ranges**   The range of the constant function $p(x) = 10$ is the one-member set $\{10\}$. The range of $q(x) = x^2 + 3$ is $[3, \infty)$, an infinite interval. (The q-graph is a parabola with vertex at $(0, 3)$.) The range of $r(x) = x^3 - 2x^2$ is less obvious and needs a closer look.

- **Blowing up and down**   The graph of r suggests that $r(x)$ "blows up" as x becomes large and *positive* and that $r(x)$ "blows down" for large *negative* values of x. ➡ (Plotting r over a larger x-interval, say $[-1000, 1000]$, would show this even more clearly.) The shorthand notations

$$r(x) \to \infty \quad \text{as} \quad x \to \infty \quad \text{and} \quad r(x) \to -\infty \quad \text{as} \quad x \to -\infty$$

  are convenient to express these properties. ➡ In particular, $r(x)$ assumes *all* real values, so its range is $(-\infty, \infty)$.

- **No breaks**   Polynomial graphs are smooth everywhere, without breaks or kinks. This reflects the fact that polynomials are among the simplest and best-behaved functions from the calculus point of view.

Characteristic shapes   Constant and linear functions have straight-line graphs. **Quadratic** and **cubic** polynomials—those with degree 2 and 3—also have standard shapes. (Quadratic graphs are parabolas.) Figures 2(a) and 2(b) show three quadratic and three cubic curves:

"Blows up" is informal talk; it means that the graph spikes upward.

We discuss limits at infinity and infinite limits in Chapter 4. Here, the discussion is informal.

In Chapter 4 we'll interpret these properties more precisely using limits.

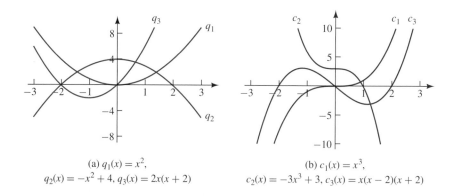

(a) $q_1(x) = x^2$,
$q_2(x) = -x^2 + 4$, $q_3(x) = 2x(x + 2)$

(b) $c_1(x) = x^3$,
$c_2(x) = -3x^3 + 3$, $c_3(x) = x(x - 2)(x + 2)$

FIGURE 2
Quadratics and cubics

Although similar to each other, the graphs in each picture can be distinguished by such differences as where and how often they cross the x-axis.

Polynomial graphs come in many shapes, but some restrictions do exist. For instance, a polynomial p of degree n can have at most n roots; thus, the graph of p can have at most n different x-intercepts.

Rational functions   Adding or multiplying two polynomials always creates a new polynomial. *Dividing* two polynomials doesn't (usually) give another polynomial; it gives a rational function. Formally:

> **DEFINITION**   A **rational function** is a function whose rule can be written as the quotient of two polynomials.

Of the functions

$$f(x) = \frac{x^2}{x^2 - 1}, \quad g(x) = 3x^{-2} = \frac{3}{x^2},$$
$$h(x) = \sqrt{2 + x} = (x + 2)^{1/2}, \quad k(x) = \frac{2}{x} + \frac{3}{x + 1},$$

the first two are clearly rational. The function $h(x)$ is not rational because it involves a fractional power. The function $k(x)$ is the *sum* of two rational functions, but is $k(x)$ itself rational? Yes it is, because, we can use basic algebra to rewrite $k(x)$ as a single quotient of polynomials. (See Example 5 in Appendix D, page A-31, for the algebraic details.)

Rational functions, unlike polynomials, have an important new graphical feature: the possibility of **horizontal** and **vertical asymptotes**—straight lines toward which a graph tends "in the limit." ◄ The function $f(x)$ above appears graphically in Example 6 in Appendix D, page A-32; the graph has one horizontal and two vertical asymptotes.

We'll study limits and asymptotes and relations between them in Chapters 2 and 4.

Other algebraic functions   Polynomials and rational functions involve only the *arithmetic* operations: addition, subtraction, multiplication, division, and raising to integer powers.

"Other" algebraic functions include ones such as

$$f(x) = \sqrt{x}, \quad g(x) = \sqrt{x + \sqrt{x}}, \quad \text{and} \quad h(x) = \sqrt{\sqrt[3]{x^2 + 1} + x^{6/7}},$$

all of which involve *fractional* powers.

Exponential functions

Understanding exponential and logarithm functions requires, first of all, some basic facility with the *algebra* of exponentials and logarithms. �']➤ The following facts are key:

Many students need practice and review with the algebra of exponential and log functions — Appendices E and F can serve this purpose.

See Appendix E for quick reviews of the necessary basics.

$$b^x b^y = b^{x+y}; \qquad\qquad (b^x)^r = b^{xr};$$
$$\log_b xy = \log_b x + \log_b y; \qquad \log_b(x^r) = r \log_b x;$$
$$e^{\ln x} = x; \qquad\qquad \ln e = 1.$$

In each line, b must be positive. In the top two equations, x and y can take any real values. In the bottom two, x and y must be positive.

> **DEFINITION**   An **exponential function** is defined by an expression of the form
> $$f(x) = b^x,$$
> where b, the **base**, is a fixed positive number.

Each of the expressions 2^x, 4^t, 0.5^z, and e^x defines an exponential function. ➤ None of the expressions x^2, z^3, $(w+1)^{15}$, and x^π defines an exponential function because each involves a fixed power of a variable base.

The base is fixed and the exponent varies — hence the name.

Why base e?   Among all exponential functions, the one with base e turns out to be especially useful and convenient; it's also the default base on most scientific calculators. The number e is irrational; its decimal expansion begins $e = 2.71828182\ldots$. What makes base e special — for both exponential and logarithm functions — will become clearer soon, when we study derivatives.

The base-e exponential function $f(x) = e^x$ is often called the **exponential function** or, sometimes, the **natural exponential function**. ➤ Alternative notations include $\exp(x)$, $\exp x$, and e^x.

The name is a bit unfortunate because other functions with other bases are also exponential.

No parentheses?   Trigonometric, exponential, and logarithm expressions are often typeset without parentheses. For example,

$$\sin(x), \quad \ln(x), \quad \sin x, \quad \text{and} \quad \ln x$$

are all syntactically correct, but the last two are typographically simpler. When confusion seems possible, we'll use parentheses.

Students are sometimes confused by the fact that expressions like $\sin x$ and $\ln x$ are often written without parentheses. This might need explicit mention — as might the fact that calculators and computers normally do require parentheses.

Graphs   Figure 3 shows graphs of several functions of the form b^x — only the base b varies. Points of special interest are shown bulleted.

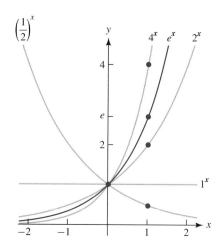

FIGURE 3
Exponential functions with various bases

- **Legal bases** Every positive number b defines a sensible exponential function. In practice, however, $b = 2$, $b = e$, and $b = 10$ are most useful.
- **Domain and range** Exponential functions accept all real inputs, so all have domain $(-\infty, \infty)$. The graphs of Figure 3 illustrate that, unless $b = 1$, the range of the exponential function $f(x) = b^x$ is $(0, \infty)$.
- **Shapes** The shape of an exponential graph $y = b^x$ depends on b: The greater the value of b, the faster b^x increases for positive x. (If $b < 1$, b^x decreases. If $b = 1$, then b^x is constant.)
- **A common point** Every graph $y = b^x$ passes through the point $(0, 1)$. (See the graphs in Figure 3.) In functional language: *If $f(x) = b^x$, then $f(0) = b^0 = 1$.* The input $x = 1$ is also of interest. For any function $f(x) = b^x$, $f(1) = b^1 = b$. (See the bulleted points in Figure 3.)

Logarithm functions

Exponential and logarithm functions come in pairs. An *exponential* function with base b corresponds to a *logarithm* function with the same base. The following table collects values of one such "matched pair" of functions, here with base $b = 2$.

Exponential and logarithm function values							
Values of 2^x							
x	-2	-1	0	1	2	3	10	13.28771
2^x	1/4	1/2	1	2	4	8	1024	10,000
Values of $\log_2 x$							
x	1/4	1/2	1	2	4	8	1024	10,000
$\log_2 x$	-2	-1	0	1	2	3	10	13.28771

Notice especially the "mirror symmetry" in the table: if $2^x = y$, then $\log_2 y = x$, and vice versa. The following definition describes precisely the connection between the logarithm and exponential functions with any given base b; it says that the two functions are **inverses** of each other: ➡

We'll revisit the idea of inverse functions in the next two chapters.

> **DEFINITION** The **logarithm function with base** b, denoted by
> $$f(x) = \log_b x,$$
> is defined by the condition
> $$y = \log_b x \iff b^y = x.$$

Each of the expressions $\log_2 x$, $\log_4 x$, $\log_{1/2} x$, and $\log_e x$ defines a logarithm function for some base b. The logarithm function with base e is called the **natural logarithm function**; in print and in computerese, it's usually denoted by $\ln(x)$ or just $\ln x$. Figure 4 shows graphs of logarithm functions with various bases; several interesting points are shown bulleted.

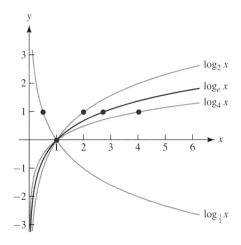

FIGURE 4
Logarithm functions with various bases

Notice especially the resemblance to the graphs of exponential functions (with the same bases) in Figure 3. The preceding definition means that a point (p, q) lies on the graph of $y = \log_b x$ if and only if the "mirror image" point (q, p) lies on the graph of $y = b^x$. Not surprisingly, properties of logarithm functions reflect ➡ analogous properties of exponential functions.

Pun intended.

- **Legal bases** Every positive number b except $b = 1$ can be used as the base for a logarithm function. (As with exponentials, $b = 2$, $b = e$, and $b = 10$ are the most useful bases.)

- **Domain and range** The graphs illustrate that, for any legitimate base b, the logarithm function accepts *positive* inputs; outputs take on *all* real values. Thus, every logarithm function has domain $(0, \infty)$ and range $(-\infty, \infty)$.

- **Shapes** Like exponential graphs, all logarithmic graphs have similar basic shapes. As the preceding graphs show, logarithm functions with base $b > 1$ increase with x, but they rise less steeply as x increases. The precise shape of a logarithmic graph depends on the particular base b. The larger the base b, the *slower* $\log_b x$ increases with x. ➡

Compare the graphs with various bases to see this.

- **A common point**   The graph of every logarithm function passes through the point $(1, 0)$. (See the graphs in Figure 4.) In functional language: *If* $f(x) = \log_b x$, *then* $f(1) = \log_b 1 = 0$. Similarly, for any $b > 0$, $f(b) = \log_b b = 1$.

Trigonometric functions

See Appendix F to review trigonometric basics.

The most important property of the trigonometric functions is their repetitive (or periodic) behavior. ◄ The familiar graphs of the sine and cosine functions (Figure 5) reflect this wavelike character:

FIGURE 5
Sine and cosine graphs

As usual, we see only part of the graphs, but in this case that's enough—the full graphs of the sine and cosine functions repeat the same pattern infinitely often.

We use u and v here to save x and y for later.

Many students are strongly wedded to the "triangular" idea of trigonometric functions. They may need help reconciling the "circular" view with the triangular.

Circular functions   In calculus, it's usually best to think of trigonometric functions in terms of circles, not triangles. As a result, the sine and cosine functions are sometimes called **circular functions**. The simplest circle, known as the **unit circle**, has radius 1 and center $(0, 0)$. In the uv-plane, the unit circle has equation $u^2 + v^2 = 1$. ◄ Imagine a point P moving *counterclockwise* around the unit circle, starting from the "east pole" $(1, 0)$, as in Figure 6.

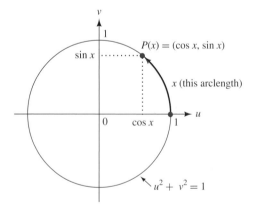

FIGURE 6
Defining sin x and cos x

As P moves endlessly around the unit circle, many related quantities vary as well: the u-coordinate of P, the v-coordinate of P, the slope of the segment from P to the origin, and others. All the trigonometric functions can be derived from these varying quantities.

> **DEFINITION** For any real number x, let $P(x)$ be the point reached by moving x units of distance counterclockwise around the unit circle in the uv-plane, starting from $(1, 0)$. (If $x < 0$, go clockwise.) Then
> $$\cos x = u\text{-coordinate of } P(x);$$
> $$\sin x = v\text{-coordinate of } P(x).$$

The definitions, the unit-circle picture, and the sine and cosine graphs themselves reveal key properties of these functions:

- **Domain and range** For any real number x, $\cos x$ and $\sin x$ are the coordinates of $P(x)$, the point x units of distance, measured counter clockwise, from $(1, 0)$. ➥ Thus, every real number x is a legal input; the domain of both the sine and cosine functions is $(-\infty, \infty)$.

  Recall: If $x < 0$, measure clockwise.

  As the point $P(x)$ wanders the unit circle, its u-and v-coordinates vary, but only between -1 and 1. Thus, both functions have the same range: the closed interval $[-1, 1]$. In other words, for all x, $-1 \le \cos x \le 1$ and $-1 \le \sin x \le 1$.

- **Famous values** The following table collects some important values of the sine and cosine functions. ➥

  Appendix F has hints for finding other useful values of the sine and cosine functions.

Famous sines and cosines						
x	0	$\pi/4$	$\pi/2$	π	$3\pi/2$	2π
$P(x)$	$(1, 0)$	$(\sqrt{2}/2, \sqrt{2}/2)$	$(0, 1)$	$(-1, 0)$	$(0, -1)$	$(1, 0)$
$\cos x$	1	$\sqrt{2}/2$	0	-1	0	1
$\sin x$	0	$\sqrt{2}/2$	1	0	-1	0

- **Odd and even** The sine function is odd, and the cosine function is even; in symbols,

$$\sin(-x) = -\sin x \quad \text{and} \quad \cos(-x) = \cos x.$$

These properties follow from the definitions and from the symmetry of the unit circle.

- **Periodic properties** The sine and cosine functions are 2π-**periodic**: they repeat themselves on intervals of length 2π. In symbols,

$$\sin(x + 2\pi) = \sin x \quad \text{and} \quad \cos(x + 2\pi) = \cos x.$$

This is so because for every real number x, $P(x)$ and $P(x + 2\pi)$ are *identical* points on the circumference of the unit circle.

- **A famous identity** For any real number x, the point $P(x) = (\cos x, \sin x)$ lies on the unit circle, so the coordinates of P must satisfy the defining equation $u^2 + v^2 = 1$. Therefore,

$$(\sin x)^2 + (\cos x)^2 = 1.$$

(This is often written without parentheses, as $\sin^2 x + \cos^2 x = 1$.) Equations that relate various trigonometric functions to each other are called **trigonometric identities**. There are many trigonometric identities; Appendix F contains some examples.

Other trigonometric functions Four additional trigonometric functions are defined in terms of the sine and cosine functions.

For the moment we mainly just mention these "other" trigonometric functions; we revisit them in Chapters 2 and 3, when we find derivatives.

> **DEFINITION** For real numbers x,
>
> $$\tan x = \frac{\sin x}{\cos x}; \qquad \cot x = \frac{\cos x}{\sin x};$$
>
> $$\sec x = \frac{1}{\cos x}; \qquad \csc x = \frac{1}{\sin x}.$$

Pieces of the graphs of these functions follow. Pieces are enough: Like the sine and cosine functions, these new functions repeat on *every* interval of length 2π. (In fact, as Figures 7(a) and 7(b) show, the tangent and cotangent functions repeat even on intervals of length π.) ◄

Appendix F explains why.

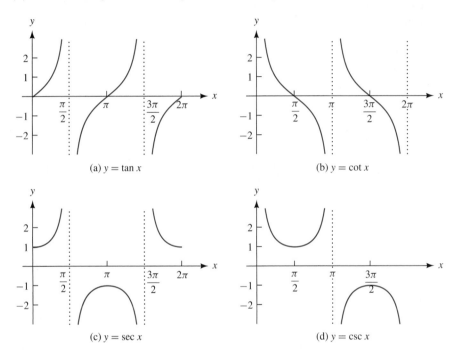

(a) $y = \tan x$

(b) $y = \cot x$

(c) $y = \sec x$

(d) $y = \csc x$

FIGURE 7
"Other" trigonometric functions

The tangent, cotangent, secant, and cosecant functions inherit certain traits from their parents, the sine and cosine functions. But they have their own personalities, too.

- **Domains and ranges** Because the sine and cosine functions are defined for *all* real numbers, the remaining trigonometric functions are also defined for all real inputs except those at which a denominator is 0. The domain of the cosecant function, for instance, consists of all real numbers *other than* integer multiples of π. The graphs illustrate these functions' ranges as well.

- **Asymptotes** The tangent, cotangent, secant, and cosecant functions all have vertical asymptotes; see Appendix F for details on asymptotes of the tangent function.

- **Functional properties** The following properties of the "other" trigonometric functions follow directly from their definitions and from basic properties of the sine and cosine functions. (Notice how the graphs reflect each property.) Each property holds for all inputs x in the given function's domain.

$$|\sec x| \geq 1; \quad |\csc x| \geq 1; \quad \tan(-x) = -\tan x; \quad \sec(-x) = \sec x.$$

- **The tangent function and the unit circle** Like the sine and cosine functions, the tangent function has a useful and pleasing geometric interpretation in terms of the unit circle:

$$\tan x = \frac{\sin x}{\cos x} = \text{slope of the line from the origin to } P(x).$$

This simple and pleasing property of the tangent function seems too little known; it may deserve emphasis. Knowing it can help students remember such facts as
$\tan(\pi/4) = 1$ and
$\tan(-x) = -\tan x$.

This interpretation helps explain, for instance, why $\tan(\pi/4) = 1$ and why $\tan x$ "blows up" as x approaches $\pi/2$.

No algebraic formulas. Do the sine and cosine functions have simple algebraic formulas? Alas, no: Trigonometric functions are called **transcendental** because they *can't* be written as algebraic combinations of powers, roots, sums, and products. Still, these functions are far from mysterious; they've been studied and used for centuries. Today, even cheap calculators produce highly accurate values of these functions. How do they do it? That's a good question, and we'll return to it later in this book.

BASIC EXERCISES

1. Explain why $3x^{1/2} + 4x^5$ is not a polynomial.

2. Is $\sqrt{2} + x^2/\sqrt{3}$ a polynomial? Justify your answer.

3. Explain why $(1 + 2x)/4x^3$ is not a polynomial.

4. Show that $(x^4 - 1)/(x^2 + 1)$ is a polynomial.

5. Is $(x^3 + 1)/(x + 1)$ a polynomial? Justify your answer.

6. Suppose that $P(x)$ is a polynomial of degree 5.
   - **(a)** What is the natural domain of P?
   - **(b)** How many x-intercepts can the graph of P have?
   - **(c)** How many y-intercepts can the graph of P have?
   - **(d)** Is it possible that P has no real roots? Justify your answer.
   - **(e)** Is it possible that $P(x) \leq 11$ for all x? Justify your answer.
   - **(f)** Is it possible that $|P(x)| \leq 11$ for all x? Justify your answer.

7. Suppose that $Q(x)$ is a polynomial of degree 6.
   - **(a)** What is the natural domain of Q?
   - **(b)** How many x-intercepts can the graph of Q have?
   - **(c)** How many y-intercepts can the graph of Q have?
   - **(d)** Is it possible that Q has no real roots? Justify your answer.
   - **(e)** Is it possible that $Q(x) \leq 11$ for all x? Justify your answer.
   - **(f)** Is it possible that $|Q(x)| \leq 11$ for all x? Justify your answer.

8. Let k be the function $k(x) = \dfrac{2}{x} + \dfrac{3}{x+1}$. Show that k is a rational function by finding polynomials p and q such that $k(x) = p(x)/q(x)$.

9. Let m be the function $m(x) = \dfrac{3x}{x^2 + 1} + \dfrac{4}{5x + 6}$. Show that m is a rational function by finding polynomials p and q such that $m(x) = p(x)/q(x)$.

10. Is $\left(\sqrt{2}\right)^x$ an exponential function? Justify your answer.

11. Explain why the expression π^x defines an exponential function but the expression x^π does not.

12. What two points are on the graph of $y = x^b$ for every positive number b?

13. What point is on the graph of $y = b^x$ for every positive number b?

14. What point is on the graph of $y = \log_b x$ for every positive number b?

15. Let $f(x) = e^x$.
    - **(a)** What is the natural domain of f?
    - **(b)** What is the range of f?
    - **(c)** Where is f increasing?
    - **(d)** Does f have any local maximum or local minimum points? If so, where are they located?
    - **(e)** Where is f concave up?
    - **(f)** Does f have any inflection points? If so, where are they located?
    - **(g)** Does f have any roots? If so, where are they located?

16. Let $F(x) = \ln x$.
    - **(a)** What is the natural domain of F?
    - **(b)** What is the range of F?
    - **(c)** Where is F increasing?
    - **(d)** Does F have any local maximum or local minimum points? If so, where are they located?
    - **(e)** Where is F concave up?

(f) Does F have any inflection points? If so, where are they located?

(g) Does F have any roots? If so, where are they located?

17. Let $f(x) = \cos(x/2)$.

(a) What is the natural domain of f?

(b) What is the range of f?

(c) Is f an even function?

(d) Is f periodic? If so, what is its period?

(e) Where in the interval $(0, 2\pi)$ is f increasing?

(f) Does f have any local maximum or local minimum points in the interval $(0, 2\pi)$? If so, where are they located?

(g) Where in the interval $(0, 2\pi)$ is f concave up?

(h) Does f have any inflection points in the interval $(0, 2\pi)$? If so, where are they located?

(i) Does f have any roots in the interval $(0, 2\pi)$? If so, where are they located?

18. Let $f(x) = \sin(2\pi x)$.

(a) What is the natural domain of f?

(b) What is the range of f?

(c) Is f an even function?

(d) Is f periodic? If so, what is its period?

(e) Where in the interval $(0, 3)$ is f increasing?

(f) Does f have any local maximum or local minimum points in the interval $(0, 3)$? If so, where are they located?

(g) Where in the interval $(0, 3)$ is f concave up?

(h) Does f have any inflection points in the interval $(0, 3)$? If so, where are they located?

(i) Does f have any roots in the interval $(0, 3)$? If so, where are they located?

19. Let $f(x) = \tan x$.

(a) What is the natural domain of f?

(b) What is the range of f?

(c) Use properties of the sine and cosine functions to show that f is an odd function.

(d) Is f periodic? If so, what is its period?

(e) Where in the interval $(0, 2\pi)$ is f increasing?

(f) Does f have any local maximum or local minimum points in the interval $(0, 2\pi)$? If so, where are they located?

(g) Where in the interval $(0, 2\pi)$ is f concave up?

(h) Does f have any inflection points in the interval $(0, 2\pi)$? If so, where are they located?

(i) Does f have any roots in the interval $(0, 2\pi)$? If so, where are they located?

(j) Where in the interval $(0, 2\pi)$ does f have vertical asymptotes?

20. Let $g(x) = b^x$, where $b > 1$ is a constant.

(a) What is the natural domain of g?

(b) What is the range of g?

(c) Is g periodic? If so, what is its period?

(d) Where is g increasing?

(e) Does g have any local maximum or minimum points? If so, where are they located?

(f) Where is g concave up?

(g) Does g have any inflection points? If so, where are they located?

(h) Does g have any roots? If so, where are they located?

(i) How is the graph of g related to the graph of $f(x) = e^x$?

21. Let $h(x) = b^x$, where $0 < b < 1$ is a constant.

(a) What is the natural domain of h?

(b) What is the range of h?

(c) Where is h increasing?

(d) Does h have any local maximum or minimum points? If so, where are they located?

(e) Where is h concave up?

(f) Does h have any inflection points? If so, where are they located?

(g) Does h have any roots? If so, where are they located?

22. Let $G(x) = \log_b x$, where $b > 1$ is a constant.

(a) What is the natural domain of G?

(b) What is the range of G?

(c) Is G periodic? If so, what is its period?

(d) Where is G increasing?

(e) Does G have any local maximum or minimum points? If so, where are they located?

(f) Where is G concave up?

(g) Does G have any inflection points? If so, where are they located?

(h) Does G have any roots? If so, where are they located?

(i) How is the graph of G related to the graph of $f(x) = \ln x$?

23. Let $H(x) = \log_b x$, where $0 < b < 1$ is a constant.

(a) What is the natural domain of H?

(b) What is the range of H?

(c) Where is H increasing?

(d) Does H have any local maximum or minimum points? If so, where are they located?

(e) Where is H concave up?

(f) Does H have any inflection points? If so, where are they located?

(g) Does H have any roots? If so, where are they located?

In Exercises 24–33, find the natural domain and range of each function. Express your answers using interval notation (see Appendix B).

24. $f(x) = \sin(3x) - 1$

25. $f(x) = \cos(3x - 1)$

26. $f(x) = e^{-x}$

27. $f(x) = -e^{x^2}$

28. $f(x) = e^{-x^2}$

29. $f(x) = e^{\sin x}$

30. $f(x) = \ln(x^2)$

31. $f(x) = \ln(x^3 + 1)$

32. $f(x) = \sqrt{1 + \cos x}$

33. $f(x) = (2 + \sin x)^{-1/3}$

In Exercises 34–39, find the period of the function.

34. $f(x) = 2 - \cos x$

35. $f(x) = \sin(x - 1)$

36. $f(x) = \sin(2x)$

37. $f(x) = \sin(x/2)$

38. $f(x) = \cos(2\pi x)$

39. $f(x) = \cos(x/\pi)$

F U R T H E R   E X E R C I S E S

40. Let $f(x) = 10^x$.
  (a) What is the natural domain of f?
  (b) Find a number k such that $f(x) = e^{kx}$.
  (c) Explain how to obtain the graph of f from the graph of e^x.

41. Let $g(x) = \log_{10} x$.
  (a) What is the natural domain of g?
  (b) Show that there is a number k such that $g(x) = k \ln x$.
  (c) Explain how to obtain the graph of g from the graph of $\ln x$.

42. Suppose that A is a positive real number and that $B = \log_5 A$. Write 5^B in terms of A as simply as possible.

43. Suppose that A is a positive real number and that $B = 2 \ln A$. Write e^B in terms of A as simply as possible.

44. Suppose that $A > 0$ is a real number and that $B = \ln A$. Find k so that $3^B = A^k$.

45. Suppose that the point (A, B) is on the graph of the exponential function b^x for some positive number b. Show that the point (B, A) is on the graph of the logarithm function $\log_b x$.

46. Suppose that the point (A, B) is on the graph of the logarithm function $\log_b x$ for some positive number b. Show that if $c = b^2$, then the point (B, A^2) is on the graph of the exponential function c^x.

47. Suppose that the line $y = 2$ is a horizontal asymptote of the function f.
  (a) Explain why the line $y = 5$ is a horizontal asymptote of the function $g(x) = f(x) + 3$.
  (b) Find the equation of a horizontal asymptote of the function $g(x) = f(x + 1)$.

  (c) Find the equation of a horizontal asymptote of the function $g(x) = 3f(x + 4) + 1$.

48. Suppose that the line $x = -3$ is a vertical asymptote of the function f.
  (a) Explain why the line $x = -3$ is a vertical asymptote of the function $g(x) = f(x) + 3$.
  (b) Find the equation of a vertical asymptote of the function $g(x) = f(x + 1)$.
  (c) Find the equation of a vertical asymptote of the function $g(x) = 3f(x + 4) + 1$.

49. Let $f(x) = \dfrac{x - 3}{x^2 - 9}$ and $g(x) = \dfrac{1}{x + 3}$.
  (a) Show that $f(x) = g(x)$ for all x such that $x \ne \pm 3$.
  (b) Find the domain and range of f.
  (c) Find the domain and range of g.
  (d) How are the graphs of f and g related?
  (e) Does the graph of f have a horizontal asymptote? If so, find an equation for this asymptote.
  (f) Does the graph of f have a vertical asymptote? If so, find an equation for this asymptote.

50. Let $f(x) = \dfrac{\sqrt{x} - 3}{x - 9}$ and $g(x) = \dfrac{1}{\sqrt{x} + 3}$.
  (a) Show that $f(x) = g(x)$ for all $x \ge 0$ such that $x \ne 9$.
  (b) Find the domain and range of f.
  (c) Find the domain and range of g.
  (d) How are the graphs of f and g related?
  (e) Does the graph of f have a horizontal asymptote? If so, find an equation for this asymptote.
  (f) Does the graph of f have a vertical asymptote? If so, find an equation for this asymptote.

1.4 AMOUNT FUNCTIONS AND RATE FUNCTIONS: THE IDEA OF THE DERIVATIVE

The **derivative** is one of the two most important concepts in calculus. ➤ We'll devote much time and effort to derivatives; various subtleties and puzzles will arise along the way. But the basic idea behind derivatives is simple: *For a given function f, the derivative*

The other is the integral, which we'll study later.

Read f′ aloud as "eff prime."

This section introduces the idea of a derivative function: "any" function f has an associated "rate function" f′ that tells how fast f varies. We interpret this rate function both as a rate of change and in terms of slope. For the moment we treat these ideas as intuitively natural—students have little trouble believing that velocity and slope exist. We treat questions of existence and the analytic definition in Chapter 2, when students have more context.

function, denoted by f′, tells the rate of change of f.◄ This principle, suitably interpreted, lies behind all our calculations and applications of the derivative.

Who invented the derivative? No one person—related ideas and methods appear through at least 2000 years of mathematical history. The European study of derivatives happened mainly in the 17th and 18th centuries, ranging from Pierre de Fermat (1601–1665; French) through Isaac Newton (1642–1727; English) and Gottfried Leibniz (1646–1716; German)—generally considered the cofounders of modern calculus—to Leonhard Euler (1707–1783; Swiss) and Joseph-Louis Lagrange (1736–1813; French). Lagrange, building on Euler's idea of function, may have been first to use both the phrase "derivative function" (*fonction dérivée*, in French) and the prime symbol to denote it.

The rest of this chapter is about the concept of the derivative function. We'll study what it means for f' to be the rate function derived from f, what each function says about the other, and how graphs of f and f' are related. Formal definitions and symbolic techniques for calculating derivatives appear in the next two chapters. Here is an informal description:

DEFINITION (The derivative, informally, as a rate function) Let f be a function. The new function f', called the **derivative** of f, is defined by the rule

$$f'(x) = \text{instantaneous rate of change of } f \text{ at } x.$$

We'll sometimes use "derivative" and "rate function" interchangeably to describe f'. When we do, we'll call f an **original function** or an **amount function**. We'll revisit and improve this definition in later sections. We'll explain, for instance, just what "instantaneous" means, and we'll consider whether a given function f *has* a derivative f'. But first we'll take derivatives out for a drive.

Rates, amounts, and cars: derivatives on the road

Cars are for students the most familiar setting in which the concept and language of rates arise naturally. The Bismarck highway story aims to use and also sharpen this intuition.

At noon on October 1, 2000, a car enters Interstate Highway 94 from the State Capitol on-ramp in Bismarck, North Dakota. For several hours, the car moves—sometimes east, sometimes west—at varying speeds.

Functions, derivatives, and the prime notation offer a powerful language for describing the situation. First, we define some symbols:

- t: the elapsed time, measured in hours since noon;
- $P(t)$: the car's position at time t, measured in miles *east* of the State Capitol on-ramp;
- $V(t)$: the car's *eastward* velocity at time t, measured in miles per hour (mph).

Figures 1(a) and 1(b) show possible graphs of the car's position and velocity functions.

(a) Position vs. time

(b) Velocity vs. time

FIGURE 1
Position and velocity

- **Position and velocity as functions of time**   Both P and V are functions of t: At any sensible input time t the car has position $P(t)$ and velocity $V(t)$. For example,

$$P(2) = 100 \quad \text{and} \quad V(2) = 70$$

because at 2 P.M., the car is 100 miles *east* of Bismarck, moving *east* at 70 mph.

- **Amount functions and rate functions**   Amount functions and rate functions come in pairs—every *rate* function describes how fast some *amount* function changes. For the Bismarck car, V is the rate function associated to P, the amount function. �']
   At any time t, $V(t)$ gives the *instantaneous rate of change of position with respect to time*. In symbols, $V(t) = P'(t)$ (or, simply, $V = P'$).

The units of V (miles per hour) and P (miles) suggest that V measures how fast P changes.

- **Positive and negative values**   Both P and V can take either positive or negative values. For example,

$$P(6.5) = -40 \quad \text{and} \quad V(6.5) = -60$$

mean that at 6:30 P.M. the car is 40 miles *west* of Bismarck traveling *west* at 60 mph. More generally, $P(t) > 0$ means that the car is *east* of the state capitol; $V(t) > 0$ means that the car is headed *east*.

- **Position vs. distance, velocity vs. speed**   The functions P and V describe the car's *position* and *velocity*. Why not use *distance* and *speed* instead? The differences are subtle but important. In the language of physics, distance and speed connote *nonnegative* quantities. (Speedometer readings are always nonnegative.) Because position and velocity can take either positive or negative values, they can convey information about direction.

Students often conflate speed with velocity and distance with position. Some explicit mention of the useful distinction is recommended.

- **What the speedometer tells; what it doesn't**   A speedometer reading of 70 mph at $t = 4$ means that $V(4) = \pm 70$. (Figure 1(b) shows that, in fact, $V(4) = -70$.) The speedometer, moreover, tells *instantaneous* speed—the car's speed at a particular moment. ➤

A 70 mph reading means that if the car maintains the same speed for a full hour, it will travel 70 miles.

- **Acceleration: another rate**   Velocity, like position, has its own rate function, called **acceleration**. Acceleration is the rate of change of velocity with respect to time; in symbols: $A(t) = V'(t)$.
   Like position and velocity, acceleration can take both positive and negative values. For the Bismarck car, for instance, $A(2) > 0$; this means that at time $t = 2$ the car's eastward velocity is *increasing*. Similarly, $A(1) < 0$ means that the car's eastward velocity is *decreasing* at time $t = 1$.

Students are quite comfortable with the idea of acceleration as rate of change of velocity. One might ask about the physical meaning of the rate of change of acceleration; it's called "jerk."

- **Velocity—rate or amount?**   Earlier we viewed V as a *rate* function, the one derived from the *amount* function P. With the acceleration A in the picture, we can also think of V as an *amount* function, for which the associated rate function is A. The moral is that almost *any* function can be thought of either as a rate or as an amount, depending on the situation.

- **Units for rates**   Every rate involves *two* varying quantities—the rate tells how fast something varies with respect to *something else*. The proper units for measuring rates must therefore reflect both of the quantities at hand. In the case at hand, velocity is the rate of change of position (measured in miles) with respect to time (measured in hours), so the unit of velocity is *miles per hour*. The appropriate unit of acceleration is therefore miles per hour per hour—the ratio of the unit of velocity to the unit of time.

Amount and rate functions in other contexts

The notions of "amount function" and "rate function" make sense in many contexts. Indeed, for *any* function f and any input t we can think of $f(t)$ as an amount, and $f'(t)$ as the corresponding rate of change. (The letter t suggests time, but this is only a convenience; mathematical "rates" need not involve time.) How one interprets $f'(t)$ as a rate depends on the situation; so do the appropriate units of measurement.

EXAMPLE 1   At time t, $f(t)$ is the *altitude* of a balloon, $g(t)$ is the *value* of a bank deposit, and $h(t)$ is the *volume* of water in a tank. What do the rate functions f', g', and h' mean? What are reasonable units for the quantities in question? What do the statements $f'(3) = -5$, $g'(3.5) = 4.2$, and $h'(3) = -4$ mean in context?

Solution   The derivative version of each function describes that function's rate of change with respect to time. Thus, at time t, $f'(t)$ tells the balloon's rate of ascent or descent; $g'(t)$ describes how fast the bank balance rises or falls; and $h'(t)$ describes the rate of water flow into or out of the tank.

   Many sensible choices are available for units. For the balloon we might choose *minutes after noon* for time, and *meters above sea level* for altitude. With these units, the statement $f'(3) = -5$ means that, at 12:03 P.M. the balloon was descending gently, at 5 *meters per minute*. (Had we chosen *seconds* for time, then $f'(3) = -5$ would mean that, at 3 seconds after noon, the balloon was falling at an alarming 5 meters per *second*.)

   For the bank deposit we might measure time in months since an initial deposit and the balance in dollars. With these choices, $g'(3.5) = 4.2$ means that after three months and two weeks, the balance is increasing at the rate of $4.20 per month. Similarly, with time in minutes and water volume in liters, $h'(3) = -4$ means that water is flowing *out* of the tank at 4 liters per minute.   ■

Slope: the derivative seen graphically

In each setting discussed above (cars, balloons, money, and water), the amount function f and the rate function f' had the same relationship: f' measures how fast *outputs* from f increase with respect to *inputs* to f. ◄

For the bank balance function, outputs are dollars, inputs are months, and the rate function tells dollars per month.

   The same ideas apply to "pure" mathematical functions—irrespective of cars, balloons, money, or other real phenomena. If f is *any* function and $y = f(x)$, then the rate function f' tells how fast y increases with respect to x. The statement $f'(3) = 5$, for example, means that if $x \approx 3$, then a small increase Δx in x causes y to increase about 5 times as much. In symbols, $\Delta y \approx 5 \Delta x$. (The Δ-symbol traditionally denotes a *change* in a variable.)

   Slope is the important geometric concept that brings functions, rates, and derivatives together—with or without a real-world setting in the background. Slope is by its very definition a rate: it's the *ratio* of two changes, Δy (a rise) and Δx (a run). ➤ The slope of the graph of $y = f(x)$ at a point (x, y) is a natural measure of how fast y changes with respect to x, so we make the following informal definition:

"Rate" and "ratio" have common linguistic roots.

DEFINITION (The derivative, informally, as slope) Let f be a function. The derivative function f' is given by the rule

$$f'(x) = \text{slope of the } f\text{-graph at } x.$$

The limit-based definition comes early in Chapter 2.

Like the earlier informal definition of derivative in terms of rates, this one needs refinement and discussion. We'll have to say, for instance, how to calculate a curved graph's slope at a point. But first let's see what the definition means in the simplest case.

Derivatives of linear functions   It's easiest to find derivatives of linear functions—those with straight-line graphs. ➤

Appendix C reviews the basics on lines and their slopes.

EXAMPLE 2 Let f be the linear function $f(x) = 3x + 1$. Explain, graphically and in terms of rates, why the derivative is the *constant* function $f'(x) = 3$.

Solution The graph of f is a straight line, so its slope (in this case, 3) is the same at *every* x-value. In symbols: $f'(x) = 3$ for all x. Graphs of f and f' appear in Figures 2(a) and 2(b).

Since linear functions have such simple derivatives we use them to start the theme of relating f and f'.

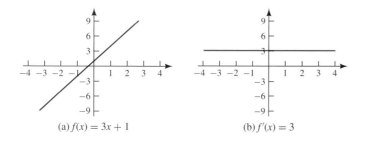

(a) $f(x) = 3x + 1$ (b) $f'(x) = 3$

FIGURE 2
A linear function and its derivative

In rate language, f increases everywhere at the rate of 3 y-units per x-unit.   ∎

The example illustrates the first part of a useful general fact:

FACT If f is the linear function $f(x) = ax + b$, then the derivative function is constant: $f'(x) = a$. Conversely, if f' is constant, then f is linear.

The second statement above—that *only* linear functions have constant derivatives—should sound reasonable. Surprisingly, it takes some work to prove. We'll return to the matter in Chapter 4.

The slope of a graph at a point: tangent lines

For straight lines, the idea of slope is simple: A line has just one slope, and any two points on the line can be used to compute it. But how could we measure the slope at a point on a *curved* graph? Does every graph *have* a slope at every point? How can we use formulas (if they're available) to find the slope at a point?

Here we acknowledge that finding the slope of a curve takes some thought, but that we can often estimate an answer from basic graphical intuition. We approach the same problem by "zooming in" in Section 1.5.

We'll tackle these important questions gradually, refining our answers over several chapters. In this chapter our approach is mainly graphical.

The slope of a *curve* at a point P can be thought of as the slope of a certain straight line through P, called the **tangent line at P**. Roughly speaking, the tangent line "points in the direction of the curve" at P. ← Here is the idea in car talk:

The words in quotes are an intuitive description; they mean that the tangent line "fits" the curve at P.

> *The curve is a highway, seen from above at night. A car, headlights piercing through fog, follows the road. When the car is at P, its headlights point along the tangent line at P.* ←

If the driver loses control at P, the car will—literally—go off on a tangent.

Using these basic ideas we can usually draw reasonably accurate tangent lines, estimate their slopes, and find their equations. For example, Figure 3 shows pieces of approximate tangent lines at several points along a curve.

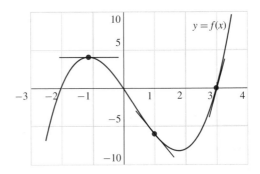

FIGURE 3
Examples of tangent lines

E X A M P L E 3   Find equations for the tangent lines shown in Figure 3.

Solution   With only a graph at hand we'll have to estimate. The leftmost tangent segment (at about $x = -1.1$) looks horizontal, so its slope is zero—in function notation, $f'(-1.1) \approx 0$. Because the line passes through $(-1.1, 4)$, its equation is $y = 4$.

Eyeball estimates for the slopes of the other two tangent segments give $f'(1) \approx -5$ and $f'(3) \approx 15$. The middle and rightmost bulleted points have approximate coordinates $(1, -6)$ and $(3, 0)$, respectively, so the corresponding tangent lines have the following point-slope equations: ←

Appendix C reviews point-slope equations for lines and how to translate them to other standard forms.

$$y = -5(x - 1) - 6 \quad \text{and} \quad y = 15(x - 3) + 0.$$ ∎

Relating amounts and rates

Relations between amount and rate functions is a crucial theme in much of what follows; we broach it here.

How are an amount function f and its rate function f' related to each other? What can either function say about the other? These questions are at the heart of calculus. We'll revisit them often, in graphical, numerical, and symbolic forms. We finish this section with two applications, one to falling objects and the other to speed limits, that illustrate this crucial connection.

Free fall   Many real-world phenomena naturally involve rate and amount functions; derivatives are just what's needed to describe and predict their behavior. We end this section by illustrating derivatives in action. We'll *calculate* derivatives later on.

A moving object is said to be in **free fall** if it is affected only by gravity. Other possible forces—air resistance, engine thrust, and so forth—are ignored. Under these circumstances, gravity produces the same downward acceleration on *all* falling objects, regardless of their size, weight, initial velocity, or other characteristics. For objects near the surface of the earth, this acceleration is essentially constant. The Florentine visionary Galileo Galilei (1564–1642) is said to have tested these claims by tossing various objects from the Leaning Tower of Pisa and observing that all of them landed at about the same time.

Does air drag matter? In practice, yes. Parachutists rely on air drag for survival; cannonballs fall faster than live chickens. Exactly what Galileo dropped isn't known; indeed, the whole Pisa story seems unlikely, with all those tourists milling around below. Nevertheless, air resistance is usually negligible for small, dense objects moving at moderate speeds, as when a coin falls to the floor.

A falling object has, at any time t, a height h, an upward velocity v, and an upward acceleration a. Given appropriate measurement scales for time and distance, $h(t)$, $v(t)$, and $a(t)$ are all functions of t, and the derivative relations $v = h'$ and $a = v'$ hold. In other words, v is the rate function of h, and a is the rate function of v. Galileo's discovery that an object in free fall has constant downward acceleration says symbolically that $a(t) = -g$ or, equivalently, that

$$v'(t) = -g$$

for some positive constant g. ➡ (The negative sign is there because the object accelerates downward.) In metric units, $g \approx 9.8$ meters per second per second; in the English system, $g \approx 32$ feet per second per second.

The g stands for gravity.

Formulas for position and velocity In the late 1600s Isaac Newton used Galileo's discovery to derive his laws of motion. Newton reasoned that if (as in free fall) the acceleration function $a(t)$ is *constant*, then the velocity function must be linear. (This is also the point of the second part of the Fact on page 39.)

Suppose that, at time $t = 0$ seconds, an object is h_0 feet above ground level and has *upward* velocity v_0. ➡ Newton's laws of motion imply rather simple formulas for the height and vertical velocity functions. With distance measured in meters, time in seconds, and velocity in meters per second, the formulas turn out to be

$v_0 > 0$ means that the object rises initially, perhaps by having been thrown upward.

$$h(t) = h_0 + v_0 t - 4.9t^2; \quad v(t) = v_0 - 9.8t.$$

With *feet* as the distance unit, we get

$$h(t) = h_0 + v_0 t - 16t^2; \quad v(t) = v_0 - 32t.$$

(We'll derive these formulas in Section 2.5.)

EXAMPLE 4 The Hubert H. Humphrey Metrodome, home of the Minnesota Twins, has a 195-foot ceiling. Could a major league pitcher throw a ball to the ceiling?

Solution Not likely—even if we ignore air drag. A pitcher throws a fast ball with an initial horizontal velocity of around 95 mph, or 140 feet per second. Throwing straight up is awkward, so let's assume a smaller initial *vertical* velocity, say 100 feet per second. If the ball starts from an initial height of 6 feet, then the preceding formulas say that

$$h(t) = 6 + 100t - 16t^2; \quad v(t) = 100 - 32t.$$

Figures 4(a) and 4(b) show graphs of h and v.

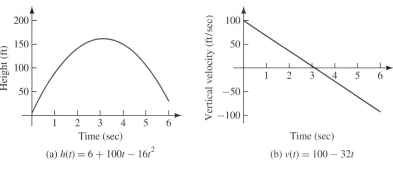

(a) $h(t) = 6 + 100t - 16t^2$ (b) $v(t) = 100 - 32t$

FIGURE 4
A baseball's height and velocity   ■

Height is greatest at the instant when upward velocity is zero, that is, when

$$v(t) = 100 - 32t = 0 \iff t = \frac{100}{32}.$$

At that time, the height is $h(100/32) = 162.25$ ft, which is lower than the Metrodome's ceiling.

Most students find the speed limit law itself plausible-sounding, once they understand what it says. But many will find it difficult to apply in problems, perhaps because of its use of various symbols with different meanings. Working carefully through simple examples may be helpful.

The speed limit law   The speed limit on Interstate Highway 94 near Bismarck, North Dakota, is 70 mph. Here's a safe bet for law-abiding drivers:

If a car never exceeds the speed limit for a full hour, then the car travels no more than 70 miles.

(If the driver remains law-abiding for two full hours, then the car covers no more than 140 miles, and so on.)

This simple-sounding principle is surprisingly useful when rephrased in the language of rate and amount functions:

FACT (The speed limit law)   Let f be a function defined for x in $[a, b]$, and let M be any real number. If

$$f'(x) \le M$$

for all x in $[a, b]$, then

$$f(b) - f(a) \le M(b - a).$$

What does the Fact have to do with cars and speed limits? We'll pick it apart to see.

- **Position and velocity**   The functions $f(x)$ and $f'(x)$ represent the car's *position* and *velocity*, respectively, at time x.

- **The speed limit**   The constant number M is our "speed limit." Requiring that $f'(x) \le M$ for all x in $[a, b]$ means, graphically, that the slope of the f-graph never exceeds M for x in $[a, b]$.

- **Displacement**   The quantity $f(b) - f(a)$ is the "displacement" (the difference in the car's position) over the time interval $[a, b]$. ← The speed limit law says that this displacement cannot exceed the product of the speed limit, M, and the time elapsed, $b - a$.

If the car's velocity is always positive, then $f(b) - f(a)$ is just the distance traveled.

- **Scofflaw** If a car *always* exceeds 70 mph for a full hour, then it must cover *at least* 70 miles. ➡ We could call this the **scofflaw principle**: *Don't try this at home.*

$$\text{If } f'(x) \geq M \text{ for all } x \text{ in } [a, b], \text{ then } f(b) - f(a) \geq M(b - a).$$

- **Strict inequalities** A "strict" version of the speed limit law also holds (where "<" replaces "≤"):

$$\text{If } f'(x) < M \text{ for all } x \text{ in } [a, b], \text{ then } f(b) - f(a) < M(b - a).$$

Bad cop In the following examples we enforce the speed limit law.

EXAMPLE 5 Let f be a function such that (i) $f(0) = 0$, and (ii) $f'(x) \leq 10$ for all $x \geq 0$. Show that $f(1) \leq 10$. What can be said about $f(1000)$?

Solution We apply the speed limit law on the interval $[0, 1]$, with $M = 10$:

$$f'(x) \leq 10 \Longrightarrow f(1) - f(0) \leq 10 \cdot (1 - 0) = 10.$$

Because $f(0) = 0$, $f(1) \leq 10$. Similar reasoning shows that $f(1000) \leq 10000$.

In rate language, condition (ii) above means that, for $x \geq 0$, $y = f(x)$ increases no faster than 10 y-units per x-unit. In graphical language, (ii) says that the slope of the f-graph never exceeds ten, so a 1-unit "run" (from $x = 0$ to $x = 1$) produces no more than a 10-unit "rise" (from $y = 0$ to $y = 10$). Either way, we conclude that $f(1) \leq 10$. ∎

EXAMPLE 6 Suppose that $f(0) = 3$ and $f'(x) \leq 2$ for all x. What can be said about $f(2)$ and $f(-4)$? What if $f'(x) \geq 2$ for all x?

Solution First we apply the speed limit law on the interval $[0, 2]$. Because the speed limit $f'(x) \leq 2$ holds on this interval, we have

$$f(2) - f(0) \leq 2 \cdot (2 - 0) = 4.$$

We also know that $f(0) = 3$; it follows that $f(2) \leq 7$.

Now $f'(x) \leq 2$ also holds for x in $[-4, 0]$, so the law says that

$$f(0) - f(-4) = 3 - f(-4) \leq 2 \cdot \big(0 - (-4)\big) = 8,$$

which implies that $f(-4) \geq -5$.

If $f'(x) \geq 2$ for all x, then the scofflaw principle, applied on $[0, 2]$, says that $f(2) - f(0) \geq 2 \cdot 2 = 4$, so $f(2) \geq 7$. Applying the same principle on $[-4, 0]$, we get $f(0) - f(-4) \geq 2 \cdot 4 = 8$; consequently, $f(-4) \leq f(0) - 8 = -5$. Thus, we've shown $f(-4) \leq -5$ and $f(2) \geq 7$. ∎

EXAMPLE 7 Suppose (as in Example 6) that $f(0) = 3$ and that $f'(x) \leq 2$ for all x. What can be said about $f(x)$ for *any* value of x? What does the result mean graphically?

Solution In Example 6 we used the speed limit law (twice) to find that $f(-4) \geq -5$ and $f(2) \leq 7$. But there's nothing really special about the inputs $x = -4$ and $x = 2$. Since the "speed limit" $f'(x) \leq 2$ holds for *all* x, the same sort of reasoning applies to *any* input interval. Consider, for instance, the interval $[0, b]$, where b is any positive number. Then the speed limit law says that

$$f(b) - f(0) \leq 2 \cdot (b - 0),$$

Remember: f(0) = 3.

which implies that $f(b) \leq 2b + 3$. ◄ Similarly, for $a < 0$, the speed limit law applied on the interval $[a, 0]$ gives

$$f(0) - f(a) \leq 2 \cdot (0 - a),$$

which implies that $f(a) \geq 2a + 3$.

These inequalities have a nice geometric meaning. Let g be the linear function $g(x) = 2x + 3$; note that g always sticks *exactly* to the speed limit. ◄ The inequalities above say that f and g are related to each other as illustrated in Figure 5.

Here the speed limit is 2, since f'(x) ≤ 2.

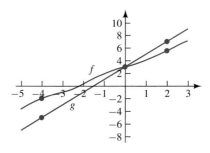

FIGURE 5
Racing functions

The picture shows that f and g "agree" at $x = 0$, and that f never rises faster than g. Our work above says that f lies *above* g before $x = 0$, and that f lies *below* g after $x = 0$. (The marked points at $x = -4$ and $x = 2$ illustrate these properties.) ■

BASIC EXERCISES

Exercises 1–10 refer to the functions P, V, and A defined on pages 36 and 37.

1. What does the statement $P(2) = 100$ mean?

2. What does the statement $P(7) < 0$ mean?

3. What does the statement $V(2) = 70$ mean?

4. What does the statement $V(6.5) = -60$ mean?

5. What does the statement $V(t) = P'(t)$ say about the relationship between the functions P and V?

6. What does the statement $A(t) = V'(t)$ say about the relationship between the functions V and A?

7. Suppose that P is measured in kilometers rather than miles. In this case, what units are associated with $V = P'$?

8. Suppose that t is measured in seconds rather than hours. In this case, what units are associated with $A = V'$?

9. What is the slope of the line tangent to the graph of $P(t)$ at $t = 2$?

10. Find an equation of the line tangent to the graph of $P(t)$ at $t = 6.5$.

11. Suppose that $B(t)$ is the balance in a bank account (in

dollars) t years after the account was established. What is the meaning of $B'(t)$?

12. Suppose that f is the linear function $f(x) = 2 - 5x$. Explain why f' is the constant function $f'(x) = -5$.

13. Suppose that g is the linear function $g(x) = 3x - 1$.
   (a) If x increases by Δx, by how much does the value of g increase?
   (b) Evaluate $g'(x)$.

14. Let f be the function shown graphically in Figure 3. Use the grid on the graph to estimate $f'(0)$.

15. Let f be the function shown graphically in Figure 3. Use the grid on the graph to estimate $f'(-2)$.

16. Let $v(t)$ be the velocity of an object in free fall at time t. What is the physical meaning of the statement $a(t) = v'(t) = -9.8$?

17. Let $v(t)$ be the velocity of an object in free fall at time t.
   (a) Explain why $v'(t) = -9.8$ implies that $v(t) = v_0 - 9.8t$, where v_0 is a constant.
   (b) What is the physical significance of the constant v_0 in part (a)?

18. What is the physical significance of the minus signs that appear in the equations for the height and velocity of an object in free fall given on page 41? [HINT: Compare graphs of the expressions $v_0 - 9.8t$ and $v_0 + 9.8t$.]

19. Example 4 claims "Height is greatest at the instant when upward velocity is zero." Explain why this statement is true.

20. Suppose that the pitcher in Example 4 throws the ball with an initial vertical velocity of 110 feet per second. Will the ball hit the ceiling of the Metrodome?

21. What are the formulas for the height and velocity of a ball thrown from an initial height of 5 feet with an initial vertical velocity of 30 ft/sec?

22. What are the formulas for the height and velocity of a ball thrown *downward* from a height of 100 feet at a speed of 40 ft/sec?

23. Interpret Example 5 in "car talk."

24. Let f be the function described in Example 5.
   (a) Show that $f(3) \leq 30$.
   (b) Is $f(25) < 300$? Justify your answer.

25. Let h be a function such that (i) $h(0) = 0$, and (ii) $h'(x) \leq -2$ for all $x \geq 0$.
   (a) Show that $h(5) \leq -10$.
   (b) Explain why $h(3) \leq 5$ must be true.
   (c) Explain parts (a) and (b) in "car talk."

26. Let g be a function such that $g(0) = 5$, and $g'(x) \leq 10$ if $x \geq 0$. Show that $g(1) \leq 15$.

27. Suppose that $f(0) = 2$ and $f'(x) \leq 4$ for all x. What can be said about the values $f(1)$ and $f(-3)$? [HINT: See Example 6.]

28. Suppose that $f(0) = 2$ and $f'(x) \geq 4$ for all x. What can be said about the values $f(1)$ and $f(-3)$?

29. Suppose that $g(0) = 1$ and $g'(x) \geq 3$ for all x.
   (a) What can be said about $g(x)$ for *any* value of x? [HINT: See Example 7.]
   (b) What does the result in part (a) mean graphically?

30. Suppose that $g(0) = 1$ and $g'(x) \leq 3$ for all x.
   (a) What can be said about $g(x)$ for *any* value of x?
   (b) What does the result in part (a) mean graphically?

In Exercises 31–39, suppose that an object can move only along the positive x-axis. Sketch the object's

   (a) *position vs. time graph;*
   (b) *velocity vs. time graph; and,*
   (c) *acceleration vs. time graph,*

31. if the object is standing still.

32. if the object is moving away from the origin at a constant velocity.

33. if the object is moving towards the origin at a constant velocity.

34. if the object first moves to the left, then to the right.

35. if the object first moves to the right, then to the left.

36. if the object is moving away from the origin at a steadily increasing speed.

37. if the object is moving towards the origin at a steadily increasing speed.

38. if the object is moving away from the origin at a steadily decreasing speed.

39. if the object is moving towards the origin at a steadily decreasing speed.

40. Suppose that $D(t)$ represents the depth (in meters) of the water in the deep end of a swimming pool t hours after noon on the day after Labor Day.
   (a) Interpret the statement $D(1) = 3$.
   (b) Interpret the statement $D'(1) = -0.5$.

41. Let $H(t)$ represent the time (in hours) between sunrise and sunset t days after January 1.
   (a) Interpret the statement $H'(100) = 0.05$.
   (b) For which values of t is $H'(t) < 0$? Justify your answer.

Exercises 42–44 refer to the function f whose graph is shown below.

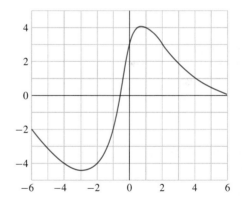

42. Rank $f'(-3)$, $f'(-2)$, $f'(0)$, $f'(1)$, and $f'(4)$ in increasing order.

43. Is $f'(-1) > 1$? Justify your answer.

44. Is $f'(3) < -2$? Justify your answer.

45. Let $f(x) = 5$.
   (a) Evaluate $f'(11)$.
   (b) Find a formula for $f'(x)$.

46. Let $g(z) = -2z$.
   (a) Evaluate $g'(37)$.
   (b) Find a formula for $g'(z)$.

Exercises 47 and 48 refer to a function f whose derivative function f′ is graphed below. [NOTE: The graph of f is not shown.]

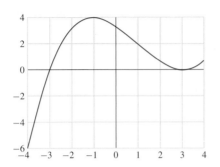

47. Suppose that $f(1) = 5$. Find an equation of the line tangent to the graph of f at the point $(1, 5)$.

48. Suppose that $f(-3) = -6$. Find an equation of the line tangent to the graph of f at the point $(-3, -6)$.

49. Suppose that the slope of the curve $y = g(x)$ at $x = 4$ is -2 and that $g(4) = 3$.
  (a) Evaluate $g'(4)$.
  (b) Find an equation of the line tangent to the curve at the point $(4, 3)$.

50. Suppose that $y = 3x + 1$ is an equation of the line tangent to the curve $y = F(x)$ at the point $(2, F(2))$.
  (a) Explain why $F(2) = 7$.
  (b) Explain why $F'(2) = 3$.

FURTHER EXERCISES

In Exercises 51 and 52, interpret the sentence as a statement about a function and its derivative. Indicate clearly what the function is, what the variable means, and appropriate units for each; then sketch a possible graph of the function.

51. The work force is growing more slowly now than it was 5 years ago.

52. Health care costs continue to rise but at a slower rate than 3 years ago.

53. Suppose that hot coffee is poured into a cup in a $25\,°C$ room. Let $T(t)$ represent the temperature (in $°C$) of the coffee in the cup at time t minutes after it was poured.
  (a) Sketch a graph of $T(t)$.
  (b) What units are associated with $T'(t)$?
  (c) Is $T(5) > 0$? Justify your answer.
  (d) Is $T'(5) > 0$? Justify your answer.
  (e) Explain why $T(300) \approx 25$.
  (f) Explain why $T'(300) \approx 0$.

54. The height of a ball (in feet) t seconds after it is thrown is given by $h(t) = -16t^2 + 38t + 74$; its (upward) velocity at time t is $v(t) = -32t + 38$.
  (a) From what height was the ball thrown?
  (b) What was the ball's initial velocity? Was it thrown up or down? How can you tell?
  (c) Was the ball's height increasing or decreasing at time $t = 2$?
  (d) At what time did the ball reach its maximum height? How high was it then?
  (e) How long was the ball in the air?

55. Suppose that $f'(x) = 1$ for all x. Find an algebraic expression for $f(x)$ if $f(0) = 2$.

56. Suppose that $f'(x) = 1$ for all x. Find an algebraic expression for $f(x)$ if $f(1) = 2$.

57. Suppose that $f'(x) = -3$ for all x. Find an algebraic expression for $f(x)$ if $f(0) = -2$.

58. Suppose that $f'(x) = -3$ for all x. Find an algebraic expression for $f(x)$ if $f(-1) = -2$.

59. Suppose that the line tangent to f at $(5, 2)$ passes through the point $(0, 1)$. Find $f(5)$ and $f'(5)$. Justify your answers.

60. Suppose that the line tangent to the curve $y = f(x)$ at $x = 3$ passes through the points $(-2, 3)$ and $(4, -1)$. Find $f(3)$ and $f'(3)$.

61. If $f'(x) = g'(x)$ for all x, must $f(x) = g(x)$ for all x?

62. Suppose that $f'(x) > 0$ for all x in the interval $(2, 7)$. Explain why $f(4) < f(5)$.

63. Suppose that $f'(x) \le 0$ for all x in the interval $(2, 7)$. Explain why $f(3) \ge f(6)$.

64. (a) Suppose that $f'(x) \le 0$ for all x in $[a, b]$ and $f(a) = c$. Use the speed limit law to show that $f(x) \le c$ for all x in $[a, b]$.
  (b) Suppose that $f'(x) \ge 0$ for all x in $[a, b]$ and $f(a) = c$. Use the speed limit law to show that $f(x) \ge c$ for all x in $[a, b]$.
  (c) Use parts (a) and (b) to prove that if $f'(x) = 0$ for all x in $[a, b]$, then f is a constant function on the interval $[a, b]$.

Here we estimate derivatives by "zooming in until the graph looks straight." We're usually more interested here in specific values of f′ than in f′ as a function, though we do use the zooming technique to "discover" some functional properties, such as that f′ = f when f(x) = e^x.

1.5 ESTIMATING DERIVATIVES: A CLOSER LOOK

In the preceding section we gave two informal descriptions of the derivative, one with rates and the other with slopes. This section is—quite literally—a closer look at the slope interpretation of the derivative. By "zooming in" on a function near an input value $x = a$, we'll both estimate numerical values of f' and see more clearly what the derivative means.

The slope of a graph at a point

As we've seen, the slope of a curve at a point P can be thought of as the slope of the **tangent line** at P—that is, the straight line through P that "fits" the curve at P. ➡ With this description, informal as it is, we can estimate derivatives for many calculus functions.

Remember the headlights-through-fog analogy? See page 40.

EXAMPLE 1 Let $f(x) = x^2$. Use tangent lines to estimate $f'(1)$ and $f'(-1.5)$. Interpret the results as rates of change.

Solution Figure 1 shows the graph of f together with reasonable candidates for tangent lines at $x = 1$ and $x = -1.5$.

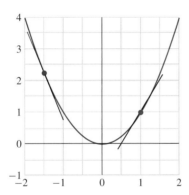

FIGURE 1
$y = x^2$ and two tangent lines

We can use the graph to estimate the slope of each tangent line. The line at $x = 1$, for instance, seems to rise 2 units as it runs 1, so its slope is 2. Similarly, the tangent line at $x = -1.5$ seems to have slope about -3. We conclude: $f'(1) \approx 2$; $f'(-1.5) \approx -3$.

In the language of rates, the results mean that (i) at $x = 1$, y is increasing twice as fast as x; and (ii) at $x = -1.5$, y *decreases* three times as fast as x *increases*. ∎

Zooming in Drawing a tangent line is one way to estimate the graph's slope at a point. The method works because, near the point in question, the graph and the tangent line are almost indistinguishable.

Another strategy for estimating slope is to "zoom in" on the point in question, perhaps repeatedly, until the graph *itself* looks like a straight line. Once the graph looks straight, it's easy to estimate the slope. One can also "zoom in numerically" on the point in question, using a table of values. We illustrate both types of zooming in the next example.

EXAMPLE 2 Let $f(x) = x^2$, as in Example 1. Estimate $f'(1)$ again, this time by zooming in on the graph. Estimate $f'(-1.5)$ by zooming in numerically. Find equations for both tangent lines.

Solution Zooming in successively on the f-graph near $(1, 1)$ gives the results shown in Figures 2(a) and 2(b).

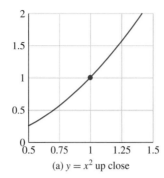

(a) $y = x^2$ up close

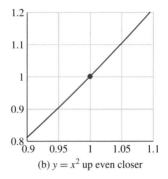

(b) $y = x^2$ up even closer

FIGURE 2
Closer and closer looks

With a calculator it's easy to produce tables of function values. Doing so with a small x-increment amounts to a numerical form of zooming. This is a nice classroom exercise, and gives another view of what "locally linear" means.

In the right-hand picture the graph looks virtually straight; its slope seems to be about 2. Thus, the (approximate) tangent line has slope 2 and passes through $(1, 1)$; its point–slope equation is therefore $y = 2(x - 1) + 1$.

To "zoom in numerically" near $x = -1.5$, we can look at a table of closely-spaced values of f: ◄

We could zoom in further by taking even more closely-spaced values.

Values of $f(x) = x^2$ near $x = -1.5$						
x	-1.8	-1.7	-1.6	-1.5	-1.4	-1.3	-1.2
$f(x)$	3.24	2.89	2.56	2.25	1.96	1.69	1.44

We got the same result graphically in Example 1.

Notice the trend: An *increase* of 0.1 in x produces a *decrease* of about -0.3 in $f(x)$, so the rate of change of $f(x)$ with respect to x seems to be -3. ◄ Because the tangent line passes through the point $(-1.5, 2.25)$ with slope -3, its point–slope equation is $y = -3(x + 1.5) + 2.25$. ∎

When zooming works: local linearity

The simple strategy just illustrated works remarkably well. Zooming in either graphically or numerically on almost any calculus function f, at almost any point $(a, f(a))$ eventually produces what looks like a straight line with slope $f'(a)$. We'll call a function with this property **locally linear** (or **locally straight**) at $x = a$. ◄ Local linearity means that f "looks like a line" near $x = a$ and therefore has a well-defined slope at $x = a$.

These are informal descriptions, not "official" math language.

Example 2 showed that the quadratic function $f(x) = x^2$ is locally linear at $x = 1$. Now let's zoom in on a trigonometric function.

EXAMPLE 3 Is $f(x) = \sin x$ locally linear at $x = 1.4$? What does the answer say about f'?

Solution Figures 3(a) and 3(b) give two views of the sine graph near the target point $P = (1.4, \sin 1.4) \approx (1.4, 0.9854)$.

(a) $y = \sin x$ near $P = (1.4, \sin 1.4)$ (b) Zooming in near $P = (1.4, \sin 1.4)$

FIGURE 3
Two views of the sine graph

In Figure 3(b), the sine graph is almost straight. To estimate the slope at P we can use any two points from the graph. Using $x = 1.38$ and $x = 1.42$, we find (approximately, of course) a slope of 0.17. In function notation, $f'(1.4) \approx 0.17$. (We'll see in Chapter 2 that the *exact* answer is $\cos 1.4 \approx 0.169967$, which is very close to our graphical estimate.) ∎

When zooming fails Not every function is locally linear at every point. A "kinked" graph, for instance, can't be straightened by repeated zooming.

EXAMPLE 4 Let $f(x) = |x|$. Does $f'(0)$ exist? Does $f'(a)$ exist if $a \neq 0$?

Solution Figures 4(a) and 4(b) show results of zooming near the origin:

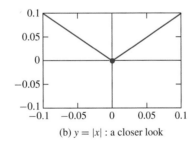

(a) $y = |x|$ (b) $y = |x|$: a closer look

FIGURE 4
Two looks at a graph

There's no mistake in the pictures—zooming has no effect at all on the kink at the origin. In mathematical terms, $f'(0)$ *does not exist*.

For $a \neq 0$, on the other hand, the graph is *already* straight, with slope ± 1, so there's no problem with derivatives: $f'(a) = 1$ if $a > 0$, and $f'(a) = -1$ if $a < 0$. In short, $f(x) = |x|$ is *not* locally linear at $x = 0$, but *is* locally linear everywhere else. ∎

Students may assume that any type of zooming is good enough to detect local linearity. But zooming repeatedly with different zoom factors in the coordinate directions can straighten out a kink—see the aside on zoom factors and distortion. (One view of continuity at a point is that zooming repeatedly in the x-direction only produces a horizontal line.)

Zoom factors and distortion. Throughout this section, "zooming in" means "zooming in with equal zoom factors in both coordinate directions." Zooming repeatedly with *different* zoom factors can so distort the picture that all information is lost.

Consider, for example, the kink at $x = 0$ on the graph $y = |x|$, as in Example 4. Zooming in repeatedly—but *only* in the x-direction (say with zoom factors 4 in x and 1 in y)—gradually flattens out the vee. Eventually, the graph looks horizontal. Try it.

Vertical tangent lines For most graphs we'll see, the zooming-until-straight strategy works fine; it gives a line whose slope is (approximately, at least) the derivative in question. But here is one important exception: For some graphs, at some points, zooming reveals a *vertical* tangent line; vertical lines have undefined slope. A graph of the cube root function (Figure 5) shows what can happen:

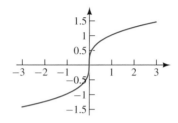

FIGURE 5
$f(x) = \sqrt[3]{x}$

As the picture shows, the y-axis is tangent to the curve at $(0, 0)$. Because the (vertical) y-axis has undefined slope, the derivative $f'(0)$ doesn't exist. (In Section 2.3 we'll give another reason, using a symbolic calculation, why $f'(0)$ does not exist.)

Plotting slope information at various points helps students see the derivative as a function rather than only pointwise.

Plotting the rate function

Zooming in or drawing tangent lines to the graph of f lets us estimate $f'(a)$ for various values of a. By pooling such information we can *plot* an estimated derivative function. The results can be surprising.

EXAMPLE 5 For $f(x) = x^2$, plot $f'(x)$. Then guess a formula for $f'(x)$.

Solution In Example 1 we estimated that $f'(1) = 2$ and $f'(-1.5) = -3$. From the mirror symmetry of the graph $y = x^2$, a few more values come easily:

x	-1.5	-1	0	1	1.5
$f'(x)$	-3	-2	0	2	3

Plotting these points (Figure 6) suggests that the graph of f' is a straight line through the origin, with slope 2. In other words, it appears that f' is a *linear* function, with equation $f'(x) = 2x$. (Our guess *is* correct, as we'll soon verify by symbolic calculation.) ∎

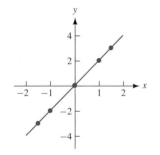

FIGURE 6
Graph of f'

If we apply the technique just illustrated to the natural exponential function $y = e^x$, we get an interesting surprise—one that helps explain the adjective "natural."

EXAMPLE 6 Let $f(x) = e^x$. Use tangent lines to plot f'; then guess a formula for f'.

Solution Figure 7 shows the graph of f (drawn dotted) with several small segments of tangent lines (drawn solid):

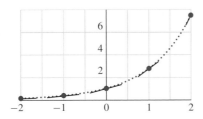

FIGURE 7
Tangent segments to $y = e^x$

Using a ruler or any convenient plotting technology, one can estimate the slope of each tangent segment. Several such results (rounded to one decimal place) are tabulated below.

The derivative of $f(x) = e^x$—graphical estimates					
x	-2	-1	0	1	2
y	0.135	0.368	1.000	2.718	7.389
Slope at (x, y)	0.1	0.4	1.0	2.7	7.4

Joining the slope data with a smooth curve (Figure 8) gives a striking result.

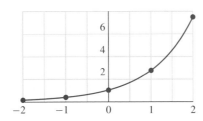

FIGURE 8
Derivative of $f(x) = e^x$

The graphs suggest that f and f' are identical! Indeed they are: ➡

If $f(x) = e^x$, then $f'(x) = e^x$. The natural exponential function is its own derivative.

Another way to say the same thing is to observe that $f(x) = e^x$ is a solution of the **differential equation** $f'(x) = f(x)$. (A differential equation, or **DE**, is any equation that involves derivatives. We'll return to the important topic of DEs in later chapters.) This striking property makes the natural exponential function one of the most important in all of mathematics. ∎

We'll prove this symbolically in Chapter 2.

This is the book's first allusion to DEs, an idea we allude to often but informally, and only as the opportunity arises naturally. This is no DE course, but we want students to see the DE formalism and how it naturally expresses properties of functions and their derivatives.

BASIC EXERCISES

Exercises 1–11 refer to the function $f(x) = x^2$ discussed in Examples 1 and 2.

1. Use the grid on the graph of f in Figure 1 to estimate the slope of the tangent line at $x = 1$.

2. Use the grid on the graph of f in Figure 1 to estimate the slope of the tangent line at $x = -1.5$.

3. Find an equation of the line tangent to f at $x = 1$.

4. Find an equation of the line tangent to f at $x = -1.5$.

5. What does the statement $f'(-1) = -2$ mean in the language of rates of change?

6. By estimating the coordinates of two points on the graph in Figure 2(b), show that the slope of the "line" is about 2.

7. Explain why the graphs of f and $\ell(x) = 2x - 1$ are visually indistinguishable when drawn in the plotting window $[0.9, 1.1] \times [0.9, 1.1]$.

8. Explain why the graphs of f and $L(x) = -3x - 2.25$ are visually indistinguishable when drawn in the plotting window $[-1.6, -1.4] \times [1.9, 2.6]$.

9. (a) Fill in the missing entries in the table below.

x	0.7	0.8	0.9	1.0	1.1	1.2	1.3
$f(x)$	0.49			1.00		1.44	

(b) Use the table in part (a) to estimate $f'(1)$.

10. Estimate $f'(1.5)$ by zooming in numerically.

11. Estimate $f'(-1)$ by zooming in numerically.

12. Suppose that f is locally linear at $x = 3$. Explain what this means about f.

13. Let $f(x) = \sin x$. Using $x = 1.38$ and $x = 1.42$, show that $f'(1.4)$ is approximately 0.17. [HINT: See Example 3.]

14. Let $f(x) = \sin x$
   (a) Find a viewing window centered at the point $(3, f(3))$ in which the graph of f appears to be linear.
   (b) Estimate $f'(3)$.

15. Let $f(x) = \sin x$.
   (a) Fill in the missing entries in the table below.

x	1.37	1.38	1.39	1.40	1.41	1.42	1.43
$f(x)$	0.97991			0.98545		0.98865	

(b) Use the table in part (a) to estimate $f'(1.4)$.

16. Let $f(x) = \sin x$. Use numerical zooming to estimate $f'(-1.4)$.

17. Let $f(x) = |x|$. [See Example 4.]
   (a) Evaluate $f'(2)$.
   (b) Evaluate $f'(-3)$.
   (c) Explain why $f'(0)$ does not exist.

18. Let $g(x) = 1 - |x|$.
   (a) Evaluate $f'(2)$.
   (b) Evaluate $f'(-3)$.
   (c) Does $f'(0)$ exist?

19. Let $f(x) = x^2$. Use the symmetry of the graph of f and the fact that $f'(1) = 2$ to explain why $f'(-1) = -2$. [HINT: See Example 5.]

20. Let $f(x) = x^2$. Explain why $f'(-1.5) = -3$ implies that $f'(1.5) = 3$.

21. Let $f(x) = x^3$. Use the symmetry of the graph of f and the fact that $f'(-1) = 3$ to explain why $f'(1) = 3$.

22. Let $f(x) = x^5$. Use the symmetry of the graph of f and the fact that $f'(2) = 80$ to find the value of $f'(-2)$.

23. Let $f(x) = x^2$.
   (a) Example 5 suggests that f' is the linear function $f'(x) = 2x$. Use this to "predict" $f'(3)$.
   (b) Use numerical or graphical zooming to estimate $f'(3)$. Is the result consistent with the prediction in part (a)?

24. Let $f(x) = e^x$.
   (a) Fill in the missing entries in the table below; then use the tabulated values to estimate $f'(0.98)$, $f'(1)$, and $f'(1.03)$.

x	0.97	0.98	0.99	1.00	1.01	1.02	1.03
$f(x)$	2.63794			2.71828		2.77319	

(b) Are your results in part (a) consistent with the assertion made in Example 6 that $f'(x) = f(x)$? Justify your answer.

25. Let $f(x) = e^x$.
   (a) Use zooming to estimate $f'(0.5)$.
   (b) Is your result in part (a) consistent with the assertion made in Example 6 that $f'(x) = f(x)$? Justify your answer.

26. Let $f(x) = e^x$.
   (a) Fill in the missing entries in the table below; then use the table to estimate $f'(1.48)$, $f'(1.5)$, and $f'(1.53)$.

x	1.47	1.48	1.49	1.50	1.51	1.52	1.53
$f(x)$	4.34924			4.48169		4.57223	

(b) Are your results in parts (a) consistent with the assertion made in Example 6 that $f'(x) = f(x)$? Justify your answer.

27. The graph of a function f is shown below.

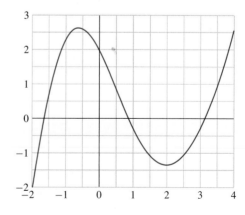

(a) Fill in the missing entries in the table below. [*NOTE: Because f is given graphically, your answers will be estimates. However, your answers should approximate the exact values within ±0.5.*]

x	−2	−1	0	1
$f'(x)$	6.0			−2.0

x	2	2.5	3	4
$f'(x)$		1.0		3.5

(b) Use your answers to part (a) to sketch a graph of f'.

28. The graph of a function f is shown below.

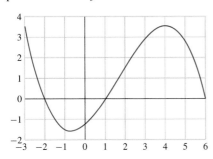

(a) Fill in the missing entries in the table below.

x	−3	−2	−1	0	1
$f'(x)$	−4.9			0.8	

x	2	3	4	5	6
$f'(x)$		1.1			−4.0

(b) Sketch a graph of f'.

29. Let $f(x) = \sqrt{x}$.
   (a) Use zooming to estimate $f'(1/4)$, $f'(1)$, $f'(9/4)$, $f'(4)$, $f'(25/4)$, and $f'(9)$.
   (b) Use your results from part (a) to sketch a graph of f' over the interval $[0, 9]$.

30. Let $f(x) = \sqrt{x}$.
   (a) Why is $f'(0)$ undefined?
   (b) Why is $f'(-1)$ undefined?

31. Let $f(x) = e^{-x}$.
   (a) Use zooming to estimate $f'(-1)$, $f'(0)$, $f'(1)$, $f'(1.5)$, and $f'(2)$.
   (b) Use your results from part (a) to sketch a graph of f' over the interval $[-1, 2]$.

32. Let $f(x) = \ln x$.
   (a) Use zooming to estimate $f'(1/10)$, $f'(1/5)$, $f'(1/2)$, $f'(1)$, $f'(2)$, and $f'(5)$.
   (b) Use your results from part (a) to sketch a graph of f' over the interval $[0, 5]$.

33. Do the points shown in the following table lie on a line? If so, find an equation of the line. If not, explain how you know that they do not.

x	5.2	5.3	5.4	5.6	5.9	6.5
y	27.8	29.2	30.6	33.4	37.6	46.0

34. Do the points shown in the following table lie on a line? If so, find an equation of the line. If not, explain how you know that they do not.

x	0	1	3	6	10	15
y	0.000	0.785	1.249	1.406	1.471	1.504

FURTHER EXERCISES

35. Let $f(x) = x^3$.
   (a) Use zooming to estimate $f'(0)$, $f'(1/2)$, $f'(1)$, $f'(3/2)$, and $f'(2)$.
   (b) Explain why $f'(-x) = f'(x)$ for all x.
   (c) Use your results from parts (a) and (b) to sketch a graph of f' over the interval $[-2, 2]$.

36. Let $g(x) = x^{1/3}$.
   (a) Estimate $g'(-1)$ and $g'(1)$.
   (b) Why is $g'(0)$ undefined?
   (c) Sketch a graph of g' over the intervals $[-3, 0)$ and $(0, 3]$.

37. Let $f(x) = 1/x$.
   (a) Use zooming to estimate $f'(1/4)$, $f'(1/2)$, $f'(1)$, $f'(2)$, and $f'(3)$.
   (b) Use symmetry to explain why $f'(-x) = f'(x)$ for all $x \neq 0$.

   (c) Use your results from parts (a) and (b) to sketch a graph of f' over the intervals $[-3, 0)$ and $(0, 3]$.

38. Let $f(x) = \sin x$.
   (a) Use zooming to estimate $f'(0)$, $f'(\pi/6)$, $f'(\pi/4)$, $f'(\pi/3)$, $f'(\pi/2)$, and $f'(\pi)$.
   (b) Use the symmetry of the sine function and your answers from part (a) to estimate $f'(2\pi/3)$, $f'(3\pi/4)$, and $f'(5\pi/6)$. Check your answers using zooming.
   (c) Sketch a graph of f' over the interval $[0, 2\pi]$.

39. Let $f(x) = \cos x$.
   (a) Use zooming to estimate $f'(0)$, $f'(\pi/6)$, $f'(\pi/4)$, $f'(\pi/3)$, $f'(\pi/2)$, and $f'(\pi)$.
   (b) Sketch a graph of f' over the interval $[0, 2\pi]$.

40. (a) Zoom in on the graph of $y = e^x$, near the point $(0, 1)$, until the graph looks like a straight line. What's the slope of this line?

(b) Zoom in on the graph of $y = 5^x$ near the point $(0, 1)$ until the graph looks like a straight line. Estimate the slope of this line as accurately as possible.

(c) Zoom in on the graph of $y = 10^x$ near the point $(0, 1)$ until the graph looks like a straight line. Estimate the slope of this line as accurately as possible.

(d) How are the numbers $\ln e$, $\ln 5$, and $\ln 10$ related to your answers to parts (a)–(c)?

41. (a) Zoom in on the graph of $y = \ln x$, near the point $(1, 0)$, until the graph looks like a straight line. What's the slope of this line?

(b) Zoom in on the graph of $y = \log_5 x$ near the point $(1, 0)$ until the graph looks like a straight line. Estimate the slope of this line as accurately as possible.

(c) Zoom in on the graph of $y = \log_{10} x$ near the point $(1, 0)$ until the graph looks like a straight line. Estimate the slope of this line as accurately as possible.

(d) How are the numbers $\ln e$, $\ln 5$, and $\ln 10$ related to your answers to parts (a)–(c)?

42. Estimate the slope of the line tangent to the graph of $y = e^x$ at $x = 0$, $x = 1$, and $x = 2$. What is the constant of proportionality that relates y and y'?

43. (a) Estimate the slope of the line tangent to the graph of $y = 2^x$ at $x = 0$, $x = 1$, and $x = 2$. What is the constant of proportionality that relates y and y'?

(b) How is $\ln 2$ related to the constant of proportionality you found in part (a)?

44. (a) Estimate the slope of the line tangent to the graph of $y = 3^x$ at $x = 0$, $x = 1$, and $x = 2$. What is the constant of proportionality that relates y and y'?

(b) How is $\ln 3$ related to contant of proportionality you found in part (a)?

45. (a) Estimate the slope of the line tangent to the graph of $y = 10^x$ at $x = 0$, $x = 1$, and $x = 2$. What is the constant of proportionality that relates y and y'?

(b) How is $\ln 10$ related to the constant of proportionality you found in part (a)?

46. Estimate the slope of the line tangent to the graph of $y = \ln x$ at $x = 1/2$, $x = 2$, and $x = 10$. What is the constant of proportionality that relates x^{-1} and y'?

47. (a) Estimate the slope of the line tangent to the graph of $y = \log_2 x$ at $x = 1/2, x = 2$, and $x = 10$. What is the constant of proportionality that relates x^{-1} and y'?

(b) How is $\ln 2$ related to the constant of proportionality you found in part (a)?

48. (a) Estimate the slope of the line tangent to the graph of $y = \log_3 x$ at $x = 1/2, x = 2$, and $x = 10$. What is the constant of proportionality that relates x^{-1} and y'?

(b) How is $\ln 3$ related to the constant of proportionality you found in part (a)?

49. (a) Estimate the slope of the line tangent to the graph of $y = \log_{10} x$ at $x = 1/2, x = 2$, and $x = 10$. What is the constant of proportionality that relates x^{-1} and y'?

(b) How is $\ln 10$ related to the constant of proportionality you found in part (a)?

50. Let $g(x) = \sin x$. Estimate the rate of growth of g at each of the following points: $x = -3$, $x = 0$, $x = 1$, $x = 2$.

51. Let $h(x) = \cos x$. Estimate the rate of growth of h at each of the following points: $x = -3$, $x = 0$, $x = 1$, $x = 2$.

52. Suppose that $g'(1) = 2$. If $x \approx 1$ increases by the small amount Δx, approximately how much does g increase? Justify your answer.

53. Suppose that $h'(2) = -3$. If $x \approx 2$ increases by the small amount Δx, approximately how much does h decrease? Justify your answer.

54. Let $f(x) = x^2$ and $g(x) = 3x$. Find the value of x for which $f'(x) = g'(x)$.

55. Let $f(x) = x^2$ and $g(x) = -2x$. Find the value of x for which $f'(x) = g'(x)$.

56. Let $f(x) = x^{-1}$ and $g(x) = 2x$. Find the value of x for which $f'(x) = g'(x)$.

57. Let $f(x) = x^{-2}$ and $g(x) = -2x$. Find the value of x for which $f'(x) = g'(x)$.

58. Graph $f(x) = \pi/2 - x$ and $g(x) = \cos x$ on the same axes. What does the result suggest about $g'(\pi/2)$?

59. Graph $f(x) = \sin x$ and $g(x) = \pi - x$ on the same axes. What does the result suggest about $f'(\pi)$?

60. Let $f(x) = \sin x$. It is a fact that that $f'(0) = 1$. Use this fact and the symmetry of the sine function to explain why
(a) $f'(2\pi) = 1$
(b) $f'(\pi) = -1$

61. Let $g(x) = \cos x$. It is a fact that that $g'(\pi/4) = -\sqrt{2}/2$. Use this fact and the symmetry of the cosine function to evaluate
(a) $g'(9\pi/4)$
(b) $g'(-\pi/4)$
(c) $g'(3\pi/4)$

1.6 THE GEOMETRY OF DERIVATIVES

The geometric relationship between a function f and its derivative f' is easy to state:

For any input a, $f'(a)$ is the slope of the f-graph at $x = a$.

This statement—innocent as it appears—is as important as any in this book. This section and the next explore its geometric meaning and implications.

This important section treats the geometric relationship between a function f and the derivative f'. We want students to reason both from properties of f to properties of f' and vice versa. The section also revisits and refines important vocabulary terms: increasing/decreasing, concavity, extrema, etc. Technical hypotheses (e.g., continuity of f') are mentioned but not emphasized for the moment.

Graphs of f and f': an extended example

Graphs of a function f and its derivative f' appear in Figures 1(a) and 1(b). Three interesting points are labeled on each. Corresponding points (e.g., A and A') have the same x-coordinate.

(a) $y = f(x)$

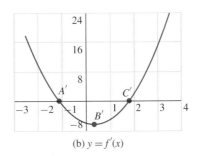
(b) $y = f'(x)$

FIGURE 1
A function and its derivative

The f'-graph describes slopes on the f-graph. At B, for instance, the f-graph seems to have slope around -6; for this reason, the f'-graph has height -6 at B'. First let's observe several straightforward geometric relationships between the two graphs, introducing some useful new terminology in the process.

- **The sign of f'**   The graph of f rises to the left of A, falls between A and C, and rises again to the right of C. This information is reflected in the *sign* of $f'(x)$: the f-graph rises where f' is positive; the f-graph falls where f' is negative. At A' and C', f' changes sign, so f itself changes direction at A and C. ➔

  A' and C' correspond to roots of f'.

- **Stationary, maximum, and minimum points**   The points A and C, with approximate coordinates $(-1.1, 4)$ and $(1.8, -8)$, are at high and low spots on the f-graph. To avoid confusion later, it will pay to be picky about language now—especially about the distinction between *inputs* to f and *outputs* from f.

  Here is the situation at $A \approx (-1.1, 4)$. The input point $x = -1.1$ is called a **local maximum point** of f; the corresponding output ($f(-1.1) \approx 4$) is called a **local maximum value** of f. At C, the graph's low spot, the situation is similar: $x = 1.8$ is a **local minimum point** of f, and $f(1.8) \approx -8$ is the corresponding **local minimum value** of f. The x-coordinates of both A and C are called **stationary points** of f. ➔ We say "local," not "global," because elsewhere in its domain (outside the picture, perhaps), f might assume larger or smaller values. The corresponding points A' and C' occur where the f'-graph crosses the x-axis (at **roots** of f').

  Careful definitions of all these terms will follow.

- **Concavity and inflection**   At the point B, the f-graph's **direction of concavity** changes from concave down to concave up. The x-coordinate of B (about $x = 0.3$) is called an **inflection point** of f. ➔ Notice another property of the inflection point: at B, the graph of f points *most steeply downward*.

  The corresponding position on the f'-graph, labeled B', is easier to see; it occurs at a local minimum point of f'. Later we'll use this property and some algebra to find the *exact* location of B. (Locating B or B' precisely by magnifying either graph doesn't work very well. Viewed closely, both graphs look like straight lines.)

We'll introduce the second derivative's link to concavity in the next section. Here it's seen in the graphs of f and f'.

Some authors call B itself an inflection point of the f-graph. For us, an inflection point is an input to f.

- **In the long run** The graph suggests that f blows up to the right of C and blows down to the left of A. In geometric terms, as $x \to \infty$, the graph of $f(x)$ rises more and more steeply. What happens over the same intervals on the f'-graph? To the right of C', f' is positive and increasing. To the left of A', f' is positive and decreasing.

What f' says about f

What the derivative function f' tells about slopes on the f-graph has many important geometric implications. We summarize several below.

Well-behaved functions. Many ideas in this section depend on both f and f' being reasonably "nice," or "well behaved." "Nice enough" means, roughly, that neither f nor f' displays sudden jumps or breaks. Any function f whose derivative function f' is continuous (i.e., without breaks) is nice enough for us. Fortunately, most calculus functions *are* nice in this sense. As we proceed we'll see more of what "nice" means and why it matters.

Increasing or decreasing? A function f is said to **increase** where its graph rises (from left to right!) and to **decrease** where its graph falls. The following definition captures these natural ideas in analytic language.

> **DEFINITION** Let I denote the interval (a, b). A function f is **increasing** on I if
>
> $$f(x_1) < f(x_2) \qquad \text{whenever} \qquad a < x_1 < x_2 < b.$$
>
> f is **decreasing** on I if
>
> $$f(x_1) > f(x_2) \qquad \text{whenever} \qquad a < x_1 < x_2 < b.$$

In these definitions, $\le$ and $\ge$ replace $<$ and $>$.

Students may find terms like "nonincreasing" pedantic, but mastering these minor subtleties now will pay off later.

If $f(x_1) \le f(x_2)$ for $x_1 < x_2$, then f is **nondecreasing** on I; if $f(x_1) \ge f(x_2)$ for $x_1 < x_2$, then f is **nonincreasing** on I. ◄ In all four cases, f is called **monotonic** on I.

The derivative function f' detects whether f increases or decreases on an interval I. This crucial fact deserves emphasis:

> **FACT** If $f'(x) > 0$ for all x in I, then f increases on I. If $f'(x) < 0$ for all x in I, then f decreases on I.

It's surprising that such an innocuous claim is not trivial to prove.

The Fact certainly sounds reasonable. To say that $f'(x) > 0$ means that the f-graph has *positive* slope—that is, that the tangent line at x points upward. The Fact sounds even simpler when applied to cars: If a car f has *positive* velocity, then f always moves *forward*. Simple as all this sounds, a rigorous proof of the Fact requires one of calculus's "big theorems"—the mean value theorem, which we'll see in Chapter 4.

Behavior at a point Functions are often said to increase or decrease *at a point*. To say, for example, that f increases *at $x = 3$* means that f increases on some open interval—perhaps a small one—containing $x = 3$. ◄

An open interval does not contain its endpoints; Appendix B has details on intervals.

Now we can restate the preceding Fact (again we assume that both f and f' are smooth functions):

> **FACT** If $f'(a) > 0$, then f is increasing at $x = a$. If $f'(a) < 0$, then f is decreasing at $x = a$.

At $x = 1$, for instance, $f'(1) < 0$. The Fact says (and Figure 1 on page 55 agrees) that at $x = 1$ the f-graph is decreasing.

Derive carefully: a dangerous curve The preceding Fact has a tempting **converse:** ➤ If f is increasing at $x = a$, then $f'(a) > 0$. The converse statement is *false*, as the following example illustrates.

"Converse" is a technical word from logic. The converse of the implication $P \Rightarrow Q$ is the implication $Q \Rightarrow P$.

EXAMPLE 1 Where is the function $f(x) = x^3$ increasing? Where is $f'(x) > 0$? What happens at $x = 0$?

Solution As its graph (Figure 2) shows,

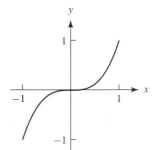

The graph is "flat" at $x = 0$ but has no maximum or minimum value.

FIGURE 2
$y = x^3$: **flat at the origin**

the function $f(x) = x^3$ increases *everywhere*. The graph also shows that $f'(x) > 0$ if $x \neq 0$ but that $f'(0) = 0$. The graph illustrates the important moral:

> *A stationary point may be* neither *a local maximum point nor a local minimum point.*

The graph in Figure 2 has a flat spot at $x = 0$ but neither a peak nor a valley there. Such a point is sometimes called a **terrace point**. ➤   ■

"Terrace point" isn't official math jargon. But maybe it should be because it meets a need.

What *can* be said about f' where f increases? This:

> **FACT** If f increases at $x = a$, then $f'(a) \geq 0$; if f decreases at $x = a$, then $f'(a) \leq 0$.

Thus, the derivative of an increasing function must be *nonnegative* but not necessarily *strictly positive*.

Maximum points, minimum points, and stationary points: definitions

The point A in Figure 1 corresponds to a local, but not a global, maximum value of f. Successful use of such technical language requires clear definitions.

> **DEFINITION** Let f be a function and x_0 a point of its domain.
>
> - x_0 is a **stationary point** of f if $f'(x_0) = 0$.
> - x_0 is a **local maximum point** of f if $f(x_0) \geq f(x)$ for all x in some open interval containing x_0. The number $f(x_0)$ is a **local maximum value** of f.
> - x_0 is a **global maximum point** of f if $f(x_0) \geq f(x)$ for all x in the domain of f. The number $f(x_0)$ is the **global maximum value** of f.
>
> (Local and global **minimum points** are defined similarly.)

Observe some linguistic subtleties:

The "point" terminology is potentially tricky for several reasons. One is the fact that (in our usage) a stationary point is a "point" of the domain of f, not a "point" on the graph of f.

- **Points vs. values** Local and global maximum *points* are inputs to a function; local and global maximum *values* are the corresponding outputs. The difference, although important, is sometimes blurred in informal speech. (The first full sentence following this one is impeccably correct.)

- **Local or global?** At a *local* maximum point, a function f may or may not assume a *global* maximum value. Minimum points, too, may be local, global, or both.

- **Extreme values** The word **extremum** (plural **extrema**) means "either a maximum or a minimum value." We'd say, for instance, that for the function f at the beginning of this section, both points A and C correspond to extrema of f.

The terminology is not completely standard.

- **Getting critical** Some authors use the term **critical point** in place of our **stationary point**. ◄ We like the latter because it suggests a graph's "flatness" at such a point. In Chapter 4, moreover, we'll use **critical point** in a slightly different way: to describe a point $x = a$ at which either $f'(a) = 0$ or $f'(a)$ is undefined.

See A and C on the graphs in Figure 1.

Finding maximum and minimum points Geometric intuition says that local maximum and local minimum values should occur at "flat" spots on a graph. ◄ This is indeed the case, assuming that f' exists at all points in question:

> **FACT** Suppose that f' exists for all x in the domain of f. Every local maximum or local minimum point x_0 of f is a root of f'—that is, $f'(x_0) = 0$.

This Fact is simple but very useful—it says that, when finding maximum and minimum values of a well-behaved function f, we can consider only a few candidates: the roots of f' and the endpoints (if any) of the domain of f. Every root of f' is a stationary point and so *possibly* a maximum or minimum point. But it's not a sure thing. We saw in Example 1 that a stationary point might be only a "terrace point"—a flat spot but neither a maximum point nor a minimum point.

The next (important) example shows how to sort through the possibilities.

This example is important—it helps students sort out for themselves the different types of stationary points.

EXAMPLE 2 Figure 3 shows the graph of a function f'; the graph of f is *not* shown (for the moment). Three points of interest are bulleted. Where, if anywhere, does f have local maximum or local minimum points? Why?

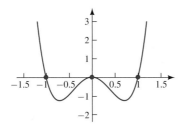

FIGURE 3
$y = f'(x)$

Solution   The three bullets (at $x = -1$, $x = 0$, and $x = 1$) are at stationary points of f. What type of stationary point is each one: a local maximum, a local minimum, or neither? To decide, we can check the sign of f' just *before* and just *after* each stationary point.

- **At $x = -1$**   Just before (to the left of) $x = -1$, we have $f'(x) > 0$. Therefore (by an earlier Fact), f increases until $x = -1$. Just after $x = -1$, $f'(x) < 0$, so f decreases immediately after $x = -1$. This means that f has a local *maximum* at $x = -1$.

- **At $x = 1$**   Consider values of x near $x = 1$. The graph shows that if $x < 1$, then $f'(x) < 0$; if $x > 1$, then $f'(x) > 0$. Therefore, reasoning as above, we see that f decreases before $x = 1$ and increases after $x = 1$, so f has a local *minimum* at $x = 1$.

- **At $x = 0$**   This time the graph shows that $f'(x) < 0$ on both sides of $x = 0$. Thus, f must decrease before *and* after $x = 0$; therefore $x = 0$ is neither a maximum nor a minimum point but just a flat spot in the f-graph.

Here, finally, is a possible f-graph (Figure 4):

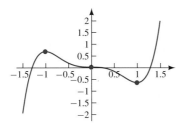

FIGURE 4
A graph with three interesting points   ■

The next Fact summarizes what we know about stationary points.

FACT (First derivative test)   Suppose that $f'(x_0) = 0$.

- If $f'(x) < 0$ for $x < x_0$ and $f'(x) > 0$ for $x > x_0$, then x_0 is a local minimum point.
- If $f'(x) > 0$ for $x < x_0$ and $f'(x) < 0$ for $x > x_0$, then x_0 is a local maximum point.

What about maximum and minimum values on a "crooked" graph? The next example illustrates one possibility.

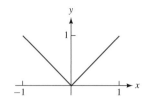

FIGURE 5
A graph with a kink

Students may be able to "feel" concavity and inflection by moving a ruler along the curve, keeping the ruler tangent to the curve at all times. The curve is concave down or up depending on whether the ruler turns clockwise or counterclockwise. At an inflection point the ruler changes direction.

EXAMPLE 3   The function $f(x) = |x|$ (see Figure 5) has a local (and global) minimum point at $x = 0$ but not a stationary point. The graph is "kinked" at $x = 0$ and thus has no tangent line and no well-defined slope there. In functional language, $f'(0)$ does not exist. Nevertheless, $x = 0$ is a local minimum point for f.   ■

Derivatives, concavity, and inflection points

So far we've described concavity and inflection points in graphical language. Here's a more formal definition:

> **DEFINITION**   The graph of f is **concave up** at $x = a$ if the slope function f' is increasing at $x = a$. The graph of f is **concave down** at $x = a$ if f' is decreasing at $x = a$. An input value at which a graph's direction of concavity *changes* is an **inflection point** of the graph.

The graphs of f and f' (Figure 1) illustrate all the possibilities:

- To the left of B, the f-graph is *concave down*; to the left of B', the f'-graph is decreasing.
- To the right of B, the f-graph is *concave up*; to the right of B' the f'-graph is increasing.
- B corresponds to an *inflection point* of f, and f' has a minimum point at B'.

The direction of concavity of the graph of f depends, as the definitions show, on whether f' increases or decreases. An inflection point of f occurs wherever f' *changes direction*—that is, wherever f' has a local minimum or a local maximum. In particular, the "terrace point" at the origin in Example 1 is also an inflection point of the function $f(x) = x^3$.

EXAMPLE 4   Discuss concavity of the sine function. Find all inflection points; explain the results in derivative language.

We'll show this carefully in Chapter 2.

Solution   It's a fact that if $f(x) = \sin x$, then $f'(x) = \cos x$. ◄ Graphs of f and f' (Figure 6) make this claim plausible.

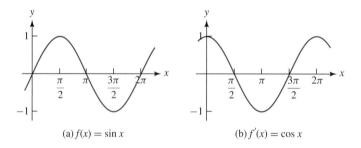

(a) $f(x) = \sin x$ (b) $f'(x) = \cos x$

FIGURE 6
Investigating concavity

Observe:

In this case the local maximum and minimum points are global, too.

- **Stationary points** f has stationary points (a local maximum point and a local minimum point) at $x = \pi/2$ and at $x = 3\pi/2$—exactly the roots of f'. ◄

- **Increasing or decreasing?** f increases on the intervals $(0, \pi/2)$ and $(3\pi/2, 2\pi)$; on the same intervals, f' is positive.

- **Concavity** f is concave *down* on $(0, \pi)$—where f' decreases—and concave *up* on $(\pi, 2\pi)$—where f' increases. In fact, f illustrates every possible combination of increasing or decreasing and concavity behavior.

- **Inflection points** f has an inflection point at each multiple of π—precisely where f' assumes a local maximum or local minimum. ∎

BASIC EXERCISES

1. Refer to the graphs of f and f' shown in Figure 1.

   (a) Draw the line that is tangent to the graph of f at A; then use the grid to estimate the slope of this line.

   (b) Is your result in part (a) consistent with the placement of the point A' on the graph of f' shown in Figure 1(b)? Justify your answer.

2. Refer to the graphs of f and f' shown on shown in Figure 1.

   (a) Draw the line that is tangent to the graph of f at B; then use the grid to estimate the slope of this line.

   (b) Is your result in part (a) consistent with the placement of the point B' on the graph of f' in Figure 1(b)? Justify your answer.

3. Explain why the point A shown in Figure 1(a) does not correspond to a global maximum value of f.

4. Suppose that $h(0) = -1$ and $h'(w) = 2$ for all w.

   (a) Is h decreasing on the interval $(0, \infty)$? Justify your answer.

   (b) Describe the graph of h as precisely as possible.

5. Suppose that a function g has a local minimum point at 2. What does this say about g?

6. Suppose that 3 is a local minimum value of a function h. What does this say about h?

7. Explain the difference between a local maximum point and a global maximum point.

8. Suppose that 5 is a local minimum point of a function f. Can 5 also be a global minimum point of f? Justify your answer.

9. What is a stationary point? (Give a graphical description.)

10. What is the relationship between the stationary points of a function and the function's extreme values?

11. Suppose that $f'(x) < 0$ for $-\infty < x < 3$, $f'(3) = 0$, and $f'(x) > 0$ for $x > 3$. Is $x = 3$ a local minimum point of the function f? Justify your answer.

12. Suppose that f' is increasing at $x = -2$. What does this imply about f?

13. What is an inflection point? (Give a graphical description.)

14. Explain how a graph of f' can be used to locate the inflection points of a function f.

15. Consider the function f whose derivative was shown in Figure 3. If $f(0) = 3$, sketch a graph of f.

In Exercises 16–20, f is the function shown below with several points labeled.

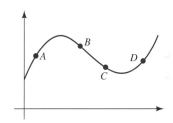

16. At which labeled points is f' positive? Justify your answer.

17. Between which pairs of labeled points does f have a stationary point?

18. Between which pair of labeled points does f have an inflection point?

19. Between which pair of labeled points is f' increasing?

20. Between which pair of labeled points does f' achieve its minimum value?

In Exercises 21–24, f is the function shown below.

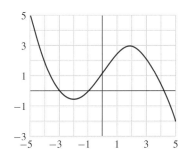

21. (a) On which intervals is f' negative? Justify your answer.

   (b) On which intervals is f' decreasing? Justify your answer.

22. (a) On which intervals is f' positive? Justify your answer.

   (b) On which intervals is f' increasing? Justify your answer.

23. Where does f' achieve its maximum value? Estimate this value of f'.

24. Sketch a graph of f'.

Exercises 25–36 concern a function g whose derivative is shown below. Use the graph of g' to answer the questions about g. [NOTE: The graph of g is not shown.]

25. On which intervals is g increasing?

26. On which intervals is g decreasing?

27. Where does g have stationary points?

28. Where does g have local maximum points?

29. Where does g have local minimum points?

30. Is g concave up at $x = 3$? Justify your answer.

31. Is g concave up at $x = 6$? Justify your answer.

32. The graph of g' has a local maximum point at $x = 3.8$ and a local minimum point at $x = 7.4$. What do these facts say about the graph of g?

33. Suppose that $g(0) = 0$. Sketch a graph of g.

34. Suppose that $g(3) = 4$. Find an equation of the line tangent to g at $x = 3$.

35. Suppose that $g(9) = -1$. Find an equation of the line tangent to g at $x = 9$.

36. Could g be the function $g(x) = x \sin x$? Justify your answer.

Exercises 37–45 concern a function f whose derivative is shown below. Use the graph of f' to answer the questions about f. [NOTE: The graph of f is not shown.]

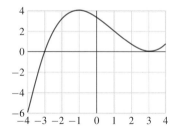

37. On which intervals is f increasing?

38. On which intervals is f decreasing?

39. Where does f have stationary points?

40. Where does f have local maximum points?

41. Where does f have local minimum points?

42. Is f concave up at $x = 2$? Justify your answer.

43. Where does f have points of inflection?

44. Suppose that $f(-3) = 2$. Find an equation of the line tangent to f at $x = -3$.

45. Suppose that $f(1) = 3$. Find an equation of the line tangent to f at $x = 1$.

In Exercises 46–49, use a graph of f to answer the following questions about f'.

   (a) How many roots does f' have? Where are they located?

   (b) On which intervals is f' positive?

   (c) Is f' increasing at $x = 2$?

   (d) Sketch a graph of f'.

46. $f(x) = 3 - x^2$

47. $f(x) = \dfrac{1}{1 + x^2}$

48. $f(x) = \dfrac{x - 2}{x^2 + 5}$

49. $f(x) = \ln x$

In Exercises 50–53, use the expression for f' to answer the following questions about f.

   (a) On which intervals, if any, is f increasing?

   (b) At which values of x, if any, does f have a stationary point?

   (c) At which values of x, if any, does f have a local minimum point?

   (d) On which intervals, if any, is f concave down?

   (e) Sketch a graph of f.

50. $f'(x) = x + 2$

51. $f'(x) = (x - 2)(x + 4)$

52. $f'(x) = \dfrac{x - 2}{x^2 + 5}$

53. $f'(x) = e^{-x^2}$

FURTHER EXERCISES

54. In the left-hand column below are graphs of several functions. In the right-hand column—in a different order— are graphs of the associated *derivative* functions. Match each function with its derivative.

[*Note: The scales on the graphs are not all the same.*]

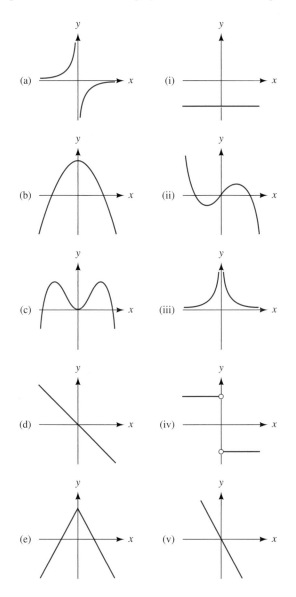

55–59. Sketch a graph of the derivative of each function labeled (i)–(v) in the right column of Exercise 54.

60. Sketch the graph of a function f for which $f(x) > 0$ and $f'(x) > 0$ for all x.

61. Sketch the graph of a function g for which $g(x) > 0$ and $g'(x) < 0$ for all x.

62. Sketch the graph of a function h for which $h(x) < 0$ and $h'(x) > 0$ for all x.

63. Sketch the graph of a function k for which $k(x) < 0$ and $k'(x) < 0$ for all x.

64. Let $f(x) = e^{\sin x}$. How many roots does f' have in the interval $[0, 2\pi]$? Where are they located? Justify your answers.

1.7 THE GEOMETRY OF HIGHER-ORDER DERIVATIVES

The derivative of a nice function f is another nice function, f'. ➡ Given the many uses of f', the next step is natural: **Differentiate** f'. ("Differentiate" means "find the derivative of.") The resulting function, denoted by f'', is called the **second derivative** of f.

Like f', the second derivative f'' carries useful information about f. What information? How do we read it? We discuss these questions in this section. But first, some friendly advice: With several functions (f, f', and f'') in the picture, it's easy to lose one's bearings. One organizing principle helps:

The derivative of any *function tells how fast that function increases or decreases.*

As before, "nice" means that all the functions and derivatives mentioned exist and have smooth, unbroken graphs.

We assume implicitly in much of this section that all the derivatives in question exist. We discuss existence (and the possibility of non-existence) in Chapter 2; here the point is to understand what f' and f'' say about f, not to worry unduly about their existence.

What f'' says about f: concavity revisited

The graph of f is concave up or down at $x = a$, depending on whether f' is increasing or decreasing at $x = a$. The preceding principle, applied to f', reads as follows:

If $f''(a) > 0$, then f' increases at $x = a$. If $f''(a) < 0$, then f' decreases at $x = a$.

This leads, in turn, to a useful test for concavity of f:

> **FACT**   The f-graph is concave up where $f'' > 0$; the f-graph is concave down where $f'' < 0$.

Observe:

This is a subtle point for students; they can discover or explore it for themselves with functions like x^3 and x^4.

- **What if $f'' = 0$?**   The Fact gives no information if $f''(a) = 0$. In that case, as we'll see, f may be concave up, concave down, or neither at $x = a$.
- **Concavity and acceleration**   Concavity has a nice physical interpretation in terms of acceleration. Suppose, for instance, that $f(x)$ represents a car's *position* east of a reference point at time x hours (as in the Bismarck car discussion on page 36). Then $f'(x)$ tells the car's *eastward velocity* at time x. Now $f''(x)$, being the rate of change of velocity, represents the car's *eastward acceleration*. Thus $f''(x) > 0$ when the car accelerates (eastward); $f''(x) < 0$ when the car decelerates.

Here is the automotive version of the Fact for an eastward-moving car:

The f-graph is concave up when the car speeds up; the f-graph is concave down when the car slows down.

See page 42 for more on the speed limit law.

(We'll revive our automotive metaphor—and enforce the speed limit law—in a page or two.) ◂

EXAMPLE 1   Interpret the concavity of the sine function using the second derivative. (We considered the same question in Example 4 in the previous section but used only the first derivative.)

Solution   If $f(x) = \sin x$, then $f'(x) = \cos x$ and $f''(x) = -\sin x$. (We'll derive both of these formulas carefully in Chapter 2. Here, we'll simply assume that they hold.) Figure 1 shows graphs of f and f'' on the same axes.

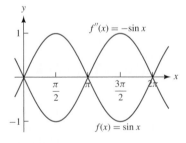

FIGURE 1
Graphs of f and f''

It's easy to see that the advertised relationship holds: f is concave up precisely where $f'' > 0$ and is concave down where $f'' < 0$. (These are also the places where the f-graph appears to be "accelerating upward.")   ■

Finding inflection points   A function f has an inflection point wherever the *sign* of f'' changes. It follows that, for smooth functions, *if $x = a$ is an inflection point of f, then* $f''(a) = 0$. On the sine graph, for instance, inflection points occur at all integer multiples of π, that is, at all roots of f''.

Inflection points of f must be roots of f'', but beware: $f''(a)$ may *be zero even if no inflection occurs at $x = a$*. The next example illustrates why: If $f''(a) = 0$, then a is a stationary point of f' but not necessarily a local maximum point or local minimum point of f'.

EXAMPLE 2   Graphs of a function f and its derivatives f' and f'' appear in Figure 2. ➤ Discuss concavity and inflection points of f.

The functions shown have simple formulas: $f(x) = x^4$, $f'(x) = 4x^3$, and $f''(x) = 12x^2$. We hid the formulas here in the margin because they're not needed in this problem.

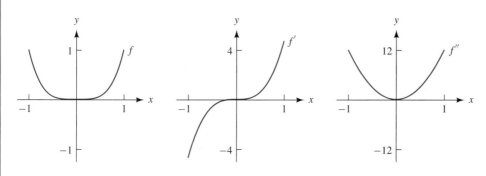

FIGURE 2
Graphs of f, f', and f''

Solution   The graph of f is concave up *everywhere* because f' is everywhere increasing. Notice also how the shape of the f-graph reflects the fact that $f(0) = f'(0) = f''(0) = 0$. If *several* derivatives of a function are zero at a point $x = a$, the graph of f looks flat near $x = a$. (The more derivatives vanish at $x = a$, the flatter the graph.)   ■

Concavity, inflection, and tangent lines   Concavity and inflection have nice interpretations in terms of tangent lines.

"Convexity" may sound more mathematical than "concavity," but the latter seems standard at this level. One reason may be the connection between upward concavity and a positive second derivative. In any event, it won't hurt students to hear "convexity" mentioned.

> **FACT (Concavity and tangent lines)**   Let f be a smooth function and let ℓ be the line tangent to the f-graph at $x = a$. If f is concave *down* on an interval I containing $x = a$, then the f-graph lies *below* ℓ for x in I. If f is concave *up* on I, then the f-graph lies *above* ℓ for x in I.

The Fact should be geometrically reasonable, but observe:

- **Why it holds: the speed limit law**   The Fact is essentially the speed limit law—but in geometric disguise. If we write $f'(a) = M$ (which is also the slope of ℓ), then the concavity assumption means that $f'(x)$ is decreasing, so $f'(x) < M$ for $x > a$. Reasoning as in Example 6 in the previous section, we see that for $x > a$, the f-graph lies *below*

Students may need help unraveling the connection with the speed limit law.

the line ℓ, which has constant slope M. Similar reasoning explains why the f-graph is also below the line ℓ for $x < a$.

- **Inflection and tangent lines**   If $x = a$ is an inflection point of f, then neither of the situations described in the Fact holds, and the tangent line *crosses* the f-graph at $x = a$. (On the sine graph, for instance, this occurs when x is any integer multiple of π.)

Concave or convex?   Is the function $f(x) = x^2$ *concave up* or *convex down*? Both names make sense, but—except in calculus courses—mathematicians generally prefer the "convex" terminology. A plane figure is called *convex* if, given any two points in the figure, the line segment joining the points also lies inside the figure. Disks and rectangles are convex, as is the plane region that lies *above* the parabola $y = x^2$. Other figures, such as a 5-pointed star, a disk with a hole removed, and the region below the parabola $y = x^2$ are nonconvex.

Classifying stationary points: the second derivative test

A stationary point on the graph of a function f may be a local maximum point, a local minimum point, or neither. It's usually obvious which case applies—*if* an accurate graph of f is available. If not, concavity may help us distinguish among these alternatives. The basic idea is easy:

> *At a local* minimum *point, the graph of f is concave* up.
> *At a local* maximum *point, the graph of f is concave* down.

The following Fact, known as the **second derivative test**, puts the pieces together. (We must assume, of course, that all the derivatives mentioned exist.)

FACT (Second derivative test)   Suppose that $f'(a) = 0$.

- If $f''(a) > 0$, then f has a local minimum at $x = a$.
- If $f''(a) < 0$, then f has a local maximum at $x = a$.
- If $f''(a) = 0$, anything can happen: f may have a local maximum, a local minimum, or neither at $x = a$, and the f-graph may be concave up, be concave down, have an inflection point, or have none of these properties.

Stirring in the formulas

We haven't yet explained how to find the derivative formulas, but that will soon be a routine exercise.

We return, finally, to the functions f, f', and f'' we first met on page 55—this time with algebraic formulas added. Here are the three formulas: ◂

$$f(x) = x^3 - x^2 - 6x; \quad f'(x) = 3x^2 - 2x - 6; \quad f''(x) = 6x - 2.$$

Figure 3 shows the graphs:

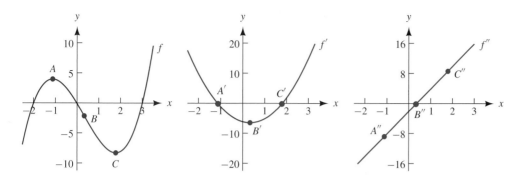

We've worked with these functions, mostly geometrically, for two sections—now it's time to see their formulas. Doing so hints at some of the advantages of having formulas to work with, as generally we will in Chapter 2.

FIGURE 3
Graphs of f, f', and f''

Combining graphs and formulas, we can sharpen our earlier observations:

- **Stationary points** The f-graph has horizontal tangent lines at the stationary points A and C. According to the derivative formula, stationary points occur at values of x for which

$$f'(x) = 3x^2 - 2x - 6 = 0$$

By the quadratic formula, f' has roots at $x = (1 \pm \sqrt{19})/3$, or, in decimal form, at $x_1 \approx -1.1196$ and $x_2 \approx 1.7863$.

- **How many stationary points?** The preceding calculation shows that f' has only two roots, so A and C are the *only* stationary points of f.

- **Concavity and an inflection point** The inflection point B seems to be somewhere near $x = 0.3$. With the formula for f'', we can locate B *exactly*. Because $f''(x) = 6x - 2 = 0$, the only root of f'' is at $x = 1/3$. As its graph shows, f'' changes sign at $x = 1/3$, so f changes its direction of concavity there, and only there.

A sample problem The following problem uses ingredients from this section.

Problems like this one make excellent discussion topics for students in small groups. Many students find verbalizing their ideas successfully to each other to be challenging but worthwhile.

EXAMPLE 3 Figure 4 shows the graph of f'; the f-graph is not shown.

FIGURE 4
Graph of f'

(a) Estimate $f''(-3)$.
(b) Where is f concave up? Concave down?
(c) Where does f have inflection points?

Solution   Looked at properly, the graph of f' answers all our questions.

(a) By definition, $f''(-3) = (f')'(-3)$, that is, the slope of the pictured graph at $x = -3$. A careful look shows this slope to be about 5.

(b) Because $f''(-3) > 0$, f is concave up at $x = -3$. More generally, f is concave up wherever $f'' > 0$, that is, where f' is increasing. Figure 4 shows that this occurs for $-4 \leq x \leq -1$ and for $3 \leq x \leq 4$. For the same reason, f is concave down for $-1 \leq x \leq 3$.

(c) The function f has an inflection point wherever its direction of concavity changes. Part (b) shows that this happens at $x = -1$ and at $x = 3$.   ■

BASIC EXERCISES

1. Suppose that $f''(-1) = 2$. What, if anything, does this imply about
   (a) f?
   (b) f'?

2. Suppose that $g''(1) = 0$. What, if anything, does this imply about
   (a) g?
   (b) g'?

3. Suppose that the function h has an inflection point at $x = 2$. What, if anything, does this imply about
   (a) h''?
   (b) h'?

4. Suppose that the function j' has a local maximum at $x = 2$. What, if anything, does this imply about
   (a) j''?
   (b) j?

5. Suppose that $f(-3) = -1$, $f'(-3) = 0$, and $f''(-3) = 2$. Is $x = -3$ a local minimum point of f? Justify your answer.

6. Suppose that $g(3) = 1$, $g'(3) = 2$, and $g''(3) = -2$. Is $x = 3$ a local maximum point of g? Justify your answer.

7. Explain why $f'(x) = 3x^2 - 2x - 6$ implies that f has exactly two stationary points.

8. Explain why $f''(x) = 6x - 2$ implies that f has only one inflection point.

9. Let f be the function shown in Figure 4. Rank the values $f''(-3)$, $f''(-2)$, $f''(1)$, and $f''(3)$ in increasing order.

10. Let f be the function described in Figure 4. Estimate the values of $f''(-3)$, $f''(-2)$, $f''(1)$, and $f''(3)$. Use these values to sketch the graph of $f''(x)$.

11. Suppose that g is increasing and concave down over the interval $[1, 5]$ and that $\ell(x) = 3x + 4$ is an equation of the line tangent to g at $x = 2$.
    (a) Sketch graphs of g and ℓ on the same axes.
    (b) Explain why $g(3) < \ell(3)$.
    (c) Is $g(1.5) > \ell(1.5)$? Justify your answer.

12. Suppose that h is decreasing and concave up over the interval $[-4, 4]$ and that $L(x) = 3 - 2x$ is an equation of the line tangent to h at $x = 1$.
    (a) Sketch graphs of h and L on the same axes.
    (b) Is $h(3) - L(3)$ positive? Justify your answer.
    (c) Is $h(-1) > L(-1)$? Justify your answer.

13. The graph of a function f appears below. [NOTE: f has an inflection point at $x = 1$; it has stationary points at $x = -4$ and $x = 6$.]

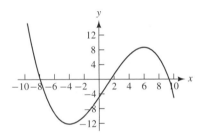

For which values of x, if any, is $f''(x)$
    (a) positive?
    (b) negative?
    (c) zero?

14. The graph of a function f appears below. [NOTE: f has points of inflection at $x = 5/6$ and at $x = 2$; f has stationary points at $x = 1/2$, $x = 5/4$, and $x = 5/2$.]

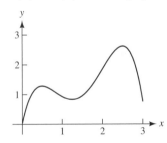

For which values of x, if any, is $f''(x)$
    (a) positive?
    (b) negative?
    (c) zero?

In Exercises 15–21, use the graph of g″ shown below to answer the questions about g and g′.

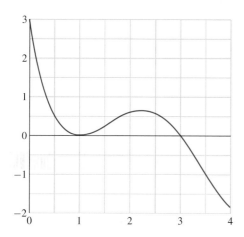

15. On which intervals is g concave up?

16. On which intervals is g' decreasing?

17. Does g have a point of inflection at $x = 1$? Justify your answer.

18. Does g have a point of inflection at $x = 3$? Justify your answer.

19. Rank the four numbers $g'(0)$, $g'(1)$, $g'(2)$, and $g'(3)$ in increasing order.

20. Is $g'(\pi) > g'(3.5)$? Justify your answer.

21. Suppose that $g'(1) = -4$. Is g decreasing at $x = 3$? Justify your answer.

22. Suppose that the functions f, f', and f'' are continuous on $(-\infty, \infty)$, that $f'(2) = -1$, and that $0.1 < f''(x) < 0.5$ if $2 < x < 4$. Find upper and lower bounds on the value of $f'(3)$. [HINT: Apply the speed limit law.]

FURTHER EXERCISES

23. Use the graph of g' shown below to answer the following questions about g''.

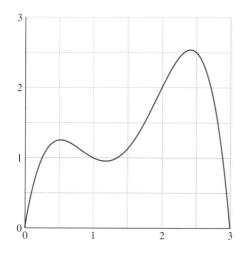

(a) Estimate $g''(0.5)$, $g''(1)$, $g''(1.5)$, and $g''(2)$.

(b) Sketch a graph of g'' over the interval $[0, 3]$.

24. Suppose that f is a linear function. Explain why f'' is the constant function $f''(x) = 0$.

25. In the left-hand column below are graphs of several functions. In the right-hand column—in a different order—are graphs of the *second* derivatives of these functions. Match each function with its second derivative function. [NOTE: The scales on the graphs are not the same.]

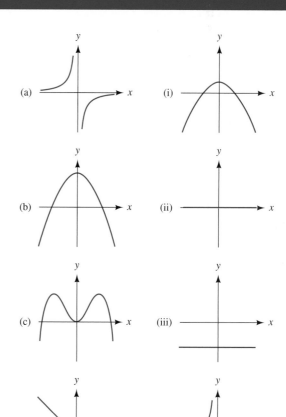

26. Graphs of f, f', and f'' appear below. Which is which? Justify your answer.

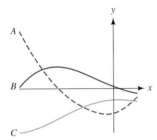

27. Graphs of f, f', and f'' appear below. Which is which? How can you tell?

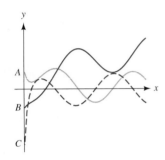

28. Water flows at a constant rate into a large tank that is a cylinder with a circular base. Let $V(t)$ be the volume of water in the tank at time t and $H(t)$ be the height of the water in the tank at time t. Give a physical interpretation of each of the following expressions and indicate whether each is positive, negative, or zero at the time t^* when the tank is one-quarter full:

(a) $V''(t)$

(b) $H''(t)$

29. Repeat Problem 28 for a tank that is a cone with its vertex pointing down.

In Exercises 30 and 31, interpret the sentence as a statement about the value of a function and its first and second derivatives. Be sure to indicate the units associated with each derivative.

30. The cost of a new car is increasing at an increasing rate.

31. The child's temperature is still rising, but the penicillin seems to be taking effect.

32. Sketch the graph of a function f for which $f(x) > 0$, $f'(x) > 0$, and $f''(x) > 0$ for all x.

33. Sketch the graph of a function f for which $f(x) > 0$, $f'(x) < 0$, and $f''(x) > 0$ for all x.

34. Assume that f is a continuous function defined on the closed interval $[-3, 3]$ such that $f(-3) = 4$ and $f(3) = -1$. Furthermore, assume that f' and f'' are continuous on $(-3, 3)$ and that the information in the table below is known about these functions.

x	$-3 \le x < -1$	-1	$-1 < x < 0$	0
$f'(x)$	$+$	0	$-$	$-$
$f''(x)$	$-$	$-$	$-$	0

x	$0 < x < 1$	1	$1 < x \le 3$
$f'(x)$	$-$	0	$-$
$f''(x)$	$+$	0	$-$

(a) Sketch the graph of a function that has the given properties.

(b) Where does f achieve its maximum and minimum values on the interval $[-3, 3]$? Justify your answer.

35. If f is an even function, then f' is an odd function; if f is an odd function, then f' is an even function. Use these facts to show that if f is an even function, then f'' is an even function.

36. Suppose that the line $y = 2x - 1$ is tangent to the graph of f at $x = 3$ and that $f''(x) > 0$ if $0 < x < 5$.

(a) Explain why $7 < f(4)$ must be true.

(b) Find a lower bound on the value of $f(2)$.

37. Suppose that $f(2) = 5$, $f'(2) = 2$, and that f is concave up everywhere.

(a) How many roots could f have? What can you say about the location of these roots?

(b) Find a lower bound on the value of $f(0)$.

(c) Suppose that $f(-2) = -1$. Show that $f(0) < 3$.

In Exercises 38–41, use the expression for f' to answer the following questions about f''.

(a) Estimate $f''(-1)$, $f''(0)$, and $f''(2)$ by zooming.

(b) How many roots does f'' have?

(c) On which intervals is $f''(x) > 0$?

(d) Sketch a graph of f''.

38. $f'(x) = \dfrac{1}{1 + x^2}$

39. $f'(x) = (x - 2)(x + 4)$

40. $f'(x) = \dfrac{x - 2}{x^2 + 5}$

41. $f'(x) = \ln(1 + |x|)$

In Exercises 42–45, use the expression for f'' to answer the following questions about f.

(a) Where, if anywhere, is f concave up?

(b) Where, if anywhere, is f' decreasing?

(c) How many stationary points does f' have? Where are they located?

(d) Does f have any inflection points? If so, where are they located?

(e) Sketch a graph of f'.

42. $f''(x) = 2x + 3$

43. $f''(x) = (x+1)^2(x-2)$

44. $f''(x) = e^{-x}$

45. $f''(x) = \dfrac{x+1}{\sqrt{x^2+1}}$

In Exercises 46–49, use the expression for f'' to answer the following questions about f.

    (a) Suppose that $f'(1) = 0$. Does f have a local minimum point at $x = 1$? Justify your answer.

    (b) Let ℓ be the line tangent to f at $x = -1$. Does f lie below ℓ over the interval $(-1, 1)$? Justify your answer.

46. $f''(x) = 1 + x^3$

47. $f''(x) = (x-2)^2(x+4)$

48. $f''(x) = e^{-x} - 3$

49. $f''(x) = \dfrac{x-2}{x^2+5}$

50. Suppose that $f'(x) = x^2$. Guess a formula for $f''(x)$.

51. Suppose that $f'(x) = 3x + x^2$. Guess a formula for $f''(x)$.

Summary

Summary sections aim both to overview the chapter's main ideas and vocabulary, and also to collect examples and exercises that may use ideas from several parts of the chapter. The section has a huge number of exercises; some might be used for testing.

Chapter 1 introduced the main objects of calculus—functions and derivatives—mainly from the graphical point of view.

Functions, calculus style Functions are the main objects of study in calculus. Readers may be most familiar with "formula" functions, such as $f(x) = x^2$, and we'll study them carefully in later chapters. More typical of Chapter 1, however, are functions defined in other ways: by graphs, by tables of data, in words, and so forth. In Section 1.1 we surveyed some of this variety and then reviewed some of the theory of functions in general. The function idea has three main parts: **rule**, **domain**, and **range**. We reviewed all of them, with appropriate examples.

Graphs Formulas, even simple ones, often reveal less than graphs do about how functions behave. Graphs give functions geometric meaning. Most important, graphs show how functions *vary*—whether they rise or fall, whether they're concave up or down, and how they're changed by such operations as adding or multiplying constants in inputs or outputs. (**Translation**, **compression**, and **stretching** are all possible, depending on the operation applied.) Section 1.2 reviewed a little of the huge variety of graphs and their uses.

A field guide to elementary functions Section 1.3 introduced the cast of leading functional characters in calculus. Many of the functions we'll treat in calculus are **elementary functions**—functions built up by combining members of the main function families: algebraic, trigonometric, exponential, and logarithm functions. We met these function families briefly in Section 1.3; further details about each family appear in the Appendices.

Amount functions, rate functions, slope functions Section 1.4 introduced the **derivative**, calculus's most important idea, interpreting it using both **rates** and **slopes**. The relationship between **amount functions** (those we start with) and **rate functions** (the derivatives of amount functions) is key to much that follows. If, say, $s(t)$ describes the **position** of a moving object at time t, then its rate function $s'(t)$ describes the object's **velocity**. Among the simplest functions are **linear functions**; their derivatives are **constant functions**.

    The **speed limit law** relates properties of rate functions to properties of amount functions. In its simplest form it asserts that if a rate function f' obeys the "speed limit" $f'(x) \le M$ for all x in an interval $[a, b]$, then the difference $f(b) - f(a)$ cannot exceed the product $M(b-a)$.

Estimating derivatives: a closer look   For any function f and input $x = a$, the derivative $f'(a)$ is the slope of the f-graph at the point $(a, f(a))$. Finding $f'(a)$ is simplest if the f-graph is a straight line, but in Section 1.5 we developed a strategy for handling curved graphs. The slope of a *curve* at a point is the slope of the **tangent line** (a straight line that "fits" the curve) at the point in question. Zooming helps us find this slope:

> *To find the slope of a* curve *at a point, zoom in until the curve "looks straight"; then find the slope.*

This trick works—even for nonlinear functions—because almost all calculus functions are "locally straight."

The geometry of derivatives   Section 1.6 described in detail how a function f and its derivative function f' are related, and what each tells about the other. For instance, a function f is **increasing** where the derivative f' is **positive**, and the f-graph has **stationary points** where the derivative f' has **roots**. **Concavity** is another important geometric concept linked to derivatives: the f-graph is concave up where the f'-graph is increasing. A graph's concavity changes at an **inflection point.**

The geometry of higher-order derivatives   Section 1.7 revisited themes of Section 1.6 but added the perspective of the **second derivative** f'', which measures the rate of change (or slope) of the first derivative. The second derivative is closely connected to concavity: the f-graph is concave up or down depending on whether $f'' > 0$ or $f'' < 0$. These properties can help us distinguish among the several possible types of stationary points: If $f'(a) = 0$, then f may have a **local maximum**, **local minimum**, or just a flat spot (a **terrace point**) at $x = a$.

Summary problems

The following examples use ideas from throughout Chapter 1.

"Elementary" functions are the ones reviewed in Section 1.3—and known to your calculator.

EXAMPLE 1   In each case, decide whether a function with the given properties exists. If so, sketch the graph of such a function; if possible, find a suitable elementary function. ◄ If no such function exists, explain why.

(a) $f(x) > 0$ and $f'(x) > 0$ for all x.

(b) $f(x) < 0$ and $f'(x) < 0$ for all x.

(c) $f''(x) > 0$ and $f(x) > 0$ for all x.

(d) $f''(x) > 0$ and $f(x) < 0$ for all x.

(e) $f(x) > 0$, $f'(x) > 0$, and $f''(x) < 0$ for $x > 0$.

Read the solutions with graphing technology at hand.

Solution   Most parts have many possible solutions; here are several. ◄

(a) The conditions say that f should be *positive* and *increasing* for all x. The exponential function $f(x) = e^x$ has these properties.

(b) The conditions say that f should be *negative* and *decreasing* for all x. The function $f(x) = -e^x$ has these properties.

The parabola $y = x^2$ doesn't quite work because it grazes the x-axis.

(c) The conditions require that f be *concave up* and *positive* for all x. There are many possibilities, including the upward-opening quadratic $f(x) = x^2 + 1$. ◄

(d) The conditions require that f be *concave up* and *negative* for all x. This is impossible. A graph that's concave up can't stay below the x-axis forever.

(e) The conditions mean that f is *positive*, *increasing*, and *concave down* for positive inputs x. The function $f(x) = \ln(x + 1)$ has all these properties. ∎

E X A M P L E 2   Figure 1 shows a derivative function f'; the graph of f is not shown.

(a) The equation $f(x) = 0$ can have no more than two solutions in the interval $[-3, 3]$. Explain why.

(b) Explain why f cannot have two roots in the interval $[0, 3]$.

(c) Suppose that $f(0) = 1$. How many solutions does the equation $f(x) = 0$ have in the interval $[-3, 3]$? Explain.

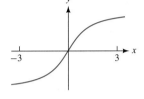

FIGURE 1
Graph of f'

Solution   Because f' is negative on the interval $(-3, 0)$ and positive on the interval $(0, 3)$, f itself must decrease on $(-3, 0)$ and increase on $(0, 3)$. Thus f has a local minimum at $x = 0$ and no other stationary points. Therefore:

(a) The graph of f is U-shaped, so it can intersect the interval $[-3, 3]$ in at most two places.

(b) The graph of f increases on the interval $(0, 3)$, so it can cross the x-axis no more than once on that interval.

(c) If $f(0) = 1$, then f has no roots in the interval $[-3, 3]$ because f has its minimum value at $x = 0$. ∎

REVIEW EXERCISES

1. Suppose that $f'(x) = 3$ (i.e., f' is a constant function). What can you say about f?

2. Let $f(x) = 5$, $g(x) = x$, and $h(x) = -2x$. Evaluate $f'(11)$, $g'(-53)$, and $h'(37)$.

3. Suppose that $g(x) = f(x) + 3$ and that $f'(x)$ exists for all x.
  (a) Explain how the graphs of f and g are related.
  (b) How is the graph of g' related to the graph of f'? Explain.
  (c) If $f'(1) = 5$, what is $g'(1)$?

4. Suppose that $g(x) = f(x) - 2$ and that $f'(x) = (x^2 + 3)^{-1}$. Evaluate $g'(1)$.

5. Suppose that $h(x) = f(x) + 1$ and that the line tangent to the graph of f at the point $(2, f(2))$ is described by the equation $y = 3x - 4$. Find an equation of the line tangent to the graph of h at the point $(2, h(2))$.

6. Let $g(x) = f(x + 3)$ and suppose that $f'(x)$ exists for all x.
  (a) Explain how the graphs of f and g are related.
  (b) How is the graph of g' related to the graph of f'? Explain.
  (c) If $f'(2) = 4$, what is $g'(-1)$?

7. Suppose that $g(x) = f(x - 2)$ and that $f'(x) = (x^2 + 3)^{-1}$. Evaluate $g'(0)$.

8. Suppose that $h(x) = f(x + 1)$ and that the line tangent to the graph of f at the point $(2, f(2))$ is described by the equation $y = 3x - 4$.
  (a) Evaluate $h(1)$.
  (b) Evaluate $h'(1)$.

9. Suppose that f is periodic with period 5 and that $f'(x)$ exists for all x. Explain why f' is also a periodic function with period 5.

10. Let $f(x) = \cos x$. Rank the three values $f'(-\pi/4)$, $f'(0)$, and $f'(\pi/4)$ in ascending order.

11. Let $f(x) = e^{-x}$. Rank the four values $f'(-1)$, $f'(0)$, $f'(2)$, and $f'(10)$ in ascending order.

12. Let $f(x) = x^2$ and $g(x) = e^x$. Indicate which function is growing faster at each of the following points: $x = -1$, $x = 0$, $x = 1$, $x = 3$.

13. Let $f(x) = x$ and $g(x) = \ln x$. Indicate which function is growing faster at each of the following points: $x = 1/10$, $x = 1/2$, $x = 2$, $x = 7$.

14. Let f be the function whose graph is shown below.

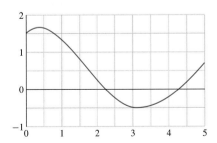

  (a) Estimate $f'(0)$, $f'(1)$, $f'(2)$, $f'(3)$, $f'(4)$, and $f'(5)$.
  (b) Use your results from part (a) to sketch a graph of the function f'.

15. Graphs of f, f', and g (not the derivative of f) are shown below. Which is which? Explain how you can tell.

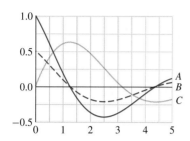

In Exercises 16–22, use the graph of f' shown below to answer the question about f. [NOTE: The graph of f is not shown.]

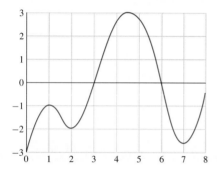

16. On which intervals is f increasing?

17. Where does f have stationary points?

18. Where does f have a local maximum point?

19. On which intervals is f concave down?

20. Where does f have an inflection point?

21. Where does f achieve its maximum value on the interval $[0, 2]$? Justify your answer.

22. Where does f achieve its minimum value on the interval $[3, 6]$? Justify your answer.

23. The graph of the *derivative* of a function f is shown below.

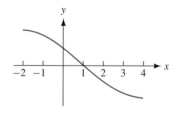

(a) Where in the interval $[-2, 4]$ is f increasing? Justify your answer.

(b) Does f have a stationary point in the interval $[-2, 4]$? If so, is it a local maximum point, a local minimum point, or neither? Justify your answers.

(c) Describe in words the general shape of the f-graph over the interval $[-2, 4]$.

24. Suppose that $f'(x) = \sin x$.

(a) Where in the interval $[0, 2\pi]$ does f have a stationary point?

(b) Where in the interval $[0, 2\pi]$ is f increasing?

(c) Where in the interval $[0, 2\pi]$ does f have a local maximum point?

(d) Where in the interval $[0, 2\pi]$ is f concave down?

(e) Where in the interval $[0, 2\pi]$ does f have an inflection point?

25. Suppose that $f'(x) = (x - 1)(x + 2)^2$.

(a) Explain why $x = 1$ is a local extreme point of f.

(b) Is $x = 1$ a local maximum point of f? Justify your answer.

(c) Is $x = -2$ a local extreme point of f? Justify your answer.

(d) Where is f increasing?

(e) Where is f concave down?

(f) Where does f have inflection points?

26. Suppose that $g(x) = 3f(x)$ and that $f'(x)$ exists for all x.

(a) Explain how the graphs of f and g are related.

(b) How is the graph of g' related to the graph of f'?

(c) If $f'(-1) = 2$, explain why $g'(-1) = 6$.

27. Suppose that $f(2) = 4$ and $f'(x) = \sqrt{x^3 + 1}$ for $x \geq -1$.

(a) Find an equation for the line tangent to f at $x = 2$.

(b) Let ℓ be the tangent line from part (a). Does $\ell(0)$ underestimate $f(0)$? Justify your answer.

(c) Estimate $f(2.1)$. Is your estimate too big? Justify your answer.

In Exercises 28–33, suppose that $f(1) = -2$ and $f'(x) \leq 3$ for all x in $[-10, 10]$.

28. Show that $f(2) \leq 1$.

29. Show that $f(5) \leq 10$.

30. Is $f(9) < 31$? Justify your answer.

31. Is $f(-5) > -23$? Justify your answer.

32. Could $f(4) = 8$? Justify your answer.

33. Could $f(8) = -25$? Justify your answer.

34. Suppose that $f(0) = 2$ and $\left| f'(x) \right| \leq 1$ for all x in $[-5, 5]$.

(a) Find upper and lower bounds on the value of $f(1)$.

(b) Find upper and lower bounds on the value of $f(-3)$.

35. Graphs of f, f', f'', and g (not a derivative of f) are shown below. Which is which? How can you tell?

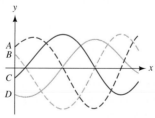

36. Sketch the graph of a function f for which $f(x) < 0$, $f'(x) < 0$, and $f''(x) < 0$ for all x.

37. Sketch the graph of a function f for which $f(x) < 0$, $f'(x) > 0$, and $f''(x) < 0$ for all x.

38. Is there a function f for which $f(x) > 0$, $f'(x) < 0$, and $f''(x) < 0$ for all x? If so, sketch the graph of such a function. If not, explain why no function can have all of these properties.

39. Is there a function f for which $f(x) < 0$ and $f''(x) > 0$ for all x? If so, sketch the graph of such a function. If not, explain why no function can have all of these properties.

40. Suppose that $f'(c) = f''(c) = 0$, but $f'''(c) > 0$. Does f have a local minimum point, a local maximum point, or an inflection point at c? Justify your answer.

In Exercises 41–46, suppose that g and g' are continuous functions, that 2 is a local maximum point of g, and that 3 is an inflection point of g.

41. Is it possible that $g(2) = 1$? If not, explain why not. Justify your answer.

42. Is it possible that $g'(2) = 1$? If not, explain why not. Justify your answer.

43. Is it possible that $g''(2) = 1$? If not, explain why not. Justify your answer.

44. Is it possible that $g(3) = 1$? If not, explain why not. Justify your answer.

45. Is it possible that $g'(3) = 1$? If not, explain why not. Justify your answer.

46. Is it possible that $g''(3) = 1$? If not, explain why not. Justify your answer.

Suppose that $f(-2) = -3$ and that f' is the function shown below. Use the speed limit law to answer the questions about f in Exercises 47–51. [NOTE: The graph of f is not shown.]

47. Could $f(3) = -6$? Justify your answer.

48. Could $f(3) = 1$? Justify your answer.

49. Show that $f(0) \geq 1$.

50. Explain why f achieves its largest value in the interval $[-2, 2]$ at $x = 2$.

51. Where in the interval $[-2, 2]$ does f achieve its smallest value?

52. Suppose that the position of a particle moving along the x-axis is given by $x(t) = \cos t$.

(a) Is the particle moving to the left at time $t = 1$? Justify your answer.

(b) Is $x'(1) > 0$? Justify your answer.

53. Suppose that the position of a particle moving along the y-axis is given by $y(t) = \sin t$.

(a) Is the particle moving up at time $t = 1$? Justify your answer.

(b) Is $y'(1) > 0$? Justify your answer.

54. Suppose that the line tangent to the curve $y = f(x)$ at $x = 2$ has slope -1 and crosses the x axis at $x = 5$. Find $f(2)$ and $f'(2)$.

55. Suppose that the line tangent to the curve $y = f(x)$ at $x = -2$ is described by the equation $y = 4x + 3$. Find $f(-2)$ and $f'(-2)$.

Exercises 56–60 refer to the graph of the derivative of a function g shown below. [NOTE: The graph of g is not shown.]

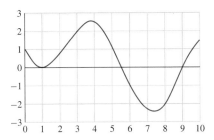

56. Suppose that $g(3) = 11$. Find an equation of the line tangent to g at the point $(3, 11)$.

57. Let ℓ be the line tangent to g at $x = 2$. Is $g(5) \leq \ell(5)$? Justify your answer.

58. Let h be the line tangent to g at $x = 6$. Explain why $g(x) \leq h(x)$ if $6 \leq x \leq 8$.

59. Is $g(3) < g(5)$? Justify your answer.

60. Is $g(6) > g(8)$? Justify your answer.

61. Let $P(t)$ be the population (in millions) of the United States t years after 1800. What does the statement $P'(10) \approx 2.3$ mean in this context?

62. Let f be the function shown below.

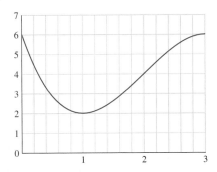

(a) Estimate $f'(1)$.

(b) Is $f'(2) > 2$? Justify your answer.

In Exercises 63–72, suppose that $g(0) = -2$ and that $g'(r) = 1/2 - \sin(r^2/4)$ for $0 \le r \le 5$.

63. Is g increasing at $r = 3$? Justify your answer.

64. Is $g''(4) < 0$? Justify your answer.

65. Is g concave up at $r = 2$? Justify your answer.

66. How many stationary points does g have in the interval $[0, 5]$? Where are they located?

67. How many local minimum points does g have in the interval $[0, 5]$? Where are they located?

68. How many local maximum points does g' have in the interval $[0, 5]$? Where are they located?

69. The function g has an inflection point in the interval $[0, 3]$. Where is it located?

70. Find an equation for the line tangent to the graph of g at $r = 0$.

71. Let $\ell(r)$ be the line tangent to the graph of g at $r = 1$. Explain why $\ell(1.1) \ge g(1.1)$.

72. Is there a number r_0 in the interval $[0, 5]$ such that $g(r_0) = 10$? Justify your answer.

73. Let $h(z) = 3z - 2$.

    (a) Evaluate $h'(1)$.

    (b) Evaluate $h''(4)$.

74. Suppose that $\ell(s) = 3s + 4$ is the line tangent to the curve $y = W(s)$ at $s = 2$.

    (a) Evaluate $W(2)$.

    (b) Evaluate $W'(2)$.

75. Suppose that $G(1) = 0$ and that G' is the function graphed below. Sketch a qualitatively correct graph of G over the interval $[1, 3]$.

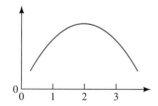

76. Suppose that $S(t)$ is the depth (in inches) of the snow on the ground t hours after midnight on Christmas (i.e., $t = 1$ is 1 A.M.). Write an expression that represents the rate it was snowing (in inches per hour) at 9 A.M. on Christmas day.

77. Suppose that f is the function whose graph is shown below.

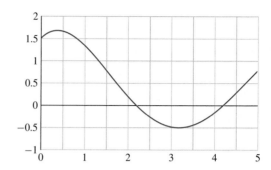

Rank the six values $-2, 0, 0.5, f'(1.5), f'(3)$, and $f'(4.5)$ in increasing order.

78. Suppose that $f''(1) = -2$.

    (a) What, if anything, does this imply about f?

    (b) What, if anything, does this imply about f'?

79. Suppose that -2 and 1 are the only roots of f' in the interval $I = [-5, 5]$. Is it possible that the maximum value of f on I occurs at 4? Justify your answer.

80. Suppose that $C(T)$ is the cost to heat a house, in dollars per day, when the average outside temperature is T degrees. Interpret the statement $C'(23) = -0.17$ in this context.

81. Let f be the function graphed below.

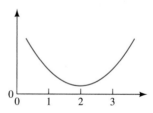

    (a) Sketch a qualitatively correct graph of f' over the interval $[1, 3]$.

    (b) Suppose that $F' = f$ and that $F(1) = 0$. Sketch a qualitatively correct graph of F over the interval $[1, 3]$.

82. Let h be the function graphed below.

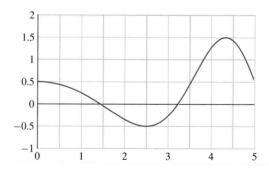

    (a) Is h increasing at $x = 2$? Justify your answer.

    (b) Is h' increasing at $x = 2$? Justify your answer.

(c) Does h have any stationary points in the interval $[1, 5]$? If so, where?

(d) Does h' have any local maximum points in the interval $[0, 5]$? If so, where?

(e) Suppose that $H' = h$ and that $H(0) = 1$. Is $H(3) > 2$? Justify your answer.

83. Suppose that $h'(w) = \sqrt{w} - 3$.

(a) Is h increasing at $w = 1$? Justify your answer.

(b) Is h concave up at $w = 4$? Justify your answer.

(c) The function h has a stationary point at $w = 9$. Is it a local minimum point, a local maximum point, or neither? Justify your answer.

84. Suppose that hot coffee $(90\,°C)$ is poured into a cup and then left in a $25\,°C$ room. Let $T(t)$ be the temperature (in $°C$) of the coffee in the cup at time t minutes after it was poured. Is $T''(5) > 0$? Justify your answer.

85. Suppose that $g(1) = 2$ and that $g'(t) = -3$ for all t. Evaluate $g(4)$.

*In Exercises 86–90, suppose that $G''(w) = w^3 + 8$ for all w. Indicate whether the statement **must** be true, **might** be true, or **cannot** be true. Justify your answers.*

86. $G(3) = 17$.

87. $w = -2$ is an inflection point of G.

88. G is concave up over the interval $[-1, 1]$.

89. G is decreasing over the interval $[0, 2]$.

90. G' is increasing at $w = -3$.

91. Let $U(t)$ be the number of people unemployed in a country t months after the election of an economically conservative president. Translate each of the following facts about the graph of $U(t)$ into statements about the unemployment situation. (Don't forget to specify units in your answers.)

(a) The y-intercept of $U(t)$ is 2,000,000.

(b) $U(2) = 3,000,000$.

(c) $U'(20) = 10,000$.

(d) $U''(36) = 800$ and $U'(36) = 0$.

In Exercises 92–97, suppose that $g'(w) = 1/2 - \cos(w^2)$.

92. Is $g''(\pi/2) > 0$? Justify your answer.

93. (a) Explain why g has an inflection point at $w = \sqrt{\pi}$.

(b) Does g have any other inflection points in the interval $[1, 3]$? If so, find them.

94. How many stationary points does g have in the interval $[1, 3]$? If there are any, find them.

95. Where in the interval $[1, 3]$ is g concave down?

96. Where in the interval $[1, 3]$ is g decreasing?

97. How many local maximum points does g have in the interval $[1, 3]$? If there are any, find them.

98. Suppose that $f'(3) = -2$.

(a) Assume that f is an *even* function. Give a graphical argument that explains why $f'(-3) = 2$.

(b) Now assume that f is an *odd* function. What is $f'(-3)$?

99. After a braking test on a straight track on the Utah Salt Flats, the driver reported:

> I accelerated smoothly from rest. After 15 seconds, I was cruising at 60 mph. After 90 seconds, I hit the brakes. The car decelerated, but I couldn't stop in time. I hit the crash barrier 10 seconds later at 10 mph.

(a) Draw a plausible graph of the distance traveled by the car as a function of time.

(b) Draw a plausible graph of the car's speed as a function of time.

(c) Draw a plausible graph of the car's acceleration as a function of time.

(d) What features of each of the graphs in parts (a)–(c) reflect the information given about the car's positive acceleration over the time interval $0 \le t < 15$, zero acceleration over the time interval $15 \le t < 90$, and deceleration over the time interval $90 \le t \le 100$?

100. An airplane takes off from one airport and, 45 minutes later, lands at another airport 300 miles away. Let t represent the time since the airplane took off, $x(t)$ the *horizontal* distance traveled, and $y(t)$ the *altitude* of the airplane.

(a) What is the physical meaning of $x'(t)$? Sketch plausible graphs of x and x'.

(b) What is the physical meaning of $y'(t)$? Sketch plausible graphs of y and y'.

Zooming in on Differences

The derivative $f'(a)$ is the slope of the *tangent line* to the graph of f at the point $(a, f(a))$. This tangent line has two main properties: (i) it passes through the point $(a, f(a))$; (ii) it "fits" the f-graph as closely as possible at $(a, f(a))$. The first property is no big deal—it's easy to find lines through a given point. The second property is trickier; in this interlude we explore further how to recognize the line that best "fits" a (curved) graph at a point.

See the pictures in Example 1, page 47.

In Example 1, page 47, we estimated that the tangent line to the graph of $y = f(x) = x^2$ at the point $(1, 1)$ has slope 2, that is, that $f'(1) \approx 2$. This estimate looks reasonable, ← but graphs alone only yield *estimates*. Do we *really* prefer $f'(1) \approx 2$ to, say, $f'(1) \approx 1.9$ or $f'(1) \approx 2.1$?

These three guesses correspond, respectively, to three linear functions, with equations ←

These equations are in point–slope form—it's often convenient in calculus.

$$\ell_2(x) = 2(x - 1) + 1, \quad \ell_{2.1}(x) = 2.1(x - 1) + 1, \quad \text{and} \quad \ell_{1.9}(x) = 1.9(x - 1) + 1.$$

(The letter ℓ stands for "linear"; the subscripts correspond to slopes.) Which guess is best? To decide, we might plot all three linear functions *and* f together; the linear graphs are "candidate tangent lines." Figure 1 shows two pictures in different windows: ←

Can you tell which graph is which in each picture?

Interludes present "enrichment" material; they're optional in the sense that later work is independent of their content. Interludes are designed for use either as "short sections" to be covered in class or as "projects" for individual or group work (and perhaps group presentation). This interlude explores somewhat further the zooming idea first met in Section 1.5.

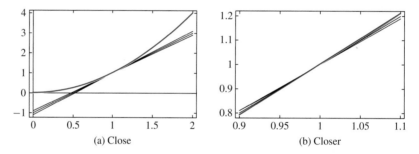

(a) Close   (b) Closer

FIGURE 1
Tangent line candidates: graphs of f, ℓ_2, $\ell_{2.1}$, and $\ell_{1.9}$

Alas, neither picture helps much—all three lines look like reasonable tangent line candidates.

A better way: look at differences   A better way to select the best candidate and to reject the duds is to compare the *errors* each candidate commits. ← To this end, we consider the **error functions**

This strategy sometimes works in politics, too.

$$f(x) - \ell_2(x), \quad f(x) - \ell_{2.1}(x), \quad \text{and} \quad f(x) - \ell_{1.9}(x),$$

which measure the *difference* between the candidate functions and the "target" function f. (This difference is the "error" committed by each tangent-line candidate in approximating the target function.) The best candidate is the linear function whose error function stays closest to zero near $x = 1$. Figure 2 shows graphs (in two different windows) of our three error functions; the dashed curve is the function $f(x) - \ell_2(x)$ (which corresponds to the estimate $f'(1) \approx 2$).

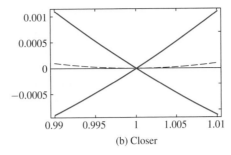

(a) Close   (b) Closer

FIGURE 2
Three error functions: $f - \ell_2$ (dashed), $f - \ell_{2.1}$, and $f - \ell_{1.9}$

All three graphs pass through the point, $(1, 0)$—not surprisingly, since all three tangent line candidates were chosen to agree with f at $x = 1$. What we really care about is how the curves behave near *but not at* $x = 1$. Observe:

- The dashed curve "wins"; it's *much* closer than the others to the line $y = 0$ for values of x near 1. (This is most obvious in the second picture; zooming in yet again would make the difference even more striking.)

- The two solid curves *cross* the x-axis at $x = 1$, so the two error functions $f(x) - \ell_{2.1}(x)$ and $f(x) - \ell_{1.9}(x)$ *change sign* at $x = 1$. This implies, in turn, that the lines $\ell_{1.9}$ and $\ell_{2.1}$ *cross* the curve $y = x^2$ at $x = 1$. (The upward concavity of the parabola $y = x^2$ suggests that the "true" tangent line should *not* cross the curve at $x = 1$.) In the second picture, the two solid curves resemble *straight lines* that cross the x-axis at the point $x = 1$.

- The dashed curve looks like a *parabola* with its vertex on the x-axis at $x = 1$. (In the second picture, the choice of vertical units "flattens"—but doesn't destroy—the parabolic shape.)

Numerical differences   Zooming in numerically on the error functions can also help reveal the best linear approximation. Here are some sample values:

Values of three error functions near $x = 1$							
x	1.000	1.001	1.002	1.003	1.004	1.005	1.006
$f(x) - \ell_2(x)$	0	0.000001	0.000004	0.000009	0.000016	0.000025	0.000036
$f(x) - \ell_{2.1}(x)$	0	−0.000099	−0.000196	−0.000291	−0.000384	−0.000475	−0.000564
$f(x) - \ell_{1.9}(x)$	0	0.000101	0.000204	0.000309	0.000416	0.000525	0.000636

Notice the big difference between the best linear approximation ℓ_2 and the two "also-rans." Values of $f - \ell_2$ are less than those of the other two error functions throughout the table; even more striking is the relative advantage of $f - \ell_2$ when x is near $x = 1$. At $x = 1.001$, for instance, ℓ_2 commits only about 1/100 the error committed by $\ell_{1.9}$ and $\ell_{2.1}$. The key advantage of ℓ_2 can be seen in the numbers: the error function $f - \ell_2$ appears to be *quadratic*, with vertex at $x = 1$, while $f - \ell_{1.9}$ and $f - \ell_{2.1}$ behave like *linear* functions.

The key point is that the difference function $f - \ell$ (where ℓ is the "true" tangent-line approximation at a point) typically looks quadratic at small scale near the point of tangency. If ℓ is chosen even slightly wrong, the difference $f - \ell$ usually looks linear, with an x-intercept at the point of tangency.

But see the exercises for some exceptions, which involve inflection points.

A zooming strategy   Here's an informal strategy that often works: ◄

Let f be a well-behaved function and $(a, f(a))$ a point on its graph. Let ℓ be a linear function whose graph passes through $(a, f(a))$. To decide whether ℓ is the "right" tangent line function for f at $x = a$, define the error function $e(x) = f(x) - \ell(x)$ and zoom in (graphically or numerically) on $e(x)$ near $x = a$. If the result looks like a line that *crosses* the x-axis at $x = a$, then ℓ is probably wrong. If the result resembles a *parabola* with vertex $(a, 0)$, then $\ell(x)$ is probably right.

FURTHER EXERCISES

1. Let $f(x) = \sqrt{x}$. The estimates $f'(1) \approx 0.5$, $f'(1) \approx 0.4$, and $f'(1) \approx 0.6$ are all reasonable, but only one is correct.

   (a) Write equations for the three linear functions and the three error functions associated with the estimates above.

   (b) Use graphical zooming (as shown above) to identify the "true" value of $f'(1)$.

   (c) Tabulate some numerical values of the three error functions near $x = 1$. How do the the numbers support your answer in the preceding part?

2. Repeat the first problem, using the function $f(x) = x^2$ and the estimates $f'(3) \approx 5.9$, $f'(3) \approx 6.0$, and $f'(3) \approx 6.1$.

3. Repeat the first problem, using the function $f(x) = e^x$ and the estimates $f'(0) \approx 0.99$, $f'(0) \approx 1.00$, and $f'(0) \approx 1.01$.

4. The strategy outlined above doesn't always work the same way. To see this, apply the zooming strategy to the function $f(x) = \sin x$, the estimates $f'(0) \approx 0.9$ and $f'(0) \approx 1.1$, and the exact answer, $f'(0) = 1.0$. What do you see? What accounts for the difference? (Hint: The function $f(x) = \sin x$ has an inflection point at $x = 0$.)

5. Apply the strategy outlined above to the function $f(x) = x^3$ at $x = 0$ (which happens to be an inflection point). Use the estimates $f'(0) = 0$, $f'(0) = 0.01$, and $f'(0) = -0.01$. What do you see?

2

FUNCTIONS AND DERIVATIVES: THE SYMBOLIC VIEW

2.1 DEFINING THE DERIVATIVE

In Chapter 1 we studied derivatives from the *graphical* point of view, interpreting them mainly in terms of slope. In this chapter we stress the *symbolic* point of view; an important goal is to use a given symbolic formula for a function f (if one exists) to find another formula for f'.

Before we can *find* derivatives symbolically, we need to *define* them symbolically. A useful definition should, of course, "agree" with our graphical view of derivatives as slopes, but it should do more: It should let us use the formula for f to find a formula for f'.

We approach the definition through two parallel problems:

In this chapter we expand on ideas of Chapter 1—now in the symbolic setting. The ideas of antiderivative and differential equation appear for the first time—systematic treatments appear later. Sections 5, 6, and 7 describe some classical applications (linear motion, growth, and oscillation) in connection with finding derivatives and (in the simplest cases) antiderivatives of polynomial, exponential, and trigonometric functions. Doing so also adds a little "modeling" flavor to the package.

- **The rate-of-change problem**   Let the function $D(t)$ give the distance, in miles, traveled by a car up to time t, in hours. Find $D'(2)$, the instantaneous speed (the rate of change of distance with respect to time) at time $t = 2$.

- **The tangent-line problem**   Let $y = f(x)$ be a function. Find $f'(2)$, the slope of the tangent line at $x = 2$.

The rate-of-change problem

EXAMPLE 1   At exactly noon, Professor X ➤ began a 2.5-hour trip in her trusty but aging automobile. The clock and trip mileage meter still work, but the speedometer gave out long ago. Worried about speeding (the limit is 70 mph), the compulsive professor recorded her travel time t (in hours) and her distance traveled $D(t)$ (in miles) every 3 minutes during the trip. Here are some of her data:

She spoke off the record.

Professor X's time and distance data								
t (hours)	1.80	1.85	1.90	1.95	2.00	2.05	2.10	2.15	2.20
$D(t)$ (miles)	66.60	69.84	73.15	76.54	80.00	83.54	87.15	90.84	94.60

Safely arrived at her desk, Professor X plotted some of her data (Figure 1).

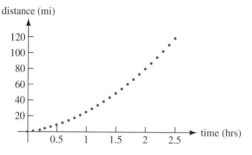

The dots are spaced at 6-minute intervals—10 to the hour.

FIGURE 1

Professor X's trip

"Was I legally under 70," she wondered, "when I passed that patrol car at 2:00 P.M.? That officer looked at me pretty hard."

Think a moment about this important point before reading on.

How can Professor X calculate or estimate $D'(2)$, her speed at 2:00 P.M.? The trip odometer showed 80 miles at 2:00 P.M., so her *average* speed was 40 mph over the first 2 hours. But what about her speed at the *instant* $t = 2$? Professor X reasons that her *average* speed over a short time interval that contains $t = 2$ should be close to her *instantaneous* speed at $t = 2$. ◄ In the 0.1-hour interval from $t = 1.90$ to $t = 2.00$, for instance, she traveled $D(2.00) - D(1.90) = 80.00 - 73.15 = 6.85$ miles; so her average speed was

$$\frac{6.85 \text{ miles}}{0.1 \text{ hours}} = 68.5 \text{ mph.}$$

"Looks perfectly legal to me," thinks Professor X with relief. "My best guess is $D'(2) = 68.5$. But just to be sure, I'll try the interval from $t = 2.00$ to $t = 2.05$."

Consulting her data, Professor X calculates as follows:

$$\text{average speed} = \frac{D(2.05) - D(2.00)}{0.05} = \frac{3.54 \text{ miles}}{0.05 \text{ hours}} = 70.8 \text{ mph.}$$

"Now it seems that $D'(2) = 70.8$. Could I be guilty?" wonders Professor X, aghast. "I'm glad I use an alias." ■

The tangent-line problem

EXAMPLE 2   Figure 2 shows part of the graph of $f(x) = x^2 + x$ along with a reasonable candidate for the tangent line at $x = 2$ (we'll call it L):

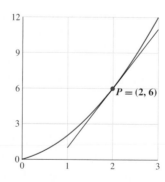

$P = (2, 6)$

FIGURE 2

A line tangent to the graph of
$y = x^2 + x$

Estimate $f'(2)$ (the slope of L) as accurately as possible; use the result to write a point–slope equation for L.

Solution An eyeball estimate puts the slope of L at 5; with this assumption a point–slope equation for L is $y = 5(x - 2) + 6$.

Finding the slope of L *exactly* is harder because we know for certain only one point $(P = (2, 6))$ on L. As a start, we might consider another line L' that passes through P and through *another* nearby point (such as the point at $x = 2.01$) on the graph of $y = x^2 + x$; we expect L and L' to have about the same slope.

Knowing *two* points on L', we can easily find its slope:

$$\frac{\Delta f}{\Delta x} = \frac{f(2.01) - f(2)}{2.01 - 2} = \frac{6.0501 - 6}{0.01} = 5.01,$$

which fits well with our graphical guess that $f'(2) = 5$.

To see graphically how f, L, and L' are related, we can plot all three together and zoom in closely (Figure 3):

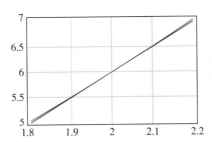

The lines L and L' look identical at this scale.

FIGURE 3
Graphs of f, L, and L'

There's no mistake: All three graphs are shown, but at this scale they're virtually identical. All three, moreover, have slopes near 5. By all available evidence so far, $f'(2) = 5$. ∎

Solving both problems—with limits

The methods we've seen (zooming, eyeballing graphs, and finding slopes or rates over small intervals) all give useful *estimates* for slopes and rates. To get *precise* answers, however, we need a sharper mathematical tool: the **limit**. Roughly speaking, the limit describes how a function $f(x)$ behaves for x *near* a specific input value $x = a$. For the moment we'll treat limits informally, showing mainly how they can help us calculate derivatives. We'll revisit limits more formally and in more detail later in this chapter.

Most students seem unbothered by abstract questions of existence of a derivative or tangent line. More "live" are questions of how to find formulas for these objects.

Average speeds, instantaneous speeds, and limits Professor X has no trouble using distance data to find *average* speeds over short time intervals. What she really wants, though, is her *instantaneous* speed at $t = 2$.

Physical intuition suggests that the instantaneous speed of a car at any instant $t = t_0$ should be closely approximated by average speeds over short time intervals that contain t_0. The shorter the interval, moreover, the better we expect our estimate to be. The concept of limit helps make this natural connection between average and instantaneous speeds precise, and it lets us use formulas to do exact calculations.

For example, let's consider the interval from $t = 2$ to $t = 2 + h$ hours, where h represents a small positive or negative increment (or change) in time. Professor X's *average* speed

over this interval is

$$\frac{\Delta D}{\Delta t} = \frac{D(2+h) - D(2)}{(2+h) - 2} = \frac{D(2+h) - D(2)}{h}.$$

This is the first appearance of limit notation. Here it should be understood from context. We study limits in their own right in Section 2.3.

If h is near 0, then the time interval is short, and we expect the preceding quotient to be near the *instantaneous* speed at $t = 2$. The limit notation gives us a compact symbolic way of saying the same thing:

$$\lim_{h \to 0} \frac{D(2+h) - D(2)}{h} = D'(2).$$

In the real world—unlike calculus texts—cars don't obey formulas exactly.

To help Professor X with limits, we'll need a formula for $D(t)$. Suppose, for instance, that $D(t) = 10t + 15t^2$ (the formula fits the data in Figure 1). ◄

Finding the speed at $t = 2$ hours is now mainly a matter of algebra:

$$\lim_{h \to 0} \frac{D(2+h) - D(2)}{h} = \lim_{h \to 0} \frac{\left(10(2+h) + 15(2+h)^2\right) - 80}{h}$$

If the formula D(t) applies after t = 2, then Professor X is a speeder after all.

$$= \lim_{h \to 0} \frac{70h + 15h^2}{h}$$
$$= \lim_{h \to 0} (70 + 15h)$$
$$= 70.$$

Thus, at precisely 2:00 P.M., Professor X's speed was *exactly* 70 mph. Absolved of guilt (at least at time 2 hours), she considers dropping her alias.

Let's review the preceding calculation, since we'll repeat it often: First, we used the formula for $D(t)$ to write the average speed as a rather complicated expression in h. Then we simplified the average speed expression algebraically until its limit as h tends to 0 became clear at a glance.

Secant lines, tangent lines, and limits Given two points P and Q on a curve C, we can draw the line through P and Q. If P and Q are close together, it's reasonable to expect this **secant line** to resemble the tangent line at P. Figure 4 illustrates the idea of secant lines approximating the tangent line (shown bold) to a curve (also bold) at the dotted point:

FIGURE 4
Secant lines approaching a tangent line

Finding slopes of secant lines is easy because we have two points to work with. If $P = \left(a, f(a)\right)$ and $Q = \left(b, f(b)\right)$ are points on the graph of $y = f(x)$, then (see Figure 5) the slope of the secant line from P to Q (i.e., from $x = a$ to $x = a + h$) is

$$\frac{f(a+h) - f(a)}{h}.$$

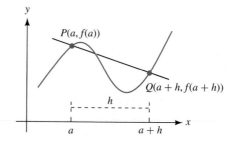

FIGURE 5
The secant line from $x = a$ to $x = a + h$

We calculated in Example 2 that the secant line to the graph of $f(x) = x^2 + x$ from $x = 2$ to $x = 2.01$ has slope 5.01. A similar calculation (details are in the next example) shows that the secant line from $x = 2$ to $x = 2.001$ has slope 5.001. These results suggest a strategy: Find the slope of the tangent line as the *limit* of slopes of secant lines over shorter and shorter intervals.

EXAMPLE 3 Compute slopes of several secant lines to the graph of $f(x) = x^2 + x$ over small intervals ending at $x = 2$. Use a limit to draw a conclusion about $f'(2)$.

Solution Results for several small intervals appear below. ➡

The symbols Δf and Δx denote changes in inputs and outputs.

Slopes of secant lines over small intervals						
Interval	$[1.9, 2]$	$[1.99, 2]$	$[1.999, 2]$	$[2, 2.001]$	$[2, 2.01]$	$[2, 2.1]$
Δx	0.1	0.01	0.001	0.001	0.01	0.1
Δf	0.49	0.049	0.004999	0.005001	0.0501	0.51
Slope $= \frac{\Delta f}{\Delta x}$	4.9	4.99	4.999	5.001	5.01	5.1

The slopes in the last line certainly seem to approach 5 as Δx approaches 0, but we'll use limits to clinch the case symbolically. For any nonzero increment h, the secant line from $x = 2$ to $x = 2 + h$ has slope

$$\frac{\Delta f}{\Delta x} = \frac{f(2+h) - f(2)}{(2+h) - 2} = \frac{f(2+h) - f(2)}{h}.$$

Now we use the formula $f(x) = x^2 + x$ to find an algebraic expression for this slope:

$$\frac{f(2+h) - f(2)}{h} = \frac{((2+h)^2 + (2+h)) - 6}{h} = \frac{5h + h^2}{h} = 5 + h.$$

Students should follow this derivation carefully; functional expressions like $f(2+h)$ may baffle some. Exercises reinforce these ideas.

The last expression shows why the slope of the tangent line at $x = 2$ is indeed exactly 5:

$$f'(2) = \lim_{h \to 0} \frac{f(2+h) - f(2)}{h} = \lim_{h \to 0} (5 + h) = 5. \qquad \blacksquare$$

The derivative, formally defined

The rate-of-change and tangent-line problems turned out to involve the same mathematical idea. Both problems—and many others—lead to limits of the form that appears in the following key definition.

> **DEFINITION** Let f be a function defined near and at $x = a$. The **derivative of** f **at** $x = a$, denoted by $f'(a)$, is defined by the limit equation
>
> $$f'(a) = \lim_{h \to 0} \frac{f(a+h) - f(a)}{h}.$$

Such an important definition deserves comment:

- **Other forms** The limit in the preceding definition can be written in other, equivalent, forms. Here are several possibilities:

$$\lim_{h \to 0} \frac{f(a+h) - f(a)}{h} \qquad \lim_{\Delta x \to 0} \frac{f(a + \Delta x) - f(a)}{\Delta x}$$

$$\lim_{x \to a} \frac{f(x) - f(a)}{x - a} \qquad \lim_{\Delta x \to 0} \frac{\Delta f}{\Delta x}$$

  Depending on the circumstances, one form may be simpler or more convenient than another, but all convey the same information.

- **Dividing by zero?** The limit in the derivative definition *always* involves a denominator tending to zero; evaluating it usually requires some trick or other. In practice, things often work out as in the preceding examples: After some careful algebra in the numerator, the troublesome denominator disappears.

- **Must $f'(a)$ exist?** In a word, no—the limit in the definition need not exist. If the limit *does* exist, we say that f **is differentiable at** $x = a$ or that f has a derivative at $x = a$. Most of the functions we treat in calculus are differentiable wherever they make sense, but there are exceptions. One is the absolute value function $g(x) = |x|$; the kink in the graph at $x = 0$ means that g has no tangent line—and hence no derivative—at $a = 0$.

Students should understand that the difference quotient (or ratio) represents a rate of change; so does its limit.

Difference quotients: a closer look

Difference quotients, no matter how they're written, have the same general form:

> **DEFINITION** For any function f, the ratio
> $$\frac{f(a+h) - f(a)}{h} = \frac{\Delta f}{\Delta x}$$
> is a **difference quotient**. It measures the *average rate of change* of the function f from $x = a$ to $x = a + h$.

To understand what the difference quotient tells, we'll analyze its parts separately.

- **The denominator** The difference $\Delta x = h = (a + h) - a$ represents a change (positive or negative) in the input variable, from $x = a$ to $x = a + h$.

- **The numerator** As x changes from $x = a$ to $x = a + h$, the output $f(x)$ changes too, from $f(a)$ to $f(a + h)$. The numerator $\Delta f = f(a + h) - f(a)$ measures this change; Δf may be positive, negative, or zero.

- **The quotient** The difference quotient is the *ratio* of the two changes Δf and Δx, so it represents a *rate* of change. Because the changes occur over an *interval* in x, the quotient represents an *average* rate of change.

- **From average to instantaneous** The difference quotient is an *average* rate of change over the interval from $x = a$ to $x = a + h$; its limit as h tends to zero is the *instantaneous* rate of change at the instant $x = a$.

Speaking of rates. In calculus, the phrase "rate of change" need not involve quantities varying in *time*. If f is *any* function, the difference quotient $\Delta f / \Delta x$ and the derivative can be thought of as rates because they compare changes in outputs to changes in inputs.

Another linguistic note: Replacing the phrase "rate of *change*" with "rate of *increase*" sometimes simplifies mental bookkeeping. If $\Delta f / \Delta x > 0$, the rate of increase of $f(x)$ with respect to x is *positive*; this means that $f(x)$ increases as x does. If $\Delta f/\Delta x < 0$, the rate of increase is *negative*, so $f(x)$ decreases as x increases.

Difference quotients and derivatives in context

Every function f has many possible interpretations. Any particular interpretation of f leads to corresponding interpretations of the difference quotient and the derivative.

In particular, rates of change may have nothing to do with time — they're simply ratios of two changes.

EXAMPLE 4 Let $g(x)$ tell the miles traveled by a test vehicle on x gallons of fuel. (Professor X's old car isn't capable of such precision.) The table shows several readings.

x (gallons)	0	1.50	1.90	1.99	2.00
$g(x)$ (miles)	0	43.2725	55.4993	58.3969	58.7206

The difference quotient

$$\frac{g(2) - g(0)}{2 - 0} = \frac{58.7206 \text{ miles}}{2 \text{ gallons}} = 29.3603 \text{ miles per gallon}$$

represents the *average* rate of gas consumption over the interval in which the first two gallons of gas were consumed. The *instantaneous* rate of gas consumption varies from moment to moment. To find an instantaneous rate we'd need a limit, and that would require an explicit formula for g. Even without such a formula, we can estimate. A difference quotient like that above, but over the short interval $[1.99, 2.00]$, gives 32.4 mpg as a reasonable estimate for the gas mileage at the moment the second gallon is consumed.   ■

Units What units to use for difference quotients and derivatives depends on the units used for x and y. For Professor X we measured distance in miles and time in hours, so the natural rate unit was *miles per hour*. In Example 4 we started with miles and gallons, so fuel consumption rates were measured in *miles per gallon*. With another vehicle (horse) and other units for distance (leagues) and fuel (bales), the appropriate rate unit would have been different: *leagues per bale*.

BASIC EXERCISES

1. Let $D(t)$ be the function in Example 1. Estimate $D'(2)$ using $D(1.95)$ and $D(2.05)$.

2. Let f, L, and L' be as in Example 2. Explain why the slope of L' is greater than the slope of L.
   [HINT: What property of the graph of f makes the statement true?]

3. Let f, L, and L' be as in Example 2, and let M be the line through the points on the graph of f where $x = 2$ and $x = 2.005$, respectively.
   (a) What is the slope of M?
   (b) Does the slope of M overestimate the slope of L? Justify your answer.
   (c) Explain why the slope of M is a better estimate of $f'(2)$ than is the slope of L'.

4. Let f, L, and L' be as in Example 2, and let M' be the line through the points on the graph of f where $x = 1.995$ and $x = 2$, respectively.
   (a) What is the slope of M'?
   (b) Does the slope of M' overestimate the slope of L? Justify your answer.
   (c) Explain why the slope of M' is a better estimate of $f'(2)$ than is the slope of L'.

5. Explain how the graphs of f and L in Figure 3 support the guess that L is the line tangent to the graph of $f(x) = x^2 + x$ at $x = 2$.

6. Find an equation for the line that is tangent to the curve $y = 10t + 15t^2$ at the point $(2, 80)$.

7. Let $f(x) = x^2 + x$. Evaluate $f'(-1)$ by mimicking the computations in Example 3.

8. How are average and instantaneous rates of change related? (Your answer should involve the word "limit"!)

9. What does the difference quotient $\dfrac{f(a+h) - f(a)}{h}$ represent graphically?

10. Suppose that $w(t)$ is the weight in ounces of a kitten t days after it is born. Use the definition of the derivative to explain why the units associated with $w'(t)$ are ounces per day.

Exercises 11 and 12 are based on the graph below, which shows how the price of a certain stock varied over a recent trading day.

11. (a) Find the average rate of change of the stock's price between 8:00 A.M. and 2:00 P.M.

   (b) Find the average rate of change of the stock's price between 9:00 A.M. and 1:00 P.M.

   (c) Estimate the instantaneous rate of change of the stock's price at 9:15 A.M.

12. (a) Find the average rate of change of the stock's price between 11:00 A.M. and 1:00 P.M.

   (b) Estimate the instantaneous rate of change of the stock's price at 10:30 A.M.

   (c) Estimate the instantaneous rate of change of the stock's price at 1:00 P.M.

In Exercises 13–16, estimate the value of f' at the given point using a difference quotient with $h = 0.001$. Compare each answer with the value obtained by zooming in on the graph of f at the point.

13. $f(x) = x^2 - 3x$ at $x = 3$

14. $f(x) = x^{-2}$ at $x = 1$

15. $f(x) = \sin x$ at $x = 0$

16. $f(x) = \cos(3x)$ at $x = \pi/2$

In Exercises 17–20, suppose that f has the values shown in the table.

x	1.9	1.99	1.999	2.0
$f(x)$	25.34	33.97	34.896	35

x	2.001	2.01	2.05	2.1
$f(x)$	35.104	36.05	40.37	46.18

Use the tabulated values of f to estimate

17. $f'(1.99)$

18. $f'(2)$

19. $f'(2.01)$

20. $f'(2.1)$

In Exercises 21–24, suppose that f has the values shown in the table.

x	1.9	1.97	2.0	2.02	2.2
$f(x)$	6.6	6.905	7	7.059	7.5

Use the tabulated values of f to estimate

21. $f'(1.9)$

22. $f'(1.97)$

23. $f'(2)$

24. $f'(2.2)$

In Exercises 25–28, use the values $f(1.9)$, $f(1.95)$, $f(2.0)$, and $f(2.01)$ to estimate

   (a) $f'(1.9)$

   (b) $f'(2.0)$

   (c) $f'(2.01)$

25. $f(x) = x^2$

26. $f(x) = \sin x$

27. $f(x) = e^x$

28. $f(x) = \ln x$

29. Let $f(x) = x^2$. Carefully explain each step in the following evaluation of $f'(3)$:

   (a) $f'(3) = \lim\limits_{h \to 0} \dfrac{f(3+h) - f(3)}{h}$

   (b) $ = \lim\limits_{h \to 0} \dfrac{(3+h)^2 - 9}{h}$

   (c) $ = \lim\limits_{h \to 0} \dfrac{6h + h^2}{h}$

   (d) $ = \lim\limits_{h \to 0} (6 + h)$

   (e) $ = 6$.

30. Let $f(x) = x^2$. Evaluate $f'(2) = \lim\limits_{\Delta x \to 0} \dfrac{f(2 + \Delta x) - f(2)}{\Delta x}$.

31. Let $f(x) = x^2$. Carefully explain each step in the following evaluation of $f'(1)$:

   (a) $f'(1) = \lim\limits_{x \to 1} \dfrac{f(x) - f(1)}{x - 1}$

   (b) $ = \lim\limits_{x \to 1} \dfrac{x^2 - 1}{x - 1}$

   (c) $ = \lim\limits_{x \to 1} (x + 1)$

   (d) $ = 2$.

32. Let $f(x) = x^2$. Evaluate $f'(-1) = \lim\limits_{x \to -1} \dfrac{f(x) - f(-1)}{x + 1}$.

In Exercises 33–36, the limit shown is $f'(a)$ for some function f and some number a. First, identify f and a. Then estimate the value of $f'(a)$ by examining a graph of the difference quotient.

33. $\lim\limits_{x \to 4} \dfrac{\sqrt{x} - 2}{x - 4}$

34. $\lim\limits_{\Delta x \to 0} \dfrac{\sqrt{9 + \Delta x} - 3}{\Delta x}$

35. $\lim\limits_{h \to 0} \dfrac{\cos h - 1}{h}$

36. $\lim\limits_{x \to 1} \dfrac{2^x - 2}{x - 1}$

FURTHER EXERCISES

37. If $f(1) = 2$ and the average rate of change of f from $x = 1$ to $x = 5$ is 3, what's $f(5)$?

38. If $f(2) = 1$ and the average rate of change of f from $x = -3$ to $x = 2$ is 4, what's $f(-3)$?

39. Let $f(x) = \sqrt{x}$. Tabulate $f(x)$ at $x = 1.998$, 1.999, 2.000, 2.001, and 2.002 and use your results to answer the following questions. (Round numerical values of $f(x)$ to seven decimal places.)

    (a) Explain how these tabulated values show that f is "locally linear" near $x = 2$.

    (b) Estimate $f'(1.999)$, $f'(2)$, and $f'(2.001)$ using the tabulated values of f.

    (c) Does $(f(2.001) - f(2))/0.001$ overestimate the exact value of $f'(2)$? Justify your answer.
    [HINT: Look at a graph of $f(x)$ near $x = 2$.]

    (d) Estimate $f''(2)$ using the results from part (b).

40. Let $f(x) = 2^x$.

    (a) Find the average rate of change of f between $x = 0$ and $x = 0.01$. Explain why this estimate of $f'(0)$ is too large.

    (b) Find the average rate of change of f between $x = -0.01$ and $x = 0$. Explain why this estimate of $f'(0)$ is too small.

    (c) Find the average rate of change of f between -0.01 and 0.01.

    (d) Why is the estimate of $f'(0)$ found in part (c) more accurate than the estimates computed in parts (a) and (b)?

In Exercises 41–44, use the limit definition of the derivative to compute $f'(4)$ for each function.

41. $f(x) = 2x + 1$

42. $f(x) = x^2 - 3x$

43. $f(x) = x^3$

44. $f(x) = 2/x$

45. Suppose that f is increasing and concave up on the interval $[0, 10]$ and that m is the slope of the line through the points $(3, f(3))$ and $(5, f(5))$.

    (a) Is $m < f'(3)$? Justify your answer with words and a picture.

    (b) Is $m > f'(5)$? Justify your answer with words and a picture.

46. Suppose that f is decreasing and concave up on the interval $[0, 10]$, and that m is the slope of the line through the points $(3, f(3))$ and $(5, f(5))$.

    (a) Is $m < f'(3)$? Justify your answer with words and a picture.

    (b) Is $m > f'(5)$? Justify your answer with words and a picture.

47. Suppose that g is increasing and concave down on the interval $[0, 10]$. Let a be the average rate of change of g over the interval $[5, 8]$. Is $a > g'(5)$? Justify your answer with words and a picture.

In Exercises 48–51, h is a function such that $h(0) = 1$, $h(2) = 7$, $h(4) = 5$, $h'(0) = -2$, $h'(2) = 3$, and $h'(4) = -1$.

48. What is the average rate of change of h over the interval $[0, 4]$?

49. Evaluate $\lim\limits_{t \to 2} \dfrac{h(t) - h(2)}{t - 2}$.

50. Evaluate $\lim\limits_{w \to 0} \dfrac{h(w) - 1}{w}$.

51. Evaluate $\lim\limits_{\Delta x \to 0} \dfrac{h(4 + \Delta x) - 5}{\Delta x}$.

In Exercises 52–53, g is a function such that g' is the function shown below.

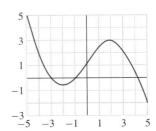

52. Evaluate $\lim\limits_{h \to 0} \dfrac{g(-4 + h) - g(-4)}{h}$.

53. Evaluate $\lim\limits_{x \to 3} \dfrac{g(x) - g(3)}{x - 3}$.

54. Suppose that $y = 3 - 2x$ is an equation of the line through the points $P = (1, g(1))$ and $Q = (4, g(4))$. What is the average rate of change of g over the interval $[1, 4]$?

55. Suppose that the average rate of change of h over the interval $[-3, 5]$ is 4. Is it possible that the line $y = 4x - 4$ passes through the points $(-3, h(-3))$ and $(5, h(5))$? Justify your answer.

56. Suppose that the average rate of change of g over the interval $[2, 2+h]$ is $4e^h$.

(a) What is the slope of the line through the points $(2, g(2))$ and $(2.05, g(2.05))$?

(b) Evaluate $g(2.1) - g(2)$.

(c) Evaluate $g(1.99) - g(2)$.

(d) Evaluate $g'(2)$.

57. Suppose that $f(2) = 3$ and that the average rate of change of f over the interval $[2, 6]$ is 5. Find an equation of the line through the points $(2, f(2))$ and $(6, f(6))$.

2.2 DERIVATIVES OF POWER FUNCTIONS AND POLYNOMIALS

In this section we start in earnest to look at derivatives symbolically. After finding the "general" power rule (x^k)' = kx^{k-1}, we apply sum and constant multiple rules to differentiate polynomials and other related functions. We see, too, how operations with constants affect derivatives.

In the preceding section we studied $f'(a)$, the derivative of the function f at the input point $x = a$. In this section we consider the derivative f' as a function in its own right. The following definition is much like that of $f'(a)$ on page 85; we use the generic x in place of the specific a to emphasize that f' is a function.

> **DEFINITION** Let f be a function. The derivative of f, denoted by f', is the function defined for an input x by
> $$f'(x) = \lim_{h \to 0} \frac{f(x+h) - f(x)}{h}.$$

Observe:

- **Can we just let $h = 0$?** The limit in the definition cannot be found just by plugging in $h = 0$. Some algebraic manipulation or trick is needed to cancel out the troublesome h in the denominator.

- **If algebra fails** The limit in the definition may be hard or impossible to find exactly, especially if f has a complicated formula. In such cases, graphical or numerical estimates of the derivative may be our only recourse.

As we do for "original" functions, we'll usually consider the "natural domains" of derivatives functions.

- **The domain of the derivative function** The domain of f' is the set of inputs x for which the limit exists. In many cases the domain of f' is the full domain of f. But not in every case: If $f(x) = |x|$, for example, then $f'(0)$ does not exist, so the domain of f' is *smaller* than the domain of f. ◄

The graph of $f(x) = |x|$ has a kink, and therefore no derivative, at $x = 0$.

Other notations for the derivative

The prime notation for the derivative function is typographically convenient, and it reminds us of a derivative's "ancestry": Every derivative function f' comes from some "original function" f. There are alternatives to the prime notation; depending on context, one may be more convenient than another. The following notations all say the same thing about the function $y = f(x) = x^2$:

$$f'(x) = 2x; \qquad \frac{dy}{dx} = 2x; \qquad \frac{d}{dx}\left(x^2\right) = 2x; \qquad \frac{df}{dx} = 2x.$$

So do these:

$$f'(3) = 6; \qquad \frac{dy}{dx}\bigg|_{x=3} = 6; \qquad \frac{d}{dx}\left(x^2\right)\bigg|_{x=3} = 6; \qquad \frac{df}{dx}\bigg|_{x=3} = 6.$$

(We'll soon see *why* these statements are true. Here, the point is the notation.) The dy/dx form of the derivative is known as **Leibniz notation**, after Gottfried Wilhelm Leibniz (1646–1716), a contemporary of Isaac Newton. The "fractional" appearance of Leibniz notation recalls the definition of the derivative as a limit of difference *quotients*:

$$\frac{dy}{dx} = \lim_{\Delta x \to 0} \frac{\Delta y}{\Delta x}.$$

Higher derivatives Both prime and Leibniz notations are available for second, third, and higher derivatives. The following notations all say the same thing about the function $y = g(x) = x^3$:

$$g''(x) = 6x; \quad \frac{d^2 y}{dx^2} = 6x; \quad \frac{d^2}{dx^2}\left(x^3\right) = 6x; \quad \frac{d^2 g}{dx^2} = 6x; \quad \frac{d^2}{dx^2}g(x) = 6x.$$

We'll use both the prime and the Leibniz notations in this book.

What's ahead: finding derivative formulas If a function f has a symbolic formula, then it's natural to search for a corresponding symbolic formula for the derivative f'. We'll succeed nicely in this quest: We'll soon be able to find symbolic derivatives even for such monsters as

$$f(x) = \ln\left(\frac{\sin(2x)}{1 + \tan^4(e^x)}\right).$$

The first step, however, is to find derivative formulas for the most basic functions: polynomial, exponential, logarithmic, and trigonometric functions. Then we'll see how to combine these answers to find derivatives of more complicated functions.

The first step is this chapter's main agenda; the second step is completed in Chapter 3.

Derivatives of power functions

Our first task is to find derivatives of **power functions**—functions of the form $f(x) = x^k$, where k is any constant (not necessarily an integer). Each of the following expressions defines a power function:

$$x, \quad x^2, \quad \sqrt{x}, \quad \frac{1}{\sqrt{x}}, \quad \frac{x^5}{\sqrt{x^3}}, \quad x^\pi.$$

We start with the easiest case: nonnegative integer powers.

EXAMPLE 1 Find derivative formulas for the linear, quadratic, and cubic power functions $l(x) = x$, $q(x) = x^2$, and $c(x) = x^3$. Interpret the results graphically.

Solution The function l has a straight-line graph with slope 1, so its derivative is the constant function $l'(x) = 1$. It's reassuring to see that the limit definition says the same thing:

$$l'(x) = \lim_{h \to 0} \frac{l(x+h) - l(x)}{h} \qquad \text{(by definition)}$$

$$= \lim_{h \to 0} \frac{(x+h) - x}{h} \qquad \text{(use formula } l(x) = x\text{)}$$

$$= \lim_{h \to 0} \frac{h}{h} = \lim_{h \to 0} 1 = 1. \qquad \text{(simplify quotient; substitute } h = 0\text{)}$$

Higher powers of x require a little more algebraic work. For $q(x) = x^2$:

$$q'(x) = \lim_{h \to 0} \frac{q(x+h) - q(x)}{h}$$

$$= \lim_{h \to 0} \frac{(x+h)^2 - x^2}{h} \qquad \text{(use formula } q(x) = x^2)$$

$$= \lim_{h \to 0} \frac{(x^2 + 2xh + h^2) - x^2}{h} = \lim_{h \to 0} \frac{2xh + h^2}{h} \qquad \text{(simplify)}$$

$$= \lim_{h \to 0} (2x + h) = 2x. \qquad \text{(cancel } h; \text{ substitute } h = 0)$$

Students should work through this algebra for themselves.

The cubic function c yields to similar algebra:

$$c'(x) = \lim_{h \to 0} \frac{c(x+h) - c(x)}{h}$$

$$= \lim_{h \to 0} \frac{(x+h)^3 - x^3}{h}$$

$$= \lim_{h \to 0} \frac{(x^3 + 3x^2h + 3xh^2 + h^3) - x^3}{h} \qquad \text{(expand the third power)}$$

$$= \lim_{h \to 0} (3x^2 + 3xh + h^2) \qquad \text{(simplify; cancel } h)$$

$$= 3x^2. \qquad \text{(substitute } h = 0)$$

Figures 1 and 2 show graphs of all three functions and their derivatives:

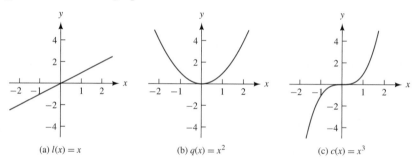

(a) $l(x) = x$ (b) $q(x) = x^2$ (c) $c(x) = x^3$

FIGURE 1
Graphs of three power functions

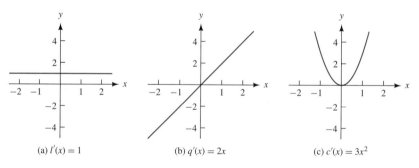

(a) $l'(x) = 1$ (b) $q'(x) = 2x$ (c) $c'(x) = 3x^2$

FIGURE 2
Derivatives of three power functions

The general shapes of the derivative graphs aren't surprising—or new. For example, we guessed in Example 5, page 50, that the derivative of $q(x) = x^2$ is $q'(x) = 2x$. The symbolic calculation tells us, for the first time, that this guess was correct. We could also have guessed back in Chapter 1 that the derivative of c is roughly parabolic in shape, but now we know more: the derivative's *exact* formula is $c'(x) = 3x^2$. ∎

Derivatives of other power functions We used basic algebra in Example 1 to differentiate x^1, x^2, and x^3. In Example 2 we apply similar (but slightly trickier) methods to two functions whose powers are *not* positive integers.

EXAMPLE 2 Differentiate the power functions $s(x) = \sqrt{x} = x^{1/2}$ and $n(x) = 1/x = x^{-1}$. What are the domains of s' and n'? Express results graphically.

Solution Handling s and n takes some careful algebra. For s:

$$
\begin{aligned}
s'(x) &= \lim_{h \to 0} \frac{s(x+h) - s(x)}{h} \\[2mm]
&= \lim_{h \to 0} \frac{\sqrt{x+h} - \sqrt{x}}{h} && \text{(use formula } s(x) = \sqrt{x}) \\[2mm]
&= \lim_{h \to 0} \frac{\sqrt{x+h} - \sqrt{x}}{h} \cdot \frac{\sqrt{x+h} + \sqrt{x}}{\sqrt{x+h} + \sqrt{x}} \\
&&&\text{(multiply top and bottom by ``conjugate'' of numerator)} \\[2mm]
&= \lim_{h \to 0} \frac{(x+h) - x}{h(\sqrt{x+h} + \sqrt{x})} = \lim_{h \to 0} \frac{1}{\sqrt{x+h} + \sqrt{x}} && \text{(simplify)} \\[2mm]
&= \frac{1}{2\sqrt{x}} = \frac{1}{2}x^{-1/2}. && \text{(substitute } h = 0; \text{ rewrite)}
\end{aligned}
$$

For the function n,

$$
\begin{aligned}
n'(x) &= \lim_{h \to 0} \frac{n(x+h) - n(x)}{h} \\[2mm]
&= \lim_{h \to 0} \frac{\frac{1}{x+h} - \frac{1}{x}}{h} && \text{(use formula } n(x) = 1/x) \\[2mm]
&= \lim_{h \to 0} \frac{\frac{x}{x(x+h)} - \frac{x+h}{x(x+h)}}{h} && \text{(rewrite with common denominator)} \\[2mm]
&= \lim_{h \to 0} \frac{x - (x+h)}{h} \cdot \frac{1}{x(x+h)} = \lim_{h \to 0} \frac{-h}{h\,x\,(x+h)} && \text{(algebra)} \\[2mm]
&= \lim_{h \to 0} \frac{-1}{x(x+h)} = \frac{-1}{x^2} = -x^{-2}. && \text{(cancel common } h; \text{ then set } h = 0)
\end{aligned}
$$

Graphs of s, n, and their derivatives appear in Figures 3 and 4. Observe the derivatives' *domains*: The derivative s' is defined wherever s is defined *except* at $x = 0$, where the graph of s has a vertical tangent line. The derivative n' has the same domain (all nonzero real numbers), as does n itself.

Note that s' has a strictly smaller domain than does s.

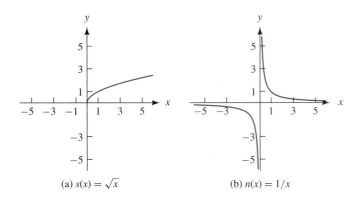

(a) $s(x) = \sqrt{x}$ (b) $n(x) = 1/x$

FIGURE 3
Graphs of $s(x) = \sqrt{x}$ and $n(x) = 1/x$

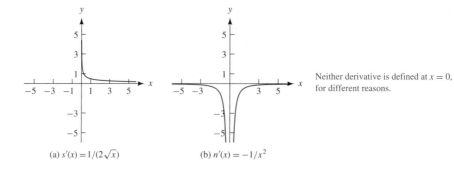

(a) $s'(x) = 1/(2\sqrt{x})$ (b) $n'(x) = -1/x^2$ Neither derivative is defined at $x = 0$, for different reasons.

FIGURE 4
Graphs of s' and n'   ∎

A general power rule   We've just found—with some algebraic effort—derivative formulas for several power functions:

$f(x)$	x^1	x^2	x^3	x^{-1}	$x^{1/2}$
$f'(x)$	1	$2x$	$3x^2$	$-1x^{-2}$	$\frac{1}{2}x^{-1/2}$

The following theorem says that all of our results so far are instances of a more general rule—one that holds for *all* real powers k:

THEOREM 1 (Power rule for derivatives)   Let k be any real constant. If $f(x) = x^k$, then $f'(x) = kx^{k-1}$.

We won't prove the theorem in its most general form (which includes even such peculiar functions as $f(x) = x^{\sqrt{2}}$ and $g(x) = x^\pi$). However, at the end of this section we show how the **binomial theorem** can be used to prove the theorem for positive integer powers. ◄

Derivative methods we'll develop in Chapter 3 will also show why the power rule holds for negative and other powers.

New derivatives from old: combining power functions

Theorem 1 gives derivatives for "pure" power functions, such as $f(x) = x^{10}$ and $g(x) = x^{-13/2}$. The next example shows how to differentiate functions built by *combining* power functions. (After illustrating the methods, we'll worry about their legality.)

EXAMPLE 3   Let $p(x) = 3x^5 + 7x^4 - x^2/3 + 11$. Find $p'(x)$.

Solution   We break p apart, differentiate each piece separately, and then reassemble the results, as follows:

$$p'(x) = \frac{d}{dx}\left(3x^5 + 7x^4 - \frac{1}{3}x^2 + 11\right) \qquad \text{(note the leibniz notation)}$$

$$= \frac{d}{dx}\left(3x^5\right) + \frac{d}{dx}\left(7x^4\right) - \frac{d}{dx}\left(\frac{1}{3}x^2\right) + \frac{d}{dx}(11) \qquad \text{(separating summands)}$$

$$= 3\frac{d}{dx}\left(x^5\right) + 7\frac{d}{dx}\left(x^4\right) - \frac{1}{3}\frac{d}{dx}\left(x^2\right) + 11\frac{d}{dx}(1) \qquad \text{(pulling constants outside derivatives)}$$

$$= 3 \cdot 5x^4 + 7 \cdot 4x^3 - \frac{1}{3} \cdot 2x + 11 \cdot 0 \qquad \text{(calculating derivatives)}$$

$$= 15x^4 + 28x^3 - \frac{2}{3}x. \qquad \text{(recombining results)}$$

Are these operations legal? We'll see in a moment that they are, but let's look first at their graphs (Figures 5(a) and (b)).

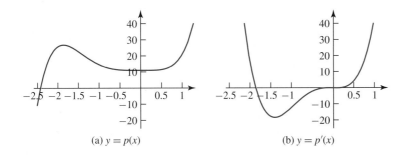

(a) $y = p(x)$ (b) $y = p'(x)$

FIGURE 5
A polynomial and its derivative

The pictures suggest that we're on the right track. In particular, the roots of p' seem to be in the right places—where the p-graph is flat.   ∎

We made two reasonable-seeming assumptions in Example 3: one about sums and one about constant multiples. The next two theorems justify these assumptions.

THEOREM 2 (The sum rule for derivatives)   Let f and g be differentiable functions, and let $h = f + g$. Then
$$h'(x) = (f + g)'(x) = f'(x) + g'(x).$$

THEOREM 3 (The constant multiple rule for derivatives)   If k is any constant, f is any differentiable function, and $g(x) = k \cdot f(x)$, then
$$g'(x) = (k \cdot f)'(x) = k \cdot f'(x).$$

The sum and constant multiple rules aren't surprising—they confirm what we'd probably guess anyway. We'll see in the next chapter, however, that differentiating *products* and *quotients* of functions takes more care.

The sum and constant multiple rules for *derivatives* follow directly from similar rules for *limits*. We'll return to this subject in the next section, where we consider limits in more detail.

EXAMPLE 4   The sum rule says that the derivative of a sum is the sum of the derivatives. Does something similar hold for *differences*?

Solution   Yes—the derivative of a difference is the difference of the derivatives. The following calculation illustrates the reason:

$$\begin{aligned}
\big(3\,f(x) - 4\,g(x) \big)' &= \big(3\,f(x) + (-4)\,g(x) \big)' && \text{(rewrite difference as sum)} \\
&= 3\,f'(x) + (-4)g'(x) && \text{(sum and constant multiple rules)} \\
&= 3\,f'(x) - 4\,g'(x).
\end{aligned}$$ ∎

More new derivatives from old: operations with constants

We'll apply ideas from this subsection later in this chapter when we find derivatives of exponential and logarithmic functions.

Given a function f and a constant a, we can form such new functions as

$$f(x+a), \quad f(x)+a, \quad f(a \cdot x), \quad \text{and} \quad a \cdot f(x).$$

In Section 1.2 we discussed how attaching these constants alters f and its graph—by translating, stretching, squashing, and reflecting across axes. How do these operations affect *derivatives*? The following fact will be useful:

This fact deserves emphasis: Stretching, squashing, translation, and reflection take "old" tangent lines to "new" tangent lines.

> **FACT**   Suppose that a line L is tangent to a curve C at a point P. Stretching, squashing, translation, and reflection may change L, C, and P, but the new L *remains tangent* to the new C at the new P.

The following example illustrates the possibilities.

EXAMPLE 5   Figure 6 shows part of the graph of a function f. The tangent line at $x = 4$ shows that $f'(4) = -2$.

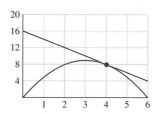

FIGURE 6
$f(x); f'(4) = -2$

Using the constant $a = 2$, form the new functions

$$g(x) = f(x+2); \quad h(x) = f(x)+2; \quad k(x) = f(2 \cdot x); \quad l(x) = 2 \cdot f(x).$$

Use graphs to decide what $f'(4) = -2$ means about the derivatives g', h', k', and l'.

Students should think carefully through what these graphs say about derivatives; the k-graph may be the subtlest.

Solution   Figure 7 shows graphs of g, h, k, and l; the transformed tangent line is shown with each.

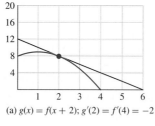

(a) $g(x) = f(x+2); g'(2) = f'(4) = -2$

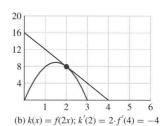

(b) $k(x) = f(2x); k'(2) = 2 \cdot f'(4) = -4$

(c) $h(x) = f(x)+2; h'(4) = f'(4) = -2$

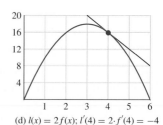

(d) $l(x) = 2f(x); l'(4) = 2 \cdot f'(4) = -4$

FIGURE 7
Four transformed graphs

Here's what the graphs say:

- **Graph of g:** The graph of $g(x) = f(x+2)$ is a *horizontal translation* of the f-graph. Like the graph itself, the tangent line moves two units *left*, but its *slope* remains unchanged, so $g'(2) = f'(4) = -2$.
- **Graph of h:** The graph of $h(x) = f(x) + 2$ is a *vertical translation* of the f-graph. The tangent line, too, moves two units *up*, but its *slope* remains unchanged, so $h'(4) = f'(4) = -2$. �

  The sum rule says the same thing about h.

- **Graph of k:** The graph of $k(x) = f(2 \cdot x)$ is a *horizontal compression* of the f-graph, with factor 2. The tangent line at $x = 4$ is compressed in the same way: The new tangent line is at $x = 2$, and its slope is doubled. Thus, $k'(2) = 2 \cdot f'(4) = -4$.
- **Graph of l:** The graph of $l(x) = 2 \cdot f(x)$ is obtained by a *vertical stretch* of the f-graph, with stretch factor 2. The tangent line at $x = 4$ is stretched in the same way: Stretching doubles its slope. Therefore, $l'(4) = 2 \cdot f'(4) = -4$. ➣ ∎

  The constant multiple rule says the same thing about l.

Example 5 concerned a specific function f, a specific constant $a = 2$, and a specific input $x = 4$, but the facts illustrated there hold in general. We summarize them briefly in a theorem:

THEOREM 4 (**How constants affect derivatives**) Let f be a differentiable function and a any constant. Then,

$$\text{(i)} \quad \big(f(x+a)\big)' = f'(x+a);$$
$$\text{(ii)} \quad \big(f(x)+a\big)' = f'(x);$$
$$\text{(iii)} \quad \big(a \cdot f(x)\big)' = a \cdot f'(x);$$
$$\text{(iv)} \quad \big(f(a \cdot x)\big)' = a \cdot f'(a \cdot x).$$

We won't prove this theorem. Parts (ii) and (iii) are simple cases of the sum and constant multiple rules; the other two parts are special cases of the ***chain rule***, which we'll see in Chapter 3.

Parts (i) and (especially) (iv) are most challenging.

Using Theorem 4 We said informally in Chapter 1 that

$$(\sin x)' = \cos x \quad \text{and} \quad (e^x)' = e^x.$$

Assuming these facts for the moment (we'll derive them carefully in later sections), we can find new, related derivatives.

EXAMPLE 6 Find derivatives of the functions defined by $3 \sin x$, $\sin(3x)$, and $\cos x$.

Solution By Theorem 4(iii),

$$(3 \sin x)' = 3(\sin x)' = 3 \cos x.$$

To differentiate $\sin(3x)$, let $f(x) = \sin x$ and $a = 3$ in Theorem 4(iv). Then $f'(x) = \cos x$, so

$$(\sin(3x))' = (f(3x))' = 3 f'(3x) = 3 \cos(3x).$$

To differentiate $\cos x$, first recall two relations between sines and cosines: For all x, $\cos x = \sin(x + \pi/2)$ and $-\sin x = \cos(x + \pi/2)$. Combining these facts with Theorem 4(i) gives

$$(\cos x)' = (\sin(x + \pi/2))' = \cos(x + \pi/2) = -\sin x. \qquad ∎$$

Recall: exp(*x*) *is an alternative notation for e^x.*

EXAMPLE 7 For k a constant, let $f(x) = e^{kx} = \exp(kx)$. What's $f'(x)$? ◂

Solution Let $g(x) = e^x$; then $g'(x) = e^x$. By Theorem 4(iv),

$$f'(x) = \big(g(kx)\big)' = k \cdot g'(kx) = k \cdot e^{kx}.$$ ∎

The power rule and the binomial theorem

See any college algebra book for more details on the binomial theorem.

The **binomial theorem** gives an explicit formula for a **binomial**—an expression of the form $(a + b)^n$, where n is a positive integer. ◂ For $n = 2$ and $n = 3$, for instance, we know these formulas (or we can check them by expanding the left sides):

$$(a + b)^2 = a^2 + 2ab + b^2; \qquad (a + b)^3 = a^3 + 3a^2b + 3ab^2 + b^3.$$

Students may need help remembering the binomial theorem. An alternative proof could be based on factoring $a^n - b^n$ rather than on expanding $(a + b)^n$.

The binomial theorem gives a similar formula for *any* positive integer n. It says, in brief, that

$$(a + b)^n = a^n + na^{n-1}b + \frac{n(n-1)}{2}a^{n-2}b^2 + \cdots + \frac{n(n-1)}{2}a^2b^{n-2} + nab^{n-1} + b^n.$$

What the "..." on the right side stands for is crucial to understanding the theorem algebraically. (For the record, the kth term of the sum has the form $C(n, k)a^k b^{n-k}$, where $C(n, k) = \dfrac{n!}{k!(n - k)!}$. The constant $C(n, k)$ is important in its own right—it counts the number of ways of choosing k objects from an n-member set.) For our purposes, however, only the first few summands in the binomial theorem matter, as the following example shows.

EXAMPLE 8 Let $f(x) = x^n$, where n is any positive integer. Use the binomial theorem to show that $f'(x) = nx^{n-1}$.

Solution By definition, $f'(x) = \lim\limits_{h \to 0} \dfrac{(x + h)^n - x^n}{h}$. Applying the binomial theorem in the numerator helps us evaluate the limit:

$$f'(x) = \lim_{h \to 0} \frac{\left(x^n + nx^{n-1}h + \frac{n(n-1)}{2}x^{n-2}h^2 + \cdots + h^n\right) - x^n}{h}$$

$$= \lim_{h \to 0} \frac{nx^{n-1}h + \frac{n(n-1)}{2}x^{n-2}h^2 + \cdots + h^n}{h} \qquad \text{(by algebra)}$$

$$= \lim_{h \to 0} \left(nx^{n-1} + \frac{n(n-1)}{2}x^{n-2}h + \cdots + h^{n-1}\right) \qquad \text{(canceling } h\text{)}$$

$$= \lim_{h \to 0} \left(nx^{n-1} + h\left(\frac{n(n-1)}{2}x^{n-2} + \cdots + h^{n-2}\right)\right) \qquad \text{(factoring)}$$

$$= nx^{n-1}. \qquad \text{(substitute } h = 0\text{)}$$

The key idea is that all terms after the first two involve at least the second power of h, and so these terms vanish in the limit—even after we divide by the original denominator. ∎

BASIC EXERCISES

1. Why can't the limit in the definition of $f'(x)$ be evaluated by plugging $h = 0$ into the difference quotient?

2. Is the domain of f' always the same as the domain of f? Justify your answer.

3. Express the statement $f'(x) = \sin(2x)$ in Leibniz notation.

4. Express the statement $f'(x) = e^{-x}$ in Leibniz notation.

5. Express the statement $\left.\dfrac{df}{dx}\right|_{x=-1} = 3$ in prime notation.

6. Express the statement $\left.\dfrac{dg}{dx}\right|_{x=1} = 4$ in prime notation.

7. Let k be the constant function $k(x) = 3$. Use the limit definition of the derivative to show that $k'(x) = 0$.

8. Let l, q, and c be the functions defined in Example 1. Find expressions for l'', q'', and c''.

9. Let l, q, and c be the functions defined in Example 1. Evaluate $l''(1)$, $q''(2)$, and $c''(3)$.

10. Let $g(x) = x^2 + x$. Use the limit definition of the derivative to show that $g'(x) = 2x + 1$.

11. Let $f(w) = w^{1/2}$. Evaluate $f'(9)$. [HINT: See Example 2.]

12. Let $g(t) = t^{-1}$. Evaluate $g'(2)$. [HINT: See Example 2.]

13. Each of the six expressions displayed just before Example 1 can be written in the form x^k for some value of the constant k.
   (a) Identify the appropriate value of k for each expression.
   (b) Differentiate the function defined by each expression.

14. Let $g(x) = 2^x$. Explain why Theorem 1 *cannot* be used to find an expression for $g'(x)$.

15. Let $s(x) = \sqrt{x}$. Find a formula for $s''(x)$.

16. Let $n(x) = 1/x$. Find a formula for $n''(x)$.

In Exercises 17–24, find a formula for f'. Check your answer for reasonableness by comparing graphs of f and f'.

17. $f(x) = 3x^2 + 4$

18. $f(x) = 7x^{-4} - 4x^7$

19. $f(x) = 4x^5 + 3x^2 - x$

20. $f(x) = 4\sqrt{x} + 1/x^3$

21. $f(x) = x^3 - \sqrt[3]{x}$

22. $f(x) = 3x^{-1/2} + 4x^{3/2}$

23. $f(x) = 4\sqrt{x^3} - 5x^{-2/3}$

24. $f(x) = 4\sqrt[5]{x^3} + 5/\sqrt[3]{x^4}$

25–32. Find the second derivative of each function in Exercises 17–24. In each case, check your answer for reasonableness by comparing graphs of f and f''.

In Exercises 33–36, find an expression for f'. Check your answers for reasonableness by comparing graphs of f and f'.

33. $f(x) = (x+2)^3$

34. $f(x) = \sqrt{x-1}$

35. $f(x) = \dfrac{1}{x+4}$

36. $f(x) = \dfrac{3}{(x+1)^2}$

37. Find an equation of the line tangent to the curve $y = x^3 - 4x$ at $x = 2$.

38. Find an equation of the line tangent to the curve $y = \sqrt{x} - 2/x$ at $x = 4$.

Let f, g, h, k, and l be the functions defined in Example 5. It is a fact that $f'(1) = 4$. In Exercises 39–43, find an equation of the line tangent to the curve.

39. $y = f(x)$ at $x = 1$

40. $y = g(x)$ at $x = -1$

41. $y = h(x)$ at $x = 1$

42. $y = k(x)$ at $x = 1/2$

43. $y = l(x)$ at $x = 1$

FURTHER EXERCISES

44. The function $f(x) = \dfrac{(x+0.00001)^8 - x^8}{0.00001}$ is closely approximated by the function $g(x) = ax^b$ for appropriate values of a and b (i.e., for any x, $|f(x) - g(x)|$ is a "small" number). What are these values? Explain why g approximates f so well.

In Exercises 45–48, find an algebraic expression for f'. [HINT: Start by rewriting the expression for f in a simpler form.]

45. $f(x) = (x+2)(3x-4)$

46. $f(x) = \dfrac{\sqrt{x}-3}{x}$

47. $f(x) = \dfrac{x^3 - 4x + 1}{\sqrt{x}}$

48. $f(x) = \left(\dfrac{x-1}{x}\right)^2$

49. Find an equation of the line tangent to the curve $y = x^3 - 6x^2$ at its point of inflection.

50. Show that the rate of change of the area of a circle with respect to its radius is equal to its circumference.

51. What is the rate of change of the volume of a sphere with respect to its radius?

52. What is the rate of change of the volume of a cube with respect to its edge length?

53. If a fixed quantity of gas in a container is maintained at a constant temperature T, the pressure P is related to the volume V by the formula

$$\left(P + \frac{n^2 a}{V^2}\right)(V - nb) = nRT,$$

where a, b, n, and R are positive constants.

   (a) Find $\dfrac{dP}{dV}$. [HINT: Start by writing P as a function of V.]

(b) For an **ideal gas**, $a = 0$ and $b = 0$. Does your result in part (a) predict that the pressure of an ideal gas decreases if the volume increases? Justify your answer.

54. (a) Over which intervals is $f(x) = (1000 - x)^2 + x^2$ decreasing? [HINT: $(1000 - x)^2 = (x - 1000)^2$.]

(b) Explain how to use part (a) to determine whether 1000^2 is bigger or smaller than $998^2 + 2^2$.

(c) Is $10,000^{100}$ smaller than $9000^{100} + 1000^{100}$? Justify your answer. [HINT: Generalize your result from part (a) to the function $f(x) = (c - x)^n + x^n$, where c is any positive number and n is an *even* positive integer.]

55. Show that $(1 + x)^r \geq 1 + rx$ if $x \geq 0$ and $r \geq 1$. [HINT: Use the speed limit law and the fact that $(1 + x)^{r-1} \geq 1$ if $x \geq 0$ and $r \geq 1$.]

56. Let $f(x) = 3x^2 - 8x^{-2}$. Evaluate $\lim\limits_{h \to 0} \dfrac{f(2 + h) - f(2)}{h}$.

57. Let $g(w) = 2/w + 3w^4$. Evaluate $\lim\limits_{w \to 1} \dfrac{g(w) - g(1)}{w}$.

58. Find a symbolic expression for the nth derivative of $f(x) = 1/x$.

59. Find a symbolic expression for the nth derivative of $f(x) = \sqrt{x}$.

60. Let $f(x) = e^x$. Use a graph of f to explain why $f'(x) \neq xe^{x-1}$.

61. How many points of inflection does the graph of $y = 2x^6 + 9x^5 + 10x^4 - x + 2$ have? Where are they located?

62. Let $f(x) = x^n$ where $n \geq 2$ is an integer.

(a) Show that f is concave up on the interval $(0, \infty)$.

(b) What can be said about the concavity of f on the interval $(-\infty, 0)$. [HINT: Does it matter whether n is even?]

63. Explain why $f(x) = x^{7/2}$ does not have a derivative at $x = 0$.

64. Let $f(x) = x^{2/3}$. Explain why $f'(0)$ does not exist.

65. Is the derivative of a polynomial always another polynomial? Justify your answer.

66. Suppose that g is an nth degree polynomial. Explain why $\dfrac{d^{n+1}}{dx^{n+1}} g(x) = 0$.

67. Let $p(x) = x^n + a_{n-1}x^{n-1} + a_{n-2}x^{n-2} + \cdots + a_1x + a_0$.

(a) Show that $\dfrac{d^n}{dx^n} p(x)$ is a constant.

(b) Show that if k is an integer such that $1 \leq k < n$, $p^{(k)}(0) = k! \, a_k$.

In Exercises 68–71, use the limit definition of the derivative function to find an expression for $f'(x)$.

68. $f(x) = \sqrt{x + 3}$

69. $f(x) = \dfrac{1}{x + 5}$

70. $f(x) = \dfrac{4}{(x + 3)^2}$

71. $f(x) = (x + 2)^3$

2.3 LIMITS

Roughly speaking, a continuous function is one whose graph is unbroken.

This relatively long section treats limits as objects in themselves: definitions, properties, numerical and geometric interpretations, basic techniques of calculation, and connections with continuity.

Our use of limits so far has been mainly to calculate derivatives. In this section we study limits in their own right, and use them to make precise the idea of a **continuous function**. ◄ We'll be informal because we need limits mainly as tools for calculation. We should add, however, that a careful theoretical study of limits is essential to any fully rigorous study of calculus; this is why courses in advanced calculus and real analysis usually start with a long chapter or two on limits.

The basic idea of a limit

The basic idea behind limits is simple. Let f be a function and L a number. To say that

$$\lim_{x \to a} f(x) = L$$

Recall: The → symbol means "approaches" or "tends to."

means, informally, that $f(x)$ approaches L as x approaches a. In other symbols, $f(x) \to L$ as $x \to a$. ◄ In other words,

As inputs to f approach a, outputs from f approach L.

In *still* other words and symbols,

$$f(x) \approx L \quad \text{whenever} \quad x \approx a.$$

Intuitive notions (such as the word "approaches" and the symbol "≈") aren't mathematical definitions. We'll give more formal definitions after some examples. They illustrate, among other things, the fact that $f(x)$ need *not* be defined at the "target point" $x = a$.

EXAMPLE 1 What is $\lim_{x \to 3} x^2$? Why?

Solution The answer is no surprise: $\lim_{x \to 3} x^2 = 9$. The squaring function $f(x) = x^2$ behaves predictably near $x = 3$: If x is near 3, then $f(x)$ is near 9. Of course, $f(x)$ *equals* 9 when $x = 3$. But the limit depends only on inputs *near* $x = 3$, not *at* $x = 3$. ■

The fact that limits "don't see" the function's value at the target point is a bit subtle; drawing functions with isolated discontinuities may help.

EXAMPLE 2 The statement

$$\lim_{x \to 3} \frac{x^2 - 9}{x - 3} = 6$$

is about the limit of a certain function at a certain x-value. Which function? Which x-value? What does the statement say? Is it true?

Solution The function (we'll call it g) is defined by the expression inside the limit sign: $g(x) = (x^2 - 9)/(x - 3)$. The x-value in question is $x = 3$.

Notice that $g(3)$ is not defined but that the rule for g makes good sense for all *other* inputs. The limit statement says that, although g has no *value* at $x = 3$, it does the next best thing: $g(x)$ approaches 6 as x approaches 3. In symbols, the limit statement says that $g(x) \to 6$ as $x \to 3$.

Is the limit statement true? The formula for g doesn't say, because $g(3)$ is not defined. But numerical evidence suggests that the limit is indeed 6:

x	2.9	2.99	2.999	2.9999	3	3.0001	3.001	3.01	3.1
$g(x)$	5.9	5.99	5.999	5.9999		6.0001	6.001	6.01	6.1

The graph (Figure 1) points to the same conclusion.

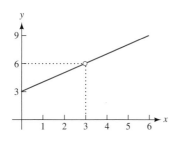

The hole in the graph reflects a gap in the domain.

FIGURE 1
$g(x) = \frac{x^2 - 9}{x - 3}$

The graph of g (except at $x = 3$) looks suspiciously like the line $y = x + 3$. A little factoring algebra resolves the mystery:

$$g(x) = \frac{x^2 - 9}{x - 3} = \frac{(x - 3)(x + 3)}{x - 3} = x + 3.$$

The last equality holds only for $x \ne 3$, but that's good enough because the limit depends on $g(x)$ only for values of x *near* $x = 3$. Now it's clear that, indeed,

$$\lim_{x \to 3} g(x) = \lim_{x \to 3}(x + 3) = 6.$$

■

Graphical and numerical views   If $\lim_{x \to a} f(x) = L$, then $f(x) \approx L$ whenever $x \approx a$. Therefore, in order to guess or estimate L, we look at values of f near $x = a$. We can do this either numerically, by plugging in numbers, or graphically, by plotting f near $x = a$, as we did in Example 2. Technology makes both approaches almost painless, and we'll use both freely. ◄

But caution is needed: graphs and numbers can mislead.

The word "approach" seems to carry confusing baggage for some students; hence this discussion. For example, some students seem to think "approach" implies "never arrive." We hope to sharpen students' intuition a little without obscuring what's simple about the idea.

Approaching clarity   In discussing limits, we often describe one quantity as "approaching" or "tending to" another. What these words mean in calculus isn't quite what they mean in everyday speech. For instance, two cars can "approach" each other on the road without coming close to colliding—and a good thing, too.

The mathematical notion of "approaching" means more than just "getting closer." When we say that $f(x) = x^2$ approaches 9 as x approaches 3, for example, we mean that $f(x)$ differs from 9 by no more than *any* desired tolerance, once x is close enough to 3. For instance, we can ensure that $f(x)$ stays between 8.999 and 9.001 by insisting that x stay between 2.9999 and 3.0001.

Filling gaps in functions' domains (when that's possible) seems to provide students some motivation for looking for limits.

Functions with gaps in their domains

One reason limits matter is that they help us handle functions with gaps in their domains. The key fact is that $\lim_{x \to a} f(x)$ may exist *even if $f(a)$ is undefined*. Indeed, such domain gaps occur often in calculus. Each of the functions in the following limits is "undefined at a":

$$\lim_{x \to 4} \frac{\sqrt{x} - 2}{x - 4}; \qquad \lim_{x \to 4} \frac{x^2 - 16}{x - 4}; \qquad \lim_{x \to 0} \frac{\cos x - 1}{x}.$$

In effect, limits can help us *find* a suitable value for $f(a)$—if one exists. The next example illustrates how (and why) we do this.

> **EXAMPLE 3**   Let $f(x) = x^2$. Use a limit to find $f'(3)$. What does the answer mean graphically?
>
> **Solution**   By definition of the derivative,
>
> $$f'(3) = \lim_{x \to 3} \frac{f(x) - f(3)}{x - 3} = \lim_{x \to 3} \frac{x^2 - 9}{x - 3}.$$
>
> We found in Example 2 that $f'(3) = 6$, so the curve $y = x^2$ has slope 6 at $x = 3$.   ∎

Definitions: formal and informal

The limit expression $\lim_{x \to a} f(x) = L$ has two kinds of ingredients:

(i) two real numbers, a and L;
(ii) a function f, defined for all x *near* $x = a$ but not necessarily *at $x = a$.*

The next two definitions say more precisely what we mean, first informally and then rigorously. (The informal definition will suffice for our use in this book.)

> **DEFINITION (Limit, informally)**   If $f(x)$ tends to a single number L as x approaches a, then $\lim_{x \to a} f(x) = L$.

Math majors: You'll see this definition again.

The following formal definition appears here mainly for comparison, but the definition and the theory behind it are key subjects in any real analysis course. ◄

> **DEFINITION (Limit, formally)** Suppose that for every positive number ϵ (epsilon) there is a positive number δ (delta) so that
> $$\left|f(x)-L\right| < \epsilon \quad \text{for all } x \text{ such that} \quad 0 < |x-a| < \delta.$$
> Then
> $$\lim_{x \to a} f(x) = L.$$

An Interlude at the end of this chapter unpacks the $\epsilon - \delta$ idea a little further.

Seeing ghosts. The modern idea of limit stems from the work of the French mathematician Augustin-Louis Cauchy around 1820—over 150 years after Isaac Newton and Gottfried Leibniz developed calculus. Newton's and Leibniz's own understanding of limit could not have been rigorous by modern standards. Sensing this, Bishop Berkeley satirized the intellectual pretensions of mathematicians in his 1734 philosophical treatise *The Analyst: A Discourse Addressed to an Infidel Mathematician*, which ridiculed Newton's limits as "ghosts of departed quantities."

Limits may not exist

A function f need not *have* a limit at a given point $x = a$. The following examples illustrate what can go wrong, and why it can matter for derivatives.

EXAMPLE 4 Let $f(x) = |x|$. The kink at $x = 0$ suggests trouble with the derivative. Use a limit to show exactly what goes wrong.

Solution By definition,
$$f'(0) = \lim_{x \to 0} \frac{f(x) - f(0)}{x - 0} = \lim_{x \to 0} \frac{|x|}{x},$$

but *only* if the limit exists. To see that the limit *doesn't* exist, consider the function $h(x) = |x|/x$. Figure 2 shows a graph; note that $h(0)$ is undefined.

The picture reveals the problem: There is no *single* number to which $h(x)$ tends as x tends to 0. If x approaches 0 from the *left* (that is, x takes negative values), then $h(x) = -1$ for all such x, so $h(x)$ approaches -1. But if x approaches 0 from the *right*, then $h(x) = 1$ for all such x, and so $h(x)$ approaches 1. These conflicting tendencies mean that the limit that defines $f'(0)$ doesn't exist.   ∎

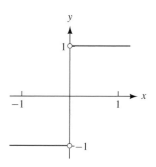

FIGURE 2
$h(x) = \frac{|x|}{x}$

EXAMPLE 5 Consider the function $f(x) = \sqrt[3]{x}$; see Figure 3:

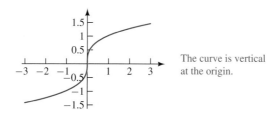

The curve is vertical at the origin.

FIGURE 3
$f(x) = \sqrt[3]{x}$

We said in Section 1.5 that $f'(0)$ does not exist because the tangent line at $x = 0$ is vertical. Use a limit to draw the same conclusion.

Solution   By definition,

$$f'(0) = \lim_{x \to 0} \frac{f(x) - f(0)}{x} = \lim_{x \to 0} \frac{\sqrt[3]{x}}{x},$$

if the limit exists. To see that the limit does *not* exist, note first that

$$\frac{\sqrt[3]{x}}{x} = \frac{x^{1/3}}{x^1} = \frac{1}{x^{2/3}} = \frac{1}{\sqrt[3]{x^2}}.$$

This mirrors the fact that the tangent line is vertical. We'll say much more about infinite limits in Chapter 4.

Now as x tends to zero, the (positive) denominator of the last fraction also tends to zero, so the fraction itself tends to infinity. ◄ Therefore, there is no finite limit, and so the derivative $f'(0)$ doesn't exist.   ■

The next example shows another limit that fails—quite spectacularly—to exist.

E X A M P L E 6   Let $g(x) = \sin(1/x)$. Discuss $\lim\limits_{x \to 0} g(x)$.

Solution   For this function both the graph (Figure 4) and a sample of numbers look suspiciously chaotic near $x = 0$:

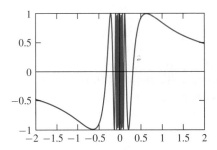

The graph looks ragged because the function oscillates wildly.

FIGURE 4
$y = \sin(1/x)$

x	-0.1	-0.05	-0.025	0	0.001	0.0025	0.0075
$g(x)$	0.544	-0.913	-0.745	$\cdots$	0.827	-0.851	0.983

In fact, the limit does not exist. As x approaches 0 (from either left or right), $1/x$ "blows up" in magnitude, so $\sin(1/x)$ oscillates faster and faster, taking values between -1 and 1. Because $\sin(1/x)$ approaches no single value, no limit can exist.   ■

Other types of limits

The simplest and most important limit idea is the one just studied: the (two-sided) limit of a function at a point. However, several variants on the same idea (with slightly different definitions) arise often enough to deserve mention. One is the notion of limits such as

$$\lim_{x \to \infty} \frac{1}{x} = 0 \quad \text{and} \quad \lim_{x \to 0} \frac{1}{x^2} = \infty,$$

Plotting or tabulating values is one way to guess the limits.

both of which involve the ∞ symbol. We'll return to these limits in Chapter 4, where they'll arise naturally. But even without formal definitions both of these limits are easy to guess. ◄

One-sided limits "One-sided" limits are another slight variant on the basic limit idea. Informal versions will be enough for our purposes: ➡

Notice the unusual use of "+" and "−" as superscripts.

> **DEFINITION (Right-hand limit)** $\lim\limits_{x \to a^+} f(x) = L$ means that $f(x) \to L$ as $x \to a$ from the right (i.e., $x \to a$ and $x > a$).

> **DEFINITION (Left-hand limit)** $\lim\limits_{x \to a^-} f(x) = L$ means that $f(x) \to L$ as $x \to a$ from the left, (i.e., $x \to a$ and $x < a$).

EXAMPLE 7 In Example 4 we saw that if $h(x) = |x|/x$, then $h(x)$ tends either to 1 or to -1 depending on whether x tends to 0 from the right or from the left. In one-sided limit notation,

$$\lim_{x \to 0^-} h(x) = -1 \quad \text{and} \quad \lim_{x \to 0^+} h(x) = 1.$$ ∎

Because these one-sided limits aren't equal, we concluded that the ordinary limit $\lim\limits_{x \to 0} h(x)$ does not exist. There's a useful principle lurking here:

> **FACT** The *ordinary* limit $\lim\limits_{x \to a} f(x)$ exists if and only if both corresponding *one-sided* limits exist and have the same value. In symbols,
> $$\lim_{x \to a} f(x) = L \iff \lim_{x \to a^+} f(x) = L = \lim_{x \to a^-} f(x).$$

Continuity

We study continuity and its advantages in more detail in Section 4.8. The point here is mainly to link continuity to limits.

Plot or visualize their unbroken graphs.

To say that f is **continuous** on an interval I means—informally—that the graph of f is "unbroken" for inputs x in I. For example, each of the following functions is continuous on the full set $(-\infty, \infty)$ of real numbers: ➡

$$f(x) = x^2; \qquad g(x) = \sin x; \qquad h(x) = \frac{x^2}{x^2+1}; \qquad k(x) = |x|.$$

(The graph of k has a kink at $x = 0$, but no break, so k is continuous at $x = 0$.) By contrast, $s(x) = \sqrt{x}$ is continuous on the interval $[0, \infty)$, but $s(x)$ is not defined for negative x. The function $m(x) = 1/x$ is continuous on $(0, \infty)$ and on $(-\infty, 0)$, but m is discontinuous at $x = 0$, where the function is undefined.

The graphical idea of "unbrokenness" is useful, but it's not fully precise. Limits turn out to be exactly what's needed to capture precisely the geometric idea of "unbrokenness."

> **DEFINITION (Continuity)** Let f be a function defined on an interval I containing $x = a$. If
> $$\lim_{x \to a} f(x) = f(a),$$
> then f is continuous at the point $x = a$. If f is continuous at each point of I (including endpoints, if any), then f is continuous on the interval I.

Here are some notes on the definition:

- **No surprises** The definition says that f is continuous at a if $f(x)$ approaches $f(a)$ whenever x approaches a. In short, f "behaves predictably" at $x = a$. In particular, finding limits of continuous functions is as easy as can be: If f is continuous at $x = a$, then the *limit* of f as x approaches a is simply the *value* of f at a.

- **Continuous where?** A function f may be continuous at some domain points and discontinuous at others, so the common phrase "f is continuous" is technically ambiguous; it doesn't say *where* f is continuous. In practice, this causes little trouble, and we'll use the following rule of thumb: *Unless otherwise qualified, "continuous" means "continuous throughout the domain of f."*

- **Continuity at endpoints** If a happens to be the left or right endpoint of the domain of f, then a right-hand limit or a left-hand limit replaces the two-sided limit in the definition. For instance, the square root function is continuous at zero because

$$\lim_{x \to 0^+} \sqrt{x} = \sqrt{0} = 0.$$

Careful proofs of such facts are important in higher analysis; they appear in advanced calculus texts.

Continuity is the rule The standard elementary functions of calculus (algebraic, exponential, logarithmic, and trigonometric functions) are all continuous wherever they're defined. For example, $\ln(x)$ is continuous everywhere on its natural domain (the set of positive numbers). Similarly, every polynomial function $p(x)$ is continuous on the full set of real numbers. ◄ These facts make basic limits very easy to find.

EXAMPLE 8 Find $\lim_{x \to 2}(x^2 + 3x + 5)$ and $\lim_{x \to 2} \ln(x)$.

Solution Because $p(x) = x^2 + 3x + 5$ and $\ln(x)$ are both continuous at $x = 2$,

$$\lim_{x \to 2} p(x) = p(2) = 15 \quad \text{and} \quad \lim_{x \to 2} \ln(x) = \ln(2) \approx 0.6931.$$

In other words, each function's *limit* as x approaches 2 is simply the function's *value* at $x = 2$. ∎

Discontinuity: three possible problems A function f is **discontinuous** at $x = a$ if—for any reason—the limit condition in the definition doesn't hold. Three things can go wrong:

1. $f(a)$ may not be defined;
2. the limit $\lim_{x \to a} f(x)$ may not exist;
3. the limit $\lim_{x \to a} f(x)$ may exist but not equal $f(a)$.

The next example exhibits all three pathologies.

EXAMPLE 9 A function f appears in Figure 5.

Hollow dots indicate holes in the graph; solid dots indicate values of f.

FIGURE 5

A function with discontinuities

The function f looks artificially concocted, and it is—most calculus functions are continuous almost everywhere.

Where is f continuous? Where is f discontinuous? ◄

Solution Nothing suspicious occurs away from integer x-values, so f is continuous at all such points. The "holes" at $x = -1$ and $x = 1$ mean that $f(-1)$ and $f(1)$ are not defined, so we have discontinuities of type 1. The "jump" at $x = 0$ leads to a discontinuity of type 2: Because $\lim_{x \to 0^-} f(x) = 1$ but $\lim_{x \to 0^+} f(x) = 0$, the limit $\lim_{x \to 0} f(x)$ does not exist. A type 3 discontinuity occurs at $x = 2$, since $\lim_{x \to 2} f(x) = 0$, but $f(2) = 1$. The function is continuous at the right-hand endpoint because $\lim_{x \to 3^-} f(x) = 1 = f(3)$. ■

New limits from old

Complicated limits can often be found by combining simpler limits. The next example illustrates the process.

EXAMPLE 10 Let $f(x) = x^2 + \sqrt{x}$. Use limits to find $f'(3)$.

Solution By definition,

$$f'(3) = \lim_{x \to 3} \frac{f(x) - f(3)}{x - 3} = \lim_{x \to 3} \frac{(x^2 + \sqrt{x}) - (9 + \sqrt{3})}{x - 3}.$$

The right-hand limit can be broken into a *sum* of two simpler limits:

$$\lim_{x \to 3} \frac{(x^2 + \sqrt{x}) - (9 + \sqrt{3})}{x - 3} = \lim_{x \to 3} \frac{x^2 - 9}{x - 3} + \lim_{x \to 3} \frac{\sqrt{x} - \sqrt{3}}{x - 3}.$$

We've seen the first limit on the right side already; in Example 2 we got 6. To find the second limit, we use algebra (multiplying numerator and denominator by an appropriate "conjugate") to eliminate a pesky denominator: ➤

We did the same thing in Example 2, page 93.

$$\frac{\sqrt{x} - \sqrt{3}}{x - 3} = \frac{\sqrt{x} - \sqrt{3}}{x - 3} \cdot \frac{\sqrt{x} + \sqrt{3}}{\sqrt{x} + \sqrt{3}} = \frac{1}{\sqrt{3} + \sqrt{x}}.$$

The rightmost expression has no vanishing-denominator problem at $x = 3$, so we can just plug $x = 3$ into the last expression:

$$\lim_{x \to 3} \frac{\sqrt{3} - \sqrt{x}}{x - 3} = \lim_{x \to 3} \frac{1}{\sqrt{3} + \sqrt{x}} = \frac{1}{2\sqrt{3}}.$$

Now we reassemble the pieces to get our answer:

$$f'(3) = \lim_{x \to 3} \frac{f(x) - f(3)}{x - 3} = \lim_{x \to 3} \frac{x^2 - 9}{x - 3} + \lim_{x \to 3} \frac{\sqrt{3} - \sqrt{x}}{x - 3} = 6 + \frac{1}{2\sqrt{3}}.$$ ■

In the preceding example we used the plausible fact that the limit of a sum is the sum of the limits. The following theorem justifies such steps.

THEOREM 5 (Algebra with limits) Suppose that

$$\lim_{x \to a} f(x) = L \quad \text{and} \quad \lim_{x \to a} g(x) = M,$$

where L and M are finite numbers. Let k be any constant. Then

(i) $\lim_{x \to a} kf(x) = kL$;

(ii) $\lim_{x \to a} \big(f(x) + g(x)\big) = L + M$;

(iii) $\lim_{x \to a} \big(f(x) \cdot g(x)\big) = L \cdot M$;

(iv) $\lim_{x \to a} \frac{f(x)}{g(x)} = \frac{L}{M}$ (if $M \neq 0$).

The rules are all intuitively reasonable, but rigorous proofs depend on the formal definition and involve careful work with ϵ's and δ's. We'll skip these proofs here; one typical proof appears in Appendix I.

Combining "obvious" limits The theorem lets us find lots of new limits—but only if we know some old limits to begin with. To get such a foothold, we'll take as obvious limits such as these: ◄

To be fully rigorous we'd have to prove even these limits.

$$\lim_{x\to 3} x = 3; \quad \lim_{x\to 3} 5 = 5; \quad \lim_{x\to 0} |x| = 0;$$

Combining such basic limits and the rules of Theorem 5, we can justify calculations like the following:

$$\lim_{x\to 3}\left(\frac{x^2+2x}{5+x}+\frac{1}{x}\right) = \frac{3^2+2\cdot 3}{5+3}+\frac{1}{3} = \frac{53}{24}.$$

From limit rules to derivative rules The sum and constant multiple rules for *derivatives* follow from the analogous rules for *limits*—after all, derivatives *are* limits. The argument for the sum rule runs as follows:

$$\big(f(x)+g(x)\big)' = \lim_{h\to 0}\frac{\big(f(x+h)+g(x+h)\big)-\big(f(x)+g(x)\big)}{h}$$
$$= \lim_{h\to 0}\frac{f(x+h)-f(x)}{h}+\lim_{h\to 0}\frac{g(x+h)-g(x)}{h}$$
$$= f'(x)+g'(x).$$

Here's the main point: Because the *limit* of a sum is the sum of the limits, the same is true for *derivatives*. The constant multiple rule for derivatives can be proved in the same way.

New continuous functions from old

Algebraic combinations Because $\sin x$ and $\cos x$ are continuous functions, we'd expect $\sin x + \cos x$ to be continuous, too. More generally, if f and g are continuous functions, it's reasonable to expect such algebraic combinations as $f+g$, f/g, and $3f-2g$ to be continuous as well. As a rule, they are; because continuity is defined via limits, it's natural that properties of limits are reflected in properties of continuous functions. The next theorem gives the fine print.

> **THEOREM 6 (Algebra with continuous functions)** Suppose that both f and g are continuous at $x=a$. Then each of the functions
> $$f+g, \qquad f-g, \qquad \text{and} \qquad fg$$
> is also continuous at $x=a$. If $g(a)\neq 0$, then f/g is continuous at $x=a$.

Proof. Each property of continuous functions follows directly from the analogous property of limits. The first claim goes like this:

$$\lim_{x\to a}(f+g)(x) = \lim_{x\to a}f(x)+g(x) = \lim_{x\to a}f(x)+\lim_{x\to a}g(x) = f(a)+g(a) = (f+g)(a).$$

The result is just what's needed to show that $f+g$ is continuous at $x=a$. □

We treat composition in much more detail in Chapter 3, but before then we'll need a few simple built-up limits, like those illustrated here.

Composing continuous functions Functions like $\cos(\ln x)$ and $\sin(1/x)$ are built by "nesting" one function inside another. The technical term is **composition**: If f and g are functions, then the composition $f\circ g$ is the new function defined by the rule $(f\circ g)(x)=f\big(g(x)\big)$.

We'll study composite functions and their properties carefully in Chapter 3, but we remark here that if f and g are *continuous* functions, then so is $f \circ g$ (provided that the composition makes sense). For instance, $\cos(\ln x)$ is continuous for $x > 0$ (but not for $x \leq 0$, where $\ln x$ is undefined). Similarly, $\sin(1/x)$ is continuous wherever $x \neq 0$. These facts mean that we can calculate simple limits like the following:

$$\lim_{x \to 3} \sin(1/x) = \sin(1/3) \approx 0.3272; \qquad \lim_{x \to 3} \cos(\ln x) = \cos(\ln 3) \approx 0.4548.$$

Limits and inequalities: the squeeze theorem

For some limits, the algebraic methods of Theorem 5 don't help. For

$$\lim_{x \to 0} x \cdot \sin\left(\frac{1}{x}\right),$$

for example, the product-of-limits rule doesn't apply because the second factor, $\sin(1/x)$, has *no* limit as x approaches 0. → A graph (Figure 6) makes the limit easy to guess, but let's see how to calculate it directly.

We saw this in Example 6, page 104.

The idea is to choose inequalities that "squeeze" the function of interest between two simpler functions—ones with limits we *can* evaluate. For the case at hand, we can use the squeezing inequalities

$$-|x| \leq x \sin\left(\frac{1}{x}\right) \leq |x|,$$

which hold for all x, as Figure 6 illustrates.

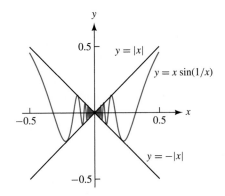

FIGURE 6
Finding a limit by squeezing

To show symbolically that the squeezing inequalities hold, note first that $\left|\sin(1/x)\right| \leq 1$ for all x. Therefore,

$$|x \sin(1/x)| = |x| \cdot |\sin(1/x)| \leq |x|,$$

which implies that $-|x| \leq x \sin(1/x) \leq |x|$, as desired.

Now we let x approach 0; then both the left and the right sides of the squeezing inequality tend to 0. Squeezed in between, the middle quantity $x \sin(1/x)$ must also tend to zero. A table of numerical values (rounded to 4 decimal places) gives the same message.

x	-0.1	-0.01	-0.001	0	0.001	0.01	0.1
$f(x)$	-0.0544	-0.0051	0.0008		0.0008	-0.0051	-0.0544

There's a general theorem here. The preceding discussion makes it reasonable; we omit the formal proof.

THEOREM 7 (The squeeze theorem)   Suppose that

$$f(x) \le g(x) \le h(x)$$

for all x in an interval containing $x = a$. If $f(x) \to L$ and $h(x) \to L$ as $x \to a$, then $g(x) \to L$ as $x \to a$.

Here are two points to keep in mind:

- The theorem is good for more than computing a limit. It also guarantees that the limit $\lim_{x \to a} g(x)$ *exists*—no matter how crazily g careens between f and h.

- The squeezing *idea* is easy enough; the hard part in practice is often choosing the "bounding functions" f and h properly.

BASIC EXERCISES

1. Let $f(x) = \begin{cases} x^2 & \text{if } x \neq 3 \\ 0 & \text{if } x = 3. \end{cases}$

 (a) Evaluate $\lim_{x \to 3} f(x)$.

 (b) Does $\lim_{x \to 3} f(x) = f(3)$?

2. Let $g(x) = \dfrac{x^2 - 4}{x - 2}$ and $h(x) = x^2$.

 (a) Explain why 2 is not in the domain of g.

 (b) Evaluate $\lim_{x \to 2} g(x)$ by mimicking the algebra in Example 2.

 (c) How is the limit in part (b) related to $h'(2)$? (See Example 3.)

3. (a) Explain why $\dfrac{x^2 - 9}{x + 3} = x - 3$ for all $x \neq -3$.

 (b) Evaluate $\lim_{x \to -3} \dfrac{x^2 - 9}{x + 3}$.

 (c) Let $f(x) = x^2$. Evaluate $f'(-3)$.

4. Suppose that $\lim_{x \to 1^+} g(x) = 5$ and $\lim_{x \to 1^-} g(x) = 3$. Does this imply that $\lim_{x \to 1} g(x)$ exists? Justify your answer.

5. Let $g(x) = \sqrt[5]{x} = x^{1/5}$. Show that $g'(0)$ does not exist. (See Example 5.)

6. Let $h(x) = \sqrt[3]{x^2} = x^{2/3}$. Does $h'(0)$ exist? Justify your answer.

7. Let $f(x) = |x|$.

 (a) Evaluate $\lim_{x \to 0^+} f'(x)$.

 (b) Evaluate $\lim_{x \to 0^-} f'(x)$.

 (c) Explain why $\lim_{x \to 0} f'(x)$ does not exist.

8. Explain why $\lim_{x \to 0^+} \sqrt{x} = 0$ but $\lim_{x \to 0} \sqrt{x}$ does not exist.

In Exercises 9–11, f is the function $f(x) = \begin{cases} 1 & \text{if } x \text{ is an integer} \\ 2 & \text{if } x \text{ is not an integer.} \end{cases}$

9. (a) Draw a graph of f over the interval $[0, 5]$.

 (b) Evaluate $\lim_{x \to 4} f(x)$.

10. Evaluate $\lim_{x \to 5/2} f(x)$.

11. For which values of a does $\lim_{x \to a} f(x)$ exist? Justify your answer.

12. Let k be a constant and let $g(x) = kf(x)$. Use Theorem 5 to show that $g'(x) = kf'(x)$.

In Exercises 13–26, f is the function shown below. Use this graph to evaluate each limit or to explain why the limit does not exist. [NOTE: $f(1) = 2$.]

13. $\lim_{x \to 0} f(x)$

14. $\lim_{x \to -3} f(x)$

15. $\lim_{x \to -1} f(x)$

16. $\lim_{x \to 2^-} f(x)$

17. $\lim_{x \to 2^+} f(x)$

18. $\lim_{x \to 2} f(x)$

19. $\lim_{x \to -2^-} f(x)$

20. $\lim_{x \to 1^+} f(x)$

21. $\lim_{x \to -4^+} f(x)$

22. $\lim\limits_{x \to 4^-} f(x)$

23. $\lim\limits_{x \to 3} f'(x)$

24. $\lim\limits_{x \to -1^+} f'(x)$

25. $\lim\limits_{x \to -1^-} f'(x)$

26. $\lim\limits_{x \to -3} f'(x)$

In Exercises 27–36, g is the function shown below. Use the graph to evaluate the limit or to explain why the limit does not exist.

27. $\lim\limits_{x \to -4^+} g(x)$

28. $\lim\limits_{x \to -3} g(x)$

29. $\lim\limits_{x \to -2} g(x)$

30. $\lim\limits_{x \to -1^+} g(x)$

31. $\lim\limits_{x \to -1} g(x)$

32. $\lim\limits_{x \to 0^-} g(x)$

33. $\lim\limits_{x \to 1} g(x)$

34. $\lim\limits_{x \to 2} g(x)$

35. $\lim\limits_{x \to 3} g(x)$

36. $\lim\limits_{x \to 4^-} g(x)$

37. Let $s(t)$ be the slope of the secant line through the points $(3, f(3))$ and $(t, f(t))$ on the graph of the function $f(x) = x^2 + x$.

   (a) Find a formula for $s(t)$.

   (b) Find $\lim\limits_{t \to 3} s(t)$.

   (c) What does your answer to part (b) imply about f?

38. Let $f(x) = x/|x|$.

   (a) Sketch a graph of f over the interval $[-5, 5]$.

   (b) Explain why $f'(x) = 0$ if $x \neq 0$.

   (c) Explain why $f'(0)$ doesn't exist.

In Exercises 39–42, f is the function defined by the rule

$$f(x) = \begin{cases} 3 - x^2/2 & \text{if } x < 2 \\ 3x - 5 & \text{if } x \geq 2. \end{cases}$$

39. Evaluate $\lim\limits_{x \to 3} f(x)$.

40. Evaluate $\lim\limits_{x \to 0} f(x)$.

41. Evaluate $\lim\limits_{x \to 2} f(x)$.

42. Evaluate $\lim\limits_{x \to 1} f(x)$.

In Exercises 43–46, evaluate the limit if $\lim\limits_{x \to 1} f(x) = 5$ and $\lim\limits_{x \to 1} g(x) = -2$.

43. $\lim\limits_{x \to 1} (f(x) + g(x))$

44. $\lim\limits_{x \to 1} (2g(x) - 3f(x))$

45. $\lim\limits_{x \to 1} f(x) \cdot g(x)$

46. $\lim\limits_{x \to 1} \dfrac{f(x) + 2}{f(x)g(x)}$

47. Suppose that f is a continuous function and $f(3) = -1$. Explain why $\lim\limits_{x \to 3} f(x) = -1$ must be true.

48. Suppose that f is continuous at $x = 1$ and that $\lim\limits_{x \to 1} f(x) = -2$. Explain why $f(1) = -2$ must be true.

FURTHER EXERCISES

In Exercises 49–55, use the graphs of f and g shown below to evaluate the limit or explain why the limit doesn't exist.
[NOTE: $f(1) = 2$.]

Graph of f

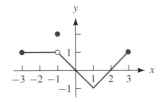

Graph of g

49. $\lim\limits_{x \to 0} (f(x) + g(x))$

50. $\lim\limits_{x \to 2} (f(x) + g(x))$

51. $\lim\limits_{x \to 1} (f(x) \cdot g(x))$

52. $\lim\limits_{x \to 2} (f(x) \cdot g(x))$

53. $\lim\limits_{x \to 0} \dfrac{f(x)}{g(x)}$

54. $\lim\limits_{x \to 0} (f(x) \cdot \cos x)$

55. $\lim\limits_{x \to -2} x^2 g(x)$

56. Suppose that g is the linear function $g(x) = mx + b$.

(a) Show that $g'(a) = \lim\limits_{h \to 0} \dfrac{g(a+h) - g(a)}{h} = m$ for every value of a.

(b) Interpret the result in part (a) in terms of slopes and rates of change.

In Exercises 57–60, use the graphs of the functions f (see Exercises 13–26, page 110) and g (see Exercises 49–55, page 111) to evaluate each limit. If a limit does not exist, explain why.

57. $\lim\limits_{x \to 0} \dfrac{f(x) - 2}{x}$

58. $\lim\limits_{x \to 3} \dfrac{f(x)}{x - 3}$

59. $\lim\limits_{h \to 0} \dfrac{g(-2 + h) - 3/2}{h}$

60. $\lim\limits_{h \to 0} \dfrac{g(2 + h)}{h}$

61. Suppose that $f(2)$ is not defined. Is it possible that $\lim\limits_{x \to 2} f(x)$ exists? Justify your answer.

62. Let $f(w) = \begin{cases} -1 & \text{if } w \text{ is an integer} \\ 2 & \text{if } w \text{ is not an integer.} \end{cases}$
Explain why $\lim\limits_{x \to 0} f(1/x)$ does not exist.

In Exercises 63–65, suppose that f is continuous at $x = 3$ and that $\lim\limits_{x \to 3} f(x) = 17$. Indicate whether the statement about f must be true, might be true, or cannot be true. Justify your answers.

63. 3 is in the domain of f.

64. $f(3) = 17$.

65. $\lim\limits_{x \to 3^-} f(x) = 17$.

66. Let $f(x) = \begin{cases} ax + 1 & \text{if } x < 2 \\ x^2 & \text{if } x \geq 2. \end{cases}$

(a) Find the value of a for which $\lim\limits_{x \to 2} f(x)$ exists.

(b) If a has the value found in part (a), does $f'(2)$ exist? Justify your answer.

67. Suppose that the function f is continuous at $x = 2$ and that f is defined by the rule

$$f(x) = \begin{cases} ax^2 + 3 & \text{if } x < 2 \\ 3x - 5 & \text{if } x \geq 2. \end{cases}$$

(a) Find the value of a.

(b) Is f differentiable at $x = 2$? Justify your answer.

68. Suppose that neither $\lim\limits_{x \to a} f(x)$ nor $\lim\limits_{x \to a} g(x)$ exists. Find functions f and g so that the following limits exist or explain why it is impossible to do so.

(a) $\lim\limits_{x \to a} \big(f(x) + g(x)\big)$

(b) $\lim\limits_{x \to a} \big(f(x) \cdot g(x)\big)$

2.4 USING DERIVATIVE AND ANTIDERIVATIVE FORMULAS

The section has two main aims: (i) to suggest why we care so deeply about derivative formulas; and (ii) to introduce the concept of antiderivative and why it matters. All systematic searching for antiderivatives comes (considerably) later.

In preceding sections we showed how to find derivative formulas for certain functions, including polynomials and other simple combinations of power functions. In later sections we'll find derivative formulas for other families of functions (including trigonometric, exponential, and logarithmic functions) and for more complicated combinations of basic functions.

Why do we bother? What are symbolic formulas good for? What can symbolic formulas tell us that graphs alone cannot? In this section, we offer some preliminary answers. We also turn the derivative problem around, looking for **antiderivative** formulas and illustrating some of their uses.

Derivatives, maxima, and minima

We return often in exercises and examples to the general idea of optimizing functions. Section 4.6 takes the "story problem" approach and adds some new twists.

Optimization—finding the biggest or smallest possible values of a varying quantity—is an important problem throughout mathematics and in applications. Derivative formulas (if they're simple) can make locating maxima and minima of a function f an easy matter. Here's the key idea:

Recall: Stationary points are roots of the derivative; critical points may be either roots or singularities.

> **FACT** Let f be differentiable on an interval I. Maximum and minimum values of f on I can occur only at stationary points of f (where $f'(x) = 0$) or at endpoints (if any) of I.

The next two examples show the Fact in action and illustrate techniques we'll use often.

EXAMPLE 1 Let $f(x) = x^2 - x$ and $I = [0, 2]$; see Figure 1. Where—exactly—on I does f take maximum and minimum values? What are these values?

Solution The graph gives immediate *estimates*, but the formulas show that our answers are *exact*. Because $f'(x) = 2x - 1$, we have $f'(x) = 0$ *only* for $x = 1/2$. The preceding Fact says that maximum and minimum values of f can occur only at $x = 1/2$ and at the endpoints of I. Checking values of f at these three points gives $f(0) = 0$, $f(1/2) = -1/4$, and $f(2) = 2$. Thus, for x in $[0, 2]$, f takes its minimum value, $-1/4$, at $x = 1/2$, and its maximum value, 2, at $x = 2$.   ■

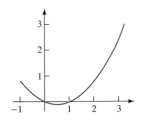

FIGURE 1
$f(x) = x^2 - x$

Students should know that for quadratic functions calculus isn't really needed to find stationary points; completing the square is an algebraic alternative.

Students should be pointed to Appendix G for general help with math–English translation.

Real-world maxima and minima Finding maximum and minimum values of real-world functions is among the most important applications of calculus. The mathematics of such story problems is often easier than the "translation" involved: restating a real-world problem in mathematical language and then translating the results back into the language of the problem. (Appendix G contains a variety of story problems and some homespun advice for solving them.)

EXAMPLE 2 A gardener wants to enclose 1000 square meters of land using as little fencing as possible. The garden is to be rectangular; one side, unfenced, lies along a river. How much fencing is needed? ➔

Solution Figure 2 shows the garden:

A similar problem and others like it are discussed in more detail in Appendix G.

FIGURE 2
A garden for fencing

Let x and y denote the lengths shown. By assumption, $xy = 1000$, so $y = 1000/x$. Let L denote the total length of fence. Then

$$L = 2x + y = 2x + \frac{1000}{x}.$$

Thus, L becomes a function of x (see Figure 3); we want to minimize L.

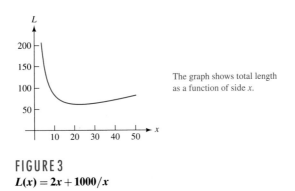

The graph shows total length as a function of side x.

FIGURE 3
$L(x) = 2x + 1000/x$

The graph suggests a minimum value somewhere near $x = 20$. With the derivative formula, we can locate this stationary point precisely. A quick calculation gives $L'(x) = 2 - 1000/x^2$, and solving $L'(x) = 0$ gives

$$2 - \frac{1000}{x^2} = 0 \iff x^2 = 500 \iff x = \pm 10\sqrt{5}.$$

(Only the positive value of x makes sense as a fence-length.) Thus, $L(10\sqrt{5}) = 40\sqrt{5} \approx 89.44$ is the smallest possible value of L. In gardening terms, we need just under 90 meters of fence, and the "best" dimensions for the desired plot are $x = 10\sqrt{5} \approx 22.36$ meters and $y = 1000/x = 20\sqrt{5} \approx 44.72$ meters. ∎

The real world? Fencing problems—perennial favorites in calculus texts—are not always fully "realistic." Few vegetable gardens *really* front directly on rivers, for example, or must be exactly 1000 square meters of area; few garden supply stores will sell exactly $40\sqrt{5}$ (an irrational number!) meters of fencing.

Still, the basic principles behind such simple problems are perfectly valid—and genuinely useful in practice. It's worth knowing, for instance, that the "best" river-fronting rectangular garden plot is twice as long as it is wide, while the best free-standing garden plot is square.

Antiderivatives

So far we've discussed differentiation—finding the derivative function f' for certain functions f. Now we consider the "reverse" problem, called **antidifferentiation**:

Given a function f, find a function F such that $F' = f$.

The function F is called an **antiderivative** of f. For instance, $F(x) = x^2$ is an antiderivative of $f(x) = 2x$.

Why antidifferentiate? If a function $f(t)$ describes a changing amount (say the position of a moving car) at time t, then the derivative $f'(t)$ describes the rate of change of f (the car's velocity) at time t. *Differentiation*, therefore, converts information about amounts to information about rates. *Antidifferentiation*, by contrast, involves reconstructing amounts from rates; for cars, this could mean finding a car's position from knowledge of its velocity, or finding velocity from knowledge of acceleration. This two-way relationship between rates and amounts is among calculus's most important and useful ideas.

Students may need to be encouraged to guess—and to check guesses by differentiation. (We exhort them often to do both.)

Although the *idea* of antiderivatives is simple, the process of *finding* symbolic antiderivatives can be difficult; we'll take up that problem systematically in several later chapters. For polynomials and power functions, however, finding antiderivatives is not much harder than finding derivatives; an educated guess may be the first step.

EXAMPLE 3 Find antiderivative functions $Q(x)$ and $S(x)$ for (a) $q(x) = x^2$ and (b) $s(x) = \sqrt{x}$. Is there more than one answer to each problem?

Solution Because $(x^3)' = 3x^2$, $Q(x) = x^3/3$ is a natural guess for (a). It's easy to check, using the constant multiple rule for derivatives, that this guess is correct:

$$Q'(x) = \left(\frac{1}{3}x^3\right)' = \frac{1}{3}(x^3)' = \frac{1}{3} \cdot 3x^2 = x^2.$$

For $s(x) = \sqrt{x} = x^{1/2}$, it's reasonable to look for an antiderivative of the form $S(x) = ax^k$, where a and k are constants. What values should a a and k have? We'll decide by differentiating our guess. By the power rule and the constant multiple rule for derivatives, $(ax^k)' = akx^{k-1}$. Now the right side can equal $x^{1/2}$ only if $k-1 = 1/2$ and $ak = 1$; these conditions force $k = 3/2$ and $a = 2/3$. This means that $S(x) = \frac{2}{3}x^{3/2}$—an answer that's easy to double-check by differentiation.

The answers we've just found are not the only ones possible. (They're not *unique*, in math-speak.) For example, all of

$$\frac{x^3}{3} + 1, \quad \frac{x^3}{3} + \frac{123}{456}, \quad \text{and} \quad \frac{x^3}{3} - \frac{\sin 3 + \cos 4}{\tan 5}$$

are antiderivatives of $q(x)$, as is *every* function of the form $x^3/3 + C$, where C is any constant. Similarly, all functions of the form $S(x) = \frac{2}{3}x^{3/2} + C$ are antiderivatives of $s(x)$.   ■

Antiderivatives are not unique Example 3 illustrates an important general principle:

Students should interpret this fact graphically.

> **THEOREM 8** If $F(x)$ is an antiderivative of $f(x)$, and C is any constant, then $F(x) + C$ is another antiderivative of $f(x)$.

The reason is simple: Adding a constant to a function $F(x)$ has no effect on F'. The implication runs the other way, too:

> **THEOREM 9** If $F'(x) = G'(x)$ for all x, then $F(x) = G(x) + C$ for some constant C.

For the particular function $q(x) = x^2$, Theorem 8 and Theorem 9 imply just what the preceding example suggests: (i) For any constant C, $Q(x) = x^3/3 + C$ is an antiderivative of q, and (ii) *every* antiderivative has this form.

A slightly more complicated (but precise) statement of the theorem might emphasize domains, which should be (finite or infinite) intervals.

Theorem 8 boils down to the easy observation that the derivative of a constant function is zero. Theorem 9 says that *only* constant functions have zero derivatives. Although this sounds simple enough, it's surprisingly tricky to prove. ➥ We'll mention the matter again in Chapter 4.

A careful proof requires the mean value theorem.

Finding formulas for antiderivatives

We've already seen how to *differentiate* any polynomial function in x: We use the power rule to differentiate each power x^k; then we combine results using the sum and constant multiple rules. We can *antidifferentiate* polynomial functions in much the same way. The power rule for derivatives, read "backwards," gets us started.

"Antiderivative rules" like this one are atypical; all systematic study of antiderivatives comes much later.

> **THEOREM 10 (Power rule for antiderivatives)** For any choice of constants C and k (where $k \neq -1$), the function $\dfrac{x^{k+1}}{k+1} + C$ is an antiderivative of x^k. *Every* antiderivative of x^k has this form.

Proof The derivative rules make it easy to verify the first assertion:

$$\frac{d}{dx}\left(\frac{x^{k+1}}{k+1} + C\right) = \frac{(k+1)x^k}{k+1} + 0 = x^k,$$

as we claimed. Theorem 9 says that *every* antiderivative has this form.   □

The exception: $k = -1$ Notice that Theorem 10 can't possibly hold for $k = -1$ because division by zero isn't allowed. Nevertheless, the exceptional function $f(x) = x^{-1} = 1/x$ *has* a well-behaved antiderivative, though not of the usual "power" form:

> **FACT**   For $x > 0$, the natural logarithm function $\ln x$ is an antiderivative of $1/x$.

Students might be asked to use the curve $y = 1/x$ to draw a possible antiderivative graph — it should look roughly log-like.

We'll prove this remarkable fact in a later section when we study logarithmic functions, but the graphs in Figure 4 make the fact plausible right now:

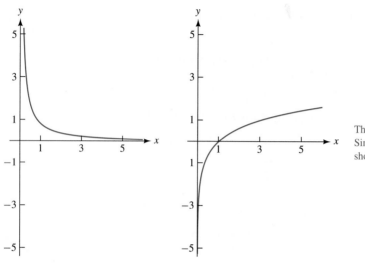

The first graph represents slopes of the second. Since $\ln x$ is defined only for $x > 0$, both graphs show only positive x.

FIGURE 4
$y = 1/x$ and $y = \ln x$

Sums and constant multiples   Antiderivatives, like derivatives, behave nicely with respect to sums and constant multiples:

> **FACT**   If $F' = f$, $G' = g$, and k is any constant, then $(F + G)' = f + g$ and $(kF)' = kf$.

This Fact is not new—it just restates the sum and constant multiple rules for derivatives in different notation.

EXAMPLE 4   Antidifferentiate $p(x) = 3x^5 + 7x^4 - x^2/3 + 11$.

Solution   We pull $p(x)$ apart, antidifferentiate the pieces separately, and then reassemble the results.

By Theorem 10, $x^6/6$, $x^5/5$, $x^3/3$, and x are antiderivatives for x^5, x^4, x^3, and 1. The preceding Fact tells us how to combine these results; we get

$$P(x) = 3 \cdot \frac{x^6}{6} + 7 \cdot \frac{x^5}{5} - \frac{1}{3} \cdot \frac{x^3}{3} + 11 \cdot x + C$$

as an antiderivative for $p(x)$—an answer that's easy to check by differentiation.   ∎

Guess and check With the power rule and the preceding Fact it's easy to piece together antiderivatives of polynomials and other power functions. *Checking* answers by differentiation is even easier still. Here's the moral:

> *When searching for antiderivatives, guess freely—but check answers carefully.*

EXAMPLE 5 Consider the function $f(x) = x^3 - x^2 - 2x$; see Figure 5(a). Figure 5(b) shows four antiderivatives of f, labeled F, G, H, and K. Find a formula for each antiderivative.

Different antiderivatives for a given function differ by vertical translation.

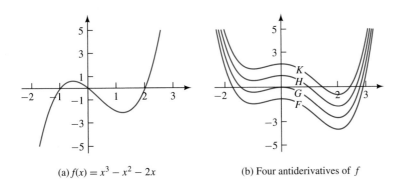

(a) $f(x) = x^3 - x^2 - 2x$ (b) Four antiderivatives of f

FIGURE 5
A function and four antiderivatives

Solution Notice the resemblance among F, G, H, and K. All four are vertical translations of each other, so they differ only by additive constants. Antiderivatives of f are functions of the form

$$g(x) = \frac{x^4}{4} - \frac{x^3}{3} - x^2 + C,$$

where C is any constant. In particular F, G, H, and K all have this form; they differ only in the value of C. Notice too that $g(0) = C$, so we can read each function's C-value from its y-intercept. A look at Figure 5(b) now shows that F, G, H, and K correspond to $C = -1$, $C = 0$, $C = 1$, and $C = 2$, respectively. ■

Easy derivatives, hard antiderivatives The concepts of derivative and antiderivative, like those of parent and child, are nothing more than different views of the same functional relationship. Perhaps surprisingly, *antidifferentiation* of elementary functions is often much harder than *differentiation*. Indeed, differentiation methods are simple enough to fit comfortably into inexpensive calculators. Finding antiderivatives is a bigger challenge—for both humans and computers.

Using derivative and antiderivative formulas: designing curves

Algebraic formulas for derivatives and antiderivatives are invaluable for applying calculus ideas to real problems. A common problem in computer graphics, for instance, is to draw a smooth curve through or near a set of data points. One way to do this is to string together separate curve pieces, called *splines*, that fit together smoothly where they meet. The following examples suggest how derivative and antiderivative formulas can be used to "build to order" curves with various geometric properties.

Splines appear in much more detail in Chapter 9, as an Interlude. But the basic ideas are simple, and work well with even modest technology at hand.

EXAMPLE 6   Figure 6 shows a line segment and part of a parabola; they meet smoothly (without a kink) at the origin. Find equations for both curve pieces.

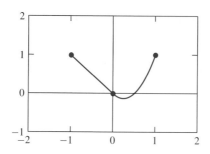

The two curves meet smoothly at the origin.

FIGURE 6
A line segment meets a parabola

Solution   The line's equation is $l(x) = -x$. The parabola's equation has form $p(x) = a + bx + cx^2$; we need specific values for a, b, and c. We'll use the picture to find these three values one by one:

1. The parabola passes through $(0, 0)$, so $p(0) = 0$. But $p(0) = a + b \cdot 0 + c \cdot 0^2 = a$, so $a = 0$. Thus, $p(x) = bx + cx^2$, with b and c still to be found.

2. At $x = 0$ the parabola and the line segment have the same slope: -1. Thus, $p'(0) = -1$; we'll use this information to find b. For any x, $p'(x) = b + 2cx$, so $p'(0) = b = -1$. Hence, $p(x) = -x + cx^2$. We still need to find c.

3. The parabola passes through $(1, 1)$, so $p(1) = 1$. But $p(x) = -x + cx^2$, and so $p(1) = -1 + c$. Therefore $-1 + c = 1$, $c = 2$, and we find that $p(x) = -x + 2x^2$.   ∎

EXAMPLE 7   We found in Example 6 that the two-part "curve" in Figure 6 has the piecewise-defined formula

$$f(x) = \begin{cases} -x & \text{if } -1 \le x \le 0 \\ -x + 2x^2 & \text{if } 0 \le x \le 1. \end{cases}$$

(The two lines agree at the common point $x = 0$.) Find and plot an *antiderivative* of f.

Solution   Because f has two well-fitting pieces, we'll look for an antiderivative F of the same form. Antidifferentiating each piece of f separately shows that F must have the form

$$F(x) = \begin{cases} -\frac{x^2}{2} + C_1 & \text{if } -1 \le x \le 0 \\ -\frac{x^2}{2} + \frac{2x^3}{3} + C_2 & \text{if } 0 \le x \le 1, \end{cases}$$

where C_1 and C_2 are constants, one for each separate antiderivative. We'll choose values for C_1 and C_2 so that the two pieces of F align properly at the common point $x = 0$. Because the first line of the definition gives $F(0) = C_1$ and the second gives $F(0) = C_2$, we must have $C_1 = C_2$, so we may as well write

$$F(x) = \begin{cases} -\frac{x^2}{2} + C & \text{if } -1 \le x \le 0 \\ -\frac{x^2}{2} + \frac{2x^3}{3} + C & \text{if } 0 \le x \le 1, \end{cases}$$

where C is any single constant. Figure 7 shows graphs of F for several values of C.

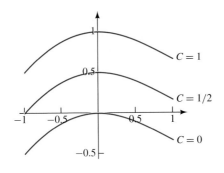

FIGURE 7
Three antiderivatives of f

The three curves are parallel; they are *not* parabolas—note the lack of reflective symmetry.

Antiderivative formulas can also be used to construct curves with prescribed stationary points and concavity properties.

EXAMPLE 8 Find some polynomial curves with exactly two stationary points: one at $x = 1$ and one at $x = -1$.

We "design" curves with given derivative properties in Section 4.7, on Taylor polynomials.

Solution Straight lines won't work: they're either horizontal (in which case every point is stationary) or they have no stationary points at all. Parabolas won't work either: they have only one stationary point, at the vertex. Thus, a cubic curve is the simplest possible answer.

Let $c(x)$ represent a cubic polynomial. The given conditions mean that $c'(x)$—a *quadratic* polynomial—must have roots at $x = \pm 1$. ➥ One possibility is $c'(x) = x^2 - 1$; antidifferentiating gives $c(x) = x^3/3 - x + C$, where C is any constant. More generally, *every* function of the form $c'(x) = k(x^2 - 1)$, where k is any nonzero constant, has its roots at $x = \pm 1$. Thus, every antiderivative of the form $c(x) = kx^3/3 - kx + C$ solves our problem. Figure 8 shows graphs of several possibilities.

The derivative of a cubic function is a quadratic function.

There are many interesting questions to ask here about links between shapes of curves and values of the constants k and C.

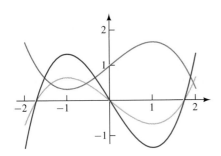

Note that all three curves have stationary points at $x = \pm 1$. Decide which curve is which.

FIGURE 8
Three cubics: $y = \frac{x^3}{3} - x$, $y = \frac{-x^3}{3} + x + 1$, $y = \frac{2x^3}{3} - 2x$

Technology is helpful in checking answers, but note that inflection points are difficult to see clearly after zooming. (Students might usefully ponder why this is.)

EXAMPLE 9 Find equations for some cubic curves with points of inflection at $x = 0$. ➥

Recall: A curve changes direction of concavity at an inflection point.

Solution We'll use antiderivatives to find an infinite family of answers. First, recall from Section 1.7 that concavity of the graph of f depends on the *second* derivative f'': the f-graph is concave up where $f''(x) > 0$ and concave down where $f''(x) < 0$. We want functions f for which $f''(x)$ changes sign at $x = 0$.

Every function of the form $f''(x) = kx$ (where k is any nonzero constant) changes sign at $x = 0$, so we can use any such function for the second derivative. To reconstruct f from f'', we antidifferentiate *twice*, picking up one arbitrary constant each time:

$$f''(x) = kx \implies f'(x) = k\frac{x^2}{2} + C_1 \implies f(x) = k\frac{x^3}{6} + C_1 x + C_2.$$

Thus, every function f of the form above has an inflection point at $x = 0$. Figure 9 shows three possibilities:

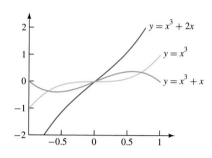

FIGURE 9
Three inflected curves

BASIC EXERCISES

1. Suppose that the only roots of f' in the interval $I = [-5, 5]$ are $x = -2$ and $x = 1$.

    (a) Is it possible that the minimum value of f on I occurs at $x = -1$? Justify your answer.

    (b) Is it possible that the maximum value of f on I occurs at $x = 5$? Justify your answer.

2. Let $g(x) = 3x - x^2$ and $I = [0, 2]$. Where on I does g take its maximum and minimum values?

In Exercises 3–12, F is an antiderivative of the function f shown below, $F(0) = 10$, and L is the line tangent to F at $x = 0$.

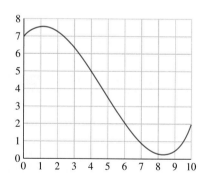

[NOTE: *f has a local maximum at $x = 1.14$, a point of inflection at $x = 4.67$, and a local minimum at $x = 8.19$.*]

3. What is the slope of F at $x = 4$? Justify your answer.

4. Where in the interval $[0, 10]$ is F increasing? Justify your answer.

5. Where in the interval $[0, 10]$ does F have points of inflection? Justify your answer.

6. Where in the interval $[0, 10]$ is F concave down? Justify your answer.

7. Estimate the value of $F''(5)$.

8. Explain why F'' achieves its minimum value over the interval $[0, 10]$ at $x = 4.67$.

9. Find an equation for L.

10. Does L lie above the curve $y = F(x)$ at $x = 1$? Justify your answer.

11. Is it possible that $F(5) = 5$? Justify your answer.

12. Is it possible that $F(5) = 15$? Justify your answer.

In Exercises 13–18, F is the antiderivative of a function f. F has a root at $x = 8.8$ and stationary points at $x = 3.2$, $x = 6$, and $x = 13.3$; F has points of inflection at $x = 4.5$ and $x = 10.5$. A graph of F is shown below.

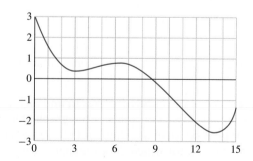

13. Where in the interval $[0, 15]$ is f positive? Justify your answer.

14. How many roots does f have in the interval $[0, 15]$? Where are they located?

15. Rank the five values -2, $f(3)$, $f(6)$, $f(9)$, and $f(14)$ in increasing order.

16. Estimate $f(10)$.

17. Where is f increasing? Justify your answer.

18. Where does f achieve its maximum value in the interval $[0, 15]$? Justify your answer.

In Exercises 19–22, answer each of the following questions about the given function. Express your answers exactly—for example, as $\sqrt{3}$—rather than in decimal form.

(a) *Where is the function increasing?*

(b) *Where is the function decreasing?*

(c) *Where does the function have local maxima?*

(d) *Where does the function have local minima?*

19. $f(x) = x^3 - 3x^2 + 5$

20. $s(t) = -8t^9 + 9t^8 - 7$

21. $g(w) = 7w^9 - 18w^7 + 63$

22. $h(r) = 5r^6 + 6r^5 - 15r^4$

In Exercises 23–26, find the maximum and the minimum value of the function over the given interval.

23. $f(x) = x^3 - 3x + 5$; $[0, 2]$

24. $f(x) = 1 + 2x^3 - x^4$; $[-1, 2]$

25. $f(x) = \sqrt{x} - 3/x$; $[0.25, 1]$

26. $f(x) = x^3 - x^2$; $[-2, 0]$

27. Show that $\frac{1}{2}x^6 + \frac{7}{5}x^5 - \frac{1}{9}x^3 + 11x + 13$ is an antiderivative of $p(x) = 3x^5 + 7x^4 - x^2/3 + 11$.

28. Suppose that C is a constant. Show that $\frac{1}{4}x^4 - \frac{1}{3}x^3 - x^2 + C$ is an antiderivative of $f(x) = x^3 - x^2 - 2x$.

29. Suppose that F is an antiderivative of $f(x) = x \sin x$. Find $F'(x)$.

30. (a) Explain why $F(x) = 2x + 1$ is an antiderivative of $f(x) = 2$.

(b) Find two other antiderivatives of f.

31. Is $G(x) = x^3 + 4$ an antiderivative of $g(x) = x^2$? Justify your answer.

32. Is $H(x) = \frac{2}{3}\sqrt{x^3} + 4$ an antiderivative of $h(x) = \sqrt{x}$? Justify your answer.

33. Suppose that $G(x) = x \sin(e^x)$ and that $G'(x) = g(x)$. Find *three* antiderivatives of g.

34. Suppose that $F'(x) = G'(x)$ for all x. Is it possible that $G(x) = F(x) + x$? Justify your answer.

35. Suppose that H is an antiderivative of $h(x) = 3x^2$.

(a) Explain why it is natural to guess that $H(x) = Ax^3 + B$, where A and B are constants.

(b) Find values of A and B such that $H'(x) = h(x)$ and $H(0) = 1$.

36. Suppose that F is an antiderivative of $f(x) = x^3$.

(a) Explain why it is natural to guess that F has the form $F(x) = Ax^4 + B$, where A and B are constants.

(b) Suppose that $F(0) = 0$. Show that $F(x) = x^4/4$.

(c) Suppose that $F(2) = 1$. Find an expression for $F(x)$.

37. Let f be the function shown graphically in Example 6.

(a) Does f have a derivative at $x = 0$? Justify your answer.

(b) Find an expression for f' and plot it.

38. Explain why a straight line has either no stationary points or infinitely many stationary points.

39. Suppose that $q(x) = ax^2 + bx + c$ is a quadratic polynomial. Show that if $a \neq 0$, q has only one stationary point.

40. Suppose that $c'(x) = k(x^2 - 1)$, where $k > 0$ is a constant. Show that c is concave down at $x = -1$ and concave up at $x = 1$.

41. Find a cubic polynomial that changes from concave up to concave down at $x = 1$.

FURTHER EXERCISES

42. Find the maximum and minimum values of the derivative of $f(x) = 6x^2 - x^4$ on the interval $[-2, 2]$.

43. Suppose that $f'(x) = Ax + x^2$, where A is a constant such that $-2 < A < 2$, and that I is the interval $[-4, 3]$. Where might the maximum value of f on I occur?

44. For which value(s) of x does the slope of the line tangent to the curve $y = -x^3 + 3x^2 + 1$ take on its largest value? Justify your answer.

45. Suppose that $q(x)$ is a polynomial of degree $n \geq 2$. Explain why q has at most $n - 1$ local extrema.
[HINT: $q'(x)$ is a polynomial of degree $n - 1$.]

46. Let $f(x) = ax^3 + bx^2 + cx + d$.

(a) Show that f has either no local extrema or a local maximum and a local minimum.

(b) Show that, if they exist, the local extrema of f are located at $x = \dfrac{-b \pm \sqrt{b^2 - 3ac}}{3a}$.

47. Is there a real number x such that $4x^3 - x^4 = 30$? Prove your answer.

48. Let p be the parabola defined by $p(x) = ax^2 + bx + c$ where $a, b,$ and c are constants. Show that the vertex of the parabola is at $x = -b/2a$.

49. (a) Find constants a and b so that the polynomial $p(x) = x^3 + ax + b$ has a local minimum at $(2, -9)$.

(b) Draw a graph of p.

50. (a) Find constants a, b, and c so that the quadratic polynomial $p(x) = ax^2 + bx + c$ is zero if $x = 1$, decreasing if $x < 2$, and increasing if $x > 2$.

(b) Draw a graph of p.

51. (a) Find a cubic polynomial $q(x) = ax^3 + bx^2 + cx + d$ that has a local maximum at $(0, 2)$ and a local minimum at $(5, 0)$.

(b) Draw a graph of q.

52. For which values of the constant k does the graph of $y = x^3 - 3x^2 + k$ have just one x-intercept? Two x-intercepts? Three x-intercepts? Justify your answers.

53. For which values of k, if any, does the function $f(x) = (8x + k)/x^2$ have a local minimum at $x = 4$?

54. A particle moves on the x-axis in such a way that its position at time $t > 0$ is given by $x(t) = 3t^5 - 25t^3 + 60t$. For which values of t is the particle moving to the left?

55. A particle moves along a straight line so that its velocity is given by $v(t) = t^2$. How far does the particle travel between $t = 1$ and $t = 3$?

56. Suppose that a rectangle has its base on the x-axis and its two upper corners on the curve $y = 2(1 - x^2)$. What is the maximum perimeter of such a rectangle?

57. Find the shortest distance from the curve $xy = 4$ to the origin. [HINT: Minimize the *square* of the distance function.]

58. What is the area of the largest rectangle whose base is on the x-axis and whose upper corners are on the curve $y = 12 - x^2$?

59. The cost of fuel for a luxury liner is proportional to the square of the speed v. At a speed of 10 km/hr, fuel costs \$3000/hr. Other fixed costs (e.g., labor) amount to \$12,000/hr. Assuming that the ship is to make a trip of total distance D, find the speed that minimizes the cost of the trip. Does this speed depend on D?

60. An open box is made by cutting squares of side w inches from the four corners of a sheet of cardboard that is $24'' \times 32''$ and then folding up the sides. What should w be to maximize the volume of the box?

61. An open box with a capacity of 36,000 cubic inches is to be twice as long as it is wide. The material for the box costs \$0.10 per square foot. What are the dimensions of the least expensive box? How much does it cost?

62. The figure below shows the graph of $f(x) = \sqrt{x}$ and its tangent line at $x = a$. Find the value of a.

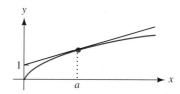

63. Find values of a and b so that the line $2x + 3y = a$ is tangent to the graph of $f(x) = bx^2$ at $x = 3$.

64. Let f be a function defined by $f(x) = Ax^2 + Bx + C$ with the following properties: (i) $f(0) = 2$; (ii) $f'(2) = 10$; (iii) $f''(10) = 4$. Find the value of $A + B + C$.

65. Find c so that the line $y = 4x + 3$ is tangent to the curve $y = x^2 + c$.

66. A fly crawls from left to right along the edge of a curved barrier on the xy-plane whose shape is the graph of $y = 7 - x^2$. A spider waits at the point $(4, 0)$. Where is the fly when the two creatures first see each other? [HINT: Draw a picture.]

67. Find an antiderivative of $1/x$ for $x < 0$.

68. Suppose that F is an antiderivative of $f(x) = e^{-x^2} = G'(x)$. Explain why $F(x) - G(x)$ is a constant.

2.5 DIFFERENTIAL EQUATIONS; MODELING MOTION

This section introduces basic ideas, vocabulary, and uses for DEs and their solutions. Physical motion (e.g., free fall) is the key example; the associated DEs are relatively simple, and they let us deduce consequences of physical laws such as Newton's laws of motion. We return to the DE theme in the following sections, where we model exponential growth and oscillation.

Algebraic equations describe relations among varying quantities. For example, the Pythagorean formula $a^2 + b^2 = c^2$ relates the side lengths of any right triangle. *Differential* equations go one step—a giant step—further: They describe relations among changing quantities and the *rates* at which they change.

Differential equations are invaluable tools for modeling real-world phenomena. As an unknown sage put it:

Nature's voice is mathematics; its language is differential equations.

The basic physical laws of motion, for instance, are essentially statements about rates of change—that is, about derivatives. Differential equations provide the proper mathematical language for expressing these laws and deducing their consequences. We'll begin to explore differential equations in this and the following two sections.

Basic ideas and examples

A **differential equation** (**DE**) is any equation that contains one or more derivatives. Here are several examples: ➤

$$f'(x) = 6x + 5; \quad y' = \frac{1}{2y}; \quad \frac{dy}{dx} = 5; \quad y''(t) = -9.8.$$

Notice the various notations and abbreviations for derivatives.

A **solution** of a differential equation is a *function* that satisfies the DE. The point bears repeating:

A solution to a DE is a function—*not a number.*

Examples of DEs will illustrate the characteristic ideas, terminology, and notational quirks.

Thinking of functions (not numbers) as solutions may baffle some students. Having families of solutions may also be a new concept. Careful use of terminology is essential.

EXAMPLE 1   Find solutions to the DE $f'(x) = 6x + 5$. How many solutions are there? How are these solutions related to each other?

Solution   This DE simply asks for an antiderivative f of the function $6x + 5$. It's easy to check that, for any constant C, the function $f(x) = 3x^2 + 5x + C$ has the desired derivative. By Theorem 9, page 115, these are the only possible derivatives. Thus, this DE has infinitely many solutions; they differ from each other only by additive constants.   ∎

EXAMPLE 2   Discuss the DE $y'(x) = \dfrac{1}{2y(x)}$. Do many solutions exist? How are they related to each other?

Solution   This DE is more challenging than the one in Example 1. This DE says that the desired function y has the property that the derivative y' is half the reciprocal of y itself. With some ingenuity and luck, one might guess that $y(x) = \sqrt{x}$ satisfies the DE. ➤ But once this guess is made, it's easily seen to be correct:

Remembering Example 2, page 93, might help too.

$$\text{If} \quad y(x) = \sqrt{x}, \quad \text{then} \quad y'(x) = \frac{1}{2\sqrt{x}} = \frac{1}{2y(x)}.$$

A similar calculation shows that $y(x) = -\sqrt{x}$ is another solution.

There are still other solutions. For any constant C, the functions $y(x) = \sqrt{x + C}$ and $y(x) = -\sqrt{x + C}$ are also solutions to the same DE:

$$\text{If} \quad y(x) = \pm\sqrt{x + C}, \quad \text{then} \quad y'(x) = \pm\frac{1}{2\sqrt{x + C}} = \frac{1}{2y(x)}.$$

(This calculation uses Theorem 4 (i), page 97.)   ∎

EXAMPLE 3   Solve the DE $y''(t) = -9.8$. How many solutions exist? How are they related to each other? (This DE is connected to the phenomenon of free fall, as we'll see later in this section.)

Solution   To find a solution function $y(t)$ from the expression for $y''(t)$, we antidifferentiate *twice*, picking up *two* constants C_1 and C_2 on the way:

$$y''(t) = -9.8 \Longrightarrow y'(t) = -9.8t + C_1 \qquad \text{(antidifferentiate } y'')$$
$$\Longrightarrow y(t) = -4.9t^2 + C_1 t + C_2. \qquad \text{(antidifferentiate } y')$$

It's easy to check by differentiation that every function of this form *is* a solution; thus, there are (as in the preceding examples) infinitely many different solutions—one for each choice of values for the two constants C_1 and C_2.   ∎

What the examples show   Following are some morals to draw from the preceding examples:

- **We don't want any arguments**   Functions that appear in DEs are often written without arguments. ("Argument" is another name for "input variable name.") For instance, all three of the DEs

$$y' = \frac{1}{2y}, \quad y'(x) = \frac{1}{2y(x)}, \quad \text{and} \quad y'(t) = \frac{1}{2y(t)}$$

  say the same thing. (In particular, the input variable name doesn't matter.) Omitting unneeded variable names unclutters a DE's appearance.

- **Choosing variable names**   The symbol t, which suggests *time*, is often used as the input variable name when stating or solving DEs. A solution function y (or $y(t)$) is then naturally thought of as a quantity that varies with time. Using t rather than, say, x, is *only* a convenience—DEs can model phenomena that have nothing to do with time.

The same is true (for the same reason) for finding antiderivatives.

- **Checking is easy; finding is hard**   *Finding* solutions to complicated DEs can be hard; many thick books treat the subject. But it's usually easy to *check* by differentiation whether a given function satisfies a DE. We'll use the guess-and-check strategy freely and often.

- **Order of a DE**   The **order** of a DE tells the number of derivatives involved. The DE $y'' = -9.8$ has **second order**, while $f'(x) = 6x + 5$ is a **first-order** DE.

Families of solutions   As the examples illustrate, a typical DE has not just one solution function but a whole **family** of solutions. Depending on the type of DE at hand, family members may differ from each other by additive or multiplicative constants, or in other ways.

Figures 1(a) and (b) show several solutions to the DEs in Examples 1 and 2:

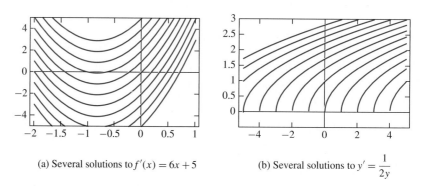

(a) Several solutions to $f'(x) = 6x + 5$ (b) Several solutions to $y' = \dfrac{1}{2y}$

FIGURE 1
Solution curves for two DEs

Notice the different families' traits: In the left-hand picture, the solution functions differ only by a *vertical* shift; in the right-hand picture, they differ by a *horizontal* shift.

Hard work, but worth doing.   Solving DEs can be much more complicated than our simple examples suggest. A huge literature and whole courses treat DE theory and solution methods. These facts attest to the depth and difficulty of the subject—but even more to its practical importance.

Initial value problems

Examples 1 and 2 concern first-order DEs; each has an *infinite family* of solutions. Family members (see Figures 1(a) and (b)) differ from each other by the value of a constant parameter.

In practice, we're often interested in *one* solution function, not a whole family. One way to specify a "unique" solution function is to require that the function have a particular output value for a particular input. ➤ Graphically speaking, this requirement means that we choose *one* solution curve by specifying a point it passes through. This extra requirement is called an **initial condition**; the combination of a DE and an initial condition is known as an **initial value problem** (**IVP**). We illustrate these ideas and jargon in the next example.

In mathematics, "unique" means "the only one."

In ordinary speech "unique" seems to mean something closer to "unusual." Mathematical usage is stricter.

EXAMPLE 4 Solve the IVP

$$f'(x) = 6x + 5; \qquad f(0) = 2.$$

(The first requirement is the DE; the second is the initial condition.)

Solution We saw in Example 1 that any function of the form $f(x) = 3x^2 + 5x + C$ is a solution of the DE. Using the initial condition $f(0) = 2$, we can find the "correct" value of C:

$$f(0) = 3 \cdot 0^2 + 5 \cdot 0 + C = 2 \implies C = 2.$$

Thus, $f(x) = 3x^2 + 5x + 2$ is the unique solution to the IVP; the graph of this function is shown in Figure 1(a)—it's the curve that passes through $(0, 2)$. ∎

EXAMPLE 5 Solve the IVP

$$y' = \frac{1}{2y}; \qquad y(1) = 2.$$

Solution We showed in Example 2 that, for any constant C, $y(x) = \sqrt{x + C}$ is a solution to the DE. The initial condition requires that $y = 2$ when $x = 1$; this means that $C = 3$, so $y = \sqrt{x + 3}$ is the unique solution to the IVP. ∎

Modeling motion: DEs in action

Modeling the motion of real-world objects is among the most important applications of calculus. We'll stick here to the simplest, one-dimensional case, in which motion occurs along a straight line. This is the case for such phenomena as a car moving on a straight east–west road (the car can travel either way), or a thrown object moving vertically under the influence of gravity. These assumptions may sound simple-minded, but the ideas they illustrate extend readily to much more general forms of motion, including those in the plane and in the three-dimensional world.

Acceleration, velocity, and position An object moving along a line has, at any instant t, an acceleration $a(t)$, a velocity $v(t)$, and a position $p(t)$, all with respect to some understood units for measuring position and time. (For a rising or falling object, the position is often denoted by h, for height.) For instance, an object moving on the x-axis might, at time $t = 2$ seconds, be 3 units to the right of the origin, have (rightward) velocity 4 units per second, and have (rightward) acceleration 5 units per second per second. In symbols,

Vehicle motion is familiar even to students who've had no physics classes.

$$p(2) = 3; \quad v(2) = 4; \quad a(2) = 5.$$

Now the functions p, v, and a are all derivatives (or antiderivatives) of each other (we saw this in Section 1.4):

$$p'(t) = v(t); \quad v'(t) = a(t); \quad p''(t) = a(t).$$

If we know formulas for any of these functions, we may be able to find formulas for the others by differentiation or antidifferentiation.

Free fall and the laws of motion   In the 1500s and 1600s Galileo, Newton, and others came to realize that forces (such as gravity, friction, and air drag) that act on an object affect the object's *acceleration*. **Newton's second law of motion** puts this more precisely:

> *A force acting on an object causes the object to accelerate in the direction of the force. The acceleration is proportional to the force. In particular,* constant *force produces* constant *acceleration.*

An important example is the case of **free fall**, in which an object is assumed to be affected only by the (constant) force of earth's gravity and so undergoes *constant* acceleration toward the center of the earth. (See Figure 2.) Physical measurements show that the magnitude of this acceleration is about 32 feet per second per second; the metric equivalent is about 9.8 meters per second per second.

FIGURE 2
An object in free fall

In typical examples of free fall we take "upward" to be the positive direction, so that "position" corresponds naturally to "height." In such cases, we write either $a(t) = -32$ or $a(t) = -9.8$, depending on the units chosen—the acceleration is taken as *negative* because the object falls *downward*.

Modeling free fall with a DE   Consider a free-falling object, with position $h(t)$, velocity $v(t)$, and constant acceleration $a(t) = -9.8$; distance and time are measured in meters and seconds, respectively. Let's model the situation with a second-order DE and then solve it.

The DE version of the story says, simply, that $h''(t) = a(t) = -9.8$. We solved this second-order DE in Example 3; we got

$$h(t) = -4.9t^2 + C_1 t + C_2,$$

where C_1 and C_2 are any real constants.

The constants C_1 and C_2 have simple physical meanings. Because $h(0) = C_2$ and $h'(0) = v(0) = C_1$, we see that C_2 represents the object's **initial height** (the height at time 0), and C_1 represents the object's **initial velocity**. For these reasons, solutions to this DE usually appear in physics texts in the form

$$h(t) = -4.9t^2 + v_0 t + h_0,$$

where the zero subscripts denote values at $t = 0$. (In the English system, with distance measured in feet, the analogous formula reads $h(t) = -16t^2 + v_0 t + h_0$.)

How many initial conditions? The preceding discussion and Example 3 involved a *second-order* DE—its solution function contained *two* constant parameters. A second-order IVP usually requires *two* initial conditions to determine a unique solution function. We illustrate the process in Example 6.

EXAMPLE 6 A cannonball (see Figure 3) is shot upward from an initial height of 5 meters, with initial velocity 98 meters per second. ➜ If free-fall conditions are assumed, how high does the cannonball rise? When does it hit the ground?

This translates to around 200 mph—possible for an old-fashioned cannon.

FIGURE 3
A predictable cannonball

Solution The problem can be stated as a second-order IVP, this time with *two* initial conditions:

$$h''(t) = -9.8; \qquad h(0) = 5; \qquad h'(0) = 98.$$

The preceding discussion showed (with $v_0 = 98$ and $h_0 = 5$) that the velocity and height functions have the formulas

$$v(t) = -9.8t + 98 \qquad \text{and} \qquad h(t) = -4.9t^2 + 98t + 5.$$

The cannonball is highest when $v(t) = 0$; solving this equation gives $t = 10$ seconds. Thus, the cannonball rises to $h(10) = 495$ meters. ➜ It remains airborne until $h(t) = -4.9t^2 + 98t + 5 = 0$; solving this quadratic equation gives $t \approx 20.05$ seconds for the time the cannonball lands. ■

Around the height of the tallest human-built structure.

Reading and writing DEs and IVPs

A DE is, in essence, a highly compressed statement about the *rate* at which some unknown function "grows." If $y(t)$ is *any* function of t, then the derivative function y' (or dy/dt) represents the instantaneous rate of change of y with respect to t. A solution to a DE is a function that "grows" in the way the DE stipulates. The DE $y' = y$, for instance, is a succinct way of saying this:

The quantity y grows at a rate equal to y itself.

This sort of translation is difficult for many students; the exercises include some basic reinforcement.

Translating to and from DE language Using DEs effectively requires one to "translate" back and forth between the symbolic language of DEs and ordinary English statements about changing quantities and rates of change. The following table illustrates several such translations. In each entry, y represents an unknown function of a variable t; k is a constant. If the input variable t denotes time, then $y = y(t)$ represents a quantity that varies with time; $y' = y'(t)$ tells how fast y grows at time t.

A DE chosen purely at random need not "model" any familiar real-world phenomenon. But many simple DEs—including all of those in the following table—*do* describe important real phenomena.

Translating between DEs and English		
DE	**English**	**Real phenomenon**
$y' = 0$	Growth rate of y is zero (so y is constant)	y is the position of a fixed object or value of a no-interest bank deposit
$y' = 0.06y$	Growth rate of y is proportional, with proportionality constant 0.06, to y itself	y is the value of a bank deposit at 6% interest, compounded continuously
$y' = kt$	Growth rate of y at time t is proportional to t	y is the height of a free-falling object
$y'' = k$	y has constant "acceleration"	y is the height of a free-falling object
$y' = k(y - 65)$	y increases at a rate proportional to the difference between y and 65	y is the temperature of a warm object in a 65 °F room

Here are some comments on the table:

- **Growth with interest** A DE of the form $y' = ky$ (like that in the second line of the preceding table) describes any quantity that grows "with interest." Financial interest (we'll discuss it further in the next section) is one example; population growth under certain conditions is another.

- **Related DEs** The DEs $y' = kt$ and $y'' = k$ in the third and fourth lines of the table are closely related; every solution to the first automatically satisfies the second—both DEs describe quantities y with constant acceleration.

- **How things cool** The DE $y' = k(y - 65)$ can model the physical principle known as **Newton's law of cooling**: If $y(t)$ is the temperature at time t of an object in a 65 °F room, then the object warms or cools at a rate *proportional to the difference between its current temperature and room temperature.*

Interpreting initial conditions A DE such as $y' = 0.06y$ tells how *quickly* a quantity y grows, but not how *large* y is at any specific time. An initial condition, such as $y(0) = 1$, adds a point of reference: It gives a value from which y "starts."

What an initial condition means in context depends on the real-world setting. An initial condition might specify, at some chosen time, the value of a bank deposit, the vertical position of a falling object, or the temperature of a cooling object. In particular, an "initial" condition need not refer specifically to time $t = 0$; *any* condition of the form $y(a) = b$ is called an initial condition. In modeling the growth of a bank account, for instance, the initial condition $y(2001) = 345.67$ could describe a balance of $345.67 on January 1, 2001.

BASIC EXERCISES

1. Is the function $f(x) = 3x^2 + 5x + 6$ the *unique* solution of the differential equation $f'(x) = 6x + 5$? Justify your answer.

2. How are the graphs of solutions of the DE $f'(x) = 6x + 5$ related to each other?

3. (a) Find a solution of the differential equation $y' = 3$.
   (b) How many solutions are there? How are they related to each other?

4. (a) Find a solution of the differential equation $f'(x) = 2x$.
   (b) How many solutions are there?

5. Is $g(x) = \sqrt{x + 4}$ a solution of the differential equation $y' = 1/2y$? Justify your answer by differentiation. (See Example 2.)

6. Consider the DE $y'(x) = -1/2y$.
   (a) Show that if C is a constant, $y(x) = \sqrt{C - x}$ is a solution of this DE.
   (b) Is $y(x) = -\sqrt{C - x}$ also a solution of this DE? Justify your answer.

7. (a) Give an example of a first-order DE.
   (b) Give an example of a second-order DE.

8. Find the unique solution of the IVP $f'(x) = 6x + 5$, $f(0) = -3$. (See Example 4.)

9. Find the unique solution of the IVP $y' = 6x + 5$, $y(1) = 2$.

10. (a) Solve the IVP $f'(x) = 3x$, $f(0) = 37$.
    (b) How many solutions of this IVP are there?

11. Find the unique solution of the IVP $y' = 1/2y$, $y(1) = -2$. (See Example 5.)

12. Find the unique solution of the IVP $y' = -1/2y$, $y(0) = 2$.

13. What is the physical significance of the minus sign in the DE for an object in free fall: $h'' = -9.8$?

14. Suppose that the cannonball in Example 6 had an initial velocity of only 90 meters per second. Write the second-order IVP that corresponds to this revised scenario.

15. Suppose that the cannonball in Example 6 was shot from a height of 3 meters (rather than 5 meters).
    (a) How high does the cannonball rise?
    (b) How long does the cannonball remain airborne?

16. The effects of air drag can't always be ignored. Suppose that for a particular falling object the air drag force is proportional to the square of the object's velocity.
    (a) Explain why this situation is described by the DE $v'(t) = -9.8 + kv(t)^2$, where k is a constant.
    (b) Explain why the constant of proportionality k is a positive number.

17. Show that $y = x^3$ is a solution of the DE $xy' = 3y$.

18. Show that $y = Cx^2$, where C is a constant, is a solution of the DE $xy' = 2y$.

In Exercises 19–22, decide whether the function given is a solution of the differential equation.

19. $y(t) = t^2/2$; $y' = t$

20. $y(t) = t^2/2$; $y' = y$

21. $y(t) = \dfrac{1}{2}t^4 + \dfrac{3}{2}t^2 + \dfrac{1}{4}$; $y' - \dfrac{2y}{t} = t^3$

22. $y(t) = \dfrac{1}{2}t^4 + \dfrac{3}{2}t^2$; $y' - \dfrac{2y}{t} = t^3$

23. Show that $\sqrt[3]{x + C}$, where C is a constant, is a solution of the DE $y' = 1/3y^2$.

24. Show that $y = x^2 - x^{-1}$ is a solution of the DE $y'' - 2y/x^2 = 0$.

25. Is $y = x^2$ a solution of the DE $y'' - 4xy' + 4y = 0$? Justify your answer.

26. Is $y = x + 1$ a solution of the DE $xy' + (y')^2 - y = 0$? Justify your answer.

27. Show that $y(x) = x^{-1} - 1$ is a solution of the differential equation $x^3y'' + x^2y' - xy = x$.

Let $h(t)$ represent the height, in meters above ground level, of an object at time t seconds, and let $v(t) = h'(t)$ represent the object's vertical velocity, in meters per second, at time t seconds. In Exercises 28–31, translate the DE into a statement about the physical situation.

28. $v'(2) = 1$

29. $h'(2) = -3$

30. $h''(1) = -2$

31. $v'(t) = -0.01(v(t))^2$

An object moves along an east–west axis; distance is measured in meters and time in seconds. Let $p(t)$, $v(t)$, and $a(t)$ denote, respectively, the object's position (in meters east of the starting point), eastward velocity (in meters per second), and eastward acceleration (in meters per second per second) at time t. Then $p' = v$ and $p'' = v' = a$. In Exercises 32–35, translate the statement into a first-order DE.

32. The object accelerates westward at a constant 5 meters per second per second.

33. The object travels eastward at a constant speed of 15 meters per second.

34. Because of friction, the object's eastward acceleration is proportional to its velocity. [NOTE: The proportionality constant is negative; explain why.]

35. The object's eastward velocity is proportional to the square root of the object's position.

In Exercises 36–38, let $h(t)$ represent the height, in meters above ground level, of an object at time t seconds, and let $v(t) = h'(t)$ represent the object's vertical velocity, in meters per second, at time t seconds.

36. (a) Solve the IVP $v'(t) = 1$; $v(0) = 0$.

   (b) Assuming the initial condition given in part (a), find the object's upward velocity at $t = 10$ seconds.

37. Find and interpret $h(10)$ if $h'(t) = -3$ and $h(0) = 100$.

38. (a) Verify by differentiation that for any constant C, $v(t) = 100/(t + C)$ is a solution of the DE $v' = -0.01v^2$.

   (b) Suppose that $v' = -0.01v^2$ and $v(0) = 5$. What is $v(30)$? What is $v(80)$? Interpret your answers in physical language.

39. An object moves along a straight line in such a way that it is slowing down with an acceleration of -8 meters per second per second. The object has an initial velocity of 14 meters per second. Find the distance the object travels during the first 3 seconds.

40. Suppose that the brakes are applied on a car traveling 50 mph and that this gives the car a constant negative acceleration of 20 ft/sec². How long will it take the car to come to a stop? How far will the car travel before stopping? [HINT: 1 mph $= 22/15$ ft/sec.]

41. First National Bank bank advertises 8% interest compounded continuously. Second National Bank advertises 10% interest compounded continuously but charges depositors a \$100 yearly administrative fee for the privilege of banking there. (For simplicity, assume that the \$100 fee is deducted continously over the full year.) Let $P(t)$ denote the value in dollars of a deposit after t years.

   (a) Explain why First National Bank's policy is modeled by the DE $P'(t) = 0.08P(t)$.

   (b) Explain why Second National Bank's policy is modeled by the DE $P' = 0.1P - 100$.

42. A flu epidemic spreads through a 3000-student college community at a rate proportional to the product of the number of members already infected and the number of those not yet infected. (This product measures the number of possible infectious contacts.) Let $P(t)$ represent the number of students infected after t days. Write a differential equation that relates P and P'.

43. The rate at which the temperature of an object changes is proportional to the difference between the temperature T of the object and the temperature S of the object's surroundings. Express this physical law as a differential equation.

44. Oil is being pumped continuously from a well at a rate proportional to the amount of oil left in the well. Write a differential equation satisfied by the function $O(t)$, the amount of oil in the tank at time t.

45. In learning theory, a "performance function" $P(t)$ may be used to measure someone's skill at a task (using units appropriate to the task) as a function of the training time t. The graph of a performance function is called a **learning curve**. For many tasks, performance improves quickly at first but tapers off (i.e., the rate of learning decreases) as the value of $P(t)$ approaches M, some maximal level of performance. Explain how the DE $P' = k(M - P)$, where k is a positive constant, describes this situation.

FURTHER EXERCISES

46. A car traveling at a constant speed of 80 mph along a straight highway fails to stop at a stop sign. Three seconds later, a highway patrol car starts from a point of rest at the stop sign and maintains a constant acceleration of 8 ft/sec². How long will it take the patrol car to overtake the speeding automobile? How far from the stop sign will this occur? What is the speed of the patrol car when it overtakes the automobile?

47. Suppose that a number of rabbits are introduced onto an island on which they have no natural enemies but that can support a maximum population of 1000 rabbits. Let $P(t)$ denote the number of rabbits at time t (measured in months) and suppose that P satisfies the differential equation

$$\frac{dP}{dt} = kP(1000 - P),$$

where k is a positive constant.

   (a) Suppose that 1000 rabbits are introduced onto the island at time $t = 0$. Does the model predict that the rabbit population will increase, decrease, or remain constant? Justify your answer.

   (b) Suppose that 1500 rabbits are introduced onto the island at time $t = 0$. Does the model predict that the rabbit population will increase, decrease, or remain constant? Justify your answer.

(c) Suppose that 250 rabbits are introduced onto the island at time $t = 0$. Does the model predict that the rabbit population will increase, decrease, or remain constant? Justify your answer.

(d) Find the value of P for which the rate of change of the rabbit population is maximal. [HINT: Evaluate $\dfrac{d}{dP}P'$.]

48. When the valve at the bottom of a cylindrical tank is opened, the depth of liquid in the tank drops at a rate proportional to the square root of the depth of liquid. (This fact, known as **Torricelli's law**, is named after Evangelista Torricelli [1608–1647], one of Galileo's contemporaries and briefly his secretary.) If $y(t)$ is the liquid's depth t minutes after the valve is opened, Torricelli's law can be expressed as the DE $y' = -k\sqrt{y}$, where k is some positive constant.

(a) Does the water level drop faster when a tank is full or when it is half full? Explain your answer.

(b) Verify by differentiation that, for any constants C and k, the function $y(t) = (C - kt)^2/4$ is a solution of Torricelli's DE $y' = -k\sqrt{y}$. (For physical reasons, it's OK to assume that $C - kt \geq 0$.)

(c) Suppose that for a certain tank, $y(0) = 9$ feet and $y(20) = 4$ feet. Find an equation for $y(t)$. Show that the tank takes 60 minutes to empty entirely.

(d) Plot $y(t)$ over the interval $0 \leq t \leq 60$.

(e) At what time is the water level dropping at a rate of 0.1 feet per minute?

49. A small-town charity fund drive aims to raise \$65,000; updated current totals are posted in the town square. According to Alfred E. Neuman's law of cooling of enthusiasm, the rate at which people contribute to such a drive is proportional to the difference between the current total and the announced target amount. Let $y(t)$ represent the current total, in thousands of dollars, t weeks after the start of the drive.

(a) Does Neuman's law of cooling sound reasonable? Why or why not?

(b) Express Neuman's law of cooling as a DE in the context of this small town's goal of raising \$65,000.

50. Find functions $f(x)$ and $g(x)$ so that $y = x$ and $y = x^2$ are both solutions of the differential equation $f(x)y'' + g(x)y' + y = 0$.

51. Consider the initial value problem $y' = 3y^{2/3}$, $y(0) = 0$.

(a) Show that $y = x^3$ is a solution of this IVP.

(b) Show that $f(x) = \begin{cases} (x+1)^3 & x \leq -1 \\ 0 & -1 < x < 2 \\ (x-2)^3 & x > 2 \end{cases}$

is also a solution of this IVP.

52. The **normal line** to the curve $y = f(x)$ at the point $P = (a, f(a))$ is the line through P that is perpendicular to the tangent line at P. Find an IVP for the curve through the point $(1, 1)$ that has the property that the normal line at any point (x, y) on the curve passes through the point $(2, 0)$.

53. A curve has the property that each point $P = (x, y)$ on the curve is the midpoint of a line segment RS, where R and S are on the coordinate axes, that is tangent to the curve at P.

(a) Show that the curve is a solution of the differential equation $y' = -y/x$.

(b) Show that the curve $y = 1/x$ is a solution of the DE in part (a).

54. A tank initially contains 100 gallons of water and 10 pounds of salt thoroughly mixed. Pure water is added at the rate of 5 gallons *per minute*, and the mixture is drained off at the same rate. (Assume complete and instantaneous mixing.) Explain why $S(t)$, the amount of salt in the tank at time t, is the solution of the IVP

$$S' = -\frac{5}{100}S; \quad S(0) = 10.$$

2.6 DERIVATIVES OF EXPONENTIAL AND LOGARITHMIC FUNCTIONS; MODELING GROWTH

In earlier sections we found derivative formulas for power functions, polynomials, and other functions with simple formulas. Such functions are called **algebraic**. We found these derivative formulas by calculating limits of difference quotients, using algebraic formulas for the functions in question. (See Example 1, page 91, for three typical derivations.)

We emphasize the fact that exponential functions model a natural type of growth behavior; equivalently, they satisfy the basic DE $y' = ky$.

In this and the following section, we differentiate exponential, logarithmic, and trigonometric functions. Doing so takes a little more effort because these functions *don't* have simple algebraic formulas. Compare, for instance, the functions

$$f(x) = x^2 + 3, \quad g(x) = e^x, \quad h(x) = \ln(x), \quad \text{and} \quad k(x) = \sin x.$$

Only f has a simple algebraic "recipe": h and k are described only by names, and g requires, at the least, a clear definition of the number e. (We'll give one in this section.) Functions

Transcendental functions are sometimes written without parentheses; there's no rigid rule.

Exponential, log, and trig functions are the most important transcendental functions, but not the only ones.

The difference between algebraic and non-algebraic formulas isn't clear to many students. One approach is to emphasize the fact that transcendental functions have names rather than formulas.

See Example 6, page 50.

(like g, h, and k) without simple algebraic formulas are called **transcendental**. ◄ To find the desired derivatives we'll use (usually without comment) basic precalculus properties of the exponential and logarithmic functions. Appendices E and F contain quick reviews of these subjects.

After finding derivatives (and some antiderivatives) of exponential and logarithmic functions, we start to suggest why the extra work is worth doing: these functions model phenomena of genuine interest in the real world.

Derivatives of exponential functions

Graphical evidence   In Section 1.5 we observed (but didn't prove) a striking fact: The natural exponential function $f(x) = e^x$ is *its own derivative*. ◄ Before proving this result symbolically, let's compare some exponential functions with various bases. Figure 1 shows three.

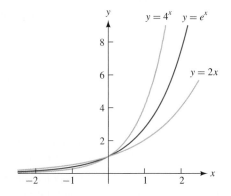

The three graphs have similar shapes, and $(0, 1)$ lies on all three.

FIGURE 1
Graphs of three exponential functions

Notice some similarities among the graphs: Each graph increases (through positive values) as we move from left to right. A similar property holds for *slopes*: On each graph, slopes increase as we move from left to right. In other ways the three graphs are different. For instance, they all pass through the common point $(0, 1)$ but with different slopes. To see more, let's zoom in on the point of interest, as in Figure 2.

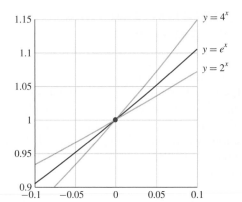

Use the grid to estimate the slopes for yourself.

FIGURE 2
Three exponential functions: a closer look

In the new window, all three "curves" look like straight lines. Here are eyeball estimates of their slopes (written as derivatives):

$$\frac{d}{dx}2^x\bigg|_{x=0} \approx 0.7; \qquad \frac{d}{dx}e^x\bigg|_{x=0} \approx 1; \qquad \frac{d}{dx}4^x\bigg|_{x=0} \approx 1.4.$$

The middle "estimate" is most important. Indeed, it's not an estimate at all—we *define* the base e so that the derivative at zero is *exactly* one:

There are other definitions for e, of course. One is the value at $t = 1$ of a solution to the IVP $y' = y$ and $y(0) = 1$.

> **DEFINITION (The number e)** The number e is the base for which the curve $y = b^x$ passes through $(0, 1)$ with slope 1. Equivalently, if $f(x) = e^x$, then $f'(0) = 1$.

Derivative formulas Exponential functions and their derivatives have much in common, as suggested by Figure 1 and our work in Section 1.5. Theorem 11 describes this relationship more precisely:

> **THEOREM 11 (Derivatives of exponential functions)**
> $$(e^x)' = e^x; \qquad (b^x)' = b^x \ln b.$$

The theorem says that the derivative of any exponential function b^x is a constant multiple of b^x; the constant is $\ln b$. If b happens to be e, then this constant is 1. In fact, the constant $\ln b$ has a nice geometric meaning for *any* value of b. Theorem 11 says that $g'(0) = g(0) \ln b = \ln b$, so the constant $\ln b$ can be seen as the slope of the curve $y = b^x$ at $x = 0$. In Figure 2 we estimated these slopes for $b = 2$, $b = e$, and $b = 4$. Note that $\ln 2 \approx 0.693$ and $\ln 4 \approx 1.386$—close to what we estimated graphically.

Proof First we prove the special case $b = e$, starting from the definition of derivative. Let $f(x) = e^x$. Then

Students should work carefully through the algebra of the limit calculation.

$$f'(x) = \lim_{h \to 0} \frac{e^{x+h} - e^x}{h} \qquad \text{(by definition of derivative)}$$

$$= \lim_{h \to 0} \frac{e^x \cdot (e^h - 1)}{h} \qquad \text{(factoring out } e^x\text{)}$$

$$= e^x \cdot \lim_{h \to 0} \frac{e^h - 1}{h} \qquad \text{(limit depends on } h\text{, so } e^x \text{ is constant)}$$

$$= e^x \cdot \lim_{h \to 0} \frac{f(h) - f(0)}{h} \qquad \text{(because } f(x) = e^x\text{)}$$

$$= e^x \cdot f'(0) \qquad \text{(by definition of } f'(0)\text{)}$$

$$= e^x \cdot 1. \qquad \text{(by definition of } e\text{)}$$

The last line above is our payoff for defining e as we did—it ensures that $f'(0) = 1$.

We've shown that $f(x) = e^x$ is its own derivative. To handle other bases b, we can rewrite $g(x) = b^x$ in terms of $f(x) = e^x$: ➡

See Appendix E for details and explanation.

$$g(x) = b^x = e^{\ln b^x} = e^{x \ln b} = f(x \ln b).$$

Thus, g is obtained from f by multiplying inputs to f by the constant $\ln b$. (In graphical terms, g is obtained from f through a horizontal compression with factor $\ln b$.) In

Section 2.2 we studied the effect on derivatives of such operations with constants. Theorem 4 (iv), page 97 implies that

$$\left(b^x\right)' = \left(f(x \ln b)\right)' = \ln b \cdot f(x \ln b) = b^x \ln b,$$

which completes the proof of Theorem 11. □

EXAMPLE 1   Find solutions of the DE $y' = y$.

Solution   The DE says that the function $y(x)$ is its own derivative. We've just shown that $y(x) = e^x$ has this property, so it is its own solution. So is *every* function of the form $y(x) = Ce^x$, where C is a constant, because (thanks to the constant multiple rule for derivatives)

$$y = Ce^x \Longrightarrow y' = Ce^x = y.$$

Figure 3 shows several of the infinitely many solution functions, each labeled with its C-value.

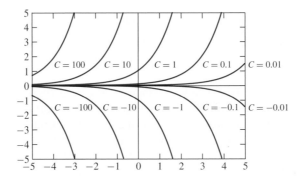

Infinitely many solutions are possible.

FIGURE 3
Solutions to $y' = y$: several curves $y = Ce^x$ ■

Derivatives of logarithmic functions

We'll revisit inverse functions more systematically in Chapter 3.

To differentiate logarithmic functions, we'll use what we've just proved about exponential functions, which are *inverses* of logarithmic functions. ← Here, in advance, are our conclusions—notice again the advantage of base e:

THEOREM 12 (Derivatives of logarithmic functions)

$$\left(\ln x\right)' = \frac{1}{x}; \quad \left(\log_b x\right)' = \frac{1}{\ln b} \cdot \frac{1}{x}.$$

"Proof" by picture   We'll explain the theorem pictorially; a more formal proof (which we omit) would amount to translating everything into symbolic form. As in the preceding proof, we start with the "natural" case, base e.

The key geometric idea is that the graphs of $y = \ln x$ and $y = e^x$ are *mirror images* of each other—each is the the reflection of the other across the line $y = x$. Figure 4 shows the situation.

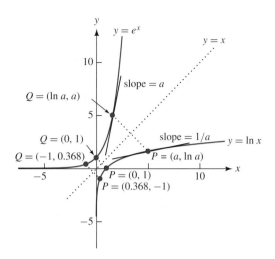

FIGURE 4
Comparing derivatives by reflection

Observe:

- **Symmetric points**   The mirror symmetry of the graphs means that a point $P = (x, y)$ lies on one graph if and only if $Q = (y, x)$ lies on the other. Several such pairs are marked with bullets.

- **Symmetric tangent lines**   Notice the two tangent segments at a pair of corresponding points P and Q. Like the graphs themselves, these two tangent segments are symmetric with respect to the line $y = x$. It follows that the tangent lines at P and Q have *reciprocal* slopes. ➤

- **Finding slopes**   The slope of the tangent line at $Q = (\ln a, a)$ is the derivative of the function $y = e^x$ evaluated at $x = \ln a$. We know that $(e^x)' = e^x$, so the tangent line at Q has slope $e^{\ln a} = a$. Hence, the tangent line at $P = (a, \ln a)$ has slope $1/a$, as the theorem asserts.

We'll use a similar picture to illustrate the derivative of any inverse function.

Convince yourself: Any two lines symmetric across $y = x$ have reciprocal slopes.

The picture and discussion show that Theorem 12 holds for the natural logarithm with base e. To see that it holds for *every* positive base b, recall that $\log_b x = \ln x / \ln b$. ➤ Applying the constant multiple rule for derivatives gives the general derivative formula:

Forgotten this fact? See Appendix F.

$$(\log_b x)' = \left(\frac{\ln x}{\ln b} \right)' = \frac{1}{\ln b} \cdot (\ln x)' = \frac{1}{x} \cdot \frac{1}{\ln b}.$$

Antiderivatives of exponential functions

The derivative rules for exponential functions are readily reversed, so the following theorem closely resembles Theorem 11.

We delay giving antiderivatives of log functions because they're not (yet) easily checked by differentiation. We fill that gap early in Chapter 3.

THEOREM 13   Let C be any constant and b any positive base.

- $e^x + C$ is an antiderivative of e^x;
- $\dfrac{b^x}{\ln b} + C$ is an antiderivative of b^x.

The theorem is easy to check by differentiation. Notice how we use the sum and constant multiple rules for the second formula:

$$\left(\frac{b^x}{\ln b} + C\right)' = \frac{1}{\ln b} \cdot (b^x)' = \frac{1}{\ln b} \cdot b^x \cdot \ln b = b^x.$$

The first formula is even easier to check (also by differentiation).

EXAMPLE 2 Solve the DE $y' = 3e^x - 3^x + 1$.

Solution The DE has the form $y' = f(x)$, so we just need an antiderivative of f. Theorem 13 gives antiderivatives of e^x and 3^x; combining them gives $3e^x - \dfrac{3^x}{\ln 3} + x$ as one possible antiderivative. (This answer is easy to check by differentiation, using the sum and constant multiple rules for derivatives.) Other antiderivatives have the form

$$3e^x - \frac{3^x}{\ln 3} + x + C,$$

where C is any constant. ∎

Modeling exponential growth

Why are exponential and logarithmic functions worth the trouble we take with them? One answer is theoretical: Because of their striking derivative properties, these functions appear everywhere in mathematics. Another answer is practical: Many important real-world quantities can be closely modeled by exponential functions. These quantities have the following key property:

*A quantity exhibits **exponential growth** if it grows at a rate proportional to its size.*

The language of DEs lets us say the same thing more precisely and succinctly:

A quantity y exhibits exponential growth if $y' = ky$, where k is a constant.

Compound-interest-bearing accounts, consumer prices, radioactively decaying masses, some biological populations—all exhibit exponential growth (at least approximately) so all can be modeled by exponential functions.

The following theorem makes the connection to exponential functions:

THEOREM 14 Let A and k be constants. Then the exponential function $y = Ae^{kt}$ solves the IVP

$$\text{(i)} \quad y' = ky; \qquad \text{(ii)} \quad y(0) = A.$$

We can prove the theorem by calculation. First, differentiating $y = Ae^{kt}$ gives

$$y'(t) = Ake^{kt} = kAe^{kt} = ky(t),$$

We found a similar derivative in Example 7, page 98.

so (i) holds as claimed. ◄ Second, $y(0) = Ae^0 = A$, so (ii) also holds, and $y = Ae^{kt}$ is indeed a solution to the given IVP. (It's also true, but harder to prove, that *every* solution has this form.)

Figures 5(a) and (b) show many functions of the form $y = Ae^{kt}$ for various values of A and k. Notice the graphs' similar shapes.

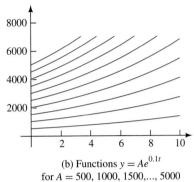

(a) Functions $y = 1000\,e^{kt}$
for $k = 0, 0.02, 0.04,..., 0.20$

(b) Functions $y = Ae^{0.1t}$
for $A = 500, 1000, 1500,..., 5000$

FIGURE 5
Two families of exponential functions

Exponential models vs. reality Theorem 14 has practical horsepower—just by choosing k and A judiciously we can model many important phenomena. On the other hand, *no* mathematical model represents real-world phenomena perfectly. One problem with exponential growth models is that many real-world quantities grow *discretely* (in small but definite jumps), while exponential functions grow *continuously*. Bank deposits, for instance, increase in steps of at least one cent, and biological populations take only integer values, while exponential functions assume fractional and irrational values. Still, exponential functions are essential and effective tools for modeling real processes. We hint at some uses of exponential models in the rest of this section; more detailed discussion appears in Chapter 4.

Interludes in Chapter 4 (when we've developed some more tools) treat growth phenomena, including exponential growth, in more detail.

EXAMPLE 3 **(Bank interest and exponential growth)** The growing balance of a savings account is modeled by the DE $y'(t) = 0.06y(t)$, with time t measured in years and the balance $y(t)$ in dollars. The account starts with $1000; what is it worth after 1 year? How long does the account take to double?

Solution We apply Theorem 14, with $k = 0.06$ and $A = 1000$, so $y(t) = 1000e^{0.06t}$. (The graph of y appears in Figure 5(a).) Hence, the value after 1 year is $y(1) = 1000e^{0.06} \approx 1061.8365$ (or $1061.84, rounded to the nearest cent). ➡ To find the doubling time we solve $y(t) = 2000$ for t:

The account grows a bit more than 6% over a year.

$$y(t) = 2000 \iff 1000e^{0.06t} = 2000 \iff e^{0.06t} = 2 \iff 0.06t = \ln 2$$

$$\iff t = \frac{\ln 2}{0.06} \approx 11.55.$$

The account doubles in about 11.55 years. ∎

EXAMPLE 4 **(Exponential population growth)** A fruit fly colony grows at the instantaneous rate of 10% per day—that is, at a rate proportional (with $k = 0.1$) to the population itself. Thus, the population $P(t)$ satisfies the IVP

$$P'(t) = 0.1P(t); \qquad P(0) = P_0,$$

where t is in days and P_0 is the population at time $t = 0$. How long does it take for the population to double? By what factor does the population increase over 10 days?

Solution Theorem 14 gives the formula: $P(t) = P_0\,e^{0.1t}$. (Graphs of $P(t)$ for various initial populations P_0 appear in Figure 5(b).) A little algebra reveals that the population doubles in just under 7 days:

$$P(t) = P_0\, e^{0.1t} = 2\, P_0 \iff 0.1t = \ln 2 \iff t \approx 6.93.$$

Over 10 days, the population is $P(10) = P_0\, e^1 \approx 2.72 P_0$—an increase by the factor e.   ∎

It can't go on forever.   Real-world biological populations can't grow exponentially forever. An initial "deposit" of 100 fruit flies, growing as just described, would number over 8 billion in a year. In a decade, the flies would outnumber earth's molecules. (That's logically—not just biologically—impossible.)

EXAMPLE 5   (Radioactive decay and carbon-14)   Three types of carbon atoms occur in the earth's atmosphere: carbon-12, carbon-13, and carbon-14. Living plants and animals contain carbon-14 in known proportions. When an organism dies, carbon-14 decays radioactively at a known rate. By measuring the proportion of carbon-14 present in a sample of organic matter (such as long-dead wood), scientists can estimate the sample's age. The method, called **carbon dating**, depends mathematically on exponential functions and their derivatives.

Suppose the carbon-14 in an organic sample weighs $W(t)$ grams at time t years and decays at a rate proportional to its weight, with $k = -0.000121$ (here k is negative because $W(t)$ decreases). If the carbon-14 weighed W_0 grams in the year 2001, how much will it weigh in 3001? What did it weigh in 1001? How long does it take the carbon-14 to lose half its weight? (This period is called the **half-life** of carbon-14.)

Solution   Let $W(t)$ represent the weight of carbon-14 t years after 2001 (so $t = 0$ corresponds to the year 2001). Then $W(t)$ satisfies the IVP

$$W'(t) = -0.000121 W(t); \qquad W(0) = W_0.$$

By Theorem 14, $W(t) = W_0 e^{-0.000121t}$ is the solution. Thus,

$$\text{weight in } 3001 = W(1000) = W_0 e^{-0.121} \approx 0.8860\, W_0\,;$$
$$\text{weight in } 1001 = W(-1000) = W_0 e^{0.121} \approx 1.1286\, W_0.$$

The carbon-14 in the sample loses about 12% of its weight over 1000 years. To find the half-life, we solve the equation $W(t) = W_0/2$ for t:

$$W_0 e^{-0.000121t} = 0.5 W_0 \iff -0.000121t = \ln(0.5) \iff t \approx 5728.$$

The half-life is about 5728 years.   ∎

BASIC EXERCISES

1. How is the number e defined?

2. Let $f(x) = 2^x$, $g(x) = e^x$, and $h(x) = 4^x$.

   (a) Use a difference quotient with increment 0.001 to estimate $f'(0)$, $g'(0)$, and $h'(0)$. (Round your answers to 3 decimal places.)

   (b) Compute $f'(0)$, $g'(0)$, and $h'(0)$ using Theorem 11.

   (c) Are the results you obtained in parts (a) and (b) consistent with each other? Justify your answer.

3. Is the function $y(t) = 2e^t$ a solution of the differential equation $y' = y$? Justify your answer.

4. Find the unique solution of the IVP $y' = y$, $y(0) = \pi$.

5. Find the unique solution of the IVP $y' = y$, $y(1) = 2e$.

6. Let $h(x) = \log_{10} x$. Use Theorem 12 to evaluate $h'(1/10)$, $h'(1)$, $h'(10)$, and $h'(100)$.

7. Let $g(x) = 3^x$ and $h(x) = \log_3 x$. If $g(a) = b$ and $g'(a) = c$, what is $h'(b)$? Justify your answer.   [HINT: $h(b) = a$.]

8. Let $g(x) = 10^x$. Use Theorem 11 to evaluate $g'(-2)$, $g'(-1)$, $g'(0)$, $g'(1)$, and $g'(2)$.

9. Use Theorem 13 to find two antiderivatives of $h(x) = 5^x$.

10. Find the solution of the IVP $y' = 3e^x - 3^x + 1$, $y(0) = 0$.

11. Find a solution of the DE $y' = 2e^x - 2^x + 2$.

12. Find the unique solution of the IVP $y' = 0.06y$, $y(0) = 100$.

13. (a) Solve the IVP $y' = 3y$, $y(0) = 37$.

(b) How many solutions are there?

14. Is $y(t) = 100 + 50e^{2t}$ a solution of the IVP $y' = 2(y - 100)$, $y(0) = 150$? Justify your answer.

In Exercises 15–20, find an expression for f'. Check your answers for reasonableness by plotting the expressions for f and f' on the same axes.

15. $f(x) = 2e^x + \pi$

16. $f(x) = e^x + x^e + e$

17. $f(x) = 2^x + x^2 + 2$

18. $f(x) = 2 \cdot 3^{x-1}$

19. $f(x) = -2 \ln x$

20. $f(x) = 3 \log_2 x$

21–26. Find the second derivative of each function in Exercises 15–20. Check your answers for reasonableness by plotting the expressions for f and f'' on the same axes.

27–30. Find an antiderivative of each function in Exercises 15–18.

31. Find an equation of the line tangent to the curve $y = e^x$ at $x = 0$.

32. Find an equation of the line tangent to the curve $y = \ln x$ at $x = 1$.

33. What is the slope of the curve $y = 3^x$ at $x = 0$?

34. What is the slope of the curve $y = \log_3 x$ at $x = 1$?

35. On January 1, 1960, the population of Boomtown was 50,000. Since then the size of the population has been accurately modeled by the function $P(t) = 50,000(0.98)^t$, where t is the number of years since January 1, 1960.

(a) What was the population of Boomtown on January 1, 2000?

(b) At what rate was the population of Boomtown changing on January 1, 2000? Was it increasing or decreasing then?

36. How long does it take for one-quarter of the carbon-14 atoms in a sample to decay?

In Exercises 37 and 38, the position of the particle on the x-axis at time $t > 0$ seconds is $x(t) = \ln t$ meters.

37. (a) Find the average velocity of the particle over the interval $1 \le t \le e$.

(b) Find the instantaneous velocity of the particle at time $t = e$.

38. Find the instantaneous acceleration of the particle at time $t = 2$.

In Exercises 39 and 40, $f(x) = \sqrt{x} - \ln x$.

39. Show that f achieves its (global) minimum value at $x = 4$.

40. Show that f has an inflection point at $x = 16$.

In Exercises 41 and 42, $f(x) = \ln x - e^{x-1}$.

41. Show that f achieves its (global) maximum value at $x = 1$. [HINT: $e^{x-1} = e^x/e$.]

42. Show that f is concave down everywhere on its domain.

In Exercises 43–46, use Theorem 14 to solve the IVP.

43. $y' = 0.1y$; $y(0) = 100$

44. $y' = -0.0001y$; $y(0) = 1$

45. $y' = (\ln 2) \cdot y$; $y(2) = 4$

46. $y' = ky$; $y(10) = 2y(0)$ [HINT: Solve for k using the initial condition.]

47. First National Bank bank advertises 8% interest, compounded continuously. Thus, if $P(t)$ denotes the value in dollars of a deposit after t years, then $P' = 0.08P$. If $2000 is deposited now in First National Bank, how much will it be worth in 10 years?

FURTHER EXERCISES

48. Let $f(x) = e^{-x} = \exp(-x)$. Use the fact that $e^{-x} = (1/e)^x$ to show that $f'(x) = -e^{-x}$.

49. Let $f(x) = e^x$.

(a) Find values of the constants a and b so that the linear function $L(x) = a + bx$ has the properties $L(0) = f(0)$ and $L'(0) = f'(0)$.

(b) Find the value of the constant c for which the quadratic function $Q(x) = L(x) + cx^2$ has the properties $Q(0) = f(0)$, $Q'(0) = f'(0)$, and $Q''(0) = f''(0)$.

(c) Find the value of the constant d for which the cubic function $C(x) = Q(x) + dx^3$ has the properties $C(0) = f(0)$, $C'(0) = f'(0)$, $C''(0) = f''(0)$, and $C'''(0) = f'''(0)$.

(d) Plot f, L, Q, and C on the same axes over the interval $[-3, 3]$.

(e) Find an interval over which $|f(x) - L(x)| < 0.1$.

(f) Find an interval over which $|f(x) - Q(x)| < 0.1$.

(g) Find an interval over which $|f(x) - C(x)| < 0.1$.

50. Let $f(x) = \ln x$.

(a) Find values of the constants a and b so that the linear function $L(x) = a + b(x - 1)$ has the properties $L(1) = f(1)$ and $L'(1) = f'(1)$.

(b) Find the value of the constant c for which the quadratic function $Q(x) = L(x) + c(x - 1)^2$ has the properties $Q(1) = f(1)$, $Q'(1) = f'(1)$, and $Q''(1) = f''(1)$.

(c) Find the value of the constant d for which the cubic function $C(x) = Q(x) + d(x-1)^3$ has the properties $C(1) = f(1)$, $C'(1) = f'(1)$, $C''(1) = f''(1)$, and $C'''(1) = f'''(1)$.

(d) Graph f, L, Q, and C on the same axes over the interval $[0.1, 3]$.

(e) Find an interval over which $|f(x) - L(x)| < 0.1$.

(f) Find an interval over which $|f(x) - Q(x)| < 0.1$.

(g) Find an interval over which $|f(x) - C(x)| < 0.1$.

51. Find the x-intercept of the line tangent to the curve $y = 2^x$ at $x = 0$. [HINT: Draw a picture.]

52. Does a real number a exist such that the line tangent to the curve $y = e^x$ at $x = a$ passes through the origin? If so, find it. If not, explain why there is no number with this property.

53. Does a real number a exist such that the line tangent to the curve $y = x - \ln x$ at $x = a$ passes through the origin? If so, find it. If not, explain why there is no number with this property.

54. Let $f(x) = \ln|x|$, $g(x) = x^{-1}$, and
$$h(x) = \begin{cases} -2 + \ln x & \text{if } x > 0 \\ 3 + \ln(-x) & \text{if } x < 0. \end{cases}$$

(a) What is the domain of f? Of g?

(b) Plot graphs of f, g, and h on the same set of axes.

(c) Show that f is an antiderivative of g.

(d) Show that h is an antiderivative of g (i.e., show that $h'(x) = g(x)$ for all $x \neq 0$).

55. Second National Bank advertises 10% interest compounded continuously, but charges depositors a $100 yearly administrative fee for the privilege of banking there. (For simplicity, assume that the $100 fee is deducted continously over the full year.) Thus, if $P(t)$ denotes the value in dollars of a deposit after t years, then $P' = 0.1P - 100$.

(a) Show that $P(t) = 1000 + Ce^{0.1t}$ is a solution of the DE $P' = 0.1P - 100$.

(b) If $2000 is deposited now in Second National Bank, how much will it be worth 10 years?

56. Suppose that A is a constant. Verify that $x(t) = 1 + t + Ae^t$ is a solution of the differential equation $x' = x - t$.

57. Suppose that A is a constant. Verify that $y(x) = Ae^x - x - 1$ is a solution of the differential equation $yy' = y^2 + xy$.

58. Suppose that A and B are constants. Verify that $y(x) = A \ln x + B + x$ is a solution of the differential equation $xy'' + y' = 1$.

59. Suppose that A and B are constants. Verify that $y(x) = Ax^{-1} + B + \ln x$ is a solution of the differential equation $x^2 y'' + 2xy' = 1$.

60. Let $f(x) = x - e \ln x$.

(a) Prove that $f(\pi) > 0$. [HINT: Show that the minimum value of f occurs at $x = e$.]

(b) Use part (a) to show that $e^\pi > \pi^e$.

61. **(a)** Show that the distance between the point $(0, 0)$ and a point (a, b) on the curve $y = e^{x/2}$ is least if a is the solution of the equation $2a + e^a = 0$.
[HINT: Minimize the square of the distance.]

(b) Estimate the distance in part (a).

62. Let $f(x) = 2^x$ and $g(x) = 7x/3 + 1$.

(a) What is the slope of the line tangent to the curve $y = f(x)$ at the point in $[0, 3]$ where the vertical distance between f and g is the greatest?

(b) What is the slope of g at the point in part (a)?

63. A certain menacing biological culture (aka The Blob) grows at a rate proportional to its size. When it arrived unnoticed one Wednesday noon in Chicago's Loop, it weighed just 1 g. By the 4:00 p.m. rush hour it weighed 4 g.

The Blob has its "eye" on the Sears Tower, a tasty morsel weighing around 3,000,000,000,000 g (i.e., 3×10^{12} g). As soon as it weighs 1000 times as much (i.e., 3×10^{15} g), The Blob intends to *eat* the Sears Tower. By what time must The Blob be stopped? Will Friday's rush-hour commuters be delayed?

64. A mold grows at a rate proportional to the amount present. Initially, its weight is 2 g; after 2 days, it weighs 5 g. How much does it weigh after 8 days?

65. A bacterial culture is placed in a large glass bottle. Suppose that the volume of the culture doubles every hour and the bottle is full after 1 day.

(a) If the culture was placed in the bottle at time $t = 0$ hours, when was the bottle half full?

(b) Assume that the bottle is "almost empty" if the culture occupies less than 1% of its volume. How long is the bottle "almost empty"?

66. A tank initially contains 100 gallons of water and 10 pounds of salt, thoroughly mixed. Pure water is added at the rate of 5 gallons per minute and the mixture is drained off at the same rate. (Assume complete and instantaneous mixing.) Thus, $S(t)$, the amount of salt in the tank at time t, is the solution of the IVP $S' = -0.05S$, $S(0) = 10$.

(a) Show that $S(t) = 10e^{-0.05t}$ is the solution of this IVP.

(b) How much salt is left in the tank after 1 hour?

67. Human skeletal fragments were brought to a laboratory for carbon dating. Analysis showed that the proportion of ^{14}C to ^{12}C was only 6.25% of the value in living tissue. How long ago did this person die?

68. **(a)** Find the minimum value of $f(x) = e^x - 1 - x$.

(b) Explain why part (a) shows that $e^x \geq 1 + x$ for all x.

Evaluate the limits in Exercises 69 and 70 by recognizing each as the definition of a derivative.

69. $\displaystyle \lim_{t \to 0} \frac{e^t - 1}{t}$

70. $\displaystyle \lim_{z \to e} \frac{\ln z - 1}{z - e}$

2.7 DERIVATIVES OF TRIGONOMETRIC FUNCTIONS: MODELING OSCILLATION

We've already guessed the sine and cosine derivatives. Here we verify those guesses symbolically and use the results to model oscillatory motion.

In Sections 1.3 and 1.5 we studied trigonometric functions and some of their derivatives graphically. In this section we take the symbolic view, finding *formulas* for derivatives and antiderivatives. Finding these formulas is a little harder (as it was for exponential and logarithmic functions) because trigonometric functions are *transcendental*, not *algebraic*—they are not defined by algebraic operations. ➡ We'll need to use some basic precalculus properties of the trigonometric functions; Appendix G offers quick reviews.

See the beginning of Section 2.6 for more on transcendental vs. algebraic functions.

Any extra trouble trigonometric functions cause is well worth taking. Like exponential and logarithmic functions, trigonometric functions have important mathematical and practical uses. The *periodic* property of trigonometric functions is their most important feature. Because of it, trigonometric functions model phenomena that exhibit repetitive or cyclical behavior—from rolling waves to bouncing springs to stock prices.

By comparison, polynomial functions model Newtonian motion and exponential functions model growth.

Derivatives of sines and cosines

Graphical and numerical evidence   Graphs tempt us to guess that $(\sin x)' = \cos x$ and that $(\cos x)' = -\sin x$ (see Figures 1(a) and 1(b)). ➡

Where f is increasing, f' is positive; where f is flat, f' is zero . . . the graphical evidence is strong.

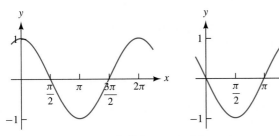

(a) $f(x) = \sin x$, $g(x) = \cos x$

(b) $f'(x) = \cos x$, $g'(x) = -\sin x$

FIGURE 1

Indeed, we've already succumbed to these temptations: We guessed these formulas in Example 4, page 60, and Example 1, page 64.

Numerical evidence for the claim that $(\sin x)' = \cos x$ is also available. The definition of the derivative as a limit suggests that, for a given input x,

$$(\sin x)' = \lim_{h \to 0} \frac{\sin(x+h) - \sin(x)}{h} \approx \frac{\sin(x+0.01) - \sin(x)}{0.01}.$$

The following table compares the last expression to $\cos x$ for several inputs x:

Numerical evidence that $(\sin x)' = \cos x$								
x	0.0	0.2	0.4	0.6	0.8	1.0	1.2	1.4
$\dfrac{\sin(x+0.01)-\sin(x)}{0.01}$	1.0000	0.9791	0.9191	0.8225	0.6931	0.5361	0.3577	0.1650
$\cos(x)$	1.0000	0.9801	0.9211	0.8253	0.6967	0.5403	0.3624	0.1700

That the last two rows are almost identical suggests we're on the right track.

Our proof uses the addition formula for sines.

Differentiating the sine: an analytic proof Graphs and tables are suggestive, but to *prove* that $(\sin x)' = \cos x$, we need to work directly with the limit that defines the derivative:

$$(\sin x)' = \lim_{h \to 0} \frac{\sin(x+h) - \sin(x)}{h}.$$

Appendix G explains this and other trigonometric identities.

To simplify the numerator we need the *addition formula for sines*: ◄

$$\sin(x+h) = \sin(x)\cos(h) + \cos(x)\sin(h).$$

In what follows we often use parentheses, as in sin(x), for added clarity.

Now we do some algebra: ◄

$$\lim_{h \to 0} \frac{\sin(x+h) - \sin(x)}{h} = \lim_{h \to 0} \frac{(\sin(x)\cos(h) + \cos(x)\sin(h)) - \sin(x)}{h}$$

$$= \lim_{h \to 0} \left(\sin(x) \cdot \frac{\cos(h) - 1}{h} + \cos(x) \cdot \frac{\sin(h)}{h} \right)$$

$$= \lim_{h \to 0} \left(\sin(x) \cdot \frac{\cos(h) - 1}{h} \right) + \lim_{h \to 0} \left(\cos(x) \cdot \frac{\sin(h)}{h} \right) \qquad \text{(sum rule for limits)}$$

$$= \sin(x) \cdot \lim_{h \to 0} \frac{\cos(h) - 1}{h} + \cos(x) \cdot \lim_{h \to 0} \frac{\sin(h)}{h}. \quad \text{(}\sin(x) \text{ and } \cos(x) \text{ are independent of } h\text{)}$$

To finish the computation we need to evaluate the two limits in the preceding line. It turns out (we'll see why in a moment) that

$$\lim_{h \to 0} \frac{\cos(h) - 1}{h} = 0 \qquad \text{and} \qquad \lim_{h \to 0} \frac{\sin(h)}{h} = 1.$$

If we assume these facts for the moment, the desired conclusion follows easily:

$$\big(\sin(x)\big)' = \sin(x) \cdot \lim_{h \to 0} \frac{\cos(h) - 1}{h} + \cos(x) \cdot \lim_{h \to 0} \frac{\sin(h)}{h}$$

$$= \sin(x) \cdot 0 + \cos(x) \cdot 1 = \cos(x).$$

We give reasonably rigorous proofs of these limits in an appendix.

Two challenging limits Both of the limits we assumed above are "nontrivial" (math-speak for "hard") mainly because we have no algebraic formulas to work with. However, each of these limits can be interpreted as the derivative of a specific function at a specific point:

- The limit

$$\lim_{h \to 0} \frac{\cos(h) - 1}{h} = \lim_{h \to 0} \frac{\cos(h) - \cos(0)}{h - 0}$$

defines the derivative of the cosine function at $x = 0$. The cosine graph is horizontal there, so the limit is zero.

- The limit

$$\lim_{h \to 0} \frac{\sin(h)}{h} = \lim_{h \to 0} \frac{\sin(h) - \sin(0)}{h - 0}.$$

defines the derivative of the sine function at $x = 0$. A close look at the curve $y = \sin x$ near $x = 0$ gives convincing graphical evidence that this derivative is indeed 1. (Appendix H presents a more rigorous symbolic proof of the same limit.)

Differentiating the cosine To show that $(\cos x)' = -\sin x$, we *could* mimic the argument just given for the sine function. Instead, we'll use what we've just proved about the sine function. Notice first that Figures 1(a) and (b) illustrate some simple relations between sines and cosines:

Since the cosine is just a translate of the sine, the respective derivatives are also translates.

$$\cos(x) = \sin(x + \pi/2) \qquad \text{and} \qquad \cos(x + \pi/2) = -\sin(x).$$

Combining these facts with Theorem 4, page 97, gives us the derivative we want:

$$\left(\cos x\right)' = \left(\sin(x + \pi/2)\right)' = \cos(x + \pi/2) = -\sin x.$$

These important results deserve an official pronouncement:

THEOREM 15 (Derivatives of sines and cosines)

$$\left(\sin x\right)' = \cos x; \qquad \left(\cos x\right)' = -\sin x.$$

Other trigonometric functions Each of the remaining trigonometric functions (tangent, secant, cotangent, and cosecant) is an algebraic combination of the sine and cosine functions. Not surprisingly, so is each derivative. With ingenious algebra we could calculate, from scratch, the derivative of each of these functions. But it's more efficient to wait until Section 3.1, where we develop explicit rules for derivatives of products and quotients.

We'll find other trigonometric derivatives later, using the quotient rule.

Antiderivatives of sines and cosines

With just a little care for signs (not *sines*), the derivative formulas of Theorem 15 can be reversed to give *antiderivative* formulas—both are easily checked by differentiation:

THEOREM 16 Let C be any constant.

If $f(x) = \sin x$, then $F(x) = -\cos x + C$ is an antiderivative of f.

If $g(x) = \cos x$, then $G(x) = \sin x + C$ is an antiderivative of g.

EXAMPLE 1 Find an antiderivative of $f(x) = 3\sin x - 4\cos x$. Is there more than one answer?

Solution Theorem 16 gives antiderivatives of $\sin x$ and $\cos x$. Combining them and using the sum and constant multiple rules tells us that $-3\cos x - 4\sin x$ is one suitable antiderivative. So, therefore, is *any* function of the form

$$F(x) = -3\cos x - 4\sin x + C,$$

where C is a constant.   ■

EXAMPLE 2   Figure 2 shows $f(x) = x + \cos x$; two points of interest are marked with bullets.

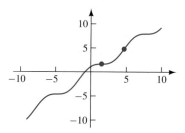

FIGURE 2

$y = x + \cos x$

Does f have any local maxima or minima? Any inflection points?

Solution   The graph appears to have flat spots (one is at the left bullet), but are they local maxima, local minima, or just flat spots? The picture alone doesn't say for sure, but derivatives settle the question easily. Because $f(x) = x + \cos x$, $f'(x) = 1 - \sin x$ and $f''(x) = -\cos x$. Therefore,

$$f'(x) = 0 \iff \sin x = 1 \iff x = \frac{\pi}{2} + 2k\pi;$$
$$f''(x) = 0 \iff \cos x = 0 \iff x = \frac{\pi}{2} + k\pi,$$

where k is any integer. In particular, the left bullet (at $x = \pi/2$) marks *both* a stationary point *and* an inflection point. Other stationary points occur at intervals of 2π, and inflection points at intervals of π. (The right bullet marks the inflection point at $x = 3\pi/2$.)

Notice also that $f'(x) = 1 - \sin x \geq 0$ for all x. Thus, the first derivative never changes sign; therefore, all the stationary points are "terrace points"—flat spots that are neither local maxima nor local minima.   ■

Modeling oscillation

Trigonometric functions model oscillation because they satisfy the simple harmonic DE $y'' = -ky$, which has a simple physical meaning.

Trigonometric functions and DEs   We saw in Section 2.6 that the exponential function $f(x) = e^x$ is its own derivative, so it satisfies the important DE $y' = y$. The sine and cosine functions behave somewhat similarly: Differentiating either of them *twice* produces the *negative* of the original function. In DE language, the sine and cosine functions satisfy the second-order DE $y'' = -y$. More generally, every function of the form $y = a \sin x + b \cos x$, where a and b are constants, is a solution of the same DE.

EXAMPLE 3   Show that $y = 2 \sin x - 3 \cos x$ satisfies the DE $y'' = -y$.

Solution   Differentiating twice shows that y is indeed a solution:

$$y = 2 \sin x - 3 \cos x \implies y' = 2 \cos x + 3 \sin x$$
$$\implies y'' = -2 \sin x + 3 \cos x = -y.$$

A similar calculation shows that $y = a \sin x + b \cos x$ solves the DE for *any* constants a and b.   ■

EXAMPLE 4   Here is an answer in search of a question: Let c be any real constant. What second-order DE does $y = \sin(cx)$ solve? Does $y = \cos(cx)$ solve the same DE?

Solution We'll differentiate twice to find out. Recall first (see Theorem 4 (iv), page 97) how multiplying the input x by a constant c affects *any* derivative:

Let f be a differentiable function. Then $\left(f(cx) \right)' = c\, f'(cx)$.

This is the "constant multiple version" of the chain rule; students may need to be reminded, and some will find the c x in the argument puzzling.

This means for the sine and cosine functions that

$$\left(\sin(cx) \right)' = c\, \cos(cx) \quad \text{and} \quad \left(\cos(cx) \right)' = -c\, \sin(cx).$$

Differentiating again gives

$$\left(\sin(cx) \right)'' = \left(c\, \cos(cx) \right)' = -c^2 \sin(cx);$$
$$\left(\cos(cx) \right)'' = \left(-c\, \sin(cx) \right)' = -c^2 \cos(cx).$$

These results show that both $y = \sin(cx)$ and $y = \cos(cx)$ satisfy the DE $y'' = -c^2 y$. ∎

EXAMPLE 5 Let $k > 0$ be a positive constant. Find solution functions for the second-order DE $y'' = -ky$.

Solution Because k is positive, $\sqrt{k}$ makes sense. By Example 4, both $y = \sin(\sqrt{k}x)$ and $y = \cos(\sqrt{k}x)$ are solutions of the DE $y'' = -kx$. ∎

The following fact—easily checked by differentiation—summarizes our results:

FACT Consider the DE $y'' = -ky$ for a positive constant k. For any constants a and b,

$$y = a \sin(\sqrt{k}x) + b \cos(\sqrt{k}x)$$

is a solution.

Why this DE matters: oscillation Why is the particular second-order DE $y'' = -ky$ worth our trouble? This DE is important because it has physical interpretations in terms of oscillation. Understanding just a little of the physics involved can help explain the mathematical behavior of the DE's solutions.

The following explanation requires a little—but just a little—physical thinking.

According to **Newton's second law of motion**, the acceleration of such an object moving along a line is proportional to the net force exerted on the object. ➜ Let's imagine $y(t)$ as the position of an object at time t; then $y''(t)$ is the object's acceleration at time t. The DE $y'' = -ky$ says that the object's acceleration at any time is *negatively* proportional to the object's position. In particular, when $y = 0$ the object has zero acceleration (and hence experiences zero force). As the magnitude $|y|$ increases, so does the force (and hence the acceleration), but in the opposite direction. In physical language, the object is said to undergo a **restoring force** (a force that tends to return the object to its rest position) that is proportional to the object's displacement from its rest position (see Figure 3):

We discussed Newton's law in the context of free -fall in Section 2.5.

The spring's restoring force is proportional to its displacement from rest.

FIGURE 3
Simple harmonic motion

This situation occurs in various real-world physical situations. A point on a plucked guitar string, for instance, is pulled back toward its "rest" position—the greater the displacement, the greater the restoring force. A weight bouncing slowly up and down on a spring is another instance of the same phenomenon. The resulting behavior in both cases is called **simple harmonic motion**: The object moves repeatedly back and forth across its rest position, continuing forever unless some other force (gravity or friction, say) intervenes.

The sine and cosine functions model simple harmonic motion; they do so because these functions satisfy the DE $y'' = -ky$. This is one (or even *the*) main reason why trigonometric functions have been studied so intensively and for so long—and remain so important.

We don't assert that the stock market really obeys physical laws. We just explore what would follow from such an assumption.

EXAMPLE 6   Some investors believe that stock price indexes (such as the Dow Jones) undergo simple harmonic motion: high prices generate an incentive to sell, thus eventually lowering prices, and vice versa. *Very* high prices generate *strong* pressure to sell, and so (the theory says) the market's "restoring force" is proportional to price.

   Not all economists buy this theory—but we can still work out its consequences. Assuming the theory, let $y(t)$ be a certain price index on day t, and suppose that historical data suggest that $y'' = -1$ when $y = 100$. On day 0, the price index is at 100 and dropping at the rate of 5 index units per day. What will the price index be 10 days later? How long is the "stock price cycle"?

Solution   The preceding examples suggest what to do. Because $y'' = -1$ when $y = 100$, the DE $y'' = -ky$ implies that $k = 0.01$. Thus, $\sqrt{k} = 0.1$, and the preceding Fact says that every function of the form $y(t) = a \sin(0.1t) + b \cos(0.1t)$ satisfies the DE. We'll use the remaining information in the problem to find numerical values for a and b. First,

$$y(0) = a \sin(0) + b \cos(0) = b = 100 \quad \Longrightarrow \quad b = 100.$$

Second,

$$y'(0) = 0.1a \sin(0) + 0.1b \cos(0) = 0.1a = -5 \quad \Longrightarrow \quad a = -50.$$

Now we have a specific formula for y:

$$y(t) = a \sin(0.1t) + b \cos(0.1t) = -50 \sin(0.1t) + 100 \cos(0.1t).$$

Figure 4 shows the graph:

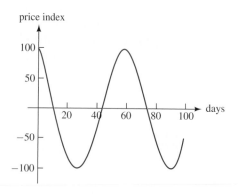

FIGURE 4
Simple harmonic stock prices

The model predicts that, on day 10, the price index is $y(10) = -50\sin(1) + 100\cos(1) \approx$ 11.96. Figure 4 shows, moreover, that price "cycles" last for about 60 days. ∎

BASIC EXERCISES

1. Let $f(x) = \sin x$. Explain why $\lim\limits_{h \to 0} \dfrac{\sin h}{h} = f'(0)$.

2. Let $g(x) = \cos x$. Explain why $\lim\limits_{h \to 0} \dfrac{\cos h - 1}{h} = g'(0)$.

3. Evaluate $\lim\limits_{x \to 0} \dfrac{\sin x}{x}$.

4. Evaluate $\lim\limits_{x \to 0} \dfrac{\cos x - 1}{x}$.

5. Let $f(x) = \sin x$, $g(x) = \sin(x + \pi/2)$, and $h(x) = \cos x$.
  (a) Explain why $f'(x) = \cos x$ implies that $g'(x) = \cos(x + \pi/2)$.
  (b) Explain why part (a) implies that $g'(x) = -\sin x$.
  (c) Explain why parts (a) and (b) imply that $h'(x) = -\sin x$.

6. Find the solution of the IVP $y'(x) = 3\sin x - 4\cos x$, $y(0) = 2$.

7. Find an antiderivative of $g(x) = 4\sin x + 3\cos x$.

8. Find a function F such that $F' = x + \cos x$ and $F(0) = 0$.

9. Find a function F such that $F' = x^2 - \sin x$ and $F(0) = 1$.

In Exercises 10–13, $g(x) = x + \sin x$ and I is the interval $[-5, 5]$.

10. Does g have any stationary points in I? If so, where?

11. Does g have any inflection points in I? If so, where?

12. Does g have any local maxima in I? If so, where?

13. Does g have any local minima in I? If so, where?

14. Let A and B be any constants. Show that $y = A\sin x + B\cos x$ is a solution of the second-order DE $y'' = -y$.

15. Let A and B be any constants, and let k be a positive constant. Show that $y = A\sin(\sqrt{k}x) + B\cos(\sqrt{k}x)$ is a solution of the second-order DE $y'' = -ky$.

16. Find the solution of the second-order IVP $y'' = -4y$, $y'(0) = 2$, $y(0) = 6$.

In Exercises 17–22, find an expression for f'. Check your answers for reasonableness by plotting graphs of the expressions for f and f' on the same axes.

17. $f(x) = 2\sin x$

18. $f(x) = 3\cos x$

19. $f(x) = \sin(3x)$

20. $f(x) = \cos(2x)$

21. $f(x) = 3\sin x - 2\cos x$

22. $f(x) = 2\cos x - 3\sin x$

23–28. Find the second derivative of each function in Exercises 17–22. Check your answers for reasonableness by plotting graphs of the expressions for f and f'' on the same axes.

29–34. Find an antiderivative of each function in Exercises 17–22.

35. Let $f(x) = x - \cos x$.
  (a) Does f have any stationary points in the interval $[0, 2\pi]$? If so, where?
  (b) Where in the interval $[0, 2\pi]$ is f increasing?
  (c) Find the maximum and minimum values of f over the interval $[0, \pi]$.
  (d) Where is f concave down?
  (e) Where is f increasing most rapidly? Evaluate f' there.

36. Repeat Exercise 35 with $f(x) = x + \cos x$.

In Exercises 37–42, draw a graph of the function over the interval $[0, 2\pi]$. Label local extrema, global extrema, and points of inflection with both coordinates. (Use exact values rather than decimal approximations for the coordinates.)

37. $f(x) = \frac{1}{2}x + \sin x$

38. $g(x) = x + \sin x$

39. $h(x) = \frac{3}{2}x + \sin x$

40. $f(x) = \sin x + \cos x$

41. $g(x) = 2\sin x - \sqrt{3}x$

42. $h(x) = \sqrt{3}\sin x + 3\cos x$

43. Let $f(x) = \sin x + \frac{1}{3}\sin(3x)$.
  (a) Does f have any stationary points in the interval $[0, \pi]$? If so, where?
  (b) Where in the interval $[0, \pi]$ is f decreasing?
  (c) Find the maximum and minimum values of f over the interval $[0, \pi]$.

44. Let $f(x) = 2\cos x + \sin(2x)$.
  (a) Does f have any stationary points in the interval $[0, \pi]$? If so, where?
  (b) Where in the interval $[0, \pi]$ is f decreasing?
  (c) Find the maximum and minimum values of f over the interval $[0, \pi]$.
  (d) Where in the interval $[0, \pi]$ is f concave up?

45. Let $f(x) = \cos x + \frac{1}{2}\cos(2x)$.

   (a) Determine where f has local maxima and minima over the interval $[0, 5]$.

   (b) Estimate where f has inflection points in the interval $[0, 5]$.

46. Repeat Exercise 45 using the function $f(x) = \sin x - \frac{1}{2}\cos(2x)$.

47. Let $f(x) = \sin(x^2)$. Use graphs of $\sin(x^2)$ and $\cos(x^2)$ to show that $f'(x) \neq \cos(x^2)$.

FURTHER EXERCISES

48. The range R of a projectile whose speed is v meters per second and whose angle of elevation is x radians is given by $R = (v^2/g)\sin(2x)$, where $g \approx 9.8$ meters per second per second is the acceleration due to gravity.

   (a) What angle of elevation gives the projectile maximum range? Justify your answer.

   (b) What is the maximum range of the projectile?

49. Let $f(x) = \sin x$.

   (a) Find values of the constants a and b so that the linear function $L(x) = a + bx$ has the properties $L(0) = f(0)$ and $L'(0) = f'(0)$.

   (b) Find the value of the constant c for which the quadratic function $Q(x) = L(x) + cx^2$ has the properties $Q(0) = f(0)$, $Q'(0) = f'(0)$, and $Q''(0) = f''(0)$.

   (c) Find the value of the constant d for which the cubic function $C(x) = Q(x) + dx^3$ has the properties $C(0) = f(0)$, $C'(0) = f'(0)$, $C''(0) = f''(0)$, and $C'''(0) = f'''(0)$.

   (d) Plot f, L, Q, and C on the same axes over the interval $[-4, 4]$.

   (e) Find an interval over which $|f(x) - L(x)| < 0.1$.

   (f) Find an interval over which $|f(x) - Q(x)| < 0.1$.

   (g) Find an interval over which $|f(x) - C(x)| < 0.1$.

50. Repeat Exercise 49 with $f(x) = \cos x$.

51. Let k be a real number. Find a trigonometric identity for $\cos(x + k)$ by differentiating both sides of the identity $\sin(x + k) = \sin x \cos k + \cos x \sin k$.

In Exercises 52–54, find the solution of the IVP.

52. $f'(z) = \cos(2z)$, $f(\pi/2) = 1$

53. $f'(x) = 2x^3 + \sin(4x)$, $f(0) = 1$

54. $g'(w) = \sin(w + 2)$, $g(0) = 3$

55. Let $h(x) = A\cos(\sqrt{k}x) + B\sin(\sqrt{k}x)$, where A, B, and $k > 0$ are constants. Choose values of A, B, and k so that $h''(x) = -4h(x)$, $h(0) = 2$, and $h'(0) = 8$.

56. Let $f(x) = A\cos x + B\sin x$, where A and B are constants. Choose values of A and B so that f is a solution of the IVP $f'' = -f$, $f'(\pi/3) = -1$, and $f(\pi/3) = \sqrt{3}$.

57. Let $f(x) = A\cos x + B\sin x$, where A and B are constants. Show that $f^{(4)}(x) = f(x)$.

58. Let $f(x) = 2 - \sin x$ and $g(x) = 1 + \cos x$.

   (a) Find the maximum vertical distance between the curves $y = f(x)$ and $y = g(x)$ over the interval $[0, 2\pi]$.

   (b) Find the slopes of the lines tangent to f and g at the point in the interval $[0, 2\pi]$ where the vertical distance between f and g is greatest.

59. Let $f(x) = \cos x$ and $g(x) = \sqrt{3}\sin x$.

   (a) Find the maximum vertical distance between the curves $y = f(x)$ and $y = g(x)$ over the interval $[0, \pi]$.

   (b) Find the slopes of the lines tangent to f and g at the point in the interval $[0, \pi]$ where the vertical distance between f and g is greatest.

60. Suppose that two sides of a rectangle are on the coordinate axes and that a corner of the rectangle lies on the curve $y = 2\cos x$, $0 \leq x \leq \pi/2$. Is it possible that the perimeter of the rectangle is $3\pi/2$? If so, find the coordinates of the corners of a rectangle with these properties. If not, find the coordinates of the corners of the rectangle with the greatest possible perimeter.

61. Suppose that one side of a rectangle is on the x-axis and that the two uppermost corners of the rectangle lie on the curve $y = 2\sqrt{2}\sin x$, $0 \leq x \leq \pi$. Among all such rectangles, find the perimeter of the one with maximum perimeter.

62. **(a)** What is the 50th derivative of $f(x) = \cos x$?

   (b) What is the 51st derivative of $g(x) = \sin x$?

   (c) What is the 52nd derivative of $g(x) = \sin x$?

63. Let $f(x) = \sin x$.

   (a) Find an equation of the line tangent to f at $x = 0$.

   (b) Find an equation of the line tangent to f at $x = \pi/3$.

   (c) Which of the tangent lines in parts (a) and (b) yields a better approximation of $\sin(\pi/6)$?

   (d) How could you have used f'' to predict which tangent line would yield the better approximation in part (c)?

Evaluate the limits in Exercises 64–67 by recognizing each as the definition of a derivative.

64. $\displaystyle\lim_{x \to \pi/2} \frac{\cos x}{x - \pi/2}$

65. $\displaystyle\lim_{x \to \pi} \frac{\sin x}{x - \pi}$

66. $\displaystyle\lim_{h \to 0} \frac{\sin(3\pi/2 + h) + 1}{h}$

67. $\displaystyle\lim_{h \to 0} \frac{2\cos(5\pi/4 + h) + \sqrt{2}}{h}$

68. Evaluate $\displaystyle\lim_{h \to 0} \frac{\cos(x - h) - \cos(x + h)}{h}$.

Chapter 2, like Chapter 1, is about derivatives. Here, however, we took the symbolic point of view, looking for derivative *formulas*. We found such formulas for several important types of functions and suggested some of their uses. We also reversed the derivative problem, finding **antiderivatives** of various functions and indicating some of their uses. We also introduced the idea of a differential equation and its solutions, suggesting how some important DEs arise in modeling motion, growth, and oscillation.

Defining the derivative   In Section 2.1 we defined the derivative formally, as a **limit**: If f is a function and $x = a$ a point of its domain, then

$$f'(a) = \lim_{h \to 0} \frac{f(a+h) - f(a)}{h},$$

if the limit exists. The expression inside the limit is called a **difference quotient**: As a quotient of differences, it measures the rate of change of $f(x)$ with respect to x over an interval of length h. As h tends to zero, the difference quotient approaches the instantaneous rate of change of f at $x = a$, that is, the derivative. In geometric terms, the difference quotient is the slope of the **secant** line to the f-graph from $x = a$ to $x = a + h$; the limit as $h \to 0$ is the slope of the **tangent** line at $x = a$.

Derivatives of power functions and polynomials   We began Section 2.2 by using the definition to find derivative formulas for power functions. Combining these results using the **sum rule** and the **constant multiple rule** for derivatives let us differentiate polynomials and other combinations of powers of x. We also studied the effects on functions and derivatives that arise from attaching constant parameters. Finally, we reviewed the binomial theorem and its use in proving a general formula for derivatives of power functions.

Limits and continuity   Having used limits informally in Section 2.2, we studied them in their own right in Section 2.3, with definitions, basic properties, standard examples, and rules for calculation. Limits are key to defining and understanding the derivative, and they'll arise again later when we define the integral—the other main concept of calculus. Limits make precise the general idea of one quantity "tending to" another, and they help us avoid such vague and imprecise terms as "infinitely small" and "infinitely close."

We used limits to define **continuity** more precisely than graphical language alone permits. Continuous functions are common in calculus, we observed. The standard elementary functions are all continuous where they're defined, and combining continuous functions algebraically or by composition produces new continuous functions.

Using the formulas   Section 2.4 introduced some important uses of the symbolic derivative formulas we've worked hard to define and calculate. Derivative formulas are essential, for example, in solving **maximum–minimum problems** symbolically and in finding *exact* solutions. The main idea—that $f'(a) = 0$ if f attains a maximum or a minimum value at $x = a$—is familiar from earlier graphical work, but symbolic formulas can both simplify calculations and make them precise.

We also considered the "inverse" problem of finding symbolic **antiderivatives**. They turn out to come in families: If $F(x)$ is any *particular* antiderivative for $f(x)$, then $F(x) + C$ is also an antiderivative, for any constant C. For the simplest functions, such as polynomials, antiderivatives are easy to find—in essence, we run the derivative rules backward. For more complicated functions the antiderivative problem is a lot harder; we'll return to it in later chapters.

Finally, we used derivative and antiderivatives to build curves "to order" with prescribed geometric properties.

Differential equations; modeling motion

Section 2.5 introduced the important idea of a **differential equation** (**DE**), an equation that involves a function $y(x)$ (or just y) and its derivatives. A **solution** to a DE is a function that satisfies the given equation. For example, if C is any constant then $y = Ce^x$ satisfies the DE $y' = y$ because differentiating y gives $y' = Ce^x = y$.

Adding an **initial condition** to a DE produces an **initial value problem** (**IVP**), which normally has only one solution. For instance, if we add the initial condition $y(0) = 5$ to the DE $y' = y$, then $y = 5e^x$ is the only solution.

Differential equations are invaluable in modeling real-world phenomena, including motion. In this section we used DEs to describe and predict the simplest sort of physical motion along a straight line.

Exponential and logarithmic derivatives; modeling growth

In Section 2.6 we found derivatives (and some antiderivatives) of exponential functions and their inverses, logarithmic functions. Exponential functions satisfy a simple but important DE: $y' = ky$, where k is a constant. The DE says that a solution function y grows at a rate *proportional to its size*. This sort of "growth with interest" occurs in many important real-world settings; we explored several briefly.

Trigonometric derivatives

In Section 2.7 we first found symbolic derivatives and antiderivatives of the sine and cosine functions. Then we observed that these functions satisfy an important **second order DE**: $y'' = -ky$, where k is a positive constant. This DE describes **periodic** or repeating phenomena, so its solutions (sines and cosines and functions built from them) are useful in modeling periodic phenomena. **Simple harmonic motion** is a key example—it occurs, for instance, for objects driven by springs.

REVIEW EXERCISES

1. Suppose that $\lim\limits_{x \to -1^+} f(x) = 3$ and $\lim\limits_{x \to -1^-} f(x) = 1$. Is it possible that $\lim\limits_{x \to -1} f(x) = 2$? Justify your answer.

2. Suppose that f is increasing and concave up on the interval $[-1, 3]$. Let m be the slope of the line between the points $(-1, f(-1))$ and $(3, f(3))$, and let a be the average rate of change of f over the interval $[-1, 3]$.

(a) Is $a < m$? Justify your answer.

(b) Is $m < f'(-1)$? Justify your answer.

In Exercises 3–6, $f(x) = x^2 - 3e^x + 4$.

3. Find $f'(x)$.

4. Find $f''(x)$.

5. Is f concave down at $x = 2$? Justify your answer.

6. Find a function F such that $F' = f$.

In Exercises 7–9, suppose that $h(0) = 1$ and that $h'(w) = 0.5 - \cos w$.

7. Find an equation for h.

8. Find an equation of the line that is tangent to h at $w = 0$.

9. Is h concave up at $w = \pi/2$? Justify your answer symbolically rather than graphically.

10. Suppose that the graphs of the functions f and $\ell(x) = 2 - x$ are visually indistinguishable in the viewing window $[-3.01, -2.99] \times [4.99, 5.01]$. Is it possible that $f(x) = x^2/6 + 7/2$? Justify your answer.

11. Explain why the statement $\lim\limits_{x \to 1} \sqrt{x - 1} = 0$ is incorrect.

12. Suppose that the average rate of change of the function $f(t)$ between $t = 3$ and $t = 3 + h$ is $3h^{-1} \sin h + he^h$.

(a) What is the slope of the line through the points $(3, f(3))$ and $(3.05, f(3.05))$?

(b) Evaluate $f'(3)$.

13. Is the antiderivative of $f(x) = x^{-2} - \sqrt[3]{x^2}$ concave down at $x = 1$? Justify your answer.

In Exercises 14–20, suppose that $g(1) = 2$ and that $g'(x) = 3x + 4/x - 5$.

14. Is $g(2) < 1$? Justify your answer.

15. Evaluate $\lim\limits_{x \to 4} \dfrac{g(x) - g(4)}{x - 4}$.

16. Evaluate $g''(3)$.

17. Is $x = 2\sqrt{3}/3$ an inflection point of g? Justify your answer.

18. Find an equation of the line that is tangent to the graph of g at $x = 2$.

19. Find the average rate of change of g over the interval $[6, 9]$.

20. Where in the interval $[0.4, 3.1]$ does g take on its minimum value? Its maximum value? Justify your answers.

21. The table below contains data about the average annual concentration in ppm (parts per million) of carbon dioxide in the atmosphere.

Year	1993	1994	1995	1996	1997
conc.	356.99	358.88	360.91	362.69	363.82

Use this data to estimate the rate at which the concentration of carbon dioxide in the atmosphere was increasing in 1995. (Be sure to include units with your answer!)

22. Let $f(x) = 2^x + x^3$. When plotted in a viewing window centered at the point $(1, 3)$, the graph of f appears to be a line through the point $(1, 3)$. Find an equation for this line.

In Exercises 23–26, find $\dfrac{df}{dx}$.

23. $f(x) = \sqrt{x^3} + 4$

24. $f(x) = 5x^6 - 7e^x$

25. $f(x) = 2\ln x + 3\cos x$

26. $f(x) = 4/\sqrt{x} + 3x^{-1}$

In Exercises 27–29, find an antiderivative of f.

27. $f(x) = \pi - x^{-3/2}$

28. $g(t) = 2e^t - 3\cos t$

29. $h(z) = 6z^5 + 5/z^{10}$

30. Suppose that the function f is increasing and concave down on the interval $[0, \infty)$. Rank the four values 0, $f'(1)$, $f(2) - f(1)$, and $\frac{1}{2}(f(3) - f(1))$ in increasing order. [HINT: Draw a picture.]

In Exercises 31 and 32, g is a function with the following properties:

    (i) $g(0) = 5$,

    (ii) $g'(0) = 4$, *and*

    (iii) $g''(x) = 1 + 2x - 3x^2$.

31. Is g concave up at $x = 2$? Justify your answer.

32. Is g increasing at $x = 2$? Justify your answer.

33. What is the *exact* value of $\lim\limits_{x \to \sqrt{2}} \dfrac{x^4 - 4}{x - \sqrt{2}}$? Justify your answer. [HINT: What is the formal definition of $f'(a)$?]

In Exercises 34–37, the functions f, f', and f'' are continuous on the interval $(-\infty, \infty)$, and f has the following properties:

    (i) f is positive on the interval $(-\infty, 1)$ and negative on the interval $(1, \infty)$.

    (ii) f is decreasing on the interval $(-\infty, 2)$ and increasing on the interval $(2, \infty)$.

    (iii) f is concave up on the interval $(-\infty, 5)$ and concave down on the interval $(5, \infty)$.

34. Rank the six values $\frac{1}{3}(f(0) - f(-3))$, $f'(0)$, $f'(2)$, $f'(5)$, $f'(7)$, and $f'(12)$ in increasing order.

35. Suppose that F is an antiderivative of f. At which value of x in the interval $[0, 10]$ does $F(x)$ attain its maximum value? Its minimum value? Justify your answers.

36. Suppose that F is an antiderivative of f. Does the graph of F have any inflection points? Justify your answer.

37. Is $F(x)$ concave up at $x = 3$? Justify your answer.

38. A fungus grows at a rate proportional to its current size. Suppose that the fungus weights 12 grams at time $t = 0$ hours and 15 grams at time $t = 6$ hours. At what time does the fungus weigh 24 grams?

39. Suppose that F is an antiderivative of $f(x) = x \sin(e^x)$. Find $F'(x)$.

40. Show that $w = 2/3$ is the global maximum point of the function $H(w) = 4w^5 - 5w^6$.

41. Let $g(w) = \pi w^2 + 4\sqrt[3]{w^2} - 1/w$. Find $g'(w)$.

42. Suppose that $q(1) = 2$ and that $q'(x) = 3x^4 + 5/x^6 + 7$. Evaluate $\lim\limits_{h \to 0} \dfrac{q(1+h) - q(1)}{h}$.

43. Let $P(t) = 3t^2 + 4\sqrt{t} + 5$. Find $P'(t)$.

44. Let $g(z) = 4^z - 2\ln z + 3z$. Is $g'(1) > 5$? Justify your answer.

45. Let $h(w) = \sin w - \cos w$. Find $\dfrac{dh}{dw}$.

46. Is $F(x) = e^x + x^2$ an antiderivative of $f(x) = e^x + x$? Justify your answer.

47. Is $y = 2x^5$ a solution of the IVP $y' = 10y/x$, $y(1) = 2$? Justify your answer.

48. Let $g(x) = e^{kx}$, where k is a real number. Use Theorem 11 (page 133) to show that $g'(x) = ke^{kx}$. [HINT: $g(x) = (e^k)^x$.]

In Exercises 49 and 50, f is a function such that $\lim\limits_{h \to 0} \dfrac{f(3+h) - f(3)}{h} = -2$, $f(0) = 0$, *and* $f(3) = 5$.

49. Is it possible that $f'(3) = 1$? Justify your answer.

50. Is it possible that $\lim\limits_{x \to 3} \dfrac{f(x) - f(3)}{x - 3} = 4$? Justify your answer.

51. (a) Let $f(x) = x^4$ and $g(x) = (x - 2)^4$. Explain why $g'(x) = 4(x - 2)^3$. [HINT: How is the graph of g related to the graph of f?]

(b) Let $h(x) = (x - c)^k$, where c and k are real numbers. Find $h'(x)$.

(c) Let $k(x) = (4 - x)^3$. Find $k'(x)$.
[HINT: $(4 - x) = -(x - 4)$.]

52. Over the interval $[0, 10]$, the maximum value of the function h occurs only once, at $x = 1$, and the minimum value of h occurs only once, at $x = 7$. Furthermore, the only root of h in the interval $[0, 10]$ is at $x = 3$. If the function H is an antiderivative of h, is it possible that the maximum value of H over the interval $[0, 10]$ occurs at $x = 5$? Justify your answer.

In Exericses 53–56, find a formula for the second *derivative of the function.*

53. $F(\theta) = \sin \theta$

54. $g(t) = e^t$

55. $U(r) = \ln r$

56. $P(v) = \sqrt[3]{v^5}$

57. The value of $\lim\limits_{x \to 1} \dfrac{x^{1000} - 1}{x - 1}$ is $f'(a)$ for a function f and a number a. Evaluate the limit by first identifying f and a and then evaluating $f'(a)$.

58. Suppose that f, f', and f'' are continous functions, that $f'(x) > 0$ for all x, and that $f''(x) < 0$ for all x. Is the average rate of change of f over the interval $[2, 5]$ greater than $f'(2)$? Justify your answer.
[HINT: Sketch a graph of f.]

59. Use calculus to prove that $f(x) = 3x^4 - 8x^3 + 17 > 0$ for every x.

60. Let $U(r) = A/r^2 - 1/r$, where A is a positive constant.

(a) On which subinterval(s) of $(0, \infty)$, if any, is U positive? Justify your answer.

(b) On which subinterval(s) of $(0, \infty)$, if any, is U decreasing? Justify your answer.

(c) On which subinterval(s) of $(0, \infty)$, if any, is U concave down? Justify your answer.

(d) Use parts (a)–(c) to sketch a qualitatively correct graph of $U(r)$ for $0 < r < \infty$.

61. A weight hangs 5 feet above the floor from a spring attached to the ceiling. If the weight is pulled down 6 inches and released at time $t = 0$ its height at time t seconds is $y(t) = 5 - \frac{1}{2} \cos(\pi t)$. Find the velocity and the acceleration of the weight 1/3 second after release.

62. (a) Use the speed limit principle and the fact that $e^x \geq 1$ for all $x \geq 0$ to show that $e^x \geq 1 + x$ for all $x \geq 0$.

(b) Use the result part (a) to show that $e^x \geq 1 + x + x^2/2$ for all $x \geq 0$.

(c) Show that $e^x \geq 1 + x + x^2/2 + x^3/6$.

In Exercises 63–66, f is a function such that $f'(x) = x^2 \cos x$.

63. Let $g(x) = f(x + \pi)$. Evaluate $g'(0)$.

64. Let $h(x) = f(2x)$. Evaluate $h'(\pi/2)$.

65. Let $j(x) = 2f(x) + 3$. Find an expression for $j'(x)$.

66. Let $k(x) = 3f(4x) + 5_x$. Find an expression for $k'(x)$.

Suppose that F is an antiderivative of the function f. In Exercises 67–70, find an antiderivative of the function.

67. $g(x) = f(x) + 3$.

68. $h(x) = f(x + 3)$.

69. $j(x) = 3f(x)$.

70. $k(x) = f(3x)$.

Tangent Lines in History

The notion of a tangent line—a straight line that "touches" a curve C at a given point P—is very old. (*Tangere* is Latin for "to touch.") Versions of the tangent line idea appear, for instance, in works of the Greek mathematicians Euclid (ca. 300 B.C.E.), Archimedes (ca. 250 B.C.E.), and Apollonius (ca. 200 B.C.E.).

For the Greeks, "tangent" seems to have meant "touches but doesn't cross," as illustrated in Figure 1.

This interlude explores how the old "touch-but-don't-cross" criterion for tangent lines stands up to the modern definition. Basic polynomial algebra is used (and reinforced).

FIGURE 1
Tangents to a circle and a spiral

Our modern, "correct" definition of the term *tangent line* involves a limit. This conclusion seems almost obvious in hindsight, but it was arrived at only after a long historical process. By 1630, the French mathematician Pierre de Fermat (better known for his "Last Theorem," proved only in 1994 by the British mathematician Andrew Wiles) had essentially the modern idea of a tangent line. He used his idea to solve problems like those that appear in calculus courses today. But not until the work of the French mathematician Augustin-Louis Cauchy in the 1820s—100 years after Newton's death—were limits understood in the modern sense.

Early mathematicians were less concerned with *description*—how to *define* tangents rigorously—than with *construction*—how, given a specific curve, to use ruler, compass, and other tools to *draw* tangent lines. If C is a circle, for instance, the situation is simple: L is the line through P that's perpendicular to the radius. The Greeks could also construct tangent lines to some other curves of classical geometry, including parabolas, ellipses, and certain spirals. (Figure 1 shows an "Archimedean spiral.")

Using the old idea

The old touch-but-don't-cross-at-P criterion for a tangent line turns out to agree with the modern idea of a tangent line for some (but not all) of the curves studied in modern calculus courses. In the following problems we compare old and new approaches to finding tangent lines—and get some algebra practice in the bargain.

The following basic idea is crucial to what follows: Consider the graph of a function $y = f(x)$, and a point $P = (a, f(a))$ on the graph of f. Every (nonvertical) straight line L through P has a point–slope equation of the form $y - f(a) = m(x - a)$, where m (the slope) is some real number. Equivalently, every such line is the graph of a function $y = L(x) = f(a) + m(x - a)$. Finding the tangent line boils down, then, to choosing the "right" value for the slope m—the one that ensures that the corresponding line does not cross the graph of f at $P = (a, f(a))$.

To find this value of m, we can look at the new function

$$h(x) = f(x) - L(x) = f(x) - (f(a) + m(x - a)),$$

which tells the *difference* between $f(x)$ and $L(x)$. The difference function has two key properties:

Algebra of quadratic functions —
especially the quadratic formula and
completing the square — is the main tool
here.

Students might look for curves that do
not have this property.

1. For *any* value of m, we get $h(a) = f(a) - L(a) = 0$. This takes care of itself because we consider only lines that pass through $(a, f(a))$.

2. The "touch-but-don't-cross at P" condition is the main challenge. For it to hold, we need to choose m so that $h(x)$ *does not change sign* at $x = a$. In other words, we need either $h(x) \geq 0$ for all x near $x = a$ or $h(x) \leq 0$ for all x near $x = a$.

Tangent lines to parabolas   The touch-but-don't-cross idea works nicely with *quadratic* functions. Parabolas have a simple property that we'll find useful: If a line ℓ intersects a parabola at two points P and Q, then ℓ *crosses* the parabola at both P and Q. Here's what this means for us:

> *The tangent line to a parabola at a point P is the line that intersects the parabola only at P.*

We'll use this condition in problems below. (The derivative rules of this chapter make some of the problems easy. The point here is to compare the old and new approaches.)

EXAMPLE 1   Consider the parabola with equation $y = f(x) = x^2$. Use the touching idea to find the tangent line at the point $(0, 0)$.

Solution   Nonvertical lines through $(0, 0)$ have equations of the form $y = L(x) = mx$. Such a line touches the parabola wherever $f(x) = L(x)$, that is, where $h(x) = f(x) - L(x) = x^2 - mx = 0$. Note that the difference function $h(x) = x^2 - mx$ is *another* quadratic equation; it can be factored as $h(x) = x(x - m)$. Thus, $h(x)$ has roots $x = 0$ and $x = m$; these roots are identical if and only if $m = 0$. Thus, the desired tangent line has slope 0, and equation $y = L(x) = 0$.   ∎

EXAMPLE 2   Use the touching idea to find the tangent line to the parabola $y = x^2$ at the point $(1, 1)$.

Solution   Nonvertical lines through $(1, 1)$ have equations of the form $y = L(x) = m(x - 1) + 1$. We want to choose m so that the quadratic equation $h(x) = f(x) - L(x) = 0$ has only one root. In this case, $h(x) = x^2 - mx + (m - 1)$. (We grouped like powers of x.) How many roots does $h(x)$ have?

Recall a useful property of quadratic functions: $Ax^2 + Bx + C$ has *one* root if and only if $B^2 - 4AC = 0$. (The following problems have more details about this fact.) For the quadratic function $h(x)$, we have $A = 1$, $B = -m$, and $C = (m - 1)$; it follows that $B^2 - 4AC = 0$ if and only if $m = 2$. Thus, the desired tangent line has slope 2; its equation is $y = L(x) = 2(x - 1) + 1$.   ∎

PROBLEM 1   Work out the details of the calculation just above; that is, show that if $A = 1$, $B = -m$, and $C = (m - 1)$, then $B^2 - 4AC = 0$ if and only if $m = 2$. For comparison, use the differentiation methods of this chapter to find an equation for the tangent line at $(1, 1)$.

PROBLEM 2   For a quadratic polynomial $p(x) = Ax^2 + Bx + C$, the quantity $D = B^2 - 4AC$ is called the **discriminant** of $p(x)$. Use the quadratic formula to explain why (i) if $D > 0$, then $p(x)$ has two roots; (ii) if $D = 0$, then $p(x)$ has one root; (iii) if $D < 0$, then $p(x)$ has no roots.   ◂

*Appendix D has details on
the quadratic formula.*

FURTHER EXERCISES

1. Take the following steps to find a point–slope equation for the tangent line to the parabola $y = f(x) = x^2$ at the point (a, a^2).

   (a) To start, use (modern) calculus ideas to find the desired tangent line. (The answer involves the symbol a of course.)

   (b) Write an equation $y = L(x)$ for the line with slope m passing through (a, a^2).

   (c) Write a (quadratic) equation for $h(x) = f(x) - L(x)$. What value of m guarantees that $h(x)$ has one root? [HINT: Use the discriminant.]

   (d) Use your answer from the preceding part to find a point–slope equation for the desired tangent line.

2. The point $P = (9, 3)$ lies on the curve with equation $x = y^2$.

   (a) Use (modern) calculus ideas to find a point–slope equation for the tangent line at P. [HINT: Differentiate the function $f(x) = \sqrt{x}$.]

   (b) Every line through P has the form $y = 3 + m(x - 9)$. Use the touching idea to find m so that the line is tangent to the graph at P. [HINT: The point is to find m so that the equations $x = y^2$ and $y = 3 + m(x - 9)$ have only one simultaneous solution.]

   (c) Reconcile your answers in the preceding parts.

3. Consider the unit circle C (with equation $x^2 + y^2 = 1$) and the "north pole" point $P = (0, 1)$. To show that the tangent line at P is horizontal, note that every (nonvertical) line through P has the form $y = mx + 1$. Show that such a line intersects C *once* if $m = 0$ and intersects C *twice* if $m \neq 0$. [HINT: A point on the line $y = mx + 1$ has the form $(x, mx + 1)$. Such a point is also on the unit circle if and only if $x^2 + (mx + 1)^2 = 1$.]

4. This problem illustrates that the touch-but-don't-cross condition doesn't always work to identify a tangent line. Consider the curve $y = f(x) = x^3$ and the point $P = (0, 0)$.

   (a) Use (modern) calculus ideas to find the tangent line at P.

   (b) Show that, in this case, *every* line through P crosses the curve at P. [HINT: Every nonvertical line through P has the form $y = L(x) = mx$. Therefore, the difference function has the form $h(x) = x^3 - mx$ and is therefore an *odd* function.]

Limit — the Formal Definition

What does the limit expression

$$\lim_{x \to a} f(x) = L$$

really mean? Informally speaking, it means that $f(x)$ "approaches" L as x "approaches" a. For the typical well-behaved functions of a beginning calculus course, this informal understanding is adequate. There's little doubt, for instance, that $\lim_{x \to 3} x^2 = 9$, whatever the legal fine print may be.

But calculus has a theoretical side, and it rests firmly on the concept of limit. Derivatives and integrals, the two main "objects" of calculus, are *defined* by means of limits, so developing a clear and unambiguous definition of limit is crucial to building a mathematically rigorous theory of calculus. The informal interpretation of limits mentioned above falls far short of this standard—the two uses of "approaches" need clearer explanation, for one thing.

Finding the "right" definition of limit is no easy matter; doing so was a serious challenge in the historical development of calculus, well into the 19th century. The following is a modern definition of limit (a definition every mathematics major encounters early and often):

DEFINITION (Limit, formally) Let $f(x)$ be defined for x in an interval containing a, except perhaps *at* $x = a$. Suppose that for every positive number ϵ (epsilon), no matter how small, there is a positive number δ (delta) so that

$$\left| f(x) - L \right| < \epsilon \quad \text{whenever} \quad 0 < |x - a| < \delta .$$

Then

$$\lim_{x \to a} f(x) = L .$$

Here are some comments on the definition:

- **In (English) words** The use of Greek letters is traditional, but the main idea can be expressed entirely in English:

  We can ensure that $f(x)$ differs from L by less than any prearranged amount ϵ by requiring that x be within δ of a.

- **In pictures** The "generic" picture (Figure 2) shows how ϵ and δ are related:

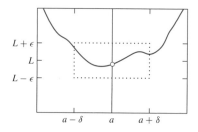

The dotted box has horizontal "radius" δ and vertical "radius" ϵ. The graph stays within the dotted box from left to right, never escaping out the top or bottom. The open dot at $x = a$ means that the value of f at $x = a$ does not appear in the limit definition.

FIGURE 2
The ϵ–δ definition of limit

This topic is optional in the sense that we don't require it explicitly in later work. It aims to "unpack" somewhat the $\epsilon - \delta$ formalism, but not to study it deeply.

Students might try to apply this graphical "nonescaping" criterion to specific limits, such as $\sin x / x \to 1$ as $x \to 0$.

Here's the definition in graphical language:

For any $\epsilon > 0$ we can choose a viewing window centered at (a, L), of width 2δ and height 2ϵ, from which the f-graph never escapes out the top or bottom, except possibly at $x = a$.

Airtight proofs Careful proofs of limit statements are essential at higher levels of mathematical analysis; inevitably, such proofs involve careful balancing of epsilons and deltas. In Appendix I, for instance, we use the definition to prove that the limit of a sum is the sum of the individual limits. The following example illustrates how the definition is used to prove a limit that seems "obvious."

It's significantly harder to show the same thing for products.

EXAMPLE 3 Show that $\lim\limits_{x \to 2} 3x = 6$.

Solution Let $\epsilon > 0$ be given. We need to find δ, also positive, such that $|f(x) - 6| < \epsilon$ whenever $0 < |x - 2| < \delta$. Note that in this case

$$|f(x) - 6| = |3x - 6| = 3|x - 2|.$$

It follows that setting $\delta = \epsilon/3$ does the job, because

$$|x - 2| < \frac{\epsilon}{3} \implies 3|x - 2| = |f(x) - 6| < \epsilon,$$

as required. (In graphical language, the idea is that the "viewing window" referred to above is three times as tall as it is wide.) ∎

FURTHER EXERCISES

1. Each of the following limits has the form $\lim\limits_{x \to a} f(x) = L$. For each, use a grapher to find a value of δ that guarantees that $|f(x) - L| < 0.001$ when $|x - a| < \delta$. (In other words, find a δ that work in the sense of the limit when $\epsilon = 0.001$.)

   (a) $\lim\limits_{x \to 2} 3x = 6$

   (b) $\lim\limits_{x \to 0} \dfrac{1 - \cos x}{x} = 0$

   (c) $\lim\limits_{x \to 1} \dfrac{x + 1}{x + 3} = 0.5$

   (d) $\lim\limits_{x \to 0} \dfrac{1 - \cos(2x)}{x^2} = 2$

   In Exercises 2–6, use the value of δ given to prove the limit. (Assume $\epsilon < 1$.)

2. $\lim\limits_{x \to 5} x = 5; \quad \delta = \epsilon$

3. $\lim\limits_{x \to 2} 6 = 6; \quad \delta = 0.2$

4. $\lim\limits_{x \to 3} x^2 - \dfrac{9}{x} - 3 = 6; \quad \delta = \epsilon$

5. $\lim\limits_{x \to 0} |x| = 0; \quad \delta = \epsilon$

6. $\lim\limits_{x \to 4} x^2 = 16; \quad \delta = \epsilon/10$

7. Use the formal definition of limit to show that $\lim\limits_{x \to 1} 0.99999x \neq 1$.

8. Let $f(x) = \begin{cases} x^2 + 1 & \text{if } x \leq 0 \\ -x & \text{if } x > 0. \end{cases}$

Use the formal definition of limit to show that f is not continuous at $x = 0$.
[HINT: $f(0) - f(x) > 1$ when $x > 0$.]

9. Let f be the function defined in the previous problem.

(a) Show that for every positive number δ, no matter how small, there is a positive number ϵ such that $|f(x) - 1| < \epsilon$ whenever $0 < |x| < \delta$.

(b) Why doesn't the result in part (a) show that f is continuous at $x = 0$?
[HINT: Compare part (a) with the formal definition of limit.]

New Derivatives From Old

3.1 ALGEBRAIC COMBINATIONS: THE PRODUCT AND QUOTIENT RULES

In Chapter 1 we studied the idea of the derivative, viewing it mainly geometrically. In Chapter 2 we viewed the derivative symbolically, finding and using explicit formulas for derivatives of the basic elementary functions. In the present chapter we find derivative formulas for more complex functions, ones built up in various ways from simpler functional pieces. An important theme throughout the chapter is "structural": just as complex functions are built from simpler functional pieces, so are complex derivatives built—not always in the "obvious" ways—from simpler derivatives.

This chapter is on "combinatorial" ideas: producing new functions and new derivatives from old. We also introduce implicit differentiation and derivatives of inverse functions; these ideas are applied to differentiate inverse trigonometric functions. Section 3.5 briefly collects miscellaneous derivative and (simple) antiderivative problems from earlier sections. Antidifferentiation is thought of here only as differentiation "in reverse." Systematic antidifferentiation appears later.

Operations on functions

A mathematical operation starts with one or more objects of some type and produces a new object of the same type. Ordinary addition, as in $2 + 3 = 5$, is an operation on *numbers*: Two old numbers are operated on to produce a new number. Subtraction, multiplication, and division are also operations on numbers. Each begins with one or more old numbers and—somehow or other—produces a new number.

This straightforward subsection can be treated quickly, but students should get the idea of functions as objects that can be combined or differentiated to produce new functions.

Operations on *functions* have similar properties. An operation on functions accepts one or more functions as input and produces a new function as output. It makes good sense, for instance, to add the two "old" functions $f(x) = x^2$ and $g(x) = \cos x$ to produce the "new" function $h(x) = x^2 + \cos x$.

Machine views Schematic diagrams like those in Figure 1 represent functions as "input–output machines"; a function accepts an input and produces an output.

Viewing function addition in machine terms may be slightly artificial, but this view is quite natural for composition.

FIGURE 1
Two function machines

From the machine point of view, operations on functions hook simple machines together to produce more complex machines. Figure 2 gives a machine view of function addition: Two function machines, f and g, are linked to form a new function machine, $f + g$:

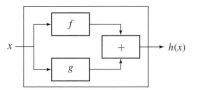

FIGURE 2
Building a new function machine: addition

The machine first duplicates an input x, sending one copy to f and one to g. The last box adds the outputs from f and g. The large outer box represents the sum function, $h = f + g$. The definition of function addition makes these ideas precise:

> **DEFINITION** Let f and g be two functions. Their sum, denoted by $f + g$, is the new function whose rule is
>
> $$(f + g)(x) = f(x) + g(x).$$

Note that inputs and outputs are functions, not numbers.

Algebraic operations—addition, subtraction, multiplication, and division—on symbolically defined functions are simple and familiar. The following table illustrates various operations applied to the functions f and g defined by $f(x) = x^2$ and $g(x) = \cos x$.

Algebraic operations on functions			
Operation	**Output**	**Rule**	**Domain**
Addition	$f + g$	$x^2 + \cos x$	$(-\infty, \infty)$
Subtraction	$f - g$	$x^2 - \cos x$	$(-\infty, \infty)$
Multiplication	$f \cdot g$	$x^2 \cos x$	$(-\infty, \infty)$
Division	g/f	$\cos(x)/x^2$	$\{x \mid x \neq 0\}$

Notice especially the domain of g/f: it is smaller than the domains of f and g because the quotient makes sense only if $f(x) = x^2 \neq 0$. Domains of built-up functions must *often* be smaller than those of the functional pieces to ensure that all the operations make sense.

Derivatives of algebraic combinations

We review composition and inversion of functions in Sections 3.2 and 3.4.

The theme of producing new functions from old runs throughout calculus. Algebraic operations, composition, inversion, and other operations all build new functions from old. ◄ How are *derivatives* of these new functions related to derivatives of the functions from which they are built?

Easy combinations: sums and constant multiples We've already seen how to find derivatives of functions built using addition and constant multiplication. The sum and constant multiple rules tell us what to do in such cases.

EXAMPLE 1 Let $f(x) = x^2 + 3 \sin x - e^x$. What's $f'(x)$? Why?

Solution By the sum and constant multiple rules,

$$f'(x) = (x^2 + 3 \cdot \sin x - e^x)' = (x^2)' + 3 \cdot (\sin x)' - (e^x)'$$
$$= 2x + 3 \cos x - e^x.$$

In this (simple) case the derivative of a combination is exactly the *same* combination of the corresponding derivatives. ■

Harder combinations Other derivative combinations are harder to handle than the preceding example might suggest. Derivatives of *products* and *quotients* of functions need special care.

Students can easily see for themselves, through simple examples, that the naive product and quotient rules aren't true.

EXAMPLE 2 Let f and g be functions, with respective derivatives f' and g'. Is $(fg)' = f'g'$? Is $(f/g)' = f'/g'$? Show by examples that these guesses, although reasonable, are *false*.

Solution Almost *any* functions f and g will do. If, say, $f(x) = x$ and $g(x) = 1$, then $f(x)g(x) = x$ and $f(x)/g(x) = x$. But

$$\big(f(x) \cdot g(x)\big)' = (x)' = 1 \neq f'(x) \cdot g'(x) = 1 \cdot 0 = 0.$$

The "false quotient rule" also produces nonsense:

$$\left(\frac{f(x)}{g(x)}\right)' = (x)' = 1 \neq \frac{f'(x)}{g'(x)} = \frac{1}{0}.$$

In fact, it takes some effort to find *any* interesting functions f and g for which $(fg)' = f'g'$. ■

But you might enjoy looking.

The (true) product and quotient rules

The product and quotient rules for derivatives follow. In each theorem, u and v are differentiable functions. ➡

It's traditional in calculus to use u and v (not f and g) in this context. We won't buck tradition.

It's not obvious that products and quotients are differentiable; we prove this for products in Appendix H.

> **THEOREM 1 (Product rule)** The product function $p(x) = u(x) \cdot v(x)$ is differentiable, and
> $$p'(x) = \big(u(x) \cdot v(x)\big)' = u'(x) \cdot v(x) + u(x) \cdot v'(x).$$
> Equivalently, $(uv)' = u'v + uv'$.

> **THEOREM 2 (Quotient rule)** The quotient function $q(x) = u(x)/v(x)$ is differentiable where $v(x) \neq 0$, and
> $$q'(x) = \left(\frac{u(x)}{v(x)}\right)' = \frac{u'(x)v(x) - u(x)v'(x)}{v(x)^2}.$$
> Equivalently, $\left(\dfrac{u}{v}\right)' = \dfrac{vu' - uv'}{v^2}$.

Notice, in particular, that the theorems say a little more than how to *calculate* derivatives—they also ensure that the derivatives in question exist.

Using the rules

Before explaining *why* the rules hold we'll show how to use them to calculate several derivatives; we'll also use the rules to tie up some loose ends from earlier sections.

EXAMPLE 3 Let $p(x) = x^2 \sin x$ and $q(x) = x^2/\sin x$. Find p' and q'.

Solution In the notation of the theorems, $u(x) = x^2$ and $v(x) = \sin x$. Thus, $u' = 2x$ and $v' = \cos x$. With u, u', v, and v' known, we just match the patterns in the theorems:

$$p'(x) = (uv)' = u'v + uv' = 2x \sin x + x^2 \cos x;$$

$$q'(x) = (u/v)' = \frac{u'v - uv'}{v^2} = \frac{(\sin x)2x - x^2 \cos x}{(\sin x)^2}.$$

We won't bother simplifying answers algebraically because our main concern is with derivatives.   ■

EXAMPLE 4   Use the product and quotient rules to differentiate e^{2x} and e^{-x}.

Solution   First, recall some basic exponential algebra:

$$e^{2x} = e^x \cdot e^x; \qquad e^{-x} = \frac{1}{e^x}.$$

Now we use the product and quotient rules, with $u = 1$ and $v = e^x$:

$$(e^x \cdot e^x)' = e^x \cdot e^x + e^x \cdot e^x = 2(e^x)^2 = 2e^{2x};$$

$$\left(\frac{1}{e^x}\right)' = \frac{-e^x}{(e^x)^2} = -\frac{1}{e^x} = -e^{-x}.$$

(Recall, by the way, that we saw earlier another way of handling the same derivatives; see Example 7, page 98.)   ■

We couldn't check this antiderivative without the product rule.

Antiderivatives of logarithmic functions   In Section 2.6 we found that $(\ln x)' = 1/x$, but we found no antiderivative. Now we can close this gap.

> **FACT**   Let C be any constant. If $f(x) = \ln x$, then $F(x) = x \ln x - x + C$ is an antiderivative of f.

The product rule makes the Fact easy to check:

$$(x \ln x - x + C)' = 1 \cdot \ln x + x \cdot \frac{1}{x} - 1 = \ln x.$$

So the Fact is indeed correct, but the antiderivative formula seems to have dropped from thin air. Where did it come from? One possibility is simple guesswork. With a little luck one *might* just stumble on the formula, and then check it using the product rule. More systematic approaches to finding antiderivatives also exist, and we'll meet some later in *A technique called integration by parts turns out to work in this case.*   this book. ◄

Graphical evidence provides another "reality check" for the Fact. Figure 3 shows graphs of $y = x \ln x - x + C$ for several values of C.

Shown are $y = x \ln x - x + C$ for $C = -1, 0, ..., 4$. Curves differ from each other only by vertical shifts—all have $y = \ln x$ as derivative.

FIGURE 3
Antiderivatives of ln x

The curves' general shape gives graphical evidence that they are indeed antiderivatives of $y = \ln x$.

Derivatives of "other" trigonometric functions In Section 2.7 we showed that $(\sin x)' = \cos x$ and that $(\cos x)' = -\sin x$, but we postponed finding derivatives of several other trigonometric derivatives. The quotient rule lets us finish the job. We'll calculate one derivative and leave the others as exercises.

EXAMPLE 5 Find and simplify the derivative of $\tan x$.

Solution Using the quotient rule, we have

$$(\tan x)' = \left(\frac{\sin x}{\cos x} \right)' = \frac{\cos^2 x + \sin^2 x}{\cos^2 x} = \frac{1}{\cos^2 x} = \sec^2 x.$$

Here, for reference, are graphs of $\tan x$ and $\sec^2 x$ (Figures 4(a) and (b)):

(a) $y = \tan x$

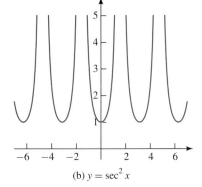

Notice the gaps in both graphs.

(b) $y = \sec^2 x$

FIGURE 4
$y = \tan x$ and its derivative

They suggest we're on the right track.   ■

The remaining trigonometric derivatives fit snugly into a table:

Derivatives of trigonometric functions					
Function	$\sin x$	$\cos x$	$\tan x$	$\cot x$	$\sec x$	$\csc x$
Derivative	$\cos x$	$-\sin x$	$\sec^2 x$	$-\csc^2 x$	$\sec x \tan x$	$-\csc x \cot x$

Evidence for the product rule

A formal proof of the product rule (one appears in Appendix H) involves difference quotients. Here we'll give two informal arguments. They don't address every detail—they don't explain, for instance, why the product of differentiable functions must be another differentiable function. ➡

Exhibit A: The product rule works for linear functions Suppose that $u(x) = ax + b$ and $v(x) = cx + d$. We'll differentiate $u \cdot v$ twice—first without and then with the product rule. To begin, notice that

$$u(x)\,v(x) = (ax + b)(cx + d) = acx^2 + (ad + bc)x + bd.$$

Either one of these exhibits should suffice to persuade, but seeing both gives a more varied view.

For more on this point, see Appendix H.

We'll give a similar (but simpler) plausibility argument for the chain rule, starting from linear functions.

The last expression is a polynomial in x. Differentiating it directly (*without* using the product rule) gives

$$(uv)' = 2acx + (ad + bc).$$

Happily, the product rule gives the same result:

$$(uv)' = u'v + uv' = a \cdot (cx + d) + (ax + b) \cdot c = 2acx + ad + bc.$$

Thus, the product rule gives the right answer for *linear* functions u and v. Most functions, of course, are not linear. But every differentiable function is "almost linear" in the sense that its graph looks straight if viewed at sufficiently small scale. This idea, made more precise here and there, can be used to deduce the product rule for *any* pair of differentiable functions.

Exhibit B: The product rule works "in practice"   Both the number of households and the mean household income in the United States vary with time; we'll denote them by $h(t)$ and $i(t)$, respectively, with t the date in years. The product function $w(t) = h(t) \cdot i(t)$ describes the *total annual U.S. household income*, another function of t.

How fast was total annual household income growing at $t = 1999$?

The U.S. Census Bureau tabulates values of these and many other related functions. Here are some samples (from www.census.gov):

U.S. household and income data					
Year	1999	1998	...	1978	1977
Households (thousands)	104,705	103,874	...	77,330	76,030
Mean household income (1999$)	54,842	53,000	...	43,760	42,441

The table gives (approximate) values for our functions: $h(1999) = 104.705$ million and $i(1999) = 54{,}842$. We can also estimate *derivatives*. For instance, the number of households grew by 831,000 from 1998 to 1999, so $h'(1999) = 0.831$ million is reasonable. For similar reasons, we can use $i'(1999) = 1842$, the change in mean income over the same year.

   To answer our question, observe first that growth in w comes from two sources: the increasing number of households and rising per-household income. The 1998–99 year produced about 0.831 million new households, earning an average of \$54,842 for a total of about

$$h'(1999) \cdot i(1999) = 0.831 \text{ million} \cdot 54842 = 45.574 \text{ billion}$$

dollars. Rising household income produced about

$$h(1999) \cdot i'(1999) = 104.705 \text{ million} \cdot 1842 = 192.866 \text{ billion}$$

new income dollars. In all, therefore, income rose at the rate of

$$h'(1999) \cdot i(1999) + h(1999) \cdot i'(1999) = 45.574 \text{ billion} + 192.866 \text{ billion}$$
$$= 238.440 \text{ billion}$$

dollars per year—exactly what the product rule predicts.

Proving the quotient rule

Quotients are closely related to products; we exploit this relationship in the following example.

EXAMPLE 6   Deduce the quotient rule from the product rule, *assuming* that the derivative of the quotient function exists. (It *does* exist, but showing this requires a proof similar to the one for the product rule given in Appendix H.)

Solution   Let u and v be differentiable functions, and let $q(x) = u(x)/v(x)$ be the quotient function. (Note that $q(x)$ is defined wherever $v(x) \neq 0$.) We want $q'(x)$. First we write $u(x) = q(x)v(x)$. Next, we differentiate $u(x)$ using the product rule (we dropped the x's for simplicity):

$$u' = (qv)' = q'v + qv' = q'v + \frac{u}{v}v'.$$

Solving the preceding equation for q' gives the quotient rule:

$$q' = \frac{u'v - uv'}{v^2}.$$ ∎

Further examples

The following examples illustrate some slightly more sophisticated uses of the rules. In particular, functions built from *several* products and quotients may require several applications of the rules.

Applying the rules to graphical and tabular functions helps force attention to the rules' structure.

EXAMPLE 7   Let u, v, and w be differentiable functions. Find a formula for $(uvw)'$.

Solution   The product rule and some clever grouping are all we need:

$$\begin{aligned}
(uvw)' &= \big((uv) \cdot w\big)' && \text{(by grouping)} \\
&= (uv)' \cdot w + (uv) \cdot w' && \text{(product rule)} \\
&= (u'v + uv') \cdot w + uvw' && \text{(product rule)} \\
&= u'vw + uv'w + uvw'.
\end{aligned}$$

Notice the pretty pattern: Each summand in the answer involves u, v, and w, with one letter primed. ∎

EXAMPLE 8   Differentiate (i) $x e^x \sin x$;   (ii) $x/(e^x \sin x)$.

Solution   The rule derived in Example 7 answers (i):

$$(x e^x \sin x)' = 1 \cdot e^x \cdot \sin x + x \cdot e^x \cdot \sin x + x \cdot e^x \cdot \cos x.$$

Differentiating (ii) takes *both* the quotient and the product rules:

$$\begin{aligned}
\left(\frac{x}{e^x \sin x}\right)' &= \frac{(e^x \sin x)(x)' - x(e^x \sin x)'}{(e^x \sin x)^2} && \text{(product rule)} \\
&= \frac{(e^x \sin x) - x(e^x \sin x + e^x \cos x)}{(e^x \sin x)^2} && \text{(taking derivatives)} \\
&= \frac{(\sin x)(1 - x) - x \cos x}{e^x \sin^2 x} && \text{(simplifying)}
\end{aligned}$$

(We won't further simplify algebraically—this form shows the answer's structure better.) ∎

EXAMPLE 9   Some values of two functions f and g appear in the following table:

This example is easily cloned with other functions f and g.

x	1.23	1.24	1.25	1.26	1.27
$f(x)$	1.5129	1.5376	1.5625	1.5876	1.6129
$g(x)$	2.7942	2.8048	2.8153	2.8258	2.8363

Estimate $f'(1.25)$, $g'(1.25)$, and $(fg)'(1.25)$.

Solution Lacking symbolic formulas for f and g, we can only *estimate* derivatives. One approach is to use the difference quotient estimates:

$$f'(1.25) \approx \frac{f(1.26) - f(1.25)}{0.01} = \frac{1.5876 - 1.5625}{0.01} \approx 2.51$$

$$g'(1.25) \approx \frac{g(1.26) - g(1.25)}{0.01} = \frac{2.8258 - 2.8153}{0.01} \approx 1.05.$$

To estimate $(fg)'(1.25)$, we can use the product rule:

$$(fg)'(1.25) = f'(1.25)g(1.25) + f(1.25)g'(1.25) \approx 2.51 \cdot 2.8153 + 1.5625 \cdot 1.05 \approx 8.71.$$

Another approach—which avoids the product rule—is to tabulate values of fg:

x	1.23	1.24	1.25	1.26	1.27
$f(x)g(x)$	4.2274	4.3127	4.3989	4.4863	4.5746

Now we can apply the difference quotient estimate directly to fg:

$$(fg)'(1.25) \approx \frac{(fg)(1.26) - (fg)(1.25)}{0.01} \approx \frac{4.4863 - 4.3989}{0.01} \approx 8.74.$$

Our two estimates of $(fg)'(1.25)$ are close but not identical—the small difference comes from roundoff errors. ∎

BASIC EXERCISES

1. Let $f(x) = 1 - x$, $g(x) = 1 + x$, $p(x) = f(x) \cdot g(x)$, and $q(x) = f(x)/g(x)$.

    (a) Explain how graphs of f, g, and p illustrate the fact that $p' \neq f' \cdot g'$.

    (b) Use zooming to show that $q'(2) \neq f'(2)/g'(2)$.

2. Let $f(x) = x^3 \cos x$. Find f'. [HINT: See Example 3.]

3. Let $g(t) = \cos t / t^4$. Find g'.

4. Find the derivative of $h(x) = 3^{2x}$ using the product rule. [HINT: See Example 4.]

5. Find the derivative of $r(x) = 2^{-x}$ using the quotient rule. [HINT: See Example 4.]

6. Let $f(w) = w/(w^2 + 1)$.

    (a) Find f' using the quotient rule.

    (b) Find f' using the product rule and the approach taken in Example 6.

7. Find the derivative of $g(z) = e^z \tan z$. [HINT: See Example 5.]

8. Find the derivative of $h(r) = r \ln r \cos r$. [HINT: See Example 7.]

In Exercises 9–14, find the derivative in two ways: (i) using the product rule, and (ii) by multiplying out before differentiating.

9. $h(x) = x \cdot x^{-1}$

10. $h(x) = x^3(x^2 - 4)$

11. $h(x) = \sqrt{x} \cdot \sqrt[3]{x}$

12. $h(x) = (x + 4)^2$

13. $h(x) = e^x \cdot e^{2x}$

14. $h(x) = \tan x \cdot \csc x$

In Exercises 15–20, find the derivative in two ways: (i) using the quotient rule, and (ii) algebraically simplifying and then differentiating.

15. $h(x) = \dfrac{x^2}{x^3}$

16. $h(x) = \dfrac{x}{\sqrt{x}}$

17. $h(x) = \dfrac{1}{e^{2x}}$

18. $h(x) = \dfrac{1 - x^2}{1 + x}$

19. $h(x) = \dfrac{1 - x^3}{1 - x}$

20. $h(x) = \dfrac{\cot x}{\csc x}$

In Exercises 21–36, find an expression for f'. Check your answers for reasonableness by comparing graphs of f and f'.

21. $f(x) = x \sin x$

22. $f(x) = x^2 \cos x$

23. $f(x) = \sqrt{x} \ln x$

24. $f(x) = x^3 e^x$

25. $f(x) = e^{2x} \ln x$

26. $f(x) = \sin x \cos x$

27. $f(x) = (x^2 + 3)e^x$

28. $f(x) = x^{3/2} \sin x$

29. $f(x) = \dfrac{\sin x}{x^2}$

30. $f(x) = \dfrac{\cos x}{x^2 + e^{2x}}$

31. $f(x) = \dfrac{(x+1)^2}{x^2+1}$

32. $f(x) = \dfrac{\sin x}{\cos(2x)}$

33. $f(x) = \cot(3x)$

34. $f(x) = \sec(x+3)$

35. $f(x) = 3\csc(2x)$

36. $f(x) = 4\tan(x+5)$

In Exercises 37–41, determine whether $G(x)$ is an antiderivative of $g(x)$.

37. $g(x) = \sec^2 x;\quad G(x) = \tan x$

38. $g(x) = (x+1)e^x;\quad G(x) = xe^x$

39. $g(x) = e^{2x}\sin x - 2e^{2x}\cos x;\quad G(x) = 2 - e^{2x}\cos x$

40. $g(x) = \dfrac{xe^x - e^x}{x^2};\quad G(x) = \dfrac{e^x}{x}$

41. $g(x) = 9x^2\ln x;\quad G(x) = 3x^3\ln x - x^3$

42. Let $h(x) = f(x) \cdot g(x)$, and $j(x) = f(x)/g(x)$. Fill in the missing entries in the table below using the information about f and g given in the table and the definitions of h and j.

x	$f(x)$	$f'(x)$	$g(x)$	$g'(x)$	$h'(x)$	$j'(x)$
-2	1	-1	-3	4		$-1/9$
-1	0	-2	1	1	-2	
0	-1	2	-2	1		
1	2	-2	-1	2	6	
2	3	-1	2	-2		1

FURTHER EXERCISES

In Exercises 43–48, f is the function shown below, $h(x) = x^2 f(x)$, and $m(x) = f(x)/(x^2+1)$.

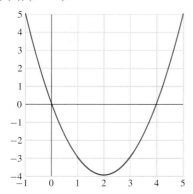

43. Estimate $h'(2)$ and $h'(4)$.

44. Show that h has a stationary point at $x = 0$.

45. Is h concave up at $x = -0.5$? Justify your answer.

46. Suppose that $f''(3) = 2$. Is $h''(3) > 0$? Justify your answer.

47. Estimate $m'(0)$ and $m'(2)$.

48. Is m increasing at $x = 3$? Justify your answer.

In Exercises 49–52, suppose that $f(1) = 2$, f' is the function shown below, and $g(x) = x^3 f(x)$.

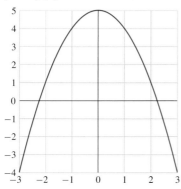

49. Estimate $g'(1)$.

50. Is g is increasing at $x = 2$? Justify your answer.

51. Estimate $g''(1)$.

52. Is g concave up at $x = -2$? Justify your answer.

In Exercises 53–68, suppose that $f(0) = 3$, f' is the function shown below, $g(x) = \sin(x)f(x)$, $h(x) = e^x f(x)$, and $k(x) = f(x) \cdot f(x) = \big(f(x)\big)^2$.

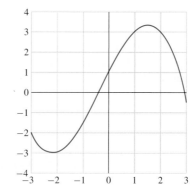

53. Evaluate $g'(0)$.

54. Is g increasing at $x = -\pi/2$? Justify your answer.

55. Is g increasing at $x = \pi/2$? Justify your answer.

56. Estimate $g''(0)$.

57. Is g concave up at $x = \pi/2$? Justify your answer.

58. Evaluate $h'(0)$.

59. Is h increasing at $x = 1$? Justify your answer.

60. Is h increasing at $x = 2$? Justify your answer.

61. Estimate $h''(0)$.

62. Is h concave up at $x = 1$? Justify your answer.

63. Is h concave up at $x = 2$? Justify your answer.

64. Evaluate $k'(0)$.

65. Is k increasing at $x = 1$? Justify your answer.

66. Is k increasing at $x = -1$? Justify your answer.

67. Estimate $k''(0)$.

68. Is k concave down at $x = 1$? Justify your answer.

69. Let $f(x) = xe^x$.

  (a) Find values of the constants a and b so that the linear function $L(x) = ax + b$ has the properties $L(0) = f(0)$ and $L'(0) = f'(0)$.

  (b) Find the value of the constant c for which the quadratic function $Q(x) = L(x) + cx^2$ has the properties $Q(0) = f(0)$, $Q'(0) = f'(0)$, and $Q''(0) = f''(0)$.

  (c) Plot f, L, and Q on the same axes over the interval $[-3, 3]$.

  (d) Find an interval over which $|f(x) - L(x)| < 0.1$.

  (e) Find an interval over which $|f(x) - Q(x)| < 0.1$.

70. Let $f(x) = \dfrac{x}{3 + x^2}$.

  (a) Find values of the constants a and b so that the linear function $L(x) = a(x - 1) + b$ has the properties $L(1) = f(1)$ and $L'(1) = f'(1)$.

  (b) Find the value of the constant c for which the quadratic function $Q(x) = L(x) + c(x - 1)^2$ has the properties $Q(1) = f(1)$, $Q'(1) = f'(1)$, and $Q''(1) = f''(1)$.

  (c) Plot f, L, and Q on the same axes over the interval $[-3, 3]$.

  (d) Find an interval over which $|f(x) - L(x)| < 0.1$.

  (e) Find an interval over which $|f(x) - Q(x)| < 0.1$.

71. Suppose that f and g are differentiable functions and that $h(x) = f(x)g(x)$. Find symbolic expressions involving only numerical constants and derivatives of f and g for

  (a) $h''(x)$.

  (b) $h'''(x)$.

72. Let $f(x) = xe^x$. Find values of the parameters A and B so that $F(x) = (Ax + B)e^x$ is an antiderivative of f.

73. Let $f(x) = (A + Bx)e^x$. Find values of the parameters A and B so that f is a solution of the IVP $y' - y = 2e^x$, $y(0) = 3$.

74. Let $g(x) = Ae^{-x} + Be^{2x}$. Find values of the parameters A and B so that g is a solution of the IVP $y' + y = 3e^{2x}$, $y(0) = -1$.

75. Let $g(x) = x^2 e^x$. Find values of the parameters A, B, and C so that $G(x) = (Ax^2 + Bx + C)e^x$ is an antiderivative of g.

76. Let $h(x) = e^{2x}\sin x$. Find values of the parameters A and B so that $H(x) = e^{2x}(A\cos x + B\sin x)$ is an antiderivative of h.

77. Consider the function $f(x) = \dfrac{\ln x}{x}$ on the interval $(1, \infty)$.

  (a) Where does f achieve its maximum value? What is this value?

  (b) Where does f have inflection points?

78. Let $f(x) = \dfrac{x + \sin x}{\cos x}$. Find an equation of the line tangent to the graph of f at $x = 0$.

79. Let $f(x) = e^x \cos x$. At which value(s) of x in the interval $[0, \pi]$ does f

  (a) achieve its maximum value?

  (b) achieve its minimum value?

  (c) have an inflection point?

80. Find the maximum and minimum values of $g(x) = e^{-x}\sin x$ over the interval $[0, \infty)$.

81. (a) Let C be a real number. Show that $y(x) = (x + C)e^{-2x}$ is a solution of the DE $y' + 2y = e^{-2x}$.

  (b) Find the solution of the IVP $y' + 2y = e^{-2x}$, $y(0) = 7$.

3.2 COMPOSITION AND THE CHAIN RULE

We study composition in some detail because the operation is relatively unfamiliar to students.

Let f and g be the functions defined by $f(x) = x^2$ and $g(x) = \cos x$. The new functions $h(x) = \cos(x^2)$ and $k(x) = (\cos x)^2$ are built from f and g by **composition**—following one function with another. In this section we study such composite (or "chained-together") functions and, especially, their derivatives.

We start with a precise definition:

> **DEFINITION**   Let f and g be functions. The **composition** of f and g, denoted $f \circ g$, is the function defined by the rule
>
> $$(f \circ g)(x) = f\big(g(x)\big).$$

Here are some basic properties of composition:

- **Order matters** The two functions $f \circ g$ and $g \circ f$ may be quite different. If, say, $f(x) = x^2$ and $g(x) = \cos x$, then

$$(f \circ g)(x) = f(g(x)) = f(\cos x) = (\cos x)^2;$$
$$(g \circ f)(x) = g(f(x)) = g(x^2) = \cos(x^2).$$

- **Repeated composition** We can compose *more than two* functions. If, say, $f(x) = x^2$, $g(x) = \cos x$, and $h(x) = e^x$, then

$$f \circ g \circ h(x) = f(g(e^x)) = f(\cos(e^x)) = (\cos(e^x))^2 = \cos^2(e^x).$$

(Notice especially the nesting and order of parentheses.)

- **Domains** The natural domain of $f \circ g$ is the set of "legal" inputs—that is, the set of inputs x for which $f(g(x))$ makes sense. For this to occur, x must first be a legal input to g so that $g(x)$ makes sense. Second, $g(x)$ must be a legal input to f so that $f(g(x))$ makes sense. These requirements mean that the domain of $f \circ g$ is a *subset* of (and may be smaller than) the domain of g.

EXAMPLE 1 Let $f(x) = x + 5$ and $g(x) = \sqrt{x}$. Find the natural domains of f, g, $f \circ g$, and $g \circ f$.

Solution Because f accepts any real number as input, while g accepts only nonnegative inputs, the domains of f and g are $(-\infty, \infty)$ and $[0, \infty)$, respectively. Composing f and g gives $f \circ g(x) = \sqrt{x} + 5$ (which makes sense for $x \geq 0$) and $g \circ f(x) = \sqrt{x + 5}$ (which makes sense for $x \geq -5$). Thus, the domains of $f \circ g$ and $g \circ f$ are, respectively, $[0, \infty)$ and $[-5, \infty)$. ■

Composition: function machines in series The machine picture of composition (Figure 1) is especially simple.

The machine picture for addition was more complicated.

FIGURE 1
A composition machine

The machines g and f are linked "in series"—an output from g is piped through f. The diagram illustrates the earlier comment about domains: A legal input x to $f \circ g$ must first pass successfully through g; then the output $g(x)$ must be acceptable to f.

Composing functions of various types

We've just seen how to compose functions described by formulas. The following examples show how the the same idea—composition—applies to functions given in other ways.

EXAMPLE 2 **(Composition with a table)** Let $f(x) = x + 2$; let g be defined by the following table:

x	-3	-2	-1	0	1	2	3	4
$g(x)$	-4	-9	-1	2	0	8	3	-2

Describe $f \circ g$ and $g \circ f$. What are their domains?

Solution Because $f(x) = x + 2$, we have

$$(f \circ g)(x) = f(g(x)) = g(x) + 2 \quad \text{and} \quad (g \circ f)(x) = g(f(x)) = g(x + 2).$$

For instance, $(f \circ g)(1) = g(1) + 2 = 0 + 2 = 2$, while $(g \circ f)(1) = g(1 + 2) = g(3) = 3$. But not just *any* input works. The quantity $(f \circ g)(10) = g(10) + 2$ is undefined because 10 is not in the domain of g. The following table gives full details on both $g \circ f$ and $f \circ g$:

x	-5	-4	-3	-2	-1	0	1	2	3	4
$g(x)$			-4	-9	-1	2	0	8	3	-2
$(f \circ g)(x)$			-2	-7	1	4	2	10	5	0
$(g \circ f)(x)$	-4	-9	-1	2	0	8	3	-2		

Notice especially the gaps in the table; they reflect gaps in the respective domains. ■

EXAMPLE 3 **(Composing graphs)** Functions f, g, and $f \circ g$ (the bold curve with several bulleted points) are shown in Figure 2. How were the bulleted values found? How was the bold graph drawn?

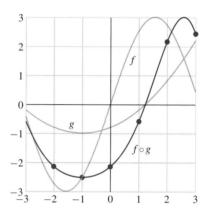

FIGURE 2
Composing graphical functions

Solution Let's find $(f \circ g)(3) = f(g(3))$. Reading approximate values from the graphs gives

$$(f \circ g)(3) = f(g(3)) \approx f(2.2) \approx 2.4.$$

Similar graphical estimates produce the following table:

	Composing graphs						
x	-3	-2	-1	0	1	2	3
$(f \circ g)(x)$	-0.6	-2.2	-2.5	-2.2	-0.6	2.2	2.4

With enough such data, we could plot $f \circ g$ (the bold curve; tabulated data points are the ones shown bulleted). ■

EXAMPLE 4 **(Composing words)** Motoring across Montana from Billings to Missoula, a driver's *altitude* varies with *distance* traveled. Distance, in turn, varies with *time*, so altitude also varies with time. Interpret the situation in the language of functions and composition.

Solution Let A, d, and t denote altitude, distance traveled, and time, measured in (say) meters above sea level, kilometers from Missoula, and hours since departure. Then altitude is a function, say f, of distance, and distance is another function, say g, of time. In function notation, $A = f(d)$ and $d = g(t)$, and the composite function $A(t) = f \circ g(t) = f(g(t))$ represents altitude as a function of time. ∎

Composing ''nice'' functions

If f and g are both "well-behaved" functions (continuous, say, or differentiable), then we naturally expect $f \circ g$ to be equally "well-behaved." This is indeed the case, but (as always) some care is needed for details.

EXAMPLE 5 Figures 3(a) and (b) show graphs of the composite functions $e^{\cos x}$ and $\sin(|x|)$. Where is each function continuous? Differentiable?

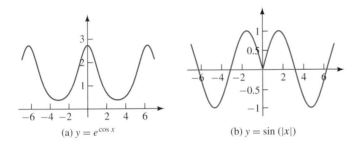

(a) $y = e^{\cos x}$ (b) $y = \sin(|x|)$

FIGURE 3

Solution As their graphs suggest, both composite functions are *continuous* for *all* inputs x. This is no surprise because all four functions involved ($\sin x$, $|x|$, $\cos x$, and e^x) are continuous for all x.

The graphs also suggest that *differentiability* is a slightly different matter. Because both $\cos x$ and e^x have derivatives for all x, so does the composition $e^{\cos x}$, and its graph is smooth. The right-hand graph, by contrast, has a cusp at $x = 0$, which reflects the fact that the function $|x|$ has *no* derivative at zero. If $x \neq 0$, on the other hand, the composite graph is smooth, since both $|x|$ and $\sin x$ have derivatives. ∎

The following theorem makes precise for continuous functions what the preceding example suggests. Because continuity was defined using limits, the proof refers to them.

> **THEOREM 3** Suppose that g is continuous at $x = a$ and f is continuous at $g(a)$. Then $f \circ g$ is continuous at $x = a$.

Proof. If $x \to a$, then $g(x) \to g(a)$ because g is continuous at a. As $g(x) \to g(a)$, $f(g(x)) \to f(g(a))$ because f is continuous at $g(a)$. Putting everything together gives

$$x \to a \implies (f \circ g)(x) \to (f \circ g)(a),$$

which is just what we needed to show. □

Exactly the same result holds with "differentiable" replacing "continuous"—this is part of the **chain rule**, to which we turn next.

The chain rule: derivatives of composite functions

With the sum, constant multiple, product, and quotient rules we can differentiate almost any *algebraic* combination of basic functions—even a mess like

$$\frac{x^2 \sin x}{\tan x} - \frac{\sin x \ln x + \cos x}{x^5 + 1} \cdot \left(2^x + \frac{3^x}{\ln x}\right).$$

Students can see through simple examples that the "naive chain rule" $(f \circ g)' = f' \circ g'$ is false.

To differentiate *any* elementary function we need just one more tool: a rule for differentiating composite (or "chained-together") functions $f \circ g$. Our experience with the product and quotient rules suggests that the rule should somehow involve f, g, f', and g'—but in what combination?

The **chain rule** is the answer. In stating it we assume that f and g are "well behaved" in the sense that f, g, f', and g' all have large enough domains to permit the desired operations.

Here is an even more compressed version of the chain rule: $(f \circ g)' = (f' \circ g) \cdot g'.$

THEOREM 4 (Chain rule)   Let f and g be functions, and let a be in the domain of g. Then

$$(f \circ g)'(a) = f'\big(g(a)\big) \cdot g'(a).$$

A fully rigorous proof of the chain rule leads to subtleties that are slightly beyond the scope of this book. Such a proof needs to explain, for example, why the derivative $(f \circ g)'(a)$ *exists* whenever both $f'\big(g(a)\big)$ and $g'(a)$ exist. We'll settle (after some comments and examples) for plausible evidence for the chain rule.

Using the variable name u avoids conflict with x.

- **Why a product?**   The theorem says that the derivative of $f \circ g$ is the *product* of $f'\big(g(a)\big)$ and $g'(a)$. (Beware: The two factors are evaluated at different inputs.) To see why a product is involved, think of derivatives as rates of change. Suppose, say, that $y = f(u)$, $u = g(x)$, $f'(u) = 3$, and $g'(x) = 2$. ◄ This means that y changes three times as fast as u and that u changes twice as fast as x. Then it's reasonable to expect that y change *six* times as fast as x.

- **The functional view**   In the theorem, we used a specific input, a, to emphasize that f' and g' are evaluated at different inputs. Because the theorem holds for *all* sensible inputs a, we can think of the chain rule as a relation among *functions*. From this point of view, we might prefer to state the chain rule as

$$(f \circ g)'(x) = f'\big(g(x)\big) \cdot g'(x)$$

This version mentions only the function names, omitting inputs entirely.

or even, equivalently, as $(f \circ g)' = (f' \circ g) \cdot g'.$ ◄

EXAMPLE 6   Use the chain rule to differentiate $\sin(3x)$ and $\sin(x + 3)$.

Solution   Let $f(u) = \sin u$, $g(x) = 3x$, and $h(x) = x + 3$. Then

$$\big(\sin(3x)\big)' = (f \circ g)'(x) = f'\big(g(x)\big) \cdot g'(x) = \cos(3x) \cdot 3.$$

Similarly,

$$\big(\sin(x + 3)\big)' = (f \circ h)'(x) = f'\big(h(x)\big) \cdot h'(x) = \cos(x + 3) \cdot 1.$$

(We found similar derivatives using Theorem 4, page 97, which applies to functions constructed using constants.)   ■

EXAMPLE 7 Do $\sin(x^2)$ and $\sin^2 x$ have the same derivative?

Solution No. Because order matters for composition, the two functions—and their derivatives—may be very different. ➡ To avoid confusion we need to keep our symbols clear. If we let $f(u) = \sin u$ and $g(u) = u^2$, then $f'(u) = \cos u$ and $g'(u) = 2u$, and thus

Plot both functions on your calculator to see how different they are.

$$\sin(x^2) = (f \circ g)(x) \qquad \text{and} \qquad \sin^2 x = (g \circ f)(x).$$

By the chain rule,

$$\left(\sin(x^2)\right)' = (f \circ g)'(x) = f'\big(g(x)\big) \cdot g'(x) = \cos\left(x^2\right) \cdot 2x;$$
$$\left(\sin^2 x\right)' = (g \circ f)'(x) = g'\big(f(x)\big) \cdot f'(x) = 2\sin x \cdot \cos x.$$ ∎

EXAMPLE 8 Differentiate the threefold composite function $\sin^3(x^2)$.

Solution We'll need our wits about us here. If we set $f(u) = u^3$, $g(u) = \sin u$, and $h(u) = u^2$, then $(g \circ h)(x) = \sin(x^2)$, and

$$(f \circ g \circ h)(x) = \left(\sin(x^2)\right)^3 = \sin^3(x^2).$$

To handle the "three-deep" composition $f \circ (g \circ h)$, we use the chain rule *twice*:

$$(f \circ (g \circ h))' = \left(f' \circ (g \circ h)\right) \cdot (g \circ h)' = \left(f' \circ (g \circ h)\right) \cdot (g' \circ h) \cdot h'.$$

For our particular f, g, and h, we get

$$\left((\sin x^2)^3\right)' = 3\left(\sin x^2\right)^2 \cdot \left(\sin x^2\right)'$$
$$= 3\left(\sin x^2\right)^2 \cdot \left(\cos x^2 \cdot 2x\right)$$
$$= 6x\left(\sin x^2\right)^2 \cos x^2.$$

(As a reality check—and some respite from all these symbols—we recommend plotting both $y = \sin^3(x^2)$ and its supposed derivative, to see that the second is indeed a plausible derivative of the first.) ∎

Work from outside in Composing two functions can be thought of as nesting one within the other. The nested parentheses on the right of $f \circ g(x) = f\big(g(x)\big)$ reflect this point of view: Here f is the "outer" function and g the "inner." In this language the chain rule says to work from outside in, one level at a time:

> To differentiate $f\big(g(x)\big)$, first differentiate the outer function, leaving the inner function alone. Then multiply by the derivative of the inner function.

This rule works for *any* level of nesting, as the next example illustrates.

EXAMPLE 9 Differentiate $\sin\big(\sin(\sin x)\big)$.

Solution Watch the step-by-step denesting:

$$\left(\sin\big(\sin(\sin x)\big)\right)' = \cos\big(\sin(\sin x)\big) \cdot \big(\sin(\sin x)\big)'$$
$$= \cos\big(\sin(\sin x)\big) \cdot \cos(\sin x) \cdot (\sin x)'$$
$$= \cos\big(\sin(\sin x)\big) \cdot \cos(\sin x) \cdot \cos x.$$ ∎

EXAMPLE 10   Differentiate $\sin^n x$, where n is any real number.

Solution   The chain rule applies, with "outer" function u^n (which has derivative nu^{n-1}) and "inner function" $\sin x$ (which has derivative $\cos x$):

$$((\sin x)^n)' = n(\sin x)^{n-1} \cdot \cos x.$$ ■

The idea of the preceding calculation works for *any* "inner" function f, and deserves its own name:

FACT (The general power rule)   Let f be a differentiable function and n a real number. Then

$$(f(x)^n)' = n f(x)^{n-1} \cdot f'(x).$$

EXAMPLE 11   Find derivatives of $(\ln x)^3$ and $\sqrt{e^x + 1}$.

Solution   Applying the general power rule (and some algebraic simplification) gives

$$((\ln x)^3)' = 3(\ln x)^2 \cdot \frac{1}{x} = \frac{3}{x}(\ln x)^2;$$

$$\left(\sqrt{e^x + 1}\right)' = ((e^x + 1)^{1/2})' = \frac{1}{2}(e^x + 1)^{-1/2} \cdot e^x = \frac{e^x}{2\sqrt{e^x + 1}}.$$ ■

The chain rule in Leibniz notation   The chain rule is especially easy to remember in Leibniz form. Here's what it says about well-behaved functions y and u:

> *Let y be a function of u and u a function of x. Then y is a function of x; the derivative of y with respect to x is*
> $$\frac{dy}{dx} = \frac{dy}{du} \cdot \frac{du}{dx}.$$

Observe the pleasant "cancellation of fractions" on the right side. (This can be a useful aid to memory, but it shouldn't be taken too literally because the derivatives in question are not ordinary fractions—they're *limits* of fractions.)

EXAMPLE 12   Differentiate $y = \sin\left(x^2\right)$ yet again, this time using Leibniz notation.

Solution   Let $y = \sin u$ and $u = x^2$. Then

$$\frac{dy}{dx} = \frac{dy}{du} \cdot \frac{du}{dx} = \cos u \cdot 2x = 2x \cdot \cos x^2.$$

(Notice how we introduced the intermediate variable $u = x^2$, and then got rid of it at the last step.)   ■

Evidence for the chain rule

Following are two "plausibility arguments" for the chain rule. The ideas can strengthened to give fully rigorous proofs. ◄

Such proofs appear in advanced calculus courses.

We gave a similar (but slightly harder) plausibility argument for the product rule. Here it's especially convenient that composing linear functions produces new linear functions.

Exhibit A: The chain rule works for linear functions   Let $f(x) = ax + b$ and $g(x) = cx + d$. We'll differentiate $f \circ g$ twice—first without and then with the chain rule. Notice first that

$$(f \circ g)(x) = a(cx + d) + b = acx + ad + b.$$

The right-hand form shows that $f \circ g$ is *another* linear function with constant derivative ac. The chain rule gives the same result. Because $f'(x) = a$ and $g'(x) = c$,

$$f'\big(g(x)\big) \cdot g'(x) = ac.$$

Exhibit B: Differentiable functions are "almost linear" If f and g are *any* differentiable functions, they're "almost linear" in the sense that f and g are closely approximated by their tangent lines near any point. In particular, near $x = a$ the function g is closely approximated by a linear function ℓ with slope $g'(a)$. In other words,

$$g(x) \approx \ell_g(x) = g'(a) \cdot x + k,$$

for some constant k (the value of k doesn't matter here).

Now let's write $g(a) = b$. Because f is differentiable at $x = b$, f is closely approximated near $x = b$ by a linear function ℓ_f, with slope $f'(b)$. Thus,

$$f(x) \approx \ell_f(x) = f'(b) \cdot x + K$$

for some other constant K. Now because $f(x) \approx \ell_f(x)$ and $g(x) \approx \ell_g(x)$, it follows that $f \circ g(x) \approx \ell_f \circ \ell_g(x)$. Since ℓ_f and ℓ_g are *linear* functions, Exhibit A applies to give

$$(\ell_f \circ \ell_g)' = f'(b) \cdot g'(a) = f'\big(g(a)\big) \cdot g'(a),$$

which is what the chain rule predicts.

Figures 4(a), (b), and (c) illustrate these ideas graphically.

The pictures need a close look. They illustrate the linear approximation approach to the chain rule.

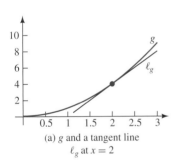

(a) g and a tangent line ℓ_g at $x = 2$

(b) f and a tangent line ℓ_f at $x = 4$

(c) $f \circ g$ and the tangent line $\ell_f \circ \ell_g$ at $x = 2$

Composing the appropriate linear approximations to f and g gives a linear approximation to $f \circ g$.

FIGURE 4
The chain rule idea in pictures

Each figure shows the graph of a function and of a tangent line at some point—in order, the functions are g, f, and $f \circ g$. The points of tangency are $x = 2$ for g and $x = g(2) = 4$ for f. Figure 4(c) shows the results of composition: the (curved) function is $f \circ g$ and the line is $\ell_f \circ \ell_g$. The message—and the main idea behind the chain rule—is this: *To find a linear function tangent to $f \circ g$, we compose two corresponding linear functions, one tangent to f and one tangent to g.*

BASIC EXERCISES

1. Let $f(x) = x^2$, $g(x) = \cos x$, and $h(x) = \cos(x^2)$.
   (a) Write h as a composition of f and g.
   (b) Find the derivative of h.

2. Let $f(x) = x^2$, $g(x) = \cos x$, and $k(x) = (\cos x)^2$.
   (a) Write k as a composition of f and g.
   (b) Find the derivative of k.

3. Find the derivative of $\cos(2x)$ using the chain rule.

4. Find the derivative of $\cos(x+2)$ using the chain rule.

In Exercises 5–20, find $f'(x)$.

5. $f(x) = (x^2 + 3)^{29}$

6. $f(x) = (1 + e^x)^{33}$

7. $f(x) = \sqrt{2 + \sin x}$

8. $f(x) = \sin\left(e^{3x}\right)$

9. $f(x) = \cos\left(x^3\right)$

10. $f(x) = \tan\left(\sqrt[3]{x}\right)$

11. $f(x) = \ln\left(4x^2 + 3\right)$

12. $f(x) = 1/\sqrt{x^2 + e^{-3x}}$

13. $f(x) = \cos\left(\sqrt{x} + e^{-x}\right)$

14. $f(x) = (x + \ln x)^{14}$

15. $f(x) = \cos^2(x^3)$

16. $f(x) = \sin^3(\sqrt{x})$

17. $f(x) = \sqrt{1 + 3x^2}$

18. $f(x) = \sqrt[3]{1 - 2x^4}$

19. $f(x) = \ln\left(x^2 + 3\sin x\right)$

20. $f(x) = \sin\left(e^{2x} + \tan(3x)\right)$

21. Let $h(x) = f\left(g(x)\right)$. Use the information about f and g given in the table below to fill in the missing information about h and h'.

x	1	2	3	4
$f(x)$	1	2	4	3
$f'(x)$	2	1	3	4
$g(x)$	4	3	1	2
$g'(x)$	3	4	2	1
$h(x)$				
$h'(x)$				

FURTHER EXERCISES

22. Let $h(x) = f\left(\dfrac{g(x)}{x^2 + 1}\right)$. If $f(1) = 3$, $f(2) = 5$, $f'(1) = 7$, $f'(2) = 11$, $g(1) = 2$, and $g'(1) = 4$, what is $h'(1)$?

In Exercises 23–25, $f(x) = \ln(2 + \cos x)$. *At which values of x does f have*

23. local maxima?

24. local minima?

25. inflection points?

In Exercises 26 and 27, f is the function shown below and $g(x) = f(x^2)$.

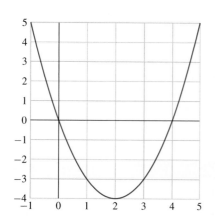

26. For which values of x is $g'(x) = 0$?

27. Is g increasing at -1?

28. Suppose that $f(1) = 2$, that f' is the function shown below, and that $k(x) = f(x^3)$. Evaluate $k'(-1)$.

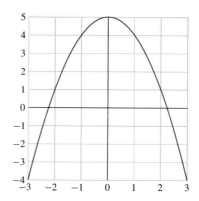

In Exercises 29–36, f and g are the functions shown below.

Graph of f

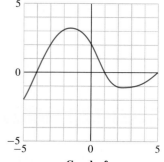

Graph of g

29. Let $h(x) = (f \circ g)(x)$.
   (a) Evaluate $h(-2)$, $h(1)$, and $h(3)$.
   (b) Estimate $h'(-2)$, $h'(1)$, and $h'(3)$.

30. Let $h(x) = (f \circ g)(x)$. Is h increasing at $x = -1$? Justify your answer.

31. Let $h(x) = (f \circ g)(x)$. What values of x correspond to stationary points of $h(x)$?

32. Let $k(x) = g(f(x))$.
  (a) Evaluate $k(0)$, $k(2)$, and $k(4)$.
  (b) Estimate $k'(0)$, $k'(2)$, and $k'(4)$.

33. Let $k(x) = g(f(x))$. Is k decreasing at $x = -4$? Justify your answer.

34. Let $j(x) = f(x^4)$. Is j increasing at $x = -1$? Justify your answer.

35. Let $k(x) = f(e^{-x})$. Determine whether k is increasing, decreasing, or stationary at $x = -1$, $x = 0$, and $x = 1$. Justify your answers.

36. Let $k(x) = f(e^{-x})$. Show that $x = -\ln 2$ is a stationary point of k and determine whether it corresponds to a local maxima or a local minima.

In Exercises 37–40, determine whether F is an antiderivative of f.

37. $f(x) = xe^{x^2}$; $F(x) = 2x^2 e^{x^2} - 4$

38. $f(x) = x^2 \sin(2x^3)$; $F(x) = \cos(2x^3)$

39. $f(x) = \dfrac{x}{\sqrt{1+x^2}}$; $F(x) = \sqrt{1+x^2}$

40. $f(x) = \dfrac{2x}{1+x^2}$; $F(x) = \ln(1+x^2)$

In Exercises 41–44, f is an antiderivative of $x \cos x$.

41. Suppose that $g(x) = f(x + \pi)$. Evaluate $g'(0)$.

42. Suppose that $h(x) = f(2x)$. Evaluate $h'(\pi/2)$.

43. Suppose that $j(x) = f(x^2) + 3x$. Find an expression for $j'(x)$.

44. Suppose that $k(x) = 3f(e^x)$. Find an expression for $k'(x)$.

45. Suppose that f is a function such that $f(\pi/2) = 17$ and $f'(x) = 2e^{x \cos x}$.
  (a) Find an equation of the line tangent to the graph of f at $x = \pi/2$.
  (b) Let $L(x)$ be the line tangent to the graph of f at $x = \pi/2$. Is $L(2) < f(2)$? Justify your answer.

46. Suppose that f is a function such that $f'(x) > 0$ for all x. If $g(x) = f(f(x))$, must g be increasing for all x? Justify your answer.

47. Suppose that f is a function such that $f'(x) < 0$ for all x. If $g(x) = f(f(x))$, must g be decreasing for all x? Justify your answer.

3.3 IMPLICIT FUNCTIONS AND IMPLICIT DIFFERENTIATION

The equation $y = -3x + 5$ defines y *explicitly* as a function, say f, of x; for an input x, the output is given by the explicit rule $f(x) = -3x + 5$. Consider, by contrast, the equation $6x + 2y = 10$ (which is equivalent to $y = 3x + 5$). Although it does not display y explicitly as a function of x, the new equation defines y *implicitly* as a function of x. Solving for y gives the same explicit formula we had before:

$$6x + 2y = 10 \iff 2y = -6x + 10 \iff y = -3x + 5.$$

The linear equation $6x + 2y = 10$ was easy to solve to find an explicit formula for y. But things aren't always so simple—more complicated equations, such as $x \sin(x + \cos y) = 5$, are much harder, or even impossible, to solve explicitly for y. Another problem is that even simple equations, such as $x^2 + y^2 = 1$, may not define y unambiguously as *one* function of x. For the same reason, the graph of an *equation* (such as the circular graph of $x^2 + y^2 = 1$) need not be the graph of a single *function*.

Despite these serious-sounding obstacles, it's surprisingly easy to find derivatives of functions defined implicitly by equations—usually without needing to solve the equations themselves. In this section we describe the process, called **implicit differentiation**, and the chain rule's special role in making it work.

We start by discussing briefly the basic objects of study: functions defined implicitly by equations rather than explicitly by functional formulas. (The difference may be new to many students.) We stress relatively simple computations, but the dependence of y' on both x and y will need comment. The graphical meaning of the implicit derivative (slope of a curve) and the connection to the chain rule are also important.

Why equations matter

Functions, not equations, are the basic objects of calculus. The main ideas of calculus—limits, derivatives, and integrals—are all defined in terms of functions, and they apply even to functions that have no convenient symbolic formulas. For these and other reasons, functions usually loom larger than equations in calculus courses.

In real-world applications of calculus, however, equations are often fully as common and as important as are functions. The laws of physics, especially, are usually stated as equations. For instance, **Kepler's third law** of planetary motion can be written as the equation

$$T^2 G M_s = 4\pi^2 r^3.$$

The equation relates the time T needed for a planet to complete one orbit around the sun to the radius r of the orbit; M_s is the mass of the sun and G is called the **gravitational constant**. (The numerical value of G depends on the choice of units.) Physicists have used calculus to derive and manipulate such equations—rather than functions—for hundreds of years.

Solving DEs (e.g, by separation of variables) often produces solutions in implicit form. We'll also use implicit differentiation in some optimization problems.

EXAMPLE 1   Does the equation $x - y^2 = 0$ define y as a function of x?

Solution   No. Solving algebraically for y shows why:

$$x - y^2 = 0 \iff y^2 = x \iff y = \pm\sqrt{x}.$$

In effect, the equation determines *two* functions: $f_1(x) = \sqrt{x}$ and $f_2(x) = -\sqrt{x}$, each defined for nonnegative inputs x. Figure 1 shows *both* of these functions:

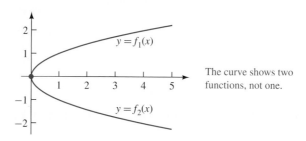

The curve shows two functions, not one.

FIGURE 1
Graph of the equation $x - y^2 = 0$

It fails the "vertical line test."

The "sideways" parabola is not the graph of a function because each nonzero value of x corresponds to *two* values of y. ← The upper and lower halves of the graph define the functions $f_1(x) = \sqrt{x}$ and $f_2(x) = -\sqrt{x}$. ∎

EXAMPLE 2   Does the equation $5x^2 - 6xy + 5y^2 = 16$ implicitly define y as a single function of x? As several functions of x?

Solution   Figure 2 shows the graph, an ellipse. The points $(2, 2)$ and $(1, -1)$ are marked with bullets:

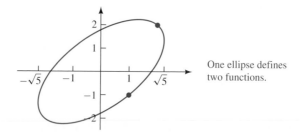

One ellipse defines two functions.

FIGURE 2
Graph of the equation $5x^2 - 6xy + 5y^2 = 16$

Like the preceding graph, this one defines two *different* functions y of x, corresponding to the upper and lower "halves" of the ellipse. (The upper and lower curves come together at the two points where the ellipse has *vertical* tangent lines.) ➡ The upper curve, passing through $(2, 2)$, defines a function g_1 for which $g_1(2) = 2$. The lower curve defines another function g_2, for which $g_2(1) = -1$. (In a moment we'll calculate derivatives at these points.) The domain of each function is the interval $[-\sqrt{5}, \sqrt{5}]$. Solving for y explicitly in terms of x is harder this time; we won't bother. ∎

Do you see these points? An exercise at the end of this section concerns finding them precisely.

Implicit functions, implicit derivatives   All three of the equations $6x + 2y = 10$, $x - y^2 = 0$, and $5x^2 - 6xy + 5y^2 = 16$ implicitly define one or more functions of x. How can we differentiate such functions?

If we can solve *explicitly* for y, there's no problem. For $x - y^2 = 0$, for instance, we get ➡

Recall: $\sqrt{x} = x^{1/2}$.

$$f_1(x) = \sqrt{x} \implies f_1'(x) = \frac{1}{2\sqrt{x}};$$

$$f_2(x) = -\sqrt{x} \implies f_2'(x) = -\frac{1}{2\sqrt{x}}.$$

What if we *can't* solve explicitly for y or don't want to take the trouble? In that case we use **implicit differentiation**; here's the idea for an equation in x and y:

Differentiate both sides of the equation, treating y as an (implicitly defined) function of x; use the chain rule. The resulting equation involves x, y, and dy/dx; it can (usually) be solved, if necessary, for dy/dx.

We'll illustrate the method with examples.

EXAMPLE 3   Let $x = y^2$. Find dy/dx by implicit differentiation.

Solution   We differentiate both sides of the equation, treating y as a function of x:

$$x = y^2 \implies \frac{d}{dx}(x) = \frac{d}{dx}(y^2) \implies 1 = 2y\frac{dy}{dx}.$$

Note the use of the chain rule in the last step: Because y is a function of x, we have $(y^2)' = 2yy'$. Solving the preceding equation for dy/dx is now easy:

$$1 = 2y\frac{dy}{dx} \implies \frac{dy}{dx} = \frac{1}{2y}.$$

We conclude that

$$y = \sqrt{x} \implies y' = \frac{1}{2y} = \frac{1}{2\sqrt{x}};$$

$$y = -\sqrt{x} \implies y' = \frac{1}{2y} = -\frac{1}{2\sqrt{x}},$$

which agrees with *both* of our earlier answers. ∎

EXAMPLE 4   Figure 2 shows that the equation $5x^2 - 6xy + 5y^2 = 16$ defines y implicitly as a function of x near the point $(2, 2)$. (Near $(2, 2)$ the graph is not vertical, and so a piece of the curve defines a function.) Find dy/dx in terms of x and y. What is its value at the point $(2, 2)$? At $(1, -1)$? What do these values mean geometrically?

Remember: y is a function of x, so the chain rule applies.

Solution   First we differentiate our equation with respect to x: ◄

$$5x^2 - 6xy + 5y^2 = 16 \implies 10x - 6y - 6x\frac{dy}{dx} + 10y\frac{dy}{dx} = 0.$$

(The middle term, $-6xy = -6x \cdot y$, is a product, so we used the product rule.) Now we solve for dy/dx:

$$10x - 6y - 6x\frac{dy}{dx} + 10y\frac{dy}{dx} = 0 \implies \frac{dy}{dx}(-6x + 10y) = 6y - 10x$$

$$\implies \frac{dy}{dx} = \frac{6y - 10x}{10y - 6x}.$$

Look at Figure 2 to check these claims.

At $(2, 2)$, therefore, $dy/dx = -1$; at $(1, -1)$, $dy/dx = 1$. Geometrically, these results mean that the curve shown has slopes -1 and 1, respectively, at the marked points $(2, 2)$ and $(1, -1)$. ◄   ∎

Implicit differentiation: pros and cons   Implicit differentiation avoids the hard problem of solving complicated equations explicitly for y. But convenience always comes at a price: derivative formulas obtained by implicit differentiation usually involve *both* x and y, not just x as with ordinary functions.

In this case implicit differentiation is a lot simpler than the explicit version.

EXAMPLE 5   Use implicit differentiation to find points on the unit circle $x^2 + y^2 = 1$ at which the tangent line has slope 1. Could the same results be found using ordinary derivatives?

Solution   Implicit differentiation with respect to x gives

$$x^2 + y^2 = 1 \implies 2x + 2y\frac{dy}{dx} = 0 \implies \frac{dy}{dx} = \frac{-x}{y}.$$

Thus, $dy/dx = 1$ if and only if $y = -x$, that is, where the line $y = -x$ intersects the unit circle. It's easy to see that these intersections occur at the points $(-\sqrt{2}/2, \sqrt{2}/2)$ and $(\sqrt{2}/2, -\sqrt{2}/2)$. (Draw your own picture to convince yourself.)

The same results can be found by "explicit differentiation," but at the cost of first solving for y in terms of x. In this case,

$$x^2 + y^2 = 1 \implies y = \pm\sqrt{1 - x^2}.$$

The functions $f_1(x) = \sqrt{1 - x^2}$ and $f_2(x) = -\sqrt{1 - x^2}$ describe the top and bottom halves of the unit circle, respectively, and their derivatives can be used to locate the same two points we found by implicit differentiation.   ∎

BASIC EXERCISES

1. This exercise refers to the equation $5x^2 - 6xy + 5y^2 = 16$ and its graph—see Examples 2 and 4.

  (a) Find the two points (x, y) on the ellipse at which the tangent line is horizontal.

  (b) Find the points (x, y) on the ellipse at which the tangent line is vertical. (At these points, the derivative dy/dx doesn't exist.)

2. This exercise refers to the equation $5x^2 - 6xy + 5y^2 = 16$ and its graph—see Examples 2 and 4.

  (a) The graph appears to be symmetric about the origin. To see that it really *is* symmetric, show that if (x_0, y_0) is on the graph, then so is the "opposite" point $(-x_0, -y_0)$.

  (b) Let (x_0, y_0) be any point on the graph. The previous part says that the "opposite" point is $(-x_0, -y_0)$. Show that the tangent lines at these two points have the same slope. (This is further evidence of the graph's symmetry.)

  (c) The line $y = -x$ intersects the ellipse at two points. Find these two points and evaluate dy/dx at each.

3. The equation $2x + 3y = 6$ implicitly defines y as a function of x.

  (a) By solving for y, find an *explicit* formula for y as a function of x. Use the result to find dy/dx.

  (b) Find dy/dx by implicit differentiation; compare your result with the previous part.

4. The equation $4x^2y - 3y = x^3$ implicitly defines y as a function of x.

    (a) Use implicit differentiation to find dy/dx.

    (b) Write y as an explicit function of x and compute dy/dx directly.

5. The equation $x^2 + y^2 = 16$ defines *two* different functions of x:

$$x^2 + y^2 = 16 \Longrightarrow y = \pm\sqrt{16 - x^2}.$$

    (a) Find dy/dx by implicit differentiation.

    (b) Find dy/dx (directly) for each of the functions $y = \pm\sqrt{16 - x^2}$. Compare your results with those found in part (a).

6. This exercise is about the equation $y^2 - x^2 = 1$ and its graph, called a **hyperbola**.

    (a) The equation $y^2 - x^2 = 1$ defines two different functions $y = f_1(x)$ and $y = f_2(x)$. Find formulas for these functions.

    (b) Plot the equation $y^2 - x^2 = 1$.
[HINT: One way is to plot both functions f_1 and f_2.]

    (c) Use implicit differentiation to find dy/dx.

    (d) Find the points on the curve $y^2 - x^2 = 1$ at which the tangent line is horizontal.

    (e) For any constant $c > 0$, the line $x = c$ intersects the hyperbola at two points. Find these two points and the slope of the hyperbola at each.

7. Repeat the previous exercise, but use the hyperbola $y^2 - 2x^2 = 1$.

8. The equation $x^5 + xy^3 + x^2y + y^5 = 32$ implicitly defines a curve. What is the slope of this curve at the point $(0, 2)$?

FURTHER EXERCISES

Exercises 9–14 refer to the curves with equations $x^2 + xy + y^2 = 1$ and $x^2 - xy + y^2 = 1$, shown below.

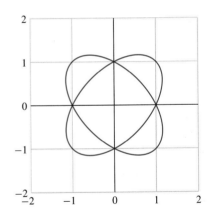

  9. Find dy/dx for each of the curves.

10. Decide which curve is which. [HINT: One way is to compare the derivatives at a common point, such as $(0, 1)$.]

11. Draw tangent lines to the curves at the four intersection points. Find the slope of each one.

12. Find and label all points at which each curve is horizontal.

13. Find and label all points at which each curve is vertical.

14. Add the line $y = x$ to the picture. Use derivatives to show that this line intersects both curves perpendicularly.

Each of the equations in Exercises 15–18 defines a curve in the xy-plane. For each equation

    (a) *Draw the curve that is implicitly defined by the equation.*

    (b) *Use implicit differentiation to find a formula for dy/dx.*

15. $x^2 + 2y^2 = 4$

16. $4x^2 - 9y^2 = 36$

17. $y^2 - x^2 = x^2y^2$

18. $y^2(2 - x) = x^3$

In Exercises 19–22, find an equation of the line tangent to the curve defined by the equation at the specified point.

19. $x^3 + y^3 = 4xy$; $(2, 2)$

20. $x^{2/3} + y^{2/3} = 2$; $(1, 1)$

21. $2\left(x^2 + y^2\right)^2 = 25xy$; $(1, 2)$

22. $\left(x^2 + y^2\right)^2 = 4x^2y$; $(-1, 1)$

23. Plot the curve defined by the equation $y^2 = x^3$ and find equations of the *two* lines tangent to the curve at $x = 1$.

24. Plot the curve defined by the equation $y^4 = 4y^2 - x^2$ and find equations of the *four* lines tangent to the curve at $x = 1$.

25. The equation $y = x + \cos(xy)$ implicitly defines y as a function of x near the point $(0, 1)$. Use this fact to estimate $y(0.025)$.

26. The square root function is implicitly defined by the equation $x = y^2$. Use implicit differentiation to show that $y'(x) = 1/(2\sqrt{x})$.

27. The natural logarithm function is implicitly defined by the equation $x = e^y$. Use implicit differentiation to show that $y'(x) = 1/x$.

In Exercises 28–30, use implicit differentiation to verify that the equation implicitly defines a solution of the differential equation.

28. $x^2 + y^2 = C$ $(C > 0)$; $y' + x/y = 0$

29. $y^2 = 1 + Ce^{-2x}$; $y(y' + y) = 1$

30. $\ln|y| + \frac{1}{2}y^2 = t + C$; $y' = y/(1 + y^2)$

3.4 INVERSE FUNCTIONS AND THEIR DERIVATIVES; INVERSE TRIGONOMETRIC FUNCTIONS

This section completes our main catalog of standard elementary functions and their derivatives. (Hyperbolic functions are treated in an Interlude.) The section appears here because we apply implicit differentiation to find the derivatives. Some instructors may prefer to defer treatment until Calculus II; for their convenience we reprint this section in Volume II.

We've seen in earlier sections how to find derivatives of new functions built from old. In this section we study how new functions can be produced by *inverting* old ones, and how to find derivatives of the new functions. The arcsine, arccosine, and arctangent functions—inverses of the standard trigonometric functions—are our most important examples.

Identities and inverses

The discussion of composition hints at the abstract ideas of operations, identities, and inverses. Math students, at least, will have seen these ideas at least informally, and will see them again in later courses.

The number 0 is an **identity** for ordinary addition because $a + 0 = a$ for all numbers a. Similarly, the number 1 is an identity for multiplication because $a \cdot 1 = a$ for all numbers a. A similar notion of "identity" applies to function composition, but in this setting the appropriate identity is a *function*:

> **DEFINITION**   The **identity function** I is defined by $I(x) = x$.

To see why I deserves the name "identity," let f be *any* real-valued function. Then, for any input x,

$$(f \circ I)(x) = f(I(x)) = f(x) \quad \text{and} \quad (I \circ f)(x) = I(f(x)) = f(x).$$

Thus, composing any function f with I (in either order) gives f.

Inversion can be thought of as an operation on functions; in machine terms, it amounts to running the function machine in reverse.

Inverse functions   The word "inverse" has several different (but related) meanings in mathematics. For instance, 3 and -3 are additive inverses because their *sum* is 0 (the additive identity), while 3 and $1/3$ are multiplicative inverses because their *product* is the multiplicative identity. Two *functions* are inverses if their *composition* is the identity function:

> **DEFINITION (Inverse functions)**   Let f and g be functions. If
> $$(f \circ g)(x) = x \quad \text{and} \quad (g \circ f)(x) = x$$
> for all x in the domains of g and f, respectively, then f and g are **inverse functions**. In this case, we write $g = f^{-1}$ (and $f = g^{-1}$).

Beware: $f^{-1}(x) \neq 1/f(x)$.

In particular, the inverse of a function f is another function f^{-1}, one that "undoes" the effect of f. ◄ Example 1 illustrates the idea.

h adds 3; h^{-1} takes 3 away.

EXAMPLE 1   If $h(x) = x + 3$, then $h^{-1}(x) = x - 3$. ◄ For any input x,
$$(h^{-1} \circ h)(x) = h^{-1}(x + 3) = (x + 3) - 3 = x = I(x);$$
$$(h \circ h^{-1})(x) = h(x - 3) = (x - 3) + 3 = x = I(x).$$
Thus, $h^{-1} \circ h = I = h \circ h^{-1}$, and so h and h^{-1} are indeed inverses.   ■

We met these functions in Sections 1.3 and 2.6.

Famous inverses: logs and exponentials   We've already studied the most important pair of inverse functions: logarithmic and exponential functions. ◄ Indeed, we *defined* logarithms as inverses of exponentials. In base e, for instance, we've seen that

$$e^{\ln x} = x \quad \text{if } x > 0; \quad \ln(e^x) = x \quad \text{for all real } x;$$

similar identities hold for other bases.

EXAMPLE 2 The functions $f(x) = 10^x$ and $g(x) = \log_{10} x$ are inverses. What does this mean when $x = 2$?

Solution Because $f(2) = 10^2 = 100$, we must have $g(100) = \log_{10} 100 = 2$. Similarly, $g(2) = \log_{10} 2 \approx 0.30103$; the inverse relationship means $f(0.30103) = 10^{0.30103} \approx 2$. �']■

Your calculator "knows" these numerical facts.

Inverse functions and symmetry If f and f^{-1} are inverse functions, then $f(a) = b \iff f^{-1}(b) = a$ for every a in the domain of f. This condition has a nice graphical meaning:

Geometric reflection is a nice way of thinking about inversion, and it appeals to students' visual intuition — which is usually stronger than their symbolic intuition.

   A point (a, b) lies on the graph of f if and only if (b, a) lies on the graph of f^{-1}.

Note that (b, a) and (a, b) are reflections of each other across the line $y = x$, as are the graphs of f and f^{-1}. Figure 1 illustrates this symmetry.

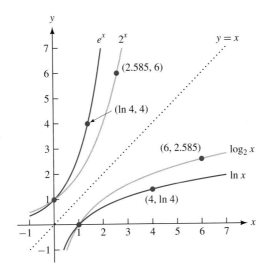

FIGURE 1
Logarithmic and exponential functions: inverses

Notice especially the three marked pairs of points: they reflect (literally!) the facts that 2^x and $\log_2 x$ are inverse functions, as are e^x and $\ln x$.

Formulas for inverse functions If a function f happens to have a simple algebraic formula, then f^{-1} may have one, too, and we may be able to find it algebraically. Here is the key idea:

   If f and f^{-1} are inverses, then $y = f^{-1}(x) \iff x = f(y)$.

Therefore, to find a formula for $f^{-1}(x)$ we can try to solve the equation $x = f(y)$ for y in terms of x. Doing so is hard for some functions but easy for others.

EXAMPLE 3 Let $f(x) = 2x + 3$. Find a formula for $f^{-1}(x)$.

Solution We solve $x = f(y)$ for y:

$$x = f(y) = 2y + 3 \implies x - 3 = 2y \implies \frac{x-3}{2} = y = f^{-1}(x).$$

The graphs of $y = 2x + 3$ and $y = (x - 3)/2$ have the expected symmetry across the line $y = x$. ➡ Notice, too, that the inverse of a linear function is linear; reflecting a line produces a new line. ■

Draw them for yourself.

Figure 2 contains all the main ideas of the inverse function theorem; it's worth a close look.

Derivatives of inverse functions

How are derivatives of f and f^{-1} related to each other? Figure 2 suggests the answer.

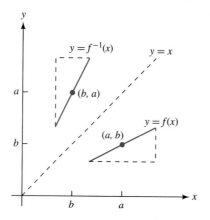

The segments through (a, b) and (b, a) have reciprocal slopes. Compare rises and runs to see why.

FIGURE 2
Comparing derivatives of f and f^{-1}

The picture shows tiny pieces of the graphs of f and f^{-1}. (The pieces look like straight lines because f is differentiable at $x = a$.) The reflective symmetry also shows that the *slopes* $f'(a)$ and $f^{-1'}(b)$ of the two pieces are *reciprocals*—the rise in one is the run in the other, and vice versa. We summarize these observations in a form we'll use later:

THEOREM 5 (Derivatives of inverse functions) Let f and g be inverse functions, and suppose $f(a) = b$. If $f'(a)$ exists and $f'(a) \neq 0$, then $g'(b)$ also exists, and $g'(b) = 1/f'(a)$. More generally,

$$g'(x) = \frac{1}{f'\big(g(x)\big)}$$

whenever the right side makes sense.

EXAMPLE 4 In Example 3 we found that $f(x) = 2x + 3$ and $g(x) = (x - 3)/2$ are inverses. It's easy to find $g'(x)$ directly, but what does Theorem 5 say?

Solution By Theorem 5, $g'(x) = 1/f'(g(x))$. But $f'(x) = 2$ for *all* inputs x, so $g'(x) = 1/2$. ∎

Of course, we could have differentiated $g(x) = (x - 2)/3$ at a glance. We'll apply Theorem 5 more impressively later in this section.

Which functions have inverses?

Does every number have an additive inverse? A multiplicative inverse?

Not every function *has* an inverse. ◂ For instance, no constant function $f(x) = k$ has an inverse because for *any* function g and any input x,

$$(f \circ g)(x) = f\big(g(x)\big) = k.$$

Thus $f \circ g$ is *still* a constant function—not the identity function.

So which functions *do* have inverses? One way to decide is to think graphically: If f has an inverse, then reflecting the curve $y = f(x)$ across the line $y = x$ should produce a new *function graph*, not just a new curve.

Questions of domain restriction are slightly subtle; many students find them mysterious. Fortunately, such questions arise infrequently in practice.

EXAMPLE 5 Does $f(x) = x^2$ have an inverse? How are square roots involved?

Solution Figure 3 shows the curves $y = x^2$ and $x = y^2$; the second is the result of reflecting the first about $y = x$.

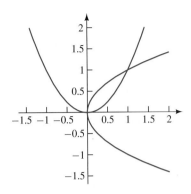

FIGURE 3
The curves $x = y^2$ and $y = x^2$

There's an important difference between the two curves: The rightward-opening parabola $x = y^2$ is *not* the graph of a function because each positive x-value corresponds to *two* different y-values. Indeed, solving $x = y^2$ algebraically for y gives *two* possible inverse functions: $y = \sqrt{x}$ and $y = -\sqrt{x}$.

Is one of these functions the "true" inverse? No—as the figure shows, $y = \sqrt{x}$ (the *upper* half of the curve $x = y^2$) and $y = -\sqrt{x}$ (the *lower* half) are, respectively, the reflections across $y = x$ of the *right* and *left* halves of the original parabola $y = x^2$. Informally speaking, $y = \sqrt{x}$ is an inverse for the "right half" of $y = x^2$, and $y = -\sqrt{x}$ is an inverse for the "left half." More formally, $y = \sqrt{x}$ is an inverse for the function $f(x) = x^2$ when we "restrict the domain" of f to nonnegative inputs. ➡   ■   *A similar description applies to $y = -\sqrt{x}$.*

One-to-one functions; restricting domains Example 5 illustrates a more general point: For a function $y = f(x)$ to have an inverse, each output y can come from only *one* input x. This condition has an official name:

> *A function f is **one-to-one** if different inputs to f give different outputs. Equivalently, $x_1 \neq x_2 \implies f(x_1) \neq f(x_2)$.*

This condition, stated graphically, is the **horizontal line test** of precalculus fame:

> *No horizontal line crosses the f-graph more than once.*

The *full* curve $y = x^2$ in Example 5 fails this test—which is why we had trouble choosing among possible inverse functions. But the right and left halves of the curve $y = x^2$ (with $x > 0$ and $x < 0$, respectively) pass the test, and so let us choose inverse functions unambiguously. A useful trick, in other words, is to **restrict the domain** of f to an interval I (perhaps infinite) on which f *is* one-to-one. The restricted function then *has* an inverse; the following Fact gives the fine print:

> **FACT** Suppose that f is one-to-one on an interval I. Then f (with domain restricted to I) has an inverse function f^{-1}, and the graphs of f and f^{-1} are reflections of each other across $y = x$.

Inverse trigonometric functions

One advantage of the "arc" form is that it avoids the possible confusion with multiplicative inverses.

Like the squaring function, the sine, cosine, tangent, and other basic trigonometric functions need their domains restricted to become one-to-one. With this taken care of, the trigonometric functions have well-behaved inverses—some rate their own buttons on scientific calculators.

Don't confuse $\sin^{-1} x$ with $1/\sin x$.

"Arc" and "inverse" notations   Two standard notations are used for inverse trigonometric functions: $\arcsin x$, $\arccos x$, and $\arctan x$ are synonyms for $\sin^{-1} x$, $\cos^{-1} x$, and $\tan^{-1} x$. ◄ We'll use both forms as convenient; the "arc" version reminds us of angles and the unit circle, while "inverse" recalls function inversion.

Domain surgery   Trigonometric functions are far from one-to-one on their full natural domains. Because they repeat themselves endlessly on intervals of length 2π, their graphs fail the horizontal line test *miserably*. (The x-axis, for instance, intersects the sine curve infinitely often.)

Many students find the domain restrictions more mysterious than other parts of the definitions.

We'll *make* the trigonometric functions one-to-one through the same "surgical" strategy we applied to the squaring function: amputate the offending part of each function's domain. Graphs will show us where to cut.

Inverting sines and cosines   The sine function is one-to-one on the interval $[-\pi/2, \pi/2]$. (We could have chosen other intervals, but this one, centered at 0, seems natural.) Figure 4(a) shows the sine curve with the part corresponding to $[-\pi/2, \pi/2]$ highlighted. Figure 4(b) shows both the (restricted) sine function and its inverse, the **arcsine** function, which is defined formally below.

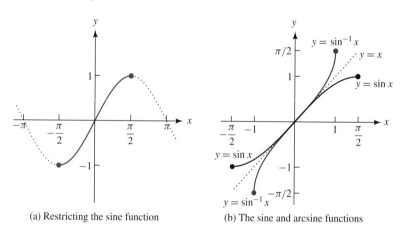

(a) Restricting the sine function   (b) The sine and arcsine functions

FIGURE 4
Constructing the arcsine

DEFINITION   For x in $[-1, 1]$, $y = \sin^{-1} x$ (or $\arcsin x$) is defined by the conditions

$$\text{(i)} \quad x = \sin y; \quad \text{(ii)} \quad -\frac{\pi}{2} \le y \le \frac{\pi}{2}.$$

In words: $\arcsin x$ is the angle between $-\pi/2$ and $\pi/2$ whose sine is x.

Restricting $\cos x$ to $[-\pi/2, \pi/2]$ wouldn't work. Do you see why not?

The **arccosine** is found in a similar way. The cosine function is one-to-one if restricted to the interval $[0, \pi]$. ◄ Reflecting this part of the cosine graph across the line $y = x$ produces the arccosine: graphs (Figure 5) and a definition follow.

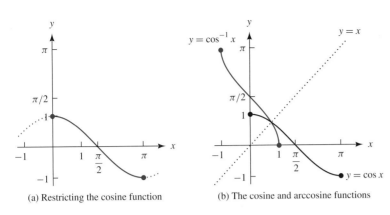

(a) Restricting the cosine function   (b) The cosine and arccosine functions

FIGURE 5
Constructing the arccosine

DEFINITION For x in $[-1, 1]$, $y = \cos^{-1} x$ (or arccos x) is defined by the conditions

(i) $x = \cos y$;   (ii) $0 \le y \le \pi$.

In words: arccos x is the angle between 0 and π whose cosine is x.

Inverting the tangent function   The ordinary tangent function becomes one-to-one if restricted to any of its "branches." We'll use the "middle" branch, through the origin; reflecting it across the line $y = x$ produces the **arctangent** function. Graphs (Figure 6) and a formal definition follow.

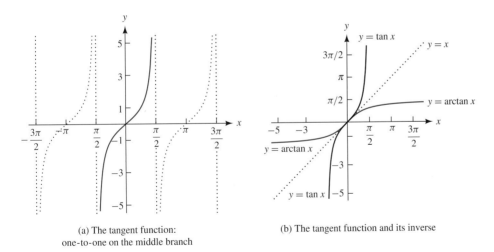

(a) The tangent function:
one-to-one on the middle branch

(b) The tangent function and its inverse

FIGURE 6
Constructing the arctangent

DEFINITION Let x be any real number. Then $y = \tan^{-1} x$ (or $y = \arctan x$) means that

(i) $x = \tan y$;   (ii) $-\pi/2 < y < \pi/2$.

Notice, in particular, that although the (restricted) tangent function has a small domain, its range is the *full* set of real numbers. Therefore, the arctangent function has range $(-\pi/2, \pi/2)$ but accepts *all* real numbers as inputs.

Domains and ranges: take care ...   The most obvious property of inverse trigonometric functions is that they "undo" trigonometric functions. A little trickier—but important for using these functions successfully—is keeping careful track of domains and ranges. A table might help (the ordinary trigonometric functions have restricted domains).

Function	sine	arcsine	cosine	arccosine	tangent	arctangent
Domain	$[-\pi/2, \pi/2]$	$[-1, 1]$	$[0, \pi]$	$[-1, 1]$	$(-\pi/2, \pi/2)$	$(-\infty, \infty)$
Range	$[-1, 1]$	$[-\pi/2, \pi/2]$	$[-1, 1]$	$[0, \pi]$	$(-\infty, \infty)$	$(-\pi/2, \pi/2)$

We include these less important functions mainly for completeness.

Other inverse trigonometric functions   All six trigonometric functions *have* inverses, but $\operatorname{arcsec} x$, $\operatorname{arccsc} x$, and $\operatorname{arccot} x$ are seldom seen in calculus courses. We'll content ourselves here with a few words about the arcsecant function.

The simplest definition of $\operatorname{arcsec} x$ starts with the connection between secants and cosines: $\sec t = 1/\cos t$ (unless $\cos x = 0$). So it's no surprise to find a related connection between the "arc" versions of both functions:

> **DEFINITION**   For any x with $|x| \ge 1$, $\operatorname{arcsec} x = \sec^{-1} x = \cos^{-1}(1/x)$.

Note that the definition does what we'd expect of an inverse function—if $y = \operatorname{arcsec} x = \arccos(1/x)$, then

$$\sec y = \frac{1}{\cos y} = \frac{1}{\cos(\arccos(1/x))} = \frac{1}{1/x} = x.$$

Figure 7 shows the secant and arcsecant functions; the dotted lines are asymptotes.

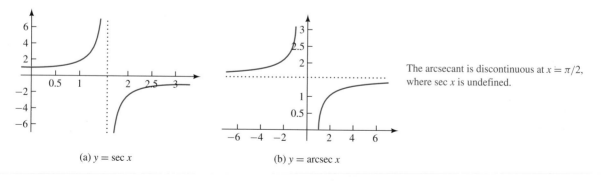

(a) $y = \sec x$

(b) $y = \operatorname{arcsec} x$

The arcsecant is discontinuous at $x = \pi/2$, where $\sec x$ is undefined.

FIGURE 7
The (restricted) secant and arcsecant functions

Working with inverse trigonometric functions

Inverse and ordinary trigonometric functions often tangle together to produce expressions like these:

$$\sin\left(\sin^{-1} x\right); \quad \cos\left(\sin^{-1} x\right); \quad \sin\left(\tan^{-1} x\right).$$

Diagrams like those in Figure 8 can help us untangle such expressions.

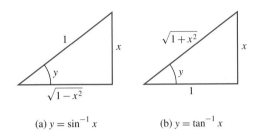

(a) $y = \sin^{-1} x$ (b) $y = \tan^{-1} x$

FIGURE 8
Relating inverse trigonometric functions

In the left-hand figure, the angle labeled y is the arcsine of x (because $\sin y = x$). The figure shows (among other things) that

$$\cos(\sin^{-1} x) = \frac{\text{adjacent}}{\text{hypotenuse}} = \sqrt{1 - x^2}.$$

In the second figure, $y = \tan^{-1} x$ (because $\tan y = x$), so

$$\sin(\tan^{-1} x) = \frac{\text{opposite}}{\text{hypotenuse}} = \frac{x}{\sqrt{1 + x^2}}.$$

Note that these equations hold only for values of x in the domains of the functions in question.

Derivatives   Ordinary trigonometric functions have trigonometric derivatives. It's a little surprising, then, that inverse trigonometric functions have *algebraic* derivatives. To find these derivatives we can use Theorem 5, the chain rule, or implicit differentiation. We'll first list the derivative formulas and then give comments, examples, and proofs.

Function	arcsin x	arccos x	arctan x	arcsec x
Derivative	$\dfrac{1}{\sqrt{1-x^2}}$	$\dfrac{-1}{\sqrt{1-x^2}}$	$\dfrac{1}{1+x^2}$	$\dfrac{1}{|x|\sqrt{x^2-1}}$

Observe:

- **Domains**   The functions arcsin x, arccos x, and arcsec x are defined on limited domains; the same is true, naturally, of their derivatives. The arcsine function, for instance, has domain $[-1, 1]$; its derivative has the (slightly) smaller domain $(-1, 1)$. ➡

This section's exercises have more details on domains.

- **Not much difference**   The derivatives of arcsin x and arccos x differ only by a sign, so $(\arcsin x + \arccos x)' = 0$ for all legal inputs x. This is no accident—

for all x in $[-1, 1]$,

$$\arcsin x + \arccos x = \frac{\pi}{2}.$$

Plot both graphs on the same axes to see how.

(The graphs of $\arcsin x$ and $\arccos x$ convey the same information.) ◄

• **Graphical evidence**   We'll show symbolically *why* these formulas hold, but graphs give immediate evidence *that* they hold. For instance, Figure 9 shows graphs of the arctangent function and its claimed derivative.

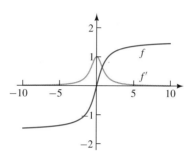

F I G U R E 9
$f(x) = \arctan x$ **and** $f'(x) = \frac{1}{1+x^2}$

The underlying ideas are similar in each case.

Proving the formulas   The derivative formulas can be proved in several different ways. ◄ We illustrate two calculations by example. The remaining derivatives of inverse trigonometric functions can be found in similar ways.

E X A M P L E 6   Use Theorem 5 to differentiate the arcsine function.

Solution   Applying Theorem 5 with $g(x) = \arcsin x$ and $f(x) = \sin x$ gives

$$(\arcsin x)' = \frac{1}{\cos(\arcsin x)} = \frac{1}{\sqrt{1 - x^2}};$$

the last equation follows from a calculation related to Figure 8.   ■

E X A M P L E 7   Use implicit differentiation to differentiate the arctangent function.

Solution   If $y = \arctan x$, then $x = \tan y$. Differentiating this equation implicitly with respect to x gives

$$1 = \sec^2 y \frac{dy}{dx}, \quad \text{or} \quad \frac{dy}{dx} = \frac{1}{\sec^2(\arctan x)}.$$

The last expression *can* be simplified using the ideas near Figure 8. For variety, we'll use instead the trigonometric identity $\sec^2 t = 1 + \tan^2 t$:

$$\frac{1}{\sec^2(\arctan x)} = \frac{1}{1 + \tan^2(\arctan x)} = \frac{1}{1 + x^2}.$$

(We used the identity $\tan(\arctan x) = x$ in the last step.)   ■

B A S I C   E X E R C I S E S

In Exercises 1–6, find the number exactly (in radians).

1. $\arcsin(1)$

2. $\arcsin\left(\sqrt{3}/2\right)$

3. $\arccos(-1)$

4. $\arccos\left(-\sqrt{2}/2\right)$

5. $\arctan(1)$

6. $\arctan\left(\sqrt{3}\right)$

In Exercises 7–12, rewrite the given expression as an algebraic expression. For example, $\cos(\arcsin x) = \sqrt{1-x^2}$.

7. $\sin(\arccos x)$

8. $\tan(\arcsin x)$

9. $\cos(\arctan x)$

10. $\arcsin(\tan x)$

11. $\cos\left(\arctan(2x)\right)$

12. $\sin\left(\arctan(2x)\right)$

In Exercises 13–24, find $f'(x)$.

13. $f(x) = \arctan(2x)$

14. $f(x) = \arctan(x^2)$

15. $f(x) = \sqrt{\arcsin x}$

16. $f(x) = \arcsin(\sqrt{x})$

17. $f(x) = \arcsin(e^x)$

18. $f(x) = e^{\arctan x}$

19. $f(x) = \arctan(\ln x)$

20. $f(x) = \arccos(2x+3)$

21. $f(x) = \operatorname{arcsec}(x/2)$

22. $f(x) = \arcsin x / \arccos x$

23. $f(x) = x^2 \arctan(\sqrt{x})$

24. $f(x) = \ln(2 + \arcsin x)$

25. Find four values of x for which $\cos x = 1/2$.

26. Use a calculator to find four values of x (two positive, two negative) for which $\tan x = 2$.

27. Suppose that the point $(-3, 5)$ is on the graph of f. Find a point on the graph of f^{-1}.

28. Suppose that $f^{-1}(2) = 3$. Find a point on the graph of f.

FURTHER EXERCISES

Let f and g be inverse functions, both defined for all x. In Exercises 29–32, explain briefly why the statement is true.

29. If f has a horizontal asymptote, then g has a vertical asymptote.

30. If $f'(x) > 0$ for all x, then $g'(x) > 0$ for all x. [HINT: Use Theorem 5, page 184.]

31. If $f'(x) < 0$ for all x, then $g'(x) < 0$ for all x.

32. If $f'(1) = 0$ and $g(3) = 1$, then $g'(3)$ is undefined.

In Exercises 33–36, $f(x) = a + bx$, where a and b are any constants, $b \neq 0$.

33. Explain why f has an inverse function g.

34. Does f have an inverse function g if $b = 0$? Justify your answer.

35. Find a formula for the inverse function $g(x) = f^{-1}(x)$.

36. Let $g(x) = f^{-1}(x)$. Find formulas for f' and g'. Are the answers consistent with Theorem 5, page 184?

The equation $\arcsin(\sin x) = x$ *suggests that the graph of* $y = \arcsin(\sin x)$, *over any interval, might be the straight line* $y = x$. *It isn't (see below). Exercises 37–39 explore this fact.*

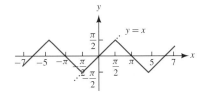

37. Explain why $\arcsin(\sin 5) \neq 5$.

38. For which values of x *does* the equation $\arcsin(\sin x) = x$ hold?

39. Let $f(x) = \arcsin(\sin x)$. Show that $f'(x) = \dfrac{\cos x}{|\cos x|}$.

40. What is the domain of the derivative of the arcsine function? Give a geometric explanation for why it is not the same as the domain of the arcsine function.

41. What is the domain of the derivative of the arctangent function? Is it the same as the domain of the arctangent function?

42. What is the domain of the derivative of the arcsecant function? Is it the same as the domain of the arcsecant function?

43. Let $f(x) = \arctan x$.
  (a) Plot graphs of f and f' on the same axes.
  (b) How is the fact that the tangent function has vertical asymptotes at $x = \pm\pi/2$ reflected in the graph of the arctangent function?
  (c) Is f even, odd, or neither?
  (d) Show that f is increasing on $(-\infty, \infty)$. How does the graph of f' reflect this fact?
  (e) Where is f concave up? Concave down? Does f have any inflection points? If so, where?

44. Let $f(x) = \arcsin x$.
  (a) Plot graphs of f and f' on the same axes.
  (b) Is f even, odd, or neither?
  (c) Show that f is increasing on $(-1, 1)$. How does the graph of f' reflect this fact?
  (d) Where is f concave up? Concave down? Does f have any inflection points? If so, where?

45. Let $f(x) = \arccos x$.
  (a) Plot graphs of f and f' on the same axes.
  (b) Is f even, odd, or neither?

(c) Show that f is decreasing on $(-1, 1)$. How does the graph of f' reflect this fact?

(d) Where is f concave up? Concave down? Does f have any inflection points? If so, where are they located?

46. (a) The function $\operatorname{arcsec} x$ accepts as inputs only values of x for which $|x| \geq 1$. Why is this restriction necessary? [HINT: What's the domain of $\arccos x$?]

(b) What's the *range* of $\operatorname{arcsec} x$? [HINT: What's the range of $\arccos x$?]

47. Let $f(x) = \operatorname{arcsec} x$.

(a) Plot graphs of f and f' using the plotting window $[-5, 5] \times [0, 5]$. [NOTE: If your calculator or computer doesn't recognize the arcsecant function, trick it by plotting $\arccos(1/x)$ instead.]

(b) Is f even, odd, or neither?

(c) Show that f is increasing everywhere in the interior of its domain. How does the graph of f' reflect this fact?

(d) Where is f concave up? Concave down? Does f have any inflection points? If so, where are they located?

48. (a) By drawing an appropriately labeled right triangle, show that $\arctan x + \arctan(1/x) = \pi/2$ if $x > 0$.

(b) Use calculus to show that $\arctan x + \arctan(1/x) = \pi/2$ for all $x > 0$. [HINT: Start by differentiating both sides of the equation.]

(c) Find an equation similar to the one in part (a) that is valid if $x < 0$.

Use calculus to prove the identities in Exercises 49–53. [HINT: Start by showing that the derivative of the expression on the left is equal to the derivative of the expression on the right.]

49. $\arcsin(-x) = -\arcsin(x)$

50. $\arccos(-x) = \pi - \arccos(x)$

51. $\arccos x = \pi/2 - \arcsin x$

52. $\arctan\left(x/\sqrt{1-x^2}\right) = \arcsin x$

53. $\arcsin\left(\dfrac{x-1}{x+1}\right) = 2\arctan(\sqrt{x}) - \pi/2$

54. (a) Show that $2\arcsin x = \arccos(1 - 2x^2)$ if $0 \leq x \leq 1$.

(b) Find an identity similar to the one in part (a) that is valid if $-1 \leq x \leq 0$.

55. Let $f(x) = \arctan\left(\dfrac{1+x}{1-x}\right)$.

(a) Assume that $x < 1$. Show that there is a constant C such that $f(x) = C + \arctan x$.

(b) Use the result in part (a) to evaluate $\lim_{x\to 1^-} f(x)$.

(c) Evaluate $\lim_{x\to 1^+} f(x)$.

56. (a) Show that $\tan(\operatorname{arcsec} x) = \sqrt{x^2-1}$ if $x \geq 1$.

(b) Find an algebraic expression for $\tan(\operatorname{arcsec} x)$ if $x \leq -1$.

57. (a) Use the identity $\tan(x+y) = \dfrac{\tan x + \tan y}{1 - \tan x \tan y}$ to derive the identity

$$\arctan x + \arctan y = \arctan\left(\frac{x+y}{1-xy}\right).$$

[HINT: Start by writing $x = \arctan u$ and $y = \arctan v$.]

(b) What conditions must be satisfied by x and y for the identity derived in part (a) to hold?

58. (a) Use the identity in part (a) of the previous exercise to show that $\pi/4 = \arctan(1/2) + \arctan(1/3)$.

(b) Show that $\pi/4 = 2\arctan(1/4) + \arctan(7/23)$. [HINT: Use the identity in part (a) of the previous exercise twice.]

59. Show that $x/(1+x^2) \leq \arctan x \leq x$ for all $x \geq 0$.

3.5 MISCELLANEOUS DERIVATIVES AND ANTIDERIVATIVES

We use this brief section to reinforce derivative ideas and methods, to review the idea of an antiderivative, and to introduce some slightly more sophisticated methods. Students should be able to read the examples independently, so little class time should be needed.

Mix and match

In this chapter we've seen techniques for differentiating functions built up from simpler functions in various ways: sums, products, quotients, and compositions. In this section's examples and exercises we mix and match methods—and suggest a few new twists—to handle an even greater variety of functions.

EXAMPLE 1 Differentiate $f(x) = \sin(e^x \sin x)$.

Solution The function involves both a composition *and* a product, so both the chain and the product rules come into play:

$$f'(x) = \cos(e^x \sin x) \cdot (e^x \sin x)' = \cos(e^x \sin x) \cdot (e^x \sin x + e^x \cos x).$$

We could check the answer for plausibility by plotting.

The answer looks complicated, but so was f itself. ◄ ∎

EXAMPLE 2 Let f be a positive function (so that $\ln f(x)$ makes sense). Show that

$$(\ln f(x))' = \frac{f'(x)}{f(x)}.$$

Use the result to show that if f is *any* differentiable function, then

$$(\ln |f(x)|)' = \frac{f'(x)}{f(x)}$$

wherever $x \neq 0$.

Solution The chain rule and the fact that $(\ln x)' = 1/x$ give

$$(\ln f(x))' = \frac{1}{f(x)} f'(x) = \frac{f'(x)}{f(x)},$$

which is the first formula. To prove the second formula, note that if $f(x) > 0$, then $|f(x)| = f(x)$, which is the case we just proved. If $f(x) < 0$, then $|f(x)| = -f(x) > 0$, and the same formula, applied to $-f(x)$, gives

$$(\ln |f(x)|)' = \frac{-f'(x)}{-f(x)} = \frac{f'(x)}{f(x)},$$

exactly as before. ➤

■ *The argument is a bit fussy, but the bottom line is easy to remember.*

EXAMPLE 3 Apply the result of Example 2 to differentiate $\ln(e^{x+5})$.

Solution Note that $f(x) = e^{x+5} > 0$ for all x and that $f(x) = f'(x)$. Thus, $f'(x)/f(x) = 1$ for all x, so Example 2 implies that $(\ln e^{x+5})' = 1$ for all x. The simple answer is surprising, but only until we recall that the natural log and exponential functions are inverses, which implies that $\ln(e^{x+5}) = x + 5$. ■

EXAMPLE 4 Consider a function f of the form $f = f_1 f_2 f_3 f_4$, where f_1 through f_4 are all positive functions. Find a formula for f' in terms of the derivatives f_1' through f_4'. Is there a pretty pattern?

Solution We *could* use the product rule, but with four factors the job might be tricky. A slicker strategy, called **logarithmic differentiation**, uses a logarithmic function to trade the product for a sum: ➤

$$\ln f = \ln f_1 + \ln f_2 + \ln f_3 + \ln f_4.$$

All the logs make sense because the functions are positive.

Example 2 says that $(\ln f)' = f'/f$; differentiating both sides of the preceding equation gives

$$\frac{f'}{f} = \frac{f_1'}{f_1} + \frac{f_2'}{f_2} + \frac{f_3'}{f_3} + \frac{f_4'}{f_4}.$$

Multiplying through by f gives

$$f' = (f_1 f_2 f_3 f_4)' = f_1 f_2 f_3 f_4 \left(\frac{f_1'}{f_1} + \frac{f_2'}{f_2} + \frac{f_3'}{f_3} + \frac{f_4'}{f_4} \right),$$

a pleasing pattern indeed. ■

Finding antiderivatives: guess and check

Techniques from this chapter let us find *derivatives*, even of quite complicated functions, relatively easily. The reverse problem, finding *antiderivatives*, is often much harder; we'll

As the examples illustrate, an initial guess may need minor fixing—perhaps with constants—before becoming precisely correct.

revisit it in later chapters. In the meantime, *guessing* antiderivative formulas—and then checking them by differentiation—is often an effective technique. It can also be a nice exercise in creative pattern recognition.

EXAMPLE 5 Finding an antiderivative from scratch for $\tan x$ isn't easy. Exhausted from searching, you fall uneasily asleep and awake later with a clear but dreamy memory of the function $\ln|\sec x|$. Was it a good dream or a cruel illusion?

Solution Example 2 lets us check:

$$(\ln|\sec x|)' = \frac{\sec x \tan x}{\sec x} = \tan x$$

It was a good dream. ■

EXAMPLE 6 Guess antiderivatives for the functions

$$f(x) = x^2 \cos x + 2x \sin x \quad \text{and} \quad g(x) = \frac{x \cos x - \sin x}{x^2}.$$

Check your guesses by differentiation.

Solution The basic forms of f and g suggest the results of applying the product and quotient rules, respectively. With this in mind, it's natural to guess

$$F(x) = x^2 \sin x + C \quad \text{and} \quad G(x) = \frac{\sin x}{x} + C$$

In each function, C stands for any constant.

as possible antiderivatives. ◄ With the product and quotient rules, it's easy to check our guesses:

$$F'(x) = (x^2 \sin x)' = x^2 \cos x + 2x \sin x;$$
$$G'(x) = \left(\frac{\sin x}{x} \right)' = \frac{x \cos x - \sin x}{x^2},$$

just as we hoped. ■

EXAMPLE 7 Antidifferentiate $f(x) = x \cos(x^2)$.

Solution The basic form of f suggests the result of applying the chain rule, perhaps to the expression $\sin(x^2)$. A check shows that our guess is *almost* correct:

$$\left(\sin(x^2) \right)' = \cos(x^2) \cdot 2x = 2x \cos(x^2).$$

To dispose of that extra factor of 2, we simply divide it out. It follows easily that, for any constant C,

$$F(x) = \frac{\sin(x^2)}{2} + C$$

is an antiderivative of f. ■

EXAMPLE 8 Antidifferentiate $\dfrac{1}{1 + 4x^2}$.

Solution The general form of the function brings the arctangent to mind, but what about that pesky 4? One tactic is to start with the function $\arctan(ax)$, where a is a constant still to be chosen. A calculation with the chain rule gives

$$(\arctan(ax))' = \frac{1}{1 + (ax)^2} \cdot a = \frac{a}{1 + a^2 x^2}.$$

Setting $a = 2$ puts the 4 in the right place:

$$(\arctan(2x))' = \frac{2}{1 + 4x^2}.$$

To remove the extra factor 2 on the right, we just divide our guess by 2 to find $\arctan(2x)/2 + C$ as the desired antiderivative. ∎

BASIC EXERCISES

In Exercises 1–61, find the derivative of the function.

1. $H(z) = e^z \cos z$

2. $w(t) = \ln(1 + t^2)$

3. $r(\theta) = \tan(3\theta)$

4. $T(u) = \dfrac{u}{\sqrt{1 + u^2}}$

5. $G(w) = w^2 e^{3w}$

6. $h(z) = \ln(\pi \sin(e^z))$

7. $W(u) = e^{u^2} \tan(\sqrt[3]{u})$

8. $f(x) = \dfrac{x^{2/3} + \ln x}{e^x \cos(4x)}$

9. $g(z) = (z^2 + 3)e^z$

10. $P(t) = \dfrac{1 - t^2}{3 + t^4}$

11. $f(w) = 3\cos(w^2)$

12. $T(\theta) = \sin(2\theta)$

13. $R(w) = w^3 \cos(4w)$

14. $A(z) = z^{-4} \tan(3z)$

15. $f(x) = x \sin x$

16. $g(t) = \sqrt{1 + t^3 \cos t}$

17. $h(r) = e^{r^2 \sin r}$

18. $f(x) = xe^{2x}$

19. $f(x) = e^{-2/x}$

20. $f(x) = x^3 e^{-x^2}$

21. $f(x) = \sin(\sqrt{x})$

22. $f(x) = e^{-x} \cos(2x)$

23. $f(x) = \tan(2x + 3)$

24. $f(x) = \pi^3$

25. $f(x) = (e^{2x} - 3\ln x)^4$

26. $f(x) = \dfrac{x}{1 + x^2}$

27. $f(x) = \dfrac{\ln x}{\sqrt{2 + \cos x}}$

28. $f(x) = \dfrac{e^{2x}}{x \ln x}$

29. $f(x) = 2\sin(e^{3x})$

30. $f(x) = 3e^{\sin(2x)}$

31. $f(x) = \sin^3(e^{-4x})$

32. $f(x) = \tan^4(3x^2)$

33. $f(x) = \dfrac{\sin(x + 1)}{e^x + e^{-x}}$

34. $f(x) = (2x + \tan(3x))^{-1}$

35. $f(x) = e^{\pi} x^e$

36. $f(x) = \dfrac{(\log_{10} x)^3}{\tan x}$

37. $f(x) = 2^x \ln x$

38. $f(x) = (x + \cos x)^{\pi}$

39. $f(x) = \log_2(\sqrt[3]{xe^x})$

40. $f(x) = \ln\left(\sqrt{\dfrac{x(x + 2)}{x + 3}}\right)$

41. $f(x) = 4^{\sqrt{\ln x}}$

42. $f(x) = \cos^3(x^4)$

43. $f(x) = \ln(e^{3x} + \sin^2 x)$

44. $f(x) = \tan(e^{x^2})$

45. $f(x) = e^{\tan(x^2)}$

46. $f(x) = \sin^5(3x^4)$

47. $f(x) = \sqrt{4 + \cos^2(3x)}$

48. $f(x) = \sqrt[3]{\sin(4x^2)}$

49. $f(x) = \cos^2(e^{3x})$

50. $f(x) = x^2(4x^3 + 5)^6$

51. $f(x) = x \ln(2 + \sin(3x))$

52. $f(x) = e^{x^3} \cos(4x^5 + 2)$

53. $f(x) = \sin^2(x \cos x)$

54. $f(x) = \sqrt{3 + x \cos x}$

55. $f(x) = e^{x/\sin x}$

56. $f(x) = \tan\left(\dfrac{\ln x}{1+x^2}\right)$

57. $f(x) = \cos\left(\dfrac{e^{2x}}{3+4x}\right)$

58. $f(x) = x^2/\sin\left(e^x \ln x\right)$

59. $f(x) = \dfrac{\ln(1+e^x)}{2x+x^3}$

60. $f(x) = (2+\cos x)^x$

61. $f(x) = x^{\ln x}$

In Exercises 62–65, use the fact that $\left(\ln(f(x))\right)' = f'(x)/f(x)$ to find an antiderivative of f.

62. $f(x) = \dfrac{4x^3}{x^4+1}$

63. $f(x) = \dfrac{2x+3}{x^2+3x+5}$

64. $f(x) = \dfrac{e^x}{1+e^x}$

65. $f(x) = \dfrac{\cos x}{2+\sin x}$

In Exercises 66–78, find an antiderivative of the function f. (Guess and check.)

66. $f(x) = \dfrac{1}{1+x^2}$

67. $f(x) = \dfrac{1}{\sqrt{1-x^2}}$

68. $f(x) = \dfrac{2}{1+4x^2}$

69. $f(x) = \dfrac{3}{9+x^2}$

70. $f(x) = \dfrac{1}{\sqrt{9-x^2}}$

71. $f(x) = \dfrac{1}{\sqrt{1-4x^2}}$

72. $f(x) = \dfrac{e^x}{1+e^{2x}}$

73. $f(x) = \dfrac{x}{\sqrt{1-x^4}}$

74. $f(x) = \dfrac{(2\arctan x)}{1+x^2}$

75. $f(x) = \dfrac{(\cos x)}{1+\sin^2 x}$

76. $f(x) = \dfrac{e^{\arcsin x}}{\sqrt{1-x^2}}$

77. $f(x) = \dfrac{1}{x(1+(\ln x)^2)}$

78. $f(x) = \dfrac{1}{(1+x^2)\arctan x}$

Summary

Combinatorial rules   This chapter does just what its title suggests: it tells how to combine (known) derivatives of basic elementary functions to produce derivatives (and, sometimes, antiderivatives) of more complicated functions. The key "combinatorial" rules are the **product and quotient rules**, for algebraic combinations, and the **chain rule**, for functions built by composition. For differentiable functions u and v, the rules read as follows:

Product: $\left(u(x)v(x)\right)' = u(x)v'(x) + u'(x)v(x);$

Quotient: $\left(\dfrac{u(x)}{v(x)}\right)' = \dfrac{v(x)u'(x) - u(x)v'(x)}{v(x)^2};$

Chain: $\left(u\bigl(v(x)\bigr)\right)' = u'\bigl(v(x)\bigr) \cdot v'(x).$

The rules make it a routine (though sometimes messy) matter to find derivative formulas, even for symbolically complicated functions. The same rules apply, of course, if u or v or both are given by graphs or tables, but applying the rules in such cases takes extra care.

EXAMPLE 1   A function u is defined symbolically: $u(x) = x^2 - 4x + 4$. Another function, v, is known *only* by its graph. Figures 1(a) and (b) show both functions.

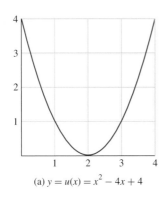
(a) $y = u(x) = x^2 - 4x + 4$

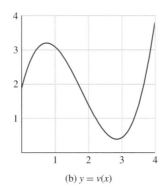
(b) $y = v(x)$

FIGURE 1
Graphs of u and v

Without a formula for v, we can hardly hope to find formulas for $(uv)'$, $(u/v)'$, and $(u \circ v)'$. But can we find, say, $(uv)'(1)$, $(u/v)'(1)$, and $(u \circ v)'(1)$? What *else* can we say about these derivatives?

Solution   The rules apply to u and v as to any other functions. Here's what they say about derivatives at $x = 1$:

$$(uv)'(1) = u(1)v'(1) + u'(1)v(1); \quad \left(\frac{u}{v}\right)' (1) = \frac{v(1)u'(1) - u(1)v'(1)}{v(1)^2};$$

$$(u \circ v)'(1) = u'\big(v(1)\big) \cdot v'(1).$$

To find the desired derivatives, we'll need numerical values for $u(1)$, $v(1)$, $u'(1)$, $v'(1)$, and $u'\big(v(1)\big)$. For v we can only read (i.e., estimate) values and derivatives directly from the graph: $v(1) \approx 3.1$ and $v'(1) \approx -0.8$. ➤ Because $u(x) = x^2 - 4x + 4$, we have $u'(x) = 2x - 4$, so $u(1) = 1$, $u'(1) = -2$, and $u'\big(v(1)\big) \approx u'(3.1) = 2.2$. Plugging these values into the formulas above gives these estimates:

Do you agree with these estimates?

$$(uv)'(1) \approx -7.0; \quad \left(\frac{u}{v}\right)' (1) \approx -0.52; \quad (u \circ v)'(1) \approx -1.76.$$

We could use the same method to find derivatives of the same three functions for inputs other than $x = 1$. The graphs can also help us better understand why we got the answers we did. For instance, the graphs show that at $x = 1$, both $u(x)$ and $v(x)$ are positive and *decreasing*. A little thought reveals that the product $u(x)v(x)$ must also be decreasing at $x = 1$; hence, the derivative $(uv)'(1) \approx -7$ is *negative*. ∎

Implicit functions and derivatives   Functions are sometimes given *implicitly*, by equations, rather than *explicitly*, by formulas. To differentiate such functions we can use the method of **implicit differentiation**, as described in Section 3.3.

EXAMPLE 2   The equation $x = e^y$ defines y implicitly as a function of x. Find dy/dx.

Solution   We differentiate both sides of the equation with respect to x:

$$x = e^y \implies 1 = e^y \frac{dy}{dx};$$

note the use of the chain rule in the last step. Finally, we solve the new equation for dy/dx:

$$1 = e^y \frac{dy}{dx} \implies \frac{dy}{dx} = \frac{1}{e^y} = \frac{1}{x}.$$

(We might have guessed the result, since $x = e^y \implies y = \ln x$.) ∎

EXAMPLE 3   Let r be any positive constant. How is the equation $x^2 + y^2 = r^2$ related to solutions of the DE

$$\frac{dy}{dx} = -\frac{x}{y}?$$

How are circles involved?

Solution   For any $r > 0$, the equation $x^2 + y^2 = r^2$ describes a circle of radius r, centered at the origin. By implicit differentiation,

$$x^2 + y^2 = r^2 \implies 2x + 2y\frac{dy}{dx} = 0 \implies \frac{dy}{dx} = -\frac{x}{y},$$

provided that $y \neq 0$. The result means that the equation $x^2 + y^2 = r^2$ implicitly defines solutions of the DE above. We can check this directly—but laboriously—by first solving the equation $x^2 + y^2 = r^2$ for y. Doing so gives the two explicit functions $y = \sqrt{r^2 - x^2}$ and $y = -\sqrt{r^2 - x^2}$. Both of these functions are solutions of the present DE, as we can check by differentiation. Here are details for the first function:

$$y = \sqrt{r^2 - x^2} \implies \frac{dy}{dx} = \frac{-2x}{2\sqrt{r^2 - x^2}} \qquad \text{(by chain rule)}$$

$$= \frac{-x}{\sqrt{r^2 - x^2}} = -\frac{x}{y} \qquad \text{(by algebra)}$$

A similar calculation shows that $y = -\sqrt{r^2 - x^2}$ is another solution. (In each case, we need $y \neq 0$ for the derivatives to exist.) Graphically speaking, the two solution functions correspond to the upper and lower halves of the circle $x^2 + y^2 = r^2$.

Notice, finally, what the DE says *geometrically*. Let (x, y) be a point on the graph of a solution function. The DE says that the solution curve has slope $-x/y$ at the point (x, y) (if $y \neq 0$). On the other hand, the line joining (x, y) to the origin has slope y/x (if $x \neq 0$). These two slopes are *negative reciprocals*, and so we see in action a well-known property of circles centered at the origin:

> *At each point (x, y) the circle is perpendicular to the line joining (x, y) to the origin.* ■

Inverse functions and derivatives; inverse trigonometric functions   Many functions have useful inverses; in Section 3.4 we explored these functions and their derivatives using tools (such as implicit differentiation and the chain rule) developed in earlier sections. Inverse trigonometric functions are useful examples; we defined and differentiated these functions and also explored some of their basic properties.

Miscellaneous derivatives and antiderivatives   In Section 3.5 we combined and collected derivative and antiderivative techniques developed in earlier sections.

REVIEW EXERCISES

1. Let $f(x)$ be any differentiable function and consider the new function $h(x) = f(x^2)$.

(a) Show that h has a stationary point at $x = 0$.

(b) Give examples to show that the stationary point of h at $x = 0$ can be either a local maximum or a local minimum.

(c) Can h have a "terrace point" (i.e., a stationary point but neither a maximum nor a minimum point) at $x = 0$? [Hint: h is an even function.]

2. Let $f(x)$ be any differentiable function, and consider the new function $g(x) = x^2 f(x)$.

(a) Show that $g(x)$ has a stationary point at $x = 0$.

(b) Show that $g(x)$ has a local minimum at $x = 0$ if f is increasing at $x = 0$ and a local maximum if f is decreasing. What can happen if $f'(0) = 0$?
[HINTS: Look at $g''(0)$. For the last question, experiment graphically with various functions f.]

3. This exercise refers to the functions u and v in Example 1.
   (a) Find $(uv)'(3)$, $(u/v)'(3)$, and $(u \circ v)'(3)$.
   (b) Explain why uv has a stationary point at $x = 2$. Is it a local maximum, a local minimum, or neither? Why?
   (c) Explain why $v \circ u$ has a stationary point at $x = 2$. Is it a local maximum, a local minimum, or neither? Why?
   (d) Find as many stationary points as possible for $u \circ v$.
   (e) Use the graph to find as many stationary points as you can for $u \circ u$. Then use the formula for $u \circ u$ to check your answers.

4. We said in Example 3 that the equation $x^2 + y^2 = r^2$ defines the *two* functions $y = \sqrt{r^2 - x^2}$ and $y = -\sqrt{r^2 - x^2}$. Show by explicit differentiation that both of these functions are solutions to the DE $dy/dx = -x/y$.

5. Show by implicit differentiation that, for any constant k, the equation $x + y = k$ defines a solution to the DE $dy/dx = -1$. What does the DE mean geometrically? What do solution "curves" look like?
[HINT: Draw several solution curves.]

6. Show by implicit differentiation that, for any constants a, b, and c, the equation $ax + by = c$ defines a solution to the DE $dy/dx = -a/b$. (Assume $b \neq 0$.) What does the DE mean geometrically? What do solution "curves" look like?

7. (This exercise resembles Example 3.) Graphs of several equations of the form $xy = k$, for various constants k, are shown below. Parts (b)–(d) refer to the DE $dy/dx = -y/x$.

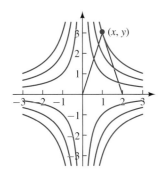

   (a) Label each curve with the appropriate value of k.
   (b) Show by implicit differentiation that the equation $xy = k$ defines solution curves of the DE above.
   (c) If $xy = k$, then $y = k/x$. Show by explicit differentiation that $y = k/x$ is a solution to the DE.

(d) What does the DE above mean about slopes?
[HINT: See the bulleted point (x, y) in the figure; it's the peak of a certain isosceles triangle.]

8. Graphs of several equations of the form $x^2 - y^2 = k$, for various constants k, are shown below. For comparison, graphs of $xy = k$ are also shown (dashed). Parts (a) and (b) refer to the DE $dy/dx = x/y$.

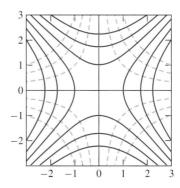

   (a) Show by implicit differentiation that the equation $x^2 - y^2 = k$ defines solution curves of the DE above.
   (b) Compare the DE above with that in the previous exercise:
   $$\frac{dy}{dx} = \frac{x}{y} \quad \text{vs.} \quad \frac{dy}{dx} = -\frac{y}{x}.$$
   How do the two DEs explain the fact that the solid and dashed solution curves shown above are perpendicular wherever they meet?
   (c) The curve $xy = 2$ passes through the point $(2, 1)$. Which curve of the form $x^2 - y^2 = k$ passes through the same point? Find the slope of each of these curves at $(2, 1)$. Are the two curves indeed perpendicular?

9. Let $h(x) = (f \circ g)(x)$ and $j(x) = f(x) \cdot g(x)$. Fill in the missing entries in the table below.

x	$f(x)$	$f'(x)$	$g(x)$	$g'(x)$	$h(x)$	$h'(x)$	$j(x)$	$j'(x)$
-1	3	2	1		0	$-1/2$	3	
0	0	$1/2$	-1	1			0	$-1/2$
1		-5	-1			2	0	

10. Use the identity $f(x)/g(x) = f(x) \cdot \left(g(x)\right)^{-1}$ together with the product and chain rules to derive the quotient rule.

11. Find an antiderivative of $g(x) = \log_b x$, where $b > 0$ is a constant.
[HINT: For any $b > 0$, $\log_b x = \ln x / \ln b$.]

Some values of a function f and its derivative f' are given in the table below.

x	−3	−2	−1	0	1	2	3
f(x)	2	−1	1	3	−2	4	5
f'(x)	1	0	2	−1	3	−3	−2

Use the tabulated values of f and f' to answer Exercises 12–16.

12. Let $g(x) = e^{f(x)}$. Evaluate $g'(-3)$.

13. Let $h(x) = f(e^x)$. Find an equation of the line tangent to h at $x = \ln 2$.

14. Let $j(x) = e^x f(x)$ and suppose that $f''(3) = 1$. Is the graph of j concave up at $x = 3$? Justify your answer.

15. Let $k(x) = f(x)/(1 + e^x)$. Is $k'(0) < -2$? Justify your answer.

16. Suppose that $R(x)$ is an antiderivative of $r(x) = x^3 f(x^2)$. Evaluate $R'(-1)$.

17. Is $G(u) = u + u \ln u$ an antiderivative of $g(u) = \ln u$? Justify your answer.

18. Is $y(x) = 3e^{x^2}$ a solution of the DE $y' = 2xy$? Justify your answer.

19. Is $y = 2x^5$ a solution of the IVP $y' = 10y/x$, $y(1) = 2$? Justify your answer.

20. Let $f(x) = \sin(|x|)$.
   (a) What is the domain of f?
   (b) Of f'?
   (c) Find an expression for $f'(x)$.

21. Suppose that $f'(x) = g(x)$ and that $h(x) = x^2$. Express $\left(f(h(x))\right)'$ in terms of g and x.

22. Evaluate $\lim\limits_{x \to \pi} \dfrac{5^{\sin x} - 1}{x - \pi}$ exactly (i.e., as a value of an elementary function).

In Exercises 23–32, express f' in terms of g and g'. Assume that g'(x) exists for all x.

23. $f(x) = \left(g(x)\right)^n$

24. $f(x) = e^{g(x)}$

25. $f(x) = \ln\left(g(x)\right)$

26. $f(x) = \sin\left(g(x)\right)$

27. $f(x) = \tan\left(g(x)\right)$

28. $f(x) = g(x^n)$

29. $f(x) = g(e^x)$

30. $f(x) = g(\ln x)$

31. $f(x) = g(\sin x)$

32. $f(x) = g(\tan x)$

33. Suppose that $N(t)$, the number of bacteria in a culture at time t, is proportional to $25 + te^{-t/20}$. At what time during the interval $0 \le t \le 100$ is
   (a) the number of bacteria the smallest?
   (b) the number of bacteria the greatest?
   (c) the rate of change of the number of bacteria a minimum?

34. Let $f(x) = \dfrac{\ln x}{k} - \dfrac{kx}{x+1}$, where k is a constant.
   (a) Show that if $0 < k \le 2$, f has no local extrema.
   (b) f has local extrema if $k > 2$. Determine how many and where they are located.

35. Suppose that f is a differentiable function, $g(x) = \left(f(x)\right)^2$, and $h(x) = \left(f(x)\right)^3$.
   (a) Use the product rule to show that $\left(g(x)\right)' = 2f(x)f'(x)$. [HINT: $\left(f(x)\right)^2 = f(x) \cdot f(x)$.]
   (b) Use part (a) and the product rule to find an expression for $\left(h(x)\right)'$.

36. Suppose that f is a differentiable function and $g(x) = \left(f(x)\right)^2$.
   (a) Show that every stationary point of f is a stationary point of g.
   (b) If x_0 is a local maximum point of f, is x_0 also a local maximum point of g? Justify your answer.

In Exercises 37 and 38, evaluate the limit by recognizing it as a derivative.

37. $\lim\limits_{x \to \pi} \dfrac{x \cos x + \pi}{x - \pi}$

38. $\lim\limits_{t \to 0} \dfrac{1}{t} \cdot \left(\dfrac{t^2 - 3t + 4}{5t + 2} - 2\right)$

39. Suppose that f, g, and h are differentiable functions and that $h(x) = f(x)g(x)$. Show that if $h'(1) \ne 0$, then $\left(f(1)\right)^2 + \left(g(1)\right)^2 > 0$.

40. Is $y(x) = (21 + 6x)^{1/3}$ a solution of the IVP $y' = 2/y^2$, $y(1) = 3$? Justify your answer.

41. Suppose that $h(w) = f(w \ln w)$ and $f'(u) = \sqrt{1 + u^3}$. Evaluate $h'(\pi)$.

42. The expression $S(t) = 0.0097 e^{-e^{-1.2t/3.0}}$ models the growth of a part of a fly within an egg before it hatches. (Size is measured in cubic millimeters, and time is measured in days.) How fast is this part of the fly growing at time $t = 2$ days?

43. Is $X(s) = ((s+1)^2 + 1)e^{-s}$ an antiderivative of $Y(s) = s^2 e^{-s}$? Justify your answer.

44. Is $X(z) = 2z^2 \ln z - z^2$ an antiderivative of $Y(z) = 4z \ln z$? Justify your answer.

45. Is $X(z) = e^z \cos z + e^z \sin z$ an antiderivative of $Y(z) = e^z \sin z$? Justify your answer.

46. Is $X(t) = \ln(2 + \sin t)$ an antiderivative of $Y(t) = \dfrac{\cos t}{t}$? Justify your answer.

47. Is $F(x) = e^{\sin x} \cos x$ an antiderivative of $f(x) = e^{\sin x}$? Justify your answer.

48. Is there a value of z such that $\arcsin z = 3$? Justify your answer.

49. For which values of θ does $\arctan(\tan \theta) = \theta$? Justify your answer.

50. Is there a value of z such that $\arctan z = 3$? Justify your answer.

51. For which values of t is $\arcsin t$ defined? Justify your answer.

52. For which values of x does $\tan(\arctan x) = \arctan(\tan x)$?

53. Suppose that the functions f and g have domain $(-\infty, \infty)$ and the following properties:
   (i) $f(x + y) = f(x)f(y)$
   (ii) $g(x + y) = g(x)g(y)$
   (iii) $f(0) \neq 0$
   (iv) $g(0) \neq 0$
   (v) $f'(0) = 1$
   (vi) $g'(0) = 1$

(a) Show that $f(0) = 1$.
   [HINT: Let $x = y = 0$ in (i); then use (iii).]

(b) Show that $f(x) \neq 0$ for all x. [HINT: Let $y = -x$ in (i).]

(c) Show that $f'(x) = f(x)$ for all x.
   [HINT: Use the definition of the derivative.]

(d) Let $k(x) = f(x)/g(x)$. Show that k is defined for all real inputs, and find an expression for $k'(x)$.

(e) Use part (d) to show that $f(x) = g(x) = e^x$.

54. (**An alternative proof of the product rule.**) Suppose that f and g are differentiable functions and that $h(x) = f(x)g(x)$.

(a) Use the definition of the derivative to show that $\left((f(x))^2 \right)' = 2f(x)f'(x)$. [HINT: Use the algebraic identity $a^2 - b^2 = (a - b)(a + b)$.]

(b) Show that

$$h(x) = \frac{1}{2} \left((f(x) + g(x))^2 - (f(x))^2 - (g(x))^2 \right).$$

(c) Use parts (a) and (b) to show that $h'(x) = f(x)g'(x) + f'(x)g(x)$.

Vibrations—simple and damped

Rhythmically repeating phenomena—vibrations—occur everywhere. Plucked strings (e.g., on a guitar) and vibrating springs (e.g., in a car's shock absorbers) are two physical examples; the rise and fall of stock prices and other economic quantities are sometimes described in similar language. In Section 2.7, we discussed **simple harmonic motion** and its natural relationship to trigonometric functions—the simplest, best known, and most useful mathematical functions that repeat rhythmically. The following graphs show some "vibrating" functions:

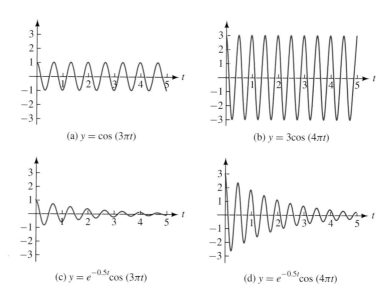

(a) $y = \cos(3\pi t)$

(b) $y = 3\cos(4\pi t)$

(c) $y = e^{-0.5t}\cos(3\pi t)$

(d) $y = e^{-0.5t}\cos(4\pi t)$

FIGURE 1
Vibrating functions

The upper two functions (cosines with some constants attached) represent relatively simple vibrations, of the sort discussed in Section 2.7. In particular, these functions' *amplitudes* stay constant with time t (shown on the horizontal axis). For the lower functions, by contrast, the amplitudes die off with time. These functions display **damped vibration**—a phenomenon we've all heard when a musical note dies away over time. **Damping** occurs when something (e.g., air drag or a sticky fluid) works against the vibration. Music *demands* damping; otherwise, every note would drone on endlessly, like a heavy metal nightmare. Shock absorbers also rely on damping; they are essentially springs immersed in a thick fluid that retards motion.

A simple DE In Section 2.7, we related *simple* harmonic motion to a nice, second-order DE. ← For any positive constant k, the DE

See the Fact on page 145 and the discussion that follows.

$$y'' = -ky$$

has solutions of the form

$$y = a\sin(\sqrt{k}\,t) + b\cos(\sqrt{k}\,t),$$

The first two functions shown above have this form, with $a = 0$.

where a and b can be any real constants. ← We observed, too, that the DE in question has a simple physical meaning. By Newton's second law, the acceleration y'' is proportional to the force on an object. Thus the DE $y'' = -ky$ describes an object that is influenced by a **restoring force** that is *negatively* proportional to the object's displacement y.

PROBLEM 1 Use the chain rule to check that, as claimed above, every function of the form $y = a \sin(\sqrt{k}\,t) + b \cos(\sqrt{k}\,t)$ satisfies the DE $y'' = -ky$. What values of k, a, and b correspond to the functions $y = \cos(3\pi t)$ and $y = 2\cos(4\pi t)$ shown above?

PROBLEM 2 Consider the DE $y'' = ky$, where k is a positive constant. Note that the trigonometric functions just discussed do *not* satisfy the DE. But consider the **hyperbolic functions**

We study hyperbolic functions in their own right in the following interlude (but this interlude is self-contained).

$$\sinh t = \frac{e^t - e^{-t}}{2} \qquad \text{and} \qquad \cosh t = \frac{e^t + e^{-t}}{2}.$$

Show that every function of the form $y = a \sinh(\sqrt{k}\,t) + b \cosh(\sqrt{k}\,t)$ satisfies the DE $y'' = ky$. Plot several solutions to $y'' = y''$ for $0 \le t \le 10$. Interpret the DE and the appearance of solutions in terms of displacement and acceleration.

Damping with DEs Damped vibration, like simple harmonic motion, is linked to a second-order DE but this time of the form

$$y'' = -ky - cy',$$

where k and c are positive constants. As before, $-ky$ represents the restoring force, while the second summand $-cy$ represents a **damping force** that is negatively proportional to the object's *velocity* y'; here c is called the **damping constant**. ➡

Air drag and other frictional forces are often negatively proportional to velocity.

Solutions of the simpler DE $y'' = -ky$ were relatively easy to guess and then check. The present DE is a little more complicated. Still, the following Fact holds:

FACT Consider the DE $y'' = -ky - cy'$, for k and c positive constants. For any constants a and b, the function

$$y = e^{-ct/2}\left(a \cos(\sqrt{k - c^2/4}\,t) + b \sin(\sqrt{k - c^2/4}\,t)\right)$$

is a solution.

Checking that the Fact holds is a matter of a straightforward (but delicate) calculation.

PROBLEM 3 Show by direct calculation that $y = e^{-ct/2} \cos(\sqrt{k - c^2/4}\,t)$ is a solution of $y'' = -ky + cy'$. (A similar calculation (one is enough!) shows that $y = e^{-ct/2} \sin(\sqrt{k - c^2/4}\,t)$ is *also* a solution.)

PROBLEM 4 Suppose that both $y = f(t)$ and $y = g(t)$ are solutions to $y'' = -ky - cy'$; let a and b be constant. Show that every function of the form $y = af(t) + bg(t)$ is also a solution. (This and the preceding problem show that the Fact holds.)

PROBLEM 5 Consider the functions $y = e^{-0.5t} \cos(3\pi t)$ and $y = 3e^{-0.5t} \cos(4\pi t)$, shown graphically above. Find the corresponding values of a, k, and c.

How might one guess the solutions in the preceding Fact? One approach is to look for solutions of the general form $y = e^{-At} \cos(Bt)$ and hope to find appropriate values for A and B. The next problem gives details.

The approach is essentially that of undetermined coefficients.

PROBLEM 6 Find values of A and B (depending on k and c) such that $y = e^{-At}\cos(Bt)$ satisfies the DE $y'' = -ky - cy'$. [HINT: Let $y = e^{-At}\cos(Bt)$; differentiate to find y' and y''. The write the equation $y'' = -ky - cy$ and equate coefficients of $\cos(Bt)$ and $\sin(Bt)$ to find two equations in the two unknowns A and B. Solve them to find that $A = c/2$ and $B = \sqrt{k - c^2/4}$.]

FURTHER EXERCISES

1. Note that for all four functions shown graphically above, the *frequencies* stay fixed over time, that is, the horizontal distance between "peaks" never changes. This is obviously true for the first two functions. Show that it holds for the second two (damped) functions also, by finding the t-coordinates of all the stationary points on the last two graphs.

2. What does it mean musically (e.g., for a plucked string) that a damped vibration has constant frequency but decreasing amplitude? How would it sound if the frequency *also* decreased with time?

3. Find and plot several solutions to the DE $y'' = -1y - y'$. Find the particular solutions for which (i) $y(0) = 1$ and $y'(0) = 0$; (ii) $y(0) = 0$ and $y'(0) = 1$.

4. What difference does it make if k is relatively big or small compared to c? To find out, set $c = 1$ and experiment graphically with solutions of the form $y = e^{-t/2}\cos(\sqrt{k - 1/4}\, t)$ for various values of k. Here are several such graphs:

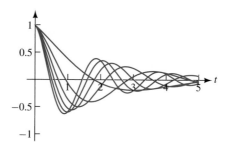

FIGURE 2
Solutions for $c = 1, k = 1, 3, 5, 7, 9, 11$

Or set $k = 1$ and try various values of c.

Hyperbolic Functions

Extended families

Exponential, logarithmic, and trigonometric functions are the best-known families of transcendental functions. Less famous—but still prominent—is the **hyperbolic** family. Its members are close cousins of both the exponential and the trigonometric families. We probe those relationships here and also explain the hyperbolic family's (at first) slightly mystifying choices for given and family names.

INTERLUDE

Hyperbolic functions are close relatives both to trigonometric and to exponential functions; we observe both forms of kinship here.

They're pronounced "cahsh" and "cinch".

Exponential ancestors   The basic hyperbolic functions are simple combinations of exponentials: ➡

> **DEFINITION** The **hyperbolic cosine** and **hyperbolic sine** functions are defined for all real x by
>
> $$\cosh x = \frac{e^x + e^{-x}}{2}; \qquad \sinh x = \frac{e^x - e^{-x}}{2}.$$

Both functions appear in Figure 1.

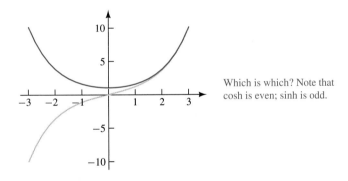

Which is which? Note that cosh is even; sinh is odd.

FIGURE 1
$y = \cosh x$ and $y = \sinh x$

Basic properties of these functions can be seen in the graphs and are easily checked from the definitions.

- **Odd and even**   The function cosh is even, while sinh is odd. For instance,

$$\cosh(-x) = \frac{e^{-x} + e^x}{2} = \cosh(x).$$

Since $\cosh x + \sinh x = e^x$, we can think of cosh as the "even part" and sinh as the "odd part" of the exponential function.

- **A familiar-looking relation**   Trigonometric functions satisfy the famous identity $\cos^2 x + \sin^2 x = 1$. Hyperbolic functions satisfy a similar identity:

$$\cosh^2 x - \sinh^2 x = 1. \qquad (1)$$

- **Derivatives**   The exponentials make derivatives easy to calculate. Here are the results—not too different from their trigonometric analogues:

$$(\cosh x)' = \sinh x; \qquad (\sinh x)' = \cosh x. \qquad (2)$$

The result means that, for all t, the point $(\cosh t, \sinh t)$ lies on the hyperbola $x^2 - y^2 = 1$. By contrast, the point $(\cos t, \sin t)$ lies on the circle $x^2 + y^2 = 1$.

- **Two striking DEs** Consider the similar-looking DEs $y'' = y$ and $y'' = -y$. The derivative formulas above imply that $y = \sinh x$ and $y = \cosh x$ are solutions of the first DE; we've already seen that $y = \sin x$ and $y = \cos x$ are solutions of the second.

PROBLEM 1 Prove Equation 1 by direct calculation. (Note that $\cosh^2 x$ means $(\cosh x)^2$.)

PROBLEM 2 Show symbolically that both parts of Equation 2 hold.

PROBLEM 3 Show that $y = \cosh x$, $y = \sinh x$, and $y = 42\cosh x - 37\sinh x$ are all solutions to the DE $y'' = -y$.

Trig-like functions Several similarities between hyperbolic and trigonometric functions appear above; there are many more. We can use cosh and sinh, for instance, to define new hyperbolic functions with suggestive names such as

$$\tanh x = \frac{\sinh x}{\cosh x} = \frac{e^x - e^{-x}}{e^x + e^{-x}}; \qquad \operatorname{sech} x = \frac{1}{\cosh x} = \frac{2}{e^x + e^{-x}}.$$

Figure 2 shows both functions.

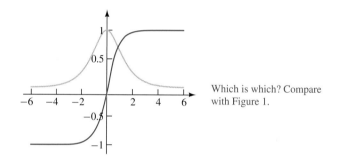

Which is which? Compare with Figure 1.

FIGURE 2
$y = \tanh x$ and $y = \operatorname{sech} x$

Basic properties of *these* functions are closely analogous to properties of their trigonometric cousins.

$$\operatorname{sech}^2 x = 1 - \tanh^2 x \tag{3}$$
$$(\tanh x)' = \operatorname{sech}^2 x \tag{4}$$
$$(\operatorname{sech} x)' = -\operatorname{sech} x \tanh x \tag{5}$$
$$\sinh(x + y) = \sinh x \cosh y + \cosh x \sinh y \tag{6}$$
$$\cosh(x + y) = \cosh x \cosh y + \sinh x \sinh y \tag{7}$$

PROBLEM 4 Prove Equations 3–6.

Hyperbolic function inverses

Because hyperbolic functions are close kin to exponential functions, inverse hyperbolic functions can be written in terms of logarithms. We pursue this in exercises.

The sinh and tanh functions are one-to-one (see their graphs) for all real numbers, and so they have inverse functions, defined as follows:

$$y = \operatorname{arcsinh} x \iff x = \sinh y; \qquad y = \operatorname{arctanh} x \iff x = \tanh y.$$

(The notations $\sinh^{-1}$ and $\tanh^{-1}$ are also used.) The arccosh and arcsech functions can be defined in similar ways. Figure 3 shows arcsinh and arctanh:

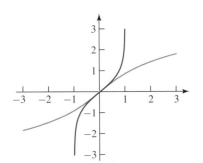

FIGURE 3
$y = \text{arcsinh } x$ and $y = \text{arctanh } x$

Which is which? Compare with
Figure 1 and Figure 2.

Yet again, properties of these functions have close trigonometric cousins. Here are two:

$$(\text{arctanh } x)' = \frac{1}{1-x^2}; \qquad (\text{arcsinh } x)' = \frac{1}{\sqrt{1+x^2}}$$

To prove the first equation, we can use Theorem 5, page 184, which relates the derivatives of functions to derivatives of their inverses. In the present case we get

$$(\text{arctanh } x)' = \frac{1}{\text{sech}^2(\text{arctanh } x)} = \frac{1}{1 - \tanh^2(\text{arctanh } x)} = \frac{1}{1-x^2}.$$

(We used Equation 3 in the second step.)

PROBLEM 5 Prove that $(\text{arcsinh } x)' = \dfrac{1}{\sqrt{1+x^2}}$.

FURTHER EXERCISES

1. Suppose that $\sinh x = 4/5$. Evaluate $\cosh x$, $\tanh x$, and $\text{sech } x$.

2. Suppose that $\tanh x = 3/4$. Evaluate $\cosh x$, $\sinh x$, and $\text{sech } x$.

3. Show that $(\cosh x + \sinh x)^k = \cosh(kx) + \sinh(kx)$ for any number k.

4. (a) Show that $y = \sinh x$ solves the initial value problem (IVP) given by the DE $y'' = y$ and the initial conditions $y(0) = 1$ and $y'(0) = 1$.

   (b) Show that $y = \cosh x$ solves the IVP $y'' = y$; $y(0) = 1$; $y'(0) = 0$.

   (c) Show that for any constants A and B the function $y = A \cosh x + B \sinh x$ solves the IVP $y'' = y$; $y(0) = A$; $y'(0) = B$.

5. (a) Show that $y = A \cosh(\sqrt{k}x) + B \sinh(\sqrt{k}x)$ solves the DE $y'' = ky$, where A, B, and k are constants, $k > 0$.

   (b) Show that $y = A \cos(\sqrt{k}x) + B \sin(\sqrt{k}x)$ solves the DE $y'' = -ky$.

6. Because $\tanh x$ can be defined using the exponential function e^x, we might guess that arctanh can be defined in terms of the natural logarithm function $\ln x$. This *is* possible; it turns out that $\text{arctanh } x = \dfrac{1}{2} \ln\left(\dfrac{1+x}{1-x}\right)$. We explore this fact in this problem.

   Let $f(x) = \dfrac{1}{2} \ln\left(\dfrac{1+x}{1-x}\right)$; note that f is defined if $-1 < x < 1$.

(a) Show that $f'(x) = \dfrac{1}{1-x^2}$.

(b) Note that $f(0) = \operatorname{arctanh}(0) = 0$ and $f'(x) = (\operatorname{arctanh} x)'$ for $-1 < x < 1$. Conclude that $f(x) = \operatorname{arctanh} x$.

(c) Solve the equation $x = \tanh y$ for y to give another derivation of the formula $\operatorname{arctanh} x = f(x)$. [HINT: Start by writing $\tanh y$ in terms of e^y and e^{-y}.]

Inbreeding. Exponential functions are related to hyperbolic functions, and hyperbolic functions to trigonometric functions. These links suggest—correctly—that exponential and trigonometric functions must be related. Indeed they are, and closely, but the strongest connection between them lives in the realm of *complex* numbers. In fact, the ordinary sine and cosine can be *defined* in terms of exponentials by the formulas

$$\cos x = \frac{e^{ix} + e^{-ix}}{2} \quad \text{and} \quad \sin x = \frac{e^{ix} - e^{-ix}}{2i},$$

where i is a (complex) square root of -1. These definitions link trigonometric functions to exponentials on the one hand and to hyperbolic functions (whose definitions look almost identical) on the other. To understand the definitions fully requires, of course, that good sense be made of expressions like e^{ix}. Doing so is one of the first tasks of any complex analysis course.

These formulas suggest several morals. One is that beautiful connections among apparently different function families can lie just below the surface. Another moral is that the exponential function—the "ancestor" of *every* function mentioned here—is one of the most important in mathematics.

---

4 USING THE DERIVATIVE

4.1 SLOPE FIELDS; MORE DIFFERENTIAL EQUATION MODELS

All derivatives can be interpreted in terms of slope. The derivatives in differential equations (DEs) and initial value problems (IVPs) are no exception. Indeed, the geometric viewpoint is essential to understanding what DEs and IVPs are really "about." Graphical views can also lead to simple but powerful techniques for finding *approximate* solutions for almost any first-order DE or IVP.

DEs, IVPs, and slopes of solution curves

Any first-order DE can be understood as a statement about slopes of solution curves. Doing so is simplest if the DE is in the form $y' = f(t, y)$, where $f(t, y)$ is an expression that depends on y or t or both. ➤ Each of the following DEs has this form:

$$y' = y; \qquad y' = 2t - 5; \qquad y' = t + y; \qquad y' = \sin(t^2 - 3y).$$

(Many DEs come ready-made in this form. Others, such as $y' + y = t^2$, can be rewritten in this form.)

> *We'll use t as the input variable in this section to suggest time, but x could have worked too.*

EXAMPLE 1 Discuss the DE $y' = y$ and its solutions in terms of slope.

Solution In slope language, the DE means this:

At any point (t, y) on a solution curve $y = y(t)$, the slope $y'(t)$ is y.

As we've seen, the DE $y' = y$ has solutions of the form $y = Ce^t$, where C is a constant. Figure 1(a) shows several solution curves, labeled with their C-values; Figure 1(b) shows the result of zooming in on one curve ($y = e^x$) at one point.

> *This chapter samples applications of the derivative and (to a lesser extent) the antiderivative. Many instructors will want to choose some proper subset of sections; the order of coverage can also be varied. Sections 4.2 and 4.4 are reprinted in Volume II.*
>
> *Technology is very helpful for plotting slope fields and families of solutions. But technology isn't absolutely essential, since figures and some graphical exercises are provided.*

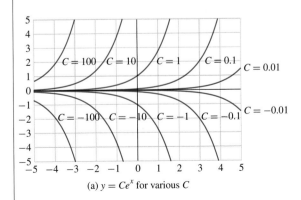

(a) $y = Ce^x$ for various C

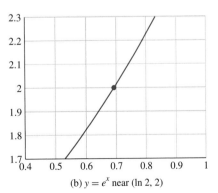

(b) $y = e^x$ near $(\ln 2, 2)$

FIGURE 1
Solutions to $y' = y$; different views

Use the grid to estimate the slope for yourself.

Figure 1(a) suggests that—as the DE requires—the solution curve through any point (t, y) has slope y at that point. Figure 1(b) gives a closer look: the solution curve through $(\ln 2, 2) \approx (0.693, 2)$ appears to have slope 2. ◂

The simple form of the DE $y' = y$ has another graphical meaning: Because y' depends only on y (and not on t), all solution curves have the same slope for any given value of y.   ∎

E X A M P L E 2   Interpret the DE $y' = 2t - 5$ graphically.

Solution   The DE says that every solution curve has slope $2t - 5$ at the point (t, y). For this DE we can check this slope property directly from symbolic formulas. In this case, solutions are simply antiderivatives of $2t - 5$, and so all solution curves have the form $y = t^2 - 5t + C$, where C is any constant. Figure 2 shows several such curves.

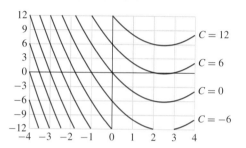

FIGURE 2
$y = t^2 - 5t + C$ **for various** C**: solutions to** $y' = 2t - 5$

Compare Figures 1 and 2. Curves in Figure 1 all have the same slope at a given y-value, while those in Figure 2 have the same slope at a given t-value. This difference occurs because y' depends only on y in the first DE; in the second DE, y' depends only on t.   ∎

In many DEs, such as $y' = y + t$, y' depends on *both* y and t. The next example shows what this means for solution curves.

We solve this and other linear DEs systematically in an Interlude to Chapter 8.

E X A M P L E 3   Interpret the DE $y' = t + y$ graphically.

Solution   For the DEs in Examples 1 and 2 we could easily find or guess solution functions. The present DE is a little harder to guess at, but it turns out that solutions have the form

$$y = Ce^t - t - 1,$$

where C is any constant. (*Checking* that these functions are solutions is a routine exercise.) Figure 3 shows graphs of several solution functions labeled by C-value:

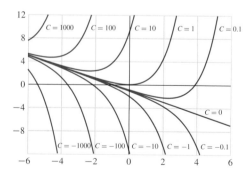

FIGURE 3
$y = Ce^t - t - 1$ **for various** C**: solutions to** $y' = t + y$

The DE $y' = y + t$ means that the solution curve through any point (t, y) has slope $t + y$ at that point. ∎

IVPs: Choosing one solution curve An IVP adds an initial condition to a DE; the result has the form

$$y' = f(t, y); \qquad y(a) = b.$$

The initial condition $y(a) = b$ means, graphically, that a solution curve must pass through the point (a, b). Thus, the initial condition lets us choose, from among *all* solution curves, the *one* that solves the IVP. ➜

In cases of interest to us there is only one solution curve through a given point.

E X A M P L E 4 Among the solution curves in Example 3, find the one that solves the IVP

$$y' = y + t; \qquad y(0) = -2.$$

For this curve, find $y(2)$, $y(10)$, and $y(-10)$.

Solution A close look at Figure 3 shows that the curve labeled $C = -1$ passes through the point $(0, -2)$. Hence, the curve $y = -1e^t - t - 1$ solves the IVP, so

$$y(2) \approx -10.4; \qquad y(10) \approx -22037.5; \qquad y(-10) \approx 8.99995.$$

Only the first result appears in Figure 3. The others are well outside the viewing window, but their general locations might be guessed from the basic shapes of solution curves. ∎

Slope fields

In the preceding examples we interpreted DEs graphically by plotting families of solution curves. To do so we had to know (or be told) *formulas* for the solution functions. Another graphical approach, called a **slope field** (also known as a **direction field**), uses only the DE itself—no solution formulas are needed. Better yet, slope fields offer a simple but powerful method of *approximating* solution curves.

Plotting a few simple slope fields by hand seems almost essential to understanding the underlying idea.

A first-order DE $y' = f(t, y)$ prescribes the slope of a solution curve through each point (t, y) in the ty-plane. A slope field captures this information by showing, centered at each of many "grid points" (t, y), a short line segment with slope $f(t, y)$. These segments "point the way" along solution curves. ➜

The short segments are tangent to solution curves.

E X A M P L E 5 Study slope fields for the DEs $y' = y$, $y' = 2t - 5$, and $y' = y + t$. How are the results related to the pictures in Examples 1–3?

Solution Figure 4 shows a slope field for the DE $y' = y$.

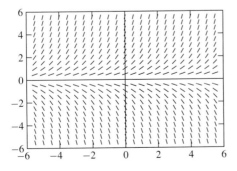

Slopes depend only on y, not on t.

FIGURE 4
Slope field for the DE $y' = y$

Plotting solution curves *on* the slope field shows clearly how the two are related (Figure 5).

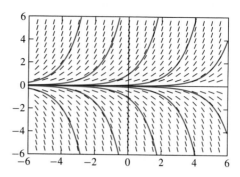

FIGURE 5
Slope field and solution curves for $y' = y$

Students should study the pictured slope fields to see that slopes may vary only with y, only with t, or with both variables.

Solution curves "go with the flow"—at each point on a solution curve, the slope field is *tangent* to the curve.

Slope fields and solution curves for the DEs $y' = 2t - 5$ and $y' = y + t$ show the same agreement (Figure 6).

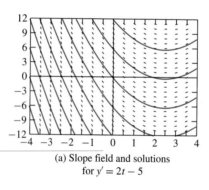

(a) Slope field and solutions
for $y' = 2t - 5$

(b) Slope field and solutions
for $y' = y + t$

FIGURE 6
Slope fields and solutions for two DEs

How to draw a slope field Given a first-order DE $y' = f(t, y)$ and a rectangle in the ty-plane, how would a person (or a computer) *draw* a slope field? The *idea* is simple:

- **Step 1** Choose a "grid" of conveniently spaced points within the rectangle. (In the preceding pictures we used a 24×24 grid—576 points in all.)
- **Step 2** At each grid point $P = (t, y)$, calculate $y' = f(t, y)$. Then use the result to draw a short line segment centered at P with slope $f(t, y)$.

Here is the result for a modest grid of points and the DE $y' = t - y$:

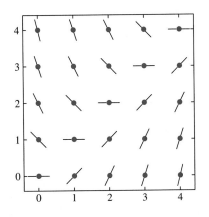

There are 25 segments in all; note the horizontal segments along the diagonal line $y = t$.

FIGURE 7
A slope field for $y' = t - y$

There's a problem, of course: No sane person wants to repeat Step 2 hundreds of times. Luckily, computers thrive on such repetitive tasks. We therefore use computer-drawn slope fields except in some exercises, and then only for simple DEs and "coarse" grids.

Go with the flow: solving DEs and IVPs graphically

Slope fields suggest a natural method of approximating solution curves for any first-order DE $y' = f(t, y)$: Start anywhere and "go with the flow." For an IVP

$$y' = f(t, y), \qquad y(a) = b,$$

the initial condition $y(a) = b$ says where to start—at the point (a, b). ➤ The resulting curve approximates *the* solution to the IVP.

The name "initial condition" is apt from this point of view.

Solution curves are usually drawn in *both* directions from the starting point—increasing t corresponds to the "future" and decreasing t to the "past." ➤ To draw additional solution curves, start somewhere else and repeat the process. The result is a collection of (approximate) solution curves for the given DE—one curve for each starting point. Sometimes these approximate solution curves help us guess exact symbolic formulas for solutions, but even without formulas the curves can be useful in practice.

"Future" and "past" are just figures of speech because DEs need not involve time.

Does every DE have solutions? How many? For every slope field we've seen in this section, one solution curve, and only one, passes through any given point in the plane. In other words, every first-order DE we've seen has infinitely many solution functions. Specifying an initial condition narrows the choice to just one solution function.

Geometric intuition suggests (and it can be shown) that the same principle holds for any DE of the form $y' = f(t, y)$, as long as $f(t, y)$ is a well-behaved function of t and y. Given such a DE and any starting point (a, b), the slope field near (a, b) prescribes exactly one curve through (a, b).

The fine points of this theory (some are very fine indeed) constitute the *existence and uniqueness theory of DEs*, a subject of more advanced study in mathematics.

More modeling with DEs

Differential equations are powerful tools for calculus-based real-world modeling. In Chapter 2, for instance, we used relatively simple DEs, and symbolic solutions, to model motion, growth, and oscillation. Adding graphical DE methods to our toolkit can both give new perspectives on old problems and let us solve new ones. We illustrate with several examples.

Air resistance: a real drag In Section 2.5 we used basic DE ideas to model "free-falling" objects—objects whose motion is influenced only by gravity and not by air drag and other forces. If $v(t)$ is the (upward) vertical velocity of a free-falling object in meters per second, then the simple DE $v'(t) = -g$ says that the (downward) acceleration due to gravity is constant; the negative sign indicates that acceleration is downward.

Ignoring air drag simplifies calculations, but air drag is a real-world fact—and a good thing too, or falling raindrops might prove fatal. The precise physics of air drag is complicated, but when small, dense objects (baseballs, say) fall at moderate speeds, air drag causes a deceleration that is proportional to the *square* of the velocity. This physical fact can be expressed as a DE:

$$v'(t) = -g + kv(t)^2,$$

Here $k > 0$ because the air drag force points upward.

where k is a positive constant and $-g$ is the (constant) downward acceleration due to gravity. ◄ The numerical value of k depends both on physical properties of the object and on units of measurement. For a falling baseball, distance in meters, and time in seconds, the ballpark value $k \approx 0.01$ makes sense, and the DE takes the form

$$v' = -9.8 + 0.01v^2.$$

The DE is separable, so it can be solved symbolically. We treat separable DEs as an application of integration in Chapter 7.

Solving this DE symbolically takes some effort, but a slope field easily gives approximate results.

EXAMPLE 6 On an outing with Dad, Bud and Sis play catch on the observation deck of the IDS Tower in Minneapolis. To Dad's horror, their baseball slips over the edge, squarely beaning a lawyer strolling along the Nicollet Mall, 200 meters below. What happens next?

Solution Thanks to air drag, Dad is sued for personal injury, not negligent homicide. Here's why.

We omit the calculations because they're not the main point here.

Without air drag the free-fall model would apply. In this case, calculations like those in Section 2.5 show that the baseball takes about 6.39 seconds to land and that it lands with a (dangerous) velocity of about 62.6 meters per second. ◄ To see why Dad isn't charged with negligent homicide, let's study a slope field (Figure 8) for the DE $v' = -9.8 + 0.01v^2$ (which applies for reasons explained above).

The analytic solution involves a hyperbolic tangent function.

The solution curve shown starts at $(0, 0)$.

FIGURE 8
A slope field for $v' = -9.8 + 0.01v^2$

The solution curve starts at $(0, 0)$, corresponding to the initial condition $v(0) = 0$. As time goes on, the velocity approaches a "terminal" value, apparently around $v = -31$ meters/second, where the slope field is horizontal. The DE itself shows the same thing: $v' = -9.8 + 0.01v^2 = 0$ when $v \approx -31.30$ meters per second.

Thus, air drag means that the ball hits the lawyer at around 31 meters per second—an unpleasant blow to be sure, but a slow pitch by major league standards. ∎

Chilling with Newton A hot object cools down at a rate that depends on the temperature difference between the object and its environment—the greater the temperature difference, the faster the cooling. **Newton's law of cooling** states this reasonable-sounding principle mathematically:

Not all physical objects really cool this way; different cooling models may lead to different DE models.

> *The object cools at a rate proportional to the temperature difference between the object and its environment.*

Newton's law mentions a rate of change, and so it *begs* for translation into DE language. If $y(t)$ is the object's temperature at time t and T_e is the temperature of the environment, then Newton's law becomes the DE

$$y' = k(y - T_e),$$

Students might think through an appropriate DE for Newtonian warming.

where k is a negative constant. (It's convenient to take $k < 0$ because the temperature of the object *decreases* when $y > T_e$.) If we also take T_0 to be the initial temperature of the object, then the temperature function $y(t)$ is a solution of the IVP

$$y' = k(y - T_e); \qquad y(0) = T_0.$$

With graphical *and* symbolic DE methods available we can solve cooling problems in two ways, and compare our results.

EXAMPLE 7 Two identical cups of dark liquid left in a $70\,°F$ laboratory cool by Newton's law. At time $t = 0$ minutes the first cup's temperature was $190\,°F$, and was dropping at $12\,°F$ per minute. When did this cup's temperature fall to $130\,°F$? The second cup was at $130\,°F$ after 10 minutes. Could the dark liquid be coffee?

Solution Lightly disguised in the words is the DE $y' = k(y - 70)$, where $y = y(t)$ denotes temperature at t minutes. We also know (for the first cup) that $y(0) = 190$ and $y'(0) = -12$; these facts and the DE let us solve for k:

$$-12 = k(190 - 70) = 120k \implies k = -0.1.$$

Thus the IVP

$$y' = -0.1(y - 70); \qquad y(0) = 190$$

describes the first cup, and

$$y' = -0.1(y - 70); \qquad y(10) = 130$$

describes the second. Figure 9 shows the associated direction fields and the appropriate solution curves in a convenient viewing rectangle.

(a) The solution to
$y' = -0.1(y - 70);\ y(0) = 190$

(b) The solution to
$y' = -0.1(y - 70);\ y(10) = 130$

FIGURE 9
Solving two IVPs

A look at the first solution curve suggests that the temperature reaches 130°F at about $t = 7$ minutes. The second curve, through (10, 130), reveals a surprise: At time $t = 0$, the liquid would have been well above 212°F—a physical impossibility for regular coffee. ◄

Perhaps the cups held motor oil, or worse . . . .

An important advantage of symbolic solutions is that by varying parameters we can solve whole families of similar DEs. The slope field method doesn't permit unevaluated parameters.

EXAMPLE 8 Let T_e, A, and k be any constants. Check that $y(t) = T_e + Ae^{kt}$ is a solution of the DE $y' = k(y - T_e)$. Use the result to re-answer the questions of Example 7.

Solution Showing that $y(t) = T_e + Ae^{kt}$ satisfies $y' = k(y - T_e)$ is a straightforward derivative calculation—we leave the details to you. In the situation of Example 7 we have $T_e = 70$ and $k = -0.1$, so $y(t) = 70 + Ae^{-0.1t}$.

To find values for A we use the initial conditions. For the first cup,

$$y(0) = 190 \implies 70 + Ae^0 = 190 \implies A = 120,$$

and so its temperature function is $y(t) = 70 + 120e^{-0.1t}$. Solving $y(t) = 130$ for t gives

$$70 + 120e^{-0.1t} = 130 \implies t \approx 6.93,$$

so the first cup was at 130°F after 6.93 minutes. For the second cup,

$$y(10) = 130 \implies 70 + Ae^{-1} = 130 \implies A = 60e \approx 163.1,$$

and so its temperature function is $y(t) = 70 + 163.1e^{-0.1t}$. Now $y(0) = 233.1$°F, which is impossible for ordinary coffee. ■

BASIC EXERCISES

1. Look again at Example 1 and its accompanying graphs. It's observed there that *all solution curves for the DE $y' = y$ have the same slope for a given value y.*

 (a) How do the shapes of the various solution curves reflect this property? (Answer in a sentence or two.)

 (b) Four of the curves shown in Example 1 pass through the level $y = 3$. Do all four curves appear to have the same slope at that level? Use a ruler and one of the curves to *estimate* this common slope as closely as you can. (The grid should help.) How could your answer have been predicted in advance?

 (c) Repeat part (b), but at the level $y = -4$.

 (d) Repeat part (b), but at the level $y = 0$.
 [HINT: Despite appearances, only one solution curve touches the line $y = 0$.]

2. Here are graphs of several functions of the form $y = Ce^t - t - 1$; all are solutions of the DE $y' = y + t$. (Compare them to the graphs in Example 3.)

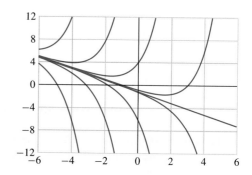

(a) One of the "curves" is a straight line. Which straight line? Label this curve with the appropriate value of C.

(b) One of the curves passes through the point $(0, 4)$. What value of C corresponds to this curve? How do you know? Label this curve with the appropriate value of C.

(c) Estimate (using the graph) the slope at $(0, 4)$ of the curve mentioned in part (b). Does your answer agree with what the DE predicts?

(d) Draw the line $y + t = 0$ (also known as $y = -t$) on the axes. This line crosses four of the solution curves at what points of special interest? Why does this occur? [HINT: What does the DE $y' = y + t$ say about points on the line $y + t = 0$?]

(e) Draw the line $y + t = -3$ (also known as $y = -t - 3$) on the axes. This line crosses four of the solution curves. What do these crossing points have in common? Explain your answer.

(f) Draw several lines with slope -1 on the axes. Each such line crosses several solution curves. What can be said about the points at which these crossings occur?

(g) The curves shown correspond to the C-values $C = \pm 500$, $C = \pm 50$, $C = \pm 5$, and $C = \pm 0.2$. Label each curve with its appropriate C-value.

3. Suppose that $f(t)$ is a solution of the DE $y' = t^2 y + t$ and that $f(1) = 2$. Explain why $y = 3t - 1$ is an equation of the line tangent to f at the point $(1, 2)$.

4. Suppose that $g(t)$ is a solution of the DE $y' = y + 2e^{-t}$ and that $g(0) = 1$. Explain why $y = 3t + 1$ is an equation of the line tangent to g at the point $(0, 1)$.

5. Suppose that $h(t)$ is a solution of the DE $y' = t^2 y$ and that $h(-2) = 1$. Find an equation of the line tangent to h at the point $(-2, 1)$.

6. Suppose that $f(t)$ is a solution of the DE $y' = e^t y$ and that $f(0) = -2$. Is $y = t - 2$ an equation of the line tangent to f at the point $(0, -2)$? Justify your answer.

In Exercises 7–14, first match the slope field to one of the differential equations (i)–(x) below. Then draw solution curves through each of the marked points on a copy of the slope field.

(i) $y' = 2t$

(ii) $y' = -2t$

(iii) $y' = ty$

(iv) $y' = -ty$

(v) $y' = y/t$

(vi) $y' = -y/t$

(vii) $y' = \cos y$

(viii) $y' = \sin t$

(ix) $y' = 1 - y$

(x) $y' = y(1 - y)$

7.

8.

9.

10.

11.

12.

13.

14.

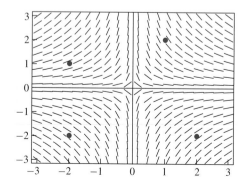

15. In Example 5 we noted that the slope field for the DE $y' = y$ varies only with y. What geometric property of the slope field in Figure 4 corresponds to "varying only with y?" [HINT: The word "parallel" should come in handy.]

16. In Example 5 we noted that the slope field for the DE $y' = 2t - 5$ varies only with t. What geometric property of the slope field in Figure 6(a) corresponds to "varying only with t?"

17. Consider the DE $y' = t/y$.
   (a) Plot a slope field for this DE for $-3 \le t \le 3$ and $-3 \le y \le 3$.
   (b) Show that if $C > 0$ is a constant, then $y = \sqrt{t^2 + C}$ and $y = -\sqrt{t^2 + C}$ are solutions of the DE.
   (c) Sketch the solution curve that satisfies the initial condition $y(0) = 1$ on the slope field from part (a).
   (d) Sketch the solution curve that satisfies the initial condition $y(1) = 0$ on the slope field from part (a).

18. Consider the DE $y' = t + 2ty$.
   (a) Plot a slope field for this DE for $-2 \le t \le 2$ and $-2 \le y \le 2$.
   (b) Show that if C is a constant, then $y = (Ce^{t^2} - 1)/2$ is a solution.
   (c) Sketch the solution curve that satisfies the initial condition $y(0) = 1$ on the slope field from part (a).
   (d) Sketch the solution curve that satisfies the initial condition $y(-1) = -1$ on the slope field from part (a).
   (e) Sketch the solution curve that satisfied the initial condition $y(0) = -1/2$ on the slope field from part (a).

19. Consider the DE $y' = e^{-t} - 2y$.
   (a) Plot a slope field for this DE for $-3 \le t \le 3$ and $-3 \le y \le 3$.
   (b) Show that the function $y(t) = e^{-t} + Ce^{-2t}$ is a solution of the DE for any value of the constant C.
   (c) Sketch the solution curve that passes through the point $(-2, 0)$ on the slope field from part (a).
   (d) Sketch the solution curve that passes through the point $(1, -1)$ on the slope field from part (a).
   (e) Sketch the solution curve that passes through the point $(1, 1)$ on the slope field from part (a).

FURTHER EXERCISES

20. Consider the DE $y' = 1 + 2ty$.

  (a) Plot a slope field for this DE for $-2 \leq t \leq 2$ and $-2 \leq y \leq 2$.

  (b) Sketch the solution curve that satisfies the initial condition $y(0) = 0.5$ on the slope field from part (a).

  (c) Sketch the solution curve that satisfies the initial condition $y(0) = -1$ on the slope field from part (a).

21. Here is a slope field for the DE $y' = t - y$. (See also Figure 7.)

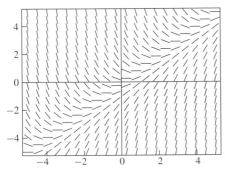

  (a) Sketch the solution curve that satisfies the initial condition $y(0) = 1$ on a copy of the slope field.

  (b) Sketch the solution curve that satisfies the initial condition $y(0) = 3$ on a copy of the slope field.

  (c) Sketch the solution curve that satisfies the initial condition $y(1) = 0$ on a copy of the slope field.

  (d) Show that if C is a constant, then $y(t) = t - 1 + Ce^{-t}$ is a solution of the DE.

  (e) Use the DE to show that $y''(t) = 1 - t + y(t)$. What does this result imply about each of the solution curves in parts (a)–(c)?

22. Newton's law of cooling is described by the DE $y' = k(y - T_e)$, where k and T_e are constants. Let $z(t) = y(t) - T_e$.

  (a) Explain why z is a solution of the DE $z' = kz$.

  (b) Find the solution of the IVP $z' = kz$, $z(0) = z_0$.

  (c) Use part (b) to show that the solution of the IVP $y' = k(y - T_e)$, $y(0) = T_0$ is $y(t) = T_e + (T_0 - T_e)e^{kt}$.

23. It's a winter day in Frostbite Falls, Minnesota—the temperature is $-10°C$. Boris and Natasha stop at a convenience store for hot (initially, $90°C$) coffee to warm them on the cold, windy walk home. Two types of cups are available: environmentally destructive foam and politically correct cardboard.

  Boris wants foam. "What do I care about the greenhouse effect?" he asks. "Besides, remember the proportionality constant k in Newton's law of cooling: $y'(t) = k \cdot (y(t) - C)$, where C is the environmental temperature, $y(t)$ is the Celsius temperature of the coffee at time t, and t is measured in minutes? Well, for foam, $k = -0.05$. For cardboard, k is a pathetic -0.08."

  "Do what you want, Boris," says Natasha. "I'd rather save the world. I'm having cardboard. And make mine decaf."

  (a) How long does Boris's coffee stay above $70°C$? How about Natasha's? How hot is each cup after 5 minutes?

  (b) Redo part (a), assuming that Boris and Natasha drink their coffee in the overheated ($25°C$) convenience store.

  (c) What value of k is needed to ensure that coffee, starting at $90°C$, is still at least $70°C$ after 5 minutes outdoors? [HINT: Use the solution function to set up an appropriate equation; then solve for k.]

24. Suppose that a cup of coffee is placed in a $65°F$ room. After 2 minutes, the coffee has cooled from $190°F$ to $180°F$. How long does the coffee stay above $100°F$?

25. In learning theory, a "performance function" $P(t)$ may be used to measure someone's skill at a task (using units appropriate to the task) as a function of the training time t. The graph of a performance function is called a **learning curve**. For many tasks, performance improves quickly at first but tapers off (i.e., the rate of learning decreases) as the value of $P(t)$ approaches M, some maximal level of performance.

  (a) Explain how the DE $P' = k(M - P)$, where k is a positive constant, describes this situation. (Notice the similarity to Newton's law of cooling!)

  (b) Verify that the function $P(t) = M - Ae^{-kt}$, where A is a constant, is a solution of the DE in part (a).

  (c) For a certain learning activity, measurements show that $P(0) = 0.1M$ and $k = 0.05$; t is measured in hours. How long does it take to reach 90% of the maximum level of performance?

26. Experience suggests that the rate at which people contribute in a charity drive is proportional to the difference between the current total and the announced goal. A fund drive is announced with a goal of \$90,000 and an initial contribution of \$10,000. One month later, \$30,000 has been contributed. What does the model predict at the end of 2 months?

27. Suppose that the resistive force on a moving object is proportional to the object's velocity—that is, that $v' = g - kv$.

  (a) If $v(0) = v_0$, find a formula for $v(t)$.

  (b) Suppose that the object is at height y_0 at time $t = 0$. Find a formula for the height of the object, $y(t)$, at any time $t > 0$.

28. Suppose that you are buying a house and that you plan to take out a \$150,000, fixed rate, 20-year mortgage. Your banker offers you two options:

  (i) An interest rate of 6.75% per year with an up-front charge of 3 points. (A "point" is 1% of the loan amount.)

  (ii) An interest rate of 7% per year.

To simplify the comparison of these two options, assume that interest is compounded continuously and that payments are made continuously. Then $M(t)$, the amount owed t years after signing the mortgage papers, is a solution of the differential equation

$$M' = iM - p,$$

where i is the interest rate and p is the annual payment (of principal and interest).

(a) Explain why the DE given models the situation described.

(b) Explain why $M(0) = 150,000$ and $M(20) = 0$.

(c) In this part, ignore the condition $M(20) = 0$ and treat p as an unknown constant. Use the initial condition $M(0) = 150,000$ to find an explicit formula for $M(t)$. [HINT: Rewrite the DE so that it has the form of a "famous" DE.]

(d) Using the formula for $M(t)$ you found in part (c) and the condition $M(20) = 0$, find a formula for p as a function of the interest rate i.

(e) Which of the two mortgage options has a lower total cost?

(f) Suppose that the $4,500 you would pay in points if you elected the first option could be invested for 20 years in an account that pays 5% annual interest compounded continuously. Would this change your answer to part (e)?

29. Consider the function f shown here.

$y = f(x)$ is a solution of one of the following differential equations. Decide which one, then explain why each of the others is not a solution.

(i) $y' = \dfrac{y - x}{x}$

(ii) $y' = \dfrac{x - y}{x}$

(iii) $y' = \dfrac{x^2 - y}{x}$

30. Suppose that a DE has the form $y' = f(t)$. Explain how you could recognize this fact from the slope field of the DE.

31. Suppose that a DE has the form $y' = g(y)$. Explain how you could recognize this fact from the slope field of the DE.

32. Suppose that a DE has the form $y' = f(t)$ and that $y(t) = te^t$ is a solution of this DE.

(a) Draw a sketch of the slope field that corresponds to the DE.

(b) Find a solution of the DE that satisfies the condition $y(0) = 2$.

33. Suppose that a DE has the form $y' = g(y)$ and that $y(t) = (t + 1)e^t$ is a solution of this DE.

(a) Draw a sketch of the slope field that corresponds to the DE.

(b) Find a solution of the DE that satisfies the condition $y(0) = 2e$.

4.2 MORE ON LIMITS: LIMITS INVOLVING INFINITY AND l'HÔPITAL'S RULE

l'Hôpital's rule is sometimes covered in Calculus II; to accommodate this choice, this section is reprinted in Volume II. But l'Hôpital's rule involves only basic derivative ideas, so it "fits" just as naturally here.

In Chapter 2 we studied limits and some of their properties and related ideas; we applied limits mainly in defining the derivative. In this section we revisit the limit theme. First we define another variant on the basic limit idea—limits that involve the ∞ symbol—and interpret results graphically in terms of asymptotes. Then we show how to use derivatives and a special result, l'Hôpital's rule, to calculate some challenging limits.

Limits at infinity and infinite limits

Read the $\to$ symbol as "approaches."

Limits at infinity and infinite limits (they're different!) describe the behavior of functions when either inputs or outputs increase or decrease "without bound." Informal definitions and examples will convey the idea. ◄

Students should distinguish carefully between the two main "types" of limits that involve infinity.

> **DEFINITION (Limit at infinity)** $\displaystyle\lim_{x \to \infty} f(x) = L$ means that $f(x) \to L$ as $x \to \infty$ (that is, as x increases without bound).

> **DEFINITION (Infinite limit)** $\displaystyle\lim_{x \to a} f(x) = \infty$ means that $f(x) \to \infty$ (that is, $f(x)$ "blows up") as $x \to a$.

Other variants exist, including limits as $x \to -\infty$ and one-sided infinite limits. Defining all of them separately would be tedious; what each means is usually clear from context.

E X A M P L E 1 Interpret the following limit statements:

$$\lim_{x \to \infty} \frac{1}{x} = 0; \qquad \lim_{x \to 0} \frac{1}{x^2} = \infty;$$

$$\lim_{x \to 0^-} \frac{1}{x} = -\infty; \qquad \lim_{x \to \infty} \sin x \text{ does not exist.}$$

S o l u t i o n   The limit $\lim_{x \to \infty} \sin x$ does not exist because the sine function oscillates forever, never settling down near any single value. The graphs in Figure 1 help explain the first three limit statements.

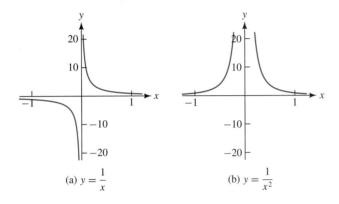

(a) $y = \dfrac{1}{x}$ (b) $y = \dfrac{1}{x^2}$

FIGURE 1

Notice especially the *graphical* meaning of each infinite limit and limit at infinity: each one corresponds to a vertical or horizontal **asymptote**. We'll refine this observation shortly. ∎

New limits from old   When calculating limits of *any* sort it's convenient to reduce complicated limits to combinations of simpler ones. The next example illustrates the process with a limit at infinity.

E X A M P L E 2 Find $\lim\limits_{x \to \infty} \dfrac{x^2 + 3}{2x^2 - 5}$.

S o l u t i o n   With a graph it would be easy to guess that the limit is 1/2. ➤ Algebra clinches the case:

Plot the function yourself if you like.

$$\lim_{x \to \infty} \frac{x^2 + 3}{2x^2 - 5} = \lim_{x \to \infty} \frac{x^2 \cdot (1 + 3/x^2)}{x^2 \cdot (2 - 5/x^2)} \qquad \text{(factor out } x^2\text{)}$$

$$= \lim_{x \to \infty} \frac{1 + 3/x^2}{2 - 5/x^2} \qquad \text{(cancel)}$$

$$= \frac{\lim\limits_{x \to \infty} 1 + \lim\limits_{x \to \infty} 3/x^2}{\lim\limits_{x \to \infty} 2 - \lim\limits_{x \to \infty} 5/x^2} \qquad \text{(separate limits)}$$

$$= \frac{1 + 0}{2 - 0} = 1/2. \qquad \text{(combine results)}$$

∎

We used several plausible facts in the preceding calculation: that $\lim\limits_{x\to\infty} 3/x^2 = \lim\limits_{x\to\infty} 5/x^2 = 0$, that the limit of a sum or quotient is the sum or quotient of the limits, and so on. Such operations are justified by Theorem 1—a version of which we saw already in Section 2.3. What's new is that the theorem applies (if the hypotheses are satisfied) to infinite limits and limits at infinity.

THEOREM 1 (Algebra with limits) Suppose that

$$\lim_{x\to a} f(x) = L \qquad \text{and} \qquad \lim_{x\to a} g(x) = M,$$

where L and M are finite numbers; a may be $\pm\infty$. Let k be any constant. Then

(i) $\lim\limits_{x\to a} kf(x) = kL;$

(ii) $\lim\limits_{x\to a} \big(f(x) + g(x)\big) = L + M;$

(iii) $\lim\limits_{x\to a} f(x) \cdot g(x) = L \cdot M;$

(iv) $\lim\limits_{x\to a} \dfrac{f(x)}{g(x)} = \dfrac{L}{M} \quad$ (if $M \ne 0$).

Observe:

- **Infinite limits**   The rules also hold for infinite limits (that is, when $L = \pm\infty$, $M = \pm\infty$, or both) but only if appropriate care is taken with uses of the infinity symbol. (We return to this question shortly.)

- **"Obvious" limits**   The theorem is useful only if we *know* some limits to start with. To get such a foothold, we'll take as "obvious" limits such as the following:

$$\lim_{x\to\infty} x^2 = \infty; \quad \lim_{x\to\infty} \frac{1}{x^2} = 0; \quad \lim_{x\to\infty} e^x = \infty; \quad \lim_{x\to-\infty} e^x = 0.$$

Asymptotes and limits

Asymptotes are not very important in themselves, but they may help student visualize functions' long-term behavior. We think of them mainly as geometric representations of limits.

The connections among asymptotes, limits at infinity, and infinite limits are easily summarized:

- **Horizontal asymptotes; limits at infinity**   The horizontal line $y = L$ is an asymptote to the graph of f if f approaches L as $x \to \pm\infty$—that is, if

$$\lim_{x\to\infty} f(x) = L \qquad \text{or} \qquad \lim_{x\to-\infty} f(x) = L.$$

- **Vertical asymptotes; infinite limits**   The vertical line $x = a$ is an asymptote to the graph of f if f blows up (or blows down) at a—that is, if

$$\lim_{x\to a^-} f(x) = \pm\infty \qquad \text{or} \qquad \lim_{x\to a^+} f(x) = \pm\infty.$$

Limits and asymptotes of rational functions   Information about asymptotes is useful for *any* function. Horizontal asymptotes describe a function's long-term behavior, while vertical asymptotes reveal sudden spikes and other anomalies. For polynomials and rational functions (quotients of polynomials) the story is especially simple.

Polynomials' asymptotes   Polynomials never have *vertical* asymptotes. A vertical asymptote occurs at a *finite* value of x near which a function's value is unbounded. Because polynomials have the pleasant form

$$p(x) = a_0 + a_1 x + \cdots + a_n x^n ,$$

free of troublesome denominators, polynomials cannot blow up (or down) except as x approaches $\pm\infty$.

Every *constant* polynomial has a horizontal asymptote—the graph itself. If, say, $p(x) = 3$, then the p-graph is the horizontal line $y = 3$. Nonconstant polynomials, on the other hand, never have horizontal asymptotes; the following Fact explains why.

The following example illustrates the Fact's value—polynomials' limits at infinity aren't really obvious without some algebraic trickery.

> **FACT**   If $p(x)$ is a nonconstant polynomial, then
> $$\lim_{x \to \infty} p(x) = \pm\infty; \qquad \lim_{x \to -\infty} p(x) = \pm\infty.$$

We won't prove this fact formally, but we'll illustrate why it holds.

EXAMPLE 3   Let $p(x) = 2x^3 - 53x^2 - 123x$. How does p behave as $x \to \infty$? What if $x \to -\infty$?

Solution   It's clear at a glance that if $x \to \infty$, then $2x^3 \to \infty$, $-53x^2 \to -\infty$, and $-123x \to -\infty$. But what about the sum? The trick is to *factor out the largest power of x*:

$$\lim_{x \to \infty} \left(2x^3 - 53x^2 - 123x \right) = \lim_{x \to \infty} x^3 \left(2 - \frac{53}{x} - \frac{123}{x^2} \right)$$
$$= \lim_{x \to \infty} x^3 \cdot \lim_{x \to \infty} \left(2 - \frac{53}{x} - \frac{123}{x^2} \right)$$
$$= \infty \cdot (2 - 0 - 0) = \infty .$$

Similarly,

$$\lim_{x \to -\infty} \left(2x^3 - 53x^2 - 123x \right) = \lim_{x \to -\infty} x^3 \cdot \lim_{x \to -\infty} \left(2 - \frac{53}{x} - \frac{123}{x^2} \right)$$
$$= -\infty \cdot (2 - 0 - 0) = -\infty .$$

Plotting $p(x)$ over a large x-interval, say $[-10, 10]$, supports our limit calculations.   ■

Algebra with the infinity symbol   In the calculations of Example 3 we breezed past two possibly suspicious claims: $\infty \cdot 2 = \infty$ and $-\infty \cdot 2 = -\infty$. Do they really make sense? Because ∞ and $-\infty$ are not numbers, their appearance in equations should always raise flags of caution. Here, fortunately, we're OK: neither $\infty \cdot 2$ nor $-\infty \cdot 2$ is really ambiguous. The following table collects some rules for proper and improper uses of the infinity symbol.

Good and bad uses of the ∞ symbol	
Expression	**What it means; remarks**
$1/\infty = 0$	Usually OK, but if we really mean, say, $\lim_{x \to \infty} 1/x = 0$, why not say so?
$3 \cdot \infty = \infty$	OK as mathematical shorthand. It means: If any quantity increases without bound, then so does three times that quantity.
$\infty + \infty = \infty$	OK again. It means: If two quantities increase without bound, then so does their sum.
$1/0 = \infty$	Wrong. Division by 0 is not defined. Worse, $1/x \to \infty$ as $x \to 0$ from the right, but $1/x \to -\infty$ as $x \to 0$ from the left.
$\infty - \infty = 0$	Wrong again. For example, as $x \to \infty$, both $x^3 \to \infty$ and $x^2 \to \infty$, but $x^3 - x^2 \to \infty$.
$\infty/\infty = 1$	Wrong. For example, as $x \to \infty$, both $x^3 \to \infty$ and $x^2 \to \infty$, but $x^3/x^2 = x \to \infty$.
$0 \cdot \infty = 0$	Wrong. For example, as $x \to \infty$, we have $x^2 \to \infty$ and $1/x \to 0$, but $x^2 \cdot 1/x = x \to \infty$.

Horizontal asymptotes of rational functions: appeal to higher powers There's a simple algebraic strategy for finding horizontal asymptotes of rational functions:

> *Factor out the highest powers of x from the numerator and denominator. Then cancel as possible.*

EXAMPLE 4 Find the horizontal asymptotes (if any) of the rational functions

$$r(x) = \frac{2x^3 - x}{x^2 - 1}, \qquad s(x) = \frac{2x^3 - x}{x^3 - 1}, \qquad \text{and} \qquad t(x) = \frac{2x^3 - x}{x^4 - 1}.$$

Solution Graphs follow soon, but let's not peek. Instead, we'll factor:

$$r(x) = \frac{2x^3 - x}{x^2 - 1} = \frac{x^3(2 - 1/x^2)}{x^2(1 - 1/x^2)} = x \cdot \frac{2 - 1/x^2}{1 - 1/x^2};$$

$$s(x) = \frac{2x^3 - x}{x^3 - 1} = \frac{x^3(2 - 1/x^2)}{x^3(1 - 1/x^3)} = \frac{2 - 1/x^2}{1 - 1/x^3};$$

$$t(x) = \frac{2x^3 - x}{x^4 - 1} = \frac{x^3(2 - 1/x^2)}{x^4(1 - 1/x^4)} = \frac{1}{x} \cdot \frac{2 - 1/x^2}{1 - 1/x^4}.$$

The last form of each function (and Theorem 1) shows that if $x \to \infty$ or $x \to -\infty$, then

$$r(x) \to \infty, \qquad s(x) \to 2, \qquad \text{and} \qquad t(x) \to 0.$$

Thus, s and t have horizontal asymptotes at $y = 2$ and $y = 0$, respectively, while r has no horizontal asymptotes. ∎

Vertical asymptotes and roots of the denominator If a rational function has vertical asymptotes, they can be located only at roots of the denominator. ← But not every root of the denominator needs to have an asymptote. If both the numerator *and* denominator have a root at $x = a$, then they have a common factor $(x - a)$, which can be canceled.

Recall: r is a root of f if $f(r) = 0$.

EXAMPLE 5 Let r, s, and t be as in Example 4. Find all vertical asymptotes.

Solution A rational function has a vertical asymptote at any x-value where the denominator is zero and the numerator isn't. To look for asymptotes, we first factor the denominator as much as possible. ← For r, s, and t, we get

Factoring polynomials can be hard, so we authors usually choose easy-to-factor polynomials, or we factor them for you.

$$r(x) = \frac{2x^3 - x}{x^2 - 1} = \frac{2x^3 - x}{(x + 1)(x - 1)};$$

$$s(x) = \frac{2x^3 - x}{x^3 - 1} = \frac{2x^3 - x}{(x - 1)(x^2 + x + 1)};$$

$$t(x) = \frac{2x^3 - x}{x^4 - 1} = \frac{2x^3 - x}{(x^2 - 1)(x^2 + 1)} = \frac{2x^3 - x}{(x - 1)(x + 1)(x^2 + 1)}.$$

The factored denominators show that, for each function, $x = 1$ and $x = -1$ are the only possible vertical asymptotes. Because the numerator $2x^3 - x$ is *not* zero at $x = \pm 1$, it follows that r and t have vertical asymptotes at $x = 1$ and at $x = -1$, and that s has a vertical asymptote at $x = 1$.

On either side of a vertical asymptote, a function may tend either to ∞ or to $-\infty$. What happens for r, s, and t? Graphs make the answers obvious, but even without graphs the question is usually easy to answer. We need only determine the *sign* of each function just to the right and just to the left of each asymptote. For $r(x)$, just to the left of $x = -1$ we see that

$$2x^3 - x < 0, \qquad x + 1 < 0, \qquad \text{and} \qquad x - 1 < 0.$$

Thus $r(x) < 0$, and so $\lim\limits_{x \to -1^-} r(x) = -\infty$. ➡ A similar sign check reveals that r blows *up* to ∞ as $x \to -1$ from the *right*.

r "blows down" to $-\infty$ as $x \to -1$ from the left.

We've waited long enough: Figure 2 shows the graphs and their vertical asymptotes.

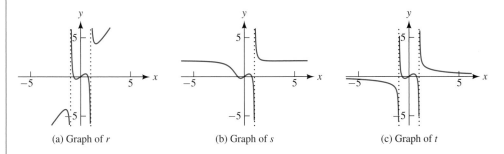

| (a) Graph of r | (b) Graph of s | (c) Graph of t |

FIGURE 2
Graphs of r, s, and t   ■

Asymptotes of other functions

Any function may have asymptotes—with the same connection to infinite limits and limits at infinity as for rational functions. Calculating these limits algebraically may take extra ingenuity.

EXAMPLE 6 Does $f(x) = \sqrt{x^2 + x} - x$ have any horizontal asymptotes?

Solution How $f(x)$ behaves as $x \to \infty$ isn't obvious from the formula. ➡ But a table of values suggests a limit of $1/2$:

A graph might help; see for yourself.

x	1	2	4	8	16	32	64	128	256
$f(x)$	0.4142	0.4495	0.4721	0.4853	0.4924	0.4962	0.4981	0.4990	0.4995

We'll use algebra to check our guess. Note the trick in the first step—multiplying numerator and denominator by a "conjugate" expression:

$$\lim_{x \to \infty} (\sqrt{x^2 + x} - x) = \lim_{x \to \infty} \frac{(\sqrt{x^2 + x} - x)(\sqrt{x^2 + x} + x)}{\sqrt{x^2 + x} + x}$$

$$= \lim_{x \to \infty} \frac{x}{\sqrt{x^2 + x} + x} \qquad \text{(multiplying out)}$$

$$= \lim_{x \to \infty} \frac{x}{x \left(\sqrt{1 + 1/x} + 1 \right)} \qquad \begin{array}{l}\text{(factor } x \text{ from denominator;} \\ \text{note that } x > 0 \text{)}\end{array}$$

$$= \lim_{x \to \infty} \frac{1}{\sqrt{1 + 1/x} + 1} = \frac{1}{2}. \qquad \blacksquare$$

Composite limits

Limits often involve functions built up by composition; consequently, it's helpful to know how the operations of composition and taking limits interact. First let's discuss some straightforward examples.

Try to guess all three limits before reading on.

EXAMPLE 7 Find and discuss each of the following limits. ◄

$$L_1 = \lim_{x \to 0} \ln(\cos x); \qquad L_2 = \lim_{x \to 0} \ln\left(\frac{\sin x}{x}\right); \qquad L_3 = \lim_{x \to \infty} \exp\left(\frac{x+1}{x+2}\right).$$

Solution The first limit is easiest. As $x \to 0$, $\cos x \to \cos 0$, so

$$\ln(\cos x) \to \ln(\cos 0) = \ln 1 = 0.$$

Why did things work so well? Because both functions involved are continuous at the points that matter: As $x \to 0$, $\cos x \to \cos 0$ because the cosine function is continuous at $x = 0$; as $\cos x \to 1$, $\ln(\cos x) \to \ln 1$ because the natural logarithm function is continuous at $x = 1$.

We've used this fact repeatedly; a formal proof appears in Appendix H.

To find L_2 we reason similarly. Recall first that as $x \to 0$, $(\sin x)/x \to 1$. ◄ Thus, as $x \to 0$,

$$\frac{\sin x}{x} \to 1 \implies \ln\left(\frac{\sin x}{x}\right) \to \ln 1 = 0.$$

(The implication holds because the function $\ln(x)$ is continuous at $x = 1$.)

The limit L_3 is "at infinity," but the same sort of reasoning applies as for L_1 and L_2: ◄

Convince yourself of the first implication.

$$x \to \infty \implies \frac{x+1}{x+2} \to 1 \implies \exp\left(\frac{x+1}{x+2}\right) \to \exp(1) = e.$$

Once again, continuity is key: the second implication holds because the exponential function is continuous at $x = 1$. ∎

Composing limits: a general principle One basic principle applies to all three limits in Example 7:

> **FACT (Limit of a composite function)** Let f and g be functions such that $\lim_{x \to a} g(x) = b$ and f is continuous at $x = b$. (The constant a may be $\pm\infty$.) Then
> $$\lim_{x \to a}(f \circ g)(x) = \lim_{x \to a} f\big(g(x)\big) = f(b).$$

A formal proof, which we omit, appeals to the ϵ–δ definition of limit.

Squeezing limits at infinity

The idea of squeezing is very easy; finding appropriate squeezing functions can be hard.

In Section 2.3 we applied the **squeeze principle** (see Theorem 7, page 110) to find some limits for which algebraic techniques don't help. Here's a version that applies to limits at infinity:

> **THEOREM 2 (The squeeze principle)** Suppose that
> $$f(x) \le g(x) \le h(x)$$
> for all large positive x. If $f(x) \to L$ and $h(x) \to L$ as $x \to \infty$, then $g(x) \to L$ as $x \to \infty$.

EXAMPLE 8 Explain why $\lim_{x \to \infty} \dfrac{\sin x}{x} = 0$.

Solution Because $-1 \le \sin x \le 1$, the inequality

$$-\frac{1}{x} \le \frac{\sin x}{x} \le \frac{1}{x}$$

holds for all $x > 0$. Because the left and the right sides tend to 0 as $x \to \infty$, so must the middle expression.   ∎

Indeterminate forms

Many limits are easy to guess "by inspection." ➤ Other limits are less susceptible to intuition. Consider these:

$$\lim_{x \to \infty} \frac{x^2}{2^x}; \qquad \lim_{x \to 0} \frac{\sin(2x)}{x}; \qquad \lim_{x \to \infty} xe^{-x}; \qquad \lim_{x \to \infty} \frac{x^2+1}{2x^2+3}.$$

This is mathematicians' jargon for "just by looking."

Indeterminate forms arise in connection with comparing growth rates of various functions.

Such limits are called **indeterminate forms** because, in each case, two conflicting tendencies operate. In the first limit, for instance, both numerator and denominator blow up:

$$x^2 \to \infty \qquad \text{and} \qquad 2^x \to \infty \qquad \text{as } x \to \infty.$$

The limit is therefore called **indeterminate of type ∞/∞**. The key question is how *fast* the numerator and denominator grow compared with each other.

The limit $\lim\limits_{x \to 0} \dfrac{\sin(2x)}{x}$ is ambiguous for another reason: Since both numerator and denominator tend to zero, their ratio is called **indeterminate of type $0/0$**. Again the question concerns the relative *rates* at which numerator and denominator tend to zero.

The limit $\lim\limits_{x \to \infty} xe^{-x}$ involves a product (not a quotient): its two factors behave in conflicting ways:

$$x \to \infty \qquad \text{but} \qquad e^{-x} \to 0.$$

Therefore, the limit is called **indeterminate of type $\infty \cdot 0$**.

The last limit, like the first, is indeterminate of type ∞/∞, but this time no big guns are needed to find the limit. Dividing numerator and denominator by x^2 does the job:

$$\lim_{x \to \infty} \frac{x^2+1}{2x^2+3} = \lim_{x \to \infty} \frac{1+1/x^2}{2+3/x^2} = \frac{1}{2}.$$

Graphical and numerical evidence   The preceding limit calculation worked because the limit happened to involve a rational function; for the other limits above we need more than algebra. Graphical and numerical approaches are a first step. The graphs in Figure 3 strongly suggest that as $x \to \infty$,

$$\frac{x^2}{2^x} \to 0 \qquad \text{and} \qquad xe^{-x} \to 0.$$

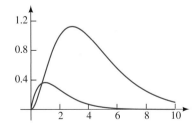

Decide which graph is which—but note that both functions have the same limit at ∞.

FIGURE 3

$y = \dfrac{x^2}{2^x}$ and $y = xe^{-x}$

The following table suggests equally convincingly that $\lim\limits_{x \to 0} \dfrac{\sin(2x)}{x} = 2$.

x	−0.1	−0.01	−0.0001	...	0.0001	0.01	0.1
$\sin(2x)/x$	1.98670	1.99987	1.99999	...	1.99999	1.99987	1.98670

l'Hôpital's rule: finding limits by differentiation

Graphics, numerics, and algebra suggested plausible values for all four of the preceding indeterminate forms. l'Hôpital's rule offers another, more powerful approach.

Comparing derivatives is "natural" in that the limiting behavior of f / g depends on the rates at f and g approach their common limit. See the explanation following Example 12.

How it works   l'Hôpital's rule says that *under appropriate conditions* (which we'll discuss in a moment) an indeterminate form can be evaluated by *differentiating the numerator and the denominator separately*. In symbols:

$$\lim_{x \to a} \frac{f(x)}{g(x)} = \lim_{x \to a} \frac{f'(x)}{g'(x)}.$$

Deferring legalities for the moment, we show l'Hôpital's rule in action.

EXAMPLE 9   Show that $\lim_{x \to 0} \dfrac{\sin(2x)}{x} = 2$.

Solution   By l'Hôpital's rule,

$$\lim_{x \to 0} \frac{\sin(2x)}{x} = \lim_{x \to 0} \frac{2\cos(2x)}{1}.$$

The right-hand limit is no longer indeterminate; simply plugging in $x = 0$ gives 2 (as we'd guessed from numerical data). ∎

EXAMPLE 10   Use l'Hôpital's rule to find $\lim_{x \to \infty} \dfrac{x^2}{2^x}$.

Solution   Assuming that the rule applies, we have

$$\lim_{x \to \infty} \frac{x^2}{2^x} = \lim_{x \to \infty} \frac{2x}{2^x \ln 2}.$$

The right-hand limit is *still* indeterminate of type ∞/∞, so we apply the rule *again*:

$$\lim_{x \to \infty} \frac{x^2}{2^x} = \lim_{x \to \infty} \frac{2x}{2^x \ln 2} = \lim_{x \to \infty} \frac{2}{2^x \ln 2 \cdot \ln 2}.$$

The rightmost limit is (at last) *not* indeterminate. Because the numerator remains constant while the denominator blows up, the last limit must be zero. So, therefore, must the first. ∎

EXAMPLE 11   Graphical evidence suggests that $\lim_{x \to \infty} xe^{-x} = 0$. Does l'Hôpital's rule agree?

Solution   Yes—but only after some algebra. To use the rule, we first rewrite the expression as a *quotient* and then differentiate:

$$\lim_{x \to \infty} xe^{-x} = \lim_{x \to \infty} \frac{x}{e^x} = \lim_{x \to \infty} \frac{1}{e^x} = 0,$$

again as expected. ∎

When it works, when it doesn't: careful statements Using l'Hôpital's rule requires care. The idea that *every* limit of quotients can be handled *à la l'Hôpital* (by differentiating top and bottom) is tempting, but wrong. For instance,

$$\lim_{x \to 0} \frac{x+42}{x+1} = 42, \qquad \text{but} \qquad \lim_{x \to 0} \frac{(x+42)'}{(x+1)'} = \lim_{x \to 0} \frac{1}{1} = 1.$$

We don't prove the Theorem, but we explain the main idea in and just before Example 13.

We erred in trying to apply the rule where it doesn't apply—to a limit that wasn't indeterminate to start with.

When *does* the rule work? The following theorem gives full details:

THEOREM 3 (l'Hôpital's rule) Let f and g be differentiable functions, such that

(a) as $x \to a$, either
    (i) $f(x) \to 0$ and $g(x) \to 0$; or (ii) $f(x) \to \pm\infty$ and $g(x) \to \pm\infty$;

(b) $\displaystyle\lim_{x \to a} \frac{f'(x)}{g'(x)}$ exists.

Then

$$\lim_{x \to a} \frac{f(x)}{g(x)} = \lim_{x \to a} \frac{f'(x)}{g'(x)}.$$

Observe:

- **Limits at infinity** The values $a = \pm\infty$ are allowed in the theorem—luckily, because we've already used the result twice with $a = \infty$. One-sided limits are also permitted.

- **Truly indeterminate** Hypothesis (a) guarantees that $\lim f/g$ is genuinely indeterminate and is of either type $0/0$ or type ∞/∞.

EXAMPLE 12 Find $\displaystyle\lim_{x \to 0^+} x \ln x$. ➡

The right-hand limit is needed because $\ln x$ is defined only for $x > 0$.

Solution The theorem involves *quotients*, so let's produce one:

$$\lim_{x \to 0^+} x \ln x = \lim_{x \to 0^+} \frac{\ln x}{1/x}.$$

The right-hand form is now indeterminate of type ∞/∞, and

$$\lim_{x \to 0^+} \frac{(\ln x)'}{(1/x)'} = \lim_{x \to 0^+} \frac{1/x}{-1/x^2} = \lim_{x \to 0^+} -x = 0.$$

By l'Hôpital's rule, the original limit is 0. ∎

Why it works: comparing rates The theorem concerns the behavior, as x tends to a, of the ratio $f(x)/g(x)$. If *both* numerator and denominator tend either to zero or to infinity, then the limit—if it exists—depends on the relative *rates* at which f and g tend to their limits. The derivatives $f'(x)$ and $g'(x)$ measure these rates. A formal proof of l'Hôpital's rule makes this general idea rigorous.

We'll omit a formal argument, but we can see the general idea symbolically and graphically. Let's suppose that f and g are differentiable functions, with $f(a) = g(a) = 0$. Then, if $x \approx a$, f and g are close to their respective tangent lines at $x = a$:

$$f(x) \approx f(a) + f'(a)(x - a) = f'(a)(x - a);$$
$$g(x) \approx g(a) + g'(a)(x - a) = g'(a)(x - a).$$

If $g'(a) \neq 0$ and $x \neq a$, then

$$\frac{f(x)}{g(x)} \approx \frac{f'(a)(x - a)}{g'(a)(x - a)} \approx \frac{f'(a)}{g'(a)},$$

so

$$\lim_{x \to a} \frac{f(x)}{g(x)} = \lim_{x \to a} \frac{f'(x)}{g'(x)} = \frac{f'(a)}{g'(a)},$$

which is l'Hôpital's rule in its simplest form.

E X A M P L E 13   By l'Hôpital's rule, $\displaystyle \lim_{x \to 0} \frac{\sin(2x)}{\sin x} = \lim_{x \to 0} \frac{2 \cos(2x)}{\cos x} = 2$. Interpret the result graphically, using tangent lines.

S o l u t i o n   Let $f(x) = \sin(2x)$ and $g(x) = \sin x$. The tangent lines to f and g at $x = 0$ are, respectively, the lines $y = 2x$ and $y = x$. Figure 4 shows graphs of f, g, and these tangent lines.

Choosing windows that show asymptotic behavior clearly can be difficult.

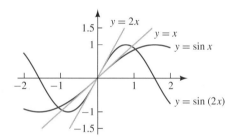

FIGURE 4
$y = \sin(2x)$, $y = \sin x$, and their tangent lines at the origin

The picture shows that, for x near 0, $f(x) \approx 2x$ and $g(x) \approx x$. Therefore,

$$\frac{f(x)}{g(x)} \approx \frac{2x}{x} = 2,$$

as claimed.   ■

B A S I C   E X E R C I S E S

1. Let $p(x) = (x + 1)(2 - x)$. Evaluate

  (a) $\displaystyle \lim_{x \to \infty} p(x)$

  (b) $\displaystyle \lim_{x \to -\infty} p(x)$

2. Let $q(x) = x^{17} - 3x^{14} + 39$. Evaluate

  (a) $\displaystyle \lim_{x \to \infty} q(x)$

  (b) $\displaystyle \lim_{x \to -\infty} q(x)$

In Exercises 3–8, use the graphs of f and g shown below to evaluate the limit or to explain why the limit doesn't exist.

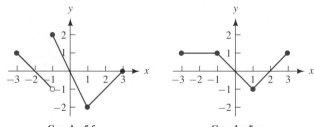

Graph of f   **Graph of g**

3. $\lim\limits_{x \to 2} \dfrac{f(x)}{g(x)}$

4. $\lim\limits_{x \to -2} \dfrac{g(x)}{f(x)}$

5. $\lim\limits_{x \to -2} \dfrac{x+2}{f(x)}$

6. $\lim\limits_{x \to -2} \dfrac{f(x)}{g(x)-1}$

7. $\lim\limits_{x \to 1} \dfrac{f(x)+2}{g(x)+1}$

8. $\lim\limits_{x \to 2} \dfrac{x^2-4}{g(x)}$

In Exericses 9–24, evaluate the limit.

9. $\lim\limits_{x \to \infty} \dfrac{3}{x^2}$

10. $\lim\limits_{x \to \infty} \dfrac{5}{\sqrt{x}}$

11. $\lim\limits_{t \to \infty} \dfrac{2t+3}{5-4t}$

12. $\lim\limits_{t \to 0} \dfrac{2t+3}{5-4t}$

13. $\lim\limits_{x \to \infty} \dfrac{x^2+1}{x}$

14. $\lim\limits_{x \to \infty} \dfrac{x^2+1}{2x^2+3}$

15. $\lim\limits_{x \to \infty} \dfrac{\sin x}{x}$

16. $\lim\limits_{x \to -\infty} \dfrac{x^3}{2+\cos x}$

17. $\lim\limits_{x \to \infty} \dfrac{2^x}{x^2}$

18. $\lim\limits_{x \to -\infty} \dfrac{2^x}{x^2}$

19. $\lim\limits_{x \to \infty} \dfrac{\ln x}{x^{2/3}}$

20. $\lim\limits_{x \to \infty} \sin\left(\dfrac{\pi}{x}\right)$

21. $\lim\limits_{x \to 0} \sin(\sin x)$

22. $\lim\limits_{x \to \infty} \exp\left((3x^2+x)/2x^3\right)$

23. $\lim\limits_{x \to 0} \cos\left(\dfrac{\tan x}{x}\right)$

24. $\lim\limits_{x \to 0^+} \arctan(x \ln x)$

In Exercises 25–30, use l'Hôpital's rule to evaluate the limit.

25. $\lim\limits_{x \to 1} \dfrac{x^3+x-2}{x^2-3x+2}$

26. $\lim\limits_{x \to 0} \dfrac{5x-\sin x}{x}$

27. $\lim\limits_{x \to 0} \dfrac{1-\cos x}{\sin(2x)}$

28. $\lim\limits_{x \to 0} \dfrac{1-\cos(5x)}{4x+3x^2}$

29. $\lim\limits_{x \to \infty} \dfrac{e^x}{x^2+x}$

30. $\lim\limits_{x \to 0} \dfrac{e^x-x-1}{x^2}$

In Exercises 31–35, use the graph of f shown to estimate the limit.

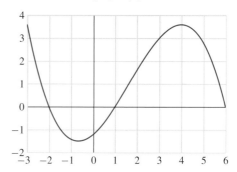

31. $\lim\limits_{x \to 1} \dfrac{f(x)}{x^2-1}$

32. $\lim\limits_{x \to 2} \dfrac{f(x)}{x^2-4}$

33. $\lim\limits_{x \to 4} \dfrac{f(x)}{(x-4)^2}$

34. $\lim\limits_{x \to 1} \dfrac{f(x)}{f(-2x)}$

35. $\lim\limits_{x \to 1} \dfrac{f(x-3)}{f(x+3)}$

36. Explain why l'Hôpital's rule can be used to evaluate $\lim\limits_{\theta \to \pi} \dfrac{\sin\theta}{\theta-\pi}$ but not $\lim\limits_{\theta \to \pi} \dfrac{\cos\theta}{\theta-\pi}$.

37. Can l'Hôpital's rule be used to evaluate $\lim\limits_{x \to \pi/2} \dfrac{\tan x}{x-\pi/2}$? Justify your answer.

38. Can l'Hôpital's rule be used to evaluate $\lim\limits_{\theta \to \infty} \dfrac{\cos\theta}{\theta}$? Justify your answer.

39. Can l'Hôpital's rule be used to evaluate $\lim\limits_{x \to \pi/2^+} \dfrac{\tan x}{x-\pi/2}$? Justify your answer.

FURTHER EXERCISES

40. Let $f(x) = \sqrt[3]{x}$. Explain why $\lim\limits_{x \to 0} f'(x) = \infty$.

41. Suppose that f is a (nonconstant) periodic function. Explain why $\lim\limits_{x \to \infty} f(x)$ does not exist.

42. Sketch the graph of a function f that has *all* of the following properties. (Be sure to label axes and indicate units on each axis.)
  (i) f has domain $(-3, \infty)$
  (ii) f has range $(-\infty, 2)$
  (iii) $f(-1) = 0;\ f(0) = 0;\ f(5) = 0$
  (iv) $\lim\limits_{x \to -3^+} f(x) = -\infty$
  (v) $\lim\limits_{x \to 2} f(x) = -3$
  (vi) $\lim\limits_{x \to \infty} f(x) = 2$

43. Sketch the graph of a function f that has *all* of the following properties:
  (a) f has domain $(-\infty, \infty)$
  (b) f has range $(-3, \infty)$
  (c) $\lim\limits_{t \to 2} f(t) = -2$
  (d) $\lim\limits_{t \to \infty} f(t) = -3$
  (e) $\lim\limits_{t \to -\infty} f(t) = 3$

44. Suppose that $r(x)$ is a polynomial of degree n such that $\lim\limits_{x \to \infty} r(x) = -\infty$ and $\lim\limits_{x \to -\infty} r(x) = -\infty$. Can you tell if n is even or odd? Explain.

45. Suppose that h has a vertical asymptote at $x = 3$, that $\lim\limits_{x \to -\infty} h(x) = \infty$, and that $\lim\limits_{x \to \infty} h(x) = -1$.
  (a) Does h have a horizontal asymptote? Justify your answer.
  (b) Could h be a rational function? Justify your answer.

46. Let $f(x) = \sqrt{x^2 + 1} - x$ and $g(x) = \sqrt{x^2 + x} - x$.
  (a) Use a calculator or a computer to complete the following table.

x	100	1,000	10,000	100,000	1,000,000
$f(x)$					
$g(x)$					

  (b) Use the results you recorded in the table above to guess $\lim\limits_{x \to \infty} f(x)$ and $\lim\limits_{x \to \infty} g(x)$.
  (c) What do your answers to part (b) imply about the graphs of f and g?
  (d) Use algebra to prove your guesses in part (b).

In Exercises 47–50, give examples of polynomials $p(x)$ and $q(x)$ such that $\lim\limits_{x \to \infty} p(x) = \infty$, $\lim\limits_{x \to \infty} q(x) = \infty$, and

47. $\lim\limits_{x \to \infty} \dfrac{p(x)}{q(x)} = \infty$.

48. $\lim\limits_{x \to \infty} \dfrac{p(x)}{q(x)} = 2$.

49. $\lim\limits_{x \to \infty} \dfrac{p(x)}{q(x)} = 0$.

50. $\lim\limits_{x \to \infty} \dfrac{p(x)}{q(x)} = 1$ and $\lim\limits_{x \to \infty} \big(p(x) - q(x)\big) = 3$.

51. Let $f(x) = \dfrac{2x^2 + x + a}{x^2 - 2x - 3}$.
  (a) Find the value of a for which $\lim\limits_{x \to 3} f(x)$ is a finite number.
  (b) For which values of a is $\lim\limits_{x \to \infty} f(x)$ a finite number?

52. Let $f(x) = \begin{cases} \dfrac{\sin x}{x} & \text{if } x \neq 0 \\ 1 & \text{if } x = 0. \end{cases}$
  Explain why f is continuous at $x = 0$.

53. Let $g(x) = \begin{cases} \dfrac{\sin x}{|x|} & \text{if } x \neq 0 \\ 1 & \text{if } x = 0. \end{cases}$
  Is g continuous at $x = 0$? Justify your answer using limits.

54. Let $h(x) = \begin{cases} \dfrac{\sin x}{\sqrt{1 - \cos^2 x}} & \text{if } x \neq 0 \\ 1 & \text{if } x = 0. \end{cases}$
  Is h continuous at $x = 0$? Justify your answer.

In Exercises 55–81, evaluate the limit.

55. $\lim\limits_{x \to \infty} e^{-x} \ln x$

56. $\lim\limits_{x \to 0} x \cot x$

57. $\lim\limits_{x \to 8} \dfrac{x - 8}{\sqrt[3]{x} - 2}$

58. $\lim\limits_{x \to 0^+} \dfrac{\sin x}{x + \sqrt{x}}$

59. $\lim\limits_{x \to 0} \dfrac{\sin x}{x - \sin x}$

60. $\lim\limits_{x \to 0} \dfrac{\tan(3x)}{\ln(1 + x)}$

61. $\lim\limits_{x \to 0} \dfrac{e^x - 1}{x}$

62. $\lim\limits_{x \to 0} \dfrac{\arctan(2x)}{\sin(3x)}$

63. $\lim\limits_{x \to 0} \dfrac{e^x - e^{-x}}{x}$

64. $\lim\limits_{x \to 0} \dfrac{\sin^2 x}{\cos(3x) - 1}$

65. $\lim\limits_{x \to 0} \dfrac{1 - \cos^2 x}{x^2}$

66. $\lim\limits_{x \to 0} \dfrac{1 - x - e^{-x}}{1 - \cos x}$

67. $\lim\limits_{x \to 1} \dfrac{\ln x}{x^2 - x}$

68. $\lim\limits_{x \to \infty} x^2 e^{-x^2/2}$

69. $\lim\limits_{x \to 1} \dfrac{\sin(\pi x)}{x^2 - 1}$

70. $\lim\limits_{x\to 0} \dfrac{1-x^2-e^{-x^2}}{x^4}$

71. $\lim\limits_{x\to 1} \dfrac{\cos^3(\pi x/2)}{\sin(\pi x)}$

72. $\lim\limits_{x\to \pi/2} \dfrac{\ln(\sin x)}{(x-\pi/2)^2}$

73. $\lim\limits_{x\to 0^+} x^2 \ln x$

74. $\lim\limits_{x\to \infty} x \sin(1/x)$

75. $\lim\limits_{x\to 0} x^2 \ln(\cos x)$

76. $\lim\limits_{x\to 0^+} \sin x \ln(\sin x)$

77. $\lim\limits_{w\to 0^+} w(\ln w)^2$

78. $\lim\limits_{\theta\to 0} \dfrac{\cos\theta}{\tan\theta}$

79. $\lim\limits_{x\to \infty} x\left(\dfrac{\pi}{2} - \arctan x\right)$

80. $\lim\limits_{x\to \pi/2} \left(\dfrac{\pi}{2} - x\right) \tan x$

81. $\lim\limits_{x\to 0} \left(\dfrac{1}{\sin x} - \dfrac{1}{x}\right)$

82. Let $f(k) = \lim\limits_{x\to 2} \dfrac{x^2 - 5x + 3k}{x^2 - 3x + k}$. Determine $f(k)$ for all k.

83. Suppose that $f(1) = 2$ and $f'(1) = 3$. Evaluate $\lim\limits_{x\to 1} \dfrac{(f(x))^2 - 4}{x^2 - 1}$.

84. Suppose that f and f' are continuous functions, that $f(0) = 0$, and that

$$\lim\limits_{x\to 0} \frac{f(x)}{\sin(2x)} = 5.$$

Evaluate $f'(0)$.

85. Suppose that f and g are differentiable functions and that $g(0) \neq 0$. Show that

$$\lim\limits_{x\to 0} \frac{xf(x)}{(e^x - 1)g(x)} = \frac{f(0)}{g(0)}.$$

86. Suppose that

$$\lim\limits_{x\to 0^+} \frac{f(x)}{g(x)} = -2 \quad \text{and} \quad \lim\limits_{x\to 0^-} \frac{f(x)}{g(x)} = 3.$$

Evaluate $\lim\limits_{x\to \infty} \dfrac{g(1/x)}{f(1/x)}$.

In Exercises 87–92, evaluate the limit.
[HINT: If $\lim\limits_{x\to a} \ln(f(x)) = A$, then $\lim\limits_{x\to a} f(x) = e^A$.]

87. $\lim\limits_{x\to 0^+} x^{2x}$.

88. $\lim\limits_{x\to \infty} (1+x)^{1/x}$

89. $\lim\limits_{x\to 0} (1+x)^{1/x}$

90. $\lim\limits_{x\to 0} (e^x + x)^{1/x}$

91. $\lim\limits_{x\to 1} (\ln x)^{\sin x}$

92. $\lim\limits_{x\to (\pi/2)^-} \sin\left(x^{\tan x}\right)$

93. l'Hôpital's rule says that if f is a differentiable function and $f(0) = 0$, then $\lim\limits_{x\to 0} \dfrac{f(x)}{x} = f'(0)$. Why isn't this a surprise?
[HINT: Review the limit definition of the derivative.]

94. Let $f(x) = \begin{cases} 3x - 1 & \text{if } x \neq 1 \\ 3 & \text{if } x = 1. \end{cases}$
Use the definition of the derivative of a function at a point (i.e., as the limit of a difference quotient) to evaluate $f'(1)$ or to explain why this derivative does not exist.

95. Let $f(x) = \begin{cases} 2x + 2 & x < 1 \\ 5 & x = 1 \\ x^2 + 3 & x > 1. \end{cases}$
Does $f'(1)$ exist? Use the limit definition of the derivative of a function at a point to justify your answer.

96. Let $L(t)$ be the length, in centimeters, of a certain species of fish when it is t years old. Suppose that the growth of this species of fish is modeled by the differential equation $L'(t) = 6.48e^{-0.09t}$.

(a) Assuming $L(0) = 0.0$, find an expression for $L(t)$.

(b) These fish mature (i.e., begin to reproduce) when they reach a length of 45 cm. At what age does the model predict that the fish mature?

(c) On the basis of this model, what is the likelihood that a lucky angler will catch one of these fish that is 75 cm long? Justify your answer.

4.3 OPTIMIZATION

We've known since Chapter 1 that roots of the derivative have something to do with maximum and minimum values. In this section we collect, summarize, and organize these ideas, and apply them to problems described in words. We also allude briefly to optimization under a constraint.

Optimization is an impressive-sounding name for a basic problem: Given a function f and a subset S of its domain, we seek the largest and smallest values of $f(x)$ for inputs x in S. By now it's clear that the derivative is involved: Anywhere f' is zero is a natural candidate for a maximum or minimum of f. But various subtleties can arise. A root of f' might, for instance, correspond to a local maximum, a local minimum, or neither. A maximum, in turn, could be global or merely local.

To help sort things out, we'll collect and summarize the language, the techniques, and a few of the subtleties involved in optimization problems.

Some authors use the words "stationary" and "critical" slightly differently.

Stationary points and critical points   Let f be a function and f' its derivative. As we've seen, f increases where $f' > 0$ and decreases where $f' < 0$, so any point x_0 at which f' changes sign is of interest. Barring bizarre circumstances (which we can safely ignore in calculus), f' can change sign at x_0 in only two ways:

(i) $f'(x_0) = 0$; *or (ii)* $f'(x_0)$ *does not exist.*

Notice the convention: "points" are inputs while "values" are outputs. Care may be needed to avoid confusion with "points" on a graph, which are 2-tuples.

The following terminology reflects the possibilities:

> **DEFINITION**   If $f'(x_0) = 0$, then x_0 is a **stationary point** of f. If *either* condition holds, then x_0 is a **critical point** of f.

Formal definitions of "local" and "global" appear in Section 2.3.

Local vs. global extreme values   *Local* maximum and minimum values of a function may or may not be *global*. ◄ The function $f(x) = x/2 + \sin(x)$ (see Figure 1) has many *local* maxima and minima on $(-\infty, \infty)$, but there is no *global* minimum or maximum because f is unbounded (both above and below) on $(-\infty, \infty)$. Figure 1 shows the graph.

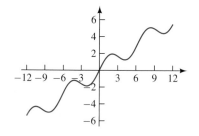

All the peaks and valleys are local—but not global—maxima or minima.

FIGURE 1
$f(x) = x/2 + \sin x$

Draw or imagine the graph of f.

EXAMPLE 1   The function $f(x) = |x|$ ◄ has no *stationary* points, because $f'(x)$ is never zero. But $x_0 = 0$ is a *critical point*, because $f'(x_0)$ does not exist. At x_0, the function f attains a local (and global) minimum value.   ■

The simplest case: continuous functions on closed intervals   As we just saw for $f(x) = x/2 + \sin(x)$ on $(-\infty, \infty)$, a function may have neither a global maximum nor a global minimum on a given interval. All is not lost—the **extreme value theorem** gives conditions under which a function *does* attain largest and smallest values on a given interval: ◄

We'll study the EVT in more detail in Section 4.8.

The main point is that actually f assumes—not just approaches—these values on the input interval.

> **THEOREM 4 (Extreme value theorem)**   If f is *continuous* on the *closed* interval $[a, b]$, then f achieves both a global maximum and a global minimum on $[a, b]$.

Another look at Figure 1 shows that on the closed interval $[-12, 12]$, the continuous function $f(x) = x/2 + \sin(x)$ does indeed take largest and smallest values (approximately ± 5.5), in this case at the interval's endpoints.

Finding maxima and minima on closed intervals   If f is continuous on interval $[a, b]$, then global maxima and minima exist; the following Fact says where to look ➡

> **FACT**   A continuous function f on a closed interval $[a, b]$ can assume its maximum and minimum values only at critical points in (a, b) or at endpoints of $[a, b]$.

We will state and prove an equivalent fact in Section 4.9.

We show in Section 4.9 that if $f'(a)$ exists and $f(a)$ is a local extremum, then $f'(a) = 0$.

The Fact says that the only possible candidates for maximum and minimum points of f are (i) the endpoints a and b; (ii) roots of f'; and (iii) points at which f' doesn't exist. In practice, this slate of candidates is usually short. Choosing among them is usually easy; with computer graphics it's often trivial.

EXAMPLE 2   Find the maximum and minimum values of $f(x) = x/2 + \sin(x)$ on $[0, 3]$.

Solution   First we find critical points. Since f' exists everywhere, we need only find roots of f'. An easy computation does the trick:

$$f'(x) = \frac{1}{2} + \cos x = 0 \iff \cos x = -\frac{1}{2}.$$

The only such x in $[0, 3]$ is $x = 2\pi/3 \approx 2.094$ The preceding Fact says that the maximum and minimum values of f on $[0, 3]$ can occur only at 0, 3, or $2\pi/3$. Evaluating f at these inputs gives

$$f(0) = 0; \quad f\left(\frac{2\pi}{3}\right) = \frac{\pi}{3} + \frac{\sqrt{3}}{2} \approx 1.91; \quad f(3) = \frac{3}{2} + \sin 3 \approx 1.64.$$

The conclusion is now clear: On $[0, 3]$, the function f assumes its minimum value, 0, at $x = 0$ and its maximum value, 1.91, at $x = 2\pi/3$. ∎

Finding maxima and minima on any interval   The preceding Fact applies only to *closed* intervals. On an arbitrary interval, f may or may not assume global maximum and minimum values. In practice, however, it's usually clear either from context or from graphics whether extreme values exist and how to find them. Critical points are still key.

Students can use technology to experiment with graphs to decide (or guess) whether maximum and minimum values exist.

EXAMPLE 3   Which point on the line $y = -2x + 2$ is closest to the origin?

Solution   Theory temporarily aside, it's intuitively clear that *some* point on the line minimizes the distance in question. To find it, let's define a function f by

$$f(x) = \text{distance from } (0, 0) \text{ to } (x, -2x + 2);$$

$f(x)$ is the dotted distance in Figure 2.

Good students may find it more natural to locate the closest point using a right-angle criterion — they should see that this gives the same result as the calculus approach.

FIGURE 2
Which point on $y = -2x + 2$ is closest to $(0, 0)$?

We can find an explicit formula for f using the distance formula:

$$f(x) = \sqrt{x^2 + y^2} = \sqrt{x^2 + (-2x + 2)^2} = \sqrt{5x^2 - 8x + 4}.$$

Intuition (or a graph) says that f has just one local (and therefore global) minimum; theory tells us to look for a stationary point. Finding one involves symbolic calculus and algebra: ◄

Use the chain rule.

$$f'(x) = \frac{10x - 8}{2\sqrt{5x^2 - 8x + 4}} = 0 \iff 10x - 8 = 0 \iff x = \frac{4}{5}.$$

Thus, the minimum distance occurs at the point $x = 4/5$. The corresponding point on the line is $(4/5, 2/5)$, and the distance itself is $\sqrt{(4/5)^2 + (2/5)^2} \approx 0.8944$.   ■

This material might be omitted if time is short, but it offers another approach and reinforces the implicit differentiation idea.

Objective functions, constraint equations, and implicit derivatives

Many optimization problems have the same general form. Some useful jargon will help us describe this form efficiently:

- **Objective function:**   Describes the quantity to be maximized or minimized. In Example 3, for instance, we minimized the distance D from the origin to a point (x, y) on a certain line. This distance—the objective function—has the form $D(x, y) = \sqrt{x^2 + y^2}$. (As written here, the objective function depends on *two* variables, x and y. In Example 3 we rewrote the objective function using just one variable, x.)
- **Constraint equation:**   Describes a condition that must be satisfied by the variables in an optimization problem. In Example 3 we required (or "constrained") the point (x, y) to lie on the line $y = -2x + 2$; this is our constraint equation, or simply the **constraint**.
- **Constrained optimization problem:**   Any optimization problem that (like Example 3) involves maximizing or minimizing some objective function subject to one or more constraint equations.

To solve Example 3 we used the constraint equation to rewrite the objective function to involve just *one* variable: $f(x) = \sqrt{5x^2 - 8x + 4}$. Then we used ordinary differentiation to minimize f. Implicit differentiation offers a slightly different (and sometimes simpler) approach to optimizing an objective function with a constraint. Two basic examples will illustrate the method and the terminology.

E X A M P L E 4   Two nonnegative numbers sum to 10. How large can their *product* be?

Solution   Let x and y be the two numbers. Then our **objective function** is $P = xy$, because we want to maximize the *product*. The **constraint equation** says that $x + y = 10$, because the two numbers sum to 10. Legal values of x are in the interval $[0, 10]$. Note that if either $x = 0$ or $x = 10$, then $P = 0$. Thus, P must be largest at some critical value of x, where $dP/dx = 0$. We find it by differentiation.

We *could* use the constraint $x + y = 10$ to solve for y and then rewrite P as a function of x alone. Instead, we differentiate both the objective function and the constraint equation

$$P = xy; \qquad x + y = 10$$

implicitly with respect to x (treating y as an implicit function of x):

$$\frac{dP}{dx} = x\frac{dy}{dx} + y; \qquad 1 + \frac{dy}{dx} = 0.$$

At a stationary point x, we have $dP/dx = 0$. This makes *three* equations in all (including the constraint equation) that must hold at a critical point:

$$0 = x\frac{dy}{dx} + y; \qquad 1 + \frac{dy}{dx} = 0; \qquad x + y = 10.$$

Substituting the second equation into the first gives

$$\frac{dy}{dx} = -1 \implies 0 = -x + y \implies x = y.$$

Thus, the objective function is greatest when the two factors x and y are equal. Because $x + y = 10$, $x = y = 5$ and $P = 25$.   ■

The answer itself isn't surprising. Neither is the answer to the following (closely related) problem.

EXAMPLE 5 Two nonnegative numbers multiply to 25. How small can their *sum* be? ➡

Solution The new objective function and the constraint equation are, respectively,

$$S = x + y \qquad \text{and} \qquad xy = 25.$$

Differentiating both of these equations implicitly with respect to x and setting $dS/dx = 0$ gives a familiar result:

$$\frac{dS}{dx} = 1 + \frac{dy}{dx} = 0; \qquad y + x\frac{dy}{dx} = 0.$$

It follows (by the same calculation as in the preceding example) that at a critical point, $x = y$. Thus (just as before) $x = y = 5$ at the critical point, and so $S = 10$ is minimum.   ■

First make a guess. (The preceding example should help.)

The best pop cans: an extended example

Real-world calculus optimization problems usually involve translating English prose into—and out of—mathematical language. Once a problem is translated into mathematical terms, more than one solution avenue may be open. Mathematical solutions, once found, require interpretation in the original context.

The next example concerns the design of ordinary 12-ounce (355-ml) aluminum soft-drink containers. Do such cans have the right dimensions? What does "right" mean? Why do other products come packed in cans of other shapes?

This example adds some verisimilitude to a shopworn example. Real-world pop cans really do have thicker tops.

EXAMPLE 6 An ordinary soft drink can has a volume of 355 cm³. Find the dimensions (radius r and height h) that minimize the surface area of such a can.

Solution We'll give two solutions, the first using ordinary derivatives and the second using *implicit* derivatives.

(Solution 1) The can's volume V and surface area A are given by

$$V = 355 = \pi r^2 h, \qquad A = 2\pi rh + 2\pi r^2.$$

These are, respectively, the constraint equation (since volume is fixed) and the objective function (since surface area is to be minimized).

From the first equation, $h = 355/(\pi r^2)$, and so

$$A = 2\pi rh + 2\pi r^2 = 2\pi r \cdot \frac{355}{\pi r^2} + 2\pi r^2 = \frac{710}{r} + 2\pi r^2.$$

Therefore,

$$\frac{dA}{dr} = -\frac{710}{r^2} + 4\pi r = 0 \implies 710 = 4\pi r^3$$

$$\implies r = \left(\frac{710}{4\pi}\right)^{1/3} \approx 3.837.$$

It's easy to check (either graphically or by taking another derivative) that at this point A has a local minimum (not a local maximum or just a flat spot). Thus, the can's optimal dimensions are $r \approx 3.84$ cm and $h = 355/\left(\pi r^2\right) \approx 7.67$ cm $= 2r$. In particular, the optimal can has a *square* profile!

(Solution 2)   We start with the same equations: $A = 2\pi rh + 2\pi r^2$ and $V = \pi r^2 h = 355$. Differentiating both equations implicitly with respect to r gives

$$\frac{dA}{dr} = 2\pi h + 2\pi r \frac{dh}{dr} + 4\pi r;$$

$$\frac{dV}{dr} = 2\pi rh + \pi r^2 \frac{dh}{dr} = 0 \implies \frac{dh}{dr} = -\frac{2h}{r}.$$

Now we substitute the last result into the expression for dA/dr and simplify:

$$\frac{dA}{dr} = 2\pi h + 2\pi r \left(-\frac{2h}{r}\right) + 4\pi r = 0 \implies h = 2r.$$

Thus, the optimal can has a square profile.   ∎

EXAMPLE 7   Example 6 showed that, to minimize surface area, a soft drink can should have a square profile. Why don't *real* cans have this shape?

Solution   One reason is that minimizing surface area does not necessarily minimize the *cost* of a can. Surface area ignores, for instance, the extra cost of the can's top, which is thicker than the sides. ◂   ∎

Look carefully at an ordinary aluminum can. Is the top obviously thicker?

EXAMPLE 8   It's reasonable to estimate that the top of a can is three times as thick as the sides and bottoms. Choose h and r to minimize the amount of aluminum in the can.

Solution   For simplicity let's pretend that the top is made of three layers of aluminum, and still minimize total area A. The argument runs as before, except that now

$$A = \text{sides} + \text{bottom} + \text{top} = 2\pi rh + \pi r^2 + 3\pi r^2 \implies A = 710/r + 4\pi r^2.$$

Now

$$\frac{dA}{dr} = \frac{-710}{r^2} + 8\pi r = 0 \implies r = \left(\frac{710}{8\pi}\right)^{1/3} \approx 3.046.$$

Therefore, the optimal dimensions are now $r \approx 3.046$ cm and $h = 12.182$ cm.   ∎

EXAMPLE 9   What are the dimensions of a *real* pop can? Are they "right"?

Solution   Measuring a real can gives $h \approx 12.5$ cm and $r \approx 3.1$ cm. These values correspond well to the numbers computed before—they're a bit greater because pop cans have some room to spare. Moreover, the tops of pop cans do seem to be about three times as thick as the sides. ∎

On beyond soda pop

Derivatives are good for more than designing aluminum cans for carbonated beverages. They work with noncarbonated beverages, too.

EXAMPLE 10 Fruit juice is often sold in 6-ounce ($\approx$ 168-cm^3) *steel* cans. Assuming that the top of such a can is no thicker than the sides, find the dimensions that minimize surface area. Are the results realistic?

Solution Mimicking the foregoing work shows, as in Example 6, that $h = 2r$ for the optimal can. From this it follows that $r \approx 2.99$ cm and $h \approx 5.98$ cm.

Actual juice cans have a more elongated profile than these numbers suggest, perhaps in order to fit the hand. ∎

BASIC EXERCISES

1. Suppose that f and f' are smooth, well-behaved functions. Furthermore, suppose that f has a root at -2 and that f' has a root at 1. If these are the only roots of f and f', respectively, in the interval $[-5, 5]$, where in this interval might f achieve its minimum value? (Identify *all* the possibilities.)

2. Suppose that 6 is the only stationary point of the function h in the interval $I = [0, 8]$ and that h has only one inflection point in this interval, at 3. Where in I could the minimum value of h occur? (Identify *all* the possibilities.)

3. Does the function $h(x) = |x - 1|$ have any critical points? If so, where are they located?

4. Which point on the line $y = -2x + 2$ is closest to $(0, 1)$? [HINT: See Example 3.]

5. This exercise offers another approach to Example 3. Let $g(x) =$ square of the distance from $(0, 0)$ to $(x, -2x + 2) = x^2 + (2 - 2x)^2$. (Instead of minimizing the distance from the origin to the line, we'll minimize the square of the distance.)

   (a) Find the minimum value of $g(x)$ and the value of x for which it occurs.

   (b) Is the answer to the previous part consistent with what was found in Example 3? Why or why not?

6. To find the point on the line $x + y = 1$ that's closest to the origin, we can minimize the objective function $D = x^2 + y^2$ subject to the constraint $x + y = 1$. Differentiating gives two equations that must hold at a critical point:

$$\frac{dD}{dx} = 2x + 2y\frac{dy}{dx} = 0 \quad \text{and} \quad 1 + \frac{dy}{dx} = 0.$$

Plugging the second equation into the first gives $x = y$. Thus, the minimum distance occurs where both $x = y$ and $x + y = 1$, that is, at the point $(1/2, 1/2)$.

In each part that follows, find the point on the given line that's closest to the origin. In all parts, $a, b,$ and c are nonzero constants.

   (a) $x + y = c$

   (b) $ax + y = c$

   (c) $ax + by = c$

7. This exercise has to do with finding the point P on the right half of the parabola $y = 1 - x^2$ that's closest to the origin.

   (a) Plot the parabola carefully in the rectangle $[0, 1] \times [0, 1]$. (Use equal-size units on both axes.) Then, use your graph to estimate the coordinates of P.

   (b) Use calculus to find the coordinates of P. [HINT: Mimic either the previous exercise or Example 3.]

   (c) Show that the line from the origin to P is perpendicular to the line that's tangent to the parabola at P. How does this property appear on your graph?

8. Repeat the previous exercise, but use the parabola $y = 1/4 - x^2$. What accounts for the difference between this exercise and the previous one?

9. Do Example 4 without using implicit differentiation. Instead, use the equations $P = xy$ and $x + y = 10$ to rewrite P as a function of only one variable, x. Then maximize P over an appropriate interval.

10. Do Example 5 without using implicit differentiation. Instead, use the equations $S = x + y$ and $xy = 25$ to rewrite S as a function of only one variable, x. Then minimize $S(x)$.

11. What is the minimum value of the expression $x^3 + y$ if $x + y = 4$ and $x \geq 0$? Justify your answer.

12. Two nonnegative numbers multiply to 10. How small can their *sum* be?

13. Show that $w = 2/3$ is the global maximum point of the function $H(w) = 4w^5 - 5w^6$.

FURTHER EXERCISES

14. Let $y = f(x)$ be a differentiable function such that $f(0) \neq 0$. This exercise is about finding the point (or points) on the f-graph that is (are) closest to the origin.

  (a) Show that if the point $(x, f(x))$ is closest to the origin among points on the graph, then x satisfies the equation $x + f(x)f'(x) = 0$.
  [HINT: One approach is to define the new function $D(x) = \sqrt{x^2 + f(x)^2}$, which gives the distance from the point $(x, f(x))$ to the origin. Then the point closest to the origin corresponds to a local minimum of $D(x)$.]

  (b) At what point is the graph of $y = \cos x$ closest to the origin? Justify your answer.

  (c) Consider the part of the graph of $y = x^2 - 1$ for $-1 \leq x \leq 1$. Find the points on this curve that are nearest to and farthest from the origin.

  (d) Which points on the graph of $y = 1/(1 + x^2)$ are closest to the origin?

15. Consider the equilateral triangle with vertices at $(-1, 0)$, $(1, 0)$, and $(0, \sqrt{3})$. (This triangle has area $\sqrt{3}$.) Describe the rectangle with largest area that can be inscribed in the equilateral triangle. What fraction of the triangle's area does this rectangle occupy?

16. Consider the isoceles right triangle with vertices at $(0, 0)$, $(1, 0)$, and $(0, 1)$. Describe the rectangle with largest area that can be inscribed in the triangle. What fraction of the triangle's area does this rectangle occupy?

17. (A version of the following exercise appeared on a 1999 entrance exam for Shanghai University in China.) Consider the part of the parabola $y = 1 - x^2$ from $x = -1$ to $x = 1$. This curve fits snugly inside an isoceles triangle with base on the x-axis and one vertex on the y-axis. (Draw your own picture.) What is the smallest possible area of such a triangle?

18. A triangle has legs on the positive x- and y-axes, and its hypotenuse passes through the point $(2, 1)$. Which such triangle has the smallest area?

19. If a projectile (such as a thrown baseball) leaves the origin with initial velocity v_0, is aimed along the line $y = mx$, and is influenced only by gravity, the projectile's path, or "trajectory," satisfies the equation

$$y = mx - \frac{g}{2v_0^2}(1 + m^2)x^2,$$

where g is the constant (downward) acceleration due to gravity.

  (a) A football is kicked with initial velocity $v_0 = 30$ meters per second and initial slope $m = 1$. (Use $g = 9.8$ meters/second^2.) How high does the football rise? Where does it land?

  (b) Plot the football's trajectory, labeling important points found in the previous part.

20. Use the trajectory formula of Exercise 19 as needed.

  (a) A baseball is thrown with initial velocity $v_0 = 128$ ft/sec and initial slope $m = 1/2$. (Use $g = 32$ ft/sec^2.) How high does the baseball rise? Where does it land?

  (b) Another baseball is thrown with initial velocity $v_0 = 128$ ft/sec, but with initial slope $m = 2$. How high does this baseball rise? Where does it land?

  (c) Plot the trajectories of both baseballs, labeling the important points found in the previous parts.

21. In the situation of Exercise 19, the projectile has range $R = \dfrac{2v_0^2}{g}\dfrac{m}{1 + m^2}$. (The range is the horizontal distance covered before landing.)

  (a) Use the formula of Exercise 19 to show why the range formula above holds.

  (b) Suppose that v_0 is fixed but m is variable. What value of m maximizes the range?

22. A farmer wants to fence a rectangular area as inexpensively as possible. Assume that fencing materials cost $1 per foot.

  (a) Suppose that $40 is available for the project. How much area can be enclosed? [HINT: Let x and y be the two dimensions of the fence so that the area A is xy and the perimeter P is $2x + 2y$. Imitate the method of Example 4 to maximize the objective $A = xy$ subject to the constraint $2x + 2y = 40$.]

  (b) Suppose that 100 square feet must be enclosed. What is the least possible cost?
  [HINT: Minimize $P = 2x + 2y$ subject to the constraint $xy = 100$.]

  (c) Discuss the relation between the two parts above. Did the two approaches give the same result?

23. A farmer wants to fence a rectangular area as inexpensively as possible. Fences must run east–west and north–south. Assume that fencing materials cost $h per foot in the east–west direction and $v per foot in the north-south direction.

  (a) Suppose that a total budget $b is available for the project. How much area can be enclosed? What are the best dimensions for the fence? [HINT: Let x and y be the east–west and north–south dimensions of the fence, respectively. Then the area is $A = xy$ and the total cost is $C = 2hx + 2vy$. Maximize $A = xy$ subject to $C = 2hx + 2vy = b$.]

  (b) Suppose that a total area of a square feet must be enclosed. What is the least possible cost? What are the best dimensions for the fence?
  [HINT: Minimize $C = 2hx + 2vy$ subject to $A = xy = a$.]

  (c) Are the two parts above consistent with each other? In each case, how much is spent for east–west fence? How much is spent for north–south fence?

24. A rectangle has its base on the x-axis, a vertex on the y-axis, and a vertex on the curve $y = e^{-x^2}$.

    (a) What choice of vertices gives the largest area?

    (b) Show that one of the vertices found in part (a) is at an inflection point of the curve.

25. Show that the optimal fruit juice can has the dimensions claimed in Example 10.

26. Soup cans are to be manufactured to contain a given volume V. No waste is involved in cutting the material for the vertical sides, but the top and bottom (circles of radius r) are cut from squares that measure $2r$ units on a side. Thus, the area A of material consumed for a can of height h is $A = 2\pi rh + 8r^2$. Find the ratio of height to diameter for the most economical can (i.e., the can requiring the least material). [HINT: Use the fact that $V = \pi r^2 h$ to express A as a function of r.]

27. A piece of wire 100 cm long is going to be cut into several pieces and used to construct the skeleton of a rectangular box with a square base.

    (a) What are the dimensions of the box with the largest volume?

    (b) What are the dimensions of the box with the largest surface area?

28. Federalist Express limits the size of a mailable parcel: The longest side plus the girth (the perimeter of a cross section perpendicular to the longest side) may not exceed 108 inches.

    (a) Which mailable cube has largest volume?

    (b) Find the dimensions of the mailable rectangular parcel with a square base that has the largest volume. [HINT: Consider two cases, depending on which side is longest.]

    (c) Among mailable right circular cylinders, which has the largest volume? [HINT: Again, consider two cases.]

    (d) Give an example of a mailable parcel with larger volume than a nonmailable parcel.

29. The water depth in Moon River x miles downstream from Hard Rock is $D(x) = 20x + 10$ feet; the width of the river is $W(x) = 10(x^2 - 8x + 22)$ feet. To create Moon Lake, a dam is to be built downstream from Hard Rock. For engineering reasons, the dam cannot be more than 130 feet high.

    (a) For which values of x is $0 \le D(x) \le 130$?

    (b) How far downstream can the dam be built? If the dam were constructed at this point, how wide would it be? How high?

    (c) What are the dimensions of the widest dam that could be constructed?

    (d) What are the dimensions of the narrowest dam that could be constructed?

    (e) If the cost of building the dam is proportional to the product of the length and the depth of the dam, where should the cheapest dam be located?

30. A truck driving over a flat interstate at a constant speed of 50 mph gets 4 miles to the gallon. Fuel costs \$1.19 per gallon. The truck loses a tenth of a mile per gallon in fuel efficiency for each mile per hour increase in speed. Drivers are paid \$27.50 per hour in wages and benefits. Fixed costs for running the truck are \$11.33 per hour. A trip of 300 miles is planned. What speed minimizes operating expenses?

31. A wire of length L is to be cut into two pieces. One piece will be used to form a square; the other, to form a circle. How should the wire be cut to maximize the sum of the areas of the pieces?

4.4   PARAMETRIC EQUATIONS, PARAMETRIC CURVES

This section is reprinted in Volume II for instructors who want to cover it later.

A point P wanders about the xy-plane, tracing its path as it goes. As P travels, its coordinates $x = f(t)$ and $y = g(t)$ are functions of time. In this situation t is called a **parameter**, f and g are **coordinate functions**, and the figure traced out by P is a **parametric curve**. ➡ The first example illustrates the idea and introduces some useful vocabulary.

Here the "parameter" is a variable. In other situations, parameters may be constants.

EXAMPLE 1 At any time t with $0 \le t \le 10$, the coordinates of P are given by the **parametric equations**

$$x = t - 2\sin t; \qquad y = 2 - 2\cos t.$$

What curve does P trace out? Where is P at time $t = 1$? In which direction is P moving at $t = 1$?

Solution A simple way to draw a curve is to calculate many points (x, y), plot each one, and "connect the dots." The first step is easy (though tedious if done by hand): For many inputs t, calculate the corresponding x and y. The following table shows a sample of results, rounded to two decimals:

t	0	0.1	0.2	0.3	...	9.8	9.9	10
x	0	−0.10	−0.20	−0.29	...	10.53	10.82	11.09
y	0	0.01	0.04	0.09	...	3.86	3.78	3.68

Note that C is not the graph of a function $y = f(x)$.

Figure 1 shows the graphical result, a curve C.

The dots appear at equal *time* intervals (not *length* intervals).

FIGURE 1
The parametric curve $x = t - 2\sin t$, $y = 2 - 2\cos t$

Notice the "dynamic" quality of the figure—the dots indicate both progress in time and a direction of motion. Ordinary function graphs, by contrast, are static objects, lying passively on the page. Let's take a closer look:

In this example, t represents time.

When is P moving fastest? Slowest?

x = 6, for instance.

- **What the bullets show**   Points corresponding to *integer* values of t are bulleted. At $t = 1$, P has coordinates $(-0.68, 0.92)$; at this instant, P is heading almost due north.
     The bullets on the graph appear at equal *time* ◄ intervals but not at equal *distances* from each other because P speeds up and slows down as it moves. ◄ We'll soon see how to calculate the speed of a parametric curve at a point.

- **Not a function graph**   The full curve C is not the graph of a function $y = f(x)$; some x-values correspond to more than one y-value. ◄ In general, parametric curves may have loops, vertical tangents, and other features not seen in function graphs. Some *pieces* of the curve C, however, do define functions; the part from $t = 2$ to $t = 5$ does so.

- **No t-axis**   The picture shows the x- and y-axes *but no t-axis*: t-values are indicated only by the bulleted points. In most parametric curves t-values don't appear at all. ◄

Most graphing calculators don't show t-values graphically, but some calculate t-values numerically.

In Calculus III we emphasize explicit parametrization of curves and properties (e.g., direction) of parametric curves.

A sampler of parametric curves

Parametric curves come in mind-boggling variety. Any choice of two equations $x = f(t)$ and $y = g(t)$ and a t-interval produces a parametric curve. Surprisingly often, the result is beautiful, useful, interesting, or all three. The next several examples hint at some of the possibilities and at connections between parametric curves and ordinary function graphs.

The curve may need a close look — the dots are not equally spaced in distance.

E X A M P L E 2   (Function graphs)   Every ordinary function graph can be written in parametric form. To produce a sine curve, for example, we can use

$$x = t; \qquad y = \sin t; \qquad -2\pi \le t \le 2\pi.$$

Figure 2 shows the curve; the dots appear at equal *time* intervals.

Is the curve traced out at constant speed? Look at the dots...

FIGURE 2
The parametric curve $x = t$, $y = \sin t$, $-2\pi \leq t \leq 2\pi$

E X A M P L E 3 (The unit circle, parametrically) If a parametric curve has *periodic* coordinate functions, then the curve's shape reflects this fact. The simplest and most important such curve is the **unit circle**, often written in xy form as $x^2 + y^2 = 1$. A simple *parametric* description of the unit circle is as follows:

$$x = \cos t; \qquad y = \sin t; \qquad 0 \leq t \leq 2\pi.$$

Figure 3 shows the curve; dots at integer multiples of $\pi/2$ are bulleted.

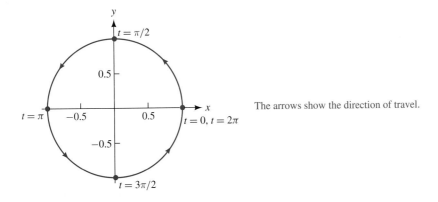

The arrows show the direction of travel.

FIGURE 3
The parametric curve $x = \cos t$, $y = \sin t$, $0 \leq t \leq 2\pi$

This important curve deserves a close look:

- **Interpreting t** The parameter t can always be thought of as time, but other useful interpretations are sometimes possible. Here, t can be thought of either as the *distance* traveled counterclockwise from $(1, 0)$, or, alternatively, as the radian measure of the *angle* (in radians) determined by the x-axis and the line from the origin to the point $P = (x, y)$.

- **Eliminating t** Because $x = \cos t$ and $y = \sin t$, we can write

$$x^2 + y^2 = (\cos t)^2 + (\sin t)^2 = 1.$$

  This shows that every point on the parametric curve satisfies the usual Cartesian (xy) equation $x^2 + y^2 = 1$ for the unit circle (as we intended).

  Notice what we just did—we traded *two* equations involving x, y and t for *one* equation involving only x and y. This process is called **eliminating the parameter**; it may or may not be possible for a given parametric curve.

- **Around and around** The circle is traced *once* as t runs from $t = 0$ to $t = 2\pi$. With a larger t-interval, the same circle would be traced repeatedly; with a smaller t-interval, the circle would be traced only partially.

EXAMPLE 4   (Other circles) The idea in Example 3 works for any circle. If (a, b) is any point in the plane and $r > 0$ is any radius, then the parametric equations

$$x = a + r \cos t; \qquad y = b + r \sin t; \qquad \text{and} \qquad 0 \le t \le 2\pi$$

produce the circle with center (a, b) and radius r.   ■

EXAMPLE 5   (Parametric art) Curves defined by periodic coordinate functions often have striking shapes. A **Lissajou curve**, for instance, is defined by the equations

$$x = \sin(5t); \qquad y = \sin(6t); \qquad 0 \le t \le 2\pi.$$

(Replacing 5 and 6 with other integers produces other Lissajou figures.) Figure 4 shows our curve.

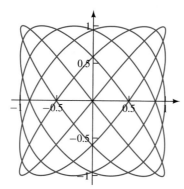

The curve crosses the x-axis 12 times. Can you find these times exactly?

FIGURE 4
The Lissajou curve $x = \sin(5t)$, $y = \sin(6t)$, $0 \le t \le 2\pi$ ■

We'll see in Calculus III that choosing a "good" parametrization can radically simplify calculations.

EXAMPLE 6   (Same curve, different equations) Different pairs of parametric equations may produce curves that look exactly the same in the xy-plane. In such cases, labeling t-values can make differences appear. For example, setting

$$x = t; \qquad y = t^2; \qquad -1 \le t \le 1$$

produces a parabolic arc. So does

$$x = t^3; \qquad y = t^6; \qquad -1 \le t \le 1.$$

Figure 5 shows both curves; the dots mark 0.25-second time intervals.

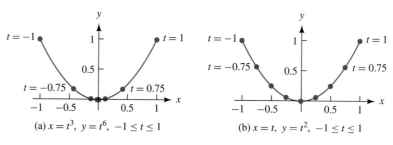

(a) $x = t^3$, $y = t^6$, $-1 \le t \le 1$ (b) $x = t$, $y = t^2$, $-1 \le t \le 1$

FIGURE 5
Two versions of the same curve

The curves themselves are geometrically identical—in each case, eliminating t gives $y = x^2$. Only the different placement of dots suggests the different coordinate functions.   ■

Calculus with parametric curves: speed and slope

Suppose that a parametric curve C has differentiable coordinate functions $x = f(t)$ and $y = g(t)$. What can the derivatives $f'(t)$ and $g'(t)$ say about the situation?

Speed If t tells time, then $\big(f(t), g(t)\big)$ gives the *position* of P in the xy-plane at time t, and it makes sense to consider the speed of P at time t. ➡ Because the derivatives f' and g' tell, respectively, how fast x and y increase, their appearance is no surprise:

As the bullets on some of the foregoing graphs show, speed varies with time.

DEFINITION (Speed of a parametric curve) Suppose that the position of a point P at time t, for $a \le t \le b$, is given by differentiable coordinate functions $x = f(t)$ and $y = g(t)$. Then the speed at time t is given by

$$\text{speed of } P \text{ at time } t = \sqrt{f'(t)^2 + g'(t)^2}.$$

Speed is measured in units of distance per unit of time.

For the speed interpretation to make good sense the units in the x- and y-directions should have equal size.

Definitions aren't subject to proof, but they *should* appeal to common sense. Does this one?

Speed, properly defined, should tell how fast the distance traveled by P increases with respect to time. Showing carefully that the preceding definition actually does so involves a subtle mathematical approach to **arclength** (distance measured along a curve). We won't study arclength in detail here, but the next example shows that the definition makes good sense for *linear* coordinate functions. ➡

We do define arclength carefully in Chapter 7.

EXAMPLE 7 At time t seconds, a point P has coordinates $x = at + b$ and $y = ct + d$, where $a, b, c,$ and d are constants. How fast is P moving at time t_0?

Solution The definition says that the speed of P is *constant*:

$$\sqrt{f'(t)^2 + g'(t)^2} = \sqrt{a^2 + c^2}.$$

To see why this result makes sense, notice first that because P has *linear* coordinate functions, *P moves along a straight line.* When $t = t_0$, the point P has coordinates $(x_0, y_0) = (at_0 + b, ct_0 + d)$; by time t_1 the point P has moved to $(at_1 + b, ct_1 + d)$, a distance of

$$\sqrt{(at_1 + b - at_0 - b)^2 + (ct_1 + d - ct_0 - d)^2} = (t_1 - t_0)\sqrt{a^2 + c^2}$$

units. The *average* speed of P from $t = t_0$ to $t = t_1$ is

$$\text{average speed} = \frac{\text{distance}}{\text{time}} = \frac{(t_1 - t_0)\sqrt{a^2 + c^2}}{(t_1 - t_0)} = \sqrt{a^2 + c^2}.$$

Thus, P has the same average speed ($\sqrt{a^2 + c^2}$) over *any* time interval, and so the *instantaneous* speed of P at any time t_0 is also $\sqrt{a^2 + c^2}$, just as the definition says. ∎

EXAMPLE 8 Consider again the parametric curve

$$x = f(t) = t - 2\sin t; \qquad y = g(t) = 2 - 2\cos t$$

of Example 1. Find the speed at $t = 3$. When is P moving fastest? Slowest?

Solution   The definition says that at any time t,

$$
\begin{aligned}
\text{speed} &= \sqrt{\left(f'(t)\right)^2 + \left(g'(t)\right)^2} = \sqrt{(1 - 2\cos t)^2 + (2\sin t)^2} \\
&= \sqrt{1 - 4\cos t + 4\cos^2 t + 4\sin^2 t} \qquad\qquad \text{(expanding)} \\
&= \sqrt{5 - 4\cos t}. \qquad\qquad\qquad\qquad\qquad (\cos^2 t + \sin^2 t = 1)
\end{aligned}
$$

The rest is easy. At $t = 3$ the speed is $\sqrt{5 - 4\cos 3} \approx 2.99$. The formula $\sqrt{5 - 4\cos t}$ also shows that the speed is greatest when $\cos t = -1$ (at $t = \pi$, for instance); the speed is least when $\cos t = 1$ (at $t = 0$ and $t = 2\pi$, for instance). Figure 1 "agrees" with these answers, for the speed is related to the distance between dots.   ∎

Slope   For an ordinary function $y = f(x)$, the derivative $f'(x)$ gives the slope of the f-graph at (x, y). Finding slopes on parametric curves also involves derivatives, but in a different way. Not all functions have derivatives; not all parametric curves have slopes. To avoid needless complications we'll work only with *smooth* curves:

DEFINITION   The parametric curve C defined by

$$
x = f(t); \qquad y = g(t); \qquad a \le t \le b
$$

is **smooth** if f' and g' are continuous functions of t, and f' and g' are not simultaneously zero.

The slope formula is nice and simple; it's easy, in particular, to detect vertical spots on the curve.

(The second requirement says that the moving point P *never stops.*) For smooth curves, the next theorem tells how to find the slope at a point.

THEOREM 5 (Slope of a parametric curve)   Consider a smooth curve with coordinate functions $x = f(t)$ and $y = g(t)$. If $f'(t) \ne 0$, then the slope dy/dx at the point $(x, y) = \left(f(t), g(t)\right)$ is given by

$$
\frac{dy}{dx} = \frac{g'(t)}{f'(t)} = \frac{dy/dt}{dx/dt}.
$$

Before proving the theorem, let's use it.

EXAMPLE 9   Consider yet again the parametric curve $x = f(t) = t - 2\sin t$, $y = g(t) = 2 - 2\cos t$ of Example 1. Find the slope at $t = 1$. Where is the curve horizontal? Where is it vertical? ◄

Guess first, by looking at the picture.

Solution   By Theorem 5, the slope at t is

$$
\text{slope at } t = \frac{g'(t)}{f'(t)} = \frac{2\sin t}{1 - 2\cos t},
$$

(unless $f'(t) = 0$, where the denominator is zero). Setting $t = 1$ gives

$$
\text{slope at time } 1 = \frac{g'(1)}{f'(1)} = \frac{2\sin 1}{1 - 2\cos 1} \approx -20.88.
$$

Figure 1 agrees: At the point marked $t = 1$, the curve has large negative slope.

The general slope formula shows that the curve is *horizontal* only when the numerator $2\sin t$ is zero—that is, when t is an integer multiple of π. Again Figure 1 agrees: At $t = \pi$ the curve appears to be horizontal.

The curve C can be *vertical* only where the denominator $(1 - 2\cos t)$ is zero—that is, when $\cos t = 1/2$. One such value is $t = \pi/3 \approx 1.05$. ➡

■ *Yet again, Figure 1 agrees.*

Proof of Theorem 5 Suppose that $f'(t_0) \neq 0$; then either $f'(t_0) > 0$ or $f'(t_0) < 0$. If $f'(t_0) > 0$, then $f'(t) > 0$ for t near t_0, and so $x = f(t)$ must be *increasing* near $t = t_0$. Similarly, if $f'(t) < 0$ then $x = f(t)$ must be *decreasing* near $t = t_0$. In either case, $f(t) \neq f(t_0)$ if $t \neq t_0$ and t is near t_0. (This ensures that denominators don't vanish unexpectedly in the following limit computations.)

By definition, the slope in question is

$$\text{slope} = \frac{dy}{dx}\bigg|_{t=t_0} = \lim_{t \to t_0} \frac{y - y_0}{x - x_0} = \lim_{t \to t_0} \frac{g(t) - g(t_0)}{f(t) - f(t_0)}.$$

We'll be done if we show that the last quantity equals $g'(t_0)/f'(t_0)$.

We start with a little trick—dividing both numerator and denominator by $(t - t_0)$. Then we'll take limits of everything in sight and see what happens. Here goes:

$$\frac{dy}{dx}\bigg|_{t=t_0} = \lim_{t \to t_0} \frac{g(t) - g(t_0)}{f(t) - f(t_0)} \qquad \text{(by definition)}$$

$$= \lim_{t \to t_0} \frac{\frac{g(t)-g(t_0)}{t-t_0}}{\frac{f(t)-f(t_0)}{t-t_0}} \qquad \text{(by our trick)}$$

$$= \frac{\lim_{t \to t_0} \frac{g(t)-g(t_0)}{t-t_0}}{\lim_{t \to t_0} \frac{f(t)-f(t_0)}{t-t_0}} = \frac{g'(t_0)}{f'(t_0)} \qquad \text{(OK since } f'(t_0) \neq 0)$$

which is what we wanted to show. □

Modeling with parametric equations

Parametric equations often help model physical processes that involve quantities that vary in both time and space. **Trajectories**—paths taken by baseballs, missiles, thrown tomatoes, and other missiles—are one such setting.

Parametric curves are much more "flexible" than ordinary function graphs, so the former are more useful for "curve design."

EXAMPLE 10 A major-league fastball leaves the pitcher's hand traveling horizontally with initial speed 150 ft/sec and initial height 7 feet. Ignoring wind resistance, ➡ describe the ball's trajectory. When and at what speed does the ball cross the plate, 60.5 feet away? Is the pitch a strike? If the batter, catcher, and umpire all miss the ball, where does it land?

Major-league batters don't ignore wind resistance.

Solution We use an xy-coordinate system with its origin at the pitcher's feet, units measured in feet, and home plate at $(60.5, 0)$; the ball starts at $(0, 7)$. Since we ignore wind resistance, the ball is influenced only by gravity. Thus, the ball's horizontal acceleration is zero, and its vertical (upward) acceleration due to gravity is -32 feet per second per second. ➡

If $x = f(t)$ and $y = g(t)$ are measured in feet and t in seconds since the ball's release, then our information boils down to this:

Recall: acceleration is the second derivative of position.

$$f(0) = 0; \quad g(0) = 0; \quad f'(0) = 150; \quad g'(0) = 0; \quad f''(t) = 0; \quad g''(t) = -32.$$

These facts lead to simple formulas for both f and g. Here is the argument for f:

$$f''(t) = 0 \implies f'(t) = a \implies f(t) = at + b,$$

We did similar "free-fall" calculations in Section 2.5.

where a and b are constants, their values as yet unknown. (We found f by antidifferentiating twice.) ◀ To find values for a and b we combine the facts that $f(t) = at + b$, $f(0) = 0$, and $f'(0) = 150$ to conclude that $f(t) = 150t$. A similar argument applies to g; the result is

$$x = f(t) = 150t; \qquad x = g(t) = 7 - 16t^2.$$

A time-lapse photo of the ball's flight would be much flatter.

These equations make sense in context, of course, only while the ball remains airborne, that is, until $y = 7 - 16t^2 = 0$, or $t = \sqrt{7}/4 \approx 0.661$ seconds. Figure 6 shows the curve for $0 \le t \le 0.661$.

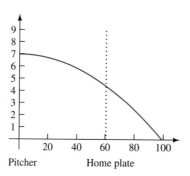

The horizontal and vertical units are different—this isn't a "photo" of the ball's flight.

Pitcher   Home plate

FIGURE 6
A baseball's trajectory: $x = f(t) = 150t$, $y = g(t) = 7 - 16t^2$, $0 \le t \le 0.661$

Notice especially the trajectory's parabolic shape. In fact, *every* free-falling object either moves vertically or follows a parabolic trajectory.

We can now answer our original questions. The ball crosses the plate when $x = f(t) = 150t = 60.5$, that is, when $t = 121/300 \approx 0.4033$ seconds. A little arithmetic shows that at this time,

$$\text{speed} = \sqrt{f'(0.4033)^2 + g'(0.4033)^2} \approx 150.55$$

This peculiar result suggests how unrealistic it is to ignore air drag.

feet per second. At the same time, the ball's height is $y = g(0.4033) \approx 4.4$ feet—high but in the strike zone for an average batter. If not hit, the ball lands at $t = 0.661$ seconds; at this time, $x = f(t) = 150 \cdot 0.661 \approx 99.2$ feet—almost 40 feet behind home plate. ■

Plot each parametric curve below. (Using a machine is fine, but then draw or copy your own curve on paper.) In each case, mark the direction of travel and label the points corresponding to $t = -1$, $t = 0$, and $t = 1$.

1. $x = t$, $y = \sqrt{1 - t^2}$, $-1 \le t \le 1$

2. $x = t$, $y = -\sqrt{1 - t^2}$, $-1 \le t \le 1$

3. $x = \sqrt{1 - t^2}$, $y = t$, $-1 \le t \le 1$

4. $x = -\sqrt{1 - t^2}$, $y = t$, $-1 \le t \le 1$

5. $x = \sin(\pi t)$, $y = \cos(\pi t)$, $-1 \le t \le 1$

6. Each parametric "curve" below is actually a line segment. In each part, state the beginning point ($t = 0$) and ending point ($t = 1$) of the segment. Then state an equation in x and y for the line each segment determines.

(a) $x = 2 + 3t$, $y = 1 + 2t$, $0 \le t \le 1$

(b) $x = 2 + 3(1 - t)$, $y = 1 + 2(1 - t)$, $0 \le t \le 1$

(c) $x = t$, $y = mt + b$, $0 \le t \le 1$

(d) $x = a + bt$, $y = c + dt$, $0 \le t \le 1$

(e) $x = x_0 + (x_1 - x_0)t$, $y = y_0 + (y_1 - y_0)t$, $0 \le t \le 1$

7. A parametric curve $x = f(t), y = g(t), a \le t \le b$ has **constant speed** if its speed is constant in t. Which of the curves in Exercises 1–5 have constant speed?

8. Show that if a curve C has linear coordinate functions $x = at + b$ and $y = ct + d$, then C has constant speed.

9. Consider the curve C shown in Example 1; suppose that t tells time in seconds.

   (a) At which bulleted points would you expect P to be moving quickly? Slowly? Justify your answers.

   (b) Use the curve to estimate the speed of P at $t = 3$. (One approach: Estimate how far P travels—i.e., the length of the curve—over the 1-second interval from $t = 2.5$ to $t = 3.5$. If d is this distance, then d distance units per second is a reasonable speed estimate at $t = 3$.)

   (c) Use the curve to estimate the speed of P at $t = 6$.

10. Plot the parametric curve

$$x = t^3; \qquad y = \sin t^3; \qquad -2 \le t \le 2.$$

What familiar curve is produced? Why does the result happen?

11. Let (a, b) be any point in the plane and $r > 0$ any positive number. Consider the parametric equations

$$x = a + r \cos t; \qquad y = b + r \sin t; \quad 0 \le t \le 2\pi.$$

   (a) Plot the parametric curve defined above for $(a, b) = (2, 1)$ and $r = 2$. Describe your result in words.

   (b) Show by calculation that if x and y are as above, then $(x - a)^2 + (y - b)^2 = r^2$. Conclude that the curve defined above is the circle with center (a, b) and radius r.

   (c) Write parametric equations for the circle of radius $\sqrt{13}$ centered at $(2, 3)$.

   (d) What "curve" results from the equations above if $r = 0$?

12. Let a and b be any positive numbers, and let a parametric curve C be defined by

$$x = a \cos t; \qquad y = b \sin t; \quad 0 \le t \le 2\pi.$$

The resulting curve is an **ellipse**.

   (a) Plot the curve defined above for $a = 2$ and $b = 1$. Describe C in words. Where is the "center" of C? Why do you think the quantities $2a$ and $2b$ are called the **major and minor axes** of C.

   (b) What curve results if $0 \le t \le 4\pi$? Why?

   (c) Write parametric equations for an ellipse with major axis 10 and minor axis 6.

   (d) Write parametric equations for another ellipse with major axis 10 and minor axis 6.

   (e) Show that for all t, $\dfrac{x^2}{a^2} + \dfrac{y^2}{b^2} = 1$.

   (f) How does the "ellipse" look if $a = b$? How does its xy-equation look?

   (g) How does an ellipse look if $a = 1000$ and $b = 1$?

   (h) How does an ellipse look if $a = 1$ and $b = 1000$?

13. Consider the Lissajou curve in Example 5.

   (a) Label the points corresponding to $t = 0$, $t = 0.1$, and $t = \pi/2$. Add some arrows to the curve to indicate direction.

   (b) How often in the interval $0 \le t \le 2\pi$ does the tracing point P return to $(0, 0)$?

   (c) How would the picture be different if the t-interval $0 \le t \le 4\pi$ were used?

14. We stated in this section that if a parametric curve C has linear coefficient functions, then C is a straight line (or part of a line). This exercise explores that fact.

   (a) Plot the parametric curve $x = 2t$, $y = 3t + 4$, $0 \le t \le 1$. Where does the curve start? Where does it end? What is its shape?

   (b) Eliminate the variable t in the two equations above to find a single equation in x and y for the line of the previous part.

   (c) Find the slope at $t = t_0$ of the parametric curve $x = 2t$, $y = 3t + 4$, $0 \le t \le 1$. Why doesn't the answer depend on t?

15. This exercise pursues the idea that if a parametric curve C has linear coefficient functions, then C is a straight line (or part of a line).

   (a) Consider the parametric curve $x = at + b$, $y = ct + d$, $t_0 \le t \le t_1$. Where does the curve start? Where does it end?

   (b) Assume that $a \ne 0$. (Don't assume that $c \ne 0$.) Eliminate the variable t in the two equations above to find one equation in x and y. What line does it describe?

   (c) Assume that $c \ne 0$. (Don't assume that $a \ne 0$.) Eliminate the variable t in the two equations above to find one equation in x and y. What line does it describe?

   (d) What happens if a and c are both zero?

16. This exercise explores the technical assumptions in the definition of smooth curves.

   (a) Consider the "curve" defined for all t by $x = 0$, $y = 0$. Plot C. Does C "deserve" to have a slope at $t = 0$? If so, what slope? If not, why not? Is C smooth in the sense of the definition?

   (b) Consider the curve defined for $-1 \le t \le 1$ by $x = t^3$ and $y = t^3$. Plot C. Does C "deserve" to have a slope at $t = 0$? What does Theorem 3 say in this case?

   (c) Consider the curve defined for $-1 \le t \le 1$ by $x = t$ and $y = t$. Plot C. Does this C "deserve" to have a slope at $t = 0$? What does Theorem 3 say about slope this time?

17. This exercise concerns Example 10.

   (a) How could the model be made more realistic? What additional information would be needed?

   (b) Use the conditions $g''(t) = -32$, $g'(0) = 0$, and $g(0) = 7$ to show that $g(t) = 7 - 16t^2$, as claimed in the Example.

   (c) Find a formula for $s(t)$, the ball's speed at time t. Plot $s(t)$ over an appropriate interval. How does the graph's shape reflect the physical situation?

18. Use parametric equations to describe the trajectory of a baseball thrown exactly as in Example 10, except that this time the initial velocity is 100 feet per second. Plot the result over an appropriate interval. Is the pitch a strike? At what speed does it cross the plate? (The strike zone is roughly from 1.5 to 4.5 feet above the ground at home plate.)

19. Consider a baseball thrown horizontally, starting from height 7 feet (as in Example 10) but with initial speed s_0.

    (a) Explain briefly why the parametric equations

    $$x = s_0 t, \quad y = 7 - 16t^2$$

    describe the ball's trajectory (ignoring wind resistance).

    (b) When does the ball reach home plate?

    (c) Is the trajectory parabolic? Why?

20. This exercise is about the situation in Example 10 but takes wind resistance into account. In practice, wind resistance *does* affect a baseball's trajectory. One possible model of wind resistance (we omit the details) leads to the parametric equations

    $$x = \frac{\ln(150 \cdot k \cdot t + 1)}{k}; \quad y = 7 - 16t^2,$$

    where the constant k can be thought of as the ball's "drag coefficient"—the smoother the ball, the lower the value of k. For a typical baseball, $k = 0.003$ is reasonable. With this value of k we get

    $$x = \frac{1000 \ln(0.45t + 1)}{3}; \quad y = 7 - 16t^2.$$

The resulting trajectory is plotted below; the curve from Example 10 is also shown.

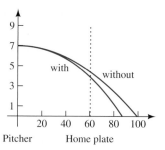

In each part below, use the graphs to give approximate answers; then use appropriate formulas to improve your results.

(a) At what time does the air-dragged ball cross the plate? How much longer does it take to reach the plate than the dragless ball?

(b) At what height does the air-dragged ball cross the plate?

(c) At what speed does the air-dragged ball cross the plate?

(d) Where does the air-dragged ball land?

21. The situation is as in the previous exercise except that, because the ball is scuffed, its "drag coefficient" is 0.005, not 0.003. Plot the new trajectory. Then answer the same questions as in the previous exercise.

4.5 RELATED RATES

No surprises here: If an equation relates several quantities (x, y, z, . . .), each varying in time, then the derivatives (x′, y′, z′, . . .) relate the rates at which these quantities vary. We try to keep it simple.

Relating amounts, relating rates Calculus was invented to describe and predict phenomena of change. In real-world settings, several quantities often vary *together* over time. Not surprisingly, the *rates* at which these quantities vary are also related to each other. Calculus lets us describe and calculate such **related rates.**

EXAMPLE 1 A point P "orbits" the origin counterclockwise on a circle of radius 2. An observer Q stands at the "east pole" of a circle of radius 1; Figure 1 gives an overhead view.

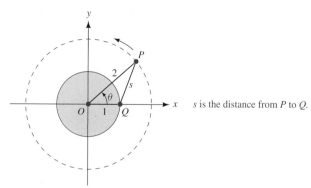

FIGURE 1
An orbiting point

Describe several quantities that vary as P moves in its orbit. Interpret derivatives of these quantities as rates of change.

Solution   *Lots* of quantities vary with time: the x- and y-coordinates of P, the distance s between P and Q, the angle θ, and others. All of them can be considered functions of time; their derivatives describe the corresponding rates. The derivative ds/dt, for example, tells how fast, in appropriate units, the distance from P to Q increases or decreases. (We'll calculate some rates in a later example.)   ■

Solving related rates problems   The typical related rates problem involves several amounts that vary together; the problem is to compute some particular rate of change, given information about one or more *other* rates of change. Solving such problems may be hard or easy (depending partly on how cleverly the needed information is camouflaged), but the underlying *idea* is quite simple: ➡

> *Write an equation that relates two or more amounts that vary with time. Differentiate both sides with respect to time, using the chain rule. The resulting equation relates the rates at which the quantities vary. Solve this equation for the desired rate.*

In some cases several amount and rate equations are needed.

A basic example illustrates the idea and the method.

The example itself isn't very interesting, but it illustrates the method about as simply as possible.

EXAMPLE 2   A point P moves from left to right along the curve $y = x^2$ at a constant *horizontal* speed of 3 units per second. ➡ How fast does the y-coordinate of P increase at the moment when P passes through $(1, 1)$? When P passes $(2, 4)$?

In other words, the shadow cast by P on the x-axis moves rightward at 3 units per second.

Solution   Several quantities vary together with time; the two of interest here are $x(t)$ and $y(t)$, the x- and y-coordinates of P at time t. The question asks that we relate an unknown rate, $y'(t)$, to the *known* rate $x'(t) = 3$.

Since P moves on the parabola $y = x^2$, the quantities x and y are related by the equation

$$y(t) = \left(x(t) \right)^2$$

for all t. Differentiating both sides with respect to t (using the chain rule) gives a relation between two rates:

$$\frac{dy}{dt} = 2x(t)\frac{dx}{dt}$$

(or just $y' = 2xx'$).

Now we can solve the problem. By assumption, $x' = dx/dt = 3$ for all t. At the point $(1, 1)$ we have $x = 1$, so

$$\frac{dy}{dt} = 2x(t)\frac{dx}{dt} = 2 \cdot 1 \cdot 3 = 6 \text{ units per second,}$$

while at $(x, y) = (2, 4)$,

$$\frac{dy}{dt} = 2x(t)\frac{dx}{dt} = 2 \cdot 2 \cdot 3 = 12 \text{ units per second.}$$

Notice, finally, a consequence of the rate equation $y' = 2xx'$: Although x increases at a *constant* rate of 3 units per second, the y-coordinate of P increases faster and faster as time goes on. ➡   ■

Would you have guessed this without any calculation?

Using favorite formulas   Textbook authors love related rates problems. The resource is infinitely renewable, and the problems let us recycle some fine old favorites: volume and area formulas, similar triangles, the law of cosines, the Pythagorean rule, and more.

Note the confession — trigonometric relations (such as similar triangles) are especially useful.

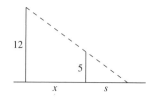

FIGURE 2
Shadows and similar triangles

Several exercises in this section concern this situation.

EXAMPLE 3 (Similar triangles come out of the shadows) A venerable family of related rates problems concerns moving shadows. Figure 2, for instance, represents (crudely) a 5-foot student, Cal, at distance x feet from a 12-foot lamp post; her shadow is s feet long. How does Cal's shadow lengthen as she moves away from the lamp post?

Solution The **similar triangles** in Figure 2 lead to a simple relation between x and s (both of which vary with time t):

$$\frac{12}{x+s} = \frac{5}{s} \implies 12s = 5x + 5s \implies 7s = 5x.$$

Differentiating with respect to t gives $7s' = 5x'$, or $s' = 5x'/7$. Thus, Cal's shadow lengthens at a rate proportional to her walking speed. If, say, Cal walks at a constant 7 feet per second away from the lamp post, then her shadow grows at a constant 5 feet per minute. ∎

EXAMPLE 4 (Orbits, angles, and the law of cosines) Suppose that the orbiting point P of Example 1 moves counterclockwise at a constant speed, making one revolution per hour. (This means that the angle θ increases at a constant 2π radians per hour, and so $d\theta/dt = 2\pi$.) Find and interpret the rates $dx/dt, dy/dt$, and ds/dt, all at the moment when $\theta = \pi/4$.

Solution The first step is to write equations relating x, y, s, and θ. Here are two simple possibilities:

$$x = 2\cos\theta; \qquad y = 2\sin\theta.$$

Differentiating each equation with respect to t (using the chain rule) gives

$$\frac{dx}{dt} = -2\sin(\theta)\frac{d\theta}{dt}; \qquad \frac{dy}{dt} = 2\cos(\theta)\frac{d\theta}{dt}.$$

Setting $\theta = \pi/4$ and $d\theta/dt = 2\pi$ gives

$$\frac{dx}{dt} = -2\sqrt{2}\pi \approx -8.89; \qquad \frac{dy}{dt} = 2\sqrt{2}\pi \approx 8.89.$$

These results mean that when $\theta = \pi/4$ the x-coordinate of P is *decreasing* at about 8.89 units per hour while the the y-coordinate of P is *increasing* at the same speed.

One way to relate s and θ is to use the **law of cosines**:

Suppose a triangle has sides of length a and b, with angle θ between these sides. Then the third side c satisfies $c^2 = a^2 + b^2 - 2ab\cos\theta$.

Applying this to the triangle OPQ in Figure 1 gives the equation $s^2 = 5 - 4\cos\theta$. Again we differentiate everything in sight with respect to t:

$$s^2 = 5 - 4\cos\theta \implies 2s\frac{ds}{dt} = 4\sin(\theta)\frac{d\theta}{dt} \implies \frac{ds}{dt} = 2\frac{\sin\theta}{s}\frac{d\theta}{dt}$$

Now when $\theta = \pi/4$ we have $s = \sqrt{5 - 4\cos\theta} = \sqrt{5 - 2\sqrt{2}}$. Plugging this into the preceding equation gives

$$\frac{ds}{dt} = 2\pi\frac{\sqrt{2}}{\sqrt{5 - 2\sqrt{2}}} \approx 6.030$$

units of distance per hour. ∎

EXAMPLE 5 (Pythagoras, Newton, and the State Patrol) It's spring break at Huxley College; the annual migration to Fort Lauderdale has begun. A State Patrol helicopter hovers 1000 feet directly above the southbound highway, with Officer Ingkvist at the radar gun.

A car with Huxley decals passes underneath and continues south. Jason and Medea, fresh from their calculus midterm, aren't watching the speedometer. Officer Ingkvist fires, and the results flash back: At the moment of firing the car was 2000 feet from the helicopter and moving away at 85 feet per second. "Got 'em!" mutters Ingkvist under her breath. What happens next?

Solution   Jason and Medea deny all wrongdoing. "The speed limit is 65 mph," they tell the judge. "We were clocked at 85 feet per second. But a simple calculation shows that 65 mph is 95 feet per second. Hence, clearly, we couldn't have been speeding." ➤

Under duress even students say "hence" and "clearly."

"Watch your language," says the judge, "but what you say makes sense. Explain yourself, Ingkvist. Use that blackboard. Be clear. And cite your sources."

Officer Ingkvist rises calmly; she's been through this before. Do judges *never* learn? She draws a diagram (Figure 3).

"In the diagram, your honor, H is the helicopter, C is the car, l is the straight-line distance from H to C, x is the horizontal distance from H to C, and 1000 feet is the constant height of the helicopter. The amounts x and l vary with time, of course. Pythagoras says, however, that at *any* time t, x and l satisfy the equation $l^2 = x^2 + 1000^2$. Newton says that differentiating this relation between l and x with respect to t relates the rates of change of l and x, as follows:

$$l^2 = x^2 + 1000^2 \implies 2l \cdot \frac{dl}{dt} = 2x \cdot \frac{dx}{dt} \implies \frac{dx}{dt} = \frac{l}{x} \cdot \frac{dl}{dt}.$$

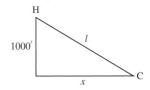

FIGURE 3
Officer Ingkvist's diagram

At the time in question dl/dt was 85 and l was 2000, and so x was $\sqrt{2000^2 - 1000^2} = 1000\sqrt{3}$. Hence, at that moment, Jason and Medea's southward speed was

$$\frac{dx}{dt} = \frac{l}{x} \cdot \frac{dl}{dt} = \frac{2000}{1000\sqrt{3}} \cdot 85 \approx 98.1495457622 \text{ feet per second,}$$

clearly a violation of law. Any questions?"

"Just one," says the judge. "Who are Pythagoras and Newton, and why won't they testify in person?"

"Never mind," say Jason and Medea, "we'll pay."   ∎

BASIC EXERCISES

1. Let $x(t)$ and $y(t)$ be variable quantities related by the equation $x + 2y = 3$. (This occurs if x and y are the coordinates of a point that moves along the line $x + 2y = 3$.)

  (a) Show that $x'(t) = -2y'(t)$ for all t.

  (b) At a certain moment, x is increasing at 1 unit/second. How fast is y increasing or decreasing at this moment?

  (c) Relate the result of the preceding part to the line $x + 2y = 3$. (Mention slope.)

2. Let $x(t)$ and $y(t)$ be variable quantities related by the equation $y = f(x)$. (This occurs if x and y are the coordinates of a point that moves along the curve $y = f(x(t))$.)

  (a) Show that $y'(t) = f'(x)x'(t)$.

  (b) At a certain moment, x is increasing at 1 unit/second. How fast is y increasing or decreasing at this moment?

  (c) Relate the result of the preceding part to the curve $y = f(x)$. (Mention slope.)

3. Let $x(t)$ and $y(t)$ be variable quantities related by the equation $x^2 + y^2 = 1$. (This occurs if x and y are the coordinates of a point that moves along the unit circle $x^2 + y^2 = 1$.)

  (a) Show that $x(t)x'(t) + y(t)y'(t) = 0$ for all t.

  (b) Suppose that $x(0) = 1$ and $y'(0) = 1$. Find $y(0)$ and $x'(0)$. Where is the moving point at this time? In what direction is it moving?

  (c) Suppose that $x(t_0) = 1/2$ and $x'(t_0) = 1$. Then there *two* possible values for $y(t_0)$. Find both of these values and the corresponding values of $y'(t_0)$.

  (d) Interpret your answers in the preceding part in terms of the moving point: Where is the point at time t_0? In which direction is it moving?

4. In the situation of Example 3, Cal's 6-foot-tall brother Hal walks away from the lamp post at 7 feet per second. How long is Hal's shadow when Hal is 10 feet from the lamp post? At what rate is Hal's shadow lengthening at this moment?

5. In the situation of Example 3, Cal's 6-foot-tall brother Hal walks away from the lamp post at 7 feet per second. How long is Hal's shadow when Hal is 30 feet from the lamp post? At what rate is Hal's shadow lengthening at this moment?

6. In the situation of Example 3, Cal and Hal's 2-foot-tall dog, Sal, runs *toward* the lamp post at 12 feet per second on an urgent canine errand. How fast is Sal's shadow lengthening or shortening when Sal is 12 feet from the post?

7. The width of a rectangle is increasing at a rate of 2 cm/sec, and its length is increasing at a rate of 3 cm/sec. At what rate is the area of the rectangle increasing when its width is 4 cm and its length is 5 cm?

8. Two cars leave an intersection simultaneously. One travels north at 30 mph, the other travels east at 40 mph. How fast is the distance between them changing after 5 minutes?

9. At a certain moment, one bicyclist is 4 miles east of an intersection traveling toward the intersection at the rate of 9 miles/hour. At the same time a second bicyclist is 3 miles south of the intersection traveling away from the intersection at the rate of 10 miles/hour. Is the distance between the bicyclists increasing or decreasing at that moment? At what rate?

10. A radio transmitter is located 3 miles from a straight section of interstate highway. A truck is traveling away from the transmitter along the highway at a speed of 65 miles per hour. How fast is the distance between the truck and the transmitter increasing when they are 5 miles apart?

11. A baseball diamond is a square 90 ft on a side. A runner travels from home plate to first base at 20 ft/sec. How fast is the runner's distance from second base changing when the runner is halfway to first base?

FURTHER EXERCISES

12. The length of the base of a right triangle is increasing at the rate of 2 inches per minute. At the same time, the height of the triangle is decreasing in such a way that the length of the hypotenuse remains 10 inches. When the length of the base is 6 inches,

(a) how quickly is the height of the triangle changing?

(b) is the area of the triangle increasing? Justify your answer.

13. Two concentric circles are expanding, the outer radius at a rate of 2 feet per second and the inner one at 5 feet per second. At a certain instant, the outer radius is 10 feet, and the inner radius is 3 feet. At this instant, is the area of the ring between the two circles increasing or decreasing? Justify your answer.

14. Boyle's law states that if the temperature of a gas remains constant, then the pressure P and the volume V of the gas satisfy the equation $PV = c$, where c is a constant. If the volume is decreasing at the rate of 10 in^3 per second, how fast is the pressure increasing when the pressure is 100 lbs/in^2 and the volume is 20 in^3?

15. Two aircraft are in the vicinity of the Erehwon air traffic control center in Neverland. Pachyderm flight 1003 from Celesteville to Paris is approaching from the south, and Peterpan flight 366 from London to Wendytown is approaching from the east. Both are at an altitude of 33,000 feet on paths that will take them directly over the air traffic control center. The Pachyderm flight is 36 nautical miles from the center and approaching it at a rate of 410 knots. The Peterpan flight is 41 nautical miles from the center and approaching it at a rate of 455 knots. [NOTE: One **nautical mile** is equal to 1852 meters. One **knot** is 1 nautical mile per hour.]

(a) How close will the planes come to each other? Will they violate the FAA's minimum separation requirement of 5 nautical miles?

(b) How many minutes before the time of closest approach?

16. Sand is being dumped on a pile in such a way that it always forms a cone whose radius equals its height. If the sand is being dumped at a rate of 10 cubic feet per minute, at what rate is the height of the pile increasing when there is 1000 cubic feet of sand in the pile?

17. A tanker accident has spilled oil in Pristine Bay. Oil-eating bacteria are gobbling 5 ft^3/hr. The oil slick has the form of a circular cylinder. When the radius of the cylinder is 500 ft, the thickness of the slick is 0.01 ft and decreasing at a rate of 0.001 ft/hr. At what rate is the area of the slick changing at this time? Is the area of the slick increasing or decreasing?

18. Oil is leaking from an ocean tanker at the rate of 5000 liters per minute. The leakage results in a circular oil slick. The depth of the oil varies linearly from a maximum of 5 cm at the point of leakage to a minimum of 0.5 cm at the outside edge of the slick. How fast is the radius of the slick increasing 4 hours after the tanker started leaking? [NOTE: 1 liter = 1000 cm^3.]

19. A spherical ball 8 inches in diameter is coated with a layer of ice of uniform thickness.

(a) If the ice melts at the rate of 10 in^3/min, how fast is the thickness of the ice decreasing when it is 2 inches thick?

(b) How fast is the outer surface area of the ice decreasing at this time?

20. Bazooka Joe is blowing a spherical bubble gum bubble. Let V be the volume of gum in the bubble, R the inside radius of the bubble, and T the thickness of the bubble; V, T, and R are functions of time t.

(a) Write a formula for V in terms of T and R. [HINT: Draw a picture.]

(b) Assume that the amount of bubble gum in the bubble is not changing. Find a formula for $V'(t)$?

(c) After 5 minutes of blowing, the bubble is 3 feet in diameter and 0.01 feet thick. If the inside radius of the bubble is expanding at a rate of 0.5 feet per minute, how fast is the thickness changing?

[HINT: Remember that the volume of gum in the bubble does not change over time.]

21. A baseball diamond is a square 90 ft on a side. A batter hits a ball along the third base line at 100 ft/sec and runs to first base at 25 ft/sec.

(a) At what rate is the distance between the ball and first base changing when the ball is halfway to third base?

(b) At what rate is the distance between the ball and the player changing when the ball is halfway to third base?

22. A highway patrol plane flies 1 mile above a straight section of rural interstate highway at a steady ground speed of 120 miles per hour. The pilot sees an oncoming car and, with radar, determines that the line-of-sight distance from the plane to the car is 1.5 miles and that this distance is decreasing at a rate of 136 miles per hour. Should the driver of the car be given a ticket for speeding? Tell it to the judge. (Assume the judge knows calculus and that the speed limit is 65 miles per hour.)

23. A coffee filter has the shape of an inverted cone. Water drains out of the filter at a rate of 10 cm³/min. When the depth of water in the cone is 8 cm, the depth is decreasing at 2 cm/min. What is the ratio of the height of the cone to its radius?

24. An inverted cone has height 10 cm and radius 2 cm. It is partially filled with liquid, which is oozing through the sides at a rate proportional to the area of the cone in contact with the liquid. Liquid is also being poured in the top of the cone at a rate of 1 cm³/min. When the depth of the liquid in the cone is 4 cm, the depth is decreasing at a rate of 0.1 cm/min. At what rate must liquid be poured into the top of the cone to keep the liquid at a constant depth of 4 cm?

25. The minute and hour hands on the face of a town clock are 7 feet and 5 feet long, respectively. How fast is the distance between the tips of the hands increasing when the clock reads 9:00?

26. A swimming pool is 15 feet wide, 40 feet long, 3 feet deep at one end, and 10 feet deep at the other end (see the sketch). Water is being added to it at the rate of 25 cubic feet per minute.

(a) How fast is the water level rising when there is 2000 cubic feet of water in the pool?

(b) How fast is the water level rising when there is 3000 cubic feet of water in the pool?

27. A rocket rises vertically from a point on the ground that is 100 m from an observer at ground level. The observer notes that the angle of elevation is increasing at a rate of 12 degrees per second when the angle of elevation is 60 degrees. Find the speed of the rocket at that instant.

28. A Ferris wheel, 50 feet in diameter, revolves at the rate of 10 radians per minute. How fast is a passenger rising when the passenger is 15 feet higher than the center of the Ferris wheel and is rising?

29. The ends of a horizontal trough 10 ft long are isosceles trapezoids with lower base 3 ft, upper base 5 ft, and altitude 2 ft. If the water level is rising at a rate of 0.25 in./min when the depth is 1 ft, how fast is water entering the trough?

30. An airplane flying east at 400 mph goes over a certain town at 11:30 A.M., and a second plane, flying northeast at 500 mph goes over the same town at noon. How fast are they separating at 1:00 P.M.? (Assume that the planes are at the same altitude.)

4.6 NEWTON'S METHOD: FINDING ROOTS

We keep things simple; an Interlude (see page 298) goes into a little more detail.

Consider these problems:

- Let $s(x) = x^2 - 2$. Find a **root** of s; that is, a number r such that $s(r) = 0$.
- Find a root of $f(x) = 2x^3 - x - 2$.

The problems aren't as easy as they look. True, the two roots of s are $\pm\sqrt{2}$, but how can we find these numbers to high *numerical* accuracy—to 10 decimal places, say? The function f poses another challenge: Although f has a simple formula, standard algebra tools (factoring, the quadratic formula, etc.) don't seem to help. ➡

See for yourself: try factoring f.

Finding roots of functions is often important in mathematics, and especially so in calculus—we do it whenever we look for a function's stationary points or vertical asymptotes, for example. In such contexts we may not say (or even think) much about the root-finding step given the bigger and flashier ideas at hand. But, glamorous or not, root-finding is often essential to using calculus effectively.

If calculus relies on root-finding, then **Newton's method** returns the favor: It uses a basic calculus idea (the tangent line) to find roots. Newton's method is simple but remarkably effective. One version of the idea may go back to ancient Babylonian and Chinese mathematicians, who calculated square roots around 2000 B.C., while modern versions are used in mathematical software. We describe Newton's method in this section and use it to make quick work of both problems above.

Roots—graphical and algebraic views

A root of a function f is an x-intercept of the f-graph, and so (given the right graph) it's easy to approximate roots just by looking.

> **EXAMPLE 1**   Figure 1 gives two views of the function $f(x) = 2x^3 - x - 2$. Use them to estimate a root.

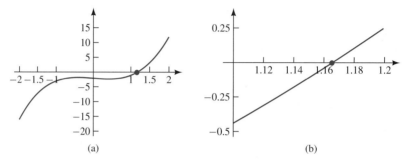

FIGURE 1
Two views of $f(x) = 2x^3 - x - 2$

> **Solution**   The first graph shows a root somewhere near $x = 1$; the second locates it more precisely, near $x = 1.165$. Further zooming might reveal additional digits, but Newton's method is more efficient.   ■

Roots can *sometimes* be found by solving equations algebraically, but only if a function has a reasonably simple formula. For one type of function—linear functions—roots are *always* easy to find.

> **EXAMPLE 2**   A line passes through the point (x_0, y_0) with slope m. Find its x-intercept algebraically. Does the method *always* work?
>
> **Solution**   The line has point–slope equation $y - y_0 = m(x - x_0)$. To find the x-intercept we set $y = 0$ and solve for x:
>
> $$-y_0 = m(x - x_0) \iff x = x_0 - \frac{y_0}{m}. \tag{1}$$
>
> This formula works with only one exception: If $m = 0$ and $y_0 \neq 0$, then the line is horizontal and has no x-intercept.   ■

Students might try, using the picture, to write the Newton iteration formula.

Newton's idea: ride the tangent line

Most functions are *not* linear, so they don't lend themselves directly to the method of Equation 1. But calculus functions are closely approximated by linear functions—this fact turns out to be the basis of Newton's method. Figure 2 illustrates Newton's idea.

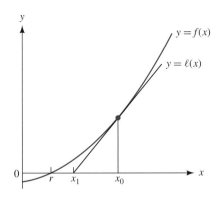

FIGURE 2
The idea of Newton's method: one step

The following picture illustrates one **Newton step**: We start with an **initial guess** (x_0 in the picture) and "ride the tangent line" to produce a new approximate root x_1. In the case shown (and in many others), the new approximation is *much* better than its predecessor. Indeed, if f happens to be a (non-horizontal) linear function, then for *any* initial guess x_0 the next estimate is an *exact* root.

Repeat...   The big idea behind Newton's method is to *repeat* (**iterate**, in math-speak) the process just outlined to produce a sequence $x_0, x_1, x_2, x_3, \ldots$ of *successive* approximations to a root. Each approximation is obtained from its predecessor in the same way:

$$x_{n+1} \text{ is the } x\text{-intercept of the tangent line at } x = x_n.$$

In many cases (as Figure 3 suggests) these successive estimates "converge" quickly toward a root.

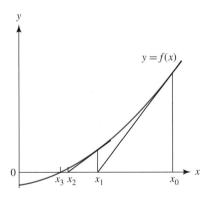

FIGURE 3
Several Newton steps: converging toward a root

Equation 1, with $m = f'(x_0)$, gives an explicit recipe for moving from one estimate to the next:

> **DEFINITION (Newton's method)** Let f be a function and x_0 any estimate to a root of f. For $n \geq 1$, the rule
>
> $$x_{n+1} = x_n - \frac{f(x_n)}{f'(x_n)} \qquad (2)$$
>
> produces a sequence $x_0, x_1, x_2, \ldots$ of estimates.

Notice:

- **An iteration function** It's convenient to express Newton's method using an **iteration function** N (for Newton), defined by

$$N(x) = x - \frac{f(x)}{f'(x)}.$$

This "iterative" view is especially convenient for machines.

Newton's method amounts to applying N repeatedly to an initial input x_0. ◂

$$x_1 = N(x_0), \quad x_2 = N(x_1), \quad x_3 = N(x_2), \quad \ldots.$$

Each iteration represents one **Newton step**.

- **Roots and fixed points** If x_n happens to *be* a root of f, and $f'(x_n) \neq 0$, then Equation 2 shows that $x_{n+1} = N(x_n) = x_n$. Thus, repeating the process has no further effect, and the process stops.

  A number r for which if $N(r) = r$ is called a **fixed point** of the function N. In the present case, fixed points of N are roots of f. (The modern theory of *dynamical systems* studies function iteration—fixed points are of special interest.)

The definition defines a sequence recursively; students might need some simpler examples (e.g., $x_{n+1} = 1 + x_n$) to understand the idea.

- **Sequences and convergence** In later chapters we'll study the ideas of **sequence** and **convergence** more carefully. For the moment, a sequence is simply a list of numbers, and "convergence" means "getting closer to."

EXAMPLE 3 We estimated graphically that $f(x) = 2x^3 - x - 2$ has a root near $x = 1.17$. Use Newton's method to do better.

Solution With $f(x) = 2x^3 - x - 2$, Newton's rule is

$$x_{n+1} = x_n - \frac{f(x_n)}{f'(x_n)} = x_n - \frac{2x_n^3 - x_n - 2}{6x_n^2 - 1}.$$

If, say, $x_0 = 1$, then a calculator gives

$$x_1 = 1.2, \quad x_2 \approx 1.1664921, \quad x_3 \approx 1.1653743, \quad x_4 \approx 1.1653730.$$

Because the first 5 digits after the decimal point appear stable, $r \approx 1.16537$ is a reasonable estimate to a root, accurate to 5 digits. ∎

How accurate? The successive Newton estimates in Example 3 appear to converge quickly to a root, with more and more digits "stabilizing" at each iteration. It's usually safe to trust these digits—as we just did. Although things *can* go wrong, the real surprise is how quickly and effectively Newton's method usually works. (It can be shown, in fact, that under good conditions each Newton step roughly *doubles* the number of correct digits.)

One way to check accuracy (if we feel the need) is to evaluate f at some nearby inputs. In the case of Example 3, for instance, we have

$$f(1.165365) \approx -0.00006 \quad \text{and} \quad f(1.165375) \approx 0.00001.$$

The sign change guarantees that, as expected, f has an x-intercept somewhere *between* $x = 1.165365$ and $x = 1.165375$.

Why bother? Isaac Newton did without computer graphics. We have them, so why do we bother with Newton's method? Why not just zoom in visually to find roots to any desired accuracy? One important reason concerns efficiency of effort. Whether done by human or machine, plotting functions requires dozens or even hundreds of function evaluations—an "expensive" proposition even for fast computers. Newton's method is *far* more efficient. For many functions, each successive Newton estimate has about twice as many correct digits as its predecessor.

Using Newton's method

Applying calculus ideas to solve problems often depends, sooner or later, on finding roots. Newton's method can speed the process. We illustrate with two examples.

EXAMPLE 4 Even a cheap calculator "knows" that $\sqrt{2} \approx 1.4142136$. How can this be? Could we find even more digits?

Solution Let's ask Newton. Our target, $\sqrt{2}$, is a root of $f(x) = x^2 - 2$. Newton's formula and a little algebra give

$$x_{n+1} = x_n - \frac{f(x_n)}{f'(x_n)} = x_n - \frac{x_n^2 - 2}{2x_n} = \frac{x_n}{2} + \frac{1}{x_n}.$$

Starting with $x_0 = 1.5$, successive estimates quickly zero in on $\sqrt{2}$:

$$x_1 \approx 1.41421568628, \quad x_2 \approx 1.41421356238, \quad x_3 \approx 1.41421356237.$$

Newton's method took only 3 steps to find 12 meaningful digits! ∎

EXAMPLE 5 Which point P on the parabola $y = x^2$ is closest to $(2, 1)$?

Solution Figure 4 shows the situation.

Another approach is to write a distance function $D(x)$, and then use Newton's method to find a root of D'.

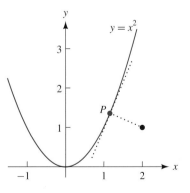

The two dotted lines are perpendicular.

FIGURE 4
Which point on $y = x^2$ is closest to $(2, 1)$?

The picture lets us estimate P crudely, but it also suggests a useful property of P:

The segment from $(2, 1)$ to P is perpendicular to the tangent line at P.

We'll write this condition as an equation we can solve to find P.

Since P lies on the parabola, its coordinates have the form (r, r^2). Now the tangent line P has slope $2r$ (because x^2 has derivative $2x$), while the segment from $(2, 1)$ to P has slope $(r^2 - 1)/(r - 2)$. The perpendicularity property means that these two slopes are negative reciprocals:

$$\frac{r^2 - 1}{r - 2} = -\frac{1}{2r}.$$

Does this result look graphically plausible?

Clearing denominators gives $2r^3 - r - 2 = 0$, which is the very equation we solved in Example 3; we got $r \approx 1.16537$. Thus, $P = (r, r^2) \approx (1.16537, 1.35809)$. ◄   ■

An Interlude (see page 298) goes into more detail on these possible problems.

Breaking Newton's method

Newton's method usually works impressively, but it *can* fail—for any of several reasons. For instance, if $f'(x_n) = 0$, then Newton's rule makes no sense, and the process stops. The following examples show other possible glitches.

EXAMPLE 6   (A near-horizontal tangent line)   Newton's method breaks down completely if $f'(x_0) = 0$. But even a *near* miss can cause trouble.
  Let $f(x) = \sin x$ and $x_0 = 1.3$. (The nearest root of f is at $x = 0$.) How does Newton's method behave?

Solution   Applying Newton's method with initial guess $x_0 = 1.3$ gives

$$x_1 \approx -2.3021; \quad x_2 \approx -3.4166; \quad x_3 \approx -3.1344; \quad x_4 \approx -3.1416.$$

We found a root at $x = -\pi$, but perhaps not the one we expected. Figure 5 explains what happened:

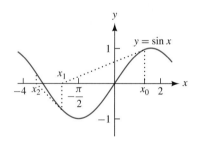

FIGURE 5

A shallow tangent: finding the "wrong" root

The tangent line at x_0 is nearly horizontal—riding it to the x-axis took us far afield.   ■

EXAMPLE 7   (Cycling)   In unusual (but interesting) circumstances, successive Newton's approximations "cycle" endlessly, never finding a root. To see this, apply Newton's method to $f(x) = x^3 - 6x^2 + 7x + 2$, with initial guess $x_0 = 1$. What happens? Why? Where are the roots of f *really* located?

Check for yourself, by hand or by calculator.

Solution   Successive Newton's estimates are an endless chain: $1, 3, 1, 3, \ldots$. ◄
Figure 6 shows why.

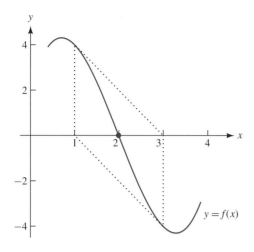

FIGURE 6
Cycling around with Newton

The graph shows one root at $x = 2$ and hints at two others not far away. (In fact, the roots turn out to be $x = 2$, $x = 2 - \sqrt{5} \approx -0.24$, and $x = 2 + \sqrt{5} \approx 4.24$.) Starting Newton's method from various initial guesses will find all three roots.

In the picture, we carefully chose our initial guess as *badly* as possible: 1 leads to 3, 3 back to 1, and so on forever. Almost any *other* initial guess would have "succeeded." With $x_0 = 1.01$, for instance, Newton's method gives

$$1.01, \quad 2.9421750, \quad 1.2842171, \quad 2.2117999, \quad 1.9960944, \quad 2.0000000.$$

Thus, moving the initial guess even *slightly* away from $x = 1$ changes the result dramatically.   ■

The butterfly effect Tiny changes in an initial guess x_0 for Newton's method can lead to very different results, as Example 7 shows. This phenomenon—small causes producing large effects—occurs often in mathematics and in the real world. It's sometimes called the **butterfly effect**: A butterfly's wing flap in Wichita could trigger a typhoon in Taiwan. Mathematicians use a more prosaic name: **sensitive dependence on initial conditions**.

BASIC EXERCISES

1. By hand, find the first three Newton estimates for $\sqrt{5}$, starting with $x_0 = 2$. Write your answers as fractions.
[HINT: First use the Definition on page 258 to write a simple formula for x_{n+1} in terms of x_n.]

2. Suppose that Newton's method is used to estimate $\sqrt[3]{28}$. If $x_0 = 3$, evaluate x_1. (Express your answer as a rational number.)

3. The function shown below has roots near -1.88, 0.35, and 1.53. Which of these roots, if any, will Newton's method converge to if $x_0 = 0.95$? Justify your answer.

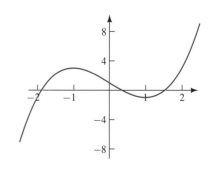

4. Use Newton's method with the value of x_0 indicated to compute approximate values of each of the following expressions. (Iterate until successive approximations agree to three decimal places.)

    (a) $\sqrt[3]{100}$; $x_0 = 4.5$

    (b) $(13)^{-2}$; $x_0 = 0.01$

5. (a) Use Newton's method to find a solution of the equation $x^5 + 4x - 3 = 0$ in the interval $[0, 1]$ to three-decimal-place accuracy.

    (b) Does the equation in part (a) have any other solutions? Justify your answer.

6. Find a solution of the equation $x \tan x = 1$ in the interval $[0, \pi/2]$ to three-decimal accuracy.

7. Throughout this problem, let $f(x) = x^2 - a$, where a is a positive number.

    (a) Calculate and simplify the Newton iteration function $N(x)$.

    (b) Show that if $x > 0$ and $x \ne \sqrt{a}$, then $\sqrt{a}$ lies *between* x and a/x.

    (c) Show that $N(x)$ can written as $N(x) = \frac{1}{2}\left(x + \frac{a}{x}\right)$. (In other words, $N(x)$ is the *average* of x and a/x—a reasonable place to look for an improved estimate to $\sqrt{a}$.)

    (d) Use the formula of the preceding part to calculate the first four Newton estimates for $\sqrt{2}$, starting with $x_0 = 1$. Write answers as *fractions*.

8. Throughout this problem, let $f(x) = x^3 - 5x$.

    (a) What does Newton's method produce if $x_0 = 1$? What if $x_0 = -1$? Why? (Use both a graph and a formula in your explanation.)

    (b) Use algebra (not Newton's method) to find all three roots of f.

    (c) Use Newton's method (choose your own initial guesses) to find all three roots to five decimal places.

9. Throughout this problem, let $f(x) = x^2 - 1$. (Yes, the roots are obvious.)

    (a) Find the first four Newton estimates to a root, starting with $x_0 = 2$. To how many decimal places is each estimate accurate?

    (b) For which starting points x_0 does Newton's method "find" the root at $x = 1$? The root at $x = -1$? For which starting points does Newton's method fail? (No proofs necessary; just experiment.)

FURTHER EXERCISES

10. Showing your work, derive Equation 1, page 256. Use the result to find the x-intercepts of each of the following lines:

    (a) Through $(1, 1)$, with slope 1.

    (b) Through $(1, 2)$, with slope 3.

    (c) The line with equation $y = mx + b$.

    (d) The line tangent to the graph $y = x^2$ at $x = 1$.

    (e) The line tangent to the graph $y = x^2 - 3$ at $x = 1$.

11. Use Equation 1 to derive Equation 2. Show all work.

12. Here's another way to find the point P on the parabola $y = x^2$ that's closest to $(2, 1)$:

    (a) Let $d(r)$ be the distance from $(2, 1)$ to $P = (r, r^2)$. Write a formula for $d(r)$.

    (b) At the desired value of r, d has a local minimum, so $d'(r) = 0$. Write out and simplify the equation $d'(r) = 0$. Does the result look familiar?

13. Let $f(x) = x^2 - a$.

    (a) Explain why the two numbers x and a/x bracket $\sqrt{a}$.

    (b) Show that Newton's method applied to f gives the iteration function $N(x) = (x + a/x)/2$—i.e., the average of x and a/x.

    (c) What happens if $x_n = \sqrt{a}$?

14. Let $f(x) = x^3 - 2x^2 - 5x + 7 = (x - 3)(x - 1)(x + 2) + 1$.

    (a) Explain why it is natural to guess that f has roots near $x = 3$, $x = 1$, and $x = -2$.

    (b) Use Newton's method to estimate the values of the roots of f to five decimal places.

15. Let $f(x) = x^3 - 10x^2 + 22x + 6$.

    (a) Find each of the three roots of f to five decimal places.

    (b) What happens when Newton's method is used with $x_0 = 2$? Explain why this happens.

    (c) Newton's method behaves oddly if $x_0 = 1.39$. How? Why?

16. Let $h(x) = 179.5x^6 - 436.8x^4 + 257.3x^2 - 1$.

    (a) $h(x)$ has three positive roots. Use Newton's method to find each one to five decimal places.

    (b) $h(x)$ has three negative roots. How are they related to the three positive roots you found in part (a)?

17. Find (approximately) the minimum value of $g(x) = 10x^{-2} + 3x^2 + x - 4$ if $1 \le x \le 10$.

In Exercises 18–20, consider the function $f(x) = x^2 \sin(x^2)$ on the interval $[0, 3]$. Use Newton's method to find (approximately, to five decimal places)

18. the minimum value of f.

19. the maximum value of f.

20. the inflection points of f.

21. Apply Newton's method to $f(x) = x^{1/3}$ starting from $x_0 = 1$. Explain what happens.

22. Apply Newton's method to $f(x) = e^{-x}$ starting from $x_0 = 0$. Explain what happens.

4.7 BUILDING POLYNOMIALS TO ORDER; TAYLOR POLYNOMIALS

A section with similar contents appears in Volume II, in connection with Taylor's theorem. The main idea here is to build polynomial functions with prescribed derivatives at a point. Technology permits useful geometric intuitions.

In this section we show how to construct polynomials with specified values and derivatives at a particular point. One reason to do so is to find polynomials (called **Taylor polynomials**) that approximate other (nonpolynomial) functions. If the original function f is complicated, ill-behaved, or poorly understood, then it may be convenient to replace f with a simpler or better understood function g. Polynomial functions are natural tools for this purpose because they're well understood and easy to work with.

Polynomials, derivatives, and coefficents

Consider the nth degree polynomial function $p(x) = a_0 + a_1(x - x_0) + a_2(x - x_0)^2 + a_3(x - x_0)^3 + \cdots + a_n(x - x_0)^n$, where x_0 and the a_i are all fixed numbers. A polynomial written this way, using powers of $(x - x_0)$, is said to be **expanded about the base point** x_0. Polynomials in this form may look strange at first compared to (say) $p(x) = 1 + 2x + 3x^2 + 4x^3$, which is expanded about $x = 0$. But the first form turns out to be more convenient for some purposes—it pays off nicely in the next (important) example.

EXAMPLE 1   Consider the following polynomial:

$$p(x) = a_0 + a_1(x - x_0) + a_2(x - x_0)^2 + a_3(x - x_0)^3 + a_4(x - x_0)^4.$$

Find $p(x_0)$, $p'(x_0)$, $p''(x_0)$, $p^{(3)}(x_0)$, and $p^{(4)}(x_0)$ (the value and first four derivatives of p at $x = x_0$).

Solution   Differentiating p is easy—but watch the coefficients: ➥

Fifth and higher-order derivatives are all zero.

$$p(x) = a_0 + a_1(x - x_0) + a_2(x - x_0)^2 + a_3(x - x_0)^3 + a_4(x - x_0)^4;$$
$$p'(x) = a_1 + 2a_2(x - x_0) + 3a_3(x - x_0)^2 + 4a_4(x - x_0)^3;$$
$$p''(x) = 2a_2 + 2 \cdot 3a_3(x - x_0) + 3 \cdot 4a_4(x - x_0)^2;$$
$$p^{(3)}(x) = 2 \cdot 3a_3 + 2 \cdot 3 \cdot 4a_4(x - x_0);$$
$$p^{(4)}(x) = 2 \cdot 3 \cdot 4a_4.$$

Now the special form of p pays off. Substituting $x = x_0$ gives

$$p(x_0) = a_0 = 1a_0 \qquad p'(x_0) = a_1 = 1a_1 \qquad p''(x_0) = 2a_2$$
$$p^{(3)}(x_0) = 2 \cdot 3a_3 = 6a_3 \qquad p^{(4)}(x_0) = 2 \cdot 3 \cdot 4a_4 = 24a_4.$$

Notice the pleasant pattern: For each i, the ith derivative $p^{(i)}(x_0)$ is a certain *constant* multiple of a_i. ➥   ■

We can think of $p(x_0)$ as the zeroth derivative at x_0.

Factorials   The constant multiples (1,1,2,6,24) in the preceding computation are **factorials**. By definition, the **factorial** of i, denoted by $i!$, is the repeated product $i \cdot (i - 1) \cdot (i - 2) \cdots 2 \cdot 1$. (By convention, $0! = 1$.) ➥ Factorials crop up often in mathematics (often enough to rate their own key on many calculators), especially around repeated operations like those in Example 1. We use factorials in the following theorem to describe the pattern just seen.

This may seem strange at first glance, but it simplifies calculations.

> **THEOREM 6**   Let $p(x) = a_0 + a_1(x - x_0) + a_2(x - x_0)^2 + \cdots + a_n(x - x_0)^n$. Then
>
> $$p(x_0) = a_0 \qquad p'(x_0) = a_1 \qquad p''(x_0) = 2a_2$$
> $$p^{(3)}(x_0) = 6a_i \qquad\qquad \ldots \qquad\qquad p^{(n)}(x_0) = n!a_n.$$
>
> Equivalently, $a_i = \dfrac{p^{(i)}(x_0)}{i!}$ for all $i \geq 0$.

Theorem 6 restates, a little more generally, what we noticed for derivatives through degree 4 in Example 1. A formal proof, which we omit, uses the technique of mathematical induction.

Read one way, the theorem is a rule for calculating certain derivatives. More important for us, the theorem offers a nice recipe for cooking up polynomials with prescribed derivatives at a point.

E X A M P L E 2   Find a quadratic function $q(x) = a_0 + a_1 x + a_2 x^2$ for which $q(0) = 1$, $q'(0) = 2$, and $q''(0) = 3$. Are there *linear* functions with all three properties? Are there cubic functions?

Solution   Theorem 6 (with $x_0 = 0$) says exactly what to do: Set $a_0 = 1$, $a_1 = 2$, and $a_2 = 3/2$. ◄ Thus, the quadratic polynomial we want is $q(x) = 1 + 2x + 3x^2/2$.

Notice the denominator in a_2.

No *linear* polynomial $\ell(x) = a_0 + a_1 x$ can work, because $\ell''(0) = 0$ for any linear polynomial. But infinitely many *cubic* polynomials satisfy all three requirements. Every function of the form $c(x) = 1 + 2x + 3x^2/2 + a_3 x^3$ satisfies all three conditions—regardless of the value of a_3. ◄ Figure 1 shows five functions of this form; the darker curve is the quadratic q (for which $a_3 = 0$):

Be sure to check this for yourself.

Another interesting set of curves might let the quadratic or linear coefficient vary, holding all other coefficients fixed.

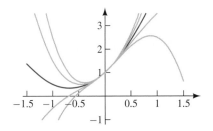

Each curve's equation is $y = 1 + 2x + 3x^2/2 + a_3 x^3$, for $a_3 = -2, -1, 0, 1, 2$. The darker curve has $a_3 = 0$, so it's quadratic.

FIGURE 1
Several functions that "match" at $x = 0$

Notice the similarity among the curves: Because all five functions shown have the same value and first two derivatives at $x = 0$, they behave similarly near $x = 0$ but spread apart elsewhere. ∎

Using made-to-order polynomials

Example 2 showed *how* to build polynomials with specified values and derivatives at a given point. But *why* do it? We illustrate several reasons by example.

Finding quadratic formulas   Sometimes we want to find an explicit formula for a function that we somehow know in advance to be quadratic.

E X A M P L E 3 We saw in Section 2.5 that if the acceleration of a moving object is *constant* in time (as in free fall), then the object's velocity function is *linear* and its position function is *quadratic*. For a certain falling object, measurements taken at time $t = 0$ seconds along a scale in meters showed

$$\text{height} = 100 \text{ m}; \quad \text{velocity} = -20\frac{\text{m}}{\text{s}}; \quad \text{acceleration} = -9.8\frac{\text{m/s}}{\text{s}}.$$

Find a formula for the position at time t. What will happen at time $t = 1$? What *was* happening at time $t = -1$? ➡

In Section 2.5 we answered similar questions by antidifferentiation.

S o l u t i o n If $p(t)$ is the position (height) at time t, then we have

$$p(0) = 100; \quad p'(0) = -20; \quad p''(0) = -9.8.$$

Now p has the form $p(t) = a_0 + a_1 t + a_2 t^2$, and Theorem 6 tells how to find the a_i:

$$a_0 = p(0) = 100; \quad a_1 = p'(0) = -20; \quad a_2 = \frac{p'(0)}{2} = -4.9.$$

Thus, the position and velocity functions are

$$p(t) = 100 - 20t - 4.9t^2; \quad v(t) = -20 - 9.8t.$$

With $t = 1$ we get $p(1) = 70.2$ and $v(1) = -29.8$, so at this time the object's height will be 70.2 meters, and its upward velocity will be -29.8 meters per second. Similar calculations with $t = -1$ show that at that time the height was 115.1 meters and the velocity was -10.2 meters per second. ■

Designer curves Another reason for tailoring polynomials to order is to construct curves with specified geometric properties. Such curves arise in computer graphics and in computer-aided design.

We treat linear, quadratic, and cubic splines more carefully in Volume II.

E X A M P L E 4 The curve in Figure 2 is built from two cubic curve segments, joined smoothly at the middle bulleted point $(1, 2)$. A curve constructed in this way is called a **cubic spline**; the separate pieces are called **spline elements**. Cubic polynomials are good for splining because, as we'll see, they let us specify two values and two derivatives—four conditions in all.

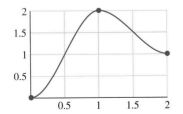

The curves meet smoothly, with zero slope, at the point $(1, 2)$.

FIGURE 2
A "splined" curve built from two cubic segments

Note the warning to students about exam possibilities!

Imagine the exam possibilities!

The curve is a calculus teacher's dream—all the "interesting" points seem to have integer or half-integer coordinates. ➡ Describe the curve symbolically.

S o l u t i o n We'll write the two cubic pieces in the form

$$p_1(x) = a_0 + a_1 x + a_2 x^2 + a_3 x^3; \quad p_2(x) = b_0 + b_1(x-1) + b_2(x-1)^2 + b_3(x-1)^3,$$

and use what we know of the functions to find the coefficients a_i and b_i. The graph shows that the first piece satisfies

$$p_1(0) = 0; \quad p_1'(0) = 0; \quad p_1(1) = 2; \quad p_1'(1) = 0.$$

Now the first two conditions and Theorem 6 tell us that $a_0 = 0$ and $a_1 = 0$, so we have $p_1(x) = a_2 x^2 + a_3 x^3$ with a_2 and a_3 still unknown. To find them, we use the last two conditions: ◂

Note that
$p_1'(x) = 2a_2 x + 3a_3 x^2.$

$$p_1(1) = 2 \implies a_2 \cdot 1^2 + a_3 \cdot 1^2 = 2 \implies a_2 + a_3 = 2$$
$$p_1'(1) = 0 \implies 2a_2 \cdot 1 + 3a_3 \cdot 1^2 = 0 \implies 2a_2 + 3a_3 = 0.$$

Solving the last two equations for a_2 and a_3 gives $a_2 = 6$ and $a_3 = -4$, so we conclude that $p_1(x) = 6x^2 - 4x^3$. Similar reasoning applies to $p_2(x)$, to give $p_2(x) = 2 - 3(x-1)^2 + 2(x-1)^3$. The piecewise definition for the full curve in Figure 2 is

$$p(x) = \begin{cases} 6x^2 - 4x^3 & \text{if } 0 \le x \le 1; \\ 2 - 3(x-1)^2 + 2(x-1)^3 & \text{if } 1 \le x \le 2. \end{cases}$$

The curve has other interesting properties, including two nicely placed inflection points. ◂

We explore some of these properties in exercises.

■

Function approximation is the main motivation for the (similar) treatment of this material in Volume II.

Polynomials that approximate other functions

Yet another important use of Theorem 6 is in finding polynomial functions (linear, quadratic, or higher-order) that *approximate* a given (nonpolynomial) function f near a given domain point $x = x_0$. If f happens to be complicated, inconvenient, or poorly understood, then having a close polynomial approximation p can reduce clutter and simplify calculations.

To achieve this approximation, we'll construct polynomials p that "match" the value and one or more derivatives of f at $x = x_0$. Example 5 illustrates the process for the square root function.

Calculators seem able to cope, but even they might need some (internal) help.

EXAMPLE 5 Let $f(x) = \sqrt{x}$. Clearly $f(64) = 8$, but $f(x)$ is inconvenient to evaluate (by hand, at least) for nearby inputs x. ◂ Which *constant* function best approximates $f(x) = \sqrt{x}$ near $x = 64$? Which *linear* function? Which *quadratic* function?

We leave the routine calculation to you.

Solution We'll find polynomials that match one or more of the following (easily found) values: ◂

$$f(64) = 8; \quad f'(64) = \frac{1}{16}; \quad f''(64) = -\frac{1}{2048}.$$

Theorem 6 says that the *quadratic* function q that matches all three of these values is

$$q(x) = 8 + \frac{1}{16}(x - 64) - \frac{1}{4096}(x - 64)^2.$$

Now we can just read off the constant and linear parts:

$$c(x) = 8; \quad \ell(x) = 8 + \frac{1}{16}(x - 64).$$

Plotting c, ℓ, q, and f together lets us compare them:

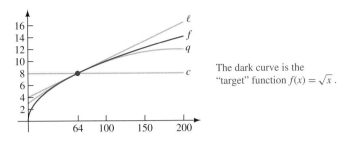

The dark curve is the "target" function $f(x) = \sqrt{x}$.

FIGURE 3
Constant, linear, and quadratic approximations to $f(x) = \sqrt{x}$

Figure 3 shows that c, ℓ, q, and f behave as claimed: (i) all four functions pass through $(64, 8)$; (ii) ℓ and q (but not c) are *tangent* to f at $x = 64$; (iii) q and f have the same concavity direction at $x = 64$. A table of values suggests how closely c, ℓ, and q approximate f near to, and far from, $x = 64$:

Three approximations to $f(x) = \sqrt{x}$							
x	35	63	63.9	64	64.1	65	100
$f(x)$	5.91608	7.93725	7.99375	8	8.00625	8.06226	8.94427
$q(x)$	5.98218	7.93726	7.99375	8	8.00625	8.06226	8.93750
$\ell(x)$	6.18750	7.93750	7.99375	8	8.00625	8.06250	9.00000
$c(x)$	8.00000	8.00000	8.00000	8	8.00000	8.00000	8.00000

The numbers give the same message as the graphs: q approximates f best, especially near $x = 64$. Indeed, the graphs of q and f "share ink" in the range $35 \le x \le 100$. ■

Linear approximation: an old story The linear approximation (or tangent-line approximation) to a function f at a point $x = x_0$ is nothing new. We observed as early as Chapter 1 that a differentiable function is "close to" its tangent line near $x = x_0$ (the point of tangency) and that this line has point-slope equation $y = f(x_0) + f'(x_0)(x - x_0)$. Theorem 6, in its simplest form, says that this linear function has the same value and the same (first) derivative as f at $x = x_0$.

One important use of linear approximation is to produce quick estimates for values of functions we don't know exactly. We saw above, for instance, that $\sqrt{65} \approx \ell(65) = 8.0625$, where ℓ is the linear approximation to $f(x) = \sqrt{x}$ based at $x = 64$. The estimate 8.0625 compares well with the *true* value $\sqrt{65} = 8.06226\ldots$.

EXAMPLE 6 Your calculator's TAN key is stuck, and you really need $\tan 31°$. You know that $\tan 30° = 1/\sqrt{3}$. What to do?

Solution We'll use a linear approximation to estimate $\tan 31°$. To this end, let $f(x) = \tan x$ (in radians!); note that $30° = \pi/6$ radians and that $31° = \pi/6 + \pi/180$ radians. Now $f'(x) = \sec^2 x$, so we have

$$f\left(\frac{\pi}{6}\right) = \frac{1}{\sqrt{3}}; \quad f'\left(\frac{\pi}{6}\right) = \sec^2\left(\frac{\pi}{6}\right) = \frac{4}{3}.$$

Our linear approximation estimate for $\tan 31°$ was too small. Students might think about how, using concavity, we might have predicted this.

Thus

$$\ell(x) = \frac{1}{\sqrt{3}} + \frac{4}{3}\left(x - \frac{\pi}{6}\right) \quad \text{and} \quad \ell(x) = \frac{1}{\sqrt{3}} + \frac{4}{3}\frac{\pi}{180} \approx 0.6006.$$

This compares well with the true value $\tan 31° \approx 0.6008\ldots$ (which you can check if your TAN key comes unstuck). ∎

Getting things straight.   **Linearization** is the generic term for replacing a nonlinear object (such as a curve or nonlinear function) with a well-chosen linear object (such as a line or linear function) that approximates the original object "well enough." Trading nonlinear for better understood linear objects makes many otherwise intractable problems solvable, at least approximately. Linearization is common in pure mathematics—and downright indispensable in applications, in which most problems are too complicated or poorly understood to be solved without some "straightening out."

Quadratic approximation: another step   Quadratic approximation takes linear approximation one step farther: we look for a quadratic polynomial that matches the value and first *two* derivatives of a given function f at a given point x_0.

Students can consider when the "tangent parabola" opens upward or downward, and what happens at a point of inflection.

The geometric result of quadratic approximation is a *parabola* (not a line, unless the quadratic term happens to be zero) that "fits" the f-graph at and near $x = x_0$. The (little) extra work done in quadratic approximation pays off nicely: The curved shape of a parabola permits a closer fit to a curved graph than any straight line allows. In particular, a quadratic approximation reflects the *concavity* of the target curve: The "tangent parabola" opens upward or downward depending on whether f is concave up or concave down at $x = x_0$. Figure 4 shows the sine function with two tangent parabolas, opening in different directions.

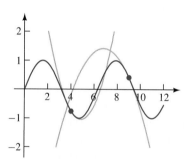

FIGURE 4
The sine curve (dark) with two "tangent parabolas"

The next example illustrates the advantage of quadratic over linear approximation.

EXAMPLE 7   Let $f(x) = 10^x$. Find ℓ and q, the linear and quadratic approximations to f, based at $x = 3$. Use each to estimate $f(3.1)$.

Solution   We need the value and two derivatives of f at $x = 3$. From $f(x) = 10^x$ we get $f'(x) = 10^x \ln 10$ and $f''(x) = 10^x (\ln 10)^2$, so

$$f(3) = 10^3 = 1000; \quad f'(3) = 1000 \ln 10 \approx 2303; \quad f''(3) = 1000(\ln 10)^2 \approx 5302.$$

Thus,

$$\ell(x) = f(3) + f'(3) \cdot (x - 3) \approx 1000 + 2303(x - 3);$$

$$q(x) = \ell(x) + \frac{f''(3)}{2} \cdot (x - 3)^2 \approx 1000 + 2303(x - 3) + 2651(x - 3)^2,$$

and plugging in numbers gives

$$\ell(3.1) \approx 1230.3; \qquad q(3.1) \approx 1256.7; \qquad f(3.1) \approx 1258.9.$$

Figure 5 shows graphically how much better q does than ℓ in fitting f near $x = 3$:

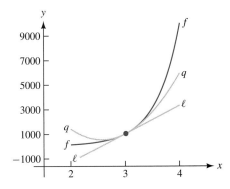

Although q does better than ℓ near $x = 3$, neither does well elsewhere. Note that q opens upward, since f is concave up.

FIGURE 5
Linear and quadratic approximations to $f(x) = 10^x$

The picture shows why ℓ fits f so poorly: f bends sharply away from ℓ, even quite near $x = 3$. The second derivative, f'', explains why. Any linear function ℓ has zero second derivative. Our target function f, by contrast, has a huge second derivative: $f''(3) \approx 5000$. Because f is so drastically nonlinear, it is badly approximated by *any* straight line—even the best-fitting one. ■

Onward and upward: Taylor-made polynomials

The TI–89 and similar tools will calculate Taylor polynomials.

There's no need to stop with quadratic polynomials in matching derivatives of a given function f at a point x_0. Higher-order matching is possible with polynomials of degree 3, 4, and higher. The following example illustrates the idea in an unusually simple setting.

EXAMPLE 8 Find a fifth-degree polynomial p_5 that matches $f(x) = e^x$ to order 5 at $x_0 = 0$—that is, such that

$$p_5(0) = f(0), \quad p_5'(0) = f'(0), \quad p_5''(0) = f''(0), \quad \dots \quad p_5^{(5)}(0) = f^{(5)}(0).$$

Solution Here $f'(x) = e^x = f(x)$, so all derivatives are the same:

$$f(0) = 1 = f'(0) = f''(0) = f^{(3)}(0) = f^{(4)}(0) = f^{(5)}(0).$$

Theorem 6 tells how to find a polynomial $p_5(x) = a_0 + a_1x + a_2x^2 + a_3x^3 + a_4x^4 + a_5x^5$ with the same derivatives—we just set $a_i = f^{(i)}(0)/i! = 1/i!$ for all $i \geq 0$. That is,

$$p_5(x) = \frac{1}{0!} + \frac{x}{1!} + \frac{x^2}{2!} + \frac{x^3}{3!} + \frac{x^4}{4!} + \frac{x^5}{5!} = 1 + x + \frac{x^2}{2} + \frac{x^3}{6} + \frac{x^4}{24} + \frac{x^5}{120}.$$

How well does p_5 approximate f near $x = 0$? Very well indeed, as Figure 6 shows.

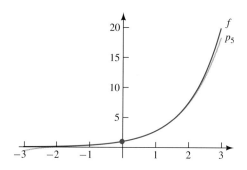

FIGURE 6

A fifth-order polynomial approximation to
$f(x) = e^x$

The graphs of f and p_5 are hard to distinguish near $x = 0$. At $x = 1$, for instance, we get

$$p_5(1) = 1 + 1 + \frac{1}{2} + \frac{1}{6} + \frac{1}{24} + \frac{1}{120} \approx 2.71667, \quad \text{while} \quad f(1) = e \approx 2.71828.$$

At $x = 5$ the match is much less impressive: $f(5) \approx 148.41$, and $p_5(5) \approx 91.42$. ∎

The formal definition The polynomial p_5 constructed in Example 8 is called the **fifth-order Taylor polynomial** for $f(x) = e^x$ based at $x = 0$; it illustrates a much more general definition:

> **DEFINITION (Taylor polynomials)**   Let f be any function whose first n derivatives exist at $x = x_0$. The **Taylor polynomial** of order n, based at x_0, is defined by
>
> $$P_n(x) = f(x_0) + f'(x_0)(x - x_0) + \frac{f''(x_0)}{2!}(x - x_0)^2$$
> $$+ \frac{f^{(3)}(x_0)}{3!}(x - x_0)^3 + \cdots + \frac{f^{(n)}(x_0)}{n!}(x - x_0)^n.$$

Observe:

- **Linear and quadratic cases**   If $n = 1$, the definition gives the familiar linear approximation; if $n = 2$ we get the quadratic approximations discussed above.

- **Maclaurin polynomials**   Taylor polynomials that happen to be based at $x = 0$ are known as **Maclaurin polynomials**. They look a little cleaner on the page:

$$P_n(x) = f(0) + f'(0)x + \frac{f''(0)}{2}x^2 + \cdots + \frac{f^{(n)}(0)}{n!}x^n.$$

In Example 8 we found the fifth-order Maclaurin polynomial for $f(x) = e^x$.

Note the (technical) distinction between order and degree.

- **Order and degree**   A Taylor polynomial P_n of **order** n is chosen so that its value and first n derivatives at $x = x_0$ agree with those of f. The definition shows that P_n also has **degree** n since it involves powers of $(x - x_0)$ up through the nth power. (If, by chance, $a_n = 0$, then the degree of P_n is less than n.)

Students sometimes stumble on this point.

- **Many symbols, just one variable**   The definition involves many symbols: $a, x, i, x_0, f,$ and n. While in this thicket, it is helpful to remember that x *is the only variable*. In specific cases all the other symbols take *numerical* values.

Taylor's idea? The idea underlying Taylor polynomials probably predates Brook Taylor (1685–1731), for whom they are named. According to some authors the idea appears in work of John Bernoulli (1667–1748), published in 1694. The same Bernoulli (one of several famous Bernoullis) is also credited with having discovered—behind the scenes—l'Hôpital's rule.

How well do Taylor polynomials fit? Taylor polynomials can be used to approximate more complicated functions. Exactly how *well* a given Taylor polynomial fits its target function depends on many factors; we'll address that question in Chapter 9. For now, we just remark that Taylor polynomials usually fit their target functions better as the order of fitting increases. We illustrate this graphically and numerically in the following example.

We take up this question in earnest in Volume II.

EXAMPLE 9 Find P_1, P_3, P_5, and P_7, the Taylor (or Maclaurin) polynomials for $f(x) = \sin x$ based at $x = 0$. Plot everything on one set of axes. How closely does each polynomial approximate $\sin 1$?

Solution To find P_7 we need the value and the first seven derivatives of $f(x) = \sin x$ at $x = 0$. Here they are in order: $0, 1, 0, -1, 0, 1, 0, -1$. ➡ Using Theorem 6 to match derivatives gives

Check the calculation.

$$P_7(x) = 0 + 1x + 0x^2 - \frac{1}{3!}x^3 + 0x^4 + \frac{1}{5!}x^5 + 0x^6 - \frac{1}{7!}x^7$$

and, therefore, that

$$P_1(x) = x; \qquad\qquad P_3(x) = x - \frac{x^3}{6};$$

$$P_5(x) = x - \frac{x^3}{6} + \frac{x^5}{120}; \qquad P_7(x) = x - \frac{x^3}{6} + \frac{x^5}{120} - \frac{x^7}{5040}.$$

Figure 7 shows all five graphs:

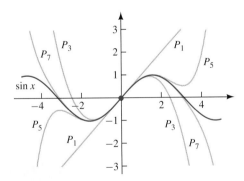

FIGURE 7
Several Taylor approximations to $f(x) = \sin x$

Observe:

- **An odd function** All the nonzero powers of x in the Maclaurin polynomials are *odd*; this reflects the fact that $\sin x$ itself is an *odd* function. (For similar reasons, all nonzero terms in Maclaurin polynomials for $\cos x$ are even.)

- **Snug fits** All four Taylor polynomials fit the sine curve well near the base point $x = 0$. Differences among the functions appear only as one moves away (to left or right) from $x = 0$.

- **Better and better**   Higher-order Taylor polynomials approximate the sine function better than lower-order ones. For instance, P_7 follows the sine curve much farther than P_1 or P_3.

Intuition suggests that P_1, P_3, P_5, and P_7 should give successively closer estimates for $\sin 1 \approx 0.84147$. So they do:

$$P_1(1) = 1; \quad P_3(1) = \frac{5}{6} \approx 0.83333;$$

$$P_5(1) = \frac{101}{120} \approx 0.84167; \quad P_7(1) = \frac{4241}{5040} \approx 0.84147.$$ ∎

BASIC EXERCISES

1. Let $f(x) = 1 + x + x^2 + x^3 + x^4 + x^5$. Find $f(0)$, $f'(0)$, $f''(0)$, $f'''(0)$, $f^{(4)}(0)$, $f^{(5)}(0)$, $f^{(6)}(0)$, and $f^{(131)}(0)$.

2. Let $f(x) = (x-1)^5$. Find $f(1)$, $f'(1)$, $f''(1)$, $f'''(1)$, $f^{(4)}(1)$, $f^{(5)}(1)$, $f^{(6)}(1)$, and $f^{(131)}(1)$.

3. Let $f(x) = x^2$ and $x_0 = 1$.

   (a) Find $P_2(x)$, the second-order Taylor polynomial based at $x = 1$.

   (b) Multiply out and simplify $P_2(x)$; explain the result.

4. Let $f(x) = x^3$. Find $P_3(x)$, the third-order Taylor polynomial for f based at $x = 1$. Then expand and simplify $P_3(x)$.

5. Find the quadratic Taylor polynomial approximation to $f(x) = \sqrt[3]{x}$ based at $x_0 = 8$. (Use rational numbers to express the polynomial's coefficients.)

6. Plot on one set of axes the cubic functions $c(x) = 1 - x + x^2 + ax^3$ for $a = -2, -1, 0, 1, 2$. What properties do all five graphs have in common? Which curve is a parabola?

7. Consider the curve in Figure 2, page 265. Show that the second cubic piece has equation $p_2(x) = 2 - 3(x-1)^2 + 2(x-1)^3$, as Example 4 claims.

8. Find the linear and quadratic Taylor approximations to $f(x) = \sqrt{x}$ expanded about the base point $x = 100$. Use each one to estimate $\sqrt{121}$. How much error does each commit in the process?

For each function in Exercises 9–13, first find the Taylor polynomial P_n of order n for the function f with base point x_0. Then plot both f and P_n on the same axes. Choose your plotting window to show clearly the relationship between f and P_n.

9. $f(x) = \dfrac{1}{1-x}, n = 3, x_0 = 0$

10. $f(x) = \sin x + \cos x, n = 4, x_0 = 0$

11. $f(x) = \ln x, n = 3, x_0 = 1$

12. $f(x) = \tan x, n = 2, x_0 = 0$

13. $f(x) = \sqrt{x}, n = 3, x_0 = 4$

In Exercises 14–19, find linear and quadratic approximations of each function at $x_0 = 0$.

14. $f(x) = \sin x$

15. $f(x) = \cos x$

16. $f(x) = \tan x$

17. $f(x) = e^x$

18. $f(x) = \arctan x$

19. $f(x) = \arcsin x$

20. The line tangent to the curve $y = g(x)$ at the point $(3, 5)$ intersects the y-axis at the point $(0, 10)$.

   (a) What is $g'(3)$?

   (b) Estimate $g(2.95)$ using a linear approximation.

FURTHER EXERCISES

21. This exercise refers to Example 9. Throughout this problem, $f(x) = \sin x$, and $P_n(x)$ is the Taylor (Maclaurin) polynomial of order n based at $x = 0$.

   (a) Every function mentioned in Example 9—f, P_1, P_3, P_5, and P_7—is odd. How is this fact "reflected" in their graphs?

   (b) Find the *even-order* Maclaurin polynomials P_2, P_4, P_6, and P_8 for $f(x) = \sin x$. How are they related to P_1, P_3, P_5, and P_7?

22. Throughout this exercise, $g(x) = \cos x$ and $P_n(x)$ is the Taylor (Maclaurin) polynomial of order n based at $x = 0$.

For use below, here are graphs of g, P_0, P_2, P_4, and P_6.

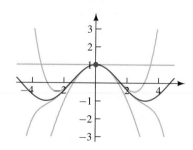

(a) Find formulas for P_0 through P_6, the Maclaurin polynomials through order 6 for g based at $x = 0$. Use your results to label the graphs shown above.

(b) Is g odd, even, or neither? What about the Maclaurin polynomials for g found in part (a)? How do the graphs "reflect" the situation?

(c) In Example 9 we found the Maclaurin polynomials P_1, P_3, P_5, and P_7 for $f(x) = \sin x$. Find the derivatives $P_1'(x)$, $P_3'(x)$, $P_5'(x)$, $P_7'(x)$, and $f'(x)$ of these functions. How are the results related to the rest of this exercise?

23. Suppose that f is a function such that $f'(x) = \sin(x^2)$ and $f(1) = 0$. [NOTE: No explicit formula for f is given.]

(a) Estimate the value of $f(0.5)$ using a linear approximation.

(b) Is the estimate you computed in part (a) greater than or less than the exact value of $f(0.5)$? Explain.

(c) Estimate the value of $f(0.5)$ using a quadratic approximation.

24. Let g be a function defined on the interval $[0, 10]$ such that the graph of g passes through the point $(5, 2)$ and the derivative of g is the function sketched below.

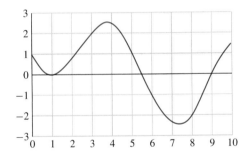

(a) Estimate $g(0)$ using a linear approximation.

(b) Estimate $g(8)$ using a quadratic approximation.

In Exericses 25–28, estimate the value of each of the following expressions using a linear approximation. How does this estimate compare with the value given by a scientific calculator?

25. $\sqrt{103}$

26. $\sqrt[3]{29}$

27. $\sin 58°$

28. 0.8^{10}

29. At time $t = 0$ seconds a car passed a reference point heading eastward at 25 meters per second, with eastward acceleration 2 meters per second per second. Let $p(t)$ be the car's eastward position at time t seconds in meters east of the reference point. (In particular, $p(0) = 0$.)

(a) Find the linear approximation function ℓ_p to p based at $t_0 = 0$. Use it to predict where the car will be at time $t = 1$ and where the car was at time $t = -1$.

(b) Find the quadratic approximation function q_p to p based at $t_0 = 0$. Use it to predict where the car will be at time $t = 1$ and where the car was at time $t = -1$.

(c) Let $v(t)$ be the car's eastward velocity, in meters per second, at time t. Find the linear approximation ℓ_v to v based at $t_0 = 0$. What does it predict at time $t = 1$ second?

30. Repeat the previous exercise but assume that at $t = 0$ the car was heading eastward at 25 meters per second and had eastward acceleration -2 meters per second per second.

31. At time $t = 0$ seconds an object was dropped from a 100-meter cliff. Its downward acceleration, was 9.8 meters/second². Let $h(t)$ be the height in meters of the object above ground level at time t seconds.

(a) Find the linear approximation ℓ to h, based at $t_0 = 0$. What does it predict for $t = 1$?

(b) Find the quadratic approximation q to h based at $t_0 = 0$. What does it predict for $t = 1$?

(c) Plot the functions ℓ and q on the same axes; use $0 \le t \le 6$. Which model—ℓ or q—seems more realistic? Does either model describe the real situation perfectly? Why or why not?

32. At a given instant, a car is traveling 50 ft/sec and accelerating 6 ft/sec². Use a second-degree Taylor polynomial to estimate how far the car travels in the next second.

33. Let f be the function graphed below.

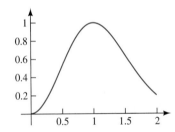

(a) Explain why $p(x) = 1$ is the first-order Taylor polynomial for f based at $x = 1$.

(b) Is it possible that $q(x) = 1 + 4x - 2x^2$ the second-order Taylor polynomial for f based at $x = 1$? Justify your answer.

(c) Is it possible that $r(x) = 3 - 2x^2$ is the second-order Taylor polynomial for f based at $x = 1$? Justify your answer.

(d) Is it possible that $s(x) = 3 - 4x + 2x^2$ is the second-order Taylor polynomial for f based at $x = 1$? Justify your answer.

34. Suppose that $p(x) = 3 - 4x + x^2$ is the quadratic Taylor polynomial approximation based at $x_0 = 1$ to a function g. Indicate whether each of the following statements *must* be true, *cannot* be true, or *might* be true. Justify your answers.

(a) $g(1) = 0$

(b) $g'(1) = -4$

(c) $g''(1) = 2$

(d) $g'''(1) = -3$

35. Suppose that $f(1) = 2$, that $f'(1)$ and $f''(1)$ exist, that f has a local maximum at $x = 1$, and that f has an inflection point at $x = -4$. Is it possible that $p(x) = 2 + 3(x - 1) - 4(x - 1)^2 = 3 - 5x + 4x^2$ is the second-degree Taylor polynomial for f based at $x = 1$? Justify your answer.

36. Suppose that $H'(x) = e^{-x} \sin x$ and that $H(0) = 1$. Estimate $H(0.1)$ using a fourth-degree Taylor polynomial approximation to H based at $x_0 = 0$.

37. Use derivatives to explain why the graphs $y = \sin x$ and $y = x - x^3/6$ are almost indistinguishable when plotted in the viewing window $[-1, 1] \times [-1, 1]$.

38. Use derivatives to explain why the graphs $y = \cos x$ and $y = \sqrt{1 - x^2}$ are almost indistinguishable when plotted in the viewing window $[-0.25, 0.25] \times [0.9, 1.1]$.

39. Use derivatives to explain why the graphs $y = \sin x$ and $y = x (\cos x)^{1/3}$ are almost indistinguishable when plotted in the viewing window $[-1, 1] \times [-1, 1]$.

40. Use derivatives to explain why the graphs $y = \sin x$ and $y = x(60 - 7x^2)/(60 + 3x^2)$ are almost indistinguishable when plotted in the viewing window $[-2, 2] \times [-1, 1]$.

41. Use derivatives to explain why the graphs $y = e^x$ and $y = \frac{5}{2} - \frac{5}{3}\cos x + \frac{1}{6}\cos(2x) + \frac{5}{3}\sin x - \frac{1}{3}\sin(2x)$ are almost indistinguishable when plotted in the viewing window $[-0.5, 0.5] \times [0.5, 2]$.

42. Use derivatives to explain why the graphs $y = \arcsin x$ and $y = 3x/(2 + \sqrt{1 - x^2})$ are almost indistinguishable when plotted in the viewing window $[-1, 1] \times [-1.6, 1.6]$.

43. In parts (a)–(c), find a quadratic polynomial with the indicated values and derivatives.
- **(a)** $q_{100}(0) = 1$, $q'_{100}(0) = 0$, $q''_{100}(0) = 0$.
- **(b)** $q_{010}(0) = 0$, $q'_{100}(0) = 1$, $q''_{100}(0) = 0$.
- **(c)** $q_{001}(0) = 0$, $q'_{100}(0) = 0$, $q''_{100}(0) = 1$.
- **(d)** Plot q_{100}, q_{010}, and q_{001} on one set of axes.
- **(e)** Show that for any constants a, b, and c, the quadratic function $q = aq_{100}(x) + bq_{010}(x) + cq_{001}(x)$ satisfies $q(0) = a$, $q'(0) = b$, $q''(0) = c$.

44. Consider again the curve in Figure 2, page 265. Find another equation for the first cubic piece, this time in the form $p_1(x) = a_0 + a_1(x - 1) + a_2(x - 1)^2 + a_3(x - 1)^3$. (In other words, expand about the base point $x = 1$.) How is the new p_1 related to the old?

45. This exercise is about the curve in Figure 2, page 265.
- **(a)** Are the points at $x = 1/2$ and $x = 3/2$ inflection points of the curve? Why or why not?
- **(b)** Note that $p''_1(1) = -12$ while $p''_2(1) = -6$. To "fix" this problem, find a *new* cubic curve $p_3(x)$ (to replace $p_2(x)$) for which $p_3(1) = 2$, $p'_3(1) = 0$, $p''_3(1) = -12$, and $p_3(2) = 1$. The curves p_1 and p_3 are shown below.

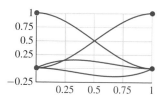

- **(c)** Where is the inflection point for the new curve p_3?

46. The following picture shows four cubic curves c_1, c_2, c_3, c_4 (labeled from top to bottom at the left edge).

All slopes at the bulleted points are either 0 or 1. For instance, $c_3(0) = 0$, $c'_3(0) = 1$, $c_3(1) = 0$, $c'_3(1) = 0$. Find a cubic equation for each curve. Check your answers by plotting.

4.8 WHY CONTINUITY MATTERS

This section and the next are brief excursions into theory. Continuity, like limits, is treated somewhat informally. We assume, for instance, that the elementary functions are continuous where they're defined. Our main goal is to explore what continuity means any what it implies.

In Section 2.3 we defined continuity in terms of limits: A function f is **continuous** at $x = a$ if

$$\lim_{x \to a} f(x) = f(a).$$

(Less formally, the condition is that $f(x) \to f(a)$ as $x \to a$.)

The standard elementary functions (algebraic, exponential, logarithmic, and trigonometric functions) are *all* continuous wherever they're defined. Combinations—sums, products, quotients, and compositions—of elementary functions are also continuous wherever *they're* defined. This is so because limits behave well with respect to combinations: the limit of a sum, for instance, is the corresponding sum of limits. (Theorem 6, page 108, treats combinations of continuous functions; its proof depends on Theorem 5, page 107, which treats combinations of limits.) Since most standard calculus functions are continuous, we need to "reach" a bit for meaningful examples.

EXAMPLE 1 Consider the function $f(x) = \begin{cases} f_1(x) = a + bx^2 & \text{if } x < 1 \\ f_2(x) = x & \text{if } x \geq 1 \end{cases}$.
For what values of the constants a and b is f continuous? For what values of a and b is f differentiable?

Solution The question of continuity comes up only at $x = 1$; everywhere else f is continuous for reasons discussed just above. For f to be continuous at $x = 1$ we need to make f_1 and f_2 "meet" properly at $x = 1$. (Doing so will ensure that

$$\lim_{x \to 1^-} f(x) = \lim_{x \to 1^+} f(x) = f(1) = 1,$$

as the definition of continuity requires.) To guarantee this we just need $f_1(1) = a + b = 1 = f_2(1)$; thus, any a and b with $a + b = 1$ "works." Figure 1 shows several functions of this form—all of which meet f_2 successfully at the point $(1, 1)$.

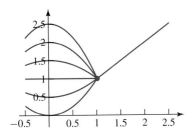

All functions shown are continuous, but only one is differentiable at $x = 1$.

FIGURE 1
A family of continuous functions at $x = 1$

For $f'(1)$ to exist we need the *slopes* of f_1 and f_2 to match at $x = 1$. Because $f_1'(x) = 2bx$, we need $f_1'(1) = 2b = 1$, so $b = 1/2$. Putting the conditions $a + b = 1$ and $b = 1/2$ together means that $a = 1/2 = b$. (The curve $y = 1/2 + x^2/2$ is among those shown.) ∎

Continuity is so much the rule in calculus courses that its importance for how calculus really "works" is easy to miss. In this section we hint at some of the consequences and advantages of continuity.

The importance of being continuous: the intermediate value theorem and the extreme value theorem

Continuity is clearly a "good thing" for calculus functions. The **intermediate value theorem (IVT)** and the **extreme value theorem (EVT)** give two reasons why. We won't prove either theorem, but we'll indicate why the property each guarantees is practically useful.

Each theorem pertains to a continuous function f on a *closed and bounded* interval $[a, b]$. (See the exercises at the end of this section for more on why the interval must be closed.)

Rigorous proofs would require more sophisticated concepts, such as connectedness or compactness. We take the "value theorems" as essentially equivalent to continuity.

The exercises give some practice with checking and using hypotheses.

THEOREM 7 (Intermediate value theorem) Let f be continuous on the closed, bounded interval $[a, b]$, and let y be any number between $f(a)$ and $f(b)$. Then, for some input c between a and b, $f(c) = y$.

> **THEOREM 8 (Extreme value theorem)**   Let f be continuous on the closed, bounded interval $[a, b]$. Then f assumes both a maximum value and a minimum value somewhere on $[a, b]$.

Existential philosophy   The EVT and the IVT are **existence theorems**. Each guarantees the existence of (at least) one point in the domain with some desirable property. Neither theorem says *where* in $[a, b]$ these points may fall or *how many* there may be. Such high-toned philosophy may suggest that these theorems, whatever their theoretical importance, have little practical use. That's wrong—and we'll see why.

The IVT in pictures   The IVT is a statement about *outputs* of f: If f is continuous on $[a, b]$, then the range of f contains not just $f(a)$ and $f(b)$, but *every number in between*. This means that the graph of a continuous function f is unbroken in the following sense:

> On the way from $\left(a, f(a)\right)$ to $\left(b, f(b)\right)$, the graph of f crosses every horizontal line between $y = f(a)$ and $y = f(b)$.

Figure 2 illustrates the situation.

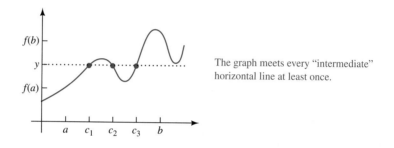

The graph meets every "intermediate" horizontal line at least once.

FIGURE 2
The IVT: f "hits" every intermediate value

The EVT in pictures   The EVT is a statement about *inputs* to f: If f is continuous on the closed interval $[a, b]$, then f achieves both a maximum and a minimum value somewhere on this interval. As shown in Figure 3, these extreme values are attained at the inputs labeled $x = x_{max}$ and $x = x_{min}$, respectively. Note that f need not achieve *global* maximum and minimum values at these points—indeed, the pictured f assumes larger values than $f(x_{max})$ just to the right of $x = 0$. What matters is that $f(x_{min})$ and $f(x_{max})$ are the biggest and smallest values of f for inputs x in the interval $[a, b]$.

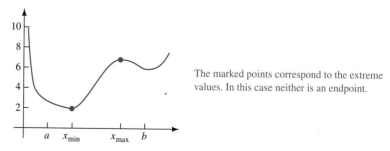

The marked points correspond to the extreme values. In this case neither is an endpoint.

FIGURE 3
The EVT: f assumes extreme values on $[a, b]$

Both hypotheses of the EVT—that f be *continuous* and that the interval be closed—are necessary. If either fails, f need not assume a maximum or a minimum. In Figure 3, for instance, f achieves neither a maximum nor a minimum on the *open* interval $(x_{\min}, x_{\max})$, even though f is continuous there.

From abstract theory, a concrete payoff

The IVT is a theoretical result, but it has useful concrete consequences. One of them, the **bisection** (or interval-halving) method, is a simple but effective technique for solving equations. First, an example to remind us of some preliminaries.

One point of this example is to review the quadratic formula—the more practice with it the better.

E X A M P L E 2   A number r is a **root** of a function f if $f(r) = 0$. The function $f(x) = x^2 - 1 = (x - 1)(x + 1)$ has *two* roots, at $x = \pm 1$. The function $g(x) = x^2$ has *one* root, at $x = 0$. Since $h(x) = x^2 + 1 \geq 1$ for all x, the function h has *no* roots. How many roots can *any* quadratic polynomial have?

Solution   The **quadratic formula**

$$r = \frac{-b \pm \sqrt{b^2 - 4ac}}{2a} = \frac{-b}{2a} \pm \frac{\sqrt{b^2 - 4ac}}{2a}$$

finds all the roots of any quadratic polynomial $p(x) = ax^2 + bx + c$. The *number* of roots (there may be 0, 1, or 2) depends on the sign of $b^2 - 4ac$. Note that the roots (if any) are evenly spaced to either side of $x = -b/2a$—the location of the parabola's vertex.   ■

The bisection method: digging systematically for roots   Finding roots algebraically is often difficult or impossible. Even when algebraic methods (such as the quadratic formula) *do* succeed, finding decimal equivalents may still be a problem. It's clear, for instance, that $x = \sqrt{2}$ is a root of $x^2 - 2$, but how could we (or a calculator) find an accurate *decimal* value? ➡

The **bisection method** will help. It's based on the following key fact, which depends in turn on the IVT:

Students might discover the basic idea of the bisection method by experiment; the main new feature here is to formalize the idea as an algorithm.

In Section 4.6 we applied Newton's method to the same problem.

> **FACT (Finding roots with continuity)**   If f is continuous on $[a, b]$, and $f(a)$ and $f(b)$ have opposite signs, then $[a, b]$ contains at least one root of f. In particular, the *midpoint* $(a + b)/2$ of $[a, b]$ differs from a root of f by no more than $(b - a)/2$—the "radius" of $[a, b]$.

The Fact follows directly from the IVT. Because f is negative at one end of $[a, b]$ and positive at the other, the IVT guarantees that $f(r) = 0$ somewhere in between—so a root r lies *somewhere* in $[a, b]$. Lacking further information, the midpoint of $[a, b]$ is as good an estimate of r as any. Figure 4 gives the generic picture.

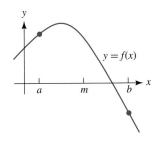

The midpoint m misses the root by no more than $(b - a)/2$, the "radius."

FIGURE 4
The idea of bisection

By applying this Fact repeatedly, we can approximate a root as closely as we wish. We illustrate the method, called the **bisection method**, by an example.

E X A M P L E 3 We use the bisection method to estimate $\sqrt{2}$ accurately. Because $\sqrt{2}$ is a root of $f(x) = x^2 - 2$ and lies somewhere in $[1, 2]$, we have all we need to get started.

Solution We'll approach an answer step by step:

- **Step 1:** Since $f(1) = -1$ and $f(2) = 2$, the Fact says that $m_1 = 1.5$ (the midpoint of $[1, 2]$) differs from a root of f by less than 0.5).
- **Step 2:** Since $f(1.5) = 0.25 > 0$, the Fact applies to the new—and shorter—interval $[1, 1.5]$. Conclusion: $m_2 = 1.25$, the new midpoint, differs from a root by less than 0.25.
- **Step 3:** Since $f(1.25) = -0.4375 < 0$, our latest interval is $[1.25, 1.50]$. Conclusion: $m_3 = 1.375$ differs from a root by less than 0.125.

    We can continue these steps as long as we like. In practice we'd continue until we were sure of some predetermined accuracy. (The next few estimates, rounded to 4 places, are 1.4375, 1.4063, 1.4219, 1.4141, 1.4180, and 1.4160—not far from $\sqrt{2} \approx 1.41421356237$.) ∎

Satisfaction guaranteed — up to a point The bisection method is sometimes called **interval-halving** for the good reason that each step cuts the length of the working interval in half. At each stage, moreover, the *midpoint* of the current interval can't miss the sought-after root by more than the *radius* of that interval. Thus the nth midpoint m_n can't miss a root r by more than the radius of the nth interval; in symbols this boils down to

$$|m_n - r| < \frac{b - a}{2^n}.$$

Students may need help with the idea of guaranteed accuracy; we return to it often in Volume II.

Note that each step of the method *doubles* the guaranteed precision of our estimate.

On the other hand, we may *never* find a root exactly. If a and b are rational numbers, for example, then so is every midpoint m_n; if the root r happens to be irrational (as $\sqrt{2}$ is) then the method will never locate r *exactly*. In real life, excellent approximations are almost always good enough.

Newton's method often finds roots much more quickly, but it assumes differentiability and requires differentiation.

A bisection algorithm The bisection method is an **algorithm**—a finite sequence of explicit instructions which, starting from appropriate inputs, reliably produces a desired output to within a predetermined level of accuracy. ("Explicit" means, roughly, "executable without really thinking." Computer programs and some cooking recipes are prime examples of algorithms.)

To emphasize the algorithmic nature of the bisection method, we'll state it explicitly in **pseudocode**—a sort of generic computer language. (Computerese is printed in the "typewriter" typeface.) Notice that the error tolerance is stated up front, as an input to the program. Once a root is found to within that tolerance, the procedure stops. (Without a stopping rule, a program might run forever.)

Students who know some programming can easily program their own bisection method.

- **Input:** A continuous function f, numbers a and b with $a < b$, and a tolerance $t > 0$. (For simplicity, we'll assume that $f(a) < 0$ and $f(b) > 0$.)
- **Output:** An approximate root of f, that is, a number m that differs from a root by less than the tolerance t.
- **Step 1:** (Find midpoint) `m:=(b+a)/2`
- **Step 2:** (Done?) `if b-a < 2t then output m; quit`
- **Step 3:** (New interval) `if f(m)<0 then a:=m else b:=m`
- **Step 4:** (Start again) `return to step 1`

A sample problem The following problem exploits several ideas from this section.

EXAMPLE 4 Let $f(x) = \sqrt{x}$.

a. What does the EVT say about f on the interval $[0, 1]$?

b. Although f is continuous on $[0, \infty)$, it has no maximum value on this interval. Does this contradict the EVT?

c. Although f is continuous on $(0, 1]$, it assumes no minimum value on this interval. Does *this* contradict the EVT?

d. Show that the IVT holds for f on $[0, 4]$ and $y = 1$.

Solution

a. The EVT says that f must achieve a maximum and a minimum somewhere on $[0, 1]$. It does: $f(0) = 0$ is the minimum value and $f(1) = 1$ is the maximum value.

b. and c. There's no contradiction in either part. The EVT applies only for closed and bounded intervals. Neither $[1, \infty)$ nor $(0, 1]$ is closed and bounded.

d. The IVT says that f must assume all values between $f(0) = 0$ and $f(4) = 2$. In particular, $y = 1$ is one such value. Sure enough, $f(1) = 1$, as the IVT requires. ■

BASIC EXERCISES

In Exercises 1–10, f and g are the functions shown below.

Graph of f   **Graph of g**

1. Over what intervals is f continuous?

2. Over what intervals is g continuous?

3. Over what intervals is $f(x) + g(x)$ continuous?

4. Over what intervals is $f(x) \cdot g(x)$ continuous?

5. Over what intervals is $\dfrac{f(x)}{g(x)}$ continuous?

6. Over what intervals is $\dfrac{g(x)}{f(x)}$ continous?

7. Does the conclusion of the IVT hold for f on $[-4, 4]$? Justify your answer.

8. Does the conclusion of the IVT hold for g on $[-4, 4]$? Justify your answer.

9. Does the conclusion of the EVT hold for f on $[-4, 4]$? Justify your answer.

10. Does the conclusion of the EVT hold for g on $[-4, 4]$? Justify your answer.

In Exercises 11–16, $f(x) = 1/x$.

11. What does the EVT say about f on the interval $[0.1, 1]$?

12. Although f is continuous on $[1, \infty)$, it has no minimum value on this interval. Why doesn't this contradict the EVT?

13. Although f is continuous on $(0, 1]$, it has no maximum value on this interval. Why doesn't this contradict the EVT?

14. What does the EVT say about f on the interval $[0, 1]$?

15. Although $f(-1) = -1$ and $f(1) = 1$, there is no value of c for which $f(c) = 0$. Why doesn't this contradict the IVT?

16. Show that the IVT holds for f on $[0.1, 1]$ and $y = 5$.

17. Use the IVT to show that $f(x) = x^5 + x^3 - 5x + 2$ has a root in $[0, 1]$.

18. The outside temperature at midnight was $13\,°C$; at 6 A.M. the temperature was $15\,°C$.

  (a) What does the IVT say about temperature during this time interval? [NOTE: Explain why the IVT's conditions are all fulfilled.]

  (b) Must there be a time between midnight and 6 A.M. when the temperature was $10\,°C$? *Could* there have been such a time?

  (c) Must there be a time between midnight and 6 A.M. when the temperature was an integer multiple of π?

  (d) What does the EVT say in this setting?

  (e) Could the temperature have been $25\,°C$ at 4 A.M.?

19. Starting with the interval $[1, 2]$, find the first four midpoint approximations to $\sqrt{3}$ by hand. Express your answers as rational numbers.

20. Use a calculator to find the first six midpoint approximations to a root of $\cos x - x$, starting with the interval $[0, 1]$. How accurate is your final approximation?

21. Suppose that f has a root in the interval $[0, 1]$. How many iterations of the bisection method are necessary to guarantee an estimate of the root within

(a) 10^{-2}?

(b) 10^{-3}?

(c) 10^{-5}?

(d) 10^{-10}?

FURTHER EXERCISES

In Exericses 22–25, explain what (if anything) the IVT says about the situation. If the answer is "nothing," explain why the IVT doesn't apply.

22. There were 37 people in this class 7 days ago; now there are 12.

23. I was 37 miles from home 7 hours ago; now I'm 12 miles from home.

24. I was driving at 37 miles per hour 7 minutes ago; now I'm driving at 12 miles per hour.

25. I had $37 in my pocket 7 days ago; today I have $12.

In Exercises 26–29, explain why the claim is true.

26. Moe was taller than Curly 7 years ago; now Curly is taller. Sometime in the last 7 years Moe and Curly were equally tall.

27. Let f be a continuous function. If $f(0) > 0$ but $f(1) < 1$, then $f(x) = x$ for some x in $(0, 1)$.

28. If f is continuous on $[0, 1]$ and $f(0) + f(1) = 0$, then $f(x) = 0$ for some x in $[0, 1]$.

29. If f is continuous on $[0, 1]$ and $f(0) \cdot f(1) < 0$, then $f(x) = 0$ for some x in $[0, 1]$.

30. Suppose that the function f is continuous at $x = 2$ and that f is defined by the rule

$$f(x) = \begin{cases} ax^2 + 3 & \text{if } x < 2 \\ 3x - 5 & \text{if } x \geq 2. \end{cases}$$

(a) Find the value of a.

(b) Is f differentiable at $x = 2$? Justify your answer.

In Exercises 31–34, indicate whether the statement must be true, might be true, or cannot be true. Assume that f is a continuous function that is defined for all real numbers and that f achieves a maximum value of 5 and a minimum value of -7.

31. The maximum value of $f(|x|)$ is 7.

32. The minimum value of $f(|x|)$ is 0.

33. The maximum value of $|f(x)|$ is 7.

34. The minimum value of $|f(x)|$ is 5.

In Exercises 35–38, indicate whether the statement must be true, might be true, or cannot be true. Justify your answer.

35. If $f(1) < 0$ and $f(5) > 0$, then there must be a number c in the interval $(1, 5)$ such that $f(c) = 0$.

36. If f is continuous on $[1, 5]$, $f(1) > 0$, and $f(5) < 0$, then there must be a number c in $(1, 5)$ such that $f(c) = 0$.

37. If f is continuous on $[1, 5]$ and there is a number c in $[1, 5]$ such that $f(c) = 0$, then $f(1) \cdot f(5) \leq 0$.

38. If f is continuous and has no roots in the interval $[1, 5]$, then $f(1) \cdot f(5) > 0$.

39. Use the IVT to find an interval in which $f(x) = x^5 + x^3 + 5x + 2$ has a root.

40. Suppose that f is defined on $[-5, 5]$, that $f(-5) = 2$ and $f(5) = -2$. If f assumes every value in $[-2, 2]$, must f be continuous? Explain. [HINT: The answer is *no*. Draw a graphical example that illustrates this.]

41. Use the IVT to prove this fixed-point theorem: If f is continuous on $[0, 1]$ and has range contained in $[0, 1]$, then f has a fixed point—that is, an input x for which $f(x) = x$. [HINT: Consider $g(x) = f(x) - x$.]

42. Let

$$f(x) = \begin{cases} x, & \text{if } x \text{ is rational} \\ 0, & \text{otherwise.} \end{cases}$$

Show that f is continuous at 0. [HINT: Use Theorem 7 to evaluate $\lim_{x \to 0} f(x)$.]

This section, like the preceding one, steps briefly into the theoretical side of the subject. We describe differentiability in terms of existence of limits; then we use it to deduce basic properties of differentiable functions.

4.9   WHY DIFFERENTIABILITY MATTERS; THE MEAN VALUE THEOREM

Graphically speaking, a function f is differentiable at $x = a$ if f is "almost linear" or "close to a line" near $x = a$. The derivative $f'(a)$ is the slope of the line in question. Such informal geometric descriptions are essential to our understanding of the derivative—but they don't tell every detail, and they lack something in precision.➡ In this section we take a somewhat more precise, analytic look at derivatives, differentiability, and their uses.

Recall the limit-based definition of derivative, from Section 2.2:

The telltale quotation marks suggest—correctly—that "almost" and "close to" are informal words.

> **DEFINITION** Let f be a function defined near and at $x = a$. Then
> $$f'(a) = \lim_{h \to 0} \frac{f(a+h) - f(a)}{h}.$$

For a given function f and $x = a$, the limit in the definition may or may not exist. If it does exist, we say that f is **differentiable** at $x = a$.

The standard elementary functions (algebraic, exponential, logarithmic, and trigonometric) are all differentiable wherever they're defined. Combinations (sums, products, quotients, and compositions) of elementary functions are also differentiable where *they're* defined; the sum, product, quotient, and chain rules tell us so. ➡

We made similar remarks (and for similar reasons) about continuity in Section 4.8.

Like continuity, differentiability is the rule in calculus—so much so, perhaps, that its true importance might be overlooked. This section aims to avoid that pitfall.

Differentiable functions are continuous

Continuity and differentiability are both "nice" properties for a function to have. How are they related to each other? The absolute value function $g(x) = |x|$ shows that continuity does not imply differentiability: $g(x)$ is continuous but not differentiable at $x = 0$. (We proved this directly from the definition in Section 2.4.) ➡ But a differentiable function *must* be continuous:

Few students would doubt this; the main point is that a careful proof requires a careful definition.

We also showed that $f(x) = \sqrt[3]{x}$ is continuous but not differentiable; see Example 5, page 103.

> **THEOREM 9** If f is differentiable at $x = a$, then f is also continuous at $x = a$.

Proof. The theorem is both graphically reasonable (it's hard to imagine a discontinuous graph having a tangent line!) and easy to prove. To prove the theorem, we need only show that

$$f(x) \to f(a) \quad \text{as} \quad x \to a.$$

(This is the formal definition of continuity of f at $x = a$.) The definition of differentiability at $x = a$ means that, as $x \to a$,

$$\frac{f(x) - f(a)}{x - a} \to f'(a).$$

From this fact it follows easily that as $x \to a$,

$$f(x) - f(a) = \frac{f(x) - f(a)}{x - a} \cdot (x - a) \to f'(a) \cdot 0 = 0,$$

as desired.   □

A day trip into theory

Calculus is more than a set of powerful methods for solving important problems. It is also a mathematical *theory*—a coherent, rigorously developed body of definitions and theorems. We don't aim here (or elsewhere) to present the theory of calculus in full detail or with full rigor. ➡ This section is, instead, a brief excursion into theory—a close look at one important theorem in its mathematical context.

In later mathematics courses, such as elementary real analysis, the theory of calculus is the main subject.

The guts of the machine. Using calculus, like driving a car, can be done effectively without perfect or constant attention to the machine's inner workings. Why bother with theory?

One good reason is that ignorance of underlying principles leaves one vulnerable in unexpected situations—no owner's manual can cover everything. A better reason concerns the difference between cars and calculus. Cars are useful tools, but calculus is a way of describing and exploring our world.

We met them in Section 4.8.

The three "value theorems" have similar forms; note that the MVT asserts that f′ (not f) assumes a special value.

The intermediate value theorem and the extreme value theorem ← guarantee that a *continuous* function assumes certain desirable values on a closed interval. The **mean value theorem** is in the same spirit: It guarantees that the derivative of a *differentiable* function assumes a certain desirable mean value at a point inside the interval.

> **THEOREM 10 (Mean value theorem)** Suppose that f is continuous on the closed interval $[a, b]$ and differentiable on the open interval (a, b). Then there is a number c between a and b for which
>
> $$f'(c) = \frac{f(b) - f(a)}{b - a}.$$

Taken out of context, the mean value theorem (MVT) is hard to see for what it is—one of the two or three *really* big theorems of calculus. The rest of this section aims to put the MVT in context. What do its words mean? What does it say? Why is the name appropriate? Are the hypotheses really necessary? What questions does the theorem answer? Why do the answers matter?

What the MVT says

The MVT says that, under appropriate hypotheses on f, the derivative f' must assume a certain mean value. Interpreting f' either as an instantaneous rate or as a slope makes the theorem comprehensible—and readily believable.

A motorist's view   If a car *averages* 60 mph over an interval of time, then at some instant during the interval the speedometer must have read *exactly* 60. The MVT says the same thing. If $f(t)$ represents a car's position in miles at time t in hours, then $f'(t)$ represents *instantaneous* velocity at time t, and $(f(b) - f(a))/(b - a)$ represents *average* velocity over the interval $a \le t \le b$. In this language the MVT equation

$$f'(c) = \frac{f(b) - f(a)}{b - a}$$

reads as follows:

> *At some time c between a and b, the instantaneous velocity is equal to the average (or "mean") velocity over the entire interval.*

The MVT in pictures   On the graph of f, each side of the MVT equation represents a *slope*—of the tangent line at $x = c$ and of the secant line from a to b, respectively. The theorem asserts that, for at least one value of c between a and b, these two slopes are equal. In the case shown in Figure 1, *two* such c's exist.

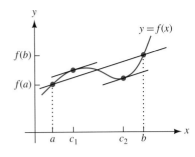

FIGURE 1
The mean value theorem

All three straight lines (two tangent lines and a secant line) have the same slope.

Why differentiability matters   The MVT requires that $f'(x)$ should exist for every x in (a, b). (Most often, $f'(x)$ exists at the endpoints, too, but that isn't strictly necessary.) ➤

This differentiability hypothesis can't be diluted. If f is not differentiable at even *one* point in (a, b), the MVT can fail. The function $f(x) = |x|$ on the interval $[-1, 1]$ illustrates this problem (the secant line over the interval is horizontal, but there's no horizontal tangent line).

Mathematicians like to state theorems as generally as possible.

Using the MVT: answering natural questions

The MVT has important theoretical uses; many amount to putting claims that sound reasonable (or even obvious) on a sound logical footing. We give several examples here, and see others later in this book.

The claims (such as Theorem 11) sound almost too simple; the surprise is that proofs take some doing.

Question 1: When is a function constant?   It's clear (from the definition of derivative or from graphical arguments) that the derivative of a constant function is the zero function:

$$\text{If } f(x) = k \text{ for all inputs } x, \text{ then } f'(x) = 0.$$

Is the *converse* true? ➤ In other words, is the following reasonable-sounding theorem true?

The exercises offer some practice with words like "converse."

THEOREM 11   If $f'(x) = 0$ for all x in an interval I, then f is constant on I.

The converse *of the statement "if P then Q" is the statement "if Q then P."*

Geometric thinking supports the claim: if a graph has a horizontal tangent line everywhere, then we expect the graph itself to be horizontal.

The theorem *is* true. The main surprise is that proving such an "obvious" fact requires a gun of the MVT's caliber.

Proof.   To show that f is constant, ➤ it's enough to show that for any two inputs $x = a$ and $x = b$, $f(a) = f(b)$. (We don't care about the specific values of $f(a)$ and $f(b)$—only that they're equal.) By the MVT there's some input c between a and b for which

We don't care which constant.

$$f'(c) = \frac{f(b) - f(a)}{b - a}.$$

We have no idea *which* c works—but it doesn't matter! By hypothesis, $f'(c) = 0$ for *every* input c between a and b, so

$$0 = f'(c) = \frac{f(b) - f(a)}{b - a} \implies f(b) - f(a) = 0 \implies f(b) = f(a),$$

as we wanted.   □

Theorem 11 has a simple but useful consequence:

Any two antiderivatives of the same function differ by a constant.

More precisely:

THEOREM 12   If $F'(x) = G'(x)$ for all x in an interval I, then $F(x) = G(x) + C$ for some constant C.

Theorem 12 can be proved by applying Theorem 11 to the difference function $F(x) - G(x)$.

Question 2: When is a function increasing?   We've often stressed—but so far never proved—that the *sign* of f' determines whether f *increases* or *decreases* over an interval. The MVT offers a simple but rigorous proof. First, a concise statement:

If a car's eastward velocity is always positive, then the car moves steadily eastward.

THEOREM 13   Suppose that $f'(x) > 0$ for all x in an interval I. Then f is increasing on I.

Proof.   We need to show that $f(a) < f(b)$ for any inputs a and b in I with $a < b$. By the MVT, there's a c somewhere in (a, b) for which

$$f(b) - f(a) = (b - a) \cdot f'(c).$$

Because both factors on the right are positive, so is $f(b) - f(a)$. But $f(b) - f(a) > 0$ implies $f(b) > f(a)$, as desired.   □

The MVT and the speed limit law   Another natural consequence of the MVT is a variant of the speed limit law: ◄

We met the speed limit law in Section 1.4.

THEOREM 14 (The racetrack principle)   If $f(a) = g(a)$ and $f'(x) \le g'(x)$ for $x \ge a$, then $f(x) \le g(x)$ for $x \ge a$.

The "racetrack" word makes sense because the theorem can be stated in racing language:

If dogs f and g are together at time $x = a$, and dog g runs at least as fast as dog f for $x \ge a$, then dog g never falls behind dog f.

The racetrack principle (like much else) can be proved by applying the MVT to the "right" function—in this case, to the function $h(x) = g(x) - f(x)$. Our hypotheses are (i) $h(a) = 0$; and (ii) $h'(x) \ge 0$ if $x \ge a$. The MVT guarantees that for each $x \ge a$ there's a number $c \ge a$ for which

$$h'(c) = \frac{h(x) - h(a)}{x - a} = \frac{h(x)}{x - a}.$$

Hypothesis (ii) gives $h'(c) \ge 0$, and the rest is easy. If $x \ge a$, then

$$g(x) - f(x) = h(x) = h(x) - h(a) = h'(c) \cdot (x - a) \ge 0 \cdot (x - a) = 0.$$

Thus, $g(x) \ge h(x)$, as desired.

EXAMPLE 1   Show, using derivatives, that if $x \geq 0$, then $\sin x \leq x$.

Solution   One approach uses Theorem 14 (the "racetrack principle"). If $f(x) = \sin x$ and $g(x) = x$, then $f(0) = g(0)$, and so "dogs" f and g start together. Also, $f'(x) = \cos x$ and $g'(x) = 1$, and so $f'(x) \leq g'(x)$ for all x (so dog g is faster). Now Theorem 14 says that dog g stays ahead: $f(x) \leq g(x)$, as desired.   ■

Root-counting with the MVT   The next example shows yet another nice use of the MVT—linking stationary points to roots.

EXAMPLE 2   Suppose that the function f is differentiable for all x and that f has 43 roots. Show that f has *at least* 42 stationary points.

Solution   We'll show that there's at least one stationary point between any two roots. If x_1 and x_2 are roots of f, then $f(x_1) = 0 = f(x_2)$, and the mean value theorem says there's a c between x_1 and x_2 with

$$\frac{f(x_2) - f(x_1)}{x_2 - x_1} = f'(c).$$

With 43 roots $x_1 < x_2 < \cdots < x_{43}$ this process generates at least 42 stationary points.   ■

The idea of the solution applies more generally, of course: If f has n roots, then f has *at least* $n - 1$ stationary points. It's possible, moreover, that f has *many more* than $n - 1$ stationary points. For instance, $f(x) = 2 + \sin x$ has *no* roots, but it has infinitely many stationary points.

Students might look for functions with, say, two stationary points but only one root.

Proving the MVT, step by step

Understood graphically, the MVT may seem obvious—what's to prove? That impression is understandable but wrong; pictures aren't proofs. A rigorous proof of the MVT involves several steps and appeals to other facts and theorems.

We'll sketch a proof that's based on two preliminary lemmas. (A **lemma** is a junior-grade or auxiliary theorem, usually used to help prove something more important or more general.)

The proof of the MVT is optional in the sense that nothing later depends on it. The proof is given largely to illustrate the nature of a step-by-step proof.

> **LEMMA 1**   Let f be any function defined on $[a, b]$. Suppose that f assumes either its maximum or its minimum value on $[a, b]$ at a point c strictly between a and b. If $f'(c)$ exists, then $f'(c) = 0$.

Proof.   We'll show what happens if $f(c)$ is a *maximum* (the minimum case is similar). If $f'(c)$ exists, then, by definition,

$$f'(c) = \lim_{h \to 0} \frac{f(c + h) - f(c)}{h} = \lim_{h \to 0^-} \frac{f(c + h) - f(c)}{h} = \lim_{h \to 0^+} \frac{f(c + h) - f(c)}{h}.$$

Since the ordinary limit exists, the left-hand and right-hand limits also exist, and all three limits are equal. Notice first that because f assumes a maximum at c, the numerator $f(c + h) - f(c)$ in all three limit expressions must be negative or zero. ➟ The denominator

Otherwise $f(c + h) > f(c)$, which means $f(c)$ is not a maximum value.

h, on the other hand, is *negative* if $h \to 0^-$ and *positive* if $h \to 0^+$. Therefore,

$$f'(c) = \lim_{h \to 0^-} \frac{f(c+h) - f(c)}{h} = \lim_{h \to 0^-} [\text{nonnegative stuff}] \geq 0.$$

(The last inequality says, in effect, that the limit of a nonnegative function is also nonnegative.) For similar reasons,

$$f'(c) = \lim_{h \to 0^+} \frac{f(c+h) - f(c)}{h} = \lim_{h \to 0^+} [\text{nonpositive stuff}] \leq 0.$$

The only possible conclusion is that $f'(c) = 0$, as desired. □

> **LEMMA 2** (**Rolle's theorem**) Suppose that f is continuous on $[a, b]$ and differentiable on (a, b) and that $f(a) = f(b)$. Then, for some c between a and b, $f'(c) = 0$.

To many students Rolle's theorem seems much simpler than the MVT. We give a relatively rigorous proof.

Remark This lemma, known as **Rolle's theorem**, is nothing more (or less) than the MVT in the special case that $f(a) = f(b)$. The picture, naturally, resembles Figure 1, which illustrates the MVT:

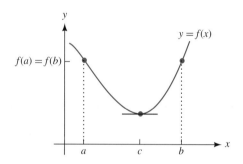

The graph is horizontal somewhere between a and b.

FIGURE 2
Rolle's theorem

Proof of Rolle's theorem. Because f is continuous on $[a, b]$, the extreme value theorem (Theorem 8, page 276) guarantees that f assumes both a maximum value and a minimum value somewhere in $[a, b]$. If both the maximum and the minimum occur at the endpoints a and b, then

$$f(x_{\max}) = f(a) = f(b) = f(x_{\min});$$

since the maximum and minimum values of f are *equal*, the function must be constant. In this strange case, there's nothing more to do—$f'(c) = 0$ for *every* c in (a, b).

The alternative is that at least one of the maximum and the minimum lies at some c *between* a and b. In this case, the preceding Lemma applies to give $f'(c) = 0$. □

All together now: proving the MVT Using Rolle's theorem to prove the MVT requires a technical step. Using f, a, and b, we create a new function to which Rolle's theorem applies.

Given f as in the MVT, consider the linear function l whose graph is the secant line to f from a to b, as shown in Figure 3.

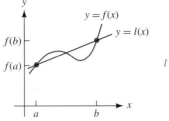

l is the secant line from $x = a$ to $x = b$.

FIGURE 3
Proving the mean value theorem: f and l

The precise formula for l isn't hard to find, but in this case it doesn't matter. What *does* matter is that

$$l(a) = f(a), \qquad l(b) = f(b), \qquad \text{and} \qquad l'(x) = \frac{f(b) - f(a)}{b - a}.$$

Finally, we consider the difference function $g(x) = f(x) - l(x)$. By design, $g(a) = 0 = g(b)$, and so Rolle's theorem applies to g. The rest is bookkeeping: For some c in (a, b),

$$0 = g'(c) = f'(c) - l'(c) = f'(c) - \frac{f(b) - f(a)}{b - a},$$

which is what we wanted to know.

BASIC EXERCISES

The converse *of the statement "if P then Q" is the statement "if Q then P." In Exercises 1–6, write (in ordinary English) the converse of the given statement. Then decide whether the statement and its converse are true.*

1. If it's raining, then it's cloudy.

2. If $f'(1) = 0$ then f has a local minimum at $x = 1$.

3. If $x > 2$ then $x > 1$.

4. If I win the lottery, then I'll get rich.

5. If $f'(x) = 2x$ then $f(x) = x^2$.

6. If $f'(x) < 0$ for all x then f is decreasing for all x.

7. Let $q(x) = Ax^2 + Bx + C$ be any quadratic polynomial (assume $A \neq 0$) and let $[a, b]$ be any interval. Show that the point c mentioned in the MVT is the *midpoint* of $[a, b]$.

In Exercises 8–14, find (i.e., plot or give a formula for) a differentiable function f with the given properties or explain why no such function can exist.

8. f has 2 roots and 1 stationary point

9. f has 3 roots and 1 stationary point

10. f has 1 root and 2 stationary points

11. f has infinitely many roots and infinitely many stationary points

12. $f'(x) = -1$ for all x and $f(0) = 137$

13. $f(0) = 0$ and $f(1) = 1$, but $f'(x) > 2$ for all x

14. f has infinitely many roots and infinitely many stationary points

In Exercises 15–18, $f(x) = |x|$.

15. Does f satisfy all hypotheses of the MVT on $[a, b] = [-1, 2]$? Explain.

16. Does f satisfy the conclusion of the MVT on $[a, b] = [-1, 2]$? Explain.

17. Does f satisfy all hypotheses of the MVT on $[a, b] = [1, 2]$? Explain.

18. Does f satisfy the conclusion of the MVT on $[a, b] = [1, 2]$? If so, find at least one suitable value of c. How many such c's exist?

19. Let $f(x) = x^7 - x^5 - x^4 + 2x + 1$. Explain why there must be a point c in the interval $(-1, 1)$ such that the line tangent to the graph of f at the point $(c, f(c))$ has slope 2.

FURTHER EXERCISES

In Exercises 20–22, $f(x) = x^2$.

20. What does the MVT say about f on $[a, b] = [-1, 1]$? Find all suitable values of c. How many are there?

21. What does the MVT say about f on $[a, b] = [1, 2]$? Find all suitable values of c. How many are there?

22. Show that for $f(x) = x^2$ and any interval $[a, b]$, the MVT's number c is the midpoint of $[a, b]$.

23. Let $g(x) = x^{2/3} - 1$. Notice that although $g(-1) = g(1) = 0$ there is no point c in the interval $(-1, 1)$ where $g'(c) = 0$. Why doesn't this contradict Rolle's theorem?

In Exercises 24–27, f is a continuous function. A portion of the graph of f is shown below.

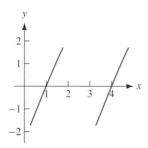

24. Explain why f must have a root in the interval $(1, 4)$.

25. Assume that f' is a continuous function. Explain why f' must have a root in the interval $(1, 4)$.

26. Assume that f' is a continuous function. Explain why the graph of f must have a horizontal tangent line somewhere between $x = 1$ and $x = 4$.

27. Why is it necessary to assume that f' is continuous in Exercises 25 and 26? [HINT: Sketch the graph of a function f that is continuous on the interval $(1, 4)$ and has the property that $f'(x) \neq 0$ anywhere in this interval.]

28. Let f be a continuous function that is positive on the interval $[0, 4]$ and differentiable on $(0, 4)$. Answer each of the following questions about f. Justify each answer by citing an appropriate theorem or by giving a counterexample.

(a) Is it always possible to find a c in $[0, 4]$ such that $f(x) \leq f(c)$ for all x in $[0, 4]$?

(b) Is it always possible to find a c in $[0, 4]$ such that the instantaneous rate of change of f at c equals the average rate of change of f over the interval $[0, 4]$?

(c) Is it always possible to find a c in $[0, 4]$ such that the line tangent to the graph of f at $(c, f(c))$ is horizontal?

29. Let f be a function such that $f(0) = 0$ and $1/2 \leq f'(x) \leq 1$ for all values of x.

(a) Use the MVT to explain why $f(2)$ cannot be equal to 3.

(b) Find upper and lower bounds for the value of $f(3)$.

(c) Find upper and lower bounds for the value of $f(-1)$.

30. Use the MVT to show that $|\sin b - \sin a| \leq |b - a|$. [HINT: $|\cos x| \leq 1$ for all x.]

31. Let f be a function that is differentiable everywhere. Furthermore, assume that the line $y = 3x - 1$ is tangent to f at $x = 1$ and that the line tangent to f at $x = 3$ passes through the points $(0, 5)$ and $(4, 1)$.

(a) Evaluate $f'(1)$ and $f'(3)$.

(b) Evaluate $f(1)$ and $f(3)$.

(c) Explain why there must be a number c in the interval $[1, 3]$ such that $f'(c) = 0$.

(d) Suppose that it is known that $f''(x) < 0$ for all x in $[1, 3]$. Explain why this implies that f has a unique maximum value over the interval $[1, 3]$.

32. Suppose that f is differentiable for all values of x, $f(-3) = -3$, $f(3) = 3$, and $|f'(x)| \leq 1$ for all x in $[-3, 3]$. Show that $f(0) = 0$.

33. At 1:00 P.M. a truck driver picked up a fare card at the entrance of a tollway. At 2:15 P.M., the trucker pulled up to a toll booth 100 miles down the road. After computing the trucker's fare, the toll booth operator issues a speeding ticket to the trucker. (The tollway speed limit is 65 mph.)

(a) The trucker claimed that he hadn't been speeding. Was he lying? Explain.

(b) The fine for speeding is $50 plus $5 for each mph above the speed limit. What is the trucker's minimum fine?

SUMMARY

This chapter offered a potpourri of applications of the derivative and antiderivative. (The sampling is a skimpy one, unfortunately—these ideas have far more uses than any textbook could possibly cover).

Slope fields   Slope fields, introduced in Section 4.1, offer a graphical interpretation of DEs of the form $y' = f(t, y)$; they also provide a graphical method of solving such DEs approximately. Starting from any point in the slope field, one "goes with the flow" to draw a curve that represents a solution. Using slope fields we can model situations more realistically than we could otherwise.

Limits involving infinity and l'Hôpital's rule   Section 4.2 is a second visit—this time with derivatives available for use as a tool—to the general theme of limits. (The first visit, in Chapter 2, had mainly to do with *defining* derivatives.) First we defined a variant on the basic limit idea, limits that involve the ∞ symbol, and interpreted results graphically in terms of asymptotes. Then we showed how to use derivatives and a special result, **l'Hôpital's rule**, to calculate some challenging limits.

Optimization   Among the derivative's most important and useful applications is finding **extreme values**—that is, maximum and minimum values—of functions. As Section 4.3 illustrated, solving optimization problems usually means identifying an appropriate function and then using the derivative to look for and classify its **critical points**. Problems posed in words received special stress—translation of English descriptions into mathematical form is crucial to applying calculus tools.

Parametric equations and parametric curves   Many interesting plane curves such as circles, are not graphs of functions. Parametrically defined curves offer much more flexibility. Defining x and y separately as **coordinate functions** of another variable—say t—lets us draw all sorts of interesting, beautiful, and complicated curves. If the coordinate functions are differentiable in t, then calculus ideas apply; we use them to define and calculate slopes and speeds.

Related rates   In practical situations, several quantities vary together in time, and the rates at which these quantities vary are themselves related. The method of **related rates** is a technique for discovering such relationships. A typical problem begins with an equation relating several quantities, all varying with time. Differentiating everything in sight—usually with respect to time—produces a new equation, one that relates the rates at which the quantities vary.

Linear and quadratic approximation   The graph of any well-behaved function is approximated—more or less closely, and near the point of tangency—by its tangent line. This means, in functional language, that f is approximated well by the linear function, called the **linear approximation** to f at x_0, whose graph is the tangent line. Section 4.6 explored the meaning and ramifications of this fact and took matters one step further, to quadratic approximation. In graphical terms, the **quadratic approximation** to f at x_0 is the function whose graph is the parabola that best fits f at x_0. Going further still, Section 4.6 introduced **Taylor polynomials**, polynomials of any degree that approximate nonpolynomial functions.

Newton's method   Finding roots of any but the simplest functions (e.g., linear functions) is difficult or impossible algebraically. **Newton's method** (like the bisection method of Section 4.8) offers a numerical alternative. To estimate a root of f near an initial guess x_0, Newton's method "rides the tangent line" from the f-graph at x_0 to the x-axis. The result is seldom *exactly* a root, but repeating Newton's method usually produces—remarkably quickly—a highly accurate approximation to a root. Section 4.6 treated the idea and typical applications of Newton's method—and suggested some ideas for "breaking" it.

Continuity and differentiability   Sections 4.8 and 4.9 are brief excursions into the theory of calculus. They explored, respectively, the mathematical significance of continuity and differentiability. The most important results are three "value theorems": the **intermediate value theorem**, the **extreme value theorem**, and, most important of all, the **mean value theorem**. All three results are implicit in much of the logical machinery of calculus.

Growth with Interest

Everyone knows that money grows "with interest." Just *how* this growth occurs is less well understood. The popular buzz-phrase "the miracle of compound interest" suggests that the phenomenon, though surely a good thing, lies well outside the sphere of human understanding.

There is nothing miraculous about bank interest. Basic calculus and some care for specialized vocabulary (watch the boldfaced words) suffice to explain what happens. Exponential growth, not divine intervention, turns out to explain compound interest nicely.

A main aim is to demystify some interest rate jargon, and relate it to calculus ideas, especially to exponential growth.

EXAMPLE 1 First National Bank (1NB) pays a **nominal annual interest rate** of 6%, compounded daily. By what percentage does a 1NB deposit increase over 1 year? (This percentage is called the **effective annual interest rate**.) What is an initial deposit of $1000 worth after a year?

Solution Let $b(t)$ denote the balance (in dollars) at time t (in years). What "nominal" means here is that, each day, the balance is multiplied by $(1 + .06/365)$. ➤ With initial balance $b(0)$, here's what happens for the first 2 days:

Our year has 365 days.

$$b\left(\frac{1}{365}\right) = b(0) \cdot \left(1 + \frac{0.06}{365}\right); \qquad b\left(\frac{2}{365}\right) = b(0) \cdot \left(1 + \frac{0.06}{365}\right)^2.$$

In general,

$$b(t) = b(0) \cdot \left(1 + \frac{0.06}{365}\right)^{365t}$$

gives the balance after t years. In particular,

$$b(1) = b(0) \cdot \left(1 + \frac{0.06}{365}\right)^{365} \approx b(0) \cdot 1.06183.$$

Thus, over one full year the balance increases by a factor of 1.06183, and so the **effective annual rate** is about 6.183%. An initial deposit of $1000 is worth 1061.83 after a year. ■

PROBLEM 1 Second National Bank (2NB) pays a **nominal annual interest rate** of 6%, but compounds interest only monthly. Find the effective annual rate. Show that an initial deposit of $1000 in 2NB is worth $1061.68 after a year.

PROBLEM 2 Show that the 1NB balance function $b(t)$ in Example 1 can be rewritten in the form

$$b(t) = b(0) \cdot \left((1 + 0.06/365)^{365}\right)^t \approx b(0) \cdot 1.06183^t.$$

Write the 2NB balance function in a similar way.

Interest rates and DEs The balance $b(t)$ of an interest-bearing financial deposit grows at a rate proportional to its current value. This is the hallmark property of exponential growth, so we expect the familiar exponential DE model

$$b' = kb$$

to apply. So it does, but some natural questions arise: How do interest rates (nominal or effective) translate into DE language? How are they related to the proportionality constant k in the DE? How does frequency of compounding play come into it? How accurate can *any* DE model be?

One approach to bank interest is to link continuous compounding to a differential equation and periodic compounding to a difference equation.

- **Discrete vs. continuous models**   In a real bank account the balance $b(t)$ rises *discretely* at regular intervals and in jumps of at least one cent. Every DE model describes *continuous* functions, and so must commit *some* error. In practice, fortunately, such errors are often small enough to ignore.

- **Frequent (and continuous) compounding**   The DE model itself represents **continuous compounding**: a sort of limiting case as the compounding becomes more and more frequent. On a time scale measured in years, one day is effectively an instant; even a month is a short time. This means that (with reasonably frequent compounding) the *nominal* interest rate can serve, without much error, as the k in the exponential DE $b' = kb$.

EXAMPLE 2   Third National Bank (3NB), feeling the competition, advertises 6% nominal interest compounded *continuously*. What effective annual rate do 3NB customers get? Should 1NB and 2NB customers jump to 3NB?

Solution   The 3NB model is the DE $b'(t) = 0.06 \cdot b(t)$; we've seen that solutions have the form

$$b(t) = b_0 e^{0.06t},$$

where the constant b_0 represents the initial value $b(0)$. The balance after one year is therefore $b(1) = b_0 \cdot e^{0.06} \approx 1.06184 b_0$, and so the effective interest rate is 6.184%. That's one extra penny a year over the 1NB return on a $1000 deposit and about 14 cents above the 2NB return—not likely to poach many calculus-savvy customers.   ∎

EXAMPLE 3   Fourth National Bank (4NB) pays $100r$% nominal annual interest, compounded continuously. (For example, $r = 0.06$ corresponds to 6%.) What's the effective annual interest rate at 4NB?

Solution   The continuous compounding policy at 4NB means that balances satisfy the DE $b'(t) = rb(t)$. As we've seen, solutions have the form $b(t) = b_0 e^{rt}$, where b_0 is the initial deposit. Hence $b(1) = b_0 e^r$, and so e^r is the annual multiplier, and $100(e^r - 1)$ is the effective annual interest rate.   ∎

PROBLEM 3   Hoping to attract wealthy depositors, Fourth National Bank (4NB; see Example 3) decides to advertise its *effective* annual interest rate, 7%, on "jumbo" deposits. Compounding is continuous. What is 4NB's *nominal* annual interest rate?

PROBLEM 4   As Example 2 illustrates, the advantage of frequent compounding isn't great for a 6% nominal annual interest rate. For higher interest rates the story is different. Find the effective annual interest rate and the value of a $1000 deposit after 1 year in each of the following cases:

(a) Nominal rate 100%, compounded yearly.

(b) Nominal rate 100%, compounded monthly.

(c) Nominal rate 100%, compounded daily.

(d) Nominal rate 100%, compounded continuously.

(e) Nominal rate 100%, compounded n times yearly.

PROBLEM 5   Why do the DE model $b' = 0.06b$ and the daily compounding model (at 1NB) give such similar results? To see why, let $b(t)$ represent the 1NB balance function.

Explain each step of the following computation:

$$b'(t) \approx \frac{b(t+1/365) - b(t)}{1/365} \qquad \text{(Step 1)}$$

$$= \left(b(t) \cdot \left(1 + \frac{0.06}{365} \right) - b(t) \right) \cdot 365 \qquad \text{(Step 2)}$$

$$= b(t) \cdot \left(1 + \frac{0.06}{365} - 1 \right) \cdot 365 = 0.06 \cdot b(t). \qquad \text{(Step 3)}$$

(The calculation shows that the 1NB balance function $b(t)$ is—approximately—a solution of the DE $b' = 0.06b$.)

Logistic Growth

We compare three reasonable-sounding population growth models: the exponential, logistic, and "warming" models. (The last model resembles Newtonian cooling.)

How do biological populations grow over time?

It depends on the organism (yeast, say, or whales) and on environmental conditions (such as food supply and physical space). Although simple mathematical models can't fully reflect the complexity of real-world population dynamics, it's interesting—and sometimes useful as a first approximation to biological reality—to compare different mathematical growth models and work out their implications.

Figure 1 shows possible population functions for three different mathematical models of population growth; we'll compare the three models (and explain their names) in what follows.

population

Appropriate units on both axes depend on the situation. For a fruit fly colony, time in days and population in thousands might make sense.

FIGURE 1
Three population growth models

Exponential growth   One curve illustrates exponential growth, in which a population grows at a rate proportional to its size. In DE language

$$P' = kP,$$

where P (or $P(t)$) denotes the population at time t and k is a (positive) constant. ◄

The exponential model is simple, but real-world populations can't grow exponentially forever. For instance, a colony of 1000 fruit flies growing exponentially at 5% per day would number over 8 billion in a year; in a decade, they'd outnumber Earth's molecules. ◄ Despite these limitations, the exponential model describes some biological populations usefully for limited periods.

We discussed exponential growth in Sections 2.6 and 4.2.

That's biologically—and logically—impossible.

PROBLEM 1   Consider the function $P(t) = Ae^{kt}$, where A and k are constants.

(a) Show that $P(t)$ is a solution of the exponential DE $y' = ky$.

(b) The exponential curve in Figure 1 has the form $P(t) = Ae^{kt}$. Use the figure to find or estimate numerical values of A and k for this curve. [HINT: Calculate $P(0)$ and $P'(0)$.]

The Rev. Malthus predicts Doomsday   The prospect of runaway growth in human population troubled the English clergyman Thomas Malthus. In *An Essay on the Principle of Population*, published in 1798, Malthus warned of an early and unpleasant end to the human race. How well the Malthusian model really describes human populations over long periods is controversial to say the least. But it's *mathematically* certain that an exponentially growing population eventually outgrows its environment's carrying capacity. Real populations cope (or don't) with this problem in various ways. Some populations (lemmings and Dungeness crabs) have boom–bust cycles; others (such as yeast in sugar solution) eat up or otherwise spoil their environments and die out completely.

''Warming'' growth   Another curve in Figure 1 illustrates a second growth model: the population grows quickly at first and then levels off as it approaches an upper bound (the environment's **carrying capacity**)—like the rising temperature of a cold object warming to room temperature. This growth model is also described by a DE (which we'll call the "warming DE"):

$$P' = k(C - P),$$

where P is the population and k and C (for "capacity") are positive constants. The DE says that the growth rate is proportional to the "available space"—the difference between the carrying capacity and the present population. (This model might apply, for instance, to a very fast-breeding population, which is limited mainly by available space.)

PROBLEM 2   Consider the function $P(t) = C - Ae^{-kt}$, where A is a constant.
(a) Show that $P(t)$ is a solution of the warming DE.

(b) The "warming curve" in Figure 1 has the form $P(t) = C - Ae^{-kt}$, with $C = 10$ and $A = 9$. Explain how these two values can be seen in the figure.

(c) For the "warming" curve in Figure 1, the value of k is 0.05. How could this value be estimated from the figure? [HINT: Estimate $P'(0)$ from the graph.]

PROBLEM 3   In Section 4.1 we used the "cooling DE" $y' = k(y - T_0)$ (where k is a negative constant) to express **Newton's law of cooling**: A warm object cools at a rate proportional to the difference between its temperature T and the environment's temperature T_0.
(a) Compare the cooling DE with the warming DE above. Why is it natural here to use a *negative* constant k?

(b) Show by differentiation that, for any constant A, the function $y = Ae^{kt} + T_0$ is a solution of the cooling DE.

Logistic growth   A third (and possibly happier) population model is **logistic growth**. The logistic curve in Figure 1 gives the idea: The population grows slowly when numbers are small, speeds up as the population grows, and then levels off as the population approaches an upper limit C. Notice that, near the beginning, the exponential and logistic curves are almost identical. This reflects the fact that when populations are small, effects of crowding are scarcely felt, and so logistic growth is essentially exponential.

Logistic growth has the following property:

The growth rate is proportional both to the population itself and to the difference between the carrying capacity and the population.

The **logistic DE** says the same thing in symbols:
$$P' = kP(C - P),$$

where P is the population, C is the carrying capacity, and k is a positive constant.

The logistic DE is separable; but requires partial fractions (a Chapter 8 topic) to antidifferentiate.

PROBLEM 4   The slow–fast–slow pattern of logistic growth also occurs in some nonbiological "populations." The number of homes with telephones, for instance, probably grew slowly when phones were new, rose faster and faster as the new technology took hold, and then leveled off as nearly every home acquired a phone. Give other examples of logistic-style growth.

PROBLEM 5   The logistic DE shows that if either $P = 0$ or $C = P$, then $P' = 0$. What does this mean in the language of population growth?

Solving the logistic DE   Searching systematically for a solution to the logistic DE $P' = kP(C - P)$ is a bit messy given our present tools. ➤ But we can readily *check* that the

It gets easier with techniques from integral calculus.

following function is a solution for any constants k, C, and d:

$$P(t) = \frac{C}{1 + d\,e^{-k \cdot C \cdot t}}.$$

PROBLEM 6 Check by differentiation that $P(t) = \dfrac{C}{1 + d\,e^{-k \cdot C \cdot t}}$ satisfies the DE $P' = kP(C - P)$. (It's a bit messy.)

Logistic flies

A colony of prudent fruit flies, eager to avoid crowding, agrees to reproduce logistically. On day 0 the population is 1000 and growing at the (net) instantaneous rate of 50 flies per day. The environment can support 10,000 flies. How will the population evolve over time? When will the population grow fastest? When will it reach 9900?

This reduces pesky zeros in calculations.

We'll model the fly population using the solution function above, measuring time t in days and population P in thousands. ← Clearly $C = 10$, so

$$P(t) = \frac{10}{1 + d\,e^{-k \cdot 10 \cdot t}}.$$

50 flies per day is 0.05 thousands per day.

To evaluate the remaining constants d and k, we can use the facts that $P(0) = 1$ and $P'(0) = 0.05$. ← The result is a fully explicit population formula:

$$P(t) = \frac{10}{1 + 9\,e^{-t/18}}.$$

PROBLEM 7 Use the facts that $P(0) = 1$ and $P'(0) = 0.05$ to show that $d = 9$ and $k = 0.05/9 = 1/180$.

The formula and the following graph (Figure 2) tell at least as much as we'd want know about logistic fly demographics.

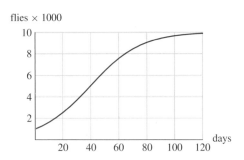

flies × 1000

FIGURE 2
Logistic flies

PROBLEM 8 Use the formula (but check answers graphically) to decide when the population reaches 5000. When is the population at 99% of capacity?

PROBLEM 9 The graph suggests that the population rises fastest around day 40, when the population is 5000—exactly *half* the carrying capacity. Verify this symbolically in two different ways:

(a) Since $P' = kP(C - P)$, growth is fastest for the value of P that maximizes $f(P) = kP(C - P)$. Show that this occurs where $P = C/2$.

(b) The maximum growth rate occurs at an *inflection point* of the P-graph. (Look for it in Figure 2.) Find this time by solving the equation $P''(t) = 0$ for t. (The calculation is messy; symbol-manipulating technology can help if necessary.)

FURTHER EXERCISES

1. Suppose that the fly population had begun exactly as above on day 0 (with 1000 members, increasing at 50 flies per day) but then bred *exponentially*.
   (a) Show that in this case (with units as above) the population function would be $P(t) = e^{0.05t}$.
   (b) When would the population be 10,000? What would the population be on day 100?

2. Suppose that the fly population had begun exactly as above on day 0 (with 1000 members, increasing at 50 flies per day) but then bred according to the *warming* model with an upper bound of 10,000 flies.
   (a) Show that in this case the population function would be $P(t) = 10 - 9e^{-t/180}$. Plot $P(t)$; how is the graph different from the others?
   (b) When will the population reach 5000? 9900? be on day 100?

3. Another population of logistic flies (this one foolish) had 1000 members on day 0, but was breeding then at the instantaneous rate of 100 flies per day (so $P'(0) = 0.1$).
   (a) Find the new population function.
   (b) When is the population at 5000? At 9900?
   (c) When does the population grow fastest? What's the population then?

4. A flu epidemic spreads throughout a 3000-student college community at a rate proportional to the product of the number of those already infected and the number of those not yet infected. Let $I(t)$ represent the number of students infected t days after the first student gets sick.
   (a) Write a differential equation that models the situation.
   (b) Suppose that $I(0) = 1$ and that $I(2) = 5$. Evaluate $I(10)$.

Digging Deeper for Roots

We introduced Newton's method of estimating roots of functions in Section 4.6. (We'll assume basic familiarity with Newton's method and that technology is available to carry it out.) In this section, we dig a little deeper and think a little harder about how to "fool" the method.

Recall the main idea: For a given function f, we form the **iteration function**

$$N(x) = x - \frac{f(x)}{f'(x)}.$$

Starting with an initial input x_0, we apply N repeatedly:

$$x_1 = N(x_0), \quad x_2 = N(x_1), \quad x_3 = N(x_2), \quad x_4 = N(x_3), \quad \dots.$$

Graphically speaking, $x_{i+1} = N(x_i)$ is the x-intercept of the tangent line to the f-graph at x_i.

Very often, the **Newton sequence** $x_0, x_1, x_2, \dots$ homes in quickly on a root of f. But not always ....

Marching on forever   Under some circumstances the Newton sequence goes on and on, never settling down.

EXAMPLE 1   Newton's method is applied to $f(x) = e^x$, starting at $x_0 = 0$. What happens? Why? Does Newton "fail"?

Solution   Figure 1 shows what happens. The Newton sequence marches left forever, one unit per step, with successive values $0, -1, -2, -3, \dots$.

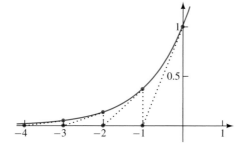

The dotted lines show 4 Newton steps.

FIGURE 1
Stepping along forever: Newton's method applied to $f(x) = e^x$

A little symbol-pushing explains this tedious behavior. Since $f(x) = e^x = f'(x)$, the iteration rule reduces to $N(x) = x - \dfrac{f(x)}{f'(x)} = x - 1$, just as the picture suggests.

Did the method "fail"? Not really. For one thing, $f(x) = e^x$ *has* no roots—and that's hardly Newton's fault. For another thing, the successive Newton's estimates $0, -1, -2, -3, \dots, -10, \dots$ actually do pretty well as *approximate* roots, as the following numbers suggest:

x	-1	-2	-3	$\ldots$	-10	$\ldots$	-20	$\ldots$
e^x	.36788	.13534	.049787	$\ldots$	.00004540	$\ldots$	.000000002	$\ldots$

So Newton's method never finds a root, but at least it marches off in the right direction. ∎

One could argue that the method does work after all, since the function is essentially zero at $-\infty$.

PROBLEM 1 How does Newton's method behave if $f(x) = e^{-2x}$, starting at $x_0 = 0$? Explain what you see in the manner of Example 1.

PROBLEM 2 Find a function $f(x)$ for which Newton's method (starting with $x_0 = 0$) produces the sequence $0, -10, -20, -30, \ldots$.

PROBLEM 3 Figure 2 shows what happens when Newton's method is applied to $f(x) = x^{1/3}$ starting from $x_0 = 2$. Explain what happens.

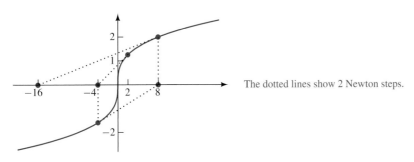

The dotted lines show 2 Newton steps.

FIGURE 2
Newton's method applied to $f(x) = x^{1/3}$

(In this case, Newton's method fails more dramatically than in Example 1: Although f has a root at $x = 0$, the Newton's sequence never comes close to it.)

Cycling Another interesting possibility is that the Newton sequence "cycles" endlessly through several values. Example 7, page 260 describes one such situation. Here is another.

EXAMPLE 2 Figure 3 shows that if Newton's method is applied to $f(x) = x^3 - 5x$, starting with $x_0 = 1$, the resulting sequence is $1, -1, 1, -1, \ldots$.

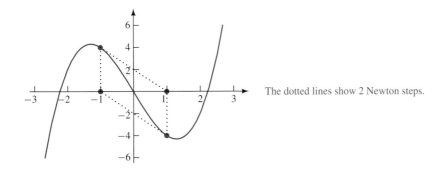

The dotted lines show 2 Newton steps.

FIGURE 3
Newton's method applied to $f(x) = x^3 - 5x$, with $x_0 = 1$

What's happening?

Solution The reason is easy to see. Since $f(x) = x^3 - 5x$, the iteration function is

$$N(x) = x - \frac{x^3 - 5x}{3x^2 - 5} = \frac{2x^3}{3x^2 - 5};$$

it's easy to check that $N(1) = -1$ and $N(-1) = 1$. ∎

PROBLEM 4 We saw in the situation of Example 2 that starting Newton's method at $x_0 = 1$ or $x_0 = -1$ leads to "cycling." Other starting points lead to very different results.

(a) Find all three roots of f *exactly* by solving the equation $f(x) = 0$ algebraically.

(b) What happens if we start Newton's method with $x_0 = 1.01$? With $x = 1.1$? With $x = 0.99$? With $x_0 = 100$?

(c) For which starting points x_0 does Newton's method blow up on the first step? Where are these points on the graph of f?

(d) Run Newton's method starting with $x_0 = 1.290$; then start with $x_0 = 1.292$. Why are the results so different? Explain in terms of the graph of f

(e) The cycling behavior in Example 2 occurred because $N(x) = -x$ for $x = \pm 1$. Are there any *other* inputs x with $x \neq 0$ but $N(x) = -x$? (If so, these inputs would also cause cycling.)

FURTHER EXERCISES

1. Cubic polynomials have an interesting algebraic property:

> Suppose that a cubic polynomial $p(x)$ has three roots a, b, and c. If we start at $x_0 = (a+b)/2$ (the average of any two roots a and b), then Newton's method finds the third root c in one step.

Explore this fact using the cubic polynomial $p(x) = x^3 - 8x^2 + 12x$. First use algebra to find the three roots of p *exactly*. Then check directly that this property holds for all three roots of p. Use a graph of p to illustrate what's happening.

2. Let $a, b,$ and c be any three real numbers. Show that the property of the preceding problem holds for the cubic polynomial $p(x) = (x-a)(x-b)(x-c)$. (Some careful algebra is needed.)

3. Let $f(x) = x^2 - 1$. (Yes, the roots of f are obvious.)

(a) Show that the iteration function N can be written as $N(x) = \dfrac{1+x^2}{2x}$. Note that $N(x)$ has a vertical asymptote at $x = 0$. What does this have to do with Newton's method? For what values of x is $N(x) = x$?

(b) The following picture shows graphs of the three functions $N(x)$, $N(N(x))$ and $N(N(N(x)))$.

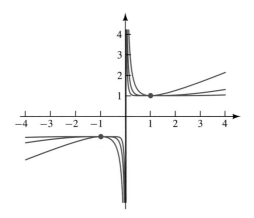

FIGURE 4

Which curve goes with which function? How are the general shapes related to Newton's method? Why are the graphs so "flat" near $x = 1$ and $x = -1$?

THE INTEGRAL

5.1 AREAS AND INTEGRALS

Two big problems The **tangent-line problem** and the **area problem** (our next main topic) are the two main geometric problems of calculus. These problems have been "big" for millennia: The ancient Greeks worked hard and ingeniously at both. Had Greek mathematicians had our algebraic advantages, they would have gone farther than they did.

We've seen that the idea of derivative, together with the rules for computing derivatives, solves the tangent-line problem. For many functions, even complicated ones, it's now easy to describe the tangent line at any point on the graph. Now we turn to the area problem and develop a new calculus tool—the integral—to solve it.

The **area problem** is about measuring the area of a region in the plane. For some special regions (like rectangles, triangles, and circles), well-known formulas do the job. Area problems are much more challenging (and interesting) for more general regions, especially for regions bounded by graphs of functions. The most important area problem of this type is to measure an area like the shaded one in Figure 1.

Our treatment of integrals is organized like that of derivatives. First we view integrals graphically, as signed areas, giving basic definitions and exploring basic properties in some detail. Later we redefine the integral (as we did the derivative) as an appropriate limit of approximating sums (as opposed to approximating differences for the derivative).

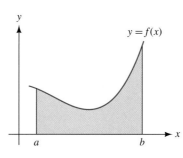

FIGURE 1
What's the shaded area?

Here is a careful statement of the problem:

Find the area of the region bounded above *by the graph of f,* below *by the x-axis, on the* left *by the vertical line x = a, and on the* right *by the vertical line x = b.*

That's a mouthful; we'll usually say just "the area under the graph of *f* from *a* to *b*." (When doubt seems possible we'll use the full form.)

The signed area idea, although not difficult, needs emphasis and repetition. The connection to ordinary area, which is always positive, puzzles a few students.

Signed area In calculus it is useful to consider **signed area** as opposed to area in the everyday sense. Signed area has the following crucial feature:

Area below the x-axis counts as negative.

In Figure 1 all the shaded area is above the x-axis, and so no sign question arises. However, a circle of radius 1 centered at the origin, for instance, has ordinary area π but *signed* area 0. ➡

Our first definition of the **integral** is in terms of signed area:

Draw your own circle to convince yourself.

DEFINITION (The integral as signed area) Let f be a function defined for $a \le x \le b$. Either of the equivalent expressions

$$\int_a^b f \quad \text{or} \quad \int_a^b f(x)\,dx$$

denotes the signed area bounded by $x = a$, $x = b$, $y = f(x)$, and the x-axis.

Here we avoid the tricky (and for most students unnatural) question of whether area exists. We mention the existence question briefly in a page or two.) In later sections we take up a question that's more real to students: how to calculate areas. We also mention integrability in Section 5.6.

Here are some comments on this crucial definition:

- **In words**   We read "the **integral** of f from a to b" for either $\int_a^b f$ or $\int_a^b f(x)\,dx$. The function f is called the **integrand**, and $[a, b]$ is the **interval of integration**. The numbers a and b are sometimes called **limits of integration**. (This phrase is a little unfortunate because "limit" has other important meanings in calculus.)

  Students need clear command of this vocabulary. Note the possibly confusing use of "limit."

- **Which notation?**   Both notations $\int_a^b f$ and $\int_a^b f(x)\,dx$ denote the same area. The first form looks a little simpler; for now, we'll usually choose it. The form containing dx has advantages that will sometimes matter later on.

  The $\int_a^b f$ form (like f' as opposed to $f'(x)$) avoids the (arguably irrelevant) variable name x.

- **More formality later**   In Section 5.6 we'll give another, more "mathematical" definition of the integral as a certain limit. (We did something similar for the derivative, defining it first geometrically and later as a limit.)

- **Is any function OK?**   Does the integral $\int_a^b f$ make sense for *every* function f defined on an interval $[a, b]$? Not quite—some very ill-behaved, highly discontinuous functions fail to have integrals. But such functions are rare in calculus courses. Elementary functions, for instance, all have integrals on any closed interval $[a, b]$ on which they're defined.

- **How to calculate integrals?**   So far, we've only *defined* the symbolic expression $\int_a^b f$ to denote a certain signed area. The problem of *calculating* areas remains. We start that project in the next example.

EXAMPLE 1   Several shaded regions labeled as integrals appear in Figure 2. Use familiar area formulas to evaluate each integral.

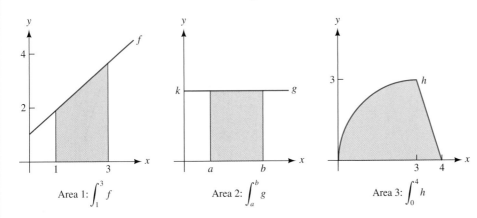

FIGURE 2
What's the shaded area?

A trapezoid with base b and heights h_1 and h_2 has area $b(h_1+h_2)/2$.

Solution   All three areas are easy to find. Area 1 is a trapezoid with base 2 and vertical sides 2 and 4, so its area ← is 6. Area 2 is a rectangle; its area is base × height = $(b-a) \cdot k$. Area 3 combines a quarter circle (of radius 3) and a triangle; a close look reveals total area $9\pi/4 + 3/2$, or about 8.569. Here are our results in integral notation:

$$\int_1^3 f = 6; \qquad \int_a^b g = k(b-a); \qquad \int_0^4 h = \frac{9\pi}{4} + \frac{3}{2}.$$

∎

Must area exist?   Signed area makes good sense for regions bounded by simple graphs, such as lines, parabolas, sinusoids, and so on. The situation is less clear for functions whose graphs are very irregular or ragged. But can the nasty curve in Figure 3 sensibly be said to bound area?

FIGURE 3
$y = \sin(\frac{1}{x})$

The answer turns out (for this curve, anyway) to be yes, but defining area (let alone computing it) takes special care in such unpromising circumstances. In Section 5.6, we'll redefine the integral using limits, partly in order to handle tough cases like this one.

Signed area: positive and negative contributions   Integrals measure *signed* area, so if an integrand f takes negative values in an interval $[a, b]$, then the integral $\int_a^b f$ may also be negative.

EXAMPLE 2   Let $f(x) = 1 - x^2$. Find or estimate values for the integrals $I_1 = \int_0^2 f$ and $I_2 = \int_{-2}^2 f$.

Solution   Figure 4 shows the areas in question; note that each grid square has area one.

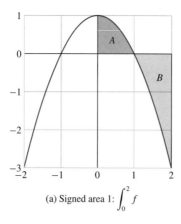

(a) Signed area 1: $\int_0^2 f$

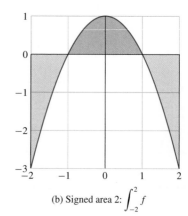

(b) Signed area 2: $\int_{-2}^2 f$

FIGURE 4
Some areas defined by $y = 1 - x^2$

Computing I_1 and I_2 *exactly* is difficult for us now, but *estimating* answers is easy. An eyeball estimate suggests that A has signed area around 2/3, while B has signed area about $-3/2$. These guesses imply that

$$I_1 = \int_0^2 f \approx \frac{2}{3} - \frac{3}{2} = -\frac{5}{6}.$$

To estimate I_2 we can just double I_1:

$$I_2 = 2 \cdot I_1 \approx -\frac{5}{3}.$$

■

EXAMPLE 3 Let $g(x) = x^3$. Find or estimate $\int_{-1}^1 g(x)\,dx$ and $\int_0^1 g(x)\,dx$.

We want students to work concretely with areas, estimating sizes by eye and exploiting symmetry.

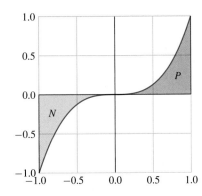

The shaded regions N and P have equal area.

FIGURE 5
Integrating an odd function: $g(x) = x^3$

The graph's symmetry means that the positive and negative areas P and N cancel, so

$$\int_{-1}^1 g(x)\,dx = 0.$$

Symmetry considerations don't help with $\int_0^1 g$, the area of P, but a close look suggests that P's area is about that of one grid square, or 0.25, so

$$\int_0^1 g(x)\,dx \approx 0.25.$$

(We'll see soon that—and why—this estimate is actually *exact*.) ■

An odd property of integrals The first part of Example 3 illustrates a general and sometimes useful fact:

FACT Let f be an *odd* function and $[-a, a]$ an interval that's symmetric about $x = 0$. Then $\displaystyle\int_{-a}^a f = 0$.

The Fact implies, for instance, that each of the following integrals is zero:

$$\int_{-5}^{5} \sin x \, dx; \quad \int_{-3}^{3} x^5 \, dx; \quad \int_{-1}^{1} \tan x \, dx; \quad \int_{-42}^{42} (x^3 + 3x + x^5) \, dx.$$

Properties of the integral

Thinking of the integral as signed area makes many of the integral's important properties simple and natural. For example, Figure 6 convincingly illustrates one simple but useful property of integrals:

If $a < c < b$, then $\int_a^b f = \int_a^c f + \int_c^b f$.

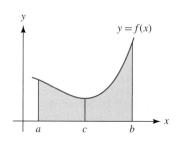

The full shaded area is the sum of two pieces.

FIGURE 6
Adding areas: $\int_a^b f = \int_a^c f + \int_c^b f$

The following theorem collects several basic properties of the integral, all in the spirit of Figure 6. (Fully rigorous proofs—even of these relatively "obvious" claims—depend on precise definitions of the sort we'll give later in this chapter.) Requiring that f and g be continuous guarantees that all the integrals in question exist.

THEOREM 1 (New integrals from old)   Let f and g be continuous functions on $[a, b]$; let k denote a real constant. Then

(i) **(Sum rule)** $\displaystyle\int_a^b \left(f(x) \pm g(x) \right) dx = \int_a^b f(x)\, dx \pm \int_a^b g(x)\, dx.$

(ii) **(Constant multiple rule)** $\displaystyle\int_a^b k f(x)\, dx = k \int_a^b f(x)\, dx.$

(iii) **(Smaller integrand, smaller integral)**   If $f(x) \le g(x)$ for all x in $[a, b]$, then $\displaystyle\int_a^b f(x)\, dx \le \int_a^b g(x)\, dx.$

(iv) **(Splitting the interval)**   If $a < c < b$, then
$$\int_a^b f(x)\, dx = \int_a^c f(x)\, dx + \int_c^b f(x)\, dx.$$

Here are some comments on parts of the theorem:

Trying to reason geometrically through parts (i) and (ii) is a good thought exercise for students.

- **Like the derivative**   Properties (i) and (ii) resemble properties of the derivative—the integral "respects" sums and constant multiples. Figure 7 illustrates the constant multiple rule for integrals.

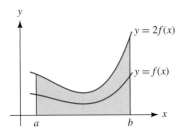

FIGURE 7
The constant multiple rule: why $\int_a^b 2f = 2\int_a^b f$

- **Bounding integrals** Property (iii) of the theorem is often used in the special case where either f or g is a *constant* function. Here is one useful version of the idea.

> **FACT (Bounding an integral)** Suppose that, for some numbers m and M, the inequality $m \le f(x) \le M$ holds for all x in $[a, b]$. Then
> $$m \cdot (b - a) = \int_a^b m\,dx \le \int_a^b f(x)\,dx \le \int_a^b M\,dx = M \cdot (b - a).$$

Figure 8 illustrates the point; the numbers m and M are lower and upper bounds for f on $[a, b]$.

The same result can be interpreted physically: If an object's speed lies between m and M, then the distance traveled lies between m(b − a) and M(b − a).

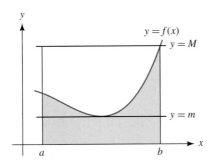

FIGURE 8
Bounding areas: why $m(b - a) \le \int_a^b f \le M(b - a)$

The picture shows that the value of the integral (the shaded area) lies between the areas of two rectangles based on the x-axis—the larger one bounded above by $y = M$ and the smaller by $y = m$.

The following examples show Theorem 1 in action.

EXAMPLE 4 The integral $I = \int_1^3 f(x)\,dx$, where $f(x) = 1/x$, measures the shaded area in Figure 9. Use the three linear functions g_1, g_2, and g_3 (also shown) to estimate I.

Students might improve the estimates using two non-constant linear functions. Note that the result gives bounds on ln 3.

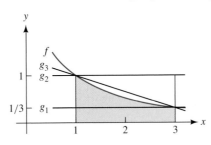

FIGURE 9
Three estimates for $\int_1^3 f$

$g_1(x) = 1/3$ *because*
$f(3) = 1/3$.

Solution   The shaded area isn't a rectangle or any other simple shape, so we can't find I exactly (for the moment). But we can estimate I using part (iii) of Theorem 1. As the picture shows, $f(x) \geq g_1(x) = 1/3$ for all x in $[1, 3]$. ◀ Therefore, by Theorem 1,

$$\int_1^3 f(x)\,dx \geq \int_1^3 g_1(x)\,dx = \frac{2}{3}.$$

(The right-hand integral is the area of a rectangle.)
    Similarly, $f(x) \leq g_2(x) = 1$ for all x in $[1, 3]$, and so

$$\int_1^3 f(x)\,dx \leq \int_1^3 g_2(x)\,dx = 2.$$

Thus, 2 is an upper bound for I, but a crude one, as the picture shows. Using g_3 in place of g_2 gives a *better* upper bound:

$$\int_1^3 f(x)\,dx \leq \int_1^3 g_3(x)\,dx = \frac{4}{3}.$$

(The right-hand integral corresponds to a *trapezoidal* area, and so an elementary area formula applies.) Combining these results gives lower and upper bounds for I:
$2/3 \leq I \leq 4/3$. ∎

EXAMPLE 5   Find $\int_0^{\pi/2} \sin x\,dx$ and $\int_0^{\pi} (3\sin x + 2\cos x)\,dx$ by using the fact (which we'll prove later) that $\int_0^{\pi} \sin x\,dx = 2$.

Draw them to convince yourself.

Solution   Symmetry of the sine and cosine graphs ◀ shows that

$$\int_0^{\pi/2} \sin x\,dx = \frac{1}{2}\int_0^{\pi} \sin x\,dx = 1; \qquad \int_0^{\pi} \cos x\,dx = 0.$$

Now the sum and constant multiple rules for integrals tell us that

$$\int_0^{\pi} (3\sin x + 2\cos x)\,dx = 3\int_0^{\pi} \sin x\,dx + 2\int_0^{\pi} \cos x\,dx = 6 + 0 = 6.$$

Students should try to count squares, keeping track of signs.

A look at of Figure 10 makes the general size of the answer plausible.

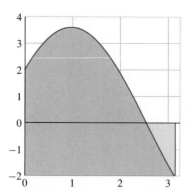

FIGURE 10
Estimating $\int_0^{\pi} (3\sin x + 2\cos x)\,dx$

Counting rectangles (each has area 1) shows that the signed area is indeed around 6. ∎

EXAMPLE 6 For any positive constant b,

$$\int_0^b 1\, dx = b \qquad \text{and} \qquad \int_0^b x\, dx = \frac{b^2}{2}.$$

Explain why. Then use Theorem 1 to find $\int_0^b (Cx + D)\, dx$ for any constants C and D.

Solution Graphs of $f(x) = 1$ and $g(x) = x$ over the interval $[0, b]$ show that the first two integrals have the claimed values. (Draw your own graphs to see why.) To finish, we use the sum and constant multiple rules:

$$\int_0^b (Cx + D)\, dx = \int_0^b Cx\, dx + \int_0^b D\, dx$$
$$= C \int_0^b x\, dx + \int_0^b D\, dx$$
$$= C\frac{b^2}{2} + Db.$$
■

Interpreting integrals

So far we've interpreted the integral $\int_a^b f$ in geometric terms, as signed area. But the integral has other useful interpretations.

Average values and integrals The rectangle in Figure 11 (below the line $y = \text{average}$) is chosen to have the same area as the shaded region.

Average value is a straightforward idea, and it points nicely to the limiting definition ahead.

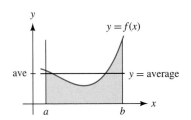

The shaded region has the same area as the rectangle under the line $y = \text{average}$.

FIGURE 11
Average value of a function

The height of that rectangle is called the **average value** of the function f over the interval $[a, b]$. The following definition puts this in analytic language:

> **DEFINITION** Let f be defined on an interval $[a, b]$. The **average value** of f over $[a, b]$ is defined by
> $$\frac{\int_a^b f(x)\, dx}{b - a} = \frac{\text{signed area}}{\text{length of interval}}.$$

The name is apt because, like other averages, the average value represents a sort of "typical value" of f for a range of inputs.

The ideas of integral and average value are closely linked. The preceding picture summarizes this two-way relationship: The average value is the *height* of a certain rectangle, while the integral is the *area* of the same rectangle.

Speed and distance   If a function $f(t)$ represents the *speed* of a moving object at time t, then the integral $\int_a^b f(t)\,dt$ represents the *distance* traveled by the object over the time interval $a \le t \le b$. Why is this true?

If the speed function $f(t)$ happens to be a constant, say k, then

$$\int_a^b f(t)\,dt = k \cdot (b - a) = \text{speed} \times \text{time} = \text{distance},$$

as claimed. Remarkably, integrating the speed function gives distance traveled even if $f(t)$ *isn't* constant. The next example isn't a proof, but it should help make the result believable.

EXAMPLE 7   The two graphs in Figure 12 show speed functions s_A and s_B for two cars A and B.

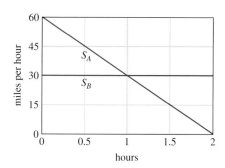

FIGURE 12
Speeds of cars A and B

What is the average value of each function over the interval $[0, 2]$? How far does each car travel over the two hours?

Solution   A look at areas shows readily that

$$\int_0^2 s_A(t)\,dt = 60 = \int_0^2 s_B(t)\,dt.$$

Thus, using the preceding definition, both speed functions have the *same* average value, 30 mph, over the interval $[0, 2]$. We expect, therefore, that the two cars cover the same total distance—60 miles—over the 2-hour period.   ■

Velocity and displacement   Speed and distance are *positive* quantities by definition. Velocity and displacement, on the other hand, can be either positive or negative, depending on the direction of motion. For an object moving along a line, for instance, we might take right as the positive direction and left as the negative direction. These conventions mean that integration of a velocity function $v(t)$ gives slightly different information from integration of a speed function. If $v(t)$ tells the *velocity* of an object moving along a left–right line at time t, then $\int_a^b f(t)\,dt$ represents the *displacement* that occurs over the time interval $a \le t \le b$. This displacement is *positive* if the net effect is *rightward* motion; otherwise, the displacement is negative.

The variable name x isn't sacred; t is another popular choice.

Integrating from right to left: a technicality   The English description of $\int_a^b f(x)\,dx$—"the integral of f from $x = a$ to $x = b$"—implies a *direction*: x starts at a and ends at b. ◄ It's usually natural to think of x as moving from left to right. Up to now, we've done just that: In every integral $\int_a^b f$ we've treated so far, we've assumed or stated that $a \le b$. For example, we've discussed $\int_0^\pi \sin x\,dx$ but not $\int_\pi^0 \sin x\,dx$.

The latter sort of "right-to-left" integrals *do* sometimes arise in calculations. The following convention handles all the possibilities with a minimum of fuss:

This annoying technicality will come up soon in practice, so it needs some comment here.

DEFINITION If $b < a$, then $\displaystyle\int_a^b f(x)\,dx = -\int_b^a f(x)\,dx.$

Why does the definition make sense? The velocity–displacement context gives a physical reason: If $f(t)$ represents velocity at time t, and $a < b$, then $\int_a^b f(t)\,dt$ gives the displacement from time a to time b. The integral $\int_b^a f(t)\,dt$ is thus the displacement over the "reversed" interval, and so is naturally opposite in sign to the first result.

The story so far, and a look ahead

Students might need some help distinguishing the forest from trees.

In this section we defined the integral $\int_a^b f$ as a certain *area*. Then we observed some properties of the integral that follow directly from the area interpretation. What's missing so far is any general technique for *measuring* areas. In the simplest cases (such as rectangles and triangles) elementary area formulas may help, but these formulas apply *only* to the simplest functions. In the rest of this chapter we offer two different practical methods of calculating integrals. In Sections 5.2 and 5.3 we'll relate the new idea of the integral to the older (and better understood) idea of the derivative. This key connection between derivative and integral, called the **fundamental theorem of calculus**, is among the most important ideas of mathematics. In Section 5.6 we'll give another definition of the integral, this time as a limit of approximating sums.

BASIC EXERCISES

1. Let g be the function shown graphically below. When asked to estimate $\int_1^2 g(x)\,dx$, a group of calculus students submitted the following answers: -4, 4, 45, and 450. Only one of these responses is reasonable; the others are "obviously" incorrect. Which is the reasonable one? Why?

In Exercises 2–4, f is the function shown below.

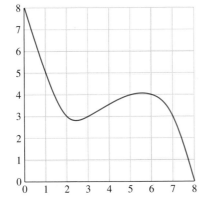

2. Which of the following is the best estimate of $\int_1^6 f(x)\,dx$: $-24, 9, 20, 38$? Justify your answer.

3. Find positive integers A and B such that $A \le \int_3^7 f(x)\,dx \le B$. Explain how you know that the values of A and B you chose have the desired properties.

4. $\int_6^8 f(x)\,dx \approx 4$. Does this approximation overestimate or underestimate the exact value of the integral? Justify your answer.

In Exercises 5–14, evaluate the integral assuming that f is the function shown below. [NOTE: The graph of f consists of two straight lines and two one-quarter circles.]

5. $\displaystyle\int_0^2 f(x)\,dx$

6. $\displaystyle\int_2^5 f(x)\,dx$

7. $\displaystyle\int_0^5 f(x)\,dx$

8. $\displaystyle\int_5^9 f(x)\,dx$

9. $\displaystyle\int_4^4 f(x)\,dx$

10. $\displaystyle\int_0^{15} f(x)\,dx$

11. $\displaystyle\int_0^{15} |f(x)|\,dx$

12. $\displaystyle\int_{15}^9 f(x)\,dx$

13. $\displaystyle\int_{12}^{15} f(x)\,dx$

14. $\displaystyle\int_9^{12} f(x)\,dx$

In Exercises 15–22, evaluate the definite integral using a graph of the integrand over the interval of integration.

15. $\displaystyle\int_{-4}^{-2} 3\,dt$

16. $\displaystyle\int_{-3}^4 \sqrt{2}\,du$

17. $\displaystyle\int_2^5 u\,du$

18. $\displaystyle\int_{-2}^1 w\,dw$

19. $\displaystyle\int_{-3}^3 |x|\,dx$

20. $\displaystyle\int_{-3}^3 |1+x|\,dx$

21. $\displaystyle\int_{-2}^2 \sqrt{4-s^2}\,ds$

22. $\displaystyle\int_{-3}^0 \sqrt{9-w^2}\,dw$

In Exercises 23–28, use the fact that $\displaystyle\int_0^\pi u^2\,du = \pi^3/3$ to evaluate the definite integral.

23. $\displaystyle\int_\pi^0 r^2\,dr$

24. $\displaystyle\int_0^\pi (3+4x^2)\,dx$

25. $\displaystyle\int_0^\pi (\pi^2 - 3t^2)\,dt$

26. $\displaystyle\int_{-\pi}^\pi w^2\,dw$

27. $\displaystyle\int_\pi^{2\pi} (v-\pi)^2\,dv$

28. $\displaystyle\int_0^\pi (\pi x + x^2)\,dx$

29. Find real numbers A and B such that $A \le \displaystyle\int_1^3 (4w - w^2)\,dw \le B$.

30. Show that $2\pi \le \displaystyle\int_0^{2\pi} \sqrt{1+3\cos^2 x}\,dx \le 4\pi$.

31. Find real numbers A and B such that $A \le \displaystyle\int_1^3 \frac{dt}{1+t^2} \le B$.

32. Find real numbers A and B such that $A \le \displaystyle\int_0^{\pi/4} \frac{d\theta}{1+\tan\theta} \le B$.

In Exercises 33–36, evaluate the integral assuming that $\displaystyle\int_{-2}^5 f(x)\,dx = 18$, that $\displaystyle\int_{-2}^5 g(x)\,dx = 5$, and that $\displaystyle\int_{-2}^5 h(x)\,dx = -11$.

33. $\displaystyle\int_{-2}^5 \big(3f(x) + 4g(x)\big)\,dx$

34. $\displaystyle\int_{-2}^5 \big(3h(x) - 4f(x)\big)\,dx$

35. $\displaystyle\int_5^{-2} f(x)\,dx$

36. $\displaystyle\int_{-2}^5 \big(h(x) + 1\big)\,dx$

FURTHER EXERCISES

37. Four students disagree on the value of the integral $\displaystyle\int_0^{\pi/2} \cos^8 x\,dx$. Jack argues for $\pi \approx 3.14$, Joan for $35\pi/256 \approx 0.43$, Ed for $2\pi/9 - 1 \approx -0.30$, and Lesley for $\pi/4 \approx 0.79$. Use the graph below to determine who is right. (One *is* right!) Explain how you know that the other values are incorrect.

38. Suppose that a car travels on an east–west road with eastward velocity $v(t) = 60 - 20t$ mph at time t hours.

   (a) Evaluate $\displaystyle\int_0^4 v(t)\,dt$. Interpret the answer in car talk.

   (b) Find the average value of $v(t)$ on the interval $[0, 4]$. Show your result graphically.

   (c) Let $s(t)$ be the car's speed at time t. Evaluate $\displaystyle\int_0^4 s(t)\,dt$ and interpret the answer in car talk.

   (d) What is the car's average speed between $t = 0$ and $t = 4$?

39. Explain why $\displaystyle\int_1^2 x^3\,dx = \int_3^4 (x-2)^3\,dx$.

40. Explain why $\displaystyle\int_1^2 x^3\,dx = \int_{-3}^{-2} (x+4)^3\,dx$.

In Exercises 41–48, evaluate the integral assuming that
(i) $\int_0^2 f(x)\,dx = 2;$ *(ii)* $\int_1^2 f(x)\,dx = -1;$ *(iii)* $\int_2^4 f(x)\,dx = 7.$

41. $\int_1^4 f(x)\,dx$

42. $\int_0^4 3f(x)\,dx$

43. $\int_0^1 f(x)\,dx$

44. $\int_0^1 \left(f(x)+1\right)dx$

45. $\int_2^4 \left(f(x)-2\right)dx$

46. $\int_0^4 \left(3-2f(x)\right)dx$

47. Explain why f must be negative somewhere in the interval $[1, 2]$. [HINT: Sketch the graph of a function that has properties (i)–(iii).]

48. Explain why $f(x) \geq 3$ somewhere in the interval $[2, 4]$.

Evaluate the integrals in Exercises 49–52 using graphical arguments.

49. $\int_0^{\pi} \cos x\,dx$

50. $\int_{\pi/2}^{3\pi/2} \sin x\,dx$

51. $\int_{-1}^1 (4x^3 - 2x)\,dx$

52. $\int_{-2}^2 (7x^5 + 3)\,dx$

Evaluate the integrals in Exercises 53–60 using graphical arguments and the fact that $\int_0^{\pi} \sin x\,dx = 2.$

53. $\int_0^{2\pi} \sin x\,dx$

54. $\int_0^{2\pi} |\sin x|\,dx$

55. $\int_0^{\pi} (1+\sin x)\,dx$

56. $\int_{-\pi/2}^{\pi/2} \cos x\,dx$

57. $\int_0^{\pi/2} (x+\cos x)\,dx$

58. $\int_0^{100\pi} \sin x\,dx$

59. $\int_0^{100\pi} |\sin x|\,dx$

60. $\int_0^{100\pi} \cos x\,dx$

61. Let $f(x) = \frac{1}{2}x + \cos x.$ Show that $1.3 \leq \int_0^3 f(x)\,dx \leq 3.5.$

62. Show that $\pi/6 \leq \int_{\pi/6}^{\pi/2} \sin x\,dx \leq \pi/3.$

63. Show that $-\pi/3 \leq \int_{2\pi/3}^{\pi} \cos x\,dx \leq -\pi/6.$

64. Show that $4.5 \leq \int_1^3 e^x \sin x\,dx \leq 15.$

65. Sketch the graph of a function f with the property that

$$\left| \int_1^5 f(x)\,dx \right| < \int_1^5 |f(x)|\,dx.$$

Explain why the function f you sketched has this property.

66. Suppose that f is a continuous function. If the average value of f over the interval $[0, 1]$ is 2 and the average value of f over the interval $[1, 3]$ is 4, what is the average value of f over the interval $[0, 3]$?

67. Suppose that f is a continuous function. If the average value of f over the interval $[-3, 1]$ is 2 and the average value of f over the interval $[-3, 7]$ is 5, what is the average value of f over the interval $[1, 7]$?

68. Suppose that f is continuous on $[a, b]$. Show that
$$\left| \int_a^b f(x)\,dx \right| \leq \int_a^b |f(x)|\,dx.$$
[HINT: $-|f(x)| \leq f(x) \leq |f(x)|.$]

69. Let $f(x) = x^2$ and $g(x) = 2x.$
   (a) Sketch the region in the xy-plane bounded by the curves $y = f(x)$ and $y = g(x).$
   (b) Explain why the area of the region in part (a) is
   $$\int_0^2 g(x)\,dx - \int_0^2 f(x)\,dx.$$

70. Let $f(x) = \sqrt{x}$ and $g(x) = x.$
   (a) Sketch the region in the xy-plane bounded by the curves $y = f(x)$ and $y = g(x).$
   (b) Express the area of the region in part (a) using integrals.

71. Let $f(x) = x + 6$ and $g(x) = x^3.$
   (a) Sketch the region in the xy-plane bounded by the curves $y = f(x),$ $y = g(x),$ and the line $x = 0.$
   (b) Express the area of the region in part (a) using integrals.

72. Let $f(x) = \ln x$ and $g(x) = 1 - x.$
   (a) Sketch the region in the xy-plane bounded by the curves $y = f(x),$ $y = g(x),$ and the line $x = e.$
   (b) Express the area of the region in part (a) using integrals.

73. Archimedes (ca. 250 B.C.E.) proved that the area under a parabolic arch is $2bh/3$, where b is the width of the base of the arch and h is the height. [NOTE: Archimedes actually proved a more general theorem about the area of any region cut off from a parabola by a line.]

(a) Use Archimedes's result to show that $\int_{-a}^{a} x^2\, dx = 2a^3/3$. [HINT: Draw the curve $y = x^2$ and the line $y = a^2$.]

(b) Use part (a) and the fact that x^2 is an even function to show that $\int_{0}^{a} x^2\, dx = a^3/3$.

[HINT: $\int_{-a}^{a} x^2\, dx = \int_{-a}^{0} x^2\, dx + \int_{0}^{a} x^2\, dx$.]

(c) Use part (b) to show that $\int_{a}^{b} x^2\, dx = (b^3 - a^3)/3$.

[HINT: $\int_{a}^{b} x^2\, dx = \int_{0}^{b} x^2\, dx - \int_{0}^{a} x^2\, dx$.]

74. Let $f(x) = 2x + 3$.

(a) Sketch a graph of f in the viewing window $[0, 3] \times [0, 9]$.

(b) Evaluate $\int_{1}^{3} f(x)\, dx$. Shade the region of the part (a) graph represented by this integral.

(c) Show that $f^{-1}(y) = (y - 3)/2$.

(d) Evaluate $\int_{5}^{9} f^{-1}(y)\, dy$ and shade the region of the part (a) graph represented by this integral.

(e) Verify that

$$\int_{1}^{3} f(x)\, dx = 3f(3) - f(1) - \int_{f(1)}^{f(3)} f^{-1}(y)\, dy.$$

75. Suppose that f is a continuous function and invertible on $[a, b]$. Then it is true that

$$\int_{a}^{b} f(x)\, dx = bf(b) - af(a) - \int_{f(a)}^{f(b)} f^{-1}(y)\, dy.$$

Give a graphical proof of this result if $0 < a < b$, and $0 < f(a) < f(b)$.
[HINT: Draw a sketch of f in the viewing window $[0, b] \times [0, f(b)]$.]

76. Use the result stated in Exercise 75 to show that $\int_{1}^{e} \ln x\, dx = e - \int_{0}^{1} e^x\, dx$.

77. Use the result stated in Exercise 75 to show that $\int_{a}^{b} \sqrt{x}\, dx = b^{3/2} - a^{3/2} - \int_{\sqrt{a}}^{\sqrt{b}} x^2\, dx$.

78. Use the results stated in Exercises 73 and 75 to show that $\int_{0}^{a} \sqrt{x}\, dx = 2a^{3/2}/3$.

5.2 THE AREA FUNCTION

For a given function f we use area to define a new function, temporarily called A_f; in the same spirit, we use slope to define the new function f'. Here we define and explore properties of the area function.

In Section 5.1 we defined the integral $\int_{a}^{b} f$ to be the signed area of the region from $x = a$ to $x = b$, bounded above or below by the graph of f. For given f, a, and b, this area is a certain fixed *number* (positive, negative, or zero). In this section we define and study a *function* based on the signed area bounded by the graph of f. This **area function**, which we'll denote by A_f, is "built" from f using the integral.

We've played the new-function-from-old game before. In the most important case, we built the derivative function f' from an "original" function f and then studied what each tells about the other. Here we repeat the process, this time with f and A_f. The relationship between f and A_f will prove remarkably similar to that between f' and f.

Defining the area function

First comes the formal definition:

One could argue for a two-parameter notation, such as $A_{f,a}$, but we fear symbol overload. Note that A_f denotes a signed (not ordinary) area, and that t is a dummy variable.

> **DEFINITION** Let f be a function and a any point of its domain. For any input x, the **area function** A_f is defined by the rule
>
> $$A_f(x) = \int_{a}^{x} f(t)\, dt.$$
>
> In words, $A_f(x)$ is the signed area defined by f from a to x.

A "generic" picture (Figure 1) illustrates the idea.

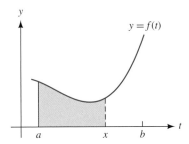

$A_f(x)$ represents *signed* area—here, all the shaded area counts as positive.

FIGURE 1
The area function: $A_f(x)$ is the shaded area

The area function idea is best approached through pictorial examples. First, some brief remarks:

- **Variable names: why so many?**   Why did we use another variable, t, in defining the expression $A_f(x) = \int_a^x f(t)\, dt$? We did it because the letter x was already taken—we used x to denote the right-hand boundary of the defining region. We introduced t to avoid using x in two different ways. Note that x, not t, is the input variable to the function A_f.

- **The domain of A_f**   For which inputs x does the rule $A_f(x) = \int_a^x f$ make sense? Barring bad behavior (such as discontinuities of f), the new function A_f has the same domain as f itself. In particular, $A_f(x)$ makes sense even if x is to the *left* of a; in this case we use the sign convention $\int_a^x f = -\int_x^a f$ (which we discussed in Section 5.1).

  See the technical note in Section 5.1 about "integrating from right to left."

- **The choice of a**   The role of a is to fix one edge (the left edge in Figure 1) of the region whose area gives $A_f(x)$. The other edge varies freely. As the definition says, *any a in the domain of f is a legal choice*. We'll soon see that different choices of a give different (but not *much* different) functions A_f.

  Students should work carefully through Examples 1–5 to get an intuition for A_f and motivation for the FTC, just ahead.

EXAMPLE 1   Let $f(x) = 3$ and $a = 0$. Describe the area function $A_f(x) = \int_0^x f(t)\, dt$ for positive inputs x. Does A_f have a simple algebraic formula?

Solution   The formula $f(x) = 3$ implies that $A_f(x) = 3x$. Figure 2(a) shows why. ➤ Figure 2(b) shows graphs of f and A_f together.

A rectangle with height 3 and base x has area $3x$.

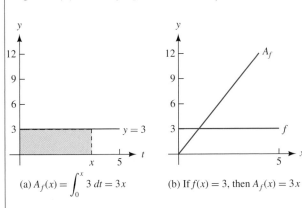

(a) $A_f(x) = \displaystyle\int_0^x 3\, dt = 3x$ (b) If $f(x) = 3$, then $A_f(x) = 3x$

Note the horizontal axes: t is the input variable in (a) while x is the variable in (b).

FIGURE 2

Notice, finally, that $A_f(x) = 3x$ is an *antiderivative* of $f(x) = 3$. This is no accident—we'll see the same pattern in later examples. ■

The example illustrates that A_f has the same formula for inputs on either side of $x = a$.

EXAMPLE 2 Let $f(x) = 3$ and $a = 0$, as in Example 1. Discuss the area function $A_f(x) = \int_0^x f(t)\,dt$ for *negative* values of x. Does the formula $A_f(x) = 3x$ from Example 1 hold here as well?

Solution Yes it does—the formula $A_f(x) = 3x$ holds for *all* inputs x. The key step is a careful look at signs; see Figure 3:

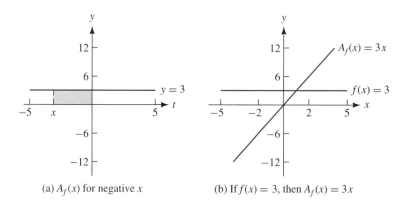

(a) $A_f(x)$ for negative x (b) If $f(x) = 3$, then $A_f(x) = 3x$

FIGURE 3

The key to the formula is to recall how we handle "right-to-left" integrals. Since $x < 0$,

$$\int_0^x f = -\int_x^0 f = -\,(\text{shaded area})\,.$$

Because $x < 0$ and the rectangle has height 3, the product $3x$ gives the *opposite* of the shaded area. Combining this result and that of Example 1 shows that if $f(x) = 3$ and $a = 0$, then $A_f(x) = \int_0^x f = 3x$ for *all* inputs x, positive or negative. ■

A happy moral The geometric meaning of $\int_a^x f$ is clear if $x \geq a$. If $x < a$, the situation looks trickier at first glance, but the moral of Examples 1 and 2 is that, when all the dust settles, the best outcome is revealed:

The same formula for $A_f(x)$ works for all x.

The same principle holds for any well-behaved function f, so we'll seldom worry about (or even mention) the issue of whether $x < a$ or $x \geq a$.

This example illustrates finding A_f for the simplest possible nonconstant f.

EXAMPLE 3 Consider the linear function $f(x) = x$ and the area function $A_f(x) = \int_0^x t\,dt$. Find the formula for A_f in this case.

Solution As Figure 4(a) shows, the region that defines $A_f(x)$ for a positive input x is a triangle with base x and height x.

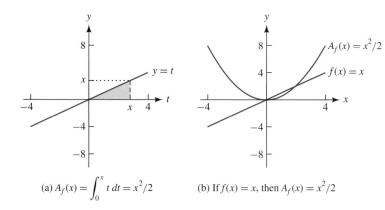

(a) $A_f(x) = \int_0^x t\, dt = x^2/2$ (b) If $f(x) = x$, then $A_f(x) = x^2/2$

FIGURE 4

The formula we want is therefore

$$A_f(x) = \frac{\text{base} \times \text{height}}{2} = \frac{x^2}{2}.$$

(The same formula holds for negative x, for reasons just mentioned.) Graphs of $f(x)$ and $A_f(x)$ appear together in Figure 4(b). Once again, A_f turns out to be an antiderivative of f.   ■

E X A M P L E 4 (Another f, same a) Consider the new linear function $f(x) = 2 - x$. Find the new area function $A_f(x) = \int_0^x f$. Is A_f *again* an antiderivative of f?

This example illustrates finding A_f for a slightly less special linear integrand f.

Solution The usual signed area picture (Figure 5) applies; note that area below the x-axis counts as negative.

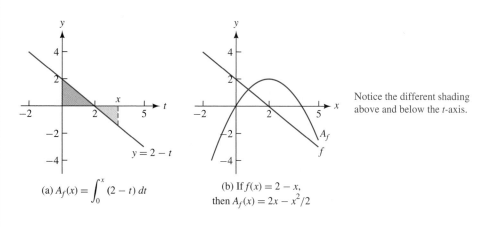

Notice the different shading above and below the t-axis.

(a) $A_f(x) = \int_0^x (2 - t)\, dt$ (b) If $f(x) = 2 - x$, then $A_f(x) = 2x - x^2/2$

FIGURE 5

With a little care, one can use triangles (or trapezoids, if $x < 2$) to find the signed area shown shaded. In Figure 5(a) the upper triangle has area 2, and the lower triangle has area $(x - 2)^2/2$, so the total signed area is

$$A_f(x) = 2 - \frac{(x - 2)^2}{2} = 2x - \frac{x^2}{2}.$$

Figure 5(a) shows a value of x greater than 2. The *picture* is different if $0 < x < 2$, but the resulting formula is the same. Figure 5(b) shows graphs of both f and A_f.

Another (perhaps easier) approach to the problem is to use additive properties of the integral (from Theorem 1, page 306) to combine results from earlier examples:

$$A_f(x) = \int_0^x (2 - t)\, dt = \int_0^x 2\, dt - \int_0^x t\, dt = 2x - \frac{x^2}{2}.$$

Either way, the conclusion is the same: $A_f(x) = 2x - x^2/2$ is an antiderivative of $f(x) = 2 - x$.   ■

EXAMPLE 5   (Same f, another a) Consider the same linear function, $f(x) = 2 - x$, as in Example 4, but now with $a = 1$, so that $A_f(x) = \int_1^x f$. Find a formula for the new area function.

Solution The only difference from Example 4 concerns the lower endpoint of integration, so the new function A_f differs from the old one only by the area of the trapezoidal region under the f-graph from $x = 0$ to $x = 1$. This area is $3/2$; see Figure 6. In symbols,

$$A_f(x) = \int_1^x f(t)\, dt = \int_0^x f(t)\, dt - \int_0^1 f(t)\, dt$$
$$= 2x - \frac{x^2}{2} - \frac{3}{2}.$$

The graphs in Figure 6 support this result.

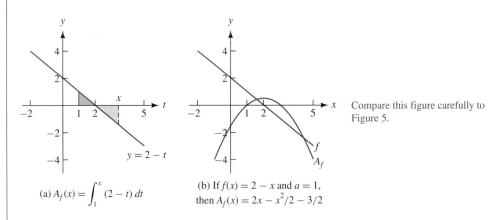

(a) $A_f(x) = \int_1^x (2 - t)\, dt$

(b) If $f(x) = 2 - x$ and $a = 1$,
then $A_f(x) = 2x - x^2/2 - 3/2$

Compare this figure carefully to Figure 5.

FIGURE 6

Two antiderivatives of the same function can differ only by an additive constant, as they do here.

As in Example 4, the area function $A_f(x) = 2x - x^2/2 - 3/2$ is an antiderivative of the original function $f(x) = 2 - x$. This time, however, A_f is the antiderivative for which $A_f(1) = 0$. ◄   ■

In Examples 1–5 we used an elementary area formula to find an explicit algebraic expression for the area function. In the next example, no such elementary area formula is available.

EXAMPLE 6 Let $f(x) = 1/x$ and $A_f(x) = \int_1^x f(t)\,dt$. Discuss the area function A_f. Does it look familiar?

Solution Figure 7(a) shows $f(x)$; the shaded area represents $A_f(3)$.

As a classroom exercise students might try to plot the area function in Figure 7(b) based on their own estimates.

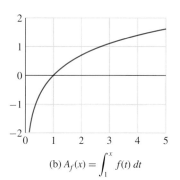

(a) $f(x) = 1/x$

(b) $A_f(x) = \int_1^x f(t)\,dt$

FIGURE 7

There's no simple area formula, but we can *estimate* values of A_f using the grid. The shaded area, for instance, seems to be a little more than one unit, so $A_f(3)$ is a little more than 1. By making and plotting many such estimates we could—laboriously—produce a graph of A_f; one appears in Figure 7(b). ➤

Note that $A_f(x) < 0$ for $x < 1$.

The graph of A_f might look familiar; in fact, it turns out that $A_f(x) = \ln x$. We'll explain this striking result in the next section, but we can see right now that it's consistent with results of earlier examples, because $A_f(x) = \ln x$ is an antiderivative of $f(x) = 1/x$. ∎

Properties of A_f: patterns in the examples The examples illustrate what's most important about an area function A_f—its relationship to the "original" function f from which it's built. In the following list we assemble several properties of this relationship that can be seen in one or more of the preceding examples. For simplicity we assume throughout that f is a continuous function defined for all real inputs; doing so ensures that A_f is also continuous and defined for all inputs.

- $A_f(a) = 0$. (See *any* example.)

- Where f is positive, A_f is increasing. Where f is negative, A_f is decreasing. (See Examples 3–5.)

- Where f is zero, A_f has a stationary point. (See Examples 3–5.)

- Where f is increasing, A_f is concave up. Where f is decreasing, A_f is concave down. (See Examples 3–6.)

These principles hold in general (not only for our example functions). We won't prove them here because all of them follow from the fundamental theorem of calculus—the main result of the next section.

Some students will guess the FTC at this point, but we haven't officially revealed the secret.

BASIC EXERCISES

1. Let $f(x) = x$ and $A_f(x) = \int_0^x f(t)\,dt$. It was shown in the text that $A_f(x) = x^2/2$ if $x > 0$. Show that this formula is correct even if $x < 0$.

2. Let $f(x) = x$ and $A_f(x) = \int_4^x f(t)\,dt$. Show that $A_f(x) = x^2/2 - 8$ for *all* values of x.

In Exercises 3–8, $A_f(x) = \int_0^x f(t)\,dt$, *where* f *is the function graphed below.*

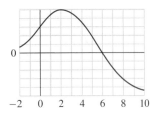

3. Which is larger: $A_f(1)$ or $A_f(5)$? Justify your answer.

4. Which is larger: $A_f(7)$ or $A_f(10)$? Justify your answer.

5. Explain why $A_f(-1) < 0$.

6. Is $A_f(8) > 0$? Justify your answer.

7. Which is larger: $A_f(-2)$ or $A_f(-1)$? Justify your answer.

8. Let $F(x) = \int_{-2}^x f(t)\,dt$. Explain why $A_f(x) = F(x) + C$, where C is a negative constant.

In Exercises 9–14, let $F(x) = \int_0^x f(t)\,dt$ *and* $G(x) = \int_5^x f(t)\,dt$. *Furthermore, suppose that* $f(t) > 1$ *for all* $t \geq 0$.

9. Explain why $F(7) > F(1)$.

10. Is $G(9) > G(5)$? Justify your answer.

11. Explain why $F(x) > F(0)$ for all $x > 0$.

12. (a) Explain why $G(x) = F(x) + C$, where C is a constant.
  (b) Is the constant C in part (a) positive? Justify your answer.

13. Explain why $F(6) \geq 6$.

14. Is it possible that $G(10) = 3$? Justify your answer.

In Exercises 15–20, let $F(x) = \int_0^x f(t)\,dt$ *and* $G(x) = \int_4^x f(t)\,dt$. *Furthermore, suppose that* $f(t) < -2$ *for all* $t \geq 0$.

15. Explain why $F(6) < F(2)$.

16. Is $G(3) > G(5)$? Justify your answer.

17. Explain why $F(x) < F(1)$ for all $x > 1$.

18. (a) Explain why $F(x) = G(x) + C$, where C is a constant.
  (b) Is the constant C in part (a) positive? Justify your answer.

19. Is it possible that $F(4) = -7$? Justify your answer.

20. Is it possible that $G(10) = -14$? Justify your answer.

In Exercises 21–28, let $f(x) = 3x + 2$, $F(x) = \int_0^x f(t)\,dt$, $G(x) = \int_1^x f(t)\,dt$, *and* $H(x) = \int_{-2}^x f(t)\,dt$.

21. Find formulas for F, G, and H.

22. Find the number C such that $G(x) = F(x) + C$.

23. Find a formula for $F(x) - H(x)$.

24. Where is F increasing? What is true about f on these intervals?

25. Where is F decreasing? What is true about f on these intervals?

26. Is F concave up anywere? If so, what is true about f on these intervals?

27. Is F concave down anywhere? If so, what is true about f on these intervals?

28. Are F, G, and H all antiderivatives of f? Justify your answer.

29–36. Repeat Exercises 21–28 using $f(x) = 2 - 3x$.

37. Suppose that F is an antiderivative of a differentiable function f.
  (a) If f is negative on $[a, b]$, what is true about F?
  (b) If f' is positive on $[a, b]$, what is true about F?

38. Suppose that $G' = g$ and that g is a differentiable function.
  (a) If G is increasing on $[a, b]$, what is true about g?
  (b) If G is concave down on $[a, b]$, what is true about g'?
  (c) Suppose that H is another function with the property $H' = g$. What relationship exists between G and H?

FURTHER EXERCISES

In Exercises 39–44, let $f(x) = 2 - |x|$ *and* $A_f(x) = \int_0^x f(t)\,dt$.

39. (a) Find a formula for A_f.
    [HINT: Write A_f as a piecewise-defined function.]
  (b) Plot f and A_f on the same axes.

40. Where is A_f increasing? What is true about f on these intervals?

41. Where is A_f decreasing? What is true about f on these intervals?

42. Where is A_f concave up? What is true about f on these intervals?

43. Where is A_f concave down? What is true about f on these intervals?

44. Where does A_f have inflection points? What is true about f at these points?

45–50. Repeat Exercises 39–44 assuming $A_f(x) = \int_3^x f(t)\,dt$.

In Exercises 51–56, $G(x) = \displaystyle\int_{-3}^{x} f(t)\,dt$ and $H(x) = \displaystyle\int_{2}^{x} f(t)\,dt$, where f is the function graphed below.
[NOTE: The graph of f is made up of straight lines and a semicircle.]

51. How are the values of $G(x)$ and $H(x)$ related? Give a graphical explanation of this relationship.

52. On which subintervals of $[-5, 5]$, if any, is H increasing?

53. Explain why G has a local minimum at $x = 1$.

54. Does H have a local maximum at $x = -3$? Justify your answer.

55. Where in the interval $[-5, -2]$ does G achieve its minimum value? Its maximum value? What are these values?

56. Where in the interval $[-5, 5]$ does H achieve its minimum value? Its maximum value? What are these values?

In Exercises 57–60, suppose that f is a continuous function and that $\displaystyle\int_{0}^{x} f(t)\,dt = \sin(x^2)$.

57. Evaluate $\displaystyle\int_{0}^{\sqrt{\pi/2}} f(t)\,dt$.

58. Show that $\displaystyle\int_{\sqrt{\pi/2}}^{x} f(t)\,dt = \sin(x^2) - 1$.

59. Find an expression for $\displaystyle\int_{-\sqrt{3\pi/2}}^{x} f(t)\,dt$.

60. Find an expression for $\displaystyle\int_{0}^{2x} f(t)\,dt$.

In Exercises 61–64, rewrite the expression in terms of F, where $F(t) = \displaystyle\int_{-1}^{t} \sqrt{1 + x^4}\,dx$.

61. $\displaystyle\int_{-1}^{4} \sqrt{1 + u^4}\,du$

62. $\displaystyle\int_{0}^{-1} \sqrt{1 + z^4}\,dz$

63. $\displaystyle\int_{-2}^{3} \sqrt{1 + t^4}\,dt$

64. $\displaystyle\int_{0}^{1} \sqrt{1 + u^4}\,du$

65. Let $F(x) = \displaystyle\int_{a}^{x} f(t)\,dt$ and $G(x) = \displaystyle\int_{a}^{x} g(t)\,dt$, where f and g are continuous functions. Suppose that $f(x) \leq g(x)$ for all $x \geq a$. Show that $F(x) \leq G(x)$ for all $x \geq a$.

66. Let $A_f(x) = \displaystyle\int_{c}^{x} f(t)\,dt$, where c is a constant and f is a continuous function.

(a) Prove that if f is positive on $[a, b]$, then A_f is increasing on $[a, b]$. [HINT: Let y and z be numbers such that $a \leq y < z \leq b$. Compare $A_f(y)$ and $A_f(z)$.]

(b) Use part (a) to show that if f is negative on $[a, b]$, then A_f is decreasing on $[a, b]$. [HINT: The function g defined by $g(x) = -f(x)$ is positive wherever f is negative.]

(c) Use parts (a) and (b) to show that A_f has a local maximum or a local minimum wherever f changes sign.

67. (a) Use the figure below to show that $\displaystyle\int_{0}^{x} \sqrt{1 - t^2}\,dt = \frac{1}{2}x\sqrt{1 - x^2} + \frac{1}{2}\arcsin x$ if $0 \leq x \leq 1$. [HINT: The area of a circular sector of radius r and angle θ is $r^2\theta/2$.]

(b) Show that $\displaystyle\int_{0}^{x} \sqrt{1 - t^2}\,dt = \frac{1}{2}x\sqrt{1 - x^2} + \frac{1}{2}\arcsin x$ if $-1 \leq x \leq 0$.

(c) Let $f(x) = \sqrt{1 - x^2}$ and let $A_f(x) = \displaystyle\int_{0}^{x} f(t)\,dt$. Show that A_f is an antiderivative of f.

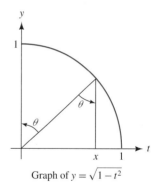

Graph of $y = \sqrt{1 - t^2}$

68. Let $f(x) = \sqrt{1 - x^2}$ and let $A_f(x) = \displaystyle\int_{-1/2}^{x} f(t)\,dt$.

(a) Use the result stated in part (a) of Exercise 67 to find a formula for A_f.

(b) Is A_f an antiderivative of f? Justify your answer.

69. Let $a > 0$ be a constant. Use a sketch similar to that given in Exercise 67 to find an expression for $\displaystyle\int_{0}^{x} \sqrt{a^2 - t^2}\,dt$ if $-a \leq x \leq a$. [HINT: Check that your answer produces the correct value if $x = a$.]

70. Let $f(x) = x^2$ and $A_f(x) = \displaystyle\int_{0}^{x} f(t)\,dt$.

(a) Use the result of Exercise 73 in Section 5.1 to find a formula for $A_f(x)$.

(b) Is A_f an antiderivative of f? Justify your answer.

71. Let $f(x) = x^2$ and $A_f(x) = \displaystyle\int_{-3}^{x} f(t)\,dt$.

(a) Use the result of Exercise 73 in Section 5.1 to find a formula for $A_f(x)$.

(b) Is A_f an antiderivative of f? Justify your answer.

5.3   THE FUNDAMENTAL THEOREM OF CALCULUS

Here we state and (somewhat informally) prove the FTC: The area function A_f is an antiderivative for f. (With any luck some students will already have guessed the result.)

What the theorem says

In the preceding section we constructed the area function A_f from an "original" function f and a base point a. All of the evidence amassed so far, both from examples and from the list on page 319 of relations between f and A_f, points to one conclusion:

THEOREM 2 (The fundamental theorem of calculus, informal version)
For any well-behaved function f and any base point a, A_f is an antiderivative of f.

The theorem's grand-sounding title is fully justified. The formal statement of this fact is the single most important theorem of elementary calculus. Here it is, complete with mathematical fine print:

THEOREM 3 (The fundamental theorem of calculus, formal version)
Let f be a continuous function defined on an open interval I containing a. The function A_f with rule

$$A_f(x) = \int_a^x f(t)\,dt$$

is defined for every x in I, and

$$\frac{d}{dx}\left(A_f(x)\right) = f(x).$$

By now, we hope, the area function A_f is familiar enough that the theorem's statement makes good sense — and might have been guessed.

We'll say much more about the FTC (our shorthand) and provide a proof at the end of this section. First, some remarks.

- **Why continuous?**   Requiring f to be continuous ensures that the integral $\int_a^x f$ exists. If f is discontinuous (if it blows up or has gaps, for instance), then A_f may have problems, too.

- **Why is I open?**   Recall that *open* intervals, such as $(-3, 10)$ and (∞, ∞), are intervals that don't contain endpoints. Working on an open interval I is a technical convenience; doing so ensures that there's "room" on both sides of a. ◄

This hypothesis rarely causes trouble in elementary calculus. We include it mainly for completeness.

- **In other symbols**   The conclusion of the FTC is sometimes written as follows:

$$\frac{d}{dx}\left(\int_a^x f(t)\,dt\right) = f(x).$$

This form avoids the symbol A_f, but the density of symbols on the left side may be mystifying. ◄

Which form seems clearer to you? Do you see that both forms say the same thing?

- **In graphical words**   The FTC means, graphically, that the *rate* of change of the area function is the *height* of the original function.

EXAMPLE 1   Let $f(x) = 2x \sin(x^2)$ and let $A_f(x) = \int_0^x f(t)\,dt$. Find a symbolic formula for A_f; interpret results graphically.

Solution   In the simple examples of the preceding section we could use elementary area formulas to find explicit formulas for A_f. Here, simple geometric formulas aren't enough. How, for instance, might we find the exact value of $A_f(2)$, the signed area shown shaded in Figure 1?

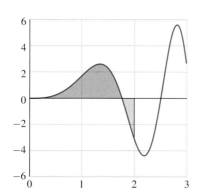

$A_f(2)$ is the net shaded area.

FIGURE 1
Finding $A_f(2)$ for $f(x) = 2x\sin(x^2)$

The FTC solves our problem. It says that A_f is *some* antiderivative of f; we need only find the right one.

Students may need reminding that a given function has many antiderivatives.

    Let's observe first that for any constant C, the function $F(x) = -\cos(x^2) + C$ is an antiderivative of $f(x) = 2x\sin(x^2)$. (This might be hard to guess, but it's easy to check.) ➥ We know too that *every* antiderivative of f—including A_f, the one we want—has this form. Thus, we must have

Do check; differentiate A_f.

$$A_f(x) = -\cos(x^2) + C$$

for some constant C. To choose the *right* value of C we use the fact that $A_f(0) = 0$. ➥ Thus,

Why? Because $\int_0^0 f = 0$ for any function f.

$$0 = A_f(0) = -\cos 0 + C \implies C = 1,$$

and we've found our formula: $A_f(x) = -\cos(x^2) + 1$. (In particular, $A_f(2) = -\cos(4) + 1 \approx 1.65364$.) The graphs of f and A_f in Figure 2 are consistent with our conclusion—the A_f-graph does appear (qualitatively, at least) to describe the behavior of signed area under the f-graph, based at 0.

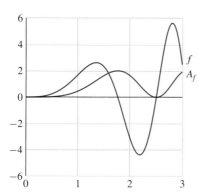

A_f is an antiderivative for f. For instance, A_f is stationary where f has x-intercepts.

FIGURE 2
If $f(x) = 2x\sin(x^2)$, then $A_f(x) = -\cos(x^2) + 1$ ■

Finding *all* antiderivatives of a function

In Example 1 we claimed that any two antiderivatives of the function $f(x) = 2x \sin(x^2)$ differ only by an additive constant. We've discussed this principle before (in Sections 2.4 and 4.9), but it's important enough here to deserve repeating:

FACT Suppose that $F'(x) = G'(x)$ for all x in an interval I. Then, for some constant C, $F(x) = G(x) + C$ for all x in I.

That all antiderivatives have this form follows from the Mean Value theorem.

The Fact means, in practice, that finding *one* antiderivative for a function f on an interval I is tantamount to finding *all* antiderivatives: If $F(x)$ is *any* antiderivative, then every other antiderivative is of the form $F(x) + C$. (We gave more details on this Fact in Section 4.11.)

Continuous functions have antiderivatives. The fundamental theorem guarantees (among other things) that every continuous function f on I *has* an antiderivative on I —namely, the area function A_f.

For the usual, nicely behaved functions of elementary calculus, this is no great surprise. For naughtier functions, such as the one in Figure 3, the situation is murkier.

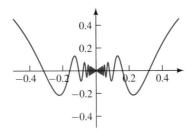

FIGURE 3
Does $f(x) = x \sin(\frac{1}{x})$ have an antiderivative?

The fundamental theorem says that every continuous function f, naughty or nice *has* an antiderivative. (*Finding* an antiderivative in symbolic form may be difficult or impossible; the FTC offers no guarantees there.)

Why the FTC is fundamental

The FTC deserves its high-sounding name for both theoretical and practical reasons. It's fundamental *theoretically* because it connects the two main concepts of calculus: the derivative and the integral. Each is a sort of inverse of the other.

The FTC's *practical* consequences are at least as important; implicitly or explicitly, we'll use them again and again. Most important, the FTC leads to a practical method of calculating specific integrals. ◄

So far, we've relied entirely on elementary area formulas.

Another version of the FTC Before proving the FTC, let's use it to prove another theorem closely related to the FTC, but handier in computations.

> **THEOREM 4 (Fundamental theorem, second version)**   Let f be continuous on $[a, b]$, and let F be *any* antiderivative of f. Then
> $$\int_a^b f(x)\,dx = F(b) - F(a).$$

This version of the FTC gives a practical method for calculating many integrals—but students shouldn't mistake it for the definition of integral.

Proof. This result follows readily from the original FTC. If F is any antiderivative of f, then $F(x)$ can differ from $A_f(x)$ (which is another antiderivative of f, according to the FTC) only by some constant C. In other words, $F(x) = A_f(x) + C$. It follows that

$$F(b) - F(a) = \big(A_f(b) + C\big) - \big(A_f(a) + C\big)$$
$$= A_f(b) - A_f(a)$$
$$= \int_a^b f - \int_a^a f = \int_a^b f,$$

just as claimed.   □

Calculating areas with antiderivatives

With Theorem 4 available it's a routine matter to calculate many signed areas.

EXAMPLE 2   In Section 5.1 we estimated—but didn't prove—that the shaded regions N and P in Figure 4 have signed areas -0.25 and 0.25, respectively. Prove it now.

Students might also consider whether every odd function has even antiderivatives and (vice versa).

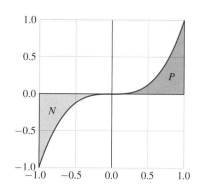

FIGURE 4
Two areas bounded by $y = x^3$

Solution   Let $f(x) = x^3$. The signed areas N and P are given by integrals:

$$N = \int_{-1}^0 f(x)\,dx; \qquad P = \int_0^1 f(x)\,dx.$$

Now $F(x) = x^4/4$ is an antiderivative of $f(x)$, and so Theorem 4 applies:

$$\int_{-1}^0 f(x)\,dx = F(0) - F(-1) = -\frac{1}{4}; \qquad \int_0^1 f(x)\,dx = F(1) - F(0) = \frac{1}{4},$$

as claimed earlier.   ■

Bracket notation The **bracket notation** offers a convenient shorthand for calculating integrals.

$$\text{For any function } F, \ F(x)\Big]_a^b \text{ means } F(b) - F(a).$$

Watch for the bracket notation in the next example.

EXAMPLE 3 Evaluate $\int_0^1 x^2 \, dx$ and $\int_0^1 x^{10} \, dx$. Interpret each integral as an area.

Solution By Theorem 4 it's enough to find *any* antiderivative, plug in endpoints, and subtract. We do just that:

$$\int_0^1 x^2 \, dx = \frac{x^3}{3}\Bigg]_0^1 = \frac{1}{3}; \qquad \int_0^1 x^{10} \, dx = \frac{x^{11}}{11}\Bigg]_0^1 = \frac{1}{11}.$$

Each integral measures an area. The lightly and darkly shaded areas in Figure 5 represent the integrals just calculated.

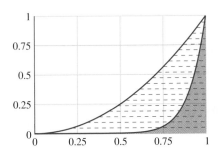

FIGURE 5
Areas under $y = x^{10}$ and $y = x^2$

■

EXAMPLE 4 Calculate the shaded area in Figure 6.

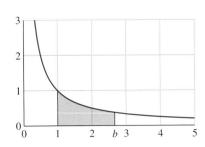

In the case shown, $b = e$ and the shaded area is 1.

FIGURE 6
Area under $y = \frac{1}{x}$ from $x = 1$ to $x = b$

Which value of b makes the shaded area 1?

Solution The shaded area is the value of the integral $\int_1^b 1/x \, dx$. Recall that the function $\ln x$ is an antiderivative for $1/x$. ◄ Now Theorem 4 says that

$$\int_1^b \frac{1}{x} \, dx = \ln x\Big]_1^b = \ln b - \ln 1 = \ln b.$$

If $b = e$ (as in the picture), the area is $\ln e = 1$.

■

From rates to amounts with the FTC

The second version of the fundamental theorem can be restated slightly (without changing its meaning) to read as follows:

The main point is that integrating any rate over an interval gives the change in amount over that interval.

> **FACT** Let f be a function defined on $[a, b]$, with continuous derivative f'. Then
> $$\int_a^b f'(t)\, dt = f(b) - f(a).$$

In words, the Fact says this:

> *Integrating f' (the rate function) over $[a, b]$ gives the change in f (the amount function) over the same interval.*

This Fact has important practical uses; with it, we can deduce *amount* information from *rate* information.

EXAMPLE 5 Demand for electricity varies predictably over the course of a day. Drawing on experience, engineers in a small town (a bedroom suburb, perhaps) use the formula

$$r(t) = 4 + \sin(0.263t + 4.7) + \cos(0.526t + 9.4)$$

to model the town's typical rate of consumption, in megawatts, t hours after midnight. Figure 7 shows the function r.

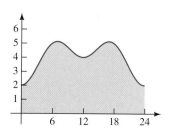

FIGURE 7
Rate of power use (megawatts) over 24 hours

Is the model reasonable? What does the shaded area represent?

Solution The graph looks generally believable. Residential demand peaks in the morning, declines during working hours, and rises again in the evening. The formula for r is complicated, but the basic ingredients—periodic functions and constants—look right.

The shaded area is the integral $\int_0^{24} r(t)\, dt$. To understand it in context, let $a(t)$ be the total *amount* of electricity consumed up to time t, starting at midnight. ➤ Then $a'(t) = r(t)$, and by the preceding Fact,

By definition, therefore, $a = 0$ when $t = 0$.

$$\int_0^{24} r(t)\, dt = a(24) - a(0) = a(24) = \text{total daily consumption.}$$

To evaluate this integral numerically we need an antiderivative for $r(t)$. The messy formula for $r(t)$ complicates the search, but we might eventually guess (and it's easy to *check* using derivative rules) that

$$4t - \frac{\cos(0.263t + 4.7)}{0.263} + \frac{\sin(0.526t + 9.4)}{0.526}$$

is an antiderivative for $r(t)$. Thanks to Theorem 4, the rest is straight (though slightly messy) calculation:

$$\int_0^{24} r(t)\,dt = 4t - \frac{\cos(0.263t + 4.7)}{0.263} + \frac{\sin(0.526t + 9.4)}{0.526} \Bigg]_0^{24}$$

$$\approx 95.781 \text{ megawatt hours.} \qquad \blacksquare$$

In Volume II we emphasize that not all integrands have simple antiderivatives — but that effective numerical methods are available as needed. (The simplest "numerical" method is visual estimation.)

When *not* to use the FTC

The FTC, useful as it is, doesn't solve *all* our integral problems. Evaluating integrals by antidifferentiation requires first finding a usable antiderivative. For a surprising number of integrands, even apparently simple ones, finding an antiderivative formula is hard or even impossible. None of the following functions, for instance, has an elementary antiderivative:

$$\sin(x^2); \qquad \frac{x}{\ln x}; \qquad 3 + \sin x + 0.3\arcsin\big(\sin(7x)\big).$$

Nevertheless, all have perfectly sensible integrals over finite intervals. For instance, the shaded area in Figure 8 shows what $\int_0^{10} f$ means for the last of the preceding functions.

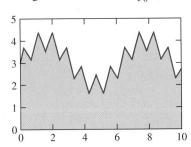

Can you estimate the shaded area? The bounding box has total area 50.

FIGURE 8
An FTC-resistant integral: $\int_0^{10} \big(3 + \sin x + 0.3\arcsin(\sin(7x))\big)\ dx$

With or without an antiderivative formula, the integral in Figure 8 certainly exists. Soon we'll study techniques that *don't* involve antiderivatives for accurately *estimating* integrals like this one.

Proving the FTC

The FTC is certainly useful, and by now, we hope, it's plausible. But why is it *true*?

The idea of the proof   Recall the setup: f is a continuous function, defined on an interval I containing $x = a$, and

$$A_f(x) = \int_a^x f(t)\,dt.$$

The theorem asserts that, for x in I,

$$\frac{d}{dx} A_f(x) = f(x).$$

By the definition of derivative

$$\frac{d}{dx} A_f(x) = \lim_{h \to 0} \frac{A_f(x+h) - A_f(x)}{h};$$

We'll work directly with the difference quotient to prove that the last limit above is $f(x)$. Figure 9 will prove useful.

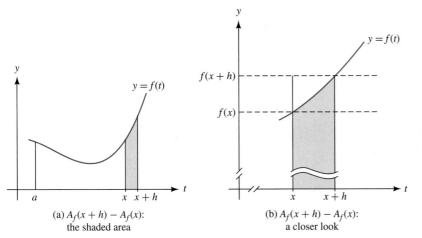

(a) $A_f(x+h) - A_f(x)$:
the shaded area

(b) $A_f(x+h) - A_f(x)$:
a closer look

Part (b) is the result of zooming in on part (a).

FIGURE 9
Proving the FTC

Notice first that $A_f(x+h) - A_f(x) = \int_a^{x+h} f - \int_a^x f = \int_x^{x+h} f$; Figure 9(a) illustrates why: the shaded region ($\int_x^{x+h} f$) is the result of subtracting the smaller region ($\int_a^x f$) from the larger ($\int_a^{x+h} f$).

Figure 9(b) shows that, for small positive values of h,

$$\int_x^{x+h} f \approx f(x) \cdot h.$$

(The last quantity is the area of the shorter rectangle.) Thus, for h near 0 we have

$$\frac{A_f(x+h) - A_f(x)}{h} \approx \frac{f(x) \cdot h}{h} = f(x),$$

and as $h \to 0$, the difference quotient tends to $f(x)$, as desired.   □

More on the proof: fine print A rigorous proof can be constructed from the preceding informal argument. The missing ingredient is a precise approach to the approximation $\int_x^{x+h} f \approx f(x) \cdot h$. It helps if f happens to be increasing near x—as it is in Figure 9. In that case, we have

$$f(x) \cdot h \leq A_f(x+h) - A_f(x) \leq f(x+h) \cdot h.$$

(Note that $A_f(x+h) - A_f(x)$ is the shaded area.) Thus,

$$f(x) \leq \frac{A_f(x+h) - A_f(x)}{h} \leq f(x+h).$$

As $h \to 0$, the quantities on both left and right tend to $f(x)$ and so, therefore, must the difference quotient. (A similar approach works if f is not increasing, although some technical details differ.)

A fully rigorous proof would depend on a limit-based definition of integral.

BASIC EXERCISES

In Exercises 1–8, $F(x) = \int_0^x f(t)\,dt$, where f is the function whose graph is shown below.

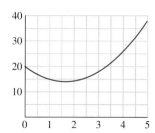

1. Is F increasing at $x = 3$? Justify your answer.

2. Is F decreasing at $x = 1$? Justify your answer.

3. Is F concave up at $x = 3$? Justify your answer.

4. Is F concave up at $x = 1$? Justify your answer.

5. Is $F'(4) > 20$? Justify your answer.

6. Is $F'(2) < 20$? Justify your answer.

7. Is $F(2) > 20$? Justify your answer.

8. Suppose that g is a function such that $g(0) = 2$ and $g'(x) = f(x)$ for all x. Explain how the graphs of F and g are related.

In Exercises 9–18, $F(x) = \int_0^x f(t)\,dt$, where f is the function graphed below. (The graph of f is made up of straight lines and a semicircle.)

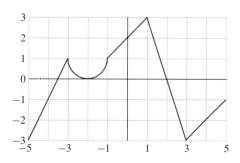

9. Identify all the stationary points of F in the interval $[-5, 5]$.

10. Identify all the critical points of F in the interval $[-5, 5]$.

11. Where in the interval $[-5, 5]$ is F decreasing? Justify your answer.

12. Where in the interval $[-5, 5]$ does F have local extrema? Justify your answer.

13. Evaluate $F(0)$, $F'(0)$ and $F''(0)$.

14. Evaluate $F(2)$, $F'(2)$ and $F''(2)$.

15. Find an equation of the line tangent to the graph $y = F(x)$ at $x = -1$.

16. Find an equation of the line tangent to the graph $y = F(x)$ at $x = 4$.

17. Identify all the inflection points of F in the interval $[-5, 5]$.

18. Let $G(x) = \int_0^x F(t)\,dt$. On which subintervals of $[-5, 5]$, if any, is G concave upward?

In Exercises 19–30, evaluate the definite integral using the fundamental theorem of calculus.

19. $\int_1^3 x\,dx$

20. $\int_0^4 \sqrt{x}\,dx$

21. $\int_{-1}^1 x^2\,dx$

22. $\int_{-2}^2 x^3\,dx$

23. $\int_{-1}^2 e^x\,dx$

24. $\int_0^\pi \cos x\,dx$

25. $\int_{\pi/2}^\pi \sin x\,dx$

26. $\int_1^e \dfrac{dx}{x}$

27. $\int_1^4 (5x + x^{3/2})\,dx$

28. $\int_{-2}^5 \dfrac{dx}{x+3}$

29. $\int_{-\pi/2}^\pi \sin(2x)\,dx$

30. $\int_{\pi/2}^{2\pi} \cos(3x)\,dx$

31. (a) Find an equation of the line tangent to the graph of $F(x) = \int_1^x \sqrt[3]{t^2 + 7}\,dt$ at $x = 1$.

    (b) Suppose that the tangent line in part (a) is used to compute an estimate of $F(1.1)$. Is this estimate too large? Justify your answer.

32. Suppose that $G(x) = \int_a^x \sin(t)\,dt$, a is a constant, and $G(\sqrt{\pi}) = 1$.

    (a) Find an equation of the line tangent to the graph $y = G(x)$ at $x = \sqrt{\pi}$.

    (b) Suppose that the tangent line in part (a) is used to compute an estimate of $G(1.8)$. Is this estimate too large? Justify your answer.

33. (a) Show that $\dfrac{d}{dx}\sin(x^2) = 2x\cos(x^2)$.

    (b) Use part (a) and the fundamental theorem of calculus to evaluate $\int_0^3 x\cos(x^2)\,dx$.

34. (a) Let $f(x) = e^{-x^3}$. Find a formula for $f'(x)$.

    (b) Use part (a) and the fundamental theorem of calculus to evaluate $\int_0^1 x^2 e^{-x^3}\,dx$.

FURTHER EXERCISES

In Exercises 35–42, $F(x) = \int_0^x f(t)\,dt$, where $f(t)$ is the function shown below.

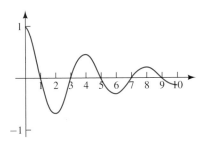

35. Does $F(x)$ have any local maxima in the interval $[0, 10]$? If so, where are they located?

36. Does $F(x)$ have any local minima in the interval $[0, 10]$? If so, where are they located?

37. At what value of x does $F(x)$ attain its minimum value on the interval $[1, 10]$?

38. On which subinterval(s) of $[0, 10]$, if any, is the graph of $F(x)$ concave up? Justify your answer.

39. Is $F'(2) < -0.4$? Justify your answer.

40. Is $F'(4) > 0.7$? Justify your answer.

41. Is $F''(7) > 1$? Justify your answer.

42. Is $F''(5) < -1$? Justify your answer.

43. Suppose that $\int_0^x f(t)\,dt = 3x^2 + e^x - \cos x$. Evaluate $f(2)$.

44. Suppose that $\int_{-1}^w g(u)\,du = \cos(\pi e^w)$. Evaluate $g(0)$.

In Exercises 45 and 46, f is a function such that $f'(x) = \sqrt[3]{1 + x^2}$ and $f(1) = 0$.

45. Explain why $f(x) = \int_1^x \sqrt[3]{1 + t^2}\,dt$.

46. Express $\int_0^3 \sqrt[3]{1 + x^2}\,dx$ in terms of f.

47. Suppose that $g(x) = b + \int_a^x f(t)\,dx$, where a and b are constants. Show that g is a solution of the IVP $g' = f$, $g(a) = b$.

48. Show that if $f(a) \neq 0$, then $\dfrac{d}{dx}\left[\int_a^x f(t)\,dt\right] \neq \int_a^x \left[\dfrac{d}{dt} f(t)\right]\,dt$.

49. Let $F(x) = \int_0^x \sqrt[3]{1 + t^2}\,dt$. Find a formula for $\dfrac{d}{dx}\left[F(x^2)\right]$.

50. Let $G(x) = \int_2^{x^3} e^{-t^2}\,dt$. Find a formula for $G'(x)$.

51. Suppose that f' is a continuous function, that $f(1) = 13$, and that $f(10) = 7$. Find the average value of f' over the interval $[1, 10]$.

52. Suppose that g' is a continuous function, that $g(-2) = 3$, and that the average value of g' over the interval $[-2, 5]$ is 1. Find $g(5)$.

53. Find the area of the region enclosed by one arch of the sine function.

54. Find the area of the region enclosed by the graphs $y = 2x$ and $y = x^2$ between $x = 0$ and $x = 2$.

In Exercises 55–58, $g(u) = \int_1^u f(x)\,dx$ where f is the function graphed below.

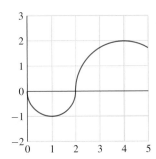

55. Evaluate $g'(4)$.

56. Does g have a tangent line at $x = 2$? Justify your answer.

57. Where in the interval $[0, 5]$ is g concave up? Justify your answer.

58. Is the average value of g' over the interval $[0, 3]$ greater than 1? Justify your answer.

In Exercises 59–63, $g(x) = \int_1^x f(t)\,dt$ and $h(x) = \int_3^x f(t)\,dt$, where f is a function with the following properties:

(i) $f'(x) \geq 0$ if $0 \leq x \leq 3$ and $6 \leq x \leq 7$; $f'(x) \leq 0$ if $3 \leq x \leq 6$.

(ii) $f''(x) \leq 0$ if $0 \leq x \leq 5$; $f''(x) \geq 0$ if $5 \leq x \leq 7$.

(iii) f has the values shown below

x	0	1	2	3	4	5	6	7
$f(x)$	0	2	4	5	4	0	-2	0

59. Evaluate $g'(4)$.

60. Where is the graph of g concave down? Justify your answer.

61. Find the value of x where $g(x)$ is maximum on the interval $[0, 7]$.

62. Find the value of x where $h(x)$ is minimum on the interval $[0, 7]$.

63. What is the average value of f' over the interval $[2, 5]$?

64. Find a polynomial function f with the following properties:
  (i) $f'(x) = ax^2 + bx$
  (ii) $f'(1) = 6$
  (iii) $f''(1) = 18$
  (iv) $\int_1^2 f(x)\,dx = 18$

65. A company is planning to phase out a product because demand for it is declining. Demand for the product is currently 800 units/month and is dropping by 10 units/month each month. To maintain customer and employee relations, the company has announced that it will continue to produce the product for one more year. At present, the company is producing the product at a rate of 900 units/month, and 1680 units of the product are in inventory.

  (a) Give expressions for the demand and production rates as functions of time t (take $t = 0$ as the present).

  (b) Let $D(t)$ be the demand rate for the product at time t. Explain why $\int_0^t D(s)\,ds$ is the total demand for the product between now and time t.

  (c) Give an expression for the inventory at time t.
    [HINT: The amount of the product in inventory is the difference between supply and demand at the end of t months.]

  (d) The company would like to reduce production at a constant rate of R units/month, with R chosen so the product inventory is zero at the end of 12 months. Find a suitable R.

66. The function $\ln x$ is sometimes *defined* for $x > 0$ by integration:

$$\ln x = \int_1^x \frac{dt}{t}.$$

Assume $a > 0$ and $x > 0$. Derive the identity $\ln(ax) = \ln a + \ln x$ by carrying out and justifying each of the following steps:

  (a) Show that $\left(\int_1^{ax} \frac{dt}{t} \right)' = \frac{1}{x}$.
    [HINT: Use the chain rule.]

  (b) Explain why the result in part (a) implies that $\ln(ax) = \ln x + C$.

  (c) By choosing an appropriate x, show that the value of the constant C in part (b) is $\ln a$.

Substitution is the simplest and most important antidifferentiation technique, and it's needed for effective use of integral tables.

5.4 FINDING ANTIDERIVATIVES; THE METHOD OF SUBSTITUTION

The fundamental theorem of calculus (FTC) makes it easy to evaluate many integrals: If f is a continuous function and F is any antiderivative of f, then

$$\int_a^b f(x)\,dx = F(x) \bigg]_a^b = F(b) - F(a).$$

In effect, finding an explicit antiderivative function F transforms an integral problem into something much easier: plugging a and b into F.

  To get anywhere with the FTC, of course, we need first to *find* a symbolic antiderivative for the given integrand f. Doing so is sometimes easy, sometimes hard, depending on f. (Finding symbolic *derivatives* is relatively easier, given the product, quotient, chain, and other "combinatorial" rules.)

  In this section, we first briefly review some familiar antiderivatives and their properties; then we present one useful method, called **substitution**, for finding antiderivatives systematically. (In Chapter 8 we return in much more detail to the problem of symbolic antidifferentiation.)

Finding antiderivatives: general ideas

Notation and terminology We'll use several standard notations and technical terms in searching for antiderivatives.

  • **Indefinite integrals** The expression

$$\int f(x)\,dx$$

is called an **indefinite integral**; f is the **integrand** and x is the **variable of integration**. For example, the equation

$$\int \cos x \, dx = \sin x + C$$

This is our first use of the antiderivative symbol; we've avoided using it to help distinguish between integrals and antiderivatives.

means that every function of the form $\sin x + C$ (where C, the **constant of integration**, may take any value) is an antiderivative of $\cos x$, and that *all* antiderivatives have this form. Notice one subtlety: Interpreted scrupulously, the indefinite integral $\int f(x) \, dx$ denotes not just one function but many—the "family" of all possible antiderivatives of f.

- **Definite integrals**   A **definite integral** is an expression of the form

$$\int_a^b f(x) \, dx,$$

with "definite" endpoints a and b (also known as **limits of integration**). Though they look much alike, definite and indefinite integrals are very different objects: the first is a real *number* and the second is family of *functions*.

Basic antiderivatives

In symbolic differentiation we start with a few known derivatives and combine them according to various rules to produce new derivatives. Antidifferentiation also requires a base of known formulas, to which more complicated problems can be reduced. The following table collects a few very basic antiderivative formulas: ➡

Many more antiderivative formulas appear in the back of this book.

Even this rudimentary table, together with substitution, suffices to find a lot of antiderivatives.

Basic antiderivative formulas
$\displaystyle\int x^k \, dx = \frac{x^{k+1}}{k+1} + C$ (if $k \neq -1$)
$\displaystyle\int \frac{1}{x} \, dx = \ln|x| + C$
$\displaystyle\int e^x \, dx = e^x + C$
$\displaystyle\int a^x \, dx = \frac{a^x}{\ln a} + C$ (if $a \neq 1$)
$\displaystyle\int \sin x \, dx = -\cos x + C$
$\displaystyle\int \cos x \, dx = \sin x + C$
$\displaystyle\int \sec^2 x \, dx = \tan x + C$
$\displaystyle\int \frac{dx}{\sqrt{1-x^2}} = \arcsin x + C$
$\displaystyle\int \frac{dx}{1+x^2} = \arctan x + C$

Each formula is easily checked by differentiation—with one possible exception.

We explain here what accounts for the mysterious absolute value in the antiderivative. For $x < 0$ we could, instead, write $\ln(-x)$.

EXAMPLE 1   The formula $\int \dfrac{1}{x}\,dx = \ln|x| + C$ has an unexpected ingredient: the absolute value. Because $\ln x$ itself is an antiderivative for $1/x$ (as we showed in Section 2.6), why do we bother with the absolute value?

Solution   The answer has to do with domains. The function $f(x) = 1/x$ is defined for all $x \neq 0$; ideally, an antiderivative should have the same domain. Unfortunately, the ordinary logarithm function $\ln x$ accepts only *positive* inputs x. The related function $\ln|x|$ solves this problem neatly—it has both the correct domain (positive *and* negative numbers) and the correct derivative. The graphs in Figure 1 give convincing evidence.

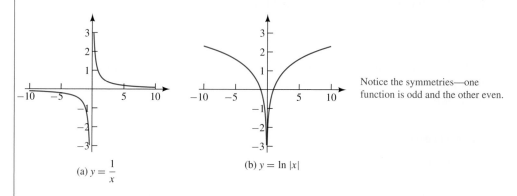

Notice the symmetries—one function is odd and the other even.

(a) $y = \dfrac{1}{x}$

(b) $y = \ln|x|$

FIGURE 1
Why $\ln|x|$ is an antiderivative for $\dfrac{1}{x}$

That $\ln|x|$ is indeed an antiderivative can be seen either in the graphs or by symbolic differentiation.   ∎

Combining antiderivatives   Every derivative rule, read backwards, says something about antiderivatives. The rules are especially simple for sums and constant multiples. We stated the following Fact in Section 2.4, but using different notation:

These are really properties of derivatives.

FACT   Let f and g be continuous functions and k any constant. Then
$$\int \big(f(x) + g(x)\big)\,dx = \int f(x)\,dx + \int g(x)\,dx;$$
$$\int k\,f(x)\,dx = k\int f(x)\,dx.$$

EXAMPLE 2   Find $\int (3\cos x - 2e^x)\,dx$.

Solution   By the Fact,
$$\int (3\cos x - 2e^x)\,dx = \int 3\cos x\,dx - \int 2e^x\,dx = 3\int \cos x\,dx - 2\int e^x\,dx$$
$$= 3\sin x - 2e^x + C,$$

an answer we can check by differentiation.   ∎

Creative guessing The next two examples illustrate educated guessing—a fully respectable but sometimes underappreciated technique in mathematics. Differentiation is easy; thus, most guesses are easy to check and incorrect guesses may be easy to fix.

We'll reiterate both points often: (i) differentiation is easier than antidifferentiation and (ii) initial guesses may be easy to fix by altering constants.

EXAMPLE 3 Find $\int \cos(2x)\, dx$ by guessing.

Solution Since $\int \cos x\, dx = \sin x + C$, we might—just guessing—try $\sin(2x)$ as an antiderivative. Differentiation shows that we missed (but only by a factor of 2).

$$\big(\sin(2x)\big)' = \cos(2x) \cdot 2 \neq \cos(2x).$$

Only a tiny alteration is needed:

$$\left(\frac{\sin(2x)}{2}\right)' = \cos(2x) \implies \int \cos(2x)\, dx = \frac{\sin(2x)}{2} + C.$$ ∎

EXAMPLE 4 Find $\int \dfrac{6}{1+4x^2}\, dx$ by creative guessing.

Solution The integrand's form and a look at the table of basic antiderivatives suggests an arctangent, perhaps with some constants attached, as in $F(x) = A\ \arctan(Bx)$. Differentiation gives ➡

Check this; use the chain rule carefully.

$$F'(x) = \big(A\ \arctan(Bx)\big)' = \frac{A}{1+(Bx)^2} \cdot B = \frac{AB}{1+B^2x^2}.$$

Our desired antiderivative therefore has $AB = 6$ and $B^2 = 4$. Setting $A = 3$ and $B = 2$ does nicely; therefore, $F(x) = 3\arctan(2x)$ is a suitable antiderivative.

This method of guessing—starting with **undetermined coefficients** A and B and then finding appropriate values for them—is common in calculus; we'll see it again.

Partial fractions may involve undetermined coefficients.

Looks can deceive Checking guesses is easy and effective, but caution is needed—some functions (the trigonometric type, especially) can be written in more than one way.

EXAMPLE 5 Is $\int \sin(2x)\, dx = \sin^2(x) + C$?

Solution Let's check. By the chain rule,

$$\left(\sin^2(x) + C\right)' = 2\sin x \cos x.$$

We hoped to get $\sin(2x)$, so we're tempted to answer no. In fact, the right answer is yes. One of the many trigonometric identities says that

$$2\sin x \cos x = \sin(2x).$$

We stand corrected. ∎

The method of substitution

The simplest and most important antidifferentiation technique is called, variously, **direct substitution**, ***u*-substitution**. or just plain **substitution**. ➡

We'll show through many examples both *how* substitution works and *that* it works; the examples will also suggest *why* it works, and at a strong link to the chain rule.

For obscure reasons, the letter u is almost invariably used for substitutions. We'll follow convention.

EXAMPLE 6   Find $\int 2x \cos(x^2)\, dx$.

Solution   Let $u = u(x) = x^2$; then

$$\frac{du}{dx} = 2x, \quad \text{so} \quad du = 2x\, dx.$$

(Whoa—can du and dx legally be separated this way? The short answer is yes; we'll return to the question later.) Substituting both u and du into the original integral gives

$$\int \cos(x^2)\, 2x\, dx = \int \cos u\, du.$$

The second integral is simpler than the first, and so we've made progress. To continue, we antidifferentiate in u and then substitute back:

$$\int \cos u\, du = \sin u + C = \sin(x^2) + C.$$

Is the answer right? An easy check, using the chain rule, shows that it is:

$$\left(\sin(x^2) + C \right)' = \cos(x^2) \cdot 2x.$$

That was easy, quick, and possibly dirty—separating du and dx might seem suspicious, for one thing. But the method—dirty or not—produced an answer we could easily check.   ∎

EXAMPLE 7   Find $\int \dfrac{x}{1+x^2}\, dx$.

Solution   If $u(x) = 1 + x^2$, then $du/dx = 2x$ and $du = 2x\, dx$. Making the substitutions gives

$$\int \frac{x}{1+x^2}\, dx = \frac{1}{2} \int \frac{2x}{1+x^2}\, dx = \frac{1}{2} \int \frac{du}{u}.$$

Notice the first step: multiplying by 2 inside the integral sign "produced" the desired du. (We paid for this convenience by dividing by 2 *outside* the integral.)

In its new form the antiderivative problem is easier:

$$\frac{1}{2} \int \frac{du}{u} = \frac{1}{2} \ln |u| + C = \frac{1}{2} \ln(1+x^2) + C,$$

where we substituted $u = 1 + x^2$ in the last step. Checking the answer is another chain-rule exercise (left to you).   ∎

Trading one integral for another   A successful u-substitution transforms one indefinite integral into another, the second simpler than the first. The process has three steps:

- **Substitute**   Choose a function $u = u(x)$, and write $du = u'(x)\, dx$. Then substitute u and du into the original integral $\int f(x)\, dx$ to produce a new integral of the form $\int g(u)\, du$.
- **Antidifferentiate in u**   Solve $\int g(u)\, du$ as an antidifferentiation problem in u; that is, find $G(u)$ such that $G'(u) = g(u)$.
- **Resubstitute**   Substitute *back* to eliminate u. The result, $F(x) = G\big(u(x)\big)$, is *one* antiderivative of f; other antiderivatives have the form $F(x) + C$.

Differentials   The symbols du and dx are called the **differentials** of u and x, respectively. If $u = u(x)$, then du and dx are related in the expected way: $du = u'(x)\, dx$.

A rigorous (and rather subtle) theory of differentials exists in higher mathematics; we won't need it in this book. For us, the differential in an integral expression (dx in $\int f(x)\, dx$, for instance) is mainly an aid to memory: it reminds us of the variable of integration. In substitution problems, trading dx's for du's (or vice versa) is a useful bookkeeping device; it helps keep us honest when we change variables.

A substitution sampler

Substitution is easy enough in theory. In practice, finding the "right" substitution is both art and science. In both realms, practice (false starts and all) makes perfect. The following examples illustrate some of the possibilities and some useful tricks of the trade.

Trying out u-substitutions mentally can be quick and effective.

Choosing u wisely   Choosing u properly is the tricky part of substitution. Things go well when (as in the preceding examples) both u and du appear conveniently in the original integrand and when the new integral is simpler than the old.

EXAMPLE 8   Find $\int \sin^3 x \cos x \, dx$.

Solution   If $u = \sin x$, then $du = \cos x \, dx$. With u and du staring us in the face, prospects look good:

$$\int \sin^3 x \cos x \, dx = \int u^3 \, du = \frac{u^4}{4} + C = \frac{\sin^4 x}{4} + C. \quad \blacksquare$$

EXAMPLE 9   Find $\int \frac{x}{1+x^4} \, dx$.

Solution   No obvious substitution suggests itself. We might try $u = 1 + x^4$, but then $du = 4x^3 \, dx$, and nothing of the sort appears in the given integrand. A better choice, it turns out, is $u = x^2$. Then $du = 2x \, dx$, and

$$\int \frac{x}{1+x^4} \, dx = \frac{1}{2} \int \frac{2x}{1+x^4} \, dx = \frac{1}{2} \int \frac{du}{1+u^2}.$$

We've made progress—the last antiderivative is an old standard:

$$\frac{1}{2} \int \frac{du}{1+u^2} = \frac{1}{2} \arctan u + C = \frac{1}{2} \arctan(x^2) + C.$$

Checking the answer involves (as usual) the chain rule. $\blacksquare$

Traveling constants   Multiplicative constants move freely (and legally) in and out of antiderivatives. We exploit this freedom in the next example, as we did in Examples 7 and 9.

EXAMPLE 10   Find $\int \frac{3x}{5x^2+7} \, dx$.

Solution   The numerator is almost (except for multiplicative constants) the derivative of the denominator; this brings $\int du/u$ to mind. If we set $u = 5x^2 + 7$, then $du = 10x \, dx$, and ➡

Watch the constants carefully.

$$\int \frac{3x}{5x^2+7} \, dx = \frac{3}{10} \int \frac{10x}{5x^2+7} \, dx = \frac{3}{10} \int \frac{du}{u}$$

$$= \frac{3}{10} \ln |u| + C = \frac{3}{10} \ln (5x^2+7) + C.$$

(Since $5x^2 + 7 > 0$ for all x, it's fair to ignore the absolute value.) $\blacksquare$

We'll do this sort of thing systematically in Chapter 8 when we study trigonometric substitutions.

Inverse substitutions: writing x and dx in terms of u and du   In the examples so far, we've written u and du in terms of x and dx. Sometimes it's simpler to write x and dx in terms of u and du. The next two examples illustrate this strategy.

EXAMPLE 11   Find $\int \dfrac{dx}{1+\sqrt{x}}$.

Solution   Let $u = \sqrt{x}$. (This is not the only possibility: $u = 1 + \sqrt{x}$ also works.) Then $x = u^2$ and $dx = 2u\,du$; substituting for x and dx gives

$$\int \frac{dx}{1+\sqrt{x}} = \int \frac{2u}{1+u}\,du.$$

The second integral is simpler than the first, but *another* substitution makes things simpler still. If $v = 1 + u$, then $dv = du$ and $u = v - 1$, so

$$\int \frac{2u}{1+u}\,du = \int \frac{2(v-1)}{v}\,dv = 2\int \left(1 - \frac{1}{v}\right)dv = 2\bigl(v - \ln|v|\bigr) + C.$$

Last, we substitute back, first for u and then for x:

$$2\bigl(v - \ln|v|\bigr) + C = 2\bigl(1 + u - \ln|1 + u|\bigr) + C = 2 + 2\sqrt{x} - 2\ln|1 + \sqrt{x}| + C.$$ ■

EXAMPLE 12   Find $\int \dfrac{x}{\sqrt{2x+3}}\,dx$.

Solution   If $u = \sqrt{2x+3}$, then $du = dx/\sqrt{2x+3}$, and substitution gives

$$\int \frac{x}{\sqrt{2x+3}}\,dx = \int x\,\frac{dx}{\sqrt{2x+3}} = \int x\,du.$$

So far so good, but what about that remaining x? To eliminate it, we write x in terms of u:

$$u = \sqrt{2x+3} \implies u^2 = 2x + 3 \implies \frac{u^2 - 3}{2} = x.$$

Now we're on our way:

$$\int x\,du = \int \frac{u^2-3}{2}\,du = \frac{u^3}{6} - \frac{3u}{2} + C = \frac{(2x+3)^{3/2}}{6} - \frac{3\sqrt{2x+3}}{2} + C.$$

For symbolic variety, let's redo the problem a little differently, again starting with $u = \sqrt{2x+3}$. Then $u^2 = 2x + 3$, and differentiating both sides gives $2u\,du = 2\,dx$; thus, $u\,du = dx$. Now we substitute for x, dx, and $\sqrt{2x+3}$—all at once:

$$\int \frac{x}{\sqrt{2x+3}}\,dx = \int \frac{u^2-3}{2u}\,u\,du = \int \frac{u^2-3}{2}\,du,$$

and the problem proceeds as before.   ■

We'll see in later chapters that substitution sometimes transforms unpleasant numerical or improper integrals into more tractable forms.

Substitution in definite integrals

The next example shows two ways of evaluating *definite* integrals by substitution.

EXAMPLE 13   Find $\int_0^{\sqrt{\pi/2}} 2x\cos(x^2)\,dx$.

Solution   We'll solve the problem in two different ways.

Method 1: Antidifferentiate in *x* and plug in endpoints If $F(x)$ is any antiderivative of $2x\cos(x^2)$, then $F(\sqrt{\pi/2}) - F(0)$ is our answer. In fact, we already found a suitable F in Example 6, where we substituted $u = x^2$ to find $F(x) = \sin(x^2)$. → Thus,

$$\int_0^{\sqrt{\pi/2}} 2x\cos(x^2)\,dx = \sin(x^2)\Big]_{x=0}^{x=\sqrt{\pi/2}} = \sin(\pi/2) - \sin 0 = 1.$$

We need just one antiderivative so we set $C = 0$.

(We wrote the symbol x in the bracket notation to emphasize which variable is in use.)

Method 2: Substitute to create a new definite integral Again, let $u = x^2$ and $du = 2x\,dx$. At the endpoints $x = 0$ and $x = \sqrt{\pi/2}$, we have $u = 0$ and $u = \pi/2$, respectively. Now we substitute for u, du, *and for the endpoints*, to get a new *definite* integral:

$$\int_0^{\sqrt{\pi/2}} 2x\cos(x^2)\,dx = \int_0^{\pi/2} \cos u\,du.$$

The last integral is easy to calculate:

$$\int_0^{\pi/2} \cos u\,du = \sin u\Big]_{u=0}^{u=\pi/2} = \sin(\pi/2) - \sin 0 = 1,$$

the same result as before. →   ∎

The u symbol in the bracket notation reminds us which variable is in play.

Another look Notice carefully the different uses of substitution in the two solutions to Example 13. In the first solution we used substitution only to find an antiderivative of the given integrand with respect to the original variable x. In the second solution we used substitution to transform the original definite integral into a *new definite integral*, with new limits of integration and a new integrand.

Why substitution works

Substitution is essentially the chain rule in action.

Substitution certainly seems to work. But *why* does it work? To see, we'll describe the process in general terms.

For any antiderivative problem $\int f(x)\,dx$, substitution means finding a function $u = u(x)$ such that $f(x)$ can be rewritten in the form

$$f(x) = g(u(x))\,u'(x).$$

To say that substitution "works" means that

$$\int f(x)\,dx = \int g(u)\,du.$$

This means, in turn, that if G is a function for which $G'(u) = g(u)$, then $G(u(x))$ is an antiderivative of f. The chain rule shows that this is indeed so:

$$\frac{d}{dx}\Big(G(u(x))\Big) = G'(u(x))\cdot u'(x) = g(u(x))\cdot u'(x) = f(x),$$

so $G(u(x))$ is indeed the antiderivative we seek.

Substitution works in *definite* integrals for essentially the same reason. The following theorem gives details.

> **THEOREM 5 (Change of variables in definite integrals)**   Let f, u, and g be continuous functions such that for all x in $[a, b]$,
>
> $$f(x) = g(u(x)) \cdot u'(x).$$
>
> Then
>
> $$\int_a^b f(x)\,dx = \int_{u(a)}^{u(b)} g(u)\,du.$$

Proof Let G be an antiderivative of g. Then, by the FTC,

$$\int_{u(a)}^{u(b)} g(u)\,du = G(u(b)) - G(u(a)).$$

We showed just above that $G(u(x))$ is an antiderivative for $f(x)$. Hence, by the FTC,

$$\int_a^b f(x)\,dx = G(u(b)) - G(u(a)),$$

so the two integrals are equal.   □

BASIC EXERCISES

In Exercises 1–10, evaluate the antiderivative using the indicated substitution. (Check your answers by differentiation.)

1. $\displaystyle\int (4x+3)^{-3}\,dx; \quad u = 4x+3$

2. $\displaystyle\int x\sqrt{1+x^2}\,dx; \quad u = 1+x^2$

3. $\displaystyle\int e^{\sin x}\cos x\,dx; \quad u = \sin x$

4. $\displaystyle\int \frac{(\ln x)^3}{x}\,dx; \quad u = \ln x$

5. $\displaystyle\int \frac{\arctan x}{1+x^2}\,dx; \quad u = \arctan x$

6. $\displaystyle\int \frac{\sin(\sqrt{x})}{\sqrt{x}}\,dx; \quad u = \sqrt{x}$

7. $\displaystyle\int \frac{e^{1/x}}{x^2}\,dx; \quad u = 1/x$

8. $\displaystyle\int x^3\sqrt{9-x^2}\,dx; \quad u = 9-x^2$

9. $\displaystyle\int \frac{e^x}{1+e^{2x}}\,dx; \quad u = e^x$

10. $\displaystyle\int \frac{x}{1+x}\,dx; \quad u = 1+x$

In Exercises 11–14, first find real numbers a and b so that equality holds; then evaluate the definite integral.

11. $\displaystyle\int_{-2}^{1} \frac{x}{1+x^4}\,dx = \frac{1}{2}\int_a^b \frac{1}{1+u^2}\,du$

12. $\displaystyle\int_{-\sqrt{\pi/2}}^{\sqrt{\pi}} x\cos(3x^2)\,dx = \frac{1}{6}\int_a^b \cos u\,du$

13. $\displaystyle\int_0^3 \frac{x}{(2x^2+1)^3}\,dx = \frac{1}{4}\int_a^b u^{-3}\,du$

14. $\displaystyle\int_1^2 x^2 e^{x^3/4}\,dx = \frac{4}{3}\int_a^b e^u\,du$

FURTHER EXERCISES

15. Example 9 says that $\displaystyle\int \frac{x}{1+x^4}\,dx = \frac{1}{2}\arctan(x^2) + C$. Verify this by differentiation.

16. Example 12 says that $\displaystyle\int \frac{x}{\sqrt{2x+3}}\,dx = \frac{(2x+3)^{3/2}}{6} - \frac{3\sqrt{2x+3}}{2} + C$. Verify this by differentiation.

17. Use the substitution $u = 1+\sqrt{x}$ to find the antiderivative $\displaystyle\int \frac{dx}{1+\sqrt{x}}$.

18. Let $a > 0$ be a constant. Derive the antiderivative formula $\displaystyle\int \frac{dx}{\sqrt{a^2-x^2}} = \arcsin(x/a) + C$ from the antiderivative formula $\displaystyle\int \frac{dx}{\sqrt{1-x^2}} = \arcsin x + C$.

19. Let a and $b > 0$ be constants. Use the substitution $u = a + b/x$ to find the antiderivative $\displaystyle\int \frac{dx}{ax^2 + bx}$.

20. Show that $\displaystyle\int \frac{dx}{1 + e^x} = x - \ln(1 + e^x) + C$.

[HINT: $\displaystyle\frac{1}{u(1+u)} = \frac{1}{u} - \frac{1}{1+u}$.]

21. Suppose that $\displaystyle\int_0^{12} g(x)\,dx = \pi$. Evaluate $\displaystyle\int_0^4 g(3x)\,dx$.

22. Let $I = \displaystyle\int \sec^2 x \tan x \, dx$.

   (a) Use the substitution $u = \sec x$ to show that $I = \frac{1}{2} \sec^2 x + C$.

   (b) Use the substitution $u = \tan x$ to show that $I = \frac{1}{2} \tan^2 x + C$.

   (c) The expressions for I in parts (a) and (b) look different, but both are correct. Explain this apparent paradox.

In Exercises 23–68, evaluate the antiderivative. (Check your answers by differentiation.)

23. $\displaystyle\int \cos(2x + 3)\,dx$

24. $\displaystyle\int \sin(2 - 3x)\,dx$

25. $\displaystyle\int (3x - 2)^4 \, dx$

26. $\displaystyle\int x \cos(1 - x^2)\,dx$

27. $\displaystyle\int \frac{2x^3}{1 + x^4}\,dx$

28. $\displaystyle\int x(3x + 2)^4 \, dx$

29. $\displaystyle\int \frac{dx}{1 - 2x}$

30. $\displaystyle\int \sqrt{3x - 2}\,dx$

31. $\displaystyle\int x\sqrt{3 - 2x}\,dx$

32. $\displaystyle\int \frac{\ln x}{x}\,dx$

33. $\displaystyle\int \frac{\sqrt{1 + 1/x}}{x^2}\,dx$

34. $\displaystyle\int x e^{x^2}\,dx$

35. $\displaystyle\int x^3(x^4 - 1)^2\,dx$

36. $\displaystyle\int \frac{x^3}{1 + x^2}\,dx$

37. $\displaystyle\int \frac{x^2}{1 + x^6}\,dx$

38. $\displaystyle\int \frac{x}{\sqrt{1 - x^4}}\,dx$

39. $\displaystyle\int x^2\sqrt{4x^3 + 5}\,dx$

40. $\displaystyle\int \frac{x}{\sqrt{1 + x^2}}\,dx$

41. $\displaystyle\int \frac{x + 4}{x^2 + 1}\,dx$

42. $\displaystyle\int x(1 - x^2)^{15}\,dx$

43. $\displaystyle\int \frac{2x + 3}{(x^2 + 3x + 5)^4}\,dx$

44. $\displaystyle\int (x + 2)(x^2 + 4x + 5)^6\,dx$

45. $\displaystyle\int \frac{x + 1}{\sqrt[3]{3x^2 + 6x + 5}}\,dx$

46. $\displaystyle\int \frac{e^{2x}}{(1 + e^{2x})^3}\,dx$

47. $\displaystyle\int \frac{e^x}{(2e^x + 3)^2}\,dx$

48. $\displaystyle\int \frac{e^{\sqrt{x}}}{\sqrt{x}}\,dx$

49. $\displaystyle\int \frac{2x + 3}{(x + 1)^2}\,dx$

50. $\displaystyle\int \frac{x^2}{x - 3}\,dx$

51. $\displaystyle\int \tan x \, dx$

52. $\displaystyle\int \sec x \tan x \, dx$

53. $\displaystyle\int \frac{\arcsin x}{\sqrt{1 - x^2}}\,dx$

54. $\displaystyle\int \sec x \tan x \sqrt{1 + \sec x}\,dx$

55. $\displaystyle\int \frac{5x}{3x^2 + 4}\,dx$

56. $\displaystyle\int \frac{\cos x}{1 + \sin^2 x}\,dx$

57. $\displaystyle\int \frac{\sec^2 x}{\sqrt{1 - \tan^2 x}}\,dx$

58. $\displaystyle\int \tan^2 x \csc x \, dx$

59. $\displaystyle\int x \tan(x^2)\,dx$

60. $\displaystyle\int x^2 \sec^2(x^3)\,dx$

61. $\displaystyle\int \frac{\cos x}{\sin^4 x}\,dx$

62. $\displaystyle\int x^4 \sqrt[3]{x^5 + 6}\,dx$

63. $\displaystyle\int \frac{(1 + \sqrt{x})^3}{\sqrt{x}}\,dx$

64. $\displaystyle\int \frac{dx}{\sqrt{x}\,\left(\sqrt{x}+2\right)^3}$

65. $\displaystyle\int x^3\sqrt{x^2+2}\,dx$

66. $\displaystyle\int \sqrt{1+\sqrt{x}}\,dx$

67. $\displaystyle\int \frac{e^x}{e^{2x}+2e^x+1}\,dx$

68. $\displaystyle\int \frac{e^{\tan x}}{1-\sin^2 x}\,dx$

In Exercises 69–74, evaluate the definite integral.

69. $\displaystyle\int_0^2 \frac{x}{\left(1+x^2\right)^3}\,dx$

70. $\displaystyle\int_{-19}^8 \sqrt[3]{8-x}\,dx$

71. $\displaystyle\int_1^e \frac{\sin\left(\ln x\right)}{x}\,dx$

72. $\displaystyle\int_e^{4e} \frac{dx}{x\sqrt{\ln x}}$

73. $\displaystyle\int_0^\pi \sin^3 x \cos x\,dx$

74. $\displaystyle\int_{-\pi/2}^\pi e^{\cos x}\sin x\,dx$

75. Suppose that the function f is continuous on the interval $[-1, 1]$. Use the substitution $u = \pi - x$ to show that

$$\int_0^\pi x f(\sin x)\,dx = \frac{\pi}{2}\int_0^\pi f(\sin x)\,dx.$$

The substitution $u^n = ax + b$ can sometimes be used to find antiderivatives of expressions involving the form $\sqrt[n]{ax+b}$. Use this substitution to evaluate the antiderivatives in Exercises 76 and 77.

76. $\displaystyle\int x\sqrt{2x+1}\,dx$

77. $\displaystyle\int \frac{dx}{\sqrt{x}+\sqrt[3]{x}}$

5.5 INTEGRAL AIDS: TABLES AND COMPUTERS

With tables and calculators, students can find many symbolic integrals. This section is about using such tools effectively and (sometimes) skeptically.

In Section 5.4 we found various symbolic antiderivatives by the method of substitution. The method worked well in the examples given, but honesty compels a tiny authorial admission: we *chose* examples for which substitution works well. For many functions—even some that look quite simple—the search for symbolic antiderivatives can be difficult, tricky, and laborious. In practice, calculus users freely resort to integral tables, computer software, roommates, or any other aids that come to hand.

Like all power tools, tables and mathematical software require careful handling. In this section, we illustrate some of their possibilities and pitfalls.

Integral tables

"Antiderivative table" would be a better name.

We added the absolute value signs.

Standard scientific reference works contain extensive integral tables. ← The *CRC Handbook of Chemistry and Physics*, 48th edition, for instance, lists nearly 600 different antiderivative formulas on more than 40 pages. (The CRC tables are relatively modest—other books contain hundreds of pages of integral formulas.) One of them reads as follows: ←

Notice the formal parameters; students may need some symbol sense to interpret them. Answers may also be reported in various symbolic forms.

> **FACT (Formula 403 from the *CRC Handbook*)**
> $$\int \frac{dx}{a+be^{px}} = \frac{x}{a} - \frac{1}{ap}\ln\left|a+be^{px}\right|$$

Notice the lack of a constant of integration on the right side; supplying one every time would be typographically tiresome.

Parameters and pattern matching Integral tables use **parameters**—letters other than the variable of integration—to stand for numerical constants that can vary from problem to problem. With this device, a single integral formula can solve an entire family of similar problems. The next few examples concern the parameters in the preceding formula.

EXAMPLE 1 Verify Formula 403 by differentiation.

Solution We differentiate the right side with respect to x; all other letters are constants. Try to follow the steps:

$$\left(\frac{x}{a} - \frac{1}{ap} \ln |a + be^{px}| \right)' = \frac{1}{a} - \frac{1}{ap} \frac{bpe^{px}}{a + be^{px}}$$

$$= \frac{1}{a} - \frac{1}{a} \frac{be^{px} + a - a}{a + be^{px}}$$

$$= \frac{1}{a} - \frac{1}{a} \left(1 - \frac{a}{a + be^{px}} \right)$$

$$= \frac{1}{a + be^{px}}.$$

That's the result we wanted; the *CRC Handbook* got it right. ■

Getting it right. Not every equation in published integral tables is correct. Integral tables change over time as new antiderivative formulas come into favor and old ones fall into disuse. With each new version of an integral table, new typographical errors may creep in; some errors have lain undiscovered for years.

Standard integral tables are sometimes used as benchmarks to check mathematical software programs for accuracy. This process sometimes uncovers errors — not in the software but in the tables. Some integral tables have been found to have error rates in the double-digit percentage range.

EXAMPLE 2 Use Formula 403 to find $\displaystyle\int \frac{5}{3 - 2e^{-x}} \, dx$.

Solution Writing

$$\int \frac{5}{3 - 2e^{-x}} \, dx = 5 \int \frac{dx}{3 - 2e^{-x}}$$

makes the parameter values in the formula directly apparent: $a = 3, b = -2, p = -1.$ ➡ *Don't forget the 5 out front.* The result is

$$\int \frac{5}{3 - 2e^{-x}} \, dx = 5 \left(\frac{x}{3} + \frac{1}{3} \ln |3 - 2e^{-x}| \right) + C.$$

■

Making the shoe fit Antiderivatives that don't appear to fit an integral template can sometimes be *made* to do so. A u-substitution, some symbolic algebra, or a combination of both often effects this Cinderella-like transformation. (Sometimes, the shoe just *won't* fit.)

EXAMPLE 3 Find $\displaystyle I = \int \frac{\cos x}{5 + 2e^{3 \sin x}} \, dx$.

Solution As it stands the integral resembles Formula 403 only vaguely. But substituting $u = \sin x$ and $du = \cos x \, dx$ reveals the familiar pattern:

$$\int \frac{\cos x}{5 + 2e^{3 \sin x}} \, dx = \int \frac{du}{5 + 2e^{3u}} \, .$$

Setting $a = 5$, $b = 2$, and $p = 3$ completes the problem:

$$I = \frac{u}{5} - \frac{\ln|5 + 2e^{3u}|}{15} + C = \frac{\sin x}{5} - \frac{\ln|5 + 2e^{3\sin x}|}{15} + C.$$

■

EXAMPLE 4 Find $I = \int \dfrac{e^x}{3e^{-x} + 2e^x}\, dx$.

Solution A touch of exponential algebra (multiplying top and bottom by e^{-x}) puts the integrand into the necessary form:

$$\frac{e^x}{3e^{-x} + 2e^x} = \frac{e^x e^{-x}}{e^{-x}(3e^{-x} + 2e^x)} = \frac{1}{2 + 3e^{-2x}}.$$

Now we can use Formula 403, with $a = 2$, $b = 3$, $p = -2$:

$$I = \int \frac{dx}{2 + 3e^{-2x}} = \frac{x}{2} + \frac{1}{4}\ln|2 + 3e^{-2x}| + C.$$

■

Handling quadratics: completing the square Quadratic expressions (of the form $ax^2 + bx + c$) appear often in antiderivative problems. Completing the square sometimes helps shoehorn such integrands into an integral table's template. ◄ We illustrate with two examples.

See Appendix D for reminders on completing the square.

Completing the square is simple, powerful, and revealing of structure. All students should know it well.

EXAMPLE 5 Find $I = \int \dfrac{dx}{x^2 + 4x + 5}$.

Solution Rummaging through an integral table (such as the one at the end of this book) turns up two likely candidates:

$$\int \frac{dx}{x^2 + a^2} = \frac{1}{a}\arctan\left(\frac{x}{a}\right) + C; \qquad \int \frac{dx}{x^2 - a^2} = \frac{1}{2a}\ln\left|\frac{x - a}{x + a}\right| + C.$$

Which formula, if either, applies? To decide we'll complete the square in the denominator:

$$x^2 + 4x + 5 = (x^2 + 4x + 4) + (5 - 4) = (x + 2)^2 + 1.$$

This, in turn, suggests the substitution $u = x + 2$, $du = dx$. Here's the result:

$$\int \frac{dx}{x^2 + 4x + 5} = \int \frac{du}{u^2 + 1} = \arctan u + C = \arctan(x + 2) + C.$$

■

EXAMPLE 6 Find $I = \int \dfrac{dx}{x^2 + 4x + 3}$.

Solution The same two possibilities suggest themselves as in Example 5. Again we complete the square:

$$x^2 + 4x + 3 = (x^2 + 4x + 4) + (3 - 4) = (x + 2)^2 - 1.$$

The rest follows easily. Substitution of $u = x + 2$ and $du = dx$ gives

$$\int \frac{dx}{x^2 + 4x + 3} = \int \frac{du}{u^2 - 1} = \frac{1}{2}\ln\left|\frac{u - 1}{u + 1}\right| + C = \frac{1}{2}\ln\left|\frac{x + 1}{x + 3}\right| + C.$$

■

Students with convenient technology can and should do this for themselves.

A graphical reality check

Results obtained by one method should sometimes be tested by another. Symbolic antiderivatives especially deserve such attention. Functions, after all, are more than purely formal expressions; they're graphical and numerical objects as well. If symbolic operations really make sense, they should stand up to graphical scrutiny. In other words, symbolically produced antiderivatives should "look right." Now and then, we'll check to make sure that they do.

Examples 5 and 6 invite such a look. Their symbolic results,

$$\int \frac{dx}{x^2+4x+5} = \arctan(x+2); \qquad \int \frac{dx}{x^2+4x+3} = \frac{1}{2}\ln\left|\frac{x+1}{x+3}\right|,$$

are a bit mysterious. Although the integrands are almost identical, the antiderivatives look surprisingly different. Could there be some mistake?

Similar-looking integrands produce very different-looking antiderivatives. Completing the square helps resolve the mystery.

Let's approach this graphically. Figure 1 shows graphs of the two integrands.

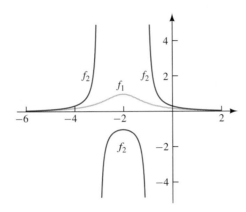

FIGURE 1

$$f_1(x) = \frac{1}{x^2+4x+5} \text{ and } f_2(x) = \frac{1}{x^2+4x+3}$$

Now the mystery begins to dissolve. Despite their typographical similarity, the two integrands are quite different: f_1 behaves tamely, while f_2 has vertical asymptotes at $x = -3$ and $x = -1$. As $x \to \pm\infty$, on the other hand, both f_1 and f_2 tend to zero.

Plots of the antiderivatives F_1 and F_2 (Figure 2) show that they, too, behave as they should.

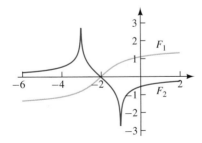

FIGURE 2

$$F_1(x) = \arctan(x+2) \text{ and } F_2(x) = 0.5\ln\left|\frac{x+1}{x+3}\right|$$

Notice these features of the graphs:

- **Asymptotes** Both f_1 and its antiderivative F_1 are tamely behaved. By contrast, f_2 and its antiderivative F_2 have vertical asymptotes at $x = -3$ and $x = -1$.

- **Long-run behavior** Both antiderivatives F_1 and F_2 appear to tend toward the horizontal as $x \to \pm\infty$. This is to be expected because the respective derivatives f_1 and f_2 both tend to zero in the long run.

The integral table in this book contains several reduction formulas. We'll explain some of them later using integration by parts.

Reduction formulas: one antiderivative in terms of another Some formulas in integral tables have antiderivatives on *both* sides of an equation. Here's another entry from the *CRC Handbook*:

FACT (Formula 311) If $n \neq 1$, then

$$\int \tan^n x \, dx = \frac{\tan^{n-1} x}{n-1} - \int \tan^{n-2} x \, dx.$$

Applying such a **reduction formula** (perhaps repeatedly) transforms one integral problem into another, the second simpler than the first.

EXAMPLE 7 Find $\int \tan^4 x \, dx$.

Solution Formula 311, with $n = 4$, says that

$$\int \tan^4 x \, dx = \frac{\tan^3 x}{3} - \int \tan^2 x \, dx.$$

The last integral may itself appear in an integral table. If so, we're finished. If not, we can apply Formula 311 *again* (this time with $n = 2$).

$$\int \tan^2 x \, dx = \frac{\tan x}{1} - \int \tan^0 x \, dx = \tan x - x.$$

Combining the results we obtain

$$\int \tan^4 x \, dx = \frac{\tan^3 x}{3} - \tan x + x + C.$$

■

Antidifferentiation by machine

Old mathematical handbooks contain vast tables of trigonometric, exponential, and logarithmic function values. Scientific calculators make such tables obsolete. To a lesser (but significant) degree, sophisticated mathematical software effectively replaces integral tables. *Maple, Mathematica*, the TI–89, and other computing tools now "know" not just integral formulas but—much more challenging—how and when to apply them.

On the other hand, some programs have clever ways of checking equality of different-looking expressions.

Symbolic camouflage Equivalent mathematical expressions can appear in radically different symbolic forms. Trigonometric expressions are especially tricky; the many "trigonometric identities" offer almost unlimited possibilities for disguise.

Computer symbolic operations often produce variant or unexpected forms of symbolic results. (What's convenient for a computer may be baffling to you and me—and vice versa.)

EXAMPLE 8   According to one integral table,

$$\int \sin^2 x \, dx = \frac{x}{2} - \frac{\sin(2x)}{4}.$$

Mathematica agrees, but here's what *Maple* says:

```
> int( sin(x)^2, x );
```

$$- 1/2 \cos(x) \sin(x) + 1/2 \, x$$

Who's right?

Solution   For once, *everybody* is right (we'll forgive everyone the omitted constant of integration). This time, the reason is simple (sometimes it's harder). Stirring the trigonometric identity $\sin(2x) = 2\sin x \cos x$ into the first formula readily produces *Maple*'s answer. (See for yourself.)   ■

When nothing works

Sometimes nothing seems to work. Symbolic methods, integral tables, algebraic tricks, and software may *all* fail to find an antiderivative in elementary form. Two reasons are possible: Either we haven't (or a computer hasn't) searched cleverly enough, or there *is* no elementary antiderivative. Some elementary functions, even simple ones, don't *have* antiderivatives with elementary formulas. None of the following functions does, for instance:

$$e^{x^2}, \qquad \sin(x^2), \qquad \frac{\sin x}{x}, \qquad \frac{x}{\ln x}.$$

Like all continuous functions, these do have antiderivatives, but not elementary ones.

The bright side   Even when symbolic methods fail, all is not lost. Numerical methods, such as those we'll study in the next chapter, often succeed. For example, numerical methods will nicely handle *definite* integrals of all the preceding "problematic" functions.

BASIC EXERCISES

Evaluate the antiderivatives in Exercises 1–10 using basic antiderivative formulas and the table of integrals in the back of the book.

1. $\int \dfrac{dx}{3 + 2e^{5x}}$

2. $\int \dfrac{dx}{x(2x+3)}$

3. $\int \dfrac{dx}{x^2(3-x)}$

4. $\int x^2 \ln x \, dx$

5. $\int \dfrac{dx}{x\sqrt{2x+1}}$

6. $\int x \sin(2x) \, dx$

7. $\int e^{2x} \cos(3x) \, dx$

8. $\int \dfrac{dx}{4 - x^2}$

9. $\int \dfrac{dx}{x\sqrt{3x-2}}$

10. $\int \dfrac{dx}{4x^2 - 1}$

FURTHER EXERCISES

Evaluate the antiderivatives in Exercises 11–40 using a table of integrals or a software package. Making simple u-substitutions or completing the square first may help.

11. $\int \dfrac{x^2}{1+x^2} \, dx$ [HINT: $\dfrac{x^2}{1+x^2} = 1 - \dfrac{1}{1+x^2}$.]

12. $\int \dfrac{4x^2 + 3x + 2}{x+1} \, dx$ [HINT: $\dfrac{4x^2 + 3x + 2}{x+1} = 4x - 1 + \dfrac{3}{x+1}$.]

13. $\int \dfrac{x-1}{x+1} \, dx$ [HINT: $x - 1 = (x+1) - 2$.]

14. $\int \dfrac{dx}{\sqrt{x-1}+\sqrt{x+1}}$
[HINT: $\left(\sqrt{x-1}+\sqrt{x+1}\right)\left(\sqrt{x-1}-\sqrt{x+1}\right)=-2.$]

15. $\int \dfrac{dx}{1+\sin x}$
[HINT: $(1+\sin x)(1-\sin x)=1-\sin^2 x=\cos^2 x.$]

16. $\int \tan^4(2x)\,dx$

17. $\int \dfrac{dx}{1+9x^2}$

18. $\int \dfrac{dx}{9+x^2}$

19. $\int \tan^3(5x)\,dx$

20. $\int x^2 e^{3x}\,dx$

21. $\int \dfrac{2x+3}{4x+5}\,dx$

22. $\int x^2\sqrt{1-3x}\,dx$

23. $\int \dfrac{4x+5}{(2x+3)^2}\,dx$

24. $\int \dfrac{dx}{(4x^2-9)^2}$

25. $\int \dfrac{x+2}{2+x^2}\,dx$

26. $\int \dfrac{3}{\sqrt{6x+x^2}}\,dx$

27. $\int \dfrac{5}{4x^2+20x+16}\,dx$

28. $\int \dfrac{dx}{\sqrt{x^2+2x+26}}$

29. $\int x^3\cos(x^2)\,dx$

30. $\int \dfrac{x}{\sqrt{x^2+4x+3}}\,dx$

31. $\int \dfrac{dx}{(x^2+3x+2)^2}$

32. $\int x^2(\cos x+3\sin x)\,dx$

33. $\int \dfrac{e^x}{e^{2x}-2e^x+5}\,dx$

34. $\int \cos x \sin x \sin^2(2\cos^2 x+1)\,dx$

35. $\int \sqrt{x^2+4x+1}\,dx$

36. $\int \dfrac{\cos x}{3\sin^2 x-11\sin x-4}\,dx$

37. $\int \dfrac{\cos x \sin x}{(\cos x-4)(3\cos x+1)}\,dx$

38. $\int \dfrac{e^{2x}}{\sqrt{e^{2x}-e^x+1}}\,dx$

39. $\int x\sin(3x+4)\,dx$

40. $\int x^3 e^{-x^2}\,dx$

5.6 APPROXIMATING SUMS: THE INTEGRAL AS A LIMIT

We first defined the integral geometrically, in terms of area. Now we define it analytically, as a limit. We treated derivatives in a similar manner. We mention, but downplay, abstract questions of integrability.

The integral $\int_a^b f$, as defined so far, is the signed area of the region bounded by the graph of f from $x=a$ to $x=b$. In Section 5.3 we saw, thanks to the FTC, that we can readily calculate any integral for which we can find an antiderivative. Sections 5.4 and 5.5 introduced some basic techniques for finding antiderivatives; we'll see more techniques in Chapter 8.

Integration and antidifferentiation are close cousins, but they are *not* the same thing. Many integrals (even simple-looking ones such as $\int_0^1 \sin(x^2)\,dx$), cannot be found using antidifferentiation because no convenient antiderivative formula exists. For such integrals we need another strategy.

For the rest of this chapter we take a different approach to the integral, defining it formally as a certain limit of "approximating sums." The limit-based definition offers new and useful perspectives on the integral and what it means. It also lends itself well—better than the FTC—to the problem of estimating integrals numerically.

This section closely mirrors Section 2.1, where we defined the derivative as a limit. There, as here, the general problem was to translate an intuitively reasonable geometric idea (the slope of a tangent line for derivatives; the area under a graph for integrals) into precise analytic language. The idea of limit is crucial for both the derivative and the integral—it links approximations to exact values.

Approximating sums

The definition of integral as a limit involves some formidable-looking terminology and notation. The underlying ideas, on the other hand, are natural and straightforward, especially when understood graphically. We'll approach the definition via a leisurely example, introducing terms and ideas as we go.

EXAMPLE 1   Figure 1 shows part of the graph of $f(x) = x^3 - 3x^2 + 8$; the shaded area represents the integral $\int_{0.5}^{3.5} f(x)\,dx$. Use the FTC to evaluate the integral *exactly*. Then use approximating sums (we explain them below) to *estimate* the same integral.

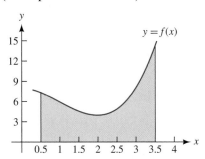

FIGURE 1
What's the area?

Solution   An exact answer is easy to find by antidifferentiation: ➡   *Check the (easy) steps.*

$$\int_{0.5}^{3.5} (x^3 - 3x^2 + 8)\,dx = \left(\frac{x^4}{4} - x^3 + 8x\right)\Bigg]_{0.5}^{3.5} = \frac{75}{4} = 18.75.$$

But suppose we hadn't known the FTC or couldn't find an antiderivative? How might we *estimate* the area in question? Figure 2 suggests four reasonable strategies.

Trapezoid sums seem especially natural to students (but they're not Riemann sums in the strict sense).

(a) Left sum, 10 subdivisions

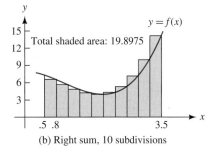

(b) Right sum, 10 subdivisions

(c) Midpoint sum, 10 subdivisions

(d) Trapezoid sum, 6 subdivisions

FIGURE 2
Four summing strategies

Which estimate looks *best to you? Which one* is *best?*

We discuss and illustrate sigma notation in some detail in the next section. Here, we emphasize the main idea more than the formalism of approximating sums. Students should work through a few very simple examples for themselves, perhaps by hand.

In each case we approximated the desired area with a sum of simpler areas, either rectangles or trapezoids; their vertical heights are determined by values of the integrand function, as shown. (We used only six trapezoids to show more clearly the difference between the integral and the trapezoid estimate.) Adding up the areas of these simpler figures gives, in each case, a natural estimate to the desired area. ◄ ■

Calculating the approximations   How, exactly, did we calculate the preceding area estimates? A close look at each picture gives the answer.

Consider first the **left approximating sum with ten subdivisions** (Figure 2(a)), which we'll denote by L_{10}. There are ten shaded rectangles, each with base 0.3 (that is, $(3.5 - 0.5)/10$). The height of each rectangle is the value of the function f at the *left* edge of the base subdivision (hence the name "left sum"). The second rectangle, for example, has the x-interval $[0.8, 1.1]$ for its base; its height is $f(0.8)$ (the value of f at the *left* endpoint). Because $f(x) = x^3 - 3x^2 + 8$, $f(0.8) = 6.592$. Therefore, for the second rectangle,

$$\text{Area} = 0.3 \cdot 6.592 = 1.9776.$$

The *total* area of all ten left rectangles is the sum

$$L_{10} = f(0.5) \cdot 0.3 + f(0.8) \cdot 0.3 + f(1.1) \cdot 0.3 + \cdots + f(3.2) \cdot 0.3$$
$$= 7.375 \cdot 0.3 + 6.592 \cdot 0.3 + 5.701 \cdot 0.3 + \cdots + 7.159 \cdot 0.3 + 10.048 \cdot 0.3 = 17.8725.$$

Think this sentence through carefully. Do you see how the picture says the same thing?

The **right approximating sum with ten subdivisions** (in Figure 2(b)), denoted by R_{10}, differs only slightly from L_{10}—this time, the height of each rectangle is the value of f at the *right* endpoint of the base interval. ◄ Hence, the total area of all ten "right" rectangles is the sum

$$R_{10} = f(0.8) \cdot 0.3 + f(1.1) \cdot 0.3 + f(1.4) \cdot 0.3 + \cdots + f(3.5) \cdot 0.3$$
$$= 6.592 \cdot 0.3 + 5.701 \cdot 0.3 + \cdots + 10.048 \cdot 0.3 + 14.125 \cdot 0.3 = 19.8975.$$

For M_{10}, the **midpoint approximating sum with ten subdivisions** (see Figure 2(c)), heights are evaluated at the *midpoint* of each subinterval. Therefore,

$$M_{10} = f(0.65) \cdot 0.3 + f(0.95) \cdot 0.3 + f(1.25) \cdot 0.3 + \cdots + f(3.35) \cdot 0.3$$
$$= 7.007 \cdot 0.3 + 6.150 \cdot 0.3 + 5.266 \cdot 0.3 + \cdots + 11.928 \cdot 0.3 = 18.6825.$$

Make a sketch to see why.

Figure 2(d) shows a **trapezoid approximating sum**, denoted by T_n. Calculating T_n is no harder than calculating L_n and R_n, thanks to a key idea: The area of each trapezoid in an approximating sum is the *average* of the left- and right-rule rectangles on the same subinterval. ◄ The same averaging applies to T_n itself: For any n, $T_n = (L_n + R_n)/2$. In the case at hand,

$$T_6 = \frac{L_6 + R_6}{2} = \frac{17.4375 + 20.8125}{2} = 19.125.$$

Getting better all the time   As the two left-rule pictures in Figure 3 (which still pertain to $\int_{0.5}^{3.5} f(x)\,dx$) suggest, we'd expect approximating sums (of any type) to approximate an integral more closely as the number of subdivisions increases.

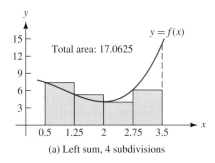
(a) Left sum, 4 subdivisions

(b) Left sum, 20 subdivisions

FIGURE 3
Two left sums

Neither approximation looks perfect, but the error committed by L_{20} appears much less than that committed by L_4. Numerical values of various sums (all computed by machine, of course) give the same message:

With even modest technology students can easily compute numbers like those in the table. We discuss errors and their estimation in Chapter 6, but students can see now that the midpoint rule appears to be most accurate.

Approximating sums for the integral $\int_{0.5}^{3.5} f(x)\,dx$				
n	L_n	R_n	M_n	T_n
2	17.0625	27.1875	17.0625	22.1250
4	17.0625	22.1250	18.3281	19.5938
8	17.6953	20.2266	18.6445	18.9609
16	18.1699	19.4355	18.7236	18.8027
32	18.4468	19.0796	18.7434	18.7632
64	18.5951	18.9115	18.7484	18.7533
128	18.6717	18.8299	18.7496	18.7508
256	18.7107	18.7898	18.7499	18.7502

As n increases (down the columns), all four types of sums approach 18.75, the answer we found earlier by antidifferentiation.

Riemann sums and the limit definition Left, right, and midpoint approximating sums are all examples of **Riemann sums**. ➤ Riemann's idea of an approximating sum is quite general. He allows rectangles with unequal bases, and their heights can be determined anywhere— even randomly—within their respective subintervals. Roughly speaking, any "rectangular" approximating sum is a Riemann sum. Figure 4 shows an "irregular" Riemann sum for our by-now-familiar integral.

Named for the German mathematician G. F. B. Riemann (1826–66), who gave the first modern definition of the integral.

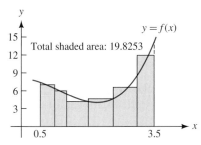
A Riemann sum, 6 (unequal) subdivisions

FIGURE 4
An irregular Riemann sum

We won't normally use such irregular sums, but the formal definition of Riemann sum (which allows for such sums) follows for the record. We'll need the following ingredients: a function f, an interval $[a, b]$, a **partition** of $[a, b]$, and a **sampling point** in each subinterval. Here is the recipe:

Students should calculate a few Riemann sums by hand — enough to get the idea.

> **DEFINITION** Let the interval $[a, b]$ be partitioned into n subintervals by any $n + 1$ points
>
> $$a = x_0 < x_1 < x_2 < \cdots < x_{n-1} < x_n = b,$$
>
> and let $\Delta x_i = x_i - x_{i-1}$ denote the width of the ith subinterval. Within each subinterval $[x_{i-1}, x_i]$, choose any **sampling point** c_i. The sum
>
> $$S_n = f(c_1)\Delta x_1 + f(c_2)\Delta x_2 + \cdots + f(c_n)\Delta x_n$$
>
> is a **Riemann sum with n subdivisions** for f on $[a, b]$.

Left, right, and midpoint sums (all shown in Figure 2) all fit this definition nicely. Each is built from a **regular partition** of $[a, b]$ (one with subintervals of *equal* length) and some simple, consistent scheme for choosing the sampling points c_i. *Trapezoid* approximating sums don't quite fit the definition, because the summands correspond to trapezoids, not rectangles. (Trapezoid sums still do a good job of approximating integrals, as we'll see.)

EXAMPLE 2 For the integral $I = \displaystyle\int_1^2 \frac{1}{x}\, dx$, find the Riemann sums L_4, R_4, and M_4. How well do they approximate the true value of I?

Solution To partition $[1, 2]$ into four subdivisions, each of length $\Delta x = 1/4$, we use

$$a = 1 < \frac{5}{4} < \frac{3}{2} < \frac{7}{4} < 2 = b.$$

Then

$$L_4 = \frac{f(1)}{4} + \frac{f(5/4)}{4} + \frac{f(3/2)}{4} + \frac{f(7/4)}{4} = \left(1 + \frac{4}{5} + \frac{2}{3} + \frac{4}{7}\right)\frac{1}{4} \approx 0.7595;$$

$$R_4 = \frac{f(5/4)}{4} + \frac{f(3/2)}{4} + \frac{f(7/4)}{4} + \frac{f(2)}{4} = \left(\frac{4}{5} + \frac{2}{3} + \frac{4}{7} + \frac{1}{2}\right)\frac{1}{4} \approx 0.6345.$$

Again the midpoint rule is much more accurate than either the left or the right rule. Students might try to understand this geometrically.

For L_4 and R_4 the sampling points in each subinterval were the left and right endpoints. For M_4 the sampling points are *midpoints* of the subintervals:

$$M_4 = \frac{f(9/8)}{4} + \frac{f(11/8)}{4} + \frac{f(13/8)}{4} + \frac{f(15/8)}{4} = \left(\frac{8}{9} + \frac{8}{11} + \frac{8}{13} + \frac{8}{15}\right)\frac{1}{4} \approx 0.6912.$$

Check for yourself by antidifferentiation.

For comparison, the exact value of I ◄ is $\ln 2 \approx 0.6931$. ∎

Sigma notation For economy and clarity, Riemann sums are usually written using **sigma (Σ) notation**. For the Riemann sum defined above, for instance, we could write

$$S_n = f(c_1)\Delta x_1 + f(c_2)\Delta x_2 + \cdots + f(c_n)\Delta x_n = \sum_{i=1}^{n} f(c_i)\, \Delta x_i.$$

The sum is taken as i, the **index variable**, ranges from 1 to n. (We'll say more about sigma notation in the next section; for the moment it's just a convenient shorthand.)

EXAMPLE 3 Find R_{10}, the right Riemann sum with ten subdivisions for the integral $I = \int_0^\pi \sin x \, dx$. (The exact value is 2.) How do R_{10} and R_{100} appear in sigma notation?

Solution A ten-member partition cuts the interval $[0, \pi]$ into ten equal subintervals. Since the interval has length π, each subinterval has width $\Delta x = \pi/10$, and the partition points are $0, \pi/10, 2\pi/10, \ldots, 9\pi/10, \pi$. Therefore, R_{10} has the form

$$R_{10} = \sin\left(\frac{\pi}{10}\right)\frac{\pi}{10} + \sin\left(\frac{2\pi}{10}\right)\frac{\pi}{10} + \cdots + \sin\left(\frac{9\pi}{10}\right)\frac{\pi}{10} + \sin(\pi)\frac{\pi}{10}.$$

To write the ten-member sum in sigma form, we set $c_i = i\pi/10$; observe that $\Delta x_i = \pi/10$ for all i (all subdivisions have the same width), and let i run from one to ten. This gives

$$R_{10} = \sum_{i=1}^{10} f(c_i)\,\Delta x_i = \sum_{i=1}^{10} \sin(i\pi/10)\frac{\pi}{10}.$$

For the right sum R_{100}, we have $c_1 = \pi/100$, $c_2 = 2\pi/100$, $\ldots$, $c_i = i\pi/100$, and $\Delta x = \pi/100$. In sigma form, this is

$$R_{100} = \sum_{i=1}^{100} f(c_i)\,\Delta x_i = \sum_{i=1}^{100} \sin(i\pi/100)\frac{\pi}{100}.$$

The sums R_{10} and R_{100} would be tedious to evaluate by hand, but a computer makes short work of both: $R_{10} \approx 1.9835$ and $R_{100} \approx 1.9998$. As we'd expect, R_{10} is close to the exact value, 2, and R_{100} is closer still. ∎

The integral defined Graphical intuition and numerical evidence ➔ suggest that, for the integral $I = \int_{0.5}^{3.5} f(x)\,dx$, all of the approximating sums—L_n, R_n, M_n, and T_n—approach the true value of I as n increases. The same holds for other integrals; the following limit-based definition makes these ideas precise:

See the table on page 351.

> **DEFINITION** Let a function $f(x)$ be defined on the interval $[a, b]$. The **integral** of f over $[a, b]$, denoted $\int_a^b f(x)\,dx$, is the number, if one exists, to which all Riemann sums S_n tend as n tends to infinity and as the widths of all subdivisions tend to zero. In symbols:
>
> $$\int_a^b f(x)\,dx = \lim_{n\to\infty} S_n = \lim_{n\to\infty} \sum_{i=1}^{n} f(c_i)\,\Delta x_i.$$

We're treating the question of "mesh"—the width of the widest subinterval—somewhat informally. For continuous functions it does no harm to assume that partitions are regular.

This important definition deserves some comment:

- **Must the limit exist?** In a word, no. A function for which the limit *does* exists is called **integrable** on $[a, b]$. In practice, being integrable on $[a, b]$ is "easy": almost every calculus-style function that's defined and bounded on $[a, b]$ is integrable. It isn't even really necessary that f be continuous on $[a, b]$—a few jumps or breaks in the f-graph are not fatal to the integral. The surprise, if any, is the difficulty of finding a *nonintegrable* function. ➔

- **Well-behaved functions** The limit in the definition, taken at face value, is a slippery customer. The ramifications of permitting arbitrary partitions and sampling points, for example, can be tricky. Luckily, the matter is much simpler for the well-behaved functions usually met in calculus courses. For such functions, almost any respectable sort of approximating sum does what we'd expect—approaches the true value of the integral as n tends to infinity.

Here's one: $f(x) = 1$ if x is rational; $f(x) = 0$ if x is irrational.

- **What's dx?**   The limit definition helps explain the somewhat mysterious dx in the notation $\int_a^b f(x)\,dx$. Consider, for example, a right approximating sum with n equal subdivisions, each of length Δx. Then, by definition,

$$\int_a^b f(x)\,dx = \lim_{n \to \infty} \sum_{i=1}^{n} f(x_i)\,\Delta x.$$

We've seen this before:
$dy/dx = \lim\limits_{\Delta x \to 0} \Delta y / \Delta x.$

Now the left side looks a lot like the right; the dx on the left (sometimes called a **differential**) corresponds naturally to the Δx (a finite difference) on the right. ← (The differential dx is sometimes described as an "infinitesimal" analogue of the finite difference Δx.)

Part of the point is that all four types of sums shown converge to the same limit.

EXAMPLE 4   The following table shows several approximating sums (rounded to 4 decimals) for the integral $I = \int_0^1 \sin(x^2)\,dx$. Can we guess a value for I? Can we tell I *exactly*?

n	L_n	R_n	T_n	M_n
8	0.2591	0.3643	0.3117	0.3096
16	0.2843	0.3369	0.3106	0.3101
32	0.2972	0.3235	0.3104	0.3102
64	0.3037	0.3169	0.3103	0.3103

We'll see in Chapter 6 how to approximate the true value to any desired accuracy.

Solution   The numbers don't identify a single obvious value for I, but something in the vicinity of 0.31 looks plausible. As we said above, $\sin(x^2)$ has no elementary antiderivative formula, and so the FTC can't help us find an exact value for I. ∎

Using the definition   The definition of $\int_a^b f(x)\,dx$ as a limit of approximating sums helps explain what an integral is and why certain sums give good approximations to integrals. But we'll seldom use the definition itself to *calculate* integrals exactly. ← Instead, we'll rely on antiderivatives when we can find them and settle for approximations when we can't.

But we will use the definition directly in examples in the next section.

B A S I C   E X E R C I S E S

In Exercises 1–6, g is the function graphed below.

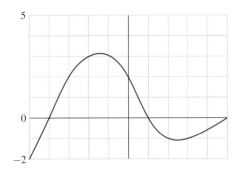

1. **(a)** Estimate the value of $\int_{-5}^{5} g(x)\,dx$ by evaluating a left sum with five equal subintervals.
   (b) Draw a sketch that illustrates the sum you computed in part (a).

2. **(a)** Estimate the value of $\int_{-5}^{5} g(x)\,dx$ by evaluating a right sum with five equal subintervals.
   (b) Draw a sketch that illustrates the sum you computed in part (a).

3. **(a)** Estimate the value of $\int_{-5}^{5} g(x)\,dx$ by evaluating a midpoint sum with five equal subintervals.
   (b) Draw a sketch that illustrates the sum you computed in part (a).

4. **(a)** Estimate the value of $\int_{-5}^{5} g(x)\,dx$ by evaluating a trapezoid sum with five equal subintervals.
   (b) Draw a sketch that illustrates the sum you computed in part (a).

5. **(a)** Estimate the value of $\int_{-1}^{4} g(x)\,dx$ by evaluating a left sum with five equal subintervals.

(b) Draw a sketch that illustrates the sum you computed in part (a).

6. (a) Estimate the value of $\int_{-3}^{2} g(x)\,dx$ by evaluating a right sum with five equal subintervals.

(b) Draw a sketch that illustrates the sum you computed in part (a).

In Exercises 7–14, f is the function graphed below.

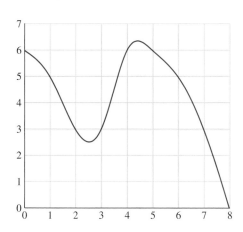

7. Estimate the value of $\int_{1}^{7} f(x)\,dx$ using a right sum with three equal subintervals.

8. Estimate the value of $\int_{1}^{7} f(x)\,dx$ using a left sum with three equal subintervals.

9. Estimate the value of $\int_{1}^{7} f(x)\,dx$ using a midpoint sum with three equal subintervals.

10. Estimate the value of $\int_{1}^{7} f(x)\,dx$ using a trapezoid sum with three equal subintervals.

11. Estimate the value of $\int_{0}^{8} f(x)\,dx$ using a right sum with four equal subintervals.

12. Estimate the value of $\int_{0}^{8} f(x)\,dx$ using a left sum with four equal subintervals.

13. Estimate the value of $\int_{0}^{8} f(x)\,dx$ using a midpoint sum with four equal subintervals.

14. Estimate the value of $\int_{0}^{8} f(x)\,dx$ using a trapezoid sum with four equal subintervals.

In Exercises 15–18, draw a sketch that illustrates the approximations L_4, R_4, M_4, and T_4. Then compute each approximation and compare it with the exact value of the integral computed using the FTC.

15. $\int_{-1}^{3} (x+1)\,dx$

16. $\int_{-1}^{3} x^2\,dx$

17. $\int_{-2}^{2} x^3\,dx$

18. $\int_{-\pi/2}^{\pi/2} \sin x\,dx$

FURTHER EXERCISES

In Exercises 19–24, construct a table like the one shown on page 351 for the integral. Do the values in the table appear to converge to the exact value of the integral (evaluated using the FTC)?

19. $\int_{-1}^{2} x\,dx$

20. $\int_{-1}^{2} x^2\,dx$

21. $\int_{0}^{1} x^3\,dx$

22. $\int_{1}^{4} \sqrt{x}\,dx$

23. $\int_{0}^{\pi} \sin x\,dx$

24. $\int_{0}^{1} e^x\,dx$

In Exercises 25–28, f is a continuous function with the values shown in the following table.

x	1	2	3	4	5	6
$f(x)$	0.14	0.21	0.28	0.36	0.44	0.54

25. Estimate $\int_{2}^{5} f(x)\,dx$ using a left sum with three equal subintervals.

26. Estimate $\int_{2}^{5} f(x)\,dx$ using a trapezoid sum with three equal subintervals.

27. Estimate $\int_{1}^{5} f(x)\,dx$ using a right sum with two equal subintervals.

28. Estimate $\int_{1}^{5} f(x)\,dx$ using a midpoint sum with two equal subintervals.

29. Find a definite integral for which $5\big(f(5) + f(10) + f(15)\big)$ is
  (a) A left Riemann sum with three equal subintervals.
  (b) A right Riemann sum with three equal subintervals.
  (c) A midpoint Riemann sum with three equal subintervals.

30. Find a definite integral for which $S = 2\big(f(2) + f(4) + f(6) + f(8)\big)$ is
  (a) A left Riemann sum with four equal subintervals.
  (b) A right Riemann sum with four equal subintervals.
  (c) A midpoint Riemann sum with four equal subintervals.

31. Explain why $f(2)\cdot 2 + f(4)\cdot 3$ is a Riemann sum approximation to $\int_2^7 f(x)\,dx$. [HINT: Draw a picture.]

32. Is $f(1)\cdot 3 + f(4)\cdot 2$ a Riemann sum approximation to $\int_1^6 f(x)\,dx$? Justify your answer.

33. Is $f(3)\cdot 1 + f(4)\cdot 4$ a Riemann sum approximation to $\int_0^5 f(x)\,dx$? Justify your answer.

34. Is $f(3)\cdot 4 + f(5)\cdot 4$ a Riemann sum approximation to $\int_0^7 f(x)\,dx$? Justify your answer.

This section lets students work with sigma notation, suggests some additional interpretations of approximating sums, and explains rigorously why some simple integrals exist as limits.

5.7   WORKING WITH SUMS

In Section 5.6 we defined the integral as a limit of approximating sums:

$$\int_a^b f(x)\,dx = \lim_{n\to\infty} \sum_{i=1}^n f(c_i)\,\Delta x_i.$$

As we said there, we'll seldom *calculate* integrals using the definition as a limit; whenever possible, we use antiderivatives instead. (Derivatives, too, are only rarely calculated directly from the definition.) But, for integrals as for derivatives, *understanding* the definition is essential to understanding what integrals are, what they measure, and what they say about functions.

In this section we focus on approximating sums themselves—their definitions, meanings, and uses. We'll also show how the limit-of-sums definition *can* be used (with effort, and for carefully chosen functions) to calculate some basic integrals.

Sums and sigma notation

The following equations illustrate some uses of the sigma notation:

$$\sum_{j=1}^{10} j^2 = 1^2 + 2^2 + \cdots + 10^2 = 385;$$

$$\sum_{k=1}^{10} (11-k)^2 = 10^2 + 9^2 + \cdots + 1^2 = 385;$$

$$\sum_{l=1}^{100} \frac{\sin(3 + l/100)}{100} = \frac{\sin(3.01) + \sin(3.02) + \cdots + \sin(4)}{100} \approx -0.3408.$$

What do the examples illustrate?

- **Different forms, same answer**   Slightly different sigma notations may produce the same result. For instance, we used j, k, and l as index variable names above, but other letters could have been used. Notice also that the first and second sums, which look quite different in sigma form, produce exactly the *same* summands.
- **Finding values**   Many-term sums can be tedious to calculate by hand, but they're easily found by computer. In *Maple*, for instance, a command of the form `sum(j^2,j=1..10)` finds the first sum above; so would `sum(i^2,i=1..10)`.

- **Algebraic properties**   The arithmetic properties of real numbers apply to many-term sums as well. For instance, the equations

$$(a_1 + b_1) + \cdots + (a_n + b_n) = (a_1 + \cdots + a_n) + (b_1 + \cdots + b_n)$$

and

$$a_1 \cdot c + a_2 \cdot c + \cdots + a_n \cdot c = c\,(a_1 + a_2 + \cdots + a_n)$$

(c is a constant) follow from the commutative and distributive properties of real numbers. Here are "sigma versions" of these facts:

Commutativity: $\displaystyle\sum_{i=1}^{n}(a_i + b_i) = \sum_{i=1}^{n} a_i + \sum_{i=1}^{n} b_i$

Distributivity: $\displaystyle\sum_{i=1}^{n} c\,a_i = c\sum_{i=1}^{n} a_i$

- **Sums vs. integrals**   Sums and integrals have similar properties. The commutative and distributive rules for sums, for instance, have close analogues for integrals:

$$\int_a^b (f + g) = \int_a^b f + \int_a^b g; \qquad \int_a^b c\,f = c\int_a^b f.$$

The similarity is no accident—integrals are *limits* of sums and so inherit many of their traits from sums. (Formal proofs of integral properties start with analogous properties of sums.)

Properties of sums are almost identical to those of integrals—hardly surprising, because integrals are "generalized sums."

EXAMPLE 1   Write sigma forms of the sums R_{10}, L_{10}, and M_{10} for $\int_2^5 \ln x\,dx$.

Solution   The interval $[2, 5]$ has length 3, and so a 10-subinterval partition has endpoints $x_0 = 2.0$, $x_1 = 2.3$, $x_2 = 2.6, \ldots x_9 = 4.7$, $x_{10} = 5.0$. In general, $x_i = 2 + 0.3i$. This gives

$$R_{10} = \big(\ln(2.3) + \ln(2.6) + \cdots + \ln(5.0)\big) \times 0.3 = \sum_{i=1}^{10} \ln(2 + 0.3i) \times 0.3;$$

$$L_{10} = \big(\ln(2.0) + \ln(2.3) + \cdots + \ln(4.7)\big) \times 0.3 = \sum_{i=0}^{9} \ln(2 + 0.3i) \times 0.3.$$

For the *midpoint* sum, the sampling points $(2.15, 2.45, \ldots, 4.85)$ have the form $2.15 + 0.3i$; therefore,

$$M_{10} = \big(\ln(2.15) + \ln(2.45) + \cdots + \ln(4.85)\big) \times 0.3 = \sum_{i=0}^{9} \ln(2.15 + 0.3i) \times 0.3.$$

The sums are easily found by machine: $R_{10} \approx 3.7961$; $L_{10} \approx 3.5212$; $M_{10} \approx 3.6620$.   ∎

Closed forms   The following equations illustrate what are called **closed forms:** ➡

c is a constant

$$\sum_{k=1}^{n} c = c + c + \cdots + c = cn;$$

$$\sum_{k=1}^{n} k = 1 + 2 + \cdots + n = \frac{n(n+1)}{2};$$

$$\sum_{k=1}^{n} k^2 = 1^2 + 2^2 + \cdots + n^2 = \frac{n(n+1)(2n+1)}{6}.$$

It's fun to observe similarities between these identities and properties of integrals: $\int_0^x c\,dk = cx;\ \int_0^x k\,dk = x^2/2,$ etc. Closed forms for sums resemble explicit antiderivatives.

The "closed forms" are the expressions on the right—easily computable expressions that calculate the less obvious sums to the left.

There are many geometric proofs of these identities, and a thriving cottage industry keeps producing more.

Formulas like these let us trade repetitive calculations for simple arithmetic. The third line says, for instance, that

$$1^2 + 2^2 + 3^2 + \cdots + 1000^2 = \frac{1000 \cdot 1001 \cdot 2001}{6} = 333{,}833{,}500;$$

calculating the left side directly would be no fun! (In a later example we'll use the same formula to calculate an integral.)

The first identity above is obvious at a glance. The third form is subtler; a formal proof appears in Appendix H, and we take another look in Example 3. The second identity is simpler, and interesting in its own right. Figure 1 (a "proof without words") suggests why it holds.

The figure shows *two* copies (one gray and one white) of the sum $1 + 2 + \cdots + n$; they "fit together" to form an $(n+1) \times n$ rectangle, and the desired equation follows. (The figure shows $n = 7$, but the same idea works for every n.) The following calculation uses the same argument, but dresses it up in sigma notation. (If the calculation looks a bit magical, refer again to the picture.)

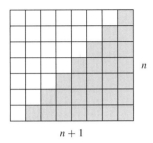

n

n + 1

FIGURE 1
Why

$$1 + 2 + \cdots + n = \frac{n(n+1)}{2}$$

EXAMPLE 2 Show that $1 + 2 + 3 + \cdots + n = \dfrac{n(n+1)}{2}$ for all positive integers n.

Solution If $S = 1 + 2 + 3 + \cdots + n$, then

$$2S = (1 + 2 + \cdots + n) + (n + (n-1) + \cdots + 1) \qquad \text{(writing } S \text{ twice)}$$

$$= \sum_{k=1}^{n} k + \sum_{k=1}^{n} (n + 1 - k) \qquad \text{(rewriting in sigma form)}$$

$$= \sum_{k=1}^{n} (k + n + 1 - k) \qquad \text{(combining the sums)}$$

$$= \sum_{k=1}^{n} (n + 1) = n(n+1),$$

as we aimed to show. ∎

EXAMPLE 3 We claimed above that, for all n,

$$1^2 + 2^2 + 3^2 + \cdots + n^2 = \frac{n(n+1)(2n+1)}{6}.$$

Why does the formula hold? How might one guess it? ◄

We haven't forgotten about calculus—we'll use the identity in a moment to calculate an integral.

Solution Let $s(n)$ denote the expression on the right side above. Clearly, $s(1) = 1$, and so the formula "works" for $n = 1$.

Now consider $s(n) - s(n-1)$. If the formula $s(n)$ is correct, we should have

$$s(n) - s(n-1) = (1^2 + 2^2 + \cdots + (n-1)^2 + n^2) - (1^2 + 2^2 + \cdots + (n-1)^2) = n^2.$$

By definition,

$$s(n) - s(n-1) = \frac{n(n+1)(2n+1)}{6} - \frac{(n-1)n(2n-1)}{6},$$

and some basic but careful algebra (multiply out both numerators; then combine results) shows that the right side does indeed reduce to n^2. This result, together with the fact that $s(1) = 1$, shows that the formula $s(n)$ "works" for all positive integers n.

Where did the formula $s(n)$ in Example 3 come from? Could we have guessed it? Not easily, perhaps, but we suggest some strategies in this section's exercises. ∎

Integrals as limits: a direct calculation

Some similar calculations are done in exercises.

By definition, $\int_a^b f(x)\,dx = \lim_{n\to\infty}\sum_{i=1}^n f(c_i)\,\Delta x_i$. The definition is inconvenient to use directly for most integrals. But a few simple cases are exceptional—and worthwhile in showing what the definition really means.

EXAMPLE 4 Use the limit definition to find $\int_0^1 x^2\,dx$.

Solution We'll work with right sums R_n. A regular partition of $[0, 1]$ into n pieces has endpoints $0, 1/n, 2/n, \ldots, 1$. Thus, $x_i = i/n$ and $\Delta x_i = 1/n$ for all i, so

$$R_n = \sum_{i=1}^n f(x_i)\Delta x = \sum_{i=1}^n f\left(\frac{i}{n}\right)\frac{1}{n} = \sum_{i=1}^n \left(\frac{i}{n}\right)^2 \frac{1}{n}$$

$$= \sum_{i=1}^n i^2 \frac{1}{n^3} = \frac{1}{n^3}\sum_{i=1}^n i^2.$$

(The last step works because n is constant with respect to i.) Next we use our closed form for the sum of squares:

$$R_n = \frac{1}{n^3}\sum_{i=1}^n i^2 = \frac{1}{n^3}\frac{n(n+1)(2n+1)}{6} = \frac{n(n+1)(2n+1)}{6n^3} = \frac{2n^3+3n^2+n}{6n^3}.$$

Last, we find the limit:➡

We found similar limits in Section 4.2.

$$\int_0^1 x^2\,dx = \lim_{n\to\infty}\frac{2n^3+3n^2+n}{6n^3} = \frac{1}{3}.$$

We could have found the same answer, of course, by antidifferentiation. The point is that the two methods agree. ∎

Three views of approximating sums

Approximating sums are *discrete* approximations to integrals of *continuously* varying functions. This relationship can be interpreted in several useful ways. We discuss three.

1. Polygonal approximations Geometrically, approximating sums represent simpler, straight-edged versions of regions with curved edges.➡ The shaded region in Figure 2, for example, could be called a **polygonal approximation** to the region under the f-graph from a to b.

Most of the pictures in this section and the last reflect this point of view.

Trapezoid sums are not (strictly speaking) Riemann sums, but they are quite natural polygonal approximations.

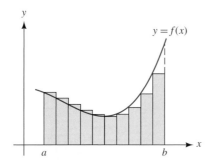

FIGURE 2
A polygonal approximation to a curved area

The total area of the polygonal region is the value of a left sum; it's apparently a reasonable approximation to $\int_a^b f$, the true area under the graph.

We defined average value in Section 5.1.

2. Average values   The average of *n numbers* is their sum divided by *n*. How is this notion related to the average value of a *function f* on an interval $[a, b]$? ◄

The relation is quite close—thanks to approximating sums. If, say, $c_1, \ldots, c_n$ are the midpoints of *n* equal subdivisions of $[a, b]$, then

$$\frac{f(c_1) + f(c_2) + f(c_3) + \cdots + f(c_n)}{n}$$

is the ordinary average of *n* equally-spaced sample values of *f*. The midpoint sum M_n is *almost* identical:

$$M_n = \left(f(c_1) + f(c_2) + f(c_3) + \cdots + f(c_n)\right) \cdot \frac{b-a}{n};$$

it differs from the preceding average only by the factor $(b - a)$. Now as $n \to \infty$, we have $M_n \to \int_a^b f(x)\,dx$, and so

$$\left(f(c_1) + f(c_2) + \cdots + f(c_n)\right)\frac{1}{n} \longrightarrow \frac{\int_a^b f(x)\,dx}{b-a},$$

which is just the average value of *f* on $[a, b]$, as defined earlier. Here is our conclusion:

The average value f over $[a, b]$ is a limit of averages taken over n-member subsets of $[a, b]$.

Trapezoid sums are not Riemann sums, but they are (unequally) weighted sums in the sense discussed here. Simpson's rule (discussed in Chapter 6) also uses unequally weighted sums. We take a quite different approach to weighted sums in a Chapter 6 interlude on Gaussian quadrature.

3. Weighted sums   An expression of the form

$$f(c_1)w_1 + f(c_2)w_2 + \cdots + f(c_n)w_n,$$

where the w_i are any positive numbers (the **weights**), is called a **weighted sum** of the function values $f(c_i)$. If $w_i = 1/n$ for all *i*, then the weighted sum is the *ordinary* average of the $f(c_i)$. Every Riemann sum $f(c_1)\Delta x_1 + \cdots f(c_n)\Delta x_n$ is a weighted sum in this sense, with weight $w_i = \Delta x_i$ and the c_i chosen depending on the type of sum at hand.

E X A M P L E 5   Write L_n, R_n, and T_n as weighted sums. What are the weights?

Solution   Let x_0 through x_n define a regular partition of $[a, b]$. Then $\Delta x = (b-a)/n$, and so

$$R_n = f(x_1)\Delta x + f(x_2)\Delta x + \cdots + f(x_n)\Delta x;$$
$$L_n = f(x_0)\Delta x + f(x_1)\Delta x + \cdots + f(x_{n-1})\Delta x.$$

Thus, both R_n and L_n are weighted sums (of different sets of values); all the weights are equal. Trapezoid sums T_n are also weighted sums, but with a little twist. Since T_n is the average $(L_n + R_n)/2$, we have

$$T_n = \left(\frac{f(x_0) + f(x_1)}{2} + \frac{f(x_1) + f(x_2)}{2} + \cdots + \frac{f(x_{n-1}) + f(x_n)}{2}\right)\Delta x$$
$$= \left(\frac{f(x_0)}{2} + f(x_1) + \cdots + f(x_{n-1}) + \frac{f(x_n)}{2}\right)\Delta x.$$

Thus, T_n is an *unequally* weighted sum of values of *f* at $n + 1$ (rather than *n*) of the partition points x_i; the first and last values have *half* the weight of the others.   ∎

Using approximating sums

Approximating sums are good for more than formally defining the integral. Indeed, compared with symbolic integrals approximating sums are often simpler conceptually, handier in applications, and easier to calculate—especially for machines. For the many integrals that involve complicated formulas or no formulas at all, approximating sums may be the only practical resort.

EXAMPLE 6 If $v(t)$ is the speed (in miles per hour) of a car at time t (in hours), then $\int_a^b v(t)\,dt =$ miles traveled from $t = a$ to $t = b$. To measure distance traveled from $t = 0$ to $t = 1$, we need the integral $\int_0^1 v(t)\,dt$.

Real cars don't adhere to explicit speed formulas. What we *can* observe, practically speaking, are numerical speed data such as those following. (Notice the irregular time intervals; real data sets *often* have gaps.)

Speed readings over one hour										
Time (min)	0	5	10	15	20	30	35	40	45	55	60
Speed (mph)	35	38	36	57	71	55	51	23	10	27	35

How far did the car travel in 1 hour?

Solution Without more information (e.g., about speeds *between* the times measured), we can't know exactly. But we can use approximating sums to estimate $\int_0^1 v(t)\,dt$. The tabulated speed data are mathematically compatible with many possible speed functions. One possibility is drawn by "connecting the dots" (see Figure 3(a)): ➤

We converted time from minutes to hours.

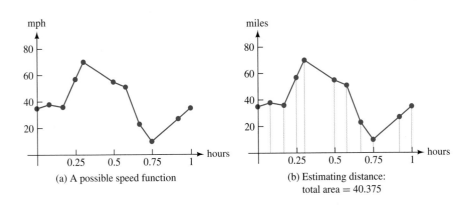

(a) A possible speed function

(b) Estimating distance: total area = 40.375

FIGURE 3
Estimating distance from speed data

The total bounded area (Figure 3(b)) can be computed using ten trapezoids. (We spare you the arithmetic.) We get 40.375—a reasonable estimate for distance traveled over the hour.

The piecewise-linear speed function just plotted isn't the only possibility. Many curves can be drawn through the known data points, but some are physically more likely than others. The important point is that the trapezoid estimate depends only on the 11 observed data points, not on the particular curve drawn through them. Figure 4 illustrates this idea.

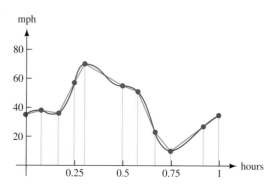

FIGURE 4

New speed function; same trapezoidal area

It shows a new speed function (better or worse than the old?) but the same trapezoid estimate (40.375 miles) for distance. ∎

BASIC EXERCISES

In Exercises 1–4, express the sum using Σ-notation.

1. $1 + 2 + 3 + \cdots + 49 + 50$

2. $\sqrt[3]{2} + \sqrt[3]{4} + \sqrt[3]{6} + \cdots + \sqrt[3]{98} + \sqrt[3]{100}$

3. $1^2 + 3^2 + 5^2 + \cdots + 97^2 + 99^2$

4. $2^1 + 2^2 + 2^3 + \cdots + 2^{14} + 2^{15}$

In Exercises 5–12, evaluate the sum.

5. $\displaystyle\sum_{k=1}^{5} k^{-1}$

6. $\displaystyle\sum_{k=1}^{4} \sqrt{k}$

7. $\displaystyle\sum_{k=1}^{6} \sin(k\pi/4)$

8. $\displaystyle\sum_{k=0}^{5} \cos(k\pi/2)$

9. $\displaystyle\sum_{k=1}^{17} k$

10. $\displaystyle\sum_{k=1}^{21} k^2$

11. $\displaystyle\sum_{k=0}^{9} (k+1)^2$

12. $\displaystyle\sum_{k=1}^{19} (k^2 + 2k)$

13. (a) Use Σ-notation to express the right sum approximation to $\displaystyle\int_{0}^{10} x^2\, dx$ with $n = 10$ equal subintervals.

   (b) Repeat part (a) using $n = 5$.

   (c) Repeat part (a) using $n = 20$.

   (d) Repeat part (a) using $n = 50$.

14. Repeat Exercise 13 for the left sum approximation.

15. (a) Use Σ-notation to express the left sum approximation to $\displaystyle\int_{1}^{11} x^2\, dx$ with $n = 10$ equal subintervals.

   (b) Repeat part (a) using $n = 5$.

   (c) Repeat part (a) using $n = 20$.

   (d) Repeat part (a) using $n = 50$.

16. Repeat Exercise 15 for the right sum approximation.

17. (a) Use Σ-notation to express the left sum approximation to $\displaystyle\int_{0}^{1} \sqrt[3]{x}\, dx$ with $n = 10$ equal subintervals.

   (b) Repeat part (a) using $n = 5$.

   (c) Repeat part (a) using $n = 20$.

   (d) Repeat part (a) using $n = 50$.

18. Repeat Exercise 17 for the right sum approximation.

19. (a) Use Σ-notation to express the right sum approximation to $\displaystyle\int_{1}^{2} \sqrt[3]{x}\, dx$ with $n = 10$ equal subintervals.

   (b) Repeat part (a) using $n = 5$.

   (c) Repeat part (a) using $n = 20$.

   (d) Repeat part (a) using $n = 50$.

20. Repeat Exercise 19 for the left sum approximation.

21. (a) Use Σ-notation to express the right sum approximation to $\displaystyle\int_{3}^{7} \sin(x^2)\, dx$ with $n = 10$ equal subintervals.

   (b) Repeat part (a) using $n = 5$.

   (c) Repeat part (a) using $n = 20$.

   (d) Repeat part (a) using $n = 50$.

22. Repeat Exercise 21 for the left sum approximation.

23. **(a)** Use Σ-notation to express the midpoint sum approximation to $\int_0^5 \sqrt{x}\, dx$ with $n = 10$ equal subintervals.

   (b) Repeat part (a) using $n = 5$.

   (c) Repeat part (a) using $n = 20$.

   (d) Repeat part (a) using $n = 50$.

24. **(a)** Use Σ-notation to express the midpoint sum approximation to $\int_2^{12} \sqrt{x}\, dx$ with $n = 10$ equal subintervals.

   (b) Repeat part (a) using $n = 5$.

   (c) Repeat part (a) using $n = 20$.

   (d) Repeat part (a) using $n = 50$.

FURTHER EXERCISES

25. Evaluate $\displaystyle\lim_{n\to\infty} \frac{1+2+3+\cdots+n}{n^2}$.

26. Evaluate $\displaystyle\lim_{n\to\infty} \frac{1^2+2^2+3^2+\cdots+n^2}{n^3}$.

27. Explain why $\displaystyle\lim_{n\to\infty} \frac{1}{n}\sum_{k=1}^{n}(4+k/n)^3 = \int_4^5 x^3\, dx$.

28. Explain why $\displaystyle\lim_{n\to\infty} \frac{1}{n}\sum_{k=1}^{n}(4+k/n)^3 = \int_0^1 (4+x)^3\, dx$.

29. Explain why $\displaystyle\lim_{n\to\infty} \frac{3}{n}\sum_{k=1}^{n}\sqrt{1+3k/n} = \int_1^4 \sqrt{x}\, dx$.

30. Explain why $\displaystyle\lim_{n\to\infty} \frac{3}{n}\sum_{k=0}^{n-1}\sqrt{1+3k/n} = \int_1^4 \sqrt{x}\, dx$.

31. Explain why $\displaystyle\lim_{n\to\infty} \frac{3}{n}\sum_{k=1}^{n}\sqrt{1+3(k-1)/n} = \int_1^4 \sqrt{x}\, dx$.

32. Explain why $\displaystyle\lim_{n\to\infty} \frac{3}{n}\sum_{k=0}^{n-1}\sqrt{1+3(2k+1)/2n} = \int_1^4 \sqrt{x}\, dx$.

33. Explain why $\displaystyle\lim_{n\to\infty} \frac{3}{n}\sum_{k=1}^{n}\sqrt{1+3(2k-1)/2n} = \int_1^4 \sqrt{x}\, dx$.

34. Evaluate $\int_0^3 x\, dx$ by computing the limit of right sums R_n.

35. Evaluate $\int_2^5 x\, dx$ by computing the limit of left sums L_n.

36. Evaluate $\int_1^4 x\, dx$ by computing the limit of midpoint sums M_n.

37. In Example 4 the integral $\int_0^1 x^2\, dx$ was evaluated by taking a limit of right sums. Find this integral by evaluating a limit of left sums L_n.

38. In Example 4 the integral $\int_0^1 x^2\, dx$ was evaluated by taking a limit of right sums. Find this integral by evaluating a limit of midpoint sums M_n.

39. Find a definite integral for which $\displaystyle\frac{2}{100}\sum_{k=1}^{100}\sin\left(\frac{2k}{100}\right)$ is a right sum approximation.

40. Find a definite integral for which $\displaystyle\frac{2}{10}\sum_{k=1}^{40}\cos\left(\frac{2k-1}{10}\right)$ is a midpoint sum approximation.

41. Evaluate $\displaystyle\lim_{n\to\infty} \frac{1}{n}\sum_{j=1}^{n}\left(\frac{j}{n}\right)^3$ by expressing it as a definite integral and then evaluating this integral using the fundamental theorem of calculus.

42. Evaluate $\displaystyle\lim_{n\to\infty} \frac{2}{n}\sum_{j=1}^{n}\left(\frac{2j}{n}\right)^3$ by expressing it as a definite integral and then evaluating this integral using the fundamental theorem of calculus.

43. Explain why $\displaystyle\lim_{n\to\infty} \frac{1}{n}\sum_{k=1}^{n}(2+5k/n)^3$ is equal to the average value of x^3 over the interval $[2,7]$.

44. Explain why $\displaystyle\lim_{n\to\infty} \frac{1}{n}\sum_{k=1}^{n}\sqrt{2(2k-1)/n}$ is equal to the average value of $\sqrt{x}$ over the interval $[0,4]$.

45. The following table gives speedometer readings at various times over a 1-hour interval.

Speed readings over one hour						
Time (min)	0	10	20	30	40	50	60
Speed (mph)	42	38	36	57	0	55	51

   (a) Draw a plausible speed graph for the 1-hour period.

   (b) Estimate the total distance traveled using

      (i) A trapezoid approximating sum, six subdivisions.

      (ii) A left approximating sum, six subdivisions.

      (iii) A midpoint approximating sum, three subdivisions.

      Which answer is most convincing? Why?

   (c) Draw a plausible distance graph for the 1-hour period.

46. At time t (measured in hours), $0 \le t \le 24$, a firm uses electricity at the rate of $E(t)$ kilowatts. The power company's rate schedule indicates that the cost per kilowatt-hour at time t is $c(t)$ dollars. Assume that both E and c are continuous functions.

   (a) Set up an N-term left sum that approximates the cost of the electricity consumed in a 24-hour period.

   (b) What definite integral is approximated by the sum you found in part (a)?

47. This exercise outlines a proof that $\displaystyle\sum_{k=1}^{n} k = \frac{n(n+1)}{2}$.

   (a) Show that $\displaystyle\sum_{k=1}^{n}\left((k+1)^2 - k^2\right) = (n+1)^2 - 1$.

(b) Show that $(k+1)^2 - k^2 = 2k+1$.

(c) Combining the results in parts (a) and (b) leads to the identity $\sum_{k=1}^{n}(2k+1) = (n+1)^2 - 1$. Use this identify to find a closed form expression for $\sum_{k=1}^{n}k$.

48. This exercise outlines a proof that $\sum_{k=1}^{n}k^2 = \dfrac{n(n+1)(2n+1)}{6} = \frac{1}{3}n^3 + \frac{1}{2}n^2 + \frac{1}{6}n$.

(a) Show that $\sum_{k=1}^{n}\left((k+1)^3 - k^3\right) = (n+1)^3 - 1$.

(b) Show that $(k+1)^3 - k^3 = 3k^2 + 3k + 1$.

(c) Use parts (a) and (b) together with the identity proved in the previous exercise to find the desired closed form expression for $\sum_{k=1}^{n}k^2$.

49. Prove that $\sum_{k=1}^{n}k^3 = \frac{1}{4}n^2(n+1)^2$.

[HINT: See the previous exercise.]

SUMMARY

This chapter introduced the **integral**. The derivative and the integral are the two most important concepts of calculus. Remarkably, they're closely related; the **fundamental theorem of calculus** describes how and why.

The integral as signed area   Section 5.1 introduced the integral graphically, as measuring **signed area**. ("Signed" means that area below the x-axis counts negatively.) The graphical viewpoint, though insufficient for *exact* calculations, explains clearly what the integral is and why some of its elementary properties hold.

The area function   Given a function f and a starting point $x = a$, we defined a related **area function** A_f:

$$A_f(x) = \int_{a}^{x} f = \text{signed area bounded by } f \text{ from } a \text{ to } x.$$

Simple examples suggest that the area function is an **antiderivative** for f. This idea, suitably embellished, is the simplest form of the **fundamental theorem of calculus**.

The fundamental theorem   Put more formally, the fundamental theorem says that if A_f is defined as we just stated, then

$$\frac{d}{dx}\left(A_f(x)\right) = f(x).$$

This result connects derivatives and integrals, the two main calculus ideas. For that reason, it deserves to be called *fundamental*.

The same idea, restated in another form, is called the **second version of the fundamental theorem**. If F is *any* antiderivative of f, then

$$\int_{a}^{b} f(x)\, dx = F(b) - F(a).$$

In other words,

To find $\int_{a}^{b} f$, find any *antiderivative, plug in endpoints, and subtract.*

Antidifferentiation by substitution   The connection between integration and antidifferentiation means that it's worth trying to find symbolic antiderivatives, even of complicated functions. The simplest and most important antidifferentiation technique is called **substitution**. Antidifferentiation by any method is nothing more than differentiation in reverse. Substitution, in particular, is the chain rule running backward. We explained this connection in Section 5.4 and used it repeatedly to find antiderivatives.

Using integral tables and computers Finding symbolic antiderivatives from scratch can be difficult. In practice, calculus users freely resort to integral tables, computer software, and other tools. Scientific reference works contain extensive integral tables—sometimes running to dozens of pages. Mathematical software such as *Maple* and *Mathematica* also produces antiderivatives quickly and easily. As with all power tools, however, using tables and mathematical software requires care, and their results require interpretation. We illustrated some of the possibilities and pitfalls in Section 5.5.

The integral as a limit of approximating sums Like the derivative, the integral is defined rigorously as a limit of approximating sums. Section 5.6 described the procedure. Although symbolically messy, approximating sums make good graphical sense. Several varieties were introduced, compared, and calculated.

Approximating sums and applications of the integral In Section 5.6 we defined the integral as a limit of approximating sums. In Section 5.7 we focused on approximating sums themselves—their definition, properties, meanings, and uses.

Thinking of the integral as a limit of sums suggests a variety of applications. One application of the integral concerns rates and amounts:

If $f(t)$ tells the rate at which a quantity varies at time t, then $\int_a^b f$ tells the amount by which the same quantity changes over the interval from $t = a$ to $t = b$.

We applied this idea using speed data for a car to estimate the distance traveled.

REVIEW EXERCISES

1. Let f be the function shown graphically below.

(a) Which of the following is the best estimate of $\int_0^{40} f(x)\,dx$: $-65, -20, 0, 30, 60$? Justify your answer.

(b) Show that the average value of f over the interval $[10, 30]$ is less than -1.

2. The graph of a function h is shown below.

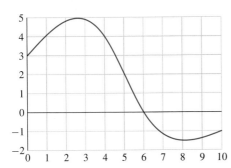

List, from smallest to largest, (i) $h'(5)$, (ii) the average value of h over the interval $[0, 10]$, (iii) the average rate of change of h over the interval $[0, 10]$, (iv) $\int_0^{10} h(x)\,dx$, (v) $\int_0^5 h(x)\,dx$, (vi) $\int_6^{10} h(x)\,dx$, and (vii) $\int_5^5 h(x)\,dx$.

3. Sketch the graph of a continuous function f such that $\int_{-2}^3 f(t)\,dt = -10$ and

(a) $\int_{-2}^3 |f(t)|\,dt = 10$.

(b) $\int_{-2}^3 |f(t)|\,dt \neq 10$.

4. Show that $0.4 \leq \int_0^1 \sin(e^x)\,dx \leq 1$.

5. Show that $\pi/2 < \int_0^{\pi} \cos(\sin x)\,dx \leq \pi$.
  [HINT: $\cos 1 > \cos(\pi/3) = 1/2$.]

6. (a) Show that $\pi(1 + 1/e) \leq \int_0^{2\pi} e^{\sin x}\,dx \leq \pi(1 + e)$.
    [HINT: If $0 \leq x \leq \pi$, $0 \leq \sin x \leq 1$. If $\pi \leq x \leq 2\pi$, $-1 \leq \sin x \leq 0$.]

  (b) Use the result in part (a) to find numbers A and B such that $A \leq \int_0^{50\pi} e^{\sin x}\,dx \leq B$.

7. (a) Let $y = f(x)$ be the line through the points $(0, \arctan 0)$ and $(1, \arctan 1)$. Explain why $f(x) \leq \arctan x$ if $0 \leq x \leq 1$. [HINT: Consider the concavity of the arctangent function.]

  (b) Find an equation of the line tangent to the curve $y = \arctan x$ at $x = 0$.

  (c) Show that $\pi/8 \leq \int_0^1 \arctan x\,dx \leq 1/2$.

8. (a) Suppose that $f(x) \geq 0$ if $0 \leq x \leq 1$. Show that $\int_0^1 x^k f(x)\, dx \leq \int_0^1 f(x)\, dx$ for all integers $k \geq 0$.

(b) Does the result in part (a) remain valid if the assumption "$f(x) \geq 0$ if $0 \leq x \leq 1$" is not made? Explain.

9. (a) Show that $\int_0^{\pi/2} \sin^2 x\, dx + \int_0^{\pi/2} \cos^2 x\, dx = \pi/2$.

(b) Explain why $\int_0^{\pi/2} \sin^2 x\, dx = \int_0^{\pi/2} \cos^2 x\, dx$.

[HINT: $\cos x = -\sin(x - \pi/2) = \sin(\pi/2 - x)$.]

(c) Use parts (a) and (b) to show that $\int_0^{\pi/2} \sin^2 x\, dx = \pi/4$.

10. (a) Show that $\int_0^{\pi/2} \sqrt{1 + \cos(2x)}\, dx = \sqrt{2} \int_0^{\pi/2} \cos x\, dx$.

[HINT: $1 + \cos(2x) = 2\cos^2 x$ for all x.]

(b) Does $\int_{\pi/2}^{\pi} \sqrt{1 + \cos(2x)}\, dx = \sqrt{2} \int_{\pi/2}^{\pi} \cos x\, dx$? Justify your answer.

11. Suppose that f is a continuous function and that $-2 \leq f(x) \leq 5$ if $1 \leq x \leq 3$. Explain why the average value of f over $[1, 3]$ must be between -2 and 5.

12. Show that the expression $\int_a^b \left(f(x) - c\right)^2 dx$ assumes its minimum value when c is the average value of f over the interval $[a, b]$.

13. Suppose that f and g are continuous on $[a, b]$ and $\int_a^b f(x)\, dx \leq \int_a^b g(x)\, dx$.

(a) Must $f(x) \leq g(x)$ for every x in $[a, b]$? If so, explain why. If not, give a counterexample.

(b) Must there be a number c such that $a \leq c \leq b$ and $f(c) \leq g(c)$? If so, explain why. If not, give a counterexample.

14. Let $F(x) = \int_a^x f(t)\, dt$ and $G(x) = \int_b^x f(t)\, dt$, where a and b are constants, and f is a continuous function. Explain why $G(x) = F(x) + C$, where C is a constant.

Some antiderivatives—trigonometric ones, especially—can be written in more than one way. In Exercises 15–17, verify the formula using the trigonometric identities $\sin^2 x + \cos^2 x = 1$, $\sin(2x) = 2\cos x \sin x$, *and* $\cos(2x) = 2\cos^2 x - 1$.

15. $\int 2 \sin x \cos x\, dx = \sin^2 x + C = -\cos^2 x + C$

16. $\int \cos(2x)\, dx = \frac{1}{2} \sin(2x) + C = \cos x \sin x + C$

17. $\int \cos^2 x\, dx = \frac{x}{2} + \frac{1}{2} \cos x \sin x + C = \frac{x}{2} + \frac{1}{4} \sin(2x) + C$

18. (a) Use the trigonometric identity $2 \sin^2 x = 1 - \cos(2x)$ to find $\int \sin^2 x\, dx$.

(b) Explain why $\int_0^{2\pi} \sqrt{1 - \cos(2x)}\, dx \neq \sqrt{2} \int_0^{2\pi} \sin x\, dx$.

Some antiderivatives are difficult to find from scratch but may be checked easily by differentiation. In Exercises 19–25, verify the antiderivative formula by differentiation.

19. $\int \ln x\, dx = x \ln x - x + C$

20. $\int \arctan x\, dx = x \arctan x - \frac{1}{2} \ln(1 + x^2) + C$

21. $\int \frac{dx}{x^2 + a^2} = \frac{1}{a} \arctan\left(\frac{x}{a}\right) + C$

22. $\int \tan x\, dx = \ln |\sec x| + C$

[HINT: Recall that $\left(\ln |x|\right)' = 1/x$ for all $x \neq 0$.]

23. $\int \sec x\, dx = \ln |\sec x + \tan x| + C$

24. $\int \frac{dx}{1 - x^2} = \frac{1}{2} \ln \left| \frac{1 + x}{1 - x} \right| + C$

25. $\int \arcsin x\, dx = x \arcsin x + \sqrt{1 - x^2} + C$

In Exercises 26–45, evaluate the antiderivative. Check your answer by differentiation.

26. $\int \left(3x^5 + 4x^{-2}\right) dx$

27. $\int \frac{dx}{3x}$

28. $\int \frac{dx}{4\sqrt{1 - x^2}}$

29. $\int \frac{3}{x^2 + 1}\, dx$

30. $\int 3e^{4x}\, dx$

31. $\int \left(2 \sin(3x) - 4 \cos(5x)\right) dx$

32. $\int 4 \sec^2(3x)\, dx$

33. $\int \left(1 + \sqrt{x}\right)^2 dx$

34. $\int (x + 1)^2 \sqrt[3]{x}\, dx$

35. $\int \frac{(3 - x)^2}{x}\, dx$

36. $\int \frac{(1 - x)^3}{\sqrt{x}}\, dx$

37. $\int e^x (1 - e^x)\, dx$

38. $\int \frac{dx}{\sqrt{2x - x^2}}$. [HINT: $2x - x^2 = 1 - (x - 1)^2$.]

39. $\int x \sin(x^2)\, dx$

40. $\displaystyle\int \frac{dx}{2x+1}$

41. $\displaystyle\int x^3 e^{x^4}\, dx$

42. $\displaystyle\int \frac{\arctan x}{1+x^2}\, dx$

43. $\displaystyle\int \frac{(\ln x)^3}{x}\, dx$

44. $\displaystyle\int \frac{dx}{1+9x^2}$

45. $\displaystyle\int \ln|\cos x|\tan x\, dx$

46. Evaluate $\displaystyle\int_0^1 x\sqrt{1-x^4}\, dx$. [HINT: Use the substitution $u = x^2$ to relate the given integral to one that can be evaluated geometrically.]

47. Use the substitution $u = 1-x$ to show that

$$\int_0^1 x^n(1-x)^m\, dx = \int_0^1 x^m(1-x)^n\, dx.$$

48. Find the flaw in the following "proof" that $I = \displaystyle\int_{-1}^1 \frac{dx}{x^2+1} = 0$:

$$I = \int_{-1}^1 \frac{dx}{x^2+1} = \int_{-1}^1 \frac{x^{-2}}{1+x^{-2}}\, dx = -\int_{-1}^1 \frac{du}{1+u^2} = -I$$

so $I = 0$.

49. Find the flaw in the following "proof" that $\displaystyle\int_0^\pi \sqrt{1-\sin x}\, dx = 0$:

$$\int \sqrt{1-\sin x}\, dx = \int \frac{\sqrt{1-\sin^2 x}}{\sqrt{1+\sin x}}\, dx$$
$$= \int \frac{\cos x}{\sqrt{1+\sin x}}\, dx$$
$$\rightarrow \int \frac{du}{\sqrt{u}}$$
$$= 2\sqrt{u}+C \rightarrow 2\sqrt{1+\sin x}+C.$$

Thus,

$$\int_0^\pi \sqrt{1-\sin x}\, dx = 2\sqrt{1+\sin \pi} - 2\sqrt{1+\sin 0} = 0.$$

50. The rate at which the world's oil is being consumed is increasing. Suppose that the rate (measured in billions of barrels per year) is given by the function $r(t)$, where t is measured in years and $t = 0$ is January 1, 1990.

 (a) Write a definite integral that represents the total quantity of oil used between the start of 1990 and the start of 1995.

 (b) Suppose that $r(t) = 32e^{0.05t}$. Find an approximate value for the definite integral from part (a) using a right sum with $n = 5$ equal subintervals.

 (c) Interpret each of the five terms in the sum from part (b) in terms of oil consumption.

 (d) Evaluate the definite integral from part (a) exactly using the FTC.

51. Suppose that the rate of change of the temperature of a cup of coffee t minutes after it is placed in a room is $T'(t) = -3.5e^{-0.05t}$ °C/minute. If the temperature of the coffee is initially 90 °C, what is the temperature of the coffee 5 minutes later?

52. Let $I = \displaystyle\int_0^5 \sqrt[3]{2x}\, dx$. Use sigma notation to write the left, right, and midpoint approximations to I. (Assume that $N = 10$ equal subintervals are used.)

53. Let $I = \displaystyle\int_0^5 \sqrt{3x}\, dx$. Use sigma notation to write the left, right, and midpoint approximations to I. (Assume that N equal subintervals are used.)

54. (a) Write the sum

$$\frac{5}{2}(2.3)^2 + \frac{5}{6}(2.8)^2 + \frac{5}{12}(3.3)^2 + \frac{5}{20}(3.8)^2$$

 using sigma notation.
 [HINT: $2 = 1\cdot 2$, $6 = 2\cdot 3$, $12 = 3\cdot 4$, and $20 = 4\cdot 5$.]

 (b) Is the sum in part (a) a Riemann sum approximation to $\displaystyle\int_0^4 x^2\, dx$? Explain.

In Exercises 55–58, rewrite the expression in terms of G, where $G(x) = \displaystyle\int_1^x g(t)\, dt.$

55. $\displaystyle\int_1^3 g(u)\, du$

56. $\displaystyle\int_0^1 g(x)\, dx$

57. $\displaystyle\int_{-2}^2 g(t)\, dt$

58. $\displaystyle\int_2^4 g(t)\, dt$

59. Suppose that f is a function such that $\displaystyle\int_0^3 f(x)\, dx = -1$.

 (a) Suppose that f is an *even* function. Explain why
$$\int_{-3}^3 f(x)\, dx = -2.$$

 (b) If f is an *odd* function, what is the value of $\displaystyle\int_{-3}^3 f(x)\, dx$? Explain.

60. Show that $0 \le \displaystyle\int_0^\pi x\sin x\, dx \le \pi^2/2$.
 [HINT: $0 \le \sin x \le 1$ if $0 \le x \le \pi$.]

In Exercises 61–64, $h(x) = \int_0^x g(t)\, dt$, where g is the function graphed below.

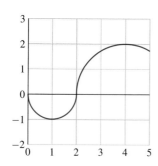

61. Rank the eight numbers $-1, 3, 5, h(1), h(4), \int_0^2 g(u)\, du,$ $\int_1^1 g(x)\, dx$, and $\int_5^3 g(t)\, dt$ in increasing order.

62. Evaluate $h'(1)$.

63. Is $h''(3) < 0$? Justify your answer.

64. How many roots does h have in the interval $[0, 5]$? Justify your answer.

65. Suppose that $\int_4^6 h(w)\, dw = 15$. Evaluate $\int_4^6 (2h(z) + 3)\, dz$.

66. Suppose that $\int_1^5 (3f(x) + 2)\, dx = 68$. Evaluate $\int_1^5 f(z)\, dz$.

In Exercises 67–70, suppose that $\int_{-3}^1 h(t)\, dt = -2$ and that $\int_{-1}^1 h(u)\, du = 4$.

67. Evaluate $\int_1^{-3} h(w)\, dw$.

68. What is the average value of h over the interval $[-1, 1]$?

69. Evaluate $\int_{-3}^{-1} h(z)\, dz$.

70. Is it possible that h is an odd function? Justify your answer.

In Exercises 71–74, H is the function $H(w) = \int_{-2}^w xe^x\, dx$.

71. Indicate whether each of the following values is positive, negative, or zero.
   (a) $H(-3)$
   (b) $H(-2)$
   (c) $H(0)$
   (d) $H(2)$

72. Show that $H(1) \geq -3e^{-1}$.

73. Evaluate $H'(1)$.

74. On which subintervals of $(-\infty, \infty)$, if any, is the graph of H concave up?

75. Show that $\lim_{n \to \infty} \left(\frac{3}{n}\right) \sum_{k=1}^n \left(1 + \frac{3k}{n}\right)^2 = 21$.

76. Is $\left(\frac{3}{5}\right) \cdot \left(-1 + 0 + \frac{1}{2} + 1 + 2\right)$ a Riemann sum approximation to $\int_{-1}^2 x\, dx$? Justify your answer.

77. Let $G(x) = \int_x^2 \cos(\pi t^2/4)\, dt$. Evaluate $G'(2)$.

78. Suppose that $\int_1^e \frac{g(\ln x)}{x}\, dx = 42$. Find values of the parameters K, a, and b so that $K \int_a^b g(u)\, du = 21$.

79. Is $\frac{2}{7} \sum_{k=0}^6 \sqrt{3 + 2k/7}$ a Riemann sum approximation of the integral $\int_3^5 \sqrt{x}\, dx$? Justify your answer.

80. What is the *exact* value of $\lim_{n \to \infty} \frac{5}{n} \sum_{k=1}^n \sqrt{4 + 5k/n}$? Justify your answer.

81. Suppose that $\int_1^4 h(w)\, dw = 17$. Evaluate $\int_4^1 (2h(z) - 5)\, dz$.

82. Suppose that $\int_{-2}^3 (f(x) + 1)\, dx = 0$.
Evaluate $\int_{-2}^3 (f(x) - x)\, dx$.

In Exercises 83–90, $S(z) = \int_1^z \sin(t^2/2)\, dt$.

83. Rank the six numbers $-0.5, 0.5, S(0), S(1), S(2)$, and $S(3)$ in increasing order.

84. Is $S(z)$ decreasing at $z = 2$? Justify your answer.

85. Is $S(z)$ concave up at $z = 3$? Justify your answer.

86. Evaluate $S''(4)$.

87. How many roots does S have in the interval $[0, 5]$? Justify your answer.

88. Where does S attain its minimum value over the interval $[0, 5]$?

89. Where does S attain its maximum value over the interval $[0, 5]$?

90. It can be shown that $S(4) \approx 0.74380$ and $S(7) \approx 0.60917$. Use this information to estimate the average value of $\sin(t^2/2)$ over the interval $[4, 7]$.

In Exercises 91–96, evaluate the integral (if possible) assuming that f is an even function such that $\int_1^2 f(t)\, dt = 3$ and $\int_1^3 f(t)\, dt = 7$. If the value of an integral cannot be determined from the information given about f, indicate this.

91. $\int_2^1 f(t)\, dt$

92. $\int_2^2 f(t)\, dt$

93. $\int_{-1}^1 f(t)\, dt$

94. $\int_{-2}^{-1} f(t)\,dt$

95. $\int_{2}^{3} f(t)\,dt$

96. $\int_{1}^{3} |f(t)|\,dt$

97. What is the average value of the function $g(z) = |1 + z|$ over the interval $[-2, 3]$?

98. Suppose that $h(t) = \sqrt{\ln(1 + e^{\sin t})}$. Evaluate $\int_{0}^{\pi} h'(x)\,dx$.

99. Explain why $\displaystyle\lim_{n \to \infty} \frac{3}{n} \sum_{j=1}^{n} \cos\left(1 + \frac{3j}{n}\right) = \sin 4 - \sin 1$.

  [HINT: What is the definition of $\int_{a}^{b} f(x)\,dx$?]

In Exercises 100–103, $F(x) = \int_{0}^{x} f(t)\,dt$, where f is a function such that f, f', and f'' are continuous on the interval $(-\infty, \infty)$ and

  (i) *f is positive on the interval $(-\infty, 1)$ and negative on the interval $(1, \infty)$.*
  (ii) *f is decreasing on the interval $(-\infty, 2)$ and increasing on the interval $(2, \infty)$.*
  (iii) *f is concave up on the interval $(-\infty, 5)$ and concave down on the interval $(5, \infty)$.*

100. Is $F(9) > F(6)$? Justify your answer.

101. Is $\int_{7}^{9} f'(x)\,dx > 0$? Justify your answer.

102. Let $F(x) = \int_{0}^{x} f(t)\,dt$. At which value of x in the interval $[0, 10]$ does $F(x)$ attain its maximum value? Justify your answer.

103. Is $F(x)$ concave up at $x = 3$? Justify your answer.

104. Suppose that $\int_{0}^{5} f(3x)\,dx = 12$. Find values of the constants K, a, and b such that
$$K \int_{a}^{b} f(u)\,du = 3.$$

105. Use the fact that $3 - 2x - x^2 = 4 - (x + 1)^2$ and the substitution $u = (x + 1)/2$ to show that $\displaystyle\int_{0}^{1} \frac{dx}{\sqrt{3 - 2x - x^2}} = \frac{\pi}{3}$.

106. Suppose that $\int_{1}^{e} f(u)\,du = 7$. Find values of the constants K, a, and b such that $K \int_{a}^{b} e^x f(e^x)\,dx = 7$.

107. Suppose that $f(t) = \sqrt{1 + t^4}$. Show that $\dfrac{d}{dx}\left(\int_{0}^{x} f(t)\,dt\right) \neq \int_{0}^{x} f'(t)\,dt$.

108. Is there a function g with the property $\int_{0}^{x} g(t)\,dt = x^2 e^x$? Justify your answer.

109. Explain why there is not a function h with the property $\int_{0}^{x} h(t)\,dt = x^2 - e^x$.

110. Show that $\dfrac{d}{dx}\left(\int_{1}^{x^3} \sin(t^2)\,dt\right) = 3x^2 \sin(x^6)$.
  [HINT: Use the chain rule.]

111. Is $f(0) \cdot 1 + f(2) \cdot 2 + f(4) \cdot 3 + f(6) \cdot 4$ a Riemann sum approximation to $\int_{0}^{10} f(x)\,dx$? Justify your answer.
  [HINT: Draw a picture.]

112. Suppose that f is a continuous function such that $\int_{-1}^{1} f(x)\,dx = 7$. Use this fact to evaluate $\int_{0}^{\pi} f(\cos x)\sin x\,dx$. Show your work.

In Exercises 113–116, $g(x) = \int_{0}^{x} \dfrac{e^{-t}}{1 + t^2}\,dt$.

113. Is $g(3) > 2$? Justify your answer.

114. Is $g(-1) > 1$? Justify your answer.

115. Is g increasing at $x = 1$? Justify your answer.

116. Is g concave up at $x = 1$? Justify your answer.

117. Suppose that $\int_{0}^{8} f(t)\,dt = 4$. Evaluate $\int_{0}^{2} x^2 f(x^3)\,dx$.

118. Explain why a trapezoid approximating sum is *not* a Riemann sum approximation.

119. Evaluate $\int_{-1}^{2} |z|\,dz$.

120. Find an antiderivative of $h(x) = \cos^3 x \sin x$.

INTERLUDE

This Interlude introduces another of the many variants on the mean value theorem, and relations between it and the "standard" version. This Interlude also gives students the chance to sort out implications, converses, and other logical details.

Mean Value Theorems and Integrals

Here are two similarly named theorems:

THEOREM 6 (Mean value theorem for derivatives) Let f be continuous on the closed interval $[a, b]$ and differentiable on the open interval (a, b). Then there is a number c in (a, b) for which

$$f'(c) = \frac{f(b) - f(a)}{b - a}.$$

THEOREM 7 (Mean value theorem for integrals) Let f be continuous on the closed interval $[a, b]$. Then there is a number c in $[a, b]$ for which

$$f(c) = \frac{\int_a^b f(x)\,dx}{b - a}.$$

Theorems 6 and 7 look (and are) closely related to each other, but the first is about derivatives and the second about integrals. In this interlude we'll call these theorems the MVTD and the MVTI, respectively. The names suggest both similarities and differences in the theorems; we explore both.

What the theorems say We met Theorem 6 in Section 4.9 (there we called it just the mean value theorem, or MVT). As the name MVTD suggests, Theorem 6 is about *derivatives* and *averages*: it says that for some c between a and b, the derivative $f'(c)$ is equal to the average rate of change of f over the interval $[a, b]$. Graphically, the MVTD says that, for at least one c between a and b, the slope of the tangent line at $x = c$ is equal to the slope of the secant line over the interval $[a, b]$; see the familiar picture in Figure 1(a).

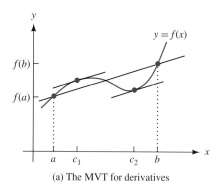

(a) The MVT for derivatives

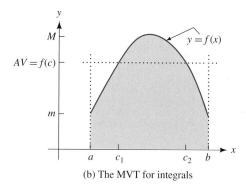

(b) The MVT for integrals

FIGURE 1

Two mean value theorems

Figure 1(b) illustrates the MVTI. It shows *two* values of c in the interval $[a, b]$ that satisfy the equation in Theorem 7. For each such c, the value $f(c)$ is the *average value* (AV) of the function f over the interval $[a, b]$. (We defined average value in Section 5.1 to be the quantity on the right side of Theorem 7.) The MVTI can thus be restated as follows:

If f is continuous on $[a, b]$, then there is at least one c in $[a, b]$ for which the value $f(c)$ equals the average value of f on $[a, b]$.

This should sound reasonable; unless f is constant we'd expect $f(x) > AV$ for some inputs x and $f(x) < AV$ for others inputs. (If f is constant then $f(x) = AV$ for *all* x, so the theorem's claim is clearly true in this case.)

The following problems explore further the MVTI and its connection to the MVTD.

PROBLEM 1 (MVTD and FTC imply MVTI) One way to prove the MVTI is to use the fundamental theorem of calculus (FTC) and the MVTD. To do so, let F be an antiderivative for f. Then we know from the FTC that $\int_a^b f(x)\,dx = F(b) - F(a)$. Use this fact and the MVTD to prove the MVTI.

Note that continuity is required of f; without it, f might "skip" its average value.

PROBLEM 2 (MVTI and FTC imply MVTD) Given the FTC, the MVTD (in a slightly weaker form) can also be proved using the MVTI, as follows: Let f be differentiable with continuous derivative f' on $[a, b]$. By the FTC, we have $f(b) - f(a) = \int_a^b f'(x)\,dx$. Now apply the MVTI to the function $g = f'$ on $[a, b]$ to conclude that the MVTD holds.

PROBLEM 3 (Proving the MVTI without the FTC) Using the FTC to prove the MVTI may be a bit of overkill, especially since the MVTD is sometimes used to prove the FTC. Fortunately, it's not hard to avoid the FTC in proving the MVTI, as follows.

There's an element of circularity in using the FTC to prove a mean value theorem. We show how to dodge that problem here.

We observed in Section 5.1 that if m and M are, respectively, the minimum and maximum values of f on $[a, b]$, then

$$m(b-a) \le \int_a^b f(x)\,dx \le M(b-a).$$

This implies (give details) that the average value of f lies *between* m and M. Use this fact and the intermediate value theorem to prove the MVTI. (You might also mention the extreme value theorem.)

PROBLEM 4 In each part following find a value of c that satisfies the MVTI for the given f and $[a, b]$.

(a) $f(x) = x$ on $[a, b] = [0, 1]$

(b) $f(x) = x^2$ on $[a, b] = [0, 1]$

(c) $f(x) = x^3$ on $[a, b] = [-1, 1]$

(d) $f(x) = e^x$ on $[a, b] = [0, 1]$

PROBLEM 5 Let $f(x) = mx + n$ be any *linear* function and $[a, b]$ any interval. Show that the MVTI holds for f on $[a, b]$ with c equal to the *midpoint* of $[a, b]$.

INTERLUDE

Numerical Integration

6.1 APPROXIMATING INTEGRALS NUMERICALLY

In Chapter 5 we defined the definite integral $\int_a^b f(x)\,dx$ as a limit of certain approximating sums. Since the fundamental theorem of calculus permits many integrals to be calculated by antidifferentiation—without any explicit reference to approximating sums—we might feel tempted to forget approximating sums entirely. That would be a serious mistake. As we'll see in this chapter, approximating sums have down-to-earth, practical value; they lead easily to good approximations for definite integrals, even ones whose "exact" values are hard or impossible to find.

In this chapter we'll see how to use approximating sums of various kinds to estimate integrals. We'll compare how well different types of sums work for this purpose, and we'll even offer "accuracy guarantees" for many of the estimates we produce. We'll also apply similar ideas to find approximate solutions to differential equations. The techniques of this chapter are called **numerical methods** (as opposed to symbolic methods) because, as we'll see, they involve direct numerical computations more than symbolic manipulation.

Students should have ready access to technology for quickly calculating left, right, trapezoid, and midpoint sums; calculators are fine. We don't explicitly expect students to program their own routines for calculating such sums. Doing so could be useful at some point, but those mechanics aren't the main point here.

A sampler of sums

In Sections 5.6 and 5.7 we described several types of approximating sums for integrals (left, right, midpoint, and trapezoid sums) and studied some of their basic properties. For a given integral $I = \int_a^b f(x)\,dx$, each such sum involves the following steps:

We mention Simpson's rule very briefly at the end of this section, and study it in detail in an Interlude. The topic is optional in the sense that Simpson's rule is not required for later work.

- **Partition:** Chop $[a, b]$ into n equal subintervals, each of length $\Delta x = (b - a)/n$, with successive endpoints $x_0 < x_1 < x_2 < \cdots < x_n$.
- **Evaluate:** Choose in each subinterval an input c_i at which to evaluate f (left endpoint, right endpoint, midpoint, etc.).
- **Sum:** Add up the contributions $f(c_i)\,\Delta x$ (one for each subinterval) to calculate the approximating sum.

We'll often write L_n, R_n, T_n, and M_n for left, right, trapezoid, and midpoint sums, each with n equal subdivisions. Here are general formulas for all of them:

$$L_n = (f(x_0) + f(x_1) + \cdots + f(x_{n-1})) \, \Delta x = \sum_{i=0}^{n-1} f(x_i) \, \Delta x$$

$$R_n = (f(x_1) + f(x_1) + \cdots + f(x_n)) \, \Delta x = \sum_{i=1}^{n} f(x_i) \, \Delta x$$

$$T_n = \left(\frac{f(x_0)}{2} + f(x_1) + \cdots + f(x_{n-1}) + \frac{f(x_n)}{2} \right) \Delta x = \sum_{i=1}^{n} \frac{1}{2}(f(x_{i-1}) + f(x_i)) \, \Delta x$$

$$M_n = (f(m_1) + f(m_1) + \cdots + f(m_n)) \, \Delta x = \sum_{i=1}^{n} f(m_i) \, \Delta x.$$

In the last line, $m_i = (x_{i-1} + x_i)/2$, the midpoint of the ith subdivision.

EXAMPLE 1 Let $I = \int_0^1 \sin x \, dx$. Write out the approximating sums R_{100} and M_{100}, both without and with sigma notation.

Many students have trouble writing sums in sigma notation; seeing both sigma and expanded forms helps explain each.

Solution Chopping the interval $[0, 100]$ into 100 equal-length subintervals gives the partition points $x_0 = 0$, $x_1 = 0.01$, $x_2 = 0.02$, ..., $x_{99} = 0.99$, $x_{100} = 1.00$, and so the right sum has the form

$$R_{100} = \big(\sin(0.01) + \sin(0.02) + \cdots + \sin(1.00) \big) \cdot \frac{1}{100}.$$

For M_{100} we evaluate f at the *midpoint* of each subinterval:

$$M_{100} = \big(\sin(0.005) + \sin(0.015) + \cdots + \sin(0.085) + \sin(0.095) \big) \cdot \frac{1}{100}.$$

To write these sums in sigma notation, we first express the right endpoints and the midpoints using an index variable i. The ith right endpoint has the form $x_i = 0.01i$ (for i from 1 to 100), whereas the ith midpoint can be written as $m_i = 0.005 + 0.01i$ (for i from 0 to 99). In sigma notation, the sums have the form

$$R_{100} = \sum_{i=1}^{100} \sin(0.01\,i) \cdot \frac{1}{100}; \qquad M_{100} = \sum_{i=0}^{99} \sin(0.005 + 0.01i) \cdot \frac{1}{100}.$$

Evaluating such monstrous sums—no matter the form—is no job fit for a human. ∎

Help from technology Computers and calculators have no trouble calculating sums like those in Example 1. Exactly *how* one uses technology to calculate such sums depends, of course, on the machine at hand. On the TI–86 calculator, for instance, commands of the form

```
sum(seq(sin(0.01*i),i,1,100))/100
sum(seq(sin(0.005+0.01*i),i,0,99))/100
```

evaluate the sums in Example 1. The results (to five decimal places) are

$$R_{100} = 0.46390 \quad \text{and} \quad M_{100} = 0.45970.$$

With the computer package *Maple*, to give another example, one might give commands something like the following to calculate the approximating sums L_{20}, R_{20}, T_{20}, and M_{20} for the integral $\int_0^1 \sin x \, dx$:

These are not "built-in" Maple commands, but they illustrate typical syntax. Maple has similar commands with names like **middlesum**.

```
left(sin(x), x=0..1, 20)        right(sin(x), x=0..1, 20)
trapezoid(sin(x), x=0..1, 20)   midpoint(sin(x), x=0..1, 20)
```

In this book we'll sometimes use *Maple*-style commands like those above—but only as illustrations, not necessarily as literal commands to be typed. It's the ideas that count—and exactly the *same* ideas apply with any form of technology.

EXAMPLE 2 Calculate several approximating sums for $\int_0^1 \sin x \, dx$. Compare results to the "exact" answer.

Solution The fundamental theorem of calculus (FTC) gives the exact answer (we rounded the numerical version to five decimal places):

$$\int_0^1 \sin x \, dx = -\cos x \Big]_0^1 = -\cos 1 + \cos 0 \approx 0.45970.$$

For comparison, here are results rounded to five decimal places:

Sum	Input	Output
L_{20}	`left(sin(x), x=0..1, 20)`	0.43857
R_{20}	`right(sin(x), x=0..1, 20)`	0.48064
T_{20}	`trapezoid(sin(x), x=0..1, 20)`	0.45960
M_{20}	`midpoint(sin(x), x=0..1, 20)`	0.45975

Notice that all four results are in the general ballpark, but the trapezoid and midpoint sums are much better estimates than the other two. Understanding how well various sums approximate integrals and why some do better than others is an important theme of this chapter. ∎

Real examples Example 2 shows nicely how (and why) approximating sums work, but in an important sense it's artificial: If we *know* the exact value of an integral, then there's little practical value in approximating it. The best use of approximating sums is in approximating integrals we *can't* evaluate exactly.

Why not? Because (for deep reasons) the antiderivative of $\sin(x^2)$ is not an elementary function.

EXAMPLE 3 Use approximating sums to estimate $I = \int_0^1 \sin(x^2) \, dx$. (The integral I can't be evaluated by antidifferentiation.) ◄ Can we say anything for *certain* about the exact value of I?

Solution With technology we can use fairly large values of n. Here are some results rounded to five decimals:

$$L_{100} = 0.30607; \quad R_{100} = 0.31448; \quad T_{100} = 0.31028; \quad M_{100} = 0.31026.$$

The four sums are close to each other, and so we can reasonably hope that they're also close to the true value of I. Without further information, we'd probably guess (but it's only a guess) that I lies somewhere near 0.310. We'll explain soon how to find a small interval (which contains 0.310) that's *guaranteed* to contain I, but it's important to realize that we may never know I exactly. ∎

Errors and error bounds

This subsection is about the idea and vocabulary of errors and error bounds; systematic error bounding comes later. The idea of an accuracy guarantee is new to many students.

Many quantities of interest, such as the integral in Example 3 or the *true* fraction of voters who prefer Smith to Jones in an election, are difficult or impossible to compute exactly; they *must* be estimated. But an approximation alone has little value. We'd also like some measure of how accurate an approximation is. A credible opinion poll, for instance, reports not only that 58% of voters surveyed prefer Smith but also that the true statistic *probably* falls between, say, 55% and 61%.

We'd like some similar measure of accuracy for approximating sums. Our wish is about to be granted—and in a much stronger way than opinion polls permit. Remarkably enough, we can often guarantee that approximating sums are accurate to within a small tolerance. We treat this theme informally in the rest of this section and in more detail in the next section.

Errors committed by approximating sums   For a given integral $I = \int_a^b f(x)\,dx$ and a large value of n, we expect the approximating sums $L_n, R_n, T_n,$ and M_n to be "close" to the exact value of I. But *how* close? Within 0.01? Within 0.000000000001? Can we be sure? Surprisingly often, we can.

The word "error" means several (mostly disagreeable) things in everyday speech. In mathematics, "error" has a simpler (and more agreeable) meaning: it's the *difference* between an exact value and an approximation. For an approximating sum T_n, for example, we call the difference $I - T_n$ the **error committed by** T_n. In the same spirit, $|I - T_n|$ is called the **absolute error** (or the **magnitude** of the error) committed by T_n. In Example 2, for instance, the error committed by M_{20} is (with numbers rounded to five decimals)

$$I - M_{20} = -\cos 1 + \cos 0 - 0.45975 = -0.00005.$$

The error is *negative* because M_{20} slightly *overestimates* I. The magnitude of the error, 0.00005, is *small* because M_{20} approximates I so closely. The following table collects a variety of error results:

\multicolumn{5}{c}{**Errors committed in approximating $I = \int_0^1 \sin(x)\,dx$**}
n	$I - L_n$	$I - R_n$	$I - T_n$	$I - M_n$
4	0.107580	−0.102787	0.002396	−0.001200
8	0.053190	−0.051993	0.000598	−0.000300
16	0.026445	−0.026146	0.000149	−0.000075
32	0.013185	−0.013111	0.000036	−0.000018

Reading down any column shows how errors tend to decrease in magnitude as n increases; reading across any row shows how one method compares with another.

Bounding errors   We can't expect (except in some contrived cases) to compute *exactly* the error a given approximation commits—doing so would be tantamount to finding the unknown quantity exactly. But it is often reasonable to ask for an **error bound**—a guarantee that the error committed by an approximation does not exceed some given amount.

Error bounds are usually stated as inequalities, sometimes involving absolute values. Here are two examples:

$$0 \leq I - L_{10} \leq 0.01; \qquad |I - M_n| \leq \frac{32}{n^2}.$$

Notice:

- **Worst-case scenarios**   Both inequalities guarantee that the error is *no worse than* the quantity on the right; the *actual* error committed may be much less.

- **An underestimate**   The first (double) inequality means that L_{10} lies within 0.01 of, but *underestimates*, the exact integral I.

We stress the idea of trapping a number between an overestimate and an underestimate.

This stands to reason; we expect more work to give a better result.

- **Size, not sign** The second inequality says that, for given n, the absolute error committed by M_n doesn't exceed $32/n^2$. We bound the *absolute* error when we care (or know) more about the size than the sign of the error.

- **Improvement as n increases** Finding and using inequalities like the second one above is the subject of the next section. But we can notice right now that the inequality depends on n: As n increases, the right side decreases toward zero, and so the absolute error committed by M_n also decreases toward zero. ◂

In general we downplay discussion of roundoff errors, which could easily become a distraction from the main thread. These paragraphs are exceptional in that sense.

Is more always better? Roundoff errors Common sense suggests that for a given integral I, L_{100} commits less error than L_{10}, T_{100} outperforms T_{10}, and so on—for more work we expect better accuracy. But more isn't *always* better. In the real world, approximating sums like L_{10000} and $T_{1000000}$ are less useful than we might expect. One drawback to using huge values of n is that adding many numbers can take a lot of time, even for a fast computer. A more serious problem is that small roundoff errors (which *always* occur in decimal arithmetic) can accumulate in repetitive calculations. In the worst cases roundoff errors can make a calculation completely meaningless.

A full treatment of roundoff errors is outside the scope of a calculus text. We'll control roundoff errors (though we'll never completely escape them) by avoiding unnecessarily large-scale computations.

Trapping the elusive integral

We pursue the "trapping" idea as a relatively simple entry point to the idea of error bounding for integrals. We take a more sophisticated, derivative-based approach in the next section.

One simple method of controlling the error committed by approximating sums is to "trap" the (unknown) exact value I *between* two approximating sums. The following example shows the basic idea.

EXAMPLE 4 Let $I = \int_0^1 \sin(x^2)\,dx$. In Example 3 we calculated the approximating sums

$$L_{100} = 0.30607; \quad R_{100} = 0.31448; \quad T_{100} = 0.31028; \quad M_{100} = 0.31026.$$

Use these numbers to "trap" I.

Solution The first key observation is that the integrand $\sin(x^2)$ is *increasing* on the interval $[0, 1]$. A useful conclusion follows:

Every left sum L_n underestimates I; every right sum R_n overestimates I.

Figure 1 illustrates the first part of our claim.

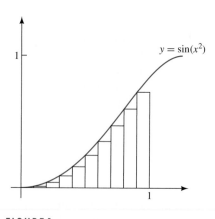

FIGURE 1
Left sums underestimate $\int_0^1 \sin(x^2)dx$

It follows that I lies somewhere *between* L_{100} and R_{100}:

$$L_{100} = 0.30607 \leq I \leq 0.31449 = R_{100}.$$

This is well worth knowing—especially because we don't know I exactly.

We could pull L_n and R_n even closer together by using larger values of n. But we can do even better, with less work, by using the trapezoid and midpoint estimates T_{100} and M_{100}. Figure 1 shows that the integrand is *concave up* on the interval $[0, 1]$. As a result the trapezoid rule T_n *overestimates* the integral for every n. ➜ It's less obvious, but also true, that M_n *underestimates* the integral; thus,

Do you see why the shape of the graph ensures this?

$$M_{100} = 0.31026 \leq I \leq 0.31028 = T_{100}.$$

This is an even "tighter" trap than we had from left and right sums.   ■

Trapping with left and right sums: monotone functions   The main trapping idea in the preceding example was that if the integrand f happens to be *increasing* on $[a, b]$, then every left sum *underestimates* $\int_a^b f(x)\,dx$, while every right sum *overestimates*. The reverse occurs if f happens to *decrease* on $[a, b]$. The following simple but useful theorem covers both possibilities: ➜

Trapping is easiest with monotone functions and left and right sums.

Recall: "monotone" means "increasing or decreasing but not both."

THEOREM 1 (Trapping the integral of a monotone function)   Suppose that f is monotone on $[a, b]$, and let $I = \int_a^b f(x)\,dx$. For any positive integers n and m, either

$$L_n \leq I \leq R_m \quad \text{or} \quad R_m \leq I \leq L_n.$$

In either case, I lies *between* L_n and R_m.

(Often we'll use $n = m$, but that's not necessary; inequalities like $L_4 \leq I \leq R_7$ are sometimes useful.)

We can't expect a simple theorem to solve *all* our problems—after all, many integrals don't involve monotone functions. Still, we can often get useful information from the theorem—sometimes with only a little extra work. We illustrate the idea with two examples.

EXAMPLE 5   (Exploiting symmetry)   Use left and right sums to find good upper and lower bounds for $I = \int_{-1}^{1} e^{x^2}\,dx$.

Solution   The integrand $f(x) = e^{x^2}$ is *not* monotone on $[-1, 1]$; it decreases on $[-1, 0]$ and increases on $[0, 1]$. But f is an *even* function and so its graph is symmetric about the y-axis. Thus, we can write

$$I = \int_{-1}^{1} e^{x^2}\,dx = 2\int_0^1 e^{x^2}\,dx = 2I_0.$$

Now $I_0 = \int_0^1 e^{x^2}\,dx$ *does* satisfy the hypothesis of Theorem 1, and so we'll use technology to find some left and right sums for I_0. Following are several, rounded to five decimal places:

Again, the inputs are in Maple style, but aren't "built in" Maple commands.

Sum	Input	Output
L_{10}	left(exp(x^2), x=0..1, 10)	1.38126
R_{10}	right(exp(x^2), x=0..1, 10)	1.55309
L_{100}	left(exp(x^2), x=0..1, 100)	1.45412
R_{100}	right(exp(x^2), x=0..1, 100)	1.47130

The first two rows and Theorem 1 imply that $1.38126 \le I_0 \le 1.55309$. The last two rows say something stronger: $1.45412 \le I_0 \le 1.47130$. Thus, we've trapped I_0 in a small interval. To trap our *real* prey, $I = 2I_0$, we multiply the preceding inequality by 2:

$$1.45412 \le I_0 \le 1.47130 \implies 2.90824 \le 2I_0 = I \le 2.94260.$$

(Multiplying the weaker inequality $1.38126 \le I_0 \le 1.55309$ by 2 gives the weaker result $2.76252 \le I \le 3.10618$.) ■

We'll employ another divide-and-conquer strategy when we get to partial fractions; the general technique may deserve mention.

E X A M P L E 6 **(Divide and conquer)**   Use left and right sums to trap $I = \int_0^2 \sin(x^2)\,dx$.

This is easy to check using derivatives or by plotting.

Solution As in Example 5, the integrand is not monotone—it increases for $0 \le x \le \sqrt{\pi/2} \approx 1.2533$ and decreases for $\sqrt{\pi/2} \le x \le 2$. ◀ Thus, we can split the desired integral into two pieces, each of which *does* satisfy the hypothesis of Theorem 1:

$$I = I_1 + I_2 = \int_0^{\sqrt{\pi/2}} \sin(x^2)\,dx + \int_{\sqrt{\pi/2}}^2 \sin(x^2)\,dx.$$

Now we apply Theorem 1, first to I_1 and then to I_2. For I_1 we find

$$L_{100} = 0.54301 \quad \text{and} \quad R_{100} = 0.55554, \quad \text{so} \quad 0.54301 \le I_1 \le 0.55554.$$

For I_2,

$$L_{100} = 0.26205 \quad \text{and} \quad R_{100} = 0.24893, \quad \text{so} \quad 0.24893 \le I_2 \le 0.26205.$$

Having trapped I_1 and I_2, we can add the preceding inequalities to trap I:

$$0.54301 + 0.24893 = 0.79194 \le I_1 + I_2 \le 0.81759 = 0.55554 + 0.26205.$$ ■

The trapping idea is easy for trapezoid sums, but a bit subtle for midpoint sums. A close look at Figure 3 should be useful.

Midpoint and trapezoid traps   As we said in Example 4, some integrals can be trapped between trapezoid and midpoint sums; *concavity* is what matters.

E X A M P L E 7   Use M_4 and T_4 to approximate $I = \int_0^1 x^2\,dx$. How much error does each sum commit?

Solution By the FTC, the exact value is $I = 1/3$. Routine calculations (by hand or machine) give

$$M_4 = \frac{63}{192}; \quad T_4 = \frac{66}{192}; \quad I = \frac{1}{3} = \frac{64}{192}.$$

(We calculated with fractions for ease of comparison.) The numbers show that T_4 *overestimates* I (by $2/192$) and M_4 *underestimates* I (by $1/192$). Figure 2 illustrates these results:

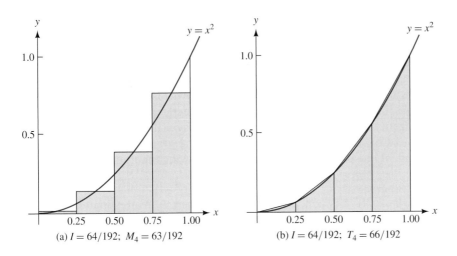

(a) $I = 64/192$; $M_4 = 63/192$

(b) $I = 64/192$; $T_4 = 66/192$

FIGURE 2
Midpoint and trapezoid estimates to $\int_0^1 x^2\, dx$

Figure 2(b) shows that (and why) T_4 overestimates I (though not by much). Upward concavity of the integrand means that the f-graph sags *below* the secant lines that define the trapezoid estimate. It's less obvious (but visible if you look *really* closely at Figure 2(a)) that M_4 underestimates I. ■

The midpoint rule and tangent lines   Thinking of the midpoint rule in a slightly different way will help explain why it underestimates the integral in Example 7. So far we've thought of M_n as a sum of *rectangular* areas, obtained by replacing the graph of f over a subinterval with a horizontal line determined at the midpoint m_i, as in Figure 3(a). An alternative, but equivalent, approach to M_n often reveals the *direction* of error more clearly. The key idea is as follows:

> *Replace the graph of f over the ith subinterval with the* tangent line *(rather than a horizontal line) at $x = m_i$.*

Figure 3(b) illustrates this view of the midpoint rule:

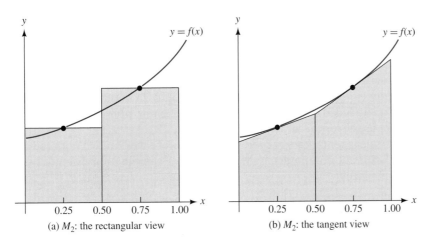

(a) M_2: the rectangular view

(b) M_2: the tangent view

FIGURE 3
Two views of the midpoint rule

From this point of view, M_n becomes a sum of *trapezoidal* areas; the tops (or bottoms if the function is negative) of the trapezoids are determined by *tangent lines*. For the trapezoid rule T_n, by contrast, the tops (or bottoms) are *secant* lines.

Why do both the rectangular and tangent approaches to M_n produce the same answer? The reason has nothing special to do with tangent lines. The fortunate fact is that the area of *any* trapezoid (with parallel vertical sides, as shown) is its base times its *height at the midpoint*. Thus, the shaded areas in Figure 3 are indeed equal.

We'll return in the next section to the connection between concavity and midpoint and trapezoid errors.

The "tangent view" of M_n explains clearly why *concavity* determines the sign of the error committed by M_n. Upward concavity of the integrand means that the f-graph lies *above* the tangent line on each subinterval. The following theorem collects what we know:

> **THEOREM 2**   If f is concave *up* on $[a, b]$, then T_n overestimates I and M_n underestimates I. If f is concave *down*, the reverse holds. In both cases, I lies between T_n and M_n.

Splitting the difference: averaging different sums

Theorem 1 says that for a monotone integrand the exact integral I lies between L_n and R_n. This suggests an obvious strategy: split the difference. Indeed, trapezoid sums can be thought of as doing exactly that:

We discussed this in Section 5.7.

$$\text{For all } n, \; T_n = \frac{L_n + R_n}{2} \text{ is the average of } L_n \text{ and } R_n. \;\blacktriangleleft$$

We can approach trapezoid and midpoint estimates in a similar way. Theorem 2 guarantees for certain integrals that T_n and M_n trap I. Therefore, it's reasonable to "compromise" between trapezoid and midpoint sums. This time, however, we'll split the difference unevenly because, as a rough rule, T_n commits about *twice* as much approximation error as M_n. (Example 7 illustrates this; so do the numbers in Example 2.) Therefore, we use, instead of the ordinary average of T_n and M_n, the number one-third of the way from M_n to T_n (called a **weighted average**). We state the result as a definition:

> **DEFINITION (Simpson's rule)**   For any positive integer n, the quantity
>
> $$S_{2n} = \frac{2}{3} M_n + \frac{1}{3} T_n$$
>
> is the **Simpson's rule approximation** with $2n$ subdivisions.

Notice the subscript on the left: It's $2n$, not n, because the subdivision endpoints x_i together with the midpoints m_i partition the interval $[a, b]$ into $2n$ subdivisions. Notice also the unequal **weights** attached to M_n and T_n; the more accurate approximation M_n gets twice as much weight as the less accurate T_n.

We say much more about Simpson's rule in an Interlude at the end of this chapter. Here we treat it only as a special average of trapezoid and midpoint estimates.

Simpson's rule is remarkably accurate and therefore well known both to humans and to many calculators and computers. Using the data in Example 2, for example, we calculate (to five decimal places)

$$S_{40} = \frac{2}{3} M_{20} + \frac{1}{3} T_{20} = \frac{2}{3} 0.45975 + \frac{1}{3} 0.45960 = 0.45970,$$

which agrees with the exact value of I to all five decimal places shown. In fact, calculating with more decimal places shows that S_{40} agrees with I to eight or nine decimal places. (We explore Simpson's rule further in an Interlude at the end of this chapter.)

BASIC EXERCISES

1. Let $I = \int_1^4 \dfrac{dx}{\sqrt{x}}$.

  (a) Use the FTC to evaluate I exactly.

  (b) Write out the approximating sums L_3, R_3, T_3, and M_3.

  (c) Compute the approximation errors $|I - L_3|$, $|I - R_3|$, $|I - T_3|$, and $|I - M_3|$.

  (d) What is the approximation error made by S_6?

2. Let $I = \int_0^1 x^3 \, dx$.

  (a) Use the FTC to evaluate I exactly.

  (b) Write out the approximating sums L_4, R_4, T_4, and M_4.

  (c) Compute the approximation errors made by L_4, R_4, T_4, M_4, and S_8.

3. Let $I = \int_0^1 \sin(x^2) \, dx$. Explain why the inequalities $L_7 \le I \le R_4$ are valid.

4. Let $I = \int_1^3 \cos(1/x) \, dx$.

  (a) Explain why the inequalities $L_7 \le I \le R_{13}$ are valid.

  (b) Explain why the inequalities $T_{11} \le I \le M_7$ are valid.

5. Let $I = \int_0^2 e^{x^2} \, dx$.

  (a) Compute L_{10}, R_{10}, T_{10}, M_{10}, and S_{20}.

  (b) Use L_{10} and R_{10} to find a bound on the approximation error made by T_{10}.

  (c) Use M_{10} and T_{10} to find a bound on the approximation error made by S_{20}.

6. Let $I = \int_1^3 e^{-x^2} \, dx$.

  (a) Compute L_{20}, R_{20}, T_{20}, M_{20}, and S_{40}.

  (b) Does L_{20} underestimate I? Justify your answer.

  (c) Does M_{20} underestimate I? Justify your answer.

7. Let $I = \int_0^1 f(x) \, dx$, where the function f has the values shown in the table:

x	0.00	0.25	0.50	0.75	1.00
$f(x)$	1.307	1.096	1.018	1.173	1.435

  (a) Compute L_4, R_4, T_4, M_2, and S_4.

  (b) A plot of the data shows that it reasonable to assume that f is concave up on the interval $[0, 1]$. Use this assumption and your results from part (a) to find upper and lower bounds on I. Justify your choices.

8. Let $I = \int_{-1}^2 f(x) \, dx$, where f has the values shown in the table.

x	−1.00	−0.25	0.50	1.25	2.00
$f(x)$	0.0000	2.6522	4.8755	6.8328	8.6790

  (a) Compute L_4, R_4, T_4, M_2, and S_4.

  (b) A plot of the data shows that it reasonable to assume that f is increasing and concave down on the interval $[0, 1]$. Use this assumption and your results from part (a) to find upper and lower bounds on I. Justify your choices.

9. Let $I = \int_0^1 \sin x \, dx$.

  (a) Use the table in Example 2 to compute the approximation errors committed by each of the approximating sums L_{20}, M_{20}, R_{20}, and T_{20}.

  (b) Why does L_{20} underestimate I?

  (c) Why does T_{20} underestimate I?

10. Let $I = \int_0^1 \sin x \, dx$. How does the table on page 375 show that, for all the methods, the approximation errors tend to decrease in magnitude as n increases?

11. Let $I = \int_0^1 \sin x \, dx$. How does the table on page 375 show that M_n overestimates I for all of the values of n shown?

12. Let I and I_0 be as in Example 5.

  (a) Compute the approximating sum T_{100} for I_0.

  (b) Use part (a) to compute an estimate of I.

13. Let $I = \int_0^1 \sin(x^2) \, dx$. Use the information in Example 3 to compute S_{200}.

14. Let $I = \int_5^7 \cos x \, dx$.

  (a) Write out the approximating sum S_4.

  (b) Compute the approximation error made by S_4.

Let $I = \int_1^5 f(x) \, dx$. In Exercises 15–18, give an example (graphical or symbolic) of a function f such that the given inequality is true for all $n \ge 1$. In each case, identify the property (or properties) of f that guarantee that the inequality is true.

15. $L_n > I$ **16.** $R_n < I$

17. $T_n < I$ **18.** $M_n > I$

19. (a) Let $I = \int_a^b f(x) \, dx$ and suppose that f is positive and concave up on the interval $[a, b]$. Use words and pictures to explain why T_n overestimates I for all $n \ge 1$.

  (b) Let I and f be as in part (a), but suppose that f is negative on some or all of the interval $[a, b]$. Does T_n still overestimate I for all $n \ge 1$? Justify your answer.

20. Let $I = \int_{-2}^5 f(x) \, dx$, where f is an increasing function over the interval $[-2, 5]$. Furthermore, suppose that $L_{10} = 9.4132$ and $R_{10} = 9.5768$.

  (a) Explain why $|I - L_{10}| \le R_{10} - L_{10}$.

  (b) Evaluate T_{10}.

  (c) Explain why $|I - T_{10}| \le 0.0818$. [HINT: $0.0818 = (R_{10} - L_{10})/2$.]

21. Let $I = \int_a^b f(x) \, dx$. Show that $T_n = (L_n + R_n)/2$.

22. Suppose that f is monotone on $[a, b]$. Explain why $|I - T_n| \leq \dfrac{|L_n - R_n|}{2}$.

23. Suppose that f does not have any inflection points in $[a, b]$. Explain why $|I - S_{2n}| \leq |M_n - T_n|$.

24. Let $I = \displaystyle\int_a^b f(x)\,dx$ and suppose that f is decreasing on $[a, b]$. Rank L_n, R_n, and T_n in increasing order.

25. Let $I = \displaystyle\int_a^b f(x)\,dx$ and suppose that f is increasing on $[a, b]$. Explain why $L_n \leq M_n \leq R_n$ for all $n \geq 1$.

26. Let $I = \displaystyle\int_a^b f(x)\,dx$, where f is the function shown below. Rank the values I, L_{30}, R_{30}, T_{30}, and M_{30} in increasing order. Justify your answer.

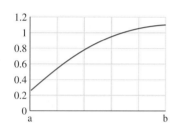

27. Suppose that f is positive, increasing, and concave down on the interval $[1, 7]$. Rank the following estimates of $\displaystyle\int_1^7 f(x)\,dx$ in increasing order: L_{100}, M_{100}, R_{100}, S_{200}, T_{100}.

28. Let f be the function shown below. Estimates of $\displaystyle\int_a^b f(x)\,dx$ computed using the left, right, midpoint, and trapezoid rules (all with the same number of equal subintervals) are 8.52974, 9.71090, 9.74890, and 11.04407. Which rule produced which estimate? Justify your answer.

Let $I = \displaystyle\int_a^b f(x)\,dx$, where f is positive and increasing over the interval $[a, b]$. In Exercises 29–34, indicate whether, for all $n \geq 1$, the statement must be true, cannot be true, or may be true. Justify your answers.

29. $L_n < I$

30. $M_n < I$

31. $L_n < R_n$

32. $L_n < M_n$

33. $L_n < T_n$

34. $T_n < M_n$

Let $I = \displaystyle\int_a^b f(x)\,dx$, where f is positive and concave up over the interval $[a, b]$. In Exercises 35–40, indicate whether, for all $n \geq 1$, the statement must be true, cannot be true, or may be true. Justify your answers.

35. $R_n \leq I$

36. $M_n \leq I$

37. $L_n \leq R_n$

38. $R_n \leq M_n$

39. $R_n \leq T_n$

40. $T_n \leq M_n$

Let $I = \displaystyle\int_a^b f(x)\,dx$, where f is positive, decreasing, and concave down over the interval $[a, b]$. In Exercises 41–46, indicate whether, for all $n \geq 1$, the statement must be true, cannot be true, or may be true. Justify your answers.

41. $R_n \leq I$

42. $T_n \leq I$

43. $L_n \leq R_n$

44. $L_n \leq T_n$

45. $R_n \leq M_n$

46. $T_n \leq M_n$

Let $I = \displaystyle\int_0^5 f(x)\,dx$, and suppose that the following inequalities are true if $0 \leq x \leq 5$:

    (i) $f(x) \geq 0$;

    (ii) $1 \leq f'(x) \leq 3$;

    (iii) $2 \leq f''(x) \leq 7$.

In Exercises 47–50, indicate whether the statement must be true, may be true, or cannot be true. Justify your answers.

47. $I - L_{10} > 0$

48. $I - T_{10} > 0.00005$

49. $M_{10} < R_{10}$

50. $S_{20} < M_{10}$

FURTHER EXERCISES

51. Explain how the "divide and conquer" strategy can be used with midpoint and trapezoid approximating sums to trap $I = \displaystyle\int_0^2 \sin(x^2)\,dx$.

52. Let $I = \displaystyle\int_0^4 xe^{-x}\,dx$.

    (a) Explain how to use left and right approximating sums to bound the value of I.

    (b) Explain how to use midpoint and trapezoid approximating sums to bound the value of I.

53. Suppose that f is a linear function and that $I = \displaystyle\int_a^b f(x)\,dx$.

    (a) Explain why $T_n = I$ for every $n \geq 1$.

    (b) Use words and pictures to show that the area of any trapezoid with parallel vertical sides is its base times its height at the midpoint.

    (c) Use part (a) to show that $M_n = T_n$ for every $n \geq 1$.

54. Show that $R_n = L_n + \big(f(b) - f(a)\big) \cdot \Delta x$, where $\Delta x = (b - a)/n$.

55. Show that $T_n = L_n + \dfrac{1}{2}\big(f(b) - f(a)\big) \cdot \Delta x$, where $\Delta x = (b - a)/n$.

56. Let $I = \int_a^b f(x)\,dx$, where f is increasing and concave up on the interval $[a, b]$. Explain why $|I - L_n| \le |I - R_n|$.

57. Let $I = \int_a^b f(x)\,dx$, where f is increasing and concave up on the interval $[a, b]$.

   (a) Explain why $|I - M_n| \le |I - L_n|$.

   (b) What can be said about the relationship between $|I - M_n|$ and $|I - R_n|$? Justify your answer.

58. Suppose that $f'(x) > 0$ and $f''(x) < 0$ if $a \le x \le b$. Use a picture to show that T_n is a more accurate estimate of $I = \int_a^b f(x)\,dx$ than L_n (i.e., $|I - T_n| < |I - L_n|$).

59. Suppose that $f'(x) > 0$ and $f''(x) > 0$ if $a \le x \le b$. Is R_n a more accurate estimate of $I = \int_a^b f(x)\,dx$ than T_n? Justify your answer.

60. Let $I = \int_a^b F(x)\,dx$, where F is an antiderivative of the function f in Exercise 26. Does T_{100} underestimate or overestimate the value of I? Explain.

In Exercises 61–64, $I = \int_a^b f(x)\,dx$ where f' is the function shown below.

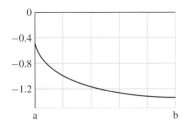

61. Rank the values I, L_n, R_n, M_n, and T_n in increasing order. Justify your answer.

62. Suppose that $f(x) \ge 0$ if $a \le x \le b$. Does L_n overestimate $\int_a^b \dfrac{dx}{1 + f(x)}$? Justify your answer.

63. Does R_n overestimate $\int_a^b \sqrt{1 + \left(f'(x)\right)^2}\,dx$? Justify your answer.

64. Does M_n overestimate $\int_a^b e^{-f(x)}\,dx$? Justify your answer.

In Exercises 65–68, f is an antiderivative of the function shown below.

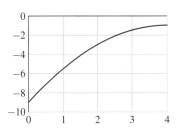

65. Let $I = \int_0^4 f(x)\,dx$. Rank the values of the approximating sums L_n, R_n, M_n, T_n, and S_{2n} in increasing order. Justify your answer.

66. Suppose that $f(0) = 0$ and that $I = \int_0^4 x f(x)\,dx$. Rank the values L_n, R_n, and I in increasing order.

67. Suppose that $f(0) = 0$ and that $I = \int_0^4 \left(f(x)\right)^2\,dx$. Rank the values L_n, R_n, and I in increasing order.

68. Suppose that $I = \int_0^4 e^{f(x)}\,dx$. Rank the values M_n, T_n, and I in increasing order.

Let $I = \int_a^b f(x)\,dx$ and suppose that f'' is the function shown below. In Exercises 69–74, indicate whether the inequality must *be true,* cannot *be true, or* may *be true. Justify your answers.*

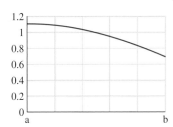

69. $I \le M_{100}$

70. $I \le L_{200}$

71. $L_{100} \le R_{100}$

72. $T_{200} \le M_{200}$

73. $M_{50} \le L_{50}$

74. $M_{100} \le S_{200}$

6.2 ERROR BOUNDS FOR APPROXIMATING SUMS

This section is optional in the sense that its contents are not required for later work. The main new idea here is that of using bounds on derivatives to create error bounds for numerical integrals.

Any estimate to an unknown quantity is most useful when it comes with an **error bound**—an ironclad guarantee that the estimate is in error by no more than some predetermined, computable amount. We develop several such guarantees in this section.

In Section 6.1 we described one approach to accuracy guarantees: "trapping" the desired integral between a known *underestimate* and a known *overestimate*. The trapping method is simple, but it works only for rather special integrals—those whose integrands are either monotone or don't change their direction of concavity on the interval of integration. Unfortunately, many useful integrals fail both these tests.

EXAMPLE 1   Estimate $I = \int_0^3 \sin(x^2)\,dx$.

Solution   As we said in Section 6.1, the integrand $\sin(x^2)$ has no elementary antiderivative formula, and so the fundamental theorem of calculus doesn't help us find I. The trapping methods of Section 6.1 don't apply either because the integrand is neither monotone nor of constant concavity on $[0, 3]$. Still, it's easy to calculate approximating sums using technology. Here are several (rounded to five decimals):

$$L_{50} = 0.75956; \quad R_{50} = 0.78428; \quad T_{50} = 0.77192; \quad M_{50} = 0.77439.$$

These nice numbers all lie in the same vicinity, and so it seems safe to guess that I lies *somewhere* nearby. But how good is each of these estimates? How much better accuracy could we expect from, say, doubling the number of subdivisions? The error bound formulas of this section let us answer such questions. For this integral I, for instance, these formulas produce the following **error bounds**: ◄

We'll give more details later; the general form of error bounds is the main point here.

$$|I - L_{50}| \le 0.54 \quad \text{and} \quad |I - M_{50}| \le 0.02.$$

We can rewrite these results as double inequalities if we prefer. For the first, we have

$$0.21956 = L_{50} - 0.54 \le I \le L_{50} + 0.54 = 1.29956.$$

This means that I, whatever its *exact* value may be, lies somewhere between 0.21956 and 1.29956. ◄

These inequalities illustrate several points:

That's a large margin of error; we'll do better with the trapezoid and midpoint rules.

- **Which does better?**   The second inequality is much "better" than the first—in practice, midpoint sums usually commit less error than left sums.

- **Ironclad promises**   Error bounds are *guarantees*, not just guesses. The second inequality, for example, means that I *must* lie within 0.02 of M_{50}, that is, somewhere in the interval $[0.75439, 0.79439]$.

The fact that an error bound may overestimate (but not underestimate) actual errors deserves emphasis.

- **Pessimistic views**   Error bounds represent worst-case scenarios; in practice, approximating sums often commit less error than their pessimistic error bounds predict.   ■

Sources of error

Different types of approximating sums commit errors for different reasons. Understanding the reasons is the key to controlling errors.

Left- and right-rule errors, constant functions, and first derivatives   Left and right sums are conceptually almost identical; left- and right-rule errors have the same source. ◄ The left and right rules "pretend," in effect, that f is *constant* on each subinterval. In particular:

For simplicity, we'll concentrate mainly on left sums, but all the important ideas apply to right sums too.

If f is constant on $[a, b]$, then the left and right rules commit zero *error in estimating $I = \int_a^b f$.*

The first derivative tells whether this situation applies: f is *constant* on an interval if and only if $f' = 0$ on that interval.

Thus, constant functions represent the best possible case for left and right sums. But most functions of interest are not constant; the more f deviates from being constant, the worse the left and right rules behave. In graphical terms, the steeper the graph of f, the more error L_n and R_n commit. (The same principle holds whether f rises or falls; the only difference is whether L_n underestimates or overestimates.)

The quantity $|f'(x)|$ measures how steeply the f-graph rises or falls at x. If $|f'|$ is large on $[a, b]$, then f is far from constant, and so we expect L_n and R_n to produce poor approximations. The following example illustrates how $|f'|$ affects left-rule errors for three linear functions.

In a nutshell: Since f' measures "non-constancy" (the source of left and right rule errors), f' determines how much error these rules commit.

EXAMPLE 2 How well does L_4 approximate each of the three integrals $\int_0^1 x\,dx$, $\int_0^1 2x\,dx$, and $\int_0^1 (4 - 4x)\,dx$? How are the results linked to first derivatives?

Solution Figure 1 shows how well or poorly L_4 works for each integral. Shaded areas represent L_4 *errors*.

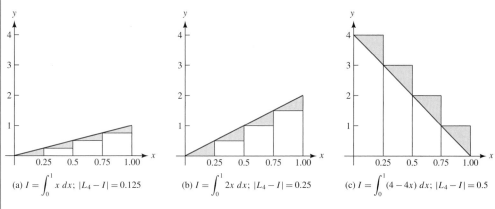

(a) $I = \int_0^1 x\,dx$; $|L_4 - I| = 0.125$ (b) $I = \int_0^1 2x\,dx$; $|L_4 - I| = 0.25$ (c) $I = \int_0^1 (4 - 4x)\,dx$; $|L_4 - I| = 0.5$

FIGURE 1
Comparing left-rule errors

Exact and approximate values of all the integrals are easily found using the FTC, technology, or hand calculation. The following table shows the results.

L_4 errors: how steepness matters			
Integral	$\int_0^1 x\,dx$	$\int_0^1 2x\,dx$	$\int_0^1 (4 - 4x)\,dx$
Exact value	0.500	1.000	2.000
L_4	0.375	0.750	2.500
$I - L_4$	0.125	0.250	-0.500
$|I - L_4|$	0.125	0.250	-0.500

Figure 1 shows, and the table confirms, that approximation errors increase in magnitude as graphs get steeper. Derivatives tell the same story: For the three given integrands, $|f'| = 1$, $|f'| = 2$, and $|f'| = |-4| = 4$, respectively. We won't be surprised, therefore, to see the first derivative f' appear in error bound formulas for left and right sums. ∎

Trapezoid- and right-rule errors, linear functions, and second derivatives   Midpoint and trapezoid sums usually do a better job than left and right sums in approximating an integral $\int_a^b f(x)\,dx$ for a simple but important reason:

> *If f is a* linear *function, then the trapezoid and midpoint rules commit* zero *error in estimating $I = \int_a^b f$.*

(This is geometrically obvious for trapezoid sums; it's not hard to see for midpoint sums as well.) This means that midpoint- and trapezoid-rule errors result not from the steepness of the f-graph but from its *concavity*:

> *The more concave (upward or downward) the graph of f, the more error M_n and T_n commit.*

If f is linear, then $f' = k$ (a constant) and $f'' = 0$. In general, the magnitude of the second derivative, $|f''|$, measures the concavity or "bulginess" of the f-graph, which in turn generates trapezoid and midpoint errors. It's no surprise, therefore, that the *second* derivative appears in the error bound theorem for trapezoid and midpoint sums.

In a nutshell: Since f'' measures "non-linearity" (the source of midpoint and trapezoid rule errors), f'' determines how much error these rules commit.

EXAMPLE 3   Let $f(x) = 1 - x^4$, and consider $I = \int_0^1 f(x)\,dx$. How is the error committed by T_4 related to the concavity of f and to f''?

Solution   Figure 2 shows I (the area under the curve), T_4 (the shaded area), and the error committed (the difference).

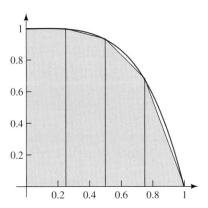

FIGURE 2
Trapezoid rule errors and concavity:
Approximating $\int_0^1 (1 - x^4)\,dx$

The figure shows that the errors committed over successive subdivisions *increase* as we move from left to right. This happens because $|f''(x)| = 4x^3$ also increases as we move from left to right along the interval of integration.   ∎

Error bound theorems

With the examples as background, we're ready for more general results. The following theorem formally presents all of the promised error bounds.

> **THEOREM 3 (Error bounds for approximating sums)** Let $I = \int_a^b f(x)\,dx$, and let L_n, R_n, T_n, and M_n denote left, right, trapezoid, and midpoint sums for I, each with n equal subdivisions.
>
> - **Left- and right-rule errors** Let K_1 be a constant such that $|f'(x)| \le K_1$ for all x in $[a, b]$. Then
>
> $$|I - L_n| \le \frac{K_1(b-a)^2}{2n}; \qquad |I - R_n| \le \frac{K_1(b-a)^2}{2n}.$$
>
> - **Midpoint- and trapezoid-rule errors** Let K_2 be a constant such that $|f''(x)| \le K_2$ for all x in $[a, b]$. Then
>
> $$|I - T_n| \le \frac{K_2(b-a)^3}{12n^2}; \qquad |I - M_n| \le \frac{K_2(b-a)^3}{24n^2}.$$

Some of the ingredients of the error bounds—the numbers 2, 12, and 24, the different powers of $(b-a)$ and n, the constants K_1 and K_2—may look mysterious. We'll explain them all soon. For the moment, we focus on the general form of the error bounds.

- **Finding K_1 and K_2: estimate** The constants K_1 and K_2 can be *any* upper bounds for $|f'|$ and $|f''|$ on $[a, b]$. Finding such bounds can be difficult, and so we usually resort to ballpark estimates, often from graphs. (We illustrate the process in examples to follow.) Doing so may seem suspect, but it's perfectly legal. *Over*estimating K_1 and K_2 is harmless—the error bounds "work" even if K_1 and K_2 are larger than necessary. ➡ The only penalty for such sloppiness is slightly weaker error bounds.

- **Inequalities** All of the formulas are inequalities. The actual errors (on the left sides) are often less than the right sides predict. ➡

- **The size, not the sign, of the error** Each inequality bounds the *absolute* error committed by a rule; the theorem doesn't distinguish overestimates from underestimates. (That distinction is sometimes clear from pictures or other information.)

- **Dependence on n** In every formula, n appears in the denominator; naturally enough, increasing n leads to decreasing error bounds. Notice, too, that for any *particular* integral I, the right side of each error bound formula depends *only* on n—all other symbols are numerical constants. In other words, the inequalities have the form

$$|I - L_n| \le \frac{C_1}{n}; \quad |I - R_n| \le \frac{C_1}{n}; \quad |I - T_n| \le \frac{C_2}{n^2}; \quad |I - M_n| \le \frac{C_3}{n^2},$$

where C_1, C_2, and C_3 are numerical constants. The last two denominators involve n^2, not n; this big advantage reflects the better performance of the trapezoid and midpoint rules.

Using error bounds

We illustrate by example what the theorem says and why it's useful. Throughout, we round numerical results to five decimals.

The ideas that K_1 and K_2 can (or must) be estimated graphically, and that overestimates are OK, may take some getting used to for students.

But not if K_1 and K_2 are too small!

But never more!

The advantage of n^2 over n for large n deserves emphasis.

It's relatively easy to bound the error committed by a given estimate, say T_{10}, for a given integral I. It's a little harder to choose n so that T_n commits no more than a given amount of error. We stress the first type of problem.

E X A M P L E 4   (A linear integrand)   How much error do L_4 and L_8 commit in estimating $I = \int_0^1 10x\,dx$? What does the error bound theorem predict?

S o l u t i o n   The FTC gives $I = 5$ (exactly!); a calculator or computer gives

$$L_4 = 3.75 \quad \text{and} \quad L_8 = 4.375.$$

Thus, the *actual* errors committed are

$$|I - L_4| = |5 - 3.75| = 1.25; \qquad |I - L_8| = |5 - 4.375| = 0.625.$$

What does Theorem 3 say? Because $f(x) = 10x$, we have $f' = 10$, and so we can take $K_1 = 10$. Now the theorem says

$$|I - L_4| \le \frac{10 \cdot 1^2}{2 \cdot 4} = 1.25; \qquad |I - L_8| \le \frac{10 \cdot 1^2}{2 \cdot 8} = 0.625.$$

In short, our worst fears are realized: L_4 and L_8 behave as badly as the theorem allows. Figure 3 illustrates this sad state of affairs.

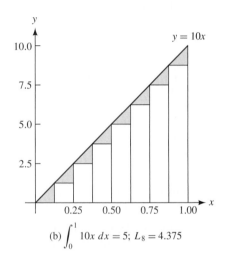

$$\text{(a)} \int_0^1 10x\,dx = 5; \ L_4 = 3.75 \qquad \text{(b)} \int_0^1 10x\,dx = 5; \ L_8 = 4.375$$

FIGURE 3
Errors committed by L_4 and L_8

E X A M P L E 5   (A quadratic integrand)   How much error do L_4 and L_8 commit in estimating $I = \int_0^1 x^2\,dx$. What do the error bounds predict?

S o l u t i o n   Easy calculations give $I = 1/3$, $L_4 = 0.21875$, and $L_8 = 0.27344$, so the errors committed are

$$|I - L_4| \approx 0.11458; \qquad |I - L_8| \approx 0.05990.$$

The first error is about twice the second—doubling n roughly halved the error committed.

To decide what Theorem 3 says here we first need a value for K_1. Because $f'(x) = 2x$, the inequality

$$|f'(x)| = |2x| \le 2$$

holds for all x in $[0, 1]$, the interval of integration. Thus, we can use $K_1 = 2$, and

Theorem 3 gives

$$|I - L_4| \le \frac{2 \cdot 1^2}{2 \cdot 4} = 0.25; \qquad |I - L_8| \le \frac{2 \cdot 1^2}{2 \cdot 8} = 0.125.$$

We're OK—the actual errors committed are safely less than the theorem's guarantees. Notice, too, that doubling n cuts the error bound in half—just as we saw for the actual errors. ➡ ■

Not all integrals behave this predictably.

Getting real Examples 4 and 5 are artificial in the sense that we could easily find *exact* values for the integrals. The following example is more realistic.

EXAMPLE 6 Use M_{10}, T_{10}, and L_{10} to approximate $I = \int_0^1 \sin(x^2)\,dx$. What do the error bound theorems predict?

Solution Here are the numbers:

$$M_{10} = 0.30982; \qquad T_{10} = 0.31117; \qquad L_{10} = 0.26910.$$

To find values for K_1 and K_2, we find first and second derivatives and plot the results. A little symbolic work with $f(x) = \sin(x^2)$ gives

$$f'(x) = 2x \cos(x^2) \quad \text{and} \quad f''(x) = -4x^2 \sin(x^2) + 2\cos(x^2).$$

It's challenging with symbolic methods to maximize $|f'(x)|$ and $|f''(x)|$ for x in $[0, 1]$, but it's easy (with technology) to *plot* f' and f''. The results are shown in Figure 4.

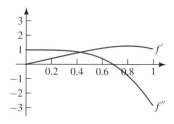

FIGURE 4
Estimating K_1 and K_2 graphically

The graphs suggest reasonable values: $K_1 = 1.5$ and $K_2 = 3$ will do. (Because we're bounding $|f'|$ and $|f''|$, negative values of the functions must be considered.)

Only arithmetic remains:

$$|I - M_{10}| \le \frac{K_2(b-a)^3}{24n^2} = \frac{3.0 \cdot 1^3}{2400} = 0.00125;$$

$$|I - T_{10}| \le \frac{K_2(b-a)^3}{12n^2} = \frac{3.0 \cdot 1^3}{1200} = 0.00250;$$

$$|I - L_{10}| \le \frac{K_1(b-a)^2}{2n} = \frac{1.5 \cdot 1^2}{20} = 0.075.$$

The errors committed by M_n, T_n, and L_n don't exceed 0.00125, 0.00250, and 0.075, respectively. ■

Choosing n in advance How many subdivisions does a given method need to approximate an integral with specified accuracy? The error-bound theorem lets us choose n in advance.

Students find this harder to do than to bound the error for a given n .

EXAMPLE 7   How large an n does each method require to approximate
$I = \int_0^1 \sin(x^2)\,dx$ with error guaranteed to be less than 0.0001? (We used the same integral in Example 6, and so the same values of K_1 and K_2 apply.)

Solution   We set each error bound less than or equal to 0.0001 and solve for n:

$$\text{For } M_n: \qquad \frac{K_2(b-a)^3}{24n^2} = \frac{3}{24n^2} \le 0.0001 \iff n \ge 35.35534;$$

$$\text{For } T_n: \qquad \frac{K_2(b-a)^3}{12n^2} = \frac{3}{12n^2} \le 0.0001 \iff n \ge 50;$$

$$\text{For } L_n: \qquad \frac{K_1(b-a)^2}{2n} = \frac{1.5}{2} \le 0.0001 \iff n \ge 7500.$$

Thus, to *guarantee* accuracy within 0.0001, the midpoint, trapezoid, and left rules require at least 36, 50, and 7500 subdivisions, respectively. Notice the striking difference in efficiency: The left rule requires almost 250 times as much work as the midpoint rule to guarantee the same accuracy!   ■

Why the theorem holds

The proofs are not used in the sequel, and so can be omitted.

We won't prove Theorem 3 in detail, but we'll outline the idea of a rigorous proof for the L_n bound and briefly indicate the analogous arguments for the other rules.

Left-rule error bounds   Let $I = \int_a^b f(x)\,dx$, and let K_1 be any upper bound for $|f'|$ on $[a, b]$. The error any approximating sum commits in approximating I is the total of the errors committed over each subinterval. (In the best cases such errors tend to cancel out; in the worst cases, they add up.)

How much error, at worst, can L_n commit over *one* subinterval $[x_{i-1}, x_i]$ of width $\Delta x = (b-a)/n$? Figure 5 illustrates the situation.

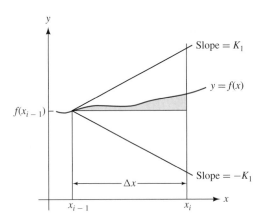

FIGURE 5
Left-rule error over one subdivision

Here's what the figure shows:

- **What the left rule pretends**   The left rule "pretends" that f is constant on $[x_{i-1}, x_i]$. The shaded area represents the error that results from this pretense.

- **What K_1 means graphically**   The derivative inequality $|f'(x)| < K_1$ means that the f-graph over $[x_{i-1}, x_i]$ must stay in the wedge between the lines with slopes $\pm K_1$. (To "escape" this wedge, f would have to increase or decrease faster than K_1 allows.) →

- **When the worst happens**   The worst possible error—positive or negative—occurs if the f-graph is either the top line or the bottom line of the wedge. A careful look at the picture shows that these errors correspond to the areas of two right triangles, one above and one below the horizontal line $y = f(x_{i-1})$. Each of these triangles has area

A rigorous proof of this fact requires the mean value theorem.

$$\frac{1}{2}\,\text{base} \cdot \text{height} = \frac{1}{2}\Delta x \cdot (K_1\,\Delta x) = \frac{1}{2}K_1\Delta x^2 = \frac{K_1(b-a)^2}{2n^2}.$$

The last quantity is the greatest possible error L_n can commit over *one* subdivision. Over all n subdivisions, therefore, the total maximum error is no more than n times as much—just what the theorem says.

Trapezoid- and midpoint-rule bounds   Again, let $I = \int_a^b f(x)\,dx$, and suppose that $|f''(x)| \le K_2$ for all x in $[a, b]$. Among all functions that satisfy this inequality, the quadratic function $q(x) = K_2 x^2/2$ represents an extreme because $q''(x) = K_2$ for all x—in other words, $|q''|$ is always as large as the inequality permits.

How much error, at worst, can M_n and T_n commit over one subinterval? We answer by computing directly with the "worst offender" function q. To simplify the algebra, we take $[0, h]$ as our subinterval.

The first step is to compare I_h (the exact integral of q over $[0, h]$) with M_h and T_h (the midpoint and trapezoid estimates over the same interval):

$$I_h = \int_0^h q(x)\,dx = \int_0^h \frac{K_2 x^2}{2}\,dx = \frac{K_2 x^3}{6}\Big]_0^h = \frac{K_2 h^3}{6};$$

$$M_h = q(h/2) \cdot h = \frac{K_2(h/2)^2}{2} \cdot h = \frac{K_2 h^3}{8};$$

$$T_h = \frac{q(0) + q(h)}{2} \cdot h = \frac{K_2 h^3}{4}.$$

The *errors* committed over $[0, h]$ are therefore

$$I_h - M_h = \frac{K_2 h^3}{6} - \frac{K_2 h^3}{8} = \frac{K_2 h^3}{24};$$
$$I_h - T_h = \frac{K_2 h^3}{6} - \frac{K_2 h^3}{4} = -\frac{K_2 h^3}{12}.$$

Notice that the trapezoid and midpoint errors have *opposite* signs as we've seen occur in examples. The mysterious constants 12 and 24 from Theorem 3 have also finally appeared.

Thus, we've found the worst-case error committed by each method over *one* subinterval. Multiplying the results by n gives the worst-case error over all n subintervals. Replacing h with $(b-a)/n$ gives the error bound formulas of Theorem 3.

BASIC EXERCISES

1. Let $\int_0^3 \sin(x^2)\,dx$.
   (a) Use Theorem 3 to show that $|I - M_{50}| \le 0.02$ as claimed in Example 1.
   (b) Explain why $0.754 \le I \le 0.795$.

2. Explain the concept of an error bound in your own words. Be sure that your explanation discusses why error bounds are "pessimistic" estimates of approximation errors.

3. Consider the three integrands in Example 2. Show that the

magnitude of the approximation error committed by L_4 is proportional to $|f'|$ for each integrand.

4. Let $I = \int_1^b f(x)\,dx$, where f is a linear function.

   (a) Show that $T_n = I$ for every $n \geq 1$.

   (b) Show that $M_n = I$ for every $n \geq 1$.

5. Let $I = \int_0^2 5x\,dx$.

   (a) What does Theorem 3 say about the error committed by R_8? (See Example 4.)

   (b) What does Theorem 3 say about the error committed by T_8?

6. Let $I = \int_0^4 3x^2\,dx$.

   (a) What does Theorem 3 say about the error committed by L_5? (See Example 5.)

   (b) What does Theorem 3 say about the error committed by M_5?

7. Let I be as in Example 6.

   (a) Explain why 2 is an acceptable value for K_1.

   (b) Is 2 an acceptable value for K_2? Justify your answer.

8. Suppose that $-4 \leq f'(x) \leq 3$ if $1 \leq x \leq 2$. Explain why Theorem 3 does *not* guarantee that $|I - L_n| \leq 3/(2n)$.

9. Let $I = \int_1^4 \dfrac{dx}{\sqrt{x}}$.

   (a) Use the FTC to evaluate I exactly.

   (b) Compute the actual approximation errors $|I - L_3|$ and $|I - R_3|$. Are these errors consistent with the error bound formulas in Theorem 3? Justify your answer.

   (c) Compute the actual approximation errors committed by T_3 and M_3. Are these errors consistent with the error bound formulas in Theorem 3? Justify your answer.

   (d) Use Theorem 3 to find a value of n that guarantees that $|I - M_n| \leq 0.005$ (i.e., that M_n has two-decimal-place accuracy).

10. Let $I = \int_0^1 x^3\,dx$.

   (a) Use the FTC to evaluate I exactly.

   (b) Compute the actual approximation errors $|I - L_4|$ and $|I - R_4|$. Are these errors consistent with the error bound formulas in Theorem 3? Justify your answer.

   (c) Compute the actual approximation errors committed by T_4 and M_4. Are these errors consistent with the error bound formulas in Theorem 3? Justify your answer.

   (d) Use the error bounds in Theorem 3 to find a value of n that guarantees that $|I - M_n| \leq 0.005$ (i.e., that M_n has two-decimal-place accuracy).

In Exercises 11–14, find a value of n for which Theorem 3 guarantees that L_n approximates the value of the integral within ± 0.005. Justify your answers.

11. $\int_0^3 e^{-x^2}\,dx$ **12.** $\int_0^2 \sin(x^2)\,dx$

13. $\int_0^1 (1+x^2)^{-1}\,dx$ **14.** $\int_1^{10} \sin(1/x)\,dx$

15–18. For each of the integrals in Exercises 11–14, find a value of n for which Theorem 3 guarantees that M_n approximates the value of the integral within ± 0.005. Justify your answers.

Let $I = \int_0^{10} f(x)\,dx$. In Exercises 19–22, give an example of a function f with the given property.

19. L_{200} underestimates I, and the magnitude of the approximation error made is as large as Theorem 3 allows.

20. L_{200} overestimates I, and the magnitude of the approximation error made is as large as Theorem 3 allows.

21. M_{200} underestimates I, and the magnitude of the approximation error made is as large as Theorem 3 allows.

22. M_{200} overestimates I, and the magnitude of the approximation error made is as large as Theorem 3 allows.

FURTHER EXERCISES

23. (a) According to Theorem 3, how much smaller is the error bound when the number of subdivisions used in a left sum estimate of an integral is doubled?

   (b) Repeat part (a) for a midpoint sum estimate.

   (c) What do parts (a) and (b) suggest about the practical utility of these two numerical integration methods?

24. (a) Compare the error bound for L_n to the error bound for L_{10n}. Approximately how many additional decimal places of guaranteed accuracy are gained by using 10 times as many subintervals?

   (b) Repeat part (a) for M_n and M_{10n}.

   (c) What do parts (a) and (b) suggest about the practical utility of these two numerical integration methods?

25. Let $I = \int_a^b f(x)\,dx$. If $|I - L_{100}| \leq 5 \times 10^{-4}$, does Theorem 3 guarantee that $|I - L_{1000}| \leq 5 \times 10^{-5}$? Justify your answer.

26. Let $I = \int_a^b f(x)\,dx$. If $|I - T_{100}| \leq 5 \times 10^{-4}$, does Theorem 3 guarantee that $|I - M_{100}| \leq 2.5 \times 10^{-5}$? Justify your answer.

27. Let $I = \int_1^{11} f(x)\,dx$, where $f(x) = \cos(1/x)$.

(a) What is the smallest value of n for which Theorem 3 guarantees that $|I - L_n| \le 0.005$?

(b) What is the smallest value of n for which Theorem 3 guarantees that $\left| \int_1^6 f(x)\,dx - L_n \right| \le 0.004$?

(c) What is the smallest value of n for which Theorem 3 guarantees that $\left| \int_6^{11} f(x)\,dx - L_n \right| \le 0.001$?

(d) Show that the estimates computed in parts (b) and (c) can be combined to produce an estimate of I that is guaranteed to be within 0.005 of the true value.

(e) The values in parts (a) and (d) are both estimates of I with two-decimal-place accuracy. How does the amount of computational effort necessary to compute the estimate in part (d) compare with that needed to compute the estimate in part (a)? (The number of values of f used is a reasonable measure of computational effort.)

28. Let $I = \int_0^5 f(x)\,dx$, where $f(x) = e^{-x^2}$.

(a) What is the smallest value of n for which Theorem 3 guarantees that $|I - R_n| \le 0.01$?

(b) What is the smallest value of n for which Theorem 3 guarantees that $\left| \int_0^2 f(x)\,dx - R_n \right| \le 0.005$?

(c) What is the smallest value of n for which Theorem 3 guarantees that $\left| \int_2^5 f(x)\,dx - R_n \right| \le 0.005$?

(d) Show that the estimates computed in parts (b) and (c) can be combined to produce an estimate of I that is guaranteed to approximate I within 0.01 of its true value.

(e) The estimates in parts (a) and (d) both estimate I within 0.01. How does the amount of computational effort necessary to compute the estimate in part (d) compare with that needed to compute the estimate in part (a)? (The number of values of f used is a reasonable measure of computational effort.)

29. Let $I = \int_0^2 \sqrt{4 - x^2}\,dx$.

(a) Explain why $I = \pi$. [HINT: Draw a picture.]

(b) Compute $|I - L_{10}|$.

(c) Why doesn't Theorem 3 provide a useful bound on the magnitude of the approximation error?

In Exercises 30–32, f is an antiderivative of the function shown below.

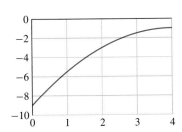

30. Find a value of n that guarantees that $\left| \int_0^4 f(x)\,dx - L_n \right| \le 0.0001$.

31. Suppose that F is an antiderivative of f. Find a value of n such that $\left| \int_1^2 F(x)\,dx - M_n \right| \le 0.01$.

32. Suppose that F is an antiderivative of f and that $f(2) = 0$. Find a value of n such that
$$\left| L_n - \int_2^4 F(x)\,dx \right| \le 0.01.$$

33. Suppose that $f''(x) = \dfrac{e^x \cos x}{1 + x^2}$. Find an integer n such that T_n approximates $\int_0^5 f(x)\,dx$ within 0.001.

34. Let $I = \int_{-1}^2 f(x)\,dx$, where f is a function with the following properties:

   (i) f is increasing on the interval $[-1, 2]$;

   (ii) f'' is the function shown;

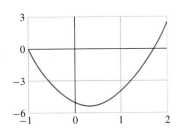

   (iii) f has the values shown in the table.

x	-1.00	-0.25	0.50	1.25	2.00
$f(x)$	2.0000	26.522	48.755	68.328	86.790

(a) Compute R_4 and an upper bound on the value of $|I - R_4|$.

(b) Compute T_4 and an upper bound on the value of $|I - T_4|$.

Let $I = \int_{-4}^6 h(x)\,dx = 9$, where h is a function with the following properties:

   (i) $-7 \le h(x) \le 3$ if $-4 \le x \le 6$,

   (ii) $-5 \le h'(x) - 2$ if $-4 \le x \le 6$, and

   (iii) $0 \le h''(x) \le 4$ if $-4 \le x \le 6$.

In Exercises 35–38, indicate whether the statement must be true, cannot be true, or may be true. Justify your answers.

35. $L_{100} = 11.75$

36. $M_{100} = 8.98$

37. $T_{100} = 8.99$

38. $I - T_{100} \le 5 \times 10^{-6}$

39. Let $I = \int_a^b f(x)\,dx$ and suppose that f is monotone on the interval $[a, b]$. Show that $|I - L_n| \le |f(b) - f(a)| \cdot \dfrac{b - a}{n}$.

40. Let $I = \int_a^b f(x)\,dx$ and suppose that f is monotone on the interval $[a, b]$. Show that $|I - M_n| \le |f(b) - f(a)| \cdot \dfrac{b-a}{n}$.

41. Let $I = \int_a^b f(x)\,dx$ and suppose that f is monotone on the interval $[a, b]$. Show that $|I - T_n| \le |f(b) - f(a)| \cdot \dfrac{b-a}{2n}$.

Euler's method is essentially a numerical version of the slope field idea: start anywhere and "go with the flow." Having access to some technology is very helpful, but not absolutely essential.

6.3 EULER'S METHOD: SOLVING DEs NUMERICALLY

The problem of solving differential equations (DEs) resembles the problem of integrating functions. In each case, symbolic (or "exact") methods are sometimes—but not always—available. When symbolic methods fail, graphical and numerical methods are often the best recourse. For DEs as for integrals, the key idea is to take small steps toward a destination, adding up small contributions as we go.

In Section 4.1 we showed how to solve a first-order initial value problem (IVP)

$$y' = f(t, y), \qquad y(a) = b$$

graphically, using its slope field:

> *Starting at (a, b), move through the slope field, "going with the flow." The result is a solution curve (i.e., the graph of a solution function) for the IVP.*

The numerical version of this idea is known as **Euler's method**. It tells exactly *how* to move step by step through a slope field to approximate a solution curve. We illustrate with another look at an example from Section 4.1.

Time $t = 0$ can denote any convenient reference time.

EXAMPLE 1 Let $y(t)$ denote the temperature (in degrees Fahrenheit) of a cup of coffee at time t (in minutes). Room temperature is $70°$F; the coffee starts at $190°$F. The coffee's temperature is described by the IVP

$$y' = -0.1(y - 70); \qquad y(0) = 190.$$

How hot is the coffee after 10 minutes? After 20 minutes?

The bulleted starting point represents the initial condition.

Solution Figure 1 shows the slope field and one plausible solution curve.

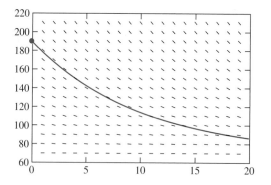

FIGURE 1
Graphically solving the IVP $y' = -0.1(y - 70)$;
$y(0) = 190$

The solution curve shows that the temperature at 10 minutes is a little over $110°$F. After 20 minutes, the temperature is about $84°$F. ■

Improving on the graphical approach Drawing a solution curve by "going with the flow" is simple and natural. Any two humans, given the slope field and initial condition shown in Figure 1, would draw similar solution curves and thus arrive at similar estimates for $y(10)$ and $y(20)$. This graphical approach, for all its simplicity, has two main flaws:

Euler's method may be harder to visualize than the slope field method, but it's easier to describe to a machine.

(i) it gives approximate answers (as do all graphical methods); and

(ii) "drawing a curve" isn't precisely defined as a mathematical process.

Of these flaws, (ii) is worse than (i). Approximate answers are fully respectable, and often they're the best available. To have any idea how *accurate* estimates are, however, we must first describe precisely, in mathematical terms, how we *produce* the estimates. A precise description is also essential if we want (as we do now) to use technology to produce and improve our estimates.

Let's describe—in terms a computer can understand—one sensible way to move through the slope field of Example 1, starting from $(0, 190)$ and ending at $t = 10$. We'll take 10 *straight-line steps, each of horizontal length 1*. The slope of each linear step is determined by the slope field at the *beginning* of the step. To make a "curve," we join successive linear steps. Figure 2 shows the result, with a dot at each successive **Euler point**.

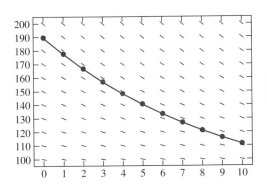

Each step corresponds to a 1-second time interval. Notice that the "curve" is really 10 straight-line segments.

FIGURE 2
Ten Euler steps through a slope field

Here's how we found the successive Euler points:

Describing Euler's method takes quite a few words, but students seem to find the idea accessible.

*   **Step 1**   The first linear step starts at the point $(0, 190)$ and ends one unit to the right, at the point $(1, 178)$. The *slope* of this line segment is given by the DE, as follows: When $t = 0$ and $y = 190$, the DE $y' = -0.1(y - 70)$ says

$$y'(0) = -0.1\big(y(0) - 70\big) = -0.1(190 - 70) = -12.$$

    Thus, the segment has slope -12, and our estimate is

$$y(1) \approx y(0) + y'(0) \cdot 1 = 190 - 12 \cdot 1 = 178.$$

*   **Step 2**   The second step begins at $(1, 178)$ and moves one unit to the right. As before, its slope is determined by the DE, but with the *updated* y-value. With $t = 1$ and $y = 178$, we get

$$y'(1) = -0.1(178 - 70) = -10.8,$$

    and so

$$y(2) \approx y(1) + y'(1) \cdot 1 \approx 178 - 10.8 \cdot 1 = 167.2.$$

Each step of the type just described is an **Euler step** with **step size** 1. It takes 10 Euler steps to reach $t = 10$. In practice, of course, such repetitive calculations are usually exported to machines. The following table (with most entries rounded to two decimals) summarizes our numerical work:

From $t = 0$ to $t = 10$ in ten Euler steps											
Step	**0**	**1**	**2**	**3**	**4**	**5**	**6**	**7**	**8**	**9**	**10**
t	0	1	2	3	4	5	6	7	8	9	10
$y'(t)$	−19.00	−10.80	−9.72	−8.75	−7.87	−7.09	−6.34	−5.74	−5.17	−4.65	−4.18
$y(t)$	190.00	178.00	167.20	157.48	148.73	140.86	133.77	127.40	121.66	116.49	111.84

We estimate, therefore, that the coffee is at about 112°F after 10 minutes.

How good is Euler's method?

Euler's method and the left-rule method are closely related. Both methods find approximate answers, and the errors each method commits come from the same source: The left rule "pretends" that the integrand function is constant over short intervals, while Euler's method "pretends" that the *slope of a solution curve* remains constant over short intervals. Neither of these conditions is likely to hold *exactly*, but in many cases these quantities are "close enough" to being constant that the resulting error stays small.

In some cases, including that of Example 1, we can tell *exactly* how "good" our Euler's method results are. It turns out (as an easy calculation shows) that the function $y(t) = 70 + 120e^{-0.1t}$ is a solution of the IVP $y' = -0.1(y - 70)$; $y(0) = 190$. In particular,

$$y(10) = 70 + 120e^{-1} \approx 114.15.$$

Note that this result is significantly different from what Euler's method predicted (see the preceding table). Plotting both the Euler "curve" and the exact solution curve together (Figure 3) shows how errors in Euler's method accumulate over the time interval.

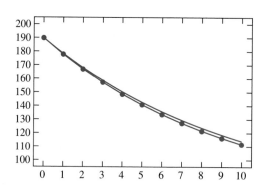

FIGURE 3
Exact vs. Euler's method solutions

The two "curves" aren't terribly different, but they spread apart slightly as time goes on.

Shorter steps, better accuracy We've seen for integrals that the left rule's accuracy improves as the number of subdivisions increases (or as the step size decreases). Euler's method is similar: More (and smaller) steps usually give more accurate results. But at a price—more steps mean more work.

What happens in the coffee situation if we use 100 steps of size 0.1 rather than 10 steps of size 1? Carrying out 100 steps by hand would be tedious, but computers don't complain. Following are some sample results; *exact* values of y appear for comparison in the last row.

From $t = 0$ to $t = 10$ in 100 Euler steps									
step	**0**	**1**	**2**	**3**	**10**	**20**	**30**	**90**	**100**
t	0	0.1	0.2	0.3	1.0	2.0	3.0	9.0	10.0
y'	−12.00	−11.89	−11.76	−11.64	−10.85	−9.82	−8.88	−4.86	−4.39
y_{Euler}	190.00	188.80	187.61	186.43	178.53	168.15	158.76	118.57	113.92
y_{exact}	190.00	188.81	187.62	186.45	178.58	168.25	158.90	118.79	114.15

The Euler estimates are better this time.

We might think of using even smaller step sizes, with thousands or millions of Euler steps. As with numerical integration, however, this strategy is computationally foolish. For one thing, roundoff error eventually becomes significant. For another, more efficient numerical strategies are available. We won't pursue such "smart" strategies except to drop the name of one of the most popular, the **Runge–Kutta method**. This method is related to Simpson's rule in the same way as Euler's method is related to the left rule. ➔

We met Simpson's rule in Section 6.1.

Euler's method in general

Suppose that we're given a first-order DE $y' = f(t, y)$ and an initial condition $y(a) = y_0$ and that we estimate $y(b)$ using Euler's method with n steps on the interval $a \le t \le b$. What exactly does Euler's method give? The answer depends on our point of view.

Like the left rule, Euler's method takes steps determined at the "left" endpoint. The Runge–Kutta method uses an averaging method similar to that of Simpson's rule.

- **The graphical view:** Euler's method says how to move step by step through the DE's slope field starting at (a, y_0) and ending when $t = b$. Each Euler step has *horizontal* length (or **step size**) $\Delta t = (b - a)/n$. Each step goes in the direction of the slope field at the *beginning point* of the step. Joining successive **Euler points** with line segments (connecting the dots, in other words) produces a piecewise–linear curve. ➔ This curve is the graph of an approximate solution function $Y(t)$ for the DE. (We'll reserve the lowercase $y(t)$ for the exact solution.)

Mathspeak for a "curve" built from linear pieces.

- **The numerical view:** Euler's method produces a list

$$Y(t_0), \ Y(t_1), \ Y(t_2), \ Y(t_3), \ \ldots, Y(t_n)$$

of numerical values of an approximate solution function $Y(t)$, for equally spaced inputs

$$a = t_0 < t_1 < t_2 < t_3 < \cdots < t_n = b;$$

each t_i is Δt units greater than its predecessor. Plotting these values and joining successive points with line segments produces the graph just mentioned.

No formulas Euler's method uses—and produces—only *numerical* information. Thus, we can use Euler's method to produce a graph or a table of values but not a *formula* for a solution function. (The same principle holds if the left rule is applied to an integral $\int_a^b f(x)\,dx$.)

The numerical nature of Euler's method is a mixed bag. To its credit, Euler's method works with almost *any* DE, no matter how complicated. On the debit side, Euler's method produces *only* approximate results—even for simple DEs that can easily be solved exactly.

Symbolic solutions—when they exist—are especially valuable because they may allow symbolic parameters, as numerical methods do not.

A general recipe for Euler's method   Here is a general description—rather than an example—of how Euler's method works.

- **Step 1:**   The starting point $Y(t_0) = y_0$ comes from the initial condition. The DE $y' = f(t, y)$ says that a solution curve through (t_0, y_0) has slope $m_0 = f(t_0, y_0)$. Thus, the first Euler step has slope m_0, and its rise (or fall) is $m_0 \cdot \Delta t$ vertical units. That is,

$$Y(t_1) = Y(t_0) + m_0 \Delta t,$$

where $t_1 = t_0 + \Delta t$.

- **Step 2:**   The second Euler step starts at $(t_1, Y(t_1))$, where the first step ended. At $(t_1, Y(t_1))$, says the DE, the solution curve has slope $m_1 = f(t_1, Y(t_1))$. Thus, the second Euler step rises (or falls) $m_1 \cdot \Delta t$ vertical units, and so

$$Y(t_2) = Y(t_1) + m_1 \Delta t.$$

- **Continue:**   The pattern should now be clear. At each Euler step we do two things: (1) use the DE to "update" the slope m_i; and (2) move with slope m_i from $(t_i, Y(t_i))$ to $(t_{i+1}, Y(t_{i+1}))$. After n steps, we arrive at $t_n = b$.

Reduced entirely to symbols, Euler's recipe for assembling an approximate solution $Y(t)$ looks like this:

$$
\begin{aligned}
Y(t_0) &= y_0 \\
Y(t_1) &= Y(t_0) + f\big(t_0, Y(t_0)\big) \cdot \Delta t \\
Y(t_2) &= Y(t_1) + f\big(t_1, Y(t_1)\big) \cdot \Delta t \\
&\;\;\vdots \\
Y(t_{i+1}) &= Y(t_i) + f\big(t_i, Y(t_i)\big) \cdot \Delta t \\
&\;\;\vdots \\
Y(t_n) &= Y(t_{n-1}) + f\big(t_{n-1}, Y(t_{n-1})\big) \cdot \Delta t
\end{aligned}
$$

Simple but powerful.   It is striking that Euler's method—the idea of which could hardly be simpler—should be named after one of history's greatest mathematicians. One lesson may be the surprising power of simple ideas. Another lesson may be that powerful ideas, properly understood, *become* simple.

Leonhard Euler (1707–1783), born in Switzerland, is among the most influential and prolific mathematicians in history. His contributions to calculus are especially notable: Combining key ideas of Newton and Leibniz, Euler established the field of mathematical analysis. To gauge Euler's importance to our field, consider just a few of the now familiar symbols and notations he introduced: $f(x)$, π, e, i, $\sum$, and Δx.

We mention logistic growth again in Section 7.4, in connection with separable DEs.

The same flies and more discussion of logistic growth appear in an Interlude in Chapter 4, but what follows is self-contained.

Euler's method in action: modeling logistic growth

To show Euler's method in action we apply it to model a population of fruit flies living in a controlled environment. ← We assume that the fly population grows **logistically**. More precisely:

> *The population's growth rate is proportional both to the population itself and to the difference between the environment's carrying capacity and the population.*

This condition is nicely expressed symbolically as a DE:

$$P' = kP(C - P),$$

where P represents the population, P' the population's growth rate, and C the carrying capacity of the environment; k is a constant of proportionality. ➡

P and P' vary with time; k and C are constants.

E X A M P L E 2 Through empirical measurements, researchers determine that their captive fly population, initially 1000 members strong, satisfies the logistic IVP

$$P' = 0.00000556\,P(10000 - P); \qquad P(0) = 1000.$$

(Here t measures time in days since the original measurement, $P = P(t)$ is the population at time t, and $P' = P'(t)$ is the growth rate in flies per day at time t.)

What will the population be in 10 days? How will the population evolve in the long run?

Solution To estimate $P(10)$, we take 10 (1-day) Euler steps. The numbers are clumsy, so we get technological help.

- **Step 1:** When $t = 0$, $P = 1000$, and so

$$P'(0) = 0.00000556 \cdot 1000 \cdot 9000 \approx 50.04 \text{ flies per day.}$$

After 1 day, therefore, we estimate a population of
$P(1) \approx 1000 + 50.04 = 1050.04$ flies.

- **Step 2:** When $t = 1$, $P \approx 1050.04$, and so

$$P'(1) \approx 0.00000556 \cdot 1050.04 \cdot (10000 - 1050.04) \approx 52.25 \text{ flies per day.}$$

Therefore, we estimate

$$P(2) \approx P(1) + P'(1) \cdot 1 \approx 1050.04 + 52.25 = 1102.29 \text{ flies.}$$

The idea should now be clear, so we'll let a computer do the rest. Here are the results with most numbers rounded to two decimal places:

Flies: From $t = 0$ to $t = 10$ in 10 Euler steps						
step	0	1	2	3	4	5
t	0	1	2	3	4	5
$P'(t)$	50.04	52.25	54.53	56.88	59.29	61.77
$P(t)$	1000.00	1050.04	1102.29	1156.82	1213.70	1272.99

step	6	7	8	9	10
t	6	7	8	9	10
$P'(t)$	64.31	66.91	69.56	72.27	75.02
$P(t)$	1334.76	1399.07	1465.97	1535.53	1607.80

Beware... The tabulated estimate $P(10) \approx 1607.80$ should be viewed cautiously:

- **Whole flies** The decimal numbers look impressive, but flies don't come in fractions. Our best guess in context is 1608 flies on day 10. (Such estimation comes with the territory. Real populations don't adhere *precisely* to mathematical models.)

- **Too big or too small?** The tabulated figure 1607.80 for day 10 *underestimates* the number of flies that would exist if the population behaved *exactly* as the DE predicts. The reason is related to step size: Taking 1-day Euler steps amounts to pretending that the growth rate remains constant over 1-day periods. In reality, the growth rate *increases* along with the population. (With symbolic techniques [coming in Chapter 7] it can be shown that an *exact* solution to the DE satisfies $P(10) = 1638.09$.)

- **Smaller steps**   Using a smaller step size would update the growth rate more often than daily and so might better estimate the true population on day 10. With 100 Euler steps, each 0.1 days long, the computer gives

$$P(0.1) \approx 1005.00, \quad P(0.2) \approx 1010.03, \quad \ldots \quad P(10) \approx 1621.43.$$

The last estimate is *still* below what the DE model predicts, but it's better than before.

In the long run   With machine help, it's easy to use Euler's method to project the fly population far into the future—if one remembers, of course, that errors accumulate over time. Figure 4 shows our results for a 150-day period using a step size of 0.1 day. ◂

The graph looks smooth because it's made from 1500 dots.

FIGURE 4
Flies in the long run

The graph's general shape looks reasonable. The population rises slowly at first, speeds up as the population increases, and then tapers off as the population nears the environment's carrying capacity. ■

BASIC EXERCISES

1. Consider the IVP in Example 1. Show how the estimate $y(3) \approx 157.48$ shown in the table on page 396 was computed.

2. Consider the IVP in Example 1. Show how the estimate $y(8) \approx 121.66$ shown in the table on page 396 was computed.

3. Show that $y(t) = 70 + 120e^{-0.1t}$ is the exact solution of the IVP in Example 1.

4. Consider the IVP in Example 1.
   (a) Use the DE to show that $y''(t) > 0$ for all $t > 0$. [HINT: $y'' = -0.1y'$.]
   (b) Use part (a) to explain why Euler's method underestimates the exact solution at each step.

5. Consider the DE in Example 2 but suppose that $P(0) = 6000$.
   (a) Use the DE to show that $P(t)$ is concave down for all $t \geq 0$.
   (b) Will Euler's method underestimate $P(100)$? Justify your answer.

6. Consider the DE in Example 2 but suppose that $P(0) = 0$.
   (a) Carry out three Euler steps by hand; use step size 1 day.
   (b) Estimate the population on day 200. Explain what's going on in biological terms.

7. Consider the DE $y' = f(t, y)$. Suppose that the slope of the line segment joining the successive Euler points $(t_i, Y(t_i))$ and $(t_{i+1}, Y(t_{i+1}))$ is m_i.
   (a) What, if anything, does this imply about $f(t_i, Y(t_i))$?
   (b) What, if anything, does this imply about $f(t_{i+1}, Y(t_{i+1}))$?

8. Consider the IVP $y' = 3$, $y(0) = 2$.
   (a) Find the exact solution $y(t)$ to this IVP. [HINT: What functions have constant derivatives?]
   (b) Use Euler's method, with step size 1, to estimate $y(1)$, $y(2)$, $y(3)$, $y(4)$, and $y(5)$. How accurate are these estimates?
   (c) What accounts for the accuracy of Euler's method in this case?

FURTHER EXERCISES

9. The number e is sometimes defined as $y(1)$, where $y(t)$ is the solution to the IVP $y' = y$, $y(0) = 1$.

  (a) Use Euler's method with one subdivision to estimate e. Why is the answer an underestimate?

  (b) Repeat part (a) with four subdivisions.

  (c) Imagine that Euler's method with 10,000 steps is used to estimate $y(1)$. Will the result underestimate e? Justify your answer.

  (d) Show that Euler's method with n steps produces the estimate $y(1) \approx \left(1 + \dfrac{1}{n}\right)^n$.

10. Consider the IVP $y' = 1 + t - y$, $y(0) = 0$.

  (a) Use Euler's method with five steps of size 0.4 to estimate $y(2)$.

  (b) Use Euler's method with 10 steps of size 0.2 to estimate $y(2)$.

  (c) Show that the exact solution of the IVP is $y(t) = t$.

  (d) How does the exact value of $y(2)$ compare with the estimates you computed in parts (a) and (b)? Explain how you could have predicted this from the slope field for the DE.

11. Consider the IVP $y' = 1 + t - y$, $y(0) = 1$.

  (a) Use Euler's method with five steps of size 0.4 to estimate $y(2)$.

  (b) Use Euler's method with 10 steps of size 0.2 to estimate $y(2)$.

  (c) Show that the exact solution of the IVP is $y(t) = t + e^{-t}$.

  (d) How does the exact value of $y(2)$ compare with the estimates you computed in parts (a) and (b)? Explain how you could have predicted this from the slope field for the DE.

12. Consider the IVP $y' = 1 + t - y$, $y(0) = -1$.

  (a) Use Euler's method with five steps of size 0.4 to estimate $y(2)$.

  (b) Use Euler's method with 10 steps of size 0.2 to estimate $y(2)$.

  (c) Show that the exact solution of the IVP is $y(t) = t - e^{-t}$.

  (d) How does the exact value of $y(2)$ compare with the estimates you computed in parts (a) and (b)? Explain how you could have predicted this from the slope field for the DE.

13. Consider the IVP $y' = y - 2$, $y(0) = 1$.

  (a) Use Euler's method with 10 steps of size 0.1 to estimate $y(1)$.

  (b) Use Euler's method with 20 steps of size 0.05 to estimate $y(1)$.

  (c) Show that the exact solution of the IVP is $y(t) = 2 - e^t$.

  (d) How does the exact value of $y(1)$ compare with the estimates you computed in parts (a) and (b)? Explain how

you could have predicted this from the slope field for the DE.

14. Consider the IVP $y' = xy$, $y(0) = 1$.

  (a) Use Euler's method with one step of size 1 to estimate $y(1)$.

  (b) Use Euler's method with two steps of size 0.5 to estimate $y(1)$.

  (c) Use Euler's method with four steps of size 0.25 to estimate $y(1)$.

  (d) Use Euler's method with eight steps of size 0.125 to estimate $y(1)$.

  (e) Show that the exact solution of the IVP is $y(x) = e^{x^2/2}$.

  (f) Show that the results in parts (a)–(d) suggest that the error made by Euler's method is proportional to $1/n$, where n is the number of steps.

15. Consider the IVP $y' = y^2$, $y(0) = 1$.

  (a) Use Euler's method with four steps of size 0.2 to estimate $y(0.8)$.

  (b) Show that the exact solution of the IVP is $y(t) = (1 - t)^{-1}$.

  (c) Explain why Euler's method doesn't provide a good estimate of $y(0.8)$.

16. Consider the IVP $y' = \sin t$, $y(0) = 0$.

  (a) Show that $y(t) = 1 - \cos t$ is the exact solution of this IVP.

  (b) Carry out Euler's method with four steps to estimate $y(1)$. Do all steps by hand.

  (c) Let $y(t)$ be the *exact* solution function, and let $Y(t)$ be the *approximate* solution function constructed by Euler's method. Plot $y(t)$ and $Y(t)$ on the same axes for $0 \le t \le 1$.

  (d) Explain why $y(t) - Y(t) \ge 0$ for any n.

17. Consider the IVP $y' = e^{-t}$, $y(0) = 0$.

  (a) Show that $y(t) = 1 - e^{-t}$ is the exact solution of this IVP.

  (b) Estimate $y(1)$ by carrying out Euler's method with five steps. Do all steps by hand.

  (c) Let $y(t)$ be the *exact* solution function, and let $Y(t)$ be the *approximate* solution function constructed by Euler's method. Plot $y(t)$ and $Y(t)$ on the same axes for $0 \le t \le 1$.

  (d) Explain why $y(t) - Y(t) \le 0$ for any n.

18. Consider the IVP $y' = f(t)$, $y(t_0) = 0$.

  (a) Show that the exact solution of this IVP is $y(t) = \displaystyle\int_{t_0}^{t} f(x)\, dx$.

  (b) Explain why the Euler's method estimate of $y(t)$ computed using n steps is equal to the left-sum estimate, L_n, of $\displaystyle\int_{t_0}^{t} f(x)\, dx$.

Simpson's Rule

On beyond trapezoid and midpoint sums   Recall the following properties of left, right, trapezoid, and midpoint approximations to a definite integral $I = \int_a^b f(x)\,dx$:

- **Constant functions**   The **left and right rules** find I exactly (i.e., commit zero error) if f is a *constant* function. The error bounds

$$|I - L_n| \le \frac{K_1(b-a)^2}{2n} \quad \text{and} \quad |I - R_n| \le \frac{K_1(b-a)^2}{2n}$$

reflect this property: If f is any *constant* function, then K_1 (an upper bound for $|f'|$ on $[a, b]$) is zero.

- **Linear functions**   The **trapezoid and midpoint rules** find I exactly (i.e., commit zero error) if f is a *linear* function (and therefore for constant functions, too). Again, the error bounds

$$|I - T_n| \le \frac{K_2(b-a)^3}{12n^2} \quad \text{and} \quad |I - M_n| \le \frac{K_2(b-a)^3}{24n^2}$$

reflect this property: If f is any *linear* function, then K_2 (an upper bound for $|f''|$ on $[a, b]$) is zero.

- **Quadratic and cubic functions**   In this unit we explore **Simpson's rule**, also known as the **parabolic rule**. As we'll discover, Simpson's rule represents two *steps* in the right direction: Simpson sums (which we denote by S_n) commit zero error if f is a *cubic* function. (Therefore, the error is zero for constant, linear, and quadratic functions, too.) Once again, an error bound formula reflects this property. Here is the formula for Simpson's rule: ◄

$$|I - S_n| \le \frac{K_4(b-a)^5}{180n^4}.$$

Here, the constant K_4 is an upper bound for $|f^{(\text{iv})}(x)|$, the magnitude of the *fourth* derivative of f for x in $[a, b]$. It's easy to see that $K_4 = 0$ for any for constant, linear, quadratic, or cubic function.

The definition   Simpson's method of approximating $I = \int_a^b f$ starts with a partition $a = x_0 < x_1 < x_2 < \cdots < x_n = b$ of $[a, b]$ into an *even* number, $n = 2m$, of subdivisions, each of length $\Delta x = (b-a)/n$. ◄ Simpson's rule is defined as follows:

DEFINITION   Simpson's approximation to I is the sum

$$S_n = \frac{\Delta x}{3}\big(f(x_0) + 4f(x_1) + 2f(x_2) + 4f(x_3) + 2f(x_4) + \cdots + 4f(x_{n-1}) + f(x_n)\big).$$

In sigma notation,

$$S_n = S_{2m} = \frac{\Delta x}{3} \sum_{i=1}^{m} \big(f(x_{2i-2}) + 4f(x_{2i-1}) + f(x_{2i})\big).$$

The definition raises obvious questions: What accounts for the coefficient pattern $1, 4, 2, 4, \ldots, 1$ in the summation, and for the division by 3? How is all this related to quadratic functions? We'll explore these questions in what follows.

Simpson sums as weighted averages   In Section 6.1 we described Simpson's rule as a **weighted average** of the trapezoid and midpoint sums: if $n = 2m$, then

$$S_n = \frac{T_m + 2M_m}{3}.$$

PROBLEM 1   Let $I = \displaystyle\int_0^1 \sin x \, dx$. By the definition above,

$$S_6 = \frac{1}{18}\left(\sin(0) + 4\sin\left(\tfrac{1}{6}\right) + 2\sin\left(\tfrac{2}{6}\right) + 4\sin\left(\tfrac{3}{6}\right) + 2\sin\left(\tfrac{4}{6}\right) + 4\sin\left(\tfrac{5}{6}\right) + \sin(1)\right).$$

Write out T_3 and M_3 in the same form and check directly that $S_6 = (T_3 + 2M_3)/3$. Then find numerical values for all three approximating sums. How close is each to the exact answer?

Simpson's rule and parabolic approximation   A geometric approach to Simpson's rule involves *parabolas*—in effect, Simpson's rule pretends that an integrand f is *quadratic* on successive pairs of subintervals. Figure 1 illustrates the idea; the shaded area represents S_6. ➔

Notice that S_6 involves three parabola arcs, not six.

The area under the (blue) graph is approximated by three parabola-topped regions.

FIGURE 1
Simpson's rule: The idea

Understanding Simpson's rule geometrically is a three-step process:

1. Partition $[a, b]$ into an even number n of equal subdivisions, each of width $\Delta x = (b - a)/n$. Consider successive *pairs* of subdivisions.

2. Each pair of subdivisions involves *three* equally-spaced partition points: x_{2i-2}, x_{2i-1}, and x_{2i}. Over each such double subinterval, imagine replacing the integrand f with a *quadratic* function q—the one whose graph (a parabola) passes through the three points $\left(x_{2i-2}, f(x_{2i-2})\right)$, $\left(x_{2i-1}, f(x_{2i-1})\right)$, and $\left(x_{2i}, f(x_{2i})\right)$. For algebraic reasons, only *one* such function q exists. If the three points happen to be collinear, then q turns out to be a linear function.

3. The area under (or over, if $f < 0$) each small parabolic arc turns out to be

$$\text{area} = \frac{\Delta x}{3}\left(f(x_{2i-2}) + 4f(x_{2i-1}) + f(x_{2i})\right);$$

summing all $n/2$ such contributions gives S_n as in the definition. (Notice the sudden appearance of the once mysterious coefficients 4 and 3.)

The claim about areas in the last step isn't obviously true, but it's not terribly difficult to defend. The following problem explores a special case.

PROBLEM 2 Let f be a function, and suppose that $f(-1) = 23$, $f(0) = 41$, and $f(1) = 11$. Find a quadratic function $q(x) = a + bx + cx^2$ with these same values. Then show by direct calculation that the area under the q-graph from $x = -1$ to $x = 1$ satisfies

$$\text{area} = \frac{1}{3}(f(-1) + 4f(0) + f(1)).$$

In general, one considers any three points of the form $(x_{2i-2}, f(x_{2i-2}))$, $(x_{2i-1}, f(x_{2i-1}))$, and $(x_{2i}, f(x_{2i}))$ on the graph of f, with equally-spaced x-coordinates. Then one finds a quadratic function q whose graph passes through these points. Integrating q over the double subinterval $[x_{2i-2}, x_{2i}]$ turns out, when the dust settles, to give

$$\frac{\Delta x}{3}(f(x_{2i-2}) + 4f(x_{2i-1}) + f(x_{2i})),$$

as desired.

Zero error on quadratics

Simpson's rule is—by design—error free for constant, linear, and quadratic integrands. The following problems give further evidence of this.

PROBLEM 3 In each part, show that S_2 evaluates the integral exactly.

$$\text{(a) } \int_a^b 1\,dx \qquad \text{(b) } \int_a^b x\,dx \qquad \text{(c) } \int_a^b x^2\,dx.$$

Do each part by calculating both the exact integral and S_2. (For S_2, use the partition $x_0 = a$, $x_1 = (a+b)/2$, $x_3 = b$.)

Problem 3 implies that Simpson's rule (even with $n = 2$) commits zero error for *every* integrand of the form $Ax^2 + Bx + C$ because

$$\int_a^b (Ax^2 + Bx + C)\,dx = A\int_a^b x^2\,dx + B\int_a^b x\,dx + C\int_a^b 1\,dx,$$

and S_2 evaluates each summand on the right side exactly.

This is a rather striking property of Simpson's rule. It accounts for the presence of a fourth (rather than third) derivative in Theorem 4.

One free degree: zero error for cubics By a stroke of good luck, Simpson's rule commits zero error even for *cubic* integrands. The following example shows that this is true for $f(x) = x^3$; arguing as in the preceding paragraph shows that the same result holds for *every* cubic function.

EXAMPLE 1 Let $I = \int_a^b x^3\,dx$; show that S_2 commits *zero* error.

Solution Direct calculation (with $x_0 = a$, $x_1 = (a+b)/2$, and $x_2 = b$) gives

$$I = \int_a^b x^3\,dx = \frac{b^4 - a^4}{4}; \qquad S_2 = \frac{b-a}{6}\left(a^3 + 4\left(\frac{a+b}{2}\right)^3 + b^3\right).$$

Straightforward algebra (see the following problem) shows that $I = S_2$. ∎

PROBLEM 4 Expand and simplify S_2 in Example 1 to show that $S_2 = I$.

An error bound It's no surprise, given Example 1, that the error committed by Simpson's rule involves the *fourth derivative* $f^{(4)}$ on $[a, b]$; the fourth derivative detects how much f differs from being cubic. ➡

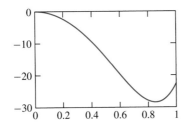

> **THEOREM 4 (Error bound for Simpson's rule)**
> Let $I = \int_a^b f(x)\,dx$, and let K_4 be any upper bound for $|f^{(4)}|$ on $[a, b]$. Then
> $$|I - S_n| \le \frac{K_4(b-a)^5}{180n^4}.$$

Notice:

*   As with K_1 and K_2 in earlier theorems, K_4 may be *any* upper bound for $|f^{(4)}|$. As before, rough estimates are best found graphically.
*   Notice that n^4 appears in the denominator; this high power of n accounts for the remarkable efficiency of Simpson's rule.

PROBLEM 5 Earlier we calculated that if $I = \int_0^1 \sin x\,dx$, then $S_6 = 0.45969967$. What does the error formula predict? How much *actual* error does S_6 commit?

Finally, we estimate an unknown quantity.

> **EXAMPLE 2** Use S_{10} to estimate $I = \int_0^1 \sin(x^2)\,dx$. How much error, at worst, might S_{10} commit? How many subdivisions would be needed to approximate I with error less than 10^{-8}?
>
> **Solution** Any convenient technology gives $S_{10} = 0.310260$ (rounded to six decimals). A slightly tedious hand calculation (it's much easier with symbol-manipulating software) finds the fourth derivative of $f(x) = \sin(x^2)$:
> $$f^{(iv)}(x) = 16\,\sin(x^2)x^4 - 48\,\cos(x^2)x^2 - 12\,\sin(x^2).$$
>
> Bounding the fourth derivative is best done graphically, as in Figure 2:

FIGURE 2
Bounding $|f^{(iv)}(x)|$ on $[0, 1]$

For a cubic function, the first four derivatives are all zero.

Graphical bounding of $f^{(4)}$ is essential for all but the simplest functions f.

K_4 is positive because of the absolute value.

The graph suggests that $K_4 = 30$ looks safe. ← The rest is arithmetic. By the theorem,

$$|I - S_{10}| \le \frac{30 \cdot (1 - 0)^5}{180 \cdot 10^4} \approx 0.000017.$$

The error, if any, enters around the fifth decimal place, and so 0.3103 is a meaningful estimate for I.

To ensure error less than 10^{-8}, we need n so that

$$|I - S_n| \le \frac{30 \cdot (1 - 0)^5}{180 \cdot n^4} < 10^{-8}.$$

Solving the last inequality for n gives

$$\frac{1}{6 \cdot n^4} < 10^{-8} \iff n^4 > \frac{10^8}{6} \iff n > \frac{100}{\sqrt[4]{6}} \approx 63.9,$$

and we conclude that any even $n \ge 64$ will do. ∎

FURTHER EXERCISES

1. Let $I = \int_0^2 e^{x^2}\, dx$.

   (a) Compute S_4 (use technology).

   (b) Bound the approximation error made by S_4.

   (c) Use the error bound formula for Simpson's rule to find a value of n so that S_n is guaranteed to approximate I within 10^{-5}.

2. Let $I = \int_0^1 \cos(100x)\, dx$.

   (a) Compute the value of I exactly, using the FTC.

   (b) Compute S_{10}. Show that the *actual* approximation error is less than 0.05.

   (c) Find an upper bound on the magnitude of the approximation error. Why is this upper bound so enormous?

   (The moral of this problem is that the error bound of Theorem 4 sometimes *vastly* overstates the actual error committed.)

3. Let $I = \int_5^7 \cos x\, dx$.

   (a) Compute S_4.

   (b) What does the error bound formula say about the error made if I is approximated by S_4? How much error does S_4 actually commit?

4. Let $I = \int_{-1}^2 f(x)\, dx$, where f is a function such that $1 \le f^{(4)}(x) \le 8$ if $-1 \le x \le 2$ and f has the values shown in the table.

x	-1.00	-0.25	0.50	1.25	2.00
$f(x)$	2.000	26.522	48.755	68.328	86.790

   Compute S_4 and an upper bound on the value of $|I - S_4|$.

5. Compute an estimate of $\int_0^2 xe^{-x^3}\, dx$ that is guaranteed to be correct within ± 0.001. Explain carefully why your estimate has the desired accuracy.

Gaussian Quadrature: Approximating Integrals Efficiently

Gaussian quadrature offers impressive accuracy in approximating integrals, at surprisingly little cost. Studying the topic gives students a different perspective on numerical integration, and some good practice in algebraic manipulation.

Calculations have costs. Even fast computers require time and other resources to complete calculations. In estimating a definite integral $\int_a^b f(x)\,dx$, for example, it may be "expensive" to find many values of the integrand f. In such cases we want an approximate method that uses relatively few evaluations of the integrand and makes the best possible use of whatever values are computed. The method called **Gaussian quadrature** works efficiently in this sense.

Special integrals—for now To avoid symbolic clutter, we'll focus mainly on integrals of the form

$$\int_{-1}^{1} f(x)\,dx,$$

for which the interval of integration is $[-1, 1]$. At the end we'll show how to extend the ideas developed here to definite integrals defined on *any* interval.

Quadrature formulas All of the approximate integration methods (left, right, midpoint, and trapezoid rules) we've studied have similar symbolic forms. Here are several examples for an integrand f on $[-1, 1]$: ➤

$$L_2 = 1\,f(-1) + 1\,f(0)$$

$$M_4 = \frac{1}{2}\,f\left(-\tfrac{3}{4}\right) + \frac{1}{2}\,f\left(-\tfrac{1}{4}\right) + \frac{1}{2}\,f\left(\tfrac{1}{4}\right) + \frac{1}{2}\,f\left(\tfrac{3}{4}\right)$$

$$T_3 = \frac{1}{3}\,f(-1) + \frac{2}{3}\,f\left(-\tfrac{1}{3}\right) + \frac{2}{3}\,f\left(\tfrac{1}{3}\right) + \frac{1}{3}\,f(1)$$

L, M, and T stand for left, midpoint, and trapezoid.

All of these rules have the same general form:

$$w_1 f(x_1) + w_2 f(x_2) + \cdots + w_n f(x_n), \tag{1}$$

where $x_1, x_2, \ldots, x_n$ are specific input points (called the **nodes**) in the interval of integration (in this case, that's $[-1, 1]$) and the $w_1, w_2, \ldots, w_n$ are positive numbers (called the **weights**).

Any expression of the form (1) is called a **quadrature formula** on the interval $[-1, 1]$. All three of the expressions M_2, L_4, and T_3 above are examples of quadrature formulas. For a given integrand function f, a quadrature formula combines values of f at the nodes with the weights to produce a *number* that (with any luck) should approximate the definite integral $\int_{-1}^{1} f(x)\,dx$. Thus, a *good* quadrature formula is one that approximates such integrals closely for many integrand functions f.

EXAMPLE 1 Let $f(x) = \cos x$. What do the quadrature formulas M_2, L_4, and T_3 give? How do these numbers compare with the "true value" of $\int_{-1}^{1} \cos x\,dx$? Which quadrature formula is "best"?

Solution Applying the quadrature formulas to $f(x) = \cos x$ gives

$$L_2 = 1\,\cos(-1) + 1\,\cos(0) \approx 1.5403;$$

$$M_4 = \frac{1}{2}\,\cos\left(-\tfrac{3}{4}\right) + \frac{1}{2}\,\cos\left(-\tfrac{1}{4}\right) + \frac{1}{2}\,\cos\left(\tfrac{1}{4}\right) + \frac{1}{2}\,\cos\left(\tfrac{3}{4}\right) \approx 1.7006;$$

$$T_3 = \frac{1}{3}\,\cos(-1) + \frac{2}{3}\,\cos\left(-\tfrac{1}{3}\right) + \frac{2}{3}\,\cos\left(\tfrac{1}{3}\right) + \frac{1}{3}\,\cos(1) \approx 1.6201.$$

The exact value, by comparison, is $\int_{-1}^{1} \cos x \, dx = \sin(1) - \sin(-1) \approx 1.6829$. In this case, at least, M_4 comes closest to the exact value and so might be considered "best" among the three quadrature formulas. On the other hand, M_4 used *four* values of the cosine, whereas L_2 used only two, and thus the better approximation came at a higher price. ∎

PROBLEM 6 In each of the following parts apply the quadrature formulas L_2, M_4, and T_3 to the given function f on $[-1, 1]$. Compare results to the "true value" of $\int_{-1}^{1} f(x) \, dx$. Try to explain any "surprises" that appear.

(a) $f(x) = e^x$

(b) $f(x) = x$

(c) $f(x) = 1$

(d) $f(x) = \sin x$

PROBLEM 7 Suppose that f is an *odd* function (i.e., $f(-x) = -f(x)$). Explain why (a) $\int_{-1}^{1} f(x) \, dx = 0$; and (b) all three quadrature formulas L_2, M_4, and T_3 give 0 (the exact answer) when applied to f.

PROBLEM 8 Suppose that f is a *constant* function (i.e., $f(x) = k$ for some real number k). Explain why all three quadrature formulas L_2, M_4, and T_3 give the *exact* value of $\int_{-1}^{1} f(x) \, dx$.

PROBLEM 9 Suppose that f is a *linear* function (i.e., $f(x) = ax + b$ for some real numbers a and b). Which (if any) of the three quadrature formulas L_2, M_4, and T_3 give the *exact* value of $\int_{-1}^{1} f(x) \, dx$? Why?

PROBLEM 10 Write out the quadrature formulas M_5 and T_5 on $[-1, 1]$. What estimate does each formula produce for $\int_{-1}^{1} \cos x \, dx$?

PROBLEM 11 Consider any quadrature formula

$$Q = w_1 f(x_1) + w_2 f(x_2) + \cdots + w_n f(x_n)$$

on $[-1, 1]$. For any function g, we'll write $Q(g)$ for the result of applying Q to g. Let g and h be any functions defined on $[-1, 1]$, and let C be any constant. Show:

(a) $Q(g + h) = Q(g) + Q(h)$

(b) $Q(Cg) = C \, Q(g)$.

(The point of the problem is that quadrature formulas behave like definite integrals in the sense that both operations "respect" sums and constant multiples.)

Gaussian quadrature formulas In all three quadrature formulas, L_2, M_4, and T_3 (and in such close relatives as L_5, M_{237}, and T_{79}), the nodes are evenly spaced—all nodes are endpoints or midpoints of *equal-length* subdivisions of the interval $[-1, 1]$.

Choosing nodes this way seems natural, but it's not the only possibility. In the early 1800s the German mathematician Carl Friedrich Gauss found that placing the nodes elsewhere can give even better results. Here are two of Gauss's quadrature formulas:

$$GQ_2 = 1 \, f\left(-1/\sqrt{3}\right) + 1 \, f\left(1/\sqrt{3}\right) \approx f(-0.5774) + f(0.5774);$$

$$GQ_3 = \frac{5}{9} f\left(-\sqrt{3/5}\right) + \frac{8}{9} f(0) + \frac{5}{9} f\left(\sqrt{3/5}\right)$$

$$\approx 0.5556 f(-0.7746) + 0.8889 f(0) + 0.5556 f(0.7746).$$

Here, GQ stands for **Gaussian quadrature**, and the subscript reflects the number of nodes. With $f(x) = \cos x$, for example, the rules give

$$GQ_2 = \cos\left(-1/\sqrt{3}\right) + \cos\left(1/\sqrt{3}\right) \approx 1.6758;$$

$$GQ_3 = \frac{5}{9}\cos\left(-\sqrt{3/5}\right) + \frac{8}{9}\cos(0) + \frac{5}{9}\cos\left(\sqrt{3/5}\right) \approx 1.6830.$$

These results agree to two or three decimal places with the exact value of $\int_{-1}^{1}\cos x\,dx$—a remarkable result given that only two or three values of the integrand were used.

We'll explore in a moment how formulas GQ_2 and GQ_3 can be found, but first let's see how well they work.

PROBLEM 12 In each of the following parts, apply the Gaussian quadrature formulas GQ_2 and GQ_3 to the given function f on $[-1, 1]$. Compare results to the "true value" of $\int_{-1}^{1} f(x)\,dx$. (Do these by hand to be sure you see the patterns.)

(a) $f(x) = 1$

(b) $f(x) = x$

(c) $f(x) = x^2$

(d) $f(x) = x^3$

(e) $f(x) = x^4$

(f) $f(x) = x^5$

What the problems show Results of Problem 12 are worth emphasizing:

Formula GQ_2 gives the exact value of the integral $\int_{-1}^{1} f(x)\,dx$ if $f(x) = 1$, $f(x) = x$, $f(x) = x^2$, and $f(x) = x^3$. Formula GQ_2 gives the exact value of $\int_{-1}^{1} x^k\,dx$ for $k = 0, 1, \dots, 5$.

Because quadrature formulas "respect" sums and constant multiples (see Problem 11), we can say more:

> **FACT** Formula GQ_2 gives the *exact* value of $\int_{-1}^{1} f(x)\,dx$ if $f(x)$ is any polynomial of degree *three* or lower; GQ_3 gives the exact value if $f(x)$ is any polynomial of degree *five* or lower.

PROBLEM 13 In each of the following parts, apply GQ_2 and GQ_3 to the given function f on $[-1, 1]$. Compare results to the "true value" of $\int_{-1}^{1} f(x)\,dx$.

(a) $f(x) = e^x$

(b) $f(x) = \ln(x + 2)$

(c) $f(x) = x^6$

Finding Gauss's weights and nodes Quadrature formulas GQ_2 and GQ_3 seem to work very well, but how were the weights and nodes in formulas GQ_2 and GQ_3 found? Problem 12 suggests how Gauss might have reasoned:

- **For GQ_2:** Choose weights w_1 and w_2 and nodes x_1 and x_2 to ensure that the formula gives exact answers for integrands 1, x, x^2, and x^3.

- **For GQ_3:** Choose weights w_1, w_2, and w_3 and nodes x_1, x_2, and x_3 to ensure that the formula gives exact answers for integrands 1, x, x^2, x^3, x^4, and x^5.

We work out the details in the next two problems.

PROBLEM 14 **(Finding the formula GQ_2)** Formula GQ_2 has the general form

$$GQ_2 = w_1 f(x_1) + w_2 f(x_2).$$

Find numerical values for w_1, x_1, w_2, and x_2 by working through the following steps. (Explain anything that needs explanation.)

(a) Assume (it's reasonable to do so) that the two weights are equal and that the nodes are symmetrically placed with respect to the origin. This leads (explain how) to the simpler form $GQ_2 = wf(-n) + wf(n)$, where w and n are positive numbers still to be found.

(b) Use the fact that GQ_2 gives the exact integral for $f(x) = 1$ to show that $w = 1$, and hence that $GQ_2 = f(n) + f(-n)$, for some n still to be found.

(c) Use the fact that GQ_2 gives the exact integral for $f(x) = x^2$ to show that $n = 1/\sqrt{3}$, and hence that $GQ_2 = f(-1/\sqrt{3}) + f(1/\sqrt{3})$, as above.

(d) Check that $GQ_2 = f(-1/\sqrt{3}) + f(1/\sqrt{3})$ gives the exact integral for both $f(x) = x$ and $f(x) = x^3$, as desired.

PROBLEM 15 **(Finding the formula GQ_3)** Because GQ_3 has three nodes and three weights, it has the general form

$$GQ_3 = w_1 f(x_1) + w_2 f(x_2) + w_3 f(x_3).$$

Find numerical values for the weights and nodes by working through the following steps. (Explain anything that needs explanation.)

(a) It's reasonable to assume (or guess) that the nodes are symmetrically placed with respect to the origin; this means that $x_2 = 0$ and that $x_3 = -x_1$. It's also reasonable to suppose (again for reasons of symmetry) that the leftmost and rightmost nodes have the same weights. This leads (explain how) to the simpler form

$$GQ_3 = w_1 f(x_1) + w_2 f(0) + w_1 f(-x_1),$$

where w_1, w_2, and x_1 are still to be found.

(b) Use the fact that GQ_3 gives the exact integral for $f(x) = 1$ to show that $2w_1 + w_2 = 2$.

(c) Use the fact that GQ_3 gives the exact integral for $f(x) = x^2$ to show that $2w_1 x_1^2 = 2/3$.

(d) Use the fact that GQ_3 gives the exact integral for $f(x) = x^4$ to show that $2w_1 x_1^4 = 2/5$.

(e) Use results from earlier parts to show that $x_1 = \sqrt{3/5}$ and $w_1 = 5/9$.

(f) Use parts (b) and (e) to show that $w_2 = 8/9$. Conclude that GQ_3 has the desired form.

Integration over any interval These ideas would be of little value if they applied *only* to integrals over the interval $[-1, 1]$. The following example suggests how to use a linear change of variable to apply the Gaussian quadrature idea to an integral over *any* finite interval.

EXAMPLE 2 Use Gaussian quadrature to approximate the integral $I = \int_2^5 \cos x \, dx$. (The exact value is $\sin 5 - \sin 2 \approx -1.8682$.)

Solution First, we find a linear function $u(x) = Ax + B$ so that $u(2) = -1$ and $u(5) = 1$. A little algebra shows that $u(x) = 2x/3 - 7/3$ does the trick. Second, we make the u-substitution $u = 2x/3 - 7/3$ in the integral I (note that $x = 3u/2 + 7/2$ and $dx = 3 \, du/2$) to get the new integral

$$I = \int_2^5 \cos x \, dx = \int_{-1}^1 \frac{3}{2} \cos\left(\frac{3}{2}u + \frac{7}{2}\right) du.$$

Finally, we apply GC_2 and GC_3 to the *new* integrand function (on the right) to get

$$GC_2(g) = -1.8201 \quad \text{and} \quad GC_3(g) = -1.8692,$$

both of which compare respectably to the exact integral. ∎

PROBLEM 16 In each part, mimic the preceding example to apply GC_3 to the given integral. Compare results to the exact integral values.

(a) $\displaystyle\int_0^1 e^x \, dx$

(b) $\displaystyle\int_1^5 \frac{1}{x} \, dx$

7

USING THE INTEGRAL

7.1 MEASUREMENT AND THE DEFINITE INTEGRAL; ARC LENGTH

Introduction

This chapter is mainly about applications, so we de-emphasize complicated symbolic calculations. Technology (symbolic, numerical, or both) can help evaluate some integrals. This section is relatively long, but much of it reviews "familiar" applications such as area.

Many important applications of calculus involve measuring something, such as the *area* of a plane region, the *volume* of a solid object, the *length* of a curve from one point to another, the *net distance* a moving object travels over an interval of time, the *work* done against gravity in raising a satellite into orbit, or the *present value* of an income stream. ◄

We'll define quantities such as work and present value as we go along.

In the simplest cases such quantities can be measured using basic formulas. For example, measuring the area of a rectangular region, the length of a straight line segment, or the distance covered by an object moving at constant speed requires no big ideas or clever techniques from calculus. In practice, though, most regions are not rectangular, most curves are not straight, and most speeds are not constant. In these more usual and more interesting situations, the definite integral turns out to be an essential tool.

In Chapter 5 we defined integrals informally in terms of signed area.

The link between integrals and areas is nothing new—we've exploited it from the beginning. ◄ But if definite integrals measured *only* area, they wouldn't deserve the fuss we make over them. In fact, as we'll see, measurement problems of *many* kinds boil down to definite integrals. The last step—evaluating a definite integral—is often relatively easy. We can use the FTC if an antiderivative is readily available; if not, we can use the numerical methods developed in Chapter 6. For many measurement problems, the main step is choosing *which* definite integral to evaluate—both the integrand and the limits of integration may take some thought to decide upon. Because our main interest in this chapter is usually in setting up integrals, we'll sometimes skip (or leave to a machine) the details of routine calculations.

Technical note: assuming good behavior   To avoid unhelpful distractions, we assume that all the integrals $\int_a^b f(x)\,dx$ we meet in this chapter make good mathematical sense. To guarantee this, it's enough to assume that every integrand f is *continuous* on $[a, b]$. We will assume this from now on unless something explicit is said to the contrary. (In fact, discontinuous integrands *do* sometimes arise in practical applications. Even in such cases, however, the basic ideas of this section often apply, although perhaps in slightly modified forms.)

Some applications lead to piecewise-continuous integrands. This occurs, for instance, in measuring arc length of a kinked curve.

Two views of the definite integral

In applying the integral in varied settings, it's useful to remember two different but closely related interpretations of a definite integral $\int_a^b f(x)\,dx$.

- **A limit of approximating sums**   The integral is defined formally as a limit of approximating sums. Chapter 6 discusses and compares several kinds of approximating sums: left, right, trapezoid, midpoint, and so on. Using right sums, for instance, we can write

$$\int_a^b f(x)\,dx = \lim_{n\to\infty} \sum_{i=1}^{n} f(x_i)\Delta x,$$

where the inputs x_i are the right endpoints of n equal-length subintervals of $[a, b]$. From this point of view, the integral "adds up" many contributions, each of the form $f(x_i)\Delta x$.

- **Accumulated change in an antiderivative**   The FTC says that

$$\int_a^b f(x)\,dx = F(b) - F(a),$$

where the function F on the right can be *any* antiderivative of f on $[a, b]$. ➙ The difference $F(b) - F(a)$ represents, in a natural way, the **accumulated change** (or net change) in F over the interval $[a, b]$. In other words, to find the net change in F over $[a, b]$, integrate f—the *rate function* associated with F—over $[a, b]$.

Students should see the pattern: Integrating speed gives change in distance; integrating velocity gives change in position; integrating any f' gives change in f.

Remember: Antiderivatives are not unique. If F is one antiderivative of f, then so is $F + k$, where k is any constant.

These two approaches to the integral are mathematically equivalent. The FTC guarantees that both methods give the same "answer." Having two different ways to think about the integral makes it more versatile in applications. Which viewpoint is "better" depends on the situation. The following example illustrates both viewpoints.

EXAMPLE 1   The function $v(t) = 10 + 20t - 10t^2$ gives a car's eastward velocity, in miles per hour at time t hours, for $0 \le t \le 3$. Calculate $I = \int_0^3 v(t)\,dt$; interpret I both as a limit of sums and as accumulated change in an antiderivative.

Solution   Calculating I symbolically is easy:

$$I = \int_0^3 v(t)\,dt = 10t + 10t^2 - \frac{10t^3}{3}\bigg]_0^3 = 30.$$

What does the answer mean? Figure 1 gives two different views.

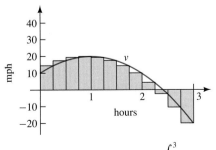

(a) An approximating sum for $\int_0^3 v(t)\,dt$

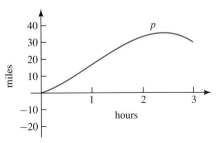

(b) An antiderivative p

FIGURE 1
Two views of one answer

Figure 1(a) suggests the limit-of-sums view of I. It shows R_{12}, the right approximating sum for I with 12 subdivisions. The signed area of each rectangle approximates the *eastward* distance covered by the car over that subinterval. The three rightmost rectangles contribute *negative* eastward distance (i.e., *westward* distance). Therefore, the right sum R_{12} approximates the *net* eastward distance covered over the entire interval $0 \le t \le 3$. As the limit of such approximating sums, I represents the *exact* net eastward distance covered over $[0, 3]$—precisely 30 miles. Numerical evidence supports this idea:

$$R_{12} \approx 25.938; \quad R_{50} \approx 29.082; \quad R_{200} \approx 29.774; \quad \ldots \quad I = 30.$$

Figure 1(b) illustrates the accumulated-change view of I. Because the function v describes the car's eastward *velocity*, an antiderivative function p describes the car's east–west *position* given appropriate units and points of reference. Since $v(t) = 10 + 20t - 10t^2$, we can choose the antiderivative function $p(t) = 10t + 10t^2 - 10t^3/3$. Then $p(0) = 0$, so the car starts at position 0 and $p(t)$ represents the car's position at time t measured in miles east of the starting point. The graph of v in Figure 1(b) shows a net movement of 30 miles east—the accumulated change in *position* over the 3-hour interval. ∎

Measuring areas in the plane

Recall the familiar interpretation of the integral as *signed* area: ◄ For any continuous function f on $[a, b]$,

$$\int_a^b f(x)\, dx = \text{signed area bounded by the } f\text{-graph for } a \le x \le b.$$

Keeping track of positive and negative contributions to signed area takes a little care. Here's a simple example to bring the issue back to mind.

EXAMPLE 2 Easy calculations give

$$I_1 = \int_0^\pi \sin x\, dx = 2 \quad \text{and} \quad I_2 = \int_0^{2\pi} \sin x\, dx = 0.$$

What do these results say about ordinary and signed areas?

Solution Because $\sin x \ge 0$ on $[0, \pi]$, the integral I_1 gives the ordinary area—2 square units—under one arch of the sine curve. That $I_2 = 0$ means that the *signed* area over $[0, 2\pi]$ is zero. This makes good geometric sense: The symmetry of the sine graph means that areas above and below the x-axis exactly cancel each other out. ∎

Areas defined by more than one curve The connection between areas and integrals can be used, with only minor changes, to measure areas defined by more than one function graph. The shaded part of Figure 2 is one such region; it is bounded above and below by function graphs and on the left and right by vertical lines.

FIGURE 2

A region defined by two curves

Notice that the shaded area in Figure 2 is the *difference* between the areas associated with $\int_a^b g(x)\,dx$ and $\int_a^b f(x)\,dx$. Therefore,

$$\text{shaded area} = \int_a^b g(x)\,dx - \int_a^b f(x)\,dx = \int_a^b \big(g(x) - f(x)\big)\,dx. \qquad (1)$$

EXAMPLE 3 Measure the shaded area in Figure 3.

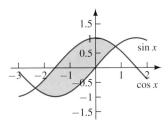

FIGURE 3
Area between sine and cosine curves

Solution The sine and cosine curves intersect at $x = -3\pi/4$ and $x = \pi/4$, and thus Formula 1 gives

$$\text{area} = \int_{-3\pi/4}^{\pi/4} (\cos x - \sin x)\,dx = 2\sqrt{2} \approx 2.82843.$$

The numerical result looks graphically reasonable, but attentive readers may wonder: Does Formula 1 apply even when (as here) one or both curves dip below the x-axis. The answer, fortunately, is yes: Formula (1) requires only that $g(x) \ge f(x)$ when $a \le x \le b$.   ■

Here's one nice way to see that the answer is yes: Add a large positive constant, say 100, to both f and g to move both graphs safely above the x-axis. Doing so leaves the area unchanged, and the constant vanishes in the integral $\int f - g$.

So that $g(x) - f(x) \ge 0$.

Other regions; integrating in x or in y In practice, plane regions of interest may be bounded by various types of curves—not necessarily graphs of the standard $y = f(x)$ style. Figure 4 illustrates two common types. ➡

More complicated regions may be combinations of these two types.

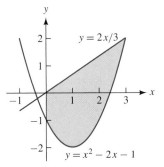

Region 1: top and bottom curves

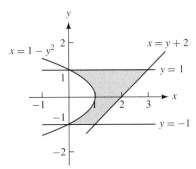

Region 2: left and right curves

FIGURE 4
Two types of plane regions

The following formulas apply to finding areas such as those in Figure 4.

FACT   Let f and g be continuous functions.

- **Integrating in x**   Let R be the region bounded above by $y = g(x)$, below by $y = f(x)$, on the left by $x = a$, and on the right by $x = b$. Then R has area

$$\int_a^b \big(g(x) - f(x)\big)\, dx. \qquad (2)$$

- **Integrating in y**   Let R be the region bounded on the right by $x = g(y)$, on the left by $x = f(y)$, below by $y = c$, and above by $y = d$. Then R has area

$$\int_c^d \big(g(y) - f(y)\big)\, dy. \qquad (3)$$

Instead of integrating in y, one could (i) interchange the variables x and y; (ii) observe that doing so amounts to a reflection, and so leaves area unchanged; and (iii) integrate in x.

Depending on the region, one or the other formula may be simpler; some areas can be calculated by integration either in x or in y. We illustrate the possibilities by example.

EXAMPLE 4   Measure the two shaded areas in Figure 4.

Solution   The two graphs in Figure 4(a) intersect at $x = 3$ and $x = -1/3$, as Figure 4 suggests—and the quadratic formula confirms. (The intersection at $x = -1/3$ is outside Region 1 and therefore doesn't appear in the calculation.) Now Formula (2) gives

$$\text{area} = \int_0^3 \left(\tfrac{2}{3}x - (x^2 - 2x - 1)\right) dx = 6.$$

Integration in x seems impractical for Region 2, because defining upper and lower curves is troublesome. But Formula (3) applies conveniently:

$$\text{area} = \int_{-1}^1 \left(y + 2 - (1 - y^2)\right) dy = \frac{8}{3}.\qquad\blacksquare$$

EXAMPLE 5   Use *both* Formulas (2) and (3) to find the area of the region bounded by the curves $x = 0$, $y = 2$, and $y = e^x$, shown shaded in Figure 5.

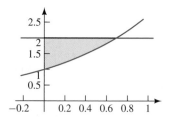

FIGURE 5
Curves $y = e^x$ and $y = 2$

Solution   The two curves intersect where $e^x = 2$ or $x = \ln 2$. Integrating in x gives

$$\text{area} = \int_0^{\ln 2} (2 - e^x)\, dx = 2\ln 2 - 1 \approx 0.3863.$$

To find the same area in terms of y, we rewrite the equation $y = e^x$ in the equivalent form $x = \ln y$. This curve is the *right* boundary; $x = 0$ is the left boundary. Integrating in y now gives

$$\text{area} = \int_1^2 (\ln y - 0) \, dy = 2\ln 2 - 1,$$

just as above.   ∎

Arc length

Arc length offers a good example of using integrals to measure geometric quantities *other* than area; arc length integrals also show the role of approximating sums.

Students often equate integrals with area, so it's helpful to see integrals used to measure another geometric quantity. Arc length integrals are often symbolically unpleasant, but technology can help.

EXAMPLE 6   How long is the curve $y = \sin x$ from $x = 0$ to $x = \pi$? (First try to estimate the length—draw your own graph.)

Solution   Straight line segments are easy to measure using the distance formula. In the spirit of approximating sums, a natural strategy suggests itself for measuring *curves*:

Approximate the curve with straight line segments and add up their lengths.

Figure 6 shows a four-segment piecewise-linear approximation to the sine curve.

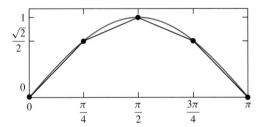

The endpoints of each line segment are shown with black dots.

FIGURE 6
Estimating the length of one arch

Knowing the coordinates of the segments' endpoints, we can readily (if tediously) calculate the total length of the four-segment chain; it's about 3.79. With more and shorter line segments, we expect increasingly better approximations to the curve's true length L. In other words, we expect L to be the *limit* of polygonal lengths as the number of subdivisions tends to infinity. This language suggests—rightly—the presence of a definite integral, and, indeed, we'll derive one in a moment. But first let's see the limiting principle in action numerically, by tabulating lengths (computed electronically, of course) of several piecewise-linear approximations to the elusive L. Each length corresponds to subdividing the x-interval $[0, \pi]$ into n equal subintervals.

Most students don't need convincing that these approximations converge to a limit, but seeing it happen numerically makes the idea concrete.

Approximating the length of a curve					
Number of segments	4	8	16	31	100
Polygonal length	3.7901	3.8125	3.8183	3.8197	3.8201

For now, 3.8201 is our best guess.   ∎

Arc length in general   A general arc length problem reads as follows:

Find the length of the f-graph from x = a to x = b.

The preceding example suggests a general strategy:

Approximate with piecewise–linear arcs and then take a limit.

How does this work in practice? How is an integral involved? *Which* integral is involved? To describe the situation more precisely, we need a more general picture.

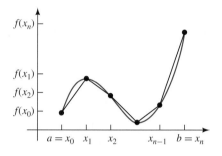

FIGURE 7
Approximating a curve C with a polygonal arc C_n

Figure 7 has three main ingredients:

1. C, the graph of f from $x = a$ to $x = b$;

2. A partition of $[a, b]$ into n subintervals with endpoints $x_0, x_1, \ldots, x_n$;

3. A **polygonal arc** C_n made from n line segments joining the points $(x_0, f(x_0))$, $(x_1, f(x_1)), \ldots, (x_n, f(x_n))$ on C.

Now we can put the idea succinctly: Length of $C = \lim_{n \to \infty} (\text{length of } C_n)$.

Interpreting the arc length estimate as an approximating sum is a bit clumsy thanks to the square roots. But the "algebraic trick" offers a nice reminder of the meaning of derivatives.

How long is C_n? A useful estimate   To measure C_n we add the lengths of its n segments. The ith segment joins $(x_{i-1}, f(x_{i-1}))$ to $(x_i, f(x_i))$, and so its length is

$$\sqrt{\left(f(x_i) - f(x_{i-1})\right)^2 + (x_i - x_{i-1})^2}.$$

Thus,

$$\text{total length of } C_n = \sum_{i=1}^{n} \sqrt{\left(f(x_i) - f(x_{i-1})\right)^2 + (x_i - x_{i-1})^2}. \tag{4}$$

We'll rewrite Equation 4 as an approximating sum for an integral. The first step is an algebraic trick—factoring out $(x_i - x_{i-1})$:

$$\text{length of } C_n = \sum_{i=1}^{n} \sqrt{\left(f(x_i) - f(x_{i-1})\right)^2 + (x_i - x_{i-1})^2}$$

$$= \sum_{i=1}^{n} \sqrt{\left(\frac{f(x_i) - f(x_{i-1})}{x_i - x_{i-1}}\right)^2 + 1} \cdot (x_i - x_{i-1}).$$

This clumsy expression can be simplified. By the definition of derivative, the approximation

$$\frac{f(x_i) - f(x_{i-1})}{x_i - x_{i-1}} \approx f'(x_i)$$

holds if $x_i - x_{i-1}$ is small. Putting the pieces together and writing Δx_i for $(x_i - x_{i-1})$, we get

$$\text{Length of } C_n = \sum_{i=1}^{n} \sqrt{\left(\frac{f(x_i) - f(x_{i-1})}{x_i - x_{i-1}}\right)^2 + 1} \cdot (x_i - x_{i-1})$$

$$\approx \sum_{i=1}^{n} \sqrt{(f'(x_i))^2 + 1} \cdot \Delta x_i.$$

The final line rewards our work: It is an approximating sum for an integral. We state the conclusion as a Fact:

We take the same tack later to derive integral formulas for measuring volume, work, present value, etc. — a reasonable discrete approximation to the desired measurement turns out to be an approximating sum for an integral.

> **FACT (Arc length by integration)**   The integral
>
> $$\int_a^b \sqrt{(f'(x))^2 + 1} \; dx$$
>
> gives the length of the f-graph from $x = a$ to $x = b$.

EXAMPLE 7   Write the length of the sine curve from $x = 0$ to $x = \pi$ as an integral. Estimate its value.

Solution   By the Fact, the length is

$$I = \int_0^\pi \sqrt{(\cos x)^2 + 1} \, dx.$$

The FTC won't help us evaluate I because there's no convenient antiderivative. But we can estimate I by using (say) the midpoint rule with 100 subdivisions: $I \approx M_{100} \approx 3.8202$, which is close to our earlier estimate.   ■

Do curves have length?   Do piecewise-linear approximations successfully approximate a curve's arc length, as we claimed?

With modern computer graphics, the answer seems obvious. Almost every "curve" in this book, for instance, is really a collection of short line segments— shorter than the eye can perceive individually—strung end to end. In this case, appearances don't deceive: All but the very worst-behaved curves *can* be approximated in the sense just discussed.

Curves do have length.

EXAMPLE 8   Interpret the integral $I = \int_0^1 \sqrt{1 + 4x^2} \, dx$ in two different ways: (i) as the *length* of an appropriate curve and (ii) as the *area* of something. Describe these quantities and evaluate them numerically.

This example is partly "cautionary": Integrals themselves are just numbers not forever bound to particular interpretations.

Solution   The integral I fits the arc length "template" if $f'(x) = 2x$. Clearly, $f(x) = x^2$ has this property. Therefore, I gives the length of the curve $y = x^2$ from $x = 0$ to $x = 1$. ➡

Any definite integral measures the signed area bounded by its integrand. In this case, therefore, I measures the area under the curve $y = \sqrt{1 + 4x^2}$ from $x = 0$ to $x = 1$.

Important note: The curve we're measuring is not *the integrand.*

How large, numerically, is I? Antidifferentiation is algebraically messy, and so we'll find M_{20}, the midpoint estimate with 20 subdivisions. Reported to three decimal places:

$$I \approx M_{20} \approx 1.479.$$

Thus, both quantities (length and area) have the same approximate numerical value: 1.479 units of *length* and 1.479 units of *area*, respectively. ◄

The respective units might be inches and square inches.

Figure 8 illustrates both interpretations of I.

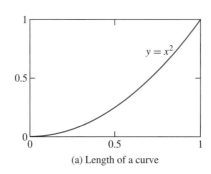

(a) Length of a curve

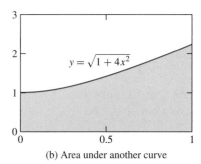

(b) Area under another curve

FIGURE 8

$\displaystyle\int_0^1 \sqrt{1+4x^2}\,dx \approx 1.479$: One value, two meanings ■

BASIC EXERCISES

1. Let R be the region between the curves $y = x$ and $y = x^2$.

  (a) Draw a sketch of the region R.

  (b) Use five left-rule rectangles to approximate the area of R. (Give a numerical answer.)

  (c) Draw a picture that illustrates the sum you computed in part (b). Use this picture to decide whether your answer in part (b) overestimates or underestimates the area of R.

  (d) Find the area of R *exactly* using the FTC.

2. Let A be the region bounded by the curves $y = \sin x$ and $y = \cos x$ and the lines $x = 1$ and $x = 3$.

  (a) Draw a sketch of the region R.

  (b) Use five midpoint-rule rectangles to approximate the area of R. (Give a numerical answer.)

  (c) Explain why M_n overestimates the area of R for every $n \geq 1$.

  (d) Find the area of R *exactly* using the FTC.

3. In this exercise, integration in x is used to find the area of Region 2 in Figure 4.

  (a) Find the area of the region bounded below by the x-axis, above by the line $y = 1$, on the right by the line $x = 1$, and on the left by the curve $x = 1 - y^2$.

  (b) Find the area of the region bounded above by the x-axis, below by the line $y = -1$, on the right by the line $x = 1$, and on the left by the curve $x = 1 - y^2$.

  (c) Find the area of the region bounded by the lines $x = 1$, $x = y + 2$, and $y = 1$.

  (d) Use the results of parts (a), (b), and (c) to find the area of Region 2.

4. This exercise provides yet another approach to finding the area of Region 2 in Figure 4.

  (a) Find the area of the region bounded by the line $x = 0$ and the curve $x = 1 - y^2$.

  (b) Find the area of the region bounded by the lines $x = y + 2$, $y = -1$, and $x = 3$.

  (c) Find the area of the region bounded by the lines $x = 0$, $x = 3$, $y = 1$, and $y = -1$.

  (d) Use the results of parts (a), (b), and (c) to find the area of Region 2.

5. Let $I = \displaystyle\int_0^1 \sqrt{1+4x^2}\,dx$. (See Example 8.)

  (a) Use a trapezoid sum with $n = 20$ subintervals to estimate I.

  (b) Explain why $M_{20} < I < T_{20}$.

6. Write an integral I that gives the length of the curve $y = x^2 + 1$ from $x = 0$ to $x = 1$.

  (a) Use a midpoint sum with $n = 20$ equal subintervals to estimate I.

  (b) Evaluate I exactly. [HINT: Use the table of integrals.]

7. Write an integral I that gives the length of the curve $y = 2 + \sin x$ from $x = 0$ to $x = \pi$. Use a midpoint sum with $n = 20$ subintervals to estimate I.

8. Compute the length of the line $y = mx + b$ from $x = A$ to $x = B$. Does the answer agree with the usual distance formula?

9. A moral of Example 8 is that a given integral can be interpreted in various ways. In each of the following parts, interpret the numerical value of the integral in the stated context using appropriate units of measurement.

(a) $\int_0^3 f(t)\,dt$, where the function $f(t) = 5t^2 - 20t + 50$ tells a certain car's speed, in miles per hour, t hours after midnight

(b) $\int_0^3 f(t)\,dt$, where the function $f(t) = 5t^2 - 20t + 50$ tells a certain car's speed, in feet per second, t seconds after midnight

(c) $\int_0^3 f(t)\,dt$, where the function $f(t) = 5t^2 - 20t + 50$ tells a certain car's acceleration, in feet per minute per minute, t minutes after midnight

10. Interpret the integral $\int_1^3 f(t)\,dt$ in each of the following situations and comment on what it means in each case if the integral is negative. For instance, if $f(t)$ is the eastward velocity of a car in miles per hour at time t hours, then $\int_1^3 f(t)\,dt$ gives the car's net eastward distance traveled between $t = 1$ and $t = 3$. If the integral is negative, the car's position at time 3 is west of its position at time 1.

(a) $f(t)$ is an object's upward velocity, in feet per second, at time t seconds.

(b) $f(t)$ is an object's upward acceleration, in feet per second per second, at time t seconds

(c) $f(t)$ is the net rate of flow of water into a tank, in liters per minute, at time t minutes.

(d) $f(t)$ is the slope at $x = t$ of the graph of $y = g(x)$.

11. Values of a function f are given in the following table:

t	0.9	1.0	1.1	1.2	1.3	1.4	1.5	1.6
$f(t)$	0.974	0.909	0.808	0.675	0.516	0.335	0.141	−0.058

t	1.7	1.8	1.9	2.0	2.1
$f(t)$	−0.256	−0.443	−0.612	−0.757	−0.872

(a) Use the table to estimate values of $f'(t)$ for $t = 1.0, 1.1, \ldots, 2.0$.

(b) Use the result of part (a) to approximate $\int_1^2 f'(t)\,dt$. Compare your result with $f(2) - f(1)$.

(c) Use the table to estimate $\int_1^2 f(t)\,dt$. What does the answer mean geometrically?

(d) Use the table to estimate $\int_1^2 \sqrt{f'(t)^2 + 1}$. What does the answer mean geometrically?

(e) In fact, $f(t) = \sin(2t)$. Use this information to find exact values of the integrals in parts (b) and (c).

12. Let $I = \int_0^1 \sqrt{1 + x}\,dx$.

(a) Calculate I exactly by antidifferentiation.

(b) I can be thought of as the area under some curve. Decide which curve and draw the region in question.

(c) I can also be thought of as the length of a graph $y = f(x)$, $x = 0$ to $x = 1$. Find a function f with this property.

FURTHER EXERCISES

In Exercises 13–24, sketch the region bounded by the given curves and find the area of this region by evaluating integrals of the form $\int_a^b \big(f(x) - g(x)\big)\,dx$.

13. $y = x^4, \quad y = 1$

14. $y = x, \quad y = x^3$

15. $y = x^2, \quad y = x^3$

16. $y = x^2 - 1, \quad y = x + 1$

17. $y = \sqrt{x}, \quad y = 0, \quad x = 4$

18. $y = \sqrt{x}, \quad y = x^2$

19. $y = 9(4x + 5)^{-1}, \quad y = 2 - x$

20. $y = 9(4x^2 + 5)^{-1}, \quad y = 2 - x^2$

21. $y = e^x, \quad y = 0, \quad x = 0, \quad x = 1$

22. $y = 2^x, \quad y = 5^x, \quad x = -1, \quad x = 1$

23. $x = y^2 - 4, \quad y = 2 - x$

24. $x = 9 - y^2, \quad y = -3 - x$

25–36. Find the area of each region in Exercises 13–24 by evaluating integrals of the form $\int_a^b \big(f(y) - g(y)\big)\,dy$.

37. Suppose that a 12-in.-diameter pizza is cut into "thirds" by making vertical cuts 4 inches on either side of the center. How much bigger is the center piece than the other two pieces?

38. Let $g(x) = f(x) + C$, where C is a constant, L_f be the length of the curve $y = f(x)$ from $x = a$ to $x = b$, and L_g be the length of the curve $y = g(x)$ from $x = a$ to $x = b$.

(a) Use the arc length formula to show that $L_f = L_g$.

(b) Give a geometric explanation of the result in part (a).

In Exercises 39–53, find the length of the curve $y = f(x)$ from $x = a$ to $x = b$.

39. $f(x) = \sqrt{1 - x^2}, \quad a = -1/2, b = \sqrt{3}/2$

40. $f(x) = \sqrt{4 - x^2}, \quad a = 0, b = 1$

41. $f(x) = x^2 \quad a = 1, b = 2$

42. $f(x) = e^x, \quad a = 0, b = 1$

43. $f(x) = x^{3/2}, \quad a = 1, b = 4$

44. $f(x) = x^{2/3}, \quad a = 0, b = 8$

45. $f(x) = 4x^{5/4}/5, \quad a = 1, b = 16$

46. $f(x) = \dfrac{\ln x}{2} - \dfrac{1}{4x^2}, \quad a = 1/4, b = 4$

47. $f(x) = \dfrac{x^2}{2} - \dfrac{\ln x}{4}, \quad a = 3, b = 9$

48. $f(x) = \dfrac{x^3}{6} + \dfrac{1}{2x}, \quad a = 1/2, b = 2$

49. $f(x) = \dfrac{x^3}{3} + \dfrac{1}{4x}, \quad a = 1/2, b = 2$

50. $f(x) = \dfrac{x^4}{4} + \dfrac{1}{8x^2}, \quad a = 1, b = 3$

51. $f(x) = \dfrac{1}{2x^2} + \dfrac{x^4}{16}, \quad a = 1, b = 3$

52. $f(x) = \dfrac{x^5}{5} + \dfrac{1}{12x^3}, \quad a = 2, b = 4$

53. $f(x) = \cosh x, \quad a = 1, b = 4$

54. Let L_1 be the length of the curve $y = f(x)$ from $x = 0$ to $x = a$, L_2 be the length of the curve $y = 2f(x)$ from $x = 0$ to $x = a$, and L_3 be the length of the curve $y = f(2x)$ from $x = 0$ to $x = a/2$. Rank the values of L_1, L_2, and L_3 in increasing order.

55. Let I be the length of the curve $y = f(x)$ from $x = a$ to $x = b$. Suppose that the function f is increasing and concave down on the interval $[a, b]$. Show that L_n, the left-sum approximation computed with n equal subintervals, overestimates the value of the arc length integral.

56. Let J be the length of the curve $y = f(x)$ from $x = 0$ to $x = 4$, where f is an antiderivative of the function shown.

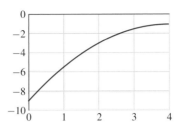

(a) Estimate J using a left-sum approximation with $n = 4$ equal subintervals.

(b) Is $L_4 < J$? Justify your answer.

57. At time $t = 0$, a bug starts crawling along the path $y = \frac{1}{3}(x^2 + 2)^{3/2}$ with constant speed $v = 6$ ft/min. If the bug starts its journey at the point $(1, \sqrt{3})$, where is it 5 minutes later?

58. A snail crawls along the curve $y = \sqrt{x^3}$ at a speed of 3 ft/h. How long does it take the snail to travel from the point $(1, 1)$ to the point $(4, 8)$? (Assume that both x and y are measured in feet.)

59. Suppose that g is a function with the property $g'(t) \geq 1$ if $a \leq t \leq b$. Let $f(x) = \displaystyle\int_a^x \sqrt{(g'(t))^2 - 1}\, dt$. Show that the length of the curve $y = f(x)$ from $x = a$ to $x = b$ is $g(b) - g(a)$.

60. Suppose that $h(x) = (f(x) + g(x))/2$, where f and g are functions with the property that $f'(x) \cdot g'(x) = -1$ if $a \leq x \leq b$. Show that the length of the curve $y = h(x)$ from $x = a$ to $x = b$ is $L = \dfrac{1}{2} \displaystyle\int_a^b |f'(x) - g'(x)|\, dx$.
[HINT: For any real number a, $\sqrt{a^2} = |a|$.]

7.2 FINDING VOLUMES BY INTEGRATION

The main idea is that integrating the "cross-sectional area function" over an appropriate slicing axis gives volume. "Slicing" at x reveals the cross-sectional area A(x).

Slicing the loaf

Imagine a solid object—a long loaf of French bread, say—lying along the x-axis in the xy-plane, between $x = a$ and $x = b$. The usual way to slice such a loaf is with cuts perpendicular to the x-axis. Mathematically speaking, the "knives" that cut such slices are vertical planes, each of the form $x = k$ for some constant k. Figure 1 shows one such cut viewed from overhead.

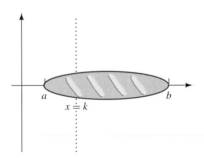

FIGURE 1
Slicing a loaf: an overhead view

The loaf's total volume is, of course, the sum of the volumes of all the slices. This obvious fact is surprisingly useful mathematically. We'll use it to compute volumes by integration for various solid objects.

The cross-sectional area function   If the loaf is irregular, different slices have different volumes even if all have the same thickness. This difference arises because slices from the middle of the loaf have larger **cross-sectional area** (where the butter goes) and, hence, more volume than slices from the narrow ends.

Students might consider how slices behave under different choices of the "slicing axis." For many solids one slicing axis is a natural choice.

For any value of x between a and b, let $A(x)$ denote the cross-sectional area revealed by a knife cut at x (i.e., the area of the intersection of the loaf with the "vertical" plane at x, perpendicular to the x-axis). For an irregular loaf, $A(x)$ varies with x, rising and falling with the loaf's thickness.

The *exact* volume of one slice of bread is hard to compute because the cross section $A(x)$ varies with x. If it happens that $A(x)$ is constant, then the following simple but important fact applies:

> *If a slice with thickness Δx has* constant *cross-sectional area A, then the slice has volume $A \cdot \Delta x$.*

In a small x-interval (i.e., for a very thin slice), the cross-sectional area $A(x)$ is *nearly* constant, and so we can approximate the volume of a slice of thickness Δx as follows:

$$\text{Volume of one slice} \approx A(x)\Delta x,$$

where $A(x)$ is the cross-sectional area at any convenient value of x within the slice.

Reassembling Riemann's loaf: estimating volume   To estimate the volume of the loaf, let's slice it into n slabs of equal thickness $\Delta x = (b-a)/n$ with cuts at $x = x_0 = a$, $x = x_1$, $x = x_2, \ldots, x = x_n = b$. (Cuts are crumbless in this ideal world.) Figure 2 gives an overhead view with $n = 4$: ➡

Approximating sums for the volume turn out to be approximating sums for the integral $\int_a^b A(x)\, dx$.

Cut on the dotted lines.

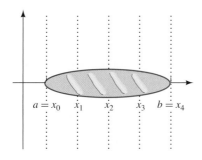

FIGURE 2
Four slices from the loaf

Using the cross-sectional area $A(x_i)$ for the ith slab leads to an estimate for *total* volume:

$$\text{Total volume} \approx A(x_1)\Delta x + A(x_2)\Delta x + \cdots + A(x_n)\Delta x. \qquad (1)$$

Here is the crucial observation: The right side of Equation (1) is an approximating sum (a right sum) for the integral $\int_a^b A(x)\, dx$ of the cross-sectional area function.

Now we play the standard limit game: As n tends to infinity, the slab thickness Δx tends to zero, and so the volume estimate tends to the true volume of the loaf. Meanwhile, the approximating sums tend to the true value of the integral. We state our conclusion as a general theorem:

> **THEOREM 1** A solid lies with its base on the xy-plane between the vertical planes $x = a$ and $x = b$. For all x in $[a, b]$, let $A(x)$ denote the area of the cross section at x perpendicular to the x-axis. If $A(x)$ is a continuous function, then
>
> $$\text{Volume} = \int_a^b A(x)\, dx.$$

Observe:

The function A can be discontinuous even for simple solids, such as a thread spool or a tower of disks as in Figure 3(b).

- **Why continuous?** Requiring that $A(x)$ be a continuous function of x ensures that the integral exists. For simple, smooth, solid objects, A *is* continuous; more complicated objects can often be handled by (mentally) breaking them up into simpler objects to which the formula of Theorem 1 applies.

- **Which axis?** Although the theorem mentions the x-axis, which is usually shown "horizontal," there is nothing sacred about these choices. For objects such as trees and Egyptian pyramids, the convenient "slicing axis" may well be vertical. In context this causes little trouble.

The simplest case: constant cross sections For solids with *constant* cross sections, called **prisms** (sticks of butter, glasses of milk, and some mass-produced bread loaves are all prisms), the theorem merely restates elementary volume formulas.

The example shows that integration succeeds in the simplest and most familiar case.

EXAMPLE 1 A rectangular parallelepiped (or "brick") has edge lengths L cm, W cm, and H cm, so its volume is LWH cm³. Does Theorem 1 agree?

Solution We certainly hope so.

If we place the brick anywhere in the xy-plane with one edge (let's use the edge of length L) parallel to the x-axis, then the brick lies between $x = a$ and $x = a + L$. All cross sections perpendicular to the x-axis are rectangles with area WH cm², and so $A(x) = WH$ for all x with $a \le x \le a + L$; the theorem gives

$$\text{Volume} = \int_a^{a+L} A(x)\, dx = \int_a^{a+L} WH\, dx = LWH$$

as we expect. Notice, too, that there's nothing special about the L-edge; we could have aligned *any* edge parallel to the x-axis. ∎

With numerical methods the shape of the cross section makes no difference as long as area can be found or estimated.

No formula? Think numerically Using the theorem directly requires an explicit formula for the area function $A(x)$—we need something to integrate. Finding such formulas isn't difficult for simple solids, but for complicated or irregular solids it may be hard or impossible. In this case, however, we can still use numerical methods to estimate the volume integral.

EXAMPLE 2 Hoping to estimate the volume of wood in a 20-meter log, Ranger Rick uses a tape measure to gauge the log's girth (circumference) at 5-meter intervals, starting from the big end. Here are Rick's results:

Measuring a natural log				
distance from end (m)	0	5	10	15	20
circumference (m)	4.0	3.6	3.2	2.6	2.0

What does Rick do next?

Solution Recalling Theorem 1, Rick defines $A(x)$ to be the tree's cross-sectional area (in square meters) x meters from the big end. Because tree cross sections are roughly circular, a section with circumference C has area $C^2/(4\pi)$, and Rick tabulates the following approximate values of A:

The log's cross-sectional areas				
x	0	5	10	15	20
$A(x)$	1.27	1.03	0.81	0.54	0.32

The left, right, or Simpson rules might have been used, but the data don't support M_4.

Finally, Rick uses these values to calculate T_4, the trapezoid-rule estimate with four subdivisions for the integral in Theorem 1: ➤

See the definition of T_4 in Section 6.1.

$$\int_0^{20} A(x)\,dx \approx T_5 = (1.27 + 2 \cdot 1.03 + 2 \cdot 0.81 + 2 \cdot 0.54 + 0.32)\frac{20}{8} \approx 15.88,$$

or just under 16 cubic meters.   ∎

Solids of revolution

Real-world solid objects come in all shapes and sizes. Vastly overrepresented in calculus books, however, are **solids of revolution**—solids formed by "revolving" some region in the xy-plane about an axis (often the x-axis). ➤

Solids of revolution could be made on a lathe or a potter's wheel.

Solids of revolution are convenient in calculus for one main reason: their cross sections perpendicular to the axis of rotation are *circular*. Thin slices of such solids are either circular **disks** or, for hollow solids, **washers** (disks with holes in the middle). This property simplifies calculating cross-sectional areas—and explains these solids' popularity.

Solids of revolution are fully described by a one-variable function—the cross-sectional radius—and so lend themselves to one-variable integral treatment.

Figure 3(a) shows one such solid; Figure 3(b) shows five disk-shaped slices that approximate the solid. (We calculate the solid's volume in Example 3.)

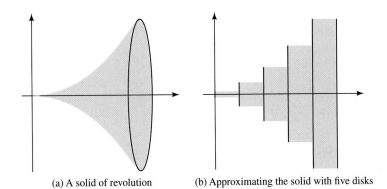

(a) A solid of revolution   (b) Approximating the solid with five disks

FIGURE 3
Disks approximating a solid

EXAMPLE 3 Find the volume of the solid formed by revolving the shaded region shown in Figure 4 about the x-axis.

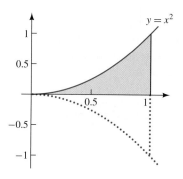

FIGURE 4
Rotate the shaded region about the
x-axis

Solution   For any x in $[0, 1]$, the cross section at x is a circle with radius $y = x^2$. Thus,

$$A(x) = \pi (x^2)^2 = \pi x^4.$$

By Theorem 1,

$$\text{Volume} = \int_0^1 A(x)\,dx = \int_0^1 \pi x^4\,dx = \frac{\pi}{5} \approx 0.628.$$ ∎

A similar computation applies whenever the region under the graph of a positive function $y = f(x)$, from $x = a$ to $x = b$, is revolved around the x-axis.

A long-known but little understood formula is explained at last.

EXAMPLE 4   Find the volume of the sphere of radius r.

Solution   The sphere is the result of revolving the area under the curve $f(x) = \sqrt{r^2 - x^2}$, from $x = -r$ to $x = r$, about the x-axis. The cross section at x, therefore, is a circle with radius $f(x)$. Hence,

$$A(x) = \pi \left(f(x) \right)^2 = \pi (r^2 - x^2).$$

Therefore,

$$\text{Volume} = \pi \int_{-r}^{r} (r^2 - x^2)\,dx = \pi \left(r^2 x - \frac{x^3}{3} \right) \Bigg]_{-r}^{r} = \frac{4\pi r^3}{3},$$

which is the well-known volume formula.   ∎

Other axes of rotation   Rotation around the x-axis is not the only possibility. Whatever the axis, the principle of Theorem 1 applies: Volume is found by integrating the cross-sectional area.

EXAMPLE 5   Find the volume of the solid formed by rotating the shaded region in Figure 4 about the axis $y = -1$.

Solution   The solid formed in this way is a *hollow* "horn." For any x in $[0, 1]$ the cross section at x is a **washer** with inner radius 1 and outer radius $1 + x^2$. The area $A(x)$ of such a washer is

$$A(x) = \pi \,(\text{outer radius})^2 - \pi \,(\text{inner radius})^2$$
$$= \pi (1 + x^2)^2 - \pi 1^2 = \pi (2x^2 + x^4).$$

By Theorem 1,

$$\text{Volume} = \int_0^1 A(x)\,dx = \pi \int_0^1 (2x^2 + x^4)\,dx = \frac{13\pi}{15} \approx 2.723.$$ ∎

EXAMPLE 6 Find the volume of the dish-shaped solid formed by rotating the shaded region in Figure 4 about the y-axis.

Solution We slice the solid *horizontally* (with slices perpendicular to the y-axis). The slice at height y is a washer with cross-sectional area $A(y)$; it has outer radius determined by the line $x = 1$ and inner radius determined by the curve $y = x^2$. To express $A(y)$ as a function of y, it's convenient to rewrite the curve equation $y = x^2$ in the form $x = \sqrt{y}$. Now the washer at height y has area

$$A(y) = \pi \, (\text{outer radius})^2 - \pi \, (\text{inner radius})^2 = \pi \, (1 - y),$$

and so the volume in question is (by an easy calculation)

$$\int_0^1 A(y) \, dy = \pi \int_0^1 (1 - y) \, dy = \frac{\pi}{2}. \qquad \blacksquare$$

Noncircular cross sections

For solids with noncircular cross sections, $A(x)$ may be harder to find; otherwise, the idea is exactly the same.

Students may find handling these solids quite challenging, but it's worth emphasizing that the additional difficulty is entirely in finding the area function $A(x)$.

EXAMPLE 7 A pyramid of height 1 has square horizontal cross sections; at the bottom, the edge length is 1. Find its volume.

Solution Let the x-axis run vertically from $x = 0$ to $x = 1$. Because the edge length decreases *linearly* from 1 (at the base) to 0 (at the apex), the edge length $\ell(x)$ at height x is $1 - x$. Thus, the cross-sectional area at height x is

$$A(x) = \ell(x)^2 = (1 - x)^2 = 1 - 2x + x^2,$$

and the volume is

$$\text{Volume} = \int_0^1 A(x) \, dx = \int_0^1 (1 - 2x + x^2) \, dx = \frac{1}{3}.$$

(Note that the pyramid has 1/3 the volume of the rectangular prism with the same base.) $\qquad \blacksquare$

This subsection is not needed in the sequel, but it addresses a possibly mystifying question: Where does the divisor 3 come from in the volume formulas for cones, pyramids, and similar solids?

Prisms and "hats": a general volume formula It is well known that if a **prism** has base area A and height h, then the volume is just the product Ah. This simple formula applies, as we saw in Example 1, because, for prisms, the cross-sectional area function is *constant*.

A similar but not identical volume formula applies to solids we'll call **hats**. ➤ These are solids that start from a base and "taper linearly to a point." In Figure 5, for example, the solid's base is a rectangle; the intermediate slices (smaller but similar rectangles) taper linearly to a point.

The name isn't official, but it suggests the shape.

FIGURE 5
Five slices from a "hat" solid

A number of well-known solids can be thought of as hats; they include square pyramids (such as in Example 7), tetrahedra (triangular pyramids), and circular cones. (We do *not* require that the "point" of a hat be "centered" above the base, though this does occur for Egyptian pyramids and for ordinary funnel-shaped cones.)

How is the volume of a hat with base area A and height h related to the volume of a *prism* with the same base area and height? The answer is surprisingly simple:

> **FACT (Hat sizes)**   Suppose that a hat solid has base area A and height h measured perpendicular to the base. Then the hat's volume is
>
> $$\text{Volume} = \frac{1}{3}\,Ah = \frac{1}{3}\,\text{base} \times \text{height}.$$

Figure 5 shows how the area decreases with "altitude."

The Fact holds because of a special property of slices parallel to the base. If $A(x)$ denotes the area of the slice at height x, then $A(x)$ decreases from $A(0) = A$ (at the bottom) to $A(h) = 0$ (at the top). ◄ The special geometry of hats lets us be more specific:

The area of the slice at height x is $A(x) = \left(\dfrac{h-x}{h}\right)^2 \cdot A.$

Figure 5 suggests why this particular formula holds (notice especially the power 2). In the figure, the base and all four slices shown are similar rectangles. These rectangles have edge lengths that decrease *linearly* to zero as x (the height) runs from 0 to h. If, say, the base rectangle has dimensions a and b (so $A(0) = ab$), then the rectangle at height x has dimensions $a(h-x)/h$ and $b(h-x)/x$, ◄ and thus its area is $A(x) = ab(h-x)^2/h^2 = A(h-x)^2/h^2$. A similar argument applies to *any* hat-shaped solid.

The multiplier $(h-x)/h$ represents a "fraction" of the total height.

Now Theorem 1 lets us calculate the hat's volume:

$$\text{Volume} = \int_0^h A(x)\,dx = \int_0^h A\frac{(h-x)^2}{h^2}\,dx = \frac{1}{3}Ah.$$

(The last step is a straightforward calculation.)

BASIC EXERCISES

1. (See Example 2.) Ranger Rick's apprentice, Nick, is a city kid unfamiliar with forest lore. Nick used Rick's circumference data and the trapezoid rule—but he assumed that cross sections of the tree were squares. What's Nick's volume estimate?

2. Seeing his calculator battery dying, Rick decides to use only two of his measurements, at $x = 5$ and $x = 15$, to estimate the volume using the midpoint rule. What is his estimate now?

3. Yet another way to estimate the volume of a log is to regard the log as part of a circular cone (the entire tree trunk) with radius decreasing linearly from a maximum at the bottom to zero at the top. Rick's log has circumference 4.0 m at the bottom and 2.0 m at height 20 m. Use these measurements to estimate the log's volume yet again.

4. Let V be the volume of a circular cone with base radius r and height h.

   (a) Use the Fact about hat sizes on page 428 to explain the formula $V = \pi r^2 h/3$.

   (b) Find the formula for V in part (a) by evaluating an integral of the form $V = \int_0^h A(y)\,dy$.

5. Let V be the volume of a square pyramid with base side s and height h.

   (a) Use the Fact about hat sizes on page 428 to find a formula for V.

   (b) Find the formula for V in part (a) by evaluating an integral of the form $V = \int_0^h A(y)\,dy$.

6. (a) Imagine a circular cone with base radius r and height h. Now lop off the top part of the cone with a horizontal cut at height $h/2$. What fraction of the cone's *volume* did you cut off?

   (b) Imagine a square pyramid with base side s and height h. Now lop off the top part of the pyramid with a horizontal cut at height $h/2$. What fraction of the pyramid's *volume* did you cut off?

(c) Consider *any* hat solid with base area A and height h. What proportion of the total volume is contained in the top half of the solid (i.e., the part with "altitude" $h/2$ or greater)?

7. Imagine a circular cone with base radius r and height h. At what vertical height would you have to cut off the cone's top to get two pieces of equal volume?

8. Imagine a square pyramid with base side s and height h. At what vertical height would you have to cut off the pyramid's top to get two pieces of equal volume?

9. Let V be the volume of the solid obtained by rotating about the x-axis the region R bounded above by the curve $y = f(x)$, below by the x-axis, on the left by the vertical line $x = a$, and on the right by the vertical line $x = b$. Furthermore, suppose that $a = x_0 < x_1 < \ldots x_{n-1} < x_n = b$ and that $x_{j-1} \le t_j \le x_j$ if $0 \le j \le n$.

(a) Explain why $V \approx \pi \sum_{j=1}^{n} \left(f(t_j)\right)^2 (x_j - x_{j-1})$.

(b) Suppose that f is decreasing over the interval $[a, b]$ and that $t_j = x_j$. Does the approximating sum in part (a) underestimate V? Justify your answer.

(c) Suppose that $f(x) = x^2$, $a = 0$, and $b = 2$. Explain why
$$\lim_{n \to \infty} \pi \sum_{j=1}^{n} \left(f(t_j)\right)^2 (x_j - x_{j-1}) = \frac{32\pi}{5}.$$

10. Let V be the volume of the solid obtained by rotating about the y-axis the region R bounded on the right by the curve $x = g(y)$, on the left by the y-axis, on the bottom by the horizontal line $y = a$, and on the top by the horizontal line $y = b$.

Furthermore, suppose that $a = y_0 < y_1 < \ldots y_{n-1} < y_n = b$, and that $y_{j-1} \le t_j \le y_j$ if $0 \le j \le n$.

(a) Explain why $V \approx \pi \sum_{j=1}^{n} \left(g(t_j)\right)^2 (y_j - y_{j-1})$.

(b) Suppose that g is decreasing over the interval $[a, b]$ and that $t_j = x_{j-1}$. Does the approximating sum in part (a) overestimate V? Justify your answer.

(c) Suppose that $g(y) = \sqrt{y}$, $a = 0$, and $b = 4$. Explain why
$$\lim_{n \to \infty} \pi \sum_{j=1}^{n} \left(g(t_j)\right)^2 (x_j - x_{j-1}) = 8\pi.$$

In Exercises 11–14, sketch the region in the first quadrant bounded by the given curves and find the volume of the solid that is formed when this region is revolved around the x-axis.

11. $y = x^3$, $y = 0$, $x = 8$

12. $y = x^4$, $y = 1$, $x = 0$

13. $y = x + 6$, $y = x^3$, $x = 0$

14. $y = x^2$, $y = x^3$

In Exercises 15–18, sketch the region bounded by the given curves and find the volume of the solid of revolution formed when the region is revolved around the y-axis.

15. $y = \sqrt{x}$, $y = 0$, $x = 4$

16. $y = \sqrt{x}$, $y = x^2$

17. $y = x^2$, $y = 2^x$, $x = 0$

18. $y = e^x$, $y = 0$, $x = 0$, $x = 1$

FURTHER EXERCISES

19. The base of a solid object is the circle $x^2 + y^2 = 4$; cross sections of the object perpendicular to the x-axis are squares with one side in the xy-plane. What is the volume of the object?

20. The base of a solid object is the region bounded by the parabola $y = x^2/2$ and the line $y = 2$; cross sections of the object perpendicular to the y-axis are semicircles. What is the volume of the object?

21. The base of a solid object is the region bounded by the parabola $y^2 = 3x$ and the line $x = 3$; cross sections of the object perpendicular to the x-axis are equilateral triangles. What is the volume of the object?

22. The base of a certain solid is the region enclosed by $y = 1/x$, $y = 0$, $x = 1$, and $x = 4$. Every cross section of the solid taken perpendicular to the x-axis is an isosceles right triangle with its hypotenuse across the base. Find the volume of the solid.

23. Consider a right circular cylinder with radius r and height h.
  (a) Compute the volume of the cylinder using circular cross sections.

(b) Compute the volume of the cylinder using rectangular cross sections.

24. Suppose that a 45° wedge is cut out of a circular cylinder with radius r. (One edge is horizontal and the other is inclined to the horizontal at an angle of 45°.)
  (a) Find the volume of the wedge using cross sections that are isosceles right triangles.
  (b) Find the volume of the wedge using cross sections that are rectangles.

25. A drinking glass has circular cross sections. The glass has height 5 inches, bottom diameter 2 inches, and top diameter 3 inches. How much liquid can the glass hold?

26. A pie dish has base diameter 8 in., top diameter 10 in., and height 2 in. What is the volume of the dish?

27. Assume that the Earth is a sphere with circumference $C \approx 24{,}900$ mi.
  (a) Find the volume of the Earth north of latitude 45°.
  (b) Find the volume of the Earth between the equator and latitude 45°.

28. A spherical balloon with radius 3 in. is partially filled with water. If the water in the balloon is 4 in. deep at the deepest point, how much water is released when the balloon hits the wall and breaks?

29. A cylindrical gasoline tank with radius 4 ft and length 25 ft is buried on its side under a service station (i.e., its flat ends are perpendicular to the ground surface). If the gasoline in the tank is 6 ft deep, what is the volume of gasoline in the tank?

30. Suppose that a hemispherical bowl of radius r, initially full of a liquid, is tilted 45°. How much liquid remains in the bowl?

31. Cross sections of a table leg are squares. The following table gives the width (in inches) of cross sections at several heights (also in inches). Use numerical integration (e.g., the midpoint rule) to estimate the volume of the table leg.

Height	0	5	10	15	20	25	30
Width	1.6	1.4	1.2	1.0	0.8	0.6	0.4

32. Suppose that the volume of water required to fill a hollow object to a depth of h inches is $V(h) = 1.5h + \sin h$ cubic inches. What is the cross-sectional area of the object 1 inch above its base?

33. A fuel-oil tank is 10 ft long and has flat ends that are perpendicular to the ground surface. Cross sections parallel to the flat ends have the shape of the ellipse $x^2/9 + y^2/36 = 1$. If the fuel oil in the tank is 9 ft deep, what is the volume of the fuel oil in the tank?

34. Suppose that two circular cylinders of radius R intersect in such a way that their axes meet at right angles. Find the volume of the space that is inside both cylinders. [HINT: Draw a sketch. The space that is inside both cylinders has an axis perpendicular to the axes of the cylinders. Furthermore, any cross section of the space perpendicular to this axis is a square.]

35. Let R be a rectangle with vertices at the points $(a, 0)$, (a, h), $(b, 0)$, and (b, h), where $h > 0$ and $b > a$.
   (a) What is the area of R?
   (b) What is the volume of the solid obtained by rotating R about the x-axis?
   (c) What is the volume of the solid obtained by rotating R about the line $y = -c$, where $c \geq 0$?
   (d) What is the volume of the solid obtained by rotating R about the line $y = c$, where $c \geq h$?

36. Let R denote the region bounded by the curves $y = x^2$, $y = 6 - x$, and $y = 0$. Write an integral for the volume of the solid that is obtained when R is rotated about the line
   (a) $x = -2$
   (b) $y = -1$

In Exercises 37–40, sketch the region bounded by the given curves and find the volume of the solid of revolution formed when the region is revolved around the line $y = a$.

37. $y = \sqrt{x}$, $y = 0$, $x = 1$, $a = 1$

38. $y = x^2 - 1$, $y = x + 1$, $a = -1$

39. $x = y^2 - 4$, $y = 2 - x$, $a = 2$

40. $y = \sqrt{x}$, $y = x^2$, $a = -2$

41. Find the volume of the solid formed when the region bounded by the curves $y = \arctan x$, $y = 0$, and $x = 1$ is revolved around the y-axis.

42. Let V be the volume of the solid formed when the region bounded by the curves $y = \arctan x$, $y = 0$, $x = -3$, and $x = -1$ is revolved around the x-axis.
   (a) Express V as a definite integral.
   (b) If the integral in part (a) is estimated using a left sum with $n = 10$ subintervals, does the result underestimate V? Justify your answer.

*Exercises 43–55 provide an introduction to the **method of cylindrical shells**: the volume of the region formed when the area below the curve $y = f(x) \geq 0$ from $x = a$ to $x = b$ is rotated around the y-axis is $V = 2\pi \int_a^b xf(x)\,dx$.*

43. Let R be a rectangle with vertices at the points $(a, 0)$, (a, h), $(b, 0)$, and (b, h), where $0 \leq a < b$ and $h > 0$. If R is rotated about the y-axis, the resulting solid is a **cylindrical shell**. Find a formula for the volume of this solid of revolution in terms of a, b, and h.

44. Let f be a function that is continuous and nonnegative on the interval $[a, b]$ and R be the region bounded above by the curve $y = f(x)$, below by the x-axis, on the left by the vertical line $x = a$, and on the right by the vertical line $x = b$. Furthermore, suppose that $0 \leq a = x_0 < x_1 < \ldots x_{n-1} < x_n = b$, $m_j = (x_{j-1} + x_j)/2$, and that V is the volume of the solid obtained by rotating R about the y-axis.
   (a) Explain why $V \approx \pi \sum_{j=1}^{n} f(m_j)\big((x_j)^2 - (x_{j-1})^2\big)$.
   (b) Show that $f(m_j)\big((x_j)^2 - (x_{j-1})^2\big) = 2m_j f(m_j)(x_j - x_{j-1})$. [HINT: $u^2 - v^2 = (u + v)(u - v)$.]
   (c) Use parts (a) and (b) to justify the formula $V = 2\pi \int_a^b xf(x)\,dx$.

45. Find the volume of the solid of revolution formed when the region bounded by the curve $y = \sin x$ between $x = 0$ and $x = \pi$ is rotated around the y-axis.

46. Find the volume of a hemisphere with radius R by rotating the region enclosed by the curve $y = \sqrt{R^2 - x^2}$, the x-axis, and the y-axis around the y-axis.

47. Find the volume of the cone formed by rotating the region enclosed by the line $y = 1 - x/2$, the x-axis, and the y-axis around the y-axis.

48. Find the volume of the solid of revolution formed when the region bounded by the curve $y = e^{-x^2}$ and the lines $x = 0$ and $x = 1$ is rotated around the y-axis.

49. Find the volume of the solid of revolution formed when the region bounded by the curve $y = \ln x$ and the lines $x = 1$ and $x = e$ is rotated around the y-axis.

50. Suppose that a circular hole of radius 2 cm is bored through the center of a sphere of radius 3 cm. What is the volume of the portion of the sphere that remains?

51. Suppose that a circular hole of radius a is bored through the center of a cone of height h and radius r. What is the volume of the portion of the cone that remains?

52. Let V be the volume of the solid of revolution formed when the region bounded by the curve $y = x^{1/3}$ and the lines $y = 0$, $x = 0$, and $x = 8$ is revolved around the y-axis.

   (a) Compute V using the method of disks and washers.

   (b) Compute V using the method of cylindrical shells.

53. Let V be the volume of the solid of revolution formed when the region bounded by the curve $y = x\sqrt{1 - x^2}$ and the lines $y = 0$, $x = 0$, and $x = 1$ is revolved around the y-axis.

   (a) Use the method of disks and washers to show that

$$V = \int_0^{1/2} \frac{\pi}{2} \left(1 + \sqrt{1 - 4y^2}\right) dy - \int_0^{1/2} \frac{\pi}{2} \left(1 - \sqrt{1 - 4y^2}\right) dy.$$

   (b) Use the method of cylindrical shells to show that

$$V = \int_0^1 2\pi x^2 \sqrt{1 - x^2}\, dx.$$

   (c) Show that $V = \pi^2/8$.

54. The rate at which a viscous fluid (e.g., water or blood) moves through a tube is not uniform. The fluid moves fastest near the center and slowest along the wall.

Suppose that a fluid is flowing in a circular pipe of radius R centimeters and that the velocity of the fluid r centimeters from the center of the pipe is $v(r)$ centimeters per second. Explain why the rate (in cubic centimeters per second) at which the liquid is flowing through the pipe is the value of the integral

$$2\pi \int_0^R r v(r)\, dr.$$

55. Suppose that a city is circular and that the population density decreases linearly to zero from the center to the rim.

   (a) Let K be the population density (in people per square mile) at the center of the city, and let R be the radius of the city. Explain why the population density at a distance r from the center of the city is $p(r) = K(1 - r/R)$ people/mi^2.

   (b) What is the population of the city?
   [HINT: Use an integral.]

7.3   WORK

Although perhaps unfamiliar to students in the physical sense, work leads naturally to integral calculations, and it illustrates one important non-geometric use of the derivative. Mass and center-of-mass calculations are done in an Interlude.

How much work does a rocket do in lifting a satellite into orbit? How much work does a car do on the 934-mile drive from Perham, Minnesota to Durham, North Carolina? How much work does a horse do in plowing the back 40? Is it more work to raise a 60-lb bucket from a 60-ft well or a 50-lb bucket from a 70-ft well?

Those are all good questions, with thoroughly practical consequences. Any kind of work requires fuel (hydrogen, gasoline, hay, cheeseburgers, ...), and it's important to know how much is needed "on board." **Work** is the common ingredient (and the common word) in each situation mentioned. We need a mathematically useful definition.

The meaning of work

The everyday meaning of "work" is all too familiar; the word covers everything from completing tax returns to digging ditches. Physicists have a narrower, more precise definition. (To a physicist, digging ditches is a lot of work; filing tax returns is almost none.) Work is done when a *force acts through a distance*. Without movement, *no* work is done; for instance, a house does no work by holding up its roof. Even Atlas, the Titan forced to bear the world on his shoulders, accomplished no work (except, perhaps, in *lifting* the globe)—fatiguing though his labors must have been.

Simplifying assumptions: Are they reasonable? Throughout this section, we assume the following:

> *A force (either constant or variable) acts along a straight line; movement occurs along the same line.*

These assumptions are convenient, but are they reasonable? After all, few real-life physical phenomena are that simple. Forces may act at *angles* to the direction of motion, and motion may occur along *curves*. Moving cars, for instance, encounter many forces—gravity, air drag, rolling resistance, crosswinds—all of which vary over the course of a trip. Can anything useful survive our simplifying assumptions?

In fact, much *does* survive. Some interesting physical phenomena conform to our "straight-line" assumptions. Complicated combinations of forces, moreover, can often be understood as *sums* of simpler forces, each acting as we have assumed.

Work done by a constant force

In the simplest instance, the force is constant along its line of action, and the "obvious" definition applies:

$$\text{Work} = \text{force} \times \text{distance}.$$

The *units* of work reflect this definition. In the United States, lifting a 30-pound toddler 3 feet to hip height takes

$$30 \text{ pounds} \cdot 3 \text{ feet} = 90 \text{ foot-pounds}$$

of work. A common unit of force in the metric system is the **newton**(N)—about 0.225 lb. ◄ Thus, lifting the same child to the same hip in Canada takes

$$133.44 \text{ newtons} \cdot 0.914 \text{ m} \approx 121.964 \text{ newton-meters}$$

of work. (Newton meters are known in physics as **Joules**.) ◄

Other units of work, such as the inch-ounce and the mile-pound are possible, but all have the same "dimension": units of *distance* times units of *force*.

Work done by a variable force

In typical physical situations work is performed by a force that *varies* along its line of action. Even hoisting a toddler can be construed this way: On the way up, the child moves away from the center of the Earth and so becomes "lighter." For practical purposes this effect is usually small enough to ignore. (But see Example 4, just ahead.) In more interesting situations, the force varies more dramatically:

- **Springs**   The farther a spring is stretched from its "natural length," the greater the force with which it pulls back. According to **Hooke's law**, an ideal spring's **restoring force** $F(x)$ is proportional to x, the distance the spring is stretched. That is,

$$F(x) = kx$$

  for some constant k, called the **spring constant**. ◄

- **Gravity**   An object's weight decreases as it moves away from the Earth. **Newton's law of universal gravitation** sharpens this commonplace observation:

  The force of Earth's gravity on an object is inversely proportional to the square of the distance from the object to the center of the Earth.

  Thus, the force F required to lift an object (i.e., to counteract gravity) is $F(x) = k/x^2$, where x is the object's distance from the center of the Earth. The value of the proportionality constant k depends on the object and on the units used to measure force and distance.

- **Buckets and ropes**   The force required to draw water from a well *decreases* as the bucket rises—the higher the bucket, the less rope to be pulled up. (We pursue this observation in Example 5.)

- **Pumping iron**   One way to "press" a heavy barbell is to exert a *constant* upward force (equal to the barbell's weight) all the way from shoulder level to the top of one's reach. This strategy is mathematically simple but not physiologically ideal. The mechanics

Students who know some physics might be told that for a force acting obliquely one can consider the component in the direction of motion.

A small advantage of the British unit system is that the force unit—the pound—is more familiar to students than the metric unit, the newton.

One pound is about 4.44 newtons.

James P. Joule was a 19th-century British physicist.

Physics students may know that the position $x(t)$ of a "bouncing" ideal spring is a sinusoidal function of time. Hooke's law implies that the acceleration $x''(t)$ is negatively proportional to the spring's displacement $x(t)$.

The numerical value of k depends on the units of measurement and on the "stiffness" of the spring.

Here is a chance to reinforce the important but too-little-understood ideas of proportionality and inverse proportionality.

of the human body make it easier to exert more upward force at some levels of arm extension than at others. Therefore, to the extent that the rules permit, a human weight lifter exerts a *varying* upward force through a barbell's travel. (But note: Whatever the weight lifter's strategy, the *work* of lifting is the same: the barbell's weight times the distance lifted.)

Handling such examples requires a definition that permits *variable* forces.

> **DEFINITION (Work)**   Let F be a continuous function. If the force $F(x)$ acts along an axis from $x = a$ to $x = b$, then the work done by the force F is
>
> $$\int_a^b F(x)\,dx.$$

After a simple example we'll discuss why this definition is reasonable.

EXAMPLE 1   Stretching a spring 1 ft beyond its natural length requires 10 lb of force. How much work is done in stretching the spring from rest to 1 ft? From rest to a ft? How does the answer depend on a?

Solution   By Hooke's law, $F(x) = kx$. The given conditions say that $F(1) = 10$, and so $k = 10$. By the preceding definition,

$$\text{Work to stretch 1 ft} = \int_0^1 10x\,dx = 10\frac{x^2}{2}\bigg]_0^1 = 5 \text{ ft-lb};$$

$$\text{Work to stretch } a \text{ ft} = \int_0^a 10x\,dx = 10\frac{x^2}{2}\bigg]_0^a = 5a^2 \text{ ft-lb}.$$

The last answer reveals an interesting relationship between force and work:

The force *required to stretch a spring a feet from rest is proportional to a; the* work *done in the process is proportional to a^2.*   ∎

Work as an integral

Why is it "right" to define work as an integral? Does the integral really represent a physically meaningful quantity, one that deserves the name "work"? Any sensible definition of work done by a *variable* force should, at least, agree with the simpler definition of work done by a *constant* force. Ours does: If $F(x) = k$, then

$$\text{Work} = \int_a^b F(x)\,dx = \int_a^b k\,dx = k(b-a) = \text{force} \times \text{distance}.$$

So far so good. But why is this definition right for variable forces? We'll give two arguments.

Adding small contributions: the integral as a sum   The work integral $\int_a^b F(x)\,dx$ can be thought of as a limit of approximating sums. Specifically, let's slice the interval $[a, b]$ into n equal subintervals, each of length Δx, and let x_i be the right endpoint of the ith subinterval. ➤ Then

As in other applications, discrete approximations prove to be integral approximating sums.

Left endpoints or midpoints would have done as well.

$$\int_a^b F(x)\,dx = \lim_{n \to \infty} \sum_{i=1}^n F(x_i)\,\Delta x.$$

Figure 1 should look familiar from earlier work:

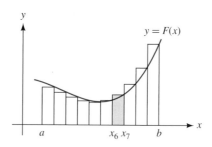

FIGURE 1
Approximating work: a right sum

The sum $\sum_{i=1}^{n} F(x_i)\,\Delta x$ is the key quantity. Each summand $F(x_i)\,\Delta x$ represents the work done by the *constant* force $F(x_i)$ over the subinterval $[x_{i-1}, x_i]$. (The shaded area in Figure 1 represents the work done over the subinterval $[x_6, x_7]$.) The sum adds up these contributions; the entire polygonal area represents this total. Here is the punch line:

> *Each approximating sum is an estimate of the total work done over the interval* $[a, b]$.

Now as $n \to \infty$, the sums tend (by definition of the integral) to $\int_a^b F(x)\,dx$, and so the integral plausibly measures the "true" work done.

These observations, although not mathematically rigorous, are useful and usually reliable intuitively. Physics and engineering students may find them useful in linking other courses to calculus.

Increments and elements   As further evidence for the integral definition of work, we offer the following mnemonic argument using "increments" and "elements." Let x be any point in the interval $[a, b]$. Consider the tiny interval $[x,\ x + \Delta x]$, with **increment of distance** Δx. Because F remains essentially constant over any tiny interval, the work ΔW done over the interval $[x,\ x + \Delta x]$ satisfies

$$\Delta W \approx F(x)\,\Delta x.$$

Letting Δx tend to zero now gives

$$dW = F(x)\,dx;$$

We use the "work element" idea again in Example 6.

dW is called the **element of work.** "Adding up" these elements by integration gives the total work done from $x = a$ to $x = b$:

$$\text{Total work} = W = \int dW = \int_a^b F(x)\,dx.$$

(The equation $W = \int dW$ should be understood informally; it means that the integral "adds up small contributions.")

Calculating work: Miscellaneous examples

The definition of work as an integral is simple enough. Deciding *what* to integrate, and over what *interval*, is usually the hardest part of applying the definition. We illustrate the process with several examples.

EXAMPLE 2   (Working against gravity)   Earth's gravity affects even very distant objects; it never dies out completely. How, then, is it possible to put objects into orbit? Calculus gives the answer.

Communications satellites weigh around 4000 newtons and orbit the Earth at altitudes of about 25,000 kms. How much work is done against Earth's gravity in lifting such a satellite into orbit?

Solution By Newton's law of gravitation, the (variable) force F needed to counteract Earth's gravity is

$$F(x) = \frac{k}{x^2},$$

where k is a constant and x denotes the distance from Earth's center. That the satellite weighs 4000 N on Earth's surface—about 6000 km from Earth's center—means (allowing for approximation)

$$4000 = \frac{k}{6000^2} \implies k = 1.44 \times 10^{11} \implies F(x) = \frac{1.44 \times 10^{11}}{x^2},$$

where force is measured in newtons. Therefore, the work done (in newton-kilometers) in moving from $x = 6000$ to $x = 31{,}000$ ➡ is found by an easy integral calculation:

$x = 31{,}000$ *corresponds to an "altitude" of 25,000 km above Earth's surface.*

$$\int_{6000}^{31000} \frac{1.44 \times 10^{11}}{x^2} \, dx = -\frac{1.4 \times 10^{11}}{x}\bigg]_{6000}^{31000} \approx 19{,}350{,}000 \text{ N-km}.$$

(In more conventional physical units, this is about 1.9×10^{10} Joules.) That's heavy lifting to be sure, but not impossibly heavy. A loaded Boeing 747 airplane accomplishes about the same work against gravity to reach cruising altitude. ∎

EXAMPLE 3 **(Flying to infinity)** How much *additional* work is required to lift the satellite another 75,000 km to an altitude of 100,000 km? Is there *any* upper limit on altitude?

This problem hints at the fact that the improper integral $\int 1/x^2 \, dx$ converges. We study improper integrals formally in Chapter 10.

Solution The next 75,000 km of altitude come almost for free. The work done in raising the satellite from $x = 31{,}000$ to $x = 106{,}000$ km is a relatively trifling

$$\int_{31000}^{106000} \frac{1.44 \times 10^{11}}{x^2} \, dx \approx 3{,}290{,}000 \text{ N-km}.$$

which is only about 17% of the work required to gain the first 25,000 km of altitude. A computation similar to those above gives the work $W(a)$ done in lifting the satellite from Earth's surface to *any* altitude a:

$$W(a) = \int_{6000}^{a} \frac{1.44 \times 10^{11}}{x^2} \, dx = 2.4 \times 10^7 \left(1 - \frac{6000}{a} \right).$$

A close look at the last expression reveals a surprising conclusion that has important consequences for space flight:

> *Lifting the satellite to* any *altitude a, no matter how great, requires no more than 2.4×10^7 N-km of work.*

Plotting W against a (Figure 2) shows that W is bounded above—and suggests why space flight is possible.

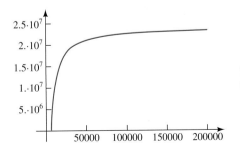

The graph has a horizontal asymptote at height 2.4×10^7.

FIGURE 2
Work (N-km) as a function of altitude (km)

EXAMPLE 4 Gravity's force diminishes—very slightly—when a 30-lb toddler is lifted 3 ft to hip height. We said earlier that this effect is negligible. Is it?

Solution If we *ignore* diminishing gravity, the work done is simply 30 lb times 3 ft, or 90 ft-lb.

Now let's take Newton's law into account. The computations resemble those of Example 2 but with different numbers. We'll need these facts:

- The Earth's radius is about 21 million ft, and so the toddler's vertical travel is from $x = 21,000,000$ to $x = 21,000,003$ ft.
- At $x = 21,000,000$, $F(x) = k/x^2 = 30$, and so $k \approx 1.323 \times 10^{16}$.

All ingredients are now ready; the total work is found by integration:

$$\int_{21000000}^{21000003} \frac{1.323 \times 10^{16}}{x^2}\, dx = -\frac{1.323 \times 10^{16}}{x} \Bigg]_{21000000}^{21000003} \approx 89.99998714.$$

A medium-sized raindrop weighs about 0.00001 pounds, or about 0.005 gm.

Thus, the "work savings" from diminishing gravity is therefore only 0.00001286 ft-lb—about the work done when a medium-sized raindrop falls one foot. ■

Have students guess first. Note that the total work has two summands: the work done on the bucket and the work done on the rope.

EXAMPLE 5 Is it more work to raise a 70-lb bucket of water from a 50-ft well or a 50-lb bucket from a 70-ft well? Rope weighs 0.25 pounds per foot.

Solution Let x denote "height," that is, the distance (in feet) from either bucket to the bottom of its well. As the first bucket travels from $x = 0$ to $x = 50$, the force required to raise it varies with x. At height x, this force must counteract both the weight of the bucket and the weight of $50 - x$ ft of rope. Thus, the first bucket's force function is

$$F(x) = 70 + 0.25 \cdot (50 - x) = 82.5 - 0.25x,$$

and the work done is

$$\int_0^{50} F(x)\, dx = \int_0^{50} (82.5 - 0.25x)\, dx = 3812.5 \text{ ft-lb.}$$

The second bucket's computation is almost identical. This time,

$$F(x) = 50 + 0.25 \cdot (70 - x) = 67.5 - 0.25x,$$

and the work done is

$$\int_0^{70} F(x)\, dx = \int_0^{70} (67.5 - 0.25x)\, dx = 4112.5 \text{ ft-lb.}$$

Note, finally, that the answer might have been guessed. The same amount of work (350 ft-lb) is done on each *bucket*, but drawing up the longer rope takes more work. ■

The idea of force acting through distance is less natural in pumping problems; hence the slicing strategy. But one can imagine a force "pushing" the water upward from the bottom, spilling it out the top of the tank.

EXAMPLE 6 **(Pumping water)** A conical tank with radius r feet and depth h feet is full of water; the cone "points" downward. How much work is needed to pump all the water out the top of the tank? (Water weighs 62.4 lb per cubic foot.)

Solution Here it's hard to visualize a force acting through a distance, and so we take a slightly different tack: We "slice the tank" horizontally into thin circular layers, calculate the work done on each layer, and "add up" our results using an integral. Figure 3 shows a side view of the tank and a typical thin layer.

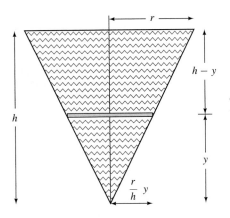

The "layer" at height y is shaded. Use similar triangles to find its radius.

FIGURE 3
Slicing a conical tank: a side view

Let y be the height (in feet) above the tank's bottom; then the tank itself lies between $y = 0$ and $y = h$. The layer at height y (shown shaded) is essentially a disk of radius ry/h with thickness Δy, and thus its approximate *volume* is

$$\text{area} \times \text{thickness} = \pi \left(\frac{r}{h} y\right)^2 \cdot \Delta y = \pi \frac{r^2}{h^2} y^2 \, \Delta y \quad \text{cubic feet.}$$

Thus, its approximate *weight* is

$$62.4 \cdot \pi \frac{r^2}{h^2} y^2 \, \Delta y \text{ lb.}$$

This layer is lifted $h - y$ feet in pumping, and so the work done on this layer is approximately

$$\Delta W = (h - y) \cdot 62.4\pi \frac{r^2}{h^2} y^2 \, \Delta y \text{ ft-lb.}$$

This means that the **element of work** in this situation is

$$dW = 62.4\pi \frac{r^2}{h^2} y^2 (h - y) \, dy;$$

the total work done (in foot-pounds) is the integral

$$\int dW = 62.4\,\pi \frac{r^2}{h^2} \int_0^h y^2 (h - y) \, dy = 62.4 \frac{\pi}{12} r^2 h^2.$$

It could be remarked now (or later, if center of mass is covered) that the same total work is done if all the mass were concentrated at the center of mass, which lies 3/4 of the way up the cone.

Notice, finally, that the *entire* tank of water weighs $62.4\pi r^2 h/3$ lb, so the work just calculated is the same as that required to lift the entire tank of water a distance of $h/4$ ft—one fourth the height of the cone. ∎

BASIC EXERCISES

1. A certain spring has a natural length of 18 in; a force of 10 lb is enough to compress it to a length of 16 in.
   (a) What is the value of the spring constant k?
   (b) How much work is done in compressing the spring from 16 to 12 in.?

2. It takes $40x$ lb of force to keep a certain spring stretched x feet from rest.
   (a) Find the work done in stretching the spring 2 ft, starting from rest.
   (b) Find the work done in stretching the same spring s ft from rest. (The answer depends on s.)
   (c) Farmer Ole's aging plow horse, Sven, can do only 10,000 ft-lb of work on his daily oats ration. Ole hitches Sven to the spring described above. How far can Sven pull?

3. It takes kx pounds of force to keep a spring stretched x feet from rest.

   (a) How much work is done in stretching the spring 10 ft from rest? (The answer depends on k.)

   (b) How much work is done in stretching the spring from $x = a$ ft to $x = a + 10$ ft? (The answer depends on both k and a.)

4. Redo Example 2, but assume that the orbit is 30,000 km from Earth's center.

5. The cable attached to an elevator car weighs 5 lb/ft. If 200 ft of cable must be wound onto a pulley to lift the car from the bottom floor to the top floor of a building, how much work is done in lifting just the cable?

6. A cylindrical tank with radius 5 ft and height 10 ft is half filled with water. How much work must be done to pump all the water over the top rim of of the tank?

7. Is it more work to raise a 60-lb bucket from a 60-ft well or a 50-lb bucket from a 70-ft well? Assume that the rope weighs 0.25 lb/ft.

FURTHER EXERCISES

8. In some situations, the force required to stretch a "spring" is not linear. Consider a simple model of a bow and arrow in which the force required to draw the arrow a distance x is $F(x) = ax + bx^2$.

   (a) If a force of 15 pounds is required to draw the arrow one foot and a force of 50 pounds is required to draw the arrow two feet, find the constants a and b.

   (b) How much work is required to draw the arrow 1 foot?

   (c) How much work is required to draw the arrow 2 feet?

9. A hemispherical tank with radius r is filled with a fluid of density ρ. How much work must be done to pump all the fluid over the top rim of the tank?

10. Suppose that a tank in the shape of the frustum of a cone is filled with a fluid of density ρ kilograms per cubic meter. If the radius of the top of the tank is 2 m, the radius of the bottom of the tank is 1 m, and height of the tank is 1 m, how much work must be done to pump all the fluid over the top rim of the tank?

11. A cylindrical gasoline tank with radius 4 ft and length 15 ft is buried under a service station. The top of the tank is 10 ft underground; its flat ends are perpendicular to the ground surface. Find the amount of work needed to pump all the gasoline in the tank to a nozzle that is 3 ft above the ground. (Gasoline weighs 42 lb/ft^3.) [HINT: Each horizontal cross section of the tank is a rectangle, one side of which has length 15 ft.]

12. A bucket that weighs 80 lb when filled with water is lifted from the bottom of a well that is 75 ft deep. However, the bucket has a hole in it, and so it weighs only 40 lb when it reaches the top of the well. Suppose that water leaks from the bucket at a constant rate and that the rope weighs 0.65 lb/ft. Find the work required to lift the bucket from the bottom of the well to the top.

13. A certain spring exerts $4x$ pounds of force when stretched x feet from rest. One end is fixed to the ceiling. A chain that is 10 ft long and weighs 2 lb/ft hangs from the other end. The end of the chain just brushes the floor. Find the work done in pulling down on the chain a distance of 2 ft. (Don't ignore the weight of the chain!)

14. An object weighing k pounds slides without friction along the graph of $y = f(x)$. (The x and y units are feet.) A horizontal force $F(x)$ is applied to move the object from $x = a$ to $x = b$. Physical intuition says that at x, the horizontal force $F(x)$ required is proportional to the slope of the graph: $F(x) = kf'(x)$.

   (a) Find the work done if $k = 10$, $a = 0$, $b = 1$, and $f(x) = x$.

   (b) Find the work done if $k = 10$, $a = 0$, $b = 1$, and $f(x) = x^3$.

   (c) Find the work done if $k = 10$, $a = 0$, $b = 1$, and $f(x) = x^n$, for n any positive integer.

   (d) Explain the relations among your answers to parts (a)–(c).

15. Suppose that an object moves along the x-axis and that the force on the object varies with x. Explain how the work done by the force F as the object moves from $x = a$ to $x = b$ can be determined from a graph of $F(x)$.

16. The force between two molecules can be modeled by a function of the form $A/x^7 + B/x^{13}$, where A and B are constants and x is the distance between the molecules. Find the work done if the distance between the molecules changes from $x = a$ to $x = b$.

17. The cross-sectional area of a tank at height y above its base is $A(y)$; the top of the tank corresponds to $y = h$.

   (a) What does the expression $\int_0^h A(y)\,dy$ represent in this context?

   (b) Suppose that the tank is filled with water to depth $y = a$. Find an expression for the work required to pump all of the water out the top of the tank.

18. A conical tank with radius r and depth h feet is full of water; the cone "points" upward.

   (a) Suppose that all of the water is pumped out the top of the tank. Explain why the work necessary is *greater* than in Example 6.

   (b) Compute the work needed to pump all of the water out the top of the tank.

7.4 SEPARATING VARIABLES: SOLVING DEs SYMBOLICALLY

We solved DEs graphically in Chapter 4 and numerically in Chapter 6; now we take a symbolic view.

The idea—an example and remarks

In earlier sections we approached DEs and IVPs graphically (with slope fields) and numerically (with Euler's method). Now we solve DEs *symbolically*, by **separating variables**. Before describing the method in general terms, we illustrate how it works—when it works—with another look at cooling coffee.

EXAMPLE 1   Let $y(t)$ denote the temperature (in degrees Fahrenheit) of a cup of coffee at time t (in minutes). Room temperature is $70°$F; the coffee starts at $190°$F. The coffee's temperature is described by the IVP

$$y' = -0.1(y - 70); \quad y(0) = 190.$$

How hot is the coffee after 10 min? How hot is the coffee at *any* time t? (We addressed similar questions in Example 1 of Section 6.3, page 394.)

Solution   First we rewrite the DE using the Leibniz notation for y':

$$\frac{dy}{dt} = -0.1(y - 70).$$

Next comes the key step: *Separate the y's and dy's from the t's and dt's.* The result is

$$\frac{dy}{y - 70} = -0.1 \, dt;$$

antidifferentiating both sides gives

$$\int \frac{dy}{y - 70} = \int -0.1 \, dt.$$

Separable DEs often lead to implicit solutions (given by equations) rather than to explicit solution functions.

Working out the antiderivatives is straightforward; the result is

$$\ln|y - 70| + C_1 = -0.1t + C_2,$$

where C_1 and C_2 are constants. Because both C_1 and C_2 can take *any* value, it's convenient (and legal) to combine the two constants into one:

$$\ln|y - 70| = -0.1t + C.$$

To solve for y, we exponentiate both sides:

$$\ln|y - 70| = -0.1t + C \Longrightarrow |y - 70| = e^{-0.1t+C} \Longrightarrow y = \pm e^C e^{-0.1t} + 70.$$

One more simplification helps reduce clutter. Because C is an arbitrary constant, so is $K = \pm e^C$; thus, y has the form

$$y = Ke^{-0.1t} + 70.$$

Finally, we use the initial condition to assign K a numerical value:

$$y(0) = 190 \implies 190 = Ke^0 + 70 \implies K = 120.$$

The problem is now completely solved. The function $y(t) = 120e^{-0.1t} + 70$ solves the IVP *exactly* for any time t. ➧ At $t = 10$, for example,

$$y(10) = 120e^{-1} + 70 \approx 114.146°\text{F}. \qquad \blacksquare$$

A plot of $y(t)$ appears on page 394.

A legal separation?   It's easy to check by differentiation that $y(t) = 120e^{-0.1t} + 70$ is a solution of the preceding IVP. But does the method really make sense? Can we really "separate" dy from dt as we just did?

That's a good question; dy/dt normally denotes *one* quantity, not the quotient of two separate quantities. The bottom line is that, although care with symbols is always wise, things work out all right in this case. The mathematical reason, roughly speaking, is that the antiderivative notations $\int f(t)\,dt$ and $\int g(y)\,dy$ are designed to ensure that dt and dy can be handled separately if appropriate care is taken.

Our best defense of the separation method, however, is that it works—and can be verified to work by an easy direct check. The same important principle applies to solving DEs and to finding antiderivatives: *Finding* answers may be difficult, but *checking* answers is (relatively) easy.

Symbolic solutions: from one, many   Solving the preceding DE by symbolic antidifferentiation was easy. Solving more complicated DEs symbolically can be *much* harder, if not impossible. Symbolic methods—when they work—have two important advantages over numerical and graphical approaches:

1. They produce *exact* solutions, not approximations.

2. They handle DEs that include parameters (symbols that can stand for any constant).

The second property means that solving *one* DE symbolically can amount, in effect, to solving whole families of DEs. The next example illustrates this advantage.

Time $t = 0$ can denote any convenient reference time.

EXAMPLE 2   Let $y(t)$ denote the temperature (in degrees Fahrenheit) of a cup of coffee at time t (in minutes). ◄ Room temperature is T_r °F; at time $t = 0$ the coffee is at T_0 °F. The coffee's temperature is described by the IVP

$$y' = -0.1(y - T_r); \quad y(0) = T_0.$$

How hot is the coffee after 10 minutes? How hot is it at *any* time t?

Symbolic methods, when available, can solve whole families of problems at once. Numerical methods don't allow unevaluated parameters.

Solution   (Notice first that neither slope fields nor Euler's method would be any use here because both require numerical data.)

This example and the last are virtual clones. So are their solutions; we need only replace 70 with T_r, 190 with T_0, and 0 with t_0 wherever they appear in the preceding solution. Here's the result:

$$y(t) = (T_0 - T_r)e^{-0.1t} + T_r.$$

The beauty of this solution is that it applies for *all* values of the parameters T_0 and T_r. Figure 1(a) shows several solution curves, all with $T_r = 70$ but with various values of T_0. Figure 1(b) shows another set of solution curves, all with $T_0 = 190$ but with various values of T_r.

(a) Different starting temperatures

(b) Different room temperatures

FIGURE 1

Cups of coffee; how they cool

The method in general: when it works, when it doesn't

Separable and inseparable DEs Separating variables can "work" only with separable DEs—those in which the t and y variables *can* be separated. Following are several **separable** DEs, each with its "separated" form:

It can be hard to tell whether or not a DE is separable. We stick to cases in which it's fairly obvious.

$$\frac{dy}{dt} = ty \quad \Longrightarrow \quad \frac{dy}{y} = t\,dt;$$

$$\frac{dy}{dt} = \frac{\sin t}{y} \quad \Longrightarrow \quad y\,dy = \sin t\,dt;$$

$$\frac{dy}{dt} = \frac{\sin(t^2)}{y} \quad \Longrightarrow \quad y\,dy = \sin(t^2)\,dt.$$

Separable DEs often have, or can be written in, one of the forms

$$\frac{dy}{dt} = f(t)g(y) \quad \text{or} \quad \frac{dy}{dt} = \frac{f(t)}{g(y)}$$

and thus either

$$\frac{dy}{g(y)} = f(t)\,dt \quad \text{or} \quad g(y)\,dy = f(t)\,dt.$$

(This is the case in all three examples above.)

In some DEs (called **inseparable**), the t and y variables *cannot* be separated. Here are two simple-looking examples:

$$\frac{dy}{dt} = t + y; \quad \frac{dy}{dt} = \sin(t + y).$$

Both DEs *can* be solved—but not by separating variables.

Antiderivative problems Even if t and y can be separated, the antiderivative problems

$$\int \frac{dy}{g(y)} = \int f(t)\,dt \quad \text{or} \quad \int g(y)\,dy = \int f(t)\,dt$$

remain. Again, trouble may loom: Some elementary functions cannot be antidifferentiated in elementary symbolic form. One of the separable DEs seen earlier poses just this problem; the right-hand antiderivative

$$\int y\,dy = \int \sin(t^2)\,dt$$

has no elementary solution.

The big picture and two morals The separation of variables method applies only to separable DEs. In practice, DEs take many other symbolic forms; fortunately, other symbolic methods exist to solve them. For example, many practically useful DEs have the form

$$y' = a(t)y + b(t);$$

they're called **first-order linear DEs.** General methods exist for solving first-order (and higher-order) linear DEs. (We describe some in an Interlude in Chapter 8.) If $a(t)$ and $b(t)$ are suitably simple functions, solutions can be found explicitly in terms of elementary functions.

We discuss solving first-order linear DEs in an Interlude in Chapter 8.

For example, the DE $y' = y + t$ is not separable, but using other methods one can produce the (easily checked) solution $y = Ce^t - t - 1$; C can be any constant.

There are two main morals: First, if separating variables fails, other methods may succeed. Second, solving DEs symbolically, like finding antiderivatives symbolically, is art as well as science; there is no fail-safe route to a solution.

Rumors, separable DEs, and logistic growth

In earlier work we used the logistic DE

$$\frac{dP}{dt} = kP(C - P) = kP(t)(C - P(t))$$

to model populations that grow logistically. Both constants k and C can be interpreted in biological terms: C represents the environment's long-run carrying capacity, and k measures the population's reproduction rate.

Biological populations come first to mind, but the logistic DE works elsewhere, too. Translating the logistic DE into words gives the key property of *any* quantity that grows logistically toward a long-run value C:

> *The quantity P grows at a rate that is proportional* both *to P itself* and *to C − P, the "room available" for further growth.*

We treat the logistic DE in detail partly to illustrate the use and meaning of formal parameters.

Solving the logistic DE   For later use, let's solve the logistic DE in general form. Separating variables sets up the antiderivative problem:

$$\frac{dP}{dt} = kP(C - P) \Longrightarrow \int \frac{dP}{P(C - P)} = \int k\, dt.$$

See Formula 23.

The right side of the last equation is easy to integrate. The left side is stickier, but it can be found in an integral table ◂ by using technology or by symbolic methods we'll study in the next chapter. In any event, the answer works out to this:

$$\int \frac{dP}{P(C - P)} = \frac{1}{C} \ln \left| \frac{P}{C - P} \right|.$$

We can drop the absolute value signs if we assume—as we will—that $0 < P < C$.

Putting everything together and isolating P solves the logistic DE. The steps are a bit messy:

$$\frac{dP}{dt} = kP(C - P) \Longrightarrow \int \frac{dP}{P(C - P)} = \int k\, dt$$

$$\Longrightarrow \ln \frac{P}{C - P} = C(kt + D)$$

$$(D \text{ is a constant of integration})$$

$$\Longrightarrow \frac{P}{C - P} = e^{Ckt} e^{CD} \qquad \text{(exponentiate both sides)}$$

$$\Longrightarrow \frac{C - P}{P} = e^{-Ckt} e^{-CD} \qquad \text{(invert both sides)}$$

$$\Longrightarrow \frac{C}{P} = e^{-Ckt} e^{-CD} + 1$$

$$\Longrightarrow P = \frac{C}{de^{-Ckt} + 1}. \qquad (d = e^{-CD})$$

Other authors use slightly different parameters.

(Because D is an arbitrary constant, so is $d = e^{-CD}$.) The result is prettier than the calculation:

> **FACT**   For any positive constants C, d, and k, the function
> $$P(t) = \frac{C}{de^{-Ckt} + 1}$$
> solves the logistic differential equation $P' = kP(C - P)$.

To apply this result, we need only choose appropriate values for the constants.

Rumors and logistic growth

Here we apply logistic analysis to a "non-biological" population.

A rumor spreads as "tellers" pass it on to "hearers." (All hearers immediately become tellers.) The rumor spreads slowly at first, when tellers are few. It spreads faster when both tellers and hearers are plentiful, slows down again as hearers become scarce, and stops when everyone knows the rumor. The teller population, in other words, grows as shown in Figure 2.

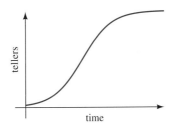

FIGURE 2
Logistic rumor-spreading

As the shape of the graph suggests, logistic growth is one plausible model for rumor-spreading. ➤

It's not the only possible model, as we'll see.

EXAMPLE 3   Riverdale High has 1000 students. On day 0, Archie, Jughead, Betty, Veronica, and 16 of their friends start a rumor that spreads logistically. A day later, 50 students know it. What happens over the next 10 days? When is the rumor spreading fastest?

Solution   Let $P(t)$ denote the number of tellers (people who know the rumor) after t days. Then $P(t)$ satisfies the logistic DE and two additional conditions:

$$\frac{dP}{dt} = kP(1000 - P); \quad P(0) = 20; \quad P(1) = 50.$$

From the preceding Fact (with $C = 1000$) we get

$$P(t) = \frac{1000}{de^{-1000kt} + 1}$$

for appropriate constants d and k. The other given conditions let us evaluate d and k:

$$P(0) = \frac{1000}{d + 1} = 20 \quad \Longrightarrow \quad d = 49;$$

$$P(1) = \frac{1000}{49e^{-1000k} + 1} = 50 \quad \Longrightarrow \quad k \approx 0.000947.$$

We've found our solution function:

$$P(t) = \frac{1000}{49e^{-0.947t} + 1}.$$

Figure 3 shows the graph.

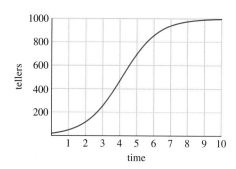

FIGURE 3
A rumor at Riverdale

By 10 days, almost everyone knows the rumor. The rumor seems to spread fastest, moreover, when $P = 500$, just after day 4, where the graph is steepest. (With elementary calculus we can find this time exactly.) ◂

The answer is $t \approx 4.11$—see the exercises.

E X A M P L E 4   Chagrined that bad news travels so fast, Archie, Jughead, Betty, and Veronica start the next rumor all by themselves. It travels through Riverdale with the same "transmission coefficient" $k = 0.000947$. What happens this time?

Solution   Except for the new initial condition, the situation is exactly as in the preceding example. Thus,

$$P(0) = \frac{1000}{d+1} = 4 \quad \Longrightarrow \quad d = 249 \quad \Longrightarrow \quad P(t) = \frac{1000}{249e^{-0.947t} + 1}.$$

Figure 4 shows the new rumor graph; the old one appears for comparison.

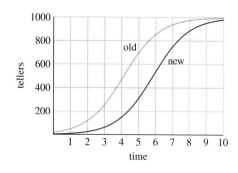

FIGURE 4
Two rumors at Riverdale

The main point is to show how enriching the model slightly leads to different predictions.

Yesterday's news: non-logistic rumors

Not all rumors spread logistically. One possible flaw in the logistic model $P' = kP(C - P)$ concerns the "transmission coefficient" k. In the logistic model, k remains constant over time. In practice, however, k probably *shrinks* over time; as a rumor ages, people care less and less.

A more realistic rumor model might somehow reflect this "staling" process. One approach is to replace the constant k in the logistic DE with a *decreasing function of t*. Here's one possibility. If

$$k(t) = \frac{K}{1+t},$$

where K is any positive constant, then (as we'd hope) $k(t) \to 0$ as $t \to \infty$. Then, the new differential equation would have the form

$$\frac{dP}{dt} = k(t)P(t)\big(C - P(t)\big) = \frac{K}{1+t} P(C - P).$$

E X A M P L E 5   Still another Riverdale rumor spreads according to the preceding DE. When the principal hears the rumor at time 0, 100 students know the rumor, and it's spreading at the rate of 100 students per day. What happens as time goes on?

Solution   As before, let $P(t)$ denote the number of students who know the rumor at time t. The new DE, like the old, is separable:

$$\frac{dP}{dt} = \frac{K}{1+t} P (1000 - P) \Longrightarrow \int \frac{dP}{P(1000 - P)} = \int \frac{K}{1+t} \, dt.$$

Both sides can be antidifferentiated and the resulting equation solved (with some effort) for P. When the dust settles the result is

$$P(t) = \frac{1000}{d(1+t)^{-1000K} + 1}.$$

The additional information lets us find the constants K and d. From $P(0) = 100$ it follows that $d = 9$. To find K we use the DE itself:

$$P'(0) = 100 = \frac{K}{1+0} 100(1000 - 100) \Longrightarrow K = \frac{1}{900}.$$

All the numbers are now in place. Here's the formula:

$$P(t) = \frac{1000}{9(1+t)^{-10/9} + 1}.$$

Figure 5 shows what happens over a 100-day interval.

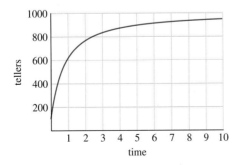

FIGURE 5

Stale news: a non-logistic rumor

Stale news travels slowly.   ■

BASIC EXERCISES

Exercises 1–4 are based on the five curves shown in Figure 1(a); label them C_1 through C_5, from top to bottom. Each curve describes the temperature "evolution" of a different cup of coffee.

1. **(a)** What values of T_0 correspond to each curve?

   (b) What does this mean in the context of Example 2?

2. Curve C_2 is the solution the IVP $y' = -0.1(y - 70)$, $y(0) = 160$. What IVP corresponds to curve C_1?

3. What IVP corresponds to curve C_4?

4. Another cup of coffee is $100°F$ after 10 minutes. Find the temperature of the coffee at time $t = 0$.

Exercises 5–8 are based on the nine curves shown in Figure 1(b); label them C_1 through C_9, from top to bottom. Each curve describes the temperature "evolution" of a different cup of coffee.

5. **(a)** What values of T_r correspond to C_1, C_4, and C_9?

   (b) What does this mean in the context of Example 2?

6. Curve C_4 is the solution the IVP $y' = -0.1(y - 70)$, $y(0) = 190$. What IVP corresponds to curve C_1?

7. What IVP corresponds to curve C_9?

8. Another cup of coffee, initially at $190°F$, is $100°F$ after 20 minutes. Find the room temperature.

Exercises 9–13 explore the IVP $y' = -0.1(y - T_r)$, $y(0) = T_0$ from Example 2.

9. Show, by differentiation that $y(t) = (T_0 - T_r)e^{-0.1t} + T_r$ is the solution of the IVP.

10. Suppose that $T_0 = 200$ and $y(10) = 100$. Find T_r.

11. Suppose that $T_r = 80$ and $y(10) = 120$. Find T_0.

12. Suppose that $y(10) = 100$ and $y(20) = 80$.

   (a) How hot was the coffee at time $t = 0$?

   (b) What's the room temperature?

13. **(a)** It's true that $\lim_{t \to \infty} e^{-0.1t} = 0$. Use this fact to find $\lim_{t \to \infty} y(t)$.

   (b) Interpret part (a) in coffee terms.

14. In Example 3, we said that $k \approx 0.00947$. Verify this claim by finding the *exact* value of k.

15. In Example 3, we said that the rumor spreads fastest when the population is 500. Show that this is true by showing that the maximum value of P' occurs when $P = C/2$.

16. In Example 3, we said that the rumor spreads fastest just after day 4. Verify this claim by finding the value of t for which $P(t) = 500$.

In Exercises 17–22, find the solution of the IVP.

17. $y' = y^2$, $y(1) = 1$

18. $y' = 2e^{-y}$, $y(0) = 1$

19. $y' = x^2 y$, $y(0) = -2$

20. $y' = \dfrac{x}{1 + y^2}$, $y(2) = 3$

21. $y' - xy^2 = 0$, $y(1) = 1$

22. $y' = x/y$, $y(2) = 3$

FURTHER EXERCISES

23. Consider the DE $y' = xy$.

   (a) Find functions f and g such that this DE can be written as $f(y)y' = g(x)$.

   (b) Find functions F and G such that $F' = f$ and $G' = g$.

   (c) Explain why $F(y) = G(x) + C$ implicitly defines a solution y of the DE.

   (d) Use part (c) to show that $y(x) = Ce^{x^2/2}$ is a solution of the DE.

24. Consider the logistic DE $P'(t) = kP(t)\big(C - P(t)\big)$, where k and C are positive constants. Show that $\lim_{t \to \infty} P(t) = C$. What does this mean in biological terms?

25. Here are plots of four variants on the logistic-rumor graph of Example 4. In each case, 50 people know the rumor on day 0.

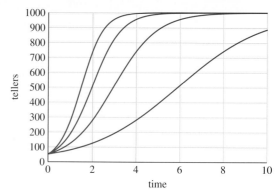

   (a) Label the curves P_1 through P_4 from top to bottom. Each curve's equation is of the form $P(t) = 1000/(19e^{-kt} + 1)$ for some value of k. Use the graph to estimate a value of k for each curve P_1 through P_4.

(b) In this context, the parameter k can be thought of as the rumor's "transmission coefficient." It measures how likely a given teller is to pass the rumor on to a given hearer. Alternatively, k can be thought of as a measure of how "interesting" the rumor may be. Which rumor curve corresponds to the hottest rumor? Which corresponds to the dullest rumor? Justify your answers.

In Exercises 26–31, find a solution of the DE.

26. $y' = \sqrt{1 - y^2}$

27. $y' = 1 + y^2$

28. $y' = 1 - y$

29. $y' = 4 - y^2$

30. $y' = y \ln |y|$

31. $y' = x^2 \cos y$

32. Find an equation of a curve $y = f(x)$ that passes through the point $(0, 1)$ and has the property that the length of any segment of the graph is the same as the area under that segment of the graph (ignore units).

(a) Show that f must satisfy the equation $\sqrt{1 + \left(f'(x) \right)^2} = f(x)$.

(b) Use the fact that $\int \dfrac{du}{\sqrt{u^2 - 1}} = \cosh^{-1} x$ to find the solution function $f(x)$.

7.5 PRESENT VALUE

This section presents an economic application of the integral. Because of the exponential factor, some of the integrals that arise are symbolically complicated; technology may be useful.

Money grows

Anyone, given the choice, would prefer a dollar today to a dollar tomorrow. This makes excellent sense. A dollar tomorrow is worth less than a dollar today because today's dollar, prudently invested, can earn some interest by tomorrow.

But *how much* less is a dollar tomorrow worth than a dollar today? What is an advertised $1 million lottery prize really worth if it's paid in 20 yearly $50,000 installments? Given the choice, should I collect my salary in annual, monthly, or weekly installments, or does it matter? How much should I deposit now to cover 4 years of college tuition starting in 10 years?

All these questions concern what economists call **present value**, that is, the value *now* of a future payment or "stream" of payments. Present-value calculations using integral calculus are vital in economic decision-making, such as in choosing among competing investment options.

The present value of one future payment   The first and most important example illustrates the simplest case: the present value of *one* future payment. Notice especially that exponential functions are involved and that present value depends on an interest rate.

Most students are new to the idea of present value, so we go into some detail about the discrete case.

EXAMPLE 1   A savings bond will pay $1000 on its maturity date 10 years from today. What is it worth now if 5% compound interest is available? What if 10% interest were available?

This example reviews basics of exponential growth.

Solution   Let $V(t)$ denote the bond's value t years from now. We're given that $V(10) = 1000$; we want to find $V(0)$.

To start, recall this important fact: If interest is continuously compounded, the value V grows *exponentially*. In other words, $V(t)$ has the form

$$V(t) = V(0)e^{rt},$$

where r is the annual interest rate. Remember why? Here's a quick refresher. Growth at continuously compounded interest rate r means, in differential equation language, that for all t,

$$V'(t) = rV(t).$$

It's easy to check that for any constant C, the function $V(t) = Ce^{rt}$ solves this DE. Because $V(0) = Ce^0 = C$, it follows that $V(0)$ is the "right" value for C.

Knowing that $V(10) = 1000$, we can solve for $V(0)$. For any interest rate r,

$$V(10) = V(0)e^{10r} = 1000 \implies V(0) = 1000e^{-10r}.$$

Thus, if $r = 0.05$, $V(0) = 1000e^{-0.5} \approx 606.53$; if $r = 0.1$, $V(0) = 1000e^{-1.0} \approx 367.88$. These calculations mean that the **present value** of a single \$1000 payment 10 years in the future is about \$607 based on 5% annual interest, or about \$368 with 10% interest. ∎

The preceding example prompts three general remarks:

- **A negative exponential**   The present value PV of one future payment depends on three things: P, the size of the payment; t, the time until the payment is made; and r, the interest rate. We found that

$$PV = Pe^{-rt}.$$

  The general form of this expression will reappear soon. The negative exponent reflects the fact that the present value of a future payment is normally *less* than the future payment itself.

- **Backward in time**   The present value of a future payment P can be thought of as the amount to be deposited now, at interest rate r, to accrue to value P after time t. Equivalently, one can think of following an investment's value *backward* in time from value P at time t to value PV at time zero.

- **Simplifying assumptions**   Present-value calculations are simplest if we assume that (1) the interest rate r remains constant over time, and (2) interest is compounded continuously. (The first assumption is just for convenience; the second lets us use calculus.) We make both of these assumptions in most of what follows.

The discrete case: present value of several future payments   Many real life cases involve several payments occurring at future times. The *total* present value of a sequence of payments is found, naturally, by addition.

E X A M P L E 2   A lottery jackpot, although advertised as \$1 million, is paid in 20 annual installments of \$50,000. What's the present value of the prize given 6% annual interest? What if 8% interest were available?

Solution   By the preceding formula, the present value of one \$50,000 payment k years in the future is $50{,}000e^{-0.06k}$. Thus, the total present value of all 20 payments is

$$50{,}000 \left(e^{-0.06 \times 0} + e^{-0.06 \times 1} + e^{-0.06 \times 2} + \cdots + e^{-0.06 \times 19} \right) \approx \$599{,}983.$$

That's much less than the advertised million. At 8% interest, the computation is similar; the present value is

$$50{,}000 \left(e^{-0.08 \times 0} + e^{-0.08 \times 1} + e^{-0.08 \times 2} + \cdots + e^{-0.08 \times 19} \right) \approx \$519{,}033,$$

still farther from the advertised million-dollar payoff. ∎

Several payments: the general form   Example 2 illustrated the general picture. If r is the interest rate and payments $P_1, P_2, \ldots, P_n$ are made at times $t_1, t_2, \ldots, t_n$, then the present value of all n payments is found by summation:

$$PV = \sum_{i=1}^{n} P_i e^{-rt_i}. \tag{1}$$

The continuous case: Present value of an income stream

The term "stream" suggests the approximate continuity of money flow—an idealization, but a useful one.

In real life, financial transactions occur at specific moments—the beginning of a month, the end of a pay period, 11:59 P.M. on April 15, and so on. Nevertheless, economists often picture income as an unbroken "stream," flowing continuously in time (hence, for instance, the term "cash flow"). The next example—in which all three graphs are drawn as continuous, unbroken curves—illustrates this point of view. Notice that the graphs show the *rates* of income flow as functions of time.

EXAMPLE 3 The graphs in Figure 1 show rates of daily income, over a 360-day "year," for three idealized workers: a tax consultant, an ice-cream vendor, and a factory worker. (Which is which? Day 0 is January 1; U.S. tax returns are due April 15.) How much does each worker earn over the whole year? Who's best off? Why?

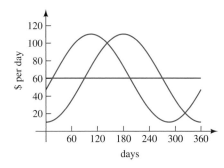

FIGURE 1
Three income streams

Solution First, which graph is which? Judging from their peaks (around April 15 = day 105 and July 1 = day 180), we'd guess that the two sinusoidal graphs represent the tax consultant and the ice-cream vendor. ➡ The straight-line graph therefore represents the factory worker's constant $60 daily wage. Label the graphs T, I, and F.

Our fable occurs north of the equator. How do the graphs show this?

The factory worker's total annual income is easiest to calculate. At $60 per day for a 360-day year, the factory worker earns $21,600—the area under the F-graph from $t = 0$ to $t = 360$. The total incomes of the other two workers can also be found as areas under the T- and the I-graphs, respectively. A close look reveals a mild surprise. All three graphs enclose the *same* total area; all three workers earn the same total annual income: $21,600.

Nevertheless, the workers are not (quite) equally well off. The tax consultant is luckiest, because T receives more income early in the year than I and F do. For now that's all we can say. Soon we'll *quantify* T's advantage by calculating the present value of each income stream at $t = 0$. ∎

Fair assumptions? We made several simplifying assumptions in Examples 1–3: that interest rates remain constant over time, that interest is compounded continuously, that daily earnings follow simple patterns, and so on. None of these assumptions need be literally true. For instance, few factory workers are paid by the day, including weekends. Ice-cream sales rise and fall with temperature, not just with the time of year.

Do such simplifications render our results useless? Certainly not. *All* economic decisions require some combination of calculation and guesswork. To some extent, the future is always unknowable. In practice, making sensible simplifying assumptions is inevitable—and it's standard operating procedure.

Why treat income as a stream?   Treating income as a continuous stream lends itself nicely to calculus; functions, derivatives, and integrals all arise naturally. From this point of view, an income stream is a function p of time: At time t, $p(t)$ is the (instantaneous) *rate* at which income "flows" to the recipient. It follows, then, that the integral $\int_a^b p(t)\,dt$ is the total income received over the time interval $a \le t \le b$. (That's why we looked at areas under the curves in Example 3.)

Present value as an integral

Building on the preceding examples, let's define the present value of a continuous income stream. Three ingredients are involved:

- A time scale t; $t = 0$ corresponds to the *present time*.
- An interest rate r, usually taken as a constant.

The income stream starts at time a and ends at time b.

- A continuous income-stream function $p(t)$ defined for $a \le t \le b$. ◄ At time t, $p(t)$ tells the rate of income flow with respect to time.

Finally, an important caution about compatible units of measurement:

> *The quantities t, r, and p must use the same time unit.*

For example, if t measures days, then r is the *daily* interest rate and $p(t)$ is measured in money units per *day*.

> **DEFINITION**   Let t, r, and p be as before. The **present value of the income stream** p is defined by the integral
> $$PV = \int_a^b p(t)e^{-rt}\,dt.$$

First we'll use the definition and then defend it as sensible. In the meantime, notice the similarity to Equation (1), page 448.

EXAMPLE 4   Given a 5% annual interest rate, find the present value (at the beginning of the 360-day year) of the income stream of each of the three workers T, I, and F in Example 3. How different are the results if 10% interest is available?

Solution   Let t denote time in days; then $t = 0$ is the present time, and the income flow lasts from $t = 0$ to $t = 360$. Because t involves days, r should measure the daily, not yearly, interest rate. Here, therefore, $r = 0.05/360$.

The three stream functions—we'll call them p_T, p_I, and p_F—are shown graphically on page 449. To find present values we need formulas for p_T, p_I, and p_F. One formula can be "read" easily from the graphs: $p_F(t) = 60$. The other two graphs look periodic; with some effort we could produce their formulas from trigonometric ingredients. Here we just state them:

$$p_T(t) = 50\cos\left(\pi \cdot \frac{t - 105}{180}\right) + 60; \quad p_I(t) = 50\cos\left(\pi \cdot \frac{t - 180}{180}\right) + 60.$$

The rest of the solution consists of straightforward (though messy) calculation. Here are the results. With $r = 0.05/360$,

Technology might help evaluate these integrals.

$$PV_\text{F} = \int_0^{360} 60e^{-0.05t/360}\, dt \approx 21068.89;$$

$$PV_\text{T} = \int_0^{360} \left(50\cos(\pi(t-105)/180) + 60\right)e^{-0.05t/360}\, dt \approx 21203.55;$$

$$PV_\text{I} = \int_0^{360} \left(50\cos(\pi(t-180)/180) + 60\right)e^{-0.05t/360}\, dt \approx 21067.78.$$

As predicted, T comes out on top, about \$135 ahead of the others.

At a 10% annual interest rate ($r = 0.1/360$) the tax consultant's advantage is a little greater:

$$PV_\text{F} = \int_0^{360} 60e^{-0.1t/360}\, dt \approx 20555.12;$$

$$PV_\text{T} = \int_0^{360} \left(50\cos(\pi(t-105)/180) + 60\right)e^{-0.1t/360}\, dt \approx 20817.26;$$

$$PV_\text{I} = \int_0^{360} \left(50\cos(\pi(t-180)/180) + 60\right)e^{-0.1t/360}\, dt \approx 20550.78. \qquad\blacksquare$$

Why the integral definition makes sense The typographical similarity between

$$\sum_{i=1}^n P_i e^{-rt_i} \quad \text{and} \quad \int_a^b p(t)e^{-rt}\, dt$$

(the formulas for present value in the discrete and continuous cases, respectively) is no accident. Roughly speaking, the integral is the continuous version of the discrete sum.

To relate the integral and the sum more precisely, we approximate a continuous income stream with a discrete sequence of payments. Suppose, then, that for $a \le t \le b$, $p(t)$ describes a continuous income stream, and let $a = t_0 < t_1 < t_2 < \cdots < t_n = b$ partition the interval $[a, b]$ into n short subintervals. We approximate the income stream p with a finite sequence of payments $P_1, P_2, \ldots, P_n$ occurring at times $t_1, t_2, \ldots, t_n$, respectively. ➡

Payments P_i occur at the end of each subinterval.

How large should each payment P_i be? Over a (short) subinterval $[t_{i-1}, t_i]$, the function p doesn't change much (because p is continuous), and so the estimate $p(t) \approx p(t_i)$ is reasonable. ➡ Thus, the *total income* received over the time interval $[t_{i-1}, t_i]$ is approximately $p(t_i)\,\Delta t_i$. In our (approximate) discrete version, therefore, it's natural to use $P_i = p(t_i)\,\Delta t_i$. In summary, we approximate the continuous stream p, defined for $a \le t \le b$, with n separate payments; at time t_i, the payment is $P_i = p(t_i)\Delta t_i$. As n tends to infinity, we expect our approximation to improve.

We pretend, in effect, that $p(t)$ is constant on each subinterval.

We saw earlier that the total present value of these n payments, given interest rate r, is

$$\sum_{i=1}^n P_i e^{-rt_i} = \sum_{i=1}^n p_i e^{-rt_i}\,\Delta t_i.$$

The key point is that the right side is an approximating sum for $\int_a^b p(t)e^{-rt}\, dt$—just the integral we've been waiting for. Therefore, as n tends to infinity, the approximation tends both to the desired integral and to the desired present value.

BASIC EXERCISES

1. Al and Bob, both 42 years old, hope to retire as millionaires. To that end, they'll deposit money now to accrue to $1 million by the time they're 65.

    (a) How much should Al deposit now if 6% interest is available?

    (b) How much should Al deposit now if 8% interest is available?

    (c) Bob has $100,000 on hand. What interest rate will he need to meet his retirement goal?

2. Christine, now 20, wants to retire at 65 with a $1 million nest egg. How much should she deposit now at 6%? At 8%? How much should she invest in speculative junk bonds that pay 20%?

3. **Real interest rates.** Inflation, the rise of prices over time, reduces the buying power of future money. In effect, inflation imposes negative interest on a deposit. Economists "control for inflation" by defining the real interest rate as

    real interest rate = nominal rate − inflation rate.

    Predicting future inflation necessarily involves guesswork; so, therefore, must the real interest rate. Historically, real interest rates have tended to hover in the range 2–4%.

    Anne and Betty, now 42 years old, hope to retire as *real* millionaires, that is, as millionaires after inflation. They can accomplish this by depositing enough money now to accrue—at real interest rate r—to $1 million by the time they're 65.

    (a) How much should Anne deposit now if 2% real interest is available?

    (b) How much should Anne deposit now if 4% real interest is available?

    (c) Betty has $200,000 on hand. What real interest rate will she need to meet her retirement goal?

4. Christopher, now 20, wants to retire at 65 with a $1 million real nest egg. How much should he deposit now at 2% real interest? At 4%? How much should he invest in speculative junk bonds that pay 15% real interest?

5. A child born in 1993 will typically start college in 2011 and graduate in 2015. Nobody really knows what college tuitions will be then. However, St. Lena College offers an "early decision" guarantee for the class of 2015: Enroll as an infant and lock in yearly tuition payments of $40,000, $42,000, $44,000, and $46,000 payable in 2011, 2012, 2013, and 2014. How much should new parents deposit in 1993 to cover these future payments if 6% annual interest is available? What if 8% interest is available?

6. Consider again the college tuition scenario in Exercise 5. This time we take a continuous point of view. Over the 4 years 2011–2015, total tuition paid is $172,000. Suppose, now, that this money is paid continuously at the *constant* rate of $43,000 per year. How much difference does the continuous point of view make? To decide, answer the same questions as in Exercise 5.

7. Consider carefully the two wavy graphs in Example 3. We claimed that their formulas are

$$p_T(t) = 50\cos\left(\pi\,\frac{t-105}{180}\right) + 60;$$

$$p_I(t) = 50\cos\left(\pi\,\frac{t-180}{180}\right) + 60.$$

    (a) Which graph goes with which formula? Explain briefly, in words, how you know.

    (b) The functions $\cos t$, p_T, and p_I are all periodic functions; that is, they repeat themselves on time intervals of a fixed length. How long is the period of each of these functions?

    (c) The formulas for p_T and p_I are "built" from $\cos t$ using various constants: 50, 60, 105, 180, and so on. Briefly discuss the effect each constant has on the corresponding graph.

FURTHER EXERCISES

8. Find the present value of the income stream in parts (a)–(e). In each case, treat income as a continuous stream. (Thus, for instance, think of yearly income of $12,000 as flowing in at the *constant rate* of $12,000 per year.)

    (a) A yearly income of $12,000 beginning 10 years in the future and lasting for 10 years. Assume annual interest rate $r = 0.06$.

    (b) A yearly income of $12,000 beginning 10 years in the future and lasting for 10 years. Assume annual interest rate $r = 0.08$.

    (c) A yearly income of $12,000 beginning 10 years in the future and lasting for 10 years. Assume annual interest rate $r = 0$. (This investor doesn't trust banks; he "deposits" the money under the floorboards.)

    (d) At time t years, with $10 \leq t \leq 20$, income flows at the rate $p(t) = 12,000e^{0.04t}$. Assume annual interest rate $r = 0.08$. [NOTE: In practice, many income streams do increase over time—for example, to correct for inflation. This one rises at a 4% instantaneous rate.]

    (e) Repeat part (d), but assume an annual interest rate of $r = 0.1$.

9. Suppose that an investment that pays a continuous return of $5000 per year for 8 years is offered for sale at $30,000. If the current interest rate is 6%, should you invest?

10. Symbolic calculation of the integrals in Example 4 is a rather messy affair. Instead, use the midpoint rule with 50 subdivisions to estimate the first three integrals there.

11. Symbolic calculation of the integrals in Example 4 is messy, but it can be done. One way is to use this antiderivative formula:

$$\int e^{ax} \cos(bx)\, dx = \frac{e^{ax}}{a^2 + b^2} \big(a \cos(bx) + b \sin(bx)\big)$$

(a) Verify by differentiation that the antiderivative formula really holds.

(b) Use the integral formula to show symbolically (as claimed in Example 4) that

$$\int_0^{360} \left(50 \cos\left(\pi \cdot \frac{t - 180}{180}\right) + 60\right) e^{-0.1t/360}\, dt \approx 20{,}550.78.$$

12. Suppose that an acquaintance offers to sell you an investment that will produce income at a continuous rate of $1000/(1 + t)$ dollars per year for 10 years. The asking price is $2000. If 10-year bank certificates of deposit that pay 5% per year compounded continuously are available, should you purchase this investment from your acquaintance?

13. Suppose that an income stream p is continuously invested at the same continuously compounded interest rate r that is currently available. Show that the total income accrued between $t = 0$ and $t = T$ is

$$e^{rT}\, PV = e^{rT} \int_0^T p(t) e^{-rt}\, dt.$$

Mass and Center of Mass

This relatively simple interlude offers a second physical application of the integral (to add to work). The one-variable setting requires that the figures considered be relatively simple.

Density and mass In many situations it's possible to consider a quantity, such as mass, as being "distributed" along the x-axis from $x = a$ to $x = b$. For example, imagine a straight piece of wire laid along the x-axis from $x = a$ to $x = b$. If the wire has constant thickness and is made of some homogeneous material such as pure copper, then the wire's mass is *evenly* distributed along the interval $[a, b]$ and the wire's **density** is constant. In this case the wire's total mass is simply the product of the density and the length. If, say, the wire has constant density 0.3 grams/centimeter (g/cm) and lies between $x = 0$ and $x = 5$ cm, then the wire's mass is $0.3 \times 5 = 1.5$ g.

If the wire has *varying* thickness or is made of some inhomogeneous material, then the wire's mass is *unevenly* distributed along the interval $[a, b]$. In this case the wire's density is *not* constant—the density is large where the wire is "fat" or "heavy" and small where the wire is "thin" or "light." In this case it's convenient to think of a **density function**, which is often denoted by $\rho(x)$. (Numerical values of $\rho(x)$ depend on the units of measurement.)

In general, the **linear density** of a distribution is *defined* as a derivative: If $Q(x)$ is the total quantity (e.g., the total mass of wire) over the interval $[a, x]$, then the density function $\rho(x)$ is defined by $\rho(x) = Q'(x)$, the rate of change of Q at x. (Note that $Q(a) = 0$ by our definition.) In the case of a wire, for instance, the statement $\rho(2) = 0.345$ could mean (depending on the units) that at $x = 2$ cm, the wire's density is 0.345 g/cm.

Now the FTC says that

$$\int_a^b \rho(x)\,dx = Q(b) - Q(a) = Q(b);$$

the right side is the total quantity in question from $x = a$ to $x = b$. Here is the formal result:

FACT (Measuring mass) Suppose that a mass distribution from $x = a$ to $x = b$ has density function $\rho(x)$. Then the total mass over the interval $[a, b]$ is given by the integral

$$\int_a^b \rho(x)\,dx.$$

EXAMPLE 1 A wire laid along the x-axis from $x = 0$ to $x = 2$ has density function $\rho(x) = x^2$. Find (and interpret) the total mass.

Solution By the preceding Fact, the total mass is

$$\int_0^2 \rho(x)\,dx = \int_0^2 x^2\,dx = \frac{8}{3}.$$

What the answer means depends on the units. If length (along the x-axis) is measured in centimeters and mass is measured in grams, then the density $\rho(x)$ is in grams per centimeter and the wire's total mass is 8/3 g. ∎

PROBLEM 1 A wire laid along the x-axis from $x = 0$ to $x = 10$ has density function $\rho(x) = 2 + \sin x$. Find the total mass if x is measured in feet and $\rho(x)$ in ounces per foot. What are the units of the answer?

For an object made of homogeneous material, mass is proportional to volume; this gives a slightly different perspective on the volume formulas of Section 7.2.

Beyond wires The wire of Example 1 can be thought of as essentially a one-dimensional object. In other cases a mass distribution along the x-axis may arise from a three-dimensional figure.

EXAMPLE 2 Consider the horn-shaped solid of revolution formed by revolving the shaded region shown in Figure 1 about the *x*-axis. (We saw in Section 7.2 how to find the solid's volume by integration; see Example 3, page 425.)

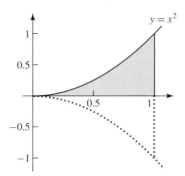

FIGURE 1
**Revolve the shaded region about
the *x*-axis**

Now imagine that the solid is made of some homogeneous material (such as plastic) that weighs 1 g/cm^3. Use the distribution idea discussed here to find the solid's mass (and hence also its volume).

Solution We can think of the solid as determining a distribution of mass along the *x*-axis from $x = 0$ to $x = 1$. The horn's outward-flaring shape means that the mass distribution is not constant along the *x*-axis. If $M(x)$ denotes the mass of the part of the solid over the interval $[0, x]$ and $V(x)$ denotes the volume of the same object, then $M(x)$ and $V(x)$ increase faster and faster as *x* moves from 0 to 1.

The linear density $\rho(x)$ of this mass distribution is the derivative $M'(x)$. In this case mass and volume have the same numerical value, and so $M'(x) = V'(x)$. We observed in Section 7.2 that $V'(x)$ is the solid's cross-sectional area (perpendicular to the *x*-axis) at *x*. (This is essentially the content of Theorem 1, page 424.) In the present case, the cross section at *x* is a disk with radius x^2, and thus we see that the linear density is $M'(x) = \pi x^4$. Integrating the density function gives the answer we want:

$$\int_0^1 \pi x^4 \, dx = \frac{\pi}{5}.$$

The numerical answer (the same as we found in Section 7.2) can be interpreted either as mass (in grams) or as volume in cubic centimeters. ∎

PROBLEM 2 Mimic the preceding example to find the mass of a cone of height *h* cm and radius *r* cm. Assume that the cone is made of some material that weighs 1 g/cm^3.

Center of mass Given a distribution of mass along the *x*-axis (as considered above), how can we find its **center of mass**—the point at which the distribution balances? For a *uniform* mass distribution from $x = a$ to $x = b$ there's no problem: The system balances at the midpoint $x = (a + b)/2$. For a general distribution, the center of mass, like mass itself, is found by integration.

To get started, imagine several **point masses**, say $m_1, m_2, \ldots, m_n$ arranged along the *x*-axis at positions $x_1, x_2, \ldots, x_n$, as in Figure 2:

Think of the masses as lead weights hanging from threads.

FIGURE 2
Five (unequal) point masses along an axis

(A point mass is a mass that can be thought of as located at one point, as can the hanging masses in Figure 2.) For a fixed value of x, say $x = p$, the quantity

$$m_1(x_1 - p) + m_2(x_2 - p) + \cdots m_n(x_n - p)$$

is called the **moment** of the system about $x = p$. It's a fact of physics that the system *balances* at p if this moment is zero. (This means, in particular, that $(x_i - p)$ must be positive for some i and negative for others—hardly surprising to anyone who's ridden a seesaw.) To find the center of mass (denoted by $\bar{x}$) one sets the moment about p equal to zero and solves for p.

PROBLEM 3 A mass distribution consists of two point masses: $m_1 = 5$ at $x_1 = -1$ and $m_2 = 5$ at $x_2 = 1$. Find the center of mass by setting the moment about p equal to zero and solving for p.

PROBLEM 4 Another mass distribution consists of two point masses: $m_1 = 5$ at $x_1 = -1$ and $m_2 = 10$ at $x_2 = 1$. Where is the center of mass now?

PROBLEM 5 Yet another mass distribution consists of three point masses: $m_1 = 1$ at $x_1 = 0$, $m_2 = 2$ at $x_2 = 2$, and $m_3 = 3$ at $x_3 = 3$. Find the center of mass.

The continuous case is derived as a limit of discrete approximations. Note that $\bar{x}$ is a fixed number—not a variable.

Continuous distributions The situation for a continuous mass distribution is similar to that just described. If the mass distribution has density $\rho(x)$ from $x = a$ to $x = b$, then the system's **moment** about $x = p$ is an *integral* rather than a sum:

$$\text{moment} = \int_a^b (x - p)\rho(x)\,dx.$$

As before, the **center of mass** is the number $\bar{x}$ for which

$$\text{moment} = \int_a^b (x - \bar{x})\rho(x)\,dx = 0.$$

PROBLEM 6 Solve the preceding equation to show that the center of mass $\bar{x}$ satisfies the equation

$$\bar{x} = \frac{\int_a^b x\rho(x)\,dx}{\int_a^b \rho(x)\,dx}.$$

(Notice that, by the discussion above, the denominator is just the total mass of the system.)

PROBLEM 7 Find the center of mass of the wire in Example 1.

PROBLEM 8 Find the center of mass of a circular cylinder (made of a homogeneous material) of radius r and "height" h. [HINT: Visualize the cylinder as running from $x = 0$ to $x = h$. Then, as discussed in Example 2, the density function $\rho(x)$ can be taken as the cross-sectional area function—which is constant in this case.]

P R O B L E M 9 Find the center of mass of a cone (made of a homogeneous material) of radius r and "height" h. [HINT: Visualize the cone as running from $y = 0$ to $y = h$ with the big end up. Then the density function $\rho(y)$ can be taken as the cross-sectional area function. (Integrate in y, not in x.)]

P R O B L E M 10 In Example 6 of Section 7.3 (page 436), we found the work needed to pump all the water out the top of a conical tank of radius r feet and height h feet. Show that this is the same amount of work as is needed to raise the entire mass of the cone from the center of gravity of the cone to the top of the cone.

SYMBOLIC ANTIDIFFERENTIATION TECHNIQUES

8.1 INTEGRATION BY PARTS

We discussed u-substitution in Chapter 5 and will use it freely in this chapter. Students may need some reminding.

Introduction

In this chapter we return to an old project—finding, for a given elementary function f, a new elementary function F for which $F' = f$. (Recall: An *elementary* function is one built from the standard basic "elements"—power functions, exponential and logarithmic functions, trigonometric functions, and so on.) ◂

Roughly speaking, an elementary function is one that has a "formula."

As we said in Chapter 5, finding elementary *antiderivatives* is, as a rule, harder than finding *derivatives*. Sometimes it is even impossible; some elementary functions do not *have* elementary antiderivatives. The function $f(x) = \sin(x^2)$ is one simple-looking example. (That's one reason we took so much trouble in Chapter 6 to approximate integrals like $\int_0^1 \sin(x^2)\,dx$.)

Many important elementary functions *do* have elementary antiderivatives, however, and in this chapter we describe several methods for finding them. If we combine the symbolic methods discussed here with a moderate-sized integral table, we can handle many of the integrals that arise in practical applications. With additional help from modern mathematical software, we can do better still.

If students have access to symbolic computing, this chapter can serve, at least in part, to demystify computer results. It also shows important and sometimes unexpected connections among families of functions.

Why bother? Elementary antiderivative formulas are obviously useful; they let us calculate definite integrals exactly, for one thing. But why do we take the trouble to *calculate* antiderivatives? Why not just "ask" an integral table or mathematical software for an answer? One answer is that, as sentient beings, we'd like to know *something* about where tabulated or computer-generated answers come from. Another answer is that looking for antiderivatives, with or without technology, reveals important—and sometimes surprising—relations among the key functions of calculus.

This section's many examples generally ramp up in sophistication.

EXAMPLE 1 Find $\int \left(\dfrac{1}{x^2} + \dfrac{1}{x^2+1} + \dfrac{2x}{x^2+1} \right) dx$. Are there any surprises?

Solution An answer is easy to find (and to check by differentiation):

$$\int \left(\frac{1}{x^2} + \frac{1}{x^2+1} + \frac{2x}{x^2+1} \right) dx = -\frac{1}{x} + \arctan x + \ln(x^2+1) + C.$$

The calculation isn't especially interesting, but notice the somewhat surprising *form* of the result. All three summands of the integrand are simple rational functions, but the antiderivative has three quite different pieces—a power of x, an arctangent, and a logarithm. One goal of this chapter is to explain how such similar parents can produce such different offspring. ∎

Integration by parts and the product rule

Integration is more than a method of integration; it also illustrates a general principle about trading derivatives and integrals.

We saw in Section 5.6 that the method of substitution is a "reversed" version of the *chain rule* for derivatives. In a similar sense, the method of **integration by parts** reverses the *product rule* for derivatives. The product rule says that, for differentiable functions u and v,

$$(u \cdot v)' = u \cdot v' + v \cdot u'.$$

The product rule can also be understood as a statement about *anti*derivatives; it says that uv is an antiderivative of $uv' + vu'$. In symbolic language, the product rule says

$$u(x) \cdot v(x) = \int \big(u(x) \cdot v'(x) + v(x) \cdot u'(x)\big)\, dx.$$

Rearranging terms gives an equivalent equation:

$$\int u(x) \cdot v'(x)\, dx = u(x) \cdot v(x) - \int v(x) \cdot u'(x)\, dx.$$

This last identity is worth a closer look. Notice especially how derivatives and antiderivatives are swapped inside the two integral signs. ➔ This simple but useful idea appears often in mathematics. In calculus, this equation is known as the **integration-by-parts formula**. As we'll see, this formula sometimes lets us trade a difficult integration problem for an easier one.

We trade $u \cdot v'$ for $v \cdot u'$.

If we write

$$u = u(x), \quad v = v(x), \quad du = u'(x)\, dx, \quad \text{and} \quad dv = v'(x)\, dx,$$

the formula looks simpler still. We state the result as a theorem; it applies both to definite and to indefinite integrals. ➔

The FTC explains why the formula applies to definite integrals.

THEOREM 1 (Integration by parts)   If u and v are differentiable functions, then

- $\displaystyle \int u\, dv = uv - \int v\, du;$
- $\displaystyle \int_a^b u\, dv = uv \Big]_a^b - \int_a^b v\, du.$

First we illustrate how the method works under ideal conditions. (Later we'll see what can go wrong . . . .)

EXAMPLE 2   Find $\displaystyle \int x\, e^x\, dx$ and $\displaystyle \int_0^1 x\, e^x\, dx$.

Solution   Setting $u = x$ and $dv = e^x\, dx$ fits the theorem's template:

$$\int x\, e^x\, dx = \int u\, dv.$$

To use the formula, we need values for du and v. The first is simple: Since $u = x$, $du = dx$. Finding a suitable v is sometimes a hard problem in its own right, but in this case it's easy: If $v = e^x$, then it's easy to check that $dv = e^x\, dx$, as desired. Now the integration-by-parts formula kicks in:

$$\int x\, e^x\, dx = \int u\, dv = uv - \int v\, du = x\, e^x - \int e^x\, dx = x\, e^x - e^x + C.$$

Checking antiderivatives produced by u-substitution involves the chain rule.

Is the answer correct? Checking the answer by differentiation involves—as we might have guessed—the product rule: ◄

$$(x\, e^x - e^x + C)' = e^x + x\, e^x - e^x = x\, e^x.$$

Thus, our "candidate" antiderivative behaves as it should.

Evaluating the *definite* integral is now a routine calculation:

$$\int_0^1 x\, e^x\, dx = x\, e^x \Big]_0^1 - \int_0^1 e^x\, dx = x\, e^x - e^x \Big]_0^1 = 1. \qquad \blacksquare$$

EXAMPLE 3 Find $\displaystyle\int x^2 \ln x\, dx$.

Solution If we set $u = \ln x$, then

$$dv = x^2 dx, \quad du = \frac{1}{x}\, dx, \quad v = \frac{x^3}{3},$$

and everything works nicely:

$$\int x^2 \ln x\, dx = \int u\, dv$$

$$= uv - \int v\, du$$

$$= \frac{x^3}{3} \ln x - \int \frac{x^2}{3}\, dx$$

$$= \frac{x^3}{3} \ln x - \frac{x^3}{9} + C.$$

The answer is easy to check by differentiation. $\qquad \blacksquare$

Tricks of the trade: Wise and foolish choices

How to choose u and dv successfully isn't always obvious. Setting $u = \ln x$ and $dv = x^2\, dx$ in Example 3, for instance, was natural enough, but not the only possibility. We might have tried, say, $u = x^2$ and $dv = \ln x\, dx$. These latter choices are not incorrect, but they turn out to be unhelpful. ◄

Try them to see why they're unhelpful.

Sometimes, surprising choices of u and dv turn out to work.

EXAMPLE 4 Find $\displaystyle\int \ln x\, dx$.

Solution At first glance the problem seems not to fit the mold at all. Yet it does fit. If we set $u = \ln x$, then

$$dv = dx, \quad du = \frac{1}{x}\, dx, \quad v = x;$$

fitting things into the formula gives

$$\int \ln x\, dx = x\, \ln x - \int 1\, dx = x\, \ln x - x + C.$$

The answer is easy to check by differentiation, using the product rule. $\qquad \blacksquare$

When things go wrong Integration by parts trades one integral expression, $\int u\,dv$, for another, $uv - \int v\,du$. The bargain is worth making only if the second expression is simpler or more cooperative than the first. In practice, such satisfaction cannot be guaranteed. Indeed, choosing u and dv unwisely can make things *worse*, not better.

EXAMPLE 5 **(A step in the wrong direction)** What's wrong with choosing $u = e^x$ and $dv = x\,dx$ for the indefinite integral $\int x\,e^x\,dx$?

Solution Our choices aren't *wrong*, but they don't help with the problem at hand. Setting

$$u = e^x, \quad dv = x\,dx, \quad du = e^x\,dx, \quad \text{and} \quad v = \frac{x^2}{2}$$

gives

$$\int x\,e^x\,dx = uv - \int v\,du = e^x\,\frac{x^2}{2} - \int \frac{x^2}{2}\,e^x\,dx.$$

The new integral (on the right) looks harder than the old one (on the left). This time we struck out. ∎

Once u and dv are chosen, we need corresponding expressions for du and v. Finding du from u is *always* straightforward because it involves only differentiation. But finding v from dv is an antidifferentiation problem in its own right; it may be hard or even impossible.

Integration by parts works only when all the subproblems can be solved; there are no guarantees . . .

EXAMPLE 6 Find $\displaystyle\int 2x\,\exp(x^2)\,dx$. ➡

Recall: $\exp(u)$ is another notation for e^u.

Solution The integrand is a product and so looks like a candidate for integration by parts. Let's try $u = 2x$ and $dv = \exp(x^2)\,dx$. It's clear that $du = 2\,dx$, but what's v? The answer: Nothing useful—$\exp(x^2)$ *has* no elementary antiderivative. We can't even write v down, let alone use it to solve our problem.

Did we choose u and dv unwisely? Or is integration by parts the wrong tool for this job? In this case the latter alternative holds. In fact, the ordinary u-substitution $u = x^2$, $du = 2x\,dx$ works nicely:

$$\int 2x\,\exp(x^2)\,dx = \int e^u\,du = \exp(x^2) + C.$$

There's a moral here: Try easy methods first—especially substitution. ∎

When things go right Mishaps are certainly possible, but for surprisingly many antiderivatives—even ones that don't appear to be products—integration by parts is effective. The trick is to choose u and dv successfully, where "successfully" means two things:

(i) dv can be antidifferentiated to give v;

(ii) $\int v\,du$ is simpler or more familiar than $\int u\,dv$.

Not *every* choice of u and dv succeeds, but if one choice fails, another may work. Intuition for recognizing good and bad choices comes with practice.

LIATE: A mnemonic for choosing *u* and *dv* Whether an attempt at integration by parts succeeds or fails usually depends on the choices of u and dv.

In his article "A Technique for Integration by Parts" (*American Mathematical Monthly* 90 (1983), pp. 210–211), Herbert E. Kasube proposes the LIATE rule for choosing u. (Choosing u is enough; given u, dv must be "everything else.")

He observes that most integrands are built from functions of five types: logarithmic (L), inverse (I) trigonometric, algebraic (A), trigonometric (T), and exponential (E). The LIATE rule says the following:

Choose u in the order LIATE.

In other words, *u* should be a function of the *first* available type in the list L, I, A, T, E. In Example 1, for instance, the choice $u = x$ was of type A (algebraic) because neither logarithmic (L) nor inverse trigonometric (I) functions were present.

Not every indefinite integral succumbs to integration by parts. For those that do, the LIATE method usually seems to work.

Mixing methods Some problems require more than one antidifferentiation method.

What does LIATE say here?

EXAMPLE 7 Find $\int \arctan x \, dx$. ◄

Solution Let $u = \arctan x$ and $dv = dx$. Then $du = (1+x^2)^{-1} dx$, $v = x$, and integration by parts gives

$$\int \arctan x \, dx = uv - \int v \, du = x \arctan x - \int \frac{x}{1+x^2} \, dx.$$

We're nearly finished—the last integral yields to the ordinary substitutions $u = 1 + x^2$ and $du = 2x \, dx$:

$$x \arctan x - \int \frac{x}{1+x^2} \, dx = x \arctan x - \frac{1}{2} \int \frac{du}{u}$$

$$= x \arctan x - \frac{1}{2} \ln |u| + C$$

$$= x \arctan x - \frac{1}{2} \ln(1+x^2) + C. \qquad ■$$

Beyond the basics

There are several useful variations on the basic integration-by-parts theme; two of them appear in the following examples.

Alternatively, one might guess that an antiderivative has the form $a\,e^x + b\,x\,e^x + c\,x^2 e^x$, and try to solve for the constants.

EXAMPLE 8 **(Do it again)** Find $\int x^2 e^x \, dx$.

Solution If $u = x^2$, then $dv = e^x \, dx$, $du = 2x \, dx$, $v = e^x$, and

$$\int x^2 e^x \, dx = x^2 e^x - 2 \int x e^x \, dx.$$

With $u = x$, $dv = e^x dx$.

Did we get anywhere? Yes! We've already seen that the last integral can be handled by *another* integration by parts. ◄ We won't redo the problem. Here's the result:

$$\int x^2 e^x \, dx = x^2 e^x - 2 \int x e^x \, dx = x^2 e^x - 2\,(x\,e^x - e^x) + C. \qquad ■$$

Alternatively, one might guess that an antiderivative has the form $a\,e^x \sin x + b\,e^x \cos x$, and try to solve for the constants.

EXAMPLE 9 **(Integrate twice; then solve)** Find $\int e^x \sin x \, dx$.

Solution If we set $u = \sin x$, then

$$dv = e^x \, dx, \quad du = \cos x \, dx, \quad v = e^x,$$

and we get

$$I = \int e^x \sin x\, dx = e^x \sin x - \int e^x \cos x\, dx.$$

Not much progress yet; let's try the method *again* on the last integral. If $u = \cos x$, then

$$dv = e^x\, dx, \quad du = -\sin x\, dx, \quad \text{and} \quad v = e^x,$$

and so

$$I = e^x \sin x - \int e^x \cos x\, dx = e^x \sin x - \left(e^x \cos x + \int e^x \sin x\, dx \right).$$

(Watch the signs carefully.) The original integral I has reappeared! It might seem that we're chasing our tail, but in fact we can *solve* the last equation for I:

$$I = e^x \sin x - (e^x \cos x + I) \implies 2I = e^x \sin x - e^x \cos x$$

$$\implies I = \frac{e^x}{2}(\sin x - \cos x) + C.$$

The result is easy to check by differentiation.   ■

Reality check   The "wraparound" trick in Example 9 seems almost too good to be true. Let's check the result graphically. Figure 1 shows graphs of $f(x) = e^x \sin x$ and $F(x) = e^x(\sin x - \cos x)/2$, which supposedly is an antiderivative:

We do a similar reality check for the partial fractions method. One could check derivatives instead, but this method brings graphical intuition to bear.

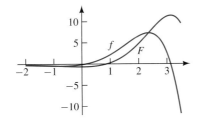

FIGURE 1
$f(x) = e^x \sin x$ and $F(x) = \dfrac{e^x}{2}(\sin x - \cos x)$

The graphs look reasonable—f appears to be the derivative of F. In particular:

- **Asymptotes**   The integrand $f(x)$ tends quickly to zero as $x \to -\infty$. Properly, therefore, the antiderivative F looks nearly horizontal toward the left of the picture.
- **Wild swings in the long run**   As $x \to \infty$, $f(x)$ changes sign at each multiple of π, oscillating between larger and larger positive and negative values. The antiderivative F therefore also oscillates dramatically, with peaks and valleys at multiples of π. Figure 1 just begins to suggest this behavior; a larger window would show it more clearly.

Reduction formulas: Stepping down to a solution

Integration by parts generates many of the reduction formulas in integral tables; it also illustrates the important idea of "stepping" toward a solution.

The equation

$$\int x^n e^x\, dx = x^n e^x - n \int x^{n-1} e^x\, dx, \tag{1}$$

which holds for all integers $n > 0$, is called a **reduction formula**. (The name makes sense because the power of x is "reduced" by one on the right-hand side.) It expresses the left-hand indefinite integral in terms of another, slightly "reduced" integral. We'll first use the formula and then explain why it holds.

EXAMPLE 10 Use reduction formula (1) to find $\int x^3 e^x \, dx$.

Solution The formula says, for $n = 3$, that

$$\int x^3 e^x \, dx = x^3 e^x - 3 \int x^2 e^x \, dx.$$

In Example 8 we found a value for the last integral; plugging that result into the formula gives the answer:

$$\int x^3 e^x \, dx = x^3 e^x - 3 \int x^2 e^x \, dx$$
$$= x^3 e^x - 3 \left(x^2 e^x - 2x e^x + 2e^x + C \right)$$
$$= x^3 e^x - 3x^2 e^x + 6x e^x - 6e^x - 3C.$$

Because C is an arbitrary constant, $-3C$ is arbitrary too, and we write simply

$$\int x^3 e^x \, dx = x^3 e^x - 3x^2 e^x + 6x e^x - 6e^x + C.$$

A routine check by differentiation shows that the answer is right. ■

Why the formula holds Example 10 shows that the reduction Formula (1) works, at least for $n = 3$. But *why* must it hold? How might we discover it? Integration by parts gives some answers. If we set

$$u = x^n, \quad dv = e^x \, dx, \quad du = n x^{n-1} \, dx, \quad \text{and} \quad v = e^x,$$

then integration by parts yields what we want:

$$\int x^n e^x \, dx = x^n e^x - n \int x^{n-1} e^x \, dx.$$

Integral tables contain many reduction formulas; most can be found using integration by parts.

BASIC EXERCISES

1. (a) Show that $\dfrac{d}{dx} x \ln x = 1 + \ln x$.

   (b) Explain why part (a) implies that $\int \ln x \, dx = x \ln x - x + C$.

2. (a) Show that $\dfrac{d}{dx} x^4 \ln x = x^3 + 4x^3 \ln x$.

   (b) Explain why part (a) implies that $\int x^3 \ln x \, dx = \dfrac{x^4 \ln x}{4} - \dfrac{x^4}{16} + C$.

   (c) Find $\int x^3 \ln x \, dx$ using integration by parts with $u = \ln x$ and $dv = x^3 \, dx$.

3. (a) Show that $\dfrac{d}{dx} x e^{-x} = e^{-x} - x e^{-x}$.

   (b) Explain why part (a) implies that $\int x e^{-x} \, dx = -e^{-x} - x e^{-x} + C$.

   (c) Find $\int x e^{-x} \, dx$ using integration by parts with $u = x$ and $dv = e^{-x} \, dx$.

4. (a) Show that $\dfrac{d}{dx} x e^{2x} = e^{2x} + 2x e^{2x}$.

   (b) Use part (a) to show that $\int x e^{2x} \, dx = \dfrac{x e^{2x}}{2} - \dfrac{e^{2x}}{4} + C$.

   (c) Find $\int x e^{2x} \, dx$ using integration by parts with $u = x$ and $dv = e^{2x} \, dx$.

5. (a) Show that $\dfrac{d}{dx} x \arctan(2x) = \arctan(2x) + \dfrac{2x}{1 + 4x^2}$.

   (b) Use part (a) to find $\int \arctan(2x) \, dx$.

   (c) Find $\int \arctan(2x) \, dx$ using integration by parts with $u = \arctan(2x)$ and $dv = dx$.

6. (a) Show that $\dfrac{d}{dx} x \arcsin x = \arcsin x + \dfrac{x}{\sqrt{1 - x^2}}$.

   (b) Use part (a) to find $\int \arcsin x \, dx$.

   (c) Find $\int \arcsin x \, dx$ using integration by parts with $u = \arcsin x$ and $dv = dx$.

7. (a) Show that $\dfrac{d}{dx}e^{2x}\sin x = 2e^{2x}\sin x + e^{2x}\cos x$.

(b) Find $\dfrac{d}{dx}e^{2x}\cos x$.

(c) Use parts (a) and (b) to find $\int e^{2x}\sin x\,dx$.

(d) Use integration by parts twice — first with $u=\sin x$, then with $u=\cos x$ — to find $\int e^{2x}\sin x\,dx$.

8. (a) Show that $\dfrac{d}{dx}e^{x}\cos(2x) = e^{x}\cos(2x) - e^{x}\sin(2x)$.

(b) Find $\dfrac{d}{dx}e^{x}\sin(2x)$.

(c) Use parts (a) and (b) to find $\int e^{x}\cos(2x)\,dx$.

(d) Use integration by parts to find $\int e^{x}\cos(2x)\,dx$.

In Exercises 9–14, use integration by parts with the suggested u and dv to find the antiderivative. Check your answers by differentiation.

9. $\int x\sin(3x)\,dx \qquad u=x, \quad dv=\sin(3x)\,dx$

10. $\int \dfrac{\ln x}{x^2}\,dx \qquad u=\ln x, \quad dv=x^{-2}\,dx$

11. $\int x\sec^2 x\,dx \qquad u=x, \quad dv=\sec^2 x\,dx$

12. $\int x\sec x\tan x\,dx \qquad u=x, \quad dv=\sec x\tan x\,dx$

13. $\int (\ln x)^2\,dx \qquad u=\ln x, \quad dv=\ln x\,dx$

14. $\int \sqrt{x}\ln x\,dx \qquad u=\sqrt{x}, \quad dv=\ln x\,dx$

In Exercises 15–20, evaluate the definite integral using integration by parts. Check your answers by comparing them with a midpoint rule estimate computed using $n=20$.

15. $\int_0^1 xe^{-x}\,dx$

16. $\int_0^\pi x\cos(2x)\,dx$

17. $\int_1^e x\ln x\,dx$

18. $\int_{\pi/4}^{\pi/2} x\csc^2 x\,dx$

19. $\int_{-1}^{\sqrt{2}/2} x^2\arctan x\,dx$

20. $\int_1^4 e^{3x}\cos(2x)\,dx$

21. (a) Show that $\int x^2\cos x\,dx = x^2\sin x - 2\int x\sin x\,dx$.

(b) Find $\int x\sin x\,dx$.

(c) Use parts (a) and (b) to show that $\int x^2\cos x\,dx = x^2\sin x + 2x\cos x - 2\sin x$.

22. (a) Show that $\int x^2\sin x\,dx = -x^2\cos x + 2\int x\cos x\,dx$.

(b) Find $\int x\cos x\,dx$.

(c) Use parts (a) and (b) to show that $\int x^2\sin x\,dx = -x^2\cos x + 2x\sin x + 2\cos x$.

23. Use the reduction formula
$$\int (\ln x)^n\,dx = x(\ln x)^n - n\int (\ln x)^{n-1}\,dx, \quad n\ge 1$$
to find $\int (\ln x)^3\,dx$.

24. Use the reduction formula
$$\int x(\ln x)^n\,dx = \frac{1}{2}x^2(\ln x)^n - \frac{n}{2}\int x(\ln x)^{n-1}\,dx, \quad n\ge 1$$
to find $\int x(\ln x)^2\,dx$.

FURTHER EXERCISES

25. Show that if $r\ne -1$ is a constant,
$$\int x^r\ln x\,dx = \frac{x^{r+1}}{r+1}\left(\ln x - \frac{1}{r+1}\right) + C.$$

26. Derive the reduction formula
$$\int x^n e^x\,dx = x^n e^x - n\int x^{n-1}e^x\,dx.$$

27. Derive the reduction formula in Exercise 23.

28. Derive the reduction formula in Exercise 24.

29. (a) Use the substitution $u=x^3$ to find $\int x^2\ln(x^3)\,dx$.

(b) Use integration by parts to find $\int x^2\ln(x^3)\,dx$. [HINT: $\ln(x^3)=3\ln x$.]

30. (a) Use the substitution $u=a+bx$ to find $\int x\sqrt{a+bx}\,,dx$.

(b) Use integration by parts with $u=x$ and $dv=\sqrt{a+bx}\,dx$ to find $\int x\sqrt{a+bx}\,,dx$.

31. Use the substitution $u=x^2$ and integration by parts to find $\int x^3 e^{x^2}\,dx$.

32. Use the substitution $u=-x^3$ and integration by parts to find $\int x^5 e^{-x^3}\,dx$.

33. (a) Show that $\int \sin^2 x\,dx = -\sin x\cos x + \int \cos^2 x\,dx$.

(b) Use part (a) and the trigonometric identity $\sin^2 x + \cos^2 x = 1$ to show that
$$\int \sin^2 x\,dx = \frac{1}{2}(x - \sin x\cos x).$$

34. Use integration by parts and the trigonometric identity $\sin^2 x + \cos^2 x = 1$ to find $\int \cos^2 x\,dx$.

35. Find $\int x\cos^2 x\,dx$ using integration by parts. [HINT: $\cos^2 x = \frac{1}{2}(1+\cos(2x))$.]

36. Find $\int x\sin^2 x\,dx$. [HINT: $\sin^2 x = \frac{1}{2}(1-\cos(2x))$.]

In Exercises 37–58, find the antiderivative. Check your results by differentiation.

37. $\int x^2 \cos x \, dx$

38. $\int x \sin x \cos x \, dx$

39. $\int x \csc x \cot x \, dx$

40. $\int \arccos x \, dx$

41. $\int \sqrt{x} \ln \left(\sqrt[3]{x} \right) dx$

42. $\int x e^x \sin x \, dx$

43. $\int \arctan(1/x) \, dx$

44. $\int x^3 (\ln x)^2 \, dx$

45. $\int e^{\sqrt{x}} \, dx$

46. $\int x^5 \sin \left(x^3 \right) dx$

47. $\int \sin (\ln x) \, dx$

48. $\int \sqrt{x} e^{-\sqrt{x}} \, dx$

49. $\int \sin \left(\sqrt{x} \right) dx$

50. $\int \dfrac{\arctan \left(\sqrt{x} \right)}{\sqrt{x}} \, dx$

51. $\int \sqrt{x} \arctan \left(\sqrt{x} \right) dx$

52. $\int x^2 \arcsin x \, dx$

53. $\int \cos x \ln(\sin x) \, dx$

54. $\int x^5 e^{-x^2} \, dx$

55. $\int x \sinh x \, dx$

56. $\int x \cosh(2x) \, dx$

57. $\int x^2 \sinh x \, dx$

58. $\int \cosh(\sqrt{x}) \, dx$

59. Let $I_n = \int_1^e (\ln x)^n \, dx$, where $n \geq 1$ is an integer.

    (a) Show that $I_1 = 1$.

    (b) Use the reduction formula in Exercise 23 to show that $I_2 = e - 2I_1 = e - 2$.

    (c) Show that $I_3 = e - 3I_2 = 6 - 2e$.

    (d) Evaluate I_5.

60. Let $I_n = \int_0^1 x^n e^x \, dx$, where $n \geq 0$ is an integer.

    (a) Show that $I_0 = e - 1$.

    (b) Use the reduction formula in Exercise 26 to show that $I_1 = e - I_0 = 1$.

    (c) Show that $I_2 = e - 2I_1 = e - 2$.

    (d) Evaluate I_5.

61. Find a function f such that

$$\int f(x) \sin x \, dx = -f(x) \cos x + \int x^3 \cos x \, dx.$$

62. Suppose that f is a continuous function, that $f(0) = 2$, and that $\int_0^\pi f(x) \sin x \, dx + \int_0^\pi f''(x) \sin x \, dx = 6$. Find $f(\pi)$.

63. Suppose that f is a continuous function, that $\int_{-\pi/2}^{3\pi/2} f'(x) \, dx = 1$, and that $\int_{-\pi/2}^{3\pi/2} f''(x) \cos x \, dx = 4$. Evaluate $\int_{-\pi/2}^{3\pi/2} f(x) \cos x \, dx$.

64. Show that v in the integration by parts formula can be *any* antiderivative of dv.

65. (a) Explain why $f(b) - f(a) = \int_a^b f'(x) \, dx$.

    (b) Use integration by parts and part (a) to show that
$$f(b) = f(a) + f'(a)(b-a) - \int_a^b (x-b) f''(x) \, dx.$$
    [HINT: Let $dv = dx$ and $v = x - b$.]

    (c) Show that $f(b) = f(a) + f'(a)(b-a) + \dfrac{1}{2} f''(a)(b-a)^2 + \dfrac{1}{2} \int_a^b (x-b)^2 f'''(x) \, dx.$

    (d) Let $p_3(x)$ be the third-degree Taylor polynomial for $f(x)$ based at $x = a$. Show that
$$f(b) - p_3(b) = -\dfrac{1}{6} \int_a^b (x-b)^3 f^{(4)}(x) \, dx.$$

8.2 PARTIAL FRACTIONS

We studied rational functions in Section 1.3; see also Appendix B.

The partial fractions method offers a nice example of divide-and-conquer strategies—difficult integrals are reduced to sums of simpler ones. The method also gives good practice with polynomial algebra.

A **rational function** is any function that can be written as a *ratio* of two polynomials. ◄ All three of the following expressions define rational functions:

$$\frac{2}{1 - x^2}; \qquad \frac{2 + 5x + 3x^2 + 3x^3}{x(1 + x^2)(x + 2)}; \qquad \frac{x^3}{1 + x^2}.$$

This section is about the problem of antidifferentiating rational functions. Notice first that there *is* a problem. Polynomials themselves are easy to antidifferentiate, but *quotients* of polynomials are another matter entirely. Derivatives of quotients can be sticky to compute; *anti*derivatives can be even worse.

The **method of partial fractions** is a systematic technique for antidifferentiating rational functions. The basic idea is to "divide and conquer": We rewrite the given rational function as a sum of simpler rational functions and then antidifferentiate the terms separately.

First examples: The method in action

Before describing the method in full theoretical regalia, we use several examples to introduce the general discussion that follows.

EXAMPLE 1 Find $\int \dfrac{2}{1-x^2}\,dx$.

Solution The problem looks hard at first glance. The integrand doesn't match any of our standard basic forms, and neither u-substitution nor integration by parts looks promising. →

Some clever substitution might succeed, but probably with more labor than necessary.

The new trick is to rewrite the integrand as a sum of two *simpler* terms, as follows:

$$\frac{2}{1-x^2} = \frac{2}{(1+x)(1-x)} = \frac{1}{1+x} + \frac{1}{1-x}. \qquad (1)$$

The last two summands are the **partial fractions** (i.e., parts of the original fraction) for which the method is named.

We'll explain soon how we *found* Equation (1). But notice now that, once written down, the equation is easy to *check*. Notice also that Equation (1) makes the antiderivative problem much easier. Each summand on the right is easy to antidifferentiate, and adding the results completes the problem. Here are the details: →

Watch the minus signs.

$$\int \frac{2}{1-x^2}\,dx = \int \frac{dx}{1+x} + \int \frac{dx}{1-x} = \ln|1+x| - \ln|1-x| + C.$$

Differentiation shows that the answer is right:

$$\left(\ln|1+x| - \ln|1-x| + C\right)' = \frac{1}{1+x} - \frac{-1}{1-x} = \frac{2}{1-x^2}$$

as claimed. ∎

The TI-89 and other computer tools will expand rational functions in partial fractions; the ideas here can help demystify the process.

EXAMPLE 2 Find $\int \dfrac{2+5x+3x^2+3x^3}{x(1+x^2)(x+2)}\,dx$.

Solution It's easy to *check* (but harder to guess) that

$$\frac{2+5x+3x^2+3x^3}{x(1+x^2)(x+2)} = \frac{1}{x} + \frac{1}{1+x^2} + \frac{2}{x+2}.$$

With the integrand subdivided into partial fractions, the problem is now easy to conquer:

$$\int \frac{2+5x+3x^2+3x^3}{x(1+x^2)(x+2)}\,dx = \int \frac{dx}{x} + \int \frac{dx}{1+x^2} + \int \frac{2}{x+2}\,dx$$

$$= \ln|x| + \arctan x + 2\ln|x+2| + C.$$

Notice the curious pattern, which is one we'll see repeatedly: Antidifferentiating a rational function produces a combination of logs and arctangents. ∎

EXAMPLE 3 Find $\int \dfrac{x^3}{1+x^2}\,dx$.

Solution In this case the denominator cannot be factored. But the numerator has degree three and the denominator only two, and so we can long divide the numerator by the denominator. Here's the result:

Students may not know or remember how to long divide polynomials; simple examples should suffice.

$$\frac{x^3}{1+x^2} = x - \frac{x}{1+x^2}.$$

Again we've rewritten the integrand as the sum of simpler terms, each of which is relatively easy to antidifferentiate: →

For the second integral, substitute $u = 1+x^2$.

$$\int x\,dx - \int \frac{x}{1+x^2}\,dx = \frac{x^2}{2} - \frac{1}{2}\ln|1+x^2| + C.$$

∎

Authors have been known to rig problems.

Good news: The method works—in principle   We've seen that not *every* elementary function has an elementary antiderivative, but must every *rational* function have one? True, we found a nice antiderivative in each of the preceding examples, but maybe that was just luck. ◄

In fact, every rational function *does* have an elementary antiderivative, which involves *only* the ingredients seen in the preceding examples: logarithms, arctangents, and rational functions. A fully rigorous proof of this fact would take us somewhat beyond our mathematical depth, but we remark that partial fractions play a key role.

Knowing that an antiderivative formula exists is one thing; finding one explicitly is quite another. The hardest problem is usually algebraic—rewriting the given rational function as a sum of partial fractions. Once this is done, antidifferentiating the separate pieces is usually relatively easy. Because the method itself is our main interest, we'll arrange to keep the algebra simple.

Students should notice the analogy between rational numbers and rational functions: writing 1/6 as 1/2 − 1/3 decomposes 1/6 into numerical "partial fractions."

Rational numbers, rational functions, and partial fractions

Rational *functions* are like rational *numbers* in that both are quotients of simpler objects. Many of the standard ideas, operations, and vocabulary that apply to ordinary fractions apply to rational functions too.

Proper vs. improper   A positive rational number p/q is called **improper** if $p \geq q$. Any improper fraction can be written as the sum of an integer and a proper fraction. For example,

$$\frac{29}{6} = 4 + \frac{5}{6};$$

the numbers 4 and 5 can be found by long dividing 29 by 6.

Rational *functions* behave similarly to rational *numbers*. A rational function $r(x) = p(x)/q(x)$ is **proper** if p has lower degree than q; otherwise, r is **improper**. (The integrand in Example 3 is improper.) The analogy with rational numbers continues:

> *Any improper rational function can be written as the sum of a polynomial and a proper rational function.*

For instance,

$$\frac{x}{x+1} = 1 - \frac{1}{x+1}; \qquad \frac{x^2}{x+1} = x - 1 + \frac{1}{x+1}.$$

As with ordinary fractions, the right sides of these equations can be found by long division.

Miss Manners would approve.   Rational functions, no matter how "improper," commit no breach of morals or manners. Learning such quaint jargon is, depending on one's point of view, either part of the fun of mathematics or an annoying obstacle.

Partial fractions—of numbers and of polynomials   Any rational *number* m/n can be written as a sum or difference of fractions of a special type: fractions whose denominators are the prime factors of n or powers thereof. For example, 6 has prime factors 2 and 3, and

$$\frac{5}{6} = \frac{5}{2 \cdot 3} = \frac{1}{2} + \frac{1}{3}; \qquad \frac{5}{12} = \frac{5}{2^2 \cdot 3} = \frac{3}{4} - \frac{1}{3}.$$

The idea for rational functions is similar. Any rational function $p(x)/q(x)$ can be written as the sum of **partial fractions**—that is, other rational functions whose denominators are either **irreducible factors** of $q(x)$ or powers thereof. (An **irreducible** polynomial is one that cannot be written as a product of lower-order factors.) ➙ We used this idea when we wrote

Irreducible factors are analogous to prime numbers: neither can be factored.

$$\frac{p(x)}{q(x)} = \frac{2 + 5x + 3x^2 + 3x^3}{x(1 + x^2)(x + 2)} = \frac{1}{x} + \frac{1}{1 + x^2} + \frac{2}{x + 2}.$$

Notice especially the denominators on the right: Each one is an irreducible factor of $q(x)$.

Two basic forms   All this jargon may sound formidably abstract. Indeed, the theory of polynomials and rational functions *is* a formidable subject, but we need to examine just the tip of that iceberg. Only the following facts will matter to us:

Students may know very little polynomial algebra; this is just a taste.

- **Factoring:**   Every polynomial can be written as a product of *linear* and *quadratic* factors.
- **Recognizing irreducible factors:**   Linear polynomials are automatically irreducible, but a quadratic polynomial $q(x) = ax^2 + bx + c$ may or may not have linear factors, depending on whether or not q has roots. The quadratic formula tells which is the case: If $b^2 - 4ac < 0$, then q has no roots and so can't be factored. If $b^2 - 4ac \geq 0$, then q has roots and can be factored.
- **Proper behavior:**   Any *proper* rational function can be written as a sum of *proper* partial fractions.

Two main types   The situation boils down to the fact that any proper rational function can be written as a sum of partial fractions of just two basic types:

$$\text{Type I:} \quad \frac{A}{(ax + b)^n}; \quad \text{Type II:} \quad \frac{Ax + B}{(ax^2 + bx + c)^n}.$$

(In each case n is a positive integer; a, b, c, A, and B are real constants.) Antidifferentiating *any* rational function, therefore, reduces to antidifferentiating these two basic types.

Type I antiderivatives   Partial fractions of the first type are always easy to antidifferentiate. The substitution $u = ax + b$ succeeds; here are the results:

$$\int \frac{A}{(ax + b)^n} \, dx = \begin{cases} \dfrac{A}{a} \ln |ax + b| & \text{if } n = 1; \\[2ex] \dfrac{A}{a(1 - n)(ax + b)^{n-1}} & \text{if } n > 1. \end{cases}$$

The general formula may look forbidding, but in most actual cases antidifferentiation is easy.

EXAMPLE 4   Find $\displaystyle\int \frac{6}{2x + 1} \, dx$ and $\displaystyle\int \frac{6}{(2x + 1)^5} \, dx.$

Solution   For both integrals, substituting $u = 2x + 1$ and $du = 2 \, dx$ does the trick:

$$\int \frac{6}{2x + 1} \, dx = \int \frac{3}{u} \, du = 3 \ln |2x + 1| + C;$$

$$\int \frac{6}{(2x + 1)^5} \, dx = \int \frac{3}{u^5} \, du = -\frac{3}{4(2x + 1)^4} + C. \qquad \blacksquare$$

Type II antiderivatives   Antidifferentiating partial fractions of the form

$$\frac{Ax + B}{(ax^2 + bx + c)^n}$$

can be quite messy, especially if $n > 1$. In that case, reduction formulas can be used to reduce the exponent n.

For $n = 1$, **completing the square** in the denominator simplifies things considerably, as the next example illustrates.

EXAMPLE 5   Find $\displaystyle\int \frac{dx}{x^2 + 2x + 2}$ and $\displaystyle\int \frac{2x + 3}{x^2 + 2x + 2}\,dx$.

Solution   Because $b^2 - 4ac < 0$, the denominator is irreducible; factoring is impossible. So let's complete the square:

$$\frac{1}{x^2 + 2x + 2} = \frac{1}{x^2 + 2x + 1 + 1} = \frac{1}{(x+1)^2 + 1}.$$

Now we substitute $u = x + 1$ and $du = dx$ in both integrals. The first integral becomes

$$\int \frac{dx}{(x+1)^2 + 1} = \int \frac{du}{u^2 + 1} = \arctan(x + 1) + C.$$

The same substitution in the second integral gives

$$\int \frac{2x + 3}{x^2 + 2x + 2}\,dx = \int \frac{2(u - 1) + 3}{u^2 + 1}\,du \qquad (u = x + 1 \text{ implies } x = u - 1)$$

$$= \int \frac{2u + 1}{u^2 + 1}\,du$$

$$= \int \frac{2u}{u^2 + 1}\,du + \int \frac{du}{u^2 + 1}$$

$$= \ln|u^2 + 1| + \arctan u + C$$

$$= \ln|x^2 + 2x + 2| + \arctan(x + 1) + C,$$

which completes the problem.   ∎

We did another reality check for integration by parts.

Reality check: A graphical interlude

We've been throwing plenty of symbols around, but does it all make sense? We've seen, for instance, that antidifferentiating rational functions seems to spawn logarithms and arctangents. When the dust cleared in Example 2, for instance, we concluded that

$$\int \frac{2 + 5x + 3x^2 + 3x^3}{x(1 + x^2)(x + 2)}\,dx = \ln|x| + \arctan x + 2\ln|x + 2| + C.$$

Note that the logs in F can be "seen" in the F-graph's long-term behavior.

A look at graphs helps explain the presence of these ingredients. Figure 1 shows graphs of the integrand f and an antiderivative F.

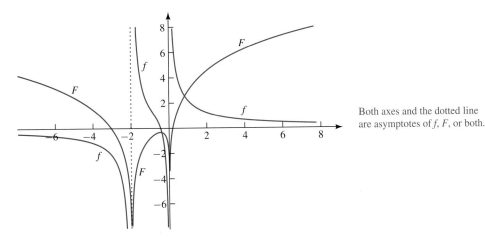

Both axes and the dotted line are asymptotes of f, F, or both.

FIGURE 1
A rational function f and an antiderivative F

The graphs are complicated (like the functions themselves), but they show the right things:

- **Two vertical asymptotes:** The integrand f has vertical asymptotes at $x = -2$ and $x = 0$; they correspond to the factors $(x + 2)$ and x in the denominator. The antiderivative F also has two vertical asymptotes, at the same places. Near these values of x, the F-graph resembles a logarithmic function. The remaining factor in the denominator, $(1 + x^2)$, is never zero, and so it contributes no vertical asymptotes either to f or to F.

- **In the long run:** The general shape of the F-graph looks roughly logarithmic as $x \to \pm\infty$. As $x \to \infty$, for instance, the F-graph is increasing and concave down just like a logarithmic function. Here's an intuitive explanation for this "log-like" behavior. Expanding the denominator of f gives

$$f(x) = \frac{2 + 5x + 3x^2 + 3x^3}{x(1 + x^2)(x + 2)} = \frac{2 + 5x + 3x^2 + 3x^3}{2x + x^2 + 2x^3 + x^4}.$$

For large $|x|$ the highest powers in the numerator and denominator "dominate," and so

$$f(x) = \frac{2 + 5x + 3x^2 + 3x^3}{2x + x^2 + 2x^3 + x^4} \approx \frac{3x^3}{x^4} = \frac{3}{x}.$$

Thus, for large positive x we have

$$F(x) \approx \int \frac{3}{x}\,dx = 3\ln|x| + C,$$

which corresponds to the log-like shape of F to the right of Figure 1.

Last, not least: How to find the partial fractions

We've seen *why* we'd want to write a rational function as a sum of partial fractions but not yet *how* to do so. How, for instance, did we arrive at the equation

$$\frac{2 + 5x + 3x^2 + 3x^3}{x(1 + x^2)(x + 2)} = \frac{1}{x} + \frac{1}{1 + x^2} + \frac{2}{x + 2}$$

in Example 2?

Writing a rational function $p(x)/q(x)$ as a sum of partial fractions takes four steps:

- **Make it proper:** If $p(x)/q(x)$ is improper, use long division to rewrite it as the sum of a polynomial and a proper rational function.
- **Factor q:** Write the denominator $q(x)$ as a product of linear and irreducible quadratic factors; some may be repeated.
- **Write as a sum:** Write $p(x)/q(x)$ as a sum of partial fractions with **undetermined coefficients** (represented by letters) in their numerators.
- **Find the coefficients:** Solve one or more algebraic equations to find numerical values for the coefficients.

The first two steps are straightforward; the last two need elaboration.

Writing the integrand as a sum   As earlier examples show, each partial fraction summand comes from some factor of the denominator of the original rational function. For instance, we expect a partial fraction sum of the general form

$$\frac{2+5x+3x^2+3x^3}{x(1+x^2)(x+2)} = \frac{A}{x} + \frac{Bx+C}{1+x^2} + \frac{D}{x+2}$$

for the rational function on the left; note that one partial fraction corresponds to each irreducible factor of the denominator. Because the middle summand has a *quadratic* denominator, its numerator can have degree up to 1 but no higher. The other summands, which have *linear* denominators, can have only constant numerators. (Otherwise, a summand would be improper.)

We deemphasize repeated factors to avoid undue distraction.

Repeated factors   The general form of an answer is slightly different if the denominator has a **repeated factor**—that is, a factor that appears to a power higher than 1. Each such factor contributes several partial fractions—one for each power of the factor—to the general form. For example, the partial fraction version of

$$\frac{1}{x^3(x^2+1)^2(x+1)}$$

has the general form

$$\frac{A}{x} + \frac{B}{x^2} + \frac{C}{x^3} + \frac{Dx+E}{x^2+1} + \frac{Fx+G}{(x^2+1)^2} + \frac{H}{x+1}.$$

(These "extra" summands are necessary to guarantee that a partial fraction form exists.)

Finding values for the coefficients   Finding numerical values for the unknown constants $A, B, C, \ldots$ is a problem in *algebra*. (The calculus part comes later.) Examples of several techniques follow.

Math jargon—impress your friends.

EXAMPLE 6 (The simplest case: only linear factors) Derive the **partial fraction decomposition** ←

$$\frac{2}{(1+x)(1-x)} = \frac{1}{1+x} + \frac{1}{1-x}.$$

(We used it in Example 1, page 467.)

Solution   The denominator's factors show that we need constants A and B such that

$$\frac{2}{(1+x)(1-x)} = \frac{A}{1+x} + \frac{B}{1-x}.$$

Multiplying both sides by $(1+x)(1-x)$ clears out the denominators; we get

$$2 = A(1-x) + B(1+x). \qquad (2)$$

Now it's easy to find A and B. One way is to multiply out the right side and collect like powers of x:

$$2 = A(1-x) + B(1+x) = A - Ax + B + Bx = (A+B) + (B-A)x.$$

Equating powers of x on the far left and far right shows that $A + B = 2$ and $B - A = 0$, and so $A = B = 1$ as claimed earlier.

   Another, perhaps simpler, route to the same result is to plug cleverly chosen values of x into Equation (2). Doing so may make the appropriate values of A and B obvious. If, say, $x = 1$, then Equation (2) becomes simply $2 = 2B$, and so $B = 1$. Similarly, plugging $x = -1$ into Equation (2) yields $2 = 2A$, or $A = 1$. ■

E X A M P L E 7   (One irreducible quadratic) It's not hard to *check* that

$$\frac{2 + 5x + 3x^2 + 3x^3}{x(1+x^2)(x+2)} = \frac{1}{x} + \frac{1}{1+x^2} + \frac{2}{x+2}. \qquad (3)$$

Explain how to *find* this equation.

Solution The form of the denominator on the left means that we want constants A, B, C, and D such that

$$\frac{2 + 5x + 3x^2 + 3x^3}{x(1+x^2)(x+2)} = \frac{A}{x} + \frac{Bx+C}{1+x^2} + \frac{D}{x+2}.$$

We'll find these constants by solving an appropriate set of equations.

   Multiplying both sides by the denominator on the left and collecting powers of x gives the new equation

$$\begin{aligned}
2 + 5x + 3x^2 + 3x^3 &= A(1+x^2)(x+2) + (Bx+C)x(x+2) + Dx(1+x^2) \\
&= 2A + (A+2C+D)x + (2A+2B+C)x^2 + (A+B+D)x^3.
\end{aligned}$$

Equating coefficients of powers of x in the first and the last expressions gives *four* equations in *four* unknowns:

$$2 = 2A; \quad 5 = A + 2C + D; \quad 3 = 2A + 2B + C; \quad 3 = A + B + D.$$

Solving these equations simultaneously takes some algebraic work (by hand or by calculator), but the process is straightforward. The results are $A = 1$, $B = 0$, $C = 1$, and $D = 2$; replacing these symbols with their values produces Equation (3). ■

B A S I C   E X E R C I S E S

1. (a) Verify, by adding the terms on the right, that
$$\frac{2}{1-x^2} = \frac{1}{1+x} + \frac{1}{1-x}.$$

   (b) Use part (a) to show that $\displaystyle\int \frac{dx}{1-x^2} = \frac{1}{2}\ln\left|\frac{1+x}{1-x}\right| + C$, where C is a constant.

2. Verify, by adding the terms on the right, that
$$\frac{2 + 5x + 3x^2 + 3x^3}{x(1+x^2)(x+2)} = \frac{1}{x} + \frac{1}{1+x^2} + \frac{2}{x+2}.$$

3. Use the algebraic identity $x^3 = x(1+x^2) - x$ to find the partial fraction decomposition of $x^3/(1+x^2)$.

4. (a) Use the algebraic identity $x = (x+1) - 1$ to find the partial fraction decomposition of $x/(1+x)$.

   (b) Find the partial fraction decomposition of $x^2/(1+x)$.

5. (a) Verify, by adding the terms on the right, that
$$\frac{5x+7}{(x+1)(x+2)} = \frac{2}{x+1} + \frac{3}{x+2}.$$

   (b) Find $\displaystyle\int \frac{5x+7}{(x+1)(x+2)}\,dx.$

6. Suppose that $p(x) = \dfrac{4x^2 + 3x + 2}{x^2(x+1)}$.

   (a) Can constants A and B be chosen so that $p(x) = \dfrac{A}{x} + \dfrac{B}{x+1}$? Justify your answer.

   (b) Can constants A and B be chosen so that $p(x) = \dfrac{A}{x^2} + \dfrac{B}{x+1}$? Justify your answer.

   (c) Find constants A and B so that $p(x) = \dfrac{A}{x} + \dfrac{B}{x^2} + \dfrac{C}{x+1}$.

   (d) Find $\displaystyle\int p(x)\,dx$.

7. Let $f(x) = \dfrac{x^2 + 1}{(x-1)^2}$.

   (a) Explain why f is a rational function.

   (b) Explain why f is not a proper rational function.

   (c) Write f as the sum of a polynomial and a proper rational function.

   (d) Use part (c) to find an antiderivative of f.

8. Let $g(x) = \dfrac{(x+1)^3}{x^2 + x + 1}$.

   (a) Explain why g is a rational function.

   (b) Is g is a proper rational function? Justify your answer.

   (c) Write g as the sum of a polynomial and a proper rational function.

   (d) Use part (c) to find an antiderivative of g.

9. Suppose that $q(x) = (x-2)(x^2 + 2x + 3)$ and that $f(x) = p(x)/q(x)$ is a proper rational function. Is $\dfrac{A}{x-2} + \dfrac{Bx+C}{x^2 + 2x + 3}$ the partial fraction decomposition of f? Justify your answer.

10. Suppose that $q(x) = (x+1)(x^2 - 3x + 4)$ and that $g(x) = p(x)/q(x)$ is a proper rational function. Find the form of the partial fraction decomposition of g. (Your answer will involve unknown constant coefficients.)

11. Suppose that $q(x) = (x+1)(x^2 - 2x + 1)$ and that $g(x) = p(x)/q(x)$ is a proper rational function. Is $\dfrac{A}{x+1} + \dfrac{Bx+C}{x^2 - 2x + 1}$ the partial fraction decomposition of g? Justify your answer.

12. Suppose that $q(x) = (x+1)(x^2 + 2x + 1)$ and that $g(x) = p(x)/q(x)$ is a proper rational function. Is $\dfrac{A}{x+1} + \dfrac{Bx+C}{x^2 + 2x + 1}$ the partial fraction decomposition of g? Justify your answer.

13. Suppose that $q(x) = (x+1)^2(x^2 + 1)$ and that $h(x) = p(x)/q(x)$ is a proper rational function. Is $\dfrac{A}{(x+1)^2} + \dfrac{Bx+C}{x^2 + 1}$ the partial fraction decomposition of h? Justify your answer.

14. Suppose that $q(x) = (x+1)(x^2 + 1)^3$ and that $k(x) = p(x)/q(x)$ is a proper rational function. Is $\dfrac{A}{x+1} + \dfrac{Bx+C}{(x^2+1)^3}$ the partial fraction decomposition of k? Justify your answer.

15. Consider the partial fraction decomposition equation
$$\frac{x^2 + 3x - 1}{x(x+1)(x-2)} = \frac{A}{x} + \frac{B}{x+1} + \frac{C}{x-2}.$$

   (a) Multiply both sides of this equation by x and then substitute $x = 0$ to show that $A = 1/2$.

   (b) Multiply both sides of this equation by $x+1$ and then substitute $x = -1$ to show that $B = 1$.

   (c) Multiply both sides of this equation by $x-2$ and then substitute $x = 2$ to show that $C = 3/2$.

   (d) Find $\displaystyle\int \frac{x^2 + 3x - 1}{x(x+1)(x-2)}\,dx$.

16. (a) Use the technique illustrated in parts (a)–(c) of Exercise 15 to find values of the constants A, B, and C such that
$$\frac{6}{(x-2)(x^2-1)} = \frac{A}{x-2} + \frac{B}{x-1} + \frac{C}{x+1}.$$

   (b) Find $\displaystyle\int \frac{6}{(x-2)(x^2-1)}\,dx$.

17. Find $\displaystyle\int \frac{x^2 + 2x + 5}{(x-1)(x+1)(x+2)}\,dx$.

18. Find $\displaystyle\int \frac{x^2 + 2x + 5}{x(x^2-4)}\,dx$.

19. Consider the partial fraction decomposition equation
$$\frac{x^2 - 1}{x(x^2+4)} = \frac{A}{x} + \frac{Bx+C}{x^2+4}.$$

   (a) Multiply both sides of this equation by x and then substitute $x = 0$ to show that $A = -1/4$.

   (b) Substitute $x = 1$ into this equation to show that $B + C = 5/4$.

   (c) Substitute $x = -1$ into this equation to show that $B - C = 5/4$.

   (d) Use parts (b) and (c) to show that $B = 5/4$ and $C = 0$.

   (e) Find $\displaystyle\int \frac{x^2 - 1}{x(x^2+4)}\,dx$.

20. Find $\displaystyle\int \frac{3x^2 + 7x + 5}{(x+1)(x^2 + 2x + 2)}\,dx$.

21. Is there a quadratic polynomial $q(x)$ such that $4/(1-x) + 5\ln(3+x) + C$ is an antiderivative of $q(x)/((1-x)^2(3+x))$? If so, find it. If not, explain why no such polynomial q exists.

22. Is there a quadratic polynomial $q(x)$ such that $4/(1-x) + 5\ln(3+x) + C$ is an antiderivative of $q(x)/((1-x^2)(3+x))$? If so, find it. If not, explain why no such polynomial q exists.

23. Is there a quadratic polynomial $q(x)$ such that $2/(1-x) + \arcsin x + \ln(3+x) + C$ is an antiderivative of $q(x)/((1-x)^2(3+x))$? If so, find it. If not, explain why no such polynomial q exists.

24. Is there a quadratic polynomial $q(x)$ such that $4/(1-x)^2 + 5\ln|x+3| + C$ is $\displaystyle\int \frac{q(x)}{(1-x)^2(x+3)}\,dx$? If so find it. If not, explain why no such polynomial q exists.

FURTHER EXERCISES

25. Consider the partial fraction decomposition

$$\frac{x^2}{(x+1)^3} = \frac{A}{x+1} + \frac{B}{(x+1)^2} + \frac{C}{(x+1)^3}.$$

(a) Multiply both sides of the equation by $(x+1)^3$ and then substitute $x = -1$ to show that $C = 1$.

(b) Substitute $x = 0$ into the equation to show that $A + B = -1$.

(c) Substitute $x = 1$ into the equation to show that $2A + B = 0$.

(d) Use parts (b) and (c) to show that $A = 1$ and $B = -2$.

(e) Find $\displaystyle\int \frac{x^2}{(x+1)^3}\, dx$.

26. Find $\displaystyle\int \frac{2-x}{x^2(x+2)}\, dx$.

27. Let $p(x) = (x+1)(x-2)$.

(a) Find the partial fraction decomposition of $1/p(x)$.

(b) Find the partial fraction decomposition of $x/p(x)$.

(c) Use parts (a) and (b) to find $\displaystyle\int \frac{4-3x}{(x+1)(x-2)}\, dx$.

28. Let $p(x) = (x-2)(x+3)$.

(a) Find the partial fraction decomposition of $1/p(x)$.

(b) Find the partial fraction decomposition of $x/p(x)$.

(c) Find $\displaystyle\int \frac{4x+5}{(x-2)(x+3)}\, dx$.

29. Let $p(x) = (x-1)(x^2+1)$.

(a) Find the partial fraction decomposition of $1/p(x)$.

(b) Find the partial fraction decomposition of $x/p(x)$.

(c) Find the partial fraction decomposition of $x^2/p(x)$.

(d) Use parts (a)–(c) to find $\displaystyle\int \frac{2+3x+4x^2}{(x-1)(x^2+1)}\, dx$.

30. Let $p(x) = (x+2)(x^2+2x+5)$.

(a) Find the partial fraction decomposition of $1/p(x)$.

(b) Find the partial fraction decomposition of $x/p(x)$.

(c) Find the partial fraction decomposition of $x^2/p(x)$.

(d) Find $\displaystyle\int \frac{3-4x+5x^2}{(x+2)(x^2+2x+5)}\, dx$.

31. Evaluate $\displaystyle\int_0^1 \frac{dx}{(x-2)(x^2+1)}$.

32. Evaluate $\displaystyle\int_0^2 \frac{dx}{x^3+1}$. [HINT: $x^3 + 1 = (x+1)(x^2 - x + 1)$.]

In Exercises 33–40, find the antiderivative.

33. $\displaystyle\int \frac{2x+1}{(x-2)(x+3)}\, dx$

34. $\displaystyle\int \frac{x+1}{(x-1)(x+2)}\, dx$

35. $\displaystyle\int \frac{5x^2+3x-2}{x^3+2x^2}\, dx$

36. $\displaystyle\int \frac{4x^2-3x+2}{x\,(2x-1)^2}\, dx$

37. $\displaystyle\int \frac{x^4}{x^4-1}\, dx$

38. $\displaystyle\int \frac{x^3}{x^2+1}\, dx$

39. $\displaystyle\int \frac{x^3}{x^2-1}\, dx$

40. $\displaystyle\int \frac{3x^2-1}{(x-1)(x+2)}\, dx$

41. Use the substitution $u = \sqrt{x+1}$ to find $\displaystyle\int \frac{dx}{x\sqrt{x+1}}$.

42. Use the substitution $u = \sqrt{x-1}$ to find $\displaystyle\int \frac{dx}{x\sqrt{x-1}}$.

43. (a) Show that $\displaystyle\int \frac{dx}{x+c} = \ln|x+c|$.

(b) Let n be an integer such that $n > 1$. Show that

$$\int \frac{dx}{(x+c)^n} = \frac{1}{(1-n)(x+c)^{n-1}}.$$

(c) Use parts (a) and (b) to show that, if $a \neq 0$,

$$\int \frac{dx}{(ax+b)^n} = \begin{cases} a^{-1}\ln|ax+b| & \text{if } n = 1 \\ a^{-1}(1-n)^{-1}(ax+b)^{1-n} & \text{if } n > 1. \end{cases}$$

44. Show that $\displaystyle\int \frac{dx}{x^2+d^2} = \frac{1}{|d|}\arctan\left(\frac{x}{|d|}\right)$.

45. Show that $\displaystyle\int \frac{x}{x^2+d^2}\, dx = \frac{1}{2}\ln(x^2+d^2)$.

46. Let n be an integer such that $n \geq 1$.

(a) Use integration by parts to show that

$$\int \frac{dx}{(x^2+d^2)^n} = \frac{x}{(x^2+d^2)^n} + 2n\int \frac{x^2}{(x^2+d^2)^{n+1}}\, dx.$$

(b) Use the result in part (a) and the algebraic identity $x^2 = (x^2+d^2) - d^2$ to show that

$$\int \frac{dx}{(x^2+d^2)^{n+1}} = \frac{1}{2nd^2}\frac{x}{(x^2+d^2)^n} + \frac{2n-1}{2nd^2}\int \frac{dx}{(x^2+d^2)^n}.$$

47. Let $n \geq 2$ be an integer. Show that $\displaystyle\int \frac{x}{(x^2+d^2)^n}\, dx = \frac{1}{2(1-n)(x^2+d^2)^{n-1}}$.

8.3 TRIGONOMETRIC ANTIDERIVATIVES

First we consider integrands that are powers of trigonometric functions. Then we try to reduce integrals with radicals to this form. The section offers students a good workout with trigonometric identities and algebra.

The symbolic antidifferentiation methods we've developed so far—u-substitution, integration by parts, and partial fractions—handle many, but not all, classes of functions. In this section we consider functions that involve two special ingredients: powers of trigonometric functions and roots of quadratic expressions. Here are some examples:

$$\int \sin^2 x \cos^3 x \, dx = \frac{\sin^3 x}{3} - \frac{\sin^5 x}{5} + C;$$

$$\int \sqrt{-x^2 - 2x} \, dx = \frac{1}{2}\left((x+1)\sqrt{-x^2 - 2x} + \arcsin(x+1)\right) + C.$$

It's easy enough to *check* these answers by differentiation, but it's less obvious how they were found.

This section contains no completely new or different ideas or methods. We explore, mainly through examples, how methods of earlier sections can be combined with properties of trigonometric and algebraic functions to handle these new classes of antiderivatives—and reveal some unexpected connections between them.

Mathematica and similar technologies easily handle trigonometric antiderivatives—but answers often appear in other forms.

Powers of trigonometric functions

Consider the following antiderivatives, all of which involve positive integer powers of the six trigonometric functions:

$$\int \cos^3 x \, dx \qquad\qquad \int \cos^3 x \sin^4 x \, dx$$

$$\int \cos^2 x \sin^3 x \tan^2 x \, dx \qquad \int \sec^3 x \tan^3 x \, dx$$

Antiderivatives of all these functions can be found in elementary form by combining substitution, integration by parts, and (sometimes) well-chosen trigonometric identities.

Useful properties of trigonometric functions   Several properties of, and relations among, the trigonometric functions will be useful as we hunt for antiderivatives.

- **Two main types:** All six trigonometric functions are defined in terms of sines and cosines. It follows that *every* product of integer powers of trigonometric functions can be written in the form $\sin^n x \cos^m x$, where n and m are (not necessarily positive) integer powers. For instance,

$$\cos^4 x \sin^3 x \tan^2 x = \cos^4 x \sin^3 x \frac{\sin^2 x}{\cos^2 x} = \cos^2 x \sin^5 x.$$

In mathspeak, "in principle" means "it's possible—but probably a lot of work."

In principle, every function of the form $\sin^n x \cos^m x$ can be antidifferentiated, though the process might be tedious and messy. ◄

Finding trigonometric antiderivatives is less messy when only *nonnegative* powers are involved. If negative powers occur, it may help to rewrite a function in terms of positive powers of secants and tangents. For instance,

$$\cos^{-5} x \sin^2 x = \cos^{-3} x \frac{\sin^2 x}{\cos^2 x} = \sec^3 x \tan^2 x.$$

In this section, therefore, we mainly consider integrals of two types:

$$\int \sin^n x \cos^m x \, dx \qquad \text{and} \qquad \int \sec^n x \tan^m x \, dx,$$

where m and n are nonnegative integers.

- **Reduction formulas:** If either $n = 0$ or $m = 0$ in the preceding forms, then the integral can be handled—with care—using one of the following reduction formulas:

$$\int \sin^n x \, dx = -\frac{\sin^{n-1} x \cos x}{n} + \frac{n-1}{n} \int \sin^{n-2} x \, dx \qquad (n \neq 0)$$

$$\int \cos^n x \, dx = \frac{\cos^{n-1} x \sin x}{n} + \frac{n-1}{n} \int \cos^{n-2} x \, dx \qquad (n \neq 0)$$

$$\int \tan^n x \, dx = \frac{\tan^{n-1} x}{n-1} - \int \tan^{n-2} x \, dx \qquad (n \neq 1)$$

$$\int \sec^n x \, dx = \frac{\sec^{n-2} x \tan x}{n-1} + \frac{n-2}{n-1} \int \sec^{n-2} x \, dx. \qquad (n \neq 1)$$

Large powers may require *repeated* use of the reduction formulas.

- **Using trigonometric identities:** Many integrands can be simplified to one of the preceding forms by using either the **Pythagorean identities**

$$\sin^2 x + \cos^2 x = 1; \qquad \tan^2 x + 1 = \sec^2 x,$$

or the **double-angle formulas**

$$\sin^2 x = \frac{1}{2} - \frac{\cos(2x)}{2}; \qquad \cos^2 x = \frac{1}{2} + \frac{\cos(2x)}{2}.$$

(These could also be called *half-angle formulas*, depending on the direction in which you read the equations.) The first two identities permit us, in effect, to trade sines for cosines, secants for tangents, and vice versa. The double-angle formulas can be used to convert even *powers* of sines and cosines to cosines of even *multiples* of x.

- **Disguised results:** Trigonometric functions are masters of disguise. For example, $f(x) = 2 \sin x \cos x$ and $g(x) = \sin(2x)$ look different but are actually the same function. This ability to change appearance is often helpful, but it can also be misleading. Beware . . . .

The point about alternative forms of an answer bears repeating—especially for trigonometric functions.

Some concrete examples will illustrate the use of these facts in finding antiderivatives.

EXAMPLE 1 Find $\int \cos^3 x \, dx$.

Solution With the substitution $u = \sin x$ in mind, we reserve one power of the cosine for du and convert the other two powers to sines:

$$\int \cos^2 x \cos x \, dx = \int (1 - \sin^2 x) \cos x \, dx$$

$$= \int (1 - u^2) \, du = \sin x - \frac{\sin^3 x}{3} + C.$$

We could, instead, have used the reduction formula for powers of cosines:

$$\int \cos^3 x \, dx = \frac{\cos^2 x \sin x}{3} + \frac{2}{3} \int \cos x \, dx = \frac{\cos^2 x \sin x + 2 \sin x}{3} + C.$$

Despite first appearances, the two answers are equal. ∎

EXAMPLE 2 Find $\int \sin^4 x \, dx$.

Solution We use the double-angle formulas to rewrite the integrand in terms of $\cos(2x)$ and $\cos(4x)$, as follows:

$$\sin^4 x = (\sin^2 x)^2 = \left(\frac{1}{2} - \frac{\cos(2x)}{2} \right)^2 = \frac{1}{4} - \frac{\cos(2x)}{2} + \frac{\cos^2(2x)}{4}.$$

The first two summands are easy to integrate. To handle the last summand we can apply the double-angle formula *again* to get

$$\frac{\cos^2(2x)}{4} = \frac{1}{8} + \frac{\cos(4x)}{8},$$

which is another manageable integrand. Here's the result:

$$\int \sin^4 x \, dx = \frac{x}{4} - \frac{\sin(2x)}{4} + \frac{x}{8} + \frac{\sin(4x)}{32} + C.$$

Other approaches to the same problem may produce equivalent—but different-looking—answers. ◄

Try a TI–89 or other technology, for instance.

EXAMPLE 3 Find $\int \cos^3 x \sin^4 x \, dx$.

Solution One strategy is to convert all the sines to cosines and then attack the result with the reduction formula for powers of cosines. Instead, we substitute $u = \sin x$, $du = \cos x \, dx$. We chip off one power of $\cos x$ to use in the du factor and convert the remaining (two) powers of cosine to sines:

$$\int \cos^3 x \sin^4 x \, dx = \int (1 - \sin^2 x)(\sin^4 x) \cos x \, dx = \int (1 - u^2) u^4 \, du.$$

The last integral is simple; we'll leave it alone. ■

EXAMPLE 4 Find $\int \sec^3 x \tan^3 x \, dx$.

Solution We substitute $u = \sec x$ and $du = \sec x \tan x \, dx$ and then convert the remaining tangents to secants:

$$\int \sec^3 x \tan^3 x \, dx = \int \sec^2 x \tan^2 x (\sec x \tan x) \, dx$$

$$= \int \sec^2 x (\sec^2 x - 1)(\sec x \tan x) \, dx$$

$$= \int u^2 (u^2 - 1) \, du,$$

and the rest is easy. ■

The main strategy is to use substitution to transform antiderivatives with radicals to antiderivatives that involve trigonometric powers.

Trigonometric substitutions

Trigonometric substitution is a special case of the general idea of u-substitution, but is tailored especially to handle integrands that involve roots of quadratic expressions. The simplest such expressions are

$$\sqrt{a^2 - x^2}, \quad \sqrt{x^2 - a^2}, \quad \text{and} \quad \sqrt{a^2 + x^2},$$

where a is a positive constant. That *trigonometric* functions come up at all in such integrals may be surprising—so far there's nothing obviously trigonometric in sight. Yet it does turn out that carefully chosen substitutions, with trigonometric ingredients, can reduce integrals of the present type to powers of trigonometric functions. A simple example (well, relatively simple) illustrates the method and some of the subtleties involved.

EXAMPLE 5   According to our integral table,

$$\int \sqrt{4 - x^2} \, dx = \frac{x\sqrt{4 - x^2}}{2} + 2 \arcsin\left(\frac{x}{2}\right).$$

We could check this formula by differentiation, but how was it found?

Solution   If we substitute $x = 2\sin t$, then $dx = 2\cos t \, dt$, and a little algebra produce a simpler-looking integral:

$$\int \sqrt{4 - x^2} \, dx = 2 \int \sqrt{4 - 4\sin^2 t} \, \cos t \, dt = 4 \int \cos^2 t \, dt.$$

The last integral, a power of cosines, has the form discussed in earlier examples. Using methods just developed (or an integral table) gives

$$4 \int \cos^2 t \, dt = 2t + \sin(2t) + C. \tag{1}$$

So far so good, but the final answer (like the original problem) should involve x, not t. To achieve this end we'll need several facts, all of which follow from our having set $x = 2\sin t$ and from the double-angle formula for sines:

$$t = \arcsin\left(\frac{x}{2}\right); \quad 2\cos t = \sqrt{4 - x^2}; \quad \sin(2t) = 2\sin t \cos t = \frac{x\sqrt{4 - x^2}}{2}.$$

Substituting these results into Equation (1) gives

$$\int \sqrt{4 - x^2} \, dx = 2t + \sin(2t) + C = 2\arcsin\left(\frac{x}{2}\right) + \frac{x\sqrt{4 - x^2}}{2} + C,$$

which is our desired destination.   ■

Comments on the example   Example 5 needs a closer look:

- **Inverse substitution:**   Substituting $x = 2\sin t$ and $dx = 2\cos t \, dt$ represents an "inverse" variant of the more usual u-substitution technique. Such substitutions, although legal, require special care.

- **Which values of t?**   The equation $x = 2\sin t$ makes sense for *all* real t. In order to write $t = \arcsin(x/2)$, however, we must (and hereafter will) assume that t lies in the interval $[-\pi/2, \pi/2]$. �──

  That is, t must lie in the range of the arcsine function.

- **Absolute values:**   In the preceding calculation we used without comment the fact that

$$\sqrt{4 - x^2} = \sqrt{4 - 4\sin^2 t} = 2\,|\cos t| = 2\cos t.$$

  The last equation assumes, in effect, that $\cos t$ is nonnegative. Fortunately, that *is* the case—restricting t to the interval $[-\pi/2, \pi/2]$ guarantees this.

- **The bottom line—it works:**   Whatever the subtleties of the trigonometric substitution, the bottom line remains: The result *is* a suitable antiderivative, as differentiation can verify.

Trigonometric substitutions: Three types   Example 5 illustrates one of three types of trigonometric substitutions. The following table gives the key properties of all three types:

Trigonometric substitutions			
Radical form	**Substitution**	**t-domain**	**Result**
$\sqrt{a^2 - x^2}$	$x = a \sin t$	$[-\pi/2, \pi/2]$	$\sqrt{a^2 - x^2} = a \cos t$
$\sqrt{a^2 + x^2}$	$x = a \tan t$	$[-\pi/2, \pi/2]$	$\sqrt{a^2 + x^2} = a \sec t$
$\sqrt{x^2 - a^2}$	$x = a \sec t$	$[0, \pi],\ x \neq \pi/2$	$\sqrt{x^2 - a^2} = \pm a \tan t$

These substitutions (sometimes combined with completing the square) produce antiderivatives of many functions that involve square roots of quadratic expressions.

From t back to x: Helpful pictures A successful trigonometric substitution trades a troublesome integral in x for a simpler integral in t, but the problem of translating back to an expression in x always remains. Doing so can be slightly tricky, as Example 5 illustrated. The pictures in Figure 1 may help—both in making a useful substitution and in unraveling it at the end.

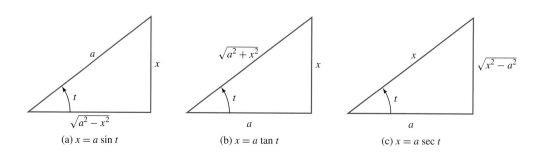

(a) $x = a \sin t$ (b) $x = a \tan t$ (c) $x = a \sec t$

FIGURE 1

Trigonometric substitutions: pictorial aids

From Figure 1(b), for instance, one can read such implications as

$$x = a \tan t \Longrightarrow \sec t = \frac{\sqrt{a^2 + x^2}}{a}.$$

We use such facts in the following examples.

EXAMPLE 6 Find $\displaystyle\int \frac{dx}{\sqrt{x^2 + 4}}$.

In the assumed t-domain (see the preceding table), $\sec t$ is nonnegative.

Solution Let $x = 2 \tan t$; then $dx = 2 \sec^2 t\, dt$ and $\sqrt{x^2 + 4} = \sqrt{4 \tan^2 t + 4} = 2 \sec t$. ◄
Therefore,

$$\int \frac{dx}{\sqrt{x^2 + 4}} = \int \frac{2 \sec^2 t}{2 \sec t}\, dt = \int \sec t\, dt = \ln|\sec t + \tan t| + C.$$

To convert the result back to an expression in x, we use the conclusion drawn just before this example:

$$\int \sec t\, dt = \ln \left| \frac{\sqrt{4 + x^2}}{2} + \frac{x}{2} \right| + C.$$ ∎

EXAMPLE 7 Find $\displaystyle\int_0^2 \frac{dx}{\sqrt{x^2+4}}$.

Solution We just calculated the antiderivative, and so the rest is algebra:

$$\int_0^2 \frac{dx}{\sqrt{x^2+4}} = \ln\left|\frac{\sqrt{4+x^2}}{2} + \frac{x}{2}\right|\Bigg]_0^2 = \ln(\sqrt{2}+1).$$

Example 6 also suggests another approach to the same goal: substitution in the *definite integral*. Notice that if $x = 2\tan t$, then $x = 0$ when $t = 0$ and $x = 2$ when $t = \pi/4$. Substituting all this into the original integral gives

$$\int_0^2 \frac{dx}{\sqrt{x^2+4}} = \int_0^{\pi/4} \sec t \, dt = \ln|\sec t + \tan t|\Bigg]_0^{\pi/4} = \ln(\sqrt{2}+1)$$

just as before. ∎

EXAMPLE 8 Find $\displaystyle\int \frac{dx}{\sqrt{x^2+2x+5}}$.

Solution Completing the square in the denominator gives

$$\int \frac{dx}{\sqrt{x^2+2x+5}} = \int \frac{dx}{\sqrt{(x+1)^2+4}}.$$

Completing the square is a simple but powerful algebraic idea. We try to remind students of it often.

Next we substitute $u = x+1$ and $du = dx$ to get $\displaystyle\int \frac{du}{\sqrt{u^2+4}}$. The result is familiar—work already done in Examples 6 and 7 completes the problem. ∎

BASIC EXERCISES

1. Find each of the following basic trigonometric antiderivatives.

  (a) $\displaystyle\int \cos x \, dx$ **(b)** $\displaystyle\int \sin x \, dx$

  (c) $\displaystyle\int \sec^2 x \, dx$ **(d)** $\displaystyle\int \sec x \tan x \, dx$

2. Find each of the following trigonometric antiderivatives.

  (a) $\displaystyle\int \sin x \cos x \, dx$ **(b)** $\displaystyle\int \tan x \, dx$

  (c) $\displaystyle\int \sec^2 x \tan x \, dx$

3. We solved Example 1 in two different ways and, apparently, got two different antiderivatives. Are these antiderivatives really different? Justify your answer.

4. **(a)** Find $\displaystyle\int \sin^4 x \, dx$ using the reduction formula for powers of sines.

  (b) Is the antiderivative you obtained in part (a) the same as the antiderivative found in Example 2? Justify your answer.

5. Let $I = \displaystyle\int \cos^3 x \sin^4 x \, dx$.

  (a) Find I by finishing Example 3.

  (b) Find I by rewriting the integrand in terms of cosines and then using the reduction formula for powers of cosines.

(c) Are the antiderivatives in parts (a) and (b) the same function? Justify your answer.

6. Find $\displaystyle\int \sec^3 x \tan^3 x \, dx$ by finishing the computations in Example 4.

7. Draw the right triangle that corresponds to the trigonometric substitution $x = a \sin t$ and use it to find an expression in a and x for

  (a) $\cos t$ **(b)** $\tan t$ **(c)** $\sin(2t)$

8. Draw the right triangle that corresponds to the trigonometric substitution $x = a \tan t$ and use it to find an expression in a and x for

  (a) $\cos t$ **(b)** $\sin t$ **(c)** $\sec(2t)$

9. Find $\displaystyle\int \frac{dx}{\sqrt{x^2+2x+5}}$ by finishing Example 8.

10. Evaluate $\displaystyle\int_{-1}^1 \frac{dx}{\sqrt{x^2+2x+5}}$.

In Exercises 11–32 find the antiderivative.

11. $\displaystyle\int \sin^2(3x) \, dx$ **12.** $\displaystyle\int \cos^2(x/3) \, dx$

13. $\displaystyle\int \sin^2 x \cos x \, dx$ **14.** $\displaystyle\int \sin^3 x \cos^3 x \, dx$

15. $\displaystyle\int \cos^2 x \sin^3 x \, dx$

16. $\displaystyle\int \cos^3(2x) \sin^2(2x) \, dx$

17. $\displaystyle\int \sin^2 x \cos^2 x \, dx$

18. $\displaystyle\int \cos^4 x \sin^2 x \, dx$

19. $\displaystyle\int \tan^4 x \, dx$

20. $\displaystyle\int \sec^4(3x) \, dx$

21. $\displaystyle\int \sec^2 x \tan^2 x \, dx$

22. $\displaystyle\int \sec^2 x \tan^4 x \, dx$

23. $\displaystyle\int \sec x \tan^2 x \, dx$

24. $\displaystyle\int \sec^3 x \tan^2 x \, dx$

25. $\displaystyle\int \sec x \tan^3 x \, dx$

26. $\displaystyle\int \frac{dx}{x^2 \sqrt{x^2 + 1}}$

27. $\displaystyle\int \frac{dx}{x^2 \sqrt{4 - x^2}}$

28. $\displaystyle\int \frac{dx}{\sqrt{1 + x^2}}$

29. $\displaystyle\int \sqrt{1 - x^2} \, dx$

30. $\displaystyle\int \frac{dx}{\left(x^2 + 4\right)^2}$

31. $\displaystyle\int x^2 \sqrt{1 - x^2} \, dx$

32. $\displaystyle\int \frac{x^2}{\sqrt{9 - x^2}} \, dx$

33. Draw the right triangle that corresponds to the trigonometric substitution $x = a \sec t$ and use it to find an expression in a and x for
  (a) $\cos t$ (b) $\sin t$ (c) $\tan(2t)$

34. When the trigonometric substitution $x = 2 \sin t$ is used, the expression $\sqrt{4 - x^2}$ becomes $2 \cos t$. When the trigonometric substitution $x = 2 \sec t$ is used, the expression $\sqrt{x^2 - 4}$ becomes $|2 \tan t|$. Why is the absolute value required in one case but not the other?

In Exercises 35–38, evaluate the integral.

35. $\displaystyle\int_3^4 \frac{dx}{x^2 \sqrt{x^2 - 4}}$

36. $\displaystyle\int_{-4}^{-3} \frac{dx}{x^2 \sqrt{x^2 - 4}}$

37. $\displaystyle\int_1^2 \frac{\sqrt{x^2 - 1}}{x} \, dx$

38. $\displaystyle\int_{-2}^{-1} \frac{\sqrt{x^2 - 1}}{x} \, dx$

FURTHER EXERCISES

In Exercises 39–46, find the antiderivative.

39. $\displaystyle\int \sec x \sin^3 x \, dx$

40. $\displaystyle\int \sin(2x) \cos^2 x \, dx$

41. $\displaystyle\int \sqrt{\cos x} \sin^5 x \, dx$

42. $\displaystyle\int \sqrt{1 + \sin x} \, dx$

43. $\displaystyle\int \sqrt{1 + x^2} \, dx$

44. $\displaystyle\int \frac{\sqrt{4 - x^2}}{x^2} \, dx$

45. $\displaystyle\int \frac{x + 2}{x \left(x^2 + 1\right)} \, dx$

46. $\displaystyle\int x \arcsin x \, dx$

47. Show that $\displaystyle\int \frac{\arctan x}{\left(1 + x^2\right)^{3/2}} \, dx = \frac{1 + x \arctan x}{\sqrt{1 + x^2}}$.
  [HINT: Start by making the substitution $w = \arctan x$.]

48. Evaluate $\displaystyle\int_{-1/2}^{1/2} \frac{\arcsin x}{\left(1 - x^2\right)^{3/2}} \, dx$.

49. (a) Use the addition formula $\cos(u + v) = \cos u \cos v - \sin u \sin v$ to show that $2 \cos u \cos v = \cos(u + v) + \cos(u - v)$.
  (b) Use part (a) to find $\displaystyle\int \cos(ax) \cos(bx) \, dx$.

50. (a) Use the addition formula $\cos(u + v) = \cos u \cos v - \sin u \sin v$ to show that $2 \sin u \sin v = \cos(u - v) - \cos(u + v)$.
  (b) Use part (a) to find $\displaystyle\int \sin(ax) \sin(bx) \, dx$.

51. (a) Use the addition formula $\sin(u + v) = \sin u \cos v + \cos u \sin v$ to show that $2 \sin u \cos v = \sin(u + v) + \sin(u - v)$.   [HINT: $\cos(-x) = \cos x$ and $\sin(-x) = -\sin x$.]
  (b) Use part (a) to find $\displaystyle\int \sin(ax) \cos(bx) \, dx$.

52. (a) Use the identity $\sec x = \dfrac{1}{\cos x} = \dfrac{\cos x}{\cos^2 x} = \dfrac{\cos x}{1 - \sin^2 x}$ to show that $\displaystyle\int \sec x \, dx = \frac{1}{2} \ln \left| \frac{1 + \sin x}{1 - \sin x} \right|$.
  (b) Show that $\displaystyle\int \sec x \, dx = \ln \left| \frac{\cos x}{1 - \sin x} \right|$.
  [HINT: Multiply the numerator and denominator in the part (a) antiderivative by $1 - \sin x$.]
  (c) Show that $\displaystyle\int \sec x \, dx = \ln |\sec x + \tan x|$.

53. (a) Assume that n is an integer. Use integration by parts with $u = \sin^{n-1} x$ and $dv = \sin x \, dx$ to show that
$$\int \sin^n x \, dx = -\sin^{n-1} x \cos x + (n - 1) \int \sin^{n-2} x \cos^2 x \, dx.$$
  (b) Use part (a) and the trigonometric identity $\sin^2 x + \cos^2 x = 1$ to show that if $n \neq 0$, then
$$\int \sin^n x \, dx = -\frac{\sin^{n-1} x \cos x}{n} + \frac{n - 1}{n} \int \sin^{n-2} x \, dx.$$

54. Use the reduction formula in part (b) of Exercise 53 to show that if $n > 0$ is an odd integer, then
$$\int_0^{\pi/2} \sin^n x \, dx = \frac{n - 1}{n} \cdot \frac{n - 3}{n - 2} \cdots \frac{4}{5} \cdot \frac{2}{3}.$$

55. Find an expression for $\displaystyle\int_0^{\pi/2} \sin^n x \, dx$ if $n > 0$ is an even integer.

56. Assume that n is a nonzero integer. Derive the reduction formula $\displaystyle\int \cos^n x \, dx = \frac{\cos^{n-1} x \sin x}{n} + \frac{n - 1}{n} \int \cos^{n-2} x \, dx$.

57. Assume that $n \neq 1$ is an integer. Derive the reduction formula $\int \tan^n x \, dx = \dfrac{\tan^{n-1} x}{n-1} - \int \tan^{n-2} x \, dx$.

58. Assume that $n \neq 1$ is an integer. Derive the reduction formula $\int \sec^n x \, dx = \dfrac{\sec^{n-2} x \tan x}{n-1} + \dfrac{n-2}{n-1} \int \sec^{n-2} x \, dx$.

Exercises 59–64 explore the substitution $x = 2 \arctan t$.

59. Let $x = 2 \arctan t$ or, equivalently, $t = \tan(x/2)$.

   (a) Show that $\sin(x/2) = t/\sqrt{1+t^2}$.

   (b) Show that $\cos(x/2) = 1/\sqrt{1+t^2}$.

   (c) Show that $\sin x$ can be written as a rational function of t.

   (d) Show that $\cos x$ can be written as a rational function of t.

60. Use Exercise 59 to show that $\int \dfrac{dx}{1 + \sin x + \cos x} = \ln|1 + \tan(x/2)| + C$.

61. Find $\int \dfrac{dx}{1 + \cos x}$.

62. Evaluate $\int_0^{\pi/2} \dfrac{dx}{2\cos x + 3 \sin x}$.

63. Evaluate $\int_{\pi/4}^{\pi} \dfrac{\sin x}{2 + \cos x} \, dx$

64. Use Exercise 59 to explain why the substitution $t = \tan(x/2)$ can be used to transform any rational expression involving only constants and powers of trigonometric functions into a rational expression in t.

65. Let $I_n = \int \dfrac{dx}{(1+x^2)^n}$, where $n \geq 1$ is an integer.

   (a) Use integration by parts to find a reduction formula for I_n.

   (b) Use a trigonometric substitution to find a reduction formula for I_n.

8.4   MISCELLANEOUS ANTIDERIVATIVES

This section collects our small kit of antidifferentiation tools and illustrates some strategies for choosing among them.

Tools for antidifferentiation   This chapter has presented several symbolic techniques for finding symbolic antiderivatives. In the following paragraphs we list our short kit of tools and some hints for which tool to use when.

We emphasize, however, that symbolic antidifferentiation is a far less "routine" problem than differentiation. Finding symbolic *derivatives* is mainly a matter of choosing and following one or more straightforward recipes. Finding *antiderivatives* successfully, by contrast, may require skill, experience, educated guesswork, judgment—and sometimes plain good luck.

There is good news, too, and a simple moral: *Checking* by differentiation that "candidate" antiderivatives really work is usually easy. So guess freely—but check carefully.

- **Substitution**   Based on the chain rule, substitution is the simplest and most powerful antidifferentiation technique. When it works, substitution transforms "hard" antiderivatives to simpler forms, which may be solvable either at a glance or by reference to an integral table. Try u-substitution *first* before resorting to more laborious methods. The method works best and most simply in cases like

$$\int 2x \cos(x^2) \, dx \quad \text{and} \quad \int e^{\sin x} \cos x \, dx,$$

where both a substitution $u = u(x)$ and its differential $du = u'(x) \, dx$ are conveniently present.

- **Integration by parts**   Based on the product rule for *derivatives*, integration by parts often succeeds with integrals like

$$\int x \sin x \, dx \quad \text{and} \quad \int x^2 e^x \, dx,$$

which involve products. (The method may succeed with other integrands, too.) As the formula $\int u \, dv = uv - \int v \, du$ suggests, the method effectively trades one integral (on the left) for another (on the right). With any luck (and with judicious choices of u and dv) the right-hand integral may be simpler or more familiar than the left-hand integral.

- **Partial fractions**   The partial fractions method applies only to *rational functions*: quotients of polynomials. The idea is first to use algebra (not calculus) to rewrite such a "total fraction" as a sum of simpler *partial fractions*, as in

$$\frac{3x+4}{(x+1)(x+2)} = \frac{1}{1+x} + \frac{2}{2+x}.$$

  The work is worth doing because the summands on the right are easy to antidifferentiate.

- **Trigonometric methods**   Section 8.3 described a variety of methods, based mainly on trigonometric identities, for antidifferentiating functions that involve powers of trigonometric functions as in

$$\int \cos^2 x \sin^3 x \, dx \quad \text{and} \quad \int \sec^3 x \tan x \, dx.$$

  Perhaps surprisingly, antiderivatives that involve squares and square roots, such as

$$\int \frac{x^2}{\sqrt{1-x^2}} \, dx \quad \text{and} \quad \int \frac{x^2}{\sqrt{1+x^2}} \, dx,$$

  can often be transformed, by means of **trigonometric substitutions**, to antiderivatives that involve powers of trigonometric functions.

Other tools   An integral table, such as the one in this book, makes finding many antiderivatives a routine matter. But not all antiderivatives yield instantly—substitutions or algebraic transformations may be needed.

Modern technology, on the other hand, makes short work of finding almost *any* symbolic antiderivative found in a calculus text. Even when such tools are available, finding *some* antiderivatives "by hand" is worthwhile as an aid to understanding and intuition.

BASIC EXERCISES

In Exercises 1–72, find the antiderivative without using the table of integrals at the back of the book (or its electronic equivalent).

1. $\displaystyle\int \frac{\sin x}{(3+\cos x)^2} \, dx$

2. $\displaystyle\int \frac{x^2}{x+1} \, dx$

3. $\displaystyle\int x\left(3+4x^2\right)^5 \, dx$

4. $\displaystyle\int \frac{dx}{\sqrt{1-x^2}}$

5. $\displaystyle\int \frac{x}{\sqrt[3]{x^2+4}} \, dx$

6. $\displaystyle\int \frac{dx}{x(3x-2)}$

7. $\displaystyle\int \frac{(\ln x)^2}{x} \, dx$

8. $\displaystyle\int e^x \sin x \, dx$

9. $\displaystyle\int \frac{\ln x}{x} \, dx$

10. $\displaystyle\int x\sqrt{x+2} \, dx$

11. $\displaystyle\int \frac{x}{3x+2} \, dx$

12. $\displaystyle\int x \cos x \, dx$

13. $\displaystyle\int \sin^2(3x) \cos(3x) \, dx$

14. $\displaystyle\int x e^{3x} \, dx$

15. $\displaystyle\int x e^{3x^2} \, dx$

16. $\displaystyle\int \frac{dx}{1+4x^2}$

17. $\displaystyle\int (2-3x)^{10} \, dx$

18. $\displaystyle\int \arctan x \, dx$

19. $\displaystyle\int \frac{\sec^2 x}{3+\tan x} \, dx$

20. $\displaystyle\int x \sin x \, dx$

21. $\displaystyle\int \frac{dx}{(x-1)(x+2)}$

22. $\displaystyle\int x^2 \ln x \, dx$

23. $\displaystyle\int \frac{2x+3}{4x+5} \, dx$

24. $\displaystyle\int \frac{x+1}{x^2+1} \, dx$

25. $\displaystyle\int \frac{e^x}{\sqrt{1-e^{2x}}} \, dx$

26. $\displaystyle\int \frac{\sin x}{2+\cos x} \, dx$

27. $\displaystyle\int \ln x \, dx$

28. $\displaystyle\int x \cos(3x^2) \, dx$

29. $\displaystyle\int \arcsin x \, dx$

30. $\displaystyle\int \frac{\sqrt{x}}{1+x} \, dx$

31. $\displaystyle\int \frac{dx}{x^2+2x+3}$

32. $\displaystyle\int \frac{x}{\sqrt{x-2}} \, dx$

33. $\displaystyle\int \frac{dx}{\sqrt{1-4x^2}}$

34. $\displaystyle\int \frac{x^3}{1+x^2} \, dx$

35. $\displaystyle\int \tan x \, dx$

36. $\displaystyle\int \cos(2x) \, dx$

37. $\displaystyle\int e^{2x}\sqrt{1+e^x} \, dx$

38. $\displaystyle\int \frac{dx}{1+x^2}$

39. $\displaystyle\int \frac{dx}{\sqrt{3-2x-x^2}}$

40. $\displaystyle\int x^2 \arcsin x\,dx$

41. $\displaystyle\int \frac{dx}{x(\ln x)^2}$

42. $\displaystyle\int x \arctan x\,dx$

43. $\displaystyle\int \frac{dx}{9x^2-4}$

44. $\displaystyle\int \frac{x+5}{x^2+3x-4}\,dx$

45. $\displaystyle\int \frac{x^3}{\sqrt{4-x^2}}\,dx$

46. $\displaystyle\int \frac{dx}{\sqrt[3]{x-1}}$

47. $\displaystyle\int \frac{x}{(x-1)(x+1)}\,dx$

48. $\displaystyle\int x^3 e^{x^2}\,dx$

49. $\displaystyle\int \frac{dx}{\sqrt{9+x^2}}$

50. $\displaystyle\int \frac{dx}{2x-x^2}$

51. $\displaystyle\int \frac{x^2}{1-3x}\,dx$

52. $\displaystyle\int \frac{x}{(x^2-1)^3}\,dx$

53. $\displaystyle\int e^x e^{2x}\,dx$

54. $\displaystyle\int \sqrt{4x-3}\,dx$

55. $\displaystyle\int \ln(1+x^2)\,dx$

56. $\displaystyle\int \sin(\sqrt{x})\,dx$

57. $\displaystyle\int x \arcsin x\,dx$

58. $\displaystyle\int \frac{dx}{9-x^2}$

59. $\displaystyle\int \frac{dx}{\sqrt{2x+3}}$

60. $\displaystyle\int \frac{dx}{(4-x^2)^{3/2}}$

61. $\displaystyle\int \frac{x}{(2x+3)^4}\,dx$

62. $\displaystyle\int x\sqrt{2x+1}\,dx$

63. $\displaystyle\int \frac{\tan x}{\sec^2 x}\,dx$

64. $\displaystyle\int \frac{x}{16+9x^2}\,dx$

65. $\displaystyle\int \frac{dx}{e^x-1}$

66. $\displaystyle\int \frac{dx}{\sqrt{2x-x^2}}$

67. $\displaystyle\int \frac{dx}{1+\sqrt{x}}$

68. $\displaystyle\int \frac{x^3}{(x^2+1)^2}\,dx$

69. $\displaystyle\int x^2 \ln(3x)\,dx$

70. $\displaystyle\int \frac{x}{9+4x^4}\,dx$

71. $\displaystyle\int \sqrt{x}\,\ln x\,dx$

72. $\displaystyle\int x \sec^2 x\,dx$

FURTHER EXERCISES

In Exercises 73–88, find the antiderivative using your ingenuity and the table of integrals at the back of the book.

73. $\displaystyle\int \frac{7-x}{(x+3)(x^2+1)}\,dx$

74. $\displaystyle\int \frac{x+6}{(x+1)(x^2+4)}\,dx$

75. $\displaystyle\int x \sin^2 x \cos x\,dx$

76. $\displaystyle\int \sin^3 x \cos^3 x\,dx$

77. $\displaystyle\int \frac{dx}{x^3+x}$

78. $\displaystyle\int \tan^4 x\,dx$

79. $\displaystyle\int (x^2+2x+3)^{3/2}\,dx$

80. $\displaystyle\int \sin(3x)\cos(5x)\,dx$

81. $\displaystyle\int \sqrt{1+e^x}\,dx$

82. $\displaystyle\int \frac{dx}{x\left(x+\sqrt[3]{x}\right)}$

83. $\displaystyle\int \frac{dx}{x^3+1}$

84. $\displaystyle\int \frac{dx}{(e^x-e^{-x})^2}$

85. $\displaystyle\int x \tan^2 x\,dx$

86. $\displaystyle\int \cos^3 x\,dx$

87. $\displaystyle\int \sin x \sin(2x)\,dx$

88. $\displaystyle\int \sin^5 x \cos^2 x\,dx$

Beyond Elementary Functions

We've remarked often in the narrative that finding antiderivatives in closed form can be hard or even impossible, but that this isn't a fatal problem — nonelementary functions can be useful and aren't necessarily difficult to study. We pursue those themes in this Interlude.

We'll use the exp *form for the exponential function in this interlude; doing so avoids towers of exponents.*

Proving rigorously from scratch that any one of these antiderivatives is not elementary is difficult. But if we assume that any one is nonelementary, we can readily deduce that others are nonelementary.

Integrability in closed form

Not every elementary function has an elementary antiderivative (i.e., an antiderivative that can be written as a combination of the usual elementary functions of calculus). Functions that *do* have elementary antiderivatives are sometimes called **integrable in closed form**; we've seen in this chapter that polynomials, rational functions, the basic trigonometric functions, and many other functions are integrable in closed form, and we've discussed several methods for finding antiderivative formulas.

Many other functions, however, are *not* integrable in closed form. None of the following antiderivatives, for instance, has a closed-form solution: ◄

$$\int \sin(x^2)\,dx; \quad \int \frac{\sin x}{\sqrt{x}}\,dx; \quad \int \exp(-x^2)\,dx; \quad \int \frac{dx}{\ln x}.$$

The problem is not that these integrands *lack* antiderivatives—the FTC guarantees that *every* continuous function has an antiderivative. The problem with these functions is that their antiderivatives are not elementary functions.

Recognizing nonelementary antiderivatives Proving from scratch that a function has no elementary antiderivative is a hard problem. Trying and failing (by hand or with technology) to find an antiderivative proves nothing—maybe we (or the software) just weren't smart enough. Given the antiderivative problem $\int \exp(-x^2)\,dx$, for instance, the TI–89 makes no progress at all; *Maple* and *Mathematica* return the strange-looking result

$$\int \exp(-x^2)\,dx = \frac{\sqrt{\pi}}{2}\operatorname{erf}(x).$$

We'll say more about the mysterious "erf" in a moment. The point here is that the right side is *not* elementary in the sense under discussion.

If we know (or take on faith) that a given function is or isn't integrable in closed form, then we can often use antiderivative methods to conclude the same thing for other functions.

EXAMPLE 1 Assume that $\exp(-x^2)$ has no elementary antiderivative. For a given nonnegative integer n, does $x^n \exp(-x^2)$ have an elementary antiderivative?

Solution For $n = 0$, no—that's our assumption. For $n = 1$, the answer is yes; substituting $u = -x^2$ and $du = -2x\,dx$ (or asking a machine) gives

$$\int x \exp(-x^2)\,dx = -\frac{\exp(-x^2)}{2} + C.$$

This case (and similar experiments with technology) might lead us to guess that the answer is yes for odd n and no for even n.

This guess is correct; integration by parts shows why. Given the integral $\int x^n \exp(x^2)\,dx$ for any $n \geq 2$, integration by parts (with $u = x^{n-1}$ and $dv = x \exp(x^2)\,dx$) gives the reduction formula

$$\int x^n \exp(x^2)\,dx = x^{n-1}\frac{\exp(x^2)}{2} - \frac{n-1}{2}\int x^{n-2}\exp(x^2)\,dx.$$

Observe:

- The left-hand integrand has an elementary antiderivative *if and only if* the right-hand integrand does.

• Applying the formula *repeatedly* reduces the power of x by 2 on each repetition. Thus, beginning with any power x^n, we eventually reach either $n = 0$ or $n = 1$, depending on whether the initial n is even or odd.

These facts imply that our guess is correct. ∎

PROBLEM 1 Make the u-substitution $u = x^2$ to relate the two integrals

$$I_1 = \int \sin(x^2)\, dx; \quad I_2 = \int \frac{\sin x}{\sqrt{x}}\, dx.$$

Conclude that if I_1 has no closed-form solution, then neither does I_2, and vice versa.

PROBLEM 2 Assume that the function $\sin(x^2)$ has no elementary antiderivative.

(a) The function $x\sin(x^2)$ has an elementary antiderivative. Find it.

(b) The function $x^3\sin(x^2)$ has an elementary antiderivative. Find it.
[HINT: Try integration by parts with $u = x^2$, $dv = x\sin(x^2)$.]

(c) Show that the function $x^2\sin(x^2)$ has no elementary antiderivative.
[HINT: Set $u = x$, $dv = x\sin(x^2)$; then imitate the argument in Example 1.]

Functions defined by integration

Lacking an elementary antiderivative is not a fatal flaw. Many useful mathematical functions are (or can be) defined not by elementary formulas but by integrals.

Logarithms as integrals In earlier work we defined the natural logarithm function as the inverse of the natural exponential function. ➤ Then, using the chain rule and the fact that the exponential function is its own derivative, we found by *calculation* that $(\ln x)' = 1/x$; that is, that $\ln x$ is an antiderivative for $1/x$.

A different approach to the logarithm is to define $\ln x$ (for $x > 0$) as the integral

$$\ln x = \int_1^x \frac{dt}{t}. \tag{1}$$

This definition avoids mentioning exponential functions; it also guarantees (by the FTC rather than by calculation) that $\ln x$ is an antiderivative of $1/x$. The following problems explore some familiar properties of $\ln x$—but from the viewpoint of the integral definition. Solve them using *only* the integral definition, forgetting anything else you may have known about logs. ➤

PROBLEM 3 Consider $\ln x$ to be defined for $x > 0$ by Equation (1).

(a) Explain why $\ln x$ is positive if $x > 1$, negative if $0 < x < 1$, and zero if $x = 1$.

(b) Why is $\ln 0$ undefined? Why is $\ln(-1)$ undefined?

(c) Draw (freehand) rough graphs of $1/x$ and $\ln x$ for $x > 0$.

(d) Use the trapezoid-rule sum T_3 (with three subdivisions) to estimate $\ln 2$. (Do this by hand to see the pattern.) Then use technology to find the trapezoid sum T_{30} for the same integral. Are your estimates too big or too small?

(e) Draw a picture to convince yourself geometrically that $\ln(1/3) = -\ln 3$. (Use the graph of $y = 1/x$ and compare appropriate areas.)

PROBLEM 4 Assume that $a > 0$ and $x > 0$. Carry out and justify each of the following steps to derive the identity $\ln(ax) = \ln a + \ln x$.

We use the natural logarithm function not as an example of a nonelementary function but as an example of a function that can be defined by integration. (This definition is arguably the "right" one, since it involves nothing more complicated than integration and the rational function $1/x$.)

Many, but not all, calculus books take this approach.

Forget only temporarily.

(a) Show that $\left(\ln(ax) - \ln(x)\right)' = \left(\displaystyle\int_1^{ax} \frac{dt}{t} - \int_1^{x} \frac{dt}{t}\right)' = 0.$ [HINT: Use the chain rule.]

(b) Explain why the result in part (a) implies that $\ln(ax) = \ln x + C$.

(c) Use an appropriate value of x to show that in part (b), $C = \ln a$.

The error function   The *error function* (erf) is defined for all real numbers x by

$$\text{erf}(x) = \frac{2}{\sqrt{\pi}} \int_0^x \exp(-t^2)\, dt. \tag{2}$$

(The name "error function" comes from probability, where the function arises in modeling "errors"—differences between expected and actual values of an observed quantity.) The function erf is well known to *Maple*, *Mathematica*, and their ilk. Figure 1 shows graphs of both erf and its derivative (the integrand). Note that one of the graphs is the proverbial "bell curve":

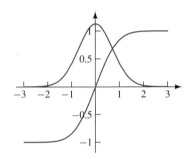

FIGURE 1
$y = \mathbf{erf}\,(x)$ **and its derivative**

PROBLEM 5

(a) Which graph in Figure 1 shows erf(x)? What is the *other* graph's formula?

(b) Use a trapezoid-rule sum T_{30} (with 30 subdivisions) to estimate erf(3). Does your answer "agree" with Figure 1? How?

(c) Use a trapezoid-rule sum T_{30} (with 30 subdivisions) to estimate erf(10) − erf(3). Does your answer "agree" with Figure 1? How?

The log integral   The **log integral function**, denoted Li, is defined for $x > 2$ by

$$\text{Li}(x) = \int_2^x \frac{dt}{\ln t}.$$

This function is useful in number theory; for large x, Li(x) closely approximates the number of primes less than x. (Slightly different definitions of Li exist in other sources.)

PROBLEM 6   In each part following, use the integral definition above.

(a) Explain why $\frac{d}{dx}\text{Li}'(x) = 1/\ln(x)$ for all $x > 2$.

(b) Use technology to plot Li$'(x) = 1/\ln(x)$ for $2 \le x \le 20$. Use your graph to draw (by hand) a rough graph of Li(x) on the same interval.

(c) Use the midpoint rule with 50 subdivisions to estimate Li(100). (The error committed is surprisingly small, even though the interval is quite large.) How many primes are there less than 100?

(d) There are 168 prime numbers less than 1000. Compare this to any convenient estimate of Li(1000).

First-Order Linear Differential Equations

INTERLUDE

This Interlude is a brief toe-dip into the deep waters of symbolic solution techniques for classes of DEs.

In the first part we explore the (nonobvious) fact that many elementary functions do not have elementary antiderivatives. But their antiderivatives are still useful functions. Indeed, many useful are (or can be) defined as integrals, including the natural logarithm.

The method "works" in a familiar case.

Separable DEs Explicit symbolic solutions to first-order DEs and IVPs are useful, but they can be difficult to find. No single method works every time. We saw in Section 7.4, for example, how to use integration to solve DEs that happen to be **separable**—that is, DEs for which the variables (y and t, say) can be "separated" on opposite sides of an equation. The following DEs are all separable:

$$\frac{dy}{dt} = 3y; \quad \frac{dy}{dt} = 2yt; \quad \frac{dy}{dt} = \cos^2(y)\cos(t); \quad \frac{dy}{dt} = \cos(t^2).$$

Even for separable DEs, finding a symbolic solution can be hard or impossible, since the work may involve one or more difficult integrals (as in the last DE above).

PROBLEM 1 Use separation of variables (as in Section 7.4) to find the solutions

$$y = Ce^{3t}; \quad y = Ce^{t^2}; \quad y = \arctan(\sin(t) + C)$$

for the first three DEs above. (In each case, C is an arbitrary constant.) What makes the fourth DE above harder than the others?

Inseparable DEs Other DEs, including all of the following samples, are **inseparable**:

$$\frac{dy}{dt} = \frac{y}{t} + 1; \quad \frac{dy}{dt} = 2y + \sin t; \quad \frac{dy}{dt} = \cos y + \cos t; \quad \frac{dy}{dt} = \cos(y + t).$$

The variables y and t in these DEs are too "entangled" to separate, and so we need other methods to solve such DEs symbolically. (We *could* use numerical or graphical methods, such as Euler's method and slope fields, but at some cost in accuracy and generality.)

First-order linear DEs A **first-order linear DE** is defined as a DE that can be written in the form

$$f(t)y' + g(t)y = h(t),$$

where f, g, and h are all functions of t. Notice especially that such a DE involves only the first power of y; expressions like y^2 and $\cos(y)$ are not allowed. Notice also that dividing by $f(t)$ and rearranging the DE slightly gives the equivalent form

$$y' = a(t)y + b(t), \tag{1}$$

where $a(t)$ and $b(t)$ are functions of t alone. Throughout this Interlude we'll use the Formula (1) and the notations $a(t)$ and $b(t)$ defined thereby.

EXAMPLE 1 Which of the four inseparable DEs above are linear? Why?

Solution The DE $y' = y/t + 1$ fits template (1), with $a(t) = 1/t$ and $b(t) = 1$, and so it's linear. The DE $y' = 2y + \sin t$ also fits, with $a(t) = 2$ and $b(t) = \sin t$. The other two inseparable DEs above don't fit the pattern and thus are not linear. ∎

PROBLEM 2 Decide whether each of the following DEs is (i) linear; (ii) separable. For each linear DE, find $a(t)$ and $b(t)$. (In all parts, k is a constant.)

(a) $y' = y^2 \sin t + \cos t$

(b) $y' = ky + 1$

(c) $y' = kty + 1$

(d) $y' = \dfrac{1}{1+t} y + k$

INTERLUDE

Solving linear DEs: a "formula" The following general solution "formula" for linear DEs is sometimes attributed to work of Euler in the early 1800s. As the quotation marks suggest, the "formula" requires some work and interpretation to produce fully explicit solutions—in particular, it involves finding antiderivatives. ◄ We'll first state the formula and then consider how to use it and how it might have been found.

FACT Consider the first-order linear DE $y' = a(t)y + b(t)$. Let $A(t)$ be any antiderivative of $a(t)$. Solutions to the DE have the form

$$y = e^{A(t)} \int e^{-A(t)} b(t)\, dt. \tag{2}$$

(The indefinite integral produces an arbitrary constant of integration.)

EXAMPLE 2 Use the formula to find solutions of the DE $y' = y + t$. Which solutions satisfy the initial conditions (1) $y(0) = 1$; (2) $y(0) = -1$?

Solution Here $a(t) = 1$ and $b(t) = t$, and so we can use $A(t) = t$ in Formula (2):

$$y = e^t \int e^{-t} t\, dt = e^t \left(-te^{-t} - e^{-t} + C\right) = -t - 1 + Ce^t.$$

Now $y(0) = C - 1$; thus, setting $C = 2$ gives the solution function $y = 2e^t - t - 1$, which satisfies $y(0) = 1$. Setting $C = 0$ gives the solution $y = -t - 1$, which satisfies the initial condition $y(0) = -1$. (Note that in this one case the solution function is linear.)

Here are two things to notice about the method:

1. The general result involves one arbitrary constant C; it came from the antiderivative $\int e^{-A(t)} b(t)\, dt$.

2. The method requires antidifferentiating two functions: $a(t)$ and $e^{A(t)}b(t)$. Either or both of these antiderivatives may be difficult to find symbolically. ■

PROBLEM 3 Check by differentiation that $y = -t - 1 + Ce^t$ is indeed a solution to $y' = y + t$. Then use technology to plot solution curves for integer values of C from -3 to 3.

PROBLEM 4 Imitate the calculations in Example 2 to find solutions for the each of following DEs. ◄ In each part, check by differentiation that your claimed solution really works, and use technology to plot solutions for several values of the arbitrary constant C.

(a) $y' = -y + t^2$

(b) $y' = -y + \cos t$

(c) $y' = -\dfrac{y}{t} + 1$ (assume $t > 0$)

(d) $y' = -\dfrac{y}{t} + \sin t$ (assume $t > 0$)

PROBLEM 5 Show by differentiation that $y = e^{A(t)} \int e^{-A(t)} b(t)\, dt$ is indeed a solution to $y' = a(t)y + b(t)$, as claimed. [HINTS: The claimed solution is a product, so the product rule applies. The first factor is a composite function, so the chain rule applies. The second factor (which involves an integral sign) is an antiderivative, and so differentiating it is especially easy.]

Why it works The preceding example and problem suggest that the method works. The following problems suggest *why* it works and how such a formula might be guessed. ◄

PROBLEM 6 (A simple case) Consider the linear DE $y' = a(t)y$ (for which $b(t) = 0$). Let $A(t)$ be any antiderivative for $a(t)$. Then the DE has solutions

$$y = Ce^{A(t)},$$

where C is an arbitrary constant. Give details for the following supporting arguments.

(a) Show by differentiation that $y = Ce^{A(t)}$ really *does* solve the DE in question.

(b) Explain why $y = Ce^{A(t)}$ is the special case $b = 0$ of Formula (2). [HINT: Antiderivatives of the zero function are constants.]

(c) Note that the DE $y' = a(t)y$ is separable. Apply the separation of variables method to find the solution claimed above. [HINT: Separating variables and integrating both sides gives $\ln|y| = A(t) + k$, where k is a constant. Solve this equation for y.]

PROBLEM 7 (The general case) The preceding problem shows that $y = Ce^{A(t)}$, where C is a *constant*, solves the linear DE $y' = a(t)y + b(t)$ in the special case that $b(t) = 0$. To handle the (more likely) case that $b(t) \neq 0$, we look for a solution of the form $y = C(t)e^{A(t)}$, where $C(t)$ is a *function* of t. Work through the following steps to find a "formula" for $C(t)$.

(a) Show by differentiation that $y = C(t)e^{A(t)}$ is a solution of the DE $y' = a(t)y + b(t)$ if and only if $C'(t) = e^{-A(t)}b(t)$. (This is another way of saying that $C(t) = \int e^{-A(t)}b(t)\,dt$.)

(b) Use the preceding part to derive Formula (2).

PROBLEM 8 Consider the DE $y' = ay + b$, where a and b are *constant* functions. Solve the DE in two ways: (i) by separating variables; (ii) using Formula (2). Show that the two answers are the same.

Population modeling with linear DEs

The first-order linear DE

$$y'(t) = a(t)y(t) + b(t)$$

can be used to model population growth under various conditions. If $y(t)$ describes a population at time t, then $y'(t)$ represents the rate of population growth, and the DE describes how growth occurs. The first summand, $a(t)y(t)$, represents growth with a *time-variable* proportionality factor $a(t)$. (This might be the population's net "birth rate.") The second summand, $b(t)$, can be thought of as a rate of *immigration* (or *emigration* if $b(t) < 0$); the latter rate depends on time but not on the population. For instance, the DE

$$y'(t) = \frac{0.1}{1+t}y(t) + 1 \tag{3}$$

could describe a population with a constant immigration rate (1 population unit per unit of time) and a birth rate $(0.1/(1+t))$ that decreases over time.

PROBLEM 9 Suppose that a population satisfies the DE (3) and the initial condition $y(0) = 50$. Find and plot a formula for $y(t)$. (Assume that $t > 0$ to avoid absolute value signs in the calculation.)

PROBLEM 10 Consider the DE

$$y'(t) = \frac{1}{1+t}y(t) + k,$$

where k is a constant, and the initial condition $y(0) = 10$.

(a) Solve the IVP given by the DE and the initial condition above. (The result involves the constant k.)

(b) Plot on one set of axes solutions to the preceding part for $k = -3, -2, -1, 0, 1, 2, 3$. (Use the time interval $0 \le t \le 20$.) Interpret the different curve *shapes* in terms of immigration or emigration.

FUNCTION APPROXIMATION

9.1 TAYLOR POLYNOMIALS

This section includes material already seen in Section 4.7, but it focuses more on approximating non-polynomial functions with polynomials. We mention trigonometric polynomials briefly in one example.

Introduction: the idea of approximation

"Function approximation"—this chapter's title phrase—suggests two possible meanings: approximation *by* functions and approximation *of* functions. In fact, we'll take *both* points of view in this chapter. A recurring problem throughout the chapter is to find (or build) "nice" functions that approximate less well behaved or well understood functions.

Why would we bother to approximate one type of function with another? What makes some functions "nicer" than others? How can we find nice functions that do what we want?

Polynomials: a nice family Polynomials form one especially nice family of functions. Calculus with polynomials is convenient; differentiation and integration could hardly be easier. Just as important, polynomial functions are easy to *evaluate*, even by hand or with crude technology. Finding values of transcendental functions, such as e^{-1}, may take much more work. ➔ The following example shows how a polynomial can approximate another function and it suggests why doing so is useful. (We'll explain later in this section how the polynomial was found.)

Could you find or estimate e^{-1} by hand? How would you try?

EXAMPLE 1 Consider the functions

$$f(x) = e^x \quad \text{and} \quad P_5(x) = 1 + x + \frac{x^2}{2} + \frac{x^3}{6} + \frac{x^4}{24} + \frac{x^5}{120}.$$

(The subscript on the polynomial P corresponds to its degree.) How closely does P_5 approximate f near $x = 0$? Use P_5 to approximate $f(-1) = e^{-1}$ and $f(2) = e^2$.

Solution The approximation is excellent near $x = 0$, as Figure 1 (page 494) shows. The graphs of f and P_5 are hard to distinguish anywhere near $x = 0$. At $x = -1$, for instance, we get ➔

Numbers are rounded to five decimal places.

$$P_5(-1) = 1 - 1 + \frac{1}{2} - \frac{1}{6} + \frac{1}{24} - \frac{1}{120} \approx 0.36667, \quad \text{while} \quad f(-1) = e^{-1} \approx 0.36788.$$

At $x = 2$ the match is less impressive but still respectable: $P_5(2) \approx 7.26667$ and

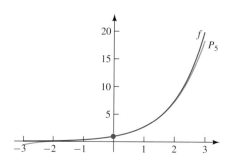

FIGURE 1
A polynomial approximation to $f(x) = e^x$

How do calculators find values of transcendental functions? They use (simpler) approximating functions.

$f(2) \approx 7.38906$. Notice, especially, that finding $P_5(-1)$ and $P_5(2)$ requires only arithmetic, whereas finding $f(-1)$ and $f(2)$ is best left to the mysterious inner workings of a calculator. ◄

We'll explain in a few pages exactly how we chose P_5 to "match" f so closely. To allay suspense, we'll mention now (and you can check easily) that f and P_5 "agree" at $x = 0$, as do their first five derivatives:

$$f(0) = P_5(0); \quad f'(0) = P_5'(0); \quad f''(0) = P_5''(0); \quad \ldots \quad f^{(5)}(0) = P_5^{(5)}(0). \quad \blacksquare$$

Approximation by ordinary polynomials is not the only possibility. Approximation by trigonometric polynomials is also possible; the process involves integration rather than differentiation.

Trigonometric polynomials: Another nice family Ordinary polynomials, simple as they are, are not *always* the best choice for approximating a given "target" function f. It may be known, for instance, that f is a **periodic function**—one that repeats itself on domain intervals of a fixed length. (Such functions arise often in modeling physical phenomena, in which repeating or rhythmic behaviors are common.) In such cases, sines and cosines—the simplest and best-understood periodic functions—are better suited for use as basic modeling elements than are ordinary polynomials, which are not periodic.

In Section 9.3 we'll meet another nice function family, the **trigonometric polynomials**, members of which are used to approximate periodic functions. Trigonometric polynomials are functions like

$$1 + 2\cos x - 4\sin(5x) \quad \text{and} \quad 2 - 3\sin x + 4\cos(2x) - 5\sin(7x);$$

that is, sums and constant multiples of the trigonometric functions

$$1, \ \cos x, \ \sin x, \ \cos(2x), \ \sin(2x), \ \cos(3x), \ \sin(3x), \ldots.$$

(In the same way, ordinary polynomials are sums and constant multiples of the power functions $1, x, x^2, x^3, \ldots$.) As a look ahead, the following example illustrates graphically how such an approximation works.

Approximation by trigonometric polynomials is more forgiving of discontinuities than is Taylor approximation.

EXAMPLE 2 A "square wave" function f is shown in Figure 2(a); the function might represent a simple alternating electric pulse. The "formula" for f is somewhat inconvenient:

$$f(x) = \begin{cases} \vdots \\ -1 & \text{if } -3\pi \leq x < -2\pi; \\ 1 & \text{if } -2\pi \leq x < -\pi; \\ -1 & \text{if } -\pi \leq x < 0; \\ 1 & \text{if } 0 \leq x < \pi; \\ \vdots \end{cases}$$

Notice that f repeats itself on intervals of length 2π.

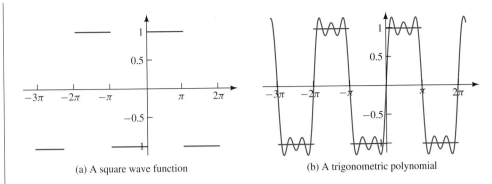

(a) A square wave function   (b) A trigonometric polynomial

FIGURE 2

Approximating a square wave

Figure 2(b) shows the square wave function again, this time together with the trigonometric polynomial

$$q(x) = \frac{4}{\pi}\left(\sin(x) + \frac{\sin(3x)}{3} + \frac{\sin(5x)}{5}\right).$$

We'll show in Section 9.3 how to find trigonometric polynomials like q, which approximate given periodic functions. We can see now, however, that q has advantages over f, including a relatively simple formula built from familiar ingredients and such "nice" properties as continuity and differentiability. ∎

Polynomials, derivatives, and coefficients

Material in this subsection essentially repeats Section 4.7.

Consider the nth degree polynomial function $p(x) = a_0 + a_1(x - x_0) + a_2(x - x_0)^2 + a_3(x - x_0)^3 + \cdots + a_n(x - x_0)^n$, where x_0 and the a_i are all fixed numbers. A polynomial written this way, using powers of $(x - x_0)$, is said to be **expanded about the base point** x_0. Polynomials in this form may look strange at first compared to (say) $p(x) = 1 + 2x + 3x^2 + 4x^3$, which is expanded about $x = 0$. But the first form turns out to be more convenient for some purposes—it pays off nicely in the next (important) example.

Expansion of polynomials about different base points is a nice algebraic technique, and it shows the value of alternate forms of the same function.

EXAMPLE 3 Consider the polynomial

$$p(x) = a_0 + a_1(x - x_0) + a_2(x - x_0)^2 + a_3(x - x_0)^3 + a_4(x - x_0)^4.$$

Find $p(x_0)$, $p'(x_0)$, $p''(x_0)$, $p^{(3)}(x_0)$, and $p^{(4)}(x_0)$ (the value and first four derivatives of p at $x = x_0$).

This example explores the relationship between polynomial coefficients and derivatives; many students can "discover" much of this for themselves by working with concrete examples.

Solution Differentiating p is easy—but watch the coefficients:

$$p(x) = a_0 + a_1(x - x_0) + a_2(x - x_0)^2 + a_3(x - x_0)^3 + a_4(x - x_0)^4;$$

$$p'(x) = a_1 + 2a_2(x - x_0) + 3a_3(x - x_0)^2 + 4a_4(x - x_0)^3;$$

$$p''(x) = 2a_2 + 2 \cdot 3a_3(x - x_0) + 3 \cdot 4a_4(x - x_0)^2;$$

$$p^{(3)}(x) = 2 \cdot 3a_3 + 2 \cdot 3 \cdot 4a_4(x - x_0);$$

$$p^{(4)}(x) = 2 \cdot 3 \cdot 4a_4.$$

Now the special form of p pays off: substituting $x = x_0$ gives

$$p(x_0) = a_0 = 1a_0; \qquad p'(x_0) = a_1 = 1a_1; \qquad p''(x_0) = 2a_2;$$
$$p^{(3)}(x_0) = 2 \cdot 3a_3 = 6a_3; \qquad p^{(4)}(x_0) = 2 \cdot 3 \cdot 4a_4 = 24a_4.$$

Notice the pleasant pattern: For each i, the ith derivative $p^{(i)}(x_0)$ is a *constant* multiple of a_i. ◄

We can think of $p(x_0)$ as the zeroth derivative at x_0.

Factorials The constant multiples (1, 1, 2, 6, 24) in the preceding computation are **factorials**. The **factorial** of i, denoted by $i!$, is defined as the repeated product $i \cdot (i-1) \cdot (i-2) \cdots 2 \cdot 1$. (By convention, $0! = 1$.) ◄ Factorials crop up often in mathematics (often enough to rate their own key on many calculators), especially around repeated operations like those in Example 3. We use factorials in the following theorem to describe the pattern just seen.

This convention looks strange at first glance, but it simplifies calculations.

THEOREM 1 Let $p(x) = a_0 + a_1(x - x_0) + a_2(x - x_0)^2 + \cdots + a_n(x - x_0)^n$. Then

$$p(x_0) = a_0; \qquad p'(x_0) = a_1; \qquad p''(x_0) = 2a_2;$$
$$p^{(3)}(x_0) = 6a_3; \qquad \cdots \qquad p^{(n)}(x_0) = n! \, a_n.$$

Equivalently, $a_i = \dfrac{p^{(i)}(x_0)}{i!}$ for all $i \geq 0$.

Theorem 1 restates, a little more generally, what we noticed for derivatives through degree 4 in Example 3. A formal proof, which we omit, uses the technique of mathematical induction.

Read one way, the theorem is a rule for calculating certain derivatives. More important for us, the theorem offers a nice recipe for cooking up polynomials with prescribed derivatives at a point.

This example explores (among other things) how the degree of a polynomial is related to the number of conditions it must satisfy.

EXAMPLE 4 Find a quadratic function $q(x) = a_0 + a_1 x + a_2 x^2$ for which $q(0) = 1$, $q'(0) = 2$, and $q''(0) = 3$. Are there *linear* functions with all three properties? Are there cubic functions?

Solution Theorem 1 (with $x_0 = 0$) says exactly what to do: Set $a_0 = 1$, $a_1 = 2$, and $a_2 = q''(0)/2 = 3/2$. Thus, the quadratic polynomial we want is $q(x) = 1 + 2x + 3x^2/2$.

No *linear* polynomial $\ell(x) = a_0 + a_1 x$ can work because $\ell''(0) = 0$ for every linear polynomial. But infinitely many *cubic* polynomials satisfy all three requirements: Every function of the form $c(x) = 1 + 2x + 3x^2/2 + a_3 x^3$ satisfies all three conditions, regardless of the value of a_3. Figure 3 shows five functions of this form; the darker curve is the quadratic q (for which $a_3 = 0$):

All five curves "agree to order 2" at $x = 0$.

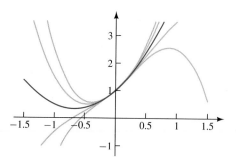

Each curve's equation is $y = 1 + 2x + 3x^2/2 + a_3 x^3$, for $a_3 = -2, -1, 0, 1, 2$. The darker curve has $a_3 = 0$, and so it's quadratic.

FIGURE 3
Several functions that "match" at $x = 0$

Notice the similarity among the curves: Because all five functions shown have the same value and first two derivatives at $x = 0$, they behave similarly near $x = 0$ but spread apart elsewhere.   ■

Polynomials that approximate other functions

An important use of Theorem 1 is for finding polynomial functions (linear, quadratic, or higher-order) that *approximate* a given (non-polynomial) function f near a given domain point $x = x_0$. If f happens to be complicated, inconvenient, or poorly understood, then having a close polynomial approximation p can reduce clutter and simplify calculations. One way to achieve this approximation is to construct polynomials p that "match" the value and one or more derivatives of the "target" function f at $x = x_0$.

Theorem 1 states how to construct polynomials with any desired derivatives at $x = x_0$. We may want to do this for reasons other than matching a target function, such as to model a physical phenomenon.

Linear approximation: An old story The linear approximation (or tangent-line approximation) to a function f at a point $x = x_0$ is nothing new. We observed as early as Chapter 1 that a differentiable function is "close to" its tangent line near $x = x_0$ (the point of tangency) and that this line has point–slope equation $y = f(x_0) + f'(x_0)(x - x_0)$. Theorem 1, in its simplest form, says that this linear function has the same value and the same (first) derivative as f at $x = x_0$. One important use of linear approximation is to produce quick estimates for values of functions we don't know exactly.

> **EXAMPLE 5** Your calculator's **TAN** key is stuck, and you really need $\tan 31°$. You know that $\tan 30° = 1/\sqrt{3}$. What to do?
>
> **Solution** We'll use a linear approximation to estimate $\tan 31°$. To this end, let $f(x) = \tan x$ (in radians!); note that $30° = \pi/6$ radians and that $31° = \pi/6 + \pi/180$ radians. Now $f'(x) = \sec^2 x$, and so we have
>
> $$f\left(\frac{\pi}{6}\right) = \frac{1}{\sqrt{3}}; \quad f'\left(\frac{\pi}{6}\right) = \sec^2\left(\frac{\pi}{6}\right) = \frac{4}{3}.$$
>
> Thus,
>
> $$\ell(x) = \frac{1}{\sqrt{3}} + \frac{4}{3}\left(x - \frac{\pi}{6}\right); \quad \ell\left(\frac{\pi}{6} + \frac{\pi}{180}\right) = \frac{1}{\sqrt{3}} + \frac{4}{3}\frac{\pi}{180} \approx 0.6006.$$
>
> This compares well with the true value $\tan 31° \approx 0.6008\ldots$ (as we can check if the **TAN** key comes unstuck).   ■

Quadratic approximation: A second step Quadratic approximation takes linear approximation a step farther: We look for a quadratic polynomial that matches the value and first *two* derivatives of a given function f at a given point x_0.

The geometric result of quadratic approximation is a *parabola* (not a line, unless the quadratic term happens to be zero) that "fits" the f-graph at and near $x = x_0$. The (little) extra work done in quadratic approximation pays off nicely: The curved shape of a parabola permits a closer fit to a curved graph than any straight line allows. In particular, a quadratic approximation reflects the *concavity* of the target curve: The "tangent parabola" opens upward or downward depending on whether f is concave up or concave down at $x = x_0$. Figure 4 shows the sine function with two tangent parabolas opening in different directions.

The "tangent parabola" is interesting in its own right because it captures aspects of concavity. Students might consider what happens geometrically when the tangent "parabola" happens to be line.

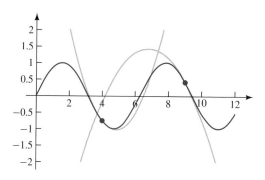

FIGURE 4
The sine curve with two "tangent parabolas"

The following example shows the advantage of quadratic over linear approximation.

EXAMPLE 6   Let $f(x) = 10^x$. Find ℓ and q, the linear and quadratic approximations to f, based at $x = 3$. Use each to estimate $f(3.1)$.

Solution   We need the value and two derivatives of f at $x = 3$. From $f(x) = 10^x$ we get $f'(x) = 10^x \ln 10$ and $f''(x) = 10^x (\ln 10)^2$, and so

$$f(3) = 10^3 = 1000; \quad f'(3) = 1000 \ln 10 \approx 2303; \quad f''(3) = 1000(\ln 10)^2 \approx 5302.$$

Thus,

$$\ell(x) = f(3) + f'(3) \cdot (x - 3) \approx 1000 + 2303(x - 3);$$

$$q(x) = \ell(x) + \frac{f''(3)}{2} \cdot (x - 3)^2 \approx 1000 + 2303(x - 3) + 2651(x - 3)^2,$$

and plugging in numbers gives the following results:

$$\ell(3.1) \approx 1230.3; \qquad q(3.1) \approx 1256.7; \qquad f(3.1) \approx 1258.9.$$

Figure 5 shows graphically how much better q does than ℓ in fitting f near $x = 3$:

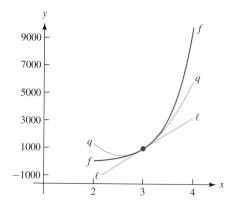

Although q does better than ℓ near $x = 3$, neither does well elsewhere. Note that q opens upward because f is concave up.

FIGURE 5
Linear and quadratic approximations to $f(x) = 10^x$

The picture shows why ℓ fits f so poorly: f bends sharply away from ℓ, even quite near $x = 3$. The second derivative, f'', explains why. Any linear function ℓ has zero second derivative. Our target function f, by contrast, has a huge second derivative:

$f''(3) \approx 5000$. Because f is so drastically nonlinear, it is poorly approximated by *any* straight line—even the best-fitting one. ∎

We see again the connection between concavity and the goodness of linear approximation. The same idea arose in bounding errors committed by (say) the trapezoid rule.

Onward and upward: Taylor-made polynomials

There's no need to stop with quadratic polynomials in matching derivatives of a given function f at a point x_0. Higher-order matching is possible with polynomials of degree 3, 4, and higher. The following example illustrates the idea in an unusually simple setting and shows where the function P_5 in Example 1 came from.

We consider Taylor series—infinite-degree polynomials—in Chapter 11.

EXAMPLE 7 Find the fifth-degree polynomial P_5 that matches $f(x) = e^x$ to order 5 at $x_0 = 0$ — that is,

$$P_5(0) = f(0), \quad P_5'(0) = f'(0), \quad P_5''(0) = f''(0), \dots P_5^{(5)}(0) = f^{(5)}(0).$$

Computing tools can find Taylor polynomials easily; even students who have such technology should find some Taylor polynomials by hand to fix ideas.

Solution Here $f'(x) = e^x = f(x)$, and so all derivatives are the same:

$$f(0) = 1 = f'(0) = f''(0) = f^{(3)}(0) = f^{(4)}(0) = f^{(5)}(0).$$

Theorem 1 tells how to find a polynomial

$$P_5(x) = a_0 + a_1 x + a_2 x^2 + a_3 x^3 + a_4 x^4 + a_5 x^5$$

with the same derivatives; we just set $a_i = f^{(i)}(0)/i! = 1/i!$ for all $i \geq 0$. That is,

$$P_5(x) = \frac{1}{0!} + \frac{x}{1!} + \frac{x^2}{2!} + \frac{x^3}{3!} + \frac{x^4}{4!} + \frac{x^5}{5!} = 1 + x + \frac{x^2}{2} + \frac{x^3}{6} + \frac{x^4}{24} + \frac{x^5}{120}.$$

Figure 1 (page 494) shows graphs of P_5 and f. ∎

The formal definition The polynomial P_5 constructed in Example 7 is called the **fifth-order Taylor polynomial** for $f(x) = e^x$ based at $x = 0$. It illustrates a more general definition:

> **DEFINITION (Taylor polynomials)** Let f be any function whose first n derivatives exist at $x = x_0$. The **Taylor polynomial** of order n, based at x_0, is defined by
>
> $$P_n(x) = f(x_0) + f'(x_0)(x - x_0) + \frac{f''(x_0)}{2!}(x - x_0)^2$$
>
> $$+ \frac{f^{(3)}(x_0)}{3!}(x - x_0)^3 + \cdots + \frac{f^{(n)}(x_0)}{n!}(x - x_0)^n.$$

Observe:

- **Linear and quadratic cases** If $n = 1$, the definition gives the familiar linear approximation; if $n = 2$, we get the quadratic approximation discussed above.

- **Maclaurin polynomials** Taylor polynomials that happen to be based at $x = 0$ are called **Maclaurin polynomials**. → They look a little cleaner on the page:

$$P_n(x) = f(0) + f'(0)x + \frac{f''(0)}{2}x^2 + \cdots + \frac{f^{(n)}(0)}{n!}x^n.$$

(In Example 7 we found the fifth-order Maclaurin polynomial for $f(x) = e^x$.)

Colin Maclaurin (1698–1746) was a Scottish contemporary of Isaac Newton. He studied the mathematics of tides, eclipses, honeycombs, and molasses barrels—along with the theory of calculus.

- **Order and degree** A Taylor polynomial P_n of **order** n is chosen so that its value and first n derivatives at $x = x_0$ agree with those of f. The definition shows that P_n also has **degree** n because it involves powers of $(x - x_0)$ up through the nth power. (If, by chance, $a_n = 0$, then the degree of P_n is less than n.)

Students sometimes lose track of what's a symbol and what's a variable in the Taylor polynomial definition.

- **Many symbols, just one variable**   The definition involves many symbols: x, x_0, f, and n. While we are in this thicket, it is helpful to remember that x *is the only variable.* In specific cases all the other symbols take *numerical* values.

Taylor's idea?   The idea underlying Taylor polynomials probably predates Brook Taylor (1685–1731), for whom they are named. According to some authors the idea appears in work of John Bernoulli (1667–1748) published in 1694. The same Bernoulli (one of several famous Bernoullis) is also credited with having discovered—behind the scenes—l'Hôpital's rule.

How well do Taylor polynomials fit?   Taylor polynomials can be used to approximate more complicated functions. Gauging *how closely* a given Taylor polynomial fits its target function is the subject of the next section. Here we simply remark that Taylor polynomials usually fit their target functions better and better as their order increases. We illustrate this principle graphically and numerically in the following example.

E X A M P L E 8   Find P_1, P_3, P_5, and P_7, the Taylor (or Maclaurin) polynomials for $f(x) = \sin x$ based at $x = 0$. Plot everything on one set of axes. How closely does each polynomial approximate $\sin 1$?

Solution   To find P_7 we need the value and the first seven derivatives of $f(x) = \sin x$ at $x = 0$. Here they are in order: 0, 1, 0, −1, 0, 1, 0, −1. Using Theorem 1 to match derivatives gives

$$P_7(x) = 0 + 1x + 0x^2 - \frac{1}{3!}x^3 + 0x^4 + \frac{1}{5!}x^5 + 0x^6 - \frac{1}{7!}x^7.$$

The formula lets us read off the lower-order Maclaurin polynomials:

$$P_1(x) = x = P_2(x); \qquad P_3(x) = x - \frac{x^3}{6} = P_4(x);$$

$$P_5(x) = x - \frac{x^3}{6} + \frac{x^5}{120} = P_6(x); \quad P_7(x) = x - \frac{x^3}{6} + \frac{x^5}{120} - \frac{x^7}{5040}.$$

Figure 6 shows all five graphs together:

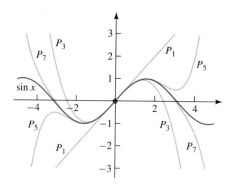

FIGURE 6
Several Taylor approximations to $f(x) = \sin x$

Observe:

- **An odd function**   All the nonzero powers of x in the Maclaurin polynomials are *odd*; this occurs because $\sin x$ itself is an *odd* function. (For similar reasons, all nonzero terms in the Maclaurin polynomials for $\cos x$ are *even*.)

- **Snug fits**   All four Taylor polynomials fit the sine curve well near the base point $x = 0$. Differences among the functions appear only as one moves away (to left or right) from $x = 0$.

- **Better and better**   Higher-order Taylor polynomials approximate the sine function better than lower-order ones. For instance, P_7 "sticks with" the sine curve much farther than P_1 or P_3.

Intuition suggests that P_1, P_3, P_5, and P_7 should give successively closer estimates for $\sin 1 \approx 0.84147$. So they do:

$$P_1(1) = 1; \quad P_3(1) \approx 0.83333; \quad P_5(1) \approx 0.84167; \quad P_7(1) \approx 0.84147. \qquad \blacksquare$$

BASIC EXERCISES

1. Let $f(x) = x^4 - 12x^3 + 44x^2 + 2x + 1$.

   (a) Find the Maclaurin series representation of f.

   (b) Find the Taylor series representation of f expanded about $x = 3$.

2. Find numbers a_0, a_1, a_2, a_3, a_4, and a_5 such that

$$x^4 - 4x^3 + 5x = a_0 + a_1(x-1) + a_2(x-1)^2$$
$$+ a_3(x-1)^3 + a_4(x-1)^4 + a_5(x-1)^5.$$

3. Let $p(x) = 9 - \dfrac{(x-1)}{8} + \dfrac{(x-1)^2}{7} + \dfrac{(x-1)^3}{6} + \dfrac{(x-1)^4}{5}$.

Evaluate

   (a) $p(1)$ **(b)** $p^{(4)}(1)$.

4. Let $q(x) = 6 + \displaystyle\sum_{k=1}^{10} \dfrac{(x-2)^k}{k^2}$. Evaluate

   (a) $q''(2)$ **(b)** $q^{(9)}(2)$.

5. Let $p(x) = \displaystyle\sum_{m=0}^{19} \dfrac{(x+3)^{2m}}{(2m+1)^4}$. Evaluate

   (a) $p^{(11)}(-3)$ **(b)** $p^{(12)}(-3)$.

6. Let $q(x) = \displaystyle\sum_{n=0}^{100} \dfrac{(x-3)^{2n+1}}{n!}$. Evaluate

   (a) $q^{(99)}(3)$ **(b)** $q^{(100)}(3)$.

In Exercises 7–12, first find the sixth-order Maclaurin polynomial of the given function; then find an interval centered at

$x = 0$ *in which the approximation error* $|f(x) - P_6(x)|$ *is less than* 0.01.

7. $f(x) = \cos x$ **8.** $f(x) = e^x$

9. $f(x) = \ln(1+x)$ **10.** $f(x) = \sqrt{1+x}$

11. $f(x) = \sinh x$ **12.** $f(x) = \cosh x$

In Exercises 13–24, first find the fifth-order Taylor polynomial for $f(x)$ *based at* x_0*; then find an interval centered at* $x = x_0$ *in which the approximation error* $|f(x) - P_5(x)|$ *is less than* 0.01.

13. $f(x) = \sin x, x_0 = \pi/4$

14. $f(x) = \cos x, x_0 = \pi/4$

15. $f(x) = \sin x, x_0 = \pi/3$

16. $f(x) = \cos x, x_0 = \pi/3$

17. $f(x) = 1/x, x_0 = 1$

18. $f(x) = 1/x, x_0 = 2$

19. $f(x) = \ln x, x_0 = 1$

20. $f(x) = 1/x^2, x_0 = 1$

21. $f(x) = \sqrt{x}, x_0 = 1$

22. $f(x) = \sqrt{x}, x_0 = 4$

23. $f(x) = 1/\sqrt{x}, x_0 = 1$

24. $f(x) = 1/\sqrt{x}, x_0 = 4$

FURTHER EXERCISES

25. Suppose that $P_n(x)$ is the nth-order Taylor polynomial for a function f. Can the degree of P_n be greater than n? Justify your answer.

26. Suppose that $P_n(x)$ is the nth-order Taylor polynomial for a function f. Can the degree of P_n be less than n? Justify your answer.

27. Suppose that $P_5(x) = 3 - x/4 - x^2/5 + 7x^3 - x^4 + 11x^5/9$ is the Taylor polynomial of order 5 for a function f. Find the Taylor polynomial of order 2 for the function f.

28. **(a)** Show that if f is an even function, then f' is an odd function.

   (b) Suppose that f is an even function. Use part (a) to show that every Maclaurin polynomial for $f(x)$ involves only *even* powers of x.

29. Suppose that f is an odd function. Show that every Maclaurin polynomial for $f(x)$ involves only *odd* powers of x.

30. Suppose that $M_n(x) = \sum_{k=0}^{n} a_k x^n$ is the nth-order Maclaurin polynomial for the function $f(x)$ and that $g(x) = f(x-b)$, where b is a constant. Show that $P_n(x) = \sum_{k=0}^{n} a_k(x-b)^n$ is the nth-order Taylor polynomial for $g(x)$ based at $x_0 = b$.

31. The fourth-order Maclaurin polynomial for $f(x) = \ln(1+x)$ is $P_4(x) = x - x^2/2 + x^3/3 - x^4/4$. Use this fact and Exercise 30 to find the fourth-order Taylor polynomial for $\ln x$ based at $x = 1$.

32. The fourth-order Taylor polynomial for $f(x) = 1/x$ based at $x_0 = 1$ is $P_4(x) = 1 - (x-1) + (x-1)^2 - (x-1)^3 + (x-1)^4$. Use this fact and Exercise 30 to find the fourth-order Maclaurin polynomial for $g(x) = 1/(1+x)$.

33. The fourth-order Taylor polynomial for $f(x) = 1/\sqrt{x}$ based at $x_0 = 1$ is $P_4(x) = 1 - (x-1)/2 + 3(x-1)^2/8 - 5(x-1)^3/16 + 35(x-1)^4/128$. Use this fact and Exercise 30 to find the fourth-order Maclaurin polynomial for $g(x) = 1/\sqrt{1+x}$.

34. Suppose that $M_n(x)$ is the nth-order Maclaurin polynomial for $f(x)$. Show that if k is a constant, then $M_n(kx)$ is the nth-order Maclaurin polynomial for $f(kx)$.

Suppose that $M_n(x)$ is the nth-order Maclaurin polynomial for $f(x)$. Use the fact stated in Exercise 34 to find the fifth-degree Maclaurin polynomial for the functions in Exercises 35–38.

35. $f(x) = \sin(x/2)$

36. $f(x) = \cos(\pi x)$

37. $f(x) = e^{-x}$

38. $f(x) = \ln(1+2x)$

Suppose that $M_n(x)$ is the nth-order Maclaurin polynomial for $f(x)$ and that m is a positive integer. It can be shown that $M_{mn}(x^m)$ is the mnth-order Maclaurin polynomial for $f(x^m)$. Use this fact to find the sixth-degree Maclaurin polynomial for the functions in Exercises 39–42.

39. $f(x) = e^{x^2}$

40. $f(x) = \sin(x^2)$

41. $f(x) = (1+x^2)^{-1}$

42. $f(x) = \sqrt{1+x^3}$

43. (a) Let $g(x) = xf(x)$. Show that $g^{(n)}(x) = nf^{(n-1)}(x) + xf^{(n)}(x)$.

(b) Suppose that $M_n(x)$ is the nth-order Maclaurin polynomial for the function $f(x)$ and that $g(x) = xf(x)$. Use

part (a) to show that $xM_n(x)$ is the Maclaurin polynomial of degree $n+1$ for $g(x)$.

44. Use part (b) of Exercise 43 to find the sixth-degree Maclaurin polynomial for $f(x) = x\sin x$.

45. Suppose that p and q are the nth-order Taylor polynomials based at x_0 for the functions f and g, respectively. Explain why $r(x) = p(x) + q(x)$ is the nth-order Taylor polynomial based at x_0 for the function $h(x) = f(x) + g(x)$.

46. Use the trigonometric identity $\cos(u+v) = \cos u \cos v - \sin u \sin v$ and the fifth-order Maclaurin polynomials for the sine and cosine functions to find the fifth-order Taylor polynomial for $\cos x$ based at $x = \pi/3$. [HINT: See Exercises 30 and 45.]

47. Suppose that $F'(x) = f(x)$ and that $P_n(x)$ is the nth-order Taylor polynomial for $F(x)$ based at x_0. Show that $\frac{d}{dx}P_n(x)$ is the Taylor polynomial of degree $n-1$ for $f(x)$ based at x_0.

48. Suppose that $F'(x) = f(x)$ and that $P_n(x)$ is the nth-order Taylor polynomial for $f(x)$ based at x_0. Show that $F(x_0) + \int_{x_0}^{x} P_n(t)\,dt$ is the Taylor polynomial of degree $n+1$ for $F(x)$ based at x_0.

Use the ideas explored in Exercises 30–48 to find the sixth-degree Maclaurin polynomial of the functions in Exercises 49–54.

49. $f(x) = \cos^2 x$
[HINT: $\cos^2 x = (1 + \cos(2x))/2$.]

50. $f(x) = \sin x \cos x$
[HINT: $\sin x \cos x = \sin(2x)/2$.]

51. $f(x) = \ln\left|\dfrac{1+x}{1-x}\right|$
[HINT: $\ln|u/v| = \ln|u| - \ln|v|$.]

52. $f(x) = \int_0^x e^{-t^2}\,dt$

53. $f(x) = \arctan x$
[HINT: $\arctan x = \int_0^x dt/(1+t^2)$.]

54. $f(x) = \arcsin x$
[HINT: $\arcsin x = \int_0^x dt/\sqrt{1-t^2}$.]

9.2 TAYLOR'S THEOREM: ACCURACY GUARANTEES FOR TAYLOR POLYNOMIALS

We state, use, and prove informally an inequality similar to Lagrange's (derivative-based) form of the difference between a function and a given Taylor polynomial. The inequality version suffices for our use, and it's a little simpler to state and prove than a corresponding equality.

In the preceding section we saw that a Taylor polynomial $P_n(x)$ approximates its target function $f(x)$ closely if x is near the base point $x = x_0$ and that the "goodness" of approximation usually improves as the degree n increases. In this section we make these useful general principles more precise: we show how to *guarantee* that Taylor polynomials approximate their target functions with specified accuracy.

Taylor's theorem lets us give such ironclad assurances. It is in the spirit of—and even resembles—the error-bound formulas for numerical integrals we studied in Chapter 6. (See, e.g., Theorem 3, page 387.) In all of these cases, the errors committed by various approximations are linked to the size of *derivatives* (first-, second-, or higher-order) of the functions in question.

Taylor errors and where they come from

A Taylor polynomial P_n is chosen to match its target function f at the base point x_0 in the sense that

$$f(x_0) = P_n(x_0); \quad f'(x_0) = P_n'(x_0); \quad f''(x_0) = P_n''(x_0); \quad \ldots \quad f^{(n)}(x_0) = P_n^{(n)}(x_0).$$

(In math jargon, f and P_n "agree to order n at x_0.") The real question about approximation, therefore, is how closely f and P_n agree *near*, rather than *at*, $x = x_0$ and how this accuracy depends on n. We focus on these questions in the following example.

EXAMPLE 1 Let $f(x) = \sqrt{x}$. Find the constant, linear, and quadratic Taylor polynomials (P_0, P_1, and P_2) for f at the base point $x_0 = 64$. ➔ How much error does each Taylor polynomial commit in approximating f near $x = 64$?

This base point is convenient because we know the exact value $f(64) = 8$.

The example shows that the goodness of approximation depends both on the degree of fitting and on the distance from the base point.

Solution Routine calculations give the following (exact) values:

$$f(64) = 8; \quad f'(64) = \frac{1}{16}; \quad f''(64) = -\frac{1}{2048}.$$

Plugging these ingredients into the recipes of Section 9.1 gives the Taylor polynomials

$$P_0(x) = 8; \quad P_1(x) = 8 + \frac{1}{16}(x - 64); \quad P_2(x) = 8 + \frac{1}{16}(x - 64) - \frac{1}{4096}(x - 64)^2.$$

Figure 1 shows P_0, P_1, P_2, and f plotted together.

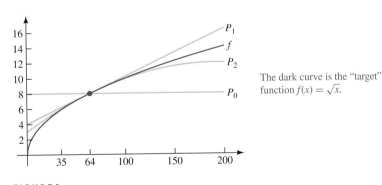

The dark curve is the "target" function $f(x) = \sqrt{x}$.

FIGURE 1
Constant, linear, and quadratic approximations to $f(x) = \sqrt{x}$

The graphs suggest, and numerical values confirm, how well or poorly P_0, P_1, and P_2 approximate f near to and far from $x = 64$:

Three approximations to $f(x) = \sqrt{x}$							
x	35	63	63.9	64	64.1	65	100
$P_0(x)$	8.00000	8.00000	8.00000	8	8.00000	8.00000	8.00000
$P_1(x)$	6.18750	7.93750	7.99375	8	8.00625	8.06250	9.00000
$P_2(x)$	5.98218	7.93726	7.99375	8	8.00625	8.06226	8.93750
$f(x)$	5.91608	7.93725	7.99375	8	8.00625	8.06226	8.94427

Students can experiment with other plotting windows.

The graphs and the numbers give the same message: P_2 approximates f best, especially near $x = 64$. Indeed, the graphs of P_2 and f "share ink" in the range $35 \le x \le 100$. ■

Sources of error   Example 1 suggests several lessons about how Taylor approximation errors arise:

- **Error committed by P_0: Look at f'**   The zero-order Taylor approximation is the *constant* function P_0. In effect, P_0 "pretends" that f itself is *constant* near x_0, or, equivalently, that $f'(x) = 0$ for x near x_0. In general, $f'(x)$ measures how much f *differs* from being constant. We expect P_0 to approximate f well if f' is near zero and poorly if f' has large positive or large negative values.

A function f is linear if and only if $f''(x) = 0$ for all x.

- **Error committed by P_1: Look at f''**   The Taylor polynomial P_1 is the familiar *linear* approximation to f at x_0; P_1 "pretends" that f is *linear* near x_0, or, equivalently, that $f''(x) = 0$ for x near x_0. ◄ Thus, $f''(x)$ measures how much f *differs* from being linear; we expect P_1 to approximate f well if f'' is near zero, and poorly if f'' takes large positive or large negative values near $x = x_0$. (In Example 1, $f''(64) = -1/2048$, and f'' takes similar small negative values near $x = 64$; this explains why P_1 commits relatively little error near $x = 64$.)

A function f is quadratic if and only if $f'''(x) = 0$ for all x.

- **Error committed by P_2: Look at f'''**   The emerging pattern continues. This time, the quadratic Taylor polynomial P_2 "pretends" that f is *quadratic* near x_0, or, equivalently, that $f'''(x) = 0$ for x near x_0. ◄ We expect P_2 to approximate f well if $|f'''(x)|$ is near zero, and poorly if $|f'''(x)|$ takes large positive values near $x = x_0$. (In Example 1, $f'''(64) = 3/262144$, and f''' takes similar small positive values near $x = 64$; this explains why P_2 approximates f so accurately near $x = 64$.)

Taylor's theorem

The preceding paragraphs suggest a moral: The error committed by P_n in approximating f is related to the magnitude of the $(n+1)^{\text{th}}$ derivative, $f^{(n+1)}(x)$. The following important theorem makes this message precise. The hypotheses ensure that all the derivatives in question exist.

The hypothesis on derivatives resembles those for numerical integral error bounds—in both cases, large derivatives correspond to larger errors.

THEOREM 2 (Taylor's theorem)   Suppose that f is repeatedly differentiable on an interval I containing x_0 and that

$$P_n(x) = a_0 + a_1(x - x_0) + a_2(x - x_0)^2 + \cdots + a_n(x - x_0)^n$$

is the nth-order Taylor polynomial based at x_0. Suppose that for all x in I,

$$\left| f^{(n+1)}(x) \right| \le K_{n+1}.$$

Then

$$\left| f(x) - P_n(x) \right| \le \frac{K_{n+1}}{(n+1)!} |x - x_0|^{n+1}. \tag{1}$$

Here are some notes on the theorem:

- **Error on the left**   The left-hand quantity in Inequality (1) is the *error* committed by $P_n(x)$ in approximating $f(x)$. Taylor's theorem guarantees that this error is no larger than the quantity on the right side.

- **Factorials**   The factorial in the denominator on the right side of Inequality (1) grows quickly with n; this helps explain why the error committed by P_n normally decreases as n increases.

- **Powers of the distance**   The positive quantity $|x - x_0|^{n+1}$ on the right side of Inequality (1) is a power of the *distance* from x to x_0. The larger this distance, the larger the possible error.

- **Other versions**   Other versions of Taylor's theorem exist. This version is relatively simple, partly because it involves an *inequality*. In other versions, Inequality (1) is replaced with an *equality* that is slightly more complicated.

- **It's OK to overestimate K_{n+1}**   *Any* upper bound for $|f^{(n+1)}|$ on I can serve as K_{n+1} in Inequality (1). Choosing K_{n+1} as small as possible improves the error bound, but the inequality holds even for larger values. →

- **Worst-case scenarios**   The right side of Inequality (1) represents the *worst* case that the hypotheses allow; in many cases the actual error committed is less than the theorem permits.

One additional complication is that the equality version involves the derivative $f^{(n+1)}(t)$ evaluated at an unknown input t.

But don't underestimate K_{n+1}.

We'll discuss the theorem's proof after exploring its meaning and some of its uses.

EXAMPLE 2   In Example 1 we found P_1 and P_2, the linear and quadratic approximations to $f(x) = \sqrt{x}$ at $x = 64$. What does Theorem 2 say about the errors these approximations commit on the interval $[50, 80]$? On the interval $[63, 65]$?

In this basic example we just work out what the theorem says.

Solution   First we need suitable values for K_2 and K_3. Calculation gives

$$f''(x) = -\frac{1}{4x^{3/2}} \quad \text{and} \quad f'''(x) = \frac{3}{8x^{5/2}},$$

and so

$$\left| f''(x) \right| = \frac{1}{4|x|^{3/2}} \quad \text{and} \quad \left| f'''(x) \right| = \frac{3}{8|x|^{5/2}}.$$

A moment's thought (or a look at graphs) shows that $|f''(x)|$ and $|f'''(x)|$ *decrease* as x increases. For the interval $[50, 80]$, therefore, we may use

$$K_2 = |f''(50)| \le 0.00071 \quad \text{and} \quad K_3 = |f'''(50)| \le 0.000022.$$

On $[63, 65]$, we may use

$$K_2 = |f''(63)| \le 0.00050 \quad \text{and} \quad K_3 = |f'''(63)| \le 0.000012.$$

All ingredients are now ready. Here's what the theorem says:

- For x in $[50, 80]$, the error bounds are

$$\left| \sqrt{x} - P_1(x) \right| \le \frac{|f''(50)|}{2}(x-64)^2 \le \frac{0.00071}{2}(80-64)^2 \approx 0.091;$$

$$\left| \sqrt{x} - P_2(x) \right| \le \frac{|f'''(50)|}{6}(x-64)^3 \le \frac{0.000022}{6}(80-64)^3 \approx 0.015.$$

(We used $x = 80$ to make $x - 64$ as large as possible.) Thus, P_1 approximates f on $[50, 80]$ to about one-decimal-place accuracy, while P_2 does considerably better.

- For x in $[63, 65]$, the largest possible errors are even less:

$$|\sqrt{x} - P_1(x)| \le \frac{|f''(63)|}{2}(x - 64)^2 \le \frac{0.00050}{2}(65 - 64)^2 = 0.00025;$$

$$|\sqrt{x} - P_2(x)| \le \frac{|f'''(63)|}{6}(x - 64)^3 \le \frac{0.000012}{6}(65 - 64)^3 = 0.000002.$$

Thus, P_1 approximates f on $[63, 65]$ to about three-decimal-place accuracy; again, P_2 does much better.

The table on page 504 shows that these error estimates are actually conservative: P_1 and P_2 behave even better than the theorem predicts. ∎

EXAMPLE 3 In Example 1 of Section 9.1 we studied the 5th-order Maclaurin polynomial

$$P_5(x) = 1 + x + \frac{x^2}{2} + \frac{x^3}{6} + \frac{x^4}{24} + \frac{x^5}{120}$$

for $f(x) = e^x$. What does Theorem 2 say about how well P_5 approximates f on the interval $[-1, 1]$? How close must $P_5(1) = 163/60$ be to the *exact* value of e?

Solution Finding derivatives of $f(x) = e^x$ is unusually easy:

$$f(x) = f'(x) = f''(x) = \cdots = f^{(6)}(x) = e^x.$$

Recall: It's OK to overestimate K_6.

Since e^x is positive and increases with x, we have $|f^{(6)}(x)| = e^x \le e^1$ for all x in $[-1, 1]$. Hence, we can take $K_6 = e$, or, for easier calculation, we can use $K_6 = 3$. ◄ Now Theorem 1 gives

$$\left| e^x - P_5(x) \right| \le \frac{3}{6!}|x|^6 = \frac{1}{240}|x|^6$$

for all x in $[-1, 1]$. With $x = 1$ we have

$$\left| e^1 - P_5(1) \right| \le \frac{1}{240} \approx 0.00412,$$

and so $P_5(1) = 163/60 \approx 2.71667$ is guaranteed to differ from e by less than about 4 in the third decimal place. (In fact, $e \approx 2.71828$—closer to $P_5(1)$ than Theorem 2 requires.) ∎

We named and studied the speed limit law long ago, in Chapter 1.

Taylor's theorem, the speed limit law, and the mean value theorem Taylor's theorem is simplest if $n = 0$. In this case, $P_0(x) = f(x_0)$, and so Taylor's theorem says that

$$\left| f(x) - f(x_0) \right| \le K_1|x - x_0|,$$

where K_1 is an upper bound for $|f'(x)|$ on I. If $x > x_0$ we can drop the absolute value signs and get

$$f(x) - f(x_0) \le K_1(x - x_0);$$

this is what we called the **speed limit law** in Chapter 1. (The name makes sense because the inequality $|f'(x)| \le K_1$ represents a "speed limit" on the growth of f.)

We studied the mean value theorem in Chapter 4.

This case of Taylor's theorem is also closely related to the **mean value theorem**. ◄ The mean value theorem says that, for some input t between x_0 and x,

$$f(x) - f(x_0) = f'(t)(x - x_0);$$

this can be seen as an "equality version" of the $n = 0$ case of Taylor's theorem.

Proving Taylor's theorem

The idea of our proof is to "integrate the inequality" $\left| f^{(n+1)}(x) \right| \leq K_{n+1}$ repeatedly.

We'll prove the theorem assuming (just for convenience) that $x_0 = 0$, and only for the specific case $n = 2$. We won't prove the general case, but the proof's main idea—integrating an inequality repeatedly—applies with only minor changes to handle *any* value of n. We'll use two familiar properties of the definite integral:

- **Bigger integrands, bigger integrals**   If g and h are functions and $g(t) \leq h(t)$ for $a \leq t \leq b$, then $\int_a^b g(t)\,dt \leq \int_a^b h(t)\,dt$.

- **Integrating a derivative**   By the FTC,

$$\int_a^b g'(t)\,dt = g(b) - g(a)$$

for any function g with a continuous derivative g'.

Proof of Taylor's theorem (for $n = 2$ and $x_0 = 0$)   We assume that $\left| f'''(x) \right| \leq K_3$ for all x in I (an interval containing zero) and need to show that

$$\left| f(x) - P_2(x) \right| \leq \frac{K_3}{6} |x|^3 \tag{2}$$

for all x in I. We'll show this for positive x; a similar argument works for negative x. Because $x > 0$, we can drop the absolute value on the right of Inequality (2); this produces the equivalent double inequality

$$-\frac{K_3}{6} x^3 \leq f(x) - P_2(x) \leq \frac{K_3}{6} x^3; \tag{3}$$

we'll show that this holds for all positive x in I.

Our assumption that $\left| f'''(t) \right| \leq K_3$ for t in I is equivalent to the double inequality

$$-K_3 \leq f'''(t) \leq K_3. \tag{4}$$

(Calling the input variable t rather than x is harmless—and it's convenient for reasons we'll see in a moment.)

The proof's first step (and main idea) is to integrate Inequality (4) over the interval $[0, x]$, using the integral properties mentioned above. Doing so gives

$$-\int_0^x K_3\,dt \leq \int_0^x f'''(t)\,dt \leq \int_0^x K_3\,dt;$$

working out the integrals gives

$$-K_3 x \leq f''(x) - f''(0) \leq K_3 x. \tag{5}$$

The second step is to integrate Inequality (5) over the interval $[0, x]$: ➤

As before we first change the variable name to t to avoid confusion with x.

$$-\int_0^x K_3 t\,dt \leq \int_0^x f''(t)\,dt - \int_0^x f''(0)\,dt \leq \int_0^x K_3 t\,dt,$$

which works out to

$$-K_3 \frac{x^2}{2} \leq f'(x) - f'(0) - f''(0)x \leq K_3 \frac{x^2}{2}. \tag{6}$$

The final step is no surprise: We Integrate Inequality (6): ➤

We leave details to the reader.

$$-\int_0^x K_3 \frac{t^2}{2}\,dt \leq \int_0^x \left(f'(t) - f'(0) - f''(0)t \right)dt \leq \int_0^x K_3 \frac{t^2}{2}\,dt.$$

Working out these integrals gives

$$-K_3\frac{x^3}{6} \le f(x) - f(0) - f'(0)x - f''(0)\frac{x^2}{2} \le K_3\frac{x^3}{6},$$

which is just another way of stating Inequality (3). This completes the proof. ☐

BASIC EXERCISES

1. Let f and P_1 be as in Example 1.

(a) Plot $|f(x) - P_1(x)|$ over the interval $[50, 80]$. What does the graph say about the maximum *actual* approximation error that occurs over this interval?

(b) In Example 2 we used Theorem 2 to show that $|f(x) - P_1(x)| \le 0.091$. Is what you observed in part (a) consistent with this result? Justify your answer.

2. Let f and P_5 be as in Example 3.

(a) Show that $|f^6(x)| \le 8$ for all x in the interval $[-2, 2]$.

(b) Use part (a) to show that Theorem 2 implies that $|f(x) - P_5(x)| \le |x|^6/90$ if $-2 \le x \le 2$.

(c) Explain why part (b) implies that $|f(x) - P_5(x)| \le 0.72$ for all x in the interval $[-2, 2]$.

(d) Plot $|f(x) - P_5(x)|$ over the interval $[-2, 2]$. What does the graph say about the maximum *actual* approximation error that occurs over this interval?

(e) Is the result in part (c) consistent with what you observed in part (d)? Justify your answer.

3. Let $f(x) = \sin x$ and $P_5(x)$ be the fifth-order Maclaurin polynomial for f.

(a) What does Theorem 2 imply about the maximum approximation error committed by P_5 over the interval $[-2, 2]$?

(b) What is the maximum *actual* approximation error committed by P_5 over the interval $[-2, 2]$?

4. Let $f(x) = \cos x$ and $P_6(x)$ be the sixth-order Maclaurin polynomial for f.

(a) What does Theorem 2 imply about the maximum approximation error committed by P_6 over the interval $[-2, 2]$?

(b) What is the maximum *actual* approximation error committed by P_6 over the interval $[-2, 2]$?

5. Let $f(x) = 1/\sqrt{x}$ and $P_4(x)$ be the fourth-order Taylor polynomial for f based at $x_0 = 1$.

(a) What does Theorem 2 imply about the maximum approximation error committed by P_4 over the interval $[1/2, 3/2]$?

(b) What is the maximum *actual* approximation error committed by P_4 over the interval $[1/2, 3/2]$?

6. Let $f(x) = \ln x$ and $P_4(x)$ be the fourth-order Taylor polynomial for f based at $x_0 = 1$.

(a) What does Theorem 2 imply about the maximum approximation error committed by P_4 over the interval $[1/2, 3/2]$?

(b) What is the maximum *actual* approximation error committed by P_4 over the interval $[1/2, 3/2]$?

FURTHER EXERCISES

7. Let $f(x) = \sin x$ and let $M_n(x)$ be the nth-degree Maclaurin polynomial for f. Explain why, for any x, n can be chosen so that $|f(x) - P_n(x)| \le 10^{-6}$.

8. Let $f(x) = e^x$ and let $M_n(x)$ be the nth-degree Maclaurin polynomial for f. Explain why, for any x, n can be chosen so that $|f(x) - P_n(x)| \le 10^{-6}$.

9. Let $f(x) = \sin(x^2)$ and $P_2(x)$ be the quadratic Maclaurin polynomial for f.

(a) Show that $P_2(x) = x^2$.

(b) Use Theorem 2 to show that if $0 \le t \le 1/2$, then $|\sin(t^2) - t^2| \le 2.5t^3/3!$.

(c) It follows from part (a) that $\int_0^{1/2} f(x)\,dx \approx \frac{1}{24}$. Show that part (b) implies that $\left|\int_0^{1/2} f(x)\,dx - \frac{1}{24}\right| \le \frac{5}{768}$.

(d) Using Theorem 2, it can be shown that if $0 \le t \le 1/2$, then $|\sin(t^2) - t^2| \le 120t^6/6!$. Use this fact to find

another bound on the approximation error committed when $\int_0^{1/2} f(x)\,dx$ is approximated $\int_0^{1/2} P_2(x)\,dx$.

10. Let $f(x) = e^{-x^2}$ and $P_2(x)$ be the quadratic Maclaurin polynomial for f. Find a bound on the approximation error committed if $\int_0^{2/3} f(x)\,dx$ is approximated by $\int_0^{2/3} P_2(x)\,dx$.

In Exercises 11–14, use Theorem 2 to evaluate the limit.

11. $\lim\limits_{x \to 0} \dfrac{x - \sin x}{x^2}$

12. $\lim\limits_{x \to 0} \dfrac{x - \sin x}{x^3}$

13. $\lim\limits_{x \to 0} \dfrac{\cos x - 1 + x^2/2}{x^3}$

14. $\lim\limits_{x \to 0} \dfrac{e^x - 1 - x}{x^2}$

15. (a) Compute the quadratic Maclaurin polynomial for $f(x) = \sqrt{1+x}$.

(b) The electrical potential V at a distance r along the axis perpendicular to the center of a uniformly charged disk of radius a and charge density σ is

$$V = 2\pi\sigma\left(\sqrt{r^2+a^2}-r\right).$$

If r is large in comparison to a, then $a/r \approx 0$. Use part (a) to find an approximation for V.

16. According to the theory of relativity, the mass m of a particle moving with velocity v is $m = m_0/\sqrt{1-(v/c)^2}$, where m_0 is the rest mass of the particle and c is the velocity of light. Show that $m \approx m_0 + m_0 v^2/2c^2$.

17. Suppose that f is a function such that $f(1) = 1$, $f'(1) = 2$, and $f''(x) = (1+x^3)^{-1}$ for $x > -1$.

    (a) Estimate $f(1.5)$ using a quadratic Taylor polynomial.

    (b) Find an upper bound on the approximation error made in part (a).

18. During an encounter with a friendly extraterrestrial, it is revealed to you that the answer to life, the universe, and everything else is $f(1)$ for some function f. It is also revealed that $f(0) = 26$, $f'(0) = 22$, $f''(0) = -16$, $f'''(0) = 12$, and $\left|f^{(4)}(x)\right| \leq 7x^4$ if $|x| \leq 3$.

    (a) Find an upper bound on the value of $f(1)$.

    (b) Find a lower bound on the value of $f(1)$.

19. Let f be a function that has continuous derivatives on an interval containing a and x.

(a) Explain why $f(x) = f(a) + \int_a^x f'(t)\,dt$.

(b) Use part (a) and integration by parts to show that

$$f(x) = f(a) + f'(a)(x-a) - \int_a^x (t-x)f''(t)\,dt$$

$$= f(a) + f'(a)(x-a) + \int_a^x (x-t)f''(t)\,dt.$$

(c) Show that repeated integration by parts leads to this alternative form of Taylor's theorem:

$$f(x) = f(a) + f'(a)(x-a) + \frac{1}{2}f''(a)(x-a)^2$$

$$+ \frac{1}{3!}f'''(a)(x-a)^3 + \cdots + \frac{1}{n!}f^n(a)(x-a)^n$$

$$+ \frac{1}{n!}\int_a^x (x-t)^n f^{(n+1)}(t)\,dt.$$

20. Let $R_n(x) = \dfrac{1}{n!}\int_a^x (x-t)^n f^{(n+1)}(t)\,dt$. (This is the integral form of the remainder in Taylor's theorem derived in Exercise 19.) Show that if $a = 0$ and $\left|f^{(n+1)}(t)\right| \leq K_{n+1}$ for all t, then

$$\left|f(x) - P_n(x)\right| = \left|R_n(x)\right| \leq \frac{K_{n+1}}{(n+1)!}\,|x|^{n+1}.$$

9.3 FOURIER POLYNOMIALS: APPROXIMATING PERIODIC FUNCTIONS

We study Fourier polynomials here; Fourier series appear briefly in an Interlude in Chapter 11. Fourier approximation builds on integrals while Taylor approximation starts with derivatives.

In earlier sections we've seen how Taylor polynomials are constructed to approximate a target function near a chosen base point x_0. Taylor polynomial approximation is "local" in the sense that it focuses attention on a single base point and its immediate vicinity.

In this section we take another approach to the problem of approximating functions, this time using **Fourier polynomials**. Our approach here is "global": We'll choose Fourier polynomials that approximate a target function as closely as possible over a full domain interval rather than at a single point. To achieve this global approximation we'll use *integrals* over the full interval rather than *derivatives* at a single point.

Trigonometric polynomials

The main tools for Taylor approximation are ordinary polynomials. The corresponding tools for Fourier approximations are **trigonometric polynomials**—functions of the form

$$q_n(x) = a_0 + a_1 \cos x + a_2 \cos(2x) + \cdots + a_n \cos(nx)$$
$$+ b_1 \sin x + b_2 \sin(2x) + \cdots + b_n \sin(nx),$$

where n is a nonnegative integer and the coefficients a_k and b_k are real numbers. Notice that trigonometric polynomials are "linear combinations" (i.e., sums and constant multiples) of the basic trigonometric functions

$$1,\ \cos x,\ \sin x,\ \cos(2x),\ \sin(2x),\ \cos(3x),\ \sin(3x),\ \ldots$$

in exactly the same way that ordinary polynomials are built from the basic power functions $1, x, x^2, x^3, \ldots$.

Trigonometric polynomials (like ordinary polynomials) may have very different shapes and properties depending on the choices of coefficients a_k and b_k. Figure 1 shows three samples, all plotted over $[-\pi, \pi]$:

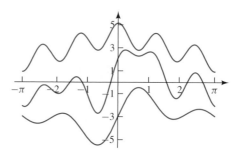

FIGURE 1
Three trigonometric polynomials

The particular formulas of the curves in Figure 1 don't matter for the moment, but observe the variety of shapes that trigonometric polynomials can assume.

Choosing the coefficients   The main idea of Fourier approximation (as for Taylor approximation) is to choose the coefficients a_k and b_k so that the resulting trigonometric polynomial closely approximates a given target function. For example, we saw in Example 2 of Section 9.1 (see especially Figure 2, page 495) the trigonometric polynomial

$$q(x) = \frac{4}{\pi}\left(\sin(x) + \frac{\sin(3x)}{3} + \frac{\sin(5x)}{5}\right)$$

approximates a certain "square wave" function. Note that in this case all the cosine coefficients a_k are zero, while the sine coefficients obey a simple rule:

$$b_k = \frac{4}{\pi}\cdot\frac{1}{k} \quad \text{(for odd } k\text{)}; \qquad b_k = 0 \quad \text{(for even } k\text{)}.$$

The main question, of course, is *how* to choose the a_k and the b_k in order to achieve a good fit with a target function. Providing and explaining an answer are the main goals of this section.

Properties of trigonometric polynomials   Understanding how to choose coefficients appropriately starts with basic properties of *all* trigonometric polynomials. We state several such properties in the following paragraphs. We'll be brief and leave some details to the reader.

- **Periodicity**   Periodicity is the most important property of trigonometric functions— and of trigonometric polynomials. Every trigonometric polynomial is 2π-periodic: it repeats itself on every interval of length 2π. This periodic behavior has a simple explanation: Each summand $a_k \cos(kx)$ and $b_k \sin(kx)$ repeats itself (k times, actually) on intervals of length 2π, and any sum of 2π-periodic functions is itself 2π-periodic. The graphs in Figure 1, for example, are shown only for inputs in the x-interval $[-\pi, \pi]$; the same shapes simply repeat themselves on intervals such as $[\pi, 3\pi]$.

  This periodicity property has two practical results: First, we may as well work just on the basic interval $[-\pi, \pi]$ because whatever happens there repeats itself elsewhere.

Second, we should expect good approximation from trigonometric polynomials only if the target function is *also* 2π-periodic.

- **Cosines are even, sines are odd**   Two simple but very useful facts follow from properties of ordinary sines and cosines:

  For each k, $\sin(kx)$ *is an odd function;* $\cos(kx)$ *is an even function.*

These properties have consequences that will save us a lot of labor in calculating integrals:

If g is an odd function, then $\int_{-\pi}^{\pi} g(x)\,dx = 0$. *If h is an even function, then* $\int_{-\pi}^{\pi} h(x)\,dx = 2\int_{0}^{\pi} h(x)\,dx.$

- **Zero integrals**   Lots of integrals arise in working with trigonometric polynomials. Luckily, many of these integrals turn out to be zero. In particular,

$$\int_{-\pi}^{\pi} \sin(kx)\,dx = 0 \quad \text{and} \quad \int_{-\pi}^{\pi} \cos(kx)\,dx = 0$$

for *every* positive integer k. Both claims are easy to check; either apply u-substitution or note that the first integrand is odd. These results make it easy to integrate *any* trigonometric polynomial. If

$$q_n(x) = a_0 + a_1 \cos x + b_1 \sin x + \cdots + a_n \cos(nx) + b_n \sin(nx),$$

then

$$\int_{-\pi}^{\pi} q_n(x)\,dx = \int_{-\pi}^{\pi} a_0\,dx + \cdots + \int_{-\pi}^{\pi} b_n \sin(nx)\,dx = 2\pi a_0.$$

(Every integral but the very first is zero, as we've just seen.)

- **More zero (and some nonzero) integrals**   Many other trigonometric integrals turn out to vanish. For instance, if m and n are any integers, then

$$\int_{-\pi}^{\pi} \cos(mx)\sin(nx)\,dx = 0$$

because the integrand is odd. Similarly, if m and n are *distinct* integers (i.e., $m \neq n$), then

$$\int_{-\pi}^{\pi} \sin(mx)\sin(nx)\,dx = 0; \quad \int_{-\pi}^{\pi} \cos(mx)\cos(nx)\,dx = 0.$$

Both of these claims are readily proved using trigonometric identities. If, on the other hand, $m = n$ in the preceding integrals, we find that

$$\int_{-\pi}^{\pi} \cos^2(mx)\,dx = \pi \quad \text{and} \quad \int_{-\pi}^{\pi} \sin^2(mx)\,dx = \pi.$$

Again, both integrals are straightforward calculations.

We'll use these facts to show how to choose trigonometric polynomials to approximate almost any target function f and to suggest why the process works. First comes the main definition:

A good understanding of evenness and oddness of functions saves a lot of labor in the Fourier setting.

DEFINITION (Fourier polynomials)   Let $f(x)$ be a function defined on $[-\pi, \pi]$. The **Fourier polynomial** of degree n for f is the trigonometric polynomial

$$q_n(x) = a_0 + a_1 \cos x + a_2 \cos(2x) + \cdots + a_n \cos(nx)$$
$$+ b_1 \sin x + b_2 \sin(2x) + \cdots + b_n \sin(nx),$$

with coefficients given by

$$a_0 = \frac{1}{2\pi} \int_{-\pi}^{\pi} f(x)\,dx;$$

$$a_k = \frac{1}{\pi} \int_{-\pi}^{\pi} f(x) \cos(kx)\,dx \qquad \text{if } k > 0;$$

$$b_k = \frac{1}{\pi} \int_{-\pi}^{\pi} f(x) \sin(kx)\,dx \qquad \text{if } k > 0.$$

Fourier and his polynomials   Fourier polynomials are named for the French mathematician Joseph Fourier (1768–1830), who used them to study the mathematics of various physical problems, including heat diffusion. Over the last 200 years, a large and still growing mathematical theory, **harmonic analysis**, has grown up around the subject.

For a given function f, the definition tells how to find the coefficients of a trigonometric polynomial that approximates f on the interval $[-\pi, \pi]$. After some examples to illustrate *that* Fourier polynomials have this approximation property, we'll suggest *why* they do. The first example illustrates, among other things, that the target function f may even have a discontinuity in the domain interval $[-\pi, \pi]$.

EXAMPLE 1   Figure 2 shows a "square wave" function f and the approximating trigonometric polynomial

$$q_9(x) = \frac{4}{\pi} \sin(x) + \frac{4}{\pi} \frac{\sin(3x)}{3} + \frac{4}{\pi} \frac{\sin(5x)}{5} + \frac{4}{\pi} \frac{\sin(7x)}{7} + \frac{4}{\pi} \frac{\sin(9x)}{9}. \qquad (1)$$

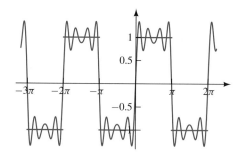

FIGURE 2

A square wave and a Fourier approximation

Figure 2(b), page 495, is similar but shows q_5 rather than q_9.

How was q_9 found? ◄

Solution   The target function's "formula" is

$$f(x) = \begin{cases} \vdots \\ -1 & \text{if } -3\pi \leq x < -2\pi; \\ 1 & \text{if } -2\pi \leq x < -\pi; \\ -1 & \text{if } -\pi \leq x < 0; \\ 1 & \text{if } 0 \leq x < \pi. \\ \vdots \end{cases}$$

To find the coefficients we use the integral-based recipes

$$a_0 = \frac{1}{2\pi} \int_{-\pi}^{\pi} f(x)\, dx; \quad a_k = \frac{1}{\pi} \int_{-\pi}^{\pi} f(x) \cos(kx)\, dx; \quad b_k = \frac{1}{\pi} \int_{-\pi}^{\pi} f(x) \sin(kx)\, dx$$

from the definition.

Our first labor-saving observation is that f is an *odd* function. This implies, at one stroke, that *all* of the integrals for a_0 and a_k are zero. As for the b_k, the fact that both $f(x)$ and $\sin(kx)$ are odd functions implies that their product is even, and so

$$b_k = \frac{1}{\pi} \int_{-\pi}^{\pi} f(x) \sin(kx)\, dx = \frac{2}{\pi} \int_0^{\pi} \sin(kx)\, dx.$$

The last integral can be found by substituting $u = kx$ and $du = k\, dx$; the result is

$$\frac{2}{\pi} \cdot \frac{-\cos(kx)}{k} \bigg]_0^{\pi} = \frac{2}{k\pi} \left(-\cos(k\pi) + \cos 0 \right).$$

The value of the last expression depends on whether k is even or odd:

$$b_k = \frac{4}{k\pi} \quad \text{if } k \text{ is odd}; \qquad b_k = 0 \quad \text{if } k \text{ is even}.$$

Thus, the b_k have the pattern

$$b_1, \ b_2, \ b_3, \ b_4, \ b_5, \ \ldots = \frac{4}{\pi}, \ 0, \ \frac{4}{3\pi}, \ 0, \ \frac{4}{5\pi}, \ \ldots,$$

which gives Formula (1).   ■

EXAMPLE 2   Find several Fourier polynomials q_n for $f(x) = x$. Plot them together with f. Do the q_n appear to approximate f? Where?

Since all trigonometric polynomials are 2π-periodic, they can't approximate nonperiodic functions well on large intervals.

Solution   We'll use the definition to find the coefficients; again, there's a simple pattern. Again the target function $f(x) = x$ is odd, and it follows as above that $a_k = 0$ for all k.

The b_k can be found using integration by parts, a table of integrals, or technology. Here's the result:

$$b_k = \frac{1}{\pi} \int_{-\pi}^{\pi} x \sin(kx)\, dx = \frac{-2\cos(k\pi)}{k}.$$

Again the numerical value depends on whether k is odd or even:

$$b_k = -\frac{2}{k} \quad \text{if } k \text{ is even}; \qquad b_k = \frac{2}{k} \quad \text{if } k \text{ is odd}.$$

Thus, the nth Fourier polynomial is

$$q_n(x) = \frac{2}{1} \sin x - \frac{2}{2} \sin(2x) + \frac{2}{3} \sin(3x) - \frac{2}{4} \sin(4x) + \cdots \pm \frac{2}{n} \sin(nx).$$

Figures 3(a) and (b) show graphs of f, q_3, and q_7 on two different domain intervals:

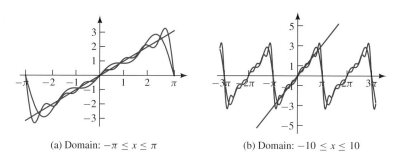

(a) Domain: $-\pi \le x \le \pi$ (b) Domain: $-10 \le x \le 10$

FIGURE 3
A function f and two Fourier polynomials

A close look at Figure 3(a) shows that q_7 (the wigglier curve) does a better job than q_3 of approximating f on $[-\pi, \pi]$. On the other hand, as Figure 3(b) shows, neither q_3 nor q_7 approximates f at all well outside the interval $[-\pi, \pi]$ because q_3 and q_7 are 2π-periodic and $f(x) = x$ is not. The figures illustrate that Fourier polynomials are effective *only* for approximating functions that, like Fourier polynomials themselves, repeat on intervals of length 2π. In the present case, we can think of q_3 and q_7 as approximations not to $f(x) = x$ itself but to the "sawtooth" function that's formed by repeating the basic shape of $y = x$ on each interval of length 2π.   ■

Why Fourier approximation works

Why do Fourier polynomials approximate a given function f on $[-\pi, \pi]$? Why are the coefficient formulas given in the definition "correct"?

Rigorous answers are well beyond our scope, but the basic idea is straightforward. The deep fact is that *every* continuous function f (and even many discontinuous functions) on $[-\pi, \pi]$ can be approximated as closely as we like by *some* trigonometric polynomial. In other words,

$$f(x) \approx q(x) = a_0 + a_1 \cos x + b_1 \sin x + \cdots + a_n \cos(nx) + b_n \sin(nx)$$

for *some* coefficients a_k and b_k. Given this, the remaining question is how to find the coefficients a_k and b_k.

Similar reasoning handles the a_k. (The case $k = 0$ is slightly different.)

Here's the answer for the b_k: ◄ Because $f(x) \approx q(x)$, we'd expect that

$$\int_{-\pi}^{\pi} f(x) \sin(kx)\,dx \approx \int_{-\pi}^{\pi} q(x) \sin(kx)\,dx$$

for all k. We'll show that the *second* integral gives πb_k. It follows (with more work) that the *first* integral has the same value.

$$\int_{-\pi}^{\pi} q(x) \sin(kx)\,dx = \int_{-\pi}^{\pi} \big(a_0 + a_1 \cos x + \cdots + b_n \sin(nx)\big) \sin(kx)\,dx$$

$$= \int_{-\pi}^{\pi} a_0 \sin(kx)\,dx + \int_{-\pi}^{\pi} a_1 \cos x \sin(kx)\,dx + \cdots + \int_{-\pi}^{\pi} b_n \sin(nx) \sin(kx)\,dx.$$

Now comes the big payoff from the integral identities discussed above: They imply that *only one* of the integrals in the last expression is nonzero. The single exception is

$$\int_{-\pi}^{\pi} b_k \sin(kx) \sin(kx)\,dx = b_k \int_{-\pi}^{\pi} \sin^2(kx)\,dx = b_k\,\pi.$$

This explains the formula for b_k given in the definition.

1. Let $f(x) = \cos(kx)$, and let $g(x) = \sin(kx)$, where k is a nonnegative integer.

   (a) Explain why, for all x, $f(x + 2\pi) = f(x)$ and $g(x + 2\pi) = g(x)$, regardless of the value of k.

   (b) Use part (a) to explain why every trigonometric polynomial is 2π-periodic.

   (c) What is the smallest period of the trigonometric polynomial $p(x) = \cos(4x) + \sin(8x)$? Show that p actually has this period. [HINT: Plot $p(x)$ first to guess the period.]

2. Let k be a positive integer.

   (a) We claimed that $\int_{-\pi}^{\pi} \cos(kx)\,dx = 0$. Use the FTC to verify this.

   (b) We also claimed that $\int_{-\pi}^{\pi} \sin(kx)\,dx = 0$. Use the FTC to verify this.

3. Suppose that m and n are distinct (i.e., $m \neq n$) positive integers. Use the FTC to show that

   (a) $\int_{-\pi}^{\pi} \cos(mx)\sin(mx)\,dx = 0$

   (b) $\int_{-\pi}^{\pi} \cos(mx)\sin(nx)\,dx = 0$

   (c) $\int_{-\pi}^{\pi} \cos(mx)\cos(nx)\,dx = 0$
   [HINT: $2\cos u \cos v = \cos(u+v) + \cos(u-v)$.]

   (d) $\int_{-\pi}^{\pi} \cos^2(mx)\,dx = \pi$

   (e) $\int_{-\pi}^{\pi} \sin(mx)\sin(nx)\,dx = 0$
   [HINT: $2\sin u \sin v = \cos(u-v) - \cos(u+v)$.]

   (f) $\int_{-\pi}^{\pi} \sin^2(mx)\,dx = \pi$

4. Let $q(x) = a_0 + a_1 \cos x + b_1 \sin x + \cdots + a_n \cos(nx) + b_n \sin(nx)$. Show that $\int_{-\pi}^{\pi} q(x)\,dx = 2\pi a_0$.

5. Let k be a positive integer and let $q(x) = a_0 + a_1 \cos x + b_1 \sin x + \cdots + a_n \cos(nx) + b_n \sin(nx)$. Show that $\int_{-\pi}^{\pi} q(x)\cos(kx)\,dx = \pi a_k$.

6. (a) Suppose that f is an odd function and that g is an even function. Show that $h = f \cdot g$ is an odd function.

   (b) Suppose that f and g are even functions. Show that $h = f \cdot g$ is an even function.

   (c) Suppose that f and g are odd functions. Show that $h = f \cdot g$ is an even function.

7. Suppose that f is an even function. Show that, for all $k > 0$, the Fourier polynomial coefficient $b_k = 0$.

8. Suppose that f is an odd function. Show that, for all $k \geq 0$, the Fourier polynomial coefficient $a_k = 0$.

9. Suppose that the Fourier polynomial of degree 5 for a function f is $q_5(x) = 2/\pi + 4\sin(3x) - \cos(5x)$.

   (a) What is the Fourier polynomial of degree 2 for f? Justify your answer.

   (b) What is the Fourier polynomial of degree 3 for f? Justify your answer.

   (c) What is the Fourier polynomial of degree 4 for f? Justify your answer.

10. Let $f(x) = 2\cos(5x) + 3\sin(4x)$ and let q_n be the Fourier polynomial of degree n for f.

    (a) Show that if $n = 3$, $q_n(x) = 0$.

    (b) Find q_4.

    (c) Explain why $q_n(x) = f(x)$ if $n \geq 5$.

11. Suppose that the Fourier polynomial of degree 5 for a function f is $q_5(x) = 3 - 7\cos x + 4\sin x - 6\cos(5x) - 2\sin(5x)$. What is the average value of f over the interval $[-\pi, \pi]$? Justify your answer.

12. Suppose that the Fourier polynomial of degree n for a function f is q_n. If $g(x) = f(x) + 1$, how is the Fourier polynomial of degree n for g related to q_n?

13. Suppose that the Fourier polynomial of degree n for a function f is q_n and that the Fourier polynomial of degree n for a function g is Q_n. Show that the nth-degree Fourier polynomial for $f + g$ is $q_n + Q_n$.

14. Let k be a positive integer. Use integration by parts to show that $\dfrac{1}{\pi}\displaystyle\int_{-\pi}^{\pi} x\sin(kx)\,dx = \dfrac{-2\cos(k\pi)}{k}$, as claimed in Example 2.

15. Consider the function $f(x)$ defined by

$$f(x) = \begin{cases} 1 & \text{if } 2m\pi < x \leq (2m+1)\pi \\ 0 & \text{if } (2m+1)\pi < x \leq (2m+2)\pi \end{cases}$$

for all integers m. This function is sometimes called a **pulse train** or a **box wave**. (Notice that, although f is discontinuous, it repeats on intervals of length 2π.)

   (a) Use the definition of Fourier polynomials to find formulas for a_k and b_k. [HINT: For any function g, $\int_{-\pi}^{\pi} f(x)g(x)\,dx = \int_0^{\pi} g(x)\,dx$.]

   (b) Use the results from part (a) to find the Fourier polynomials q_1, q_3, q_5, and q_7 for f.

   (c) Plot f and the Fourier polynomials from part (b) on the same axes.

(d) Explain the relationship between the Fourier polynomial in this exercise and the one found in Example 2.

16. Consider the function $f(x)$ defined by

$$f(x) = \begin{cases} \pi + x & \text{if } -\pi \le x < 0 \\ \pi - x & \text{if } 0 \le x \le \pi \end{cases}$$

and repeated on intervals of length 2π. This function is sometimes called a **sawtooth wave**.

(a) Use the definition of Fourier polynomials to find formulas for a_k and b_k.

(b) Use your answers from part (a) to find the Fourier polynomials q_1, q_3, q_5, and q_7 for f.

(c) Plot f and the Fourier polynomials from part (b) on the same axes.

In Exercises 17–19, find the Fourier polynomial of degree 7 for the function f.

17. $f(x) = |x|$ **18.** $f(x) = x^2$

19. $f(x) = 4 + 3x + x^2$

20. Suppose that f is a function that has period T and is defined on the interval $[-T/2, T/2]$.

(a) Let $g(x) = f(T x/2\pi)$. Show that g has period 2π and is defined on the interval $[-\pi, \pi]$.

(b) Let g be as in part (a) and let q_n be the Fourier polynomial of degree n for g. Explain why

$$f(x) \approx q_n\left(\frac{2\pi x}{T}\right) = a_0 + a_1 \cos\left(\frac{2\pi x}{T}\right)$$
$$+ a_2 \cos\left(\frac{4\pi x}{T}\right) + \cdots + a_n \cos\left(\frac{2n\pi x}{T}\right)$$
$$+ b_1 \sin\left(\frac{2\pi x}{T}\right) + \cdots + b_n \sin\left(\frac{2n\pi x}{T}\right).$$

(c) Use part (b) to show that the coefficients in the Fourier polynomial for f are

$$a_0 = \frac{1}{T}\int_{-T/2}^{T/2} f(x)\cos\left(\frac{2\pi x}{T}\right)dx;$$
$$a_k = \frac{2}{T}\int_{-T/2}^{T/2} f(x)\cos\left(\frac{2\pi kx}{T}\right)dx, \text{ if } k \ge 1;$$
$$b_k = \frac{2}{T}\int_{-T/2}^{T/2} f(x)\sin\left(\frac{2\pi kx}{T}\right)dx, \text{ if } k \ge 1.$$

Splines—Connecting the Dots

How does one draw a "curve" (perhaps with corners) through several given points in a plane? Figure 1 shows three possible curves, called **splines,** through five points:

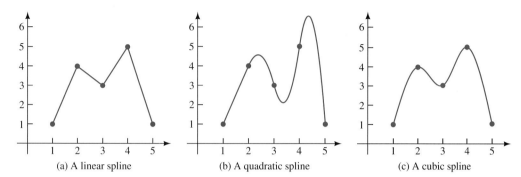

(a) A linear spline   (b) A quadratic spline   (c) A cubic spline

FIGURE 1
Three curves through given points

This Interlude fits the chapter's theme in that piecewise-defined functions are chosen to "fit" given data.

A human can choose among the many possible curves on aesthetic or other grounds. But computers need precise instructions in their own language—mathematics. Calculus provides the needed tools.

Basic ideas and key words The idea behind splines is to "tie together" small curve segments, called **spline elements**, to form a single larger curve called a **spline**. The points at which elements are tied together (shown as dots in Figure 1) are called **knots**. Figure 1(a) shows a **linear spline**, a spline formed from line segments. Figure 1(b) shows a **quadratic spline**, a spline formed from parabolic pieces. Figure 1(c) shows a **cubic spline**, a spline formed by knotting cubic arcs. ➜ In all three cases the *individual* elements are smooth and unbroken, and so any spline built from such pieces will also be smooth and unbroken *except* perhaps at the knots. By matching derivatives at the knots we'll iron out the kinks.

A cubic arc is defined by a cubic function
$y = a + bx + cx^2 + dx^3$.

PROBLEM 1 Let $S(x)$ be the linear spline function $S(x)$ in Figure 1(a). The first line segment in Figure 1(a) has equation $\ell_1(x) = 3x - 2$. Find linear formulas for ℓ_2, ℓ_3, and ℓ_4 to produce the piecewise-linear formula

$$S(x) = \begin{cases} 3x - 2 & \text{if } 1 \le x \le 2; \\ \ell_2(x) & \text{if } 2 < x \le 3; \\ \ell_3(x) & \text{if } 3 < x \le 4; \\ \ell_4(x) & \text{if } 4 < x \le 5. \end{cases}$$

Students may need to be reminded that piecewise-defined formulas do define functions.

PROBLEM 2 Give a formula for a piecewise-linear function whose graph passes through the points $(0, 0)$, $(1, 1)$, and $(2, 4)$.

Quadratic splines: smoother Linear splines, although simple, have an ugly kink at each knot (unless, by pure chance, successive slopes match up). One way to avoid such kinks is to use a quadratic spline formed by linking parabolic pieces. ➜

Each piece is defined by a quadratic equation.

What makes a curve degenerate? The graph of a quadratic polynomial $q(x) = a + bx + cx^2$, where a, b, and c are constants, is *usually* a parabola. There's one exception: If $c = 0$, then $q(x) = a + bx$ is actually a *linear* polynomial; its graph is a *line*. Any polynomial that happens to have less than its "advertised" power is sometimes called **degenerate**; a line, for instance, can be seen as a "degenerate parabola." Mathematicians are comfortable with degeneracy.

Linear splines are crooked because only *one* line segment can join one knot to the next. Quadratic segments are—literally—more flexible: Given any two successive knots, we can find a parabola that joins them with *any* desired slope at the left knot. Figure 2 shows several parabolas joining $(0, 0)$ and $(1, 1)$, each labeled with its slope at $(0, 0)$: ◄

One "parabola" is actually a straight line.

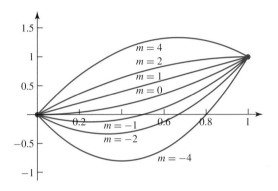

FIGURE 2
Parabolas joining two knots: m is the slope at $(0, 0)$

PROBLEM 3 Find a quadratic equation for each curve in Figure 2.

PROBLEM 4 In each part, find and plot a quadratic polynomial that satisfies the three given conditions.

(a) $Q(0) = 0$; $Q'(0) = 3$; $Q(1) = 5$.

(b) $Q(0) = 0$; $Q'(0) = 3$; $Q(10) = 5$.

(c) $Q(1) = 0$; $Q'(1) = 3$; $Q(3) = 0$.

By choosing slopes judiciously at each knot we can smooth out the resulting curve, as the next example shows.

EXAMPLE 1 Discuss how to find a piecewise-quadratic formula for the spline in Figure 1(b).

Solution To prevent kinks we'll arrange that slopes of "incoming" and "outgoing" elements match at each knot. Smoothness is no problem at the first knot, and so *any* quadratic curve joining $(1, 1)$ to $(2, 4)$ will do. Figure 1(b) starts with a straight line; a close look shows that the formula $S_1(x) = 3x - 2$ works for $1 \le x \le 2$. In particular, $S_1'(2) = 3$. For the second spline element, from $x = 2$ to $x = 3$, we need a quadratic polynomial $S_2(x)$ that joins the second and third knots and also *agrees in slope* with S_1 at $x = 2$. Thus, S_2 must satisfy three conditions:

$$S_2(2) = 4; \qquad S_2'(2) = 3; \qquad S_2(3) = 3. \qquad (1)$$

Building splines by stringing elements together from left to right is easy to describe; in practice, linear algebra is used to streamline the process.

It's easier to find such an S_2 if we first write

$$S_2(x) = a + b(x-2) + c(x-2)^2$$

and then search for a, b, and c. In this case we have $S_2(2) = a$ and $S_2'(2) = b$, and thus conditions (1) mean that $a = 4$ and $b = 3$. This gives $S_2(x) = 4 + 3(x-2) + c(x-2)^2$ with only c still to be found. The remaining condition, $S_2(3) = 3$, gives our answer. Because $S_2(3) = 7 + c$, we have

$$S_2(3) = 3 \iff 7 + c = 3 \iff c = -4.$$

All pieces are now in place: $S_2(x) = 4 + 3(x-2) - 4(x-2)^2$. ∎

PROBLEM 5 Argue as in Example 1 to show that the quadratic spline in Figure 1(b) has piecewise-quadratic formula

$$S(x) = \begin{cases} S_1(x) = 3x - 2 & \text{if } 1 \le x \le 2; \\ S_2(x) = 4 + 3(x-2) - 4(x-2)^2 & \text{if } 2 < x \le 3; \\ S_3(x) = 3 - 5(x-3) + 7(x-3)^2 & \text{if } 3 < x \le 4; \\ S_4(x) = 5 + 9(x-4) - 13(x-4)^2 & \text{if } 4 < x \le 5. \end{cases}$$

Figure 3 shows the four quadratic functions S_1 through S_4 plotted together (extended beyond the knots, this time); the spline S is the bold curve.

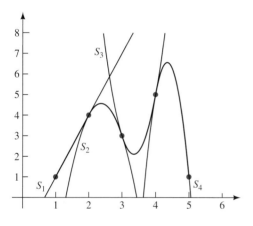

Notice how successive quadratic elements fit together smoothly at each knot.

FIGURE 3
Smooth-fitting quadratic elements

Differentiating the piecewise-quadratic formula gives a piecewise-linear formula.

The spline's second derivative S'' is discontinuous at each knot—notice the slightly bumpy look.

Formal definitions The preceding examples illustrate the first two definitions and suggest the third:

> **DEFINITION** A **linear spline** is a continuous, piecewise-linear function S. A **quadratic spline** is a continuous, piecewise-quadratic function S whose first derivative S' is also continuous. A **cubic spline** S is a continuous, piecewise-quadratic function whose first *two* derivatives, S' and S'' are also continuous.

The definition looks a bit technical, but it means simply that incoming and outgoing spline elements "agree" at each knot, both in their values and in one or more derivatives.

Counting the ways: Degrees of freedom   There is just one line through two given points, or through one point with given slope. Either way, a straight line is completely determined by *two* conditions. The algebraic reason is that the generic linear equation $y = a + bx$ involves *two* parameters, a and b. In mathematical language, we have **two degrees of freedom** in choosing a line; specifying two points (or one point and one slope) "uses up" both degrees of freedom.

By contrast, a quadratic polynomial $y = a + bx + cx^2$ involves *three* parameters, and so we have three degrees of freedom in choosing quadratics. The practical result is that a quadratic spline element can be chosen to satisfy *three* conditions. Hitting the left and right knots costs two degrees of freedom, but the third remains available. Our method "spends" the last degree of freedom in specifying a derivative at the left knot.

The pattern continues. Cubic spline elements allow *four* degrees of freedom—hitting the knots costs two, and we spend the others on matching *two* derivatives at the left knot.

Cubic splines: Still smoother   Using cubic spline elements, we can arrange that, at each knot, incoming and outgoing elements agree in their values and in their first *two* derivatives. By avoiding abrupt changes in concavity, cubic elements can produce smoother and more pleasing splines than quadratic elements can manage.

EXAMPLE 2   Construct a cubic spline through the knots in Figure 1(c).

Solution   Because smoothness is no problem at the first knot, we can start with *any* cubic curve S_1 that joins $(1, 1)$ to $(2, 4)$. Although infinitely many possibilities exist, some choices give better results than others. Moreover, the resulting spline depends very strongly on how the first element is chosen. For instance, Figure 4 shows two cubic splines through the same knots:

The figure illustrates how sensitive the splining process is to initial choices.

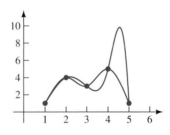

FIGURE 4
Same knots, different cubic splines

Notice that the two splines differ just slightly in the first element but much more thereafter. Given this sensitivity to initial choices, mathematicians have found various ways of choosing the first cubic spline element to produce a pleasing result. The **natural spline method**, for instance, arranges things so that $S''(x_0) = 0 = S''(x_n)$; this means that S has zero concavity at the first and last knots. (The "tamer" curve in Figure 4 is a natural spline.) Full details on natural splining are beyond our scope. ◄ We'll just say, therefore, that the unlikely looking cubic

Numerical analysis textbooks discuss natural and other splining methods.

$$S_1(x) = 1 + \frac{123}{28}(x - 1) - \frac{39}{28}(x - 1)^3$$

can be used to start things off. Given the formula, it's easy to check that

$$S_1(1) = 1, \quad S_1(2) = 4, \quad S_1'(2) = \frac{3}{14}, \quad \text{and} \quad S_1''(2) = -\frac{117}{14}.$$

The first two conditions ensure that S_1 hits the first two knots; the remaining conditions will help us determine S_2.

INTERLUDE

The second spline element is a cubic polynomial that satisfies *four* conditions: →

$$S_2(2) = 4; \quad S_2'(2) = \frac{3}{14}; \quad S_2''(2) = -\frac{117}{14}; \quad S_2(3) = 3. \tag{2}$$

The middle two conditions come from matching derivatives of S_1.

Again, writing $S_2(x) = a + b(x-2) + c(x-2)^2 + d(x-2)^3$ simplifies our quest. Because

$$S_2(2) = a, \quad S_2'(2) = b, \quad \text{and} \quad S_2''(2) = 2c,$$

conditions (2) imply that $a = 4$, $b = 3/14$, and $c = -117/28$, and so

$$S_2(x) = 4 + \frac{3}{14}(x-2) - \frac{117}{28}(x-2)^2 + d(x-2)^3$$

with only d left to find. The final condition, $S_2(3) = 3$, does the trick:

$$3 = S_2(3) = 4 + \frac{3}{14} - \frac{117}{28} + d \implies d = \frac{83}{28},$$

and we're done at last:

$$S_2(x) = 4 + \frac{3}{14}(x-2) - \frac{117}{28}(x-2)^2 + \frac{83}{28}(x-2)^3. \qquad ∎$$

PROBLEM 6 It turns out that the cubic spline in Figure 1(c) has the piecewise-cubic formula

$$S(x) = \begin{cases} S_1(x) = 1 + \frac{123}{28}(x-1) - \frac{39}{28}(x-1)^3 & \text{if } 1 \le x \le 2; \\ S_2(x) = 4 + \frac{3}{11}(x-2) - \frac{117}{28}(x-2)^2 + \frac{83}{28}(x-2)^3 & \text{if } 2 < x \le 3; \\ S_3(x) = 3 + \frac{3}{4}(x-3) + \frac{33}{7}(x-3)^2 - \frac{97}{28}(x-3)^3 & \text{if } 3 < x \le 4; \\ S_4(x) = 5 - \frac{3}{14}(x-4) - \frac{159}{28}(x-4)^2 + \frac{53}{28}(x-4)^3 & \text{if } 4 < x \le 5. \end{cases}$$

The formula is messy; some help from symbolic computing could be useful. Notice the advantage of expanding each element about its base point.

(a) Argue as in Example 2 to verify the formula for S_3.

(b) Write a piecewise-quadratic formula for $S'(x)$; check that $S'(x)$ is indeed continuous at the knots. Plot $S'(x)$ if technology permits.

(c) Write a piecewise-linear formula for $S''(x)$; check that $S''(x)$ is indeed continuous at the knots. Plot $S''(x)$ if technology permits.

Postscript The general idea of linear, quadratic, and cubic splines—our main interest in this section—is simple. Elements of the desired type are linked end to end; as many derivatives as possible are made to agree at knots. The necessary calculations, although routine, can be tedious and repetitive, especially when dozens or hundreds of knots are involved. In real-life practice such calculations are always left to machines, and specialized methods are used to speed up and simplify the machines' work.

FURTHER EXERCISES

1. Let (x_0, y_0) and (x_1, y_1) be any two points with $x_0 \ne x_1$, and let m_0 be any real number. Consider the quadratic function q defined by

$$q(x) = y_0 + m_0(x - x_0) + \frac{y_1 - y_0 - m_0(x_1 - x_0)}{(x_1 - x_0)^2}(x - x_0)^2.$$

(a) Find $q(x)$ in the case $(x_0, y_0) = (2, 4)$, $(x_1, y_1) = (3, 3)$, $m_0 = 3$. Then check that $q(2) = 4$, $q(3) = 3$, and $q'(2) = 3$.

(b) Plot your function q from the previous part. How does the graph show that $q(2) = 4$, $q(3) = 3$, and $q'(2) = 3$?

(c) Show (work with the general formula above) that $q(x_0) = y_0$, $q(x_1) = y_1$, and $q'(x_0) = m_0$. What do these properties mean about the graph of q?

(d) Give an example in which $q(x)$ turns out to be a linear function. Interpret your example in graphical terms.

2. The figure shows two quadratic splines; both pass through the three knots $(0, 1)$, $(1, -2)$, and $(2, 3)$.

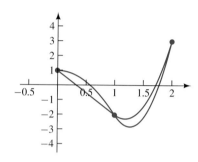

(a) For one of the splines, $S'(0) = -3$. Use this information to find formulas for both elements of this spline.

(b) For the other spline, $S'(0) = 0$. Use this information to find formulas for both elements of this spline.

3. Let (x_0, y_0) and (x_1, y_1) be any two points with $x_0 \neq x_1$, and let d_1 and d_2 be any real numbers. Consider the cubic function c defined by

$$c(x) = y_0 + d_1(x - x_0) + \frac{d_2}{2}(x - x_0)^2 +$$

$$\frac{y_1 - y_0 - d_1(x_1 - x_0) - \frac{d_2}{2}(x_1 - x_0)^2}{(x_1 - x_0)^3}(x - x_0)^3$$

Show by (careful!) calculation that c satisfies the four conditions

$$c(x_0) = y_0; \quad c'(x_0) = d_1; \quad c''(x_0) = d_2; \quad c(x_1) = y_1.$$

These four conditions mean that c is the general cubic spline element that joins (x_0, y_0) to (x_1, y_1) with first two derivatives d_1 and d_2 at (x_0, y_0).

4. In each part, either use the formula in the previous exercise or work from scratch to find a cubic function with the given properties. Plot each result.

(a) $c(0) = 0$; $c'(0) = 0$; $c''(0) = 0$; $c(1) = 0$.

(b) $c(0) = 0$; $c'(0) = 0$; $c''(0) = 0$; $c(1) = 1$.

(c) $c(0) = 1$; $c'(0) = 0$; $c''(0) = -1$; $c(1) = 1/2$.

(d) $c(0) = 1$; $c'(0) = 1$; $c''(0) = 1$; $c(1) = 8/3$.

5. The following figure shows two cubic splines; both pass through the three knots $(0, 1)$, $(1, -2)$, and $(2, 3)$.

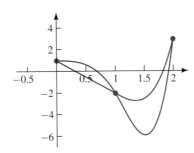

(a) For one of the splines, $S'(0) = -3$ and $S''(0) = 0$. Use this information to find formulas for both elements of this spline.

(b) For the other spline, $S'(0) = 0$ and $S''(0) = 0$. Use this information to find formulas for both elements of this spline.

10 IMPROPER INTEGRALS

10.1 IMPROPER INTEGRALS: IDEAS AND DEFINITIONS

One goal of our rather detailed treatment is to prepare for infinite series, which are improper sums in exactly the same sense that integrals can be improper. We stress the infinite interval case.

Each of the following expressions is an **improper integral**:

$$\int_1^\infty \frac{dx}{x^2} \qquad \int_1^\infty \frac{dx}{x} \qquad \int_{-\infty}^\infty \frac{dx}{1+x^2} \qquad \int_0^\infty e^{-x}\,dx \qquad \int_0^1 \frac{dx}{x^2} \qquad \int_0^1 \frac{dx}{\sqrt{x}}$$

Keep these basic examples in mind. They illustrate most of what can go right—and wrong—with improper integrals.

Improper integrals, like improper fractions, commit no breach of morals or manners. The adjective "improper" is a warning sticker attached to integrals that differ somehow from the ordinary $\int_a^b f(x)\,dx$ variety, in which $[a, b]$ is a *finite* interval and $f(x)$ is continuous on all of the interval $[a, b]$. Each of the preceding integrals, examined carefully, should raise some suspicion.

Two improprieties Integrals can commit two types of "impropriety":

- **Infinite intervals** The interval of integration may be infinite, as in the first four sample integrals. This is "improper" because the formal definition of definite integral relies on partitions of a *finite* interval.

- **Infinite integrands** The integrand may be unbounded on the interval of integration, as in the last two samples. ← This, too, is "improper" because the integrand is not defined somewhere inside, or at an endpoint of, the interval of integration.

The integrand "blows up," in other words.

Some really offensive integrals, such as $\displaystyle\int_0^\infty \frac{dx}{\sqrt{x}+x^2}$, commit *both* types of impropriety and will need especially strict handling.

Convergence and divergence: Basic ideas and examples

Some improper integrals have a sensible numerical value; they are called **convergent**. For other integrals the impropriety is fatal; these integrals have no sensible finite value and are called **divergent**. We'll give formal definitions after some concrete examples.

Later we'll exploit the analogy to $\sum 1/k^2$.

EXAMPLE 1 Make sense of $\displaystyle\int_1^\infty \frac{dx}{x^2}$.

Solution What could such an integral mean? Interpreted geometrically, the integral represents the shaded area in Figure 1:

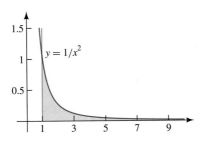

FIGURE 1

FIGURE 1

The improper integral $\int_1^\infty \dfrac{dx}{x^2}$ **as area**

The shaded region extends infinitely far to the right, but might its *area* be finite?

The answer, perhaps surprisingly, is yes; the reason involves a limit. For any number $t > 1$, consider the (proper) integral

$$I(t) = \int_1^t \frac{dx}{x^2},$$

which represents the shaded area from $x = 1$ to $x = t$. We can calculate $I(t)$ exactly:

$$I(t) = \int_1^t \frac{dx}{x^2} = \frac{-1}{x}\Bigg]_1^t = 1 - \frac{1}{t}.$$

Clearly, $I(t) \to 1$ as $t \to \infty$. Thus, the total shaded region, although infinitely long, has *finite* area. In summary,

$$\lim_{t \to \infty} \int_1^t \frac{dx}{x^2} = \lim_{t \to \infty} \left(1 - \frac{1}{t}\right) = 1;$$

we say that the integral **converges** to 1. ∎

EXAMPLE 2 Does $\int_1^\infty \dfrac{dx}{x}$ converge or diverge? Why?

Solution This integral itself resembles the one in Example 1, but a picture (Figure 2) suggests a difference:

One view of the question of convergence is whether or not the antiderivative—in this case it's ln x —has a horizontal asymptote.

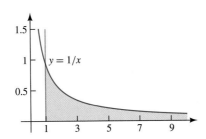

FIGURE 2

The improper integral $\int_1^\infty \dfrac{dx}{x}$ **as area**

The question, again, is whether the shaded region (unbounded on the right) has finite or infinite area. The picture alone, being finite, doesn't say. To find an answer, we'll calculate much as before. For $t > 1$, the area from $x = 1$ to $x = t$ is

$$\int_1^t \frac{dx}{x} = \ln x\Bigg]_1^t = \ln t.$$

(The shaded area shown in Figure 2 is $\ln 10 \approx 2.3026$.) In this case, $I(t) = \ln t \to \infty$ as $t \to \infty$, and so we conclude that the improper integral **diverges** to infinity. In symbolic shorthand:

$$\lim_{t \to \infty} \int_1^t \frac{dx}{x} = \lim_{t \to \infty} \ln t = \infty. \qquad \blacksquare$$

Looks can deceive Examples 1 and 2 illustrate a common subtlety of improper integrals: Although the graphs of $y = 1/x^2$ and $y = 1/x$ appear similar, the first graph bounds only *one* unit of area, while the second bounds *infinite* area. In short, graphs tell only a small part of the story for improper integrals.

EXAMPLE 3 Does $\displaystyle\int_{-\infty}^{\infty} \frac{dx}{1+x^2}$ converge? If so, to what?

Solution This integral is improper at *both* ends. Breaking the integral into two pieces lets us handle one impropriety at a time:

$$\int_{-\infty}^{\infty} \frac{dx}{1+x^2} = \int_{-\infty}^{0} \frac{dx}{1+x^2} + \int_0^{\infty} \frac{dx}{1+x^2}.$$

Let's consider the second summand first. A calculation shows that it converges to $\pi/2$:

$$\lim_{t \to \infty} \int_0^t \frac{dx}{1+x^2} = \lim_{t \to \infty} \arctan x \Big]_0^t = \lim_{t \to \infty} \arctan t = \frac{\pi}{2}.$$

A similar calculation handles the first summand, but we can avoid needless work if we first notice that the integrand is an *even* function, and thus conclude that the first and second summands have the *same* value. Putting the pieces together shows that the original integral converges to π:

$$\int_{-\infty}^{\infty} \frac{dx}{1+x^2} = \int_{-\infty}^{0} \frac{dx}{1+x^2} + \int_0^{\infty} \frac{dx}{1+x^2} = \pi. \qquad \blacksquare$$

Another impropriety: Infinite integrands

The improprieties in Examples 1–3 all involved infinite *intervals* of integration. Much the same strategy applies to integrals with finite *intervals* of integration, but whose *integrands* blow up to infinity within, or at an endpoint of, the interval.

We deemphasize integrals like I_2, with interior singularities. These integrals diverge for most of the usual calculus functions, including rational functions.

EXAMPLE 4 Does $I_1 = \displaystyle\int_0^1 \frac{dx}{x^2}$ converge? If so, to what? What about $I_2 = \displaystyle\int_{-1}^1 \frac{dx}{x^2}$?

Solution For I_1 we want to know whether the *vertically* unbounded shaded region in Figure 3 has finite or infinite area.

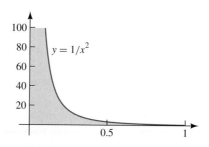

$$y = 1/x^2$$

FIGURE 3

The improper integral $\displaystyle\int_0^1 \frac{dx}{x^2}$ as area

To settle the question we find *another* limit of areas, but this time we let t tend to zero from the right. For any $t > 0$, the area from $x = t$ to $x = 1$ is finite, and it's easy to find explicitly:

$$I(t) = \int_t^1 \frac{dx}{x^2} = -\frac{1}{x}\bigg]_t^1 = \frac{1}{t} - 1.$$

Now as $t \to 0^+$, we have $I(t) \to \infty$, too. Here is our conclusion in symbols:

$$\lim_{t \to 0^+} \int_1^t \frac{dx}{x^2} = \lim_{t \to 0^+} \left(\frac{1}{t} - 1\right) = \infty.$$

In words: The integral $\displaystyle\int_0^1 \frac{dx}{x^2}$ **diverges** to infinity.

The new feature of I_2 is that the impropriety (at $x = 0$) is *inside* the interval of integration. We approach the problem in the "usual" way: We break I_2 into two integrals, each with just one impropriety, at an endpoint:

$$I_2 = \int_{-1}^1 \frac{dx}{x^2} = \int_{-1}^0 \frac{dx}{x^2} + \int_0^1 \frac{dx}{x^2}.$$

We've just shown that the second integral diverges; so, therefore, does I_2.   ∎

Convergence and divergence: Formal definitions

We applied the same basic idea in each of the preceding examples. First we located an impropriety at ∞, at $-\infty$, or at a finite endpoint of the interval of integration. Then we considered the limit as a variable endpoint tends to the troublesome value from either above or below. In the case of greatest interest, the fine print reads like this:

DEFINITION Consider the integral $I = \int_a^\infty f(x)\,dx$, where f is continuous for $x \geq a$. If the limit

$$L = \lim_{t \to \infty} \int_a^t f(x)\,dx$$

exists and is finite, then I **converges** to L. Otherwise, I **diverges**.

A similar but more general definition of convergence applies to *any* improper integral:

If $a = -\infty$ or $b = \infty$, then the one-sided limits in the definition become "ordinary" limits at $\pm infty$.

DEFINITION Let the integral $I = \int_a^b f(x)\,dx$ be improper either at a or at b. (The cases $a = -\infty$ and $b = \infty$ are allowed.) If either

$$\lim_{t \to a^+} \int_t^b f(x)\,dx \qquad \text{or} \qquad \lim_{t \to b^-} \int_a^t f(x)\,dx$$

exists and has finite value L, then I **converges** to L. Otherwise, I **diverges**.

Notice, in particular, that every convergent *improper* integral is a limit of *proper* integrals. For example,

$$\int_1^\infty f(x)\,dx = \lim_{t \to \infty} \int_1^t f(x)\,dx$$

if the limit exists.

Improprieties at both ends If an integral is improper at *both* ends, it can be broken into two summands in any convenient manner; the whole integral converges only if *both* summands converge. (We took this approach in Example 3.) The next example illustrates another "double impropriety."

> **EXAMPLE 5** Does $I = \int_0^\infty \dfrac{dx}{x^2}$ converge? If so, to what?
>
> **Solution** The integral has improprieties at both ends. To separate them, we write
>
> $$I = \int_0^\infty \frac{dx}{x^2} = \int_0^1 \frac{dx}{x^2} + \int_1^\infty \frac{dx}{x^2} = I_1 + I_2.$$

Students could be asked what happens if the break occurs at $x = 2$, not $x = 1$.

As we saw in earlier examples, I_2 *converges* to 1, but I_1 *diverges* to ∞. Hence, I itself diverges. (An integral converges only if all of its pieces converge.) ∎

Integrands that change sign: Another way to diverge In each example so far the integrand has been a *positive* function. In this case integrals are readily interpreted as areas: The integral converges if the area in question remains finite; otherwise, the integral diverges to infinity.

If the integrand *changes* sign, the area interpretation is less useful. In this case an integral may diverge without "blowing up."

> **EXAMPLE 6** Does $I = \int_0^\infty \cos x \, dx$ converge or diverge?
>
> **Solution** The definitions give a quick answer. Because
>
> $$\int_0^t \cos x \, dx = \sin x \Big]_0^t = \sin t,$$
>
> we have
>
> $$\lim_{t \to \infty} \int_0^t \cos x \, dx = \lim_{t \to \infty} \sin t.$$

The last limit doesn't exist: As $t \to \infty$, $\sin t$ oscillates endlessly between -1 and 1. Hence, I diverges. ∎

Substitution in improper integrals Simple u-substitutions sometimes allow us to trade one improper integral for another—or even for a *proper* integral.

The substitution $u = 1/x$ transforms many integrals with infinite intervals into integrals with unbounded integrands, and vice versa.

> **EXAMPLE 7** Consider $I_1 = \int_0^1 \dfrac{dx}{x^2}$ and $I_2 = \int_0^1 \dfrac{dx}{\sqrt{x}}$. How does the substitution $u = 1/x$ transform each integral?
>
> **Solution** If $u = 1/x$, then $x = 1/u$ and $dx = -1/u^2 \, du$. Also, $x = 1$ and $x = 0$ correspond, respectively, to $u = 1$ and $u = \infty$. ← Making these substitutions in I_1 and I_2 gives two *new* improper integrals:
>
> $$J_1 = \int_1^\infty 1 \, du; \quad J_2 = \int_1^\infty \frac{\sqrt{u}}{u^2} \, du = \int_1^\infty \frac{du}{u^{3/2}}.$$

As $x \to 0^+$, $u = 1/x \to \infty$.

It's easy to check by direct calculation that I_1 and J_1 diverge to infinity, whereas $I_2 = J_2 = 2$. ∎

BASIC EXERCISES

In Exercises 1–4, explain why the integral is improper.

1. $\int_0^\infty x^2 e^{-x^2}\, dx$

2. $\int_0^1 \dfrac{dx}{x^2 - 3x + 2}$

3. $\int_1^4 \dfrac{dx}{x^2 \ln x}$

4. $\int_0^{2\pi} \dfrac{\cos x}{\sqrt{1 + \cos x}}\, dx$

5. Show that $\int_0^1 \dfrac{dx}{\sqrt{x}} = 2$ as claimed in Example 7.

6. Show that $\int_1^\infty \dfrac{du}{u^{3/2}} = 2$ as claimed in Example 7.

In Exercises 7–18, use an antiderivative to evaluate the improper integral.

7. $\int_1^\infty \dfrac{dx}{x^3}$

8. $\int_0^4 \dfrac{dx}{\sqrt{x}}$

9. $\int_1^\infty \dfrac{\ln x}{x^2}\, dx$

10. $\int_e^\infty \dfrac{dx}{x\,(\ln x)^2}$

11. $\int_0^\infty e^{-x}\, dx$

12. $\int_0^\infty x e^{-x}\, dx$

13. $\int_{-\infty}^1 e^x\, dx$

14. $\int_{-\infty}^0 x e^x\, dx$

15. $\int_0^{16} \dfrac{dx}{\sqrt[4]{x^3}}$

16. $\int_0^1 \dfrac{x}{\sqrt{1 - x^2}}\, dx$

17. $\int_3^\infty \dfrac{x}{(x^2 - 4)^3}\, dx$

18. $\int_0^\infty \dfrac{\arctan x}{1 + x^2}\, dx$

19. Suppose that $\int_0^\infty f(x)\, dx = 17$. Does $\int_{100}^\infty f(x)\, dx$ converge? Justify your answer.

20. Suppose that f is continuous everywhere and that $\int_2^\infty f(x)\, dx$ converges. Explain why $\int_5^\infty f(x)\, dx$ also converges.

FURTHER EXERCISES

21. Suppose that $0 \le g(x) \le x^{-2}$ for all $x \ge 1$. Give a graphical argument that explains why $\int_1^\infty g(x)\, dx$ converges. [HINT: See Example 1.]

22. Suppose that $h(x) \ge x^{-1}$ for all $x \ge 1$. Give a graphical argument that explains why $\int_1^\infty h(x)\, dx$ diverges. [HINT: See Example 2.]

23. Suppose that f is an odd function and that $\int_0^\infty f(x)\, dx = 17$. Evaluate $\int_{-\infty}^\infty f(x)\, dx$.

24. **(a)** Show that $\lim\limits_{a \to \infty} \int_{-a}^a x\, dx = 0$.

  (b) Explain why $\int_{-\infty}^\infty x\, dx$ diverges.

25. Let $I = \int_{-1}^1 \dfrac{dx}{x^3}\, dx$.

  (a) Explain why I is an improper integral.

  (b) Does I converge? Justify your answer.

26. Does the integral $\int_0^5 \dfrac{dx}{x - 2}$ converge? Justify your answer.

27. **(a)** Show that $\int_1^\infty \dfrac{\cos(\sqrt{x})}{\sqrt{x}}\, dx$ diverges.

  (b) Does $\int_0^1 \dfrac{\cos(\sqrt{x})}{\sqrt{x}}\, dx$ also diverge? Justify your answer.

28. Let R be the region between the graphs $y = 1/x$ and $y = 1/(x+1)$ to the right of $x = 1$. Does R have finite area? Justify your answer.

29. Let S be the region between the graphs $y = 1/x$ and $y = 1/\sqrt{x}$ between $x = 0$ and $x = 1$. Does S have finite area? Justify your answer.

30. The equation $y = \sqrt{R^2 - x^2}$ describes a semicircle of radius R. Use the arc length formula to find the circumference of a circle of radius R.

31. Let $f(x) = 1/x$ and let R be the region under the graph of f and above the x-axis for $x \ge 1$ (i.e., the shaded region in Figure 2). Find the volume of the solid of revolution formed when R is rotated about the x-axis.

32. Let $f(x) = 1/x$ and let R be the region under the graph of f and above the x-axis for $x \ge 1$ (i.e., the shaded region in Figure 2). Find the volume of the solid of revolution formed when R is rotated about the y-axis.

In Exercises 33–48, use an antiderivative to determine whether the improper integral converges. If the integral converges, evaluate it.

33. $\int_0^\infty \dfrac{x}{\sqrt{1 + x^2}}\, dx$

34. $\int_1^\infty \dfrac{dx}{x(1 + x)}$

35. $\int_{-2}^2 \dfrac{2x + 1}{\sqrt[3]{x^2 + x - 6}}\, dx$

36. $\int_\pi^\infty e^{-x} \sin x\, dx$

37. $\int_2^4 \dfrac{x}{\sqrt{|x^2 - 9|}}\, dx$

38. $\int_1^3 \dfrac{dx}{\sqrt[3]{x - 2}}$

39. $\int_2^3 \dfrac{x}{\sqrt{3 - x}}\, dx$

40. $\int_0^2 \dfrac{dx}{\sqrt{4 - x^2}}$

41. $\int_1^\infty \dfrac{dx}{x(\ln x)^2}$

42. $\int_0^\infty \dfrac{dx}{(x - 1)^2}$

43. $\int_0^\infty \dfrac{dx}{e^x - 1}$

44. $\int_{-\infty}^\infty e^{-x}\, dx$

45. $\int_{-\infty}^\infty \dfrac{dx}{e^x + e^{-x}}$

46. $\int_0^1 \dfrac{e^{-\sqrt{x}}}{\sqrt{x}}\, dx$

47. $\int_0^{\pi/2} \dfrac{\cos x}{\sqrt{\sin x}}\, dx$

48. $\int_0^{\pi/2} \sec^2 x\, dx$

In Exercises 49–54, find all values of the parameter p for which the integral converges.

49. $\int_1^\infty \dfrac{dx}{x^p}$ [HINT: Consider the cases $p > 1$ and $p \le 1$.]

50. $\int_0^1 \dfrac{dx}{x^p}$

51. $\int_1^e \dfrac{dx}{x(\ln x)^p}$

52. $\int_e^\infty \dfrac{dx}{x(\ln x)^p}$

53. $\int_1^\infty x^p e^x \, dx$

54. $\int_1^\infty x^p e^{-x} \, dx$

55. (a) Explain why $\int_0^1 \dfrac{\cos x}{x} \, dx$ is an improper integral.

   (b) Explain why $\int_0^1 \dfrac{\sin x}{x} \, dx$ is *not* an improper integral.
   [HINT: Use l'Hôpital's rule.]

56. Let $f(x) = \begin{cases} x \ln x & \text{if } x > 0 \\ 0 & \text{if } x = 0. \end{cases}$ Is $\int_0^1 f(x)\,dx$ an improper integral? Justify your answer.   [HINT: Use l'Hôpital's rule.]

57. Let $f(x) = x / \ln x$. Is $\int_0^{1/e} f(x)\,dx$ an improper integral? Justify your answer.

58. Suppose that f is a differentiable function, that f' is continuous on $[1, \infty)$, and that $|f(x)| \le e^{-x} \ln x$ if $x \ge 1$. Show that $\int_1^\infty f'(x)\,dx$ converges.

In Exercises 59 and 60, find the value(s) of the parameter C for which the improper integral converges.

59. $\int_0^\infty \left(\dfrac{2x}{x^2+1} - \dfrac{C}{2x+1} \right) dx$

60. $\int_1^\infty \left(\dfrac{Cx}{x^2+1} - \dfrac{1}{2x} \right) dx$

In Exercises 61–66, use a change of variables to transform the improper integral into a proper integral with the same value. (You do not need to evaluate these integrals.)

61. $\int_1^\infty \dfrac{x}{x^3+1} \, dx$ [HINT: Let $u = x^{-1}$.]

62. $\int_0^{\pi/2} \dfrac{\cos x}{\sqrt{\pi - 2x}} \, dx$ [HINT: Let $u = \sqrt{\pi - 2x}$.]

63. $\int_1^\infty \dfrac{dx}{1+x^4}$

64. $\int_0^\infty x^3 e^{-x} \, dx$ [HINT: Let $u = e^{-x}$.]

65. $\int_0^\infty \dfrac{x \ln x}{1 + x^4} \, dx$

66. $\int_{\pi/4}^{\pi/2} \sqrt{1 + \tan x} \, dx$
   [HINT: Let $u = \tan x = 1/x^2$.]

67. Show that $\int_0^1 \dfrac{dx}{\sqrt{x + x^3}} = \int_1^\infty \dfrac{dx}{\sqrt{x + x^3}}$.

10.2 DETECTING CONVERGENCE, ESTIMATING LIMITS

Questions of convergence and divergence for integrals are almost identical to—but often easier than—the same questions for series. Intuition developed here will carry over to infinite series; comparison is the main idea.

The preceding section was about the *definitions* of convergence and divergence for improper integrals. An integral of the form $\int_1^\infty f(x)\,dx$, for example, converges to a number L if

$$\lim_{t \to \infty} \int_1^t f(x)\,dx = L;$$

the integral diverges if the limit does not exist.

   Determining whether such limits exist, and finding those that do, wasn't hard for the relatively simple integrals in Section 10.1. In more challenging cases, things may go less well. Finding a symbolic expression for $\int_1^t f(x)\,dx$ may be difficult; even if such an expression *is* found, deciding whether the limit exists—let along finding it—may be hard.

   All is not lost. As we'll see, we can often determine convergence or divergence even for integrals we can't evaluate exactly. We'll see, too, how to use numerical methods to help us *estimate* values of such integrals.

We show how to use numerical methods to estimate numerical values of convergent improper integrals. One aim is to make the ideas of convergence and divergence more concrete; another is to build intuition for estimating sums of convergent series.

Detecting convergence or divergence by comparison

Our main tool for deciding whether a given improper integral converges or diverges is called **comparison**. The underlying idea—that larger integrands give larger integrals—could hardly be simpler. It's quite clear, for instance, that if $0 \le f(x) \le g(x)$ for all x in a *finite* interval $[a, b]$, then

$$0 \le \int_a^b f(x)\,dx \le \int_a^b g(x)\,dx.$$

The following theorem says much the same thing for *improper* integrals:

THEOREM 1 (Comparison for nonnegative improper integrals) Let f and g be continuous functions. Suppose that for all $x \geq a$,

$$0 \leq f(x) \leq g(x).$$

- If $\displaystyle\int_a^\infty g(x)\,dx$ *converges*, then so does $\displaystyle\int_a^\infty f(x)\,dx$, and

$$\int_a^\infty f(x)\,dx \leq \int_a^\infty g(x)\,dx.$$

- If $\displaystyle\int_a^\infty f(x)\,dx$ *diverges*, then so does $\displaystyle\int_a^\infty g(x)\,dx.$

(A similar result holds for improper integrals with unbounded integrands.) Figure 1 illustrates both claims.

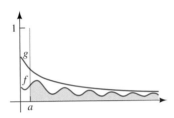

FIGURE 1
The comparison test, graphically

The graphs make both of the theorem's claims easy to believe:

- If the area under the g-graph is *finite*, then so is the (shaded) area under the "lower" f-graph, and the shaded area is less.
- If the area under the f-graph is *infinite*, then so is the area under the "higher" g-graph.

A formal proof (which we omit) makes these ideas precise.

The basic idea is extremely simple: Bigger integrands give bigger integrals.

Using the theorem   Using Theorem 1 successfully means finding appropriate "known" integrals with which to compare "unknown" integrals. Finding the "right" comparison may be the main problem.

EXAMPLE 1   Does $\displaystyle I = \int_1^\infty \frac{dx}{x^5+1}$ converge? If so, can anything be said about its limit?

Solution   By definition,

$$I = \lim_{t \to \infty} \left(\int_1^t \frac{dx}{x^5+1} \right),$$

if the limit exists. Unfortunately, the given integrand has a messy antiderivative. Even if we wrote it out, finding a limit (if one exists) would be hard.

Theorem 1 is just what we need; we'll compare I to something simpler:

$$\int_1^\infty \frac{dx}{x^5+1} \qquad \text{vs.} \qquad \int_1^\infty \frac{dx}{x^5}.$$

We can handle the second integral directly:

$$\lim_{t \to \infty} \int_1^t \frac{dx}{x^5} = \lim_{t \to \infty} \left(\frac{1}{4} - \frac{1}{4t^4} \right) = \frac{1}{4}.$$

Figure 2 shows both integrands.

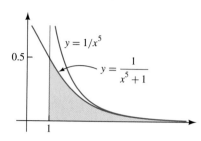

FIGURE 2

Comparing two improper integrals

The picture (or basic algebra) shows that

$$\frac{1}{x^5 + 1} < \frac{1}{x^5}$$

for all $x \geq 1$. ◄ Now Theorem 1 applies:

$$I = \int_1^\infty \frac{dx}{x^5 + 1} < \int_1^\infty \frac{dx}{x^5} = \frac{1}{4},$$

and so we conclude that I converges to *some* limit between 0 and 1/4. (We'll estimate the limit more precisely soon.) ■

Compared to what? Integrals for reference   Using Theorem 1 successfully (as we just did in Example 1) requires some "benchmark" integrals against which to compare. A few important examples (and their close relatives, such as constant multiples) go a long way:

$$\int_0^\infty e^{-x} \, dx = 1; \qquad\qquad \int_1^\infty \frac{dx}{x} \quad \text{diverges}$$

$$\int_1^\infty \frac{dx}{x^p} = \frac{1}{p-1} \quad \text{(if } p > 1\text{)}; \qquad \int_1^\infty \frac{dx}{x^p} \quad \text{diverges if } p \leq 1$$

All four claims are easily checked using the definition of convergence. ◄ The last line is sometimes summarized as the **p-test** for integrals:

$$\int_1^\infty \frac{dx}{x^p} \quad \text{converges if } p > 1 \text{ and diverges otherwise.}$$

Manipulating improper integrals   Convergent improper integrals behave just like ordinary integrals with respect to sums and constant multiples. For instance, if both $\int_1^\infty f(x) \, dx$ and $\int_1^\infty g(x) \, dx$ are convergent integrals, then we can write equations like these:

$$\int_1^\infty \big(3f(x) - 2g(x) \big) \, dx = 3 \int_1^\infty f(x) \, dx - 2 \int_1^\infty g(x) \, dx;$$

$$\int_1^\infty f(x) \, dx = \int_1^{10} f(x) \, dx + \int_{10}^\infty f(x) \, dx.$$

In particular, all of the integrals just mentioned converge.

EXAMPLE 2 Use comparison to decide whether each of the following integrals converges or diverges:

$$\int_0^\infty \frac{dx}{e^x + x}; \qquad \int_{100}^\infty \frac{dx}{\sqrt{x}}; \qquad \int_{100}^\infty \frac{dx}{10\sqrt{x} - 7}.$$

If an integral converges, find an upper bound for its value.

The second two integrals can be done by direct calculation, without using comparison, but comparison saves calculation.

Solution The first integral resembles $\int_0^\infty e^{-x}\, dx$; indeed, the comparison works well:

$$\frac{1}{e^x + x} \le \frac{1}{e^x} \quad \text{if } x \ge 0, \text{ so} \quad \int_0^\infty \frac{1}{e^x + x} \le \int_0^\infty e^{-x} = 1.$$

The second integral resembles another of our benchmarks; thus, we might guess—correctly—that it diverges. Because

$$\int_{100}^\infty \frac{dx}{\sqrt{x}} = \int_1^\infty \frac{dx}{\sqrt{x}} - \int_1^{100} \frac{dx}{\sqrt{x}}$$

and the right side diverges, the left side must also diverge. ➡

The third integral diverges too, and a little algebra with inequalities shows why. Notice first that

The right side is the sum of a divergent integral and a finite number.

$$\frac{1}{10\sqrt{x} - 7} > \frac{1}{10\sqrt{x}}$$

for $x \ge 100$. Since

$$\int_{100}^\infty \frac{dx}{10\sqrt{x}} = \frac{1}{10} \int_{100}^\infty \frac{dx}{\sqrt{x}}$$

diverges, Theorem 1 implies that the third integral must diverge too.   ∎

Integrands that change sign   Does the integral

$$I = \int_1^\infty \frac{\sin x}{x^2}\, dx$$

converge or diverge? Theorem 1 doesn't say—it applies only to *nonnegative* integrands. On the other hand, because

$$\left| \frac{\sin x}{x^2} \right| \le \frac{1}{x^2}$$

for all $x \ge 1$, it follows that

$$\int_1^\infty \left| \frac{\sin x}{x^2} \right| dx \le \int_1^\infty \frac{dx}{x^2} = 1.$$

We would therefore expect that I itself converges, and that

$$|I| = \left| \int_1^\infty \frac{\sin x}{x^2}\, dx \right| \le \int_1^\infty \left| \frac{\sin x}{x^2} \right| dx \le 1.$$

We'll see a similar theorem in Chapter 11, where we study infinite series.

The following theorem justifies these speculations. ➡

THEOREM 2 (Absolute comparison for improper integrals)   Suppose that $\int_a^\infty |f(x)|\,dx$ converges. Then $\int_a^\infty f(x)\,dx$ also converges, and

$$\left| \int_a^\infty f(x)\,dx \right| \leq \int_a^\infty |f(x)|\,dx.$$

Absolute convergence   An improper integral $\int_a^\infty f(x)\,dx$ is called **absolutely convergent** if $\int_a^\infty |f(x)|\,dx$ converges, as in the hypothesis of Theorem 2. The theorem guarantees, in effect, that if an improper integral converges *with* absolute value signs, then it also converges *without* absolute value signs. ◄

There are integrals—seldom encountered in calculus courses—that diverge with absolute values but converge without them.

Tails and estimation

Any improper integral of the form $I = \int_1^\infty f(x)\,dx$ can be rewritten as a sum like the following: ◄

We could have broken the integral elsewhere than at $x = 1000$.

$$\int_1^\infty f(x)\,dx = \int_1^{1000} f(x)\,dx + \int_{1000}^\infty f(x)\,dx.$$

The first summand on the right is an *ordinary* definite integral; we can apply either antidifferentiation or numerical methods to find or estimate its value—without any worries about convergence or divergence. The second integral on the right is called, picturesquely, an **upper tail** (or just a **tail**) of I.

We'll revisit the tail idea in the series setting. Many students find these ideas challenging, so we stick with relatively simple examples.

Convergent integrals have skinny tails   If $I = \int_1^\infty f(x)\,dx$ converges to a number L, then we must have

$$\int_1^a f(x)\,dx \approx \int_1^\infty f(x)\,dx = L$$

for large positive a. This means, in turn, that the upper tail $\int_a^\infty f(x)\,dx$ must be *near zero* for sufficiently large a.

EXAMPLE 3   Both $I = \int_0^\infty e^{-x}\,dx$ and $J = \int_1^\infty \dfrac{\sin x}{x^2}\,dx$ converge. For each integral, find an upper tail with absolute value less than 0.001. What do the answers mean about the values of I and J?

Solution   For each integral we need a number a such that

$$\left| \int_a^\infty f(x)\,dx \right| < 0.001.$$

Handling I is relatively easy. For any real number a we have

$$\int_a^\infty e^{-x}\,dx = \lim_{t \to \infty} -e^{-x} \Big]_a^t = e^{-a} = \frac{1}{e^a}.$$

Thus,

$$\int_a^\infty e^{-x}\,dx = \frac{1}{e^a} < 0.001 \iff e^a > 1000 \iff a > \ln 1000 \approx 6.908.$$

Handling J is a little trickier. Because

$$\left| \frac{\sin x}{x^2} \right| \leq \frac{1}{x^2}$$

for all x, Theorems 1 and 2 give

$$\left| \int_a^\infty \frac{\sin x}{x^2}\, dx \right| \le \int_a^\infty \frac{1}{x^2}\, dx = \frac{1}{a}.$$

Finally, $1/a < 0.001$ if $a > 1000$.

The results mean that the ordinary (proper) integrals

$$I_1 = \int_0^7 e^{-x}\, dx \quad \text{and} \quad J_1 = \int_1^{1000} \frac{\sin x}{x^2}\, dx$$

differ from I and J, respectively, by less than 0.001.   ■

Approximating improper integrals numerically   The result of Example 1—that a certain integral converges to *some* limit less than 1/4—is a bit unsatisfying. Can we say more? The next example illustrates that we can indeed, by combining skinny tails with numerical estimates.

EXAMPLE 4   Estimate the value of $I = \int_1^\infty \dfrac{dx}{x^5 + 1}$. How good is the estimate?

Solution   Symbolic methods aren't promising (as we said in Example 1), and so we'll take a numerical approach. Because numerical integration methods apply to *proper* integrals, we first break I into a finite piece I_1 and a tail I_2 (which we hope is small): ➡

We could have amputated the tail elsewhere.

$$I = \int_1^\infty \frac{dx}{x^5 + 1} = \int_1^5 \frac{dx}{x^5 + 1} + \int_5^\infty \frac{dx}{x^5 + 1} = I_1 + I_2.$$

To estimate I_1 we can use any numerical method, such as the midpoint rule with 50 subdivisions:

$$I_1 = \int_1^5 \frac{dx}{x^5 + 1} \approx M_{50} \approx 0.1799.$$

Assuming (for the moment) that the tail integral I_2 is near zero, we have our desired estimate:

$$I = I_1 + I_2 \approx 0.1799 + 0 = 0.1799.$$

The result is (as expected) a positive number less than 1/4 (the bound on I we found in Example 1), but how *good* is this estimate? Note that error can arise from two different sources:

Small roundoff errors might also be present; we ignore them here to avoid distraction from calculus ideas.

  (i) the error M_{50} commits in estimating I_1;

  (ii) the error due to ignoring the tail I_2.

We discussed the first type of error in Chapter 6; using methods discussed there we can show that this error cannot exceed 0.003. ➡

We omit the details; the idea is the point.

To gauge the second type of error (the process is called **bounding the tail**) we can use Theorem 1—which applies as readily to upper tail integrals as to any others. Because the inequality

$$\frac{1}{x^5 + 1} < \frac{1}{x^5}$$

holds for $x \ge 5$, Theorem 1 and an easy calculation give

$$I_2 = \int_5^\infty \frac{dx}{x^5 + 1} < \int_5^\infty \frac{dx}{x^5} = \frac{1}{2500} = 0.0004.$$

Having bounded *both* types of possible error, we conclude that the estimate $I \approx 0.1799$ commits *total* error less than $0.003 + 0.0004 = 0.0034$.   ■

We assemble several pieces in our last example.

EXAMPLE 5 Show that $I = \int_1^\infty e^{-x^2}\,dx$ converges and estimate its limit. How large could the error be?

Solution Because the integrand doesn't have an elementary antiderivative, we'll compare and estimate. First, I converges by comparison to one of our benchmark integrals. Since

$$e^{-x^2} \le e^{-x} \quad \text{for } x \ge 1,$$

we have

$$\int_1^\infty e^{-x^2}\,dx \le \int_1^\infty e^{-x}\,dx \le \int_0^\infty e^{-x}\,dx = 1.$$

Figure 3 shows both integrands.

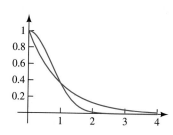

FIGURE 3
Comparing $y = e^{-x}$ and $y = e^{-x^2}$

To estimate I we'll break it into a finite piece and a tail:

$$I = \int_1^5 e^{-x^2}\,dx + \int_5^\infty e^{-x^2}\,dx = I_1 + I_2.$$

To estimate I_1 we can use the midpoint rule; $M_{100} \approx 0.1394$. The midpoint-rule error bound formula shows that M_{100} commits error less than 0.00054 in estimating I_1.

We can use the same comparison as before (this time with $a = 5$) to bound the tail integral I_2:

$$I_2 = \int_5^\infty e^{-x^2}\,dx < \int_5^\infty e^{-x}\,dx = e^{-5} \approx 0.0067.$$

Thus, the total error from *both* sources (numerical integration and ignoring the tail) in the estimate $I \approx 0.1394$ is well under 0.01. ∎

BASIC EXERCISES

1. Suppose that $1 < f(x) < g(x)$ for all $x \ge 0$.

(a) Rank the three values $1, 1/f(x)$, and $1/g(x)$ in increasing order.

(b) Suppose that $r \ge 1$. Rank the three values $1, 1/(f(x))^r$, and $1/(g(x))^r$.

(c) Suppose that $0 < r < 1$. Rank the three values $1, 1/(f(x))^r$, and $1/(g(x))^r$.

2. Suppose that $0 < f(x) < g(x) < 1$ for all $x \ge 0$.

(a) Rank the three values $1, 1/f(x)$, and $1/g(x)$ in increasing order.

(b) Suppose that $r \ge 1$. Rank the three values $1, 1/(f(x))^r$, and $1/(g(x))^r$.

(c) Suppose that $0 < r < 1$. Rank the three values $1, 1/(f(x))^r$, and $1/(g(x))^r$.

3. Let $f(x) = \dfrac{x^2+2}{x^2+1}$.

(a) Show that $f(x) > 1$ for all x.

(b) Use the inequality in part (a) to show that $\int_{-\infty}^\infty f(x)\,dx$ diverges.

4. Let $f(x) = \dfrac{e^x}{1 + e^x}$.

   (a) Show that $f(x) > 1/2$ for all $x \geq 0$.
[HINT: $e^x \geq 1$ for all $x \geq 0$.]

   (b) Use the inequality in part (a) to show that $\displaystyle\int_{-\infty}^{\infty} f(x)\,dx$ diverges.

5. Let $f(x) = x + \sin x$.

   (a) Show that $x - 1 \leq f(x)$ for all $x \geq 0$.

   (b) Use the inequality in part (a) to show that $\displaystyle\int_{2}^{\infty} \dfrac{dx}{f(x)}$ diverges.

6. Let $f(x) = x^2 + \sin x$.

   (a) Show that $x^2 - 1 \leq f(x)$ for all $x \geq 0$.

   (b) Does $\displaystyle\int_{2}^{\infty} \dfrac{dx}{f(x)}$ converge? Justify your answer.

7. Let $f(x) = x^2 + \sqrt{x}$.

   (a) Show that $x^2 \leq f(x)$ for all $x \geq 0$.

   (b) Use the inequality in part (a) to show that $\displaystyle\int_{1}^{\infty} \dfrac{dx}{f(x)}$ converges.

8. Let $f(x) = x^2 - \sqrt{x}$.

   (a) Show that $x^2/2 \leq f(x)$ for all $x \geq 2$.

   (b) Does $\displaystyle\int_{3}^{\infty} \dfrac{dx}{f(x)}$ converge? Justify your answer.

9. Does $\displaystyle\int_{2}^{\infty} \dfrac{dx}{x - \sqrt{x}}$ converge? Justify your answer.

10. Does $\displaystyle\int_{1}^{\infty} \dfrac{dx}{x + \sqrt{x}}$ converge? Justify your answer.

In Exercises 11–14, find a value for the parameter a that makes the value of the improper integral less than 10^{-5}.

11. $\displaystyle\int_{a}^{\infty} e^{-x}\,dx$ **12.** $\displaystyle\int_{a}^{\infty} x e^{-x^2}\,dx$

13. $\displaystyle\int_{a}^{\infty} \dfrac{dx}{x^2 + 1}$ **14.** $\displaystyle\int_{a}^{\infty} \dfrac{dx}{x(\ln x)^3}$

In Exercises 15–18, find a proper integral whose value approximates that of the given (convergent) improper integral within 10^{-5}.

15. $\displaystyle\int_{0}^{\infty} \dfrac{dx}{x^2 + e^x}$ **16.** $\displaystyle\int_{1}^{\infty} \dfrac{dx}{x^4\sqrt{2x^3 + 1}}$

17. $\displaystyle\int_{0}^{\infty} \dfrac{\arctan x}{(1 + x^2)^3}\,dx$ **18.** $\displaystyle\int_{0}^{\infty} \dfrac{e^{-x}}{2 + \cos x}\,dx$

19. Suppose that $f(x) \geq 0$ for all $x \geq 1$ and that $\displaystyle\int_{1}^{\infty} f(x)\,dx$ converges. Explain why there is a number a such that $\displaystyle\int_{a}^{\infty} f(x)\,dx \leq 10^{-10}$.

20. Suppose that $g(x) \geq 0$ for all $x \geq 1$ and that $\displaystyle\int_{1}^{\infty} g(x)\,dx$ diverges. Explain why there is a number b such that $\displaystyle\int_{1}^{b} g(x)\,dx \geq 10^{10}$.

21. Suppose that $I = \displaystyle\int_{0}^{\infty} f(x)\,dx$ converges and that $\left| \displaystyle\int_{a}^{\infty} f(x)\,dx \right| \leq 0.0001$. Show that $\left| I - \displaystyle\int_{0}^{a} f(x)\,dx \right| \leq 0.0001$.

22. Show that $0.8 < \displaystyle\int_{0}^{\infty} \sin\left(e^{-x}\right) dx < 1$.
[HINT: Use the substitution $u = e^{-x}$.]

FURTHER EXERCISES

23. Show that $\displaystyle\int_{0}^{\infty} e^{-x^2}\,dx$ converges. [HINT: See Example 5 but be careful; $e^{-x^2} > e^{-x}$ for some $x \geq 0$.]

24. Consider the integral $I = \displaystyle\int_{2}^{\infty} \dfrac{dx}{(\ln x)^2}$.

   (a) Show that $\ln x \leq \sqrt{x}$ for all $x \geq 2$.

   (b) Does I converge? Justify your answer.

25. Suppose that $p \geq 1$ is a constant and that $I = \displaystyle\int_{2}^{\infty} \dfrac{dx}{(\ln x)^p}$. For which values of p, if any, does I converge? Justify your answer. [HINT: $\displaystyle\lim_{x \to \infty} \dfrac{(\ln x)^p}{x} = 0$.]

26. **(a)** Show that $0 \leq x/2 \leq \sin x$ if $0 \leq x \leq 1$. [HINT: $1/2 \leq \cos x$ if $0 \leq x \leq 1$.]

   (b) Use the inequality in part (a) to show that $\displaystyle\int_{0}^{1} \dfrac{dx}{\sqrt{\sin x}}$ converges.

In Exercises 27–30, use the comparison test to determine whether the improper integral converges or diverges.

27. $\displaystyle\int_{0}^{\infty} \dfrac{dx}{x^4 + x}$ **28.** $\displaystyle\int_{1}^{\infty} \dfrac{dx}{\sqrt{x} - 1}$

29. $\displaystyle\int_{1}^{\infty} \dfrac{dx}{\sqrt[3]{x^6 + x}}$ **30.** $\displaystyle\int_{0}^{\infty} \dfrac{dx}{\sqrt{x}(1 + x)}$

31. Does $\displaystyle\int_{0}^{\infty} \dfrac{e^{-x}}{\sqrt{x}}\,dx$ converge? Justify your answer.

32. Show that the integral $\displaystyle\int_{0}^{1} \dfrac{\cos x}{x}\,dx$ diverges.

33. **(a)** Show that $\displaystyle\int_{1}^{\infty} \dfrac{\cos x}{x^2}\,dx$ converges.

   (b) Use integration by parts and part (a) to show that $\displaystyle\int_{1}^{\infty} \dfrac{\sin x}{x}\,dx$ converges.

34. Let $I = \displaystyle\int_{0}^{\infty} \dfrac{dx}{\sqrt{x + x^4}}$. Show that $0 \leq I \leq 3$.

35. Evaluate $\displaystyle\lim_{x \to \infty} \dfrac{\displaystyle\int_{1}^{x} \sqrt{1 + e^{-3t}}\,dt}{x}$.

36. Evaluate $\displaystyle\lim_{x \to \infty} e^{x^2} \displaystyle\int_{0}^{x} e^{-t^2}\,dt$.

We assume no specialized knowledge of probability; basic terms and ideas are described here.

10.3 IMPROPER INTEGRALS AND PROBABILITY

Many real-world phenomena exhibit forms of random behavior. The number of heads in 10 throws of a coin, the height of a male college student chosen at random, the actual weight of a nominally 16-oz cereal package, and the working life of a 60-watt light bulb are all examples.

Statisticians call such quantities **random variables**. A random variable that can take only *finitely* many values (such as the number of heads in 10 coin tosses) is called **discrete**. A random variable that ranges over an *interval* of real numbers is called **continuous**. Human adult height is a good example: Any number in some interval—(36, 85), say—may conceivably be someone's height in inches. We consider only continuous random variables, even though calculus methods can also be applied in the discrete case.

Random phenomena are, by nature, not perfectly predictable. But one might reasonably want to know the probability that a male college student is between 68 and 75 inches tall or the likelihood of getting less than 15 ounces of Cheerios in a package. Doing so turns out to involve integrals—many of them improper.

Basics of continuous probability

By convention, probabilities are measured on a scale from 0 to 1. An event that is certain to occur has probability 1. (It's certain, for example, that a male college student's height in inches is *some* positive number.) Because a continuous random variable X has infinitely many possible values, it's not interesting to ask for the probability that X is *precisely* equal to some number—that probability is zero. A better question concerns the probability that X lies in some *interval*, such as (68, 75). If this probability is, say, 0.78, then 78% of male college students are between 68 and 75 inches tall.

Associated with every continuous random variable X is a function f called the **probability density function**, or **pdf**, of X. The connection between f and X is given by an integral:

$$\int_a^b f(x)\,dx = \text{probability that } X \text{ lies in } (a, b).$$

The shaded region in Figure 1 represents this probability geometrically.

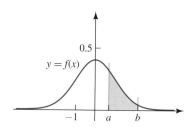

FIGURE 1
Probability that $a < X < b$

Here are some commonsense facts about f and X; some are reflected in Figure 1:

- **Domain** The domain of f is the set of possible values of X. (Often f has an infinite domain—hence the need for improper integrals.)

- **Near, not exact** For a given x, $f(x)$ measures the comparative likelihood that the value of X falls *near* x. The probability that X takes any *single* value x is zero.

- **Certainty**   Because X must take *some* real value, $\int_{-\infty}^{\infty} f(x)\,dx = 1$. (The graph in Figure 1 bounds total area 1.)
- **A positive function**   For all inputs x, $f(x) \geq 0$ (as in Figure 1).

The normal density function

Students may have some general ideas about "bell curves."

Many real-life random phenomena can be modeled by a **normal** (also called **Gaussian normal**) density function—one of the following form: ➡

Recall: $\exp(\text{stuff}) = e^{\text{stuff}}$.

$$f(x) = \frac{1}{\sqrt{2\pi}\,s} \exp\left(-\frac{(x-m)^2}{2s^2}\right).$$

A random variable whose probability density function has this form is said to be **normally distributed**.

All the constants may look scary to students, but we show that each of them has a simple geometric meaning.

The normal density function looks messy, but in practice it's not too bad. The letters s and m stand for constant parameters called, respectively, the **standard deviation** and the **mean** of the random variable. (Statisticians usually write σ and μ, but we'll stick with English.) Their numerical values depend on the situation being modeled. The mean m, as its name suggests, is a kind of average value of X. The standard deviation s is a measure of how "spread out" X's values are. The graphs in Figure 2 illustrate the geometric effects of varying m and s; all four graphs—versions of the famous "bell curve"—bound the same total (unit) area.

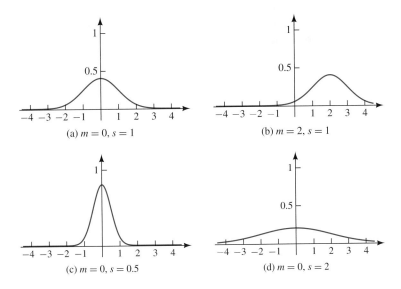

(a) $m = 0$, $s = 1$

(b) $m = 2$, $s = 1$

(c) $m = 0$, $s = 0.5$

(d) $m = 0$, $s = 2$

FIGURE 2
Four normal density functions

Integrating the normal density — properly and improperly

Using the normal density function

$$f(x) = \frac{1}{\sqrt{2\pi}\,s} \exp\left(-\frac{(x-m)^2}{2s^2}\right)$$

requires integrating it over various intervals, either finite or infinite. Because the normal density function has no elementary antiderivative, such integrals *must* be estimated numerically. The following properties of f help simplify the process.

- **Convergence**   For any values of m and s, the improper integral $\int_{-\infty}^{\infty} f(x)\,dx$ converges, and its limit is 1. Showing that the integral converges is not too difficult; we showed something similar in Example 5 of Section 10.2 (page 536). Estimating a limit is easy, but showing rigorously that it is *precisely* 1 is considerably harder; we omit the proof.

- **Symmetry**   For any values of m and s, the graph of f is "centered" on the line $x = m$; the graph bounds total area 0.5 to each side of this line. This fact can simplify area computations and improve the accuracy of numerical estimates.

We showed by comparison in Example 5, page 536, that integrating from 1 to ∞ gives a finite result.

Students should thoroughly understand the symmetry of the graph with respect to the mean; doing so aids intuition considerably.

EXAMPLE 1   Suppose that the birth weight (in pounds) of a certain population of infants is normally distributed with mean 7.5 lb and standard deviation 1 lb. What percentage of infants can be expected to weigh between 6.5 and 8.5 lb? Over 10 lb?

Solution   Both answers are areas bounded by the normal density function with parameter values $m = 7.5$ and $s = 1$. Both areas are shown shaded in Figure 3.

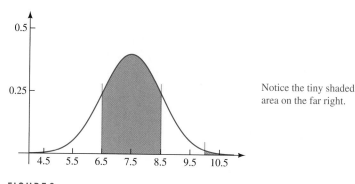

Notice the tiny shaded area on the far right.

FIGURE 3
Normal density, $m = 7.5$, $s = 1$

The answers, written as integrals, are

$$I_1 = \int_{6.5}^{8.5} f(x)\,dx \quad \text{and} \quad I_2 = \int_{10}^{\infty} f(x)\,dx.$$

Applying the midpoint rule to I_1 gives $M_{20} \approx 0.6829$. Thus, given our assumptions, about 68% of babies should weigh within one pound of the mean.

Figure 3 suggests that I_2 is small. To estimate it numerically, we use the fact that the total area to the right of $x = 7.5$ is (exactly!) 0.5. Therefore,

$$I_2 = \int_{10}^{\infty} f(x)\,dx = 0.5 - \int_{7.5}^{10} f(x)\,dx.$$

The last integral can be estimated numerically. The midpoint rule gives $M_{20} \approx 0.4938$, and so $I_2 \approx 0.0062$. Therefore, only around 0.6% of babies can be expected to weigh over 10 lb. ∎

Is life really normal?   Are real-life phenomena—baby weights, SAT scores, heights of male adults, and so on—*really* normally distributed?

In one sense, certainly not. One obvious problem is that every normal distribution is infinitely "spread out": The variable can take *any* real value—large or small, positive or negative. Few real-life phenomena behave this way. No baby has negative weight, for instance; yet, every normal distribution assigns some tiny but positive probability to this peculiar event.

In another, more practical sense, normal distributions do usefully model many phenomena. "Model" is the key word—in suitable settings the normal density function provides an effective, if imperfect, *approximation* to an underlying reality. Imperfection is no surprise; it comes with the territory of real life. Effectiveness is the real surprise.

EXAMPLE 2 Possible scores on the math and verbal parts of the Scholastic Aptitude Test (SAT) range from 200 to 800. Assume that test scores are normally distributed with mean 500 and standard deviation 100. ➡ What percentage of students score between 400 and 600? Over 750?

Historically, this assumption is not far off.

Solution The situation—and the picture—closely resemble those of Example 1. Setting $m = 500$ and $s = 100$ gives Figure 4; areas of interest are shaded.

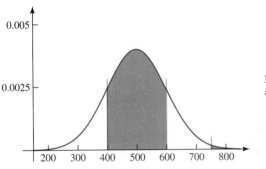

Notice the tiny shaded area on the far right.

FIGURE 4
Normal density, $m = 500, s = 100$

The shaded areas can be estimated numerically. We omit details this time because, for reasons we'll soon see, the shaded regions here have exactly the same areas as those in Example 1. We therefore conclude that about 68% of SAT scores fall between 400 and 600, that is, within one standard deviation of the mean; only 0.6% of scores are above 750. ∎

Keeping it simple: The standard normal density

Calculations are simplest if $m = 0$ and $s = 1$. With these parameter values, the **standard normal density** function takes a particularly pleasant form

$$n(x) = \frac{1}{\sqrt{2\pi}} \exp\left(\frac{-x^2}{2}\right).$$

In fact, any normal distribution can easily be "standardized"—that is, reinterpreted as a standard normal distribution. In the SAT case, for instance, we could consider how much scores differ from 500 rather than "raw" test scores themselves. Doing so moves the mean to 0; the standard deviation remains at 100. Dividing *these* results by 100 leaves the mean unchanged at 0 but cuts the standard deviation to 1. The results therefore have a *standard normal distribution*.

Statisticians call such altered data **Z-scores**. For example, raw SAT scores of 620 and 450 correspond to Z-scores of 1.20 and −0.5, that is, to scores 1.2 standard deviations above and 0.5 standard deviation below the mean, respectively. Similarly, a 10-lb baby from the population of Example 1 weighs in at 2.5 standard deviations above the mean.

To find the probability of a Z-score between -1 and 1, we integrate the standard normal density:

$$\int_{-1}^{1} \frac{1}{\sqrt{2\pi}} \exp\left(\frac{-x^2}{2}\right) dx.$$

It's worth emphasizing that the Z-score idea boils down to substitution; this also helps explain the constants in the standard normal pdf.

Also known as u-substitution.

No symbolic antiderivative is available, but numerical integration methods work fine. The midpoint rule with 20 subdivisions gives $M_{20} \approx 0.6829$. This by-now-familiar result offers evidence that Z-scores make mathematical sense.

Why Z-scores work: Substitution in definite integrals   What statisticians call Z-scores *we* call Z-substitution in a definite integral. ← We illustrate with an example.

E X A M P L E 3   Write integrals, with and without Z-scores, for the probability of an SAT score between 500 and 700. Why do both integrals give the same result?

S o l u t i o n   With raw scores we use $m = 500$ and $s = 100$; the desired probability is

$$I_1 = \frac{1}{\sqrt{2\pi} \cdot 100} \int_{500}^{700} \exp\left(-\frac{(x-500)^2}{2 \cdot 100^2}\right) dx.$$

Raw scores of 500 and 700 give Z-scores of 0 and 2.

With Z-scores we want the probability of a result between 0 and 2. ← This is the integral

$$I_2 = \frac{1}{\sqrt{2\pi}} \int_{0}^{2} \exp\left(-\frac{x^2}{2}\right) dx.$$

Numerical evidence that $I_1 = I_2$ is easily found: For both integrals, $M_{20} \approx 0.47729$. A symbolic calculation confirms the result. Substituting

$$Z = \frac{x-500}{100} \quad \text{and} \quad dZ = \frac{dx}{100}$$

in I_1 yields I_2.   ■

Z-score tables   In olden days (before computers) it was difficult to estimate the definite integrals that arise in the study of normal distributions. The only recourse was to numerical tables; part of one such table follows. For a given input x, the table entry is $A(x) = \int_{-\infty}^{x} n(t)\,dt$, the area shown graphically in Figure 5.

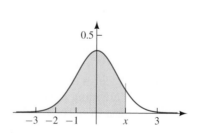

FIGURE 5
Standard normal density; $A(x) = \int_{-\infty}^{x} n(t)\,dt$

	\multicolumn{10}{c}{**Values of $A(x) = \int_{-\infty}^{x} n(t)\,dt$**}
x	0.0	0.1	0.2	0.3	0.4	0.5	0.6	0.7	0.8	0.9
$A(x)$	0.5000	0.5398	0.5793	0.6179	0.6554	0.6915	0.7257	0.7580	0.7881	0.8159
x	1.0	1.1	1.2	1.3	1.4	1.5	1.6	1.7	1.8	1.9
$A(x)$	0.8413	0.8643	0.8849	0.9032	0.9192	0.9333	0.9452	0.9554	0.9641	0.9713
x	2.0	2.1	2.2	2.3	2.4	2.5	2.6	2.7	2.8	2.9
$A(x)$	0.9773	0.9822	0.9861	0.9893	0.9918	0.9938	0.9953	0.9965	0.9974	0.9981

The numbers compare well with the graph. As we'd expect, for instance, $A(0) = 0.5$ and $A(2.9) \approx 1.00$.

BASIC EXERCISES

1. Plot the normal probability density function with the given parameter values. On each graph, shade the area corresponding to the probability that the value of a random variable having this distribution will be within one standard deviation of the mean.

   (a) $m = 1, s = 1$

   (b) $m = 2, s = 1/2$

   (c) $m = 0, s = 1/4$

2. (a) Let X be a normally distributed random variable with $m = 0$ and $s = 1$. Explain why the proportion of the possible values of X that lie within three standard deviations of the mean is $\dfrac{1}{\sqrt{2\pi}} \displaystyle\int_{-3}^{3} e^{-x^2/2}\,dx$.

   (b) Let Y be a normally distributed random variable with $m = 0$ and $s = 2$. Write a definite integral whose value is the proportion of the possible values of Y that lie within three standard deviations of the mean.

   (c) Use the substitution $u = x/2$ to show that the integrals in parts (a) and (b) are equal.

   (d) Use numerical integration to estimate the integral in part (a).

3. Let I_1 and I_2 be the integrals discussed in Example 3. Show that I_2 is the result of making the substitution $Z = (x - 500)/100$ in I_1.

4. Use the substitution $z = (x - m)/s$ to show that
   $$\frac{1}{\sqrt{2\pi}\, s} \int_{x_1}^{x_2} \exp\left(-\frac{(x - m)^2}{2s^2}\right) dx = \frac{1}{\sqrt{2\pi}} \int_{z_1}^{z_2} e^{-z^2/2}\,dz,$$
   where $z_1 = (x_1 - m)/s$ and $z_2 = (x_2 - m)/s$.

5. Let $f(x) = \dfrac{1}{\sqrt{2\pi}\, s} \exp\left(-\dfrac{(x - m)^2}{2s^2}\right)$.

   (a) We showed in Example 5 that $\displaystyle\int_{1}^{\infty} e^{-x^2}\,dx$ converges. In fact, the integral $\displaystyle\int_{0}^{\infty} e^{-x^2}\,dx$ also converges; its limit can

be shown to be $\sqrt{\pi}/2$. Use these facts to explain why $\displaystyle\int_{-\infty}^{\infty} e^{-x^2}\,dx = \sqrt{\pi}$.

   (b) Use the substitution $u = x/\sqrt{2}$ to show that if $m = 0$ and $s = 1$, then $\displaystyle\int_{-\infty}^{\infty} f(x)\,dx = 1$.

   (c) Use the result in part (b) to show that $\displaystyle\int_{-\infty}^{\infty} f(x)\,dx = 1$ for any real number m and any positive number s. [HINT: Use the substitution $u = (x - m)/s$.]

6. Suppose that an observation of a normally distributed random variable has a Z-score of -1.3.

   (a) Is this observation larger than the mean? Justify your answer.

   (b) How many standard deviations from the mean is this observation?

7. (a) What Z-score corresponds to an SAT score of 600?

   (b) What Z-score corresponds to an SAT score of 450?

   (c) Use part (b) to write an integral whose value is the probability of getting an SAT score greater than 450.

   (d) Use part (a) to write an integral whose value is the probability of getting an SAT score less than 600.

   (e) Use parts (c) and (d) to write an integral whose value is the probability of getting an SAT score between 450 and 600.

8. Let $A(x) = \displaystyle\int_{-\infty}^{x} n(t)\,dt$, where $n(t)$ is the standard normal density function. Explain why $\displaystyle\int_{z_1}^{z_2} n(t)\,dt = A(z_2) - A(z_1)$.

9. Let $A(x) = \displaystyle\int_{-\infty}^{x} n(t)\,dt$, where $n(t)$ is the standard normal density function.

   (a) Explain why $A(-z) = 1 - A(z)$.

   (b) Use part (a) and the table on page 543 to estimate $A(-1.2)$.

In Exercises 10 and 11, use the table on page 543 to compute the probability of getting an SAT score

10. greater than 600.

11. between 350 and 500.

In Exercises 12 and 13, use the table on page 543 to estimate

12. $\dfrac{1}{5\sqrt{2\pi}} \displaystyle\int_{-\infty}^{14} \exp\left(-\dfrac{(x-10)^2}{50}\right)$

13. $\dfrac{1}{5\sqrt{2\pi}} \displaystyle\int_{-\infty}^{4} \exp\left(-\dfrac{(x-10)^2}{50}\right)$

Part of the graph of the probability density function for a random variable X with values in the interval $[0, \infty)$ is shown below. In

Exercises 14–17 use the graph to estimate the probability that a random value of X lies in the interval.

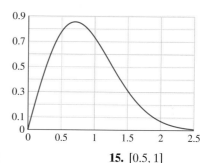

14. $[0, 0.5]$ **15.** $[0.5, 1]$

16. $[0, 1.5]$ **17.** $[1.5, \infty)$

FURTHER EXERCISES

18. How high must a student score on the SAT to have a score in the top 10%? In the top 5%? [HINT: Use the tabulated values of $A(x)$ on page 543.]

19. Suppose that the average rainfall in May is 5 inches with a standard deviation of 0.6 inch. What is the probability that the rainfall next May will differ from the average by more than 1 inch? (Assume that May rainfall amounts are normally distributed.)

20. During the grand finale of a circus, a performer is shot from a special cannon. The distance the performer travels varies but is normally distributed with a mean of 150 feet and a standard deviation of 10 feet. The landing net is 30 feet long.

(a) How far away from the cannon should the nearest edge of the net be placed?

(b) Given the net position in part (a), what is the probability that the performer will miss the landing net?

21. A stamping machine produces can tops whose diameters are normally distributed with a standard deviation of 0.01 inch. At what "nominal" (i.e., mean) diameter should the machine be set so that no more than 10% of the can tops produced have a diameter greater than 3 inches.

22. Let $A(x) = \displaystyle\int_{-\infty}^{x} n(t)\,dt$, where $n(t)$ is the standard normal probability density function. (See the table on page 543.)

(a) Since 0.75 lies midway between 0.7 and 0.8, it is reasonable to estimate that $A(0.75) \approx (A(0.7) + A(0.8))/2 = (0.7580 + 0.7881)/2 = 0.77305$. Does this approximation overestimate the exact value? Justify your answer. (Assume that the values of $A(0.7)$ and $A(0.8)$ given in the table are exact.)

(b) Use a tangent line approximation to estimate $A(0.75)$. [HINT: $A'(x) = n(x)$.]

(c) Does the estimate you computed in part (b) overestimate the exact value? Justify your answer.

23. The probability density function for the **log-normal** distribution is

$$g(x) = \begin{cases} \dfrac{1}{\sqrt{2\pi}\,\beta x}\,e^{-(\ln x - \alpha)^2/2\beta^2} & \text{if } x > 0, \\ 0 & \text{if } x \leq 0. \end{cases}$$

(a) Explain why $\beta > 0$ must be true for g to be a probability density function.

(b) Use the substitution $u = (\ln x - \alpha)/\beta$ to show that the probability that $a \leq x \leq b$ is

$$\int_a^b g(x)\,dx = A\left(\dfrac{\ln b - \alpha}{\beta}\right) - A\left(\dfrac{\ln a - \alpha}{\beta}\right),$$

where $A(x) = \displaystyle\int_{-\infty}^{x} n(x)\,dx$.

24. Let T be the number of minutes that it takes a randomly selected person to solve a certain puzzle. The probability density function of T is

$$f(x) = \begin{cases} 3/x^4 & \text{if } x \geq 1, \\ 0 & \text{if } x < 1. \end{cases}$$

(a) Show that $\displaystyle\int_{-\infty}^{\infty} f(x)\,dx = 1$.

(b) What is the probability that $T > 2$?

(c) What is the probability that $T < 1.5$?

(d) Evaluate $\displaystyle\int_{-\infty}^{\infty} x f(x)\,dx$. (This is the **mean** of the random variable T.)

(e) Find m such that 50% of the people solve the puzzle in m minutes or less. (This is the **median** of the random variable T.)

25. Find k so that $f(x) = k/(1 + x^2)$ is a probability density function. (This is the **Cauchy** distribution.)

26. Find k so that
$$f(x) = \begin{cases} k(1-x^2) & \text{if } 0 \le x \le 1, \\ 0 & \text{otherwise,} \end{cases}$$
is a probability density function.

27. Let $\lambda > 0$ be a constant, and let f be the function
$$f(x) = \begin{cases} \lambda e^{-\lambda x} & \text{if } x \ge 0, \\ 0 & \text{if } x < 0. \end{cases}$$

(a) Show that f is a probability density function.
[NOTE: f is known as the **exponential** density function.]

(b) Evaluate $\int_{-\infty}^{\infty} x f(x)\, dx$. [NOTE: If X is a random variable that has f as its probability density function, then the value of this integral is the **mean** of X.]

28. The exponential density function (see Exercise 27) is often used to model the lifespan of electrical devices. Suppose that 10% of a certain type of device fail after 6 months.

(a) What value of λ corresponds to the observed lifespan?

(b) What is the probability that a randomly selected device will still be functioning after 18 months?

(c) What is the mean lifespan of this device?

*Exercises 29–33 explore some properties of the **gamma** function:*
$$\Gamma(x) = \int_0^{\infty} t^{x-1} e^{-t}\, dt.$$

29. (a) Evaluate $\Gamma(1)$.

(b) Use integration by parts to show that if $x > 1$, $\Gamma(x) = (x-1)\Gamma(x-1)$. [HINT: For any real number z, $\lim_{t \to \infty} t^z e^{-t} = 0$.]

30. Show that $0 < \Gamma\left(\frac{2}{3}\right) < 2$. [HINT: Be careful; the integral has *two* improprieties.]

31. Use the fact that $\int_0^{\infty} e^{-x^2}\, dx = \frac{\sqrt{\pi}}{2}$ to evaluate $\Gamma\left(\frac{1}{2}\right)$.
[HINT: Let $u = \sqrt{t}$.]

32. Show that $\Gamma(z+1) = \int_0^{\infty} t^z e^{-t}\, dt = \int_0^1 \left(\ln(1/x)\right)^z dx$.
[HINT: Use the substitution $t = \ln(1/x)$.]

33. It is a fact that $\Gamma(n+1) = \int_0^{\infty} x^n e^{-x}\, dx = n!$ if $n \ge 0$ is an integer. Use this fact to show that if m and n are positive integers, then $\int_0^1 x^m (\ln x)^n\, dx = \frac{(-1)^n\, n!}{(m+1)^{n+1}}$.
[HINT: Make the substitution $x = e^{-u}$ in the second integral.]

34. Suppose that x and y are uniformly distributed random variables with values in the interval $[0, 2]$. (Uniformly distributed means that every value in the interval is equally probable.)

(a) Consider (x, y) as a point in the xy-plane. Explain why the **sample space** is the square $[0, 2] \times [0, 2]$.

(b) Explain why the probability that $x \le 1$ *and* $y \le 1$ is $1/4$.
[HINT: What proportion of the sample space is occupied by the region $[0, 1] \times [0, 1]$.]

35. Suppose that x and y are uniformly distributed random variables with values in the interval $[-2, 2]$. What is the probability that $x^2 + y^2 \le 1$? Justify your answer.

36. Suppose that x and y are uniformly distributed random variables with values in the interval $[0, 1]$. What is the probability that $x + y \le 1/2$? Justify your answer.

37. Suppose that x and y are uniformly distributed random variables with values in the interval $[0, 1]$. What is the probability that $y/x \ge 2$? Justify your answer.

38. Suppose that x and y are uniformly distributed random variables with values in the interval $[0, 2]$. What is the probability that $xy \le 2$? Justify your answer.

39. Suppose that x and y are uniformly distributed random variables with values in the interval $[0, 3]$. What is the probability that $x + y \ge xy$? Justify your answer.

11

INFINITE SERIES

11.1 SEQUENCES AND THEIR LIMITS

We raised questions of convergence and divergence for improper integrals in Chapter 10; we exploit that intuition often here. Sequence limits we treat as similar to ordinary function limits, except that here we stress Theorem 3, which guarantees convergence of a bounded, monotone sequence.

This section, on infinite *sequences*, prepares the ground for the next topic—infinite *series*. Convergent series are defined in terms of the simpler, more basic idea of convergent sequences. We start with a brief introduction to sequences—what they are, what it means for them to converge or diverge, and how to find their limits.

Terminology and basic examples

A **sequence** is an infinite list of numbers, of the general form

$$a_1, \ a_2, \ a_3, \ a_4, \ldots, a_k, \ a_{k+1}, \ldots.$$

Read "a sub three" and "a sub k."

Individual entries are called the **terms** of the sequence; a_3 and a_k, ◄ for instance, are the third term and the kth term, respectively. The full sequence is, technically speaking, an **ordered set**; the standard notation

$$\{a_k\}_{k=1}^{\infty}$$

(or simply $\{a_k\}$) uses set (wiggly) brackets to emphasize this view.

Our main interest in sequences is in their **limits**. For the simplest sequences, limits (or the lack thereof) are evident at a glance. The next three examples are of this type.

The first few examples are mainly to illustrate notation and main ideas.

EXAMPLE 1 Discuss the sequence $\{a_k\}_{k=1}^{\infty}$ defined by the formula $a_k = 1/k$. Does this sequence have a limit?

Solution Sampling some terms—

$$\frac{1}{1}, \frac{1}{2}, \frac{1}{3}, \ldots, \frac{1}{10}, \frac{1}{11}, \ldots, \frac{1}{100}, \frac{1}{101}, \ldots$$

shows (to nobody's surprise) that the sequence **converges** to zero: As k increases, the terms a_k approach zero arbitrarily closely. In symbols,

$$\lim_{k \to \infty} a_k = \lim_{k \to \infty} \frac{1}{k} = 0.$$

∎

EXAMPLE 2   Suppose that $\{b_j\}_{j=1}^{\infty}$ is defined by

$$b_j = \frac{(-1)^j}{j}, \quad j = 1, 2, 3, \ldots.$$

(We used j, not k, as our **index variable**—the choice is up to us.) What's $\lim_{j \to \infty} b_j$?

Solution   Writing out terms shows a pattern similar to that in Example 1:

$$-\frac{1}{1}, \frac{1}{2}, -\frac{1}{3}, \ldots, \frac{1}{10}, -\frac{1}{11}, \ldots, \frac{1}{100}, -\frac{1}{101}, \ldots.$$

Although the terms oscillate in *sign*, they approach zero more and more closely as j increases. Eventually, all the terms—positive or negative—remain within any specified distance from zero. (All terms past b_{1000}, for instance, are within 0.001 of zero.) Hence, the sequence $\{b_j\}$ **converges** to zero:

$$\lim_{j \to \infty} b_j = \lim_{j \to \infty} \frac{(-1)^j}{j} = 0.$$ ■

EXAMPLE 3   Does the sequence $\{c_k\}_{k=0}^{\infty}$ with general term $c_k = (-1)^k$ converge?

Solution   No; it **diverges**. Successive terms have the pattern

$$1, -1, 1, -1, 1, \ldots,$$

never settling on a single limit.   ■

EXAMPLE 4   Discuss the **Fibonacci sequence**, defined by the rules

$$F_1 = 1; \quad F_2 = 1; \quad F_{n+2} = F_n + F_{n+1};$$

each term is the sum of its two predecessors. � Such definitions are called **recursive**: Each term is defined by means of earlier terms.

Newton's method (in Chapter 4) describes another recursively defined sequence.

Solution   The first few terms of this sequence are

$$1, 1, 2, 3, 5, 8, 13, 21, 34, 55, \ldots.$$

The sequence is named for the Italian mathematician Leonardo Fibonacci (1170–1250), who related it to a rabbit population explosion under certain conditions.

As the pattern suggests, the sequence **diverges** to infinity, and we write $\lim_{n \to \infty} F_n = \infty$.   ■

Lessons from the examples

Sequences have their own notational quirks and conventions. Here are several to watch for:

- **Where to start?**   The sequence in Example 3 began with c_0, not c_1. Other starting points, such as a_2 or even b_{-3}, occasionally arise. In practice, such differences are unimportant. What matters for sequences is their long-run behavior, not the presence or absence of a few initial terms.

- **Index variable names don't matter**   We can define the squaring function by writing either $f(t) = t^2$ or $f(x) = x^2$; the *variable name* makes no difference. In the same way, a sequence's *index name* is arbitrary: $\{a_k\}_{k=1}^{\infty}$ and $\{a_j\}_{j=1}^{\infty}$ mean exactly the same thing.

The point bears repeating — a given sequence may have different symbolic representations.

- **Reindexing**   The sequence

$$\frac{1}{1}, \frac{1}{2}, \frac{1}{3}, \dots, \frac{1}{10}, \frac{1}{11}, \dots$$

of Example 1 can be described symbolically in various different-looking but still equivalent ways. Here are two:

$$a_k = \frac{1}{k}, \quad k = 1, 2, \dots \qquad \text{or} \qquad a_j = \frac{1}{j+1}, \quad j = 0, 1, 2, \dots.$$

Depending on the situation, one description or the other may be preferable.

We'll exploit this view often — e.g., when we use l'Hôpital's rule to find limits.

Sequences as functions   Sequences are closely related to functions, as expressions such as

$$a_k = \frac{\sin k}{k} \qquad \text{and} \qquad f(x) = \frac{\sin x}{x}$$

illustrate. The formal definition makes this connection precise.

> **DEFINITION**   An **infinite sequence** is a real-valued function that is defined for *positive integer inputs.*

The definition and the preceding examples give us several useful ways to think of a sequence:

- **As a list**   As an infinite list of numbers: $a_1, a_2, a_3, \dots$.
- **As a function**   As a function $a(n)$, where n takes only positive integer values. (The rule for a may or may not make sense for other inputs.) Thus, $a(1) = a_1$, $a(2) = a_2$, $a(3) = a_3$, and so on.
- **As a discrete sample**   As a "discrete sample" of values of an ordinary calculus-style function $f(x)$ defined for real $x \geq 1$. The function $f(x) = 1/x$, for example, produces the sequence $a_k = 1/k$ in Example 1.

Graphs of sequences, graphs of functions   The graph of any function f consists of the points $(x, f(x))$ for x in the domain of f. The graph of a *sequence* $\{a_k\}$ is therefore the set of points (k, a_k) as k runs through positive integer values.

EXAMPLE 5   Let a function f and a sequence $\{a_k\}$ be defined by

$$f(x) = \frac{\sin x}{x}; \qquad a_k = \frac{\sin k}{k}.$$

Plot graphs of both. What do the graphs say about limits?

Solution Figure 1 shows the graphs.

The sequence is plotted with dots.

FIGURE 1
Graphs of $f(x) = \dfrac{\sin x}{x}$ and $a_k = \dfrac{\sin k}{k}$

The graphs illustrate how the sequence $\{a_k\}$ is a "discrete sample" of the continuous function f. They show, too, that as x (or k) tends to infinity, this sequence and function, although oscillating in sign, tend to zero. ∎

Not every sequence comes naturally from a familiar calculus function. Nevertheless, graphs or tables often suggest limits.

EXAMPLE 6 A sequence $\{b_j\}$ has general term

$$b_j = 1 \cdot 2 \cdot 3 \cdot 4 \cdots (j-1) \cdot j = j!$$

(In words: b_j is j factorial.) Tabulate $\{b_j\}$; find its limit, if any.

Solution As the table suggests, $\{b_j\}$ diverges—quickly—to infinity.

As $k \to \infty$, $k! \to \infty$: explosive numerical evidence						
k	1	2	4	8	16	32	64
$k!$	1	2	24	40,320	2.092×10^{13}	2.631×10^{35}	1.269×10^{89}

Can any doubt remain? ➔

■ *Graphs work poorly for this sequence—most windows are too small.*

Sequence limits defined

Sequences are special sorts of functions; limits of sequences, therefore, are mild variants on limits at infinity. An informal definition will suffice. ➔

A formal definition describes more precisely what "approaches" means.

DEFINITION (Limit of a sequence) Let $\{a_k\}$ be a sequence and L a real number. If a_k approaches L to within any desired tolerance as k increases without bound, then the sequence **converges** to L. In symbols,

$$\lim_{k \to \infty} a_k = L.$$

Otherwise, the sequence **diverges**.

Notice:

- **Divergence to infinity**   If either $a_k \to \infty$ or $a_k \to -\infty$ as k increases without bound, then the sequence diverges to (positive or negative) infinity. We write, for instance,

$$\lim_{k \to \infty} k! = \infty.$$

- **Other divergence behavior**   Example 3 shows that a divergent sequence need not "blow up"; other patterns of "wandering" behavior (or no pattern at all) are possible.

- **Asymptotes**   A sequence, like a function, converges to a finite limit L if and only if $y = L$ is a horizontal asymptote of its graph.

Sequences, functions, and limits   For sequences that are "discrete samples" of familiar functions, we can often use what we know of the underlying function to find limits.

> **FACT**   Let f be a function defined for $x \geq 1$. If $\lim\limits_{x \to \infty} f(x) = L$ and $a_k = f(k)$ for all $k \geq 1$, then $\lim\limits_{k \to \infty} a_k = L$.

The Fact's converse is false; strong students might investigate this.

Example 5 illustrates this Fact:

$$\lim_{k \to \infty} \frac{\sin k}{k} = \lim_{x \to \infty} \frac{\sin x}{x} = 0.$$

EXAMPLE 7   Does the sequence with general term $a_k = \sin k$ converge or diverge?

Solution   Because $\lim\limits_{x \to \infty} \sin x$ does not exist, the preceding Fact doesn't help. Instead, let's look at the graph (Figure 2).

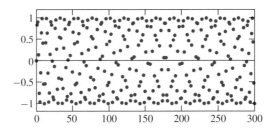

FIGURE 2
The sequence $a_k = \sin k$

Although full of interesting shapes, the graph never settles on a single limit, and so the sequence diverges.   ∎

Finding limits of sequences

Students may need reminding of l'Hôpital's rule. Note that we regard $a_k = a(k)$ as a differentiable function of k.

Many of the tools we've developed for finding limits of functions will help us find limits of sequences as well.

We studied l'Hôpital's rule in Chapter 4.

Using l'Hôpital's rule   If a sequence has a nice symbolic formula, l'Hôpital's rule can sometimes be applied to find the limit. ◀

EXAMPLE 8   Numerical evidence suggests that if $a_k = 2^k/k^2$, then $\{a_k\}$ diverges to infinity. Use l'Hôpital's rule to show this result symbolically.

Solution   l'Hôpital's rule applied to $h(x) = 2^x/x^2$ gives

$$\lim_{x \to \infty} \frac{2^x}{x^2} = \lim_{x \to \infty} \frac{2^x \ln 2}{2x} \quad \text{(differentiate top and bottom separately)}$$

$$= \lim_{x \to \infty} \frac{2^x \ln 2 \cdot \ln 2}{2} \quad \text{(apply l'Hôpital's rule again)}$$

$$= \frac{(\ln 2)^2}{2} \lim_{x \to \infty} 2^x = \infty.$$

Because $h(x) \to \infty$, $a_k \to \infty$ too; the sequence diverges.   ■

EXAMPLE 9   Show that $\lim_{n \to \infty} n^{1/n} = 1$.

Solution   l'Hôpital's rule doesn't apply directly, but applying the natural logarithm produces a fraction:

$$a_n = n^{1/n} \implies \ln(a_n) = \frac{\ln n}{n}.$$

l'Hôpital's rule *does* apply to the last quantity:

$$\lim_{n \to \infty} \frac{\ln n}{n} = \lim_{n \to \infty} \frac{1/n}{1} = 0.$$

We've shown that $\ln(a_n) \to 0$ as $n \to \infty$; it follows that $a_n \to 1$, as desired.   ■

New sequence limits from old   Limits of sequences, like limits of functions, can be combined in various symbolic ways to give new limits. We'll need some *known* limits, of course, to get started. Here are several useful and important ones:

$$\lim_{n \to \infty} n^{1/n} = 1$$

$$\lim_{n \to \infty} x^{1/n} = 1 \quad \text{(for all } x > 0)$$

$$\lim_{n \to \infty} \frac{1}{n^k} = 0 \quad \text{(for all } k > 0)$$

$$\lim_{n \to \infty} r^n = 0 \quad \text{(if } -1 < r < 1)$$

(We derived the first of these limits in Example 9, using l'Hôpital's rule. The other limits are easier.)

Calculating with limits   Plausible-seeming calculations such as

$$\lim_{k \to \infty} \left(\frac{1}{k} + \frac{3k}{k+1} \right) = \lim_{k \to \infty} \frac{1}{k} + 3 \lim_{k \to \infty} \frac{k}{k+1} = 0 + 3 = 3$$

rely implicitly on the following theorem. We've already seen it—in almost identical form—for functions.

> **THEOREM 1 (Algebra with limits)**   Suppose that
> $$a_k \to L \quad \text{and} \quad b_k \to M$$
> as $k \to \infty$, where L and M are finite numbers. Let c be any real constant. Then
> $$ca_k \to cL, \quad a_k \pm b_k \to L \pm M, \quad \text{and} \quad a_k b_k \to LM.$$
> If $M \neq 0$, then $\dfrac{a_k}{b_k} \to \dfrac{L}{M}$.

Squeezing limits   For sequences, as for functions, unknown limits can sometimes be found by "squeezing" them between known limits.

> **THEOREM 2 (The squeeze principle)**   Suppose that
> $$a_k \leq b_k \leq c_k \quad \text{for all } k \geq 1$$
> and that
> $$\lim_{k \to \infty} a_k = \lim_{k \to \infty} c_k = L.$$
> Then $\lim\limits_{k \to \infty} b_k = L$.

The hard part of squeezing, of course, is to find appropriate squeeze inequalities; graphical experiments may help.

EXAMPLE 10   We've seen graphically that $\lim\limits_{k \to \infty} \dfrac{\sin k}{k} = 0$. Use squeezing to show this legalistically.

Solution   The squeeze inequality
$$-\frac{1}{k} \leq \frac{\sin k}{k} \leq \frac{1}{k}$$
holds for all integers $k > 0$. Because both the left and the right sides tend to 0 as k tends to infinity, the middle expression must do so too.   ∎

Guaranteeing convergence: An existence theorem

The best way to show that a sequence converges is to find a limit. But doing so is sometimes hard. The following example illustrates the difficulty—and also suggests a remedy.

EXAMPLE 11   Does the sequence $a_n = \left(1 + \dfrac{1}{n}\right)^n$ converge?

Solution   The answer isn't obvious from the formula, so let's tabulate some numerical values:

Values of $(1 + 1/n)^n$						
n	16	32	64	128	256	512	1024
$(1+1/n)^n$	2.63793	2.67699	2.69734	2.70774	2.71299	2.71563	2.71696

As $n \to \infty$, the terms a_n seem to increase but not to blow up. Thus, apparently, the sequence converges to *some* limit. (The number $e \approx 2.71828$ is a tempting guess.)   ∎

A convergence theorem   The sequence in Example 11 appears from the table of numbers to be **nondecreasing**:

We'll use Theorem 3 often though implicitly — e.g., when applying comparison tests for series convergence.

$$a_1 \le a_2 \le \cdots \le a_k \le a_{k+1} \le \cdots.$$

(For this sequence, *strict* inequalities happen to hold, and so we could use the stronger adjective **increasing**.) Common sense suggests that any nondecreasing sequence should either (i) converge to a limit; or (ii) diverge to ∞. Because the sequence in Example 11 appears to be bounded above (by 3, for example), it's reasonable to guess that it converges. Theorem 3 makes these commonsense impressions precise. It applies to any **monotone** sequence (i.e., any sequence that is either nondecreasing on nonincreasing).

THEOREM 3   Suppose that the sequence $\{a_k\}$ is *nondecreasing* and *bounded above* by a number A. That is,

$$a_1 \le a_2 \le a_3 \le \cdots a_k \le a_{k+1} \le \cdots \le A.$$

Then $\{a_k\}$ converges to some finite limit a, with $a \le A$.
    Similarly, if $\{b_k\}$ is *nonincreasing* and *bounded below* by a number B, then $\{b_k\}$ converges to a finite limit $b \ge B$.

EXAMPLE 12   Consider the increasing sequence $\{a_k\}$ defined recursively by

$$a_1 = 0; \quad a_{k+1} = \sqrt{6 + a_k} \quad \text{if } k \ge 1.$$

Show that the sequence $\{a_k\}$ converges and that $\lim\limits_{k \to \infty} a_k \le 3$.

Solution   The first few terms suggest that the sequence is increasing: ➤

We'll take this for granted, though it's not hard to show.

$$a_1 = 0; \quad a_2 = \sqrt{6} \approx 2.45; \quad a_3 \approx 2.91; \quad a_4 \approx 2.98; \quad a_5 \approx 2.997.$$

The sequence also seems to be bounded above by 3. This is easy to show. If $a_k < 3$, then, by definition,

Taking limits of both sides of the recursion equation shows that the sequence limit L satisfies $L = \sqrt{6 + L}$, so $L = 3$.

$$a_{k+1} = \sqrt{6 + a_k} < \sqrt{6 + 3} = 3.$$

Thus, *no* term can exceed 3. It follows from the theorem, therefore, that the sequence converges to a limit no greater than 3. ➤ ■

The limit is 3, but that requires further proof.

BASIC EXERCISES

In Exercises 1–17, find the limit of the sequence or explain why the limit does not exist.

1. $a_k = (-3/2)^k$

2. $a_k = (-0.8)^k$

3. $a_k = (1.1)^k$

4. $a_k = \left(\sqrt{26}/17\right)^k$

5. $a_k = (1/k)^k$

6. $a_k = \sin k$

7. $a_k = \arctan k$

8. $a_k = \cos(1/k)$

9. $a_k = \sin(k\pi)$

10. $a_k = \cos(k\pi)$

11. $a_k = \dfrac{k^2}{k^2 + 3}$

12. $a_k = \sqrt{\dfrac{2k}{k+3}}$

13. $a_m = m^2 e^{-m}$

14. $a_j = \dfrac{\ln j}{\sqrt[3]{j}}$

15. $a_k = \dfrac{k!}{(k+1)!}$

16. $a_k = \ln\left(\dfrac{k}{k+1}\right)$

17. $a_k = 3^{1/k}$

18. (a) For which values of x does $\lim\limits_{n \to \infty} x^n$ exist?

    (b) Find all values of x for which $\lim\limits_{n \to \infty} x^n = 0$.

    (c) Are there any values of x for which $\lim\limits_{n \to \infty} x^n = L \ne 0$? For each such x, find the limit L.

In Exercises 19–24, give an example of a sequence that is

19. convergent but not monotone.

20. bounded but not monotone.

21. monotone but not convergent.

22. nonincreasing and unbounded.

23. nonincreasing and convergent.

24. unbounded but not monotone.

25. Use Theorem 3 to show that the sequence $0.7, 0.77, 0.777, 0.7777, 0.77777, 0.777777, 0.7777777, \ldots$ has a limit.

26. Suppose that $\lim_{k \to \infty} a_k = L$, where L is a finite number, and that the terms of the sequence $\{b_k\}$ are defined by $b_k = L - a_k$. Explain why $\lim_{k \to \infty} b_k = 0$.

FURTHER EXERCISES

In Exercises 27–32, find the limit of the sequence or explain why the limit does not exist. [HINT: l'Hôpital's rule may be useful.]

27. $a_n = n \sin(1/n)$

28. $a_k = (2^k + 3^k)^{1/k}$

29. $a_k = \int_0^k e^{-x} \, dx$

30. $a_k = \int_k^\infty \dfrac{dx}{1 + x^2}$

31. $a_k = \sqrt{k^2 + 1} - k$

32. $a_k = \sqrt{k^2 + k} - k$

In Exercises 33–36, determine the values of x for which the sequence converges as $k \to \infty$. Evaluate $\lim_{k \to \infty} a_k$ for these values of x.

33. $a_k = e^{kx}$

34. $a_k = (\ln x)^k$

35. $a_k = (\arcsin x)^k$

36. $a_k = 2^{-k}(\arctan x)^k$

37. Show that $\lim_{n \to \infty} x^{1/n} = 1$ for all $x > 0$.

38. Let $a_k = \left(1 + \dfrac{x}{k}\right)^k$, where x is a real number.

   (a) Show that $\lim_{k \to \infty} \ln(a_k) = x$.

   (b) Use part (a) to evaluate $\lim_{k \to \infty} a_k$.

39. Evaluate $\lim_{n \to \infty} \left(1 - \dfrac{1}{2n}\right)^n$.

40. Let $a_n = \displaystyle\sum_{k=1}^n \dfrac{k}{n^2}$.

   (a) Evaluate a_{10}.

   (b) Explain why $\lim_{n \to \infty} a_n = \displaystyle\int_0^1 x \, dx = 1/2$.
   [HINT: $k/n^2 = (k/n) \cdot (1/n)$.]

41. Let $a_n = \displaystyle\sum_{k=1}^n \dfrac{1}{n+k}$.

   (a) Show that this sequence is increasing (i.e., $a_{n+1} > a_n$).

   (b) Show that $a_n \le \dfrac{n}{n+1} < 1$.

   (c) What do parts (a) and (b) imply about $\lim_{n \to \infty} a_n$?

   (d) Explain why $\lim_{n \to \infty} a_n > 1/2$. [HINT: $a_1 = 1/2$.]

   (e) Show that $\lim_{n \to \infty} a_n = \ln 2$.

   [HINT: $\dfrac{1}{n+k} = \dfrac{1}{1 + k/n} \cdot \dfrac{1}{n}$, and a_n is a Riemann-sum approximation to an integral.]

42. Let $a_n = \displaystyle\sum_{k=1}^n k^2/n^3$. Evaluate $\lim_{n \to \infty} a_n$. [HINT: Think of a_n as a Riemann-sum approximation to an integral.]

43. Let $a_n = \dfrac{\sqrt[n]{n!}}{n}$.

   (a) Show that $\ln a_n = \dfrac{1}{n} \displaystyle\sum_{k=1}^n \ln k - \dfrac{1}{n} \displaystyle\sum_{k=1}^n \ln n$.

   (b) Use part (a) to show that $\ln a_n$ is a right-sum approximation to $\displaystyle\int_0^1 \ln x \, dx$.

   (c) Use part (b) to show that $\lim_{n \to \infty} a_n = e^{-1}$.

44. Let $a_n = 4^n/n!$.

   (a) Find a number N such that $a_{n+1} \le a_n$ for all $n \ge N$.

   (b) Use part (a) to explain why $\lim_{n \to \infty} a_n$ exists.

   (c) Evaluate $\lim_{n \to \infty} a_n$.

45. Suppose that $\{a_n\}$ is a sequence with the property $|a_{n+1}/a_n| \le (n+3)/(2n+1)$ for all $n \ge 1$. Show that $\lim_{n \to \infty} a_n = 0$.
[HINT: Start by showing that $|a_{n+1}/a_3| \le (6/7)^{n-2}$ for all $n \ge 3$.]

In Exercises 46–49, let $a_n = \cos 1 \cdot \cos 2 \cdot \cos 3 \cdot \cos 4 \cdots \cos n$.

46. Is the sequence $\{a_n\}$ bounded? Justify your answer.

47. Is the sequence $\{a_n\}$ monotone? Justify your answer.

48. Is the sequence $\{|a_n|\}$ bounded? Justify your answer.

49. Is the sequence $\{|a_n|\}$ monotone? Justify your answer.

50. Let $a_n = \dfrac{1 \cdot 3 \cdot 5 \cdots (2n-1)}{2 \cdot 4 \cdot 6 \cdots (2n)}$. Use Theorem 3 to show that $\lim_{n \to \infty} a_n$ exists.

51. Show that $\lim_{n \to \infty} \sin\left(\dfrac{\pi}{2^2}\right) \cdot \sin\left(\dfrac{\pi}{3^2}\right) \cdots \sin\left(\dfrac{\pi}{n^2}\right) = 0$.

   [HINT: $0 < \sin x < x$ when $0 < x < 1$.]

52. Does the sequence defined by $a_1 = 1$, $a_{n+1} = 1 - a_n$ converge? Justify your answer.

53. Does the sequence defined by $a_1 = 1$, $a_{n+1} = a_n/2$ converge? Justify your answer.

54. Consider the sequence defined by $a_1 = 1$, $a_{n+1} = \left(\dfrac{n}{n+1}\right) a_n$.

   (a) Show that the sequence converges.

   (b) Find the limit. [HINT: Write out the first few terms and look for a pattern.]

55. For which values of $x \ge 0$ does the sequence defined by $a_1 = x$, $a_{n+1} = \sqrt{a_n}$ converge? Justify your answer.

11.2 INFINITE SERIES, CONVERGENCE, AND DIVERGENCE

This section is mainly about the ideas and properties of convergence and divergence; systematic convergence testing is in the next section. Geometric series are the most important prototypes.

An **infinite series** (just **series** for short) is an expression of the form

$$\sum_{k=1}^{\infty} a_k = a_1 + a_2 + a_3 + a_4 + \cdots + a_k + a_{k+1} + \cdots.$$

(Notice the **sigma notation** on the left; we used it earlier for approximating sums for integrals.) A series results from *adding* the terms of a sequence $a_1, a_2, a_3, \ldots$. If, say, $a_k = 1/k^2$, then

$$\sum_{k=1}^{\infty} a_k = \sum_{k=1}^{\infty} \frac{1}{k^2} = \frac{1}{1} + \frac{1}{4} + \frac{1}{9} + \frac{1}{16} + \cdots.$$

If $a_k = k$, then

$$\sum_{k=1}^{\infty} a_k = \sum_{k=1}^{\infty} k = 1 + 2 + 3 + \cdots.$$

Natural questions   The notion of an infinite sum raises natural questions:

- What does it *mean* to add infinitely many numbers?
- Which series add up to a finite number? Which series blow up?
- If a series has a finite sum, how can we find (or estimate) it?
- What good are infinite series?

The rest of this chapter addresses these questions.

Improper sums vs. improper integrals   Standard examples of infinite series include

We emphasize the integral—series analogy here and later.

$$\text{(i)} \quad \sum_{k=1}^{\infty} \frac{1}{k^2}; \quad \text{(ii)} \quad \sum_{k=1}^{\infty} \frac{1}{k}; \quad \text{(iii)} \quad \sum_{k=1}^{\infty} \frac{1}{\sqrt{k}}; \quad \text{(iv)} \quad \sum_{k=1}^{\infty} \frac{1}{2^k}.$$

Notice the close typographical resemblance to improper integrals:

$$\text{(i)} \quad \int_1^{\infty} \frac{dx}{x^2}; \quad \text{(ii)} \quad \int_1^{\infty} \frac{dx}{x}; \quad \text{(iii)} \quad \int_1^{\infty} \frac{dx}{\sqrt{x}}; \quad \text{(iv)} \quad \int_1^{\infty} \frac{dx}{2^x}.$$

This is no accident; infinite series and improper integrals are closely analogous; we'll often exploit the connection. We'll see, in fact, that items (i) and (iv) of *both* preceding lists converge, whereas (ii) and (iii) diverge.

Why series matter: A look ahead

This look ahead can be left to student reading.

Understanding series takes some work. To preview why the work is worthwhile, consider the fact (we'll see later why it's true) that for any real number x,

$$\cos x = 1 - \frac{x^2}{2!} + \frac{x^4}{4!} - \frac{x^6}{6!} + \frac{x^8}{8!} - \cdots. \tag{1}$$

If, say, $x = 1$, then

$$\cos 1 = 1 - \frac{1}{2!} + \frac{1}{4!} - \frac{1}{6!} + \frac{1}{8!} - \cdots. \tag{2}$$

So what? Why would we write something familiar—the cosine function—in terms of something exotic—a series?

One good answer is that the cosine function has no *algebraic* formula, and so finding accurate numerical values of $\cos x$ for arbitrary inputs x is a genuine problem. ◄ Infinite series help solve this problem. Although not quite a formula in the ordinary sense (ordinary formulas don't include dots ...), Equation (1) gives a concrete, computable recipe for *approximating* $\cos x$: Given an input x, calculate, as far out as practically possible, the "infinite polynomial"

$$1 - \frac{x^2}{2!} + \frac{x^4}{4!} - \frac{x^6}{6!} + \frac{x^8}{8!} - \cdots.$$

Finding $\cos x$ *is easy for a few special values of* x, *such as* $x = \pi/4$.

With any luck, the result should closely approximate the "true" value of $\cos x$.

Equation (2) shows how to approximate $\cos 1$. A calculator readily gives, to seven decimals,

$$1 - \frac{1}{2!} = 0.5000000;$$

$$1 - \frac{1}{2!} + \frac{1}{4!} = 0.5416667;$$

$$1 - \frac{1}{2!} + \frac{1}{4!} - \frac{1}{6!} = 0.5402778;$$

$$1 - \frac{1}{2!} + \frac{1}{4!} - \frac{1}{6!} + \frac{1}{8!} = 0.5403026.$$

The results converge with gratifying speed to the "right" answer—the true value of $\cos 1$ (≈ 0.5403023).

Good questions   These calculations raise good questions:

> *Where did Equation (1) come from? What do all the "dots" really mean? Are similar equations available for* other *functions—sine, arctangent, logarithmic, and so on? How many terms are needed to guarantee accuracy to, say, five decimals?*

We'll answer all of these questions in this chapter.

Definitions and terminology

Working successfully with series requires some up-front investment in definitions and technical language. After stating terms and definitions, we show by example why they're reasonable.

Series language   Let

$$\sum_{k=1}^{\infty} a_k = a_1 + a_2 + a_3 + \cdots + a_k + a_{k+1} + \cdots$$

be an infinite series. (In most cases the index variable starts at 1, but sometimes it's convenient to start k at 0 or elsewhere.) ➔ The summand a_k is called the kth **term** of the series, and the nth **partial sum**, usually denoted by S_n, is the (finite) sum of all terms *through index n*:

Sometimes we'll use other names, such as j, for the index variable.

$$S_n = a_1 + a_2 + a_3 + \cdots + a_{n-1} + a_n = \sum_{k=1}^{n} a_k. \qquad (3)$$

The nth **tail**, denoted by R_n, is the (infinite) sum of all terms *beyond index n*:

We defined similar tails for improper integrals.

$$R_n = a_{n+1} + a_{n+2} + a_{n+3} + \cdots = \sum_{k=n+1}^{\infty} a_k.$$

As the notation R_n suggests, the nth tail is a *remainder*—what's left after adding terms through index n. In symbols,

$$\sum_{k=1}^{\infty} a_k = \sum_{k=1}^{n} a_k + \sum_{k=n+1}^{\infty} a_k = S_n + R_n.$$

(We did the same thing in Chapter 10 with improper integrals:

$$\int_{1}^{\infty} a(x)\,dx = \int_{1}^{n} a(x)\,dx + \int_{n}^{\infty} a(x)\,dx,$$

where the last integral is another type of upper tail.)

The crucial definition of convergence involves the partial sums S_n:

DEFINITION If $\lim\limits_{n \to \infty} S_n = S$, for some finite number S, then the series $\sum_{k=1}^{\infty} a_k$ **converges** to the limit S. (S is also called the **sum** of the series.) Otherwise, the series **diverges**.

Notice the following aspects of the definition:

- **Divergent series** A divergent series is one for which the sequence of partial sums does *not* converge to a finite limit S. One possibility is that the partial sums S_n blow up to infinity. Another possibility is that the partial sums remain bounded but never settle on a specific limit.

- **Improper integrals, improper sums** The definition says, in symbols, that

$$\sum_{k=1}^{\infty} a_k = \lim_{n \to \infty} \sum_{k=1}^{n} a_k$$

if the limit exists. Convergence for improper integrals means much the same thing:

$$\int_{x=1}^{\infty} f(x)\,dx = \lim_{n \to \infty} \int_{x=1}^{n} f(x)\,dx$$

if *this* limit exists. ➔ An infinite series is an improper sum in exactly the sense that an integral may be improper.

In each case we take the limit of something proper.

- **Convergence, partial sums, and tails** To say that $\sum a_k$ converges to the sum S means that $S_n \to S$ as $n \to \infty$. Since for all n, $S = S_n + R_n$, it follows that $R_n \to 0$ as $n \to \infty$.

The converse is true as well: If $R_n \to 0$ then the series converges.

- **Two sequences—keep them straight** Every series $\sum a_k$ involves *two* sequences: the sequence $\{a_k\}$ of *terms* and the sequence $\{S_n\}$ of *partial sums*. Keeping these related but different sequences separate is essential. We'll take special care to do so in the following examples.

EXAMPLE 1 Does the series $\displaystyle\sum_{k=0}^{\infty} \frac{1}{2^k} = 1 + \frac{1}{2} + \frac{1}{4} + \frac{1}{8} + \cdots$ converge? If so, to what limit?

Solution Because the index k begins at 0, not 1, so does the sequence of partial sums. Direct calculation yields

$$S_0 = 1 = 2 - 1;$$

$$S_1 = 1 + \frac{1}{2} = \frac{3}{2} = 2 - \frac{1}{2};$$

$$S_2 = 1 + \frac{1}{2} + \frac{1}{4} = \frac{7}{4} = 2 - \frac{1}{4};$$

$$S_3 = 1 + \frac{1}{2} + \frac{1}{4} + \frac{1}{8} = \frac{15}{8} = 2 - \frac{1}{8};$$

$$S_4 = 1 + \frac{1}{2} + \frac{1}{4} + \frac{1}{8} + \frac{1}{16} = \frac{31}{16} = 2 - \frac{1}{16}.$$

The pattern is easy to see: For any $n \geq 1$,

Technology makes producing such tables easy; seeing actual numbers may help demystify these ideas.

$$S_n = 2 - \frac{1}{2^n}.$$

This explicit formula for S_n lets us answer the question posed above: Because $S_n \to 2$ as $n \to \infty$, the series converges to 2.

$R_n = 2 - S_n$.

A numerical table of partial sums and tails supports this conclusion: ◄

n	0	1	2	3	4	5	6	7	8	9	10
S_n	1	1.5	1.75	1.875	1.938	1.969	1.984	1.992	1.996	1.998	1.999
R_n	1	0.5	0.25	0.125	0.063	0.031	0.016	0.008	0.004	0.002	0.001

Partial sums and tails of $1 + \dfrac{1}{2} + \dfrac{1}{4} + \cdots$

As the numbers show, the partial sums S_n converge to 2 while the tails R_n tend to 0. ∎

Students should understand this example thoroughly; they should see explicitly why the S_n have the claimed form.

EXAMPLE 2 Does $\displaystyle\sum_{k=1}^{\infty} (-1)^k = -1 + 1 - 1 + 1 - \cdots$ converge?

Solution No. Successive partial sums are $-1, 0, -1, 0, \ldots$. Thus, the sequence $\{S_n\}$ diverges and so does the series. ∎

EXAMPLE 3 Does the **harmonic series** $\sum_{k=1}^{\infty} \frac{1}{k}$ converge? ➤

The harmonic series will be one of our most important examples.

Solution The answer depends on the partial sums S_n. By definition,

$$S_n = 1 + \frac{1}{2} + \frac{1}{3} + \frac{1}{4} + \frac{1}{5} + \frac{1}{6} + \cdots + \frac{1}{n}.$$

Because no simple formula for S_n comes to mind (in fact, there *is* no such simple formula), we'll investigate the partial sums numerically. Here are some results, computed to three decimal places:

$$S_1 = 1; \quad S_{20} = 3.598; \quad S_{50} = 4.499; \quad S_{100} = 5.187; \quad S_{1000} = 7.485.$$

In fact, the series diverges. We'll show this fact soon by comparing the series to an integral.

The numerical evidence is ambiguous; the S_n's seem to keep growing, although slowly. Whether the sequence of partial sums $\{S_n\}$ converges or diverges is not yet clear. ➤ ■

When does a series (or an integral) converge?

Whether a given infinite series converges or diverges is a delicate question. ➤ Such series as

So was the analogous question for improper integrals.

$$\sum_{k=1}^{\infty} \frac{1}{k} = 1 + \frac{1}{2} + \frac{1}{3} + \cdots \quad \text{and} \quad \sum_{k=1}^{\infty} \frac{1}{k^2} = 1 + \frac{1}{4} + \frac{1}{9} + \cdots$$

pose the same puzzle: Although successive *terms* of both series tend to zero, the *number* of terms is infinite. Convergence or divergence hinges on which of these conflicting tendencies "wins" in the long run.

The same dilemma arose for the improper *integrals*

$$\int_1^{\infty} \frac{1}{x} \, dx \quad \text{and} \quad \int_1^{\infty} \frac{1}{x^2} \, dx,$$

and it's worth recalling exactly what happened. In each case, the "partial integral" $I(t)$ is easily found. For the first integral, we found

$$I(t) = \int_1^t \frac{dx}{x} = \ln t \to \infty.$$

For the second,

$$I(t) = \int_1^t \frac{dx}{x^2} = 1 - \frac{1}{t} \to 1.$$

Thus, the two similar-looking integrals led to opposite results: The first integral diverges to infinity and the second converges to 1. Deciding whether the corresponding *series* converge or diverge is a bit harder because no convenient formulas for S_n are available.

Convergence and divergence: Graphical views For a series $\sum a_k$, plotting both the terms $\{a_k\}$ and the partial sums $\{S_n\}$ on the same axes illustrates the connection between the two— and sometimes suggests whether the series converges or diverges. The two series $\sum 1/k$ and $\sum 1/k^2$ generate Figures 1(a) and 1(b), respectively.

In all interesting cases the a_k tend to zero, so there's little to see in the terms.

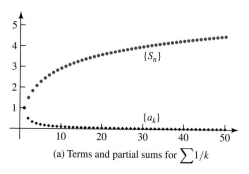
(a) Terms and partial sums for $\sum 1/k$

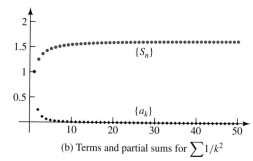
(b) Terms and partial sums for $\sum 1/k^2$

FIGURE 1
Terms and partial sums for two series

The two pictures give different impressions. The pictured behavior of partial sums suggests (but doesn't prove) that the first series diverges; the second series appears to converge because the partial sums seem to level off, perhaps approaching a limit near 1.7.

Note the generally "log-like" appearance of the partial sums in Figure 1(a).

Geometric series: The nicest kind

The most important family of infinite series are the **geometric series**. They have the form

$$\sum_{k=0}^{\infty} ar^k = a + ar + ar^2 + ar^3 + ar^4 + \cdots;$$

here a is called the **leading term** and r is the **ratio**, because each term is r times the preceding term. An especially simple example is

$$\sum_{k=0}^{\infty} \left(\frac{1}{2}\right)^k = 1 + \frac{1}{2} + \frac{1}{4} + \frac{1}{8} + \cdots,$$

with $a = 1$ and $r = 1/2$. We saw in Example 1, page 558, that this series converges to 2.

Partial sums of geometric series   Geometric series have a great advantage: It's easy to tell whether they converge and, if so, to find their sums. This is because geometric series—unlike many others—have a simple, explicit formula for the partial sums S_n. The formula depends on a beautiful algebraic fact. If $r \neq 1$ and $n \geq 0$, then

Multiplying both sides by $(1 - r)$ is one way to prove this equation. The exercises outline another approach.

$$1 + r + r^2 + r^3 + \cdots + r^n = \frac{1 - r^{n+1}}{1 - r}. \tag{4}$$

Multiplying Equation (4) by a gives a formula for S_n:

$$S_n = a + ar + ar^2 + ar^3 + \cdots + ar^n = a\frac{1 - r^{n+1}}{1 - r}. \tag{5}$$

From Formula (5) follows the whole story of convergence and divergence for geometric series. As always, the question is how the sequence $\{S_n\}$ of partial sums behaves. In this case, the issue has to do entirely with the power r^{n+1}. We'll need the following facts:

$$\lim_{m \to \infty} r^m = \begin{cases} 0 & \text{if } |r| < 1 \\ 1 & \text{if } r = 1 \\ \text{does not exist} & \text{if } |r| > 1 \text{ or } r = -1 \end{cases}$$

The conclusion for geometric series follows, and it's worth emphasizing:

> **THEOREM 4 (Convergence and divergence of geometric series)** If $|r| < 1$, the geometric series
> $$\sum_{k=0}^{\infty} ar^k = a + ar + ar^2 + ar^3 + \cdots$$
> converges to $\dfrac{a}{1-r}$. If $a \neq 0$ and $|r| \geq 1$, the series diverges.

EXAMPLE 4 The series $\dfrac{1}{3} - \dfrac{1}{6} + \dfrac{1}{12} - \dfrac{1}{24} + \cdots$ converges. To what limit?

Students should work enough examples like this one to be comfortable with such calculations.

Solution The series is geometric, with $a = 1/3$ and $r = -1/2$. By Theorem 4, it converges to

$$\frac{a}{1-r} = \frac{1/3}{1+1/2} = \frac{2}{9} \approx 0.2222222.$$

A numerical look at partial sums and tails supports this computation. ➔

$R_n = \dfrac{2}{9} - S_n$.

Partial sums and tails of $\frac{1}{3} - \frac{1}{6} + \frac{1}{12} - \frac{1}{24} + \cdots$								
n	0	1	2	3	4	5	...	10
S_n	0.3333	0.1667	0.2500	0.2083	0.2292	0.2188	...	0.2223
R_n	−0.1111	0.0555	−0.0278	0.0139	−0.0069	0.0035	...	−0.0001

Telescoping series Most series *other* than the geometric variety do *not* admit explicit formulas for partial sums. Telescoping series are among the unusual (and pleasant) exceptions. The next example illustrates how telescoping series work, and explains the name.

EXAMPLE 5 Show that $\sum_{k=1}^{\infty} \dfrac{1}{k(k+1)}$ converges and find its limit.

Note the use of partial fractions—they're good for more than integration.

Solution A little algebra inside the summation sign lets us rewrite the series in a more convenient form: ➔

$$\sum_{k=1}^{\infty} \frac{1}{k(k+1)} = \sum_{k=1}^{\infty} \left(\frac{1}{k} - \frac{1}{k+1} \right).$$

To convince yourself that the two sides are equal, find a common denominator on the right side.

Writing out some terms shows the "telescoping" pattern: ➔

$$S_n = \sum_{k=1}^{n} \left(\frac{1}{k} - \frac{1}{k+1} \right) = \left(\frac{1}{1} - \frac{1}{2} \right) + \left(\frac{1}{2} - \frac{1}{3} \right) + \left(\frac{1}{3} - \frac{1}{4} \right) + \cdots + \left(\frac{1}{n} - \frac{1}{n+1} \right)$$

$$= 1 - \frac{1}{n+1}.$$

The summands collapse like an old-fashioned spyglass.

Now it's clear that, as $n \to \infty$, $S_n \to 1$; that's the sum. Again the numbers agree: ➔

Watch the tails go to zero.

Partial sums and tails of $\sum_{k=1}^{\infty} \frac{1}{k^2+k}$								
n	1	2	3	4	5	6	...	11
S_n	0.5000	0.6667	0.7500	0.8000	0.8333	0.8571	...	0.9167
R_n	0.5000	0.3333	0.2500	0.2000	0.1667	0.1429	...	0.0833

Algebra with series

As with functions and sequences, combining series algebraically produces new series. Combining *convergent* series produces new *convergent* series, with limits related in the expected way.

> **THEOREM 5** Suppose that $\sum a_k$ converges to S and that $\sum b_k$ converges to T. Let c be any constant. Then
>
> $$\sum_{k=1}^{\infty} (a_k + b_k) \quad \text{converges to } S + T$$
>
> and
>
> $$\sum c a_k \quad \text{converges to } cS.$$
>
> In short:
>
> $$\sum (a_k + b_k) = \sum a_k + \sum b_k \quad \text{and} \quad \sum c a_k = c \sum a_k.$$

After all, the limit of a series is defined as the limit of the sequence of partial sums.

These reasonable-looking properties of convergent *series* follow directly from the analogous properties of convergent *sequences*. ◄

A little series algebra, cleverly applied, can immensely simplify finding the limits of certain series.

EXAMPLE 6 Evaluate $\sum_{k=0}^{\infty} \dfrac{4 + 2^k}{3^k}$.

Solution The series is the sum of two (convergent) geometric series. Applying Theorems 4 and 5 gives

$$\sum_{k=0}^{\infty} \frac{4 + 2^k}{3^k} = \sum_{k=0}^{\infty} \frac{4}{3^k} + \sum_{k=0}^{\infty} \left(\frac{2}{3}\right)^k = 4 \cdot \frac{3}{2} + 3 = 9. \qquad \blacksquare$$

We'll calculate or estimate tails in later work by similar methods.

EXAMPLE 7 Calculate the tail R_{10} for the geometric series $\sum_{k=0}^{\infty} \dfrac{3}{2^k}$.

Solution A little algebra is all we need:

$$R_{10} = \sum_{k=11}^{\infty} \frac{3}{2^k} = \frac{3}{2^{11}} + \frac{3}{2^{12}} + \frac{3}{2^{13}} + \cdots$$

$$= \frac{3}{2^{11}} \left(1 + \frac{1}{2} + \frac{1}{2^2} + \frac{1}{2^3} + \cdots \right) \qquad \text{(factoring out the constant)}$$

$$= \frac{3}{2^{11}} \cdot 2 = \frac{3}{2^{10}} = \frac{3}{1024}. \qquad \text{(summing the geometric series)}$$

$\blacksquare$

Detecting divergent series

We are mainly interested in *convergent* series and their limits. Theorem 5, for instance, applies only to convergent series, and so it's important to recognize *divergence* when it occurs. One strategy is to use Theorem 5 indirectly.

EXAMPLE 8 Suppose that $\sum a_k$ diverges, and let $c \neq 0$ be a constant. Explain why $\sum c \, a_k$ diverges, too.

Solution If $\sum c \, a_k$ were *convergent*, then, by Theorem 5, the series

$$\sum \frac{1}{c} \, c \, a_k = \sum a_k$$

must *also* converge, which contradicts our assumption. ∎

The *n*th term test The following theorem describes another useful divergence detector:

> **THEOREM 6 (The *n*th term test for divergence)** If $\lim\limits_{n \to \infty} a_n \neq 0$, then $\sum a_n$ diverges.

The theorem holds because, for a series $\sum a_k$ to converge, the partial sums S_n must converge to a limit. For this to occur the difference $S_n - S_{n-1}$ between *successive* partial sums must tend to zero. ➡ But this difference is just the *n*th term:

$$S_n - S_{n-1} = (a_1 + a_2 + \cdots + a_{n-1} + a_n) - (a_1 + a_2 + \cdots + a_{n-1}) = a_n.$$

Thus, the terms of a convergent series must tend to zero, as the theorem says.

Otherwise the partial sum sequence wouldn't "level off."

What the theorem does not say It's especially important to notice that the *n*th term test does *not* guarantee that $\sum a_n$ converges whenever $a_n \to 0$. For example, the harmonic series $\sum 1/k$ "passes" the *n*th term test, but it *diverges*. ➡

In practice, the *n*th term test is an effective but rather blunt instrument—it sometimes detects divergence, but it *never* detects convergence. We'll develop tools for that purpose in the next section.

We've said this several times, and we'll show it rigorously in the next section.

That the n th term test never implies convergence bears repeating.

EXAMPLE 9 Does $\displaystyle\sum_{k=1}^{\infty} \frac{k}{k+1000}$ converge?

Solution No. Because $a_k = \dfrac{k}{k+1000} \to 1$ as $k \to \infty$, the series diverges. ∎

EXAMPLE 10 Assuming that $\displaystyle\sum_{k=0}^{\infty} \frac{3^k}{k!}$ converges (as it really does), find $\lim\limits_{k \to \infty} \dfrac{3^k}{k!}$.

Solution The limit is zero: By Theorem 6, the terms of *every* convergent series must tend to zero. ∎

BASIC EXERCISES

1. Consider the series $\displaystyle\sum_{k=0}^{\infty} a_k = \sum_{k=0}^{\infty} \frac{1}{5^k}$.

(a) Evaluate $a_1, a_2, a_5, a_{10}, S_1, S_2, S_5$, and S_{10}.

(b) Show that the sequence $\{a_k\}$ is decreasing and bounded below.

(c) Show that the sequence $\{S_n\}$ is increasing and bounded above. What does this imply about the sequence of partial sums?

(d) Find the sum of the series (i.e., $\displaystyle\lim_{n\to\infty} S_n$).

(e) Evaluate R_1, R_2, R_5, and R_{10}.

(f) Show that $\{R_n\}$ is decreasing and bounded below.

(g) Evaluate $\displaystyle\lim_{n\to\infty} R_n$.

2. Consider the series $\displaystyle\sum_{k=0}^{\infty} a_k = \sum_{k=0}^{\infty} (-0.8)^k$.

(a) Evaluate $a_1, a_2, a_5, a_{10}, S_1, S_2, S_5$, and S_{10}.

(b) Find the sum of the series (i.e., $\displaystyle\lim_{n\to\infty} S_n$).

(c) Evaluate R_1, R_2, R_5, and R_{10}.

(d) Is the sequence $\{a_k\}$ decreasing? Is it bounded?

(e) Is the sequence $\{S_n\}$ increasing? Justify your answer.

(f) Show that the sequence $\{R_n\}$ is neither increasing nor decreasing.

(g) Show that the sequence $\{|R_n|\}$ is decreasing.

(h) Evaluate $\displaystyle\lim_{n\to\infty} R_n$.

3. Consider the series $\displaystyle\sum_{k=0}^{\infty} a_k = \sum_{k=0}^{\infty} \frac{1}{k+2^k}$.

(a) Show that the sequence $\{a_k\}$ is decreasing.

(b) Explain why $a_k \leq 2^{-k}$ for all $k \geq 0$.

(c) Show that the sequence $\{S_n\}$ is increasing.

(d) Use part (c) to show that $S_n \leq 2 - 2^{-n} < 2$. [HINT: $\displaystyle\sum_{k=0}^{n} 2^{-k}$ is a geometric series.]

(e) Show that $\displaystyle\sum_{k=0}^{\infty} a_k$ converges.

4. Consider the series $\displaystyle\sum_{j=0}^{\infty} a_j = \sum_{j=0}^{\infty} \frac{1}{2+3^j}$.

(a) Evaluate S_1, S_2, S_5, and S_{10}.

(b) Show that the sequence $\{S_n\}$ is increasing and bounded above.

(c) Does $\displaystyle\sum_{j=0}^{\infty} a_j$ converge? Justify your answer.

5. Consider the series $\displaystyle\sum_{k=0}^{\infty} \frac{1}{k!}$.

(a) Explain why $\dfrac{1}{k!} \leq \dfrac{1}{2^{k-1}}$ if $k \geq 1$. [HINT: Explain why $1/3! < 1/(2\cdot2)$ and $1/4! < 1/(2\cdot2\cdot2)$.]

(b) Show that the sequence of partial sums $\{S_n\}$ is increasing.

(c) Use parts (a) and (b) to show that the series converges.

6. The series $\displaystyle\sum_{k=0}^{\infty} a_k = \sum_{k=0}^{\infty} \frac{1}{k!}$ converges to $e \approx 2.718282$.

(a) Evaluate $a_1, a_2, a_5, a_{10}, S_1, S_2, S_5$, and S_{10}.

(b) Show that $\{a_k\}$ is a decreasing sequence.

(c) Show that $\{S_n\}$ is an increasing sequence.

(d) Show that $R_n > 0$ for all $n \geq 0$.

(e) Show that $\{R_n\}$ is a decreasing sequence.

(f) Find a value of n for which S_n differs from e by less than 0.001.

(g) Find a value of n for which S_n differs from e by less than 10^{-5}.

(h) Use parts (e) and (g) to show that $R_{50} < 10^{-5}$.

In Exercises 7 and 8, use the fact that $\displaystyle\sum_{m=1}^{\infty} \frac{1}{m^4} = \frac{\pi^4}{90}$ to evaluate the series.

7. $\displaystyle\sum_{i=0}^{\infty} \frac{1}{(i+1)^4}$

8. $\displaystyle\sum_{k=3}^{\infty} \frac{1}{k^4}$

9. This exercise is about partial sums of the geometric series $\displaystyle\sum_{k=0}^{\infty} ar^k$.

(a) Find a formula for S_n when $r=1$. Explain why the formula for S_n (Equation 5) does not hold in this case.

(b) Show that $S_n - rS_n = (1-r)S_n$ for any r.

(c) Use part (b) to show that Equation 5 holds if $r \neq 1$.

10. Use Equation 5 to evaluate $3+6+12+24+48+96+\cdots+3072$. [HINT: $3072 = 3\cdot2^{10}$.]

In Exercises 11–18, find the limit of the series.

11. $\dfrac{1}{16} + \dfrac{1}{32} + \dfrac{1}{64} + \dfrac{1}{128} + \cdots + \dfrac{1}{2^{i+4}} + \cdots$

12. $2 - 5 + 9 + \dfrac{1}{3} + \dfrac{1}{9} + \dfrac{1}{27} + \dfrac{1}{81} + \cdots + \dfrac{1}{3^n} + \cdots$

13. $\displaystyle\sum_{n=0}^{\infty} e^{-n}$

14. $\displaystyle\sum_{k=3}^{\infty} \left(\frac{e}{\pi}\right)^k$

15. $\displaystyle\sum_{m=2}^{\infty} (\arctan 1)^m$

16. $\displaystyle\sum_{i=10}^{\infty} \left(\frac{2}{3}\right)^i$

17. $\displaystyle\sum_{j=5}^{\infty} \left(-\frac{1}{2}\right)^j$

18. $\displaystyle\sum_{j=0}^{\infty} \frac{3^j + 4^j}{5^j}$

19. Show that $\displaystyle\sum_{k=1}^{\infty} \frac{1}{2+\sin k}$ diverges.

20. Does $\displaystyle\sum_{k=0}^{\infty} (-1)^k$ converge? Justify your answer.

In Exercises 21–24, find an expression for the partial sum S_n of the series. Use this expression to determine whether the series converges and, if so, to find its limit.

21. $\displaystyle\sum_{k=0}^{\infty} \big(\arctan(k+1) - \arctan k\big)$

22. $\displaystyle\sum_{j=1}^{\infty} \frac{j}{(j+1)!}$

23. $\displaystyle\sum_{m=1}^{\infty} \left(\frac{1}{\sqrt{m}} - \frac{1}{\sqrt{m+2}} \right)$

24. $\displaystyle\sum_{j=1}^{\infty} \ln\left(1 + \frac{1}{j}\right)$ [HINT: $\displaystyle\sum_{j=1}^{\infty}(\ln(j+1) - \ln j)$]

25. Suppose that the partial sums of the series $\displaystyle\sum_{k=1}^{\infty} a_k$ are
$$S_n = \sum_{k=1}^{n} a_k = 5 - \frac{3}{n}.$$

    (a) Evaluate $\displaystyle S_{100} = \sum_{k=1}^{100} a_k$.

    (b) Evaluate $\displaystyle\sum_{k=1}^{\infty} a_k$.

(c) Evaluate $\displaystyle\lim_{k \to \infty} a_k$.

(d) Show that $a_k > 0$ for all $k \geq 1$. [HINT: $a_{n+1} = S_{n+1} - S_n$.]

26. Let $\displaystyle H_n = \sum_{k=1}^{n} \frac{1}{k}$ and let $\displaystyle S_n = \sum_{k=0}^{n} \frac{1}{2k+1}$.

    (a) Explain why $\displaystyle\lim_{n \to \infty} H_n = \infty$.

    (b) Show that $S_n \geq \frac{1}{2} H_n$.

    (c) What do the results in parts (a) and (b) imply about
$$\sum_{k=0}^{\infty} 1/(2k+1)?$$ Justify your answer.

FURTHER EXERCISES

In Exercises 27–29, use the fact that $\displaystyle\sum_{i=1}^{\infty} \frac{1}{i^2} = 1 + \frac{1}{4} + \frac{1}{9} + \frac{1}{16} + \frac{1}{25} + \cdots = \frac{\pi^2}{6}$ *to find the limit of the series.*

27. $\displaystyle\sum_{j=1}^{\infty} \frac{1}{(2j)^2}$

28. $\displaystyle\sum_{k=0}^{\infty} \frac{1}{(2k+1)^2}$ [HINT: See the previous exercise.]

29. $\displaystyle\sum_{m=1}^{\infty} \frac{(-1)^{m+1}}{m^2} = 1 - \frac{1}{4} + \frac{1}{9} - \frac{1}{16} + \frac{1}{25} - \frac{1}{36} + \cdots$

30. Express $\displaystyle\sum_{m=3}^{\infty} \frac{2^{m+4}}{5^m}$ as a rational number.

For each of the series in Exercises 31–36, find all values of x for which the series converges, then state the limit as a simple expression involving x. (Assume that $x^0 = 1$ for all x.)

31. $\displaystyle\sum_{k=0}^{\infty} x^k$

32. $\displaystyle\sum_{m=2}^{\infty} \left(\frac{x}{5}\right)^m$

33. $\displaystyle\sum_{j=5}^{\infty} x^{2j}$

34. $\displaystyle\sum_{k=1}^{\infty} x^{-k}$

35. $\displaystyle\sum_{n=3}^{\infty} (1+x)^n$

36. $\displaystyle\sum_{j=4}^{\infty} \frac{1}{(1-x)^j}$

37. Find the limit of the sequence defined by $S_1 = 1$, $S_{n+1} = S_n + 1/3^n$. [HINT: Write out the first few terms to see the pattern.]

38. Find the limit of the sequence defined by $a_1 = 4$, $a_{n+1} = a_n - 1/2^n$.

In Exercises 39–52, determine whether the series converges or diverges. If a series converges, find its limit. Justify your answers.

39. $\displaystyle\sum_{n=0}^{\infty} \frac{n+1}{2n+1}$

40. $\displaystyle\sum_{j=0}^{\infty} (\ln 2)^j$

41. $\displaystyle\sum_{n=2}^{\infty} \frac{2}{n^2-1}$

42. $\displaystyle\sum_{n=1}^{\infty} \left(1 + \frac{1}{n}\right)^n$

43. $\displaystyle\sum_{j=1}^{\infty} \sqrt[j]{\pi}$

44. $\displaystyle\sum_{k=1}^{\infty} \frac{1}{\ln(10^k)}$

45. $\displaystyle\sum_{j=2}^{\infty} \frac{3^j}{4^{j+1}}$

46. $\displaystyle 1 - \frac{1}{2} - \frac{1}{3} - \frac{1}{4} - \frac{1}{5} - \cdots$

47. $\displaystyle\frac{1}{100} + \frac{1}{200} + \frac{1}{300} + \cdots$

48. $\displaystyle 2 - 2 + 2 - 2 + 2 - 2 + \cdots$

49. $\displaystyle\frac{3}{10} - \frac{3}{20} + \frac{3}{40} - \frac{3}{80} + \frac{3}{160} - \frac{3}{320} + \cdots$

50. $\displaystyle 1 - \frac{1}{2} + \frac{1}{2} - \frac{1}{3} + \frac{1}{3} - \cdots$

51. $\displaystyle 1 - 1 + 2 - 1 - 1 + 3 - 1 - 1 - 1 + 4 - 1 - 1 - 1 - 1 + \cdots$

52. $\displaystyle\frac{4}{7^{10}} + \frac{4}{7^{12}} + \frac{4}{7^{14}} + \frac{4}{7^{16}} + \frac{4}{7^{18}} + \cdots$

53. A rubber ball rebounds to two-thirds the height from which it falls. If it is dropped from a height of 4 feet and is allowed to continue bouncing indefinitely, what is the total distance it travels?

54. Let $\displaystyle S_n = \sum_{k=1}^{n} \frac{1}{\sqrt{k}}$.

    (a) Evaluate $\displaystyle\lim_{k \to \infty} \frac{1}{\sqrt{k}}$.

    (b) Show that $\displaystyle S_n \geq \frac{n}{\sqrt{n}} = \sqrt{n}$ for all $n \geq 1$. [HINT: If $k \leq n$, then $1/k \geq 1/n$.]

    (c) Use part (b) to show that $\displaystyle\sum_{k=1}^{\infty} \frac{1}{\sqrt{k}}$ diverges.

55. Use the previous exercise and the fact that $\ln x \le \sqrt{x}$ for all $x \ge 1$ to show that $\displaystyle\sum_{k=2}^{\infty} \frac{1}{\ln k}$ diverges.

56. Let $\{a_k\}$ be an increasing sequence such that $a_1 > 0$ and $a_k \le 100$ for all $k \ge 1$.

   (a) Does $\displaystyle\lim_{k\to\infty} a_k$ exist? Justify your answer.

   (b) Show that $\displaystyle\sum_{k=1}^{\infty} a_k$ diverges.

57. Let $\{a_k\}$ be a sequence of positive terms such that $\displaystyle\sum_{k=1}^{n} a_k \le 100$ for all $n \ge 1$. Explain why $\displaystyle\lim_{k\to\infty} a_k = 0$ must be true.

58. Suppose that the partial sums of the series $\displaystyle\sum_{j=1}^{\infty} b_j$ are
$$S_n = \sum_{j=1}^{n} b_j = \ln\left(\frac{2n+3}{n+1}\right).$$

   (a) Evaluate $\displaystyle\lim_{n\to\infty} S_n$.

   (b) Does the series converge? Justify your answer.

   (c) Show that $b_j < 0$ for all $j \ge 1$.

59. Suppose that the partial sums of the series $\displaystyle\sum_{k=1}^{\infty} a_k$ satisfy the inequality $\dfrac{6\ln n}{\ln(n^2+1)} < S_n < 3 + ne^{-n}$ for all $n \ge 100$.

   (a) Does the series converge? If so, to what limit? Justify your answers.

   (b) What, if anything, can be said about $\displaystyle\lim_{k\to\infty} a_k$? Explain.

60. Let $\displaystyle S_n = \sum_{k=1}^{n} a_k$, and suppose that $0 \le S_n \le 100$ for all $n \ge 1$.

   (a) Give an example of a sequence $\{a_k\}$ that satisfies these conditions but $\displaystyle\sum_{k=1}^{\infty} a_k$ diverges.

   (b) Show that if $a_k > 0$ for all $k \ge 1$, then $\displaystyle\sum_{k=1}^{\infty} a_k$ converges.

   (c) Show that if $a_k > 0$ for all $k \ge 10^6$, then $\displaystyle\sum_{k=1}^{\infty} a_k$ converges.

61. Suppose that $\displaystyle\sum_{k=1}^{\infty} a_k$ diverges.

   (a) Explain why $a_k > 0$ for all $k \ge 1$ implies that $\displaystyle\lim_{n\to\infty} S_n = \infty$.

   (b) Give an example of a divergent series for which $\displaystyle\lim_{n\to\infty} S_n$ does not exist.

62. Let $\displaystyle H_n = \sum_{k=1}^{n} \frac{1}{k}$, and let $\displaystyle I_n = \int_{1}^{n+1} \frac{dx}{x}$.

   (a) Let L_n be the left Riemann-sum approximation, with n equal subdivisions, to I_n. Show that $L_n = H_n$.

   (b) Use part (a) to show that the harmonic series diverges. [HINT: Start by comparing L_n and I_n.]

63. Let $\displaystyle H_n = \sum_{k=1}^{n} \frac{1}{k}$, and let $\displaystyle a_m = \sum_{j=1}^{2^{m-1}} \frac{1}{2^{m-1}+j}$. Then $\displaystyle H_{2^n} = 1 + \sum_{m=1}^{n} a_m$. [NOTE: a_m is the sum of a "block" of 2^{m-1} consecutive terms of the harmonic series—those from $n = 2^{m-1}+1$ through $n = 2^m$.]

   (a) Show that $a_1 = 1/2$, $a_2 = 7/12$, and $a_3 = 533/840$.

   (b) Show that $H_8 = 1 + a_1 + a_2 + a_3 = 761/280$.

   (c) Show that $a_k \ge 1/2$ for all $k \ge 1$.

      [HINT: $\dfrac{1}{2^{m-1}+j} \ge \dfrac{1}{2^{m-1}+2^{m-1}}$ if $1 \le j \le 2^{m-1}$.]

   (d) Use part (c) to show that $\displaystyle\lim_{n\to\infty} H_n = \infty$ (i.e., the harmonic series diverges).

64. Consider the series $\displaystyle\sum_{k=1}^{\infty} \frac{1}{k^p}$ with $p > 1$. This exercise outlines a proof that this series converges.

   (a) Let $\displaystyle S_n = \sum_{k=1}^{n} \frac{1}{k^p}$. Show that the sequence of partial sums $\{S_n\}$ is increasing.

   (b) Show that $\displaystyle S_{2m+1} = 1 + \sum_{k=1}^{m} \frac{1}{(2k)^p} + \sum_{k=1}^{m} \frac{1}{(2k+1)^p}$.

   (c) Explain why $\displaystyle S_{2m+1} < 1 + 2\sum_{k=1}^{m} \frac{1}{(2k)^p}$.

      [HINT: $1/(x+1) < 1/x$ if $x > 0$.]

   (d) Show that $S_{2m+1} < 1 + 2^{1-p} S_{2m+1}$.
      [HINT: First show that $S_{2m+1} < 1 + 2^{1-p} S_m$.]

   (e) Show that $\{S_n\}$ is bounded above.

This section is about convergence testing for positive series. Comparison (to other series or to integrals) is the main tool. We treat the concrete matter of estimating limits as well as abstract questions of convergence or divergence.

11.3 TESTING FOR CONVERGENCE; ESTIMATING LIMITS

In theory, the question of convergence is simple: The series $\sum a_k$ converges to the sum S if the sequence $\{S_n\}$ of partial sums tends to S. The trouble, in practice, is that a simple, explicit formula for S_n is often unavailable. It might seem, then, that testing for convergence—let alone finding a limit—would be difficult or impossible. Surprisingly, that isn't so. All the convergence tests of this section and the next (comparison test, integral test, ratio test, and so on) offer clever, indirect ways of testing whether $\{S_n\}$ converges.

Nonnegative series A series $\sum a_k$ for which $a_k \geq 0$ for all k is called **nonnegative**. For such a series, the sequence $\{S_n\}$ of partial sums is nondecreasing: ➤

Convince yourself; it's easy but important.

$$S_1 \leq S_2 \leq S_3 \leq \cdots \leq S_n \leq S_{n+1} \leq \cdots.$$

Nondecreasing sequences are easier to study than others for one main reason: A nondecreasing sequence either (i) converges or (ii) blows up to infinity. ➤ (An arbitrary sequence can diverge without blowing up.) This means, in practice, that the question of convergence or divergence for a *nonnegative* series $\sum a_k$ boils down to the following simpler question:

Theorem 3, page 553, says so.

Do the partial sums S_n blow up or remain bounded as $n \to \infty$?

The answer may be obvious at a glance if a simple formula for S_n is available. ➤ If not, our best strategy may be to *compare* the given series to something that is better understood (another series, an integral—whatever works). Sometimes an obvious comparison suggests itself.

We have such a formula for geometric series.

EXAMPLE 1 Does $\displaystyle\sum_{k=0}^{\infty} \frac{1}{2^k + 1}$ converge?

This example anticipates and motivates the comparison test. We estimate a limit in the following example.

Solution We saw in the preceding section that the geometric series $\sum_{k=0}^{\infty} 1/2^k$ converges to 2. For all k, it's clear that

$$\frac{1}{2^k + 1} < \frac{1}{2^k},$$

and so each partial sum of $\sum_{k=0}^{\infty} 1/(2^k + 1)$ is *less than* the corresponding partial sum of $\sum_{k=0}^{\infty} 1/2^k$. ➤ Therefore, the partial sums of the original series cannot blow up; they must tend to some limit less than 2. Numerical evidence agrees. For the original series, calculation gives

Adding smaller summands gives a smaller sum.

$$S_{10} \approx 1.263523536; \quad S_{20} \approx 1.264498827; \quad S_{100} \approx 1.264499780. \quad \blacksquare$$

The comparison test: One series vs. another

In Example 1 we showed that one series converges by comparing it to another series that is *known* to converge. The following theorem makes this idea precise.

THEOREM 7 (Comparison test for nonnegative series) Consider two series $\sum a_k$ and $\sum b_k$, with $0 \leq a_k \leq b_k$ for all k.

- If $\sum b_k$ *converges*, so does $\sum a_k$, and $\sum a_k \leq \sum b_k$.
- If $\sum a_k$ *diverges*, so does $\sum b_k$.

Observe:

- **What we'd expect** The theorem's assertions should seem reasonable. A formal proof uses the fact that *every* partial sum of $\sum a_k$ is less than the corresponding partial sum of $\sum b_k$.

The comparison test is indeed natural—smaller summands "should" give smaller sums.

- **Comparing integrals, comparing series** An almost identical comparison theorem applies to improper integrals. ◄ Theorem 1, Section 10.2, says that if $0 \le a(x) \le b(x)$ for all $x \ge 1$, then

$$\int_1^\infty a(x)\,dx \le \int_1^\infty b(x)\,dx.$$

- **Successful comparisons** In a "successful" comparison, either both series converge or both diverge. To use the comparison test, therefore, it's necessary first to *guess* whether the series in question converges or diverges. ◄

Comparing tails Theorem 7 says that if $0 \le a_k \le b_k$ for all $k \ge 1$ and $\sum b_k$ converges, then $\sum a_k$ converges too, and

$$\sum_{k=1}^\infty a_k \le \sum_{k=1}^\infty b_k.$$

A similar inequality holds for upper tails of convergent series. If N is *any* positive integer, $0 \le a_k \le b_k$ for all $k \ge N$, and $\sum b_k$ converges, then $\sum a_k$ converges too, and

$$\sum_{k=N+1}^\infty a_k \le \sum_{k=N+1}^\infty b_k.$$

We'll "compare tails" in the following example to estimate the numerical value of a limit.

EXAMPLE 2 We've seen (using comparison) that $\sum_{k=0}^\infty \dfrac{1}{2^k+1}$ converges, and a calculator gives $S_{100} \approx 1.264499781$. How closely does S_{100} approximate the *true* sum S?

Solution The error in using S_{100} to estimate the limit comes from ignoring the tail R_{100}. In symbols,

$$S = \sum_{k=0}^{100} a_k + \sum_{k=101}^\infty a_k = S_{100} + R_{100}.$$

Clearly, $\dfrac{1}{2^k+1} < \dfrac{1}{2^k}$ for all k; in particular, the inequality holds for $k \ge 101$. Now we compare tails:

$$R_{100} = \sum_{k=101}^\infty \frac{1}{2^k+1} < \sum_{k=101}^\infty \frac{1}{2^k}.$$

The comparison is worthwhile because the right side is a *geometric* series, which we can calculate exactly:

$$\sum_{k=101}^\infty \frac{1}{2^k} = \frac{1}{2^{101}} + \frac{1}{2^{102}} + \frac{1}{2^{103}} + \cdots = \frac{1}{2^{101}}\left(1 + \frac{1}{2} + \frac{1}{2^2} + \cdots\right) = \frac{1}{2^{101}} \cdot 2 = \frac{1}{2^{100}}.$$

This shows that we commit *very* little error by ignoring the tail. The error, R_{100}, is less than $1/2^{100} \approx 8 \times 10^{-31}$. ∎

The integral test: Series vs. integrals

The *idea* of comparison is easy. Harder, in practice, is deciding what to compare a series *to*. Our only reliable "benchmark" series, so far, are geometric series. The **integral test** enlarges our stock of benchmark series considerably.

Comparing areas Thinking of the terms of a nonnegative *series* $\sum_{k=1}^{\infty} a_k$ as rectangular areas, each with base 1, helps clarify the close connection with the *integral* $\int_1^{\infty} a(x)\,dx$. Figure 1 shows two ways of doing so.

Students should study the following figures very carefully; they illustrate all the main ideas of the integral test.

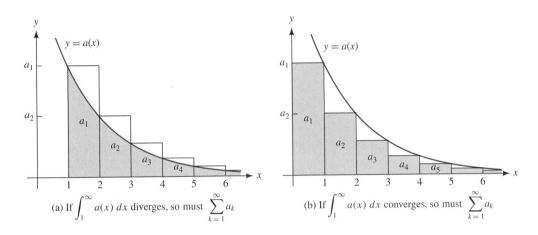

(a) If $\displaystyle\int_1^{\infty} a(x)\,dx$ diverges, so must $\displaystyle\sum_{k=1}^{\infty} a_k$ (b) If $\displaystyle\int_1^{\infty} a(x)\,dx$ converges, so must $\displaystyle\sum_{k=1}^{\infty} a_k$

FIGURE 1
Relating improper integrals to infinite series

Look closely:

- **Total areas** The successive rectangles have *heights* $a(1) = a_1$, $a(2) = a_2$, $a(3) = a_3$, and so on; each *base* is 1. The respective *areas*, therefore, are a_1, a_2, a_3, and so on. Thus,

    The series $a_1 + a_2 + a_3 + a_4 + \cdots$ represents the total "left-rule" rectangular area from 1 to ∞.

- **An important inequality** The shaded area in Figure 1(a) represents the integral $\int_1^{\infty} a(x)\,dx$. Thus, if the integral diverges, so must the series. Here is the message of Figure 1(a) in inequality form:

$$a_1 + a_2 + a_3 + \cdots \geq \int_1^{\infty} a(x)\,dx. \tag{1}$$

    If the right side diverges to infinity, then so must the left.

- **A decreasing integrand** The reasoning that led to Inequality (1) requires that $a(x)$ be *decreasing* for $x \geq 1$, as shown in the pictures. (We collect such technical hypotheses carefully in the following theorem.)

The integral test is, in effect, just another form of comparison.

• **Bounding a series from above**   Figure 1(b) shows an integral bounding a series from *above*. This time, comparing areas gives

$$a_2 + a_3 + \cdots \le \int_1^\infty a(x)\,dx,$$

or, equivalently,

$$a_1 + a_2 + a_3 + \cdots \le a_1 + \int_1^\infty a(x)\,dx. \tag{2}$$

If the right side converges, so must the left.

Combining Inequalities (1) and (2) gives *upper* and *lower* bounds for the series:

$$\int_1^\infty a(x)\,dx \;\le\; \sum_{k=1}^\infty a_k \;\le\; a_1 + \int_1^\infty a(x)\,dx. \tag{3}$$

In particular:

The integral $\int_1^\infty a(x)\,dx$ and the series $\sum_{k=1}^\infty a_k$ either both converge or both diverge.

The final picture, Figure 2, relates the tails of an integral and of a series.

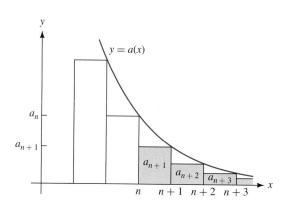

The shaded part is the tail R_n.

FIGURE 2

Comparing tails: Why $\displaystyle\sum_{k=n+1}^\infty a_k \le \int_n^\infty a(x)\,dx$

Comparing areas in Figure 2 shows that, for all n, the tail R_n satisfies

$$R_n = \sum_{k=n+1}^\infty a_k \le \int_n^\infty a(x)\,dx.$$

Lessons from the pictures   Figures 1 and 2 show a particular function $a(x)$, but the conclusions we drew hold for *any* function $a(x)$ that is both positive and decreasing. It's time to collect our observations in a theorem.

THEOREM 8 (Integral test for positive series) Suppose that, for all $x \geq 1$, the function $a(x)$ is continuous, positive, and decreasing. Consider the series and the integral

$$\sum_{k=1}^{\infty} a_k \quad \text{and} \quad \int_1^{\infty} a(x)\, dx,$$

where $a_k = a(k)$ for integers $k \geq 1$.

- If either diverges, so does the other.
- If either converges, so does the other. In this case, we have

$$\int_1^{\infty} a(x)\, dx \leq \sum_{k=1}^{\infty} a_k \leq a_1 + \int_1^{\infty} a(x)\, dx.$$

and

$$R_n = \sum_{k=n+1}^{\infty} a_k \leq \int_n^{\infty} a(x)\, dx.$$

Convergent and divergent p-series Series of the form $\sum_{k=1}^{\infty} 1/k^p$ are called **p-series**. They form an important family of examples.

EXAMPLE 3 For which p does the p-series $\sum_{k=1}^{\infty} \dfrac{1}{k^p}$ converge?

Solution We saw in Chapter 10 that the improper integral $\int_1^{\infty} dx/x^p$ converges if and only if $p > 1$. By the integral test, the same is true for the series. In particular, the harmonic series $\sum 1/k$ diverges. ∎

This useful result deserves special mention:

FACT (The p-test for series) The p-series $\sum_{k=1}^{\infty} \dfrac{1}{k^p}$ converges if and only if $p > 1$.

The Fact itself gives no information about the value of limits.

Harmonic divergence The fact that the harmonic series

$$1 + \frac{1}{2} + \frac{1}{3} + \frac{1}{4} + \frac{1}{5} + \cdots$$

diverges to infinity—even though the terms themselves tend to zero—has fascinated mathematicians for many centuries. One early proof (unrelated to integrals) is attributed to Nicole Oresme, a 14th-century French bishop, scientist, and mathematician.

EXAMPLE 4 The p-series $\sum_{k=1}^{\infty} 1/k^3$ converges to some limit S. (The integral test says so.) How large must n be to ensure that S_n differs from S by less than 0.0001?

Solution We need to choose n so that the tail R_n is less than 0.0001. By the last inequality in Theorem 8,

$$R_n \leq \int_n^\infty \frac{dx}{x^3} = \frac{1}{2n^2}.$$

(The last step is an easy calculation.) This quantity (and hence also R_n) are less than 0.0001 if $n \geq 71$. Hence, $S_{71} \approx 1.20196$ differs from the true limit by less than 0.0001. ∎

EXAMPLE 5 Does $\displaystyle\sum_{k=1}^\infty \frac{1}{10k+1}$ converge?

Solution The integral test says no.

$$\int_1^\infty \frac{1}{10x+1}\, dx = \lim_{n\to\infty} \int_1^n \frac{1}{10x+1}\, dx = \lim_{n\to\infty} \left. \frac{\ln(10x+1)}{10}\right]_1^n = \infty.$$

The comparison test *also* says no. Since $10k + 1 \leq 11k$ for all $k \geq 1$, we have

$$\frac{1}{10k+1} \geq \frac{1}{11k} \implies \sum_{k=1}^\infty \frac{1}{10k+1} \geq \sum_{k=1}^\infty \frac{1}{11k} = \frac{1}{11} \sum_{k=1}^\infty \frac{1}{k}.$$

Because the last series diverges to infinity, so must the first. ∎

The ratio test: Comparison with a geometric series

In a geometric series $a + ar + ar^2 + ar^3 + ar^4 + \cdots$, the ratio of successive terms is r; by Theorem 4, page 561, the series converges if and only if $|r| < 1$.

The **ratio test** is also based on ratios of successive terms; it amounts to a lightly disguised form of comparison with a geometric series.

Another possibility, not considered in the theorem, is that the limit doesn't exist. Strong students might be asked to show that the a series may converge even if the limit does not exist.

THEOREM 9 (Ratio test for positive series) Suppose that $a_k > 0$ for all k and that

$$\lim_{k\to\infty} \frac{a_{k+1}}{a_k} = L.$$

- If $L < 1$, then $\sum a_k$ *converges.*
- If $L > 1$, then $\sum a_k$ *diverges.*
- If $L = 1$, the test is inconclusive—either convergence or divergence is possible.

Two points deserve emphasis:

- **Best cases** The ratio test works best for series like $\sum 1/k!$, $\sum r^k$, and $\sum 1/(2^k + 3)$, in which the index k appears in an exponent or a factorial.

The limit is 1 for every p-series.

- **Other cases** For many series, unfortunately, the ratio a_{k+1}/a_k either tends to 1 or has *no* limit. ← In such cases, the ratio test tells us nothing.

EXAMPLE 6 Show that $\displaystyle\sum_{k=0}^{\infty} \frac{1}{k!}$ converges. Guess its limit.

Solution The ratio test works nicely. Since

$$\lim_{k\to\infty} \frac{a_{k+1}}{a_k} = \lim_{k\to\infty} \frac{k!}{(k+1)!} = \lim_{k\to\infty} \frac{1}{k+1} = 0,$$

the series converges. In fact, it converges very, very fast. Here are some representative partial sums:

$$S_5 \approx 2.716667; \quad S_{10} \approx 2.718281; \quad S_{30} \approx 2.718281828459045235360287471350.$$

Is e involved somehow? It certainly seems so—S_{30} agrees with e in all decimal places shown. In fact, this series can be shown to converge to e. We explore this phenomenon further in later sections. ∎

EXAMPLE 7 Does $\displaystyle\sum_{k=0}^{\infty} \frac{100^k}{k!}$ converge?

Solution Yes, by the ratio test:

$$\lim_{k\to\infty} \frac{a_{k+1}}{a_k} = \lim_{k\to\infty} \frac{100^{k+1}}{(k+1)!} \cdot \frac{k!}{100^k} = \lim_{k\to\infty} \frac{100}{k+1} = 0.$$

Notice what the result means: Even though 100^k grows very fast, $k!$ grows even faster. ∎

Why the ratio test works To illustrate the connection between the ratio test and geometric series, and to give the idea of a proof, let's suppose, for instance, that

A general argument is slightly subtle, so we discuss a special case.

$$\lim_{k\to\infty} \frac{a_{k+1}}{a_k} = \frac{1}{2}.$$

Why must $\sum a_k$ converge?

The idea is that $a_{k+1} \approx a_k/2$ for large k, and so the given series should be comparable to a *geometric* series. Suppose, for instance, that $a_{k+1} < 0.6 a_k$ for all $k \geq 1000$. ➤ Then

Such an inequality must hold for large k because the ratio limit is 1/2.

$$a_{1001} < (0.6)a_{1000}, \quad a_{1002} < (0.6)a_{1001} < (0.6)^2 a_{1000}, \quad a_{1003} < (0.6)^3 a_{1000}, \ldots.$$

Therefore,

$$a_{1000} + a_{1001} + a_{1002} + \cdots < a_{1000}\left(1 + (0.6) + (0.6)^2 + (0.6)^3 + \cdots\right).$$

The preceding inequality is the point; it shows that an upper tail of the original series $\sum a_k$ converges by comparison with the geometric series in the last line. (The divergence part of the ratio test can be proved using similar ideas.)

BASIC EXERCISES

1. Consider the series $\displaystyle\sum_{k=0}^{\infty} a_k$, where $a_k = \dfrac{1}{k + 2^k}$.

   (a) Use the comparison test to show that the series converges.

   (b) Show that $0 \leq R_{10} \leq 2^{-10}$.

   (c) Compute an estimate of the limit of the series that is guaranteed to be within 0.001 of the exact value.

   (d) Is your estimate in part (c) an overestimate? Justify your answer.

2. Consider the series $\displaystyle\sum_{j=0}^{\infty} \frac{1}{2+3^j}$.

(a) Show that the series converges.

(b) Estimate the limit of the series within 0.01.

(c) Is your estimate in part (b) an overestimate? Justify your answer.

In Exercises 3 and 4, suppose that $a(x)$ is continuous, positive, and decreasing for all $x \geq 1$ and that $a_k = a(k)$ for all integers $k \geq 1$.

3. Rank the values $\displaystyle\int_1^n a(x)\,dx, \sum_{k=1}^{n-1} a_k,$ and $\displaystyle\sum_{k=2}^{n} a_k$ in increasing order.   [HINT: Draw a picture.]

4. Rank the values $\displaystyle\int_n^{\infty} a(x)\,dx, \sum_{k=n+1}^{\infty} a_k,$ and $\displaystyle\int_{n+1}^{\infty} a(x)\,dx$ in increasing order.

Suppose that $a(x)$ is continuous, positive, and decreasing for all $x \geq 1$ and that $a_k = a(k)$ for all integers $k \geq 1$. In Exercises 5–8, draw a carefully annotated picure that shows that

5. $\displaystyle\int_1^{n+1} a(x)\,dx \leq \sum_{k=1}^{n} a_k$

6. $\displaystyle\sum_{k=2}^{n} a_k \leq \int_1^n a(x)\,dx$

7. $\displaystyle\sum_{k=n+1}^{\infty} a_k \leq a_{n+1} + \int_{n+1}^{\infty} a(x)\,dx$

8. $\displaystyle\sum_{k=n+1}^{\infty} a_k \leq \int_n^{\infty} a(x)\,dx$

In Exercises 9–12, use the integral test to find upper and lower bounds on the limit of the series.

9. $\displaystyle\sum_{k=1}^{\infty} \frac{1}{k^3}$

10. $\displaystyle\sum_{k=1}^{\infty} \frac{1}{k\sqrt{k}}$

11. $\displaystyle\sum_{j=1}^{\infty} j e^{-j}$

12. $\displaystyle\sum_{k=0}^{\infty} \frac{1}{k^2+1}$

13. Consider the series $\displaystyle\sum_{k=1}^{\infty} \frac{e^{\sin k}}{k^2}$.

(a) $\displaystyle\int_1^{\infty} \frac{e^{\sin k}}{k^2}$ is a convergent improper integral. Does it follow from this fact and Theorem 8 that the series converges? Justify your answer.

(b) Show that this series converges.

14. Use the fact that $\ln x \leq \sqrt{x}$ for all $x \geq 1$ to show that $\displaystyle\sum_{n=2}^{\infty} \frac{1}{(\ln n)^2}$ diverges.

15. Use the fact that $\ln x \leq x$ for all $x \geq 1$ to show that $\displaystyle\sum_{n=2}^{\infty} \frac{1}{(\ln n)^2}$ diverges.   [HINT: $x \ln x \geq (\ln x)^2$ if $x \geq 1$.]

16. Show that $\displaystyle\sum_{k=3}^{\infty} \frac{1}{(\ln k)^k}$ converges.   [HINT: $\ln 3 \approx 1.0986$.]

In Exercises 17–20, use the comparison test to show that the series converges. Then find upper and lower bounds on the limit of the series.

17. $\displaystyle\sum_{n=1}^{\infty} \frac{1}{n^2 + \sqrt{n}}$

18. $\displaystyle\sum_{j=0}^{\infty} \frac{1}{j + e^j}$

19. $\displaystyle\sum_{m=1}^{\infty} \frac{1}{m\sqrt{1+m^2}}$

20. $\displaystyle\sum_{k=1}^{\infty} \frac{k}{(k^2+1)^2}$

In Exercises 21–24, use the ratio test to show that the series converges.

21. $\displaystyle\sum_{j=0}^{\infty} \frac{j^2}{j!}$

22. $\displaystyle\sum_{k=1}^{\infty} \frac{2^k}{k!}$

23. $\displaystyle\sum_{n=1}^{\infty} \frac{n^2}{2^n}$

24. $\displaystyle\sum_{m=1}^{\infty} \frac{m!}{(2m)!}$

25. Consider the series $\displaystyle\sum_{k=1}^{\infty} a_k = \sum_{k=1}^{\infty} \frac{\ln k}{k}$.

(a) Use the integral test to show that the series diverges. [HINT: Be careful, the integrand is not monotone.]

(b) Use the comparison test to show that the series diverges. [HINT: $1 - x^{-1} \leq \ln x$ for all $x > 0$.]

(c) Can the ratio test be used to show that the series diverges? Explain.

26. Consider the series $\displaystyle\sum_{k=1}^{\infty} a_k = \frac{1}{2} + \frac{1}{3} + \frac{1}{2^2} + \frac{1}{3^2} + \frac{1}{2^3} + \frac{1}{3^3} + \cdots$.

(a) Explain why $\displaystyle\lim_{k\to\infty} a_{k+1}/a_k$ does not exist.

(b) What, if anything, does the ratio test say about the convergence of $\displaystyle\sum_{k=1}^{\infty} a_k$?

(c) Show that the series converges, and evaluate its limit. [HINT: Rewrite the series as the sum of two convergent series.]

27. (a) What, if anything, does the ratio test say about the convergence of the series $\dfrac{1}{2} + \dfrac{1}{2} + \dfrac{1}{4} + \dfrac{1}{4} + \dfrac{1}{8} + \dfrac{1}{8} + \cdots$?

(b) Does the series in part (a) converge or diverge? Justify your answer.

28. Give an example of a divergent series $\displaystyle\sum_{k=1}^{\infty} a_k$ such that $a_k > 0$ and $a_{k+1}/a_k < 1$ for all $k \geq 1$.

29. Use the ratio test to show that $\displaystyle\sum_{n=1}^{\infty} n^{-n}$ converges.

30. Use the ratio test to show that the series $\displaystyle\sum_{n=1}^{\infty} \frac{n^n}{n!}$ diverges.

FURTHER EXERCISES

In Exercises 31–36, determine whether the series converges or diverges. If the series converges, find a number N such that the partial sum S_N approximates the sum of the series within 0.001. If the series diverges, find a number N such that $S_N \geq 1000$.

31. $\displaystyle\sum_{k=0}^{\infty} \frac{1}{k^2 + 3}$

32. $\displaystyle\sum_{m=1}^{\infty} \frac{\arctan m}{m}$

33. $\displaystyle\sum_{k=0}^{\infty} \frac{1}{2 + \cos k}$

34. $\displaystyle\sum_{m=2}^{\infty} \frac{\ln m}{m^3}$

35. $\displaystyle\sum_{k=0}^{\infty} \frac{k}{k^6 + 17}$

36. $\displaystyle\sum_{k=2}^{\infty} \frac{1}{k (\ln k)^5}$

In Exercises 37 and 38, let $S_n = \displaystyle\sum_{k=1}^{n} a_k$, $T_n = \displaystyle\sum_{k=1}^{n} b_k$, and assume that $0 \leq a_k \leq b_k$ for all $k \geq 1$.

37. (a) Suppose that $\displaystyle\sum_{k=1}^{\infty} b_k$ converges. Explain why there is a number M such that $S_n \leq T_n \leq M$ for all $n \geq 1$.

(b) Explain why $\{S_n\}$ is an increasing sequence.

(c) Explain why parts (a) and (b) together imply that $\displaystyle\sum_{k=1}^{\infty} a_k$ converges.

38. (a) Suppose that $\displaystyle\sum_{k=1}^{\infty} a_k$ diverges. Explain why $\displaystyle\lim_{n \to \infty} S_n = \infty$.

(b) Suppose that $\displaystyle\sum_{k=1}^{\infty} a_k$ diverges. Use part (a) to show that $\displaystyle\sum_{k=1}^{\infty} b_k$ diverges.

39. Suppose that $a(x)$ is continuous, positive, and decreasing for all $x \geq 1$, that $a_k = a(k)$ for all integers $k \geq 1$, and that $\displaystyle\int_{1}^{\infty} a(x)\,dx$ converges.

(a) Explain why the sequence of partial sums $\{S_n\}$ is an increasing sequence.

(b) Explain why $\displaystyle\int_{1}^{n} a(x)\,dx \leq \int_{1}^{\infty} a(x)\,dx$.

(c) Use parts (a) and (b) to show that the sequence of partial sums $\{S_n\}$ converges.

40. (a) Where in the proof of the integral test (Theorem 8) is the assumption that $a(x)$ is a decreasing function used?

(b) Suppose that the requirement that $a(x)$ be decreasing for all $x \geq 1$ is replaced by the "weaker" requirement that $a(x)$ be decreasing for all $x \geq 10$. How does this change in assumptions affect the conclusions of Theorem 8?

41. Does the series $1 + \dfrac{1}{1 \cdot 3} + \dfrac{1}{1 \cdot 3 \cdot 5} + \dfrac{1}{1 \cdot 3 \cdot 5 \cdot 7} + \cdots + \dfrac{1}{1 \cdot 3 \cdot 5 \cdot 7 \cdots (2k + 1)} + \cdots$ converge? Justify your answer.

42. Does the series $\dfrac{1}{2} + \dfrac{1}{2 \cdot 4} + \dfrac{1}{2 \cdot 4 \cdot 6} + \cdots + \dfrac{1}{2 \cdot 4 \cdot 6 \cdots (2k)} + \cdots$ converge? Justify your answer.

43. Show that $\displaystyle\sum_{k=3}^{\infty} \frac{1}{(\ln k)^{\ln k}}$ converges.
[HINT: $\ln k > e^2$ if $k > 1619$.]

44. Suppose that $a_n \geq 0$ for all $n \geq 1$ and that $\displaystyle\sum_{n=1}^{\infty} a_n$ converges.
Show that $\displaystyle\sum_{n=1}^{\infty} |\sin a_n|$ converges.
[HINT: $|\sin x| \leq |x|$ for all x.]

In Exercises 45–52, determine whether the series converges. If it converges, find upper and lower bounds on its limit. Justify your answers.

45. $\displaystyle\sum_{n=1}^{\infty} \frac{\arctan n}{1 + n^2}$

46. $\displaystyle\sum_{m=1}^{\infty} \frac{m^3}{m^5 + 3}$

47. $\displaystyle\sum_{j=1}^{\infty} \frac{1}{100 + 5j}$

48. $\displaystyle\sum_{k=2}^{\infty} \frac{1}{k \ln k}$

49. $\displaystyle\sum_{n=1}^{\infty} \frac{1}{n\,3^n}$

50. $\displaystyle\sum_{n=2}^{\infty} \frac{1}{\sqrt[3]{n^2 - 1}}$

51. $\displaystyle\sum_{j=0}^{\infty} \frac{j!}{(j + 2)!}$

52. $\displaystyle\sum_{n=0}^{\infty} \frac{n!}{(2n)!}$

53. Suppose that $\{a_k\}$ is a sequence of positive terms and that r is a constant such that $a_{k+1}/a_k \leq r < 1$ for all $k \geq 1$.

(a) Show that $a_2 \leq a_1 r$.

(b) Show that $a_{k+1} \leq a_1 r^k$ for every $k \geq 1$.

(c) Use part (b) to show that $\displaystyle\sum_{k=1}^{\infty} a_k$ converges.
[HINT: Use the comparison test and the formula for the sum of geometric series.]

(d) Show that $R_n = \displaystyle\sum_{k=n+1}^{\infty} a_k \leq \frac{a_{n+1}}{1 - r}$.

54. Use Exercise 53 to find an integer N such that the partial sum S_N approximates the sum of the series $\displaystyle\sum_{n=1}^{\infty} n^2/2^n$ within 0.0005.

55. Use Exercise 53 to find an integer N such that the partial sum S_N approximates the sum of the series $\displaystyle\sum_{n=1}^{\infty} (n!)^2/(2n)!$ within 0.0005.

11.4 ABSOLUTE CONVERGENCE; ALTERNATING SERIES

Not-necessarily-positive series The integral, comparison, and ratio tests apply only to *nonnegative* series. Some interesting series, however, have both positive and negative terms.

Students should thoroughly understand this example as a prototype of the phenomena at hand.

EXAMPLE 1 Does the **alternating harmonic series**

$$\sum_{k=1}^{\infty} \frac{(-1)^{k+1}}{k} = 1 - \frac{1}{2} + \frac{1}{3} - \frac{1}{4} + \frac{1}{5} - \cdots$$

converge or diverge? To what limit?

Solution As always, the question is how partial sums behave. Tabulating some of them shows a pattern.

\multicolumn{11}{c}{**Partial sums of** $1 - \frac{1}{2} + \frac{1}{3} - \frac{1}{4} + \frac{1}{5} - \cdots$}										
n	1	2	3	4	5	6	7	8	9	10	...
S_n	1	0.500	0.833	0.583	0.783	0.617	0.760	0.635	0.746	0.646	...
n	51	52	53	54	55	56	57	58	59	60	...
S_n	0.703	0.684	0.702	0.684	0.702	0.684	0.702	0.685	0.702	0.685	...

Successive partial sums seem to hop back and forth across some limiting value. Plots of partial sums and terms (Figure 1) exhibit the same pattern:

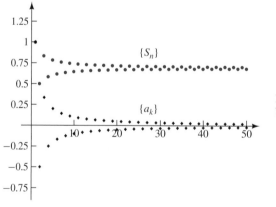

Blue dots show partial sums; black dots show terms.

FIGURE 1

Terms and partial sums for $1 - \frac{1}{2} + \frac{1}{3} - \frac{1}{4} + \frac{1}{5} - \cdots$

Because the terms alternate in sign, the partial sums successively rise and fall, alternately overshooting and undershooting the limiting value, which is apparently around 0.69. (It can be shown—with considerable effort—that the exact limit is $\ln 2 \approx 0.69315$.) ∎

Absolute vs. conditional convergence

We discussed absolute convergence of improper integrals in Chapter 10.

The alternating harmonic series illustrates the phenomenon of **conditional convergence**. Although

$$1 - \frac{1}{2} + \frac{1}{3} - \frac{1}{4} + \frac{1}{5} - \cdots$$

converges (as Example 1 suggests), the *ordinary* harmonic series

$$1 + \frac{1}{2} + \frac{1}{3} + \frac{1}{4} + \frac{1}{5} + \cdots$$

diverges, as we saw from the integral test.

EXAMPLE 2   Does $\displaystyle\sum_{k=1}^{\infty} \frac{\sin k}{k^2}$ converge? Does $\displaystyle\sum_{k=1}^{\infty} \frac{|\sin k|}{k^2}$? Estimate limits.

Solution   The first series, like the alternating harmonic series, has both negative and positive terms—although in no regular order this time. Plotting terms and partial sums (Figure 2) suggests (but doesn't prove) that this series converges.

FIGURE 2
Terms and partial sums for $\displaystyle\sum_{k=1}^{\infty} \frac{\sin k}{k^2}$

The partial sums wander up and down just slightly but still appear to approach a horizontal asymptote, perhaps near $y = 1$.

The second series also seems to converge, judging from Figure 3. This time the limit appears to be near 1.25.

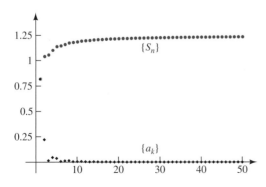

FIGURE 3
Terms and partial sums for $\displaystyle\sum_{k=1}^{\infty} \frac{|\sin k|}{k^2}$

If $\sum a_k$ is the first series, $\sum |a_k|$ is the second.

The second series comes from the first by taking the absolute value of each term. ◄ The new series is nonnegative, and so the comparison test applies. Because

$$0 \le \frac{|\sin k|}{k^2} \le \frac{1}{k^2}$$

for all $k \ge 1$ and $\sum_{k=1}^{\infty} 1/k^2$ converges, so must $\sum_{k=1}^{\infty} |\sin k| / k^2$. ∎

Examples 1 and 2 illustrate the phenomena of **conditional convergence** and **absolute convergence**, respectively. The formal definitions are as follows:

> **DEFINITION (Absolute and conditional convergence)** Let $\sum a_k$ be any series.
> - If $\sum |a_k|$ converges, then $\sum a_k$ **converges absolutely**.
> - If $\sum |a_k|$ diverges but $\sum a_k$ converges, then $\sum a_k$ **converges conditionally**.

The wacky world of conditional convergence Conditionally convergent series have some surprising properties. Here is one of the oddest:

> *Let $\sum a_k$ be conditionally convergent, and let L be any real number. Then the terms of $\sum a_k$ can be reordered in such a way that the resulting series converges to L.*

(For more details, see your instructor.) Notice how drastically this peculiar property of conditionally convergent series upsets the naive hope that addition is commutative even for infinite sums.

Pluses and minuses of pluses and minuses Let $\sum_{k=1}^{\infty} a_k$ be any series. If it happens that $a_k \ge 0$ for all k, the advantage is simplicity: The partial sums are nondecreasing. The disadvantage, as the harmonic series shows, is that the partial sums may tend to infinity.

Mixing positive and negative terms may cost something in simplicity, but it's an advantage for convergence. As the alternating harmonic series shows, positive and negative terms can offset each other, thus helping the cause of convergence.

Absolute convergence implies ordinary convergence We saw in Chapter 10 that if $\int_1^{\infty} |f(x)| \, dx$ converges, then so must $\int_1^{\infty} f(x) \, dx$, and $\left| \int_1^{\infty} f(x) \, dx \right| \le \int_1^{\infty} |f(x)| \, dx$. (See Theorem 2, page 534.) The same principle applies to infinite series:

> **THEOREM 10** If $\sum_{k=1}^{\infty} |a_k|$ converges, then so does $\sum_{k=1}^{\infty} a_k$, and
> $$\left| \sum_{k=1}^{\infty} a_k \right| \le \sum_{k=1}^{\infty} |a_k|.$$

The theorem is essentially the triangle inequality for infinite sums.

The theorem's inequality should be believable—it is the infinite version of the fact that the absolute value of a sum can't exceed the sum of the absolute values. The idea of a rigorous proof is to write the original series as a sum of two new series, one entirely positive and the other entirely negative. Using the comparison test, one can show that each of these new series converges.

The theorem shows that, as Figure 3 suggested, the series $\sum_{k=1}^{\infty} \sin k / k^2$ of Example 2 does indeed converge, because $\sum_{k=1}^{\infty} |\sin k| / k^2$ does. Our limit estimates from Example 2 are also consistent with the theorem:

$$1 \approx \left| \sum_{k=1}^{\infty} \frac{\sin k}{k^2} \right| \leq \sum_{k=1}^{\infty} \frac{|\sin k|}{k^2} \approx 1.25.$$

EXAMPLE 3   For which values of x does the **power series**

$$\sum_{k=1}^{\infty} k x^k = x + 2x^2 + 3x^3 + 4x^4 + \cdots$$

converge? (A power series is something like an "infinite polynomial"; we discuss power series carefully in the next section.)

This example anticipates systematic treatment of power series in the next section.

Solution   First we use the ratio test to check for *absolute* convergence:

$$\lim_{k \to \infty} \left| \frac{(k+1)x^{k+1}}{kx^k} \right| = \lim_{k \to \infty} \left| \frac{k+1}{k} \right| \cdot |x| = 1 \cdot |x| = |x|.$$

If $|x| < 1$, the original series converges absolutely. By Theorem 10, it also converges *without* absolute value signs.

If $|x| \geq 1$, the series fails the nth term test, and so diverges.   ∎

Students should convince themselves that the series fails the n th term test.

Estimating limits

Estimating a limit for any series—nonnegative or not—depends upon keeping the upper tail small. Theorem 10, combined with earlier estimates, can help.

EXAMPLE 4   For the series $\sum_{k=1}^{\infty} (-1)^{k+1} / k^3$, we find (using technology) that $S_{100} \approx 0.901542$. How closely does S_{100} approximate S, the true sum of the series?

Solution   Because

$$S = \sum_{k=1}^{100} \frac{(-1)^{k+1}}{k^3} + \sum_{k=101}^{\infty} \frac{(-1)^{k+1}}{k^3} = S_{100} + R_{100},$$

we need only estimate R_{100}, as follows:

$$|R_{100}| = \left| \sum_{k=101}^{\infty} \frac{(-1)^{k+1}}{k^3} \right| \leq \sum_{k=101}^{\infty} \frac{1}{k^3} \qquad \text{(by Theorem 10)}$$

$$< \int_{100}^{\infty} \frac{1}{x^3} \, dx. \qquad \text{(by the integral test)}$$

The last integral is easy to calculate:

$$\int_{100}^{\infty} \frac{1}{x^3} \, dx = \left. \frac{-1}{2x^2} \right]_{100}^{\infty} = \frac{1}{20{,}000} = 0.00005,$$

and so the estimate $S \approx S_{100} \approx 0.901542$ is good to at least four decimal places.   ∎

Alternating series

For series with both positive and negative terms, testing for absolute convergence is usually the best option. In the special (but surprisingly useful) case that the terms alternate in sign, we can sometimes do better.

DEFINITION An **alternating series** is one whose terms alternate in sign, that is, a series of the form

$$c_1 - c_2 + c_3 - c_4 + c_5 - c_6 + \cdots,$$

where each c_i is positive.

The **alternating harmonic series**

$$1 - \frac{1}{2} + \frac{1}{3} - \frac{1}{4} + \frac{1}{5} - \cdots$$

See Example 1, especially Figure 1.

illustrates the best possibility. ◄ Because successive terms alternate in sign and decrease in size, successive partial sums straddle smaller and smaller intervals. If the terms also tend to zero, then the partial sums narrow down on a limit. The following theorem makes these observations formal; it also gives a convenient error bound.

THEOREM 11 (Alternating series test) Consider the series

$$\sum_{k=1}^{\infty}(-1)^{k+1}c_k = c_1 - c_2 + c_3 - c_4 + \cdots,$$

where

(i) $c_1 \geq c_2 \geq c_3 \geq \cdots \geq 0;$ and   (ii) $\lim_{k \to \infty} c_k = 0.$

Then the series converges, and its sum S lies *between* any two successive partial sums S_n and S_{n+1}. In particular,

$$|S - S_n| < c_{n+1}$$

for all $n \geq 1$.

The last inequality is especially useful—students should understand it thoroughly, including its relation to "betweenness."

A formal proof is slightly tricky, but the underlying idea is simple: Because the limit S lies *between* successive partial sums, adding another term to any partial sum always "overshoots" the limit, which explains the final inequality.

Technology may help students generate guesses and verify numerical calculations.

Using the theorems: Miscellaneous examples

Combining Theorems 10 and 11 with results from earlier sections enables us to handle many not-necessarily-positive series, detecting convergence or divergence and estimating limits. The following examples illustrate some useful tricks of this trade.

EXAMPLE 5 (An alternating p-series: another look) What does Theorem 11 say about $\sum_{k=1}^{\infty}(-1)^{k+1}/k^3$ and its 100th partial sum, $S_{100} \approx 0.9015422$?

Solution In this context, $c_k = 1/k^3$. Now Theorem 11 says not only that the series converges—which we already knew—but also that

$$|S - S_{100}| < c_{101} = \frac{1}{101^3} \approx 0.000001.$$

Thus, $S_{100} \approx 0.9015422$ lies within 0.000001 of the true limit S. Equivalently, S lies between $S_{100} \approx 0.9015422$ and $S_{101} \approx 0.9015432$. ∎

EXAMPLE 6 Does $\displaystyle\sum_{j=1}^{\infty} (-1)^j \frac{j}{j+1}$ converge or diverge? Why?

Solution The alternating series test looks tempting at first glance. But it doesn't apply, because

$$\lim_{j \to \infty} \frac{j}{j+1} = \lim_{j \to \infty} \frac{1}{1+1/j} = 1,$$

not zero as Theorem 11 requires. The nth term test does apply, however. (Maybe we should call it the "jth term test" here.) Since

$$\frac{j}{j+1} \to 1 \quad \text{as} \quad j \to \infty,$$

it follows that the jth term has no limit as $j \to \infty$. ➤ Therefore, the given series diverges. ∎

Successive terms are alternately near 1 and −1, and so the terms diverge.

EXAMPLE 7 Does the series

$$1 + 2 + 3 + 4 + 5 - \frac{1}{6} + \frac{1}{7} - \frac{1}{8} + \frac{1}{9} - \cdots$$

converge? If so, find or estimate the limit.

A few out-of-pattern terms affect the limit, but not convergence or divergence.

Solution The alternating series test doesn't apply right out of the box because the first five terms break the desired pattern. The problem isn't fatal, however. Basic series algebra lets us group our terms into two blocks, as follows:

$$(1 + 2 + 3 + 4 + 5) - \left(\frac{1}{6} - \frac{1}{7} + \frac{1}{8} - \frac{1}{9} + \cdots \right).$$

The first block is finite, so convergence isn't an issue; its sum is 15. The second block clearly satisfies all hypotheses of the alternating series test and so converges to some limit L. Any partial sum of the second block, moreover, differs from L by less than the magnitude of the next term (by the last line of Theorem 11).

  The entire series therefore converges to $S = 15 - L$, and any partial sum differs from S by no more than the next term. The partial sum $S_9 = 1 + 2 + \cdots + 1/9 \approx 14.962$, for instance, overshoots the true limit by less than $1/10$. In other words, the exact limit S satisfies $14.862 \le S \le 14.962$. ∎

EXAMPLE 8 Does $\displaystyle\sum_{n=1}^{\infty} \frac{\sin n}{n^3 + n^2 + n + 1 + \cos n}$ converge or diverge? Why?

Solution The problem is easier than it looks. Hoping for absolute convergence, we start by taking absolute values:

$$\left| \frac{\sin n}{n^3 + n^2 + n + 1 + \cos n} \right| = \frac{|\sin n|}{n^3 + n^2 + n + 1 + \cos n}.$$

The general appearance of numerator and denominator suggests a comparison. A simple inequality make the job much easier:

$$\frac{|\sin n|}{n^3 + n^2 + n + 1 + \cos n} \leq \frac{1}{n^3}.$$

Estimating a limit isn't hard since a similar comparison applies to the tail.

Because the *p*-series $\sum 1/n^3$ converges, so must the absolute-value version of the given series. Finally, Theorem 10 guarantees that the original series also converges. ∎

BASIC EXERCISES

Exercises 1–4 are about the series in Example 7.

1. Does the series converge conditionally or absolutely? Justify your answer.

2. Does the partial sum S_{15} overestimate the limit of the series? Justify your answer.

3. $S_{60} \approx 14.902$. Use this result to find upper and lower bounds for S.

4. The alternating harmonic series can be shown to converge to ln 2. Use this fact to find the limit of the series exactly.

5. Consider the series in Example 8.

    (a) Compute S_{50}.

    (b) Explain why $|R_{50}| \leq \displaystyle\int_{50}^{\infty} \frac{dx}{x^3}$.

    (c) Use parts (a) and (b) to find upper and lower bounds for the limit of the series.

6. Suppose that $\displaystyle\sum_{k=1}^{\infty} a_k$ converges absolutely. Show that $\displaystyle\sum_{k=1}^{\infty} \frac{a_k}{k}$ also converges.

7. Suppose that $\displaystyle\sum_{k=1}^{\infty} \frac{a_k}{k}$ converges. Must $\displaystyle\sum_{k=1}^{\infty} a_k$ also converge? Justify your answer.

8. Show that $\displaystyle\sum_{k=2}^{\infty}(-1)^k \frac{k}{k^2 - 1}$ converges conditionally.

In Exercises 9–12, show that the series converges. Then compute an estimate of the limit that is guaranteed to be in error by no more than 0.005.

9. $\displaystyle\sum_{k=1}^{\infty} \frac{(-1)^k}{k^4}$

10. $\displaystyle\sum_{k=1}^{\infty} \frac{(-1)^k}{k^2 + 2^k}$

11. $\displaystyle\sum_{k=0}^{\infty} \frac{(-3)^k}{(k^2)!}$

12. $\displaystyle\sum_{k=5}^{\infty}(-1)^k \frac{k^{10}}{10^k}$

13. Suppose that $a_k \geq 0$ for all $k \geq 1$. Is it possible that $\displaystyle\sum_{k=1}^{\infty} a_k$ converges conditionally? Justify your answer.

14. Does $\displaystyle\sum_{n=2}^{\infty}(-1)^n \frac{n}{2n - 1}$ converge? Justify your answer.

FURTHER EXERCISES

15. For which values of p, if any, does $\displaystyle\sum_{k=2}^{\infty} \frac{\ln k}{k^p}$ converge? Justify your answer.

16. For which values of p, if any, does $\displaystyle\sum_{k=2}^{\infty}(-1)^k \frac{\ln k}{k^p}$ converge? Justify your answer.

17. For which values of p, if any, does $\displaystyle\sum_{k=2}^{\infty}(-1)^k \frac{\ln k}{k^p}$ converge absolutely? Justify your answer.

18. For which values of p, if any, does $\displaystyle\sum_{k=2}^{\infty}(-1)^k \frac{\ln k}{k^p}$ converge conditionally? Justify your answer.

In Exercises 19–26, determine whether the series converges absolutely, converges conditionally, or diverges. If the series converges, find upper and lower bounds on its limit. Justify your answers.

19. $\displaystyle\sum_{j=1}^{\infty} \frac{(-1)^{j+1}}{j^2}$

20. $\displaystyle\sum_{k=1}^{\infty} \frac{(-1)^k}{\sqrt{k}}$

21. $\displaystyle\sum_{n=1}^{\infty} \frac{(-3)^n}{n^3}$

22. $\displaystyle\sum_{k=4}^{\infty}(-1)^k \frac{\ln k}{k}$

23. $\displaystyle\sum_{k=0}^{\infty}(-1)^k\frac{k}{2k+1}$

24. $\displaystyle\sum_{m=0}^{\infty}(-1)^m\frac{m^3}{2^m}$

25. $\displaystyle\sum_{j=0}^{\infty}(-1)^j\frac{j!}{(j^2)!}$

26. $\displaystyle\sum_{n=1}^{\infty}(-1)^{n+1}\frac{\arctan n}{n}$

27. Consider the series $\displaystyle\sum_{k=1}^{\infty}(-1)^{k+1}a_k$. Suppose that the terms of the sequence $\{a_k\}$ are positive and decreasing for all $k\geq 10^9$ and $\lim_{k\to\infty}a_k=0$ but that $a_{10^9}>a_1$. Explain why the series converges.   [HINT: Theorem 11 doesn't apply directly.]

28. Does $\quad 1-\dfrac{1}{2^3}+\dfrac{1}{3^2}-\dfrac{1}{4^3}+\dfrac{1}{5^2}-\dfrac{1}{6^3}+\dfrac{1}{7^2}-\dfrac{1}{8^3}+\cdots\quad$ converge? Justify your answer.

29. Suppose that $\displaystyle\sum_{j=1}^{\infty}b_j$ converges to a number S and that $b_j\geq 0$ for all $j\geq 1$. Show that $\displaystyle\sum_{j=1}^{\infty}(-1)^{j+1}b_j$ also converges.

30. Suppose that $0\leq b_{j+1}\leq b_j$ for all $j\geq 1$ and that the partial sum $\displaystyle\sum_{j=1}^{100}b_j$ approximates $S=\displaystyle\sum_{j=1}^{\infty}b_j$ within 0.005. Explain why $0\leq\displaystyle\sum_{j=1}^{\infty}(-1)^{j+1}b_j-\displaystyle\sum_{j=1}^{100}(-1)^{j+1}b_j\leq 0.005$.

31. Give an example of a convergent series $\displaystyle\sum_{k=1}^{\infty}a_k$ with the property that $\displaystyle\sum_{k=1}^{\infty}(a_k)^2$ diverges.

32. Suppose that $\displaystyle\sum_{k=1}^{\infty}a_k$ diverges. Is it possible that $\displaystyle\sum_{k=1}^{\infty}|a_k|$ converges? Justify your answer.

33. **A proof of the alternating series test.** Let $S_n=\displaystyle\sum_{k=1}^{n}(-1)^{k+1}c_k$ denote the partial sum of the first n terms of a series satisfying the hypotheses of the alternating series test (Theorem 11).

   (a) Show that the sequence of even partial sums, $S_2, S_4, S_6, S_8, \ldots$ is increasing.

   (b) Show that the sequence of odd partial sums, $S_1, S_3, S_5, S_7, \ldots,$ is decreasing.

   (c) Show that $S_{2m}\leq S_{2m-1}$ for any integer $m\geq 1$.

   (d) Use part (c) to show that the sequence of even partial sums and the sequence of odd partial sums both converge. [NOTE: Although both sequences converge, we must still show that they converge to the same limit.]

   (e) Show that $\displaystyle\lim_{m\to\infty}(S_{2m+1}-S_{2m})=0$. From this it follows that there is a real number S such that $\displaystyle\lim_{n\to\infty}S_n=S$.

   (f) Explain why $0<S-S_{2m}<c_{2m+1}$ and $0<S_{2m+1}-S<c_{2m+2}$.

11.5 POWER SERIES

A main point is to decide which values of x produce convergent series; these x form the domains of useful functions.

A **power series** is a series of the form

$$a_0+a_1(x-x_0)+a_2(x-x_0)^2+a_3(x-x_0)^3+\cdots+a_n(x-x_0)^n+\cdots=\sum_{k=0}^{\infty}a_k(x-x_0)^k.$$

Here x is a variable, the constants a_k are called the **coefficients**, and the constant x_0 is called the **base point**. For convenience we'll often use $x_0=0$; in this case the appearance is slightly simpler:

$$a_0+a_1x+a_2x^2+a_3x^3+\cdots+a_nx^n+\cdots=\sum_{k=0}^{\infty}a_kx^k.$$

A power series may converge for some values of x and diverge for others. We illustrate these words and ideas with examples.

EXAMPLE 1 **(A geometric power series)** One of the simplest and most useful power series is

$$S(x)=1+x+x^2+x^3+x^4+x^5+\cdots=\sum_{k=0}^{\infty}x^k.$$

(In this case, $x_0 = 0$ and $a_k = 1$ for all $k \geq 0$.) For which real numbers x does $S(x)$ converge?

Solution   Setting $x = 1$ gives the series

$$S(1) = 1 + 1 + 1^2 + 1^3 + 1^4 + \cdots = 1 + 1 + 1 + 1 + 1 + \cdots,$$

which clearly diverges. If, instead, $x = 1/2$, then the series converges to 2:

$$S(1/2) = 1 + \frac{1}{2} + \frac{1}{4} + \frac{1}{8} + \cdots + \frac{1}{2^n} + \cdots = 2.$$

Indeed, $S(x)$ is a geometric series (in powers of x) for *any* value of x, and so the series converges if and only if $|x| < 1$. We even know the limit:

If $|x| < 1$, then $1 + x + x^2 + x^3 + x^4 + \cdots$ converges to $\dfrac{1}{1-x}$.

Thus, $S(x)$ converges if $-1 < x < 1$ and diverges otherwise.   ■

EXAMPLE 2   We'll show in the next section that, for any number x,

$$e^x = 1 + x + \frac{x^2}{2!} + \frac{x^3}{3!} + \frac{x^4}{4!} + \cdots.$$

Interpret the right side in the language of power series. For which x does the series converge?

It's very useful for students to write both the expanded and the sigma forms of series — each version reveals different aspects of structure.

Solution   Writing the series in the form

$$1 + x + \frac{x^2}{2!} + \frac{x^3}{3!} + \cdots = \sum_{k=0}^{\infty} \frac{1}{k!} x^k$$

shows the pattern of coefficients. (Here $x_0 = 0$ and $a_k = 1/k!$.)

We'll use the ratio test to decide where the series converges. (Since the ratio test applies only to *positive* series, we'll check for *absolute* convergence.) For any input x,

$$\lim_{k \to \infty} \frac{|a_{k+1} x^{k+1}|}{|a_k x^k|} = \lim_{k \to \infty} \frac{|x|^{k+1}}{(k+1)!} \cdot \frac{k!}{|x|^k} = \lim_{k \to \infty} \frac{|x|}{k+1} = 0.$$

Recall: If a series converges with absolute value signs, then it converges without.

Because $0 < 1$, the ratio test guarantees that this series converges absolutely—and therefore also in the ordinary sense—for *all* values of x. ◄   ■

Power series and polynomials   Power series are, roughly speaking, "infinite-degree" polynomials. Notice these points of similarity:

- **The terms are power functions**   For both polynomials and power series, each summand is of the form $a_k x^k$ with k a nonnegative integer.
- **Partial sums are ordinary polynomials**   Every partial sum S_n of the power series $\sum_{k=0}^{\infty} a_k x^k$ has the form

$$S_n = a_0 + a_1 x + a_2 x^2 + a_3 x^3 + \cdots + a_n x^n,$$

The same observation applies for arbitrary base points.

that is, an ordinary polynomial of degree n.

An important proviso!

- **Easy to use**   Polynomials are easy to differentiate and integrate, term by term. So are power series—if due care is taken for convergence. ◄ We'll return soon to this theme and see why it matters.

Choosing base points   The polynomial functions

$$p(x) = 1 + 2x + 3x^2 \quad \text{and} \quad q(x) = 1 + 2(x-5) + 3(x-5)^2$$

are not much different—the q-graph is found by sliding the p-graph 5 units to the right. The differences between p and q have to do with different choices of the **base point**: q is said to be **expanded** about $x = 5$ whereas p is expanded about $x = 0$.

The same notion of base point applies to power series. For example, the two power series

$$\sum_{k=0}^{\infty} 2^k x^k \quad \text{and} \quad \sum_{k=0}^{\infty} 2^k (x-1)^k$$

are written in powers of $(x - 0)$ and powers of $(x - 1)$, and so their respective base points are $x = 0$ and $x = 1$. As with polynomials, the mathematical difference is small: The second series is the result of shifting the first series one unit to the right.

Power series as functions

Any power series

$$S(x) = \sum_{k=0}^{\infty} a_k (x - x_0)^k = a_0 + a_1(x - x_0) + a_2(x - x_0)^2 + a_3(x - x_0)^3 + \cdots$$

We continue this theme in the next section, where the calculus of series functions is the main focus.

defines, in a natural way, a *function* of x. For a given input x, $S(x)$ is the limit—if one exists—of the power series.

Domains of power series   Any function given by a "formula" in x has a natural domain: the set of x for which the formula makes sense. Power series are no different. The domain of a power series function $S(x)$ is the set of inputs x for which the series converges; this set is also called the **interval of convergence**. We've seen, for instance, that $\sum_{k=0}^{\infty} x^k$ converges for x in $(-1, 1)$, whereas $\sum_{k=0}^{\infty} x^k/k!$ converges for x in $(-\infty, \infty)$.

EXAMPLE 3   A function $S(x)$ is defined by the power series

$$S(x) = \sum_{k=0}^{\infty} 2^k x^k = 1 + 2x + 4x^2 + 8x^3 + \cdots .$$

What's the domain of S? Is a simpler formula available for S?

Solution   We *could* use the ratio test. Instead, let's think of $S(x)$ as a geometric series $1 + r + r^2 + r^3 + \cdots$, with $r = 2x$:

$$S(x) = 1 + 2x + (2x)^2 + (2x)^3 + \cdots .$$

A geometric series converges if $|r| < 1$; *this* one converges, therefore, if $|2x| < 1$, that is, if $|x| < 1/2$. In that case the limit is $1/(1 - r) = 1/(1 - 2x)$. To summarize: The power series $S(x)$ has interval of convergence $(-1/2, 1/2)$; for x in that interval,

$$S(x) = 1 + 2x + (2x)^2 + (2x)^3 + \cdots = \frac{1}{1 - 2x}.$$

Thus, the function S has the simple formula $S(x) = 1/(1 - 2x)$—but the formula holds only if $|x| < 1/2$. ∎

For calculus purposes endpoint behavior is less important than intervals of convergence, but we work through some endpoint questions for completeness.

Finding the interval of convergence   Given a power series, the first task is to find its interval of convergence. For many series, the ratio test is all that's needed. We illustrate with several (important) examples.

EXAMPLE 4   Where does $S(x) = \sum_{k=0}^{\infty}(x-5)^k$ converge?

Solution   The series is geometric in powers of $r = (x-5)$:

$$S(x) = 1 + (x-5) + (x-5)^2 + (x-5)^3 + \cdots,$$

and so it converges if (and only if) $|r| = |x-5| < 1$. Thus, the convergence interval is $(4, 6)$—the result of shifting $(-1, 1)$ five units to the right.   ∎

EXAMPLE 5   Show that $1 + 2x + 3x^2 + 4x^3 + 5x^4 + \cdots = \sum_{k=1}^{\infty} kx^{k-1}$ converges only for x in $(-1, 1)$. Guess a limit.

Solution   We'll use the ratio test to check for *absolute* convergence. The ratio of successive terms is

$$\frac{|a_{k+1}x^{k+1}|}{|a_k x^k|} = \frac{(k+1)|x|^k}{k|x|^{k-1}} = |x| \cdot \frac{k+1}{k}.$$

This ratio tends to $|x|$ as $k \to \infty$, and so the series converges absolutely if $|x| < 1$.

If $|x| = 1$, the ratio test is inconclusive. But it's easy to see that if $x = \pm 1$, then

$$\left| kx^{k-1} \right| = |k| \to \infty \quad \text{as} \quad k \to \infty.$$

Thus, by the nth term test, the series *diverges* if $x = \pm 1$. (It diverges for the same reason if $|x| > 1$.) The interval of convergence is therefore $(-1, 1)$, as claimed.

To guess a limit, let's recall from Example 1 that the equation

$$S(x) = 1 + x + x^2 + x^3 + x^4 + \cdots = \frac{1}{1-x} \tag{1}$$

We'll use the series function $S(x)$ repeatedly in later examples.

holds for $|x| < 1$. Differentiating all three quantities in Equation (1) suggests a natural guess for the limit of the series at hand:

$$S'(x) = 1 + 2x + 3x^2 + 4x^3 + \cdots = \frac{1}{(1-x)^2}.$$

With $x = 1/2$, for example, our guess is that

$$\sum_{k=1}^{\infty} k\left(\frac{1}{2}\right)^{k-1} = 1 + \frac{2}{2} + \frac{3}{4} + \frac{4}{8} + \cdots = \frac{1}{(1-1/2)^2} = 4.$$

Numerical evidence is promising: For the preceding series, $S_{20} \approx 3.999958038$.   ∎

Good questions   Our guess in Example 5 is reasonable (and correct), but it raises some good questions:

- Is it legitimate to differentiate a series term by term?
- On what interval does the resulting series converge?

- Is $S'(x)$ the correct derivative of $S(x)$?
- Can we *antidifferentiate* a series function term by term?

We explore these questions informally in the following examples and return to them more formally in the next section.

EXAMPLE 6   (Antidifferentiating a power series)   Antidifferentiating the geometric series

This example anticipates the general results of the next section.

$$S(x) = 1 + x + x^2 + x^3 + \cdots = \sum_{k=1}^{\infty} x^{k-1}$$

term by term gives the new series

$$T(x) = x + \frac{x^2}{2} + \frac{x^3}{3} + \frac{x^4}{4} + \frac{x^5}{5} + \cdots = \sum_{k=1}^{\infty} \frac{x^k}{k}.$$

Where does $T(x)$ converge? Guess a limit.

Solution   Because $S(x)$ converges for $|x| < 1$, we might expect the same of $T(x)$. The ratio test supports this guess:

$$\lim_{k \to \infty} \frac{\left| a_{k+1} x^{k+1} \right|}{\left| a_k x^k \right|} = \lim_{k \to \infty} |x| \cdot \frac{k}{k+1} = |x|,$$

and so $T(x)$ converges (absolutely) on the interval $(-1, 1)$.

What happens at the endpoints? Setting $x = \pm 1$ in $T(x)$ produces two series we've seen before:

$$T(1) = \sum_{k=1}^{\infty} \frac{1}{k}; \qquad T(-1) = \sum_{k=1}^{\infty} \frac{(-1)^k}{k}.$$

As we saw earlier, the first series diverges; the second converges conditionally (by the alternating-series theorem). Thus, T converges for x in $[-1, 1)$.

Because $T(x)$ came from $S(x)$ by antidifferentiation, it's reasonable to guess a similar relationship for limits:

$$1 + x + x^2 + x^3 + \cdots = \frac{1}{1-x} \implies x + \frac{x^2}{2} + \frac{x^3}{3} + \cdots = -\ln(1-x).$$

Numerical evidence suggests that we're right. If $x = 1/2$, the series gives $S_{20} \approx 0.69314714$; that's not far from $-\ln 1/2 \approx 0.69314718$. ∎

EXAMPLE 7   Where does the power series $\sum_{k=0}^{\infty} k! \, x^k$ converge?

A power series may converge only at its base point.

Solution   Every power series converges at its base point—in this case, $x = 0$. But if $x \neq 0$, the ratio test (applied to absolute values) gives

$$\lim_{k \to \infty} \frac{\left| a_{k+1} x^{k+1} \right|}{\left| a_k x^k \right|} = \lim_{k \to \infty} \frac{(k+1)! \, |x|^{k+1}}{k! \, |x|^k} = \lim_{k \to \infty} (k+1) \cdot |x| = \infty,$$

and so the series diverges for *all* $x \neq 0$. This power series has, in a sense, the smallest possible domain: It converges *only* if $x = 0$. ∎

Lessons from the examples

The preceding examples illustrate several useful properties of power series and their convergence sets.

In Example 7 the power series converged only at the base point $x = 0$. We'll call the set $\{0\}$ an interval of radius 0.

- **Domains are intervals**   In each example we've seen, the convergence set turned out to be an *interval*, centered at the base point. ◄ This is no accident—*every* power series converges on an interval centered at the base point. The radius of this interval is called the **radius of convergence**; it can be zero, finite, or infinite.

The ratio test shows this.

- **Any radius of convergence is possible**   Every positive number R is a possible radius of convergence for a power series. Indeed, the series $\sum_{k=0}^{\infty} x^k / R^k$ has radius of convergence precisely R. ◄

- **At endpoints, anything can happen**   The series in Example 1 converges on the *open* interval $(-1, 1)$; the series in Example 6 converges on the "half-open" interval $[-1, 1)$. In fact, an interval of convergence may include either, both, or neither of its endpoints—any combination is possible. (In practice, what matters most is the *radius* of convergence; what happens at the endpoints can be interesting, but it's usually less important.)

The following theorem summarizes our observations.

THEOREM 12   Let $S(x) = \displaystyle\sum_{k=0}^{\infty} a_k (x - x_0)^k$ be a power series. The set of x for which $S(x)$ converges is an interval centered at x_0; endpoints may or may not be contained in the interval. The radius of convergence may be zero, finite, or infinite.

The proof is basically straightforward, but it's complicated somewhat by the reference to abstract boundedness.

The idea of proof   The theorem says that if $S(x)$ converges for $x = C$, then $S(x)$ also converges for $|x| < |C|$. Suppose, for instance, that $\sum_{k=0}^{\infty} a_k x^k$ converges for $x = C = 1$. Then $\sum_{k=0}^{\infty} a_k$ converges. By the nth term test, $a_k \to 0$ as $k \to \infty$, and so the a_k's must be bounded in absolute value. This means that there is a number $M > 0$ such that $|a_k| \le M$ for all k, which implies that

$$\left| a_k x^k \right| \le M |x|^k$$

for all k. Now if $|x| < 1$, then the geometric series $\sum_{k=0}^{\infty} M |x|^k$ converges; by comparison, so does $\sum_{k=0}^{\infty} \left| a_k x^k \right|$. (A general proof for any value of C isn't much harder.)

Power series convergence, graphically   The nth partial sum of the power series $S(x) = \sum_{k=0}^{\infty} a_k x^k$ is the polynomial

$$p_n(x) = a_0 + a_1 x + a_2 x^2 + a_3 x^3 + \cdots + a_n x^n.$$

To say that the power series converges for x in $(-R, R)$ means that, for any x in that interval, there's a number $S(x)$ such that $p_n(x) \to S(x)$ as $n \to \infty$.

Sorting out exactly what this means and when it happens is a worthy challenge. Figure 1 gives a graphical sense of the situation for the geometric power series $S(x) = \sum_{k=0}^{\infty} x^k$.

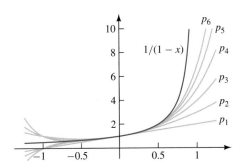

FIGURE 1

On $(-1, 1)$, $\displaystyle\sum_{k=0}^{\infty} x^k$ converges to $\dfrac{1}{1-x}$

The graphs labeled p_1 through p_6 represent the first six partial sums. Over the interval $(-1, 1)$, they appear to approach the graph of the limiting function (shown darker) more and more closely. Outside the interval $(-1, 1)$ the polynomial graphs seem to diverge, failing to approach any common limiting function.

Students can experiment graphically with partial sums of other convergent power series.

BASIC EXERCISES

1. The power series $\displaystyle\sum_{k=1}^{\infty} x^k/k$ has radius of convergence 1. Plot the partial sum polynomials of degree 1, 2, 4, 6, 8, and 10 over the interval $[-2, 2]$. Is the interval of convergence of the series apparent? Explain.

2. The power series $\displaystyle\sum_{k=1}^{\infty} (x-3)^k/k$ has radius of convergence 1. Plot the partial sum polynomials of degree 1, 2, 4, 6, 8, and 10 over the interval $[1, 5]$. Is the interval of convergence of the series apparent? Explain.

In Exercises 3–6, find the radius of convergence of the power series.

3. $\displaystyle\sum_{j=1}^{\infty} \left(\frac{x}{2}\right)^j$

4. $\displaystyle\sum_{k=1}^{\infty} \frac{x^k}{k\,3^k}$

5. $\displaystyle\sum_{k=1}^{\infty} \frac{x^k}{\sqrt{k}}$

6. $\displaystyle\sum_{n=0}^{\infty} \frac{x^n}{n!+n}$

In Exercises 7–10, find the radius and the interval of convergence of the power series.

7. $\displaystyle\sum_{n=0}^{\infty} (x-2)^n$

8. $\displaystyle\sum_{n=2}^{\infty} \frac{(x-3)^{2n}}{n^4}$

9. $\displaystyle\sum_{n=2}^{\infty} \frac{(x+5)^n}{n \ln n}$

10. $\displaystyle\sum_{n=1}^{\infty} \frac{(x+1)^n}{n}$

FURTHER EXERCISES

11. Show that $\displaystyle\sum_{k=0}^{\infty} \frac{x^k}{R^k}$ converges on $(-R, R)$, where $R > 0$ is a constant.

12. Show that $\displaystyle\sum_{k=1}^{\infty} \frac{x^k}{k R^k}$ converges on $[-R, R)$, where $R > 0$ is a constant.

13. Show that $\displaystyle\sum_{k=1}^{\infty} \frac{x^k}{k^2 R^k}$ converges on $[-R, R]$, where $R > 0$ is a constant.

14. Concoct a power series that converges on $(-R, R]$, where $R > 0$ is a constant.

In Exercises 15–20, give an example of a power series that has the given interval as its interval of convergence.
[HINT: See Exercises 11–14.]

15. $[-4, 4)$

16. $(-3, 3]$

17. $[-1, 5]$

18. $(-4, 0)$

19. $(8, 16]$

20. $[-11, -3)$

In Exercises 21–24, suppose that the power series $\sum_{k=0}^{\infty} a_k x^k$ converges only if $-2 < x \le 2$.

21. Explain why the radius of convergence of the power series is 2.

22. Explain why the power series $\sum_{k=0}^{\infty} a_k(x-1)^k$ has radius of convergence 2.

23. Show that the interval of convergence of $\sum_{k=0}^{\infty} a_k(x-3)^k$ is $(1, 5]$.

24. Find the interval of convergence of $\sum_{k=0}^{\infty} a_k(x+1)^k$.

25. Suppose that $\sum_{k=0}^{\infty} a_k(x-b)^k$ converges only if $-11 \le x < 17$.

  (a) What is the radius of convergence of the power series?

  (b) Determine the value of b.

26. Suppose that $\sum_{n=1}^{\infty} a_n$ converges and that $|x| < 1$. Show that $\sum_{n=1}^{\infty} a_n x^n$ converges absolutely.

Suppose that the power series $\sum_{k=0}^{\infty} a_k x^k$ converges if $x = -3$ and diverges if $x = 7$. In Exercises 27–32, indicate whether the statement must be true, cannot be true, or may be true. Justify your answers.

27. The power series converges if $x = -10$.

28. The power series diverges if $x = 3$.

29. The power series converges if $x = 6$.

30. The power series diverges if $x = 2$.

31. The power series diverges if $x = -7$.

32. The power series converges if $x = -4$.

Suppose that the power series $\sum_{k=0}^{\infty} a_k (x+2)^k$ converges if $x = -7$ and diverges if $x = 7$. In Exercises 33–38, indicate whether the statement must be true, cannot be true, or may be true. Justify your answers.

33. The power series converges if $x = -8$.

34. The power series converges if $x = 1$.

35. The power series converges if $x = 3$.

36. The power series diverges if $x = -11$.

37. The power series diverges if $x = 5$.

38. The power series diverges if $x = -5$.

In Exercises 39–42, let $f(x) = \sum_{n=0}^{\infty} \dfrac{2x^n}{3^n + 5}$.

39. Explain why 10 is not in the domain of f.

40. Which of the numbers 0.5, 1.5, 3, and 6 are in the domain of f? Justify your answer.

41. Estimate $f(1)$ within 0.01 of its exact value.

42. Estimate $f(-1.5)$ within 0.01 of its exact value.

In Exercises 43–46, let $h(x) = \sum_{k=0}^{\infty} \dfrac{(x-2)^k}{k! + k^3}$.

43. What is the domain of h? Justify your answer.

44. Estimate $h(0)$ within 0.005 of its exact value.

45. Estimate $h(1)$ within 0.005 of its exact value.

46. Estimate $h(3)$ within 0.005 of its exact value.

In Exercises 47–50, let $g(x) = \sum_{n=1}^{\infty} \dfrac{(x+4)^n}{n^3 5^n}$.

47. What is the domain of g?

48. Estimate $g(0)$ within 0.005 of its exact value.

49. Estimate $g(1)$ within 0.005 of its exact value.

50. Estimate $g(-5)$ within 0.005 of its exact value.

11.6   POWER SERIES AS FUNCTIONS

Here we discuss mainly the calculus of series functions. We show, too, how to find power series for some functions starting with series for other functions.

Any power series

$$S(x) = \sum_{k=0}^{\infty} a_k(x - x_0)^k = a_0 + a_1(x - x_0) + a_2(x - x_0)^2 + a_3(x - x_0)^3 + \cdots$$

can be thought of as a function of x; its domain is the series' interval of convergence—an interval centered at x_0. In this section we explore the remarkable—and useful—properties of functions defined by power series. (For simplicity we'll mainly use $x_0 = 0$.)

Calculus with power series

Given *any* power series $S(x)$, convergent or divergent, it's easy to differentiate or antidifferentiate term by term to produce *new* series we'll call $D(x)$ and $A(x)$:

$$S(x) = \sum_{k=0}^{\infty} a_k x^k = a_0 + a_1 x + a_2 x^2 + a_3 x^3 + \cdots;$$

$$D(x) = \sum_{k=1}^{\infty} k a_k x^{k-1} = a_1 + 2a_2 x + 3a_3 x^2 + \cdots;$$

$$A(x) = \sum_{k=0}^{\infty} a_k \frac{x^{k+1}}{k+1} = a_0 x + a_1 \frac{x^2}{2} + a_2 \frac{x^3}{3} + a_3 \frac{x^4}{4} + \cdots.$$

Important questions arise:

- If the series S has radius of convergence r, is the same true of D and A?
- Even if we assume that S, D, and A all converge on $(-r, r)$, must D be the derivative of S in the ordinary calculus sense? Must A be an antiderivative of S?

The following theorem answers all these questions in the affirmative. Conveniently, everything works just as we'd hope.

> **THEOREM 13 (Derivatives and antiderivatives of power series)** Let $S(x)$ be a power series with radius of convergence $r > 0$. Let $D(x)$ and $A(x)$ be defined as above.
>
> - Both D and A have radius of convergence r.
> - If $|x - x_0| < r$, $D(x) = S'(x)$.
> - If $|x - x_0| < r$, $A'(x) = S(x)$.

We omit the proof, but note that we've seen several parts of the theorem illustrated in earlier examples.

The theorem says, among other things, that a function S given by a power series is differentiable and that its derivative is another power series S' with the same radius of convergence as S. The same principle applies to S', to S'', and so on to show that S has *infinitely many* derivatives—all available by repeated term-by-term differentiation.

EXAMPLE 1 For any x, $e^x = 1 + x + \dfrac{x^2}{2!} + \dfrac{x^3}{3!} + \cdots$. Explain why.

Solution Let $S(x)$ represent the preceding series. We saw in the last section that $S(x)$ converges for *all* x. By Theorem 13, S' can be found by differentiating S term by term. In this case, differentiation produces a curious result:

Differentiating S term by term leaves S unchanged.

But *every* differentiable function S for which $S' = S$ has the form $S(x) = Ce^x$. Since $S(0) = 1$, it follows that $C = 1$; thus, $S(x) = e^x$, as claimed. ■

Students should check this derivative for themselves. Similar examples can be done with series for the sine and cosine functions, and for their hyperbolic versions.

Writing known functions as power series

In earlier examples we've written several functions, including $1/(1-x)$ and e^x, in power series form. Can *other* familiar functions be "represented" as power series? If so, how?

Theorem 13 suggests some answers. But first let's address an even *more* basic question.

Why bother? Examples with the sine function   Why write a function as a power series? What good, for instance, is the equation

$$\sin x = x - \frac{x^3}{3!} + \frac{x^5}{5!} - \frac{x^7}{7!} + \frac{x^9}{9!} - \cdots, \tag{1}$$

We'll explain in the next section why the equation holds.

One approach is to use the argument in Example 1.

which holds for all real numbers x? ◄ The next two examples suggest some answers.

Trigonometric functions lack finite algebraic formulas; power series are the next best thing. Using them lets us find approximate—but very accurate—values of trigonometric (and other transcendental) functions.

EXAMPLE 2   **(Transcendental family values)**   Use the series expression (1) to approximate $\sin 1$ accurately.

Solution   Substituting $x = 1$ into Equation (1) gives

$$\sin 1 = 1 - \frac{1}{3!} + \frac{1}{5!} - \frac{1}{7!} + \frac{1}{9!} - \frac{1}{11!} + \cdots,$$

an alternating series with terms decreasing (rapidly!) to zero. By the alternating series theorem, each partial sum S_n of such a series differs from the limit by no more than the size of the next term, a_{n+1}. In particular, the partial sum

$$1 - \frac{1}{3!} + \frac{1}{5!} - \cdots - \frac{1}{11!} \approx 0.8414709846$$

differs from $\sin 1$ by no more than $1/13! \approx 2 \times 10^{-10}$. In other words, our estimate is *guaranteed* accurate to at least nine decimal places—not bad for so little work!   ∎

As we've seen often, many integrals cannot be calculated in "closed form," by elementary antidifferentiation. Numerical methods—such as the midpoint rule—may help. Infinite series, being easy to integrate, offer another way to transcend our troubles.

EXAMPLE 3   **(Hard integrals made easy)**   Find, in series form, an antiderivative for $\sin(x^2)$. Use it to estimate $I = \int_0^1 \sin(x^2)\, dx$. (For comparison, the midpoint rule applied to I gives $M_{50} \approx 0.31025$.)

Solution   The function $\sin(x^2)$ has no *elementary* antiderivative, but it's easy to find an antiderivative in *series* form. To do so, we replace x with x^2 in the sine series (1) to produce the new series

$$\sin(x^2) = x^2 - \frac{x^6}{3!} + \frac{x^{10}}{5!} - \frac{x^{14}}{7!} + \cdots.$$

(Because the original series converges for all x, so does this one.)

It, too, converges for all x.

Antidifferentiating term by term gives yet another power series: ◄

$$\int_0^x \sin(t^2)\, dt = \frac{x^3}{3} - \frac{x^7}{7 \cdot 3!} + \frac{x^{11}}{11 \cdot 5!} - \frac{x^{15}}{15 \cdot 7!} + \cdots.$$

The result is not an elementary function, but it's an honest antiderivative for $\sin(x^2)$, and so we can find our definite integral in the obvious way:

$$\int_0^1 \sin(x^2)\, dx = \frac{x^3}{3} - \frac{x^7}{7 \cdot 3!} + \frac{x^{11}}{11 \cdot 5!} - \frac{x^{15}}{15 \cdot 7!} + \cdots \Big]_0^1$$

$$= \frac{1}{3} - \frac{1}{7 \cdot 3!} + \frac{1}{11 \cdot 5!} - \frac{1}{15 \cdot 7!} + \cdots.$$

The alternating series theorem applies to the last series, and so the estimate

$$\int_0^1 \sin(x^2)\,dx \approx \frac{1}{3} - \frac{1}{7\cdot 3!} + \frac{1}{11\cdot 5!} - \frac{1}{15\cdot 7!} \approx 0.3102681578$$

is in error by no more than $1/(19\cdot 9!) \approx 1.5 \times 10^{-7}$ (the size of the next term). The midpoint rule estimate agrees with the result through four decimal places. ∎

New series from old: Help from algebra and calculus Power series can be found for many familiar functions by applying simple algebra or calculus operations to a few standard known series. Differentiating the sine series, for instance, gives the new series

$$\cos x = 1 - \frac{x^2}{2!} + \frac{x^4}{4!} - \frac{x^6}{6!} + \cdots.$$

which, like the old one, converges for all x.

We can also start with another famous series,

$$\frac{1}{1-x} = 1 + x + x^2 + x^3 + x^4 + x^5 + \cdots, \tag{2}$$

which converges for $|x| < 1$. With a little algebraic ingenuity we can produce many other useful series, all converging on the same set. Replacing x with $-x$ in Equation (2) gives the alternating series

$$\frac{1}{1+x} = 1 - x + x^2 - x^3 + x^4 - x^5 + \cdots. \tag{3}$$

Replacing x with x^2 in Equation (3) gives still another alternating series:

$$\frac{1}{1+x^2} = 1 - x^2 + x^4 - x^6 + x^8 - x^{10} + \cdots.$$

Integrating *this* series term by term gives another striking result:

$$\arctan x = x - \frac{x^3}{3} + \frac{x^5}{5} - \frac{x^7}{7} + \frac{x^9}{9} - \cdots.$$

Setting $x = 1$ in this last series yields a *really* remarkable result:

$$\frac{\pi}{4} = 1 - \frac{1}{3} + \frac{1}{5} - \frac{1}{7} + \frac{1}{9} - \cdots.$$

(Caution is needed—these simple arguments show only that the series for $\arctan x$ is valid if $-1 < x < 1$. Showing carefully that the series converges to $\pi/4$ at the endpoint $x = 1$ requires further argument.)

Multiplying power series Convergent power series can be multiplied together, something like polynomials, to form new convergent series. As always with series, convergence is a question. Here's the answer: The product of two power series converges wherever both factors converge.

EXAMPLE 4 We've seen already that

$$\frac{1}{1-x} = 1 + x + x^2 + x^3 + \cdots \quad \text{and} \quad \frac{1}{1+x} = 1 - x + x^2 - x^3 + \cdots.$$

The final answer can also be obtained by substituting $-x^2$ for x in the first series.

Multiply these series. Where does the new series converge? What familiar function does the result represent?

Solution Symbolically, the problem looks like this:

$$\left(1 + x + x^2 + x^3 + \cdots\right) \cdot \left(1 - x + x^2 - x^3 + \cdots\right) = a_0 + a_1 x + a_2 x^2 + a_3 x^3 + \cdots .$$

We want numerical values for the constants on the right.

Both factors have infinitely many summands, and so ordinary expansion quickly gets out of hand. To avoid this, we collect like powers right from the start. It's clear, for instance, that $a_0 = 1 \cdot 1 = 1$; no other combination of factors yields a constant result. Similarly, tracking the first and second powers of x gives

$$a_1 = 1 \cdot (-1) + 1 \cdot 1 = 0; \qquad a_2 = 1 \cdot 1 + 1 \cdot (-1) + 1 \cdot 1 = 1.$$

Continuing this process reveals a simple pattern:

$$\left(1 + x + x^2 + x^3 + \cdots\right) \cdot \left(1 - x + x^2 - x^3 + \cdots\right) = 1 + x^2 + x^4 + x^6 + \cdots .$$

The result is a geometric series in powers of x^2; it converges for $|x^2| < 1$, that is, if $-1 < x < 1$.

What familiar function does the product series represent? Because the two factors represent the functions $1/(1-x)$ and $1/(1+x)$, it follows that the product *series* represents the product *function* $1/(1-x^2)$. ∎

EXAMPLE 5 Find a power series for $\ln(1+x)$; use it to estimate $\ln(1.5)$ with error guaranteed to be less than 0.0001.

Solution Integrating both sides of Equation (3) gives

$$\ln(1+x) = \int \frac{1}{1+x}\, dx = \int \left(1 - x + x^2 - x^3 + \cdots\right) dx$$

$$= x - \frac{x^2}{2} + \frac{x^3}{3} - \frac{x^4}{4} + \cdots .$$

(We used $C = 0$ as the constant of integration because our "target" function $\ln(1+x)$ has the value 0 when $x = 0$.) The new series, like the old, converges for x in $(-1, 1)$. To estimate $\ln(1.5)$ we plug in $x = 0.5$:

$$\ln(1.5) = 0.5 - \frac{0.5^2}{2} + \frac{0.5^3}{3} - \frac{0.5^4}{4} + \cdots = \sum_{k=1}^{\infty} (-1)^{k+1} \frac{0.5^k}{k} .$$

Now the alternating series theorem applies. To achieve our target accuracy, we can use any partial sum S_n for which

$$c_{n+1} = \frac{0.5^{n+1}}{n+1} < 0.0001.$$

It's easy to see that $n = 10$ works, with room to spare. In fact, $S_{10} \approx 0.405435$; this compares closely with the value $\ln 1.5 \approx 0.405465$ reported by a calculator. ∎

We'll apply Taylor's theorem in the next section; the approach of Example 1 might also be used.

A brief atlas of power series For easy reference, we collect a short list of "standard" power series for basic calculus functions. In the next section we'll see how to show rigorously that the series really converge to the stated limits.

A power series sampler		
Function	**Series**	**Convergence interval**
$\sin x$	$x - \dfrac{x^3}{3!} + \dfrac{x^5}{5!} - \dfrac{x^7}{7!} + \dfrac{x^9}{9!} - \cdots$	$(-\infty, \infty)$
$\cos x$	$1 - \dfrac{x^2}{2!} + \dfrac{x^4}{4!} - \dfrac{x^6}{6!} + \dfrac{x^8}{8!} - \cdots$	$(-\infty, \infty)$
e^x	$1 + x + \dfrac{x^2}{2!} + \dfrac{x^3}{3!} + \dfrac{x^4}{4!} + \dfrac{x^5}{5!} + \cdots$	$(-\infty, \infty)$
$\dfrac{1}{1-x}$	$1 + x + x^2 + x^3 + x^4 + x^5 + \cdots$	$(-1, 1)$
$\dfrac{1}{1+x}$	$1 - x + x^2 - x^3 + x^4 - x^5 + \cdots$	$(-1, 1)$
$\dfrac{1}{1+x^2}$	$1 - x^2 + x^4 - x^6 + x^8 - x^{10} + \cdots$	$(-1, 1)$
$\arctan x$	$x - \dfrac{x^3}{3} + \dfrac{x^5}{5} - \dfrac{x^7}{7} + \dfrac{x^9}{9} - \cdots$	$[-1, 1]$

What's next? A power series for any function

As we've seen, knowing a power series expression for one function can lead, via various manipulations, to power series for related functions. A good question remains:

Given any function f, how can we find a power series "from scratch," without knowing a related series to begin with?

We answer this question in the next section.

BASIC EXERCISES

In Exercises 1–3, $f(x) = \sum_{k=0}^{\infty} \left(\dfrac{x}{2}\right)^k$.

1. What is the radius of convergence of the power series for f?

2. According to Theorem 13, $f'(x) = \sum_{k=1}^{\infty} \dfrac{k\,x^{k-1}}{2^k}$. What is the radius of convergence of the series for f'?

3. According to Theorem 13, $F(x) = \sum_{k=0}^{\infty} \dfrac{x^{k+1}}{(k+1)\,2^k}$ is an antiderivative of f. What is the radius of convergence of the series for F?

4. Let $f(x) = \ln(1+x)$. Show that the power series for f and f' have the same radius of convergence but not the same interval of convergence.

In Exercises 5–8, use the power series representation of $1/(1-x)$ to produce a power series representation of the function f.

5. $f(x) = \dfrac{x^2}{1+x}$

6. $f(x) = \dfrac{1}{1-x^2}$

7. $f(x) = \dfrac{1}{(1+x)^2}$

8. $f(x) = \dfrac{x}{1-x^4}$

In Exercises 9–12, find a power series representation of the function and the radius of convergence of the power series. Then plot the function and the fifth-order polynomial that is a partial sum of the power series on the same axes. [HINT: Write out the first few terms of the series before trying to find the form of the general term.]

9. $f(x) = \arctan(2x)$

10. $f(x) = \cos(x^2)$

11. $f(x) = x^2 \sin x$

12. $f(x) = \ln\left(1 + \sqrt[3]{x}\right)$

13. Use the partial sum of a series to estimate $1/\sqrt{e}$ with an error less than 0.005.

14. Use the partial sum of a series to estimate $\int_0^{0.2} xe^{-x^3}\,dx$ with an error less than 10^{-5}.

15. Use power series to show that $\lim\limits_{x \to 0} \dfrac{(\sin x - x)^3}{x\,(1-\cos x)^4} = -\dfrac{2}{27}$.

16. Show that $\lim\limits_{x \to 0^+} \dfrac{x - \sin x}{(x \sin x)^{3/2}} = \dfrac{1}{6}$.

FURTHER EXERCISES

In Exercises 17–22, find a power-series representation of the function and the radius of convergence of the power series.

17. $f(x) = \dfrac{1}{2+x}$

18. $f(x) = \sin\left(\sqrt{x}\right)$

19. $f(x) = \sin x + \cos x$

20. $f(x) = \ln\left(1 + x^2\right)$

21. $f(x) = (x^2 - 1)\sin x$

22. $f(x) = \ln\left(\dfrac{1+x}{1-x}\right)$

23. Use power series to show that $y = e^x$ is a solution of the DE $y' = y$.

24. Use power series to show that $y = 2e^x$ is the solution of the IVP $y' = y$, $y(0) = 2$.

25. Use power series to show that $y = e^{3x}$ is the solution of the IVP $y' = 3y$, $y(0) = 1$.

26. Use power series to show that $y = \sin x$ is a solution of the DE $y'' = -y$.

27. Use power series to show that $y = 1/(1-x)$ is the solution of the IVP $y' = y^2$, $y(0) = 1$.

28. (a) Show that $f(x) = \tan x$ is the solution of the IVP $f'(x) = 1 + \left(f(x)\right)^2$, $f(0) = 0$.

(b) Use part (a) to find the first four nonzero terms in the power series representation of $\tan x$.

In Exercises 29–34, use power series to evaluate the limit. Check your answer using l'Hôpital's rule.

29. $\lim\limits_{x \to 0} \dfrac{\sin x}{x}$

30. $\lim\limits_{x \to 0} \dfrac{e^x - 1}{x}$

31. $\lim\limits_{x \to 0} \dfrac{1 - \cos x}{x^2}$

32. $\lim\limits_{x \to 0} \dfrac{\arctan x}{x}$

33. $\lim\limits_{x \to 0} \dfrac{\ln(1+x) - x}{x^2}$

34. $\lim\limits_{x \to 0} \dfrac{1 - \cos^2 x}{x}$ [HINT: $1 - \cos^2 x = \left(1 - \cos(2x)\right)/2$.]

35. Evaluate $\sum\limits_{n=1}^{\infty} \dfrac{n}{2^n}$ exactly. [HINT: If $f(x) = \sum\limits_{n=0}^{\infty} x^n$, then $f'(x) = \sum\limits_{n=1}^{\infty} n x^{n-1}$.]

36. Show that $\dfrac{1}{x-1} = \sum\limits_{k=1}^{\infty} \dfrac{1}{x^k}$ if $|x| > 1$.

[HINT: $1/(x-1) = x/(x-1) - 1$.]

37. (a) Use the formula for the sum of a geometric series to show that

$$\sum_{k=1}^{\infty} \dfrac{x^k}{k} = -\ln|1-x|.$$

(b) What is the interval of convergence of the series in part (a)?

(c) Show that if $N \geq 1$, then

$$0 < \ln 2 - \sum_{k=1}^{N} \dfrac{1}{k\,2^k} \leq \dfrac{1}{(N+1)2^N}.$$

[HINT: $-\ln(1/2) = \ln 2$.]

38. Use a power series to show that $x - x^2/2 < \ln(1+x) < x$ for all x in the interval $(0, 1)$.

39. Use power series to show that $1 - \cos x < \ln(1+x) < \sin x$ if $0 < x < 1$.

40. Let $f(x) = \dfrac{1}{1+x^4}$.

(a) Find a power series representation of f.

(b) What is the interval of convergence of the series in part (a)?

(c) Use the series found in part (a) to evaluate $\int_0^{0.5} f(x)\,dx$ with an error no greater than 0.001.

41. (a) Find the power series representation of an antiderivative of e^{-x^2}.

(b) Use the result from part (a) to estimate $\int_0^1 e^{-x^2}\,dx$ within 0.005 of its exact value.

42. Estimate $\int_0^1 \cos(x^2)\,dx$ with an error no greater than 0.005.

43. Estimate $\int_0^1 \sqrt{x}\,\sin x\,dx$ with an error no greater than 0.001.

44. Estimate $\int_0^{1000} \dfrac{e^{-10x}\,\sin x}{x}\,dx$ with an error no greater than 5×10^{-5}.

In Exercises 45–50, find the first four nonzero terms in the power series representation of the function.

45. $f(x) = e^{2x} \ln(1 + x^3)$

46. $f(x) = \arctan x \sin(4x)$

47. $f(x) = \dfrac{e^x}{1 - x}$

48. $f(x) = \dfrac{\cos x}{1 + x^2}$

49. $f(x) = e^{\sin x}$

50. $f(x) = \ln(1 + \sin x)$

In Exercises 51–54, find the elementary function represented by the power series by manipulating a more familiar power series (e.g., the series for $\cos x$, $\sin x$, $(1 - x)^{-1}$).

51. $\displaystyle\sum_{k=1}^{\infty} k x^{k-1}$

52. $\displaystyle\sum_{k=0}^{\infty} \dfrac{x^k}{(k+1)!}$

53. $\displaystyle\sum_{k=1}^{\infty} (-1)^{k+1} x^k$

54. $\displaystyle\sum_{k=1}^{\infty} \dfrac{(2x)^k}{k}$

11.7 TAYLOR SERIES

We discussed Taylor polynomials in Section 9.1. Here we take the next step to Taylor series (and provide some reminders).

In the preceding section we saw some of the practical advantages of writing a function as a power series. We also saw ways of using a power series for one function to derive power series for other functions. In this section we show, given a suitable function, how to find its power series "from scratch" by matching derivatives. The idea is not new—we did the same thing in Section 9.1, where we found Taylor polynomials. Here we extend these ideas to find **Taylor series**—"infinite Taylor polynomials."

Does every function have a power series? Mathematical life would be simpler if *every* function $f(x)$ could be written as a power series—ideally, a series that converges to $f(x)$ for all x. Alas, it isn't so. At least two things can go wrong:

- **Smaller domains** A power series may have a smaller domain than the function it represents. For instance, the series equation

$$\frac{1}{1 + x^2} = 1 - x^2 + x^4 - x^6 + x^8 - x^{10} + \cdots$$

holds if—but only if—$|x| < 1$, even though the left side is defined (and well behaved) for *all* real numbers x.

Students often miss this important point.

- **No series at all** A function may have no series at all. As Theorem 13 (page 591) says, every power series can be differentiated repeatedly on its interval of convergence. ➡ Thus, a function that *has* a power series with base point $x = x_0$ must itself be repeatedly differentiable at $x = x_0$. This means, for instance, that $f(x) = |x|$ (which is not differentiable at $x = 0$) has *no* power series with base point $x = 0$.

Each derivative is another power series.

Coefficients and derivatives at the base point

A simple equation relates coefficients and derivatives of a power series. (We saw the same principle at work for Taylor polynomials.) If

$$S(x) = a_0 + a_1(x - x_0) + a_2(x - x_0)^2 + a_3(x - x_0)^3 + a_4(x - x_0)^4 + \cdots,$$

then, clearly, $S(x_0) = a_0$. Differentiating S repeatedly gives

$$S'(x) = a_1 + 2a_2(x - x_0) + 3a_3(x - x_0)^2 + 4a_4(x - x_0)^3 + \cdots;$$

$$S''(x) = 2a_2 + 6a_3(x - x_0) + 12a_4(x - x_0)^2 + \cdots;$$

$$S'''(x) = 6a_3 + 24a_4(x - x_0) + \cdots;$$

$$\vdots$$

These equations show that

$$S(x_0) = a_0; \quad S'(x_0) = a_1; \quad S''(x_0) = 2a_2; \quad S'''(x_0) = 6a_3; \quad \dots.$$

*The Fact resembles
Theorem 1, page 496.*

The following Fact captures the general pattern: ◄

FACT If $S(x) = \sum_{k=0}^{\infty} a_k(x - x_0)^k$, then $a_k = \dfrac{S^{(k)}(x_0)}{k!}$ for all $k \geq 0$.

This Fact amounts to a recipe for cooking up a power series for a given function expanded about a given base point x_0.

EXAMPLE 1 Assuming that $f(x) = \sin x$ *has* a power series based at $x = 0$, *find it.*

Solution To find the desired series

$$f(x) = a_0 + a_1 x + a_2 x^2 + a_3 x^3 + \cdots,$$

we need "only" find the coefficients $a_0, a_1, a_2, a_3, \dots$. Finding infinitely many of *anything* sounds difficult, but in this case it's easier than it seems. For the sine function (and for many functions of interest) the coefficients follow a simple pattern. The first few derivatives of $f(x) = \sin x$ reveal the pattern:

$$f(0), f'(0), f''(0), f'''(0), f^{(4)}(0), \dots = 0, 1, 0, -1, 0, \dots.$$

By the preceding Fact, the series coefficients have a similar pattern:

$$a_0, a_1, a_2, a_3, a_4, a_5, a_6, \dots = 0, 1, 0, -\frac{1}{3!}, 0, \frac{1}{5!}, 0, \dots.$$

Thus, the sine series is the one we've seen before:

$$\sin x = x - \frac{x^3}{3!} + \frac{x^5}{5!} - \frac{x^7}{7!} + \cdots.$$

It's not hard (using the ratio test) to show that this series converges for *all* x, as we'd hope. ■

Taylor series

Using the preceding Fact as a recipe for the coefficients, we can write a power series for *any* function f that has repeated derivatives at $x = x_0$.

DEFINITION (Taylor series) Let f be any function with infinitely many derivatives at $x = x_0$. The **Taylor series** for f is the series $\sum_{k=0}^{\infty} a_k(x - x_0)^k$ with coefficients given by

$$a_k = \frac{f^{(k)}(x_0)}{k!}, \quad k = 0, 1, 2, \dots.$$

If $x_0 = 0$, then the series looks a little simpler; such series are called **Maclaurin series** after the 17th-century Scottish mathematician Colin Maclaurin.

EXAMPLE 2 The function $f(x) = \ln x$ is not defined at $x = 0$, and so there's no Maclaurin series. Expand f about $x = 1$.

Solution Derivatives of $f(x) = \ln x$ are easy for either a human or a machine to calculate. Here are several:

$$f'(x) = \frac{1}{x}; \quad f''(x) = -\frac{1}{x^2}; \quad f'''(x) = \frac{2}{x^3}; \quad f^{(4)}(x) = -\frac{6}{x^4}.$$

At $x = 1$, therefore, we have

$$f(1) = 0; \quad f'(1) = 1; \quad f''(1) = -1; \quad f'''(1) = 2; \quad f^{(4)}(1) = -6, \quad \ldots,$$

so the Taylor coefficients are

$$a_0 = 0; \quad a_1 = 1; \quad a_2 = -\frac{1}{2}; \quad a_3 = \frac{1}{3}; \quad a_4 = -\frac{1}{4}; \quad \ldots.$$

The Taylor series is therefore

$$(x-1) - \frac{(x-1)^2}{2} + \frac{(x-1)^3}{3} - \frac{(x-1)^4}{4} + \cdots = \sum_{k=1}^{\infty} \frac{(-1)^{k+1}}{k}(x-1)^k. \quad \blacksquare$$

Finding Taylor series: Help from technology Computing the necessary derivatives to find a Taylor series by hand can be tedious and error prone. Technology can help. The following, for instance, is how one computer algebra system finds Taylor polynomials (partial sums of Taylor series) in the cases illustrated in the preceding examples:

```
> taylorpoly( sin(x), x=0, 7 );
              3         5           7
       x - 1/6 x + 1/120 x - 1/5040 x
> taylorpoly( ln(x), x=1, 7 );
                  2         3           4
    x - 1 - 1/2 (x - 1) + 1/3 (x - 1) - 1/4 (x - 1)
                  5         6           7
      + 1/5 (x - 1) - 1/6 (x - 1) + 1/7 (x - 1)
```

Converging to the right place: Taylor's theorem

Any function f that's infinitely differentiable at $x = x_0$ has a Taylor series—ideally, one with a large radius of convergence. One possible problem remains: The series might converge at x but perhaps to a limit *other* than $f(x)$.

Taylor's theorem guarantees that this unfortunate event seldom occurs. We met Taylor's theorem in Section 9.2 (see Theorem 2, page 504); we used it there to predict how closely a Taylor polynomial approximates its "target" function f. That question is relevant here because Taylor *polynomials* are partial sums of Taylor *series*.

Having seen Taylor's theorem earlier should help students master this relatively technical circle of ideas.

THEOREM 14 (Taylor's theorem) Suppose that f is repeatedly differentiable on an interval I containing x_0 and that

$$P_n(x) = a_0 + a_1(x - x_0) + a_2(x - x_0)^2 + \cdots + a_n(x - x_0)^n$$

is the nth-order Taylor polynomial based at x_0. Suppose that for all x in I,

$$\left| f^{(n+1)}(x) \right| \le K_{n+1}.$$

Then $\left| f(x) - P_n(x) \right| \le \dfrac{K_{n+1}}{(n+1)!} |x - x_0|^{n+1}.$

Observe:

- **Estimating difference** Taylor's theorem estimates the *difference* between $f(x)$ and $P_n(x)$. Unless K_{n+1} grows very quickly with n, this difference tends to 0 as $n \to \infty$, and so the series converges to $f(x)$.

- **Why does it hold?** We discussed the theorem's proof at length in Section 9.2; an important ingredient is the mean value theorem.

EXAMPLE 3 For $f(x) = \sin x$, show that the Maclaurin series converges to $\sin x$ for *every* value of x.

Solution For $f(x) = \sin x$, derivatives of *all* orders are sines or cosines or their opposites, and so the inequality

$$\left| f^{(n+1)}(x) \right| \leq 1$$

holds for all x and for all n. Thus, we can use $K_{n+1} = 1$ for all n in Taylor's theorem:

$$\left| \sin x - P_n(x) \right| \leq \frac{1 \cdot |x|^{n+1}}{(n+1)!}.$$

The last quantity tends to 0 as $n \to \infty$, regardless of the value of x. Hence, the series converges, for all x, to $\sin x$. The graphs in Figure 1 suggest what this convergence means geometrically. ◄

The same figure appears, with additional comments, on page 500.

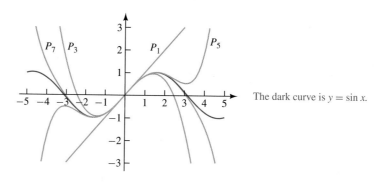

The dark curve is $y = \sin x$.

FIGURE 1
Maclaurin polynomials converging to $f(x) = \sin x$

Notice how the higher-order Maclaurin polynomials approximate the sine function better than lower-order ones. For instance, P_7, "sticks with" the sine curve much farther than P_1 or P_3. ∎

BASIC EXERCISES

1. Let $f(x) = \int_3^x \sqrt{t} e^{-t} \, dt$.

   (a) Show that if $x \approx 3$, then

$$f(x) \approx \sqrt{3} e^{-3}(x-3) - \frac{5}{12}\sqrt{3}e^{-3}(x-3)^2 + \frac{23}{216}\sqrt{3}e^{-3}(x-3)^3.$$

   (b) Use Theorem 14 to bound the error made when $f(3.5)$ is estimated using the polynomial in part (a).

2. Let $f(x) = \sqrt{1+x}$.

   (a) Find the first three nonzero terms in the Maclaurin series for f.

   (b) Use Theorem 14 to bound the approximation error made if the Maclaurin polynomial from part (a) is used to estimate $f(1)$.

3. Let $f(x) = e^{2x}$. What is the coefficient of x^{100} in the Maclaurin series representation of f?

4. Let $f(x) = \dfrac{x}{1 - x^3}$.

   (a) Find the Maclaurin series for $f(x)$.

   (b) What is the interval of convergence of the series in part (a)?

   (c) Use part (a) to find a power series for $f''(x)$.

   (d) Use part (a) to find the Maclaurin series for $\displaystyle\int_0^x f(t)\,dt$.

5. (a) Find the Maclaurin series representation of $f(x) = \dfrac{1}{2+x}$. [HINT: $\dfrac{1}{2+x} = \dfrac{1}{2} \cdot \dfrac{1}{1+(x/2)}$.]

   (b) Find $f^{(259)}(0)$ exactly.

6. Suppose that f is a function such that $f(1) = 1$, $f'(1) = 2$, and $f''(x) = 1/(1 + x^3)$ for $x > -1$.

   (a) Estimate $f(1.5)$ using a quadratic Taylor polynomial.

   (b) Find an upper bound on the approximation error made in part (a).

FURTHER EXERCISES

7. Use Theorem 14 to show that the Maclaurin series for e^x converges to e^x for all x.

8. Use Theorem 13 to show that the Maclaurin series for $1/(1 + x)$ converges to $1/(1 + x)$ if $-1/2 < x < 1$. [HINT: Consider the cases $-1/2 < x < 0$ and $0 \le x < 1$ separately.]

9. Suppose that f is a function such that $f^{(n)}$ exists for all $n \ge 1$.

   (a) Explain why the Maclaurin series for f converges to f if $\left| f^{(n)}(x) \right| \le n$ for all $n \ge 1$ and all x.

   (b) Does Theorem 13 guarantee that the Maclaurin series for f converges to f if $\left| f^{(n)}(x) \right| \le 2^n$ for all $n \ge 1$ and all x?

10. Let $f(x) = \begin{cases} \dfrac{1 - \cos x}{x^2} & \text{if } x \ne 0, \\ \dfrac{1}{2} & \text{if } x = 0. \end{cases}$ Evaluate $f^{(100)}(0)$.

11. Let $f(x) = \begin{cases} x^{-1} \sin x & \text{if } x \ne 0, \\ 1 & \text{if } x = 0. \end{cases}$

   (a) Find the Maclaurin series representation of f.

   (b) What is the interval of convergence of the power series found in part (a)?

   (c) Use the series in part (a) to estimate $f'''(1)$ with an error no greater than 0.005.

12. Let $f(x) = \begin{cases} e^{-1/x^2} & \text{if } x \ne 0, \\ 0 & \text{if } x = 0. \end{cases}$

   (a) Use the definition of the derivative (and l'Hôpital's rule) to show that $f'(0) = 0$.

   (b) Using methods similar to those in part (a), it can be shown that $f^{(k)}(0) = 0$ for all integers $k \ge 0$. Use this fact to find the Maclaurin series for f.

   (c) What is the radius of convergence of the series in part (b)?

   (d) For which values of x does the series in part (b) converge to $f(x)$?

Sequences Infinite series are formed by adding—in a special sense and with due care for convergence—the terms of an infinite **sequence**. To get started, we defined and studied sequences and their limits in their own right.

Series and convergence An infinite series **converges** if its sequence of partial sums, S_n, formed from only finitely many terms, converge to a limit S. For a given series, the sequence of partial sums may be hard to understand or handle directly. For **geometric series**, however, partial sums (and therefore limits) are easy to calculate. Geometric series are our simplest and most important examples.

Convergence tests The first question to ask about a series is whether it converges or diverges. As with improper integrals, the question can be subtle. To answer it, we developed several tests for convergence and divergence, including the **comparison test**, the **integral test**, and the **ratio test**. All of these tests apply only to series of **nonnegative** terms.

Absolute convergence Series that contain both positive and negative terms need special care; they raise the notions of **absolute** versus **conditional** convergence. The **alternating series test** handles certain series with terms that alternate in sign.

11
SUMMARY

Estimating limits Many convergent series are difficult to sum exactly. With help from technology, we can calculate specific partial sums and then estimate the error committed in ignoring the **upper tail**.

Series as functions "Infinite polynomials"—**power series**—are useful and convenient; many standard calculus functions can be written in power series form. Power series, their **intervals of convergence**, and their uses are the subjects of the last two sections of the chapter.

Taylor series; Taylor's theorem Taylor series, constructed by matching derivatives of a target function to those of a power series, give useful "formulas" for many calculus functions, including transcendental ones such as $\sin x$ and e^x. **Taylor's theorem** guarantees that, given appropriate conditions, the Taylor series of a function converges to the "right place"—the value $f(x)$.

REVIEW EXERCISES

In Exercises 1–8, find the limit of the sequence or explain why the limit does not exist.

1. $a_k = \left(\dfrac{\pi}{e}\right)^k$

2. $a_k = e^{-k}$

3. $a_k = (\arcsin 1)^k$

4. $a_k = \dfrac{k}{\sqrt{k}+10}$

5. $a_n = \dfrac{n+2}{n^3+4}$

6. $a_k = \dfrac{\ln(1+k^2)}{\ln(4+3k)}$

7. $a_k = \dfrac{\cos k}{\ln(k+1)}$

8. $a_k = e^{-k}\sin k$

In Exercises 9–34, determine whether the series converges absolutely, converges conditionally, or diverges. If the series converges, find an upper bound on its limit. If the series diverges, explain why.

9. $\displaystyle\sum_{k=0}^{\infty}\left(\dfrac{1}{k!}\right)^2$

10. $\displaystyle\sum_{n=3}^{\infty}\dfrac{1}{n(\ln n)^3}$

11. $\displaystyle\sum_{n=1}^{\infty}\left(\sum_{k=1}^{n}k^{-1}\right)$

12. $1-\dfrac{1}{2}+\dfrac{1}{2}-\dfrac{1}{4}+\dfrac{1}{3}-\dfrac{1}{6}+\dfrac{1}{4}-\dfrac{1}{8}+\dfrac{1}{5}-\dfrac{1}{10}+\cdots$

13. $\displaystyle\sum_{j=1}^{\infty}\dfrac{j}{5^j}$

14. $\displaystyle\sum_{j=1}^{\infty}\dfrac{j}{j^4+j-1}$

15. $\displaystyle\sum_{m=0}^{\infty}e^{-m^2}$

16. $\displaystyle\sum_{m=1}^{\infty}\dfrac{m^3}{m^4-7}$

17. $\displaystyle\sum_{k=1}^{\infty}\dfrac{k!}{(k+1)!-1}$

18. $\displaystyle\sum_{j=2}^{\infty}\dfrac{\ln j}{j^2}$

19. $\displaystyle\sum_{k=1}^{\infty}\dfrac{\sqrt{k}}{k^2+1}$

20. $\displaystyle\sum_{k=0}^{\infty}\dfrac{(-2)^k}{7^k+k}$

21. $\displaystyle\sum_{k=0}^{\infty}\dfrac{(-1)^k}{(k+1)\,2^k}$

22. $\displaystyle\sum_{m=8}^{\infty}\dfrac{\sin m}{m^3}$

23. $\displaystyle\sum_{n=1}^{\infty}\dfrac{\cos(n\pi)}{n}$

24. $\displaystyle\sum_{k=0}^{\infty}\dfrac{(-3)^k}{k^3+3^k}$

25. $\displaystyle\sum_{k=1}^{\infty}\dfrac{k^\pi}{k^e}$

26. $\displaystyle\sum_{m=2}^{\infty}\dfrac{1}{(\ln 3)^m}$

27. $\displaystyle\sum_{j=0}^{\infty}\left(\dfrac{1}{2^j}+\dfrac{1}{3^j}\right)^2$

28. $\displaystyle\sum_{k=1}^{\infty}\left(\int_k^{k+1}\dfrac{dx}{x^2}\right)$

29. $\displaystyle\sum_{m=0}^{\infty}\left(\int_0^m e^{-x^2}\,dx\right)$

30. $\displaystyle\sum_{n=1}^{\infty}\dfrac{\ln n}{\ln(3+n^2)}$

31. $\displaystyle\sum_{n=1}^{\infty}\sin(1/n)$

32. $\displaystyle\sum_{n=1}^{\infty}\dfrac{\sin(1/n)}{n}$

33. $\displaystyle\sum_{n=1}^{\infty}e^{-1/n}$

34. $\displaystyle\sum_{n=1}^{\infty}\left(1-e^{-1/n}\right)$

35. (a) Estimate a lower bound for $n!$ by comparing $\ln(n!)$ and $\displaystyle\int_1^n \ln x\,dx$.

(b) Let b be a positive number. Use part (a) to find an integer N such that $b^N/N! < 1/2$.

36. Let $a_k = \displaystyle\int_k^{\infty}\dfrac{dx}{2x^2-1}$.

(a) Evaluate $\displaystyle\lim_{k\to\infty} a_k$.   [HINT: $1/2x^2 \le 1/(2x^2-1) \le 1/x^2$ if $x \ge 1$.]

(b) Does $\displaystyle\sum_{k=1}^{\infty}(-1)^{k+1}a_k$ converge absolutely? Justify your answer.

(c) Does $\displaystyle\sum_{k=1}^{\infty}(-1)^{k+1}a_k$ converge? Justify your answer.

In Exercises 37–48, find the interval of convergence (endpoint behavior too!) of the power series.

37. $\sum_{m=1}^{\infty} \frac{x^m}{m^2+1}$

38. $\sum_{n=1}^{\infty} n^n x^n$

39. $\sum_{k=1}^{\infty} (3x)^k$

40. $\sum_{m=0}^{\infty} \frac{(3x)^m}{m!}$

41. $\sum_{n=1}^{\infty} \frac{(3x)^n}{n}$

42. $\sum_{j=1}^{\infty} \frac{(3x)^j}{j^2}$

43. $\sum_{m=0}^{\infty} \left(\frac{x-3}{2}\right)^m$

44. $\sum_{j=0}^{\infty} \frac{(x-2)^j}{j!}$

45. $\sum_{k=1}^{\infty} \frac{(x-1)^k}{k4^k}$

46. $\sum_{n=1}^{\infty} \frac{(x-1)^n}{\sqrt{n}}$

47. $\sum_{i=1}^{\infty} \frac{(x+5)^i}{i(i+1)}$

48. $\sum_{m=1}^{\infty} \frac{2^m(x-1)^m}{m}$

Consider a power series of the form $\sum_{k=0}^{\infty} a_k (x-1)^k$. In Exercises 49–53, indicate whether the statement **must** *be true,* **cannot** *be true, or* **may** *be true. Justify your answers.*

49. The power series converges only if $|x| > 2$.

50. The power series converges for all values of x.

51. If the radius of convergence of the power series is 3, the power series converges if $-2 < x < 4$.

52. The interval of convergence of the power series is $[-5, 5]$.

53. If the interval of convergence of the power series is $(-7, 9)$, the radius of convergence is 7.

54. (a) Evaluate $\lim_{x \to 1^-} \sum_{k=0}^{\infty} (-1)^k x^k$.

(b) Explain why the result in part (a) does *not* mean that $\sum_{k=0}^{\infty} (-1)^k$ converges.

In Exercises 55–58, use power series to evaluate the limit. Check your answers using l'Hôpital's rule.

55. $\lim_{x \to 0} \frac{1 - \cos x}{x}$

56. $\lim_{x \to 0} \frac{e^x - e^{-x}}{x}$

57. $\lim_{x \to 0} \frac{x - \arctan x}{x^3}$

58. $\lim_{x \to 1} \frac{\ln x}{x - 1}$

In Exercises 59–62, find the Maclaurin series for f and determine its radius of convergence.

59. $f(x) = 2^x = e^{x \ln 2}$

60. $f(x) = \cos^2 x = \frac{1}{2}(1 + \cos(2x))$

61. $f(x) = \frac{5+x}{x^2+x-2} = \frac{2}{x-1} - \frac{1}{x+2}$

62. $f(x) = \sin^3(x) = \frac{1}{4}(3 \sin x - \sin(3x))$

63. Determine the coefficients a_k such that $\frac{1}{1-x} = \sum_{k=0}^{\infty} a_k (x-2)^k$.
[HINT: $\frac{1}{1-x} = -\frac{1}{1+(x-2)}$.]

64. Is $1 - x + \frac{x^2}{2} - \frac{x^4}{8} + \frac{x^5}{15} - \frac{x^6}{240} + \cdots$ the Maclaurin series representation of the function f shown in the graph below? Justify your answer.

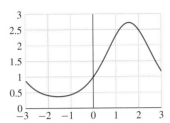

65. Suppose that f is a function that is positive, increasing, and concave down on the interval $[-2, 2]$.

(a) Is the coefficient of x^2 in the Maclaurin series representation of f positive? Justify your answer.

(b) Let $g(x) = 1/\sqrt{1 + f(x)}$. Is the coefficient of x^2 in the Maclaurin series representation of g positive? Justify your answer.

66. Let $H_n = \sum_{k=1}^{n} \frac{1}{k}$ be the nth partial sum of the harmonic series, let $a_n = H_n - \ln n$, and let $f(x) = \ln(x+1) - \ln x - \frac{1}{x+1}$.

(a) Show that $\ln(n+1) < H_n < 1 + \ln n$.
[HINT: Use the integral test.]

(b) Show that the sequence $\{a_n\}$ is decreasing.
[HINT: Explain why $\ln(n+1) - \ln n = \int_n^{n+1} x^{-1} dx > (n+1)^{-1}$.]

(c) Use part (c) to show that $\lim_{n \to \infty} a_n$ exists. (This limit, denoted by γ, is called **Euler's constant**; $\gamma \approx 0.57722$.)

(d) Show that $f(x) = -\int_x^{\infty} f'(t) dt$.

(e) Use part (d) to show that $f(x) > \frac{1}{2(x+1)^2}$.
[HINT: If $x > 0$, then $-f'(x) = \frac{1}{x(x+1)^2} > \frac{1}{(x+1)^3}$.]

(f) Show that $a_n - \gamma = \sum_{k=n}^{\infty} (a_k - a_{k+1})$.

(g) Use parts (e) and (f) to show that $\frac{1}{2(n+1)} < a_n - \gamma < \frac{1}{2n}$.
[HINT: $f(k) = a_k - a_{k+1}$.]

Exercises 67–76 explore some properties of the **binomial series**:

$$(1+x)^r = 1 + \sum_{n=1}^{\infty} \frac{r(r-1)(r-2)\cdots(r-n+1)}{n!} x^n,$$

where r is a constant.

67. Show that the binomial series converges if $|x| < 1$.

68. Show that $\sqrt{1+x} \approx 1 + \frac{1}{2}x - \frac{1}{8}x^2 + \frac{1}{16}x^3 - \frac{5}{128}x^4 + \frac{7}{256}x^5 \mp \cdots$.

In Exercises 69–72, find the first four nonzero terms of a power series representation of the function.

69. $f(x) = (1+x^4)^3$

70. $f(x) = \sqrt[3]{1-x^2}$

71. $f(x) = (1+x^2)^{-3/2}$

72. $f(x) = \arcsin x$.

73. Estimate $\int_0^{0.4} \sqrt{1+x^3}\,dx$ with an error less than 5×10^{-4}.

74. Let $f(x) = (1+x)^r$.

(a) Show that $(1+x)f'(x) = rf(x)$.

(b) Let $g(x) = (1+x)^{-r}f(x)$. Show that $g'(x) = 0$.

(c) Use part (b) to show that $f(x) = (1+x)^r$.

75. (a) Show that
$$\arcsin x = \int_0^x \frac{dt}{\sqrt{1-t^2}} = x + \sum_{n=1}^{\infty} \frac{1\cdot 3\cdot 5 \cdots (2n-1)}{2\cdot 4\cdot 6 \cdots (2n)} \frac{x^{2n+1}}{2n+1}.$$

(b) If $n \geq 1$ is an integer, then $\int_0^{\pi/2} \sin^{2n+1} x\,dx = \frac{2\cdot 4\cdot 6 \cdots (2n)}{3\cdot 5\cdot 7 \cdots (2n+1)}$. Use this fact to evaluate $\int_0^1 \frac{x^{2n+1}}{\sqrt{1-x^2}}\,dx$.

(c) Use parts (a) and (b) to show that $\int_0^1 \frac{\arcsin x}{\sqrt{1-x^2}}\,dx = \sum_{k=0}^{\infty} \frac{1}{(2k+1)^2}$.

(d) Use the substitution $u = \arcsin x$ to show that $\int_0^1 \frac{\arcsin x}{\sqrt{1-x^2}}\,dx = \frac{\pi^2}{8}$.

(e) Use parts (c) and (d) to show that $\sum_{k=1}^{\infty} \frac{1}{k^2} = \frac{\pi^2}{6}$.

76. Let $f(x) = (1+x)^r$. In this exercise we prove that the binomial series converges to f.

(a) Use part (e) of Exercise 19 in Section 9.2 to show that $R_n(x) = f(x) - P_n(x)$ is $R_n(x) = \frac{r\cdot(r-1)\cdot(r-2)\cdots(r-n)}{n!} \int_0^x \frac{(x-t)^n}{(1+t)^{n+1-r}}\,dt$.

(b) Suppose that $0 \leq t \leq x < 1$. Show that $\frac{|x-t|}{1+t} \leq |x|$.

(c) Use part (b) to show that if $0 \leq x < 1$, then $|R_n(x)| \leq \frac{|(r-1)\cdot(r-2)\cdots(r-n)|}{n!} x^n \left|(1+x)^r - 1\right|$.

(d) Use part (c) to show that the binomial series converges to f if $0 \leq x < 1$.

(e) Adapt the reasoning in parts (b)–(d) to show that the binomial series converges to f if $-1 < x < 0$.

77. **(A proof that e is irrational.)** Assume that $e = m/n$, where m and n are positive integers.

(a) Explain why $m! \left| \frac{1}{e} - \sum_{k=0}^{m} \frac{(-1)^k}{k!} \right| \leq \frac{m!}{(m+1)!} = \frac{1}{m+1}$.

(b) Explain why $m!/e$ is an integer.

(c) Explain why $m! \sum_{k=0}^{m} \frac{(-1)^k}{k!}$ is an integer.

[HINT: Start by explaining why $m!/k!$ is an integer if k is an integer and $0 \leq k \leq m$.]

(d) Parts (a)–(c) imply that $N = m! \left| \frac{1}{e} - \sum_{k=0}^{m} \frac{(-1)^k}{k!} \right|$ is an integer that is less than or equal to $1/(m+1)$. Explain why it follows that $N = 0$.

(e) Explain why the conclusion of part (d) is impossible and therefore e cannot be a rational number.

[HINT: $\sum_{k=m+1}^{\infty} (-1)^k/k! \neq 0$.]

78. **(Cauchy condensation theorem.)** Let $\sum_{n=1}^{\infty} a_n$ be a series of positive terms such that $a_{n+1} \leq a_n$ for all n.

(a) Let $m \geq 1$ be an integer. Explain why
$$2^{m-1}a_{2^m} \leq a_{2^{m-1}+1} + a_{2^{m-1}+2} + \cdots + a_{2^m} \leq 2^{m-1}a_{2^{m-1}}.$$

(b) Use part (a) to show that $\frac{1}{2} \sum_{k=1}^{m} 2^k a_{2^k} \leq \sum_{k=2}^{2^m} a_k$.

(c) Use part (b) to show that if $\frac{1}{2} \sum_{k=1}^{\infty} 2^k a_{2^k}$ diverges, then $\sum_{k=1}^{\infty} a_k$ diverges.

(d) Let m and n be integers such that $n \leq 2^m$. Use part (a) to show that $\sum_{k=2}^{n} a_k \leq \sum_{k=1}^{m} 2^{k-1} a_{2^{k-1}}$.

(e) Use part (d) to show that if $\sum_{k=0}^{\infty} 2^k a_{2^k}$ converges, then $\sum_{k=2}^{\infty} a_k$ converges.

79. Use Exercise 78 to prove that the harmonic series diverges.

80. Use Exercise 78 and the properties of geometric series to prove that $\sum_{k=1}^{\infty} 1/k^p$ converges if $2^{1-p} < 1$ (i.e., $p > 1$) and diverges otherwise.

81. Use Exercise 78 and the result of the previous exercise to show that $\sum_{k=2}^{\infty} \frac{1}{k(\ln k)^p}$ converges if $p > 1$ and diverges otherwise.

82. Use the fact that $\int_0^{\infty} t^n e^{-t}\,dt = n!$ to show that $\int_0^{\infty} e^{-t} \sin(xt)\,dt = \frac{x}{1+x^2}$ if $|x| < 1$.

83. (a) Use the trigonometric identity $\tan x = \cot x - 2\cot(2x)$ to show that
$$\sum_{k=1}^{n} \frac{1}{2^k} \tan\left(\frac{x}{2^k}\right) = \frac{1}{2^n} \cot\left(\frac{x}{2^n}\right) - \cot x.$$

(b) Use part (a) to show that
$$\sum_{k=1}^{\infty} \frac{1}{2^k} \tan\left(\frac{x}{2^k}\right) = \frac{1}{x} - \cot x.$$

84. Let $I_n = \int_0^{\pi/4} \tan^n x \, dx$ for any integer $n \geq 0$.

(a) Show that $\{I_n\}$ is a nonincreasing sequence (i.e., $I_{n+1} \leq I_n$).

(b) Show that $I_n + I_{n-2} = \dfrac{1}{n-1}$.

(c) Use parts (a) and (b) to show that $\dfrac{1}{2(n+1)} \leq I_n \leq \dfrac{1}{2(n-1)}$. [HINT: Part (b) implies that $I_{n+2} + I_n = 1/(n+1)$.]

(d) Show that, if $n \geq 2$, $I_n = \dfrac{1}{n-1} - \int_0^{\pi/4} \tan^{n-2} x \, dx$.

(e) Use part (d) to show that $I_{2n} = (-1)^n \left(\dfrac{\pi}{4} + \sum_{k=1}^{n} \dfrac{(-1)^k}{2k-1} \right)$ for all integers $n \geq 1$.

(f) Use parts (c) and (e) to show that $\sum_{k=1}^{\infty} \dfrac{(-1)^{k+1}}{2k-1} = \dfrac{\pi}{4}$.

(g) Use part (d) to show that $I_{2n+1} = (-1)^n \left(\dfrac{1}{2} \ln 2 + \sum_{k=1}^{n} \dfrac{(-1)^k}{2k} \right)$ for all integers $n \geq 1$.

(h) Use parts (c) and (g) to show that $\sum_{k=1}^{\infty} \dfrac{(-1)^k}{k} = -\ln 2$.

Fourier Series

Fourier series are the infinite analogues of **Fourier polynomials**, which we defined and explored briefly in Section 9.3. (In the same sense, Taylor series are the infinite version of Taylor polynomials.) Compare the following definition with that on page 512:

> **DEFINITION** Let $f(x)$ be a function defined on $[-\pi, \pi]$. The **Fourier series** for f is the series
>
> $$a_0 + a_1 \cos x + b_1 \sin x + a_2 \cos(2x) + b_2 \sin(2x) + \cdots$$
> $$+ a_n \cos(nx) + b_n \sin(nx) + \cdots$$
>
> with coefficients given by
>
> $$a_0 = \frac{1}{2\pi} \int_{-\pi}^{\pi} f(x)\, dx;$$
>
> $$a_k = \frac{1}{\pi} \int_{-\pi}^{\pi} f(x)\cos(kx)\, dx \qquad \text{if } k > 0;$$
>
> $$b_k = \frac{1}{\pi} \int_{-\pi}^{\pi} f(x)\sin(kx)\, dx \qquad \text{if } k > 0.$$

Naturally enough, Fourier series inherit many of their properties from Fourier polynomials.

PROBLEM 1 Let f and g be functions defined on $[-\pi, \pi]$; assume that f is odd and g is even.

(a) Show that the Fourier series of f has $a_k = 0$ for all $k \geq 0$.

(b) Show that the Fourier series of g has $b_k = 0$ for all $k \geq 1$.

PROBLEM 2 Show that the Fourier series for $f(x) = x$ has the form

$$\frac{2}{1}\sin x - \frac{2}{2}\sin(2x) + \frac{2}{3}\sin(3x) - \frac{2}{4}\sin(4x) + \frac{2}{5}\sin(5x) - \cdots.$$

What's the general "formula" for b_n?

PROBLEM 3 Show that the Fourier series for $f(x) = |x|$ has the form

$$\frac{\pi}{2} - \frac{4}{\pi}\cos x - \frac{4}{9\pi}\cos(3x) - \frac{4}{25\pi}\cos(5x) - \frac{4}{49\pi}\cos(7x) - \cdots.$$

(Note that $b_k = 0$ for all $k \geq 1$.)

Convergence and divergence of Fourier series Whether a Fourier series converges or diverges for a given value of x is, in general, a difficult question—much more so than for Taylor series. Although Taylor series converge for x in a particular *interval*, and diverge elsewhere, the convergence set of a Fourier series may be quite complicated. Under suitably strict conditions, however, a Fourier series *does* converge, and to the "right place"—to the function value $f(x)$ itself. The following theorem illustrates one set of (technical-looking) conditions under which this happens.

THEOREM 15 Let f be continuous on $[-\pi, \pi]$, with $f(-\pi) = f(\pi)$ and only finitely many local maximum and minimum points in the interval $[-\pi, \pi]$. Then the Fourier series of f converges to $f(x)$ for all x in $[-\pi, \pi]$.

PROBLEM 4 This problem is about the function $f(x) = |x|$. Observe that Theorem 15 applies to f.

(a) Apply Theorem 15 with $x = 0$ to show that

$$1 + \frac{1}{9} + \frac{1}{25} + \frac{1}{49} + \cdots = \frac{\pi^2}{8}.$$

(b) Apply Theorem 15 with $x = \pi/4$; what series identity results?

(c) Apply Theorem 15 with $x = \pi/2$; what series identity results?

PROBLEM 5 Experiment with Theorem 15, the function $f(x) = x^2$, and an appropriate value of x to show that

$$\sum_{k=1}^{\infty} \frac{1}{k^2} = 1 + \frac{1}{4} + \frac{1}{9} + \cdots = \frac{\pi^2}{6}.$$

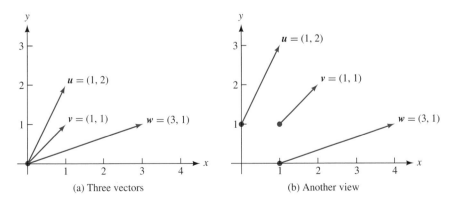

VECTORS AND POLAR COORDINATES

V.1 VECTORS AND VECTOR-VALUED FUNCTIONS

A **vector** is a quantity that has both magnitude and direction. Vectors can "live" in any dimension—in the real line, in the xy-plane, in xyz-space, or in higher-dimensional spaces. This section introduces vectors and vector-valued functions in the xy-plane.

Vectors in the plane can be thought of either as arrows (a natural metaphor for objects with length and direction) or as 2-tuples:

- **Vectors as arrows**   A vector v can be described by an arrow in the xy-plane. Two arrows with the same length and the same direction describe the same vector—regardless of where the arrows are placed in the plane.

    It's common to denote vectors either with bold type, as in v, or with an arrow on top, as in $\overrightarrow{PQ}$. ➨ Ordinary numbers (also called **scalars** when vectors are in the picture) appear in ordinary type.

- **Vectors as 2-tuples**   A vector v can be written as a 2-tuple of real numbers, as in $v = (a, b)$. The numbers a and b are called the **components** (or, alternatively, the **coordinates**) of the vector v.

Figure 1 illustrates these views of vectors and some connections between them.

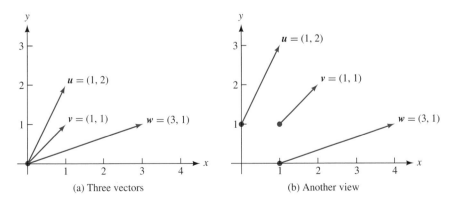

(a) Three vectors   (b) Another view

FIGURE 1
Vectors as arrows and as 2-tuples

This brief chapter introduces two "alternative" views of calculus in the plane: the vector formalism and polar coordinates. Vectors are treated informally—no formal linear algebra is presented (or assumed). Vectors are treated algebraically as 2-tuples and geometrically as arrows. The main application of vectors is physical motion in the plane, with position, velocity, and acceleration regarded as vectors.

Students sometimes miss the boldface convention for vectors.

The vector-as-arrow view can be covered quickly; most of our calculations involve 2-tuples.

The latter is convenient when writing by hand.

Following are some notes on the pictures; watch for some useful vocabulary and notation.

The point that the same vectors can be drawn in more than one place may need emphasis. A similar point is made below about interpreting components.

- **Different tail points, same vectors**   The two pictures show exactly the same vectors *u*, *v*, and *w*. The only difference concerns where in the plane the vectors are placed; the vectors' tail points are shown as dark dots in the pictures,

- **Vectors based at the origin**   In Figure 1(a) all three vectors have their tails at the origin so each vector is of the form $\overrightarrow{OP}$, where O is the origin and P is the point at the tip. In this special case, the *components* of each vector are the same as the Cartesian *coordinates* of the tip point P. For this reason a vector of the form $v = \overrightarrow{OP}$ is called the **position vector** of the point P.

- **What the components say**   In Figure 1(b), each vector's components are *not* the Cartesian coordinates of its tip point. Instead, they describe the **displacement** between the vector's head and its tail. The vector $w = (3, 1)$, for instance, involves moving 3 units to the right and 1 unit up.

- **The vector from P to Q**   If $P = (a, b)$ and $Q = (c, d)$ are any points in the plane, then the vector from P to Q, denoted by $\overrightarrow{PQ}$, has components $(c - a, d - b)$. In Figure 1(b), for instance, the vector w starts at $(1, 0)$ and ends at $(4, 1)$, and so its coordinates are indeed $(3, 1)$.

- **Finding lengths**   The **length** (or **magnitude**) of a vector is the distance between its head and its tail. If $v = (a, b)$, then, by the distance formula in the xy-plane,

$$\text{length of } v = |v| = \sqrt{a^2 + b^2}.$$

Both cases involve measuring sizes.

A vector with length 1 is called a **unit vector**. Notice the use of the absolute value notation for the length of a vector. ◂

Vector algebra is surprisingly simple, given its descriptive power. Students should be impressed.

Algebra with vectors

Vectors permit algebraic operations much like those with ordinary numbers. Here are some simple samples of operations with 2-tuples:

$$(1, 2) + (2, 1) = (3, 3); \qquad -3(1, 2) = (-3, -6); \qquad 3(1, 2) - (3, 4) = (0, 2).$$

The first operation illustrates the **sum** of two vectors; the result is another vector. The second operation illustrates **scalar multiplication**; a vector is multiplied by a scalar to produce a new vector. The third operation combines scalar multiplication with the **difference** of two vectors.

Here are the formal rules:

> **DEFINITION (Operations on vectors)**   Let $v = (a, b)$ and $w = (c, d)$ be plane vectors and let r be a scalar. Then
> $$v + w = (a, b) + (c, d) = (a + c, b + d)$$
> is **sum** of v and w. **Scalar multiplication** of v by r is defined by
> $$r\,v = r(a, b) = (ra, rb).$$

More enlightening than these simple formulas are their geometric meanings. Consider addition first.

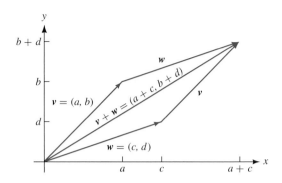

FIGURE 2
Adding vectors

Figure 2 describes addition geometrically. If $\boldsymbol{v} = (a, b)$ and $\boldsymbol{w} = (c, d)$, then the sum $\boldsymbol{v} + \boldsymbol{w} = (a + c, b + d)$ is the vector obtained by putting the tail of one vector at the head of the other. ➡ Figure 2 also illustrates the **parallelogram rule**: The sum $\boldsymbol{v} + \boldsymbol{w}$ is the *diagonal* of the parallelogram with sides $\boldsymbol{v}$ and $\boldsymbol{w}$.

The order doesn't matter; vector addition is commutative.

Figure 3 describes scalar multiplication:

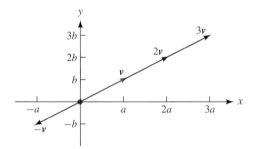

FIGURE 3
Scalar-multiplying vectors

(All vectors shown have tails at the origin.) This picture illustrates the product of a vector $\boldsymbol{v}$ with a scalar a: The result, $a\boldsymbol{v}$, is a new vector with direction either the same as $\boldsymbol{v}$ (if $a > 0$) or opposite to $\boldsymbol{v}$ (if $a \leq 0$); the length of $a\boldsymbol{v}$ is $|a|$ times the length of $\boldsymbol{v}$. ➡

In other words, multiplication by a stretches $\boldsymbol{v}$ by the factor $|a|$.

Figure 4 shows several combined vector operations:

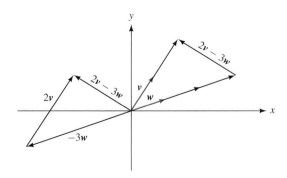

FIGURE 4
Algebra with vectors

Students may turn **v** − **w** *around. Note that* **v** − **w** *adds to* **w** *to give* **v**.

Notice, especially, how the **difference** of two vectors appears:

> *If **v** and **w** have the same tail point, then the difference **v**−**w** points from the tip of **w** to the tip of **v**.*

(The picture shows two copies of the difference vector 2**v**−3**w**.)

Vector algebraic operations enjoy many of the pleasant properties that we've come to expect of operations with ordinary numbers. Theorem 1 collects several such properties.

THEOREM 1 (Properties of vector operations)   Let u, v, and w be vectors and let r and s be scalars. The following algebraic properties hold:

    (a) $u + v = v + u$ (commutativity);

    (b) $u + (v + w) = (u + v) + w$ (associativity);

    (c) $(r + s)v = rv + sv$,   and $r(v + w) = rv + rw$ (distributivity).

All parts of the theorem can be shown to hold using similar properties of ordinary addition and multiplication.

We seldom use the **ij***-notation, but include it for completeness.*

Standard basis vectors   The two-dimensional vectors

$$i = (1, 0) \quad \text{and} \quad j = (0, 1)$$

are especially simple—but especially useful. Both i and j have length 1, and they point in perpendicular directions—along the x- and y-axes, respectively. The vectors i and j are known as the **standard basis vectors** for $\mathbb{R}^2$. They deserve this important-sounding name for a good reason:

> *Every vector $v = (a, b)$ in $\mathbb{R}^2$ can be written as a sum of scalar multiples of i and j.*

If, say, $v = (2, 3)$, then

$$v = (2, 3) = (2, 0) + (0, 3) = 2(1, 0) + 3(0, 1) = 2i + 3j.$$

A sum of the form $rv + sw$, where r and s are scalars, is called a **linear combination** of v and w. As the preceding calculation illustrates, *every* vector (a, b) in $\mathbb{R}^2$ can be written as a linear combination of i and j:

$$(a, b) = ai + bj.$$

Indeed, some authors use the ij-notation for almost all 2-vectors.

Vector-valued functions

Vector-valued functions are essentially 2-tuples of ordinary functions, or, equivalently, parametric curves. The vector notation can simplify notation, and it's especially natural in interpreting velocity.

A **vector-valued function** is one that produces vectors as outputs. Consider, for example, the function defined by the rule

$$f(t) = (\cos t, \sin t).$$

For this function, the notation $f : \mathbb{R} \to \mathbb{R}^2$ makes sense because f accepts a single number t as input and produces the vector $(\cos t, \sin t)$ as output. Notice too that, because the function is vector-valued, we use the boldface symbol f rather than an ordinary f to denote it. The two functions inside the parentheses are called **component functions**, or **coordinate functions**.

It's often helpful to think of a vector-valued function as a curve traced out by a collection of position vectors $f(t)$, one for each input t. (All tails are pinned at the origin.) Figure 5 shows several of these position vectors for the vector-valued function $f(t) = (t, 3 + \sin t)$.

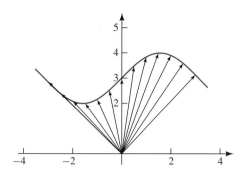

FIGURE 5
Position vectors tracing a curve

Parametric curves and vector-valued functions. Parametric curves are close kin to vector-valued functions. The following example illustrates the relationship.

EXAMPLE 1 A vector-valued function $f : \mathbb{R} \to \mathbb{R}^2$ is defined by $f(t) = (\cos t, \sin t)$. How is f related to a parametric curve? Which curve?

Solution Setting

$$x = \cos t; \qquad y = \sin t; \qquad 0 \le t \le 2\pi$$

gives a parametric form of the unit circle $x^2 + y^2 = 1$, traversed once counterclockwise starting from the "east pole" $(1, 0)$. Thus, for any input t the vector $f(t) = (\cos t, \sin t)$ can be thought of as the *position vector* for a point on the unit circle. ➤ As t ranges through the domain $(-\infty, \infty)$, the tip of the vector $f(t)$ traces the unit circle again and again, counterclockwise. ∎

The tail is pinned at the origin.

Calculus with vector-valued functions

In single-variable calculus, derivatives describe rates and directions of change. ➤ The same useful interpretation proves true for derivatives of vector-valued functions:

Positive derivatives correspond to change in the increasing direction.

> **DEFINITION (Derivative of a vector-valued function)** Consider the vector-valued function $f(t) = (f_1(t), f_2(t))$. The derivative of f, denoted f', is the vector-valued function defined by
>
> $$f'(t) = \frac{d}{dt}\big(f_1(t), f_2(t) \big) = \big(f_1'(t), f_2'(t) \big).$$

Defining the derivative this way sidesteps the slight inconvenience of defining limits of vector-valued functions. After a few pages we explain — informally — why this definition produces a vector that points in the tangent direction.

Calculating this new derivative is no harder than finding a list of *ordinary* derivatives. For example,

$$f(t) = (\cos t, \sin t) \implies f'(t) = (-\sin t, \cos t);$$

we simply differentiate each component function separately.

What the vector derivative means: Velocity The definition is easy to use symbolically, but what does the derivative *mean*?

The short answer is **velocity**. More precisely, let $f : I \to \mathbb{R}^2$ be a vector-valued function such that $f'(t) \neq (0,0)$ for all t in an interval I. (This guarantees that f traces out a curve C.) If t_0 is in I, then the derivative vector $f'(t_0)$ has two main meanings:

- **Direction** The vector $f'(t_0)$ is tangent to the curve C at the point $t = t_0$; it points in the direction of increasing t.
- **Speed** The scalar $|f'(t_0)|$ (the magnitude of the derivative vector) tells the instantaneous speed (in units of distance per unit of time t) at which $f(t)$ moves along C.

Taken together, these observations mean that if $f(t)$ describes the position of a moving particle (a vector quantity) at time t, then the derivative $f'(t)$ describes the particle's **velocity**—another vector quantity—at the same time. We'll explain in a moment *why* these interpretations hold; first, we illustrate their uses by example.

EXAMPLE 2 Find and interpret the velocity vector to the curve $p(t) = (\cos t, \sin t)$ (i.e., the unit circle) at the points where $t = 0$ and where $t = \pi/4$.

Solution The symbolic calculations are simple. Since $p'(t) = (-\sin t, \cos t)$, we have

$$p'(0) = (0, 1) \quad \text{and} \quad p'\left(\frac{\pi}{4}\right) = \left(-\frac{\sqrt{2}}{2}, \frac{\sqrt{2}}{2}\right).$$

These vectors are indeed tangent to the curve at the points in question. At $t = 0$, for instance, our function gives $p(0) = (1, 0)$. This is the circle's "east pole"; at this point, the curve is *vertical*, as is the velocity vector $p'(0) = (0, 1)$. (The velocity vector points *upward* because the curve is traversed counterclockwise.) Similarly, the derivative vector $p'(\pi/4)$ is tangent to the circle at the "northeast" point $p(\pi/4) = (\sqrt{2}/2, \sqrt{2}/2)$.

Another calculation shows that both of these vectors have the same length, 1. In fact,

$$\left| p'(t) \right| = \left| (-\sin t, \cos t) \right| = \sqrt{\sin^2 t + \cos^2 t} = 1$$

for *all* inputs t. This means that the curve is traversed at a *constant* speed of 1 unit of distance per unit of time. ∎

Speed and arc length Recall that to find the total distance an object travels over a time interval we *integrate* the object's speed function over the interval.

In the present setting, this means that we can find the length of a curve C traced out by a vector-valued position function $p(t)$ by integrating the speed function over the t-interval in question. (Note that the speed at any time t is a scalar, so the speed function is an ordinary scalar-valued function.)

Suppose, then, that a curve C is given by the position function

$$p(t) = \big(x(t), y(t)\big); \qquad a \le t \le b.$$

We said above that the speed at which C is traversed at time t is given by

$$|p'(t)| = \sqrt{x'(t)^2 + y'(t)^2}.$$

This formula shows that, for most curves, the speed is a *nonconstant* function of t. In the (rare) exceptional case, we speak of a **constant-speed parametrization**.

FACT (Arc length by integration) Consider the curve C given by the position function

$$p(t) = (x(t), y(t))$$

for $a \le t \le b$. Then

$$\text{arc length of } C = \int_a^b \sqrt{x'(t)^2 + y'(t)^2} \, dt.$$

In earlier work we defined arclength only for function graphs; with speed we can handle more general curves.

EXAMPLE 3 Find the length of the unit circle using the parametrization $p(t) = (\cos t, \sin t)$, $0 \le t \le 2\pi$.

Solution We found in Example 2 that for $p(t) = (\cos t, \sin t)$ the speed function has constant value 1. Thus, we have

$$\text{arc length} = \int_0^{2\pi} 1 \, dt = 2\pi,$$

the (familiar) circumference of a unit circle. ∎

Understanding vector derivatives It's useful and enlightening to think of vector derivatives as velocities. But why does this interpretation make sense? Why, for instance, does the derivative vector $f'(t_0)$ point in the direction *tangent* to the curve defined by f at the point $t = t_0$?

A full answer requires more theory than we're ready for now, but the general idea is not difficult. If h is a small positive number, then by the definition of derivative (written in vector form) we have

$$f'(t_0) \approx \frac{f(t_0 + h) - f(t_0)}{h}.$$

The equation deserves a close look:

- The numerator on the right is the difference between two vectors. Such a vector *difference* is a vector that *joins* the two nearby points $f'(t_0 + h)$ and $f(t_0)$ on the curve and so points "in the direction of the curve." (The denominator h is a scalar and so affects only the length, not the direction, of the difference.)

- The preceding approximate equality has a close analogue for lengths:

$$|f'(t_0)| \approx \frac{|f(t_0 + h) - f(t_0)|}{h}.$$

The numerator on the right measures the *distance* between $f'(t_0 + h)$ and $f(t_0)$, whereas the denominator measures the "time elapsed," and so the quotient gives a natural estimate of the curve's speed at time t_0.

Vector antiderivatives and integrals Vector *antiderivatives*, like derivatives, are found component-by-component. In symbols: If $f(t) = (f_1(t), f_2(t))$, then

$$\int f(t) \, dt = \int (f_1(t), f_2(t)) \, dt = \left(\int f_1(t) \, dt, \int f_2(t) \, dt \right).$$

As with vector derivatives, we avoid a limit-based definition: antiderivatives are found term by term.

EXAMPLE 4 Let $f(t) = (2t, \cos t)$. Show that

$$\int f(t) \, dt = (t^2 + C_1, \sin t + C_2),$$

where C_1 and C_2 are arbitrary constants.

Solution   We antidifferentiate separately in each component:

$$\int (2t, \cos t)\, dt = \left(\int 2t\, dt, \int \cos t\, dt\right) = (t^2 + C_1, \sin t + C_2).$$

The answer (as usual for antiderivatives) is easily checked by differentiation. ∎

Modeling motion   The vector tools and ideas we've developed allow us to model two-dimensional motion—the movement of objects in the xy-plane. The key idea is that vector-valued acceleration, velocity, and position functions are all derivatives and antiderivatives of each other.

In simple cases the acceleration is a constant vector; integrating shows easily—keeping track of constants of integration—that the corresponding position vector has quadratic component functions.

Starting with acceleration   In modeling physical motion, it's often most natural to begin with information about **acceleration** (the derivative of velocity) and to work from there to formulas for velocity and position. Acceleration arises naturally in physical settings because of its close connection to force. **Newton's second law** puts the matter like this:

> *A force acting on an object produces an acceleration that is directly proportional to the force and inversely proportional to the object's mass.*

Forces (gravitational force, air drag, sliding friction, a rocket's thrust, etc.) can often be measured directly and, thanks to Newton's law, converted into information about acceleration.

In simple cases, such as free fall, the driving force is constant; hence so is the acceleration vector.

Zero acceleration   In the simplest possible case, an object's acceleration is the zero vector. In this case it's easy to find velocity and position functions by antidifferentiation. For velocity,

$$\boldsymbol{a}(t) = (0,0) \Longrightarrow \boldsymbol{v}(t) = \int (0,0)\, dt = \left(\int 0\, dt, \int 0\, dt\right) = (C_1, C_2),$$

where C_1 and C_2 are constants. For position,

$$\boldsymbol{v}(t) = (C_1, C_2) \Longrightarrow \boldsymbol{p}(t) = \int (C_1, C_2)\, dt = \left(\int C_1\, dt, \int C_2\, dt\right)$$
$$= (C_1 t + C_3, C_2 t + C_4),$$

where C_3 and C_4 are arbitrary constants.

In specific cases, the four constants can be evaluated using additional information (such as the velocity and position of the particle at time $t = 0$). Notice, however, that regardless of the numerical values of these constants, the calculation illustrates an interesting physical fact:

> *In the absence of outside forces, an object has* zero *acceleration, constant* velocity *(and speed), and a* linear *position function.*

EXAMPLE 5   At time $t = 0$, a particle in the plane has velocity vector $(1, 2)$ and position vector $(3, 4)$. (These stipulations are called **initial conditions.**) No external force acts, so the acceleration is $\boldsymbol{a}(t) = (0, 0)$ at all times. Describe the particle's movement. Where is the particle at time $t = 100$?

Solution   As we just calculated, the particle has constant velocity function $\boldsymbol{v}(t) = (C_1, C_2)$ and linear position function $\boldsymbol{p}(t) = t(C_1, C_2) + (C_3, C_4)$. The initial conditions give $C_1 = 1$, $C_2 = 2$, $C_3 = 3$, and $C_4 = 4$, and so

$$\boldsymbol{v}(t) = (1, 2) \quad \text{and} \quad \boldsymbol{p}(t) = (3, 4) + t(1, 2).$$

Thus, the particle moves away from $(3, 4)$ with constant speed $\sqrt{5}$, in the direction of the vector $(1, 2)$. At $t = 100$ the particle's position is $\boldsymbol{p}(100) = (103, 204)$. ∎

Constant acceleration In the next simplest case, an object's acceleration is a nonzero *constant* vector. This case is especially important; it arises when a constant force (such as gravity) acts on an object, producing a constant acceleration. Suppose, then, that an object has constant acceleration vector $a(t) = (a_1, a_2)$. Then

$$v(t) = \int (a_1, a_2)\, dt = t(a_1, a_2) + (C_1, C_2),$$

where C_1 and C_2 are arbitrary constants. Because $v(0) = (C_1, C_2)$, the constants represent the object's initial velocity.

To find position we antidifferentiate again:

$$p(t) = \int \left(t(a_1, a_2) + (C_1, C_2) \right) dt = \frac{t^2}{2}(a_1, a_2) + t(C_1, C_2) + (C_3, C_4),$$

where C_3 and C_4 are again arbitrary constants. Since $p(0) = (C_3, C_4)$, these constants represent the object's initial position. In particular:

Constant acceleration begets linear velocity and quadratic position.

EXAMPLE 6 An object starts from rest at the origin and has constant acceleration $a = (1, 2)$. What happens? What are the object's position and velocity at $t = 100$ seconds?

Solution The calculations preceding this example, together with the initial conditions, mean that the object's velocity and position functions are

$$v(t) = t(1, 2) \quad \text{and} \quad p(t) = \frac{t^2}{2}(1, 2).$$

Thus, the particle moves along the curve defined by $p(t)$. At $t = 100$ the particle's velocity is $100(1, 2) = (100, 200)$; its speed is $100\sqrt{5} \approx 223.6$ units per second; and its position is $p(100) = 5000(1, 2) = (5000, 10000)$. ➔   ■   *It's gone a long way.*

Gravity and acceleration It's common knowledge that Earth's gravity pulls everything toward the center of the Earth, producing a "downward" acceleration. It's also true—but less obvious—that the acceleration due to gravity has the same magnitude for all objects. (This magnitude is usually denoted by g; it is called the **acceleration due to gravity**. In the metric system, $g \approx 9.8$ meters per second per second. In the English system, $g \approx 32$ feet per second per second.)

*An object affected only by gravity is said to be in **free fall**; for such an object the acceleration vector has constant magnitude and is often taken to point "downward." Several exercises pursue these ideas.*

As a result, gravity induces the same acceleration on all objects near the surface of the Earth. In vector language this means that the acceleration due to gravity is a *constant* vector of length g, pointing toward Earth's center.

BASIC EXERCISES

In Exercises 1–8, use the vectors $u = (1, 2)$, $v = (2, 3)$, and $w = (-2, 1)$ to find

1. $u + v$

2. $u - v$

3. $2u - 3v$

4. $u + v/2 + w/3$

5. $|u|$

6. $|w|$

7. $|3u + 2w|$

8. $|2v - 3u|$

Consider the three vectors $u = (a, b)$, $v = (c, d)$, and $w = (e, f)$, and let r be a scalar. By the definition of vector addition, $u + v = (a, b) + (c, d) = (a + c, b + d) = (c + a, d + b) = (c, d) + (a, b) = v + u$. (The middle step holds because ordinary addition of numbers is commutative.) This argument shows that

vector addition is commutative, as asserted in Theorem 1. Use a similar argument to show the claims in Exercises 9 and 10.

9. $u + (v + w) = (u + v) + w$

10. $r(v + w) = rv + rw$

11. In this section we mentioned the parallelogram rule for vector addition: The sum $v + w$ is the diagonal of the parallelogram with adjacent sides v and w.

   (a) Draw and label a picture to illustrate this fact for the vectors $v = (2, 1)$ and $w = (1, 3)$. (Base both vectors at the origin.) What are the components of the diagonal vector?

(b) The parallelogram you drew in part (a) actually has *two* diagonals. You drew a northeast-pointing diagonal in part (a). Now draw the northwest-pointing diagonal vector. What are its components? How is it related to *v* and *w*?

(c) Draw the southeast-pointing diagonal vector. What are its components? How is it related to *v* and *w*?

12. Let *v* and *w* be nonparallel vectors. What basic fact from Euclidean geometry is expressed by the relation $|v + w| \le |v| + |w|$?

*Let **u** and **v** be the vectors pictured below. In Exercises 13–16, draw the vector **w**.*

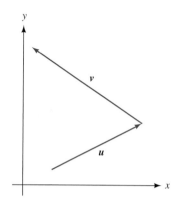

13. $w = u + v$.   **14.** $w = u - v$.

15. $w = v - u$.   **16.** $w = u + u$.

*Let **u** and **v** be the vectors pictured below. In Exercises 17–20, draw the vector **w**.*

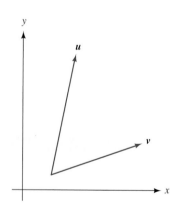

17. $w = u + v$.   **18.** $w = u - v$.

19. $w = v - u$.   **20.** $w = v + v$.

21. Let ℓ be the line through the point $P(1, 2)$ in the direction of the vector $v = (2, 3)$.

(a) The line ℓ is the image of the vector-valued function $L(t) = (1, 2) + t(2, 3)$ for all real t. Draw a picture to explain why; label the points on ℓ that correspond to $t = 0$, $t = 1$, $t = 2$, and $t = -1$.

(b) What is the image of the function $L(t) = (1, 2) + t(2, 3)$ if the domain is restricted to $t \ge 0$?

(c) What is the image of the function $L(t) = (1, 2) + t(2, 3)$ if the domain is restricted to $-1 \le t \le 1$?

22. Repeat Exercise 21, but let ℓ be the line through (a, b) in the direction of (c, d). (Assume that c and d are not both zero.)

23. Suppose that the motion of a particle is described by the parametric equations $x(t) = 1 - 2t + t^3$, $y(t) = 2t^4$. What is the particle's speed at time $t = 1$?

24. This exercise is about Example 6.

(a) By hand, sketch the "curve" defined by $p(t)$ for $0 \le t \le 100$. What very simple shape does the "curve" seem to have? [HINT: The curve is parametrized by $x(t) = p_1(t)$; $y(t) = p_2(t)$; $0 \le t \le 100$.]

(b) Eliminate the variable t in the parametric equations for the curve $p(t)$; what's the resulting equation? Does it agree with what you found in part (a)?

(c) Find the arc length of the curve $p(t)$ from $t = 0$ to $t = 100$.

25. Redo Exercise 24 but assume that the acceleration vector is $(1, -1)$.

26. At time $t = 0$ seconds a particle is at the origin and has velocity vector $(4, 4)$. It undergoes constant acceleration $a(t) = (0, -1)$.

(a) Find formulas for the velocity function $v(t)$ and the position function $p(t)$.

(b) Plot the path taken by the particle $p(t)$ for $0 \le t \le 10$. What familiar shape does the path seem to have?

(c) Eliminate the variable t in the parametric equations for the curve $p(t)$; what's the resulting equation? Does it agree with what you found in part (c)?

(d) Find the arc length of the curve $p(t)$ from $t = 0$ to $t = 10$. [HINT: Set up the integral by hand; either solve it exactly using a table of integrals or use technology to approximate the integral numerically.]

27. A projectile is at $(0, 0)$ at time 0 seconds. It has initial speed 100 meters per second, initial angle $\pi/3$, and travels under free fall conditions.

(a) Find equations for the velocity and position functions.

(b) When does the projectile touch down?

(c) Plot the projectile's trajectory from takeoff to landing.

(d) At what time is the projectile at maximum height? How high is this? [HINT: Find the time at which the velocity vector is horizontal.]

(e) Find the speed and the velocity at the moment the projectile is highest.

28. A projectile is at $(0, 0)$ at time 0 seconds. It has initial speed s_0 meters per second, initial angle α, and travels under free fall conditions.

(a) Find equations for the velocity and position functions.

(b) At what time is the projectile highest? [HINT: The answer depends on both s_0 and α.]

(c) Find the speed and the velocity at the moment when the projectile is highest.

(d) Find the speed and the velocity at the moment when the projectile lands.

29. Suppose that the velocity of an object at time t seconds is $(5t^2 + 3t - 4, 1 - t)$ meters/second. At time $t = 2$ the object is at the point with coordinates $(1, 0)$.

   (a) Find the object's acceleration vector at time $t = 1$.

   (b) Find the position of the object at time $t = 0$.

   (c) Express the distance traveled by the object between time $t = 0$ and time $t = 2$ as an integral.

30. Suppose that the motion of a particle is described by the parametric equations $x = t^3 - 3t$, $y = t^2 - 2t$.

   (a) Does the particle ever come to a stop? If so, when and where?

   (b) Is the particle ever moving straight up or down? If so, when and where?

   (c) Is the particle ever moving horizontally left or right? If so, when and where?

31. A particle moves in the xy-plane with constant acceleration vector $\boldsymbol{a}(t) = (0, -1)$. At time $t = 0$ the particle is at the point $\boldsymbol{p}(0) = (0, 0)$ and has velocity $\boldsymbol{v}(0) = (1, 0)$.

   (a) Give a formula for the particle's velocity function $\boldsymbol{v}(t)$.

   (b) Give a formula for the particle's position function $\boldsymbol{p}(t)$.

   (c) Write an integral whose value is the distance traveled by the particle between $t = 0$ and $t = 5$.

In Exercises 32–36, plot the curve and estimate its arc length by eye. Set up the arc length integral. If possible, evaluate it exactly by antidifferentiation; otherwise, estimate the answer using a midpoint approximating sum with 20 subdivisions.

32. $\boldsymbol{r}(t) = (3 + t, 2 + 3t), 0 \le t \le 1$.

33. $\boldsymbol{r}(t) = (\cos(2t), \sin(2t)); 0 \le t \le \pi$

34. $\boldsymbol{r}(t) = (\sin(3t), \cos(3t)); 0 \le t \le 2\pi/3$

35. $\boldsymbol{r}(t) = (3\sin t, \cos t); 0 \le t \le 2\pi$

36. $\boldsymbol{r}(t) = (t\cos t, t\sin t); 0 \le t \le 4\pi$

37–41. Find a formula for the speed at time t of the vector-valued functions given in Exercises 32–36.

42. Consider the vector-valued function $\boldsymbol{p}(t) = (\sin t, t)$.

   (a) Draw (by hand) a rough plot of the curve defined by $\boldsymbol{p}(t)$; let $0 \le t \le 4\pi$.

   (b) Find the position, velocity, and acceleration vectors at $t = 0$.

   (c) Find a vector equation for the tangent line ℓ at $t = \pi$ to the curve defined by $\boldsymbol{p}(t)$.

   (d) On one set of axes, plot both the curve and the tangent line from part (c).

   (e) Find the arc length from $t = 0$ to $t = 4\pi$.

43. Find the length of the logarithmic spiral $r = e^\theta$ between $\theta = 0$ and $\theta = \pi$.

V.2 POLAR COORDINATES AND POLAR CURVES

This section introduces polar coordinates themselves; all "polar calculus" is deferred to the next section. The pace is leisurely; students who have seen polar coordinates can be hurried through.

Any point P in the xy-plane has a familiar and natural "address": its **rectangular** (or **Cartesian**) **coordinates**. The point P in Figure 1(a), for instance, has rectangular coordinates $(4, 3)$.

(a) A rectangular address

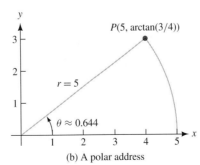
(b) A polar address

FIGURE 1
Polar and rectangular coordinates

The x- and y-coordinates of P measure the distances from P to the two perpendicular coordinate axes. To reach $P(4, 3)$ from the origin, one moves 4 units right and 3 units up.

Polar coordinates offer another way of locating a point in the plane. In the **polar coordinate system**, a point P has coordinates r and θ; they tell, respectively, the *distance* from the origin O to P and the *angle* (in radians!) from the positive x-axis to the ray from O to P. Figure 1(b) shows that the point P with rectangular coordinates $(4, 3)$ has polar coordinates $(5, \arctan(3/4)) \approx (5, 0.644)$.

Polar coordinate systems

The fact that a point has many possible sets of polar coordinates may be puzzling, but in this simple setting it seldom causes much trouble.

A **rectangular coordinate system** in the Euclidean plane starts with an origin O and two perpendicular coordinate axes. Usually the x-axis is horizontal and the y-axis is vertical; x-coordinates increase to the right and y-coordinates increase upward.

A polar coordinate system starts with different ingredients: an origin O, called the **pole**, and a ray (i.e., a half-line) beginning at the origin, called the **polar axis**. The polar axis normally points to the right, along the positive x-axis. With these ingredients and a unit for measuring distance, we can assign polar coordinates (r, θ) to any point P:

r is the distance from O to P; θ is any angle from the polar axis to the segment $\overline{OP}$.

Figure 2 shows several points with their polar coordinates, plotted on a polar grid.

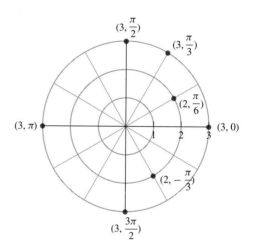

FIGURE 2
Points on a polar grid

Polar vs. rectangular grids   A rectangular coordinate system leads naturally to a rectangular grid, with vertical lines $x = a$ and horizontal lines $y = b$. In a polar system, holding the coordinates r and θ constant produces, respectively, concentric circles and radial lines. The result is a weblike polar grid. Figure 3 shows grids of both types.

It's crucial for polar coordinates that distances in the x- and y-directions are equal; circles should look round. This may be problematic for some technologies.

On the scales   In a rectangular coordinate system, the two axes often have different scales of measurement. As a result, on a graph, a vertical inch and a horizontal inch may represent different distances. In particular, "circles" may look far from round.

A polar coordinate system, by contrast, has just one axis—the polar axis. As a result, distance does not depend on direction, and circles look round.

Polar coordinates: Not unique   A point in the plane—$P(4, 3)$, for instance—has just one possible pair of *rectangular* coordinates. Different rectangular coordinate pairs (x_1, y_1) and (x_2, y_2) correspond to different points in the plane.

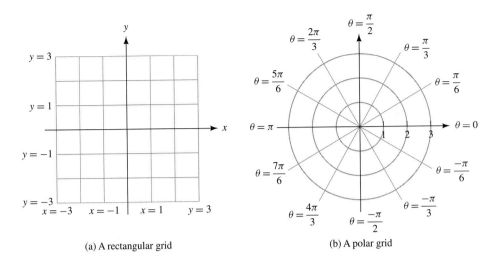

(a) A rectangular grid   (b) A polar grid

FIGURE 3
Two types of grids

Polar coordinates, by contrast, are *not* unique. Every point in the plane has many possible pairs of polar coordinates. For example, all of the polar coordinate pairs

$$\left(2, \frac{\pi}{4}\right), \quad \left(2, \frac{9\pi}{4}\right), \quad \left(2, -\frac{7\pi}{4}\right), \quad \left(2, -\frac{15\pi}{4}\right), \quad \left(-2, \frac{5\pi}{4}\right), \quad \left(-2, -\frac{3\pi}{4}\right),$$

(and many others) represent the same point—the one with rectangular coordinates $(\sqrt{2}, \sqrt{2})$. Notice especially the last two pairs: A negative r-coordinate means that, to locate the point P, one moves r units in the direction *opposite* the θ-direction. The point $(-2, 5\pi/4)$, for instance, lies 2 units from the origin on the ray $\theta = \pi/4$. (That's the ray opposite $\theta = 5\pi/4$.) The origin O allows even more freedom: It's represented by *every* pair of the form $(0, \theta)$, regardless of θ.

This ambiguity of polar coordinates arises for a simple reason. All angles that differ by integer multiples of 2π determine the same direction. In practice, this ambiguity can be annoying but is seldom a serious problem. Two simple rules help:

- **Multiples of 2π**   For any r and θ, the pairs (r, θ) and $(r, \theta + 2\pi)$ describe the same point.

- **Negative r**   For any r and θ, the pairs (r, θ) and $(-r, \theta + \pi)$ describe the same point.

The section's exercises explore these "rules" further.

Polar coordinates on Earth.   The polar grid somewhat resembles an overhead view of Earth with the observer looking "down" at the North Pole. In cartographers' language, lines of **longitude** (or **meridians**) converge at the pole; the concentric circles are lines of **latitude** (or **parallels**). For hundreds of years, the **prime meridian** (polar axis, in calculus language), for which $\theta = 0$, has been taken to be the line of longitude that passes through the Greenwich Observatory located just east of London, England. For the same reason, Greenwich Mean Time (the time of day along the prime meridian) is used worldwide as a reference point.

Why is Greenwich "prime" rather than, say, India or Arabia, where navigation and timekeeping flourished even in antiquity? There is no intrinsic reason; Greenwich just happened to be a center of attention when the terms were defined—an early (and quite literal) instance of Eurocentrism.

Polar coordinates in the *plane*, it should be said, aren't perfectly suited to measuring the (almost) spherical Earth. In practice, geographers use a related system called *spherical* coordinates.

The arbitrariness of the "prime meridian" makes an interesting discussion, with political overtones. Note that the choice of north and south poles is not arbitrary; it reflects Earth's magnetic field.

Polar graphs

The ordinary graph of an equation in x and y is the set of points (x, y) whose coordinates satisfy the equation. The graph of $x^2 + y^2 = 1$, for instance, is the circle of radius 1 about the origin. The point $(2, 3)$ does not lie on this graph because $2^2 + 3^2 \neq 1$.

The idea of a **polar graph** is similar but not quite identical. The graph of an equation in r and θ is the set of points whose *polar* coordinates r and θ satisfy the equation. For instance, the polar point $(3, 0)$ lies on the graph of $r = 2 + \cos\theta$ (because $3 = 2 + \cos 0$), but the polar point $(2, \pi)$ does not.

A warning Because a point in the plane has more than one pair of polar coordinates, polar plotting requires extra care. At first glance, for instance, the point P with polar coordinates $(-3, \pi)$ seems *not* to satisfy the polar equation $r = 2 + \cos\theta$. A closer look, however, shows that P can also be written with polar coordinates $(3, 0)$—which *do* satisfy the given equation. Here's the moral:

> *A point P lies on the graph of a polar equation if P has any pair of polar coordinates that satisfy the equation.*

Drawing polar graphs

The simplest polar graphs come from functions—usually of the form $r = f(\theta)$. Given such a function and a specific θ-domain, it's a routine matter to tabulate points and then plot them. We illustrate by example.

EXAMPLE 1 Plot the equation $r = 2 + \cos\theta$ for $0 \leq \theta \leq 2\pi$.

Solution Let $f(\theta) = 2 + \cos\theta$. We want the r–θ graph of f. First we tabulate some values.

Values of $r = f(\theta) = 2 + \cos\theta$												
θ	0	$\frac{\pi}{6}$	$\frac{\pi}{3}$	$\frac{\pi}{2}$	$\frac{2\pi}{3}$	$\frac{5\pi}{6}$	π	$\frac{7\pi}{6}$	$\frac{4\pi}{3}$	$\frac{3\pi}{2}$	$\frac{5\pi}{3}$	$\frac{11\pi}{6}$	2π
r	3	2.87	2.5	2	1.5	1.14	1	1.14	1.5	2	2.5	2.87	3

Next we plot the data (polar "graph paper" makes the job easier) and fill in the gaps smoothly. Figure 4 shows the result.

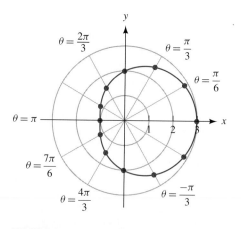

FIGURE 4

A polar graph: $r = 2 + \cos\theta$

■

Polar graphs: A sampler

Several polar graphs follow. We have already seen the simplest polar graphs of all—those of the equations $r = a$ and $\theta = b$.

The simplest Cartesian graphs are straight lines; naturally enough, the simplest polar graphs are circles and rays.

Cardioids and limaçons   Graphs of the form $r = a \pm b \cos\theta$ and $r = a \pm b \sin\theta$, where a and b are positive numbers, are called **limaçons**; if $a = b$, the term **cardioid** ("heartlike") is used. (Figure 4 shows a limaçon.) The graphs in Figure 5 illustrate the variety of limaçons and show the effects of the constants a and b.

Students should study the figure for symmetries in the graphs and in the corresponding polar equations. Differences between the "sine-based" and "cosine-based" curves are worth noting.

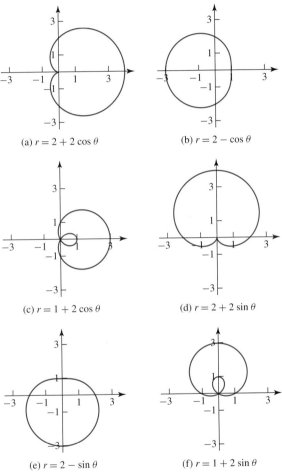

(a) $r = 2 + 2\cos\theta$

(b) $r = 2 - \cos\theta$

(c) $r = 1 + 2\cos\theta$

(d) $r = 2 + 2\sin\theta$

(e) $r = 2 - \sin\theta$

(f) $r = 1 + 2\sin\theta$

FIGURE 5
Six limaçons

Notice some features of these graphs.

- **What θ-range?**   The graphs were drawn by letting θ vary through the interval $[0, 2\pi]$. Since all functions involved are 2π-periodic, any other interval of length 2π would produce the same result. (We could have used the interval $-\pi \le t \le \pi$, for example.)

- **Symmetry**   Three of the preceding limaçons—those that involve the cosine function— are symmetric about the x-axis, that is, the line $\theta = 0$. (The other three are symmetric about the y-axis.) This symmetry occurs because the cosine function is *even*: For any θ, $\cos\theta = \cos(-\theta)$. The other graphs are symmetric about the y-axis because the sine function is odd.

Students might enjoy thinking through some non-periodic polar graphs, such as $r = \theta$; several appear in the exercises.

- **Inner loops** Each of the limaçons $r = 1 + 2\cos\theta$ and $r = 1 + 2\sin\theta$ has an inner loop. A close look at the graphs and the formulas reveals that these loops correspond to *negative* values of r. For $r = 1 + 2\cos\theta$, for instance, we have $r = 0$ when $\theta = 2\pi/3$ or $\theta = 4\pi/3$, and $r < 0$ for $2\pi/3 < \theta < 4\pi/3$. For these θ-values, therefore, the curve is drawn on the *opposite* side of the origin.

Roses Equations of the form $r = a\cos(k\theta)$ and $r = a\sin(k\theta)$, where a is a constant and k is a positive integer, produce graphs called **roses**. The graphs in Figure 6 help explain the name.

Students should try counting the petals—and accounting for the slightly surprising result.

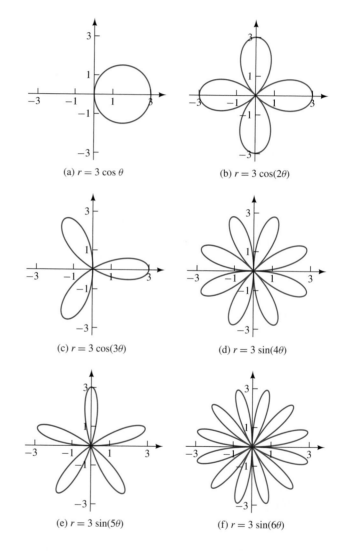

(a) $r = 3\cos\theta$

(b) $r = 3\cos(2\theta)$

(c) $r = 3\cos(3\theta)$

(d) $r = 3\sin(4\theta)$

(e) $r = 3\sin(5\theta)$

(f) $r = 3\sin(6\theta)$

FIGURE 6
A bouquet of roses

Notice the following features of the graphs:

- **Symmetry** Like limaçons (and for the same reason), all roses are symmetric about an axis—"cosine roses" about the x-axis and "sine roses" about the y-axis.
- **The rose's radius** The coefficient a in $r = a\cos(k\theta)$ and $r = a\sin(k\theta)$ determines the rose's "radius."

• **How many petals?**   The coefficient k in $r = a \cos(k\theta)$ and $r = a \sin(k\theta)$ determines the number of "petals": k if k is odd and $2k$ if k is even. But here's a subtlety best revealed by plotting some roses by hand:

If k is odd, then each petal is traversed twice for $0 \le \theta \le 2\pi$.

In other words, for odd k, the rose $r = a \cos(k\theta)$ (or $r = a \sin(k\theta)$) has k *double* petals.

Trading polar and rectangular coordinates

How are the polar coordinates (r, θ) of a point P related to the rectangular coordinates (x, y) of the same point? How can either type of coordinates be found from the other? Figure 7 gives a useful view.

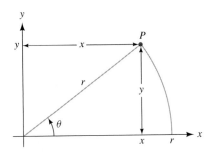

FIGURE 7
Relating polar and rectangular coordinates

The picture illustrates many relations among x, y, r, and θ. Among the simplest are these:

It's easy to translate from Cartesian to polar coordinates; going the other way is slightly messier.

$$x = r \cos\theta; \qquad y = r \sin\theta; \qquad r^2 = x^2 + y^2; \qquad \tan\theta = \frac{y}{x}.$$

(The last equation holds only if $x \ne 0$.)

These relations let us convert from one type of coordinates to the other. Equations in x and y, for instance, are easy to rewrite in terms of r and θ, as the next two examples illustrate.

EXAMPLE 2   Find a polar equation for the straight line $y = mx + b$.

Solution   Substituting $x = r \cos\theta$ and $y = r \sin\theta$ into the equation for the line gives

$$y = mx + b \iff r \sin\theta = m(r \cos\theta) + b \iff r = \frac{b}{\sin\theta - m \cos\theta}.$$

(One moral is that rectangular coordinates are better suited to straight lines than are polar coordinates!)   ∎

EXAMPLE 3   The graph of $r = 3 \cos\theta$ *looks* like a circle. Is it a circle? Which circle?

Notice the useful little algebraic trick: multiplying both sides by r.

Solution   It *is* a circle. Changing to rectangular coordinates shows why:

$$r = 3 \cos\theta \implies r^2 = 3r \cos\theta \implies x^2 + y^2 = 3x.$$

As expected, the last equation does define a circle. To decide *which* circle, complete the square:

$$x^2 + y^2 = 3x \iff x^2 - 3x + y^2 = 0 \iff \left(x - \frac{3}{2}\right)^2 + y^2 = \frac{9}{4}.$$

The circle therefore has radius $3/2$ and center at $(3/2, 0)$—just as Figure 6 suggests.   ∎

In Exercises 1–4, a point is given in rectangular coordinates. Give three different pairs of polar coordinates for the point; r should be negative for at least one pair. [NOTE: Because only familiar angles are involved, give exact answers rather than decimal approximations.]

1. $(\pi, 0)$ **2.** $(0, \pi)$

3. $(1, 1)$ **4.** $(-1, 1)$

In Exercises 5–8, a point is given in rectangular coordinates. Give three different pairs of polar coordinates for the point; r should be negative for at least one pair. [NOTE: Round your answers to four decimal places.]

5. $(1, 2)$ **6.** $(-1, 2)$

7. $(1, 4)$ **8.** $(10, 1)$

In Exercises 9–12, a point is given in polar coordinates. Plot the point and label it with its rectangular coordinates. [NOTE: Give exact answers rather than decimal approximations.]

9. $(2, \pi/4)$ **10.** $(-2, 5\pi/4)$

11. $(1, 13\pi/6)$ **12.** $(42, 0)$

In Exercises 13–16, a point is given in polar coordinates. Plot the point and label it with its rectangular coordinates. [NOTE: Round your answers to four decimal places.]

13. $(1, 1)$ **14.** $(-1, 2)$

15. $(2, \pi/4)$ **16.** $(3, \arctan 2)$

In Exercises 17–20, rewrite the equation in r and θ as an equivalent equation in x and y; then plot the graph.

17. $r = 2 \sec\theta$ **18.** $r = 4$

19. $\theta = \pi/3$ **20.** $r = 2\sin\theta$

In Exercises 21–24, rewrite the equation in x and y as an equivalent equation in r and θ; then plot the graph.

21. $x^2 + y^2 = 9$ **22.** $y = 4$

23. $y = 2x$ **24.** $(x-1)^2 + y^2 = 1$

25. We claimed in this section that for any numbers r and θ the pairs $(r, \theta), (r, \theta + 2\pi)$, and $(-r, \theta + \pi)$ all describe the same point in the plane.

(a) Show that the claim is true if $r = 1$ and $\theta = 0$.

(b) Show that the claim is true if $r = -1$ and $\theta = \pi/4$.

(c) The point with rectangular coordinates $(1, 0)$ can be written in polar coordinates as $(1, 2k\pi)$, where k is any integer, or as $(-1, (2k-1)\pi)$, where k is any integer. In the same sense, describe all the possible polar coordinates of the point with rectangular coordinates $(1, 1)$.

26. Consider the limaçon $r = 2 + \sin\theta, 0 \le \theta \le 2\pi$.

(a) Make a table of values like that in Example 1—let θ range from 0 to 2π in steps of $\pi/6$. (Round r-values to three decimals.)

(b) Plot the points calculated in part (a) on a copy of the polar grid shown in Example 1. Join the points with a smooth curve.

(c) What is the axis of symmetry of this limaçon?

(d) The r values in the table in Example 1 are symmetric about $\theta = \pi$. What similar type of symmetry does your table from part (a) show?

27. Consider the cardioid $r = 1 + \cos\theta, 0 \le \theta \le 2\pi$.

(a) Make a table of values like that in Example 1—let θ range from 0 to 2π in steps of $\pi/6$. (Round r values to three decimals.)

(b) Plot the points calculated in part (a) on a copy of the polar grid shown in Example 1. Join the points with a smooth curve.

(c) What is the axis of symmetry of this cardioid?

(d) How does the table of values in part (a) reflect the cardioid's symmetry?

28. Consider the limaçon $r = 1 - 2\cos\theta, 0 \le \theta \le 2\pi$.

(a) Make a table of values like that in Example 1—let θ range from 0 to 2π in steps of $\pi/6$. (Round r values to three decimals.)

(b) Plot the points calculated in part (a) on a copy of the polar grid shown in Figure 4. Join the points with a smooth curve.

(c) For what values of θ is $r = 0$? How do these values appear on the graph?

(d) On what θ-interval is $r < 0$? How does this interval show up on the graph?

In Exercises 29–34, draw a graph of the given polar equation. (The models of cardioids and limaçons shown in Figure 5 should be helpful. Be sure to label your graphs with appropriate units.)

29. $r = 3 + 3\cos\theta$ **30.** $r = 3 - \cos\theta$

31. $r = 1 + \sqrt{3}\cos\theta$ **32.** $r = 4 + 4\sin\theta$

33. $r = 4 - 2\sin\theta$ **34.** $r = 2 - 4\sin\theta$

In Exercises 35–40, sketch the given polar rose. (The models of roses shown in Figure 6 should be helpful. Be sure to label your graphs with appropriate units.)

35. $r = 2\sin\theta$ **36.** $r = 2\sin(2\theta)$

37. $r = 2\sin(3\theta)$ **38.** $r = 2\cos(4\theta)$

39. $r = 2\cos(5\theta)$

40. $r = 2\cos(1001\theta)$ (rough sketch is fine!)

In Exercises 41–48, plot the graph of the equation. (In each case, the graph is some sort of spiral.)

41. $r = \theta, 0 \le \theta \le 2\pi$ (an Archimedean spiral)

42. $r = 2\theta, -2\pi \le \theta \le 0$ (another Archimedean spiral)

43. $r = \ln(\theta)$, $1 \le \theta \le 4\pi$ (a logarithmic spiral)

44. $r = e^{\theta/2}$, $-\pi \le \theta \le \pi$ (an exponential spiral)

45. $r = \theta^2$, $0 \le \theta \le 2\pi$ (a quadratic spiral)

46. $r = 1/\theta$, $1/2 \le \theta \le 2$ (a hyperbolic spiral)

47. $r = \sqrt{\theta}$, $1/4 \le \theta \le 4$ (a parabolic spiral)

48. $r = 1/\sqrt{\theta}$, $1/4 \le \theta \le 4$ (a Lituus spiral)

49. The polar equation $r = a\cos\theta + b\sin\theta$, where a and b are real numbers, describes a circle. Find the radius and the center of this circle.

50. Suppose that $g(\theta) = f(\theta + \alpha)$. Describe how the graph of the polar equation $r = g(\theta)$ is related to that of $r = f(\theta)$ if $\alpha > 0$.

51. (a) Plot the curve $r = \cos^2\theta$, $0 \le \theta \le 2\pi$.

(b) Find an equation for this curve in Cartesian coordinates.

52. (a) Plot the curve $r = 1/(1 + \cos\theta)$, $0 \le \theta < \pi$.

(b) Find an equation for this curve in Cartesian coordinates.

53. Find an equation for the distance between the points (r_1, θ_1) and (r_2, θ_2).

54. This exercise concerns limaçons of the form $r = 1 + a\cos\theta$, where a is any real constant. The following questions are open-ended. Answer them by experimenting with plots for various values of a: positive, negative, large, small, and so forth.

(a) For which positive values of a does the graph have an inner loop?

(b) What happens at $a = 1$?

(c) What happens as $a \to 0$?

(d) How are the graphs for a and $-a$ (e.g., $r = 1 + 0.5\cos\theta$ and $r = 1 - 0.5\cos\theta$) related to each other?

(e) What happens as $a \to \infty$?

V.3 CALCULUS IN POLAR COORDINATES

In the last section we explored the polar coordinate system, polar equations, and the geometry of polar curves. This section is about calculus with polar curves. The two main problems that stand out for polar curves are the same as those for rectangular curves: finding the slope at a point and finding the area enclosed.

To visualize these problems, consider Figure 1:

We treat the two canonical geometric problems for polar curves: slopes and enclosed areas. The slope formula (slightly inconvenient except at the origin) is calculated with reference to parametric equations.

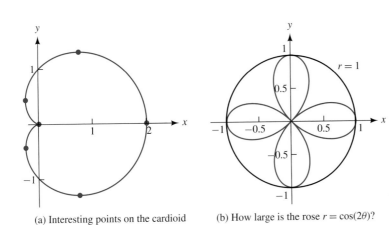

(a) Interesting points on the cardioid
$r = 1 + \cos\theta$

(b) How large is the rose $r = \cos(2\theta)$?

FIGURE 1
Two polar curves

Among the questions we'll address are these:

- **Horizontal and vertical tangents** Where—exactly—does the cardioid have horizontal and vertical tangent lines? The points marked with dots on the cardioid seem to be of interest, but what are their coordinates?

- **Slope at any point**   What's the slope of either curve at *any* point?
- **Areas**   How much area does one petal of the rose enclose? What fraction of the circular area does the rose enclose?

Slopes on polar curves

Both curves just shown are of this type.

Let's consider curves of the form $r = f(\theta)$, where f is a differentiable function. ← For a given θ_0 we want the slope at the polar point (r_0, θ_0).

An obvious (but wrong) guess   Let's acknowledge, just for the record, that the desired slope is *not* $f'(\theta_0)$. A look at either Figure 1(a) or 1(b) quickly confirms this. For $f(\theta) = 1 + \cos\theta$, for instance, $f'(\theta) = -\sin\theta$, which varies only between -1 and 1. Yet it's clear at a glance that slopes on the cardioid take *all* real values; at three points, moreover, the cardioid has vertical tangent lines. Thus, $f'(\theta)$ is not the slope we seek.

Polar curves and parametric equations   We showed in earlier work how to find the slope at a point on a curve defined by parametric equations. Here is the result, for reference:

FACT (Slope of a parametric curve)   Let a smooth curve C be given by parametric equations $x = f(t)$, $y = g(t)$, with $a \le t \le b$. If $f'(t) \neq 0$, then the slope of C at (x, y) is given by

$$\frac{dy}{dx} = \frac{g'(t)}{f'(t)} = \frac{dy/dt}{dx/dt}.$$

To *use* the result, we need first to write a polar curve $r = f(\theta)$ in parametric form. That is surprisingly easy to do. The key facts are the conversion formulas from polar to rectangular coordinates:

$$x = r\cos\theta; \qquad y = r\sin\theta.$$

For points on our polar curve $r = f(\theta)$, therefore,

$$x = r\cos\theta = f(\theta)\cos\theta; \qquad y = r\sin\theta = f(\theta)\sin\theta.$$

These are the desired parametric equations. We've rewritten the curve, originally given in r–θ form, as a pair of parametric equations with θ as a parameter. All that's left is to apply the preceding slope formula. We need $dx/d\theta$ and $dy/d\theta$; let's compute them now. By the product rule,

$$x = f(\theta)\cos\theta \implies \frac{dx}{d\theta} = f'(\theta)\cos\theta - f(\theta)\sin\theta;$$

$$y = f(\theta)\sin\theta \implies \frac{dy}{d\theta} = f'(\theta)\sin\theta + f(\theta)\cos\theta.$$

Everything is in place. Here's the result, stated with appropriate technical hypotheses:

FACT (Slope of a polar curve)   Let a curve C be given in polar coordinates by a function $r = f(\theta), \alpha \le \theta \le \beta$, where f and f' are continuous on (α, β) and not simultaneously zero. Then, for θ in (α, β), the slope of C at $(r, \theta) = (f(\theta), \theta)$ is given by

$$\frac{dy}{dx} = \frac{dy/d\theta}{dx/d\theta} = \frac{f'(\theta)\sin\theta + f(\theta)\cos\theta}{f'(\theta)\cos\theta - f(\theta)\sin\theta}$$

wherever the denominator is not zero.

The slope formula becomes much simpler where $f(\theta) = 0$. Students might think through why the answer is $\tan\theta$. This is pursued in Example 3.

Using this Fact, we can answer the questions on tangents raised at the beginning of this section. The next example shows how. It also illustrates some of the caution needed in working with polar coordinates.

EXAMPLE 1   Consider the cardioid $r = 1 + \cos\theta$ shown on page V-19. ➥ Where is the curve horizontal? Where is it vertical? What happens at the origin?

Take a close look.

Solution   Here $f(\theta) = 1 + \cos\theta$ and $f'(\theta) = -\sin\theta$, thus,

The example offers some review and practice with trigonometric equations.

$$\frac{dy/d\theta}{dx/d\theta} = \frac{f'(\theta)\sin\theta + f(\theta)\cos\theta}{f'(\theta)\cos\theta - f(\theta)\sin\theta} \qquad \text{(by the Fact)}$$

$$= \frac{(-\sin\theta)\sin\theta + (1 + \cos\theta)\cos\theta}{-\sin\theta\cos\theta - (1 + \cos\theta)\sin\theta} \qquad \text{(substituting)}$$

$$= \frac{(1 - 2\cos\theta)(1 + \cos\theta)}{(2\cos\theta + 1)\sin\theta}. \qquad \text{(by algebra)}$$

Now the cardioid can have a horizontal tangent line only if the numerator $dy/d\theta$ is zero. The preceding calculation shows when this occurs:

$$(1 - 2\cos\theta)(1 + \cos\theta) = 0 \iff \cos\theta = \frac{1}{2} \quad \text{or} \quad \cos\theta = -1.$$

For θ in $[0, \pi]$, one condition or the other holds only if $\theta = \pi/3$ or $\theta = \pi$. (By symmetry, it's enough to look only on the upper half of the cardioid.)

The figure shows that, in fact, the upper half of the cardioid is horizontal *only* at $\theta = \pi/3$, that is, at the point with polar coordinates $(3/2, \pi/3)$ and rectangular coordinates $(3/4, 3\sqrt{3}/4) \approx (0.75, 1.30)$. Symmetry dictates that the cardioid is also horizontal at $\theta = 5\pi/3$.

What happens at $\theta = \pi$, where the cardioid has a "cusp"? At $\theta = \pi$, both $dx/d\theta$ and $dy/d\theta$ are zero, and so the slope expression is undefined. It can be shown using l'Hôpital's rule, however, that the expression tends to zero as θ tends to π. Thus, the cardioid can reasonably be said to have *zero* slope at $\theta = \pi$.

A vertical tangent line can occur only where the denominator $dx/d\theta$ is zero, that is, if

$$\sin\theta\,(2\cos\theta + 1) = 0 \iff \sin\theta = 0 \quad \text{or} \quad \cos\theta = -\frac{1}{2}.$$

For θ in $[0, \pi]$, one or the other holds if $\theta = 0$ or $\theta = 2\pi/3$. As the figure shows, both $\theta = 0$ and $\theta = 2\pi/3$ correspond to points of vertical tangency on the cardioid. These points have polar coordinates $(2, 0)$ and $(1/2, 2\pi/3)$, respectively.

Superimposing the cardioid on a polar grid supports all the preceding calculations.

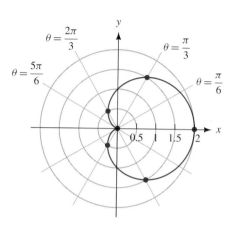

FIGURE 2

Horizontal and vertical points on the cardioid $r = 1 + \cos\theta$

The result shows that, for circles, position and tangent vectors are perpendicular.

EXAMPLE 2   Let $a > 0$ be any positive constant. What does the slope formula say about the circle $r = a$?

Solution   For the circle $r = a$, we have $f(\theta) = a$ and $f'(\theta) = 0$. Now the Fact says that

$$\frac{dy}{dx} = \frac{f'(\theta)\sin\theta + f(\theta)\cos\theta}{f'(\theta)\cos\theta - f(\theta)\sin\theta}$$

$$= \frac{a\cos\theta}{-a\sin\theta} = -\cot\theta = -\frac{1}{\tan\theta}.$$

Why perpendicular? Because the slopes are negative reciprocals.

Note what the last expression means: The tangent line to the circle at any point $P(a, \theta)$ is perpendicular to the ray from the origin to P. ◄

EXAMPLE 3   Let $r = f(\theta)$ describe a polar curve C; suppose that $f(\theta_0) = 0$. What does the formula

$$\frac{dy}{dx} = \frac{f'(\theta)\sin\theta + f(\theta)\cos\theta}{f'(\theta)\cos\theta - f(\theta)\sin\theta}$$

say about the slope of C at the point $(0, \theta_0)$?

Remember that f and f' aren't simultaneously zero.

Solution   The slope formula becomes much simpler if $f(\theta_0) = 0$. In that case, ◄

$$\frac{dy}{dx} = \frac{f'(\theta_0)\sin\theta_0}{f'(\theta_0)\cos\theta_0} = \tan\theta_0.$$

Note what this means: If a smooth polar curve passes through the origin at $\theta = \theta_0$, its tangent line is simply the ray $\theta = \theta_0$. For the rose $r = \cos(2\theta)$, for example, $r = 0$ when $\theta = \pi/4$, $\theta = 3\pi/4$, $\theta = 5\pi/4$, and $\theta = 7\pi/4$. As Figure 3 shows, the curve passes through the origin in just these directions.

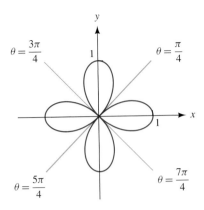

FIGURE 3
**The rose $r = \cos(2\theta)$: Tangent lines at
the origin**

Finding area in polar coordinates

The standard area problem in rectangular coordinates concerns the area defined by an ordinary $y = f(x)$-style graph for $a \leq x \leq b$. In polar coordinates, the standard area problem is a little different: to find the area bounded by a polar curve $r = f(\theta)$ for $\alpha \leq \theta \leq \beta$. Figure 4 illustrates the "generic" situations (the areas in question are striped).

Students should study the "generic" area pictures carefully; the polar picture helps explain the otherwise mysterious polar area formula.

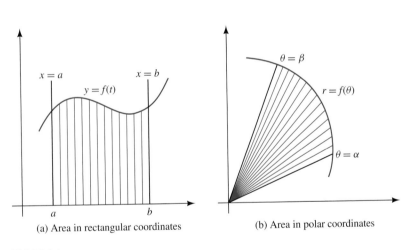

(a) Area in rectangular coordinates   (b) Area in polar coordinates

FIGURE 4
Generic areas

The different styles of shading in Figures 4(a) and (b)—one vertical, the other radial—were chosen intentionally. They reflect two slightly different approaches to finding areas. To emphasize both similarities and differences between the rectangular and polar situations, the next two subsections are written in "parallel."

Area, Cartesian-style In rectangular coordinates, area is approximated by subdividing the region into thin *vertical strips*, each one based on the x-axis. Each strip corresponds to a small subinterval—say, $[x_i, \ x_i + \Delta x]$—obtained by partitioning the domain interval $a \leq x \leq b$ into n equal pieces. If Δx is small, then the strip is approximately a rectangle with base Δx and height $f(x_i)$. Therefore,

$$\text{Area of one strip} \approx f(x_i)\,\Delta x.$$

Adding all n strips gives

$$\text{Total area} \approx \sum_{i=1}^{n} f(x_i)\,\Delta x.$$

Therefore, if we take the limit as $\Delta x \to 0$ we get

$$\text{Total area} = \lim_{n\to\infty} \sum_{i=1}^{n} f(x_i)\,\Delta x = \int_{a}^{b} f(x)\,dx.$$

Look carefully at Figure 4(b), the polar picture: it shows 20 radial wedges.

Area, polar-style   In polar coordinates, by contrast, area is approximated by subdividing the region into thin *pie-shaped wedges*, each with its vertex at the origin. ← Each wedge corresponds to a small subinterval—say, $[\theta_i, \ \theta_i + \Delta\theta]$—obtained by partitioning the domain interval $\alpha \le \theta \le \beta$ into n equal pieces. If $\Delta\theta$ is small, then each wedge is approximately a sector of a circle with radius $f(\theta_i)$; the wedge makes the angle $\Delta\theta$ at the origin.

Students should think through the circular sector area formula for themselves.

Now, a brief detour. Just ahead, we'll need to know the area of a **circular sector** as just described. The answer, although perhaps less familiar than the area of a rectangle, is easy to find. A full circle of radius R (for which θ runs from 0 to 2π) encloses total area πR^2. A wedge making angle $\Delta\theta$ at the origin represents the fraction $\Delta\theta/(2\pi)$ of the total circle, and so

$$\text{Area of wedge} = \pi R^2 \cdot \frac{\Delta\theta}{2\pi} = \frac{R^2}{2}\,\Delta\theta.$$

If, say, $R = f(\theta_i)$, then a circular wedge has area $f(\theta_i)^2 \Delta\theta/2$.

Back to the main road. Our detour showed that in the "generic" case illustrated earlier,

$$\text{Area of one wedge} \approx \frac{f(\theta_i)^2}{2}\,\Delta\theta.$$

Adding all n wedges gives

$$\text{Total area} \approx \sum_{i=1}^{n} \frac{f(\theta_i)^2}{2}\,\Delta\theta.$$

Taking the limit as $\Delta\theta \to 0$ gives

$$\text{Total area} = \lim_{n\to\infty} \sum_{i=1}^{n} \frac{f(\theta_i)^2}{2}\,\Delta\theta = \int_{\alpha}^{\beta} \frac{f(\theta)^2}{2}\,d\theta.$$

The formula is worth remembering:

FACT (Area in polar coordinates)   Let f be a continuous function, and let R be the region in the xy-plane bounded by the polar curve $r = f(\theta)$ and the rays $\theta = \alpha$ and $\theta = \beta$. Then

$$\text{Area of } R = \int_{\alpha}^{\beta} \frac{f(\theta)^2}{2}\,d\theta.$$

EXAMPLE 4   What's the area of one leaf of the polar rose $r = f(\theta) = \cos(2\theta)$? What fraction of the circle $r = 1$ does the entire rose cover?

Solution   As Figure 3 shows, the eastward-pointing leaf lies between $\theta = -\pi/4$ and $\theta = \pi/4$. To ease calculations, we integrate from $\theta = 0$ to $\theta = \pi/4$ and double the result. Here is the integral calculation:

$$\int_0^{\pi/4} \frac{\cos^2(2\theta)}{2}\, d\theta = \frac{\theta}{4} + \frac{\sin(4\theta)}{16}\Bigg]_0^{\pi/4} = \frac{\pi}{16}.$$

Thus, *one* leaf has area $\pi/8$; all four leaves have area $\pi/2$—exactly half the area of the circle $r = 1$. ■

A rose with any other *n* ...   A more general (and more surprising) result than that of the last example is true:

> *For any even n, the rose $r = \cos(n\theta)$ encloses total area $\pi/2$—half the area of the enclosing circle.*

The exercises pursue this rather striking fact further. A similar but not identical result holds for odd n .

EXAMPLE 5   How much area does the cardioid $r = 1 + \cos\theta$ enclose?

Solution   With the integral formula, the answer is easy:

$$\begin{aligned}
\text{Area} &= \frac{1}{2}\int_0^{2\pi} f(\theta)^2\, d\theta \\
&= \frac{1}{2}\int_0^{2\pi}\left(1 + 2\cos\theta + \cos^2\theta\right) d\theta \\
&= \frac{1}{2}\left(\theta + 2\sin\theta + \frac{\theta}{2} + \frac{\sin(2\theta)}{4}\right)\Bigg]_0^{2\pi} \\
&= \frac{3\pi}{2} \approx 4.71.
\end{aligned}$$

■

BASIC EXERCISES

1. We claimed in this section that

$$x = f(\theta)\cos\theta \implies \frac{dx}{d\theta} = f'(\theta)\cos\theta - f(\theta)\sin\theta;$$
$$y = f(\theta)\sin\theta \implies \frac{dy}{d\theta} = f'(\theta)\sin\theta + f(\theta)\cos\theta.$$

   Use the product rule to show that these claims are valid.

2. We claimed in Example 1 that on the cardioid $r = 1 + \cos\theta$, the slope dy/dx at (r, θ) is

$$\frac{(1 - 2\cos\theta)(1 + \cos\theta)}{(2\cos\theta + 1)\sin\theta}.$$

   Use the Fact on page V-21 to verify this.

3. Consider the spiral $r = \theta, 0 \le \theta \le 4\pi$.

   (a) Draw the spiral.

   (b) At what points does the spiral have horizontal tangent lines?

   (c) At what points does the spiral have vertical tangent lines?

   (d) Write an equation in rectangular form for the line tangent to the spiral at the polar point $(1, 1)$. Draw this tangent line on your graph.

4. Consider the limaçon $r = 1 + 2\sin\theta$.

   (a) Draw the limaçon.

   (b) Write an equation in rectangular form for the line tangent to the limaçon at the polar point $(1, 0)$. Draw this tangent line on your graph.

   (c) Find the slope of the line tangent to the limaçon at the polar point $(0, 7\pi/6)$. Draw this tangent line on your graph.

   (d) Find the slope of the line tangent to the limaçon at the polar point $(0, 11\pi/6)$. Draw this tangent line on your graph.

   (e) At what points does the limaçon have horizontal tangent lines?

In Exercises 5–8, draw the region bounded by the given polar curves and find its area.

5. $r = 1, \quad \theta = 0, \quad \theta = \pi$

6. $r = 3$, $\theta = 0$, $\theta = \pi/2$

7. $r = a$, $\theta = 0$, $\theta = \pi$

8. $r = 1$, $\theta = 0$, $\theta = \beta$

In Exercises 9–15, draw the given region and find its area.

9. The outer loop of the limaçon $r = 1 + 2\sin\theta$.

10. The inner loop of the limaçon $r = 1 + 2\cos\theta$.

11. The area enclosed by the cardioid $r = 1 - \cos\theta$ that is to the right of the vertical line $\theta = \pi/2$.

12. The area enclosed by the cardioid $r = 1 - \cos\theta$ that is to the left of the vertical line $\theta = \pi/2$ and above the horizontal line $\theta = 0$.

13. The area inside the cardioid $r = 1 + \cos\theta$ and outside the circle $r = \sin\theta$.

14. The region bounded by $r = \sec\theta$, $\theta = 0$, and $\theta = \pi/4$.

15. The region bounded by $r = \sec\theta$, $\theta = 0$, and $\theta = \arctan m$.

16. Consider the $2n$-leafed rose $r = \cos(n\theta)$, where n is even.

(a) Find the area of one leaf.

(b) Find the area of all $2n$ leaves. What fraction of the circle $r = 1$ does the entire rose fill up?

17. Consider the n-leafed rose $r = \cos(n\theta)$, where n is odd.

(a) Find the area of one leaf.

(b) Find the area of n leaves. What fraction of the circle $r = 1$ does the entire rose fill up?

18. Draw and then calculate the area bounded by one "turn" of the spiral $r = \theta$, that is, from $\theta = 0$ to $\theta = 2\pi$.

19. Draw and then calculate the area bounded by one "turn" of the exponential spiral $r = e^\theta$, that is, from $\theta = 0$ to $\theta = 2\pi$.

20. Draw and then calculate (or estimate numerically) the area bounded by one "turn" of the logarithmic spiral $r = \ln\theta$, that is, from $\theta = 2\pi$ to $\theta = 4\pi$.

21. Use polar coordinates to find the area of the region inside the circle $r = 1$ and to the right of $x = 1/2$.

22. Let $0 < a < 1$. Use polar coordinates to find the area of the region inside the circle $r = 1$ and to the right of $x = a$.

FURTHER EXERCISES

In this section we used the idea that a polar curve can also be thought of as a parametric curve. Specifically, the curve defined by the polar function $r = f(\theta)$, $\alpha \le \theta \le \beta$, can also be defined by the parametric equations $x = f(\theta)\cos\theta$, $y = f(\theta)\sin\theta$, $\alpha \le \theta \le \beta$. Consider, for example, the unit circle $r = 1$, $0 \le \theta \le 2\pi$. Then $f(\theta) = 1$, and so the parametric form is simply $x = f(\theta)\cos\theta = \cos\theta$, $y = f(\theta)\sin\theta = \sin\theta$, $0 \le \theta \le 2\pi$.

In Exercises 23–30, a curve is given in polar form. Rewrite the curve in parametric form and then plot it. Do you see the "expected" results?

23. $r = 2$, $0 \le \theta \le 2\pi$

24. $r = 2$, $0 \le \theta \le \pi$

25. $r = \sec\theta$, $-\pi/4 \le \theta \le \pi/4$

26. $r = \csc\theta$, $\pi/4 \le \theta \le 3\pi/4$

27. $r = \theta$, $0 \le \theta \le 2\pi$

28. $r = \cos\theta$, $0 \le \theta \le \pi$

29. $r = \cos(2\theta)$, $0 \le \theta \le 2\pi$

30. $r = 1 + \cos\theta$, $0 \le \theta \le 2\pi$

31. The formula for the slope of a polar curve requires that f and f' not be simultaneously zero. Show that if this condition holds, then $dy/d\theta$ and $dx/d\theta$ are not simultaneously zero.
[HINT: Recall that $dy/d\theta = f'(\theta)\sin\theta + f(\theta)\cos\theta$ and $dx/d\theta = f'(\theta)\cos\theta - f(\theta)\sin\theta$. Look at $(dy/d\theta)^2 + (dx/d\theta)^2$.]

32. This open-ended problem is about the family of limaçons of the form $r = 1 + a\cos\theta$.

(a) After plotting limaçons for various values of a, determine which ones have a "dimple" (i.e., a pushed-in section on either the right or the left) and which ones don't. [HINT: Any limaçon with a dimple has three vertical tangent lines.]

(b) The graph of $r = 1 + a\cos\theta$ has no dimple if $|a| \le 1/2$. Show this using derivatives.
[HINT: Which values of a lead to three vertical tangent lines?]

Multivariable Calculus: A First Look

M.1 THREE-DIMENSIONAL SPACE

Single-variable calculus is done mainly in the two-dimensional xy-plane. The Euclidean plane, also known as $\mathbb{R}^2$, is the natural home of such familiar calculus objects as the graph $y = f(x)$, tangent lines to that graph at various points, and the various regions whose areas we might measure by integration.

To do *multivariable* calculus, we need more room. The graph of $z = f(x, y)$, where f is a function of two input variables, lives in *three*-dimensional xyz-space. With three dimensions to work in, we will "see" not only this graph but a variety of multivariable analogues of derivatives and integrals. This section explores three-dimensional Euclidean space, or $\mathbb{R}^3$, where we'll spend most of our time.

In another sense, of course, we spend *all* of our time in $\mathbb{R}^3$. In everyday usage, "space" connotes three physical dimensions. The intuition we gain from living in three spatial dimensions is often useful in mentally picturing and manipulating the objects of multivariable calculus. Familiar as it is, however, three-dimensional space poses special problems for visualization. Two-dimensional pictures (on paper or on a computer screen) of three-dimensional objects are *always* more or less distorted or incomplete. Minimizing such problems is an active science (and an art) in its own right; doing so means carefully controlling viewpoint, perspective, shading, lighting, and other factors.

This chapter's main subject is multivariable calculus, not computer graphics (although we sometimes mention computer graphics) or technical drawing, and so we draw pictures to illustrate ideas as simply as possible, not necessarily to look as lifelike as possible. It's worth remarking, however, that many of the basic tools and methods of computer graphics draw directly on the ideas we'll develop in this chapter.

Cartesian coordinates in three dimensions

The *idea* of Cartesian coordinates is the same in both two and three dimensions, but the pictures look a little different. Compare these (Figure 1):

This chapter offers a very quick overview of multivariable topics. Students who take multivariable calculus and other mathematics courses will meet the same material in more depth there. For students who will take no further calculus, these topics may be more accessible and useful for applications than as an introduction to infinite series.

The first section introduces 3-d Cartesian space, building on students' intuition in lower dimensions. Similarities and differences are explored.

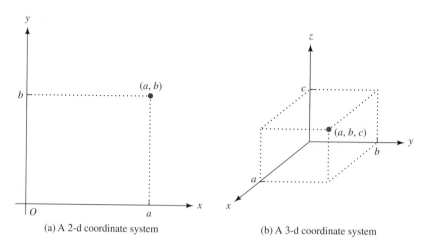

(a) A 2-d coordinate system   (b) A 3-d coordinate system

FIGURE 1
Coordinate systems

We don't mention alternative 3-d coordinate systems (e.g., cylindrical and spherical) in this chapter.

Recall the formalities in the xy-plane. A Cartesian coordinate system consists of an origin, labeled O, and horizontal and vertical coordinate axes, labeled x and y, passing through O. On each axis we choose a positive direction (usually "east" and "north") and a unit of measurement (not necessarily the same on both axes).

Given such a coordinate system, every point P in the plane corresponds to one and only one ordered pair (a, b) of real numbers, called the Cartesian coordinates of P. The pair (a, b) can be thought of as P's "Cartesian address." To reach P from the origin, move a units in the positive x-direction and b units in the positive y-direction. ◄

If a or b is negative, go the other way.

There's "room" in $\mathbb{R}^3$ for three mutually perpendicular axes. $\mathbb{R}^2$ has room for only two.

Coordinates in three-dimensional xyz-space work the same way—but with *three* coordinate axes, labeled x, y, and z. Each axis is perpendicular to the other two. ◄ To reach the point $P(a, b, c)$ from the origin, go a units in the positive x-direction, b units in the positive y-direction, and c units in the positive z-direction. As Figure 1 illustrates, the resulting point $P(a, b, c)$ can also be thought of as a corner (the one opposite the origin) of a rectangular solid with dimensions $|a|$, $|b|$, and $|c|$.

Quadrants and octants   The two axes divide the xy-plane into four **quadrants**, defined by the pattern of positive or negative x- and y-coordinates. The analogous regions in xyz-space are called **octants**. The first octant, for instance, consists of all points (x, y, z) with all three coordinates positive. In Figure 1(a), only the first octant is visible. Figure 1(b) gives another view. There are eight octants in all in xyz-space—one for each of the possible patterns of signs of the three coordinates: $(+, +, +)$, $(-, +, +)$, ..., $(-, -, -)$.

Coordinate planes   One can think of the first octant as a room, with the origin at the lower left corner of the front wall. At this point three walls meet, all at right angles. These "walls" are known as the **coordinate planes**: the yz-plane (the front wall), the xy-plane (the floor), and the xz-plane (the left wall). The coordinate planes correspond to simple equations in the variables x, y, and z. The yz-plane, for example, is the graph of the equation $x = 0$, that is, the set of all points (x, y, z) that satisfy this equation. Similarly, the xy- and xz-planes are graphs of the equations $z = 0$ and $y = 0$, respectively.

Many possible views   The xy-plane, being "flat," is relatively easy to draw. Simulating three-dimensional space on a flat page or computer screen is much harder, and there is always some price to be paid in distortion. For example, in 3-d reality, the x-, y-, and z-axes are all perpendicular to each other, but no flat picture can really show this. The axes in Figure 2, for instance, don't make right angles on the page.

The problem of drawing truly accurate figures is sticky, but we try to avoid it in this overview chapter.

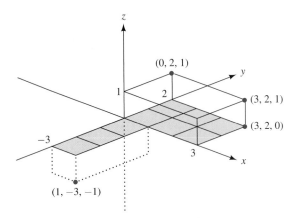

FIGURE 2
Another view of 3-d space

This figure's view of xyz-space is somewhat different from that of the last picture. Observe the following features:

- **Horizontal and vertical** The xy-plane (in which the shaded "floor tiles" lie) is drawn to appear horizontal. The z-axis is vertical; the positive direction is up. This is a standard convention; we'll follow it consistently.

- **Hidden lines** The dashed lines in Figure 2 lie "below" the xy-plane. They would be hidden from view if the xy-plane (the "floor") were opaque. How much of xyz-space is considered to be visible is a matter of choice. Sometimes only the first octant is shown.

- **Positive directions** An arrow on each axis indicates the positive direction. The 3×2 block of shaded squares lies in the first quadrant of the xy-plane. The other shaded squares lie in the plane's fourth quadrant.

- **Plotting points: Positive and negative coordinates** Any point $P(a, b, c)$ is plotted the same way: From the origin, move $a, b,$ and c units in the positive x-, y-, and z-directions, respectively. Negative coordinates cause no special problem; just move the other way.

- **Where's the viewer?** The picture is drawn as though the viewer were floating somewhere above the *fourth* quadrant of the xy-plane. In the earlier 3-d picture, by contrast, the viewer floats somewhere above the *first* quadrant. There's nothing sacred about *either* viewing angle; we'll use a variety of viewpoints as we go along. For that matter, so do the various computer plotting packages readers may have at hand.

- **No perspective** To a human viewer, rectangular boxes like the preceding ones would appear in perspective; the sides would taper toward a vanishing point. The closer the viewer, the more pronounced those effects would be. For the sake of simplicity, we ignore perspective effects in the picture. In effect, the viewer is assumed to be *very* far from the origin, perhaps looking through a telescope.

All pictures in this chapter use a similar "faraway" viewpoint. We think this is simpler, if not necessarily more "lifelike."

There is no single "best" picture of a 3-d object; choosing a good or convenient view may depend on properties of the object, what needs emphasis, or even the drawing technology at hand. ➡

Computer, calculator, pencil, sharp stick, . . .

Distance and midpoints

Concepts of distance and midpoint are straightforward generalizations of the 2-d case. Students should see, for example, that the 3-d distance formula "follows" from the ordinary Pythagorean rule.

Let $P(x_1, y_1)$ and $Q(x_2, y_2)$ be any two points in the xy-plane. Recall that the distance from P to Q (or from Q to P—it doesn't matter) is given by the familiar Pythagorean formula

$$d(P, Q) = \sqrt{(x_2 - x_1)^2 + (y_2 - y_1)^2}$$

and that the midpoint M of the segment joining P to Q has these "averaged" coordinates:

$$M = \left(\frac{x_1 + x_2}{2}, \frac{y_1 + y_2}{2} \right).$$

The formulas in three dimensions aren't much different.

DEFINITION   The distance between $P(x_1, y_1, z_1)$ and $Q(x_2, y_2, z_2)$ is

$$d(P, Q) = \sqrt{(x_2 - x_1)^2 + (y_2 - y_1)^2 + (z_2 - z_1)^2}.$$

The midpoint of the segment joining P and Q has coordinates

$$M\left(\frac{x_1 + x_2}{2}, \frac{y_1 + y_2}{2}, \frac{z_1 + z_2}{2} \right).$$

In either two or three dimensions, the distance formula reflects the Pythagorean rule. See the exercises for more details.

Both definitions are simply three-dimensional versions of the corresponding formulas in the xy-plane. In both two and three dimensions, for example, distance is computed as the square root of the sum of the squared differences in coordinates. ◄

EXAMPLE 1   Consider the points $P(0, 0, 0)$ and $Q(2, 4, 6)$. Find the distance from P to Q and the midpoint M of the segment joining them. How far is M from P and from Q?

Solution   By the distance formula,

$$d(P, Q) = \sqrt{(2 - 0)^2 + (4 - 0)^2 + (6 - 0)^2} = \sqrt{56} \approx 7.483.$$

According to the formula, the midpoint is $M(1, 2, 3)$; each coordinate of M splits the difference between the corresponding coordinates of P and Q. To see why M deserves the name "midpoint," notice that

$$d(P, M) = \sqrt{(1 - 0)^2 + (2 - 0)^2 + (3 - 0)^2}$$

$$= \sqrt{(2 - 1)^2 + (4 - 2)^2 + (6 - 3)^2} = \sqrt{14} \approx 3.742.$$

Thus, M lies halfway between P and Q, as a midpoint should.   ■

Equations and their graphs

The graph of an equation may or may not be the graph of a function. The unit circle is not a function graph.

The graph of an equation in x and y is the set of all points (x, y) that satisfy the equation. The graph of $x^2 + y^2 = 1$, for instance, is a circle of radius 1 in the xy-plane, centered at the origin. The graph of the equation $x = 0$ is the y-axis. ◄

The same idea applies for three variables: The graph of an equation in x, y, and z is the set of points (x, y, z) in space that satisfy the equation. Figure 3 presents three simple examples (only the first octant is shown).

It may be confusing that a given equation, such as $x = 3$, has very different graphs in 2-d and in 3-d.

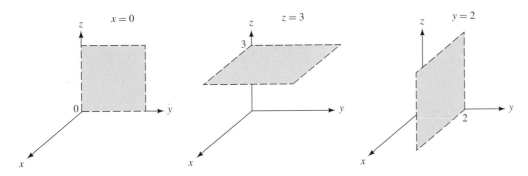

FIGURE 3
Three simple graphs

Solutions of the equation $x = 0$ are points of the form $(0, y, z)$, and so the graph is the yz-plane. Similarly, solutions of $z = 3$ are all points of the form $(x, y, 3)$, and thus the graph is a horizontal plane floating 3 units above the xy-plane. The graph of $y = 2$ is parallel to the xz-plane but moved 2 units in the positive y-direction.

Notice that in each case, the graph of an equation in x, y, and z is a plane—a *two-dimensional* object. In contrast, the graph of one equation in x and y is usually a curve or a line—a *one-dimensional* object. The pattern is the same in both cases: The graph of an equation has dimension one less than the number of variables.

A few special types of graphs in xyz-space deserve special mention.

Planes   A **linear equation** is one of the form $ax + by + cz = d$, where a, b, c, and d are constants and at least one of a, b, and c is nonzero. ➤ All three of the equations just plotted are linear. They illustrate an important general fact:

What goes wrong if $a = b = c = 0$?

> *The graph of any linear equation is a plane.*

(We explain this fact carefully in a later section.) To draw planes in xyz-space, we use the fact that a plane is uniquely determined by three points (unless the points happen to be on a straight line).

Students might guess that planes are 3-d analogues of lines in 2-d.

EXAMPLE 2   Plot the linear equation $x + 2y + 3z = 3$ in the first octant.

Solution   First we'll find some points (x, y, z) that satisfy $x + 2y + 3z = 3$. If anything, this is too easy—there are infinitely many possibilities. Given *any* values for x and y, the equation determines a corresponding value for z. If, say, $x = 1$ and $y = 1$, then $x + 2y + 3z = 3$ can hold only if $z = 0$. Similarly, setting $y = 2$ and $z = 3$ forces $x = -10$. Among all possible solutions, three of the simplest are

$$P(3, 0, 0); \qquad Q\left(0, \frac{3}{2}, 0\right); \qquad R(0, 0, 1).$$

These solutions are both easy to find (set two coordinates to zero and solve for the third) and easy to plot (they lie on the coordinate axes). Figure 4 shows the plane.

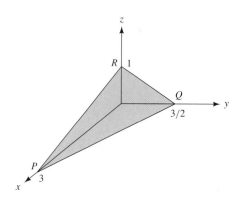

FIGURE 4

A plane in the first octant: $x + 2y + 3z = 3$

Notice the following features:

- **Intercepts**   A typical *line* in the xy-plane has x- and y-intercepts where the line intersects the coordinate axes. In a similar sense, a typical *plane* in xyz-space has x-, y-, and z-intercepts. In the figure, the intercepts are P, Q, and R. ◄

Not every line in the xy-plane intercepts both axes; not every plane in space intercepts all three axes. See the exercises at the end of the section for more on this.

- **Traces**   If we "slice" a surface in xyz-space with a plane, the intersection of the surface with the plane is called the **trace** of the surface in that plane. The plane p shown in Figure 4 meets each of the three coordinate planes in a straight line. Those three lines are therefore the traces of the surface $x + 2y + 3z = 3$ in the xy-plane, the xz-plane, and the yz-plane, respectively.

Look for this line in Figure 4.

  It's easy to find equations for these traces. For example, a point (x, y, z) lies both in the plane p *and* in the xy-plane if and only if it satisfies both $x + 2y + 3z = 3$ and $z = 0$. Setting $z = 0$ in the first equation gives $x + 2y = 3$—as expected, the equation of a line in the xy-plane. This line is therefore the trace of p in the xy-plane. ◄   ∎

Students seem to understand balls and spheres geometrically, but they struggle with the quadratic algebra involved.

Spheres   In the plane, a circle of radius $r > 0$ and center $C(a, b)$ is the set of points $P(x, y)$ at distance r from (a, b). Translating this description into symbolic language produces the familiar formula for a circle in the plane:

$$d(P, C) = \sqrt{(x - a)^2 + (y - b)^2} = r, \qquad \text{or} \qquad (x - a)^2 + (y - b)^2 = r^2.$$

(Squaring both sides does no harm and simplifies the equation's appearance.)

  The object in space that is analogous to a circle in the plane is a **sphere** of radius r. Like a circle, a sphere is "hollow," similar to an empty orange skin. Adding the interior (the edible part of the orange) produces a **ball**. Like a circle, a sphere is the set of points at some fixed distance—the radius—from a fixed center point. Given a radius $r > 0$ and a center point $C(a, b, c)$, the sphere of radius r centered at C is the set of points (x, y, z) such that

$$d(P, C) = \sqrt{(x - a)^2 + (y - b)^2 + (z - c)^2} = r,$$

or, equivalently,

$$(x - a)^2 + (y - b)^2 + (z - c)^2 = r^2.$$

The simplest example, the **unit sphere**, has center $(0, 0, 0)$ and radius 1. Its equation reduces to this simple form:

$$x^2 + y^2 + z^2 = 1.$$

For instance, circles may not look circular. Depending on the viewing angle, they may look like ellipses.

Drawing circles in the xy-plane is easy, even by hand. Drawing spheres (or any "curved" objects, for that matter) convincingly by hand is much harder. ◄ Fortunately, rough sketches usually suffice.

  Completing the square may reveal an equation's spherical form.

EXAMPLE 3 Is the graph of $x^2 - 2x + y^2 - 4y + z^2 - 6z = 0$ a sphere? Which one?

Solution Completing the square in each variable separately gives

$$x^2 - 2x + y^2 - 4y + z^2 - 6z = 0 \iff$$
$$(x^2 - 2x + 1) + (y^2 - 4y + 4) + (z^2 - 6z + 9) = 1 + 4 + 9 \iff$$
$$(x - 1)^2 + (y - 2)^2 + (z - 3)^2 = 14.$$

The last form shows that our equation describes the sphere of radius $\sqrt{14}$ centered at $(1, 2, 3)$. As the equation shows, this sphere passes through the origin. Figure 5 shows this, too.

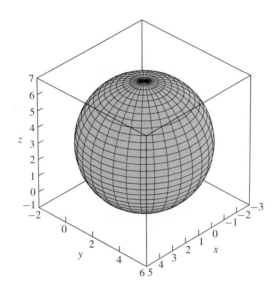

FIGURE 5
Graph of $x^2 - 2x + y^2 - 4y + z^2 - 6z = 0$ ■

Cylinders What is the graph of the equation $y = x^2$? The answer depends on where we're working. In the xy-plane, the graph is the familiar parabola—all points of the form (x, x^2). Here's the graph of the same equation in xyz-space (Figure 6).

Note that "cylinder" is used differently here from in everyday speech, where cylinders are "round."

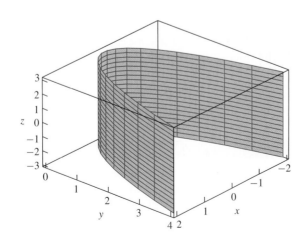

FIGURE 6
Graph of $y = x^2$ in xyz-space

Observe:

In other words, the graph has "vertical walls."

- **A missing variable** The graph is *unrestricted in the z-direction*—it contains all points that lie directly above or below the graph of $y = x^2$ in the xy-plane. ← The graph has this property because z is "missing" in the equation $y = x^2$. This means that if (x, y) satisfies the equation, then so does *every* point (x, y, z), regardless of the value of z.

- **What's a cylinder?** Graphs like this one, in which at least one of the variables is unrestricted, are called **cylinders**. Any equation that omits one or more variables— $y = z$, say—has a cylindrical graph. Plotting cylinders is comparatively simple. If the equation involves only y and z, for instance, we first plot the equation in the yz-plane and then "extend" the graph in the x-direction.

Having technology to plot many examples should help students master such subtleties as the roles of different variables.

In everyday speech, "cylinder" usually means a circular tube. As the next example illustrates, the mathematical idea of a cylinder is much more general.

E X A M P L E 4   Discuss the graph in xyz-space of the equation $z = 2 + \sin y$. Interpret the result as a cylinder.

The surface, like many graphs, continues forever; a picture shows only part of the graph.

Solution   There's no variable x in the equation, and so the graph is unrestricted in the x-direction; that is, it's a cylinder in x. Figure 7 gives a representative view: ←

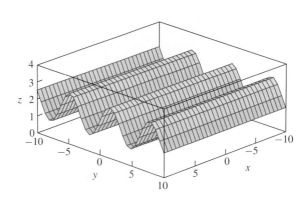

FIGURE 7
Graph of $z = 2 + \sin y$

Exercises continue some of the ideas in this example.

The graph resembles the surface of an idealized ocean with regular waves moving parallel to the y-axis. Each wave is infinitely long with its trough and crest parallel to the x-axis. Notice especially how the surface meets the yz-plane. The curve of intersection—that is, the trace of the surface in the yz-plane—is the ordinary sine curve $z = 2 + \sin y$. In fact, the entire surface can be thought of as infinitely many identical copies of this curve, one for each value of x.   ∎

B A S I C   E X E R C I S E S

1. We said in this section that the graph of $y = x^2$ is a cylinder in xyz-space unrestricted in the z-direction. (See Figure 6.)
   (a) Plot the equation $z = y^2$ in xyz-space. What is the unrestricted direction?
   [HINT: Start in yz-space.]
   (b) Plot the equation $z = x^2$ in xyz-space. What is the unrestricted direction?

2. Plot the equation $x^2 + y^2 = 1$, first in xy-space, then in xyz-space. (The second graph should resemble a vertical pipe—a cylinder in the everyday sense of the word.)

In Exercises 3–6, plot the given equation in xyz-space (a rough sketch is fine); then describe the graph in words.

3. $y^2 - z^2 = 0$ **4.** $y^2 + z^2 = 0$

5. $y^2 + z = -1$

6. $y^2 + z^2 = -1$ [HINT: Does the graph contain any points?]

In Exercises 7–11, find an equation in x, y, and z for the graph in xyz-space of

7. a sphere of radius 2, centered at the origin.

8. a sphere of radius 1, centered at $(1, 1, 1)$.

9. a circular cylinder of radius 1, centered along the y-axis.

10. a circular cylinder of radius 2, centered along the z-axis.

11. a cylindrical surface that resembles an ocean with waves rolling in the x-direction (see Example 4).

12. The equation $z = 3$ omits two variables. Therefore, its graph in xyz-space should be a cylinder in both the x-direction and the y-direction. Is it? What is the trace of the graph in each of the coordinate planes?

13. The graph of $x^2 + y^2 - 6y + z^2 - 4z = 0$ is a sphere. Find the center and radius; then draw the sphere.

14. Consider the unit sphere S with equation $x^2 + y^2 + z^2 = 1$. If we set $z = 0$ in this equation, we get $x^2 + y^2 + z^2 = x^2 + y^2 = 1$. This means, geometrically, that S intersects the xy-plane in the unit circle $x^2 + y^2 = 1$. In mathematical language, the unit circle is the trace of S in the xy-plane. (To put it another way, the unit circle is the "equator" of the unit sphere.)

(a) Set $x = 0$ in the original equation to find the equation of the intersection of S and the yz-plane.

(b) What is the intersection of S and the xz-plane? Describe the answer geometrically.

(c) Use the results in parts (a) and (b) to sketch the part of S that lies in the first octant.
[HINTS: First draw a set of coordinate axes. Then draw the traces of S in each of the three coordinate planes.]

(d) Set $z = 1/2$ in the original equation to show that S intersects the plane $z = 1/2$ in the circle of radius $\sqrt{3}/2 \approx 0.87$ centered at $(0, 0)$.

(e) What is the trace of S in the plane $z = 0.9$? In the plane $z = 1$? In the plane $z = 2$? Explain your answers.

15. The distance formula in xyz-space can be thought of as just another instance of the Pythagorean rule for right triangles. (The square of the hypotenuse is the sum of the squares of the sides.) This exercise illustrates why.

(a) Plot and label the points $O(0, 0, 0)$, $P(1, 0, 0)$, $Q(1, 2, 0)$, and $R(1, 2, 3)$ in an xyz-coordinate system. Observe that the triangles $\triangle OPQ$ and $\triangle OQR$ are both right triangles. Mark the sides OP, PQ, and QR with their lengths. (The lengths should be obvious from the picture.)

(b) Use the Pythagorean rule (not the distance formula) on the triangle $\triangle OPQ$ to find the length of OQ.

(c) Use the Pythagorean rule (not the distance formula) on the triangle $\triangle OQR$ to find the length of OR.

(d) For comparison, use the distance formula to compute the lengths of OQ and OR.

Any reasonable formula for distance should satisfy some commonsense requirements. For example, the distance $d(P, P)$ from any point P to itself should certainly be zero. So it is. If $P(x, y, z)$ is any point, then the distance formula says $d(P, P) = \sqrt{(x-x)^2 + (y-y)^2 + (z-z)^2} = 0$. In the same spirit, use the distance formula to verify the commonsense properties in Exercises 16–18. Throughout, use the points $P(x, y, z)$ and $Q(a, b, c)$.

16. If $P \neq Q$, then $d(P, Q) > 0$.

17. $d(P, Q) = d(Q, P)$.

18. If M is the midpoint of P and Q, then $d(P, M) = d(M, Q) = d(P, Q)/2$.

19. In this section we said that xyz-space contains eight different octants. List eight points, all with coordinates ± 1, one in each octant. Draw a picture showing all eight points.

In Exercises 20–23, consider the linear equation $Ax + By = C$ and its graph (a line) in the xy-plane. Here A, B, and C are constants such that $A \cdot B \neq 0$.

20. What goes wrong if $A = B = 0$?

21. Find the slope of the line $Ax + By = C$. Which lines have undefined slope?

22. Find the y-intercept of the line $Ax + By = C$. Which lines have no y-intercept?

23. Find the x-intercept of the line $Ax + By = C$. Which lines have no x-intercept?

In Exercises 24–26, consider the linear equation $Ax + By + Cz = D$ and its graph (a plane) in xyz-space. Here A, B, C, and D are constants such that $A \cdot B \cdot C \neq 0$.

24. What goes wrong if $A = B = C = 0$?

25. Find (if possible) an x-intercept of the plane $Ax + By + Cz = D$. (Set $y = 0$ and $z = 0$, then solve for x.) Give an example of a plane with no x-intercept.

26. Find (if possible) a z-intercept of the plane $Ax + By + Cz = D$. Give an example of a plane with no z-intercept.

27. The linear equation $x + 2y + 3z = 3$ defines a plane p in xyz-space. (See Figure 4.)

(a) Find the equation of the trace of p in the xz-plane. Where does the trace intercept the x- and z-axes?

(b) Find the equation of the trace of p in the yz-plane. Where does the trace intercept the y- and z-axes?

(c) Find the equation of the trace of p in the plane $x = 1$.

28. Consider the plane p with equation $4x + 2y + z = 4$.

(a) Find the x-, y-, and z-intercepts of p. Use them to draw p in the first octant.

(b) Find the traces of p in each of the three coordinate planes. How do your answers appear in the picture in part (a)?

We said in this section that, as a rule, a line in the xy-plane intercepts both coordinate axes, and a plane in xyz-space intercepts all *three coordinate axes. But exceptions are possible. Some of these are illustrated in Exercises 29–32.*

29. Give an example of a line in the xy-plane that intercepts the x-axis but not the y-axis. Write an equation for your line in the form $ax + by = c$.

30. Consider the plane $x = 1$ in xyz-space. Find all possible intercepts with the three coordinate axes.

31. Consider the plane $x + 2y = 1$ in xyz-space. Find all possible intercepts with the three coordinate axes.

32. Give the equation of a plane in xyz-space that intersects the y-axis and the z-axis but not the x-axis.

33. Suppose that $P_1(x_1, y_1, z_1)$ and $P_2(x_2, y_2, z_2)$ both lie on the plane with equation $Ax + By + Cz = D$. Show that the midpoint of P_1 and P_2 also lies on this plane.

M.2 FUNCTIONS OF SEVERAL VARIABLES

The main aim is to broaden students' view of functions and graphs. Similarities and differences between $f(x) = x^2$ and $g(x, y) = x^2 + y^2$ are explored in detail. Various ways of representing such functions geometrically are explored and compared.

Functions of one variable are the basic objects of single-variable calculus. Functions of two (or more) variables play a similar role in multivariable calculus. In this section we meet such functions and consider some of their rudimentary properties.

Functions of one or more variables

The squaring function, defined for all real numbers x by $f(x) = x^2$, is typical of the functions of beginning calculus: f accepts one number, x, as input and assigns another number, x^2, as output. If, say, $x = 2$, then $f(2) = 4$.

Consider, by contrast, the function g defined by $g(x, y) = x^2 + y^2$. Unlike f, g accepts a *pair* (x, y) of real numbers as inputs. The output is a third real number, $x^2 + y^2$. If, say, $x = 2$ and $y = 1$, then $g(2, 1) = 4 + 1 = 5$.

"One" and "two" count the input variables to f and g.

Naturally enough, f is called a function of one variable and g a function of two variables. ← The difference has to do with domains: The domain of f is the one-dimensional real number line, whereas the domain of g is the two-dimensional xy-plane.

The function f corresponds to the equation $y = x^2$; x is the **independent variable**, and y is the **dependent variable**. The function g corresponds to the equation $z = x^2 + y^2$; here both x and y are independent variables, and z is the dependent variable.

We use f and g to illustrate various similarities and differences between functions of one and two variables. Notice, however, that there's nothing sacred about *two* variables—we can (and do) discuss such functions as

$$h(x, y, z) = x^2 + y^2 + z^2 \quad \text{and} \quad k(x, y, z, w) = x^2 + y^2 + z^2 + w^2,$$

which accept three or more variables. For now, we'll keep things simple by sticking mainly to functions of two variables.

Why bother? Single-variable calculus is challenging enough. Why complicate things by adding more variables?

It's a fair question. One good practical answer is that functions of several variables are essential for describing and predicting phenomena we care about, both natural and human-made. In economics, for instance, a manufacturer's profit depends on *many* input variables: labor costs, distance to markets, tax rates, and so on. In physics, a satellite's motion through space depends on a variety of forces. In biology, populations rise and fall with variations in climate, food supply, predation, and other factors. The weather varies with both longitude and latitude. In short, our world is multidimensional, and modeling it successfully requires multivariable tools.

See the back page of your newspaper.

The National Weather Service plots multivariable functions every day. ← Here (Figure 1), for instance, are noon surface temperatures on a relatively warm (by Upper Midwest standards) winter day.

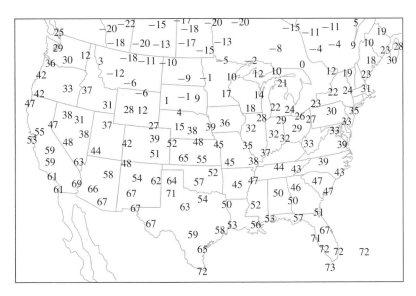

FIGURE 1
Plot of surface temperatures (Fahrenheit)

The map shows how the temperature function varies across its domain, the continental United States.

A contour map of the same data appears later in the section.

Functional vocabulary and notation   Most of the basic words and notations for functions of several variables are similar to those for functions of one variable. Roughly speaking, a function is a "machine" that accepts inputs and assigns outputs. A bit more formally:

- **Domain**   The domain of a function is the set of permissible inputs. The preceding function g, for instance, accepts *any* 2-tuple (x, y) as input, and so the domain is the set $\mathbb{R}^2$.

- **Range**   The range of a function is the set of possible outputs. For g, the range is the set $[0, \infty)$ of nonnegative real numbers.

- **Rule**   The rule of a function is the method for assigning outputs to inputs. For g, the rule is given by the algebraic formula $g(x, y) = x^2 + y^2$. Not every function has a simple symbolic rule. We often encounter functions given by tables, by graphs, or in other ways.

- **"Arrow" notations**   We used the notation $g(x, y) = x^2 + y^2$ to describe a certain function of two variables. Other notations involving arrows are sometimes convenient. The notation

$$g : \mathbb{R}^2 \to \mathbb{R}$$

says that g is a function that accepts *two* real numbers as input and produces *one* real number as output. If we want to emphasize the rule by which g sends inputs to outputs, we can write

$$g : (x, y) \to x^2 + y^2.$$

These notations remind us that a function begins with an input (a 2-tuple in this case) and ends with an output (a single number in this case).

It's crucial in this setting to keep track of the numbers of input and output variable; arrow notations may help.

Graphs in one and several variables

To an ant walking along it, the parabola looks like a (one-dimensional) straight line.

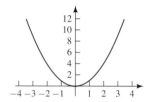

FIGURE 2
Graph of $f(x) = x^2$

It's important to count dimensions properly: The graph of a function of 2 variable is a 2-d object in 3-d space.

The graph of f is the set of all points (x, y) for which $y = f(x) = x^2$. For example, $f(2) = 4$, and so the point $(2, 4)$ lies on the graph. Geometrically, this graph is a curve—a parabola, in this case—in the xy-plane. Like a straight line, the curve $y = x^2$ is a *one*-dimensional object that lives in a *two*-dimensional space—the xy-plane. ◄ Figure 2 shows part of the familiar graph.

The graph of g is the set of all points (x, y, z) for which $z = g(x, y) = x^2 + y^2$. For example, since $g(2, 1) = 5$, the point $(2, 1, 5)$ lies on the g-graph. Figure 3 shows part of the g-graph.

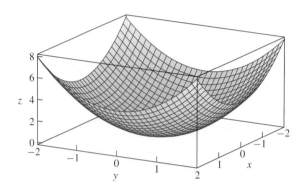

FIGURE 3
Graph of $g(x, y) = x^2 + y^2$

To an ant walking along it, the g-graph looks like a (two-dimensional) flat plane, just as Earth's surface looks flat to a human.

This graph, called a **paraboloid**, is quite different from the parabola shown earlier. Notice especially the dimensions involved: The graph of g is a *two*-dimensional surface hovering in *three*-dimensional xyz-space. ◄ As a rule, the *dimension* of any graph is the number of input variables the function accepts. (This rule of thumb applies to almost every function seen in calculus courses. For the record, however, some very ill-behaved functions do violate this rule.)

In other respects, the graphs of f and g are quite similar to each other. For both functions, the *height* of the graph above a given domain point (a typical input is x_0 for f and (x_0, y_0) for g) tells the corresponding output value. (Typical outputs are $y_0 = f(x_0)$ and $z_0 = g(x_0, y_0)$, respectively.)

Multivariable graphs: Beware   Graphs are at least as important in multivariable calculus as in elementary calculus, but multivariable graphs are usually more complicated; they need extra care in handling. Choosing a "good" viewing window, for example, takes some care even for functions of one variable, and the problem can be stickier still for functions of two variables. The fact that multivariable graphs "live" naturally in three-dimensional (or even higher-dimensional) space—not on a flat page or a computer screen—only adds to the problem. For this and other reasons, we try to look at functions from as many points of view as possible.

Sometimes this "curve" is just one point.

Level curves and contour maps   Let $f(x, y)$ be a function of two variables, and let c be a number in the range of f. Then $f(x, y) = c$ is an equation in x and y; its graph is (usually) a curve in the xy-plane. ◄ Such curves have a special name.

DEFINITION   Let $f(x, y)$ be a function, and let c be a constant. The set of all (x, y) for which $f(x, y) = c$ is called a **level curve** of f. A collection of level curves drawn together is called a **contour map** of f.

Contour maps and level curves often reveal more about functions than do "surface" graphs. For similar reasons, hikers find contour maps more useful than photos of mountainous terrain.

Observe:

- **Why "level"?**   The word "level" makes good sense here because $f(x, y)$ has the same value, namely c, at each point along the level curve. In other words, the graph of f is level above the level curve $f = c$.

- **Which level curves to draw?**   Each number c in the range of f has its own level curve. Because the range of a function is usually infinite, we cannot possibly draw *all* the level curves. In practice, we draw some convenient selection of curves, corresponding to *evenly spaced* values of c. The spacing between curves reflects how fast the function increases or decreases.

- **Labels**   We sometimes label level curves with their corresponding output values. Therefore, typical labels might be of the form $z = c$, $f = c$, or even simply c.

EXAMPLE 1   Figure 4 shows a sample of level curves for the function $g(x, y) = x^2 + y^2$. Label each level curve with the appropriate output value. Recall that the graph of g is a paraboloid. How is this shape reflected in the level curves?

Technology is almost essential for plotting nontrivial contour maps; note that plotting parameters such as the number of curves to be shown is essential for a useful result.

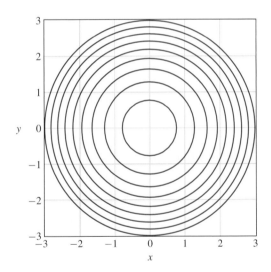

FIGURE 4
Level curves of $g(x, y) = x^2 + y^2$

Solution   Each level curve is a circle about the origin; each is the graph of an equation $x^2 + y^2 = c$ for some c. The circles, from smallest to largest, correspond to the levels $z = 1, z = 2, \ldots, z = 9$.

Notice that level curves of g get closer and closer together as we move outward from the origin. This reflects the fact that the g-graph is a paraboloid—it gets steeper and steeper as we move away from the origin.   ∎

EXAMPLE 2   Drawing level curves on a temperature map makes the map easier to read and interpret. (Newspapers usually do this.)

Figure 5 shows another version of the map in Figure 1. The boundaries of shaded regions, called **isotherms**, correspond to the level curves of the temperature function.

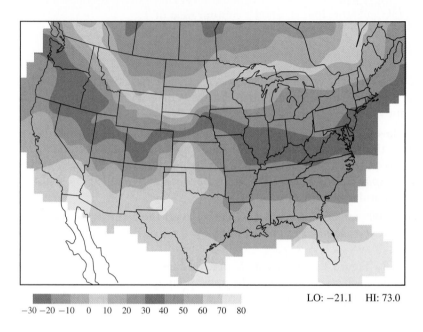

LO: −21.1   HI: 73.0

−30 −20 −10 0 10 20 30 40 50 60 70 80

FIGURE 5
A contour plot of surface temperatures (Fahrenheit)

What we call "linear" functions might be called "affine" in a linear algebra course — this slightly inconsistent terminology seems to cause little trouble.

Linear functions   A linear function of *one* variable is one that can be written in the form $L(x) = a + bx$, where a and b are constants. A linear function of *several* variables has a similar algebraic form.

> **DEFINITION**   A **linear function** of two variables is one that can be written in the form
>
> $$L(x, y) = a + bx + cy,$$
>
> where a, b, and c are constants.

Linear functions of three (or more) variables are similar. A linear function of three variables has the form $L(x, y, z) = a + bx + cy + dz$, where a, b, c, and d are constants.

Why "linear"?   Why do linear functions deserve that name? In the xy-plane, there's no mystery—the graph of a linear function $y = a + bx$ is a straight *line*. In xyz-space, however, the graph of a linear function $z = a + bx + cy$ is not a line but a plane. (In $xyzw$-space, the graph of a linear function $w = a + bx + cy + dz$ is even less like a line. It's a three-dimensional solid, called a **hypersurface**.) Nevertheless, we call any function that involves only constants and the first power of each variable *linear*, regardless of the number of variables. In the same spirit, we call a function *quadratic* (no matter how many variables are involved) if the variables appear in nonnegative integer powers, none of which exceed 2. ◄

The function $f(x, y) = x^2 + xy + y^2$ is quadratic in this sense.

Readers who have studied linear algebra will recall that the word "linear" (as in "linear transformation") is used in still another way in that subject. Like other very useful English words, "linear" seems to have spawned a whole family of related but not identical meanings.

Why linear functions matter   Linear functions are simple, useful, and easy to work with. Most important for us, linear functions are prototypes, or models, for *all* differentiable functions. Indeed, any differentiable function, in any number of variables, can be called "almost linear" or "locally linear" in much the same sense that an ordinary calculus function $y = f(x)$ looks like a straight line if we zoom in repeatedly on a typical point on its graph.

BASIC EXERCISES

In Exercises 1–5, find the domain and range of the function.

1. $g(x, y) = x^2 + y^2$

2. $h(x, y) = x^2 + y^2 + 3$

3. $j(x, y) = 1/(x^2 + y^2)$

4. $k(x, y) = x^2 - y^2$

5. $m(x, y) = \sqrt{1 - x^2 - y^2}$

6. Let $f(x, y) = y - x^2$, and let $g(x, y) = x - y^2$.

   (a) In the rectangle $[-3, 3] \times [-3, 3]$, draw and label the level curves of f that correspond to $z = -3, z = -2, \ldots,$ $z = 2$, and $z = 3$. What is the shape of each level curve?

   (b) In the rectangle $[-3, 3] \times [-3, 3]$, draw and label the level curves of g that correspond to $z = -3, z = -2, \ldots,$ $z = 2$, and $z = 3$. What is the shape of each level curve?

   (c) How are the results of parts (a) and (b) similar? How are they different?

   (d) Use technology to plot the graphs $z = f(x, y)$ and $z = g(x, y)$ for (x, y) in $[-3, 3] \times [-3, 3]$. Describe briefly, in words, how the two graphs are related to each other.

7. Let $f(x, y) = x^2 + y^2$, and let $g(x, y) = x^2 + y^2 + 1$.

   (a) In the rectangle $[-3, 3] \times [-3, 3]$, draw and label the level curves of f that correspond to $z = 0, z = 2, z = 4,$ $z = 6$, and $z = 8$. What is the shape of each level curve?

   (b) In the rectangle $[-3, 3] \times [-3, 3]$, draw and label the level curves of g that correspond to $z = 1, z = 3, z = 5,$ $z = 7$, and $z = 9$. What is the shape of each level curve?

   (c) How are the results of parts (a) and (b) similar? How are they different?

   (d) Use technology to plot the graphs $z = f(x, y)$ and $z = g(x, y)$ for (x, y) in $[-3, 3] \times [-3, 3]$. Describe briefly, in words, how the two graphs are related to each other.

8. Let f and g be the linear functions $f(x, y) = 2x - 3y$ and $g(x, y) = -2x + 3y$.

   (a) In the rectangle $[-3, 3] \times [-3, 3]$, draw and label the level curves of f that correspond to $z = -5, z = -3,$ $z = -1, z = 1, z = 3$, and $z = 5$. What is the shape of each level curve?

   (b) In the rectangle $[-3, 3] \times [-3, 3]$, draw and label the level curves of g that correspond to $z = -5, z = -3,$ $z = -1, z = 1, z = 3$, and $z = 5$. What is the shape of each level curve?

   (c) How are the results of parts (a) and (b) similar? How are they different?

   (d) What special properties do the level curves of a *linear* function have?

   (e) Use technology to plot the graphs $z = f(x, y)$ and $z = g(x, y)$ for (x, y) in $[-3, 3] \times [-3, 3]$. Describe briefly, in words, how the two graphs are related to each other.

9. Let f and g be the functions $f(x, y) = 2 + x^2$ and $g(x, y) = 2 + y^2$.

   (a) In the rectangle $[-3, 3] \times [-3, 3]$, draw and label the level curves of f that correspond to $z = 0, z = 2, z = 4,$ $z = 6$, and $z = 8$. What is the shape of each level curve?

   (b) In the rectangle $[-3, 3] \times [-3, 3]$, draw and label the level curves of g that correspond to $z = 0, z = 2, z = 4,$ $z = 6$, and $z = 8$. What is the shape of each level curve?

   (c) How are the results of parts (a) and (b) similar? How are they different?

   (d) Use technology to plot the graphs $z = f(x, y)$ and $z = g(x, y)$ for (x, y) in $[-3, 3] \times [-3, 3]$. Describe briefly, in words, how the two graphs are related to each other.

   (e) The graphs of f and g are both cylinders (in the sense defined in the text). How do the contour maps of f and g reflect this fact?

In Exercises 10–13, imagine a map of the United States in the usual position. The positive x-direction is east, and the positive y-direction is north. Suppose that the units of x and y are miles and that Los Angeles, California, has coordinates $(0, 0)$. (Several approximations are involved here. The Earth's surface is not flat, and Los Angeles occupies more than a single point.) Let $T(x, y)$ be the temperature, in degrees Celsius, at the location (x, y) at noon, Central Standard Time, on January 1, 2001.

10. What does it mean in weather language to say that $T(0, 0) = 15$?

11. What do the level curves of T mean in weather language? As a rule, would you expect level curves of T to run north and south or east and west? Why?

12. International Falls, Minnesota, is about 1400 miles east and 1100 miles north of Los Angeles. The noon temperature in International Falls on January 1, 2001, was $-15°$ C. What does this mean about $T(x, y)$?

13. Suppose that International Falls was the coldest spot in the country at the time in question. How would you expect the level curves to look near International Falls?

14. For any point (x, y) in the xy-plane, let $f(x, y)$ be the distance from (x, y) to the origin. Then f has the formula $f(x, y) = \sqrt{x^2 + y^2}$.

   (a) Find the domain and range of f.

(b) Plot f. Describe the graph in words.

(c) Draw the level curve of f that passes through $(3, 4)$.

(d) All level curves of f have the same shape. What is it?

15. For any point (x, y) in the xy-plane, let $f(x, y)$ be the distance from (x, y) to the line $x = 1$.

(a) Find a formula for $f(x, y)$.

(b) Plot f. Describe the graph in words.

(c) Draw the level curve that passes through $(3, 4)$.

(d) All level curves of f have the same shape. What is it?

16. Some values of a linear function $L(x, y)$ are tabulated below.

Values of $L(x, y)$							
y \ x	**−3**	**−2**	**−1**	**0**	**1**	**2**	**3**
3	−15	−12	−9	−6	−3	0	3
2	−13	−10	−7	−4	−1	2	5
1	−11	−8	−5	−2	1	4	7
0	−9	−6	−3	0	3	6	9
−1	−7	−4	−1	2	5	8	11
−2	−5	−2	1	4	7	10	13
−3	−3	0	3	6	9	12	15

(a) All the level curves of L are straight lines. Using this fact, draw (in the rectangle $[−3, 3] \times [−3, 3]$) and label the level curves $z = −12$, $z = −8$, $z = −4$, $z = 0$, $z = 4$, $z = 8$, $z = 12$.

(b) Find an equation in x and y for the level line $z = 0$.

(c) Because L is a linear function, its formula has the form $L(x, y) = a + bx + cy$ for some constants a, b, and c. Find numerical values for a, b, and c.
[HINT: The table says that $L(0, 0) = 0$. Therefore, $L(0, 0) = a + b \cdot 0 + c \cdot 0 = 0$, so $a = 0$. Use similar reasoning to find values for b and c.]

(d) Use technology to plot $L(x, y)$ over the rectangle $[−3, 3] \times [−3, 3]$. Is the shape of the graph consistent with the level curves you plotted in part (a)?

We stress similarities to and differences from ordinary derivatives; both are plentiful.

M.3 PARTIAL DERIVATIVES

Derivatives in one variable — interpretations

Let f be an ordinary function of one variable. Recall some familiar properties of the derivative function f': ◄

To avoid distractions, we assume that f and f' are continuous functions.

- **Slope**   For any fixed input $x = x_0$, the derivative $f'(x_0)$ tells the *slope* of the f-graph at the point $(x_0, f(x_0))$. The sign of $f'(x_0)$, in particular, tells whether f is increasing or decreasing (rising or falling, in everyday speech) at $x = x_0$.

In a specific example, we would need to specify appropriate units for everything.

- **Rate of change**   The derivative f' can also be interpreted as the *rate function* associated with f, as follows: For any input x_0, $f'(x_0)$ tells the instantaneous rate of change of $f(x)$ with respect to x. If, say, $f(x)$ gives the *position* of a moving object at time x, then $f'(x)$ gives the corresponding *velocity* at time x. ◄

- **Limit**   The derivative $f'(x_0)$ is defined as a limit of difference quotients:

$$f'(x_0) = \lim_{h \to 0} \frac{f(x_0 + h) - f(x_0)}{h}.$$

Similar interpretations hold if $h < 0$, but $h = 0$ is illegal.

For any $h > 0$, the difference quotient can be thought of either as the average rate of change of f over the interval $[x_0, x_0 + h]$ or as the slope of a secant line on the f-graph, over the same interval. ◄ Taking the limit as $h \to 0$ corresponds to finding the instantaneous rate of change of f or, equivalently, the slope of the tangent line to the f-graph at $x = x_0$.

- **Linear approximation**   At a point $(x_0, f(x_0))$ on the curve $y = f(x)$, the tangent line has slope $f'(x_0)$. This tangent line is the graph of the linear function L with equation

$$y = L(x) = f(x_0) + f'(x_0)(x - x_0).$$

The function L is called the **linear approximation** to f at x_0. The name makes sense because the graphs of f and L are close together near x_0. In symbols,

$$L(x) \approx f(x) \quad \text{when} \quad x \approx x_0.$$

We emphasize linear approximation strongly in our treatment of multivariable calculus: In any dimension, differentiable functions are "almost" linear.

Derivatives in several variables

Derivatives are just as important in multivariable calculus as in one-variable calculus, but—not surprisingly—the idea is more complicated for functions of several variables.

Take slope, for instance. The graph of a one-variable function $y = f(x)$ is a curve in the xy-plane. The slope at (x_0, y_0)—a single number—completely describes the graph's direction at (x_0, y_0). The graph of a two-variable function $z = f(x, y)$, by contrast, is a *surface*, which has no single slope at a point. A surface's steepness at a point depends on the direction (uphill, downhill, along the "contour," and so on) taken from the point. ➤ To put it another way, the graph of a one-variable function can be approximated near a given point by a one-dimensional tangent *line*. The graph of a two-variable function can be approximated near a fixed point by a two-dimensional tangent *plane*.

Every hiker knows this. How steep a mountain "feels" depends on the direction of the trail.

Here's the moral: To suit *multivariable* calculus, our notion of derivative must go beyond the simple idea of slope. The idea of linear approximation, not slope, turns out to be the key to extending the idea of the derivative to functions of more than one variable.

In this section we start to extend the derivative idea to functions of several variables. **Partial derivatives** are the simplest multivariable analogues of ordinary derivatives. ➤

"Partial" suggests— correctly—that there's more to the derivative story.

Partial derivatives: The idea   The basic idea of a partial derivative is to differentiate with respect to *one* variable, holding all the others constant. The following easy example illustrates the idea and introduces some useful terminology and notation.

E X A M P L E 1   Let $f(x, y) = x^2 - 3xy + 6$. Find $f_x(x, y)$ and $f_y(x, y)$, the partial derivatives of f with respect to x and y, respectively. Find the numerical values $f_x(2, 1)$ and $f_y(2, 1)$.

Students find the process of partial differentiation easy; interpreting results may be more challenging.

Solution   To find f_x, we differentiate $f(x, y) = x^2 - 3xy + 6$ with respect to x, *treating y as a constant*:

$$f_x(x, y) = 2x - 3y.$$

To find f_y, we *treat x as a constant*:

$$f_y(x, y) = -3x.$$

Setting $x = 2$ and $y = 1$ in these formulas gives

$$f_x(2, 1) = 2 \cdot 2 - 3 \cdot 1 = 1; \qquad f_y(2, 1) = -3 \cdot 2 = -6. \qquad ■$$

The calculations were easy, but what do the results mean? What do they say about how f behaves near $(x, y) = (2, 1)$? Can we interpret the results graphically and numerically? Understanding multivariable derivatives fully is a long-term proposition, but here are some starters.

Holding variables constant To find the partial derivative f_x of a function f with respect to x, we treat all the other variables as constants. This produces a function of just one variable, x, which we differentiate in the usual way. For example, suppose we fix $y = 3$ in $f(x, y) = x^2 - 3xy + 6$. Then $f(x, y) = f(x, 3) = x^2 - 9x + 6$, and

$$\frac{d}{dx}\big(f(x, 3)\big) = f_x(x, 3) = 2x - 9.$$

This agrees, as it should, with the general formula $f_x(x, y) = 2x - 3y$ found earlier.

Directional rates of change Partial derivatives (like ordinary derivatives) can be interpreted as rates or slopes—but with an important proviso about directions. For a function $f(x, y)$ and a point (x_0, y_0) in its domain, the partial derivative $f_x(x_0, y_0)$ tells the rate of change of $f(x, y)$ with respect to x (that's the only variable that's free to move); that is, how fast $f(x, y)$ increases as the input (x, y) moves away from (x_0, y_0) in the *positive* x-direction. The other partial derivative, $f_y(x_0, y_0)$, tells how fast f increases near (x_0, y_0) as y increases. The next example illustrates what this means numerically.

We think the numerical view deserves more attention than it usually gets. Notice that the table is "oriented" just like the xy-plane: for instance, rows correspond to fixed values of y.

EXAMPLE 2 The function $f(x, y) = x^2 - 3xy + 6$ has partial derivatives $f_x(x, y) = 2x - 3y$ and $f_y(x, y) = -3x$. What does this say about rates of change of f at $(x, y) = (2, 1)$? At $(x, y) = (1, 2)$?

Solution We start at $(2, 1)$. The formulas give $f_x(2, 1) = 1$ and $f_y(2, 1) = -6$. These numbers represent rates of change of f with respect to x and y, respectively, at $(2, 1)$. A table of f-values centered at $(2, 1)$ shows what this means. ◄

The boxed row and column meet at $(2, 1)$, our target point.

Values of $f(x, y) = x^2 - 3xy + 6$ near $(2, 1)$							
y \ x	**1.97**	**1.98**	**1.99**	**2.00**	**2.01**	**2.02**	**2.03**
1.03	3.7936	3.8022	3.8110	3.8200	3.8292	3.8386	3.8482
1.02	3.8527	3.8616	3.8707	3.8800	3.8895	3.8992	3.9091
1.01	3.9118	3.9210	3.9304	3.9400	3.9498	3.9598	3.9700
1.00	3.9709	3.9804	3.9901	4.0000	4.0101	4.0204	4.0309
0.99	4.0300	4.0398	4.0498	4.0600	4.0704	4.0810	4.0918
0.98	4.0891	4.0992	4.1095	4.1200	4.1307	4.1416	4.1527
0.97	4.1482	4.1586	4.1692	4.1800	4.1910	4.2022	4.2136

Numerical tables like this one deserve a close look; watching which digits change, and how fast, tells a lot about partial derivatives.

Reading *up* the boxed column (at each step, y increases by 0.01) shows successive corresponding values of f *decreasing* by about 0.06. Thus, -6 is the rate of change of f with respect to y at $(2, 1)$; equivalently, $f_y(2, 1) = -6$. Similarly, the fact that $f_x(2, 1) = 1$ suggests that values of $f(x, 1)$ should increase at about the same rate as x if $x \approx 2$. Reading *across* the boxed row confirms this expectation.

Similar reasoning applies at $(1, 2)$. The values $f_x(1, 2) = -4$ and $f_y(1, 2) = -3$ mean that f decreases (at different rates) with respect to both x and y near $(1, 2)$. Numerical f-values bear this out:

Values of $f(x, y) = x^2 - 3xy + 6$ near $(1, 2)$					
y \ x	0.98	0.99	1.00	1.01	1.02
2.02	1.0216	0.9807	0.9400	0.8995	0.8592
2.01	1.0510	1.0104	0.9700	0.9298	0.8898
2.00	1.0804	1.0401	1.0000	0.9601	0.9204
1.99	1.1098	1.0698	1.0300	0.9904	0.9510
1.98	1.1392	1.0995	1.0600	1.0207	0.9816

Reading either across or up shows f-values decreasing at rates of about -4 and -3, respectively. ∎

Formal definitions   Partial derivatives are defined formally as limits, in much the same way as ordinary derivatives are defined.

DEFINITION   Let $f(x, y)$ be a function of two variables. The **partial derivative** with respect to x of f at (x_0, y_0), denoted by $f_x(x_0, y_0)$, is defined by

$$f_x(x_0, y_0) = \lim_{h \to 0} \frac{f(x_0 + h, y_0) - f(x_0, y_0)}{h}$$

if the limit exists. The partial derivative with respect to y at (x_0, y_0), denoted by $f_y(x_0, y_0)$, is defined by

$$f_y(x_0, y_0) = \lim_{h \to 0} \frac{f(x_0, y_0 + h) - f(x_0, y_0)}{h}$$

if the limit exists.

The definition says, in effect, that $f_x(x_0, y_0)$ is the ordinary derivative at $x = x_0$ of an ordinary function of one variable—namely, the function given by the rule $x \to f(x, y_0)$. Some further comments and observations follow.

- **Do they exist?**   If either limit does not exist, then neither does the corresponding partial derivative. It's possible, for instance, that $f_x(0, 0)$ exists but $f_y(0, 0)$ doesn't. For most functions in this chapter, however, both partial derivatives *do* exist.

- **About domains**   For the preceding limits to exist, $f(x, y)$ must be defined at (x_0, y_0) and at nearby points (x, y). In practice, this condition seldom causes trouble. In particular, there's no problem if (x_0, y_0) lies in the interior of the domain of f, that is, if f is defined both at and near (x_0, y_0). (For the record, trouble is likeliest if (x_0, y_0) lies on the edge of the domain of f.)

- **Other notations**   As with ordinary derivatives, various notations are used to denote partial derivatives. If, say, $z = f(x, y) = x \sin y$, then all of the expressions

$$f_x, \quad \frac{\partial f}{\partial x}, \quad \frac{\partial z}{\partial x}, \quad \text{and} \quad \frac{\partial}{\partial x}(x \sin y)$$

mean the same thing, as do

$$f_x(x_0, y_0), \quad \frac{\partial f}{\partial x}(x_0, y_0), \quad \frac{\partial z}{\partial x}\bigg|_{(x_0, y_0)}, \quad \text{and} \quad \frac{\partial}{\partial x}(x \sin y)\bigg|_{(x_0, y_0)}.$$

Partial derivatives with respect to y are expressed with similar notations. Notice especially the "curly-d" symbol ∂. It's usually read aloud as "partial."

On a topographic map oriented the usual way, the partial derivatives f_x and f_y describe the steepness of the terrain in the eastward and northward directions, respectively.

Partial derivatives and contour maps   We saw in Example 2, page M-18, how to estimate partial derivatives from a table of function values. Contour maps can be used for the same purpose. Thinking of $f_x(x_0, y_0)$ and $f_y(x_0, y_0)$ as rates suggests how: Use the contour map to measure how fast $z = f(x, y)$ rises or falls near (x_0, y_0) as either x or y increases. ◄

EXAMPLE 3   Figure 1 is a contour map of the function $f(x, y) = x^2 - 3xy + 6$, centered at $(2, 1)$. Use the contour map to estimate the partial derivatives $f_x(2, 1)$ and $f_y(2, 1)$.

Contour maps give a useful alternative view to numerical tables; they emphasize where the function is constant as well as revealing "uphill" and "downhill" directions.

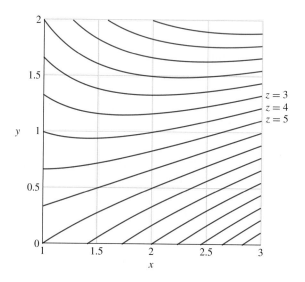

$z = 3$
$z = 4$
$z = 5$

FIGURE 1
Level curves of $f(x, y) = x^2 - 3xy + 6$

Solution   The level curves represent successive integer values of $z = f(x, y)$. In general, values of $f(x, y)$ increase as (x, y) moves toward the lower right. ◄

Look closely at the contour map to convince yourself of these claims.

First we estimate $f_x(2, 1)$. A close look at the figure suggests that $f(2.1, 1) \approx 4.1$. Increasing x by 0.1 increases f by 0.1; this suggests that $f_x(2, 1) \approx 1$. Similarly, $f(2, 1.1) \approx 3.4$, and so increasing y by 0.1 increases f by -0.6; thus, $f_y(2, 1) \approx -6$. ∎

Partial derivatives and linear approximation

The idea is simple: Find a linear function that matches value and partial derivatives at a given point. Working through the details takes some effort.

For a differentiable function $y = f(x)$ of one variable, the ordinary derivative can be interpreted in terms of linear approximation. For any point (x_0, y_0) on the f-graph, there's a certain line through this point—the tangent line—that best "fits" the graph near $x = x_0$. The derivative $f'(x_0)$ gives the slope of this tangent line. Because the slope is known, it's easy to find an equation for the tangent line in point–slope form:

$$y - y_0 = f'(x_0)(x - x_0).$$

Equivalently, we can think of the tangent line as the graph of the linear function L defined by

$$y = L(x) = y_0 + f'(x_0)(x - x_0).$$

(Recall that $f(x_0) = y_0$.) The function L is called the **linear approximation** to f at x_0. The name is appropriate for three good reasons:

(i) L is linear;   (ii) $L(x_0) = f(x_0)$;   (iii) $L'(x_0) = f'(x_0)$.

In short, L agrees with f at x_0 as closely as *any* linear function can—both functions have the same value and the same (first) derivative. ➡

The idea of quadratic approximation is similar, except that we'd require agreement in the second derivative too.

Linear approximation in several variables   The idea of linear approximation is essentially the same for functions of two (or more) variables: Given a function $f(x, y)$ and a point (x_0, y_0) in the domain of f, we look for a linear function $L(x, y)$ that has the same value and partial derivatives as does f at (x_0, y_0). In other words, we want a linear function L such that

$$L(x_0, y_0) = f(x_0, y_0), \quad L_x(x_0, y_0) = f_x(x_0, y_0), \quad \text{and} \quad L_y(x_0, y_0) = f_y(x_0, y_0).$$

In the one-variable case, the graph of a linear approximation function is called a tangent line. For a function of two variables, the graph of the linear approximation function is called a **tangent plane**. We illustrate and summarize these ideas in the next example.

EXAMPLE 4   Find the linear approximation function L to $f(x, y) = x^2 + y^2$ at $(x_0, y_0) = (2, 1)$. How are graphs of f and L related?

Solution   The partial derivatives of f are $f_x(x, y) = 2x$ and $f_y(x, y) = 2y$. Thus, at our base point, $(x_0, y_0) = (2, 1)$:

$$f(2, 1) = 5; \qquad f_x(2, 1) = 4; \qquad f_y(2, 1) = 2.$$

Let's find a linear function L to match these values.

It's easiest to start by writing L in the convenient form

$$L(x, y) = a(x - x_0) + b(y - y_0) + c = a(x - 2) + b(y - 1) + c$$

and then choosing appropriate values for a, b, and c. Because $L(x, y) = a(x - 2) + b(y - 1) + c$, it's easy to see that

$$L(2, 1) = c; \qquad L_x(2, 1) = a; \qquad L_y(2, 1) = b.$$

To match f, we must have $c = 5$, $a = 4$, and $b = 2$; therefore,

$$L(x, y) = a(x - 2) + b(y - 1) + c = 4(x - 2) + 2(y - 1) + 5.$$

Figure 2 shows graphs of f and L together:

Showing the surface and tangent plane clearly in one picture is difficult; one gets in the way of the other. The (following) contour map gives another useful view.

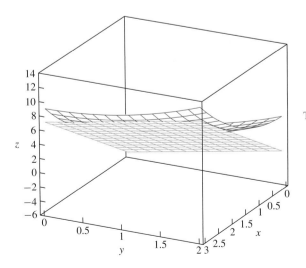

The tangent plane is shown gray.

FIGURE 2
Graphs of f and L together

Contours of any linear function are (i) straight lines, and (ii) evenly spaced. Students should understand why both properties hold.

The figure illustrates the phrases "tangent plane" and "linear approximation": The plane $z = L(x, y)$ touches the surface $z = f(x, y)$ at $(2, 1, 5)$; at this point, moreover, the flat plane fits the curved surface as well as possible. A closer look (Figure 3) at both functions near $(2, 1)$, this time using contour maps, suggests how good the fit really is.

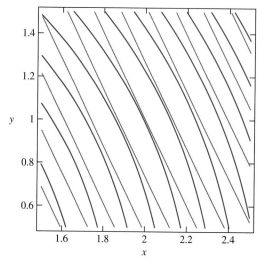

The gray lines are contours of L.

FIGURE 3
Level curves f and L together

The two contour maps are almost identical near $(2, 1)$.   ■

Linear approximation: The general formula   The procedure in Example 4 works the same way for any function of several variables as long as the necessary partial derivatives exist. The following are definitions for two and three variables. (The same idea works for any number of variables.)

DEFINITION (Linear approximation)   Let $f(x, y)$ and $g(x, y, z)$ be functions and suppose that all the following partial derivatives exist. The **linear approximation** to f at (x_0, y_0) is the function

$$L(x, y) = f(x_0, y_0) + f_x(x_0, y_0)(x - x_0) + f_y(x_0, y_0)(y - y_0).$$

The linear approximation to g at (x_0, y_0, z_0) is the function

$$L(x, y, z) = g(x_0, y_0, z_0) + g_x(x_0, y_0, z_0)(x - x_0)$$
$$+ g_y(x_0, y_0, z_0)(y - y_0) + g_z(x_0, y_0, z_0)(z - z_0).$$

Visualizing linear approximation is considerably more difficult in three dimensions.

EXAMPLE 5   Find the linear approximation to $g(x, y, z) = x + yz^2$ at $(1, 2, 3)$. Does the answer make numerical or graphical sense?

Solution   Easy calculations give

$$g(1, 2, 3) = 19; \ g_x(1, 2, 3) = 1; \ g_y(1, 2, 3) = 9; \ g_z(1, 2, 3) = 12.$$

The linear approximation function therefore has the form

$$L(x, y, z) = g(1, 2, 3) + g_x(1, 2, 3)(x - 1) + g_y(1, 2, 3)(y - 2) + g_z(1, 2, 3)(z - 3)$$
$$= 19 + 1(x - 1) + 9(y - 2) + 12(z - 3).$$

To see the situation numerically, we tabulate some values of each function.

Values of L and g near $(1, 2, 3)$						
(x, y, z)	$(1, 2, 3)$	$(1.1, 2, 3)$	$(1, 2.1, 3)$	$(1, 2, 3.1)$	$(1.1, 2.1, 3.1)$	$(3, 4, 5)$
$g(x, y, z)$	19	19.1	19.9	20.22	21.281	103
$L(x, y, z)$	19	19.1	19.9	20.2	21.2	63

As the numbers illustrate, $L(x, y, z)$ and $g(x, y, z)$ are close together if, but only if, (x, y, z) is near $(1, 2, 3)$. ➤

The last column illustrates what happens far from $(1, 2, 3)$.

To plot ordinary graphs of g and L would require four dimensions. ➤ Instead we plot, for comparison, the level surfaces $L(x, y, z) = 19$ and $g(x, y, z) = 19$, both of which pass through the base point $(1, 2, 3)$. (A **level surface** is like a level curve—it's a set of inputs along which a function has constant output value.) Figure 4 suggests again how similarly $g(x, y, z)$ and $L(x, y, z)$ behave when $(x, y, z) \approx (1, 2, 3)$.

One for each input variable and one more for the output.

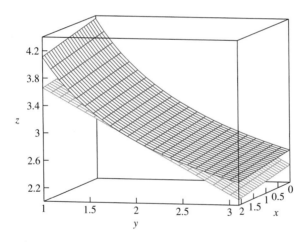

FIGURE 4
A curved surface and a linear approximation ∎

In Exercises 1–8, find the partial derivative with respect to each variable.

1. $f(x, y) = x^2 - y^2$

2. $f(x, y) = x^2 y^2$

3. $f(x, y) = \dfrac{x^2}{y^2}$

4. $f(x, y) = \cos(xy)$

5. $f(x, y) = \cos x \cos y$

6. $f(x, y) = \dfrac{\cos x}{\cos y}$

7. $f(x, y, z) = x y^2 z^3$

8. $f(x, y, z) = \cos(xyz)$

9. Let $f(x) = x^2$ and $x_0 = 3$.

(a) Let L be the linear approximation to f at x_0. Show that $L(x) = 9 + 6(x - 3)$.

(b) Plot L and f on the same axes. (Choose your own plotting window.) Supposedly, "L linearly approximates f near x_0." How do the graphs illustrate this?

(c) Find an interval $a \le x \le b$ on which $|f(x) - L(x)| < 0.01$. (On this interval, $L(x)$ approximates $f(x)$ within 0.01.) [HINT: This can be done either graphically, by zooming, or symbolically, by solving inequalities.]

10. Redo Exercise 9, but let $f(x) = \sqrt{x}$ and $x_0 = 9$.

11. Let $f(x) = x^2$.

   (a) $f'(3) = 6$. What does this mean about the graph of f? (Use a graph of $f(x)$ for $2.5 \le x \le 3.5$ to illustrate your answer.)

   (b) Plot $f(x)$ over the interval $2.5 \le x \le 3.5$. On your graph, draw the secant lines from $x = 3$ to $x = 3.5$ and from $x = 3$ to $x = 3.1$.

   (c) Find the average rate of change $\Delta y / \Delta x$ of f over the intervals $[3, 3.5]$ and $[3, 3.1]$.

   (d) Find the limit $\lim\limits_{h \to 0} \dfrac{f(3+h) - f(3)}{h}$. Interpret the answer as a derivative. Does the answer agree with other information already given?

12. Redo Exercise 11, but use $f(x) = x^2 - x$.

Some values of a function $g(x, y)$ are tabulated below. Use the table to answer the questions in Exercises 13–16.

Values of g(x, y)				
y \ x	**−0.0100**	**0.0000**	**0.0100**	**0.0200**
1.02	2.0603	2.0604	2.0603	2.0600
1.01	2.0300	2.0301	2.0300	2.0297
1.00	1.9999	2.0000	1.9999	1.9996
0.99	1.9700	1.9701	1.9700	1.9697
⋮	⋮	⋮	⋮	⋮
0.02	0.0203	0.0204	0.0203	0.0200
0.01	0.0100	0.0101	0.0100	0.0097
0.00	−0.0001	0.0000	−0.0001	−0.0004
−0.01	−0.0100	−0.0099	−0.0100	−0.0103

y \ x	**0.9900**	**1.0000**	**1.0100**	**1.0200**
1.02	1.0803	1.0604	1.0403	1.0200
1.01	1.0500	1.0301	1.0100	0.9897
1.00	1.0199	1.0000	0.9799	0.9596
0.99	0.9900	0.9701	0.9500	0.9297
⋮	⋮	⋮	⋮	⋮
0.02	−0.9597	−0.9796	−0.9997	−1.0200
0.01	−0.9700	−0.9899	−1.0100	−1.0303
0.00	−0.9801	−1.0000	−1.0201	−1.0404
−0.01	−0.9900	−1.0099	−1.0300	−1.0503

13. Use the table to estimate the partial derivatives $g_x(1, 1)$ and $g_y(1, 1)$.

14. It's true that $g_x(0, 0) = 0$ and $g_y(0, 0) = 1$. How do the table entries reflect these facts?

15. **(a)** Consider the linear function $L(x, y) = 0 + 0x + 1y = y$. Show that $L_x(0, 0) = g_x(0, 0) = 0$, $L_y(0, 0) = g_y(0, 0) = 1$, and $L(0, 0) = g(0, 0) = 0$.

   (b) Fill in the following table of values for the function L from part (a). Compare your results with the tabulated values of g. (The results show how L linearly approximates g near $(0, 0)$.)

Values of L(x, y)					
y \ x	**−0.02**	**−0.01**	**0.00**	**0.01**	**0.02**
0.02					
0.01					
0.00					
−0.01					
−0.02					

16. Find the linear function $M(x, y)$ such that (i) $M(1, 1) = g(1, 1)$, (ii) $M_x(1, 1) = g_x(1, 1)$, and (iii) $M_y(1, 1) = g_y(1, 1)$. [HINT: One approach is to write $M(x, y) = a + b(x - 1) + c(y - 1)$ and then use the conditions to find values for a, b, and c.]

17. Let $f(x, y) = \sin y + 2$. (The formula is independent of x.)

   (a) Plot f; use the domain $-5 \le x \le 5$, $-5 \le y \le 5$. How does the shape of the graph reflect the fact that f is independent of x? (In Section M.1 we called such graphs cylinders.)

   (b) Find $f_x(x, y)$ and $f_y(x, y)$. How do the answers reflect the fact that f is independent of x?

   (c) Find the linear approximation function L for f at the point $(0, 0)$. How does its form reflect the fact that f is independent of x?

18. Let f be the function in Example 3.

   (a) Use the contour map in Figure 1 to estimate the partial derivatives $f_x(1.5, 1.5)$ and $f_y(1.5, 1.5)$.

   (b) Use the formula $f(x, y) = x^2 - 3xy + 6$ to find $f_x(1.5, 1.5)$ and $f_y(1.5, 1.5)$ exactly.

   (c) Use results of part (b) to find the linear approximation $L(x, y)$ to $f(x, y)$ at $(1.5, 1.5)$.

19. Let $f(x, y) = \sin x$.

   (a) Draw a contour map of f in the rectangle $-\pi \le x \le \pi$, $-2 \le y \le 2$. Show the level curves that correspond to $z = \pm 1$, $z = \pm 0.75$, $z = \pm 0.5$, $z = \pm 0.25$, and $z = 0$.

   (b) Use the level-curve diagram to estimate $f_x(0, 0)$ and $f_y(0, 0)$.

   (c) Use the level-curve diagram to estimate $f_x(\pi/2, 0)$ and $f_y(\pi/2, 0)$.

   (d) The formula shows that $f_y(x, y) = 0$ for all (x, y). How does the contour map reflect this fact?

(e) The formula shows that $f_x(x, y)$ is independent of y. How does the contour map of f reflect this fact?

20. Let $f(x, y) = \cos y$.

(a) Draw a contour map of f in the rectangle $-\pi \le x \le \pi$, $-2 \le y \le 2$. Show the level curves that correspond to $z = \pm 1$, $z = \pm 0.75$, $z = \pm 0.5$, $z = \pm 0.25$, and $z = 0$.

(b) Use the level-curve diagram to estimate $f_x(0, 0)$ and $f_y(0, 0)$.

(c) Use the level-curve diagram to estimate $f_x(\pi/2, 0)$ and $f_y(\pi/2, 0)$.

(d) The formula for f shows that $f_x(x, y) = 0$ for all (x, y). How does the contour map of f reflect this fact?

(e) The formula for f shows that $f_y(x, y)$ is independent of x. How does the contour map of f reflect this fact?

21. Let $f(x, y) = 2x - 3y$.

(a) Draw a contour map of f in the rectangle $[-3, 3] \times [-3, 3]$. Show the level curves that correspond to $z = -5$, $z = -4, z = -3, \ldots, z = 4$, and $z = 5$.

(b) Use your contour map (not the formula) to find $f_x(0, 0)$ and $f_y(0, 0)$.

(c) The formula for f implies that both f_x and f_y are constant functions. How does the contour map of f reflect this fact?

(d) The formula for f implies that for any (x, y), $f_x(x, y) = 2$ and $f_y(x, y) = -3$. How does the contour map reflect the fact that $f_x(x, y)$ is positive but $f_y(x, y)$ is negative?

22. Let $f(x, y) = 2y - x$.

(a) Draw a contour map of f in the rectangle $[-3, 3] \times [-3, 3]$. Show the level curves that correspond to $z = -5$, $z = -4, z = -3, \ldots, z = 4$, and $z = 5$.

(b) Use your contour map (not the formula) to find $f_x(0, 0)$ and $f_y(0, 0)$.

(c) The formula for f implies that $f_x(x, y) = -1$ and $f_y(x, y) = 2$ for all (x, y). How does the contour map reflect these facts? In particular, how does the contour map show that $f_x(x, y)$ is negative but $f_y(x, y)$ is positive?

23. Let $f(x, y) = xy$.

(a) Find the linear approximation function L to f at $(x_0, y_0) = (2, 1)$.

(b) (Do this part by hand.) On one set of xy-axes, draw the level curves $L(x, y) = k$ for $k = 1, 2, 3, 4, 5$. On another set of axes, draw the level curves $f(x, y) = k$ for $k = 1, 2, 3, 4, 5$. (In each case, draw the curves into the square $[0, 3] \times [0, 3]$.)

(c) How do the contour maps in part (b) reflect the fact that L is the linear approximation to f at the point $(2, 1)$? Explain briefly in words.

(d) Use technology to plot contour maps of f and L in the window $[1.8, 2.2] \times [0.8, 1.2]$. Explain what you see.

24. Repeat Exercise 23 using the function $f(x, y) = x^2 - y^2$.

25. Let $f(x, y) = x^2 + y^2$.

(a) Use Figure 4 on page M-13 to estimate the partial derivatives $f_x(1, 2)$ and $f_y(1, 2)$.

(b) Check your answers to part (a) by symbolic differentiation.

(c) Use your answers from part (a) to find the linear approximation $L(x, y)$ to $f(x, y)$ at $(1, 2)$.

(d) On one set of axes, plot the level curves $L(x, y) = k$ and $f(x, y) = k$ for $k = 3, 4, 5, 6, 7$. (Use the window $[0, 3] \times [0, 3]$.) What's special about the point $(1, 2)$?

26. Let $f(x, y) = \sin x + 2y + xy$.

(a) Find the partial derivatives $f_x(x, y)$ and $f_y(x, y)$; then evaluate $f_x(0, 0)$ and $f_y(0, 0)$.

(b) Find a linear function $L(x, y) = a + bx + cy$ such that $L_x(0, 0) = f_x(0, 0)$, $L_y(0, 0) = f_y(0, 0)$, and $L(0, 0) = f(0, 0)$.

(c) Complete the following table (round answers to four decimals). How do the answers reflect the fact that L approximates f closely near $(0, 0)$?

(x, y)	$(0, 0)$	$(0.01, 0.01)$	$(0.1, 0.1)$	$(1, 1)$
$f(x, y)$				
$L(x, y)$				

(d) Use technology to draw contour plots of both f and L in the rectangle $-1 \le x \le 1$, $-1 \le y \le 1$. Label several contours on each. How do the pictures reflect the fact that L approximates f closely near $(0, 0)$?

In Exercises 27–30, find the linear function L that linearly approximates f at the given point (x_0, y_0). (If possible, check your answers graphically by plotting both f and L near (x_0, y_0).)

27. $f(x, y) = x^2 + y^2$; $(x_0, y_0) = (2, 1)$.

28. $f(x, y) = x^2 + y^2$; $(x_0, y_0) = (0, 0)$.

29. $f(x, y) = \sin x + \sin y$; $(x_0, y_0) = (0, 0)$.

30. $f(x, y) = \sin x \sin y$; $(x_0, y_0) = (0, 0)$.

31. Let $f(x, y)$ be a differentiable function of two variables, let (x_0, y_0) be any point in its domain, and let $L(x, y)$ be the linear approximation to f at (x_0, y_0). Show that if f is independent of one of the variables—say, x—then so is L.

32. Suppose that $f(3, 4) = 25$, $f_x(3, 4) = 6$, $f_y(3, 4) = 8$, and $f(4, 5) = 41$.

(a) Find a linear function $L(x, y)$ that approximates f as well as possible near $(3, 4)$.

(b) Use L to estimate $f(2.9, 3.9)$, $f(3.1, 4.1)$, and $f(4, 5)$.

(c) Could f itself be a linear function? Why or why not?

33. Suppose that $g(3, 4) = 5$, $g_x(3, 4) = 3/5$, $g_y(3, 4) = 4/5$, and $g(4, 5) = \sqrt{41}$.

(a) Find a linear function $L(x, y)$ that approximates g as well as possible near $(3, 4)$.

(b) Use L to estimate $g(2.9, 4.1)$ and $g(4, 5)$.

(c) Could g be a linear function? Why or why not?

34. Let $f(x, y) = |y| \cos x$. This exercise explores the fact that the partial derivatives of a function may or may not exist at a given point.

(a) Use technology to plot $z = f(x, y)$ over the rectangle $[-5, 5] \times [-5, 5]$. The graph suggests that there may be trouble with partial derivatives where $y = 0$, that is, along the x-axis. How does the graph suggest this? Which partial derivative (f_x or f_y) seems to be in trouble?

(b) Use the definition to show that $f_y(0, 0)$ does not exist. In other words, explain why the limit $\lim\limits_{h \to 0} \dfrac{f(h, 0) - f(0, 0)}{h}$ does not exist.

(c) Show that $f_x(0, 0)$ does exist; find its value. How does the result appear on the graph?

(d) Use the limit definition to show that $f_y(0, \pi/2)$ does exist; find its value.

(e) How does the graph reflect the result of part (d)? (You may need to do some experimenting with the graph to answer this.)

(f) Find a function $g(x, y)$ for which $g_y(0, 0)$ exists but $g_x(0, 0)$ does not. Use technology to plot its graph.

35. Let $f(x, y) = |x| \, y$.

(a) By experimenting with graphs (use technology!), try to guess where $f_x(x, y)$ and $f_y(x, y)$ do exist and where they don't. (No proofs are needed.)

(b) Find $f_x(0, 0)$.

(c) Explain why $f_x(0, 1)$ does not exist.

M.4 OPTIMIZATION AND PARTIAL DERIVATIVES: A FIRST LOOK

A complete account of optimization, even in two variables, takes considerable space and care. But partial derivatives play a useful and intuitive role, so we emphasize them here. In simple cases the situation is not dissimilar to that in one variable.

Optimization—finding maximum and minimum values of a function—is as important for multivariable functions as it is for one-variable functions. Functions of several variables are more complicated, but derivatives are still the crucial tool.

A one-variable review

For a one-variable differentiable function $y = f(x)$ on an interval I, finding maximum and minimum values is relatively straightforward. Maxima and minima are found only at stationary points—where $f'(x) = 0$—or at the endpoints (if any) of the interval I. Usually, only a few such "candidate" points exist, and we can check directly which one produces, say, the largest value of f.

"Extremum" (singular) means "either maximum or minimum"; "extrema" is the plural.

A simple idea lies behind all talk of derivatives and extrema: ◄ At a local maximum or minimum point x_0, the graph of a differentiable function f must be "flat," and so $f'(x_0) = 0$. However, a stationary point x_0 might be (i) a local maximum point, (ii) a local minimum point, or (iii) neither. (The function $f(x) = x^3$ at $x = 0$ illustrates the "neither" case.)

Without technology, plotting f may be hard.

For simple one-variable functions, deciding which of (i)–(iii) actually holds is easy. One strategy is to check the sign of $f''(x_0)$. If, say, $f''(x_0) < 0$, then f is concave down at x_0, and so f has a local maximum there. Alternatively, we might just plot f and see directly how it behaves near x_0. ◄

FIGURE 1
Local vs. global extrema

Local talk. When is a maximum or minimum "local"? When is it "global"? Figure 1 shows the difference:

All six bulleted points (three maximum points and three minimum points) correspond to *local* extrema. At each bulleted point $(x_0, f(x_0))$, $f(x_0)$ is either highest or lowest among *nearby* points $(x, f(x))$. (For present purposes, exactly *how* nearby doesn't matter.) Only the first and last points are *global* extrema because only they represent the largest and smallest values of $f(x)$ among all possibilities shown in the picture. On a larger domain interval—say, $-15 \leq x \leq 15$—these extrema might not be global.

Local maxima and minima are conceptually simpler than the global variety, are readily recognizable on graphs, and are often convenient to locate symbolically, using derivatives. With all these advantages, local extrema are usually the main tools used to solve optimization problems.

In several variables

If a one-variable function has a local maximum or minimum at x_0, then the ordinary derivative (if it exists) must be zero at x_0. If a two-variable function $f(x, y)$ has a local maximum at (x_0, y_0), then *both* partial derivatives (if they exist) must vanish there:

$$f_x(x_0, y_0) = 0; \qquad f_y(x_0, y_0) = 0.$$

In words, (x_0, y_0) is a stationary point of f. ➡

The result sounds plausible, but why is it true? Consider the case of a local maximum. Geometrically, the surface $z = f(x, y)$ has a "peak" above the domain point (x_0, y_0). If we slice the surface with any vertical plane, say the plane $y = y_0$, then the resulting curve—that is, the trace of the surface $z = f(x, y)$ in the plane $y = y_0$—has the equation $z = f(x, y_0)$, and this curve must have a peak at $x = x_0$. We know from one-variable calculus that if the function $x \to f(x, y_0)$ is differentiable, then its derivative must be zero at x_0. In other words,

This is the natural extension of the one-variable idea.

$$\frac{dz}{dx}(x_0) = f_x(x_0, y_0) = 0.$$

For similar reasons, $f_y(x_0, y_0) = 0$. Here's the general fact:

> **THEOREM 1 (Extreme points and partial derivatives)** Suppose that $f(x, y)$ has a local maximum or a local minimum at (x_0, y_0). If both partial derivatives exist, then
>
> $$f_x(x_0, y_0) = 0 \quad \text{and} \quad f_y(x_0, y_0) = 0.$$

Caution The theorem is useful, but what it *doesn't* say is also important. It does *not* guarantee, in particular, that at a stationary point f *must* assume either a local maximum or a local minimum value. The next example illustrates both sides of this coin.

Thinking about mountainous terrain may help students negotiate the subtleties of various possible surface "shapes" at a stationary point, including the fact that a stationary point need not be a local extremum.

EXAMPLE 1 Let $f(x, y) = x^2 + y^2$, and let $g(x, y) = xy$. Find all the stationary points of f and g. What happens at each one?

Solution Finding the partial derivatives is easy:

$$f_x(x, y) = 2x; \quad f_y(x, y) = 2y; \quad g_x(x, y) = y; \quad g_y(x, y) = x.$$

Both f and g, therefore, are stationary only at the origin $(0, 0)$. For f the origin is a *minimum* point, because $f(x, y) = x^2 + y^2 \geq 0$ for all (x, y). For g, however, the origin is neither a maximum nor a minimum point, because $g(x, y)$ assumes both positive and negative values near $(0, 0)$. (For example, $g(0.1, -0.1) < 0$, but $g(0.1, 0.1) > 0$.) Contour maps of f and g illustrate their very different behavior near the stationary point. (In

Note that darker regions are "lower."

Figures 2 through 5, the level curves are the edges of the shaded regions. Note the key to the right of each contour map.) Figure 2 shows f.

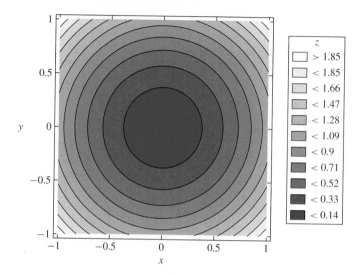

FIGURE 2
A contour map of $f(x, y) = x^2 + y^2$

Level curves of f are circles centered on the "basin" at $(0, 0)$. Thus, the figure suggests a minimum point at $(x, y) = (0, 0)$. The suggestion is correct: $f(0, 0) = 0$, and $f(x, y) \geq 0$ for all (x, y); thus, f assumes a local (and even global) minimum value at $(0, 0)$. ◄ Now look at g near its stationary point (Figure 3):

Look carefully; notice, in particular, that darker regions are "lower."

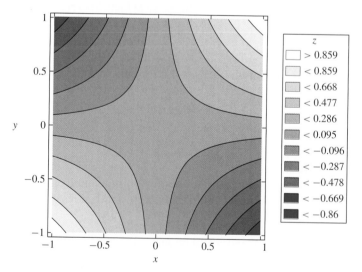

FIGURE 3
A contour map of $g(x, y) = xy$

Think about this carefully. Can you see the saddle in the contour map?

Level curves of g show a "saddle" at $(0, 0)$. (If the surface were literally a saddle, the horse would be walking either "northeast" or "southwest.") ◄ The surface rises above the first and third quadrants and falls below the second and fourth quadrants. ∎

Different types of stationary points Here is one moral of the preceding example: Although the basic strategy for optimizing a function—find the stationary points and analyze them—is exactly the same for functions of one and of several variables, the situation is usually more complicated for functions of several variables. For one thing, finding stationary points may be harder; for another, functions of several variables can behave in more complicated ways near a stationary point. This makes multivariable optimization harder, but also more interesting.

As we did for functions of one variable, we identify three main types of stationary points for a function $f(x, y)$. (The definitions for a three-variable function $g(x, y, z)$ are almost identical.)

- **Local minimum point**   A stationary point (x_0, y_0) is a **local minimum point** for f if $f(x, y) \geq f(x_0, y_0)$ for all (x, y) near (x_0, y_0). (A little more formally, $f(x, y) \geq f(x_0, y_0)$ for all (x, y) in some rectangle surrounding (x_0, y_0).) In this case, we say that f assumes a local minimum value at (x_0, y_0). In Example 1, $(0, 0)$ is a local minimum point for $f(x, y) = x^2 + y^2$.

- **Local maximum point**   A stationary point (x_0, y_0) is a **local maximum point** for f if $f(x, y) \leq f(x_0, y_0)$ for all (x, y) near (x_0, y_0). In this case, we say that f assumes a local maximum value at (x_0, y_0). Figure 4 illustrates a local maximum point for the function $h(x, y) = 1 - x^2 - y^2$.

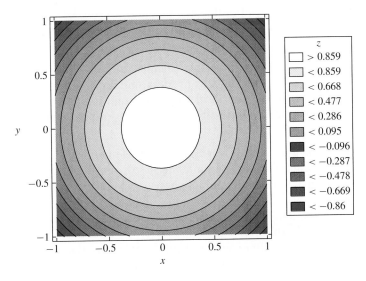

FIGURE 4
Contour plot of $1 - x^2 - y^2$

- **Saddle point**   A stationary point (x_0, y_0) is a **saddle point** for f if f assumes neither a local maximum nor a local minimum at (x_0, y_0). In Example 1, $(0, 0)$ is a saddle point for $g(x, y) = xy$.

As Figure 5 shows, all three possibilities can coexist in close quarters. The function in question is $f(x, y) = \cos(x)\sin(y)$. ➡

Saddle points seem hardest for students to visualize, but comparing contour maps shows clear differences between saddles and local extrema.

Look in the picture for a stationary point of each type just listed.

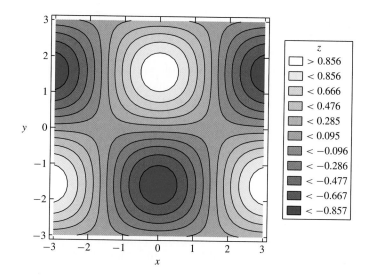

FIGURE 5
Contour plot of $\cos(x)\sin(y)$

Optimization: More to the story

There's much more to the story of optimizing functions of several variables; we've taken only a first, short look. Two main questions arise in multivariable calculus courses.

In multivariable calculus we describe how a function's "quadratic approximation" reveals the nature of a stationary point.

Second derivative tests   In single-variable calculus, the second derivative f'' is sometimes used to classify stationary points as maxima, minima, or neither. For example, if $f'(x_0) = 0$ and $f''(x_0) > 0$, then x_0 is a local minimum point for f. A similar but (necessarily) more sophisticated approach is possible for functions of two or more variables.

We just hint at the possible complications associated with edge values, and give one relatively simple example.

Extremes on the boundary   Recall what happens in elementary calculus for a differentiable function $f(x)$ defined on a closed interval $[a, b]$: f may assume its maximum and minimum values either at a stationary point (where $f'(x) = 0$) or at either of the endpoints $x = a$ and $x = b$.

The situation is similar for a function of two variables defined on a region, such as a rectangle or a circle, that has a definite "edge," or boundary: $f(x, y)$ may assume its maximum and minimum either at a stationary point or somewhere on the boundary of the region. We illustrate the situation, and one way to approach it, with a simple example.

EXAMPLE 2   Where on the rectangle $R = [-1, 1] \times [-1, 1]$ does $g(x, y)$ assume its minimum and maximum values?

Solution   We saw in Example 1, page M-27, that g has only one stationary point, a saddle point, in the interior of R. Therefore, the maximum and minimum values of g must occur somewhere on the boundary of R. A look at the contour plot of g (notice the symmetry) shows that it's enough to look along *any* boundary edge of R, such as the right edge. On this edge we have $x = 1$, and so g behaves like a function of just one variable: $g(x, y) = g(1, y) = y$. Clearly, $g(1, y) = y$ is largest at $y = 1$ and smallest at $y = -1$. We therefore conclude that $g(1, 1) = 1$ and $g(1, -1) = -1$ are, respectively, maximum and minimum values of g on R. ◼

BASIC EXERCISES

1. Let $g(x, y) = xy$. (Its contour map is shown in Figure 3.) To an ant walking along the surface $z = g(x, y)$ from lower left to upper right, the origin seems to be a low spot; another ant walking from upper left to lower right would experience the origin as a high spot.

   (a) An ant walks along the surface from $(0, -1)$ to $(0, 1)$. How does the ant's altitude change along the way?

   (b) Another ant walks along the surface from $(0.5, -1)$ to $(0.5, 1)$. How does the ant's altitude change along the way? Where is the ant highest? How high is the ant there?

2. See Figure 5, the contour map of $f(x, y) = \cos x \sin y$.

   (a) The surface $z = f(x, y)$ resembles an egg carton. Where do the eggs go?

   (b) From the figure alone, estimate the coordinates of a local minimum point, a local maximum point, and a saddle point.

   (c) Use the formula $f(x, y) = \cos x \sin y$ to find (exactly) all the stationary points of f in the rectangle $R = [-3, 3] \times [-3, 3]$.

   (d) Find the maximum and minimum values of f in the rectangle $R = [-3, 3] \times [-3, 3]$.

3. Consider the function $f(x, y) = x(x - 2) \sin y$. Here's a contour map:

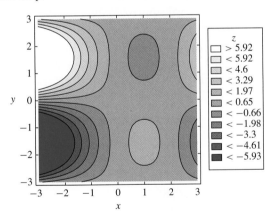

   (a) The function f has two stationary points along the line $x = 1$. Use the figure to estimate their coordinates. What type is each one?

   (b) There are four stationary points inside the rectangle $R = [-3, 3] \times [-3, 3]$. Use the formula for f to find all four.

   (c) The contour plot shows that f assumes its maximum and minimum values on $R = [-3, 3] \times [-3, 3]$ somewhere along the left boundary—that is, where $x = -3$. Find these maximum and minimum values.
   [HINT: If $x = -3$, then $f(x, y) = f(-3, y) = 15 \sin y$. This is a function of one variable, defined for $-3 \le y \le 3$.]

In Exercises 4–7, use the formula to find all stationary points of the function. Then use technology (e.g., a properly chosen contour plot or surface plot) to decide what type of stationary point each one is.

4. $f(x, y) = -x^2 - y^2$

5. $f(x, y) = x^2 - y^2$

6. $f(x, y) = 3x^2 + 2y^2$

7. $f(x, y) = xy - y - 2x + 2$

8. Consider the linear function $L(x, y) = 1 + 2x + 3y$. Does L have any stationary points? If so, what type are they? If not, why not?

9. Consider the linear function $L(x, y) = a + bx + cy$, where a, b, and c are constants.

   (a) The graph of L is a plane. Which planes have stationary points? For these planes, where are the stationary points?

   (b) Under what conditions on a, b, and c will L have stationary points? In this case, where are the stationary points? Reconcile your answers with those in part (a).

10. Let $f(x, y) = x^2$. The graph of f is a cylinder unrestricted in the y-direction.

   (a) Use technology to plot the surface $z = f(x, y)$. Where in the xy-plane are the stationary points? What type are they? [HINT: There's a whole line of stationary points.]

   (b) Use partial derivatives of f to find all the stationary points. Reconcile your answer with part (a).

In Exercises 11–13, give an example of a function with the specified properties.
[HINTS: (i) See Exercise 10 for ideas. (ii) Check your answers by plotting.]

11. Every point on the x-axis is a local minimum point.

12. Every point on the line $x = 1$ is a local maximum point.

13. $(3, 4)$ is a local minimum and the function is nonconstant.

M.5 MULTIPLE INTEGRALS AND APPROXIMATING SUMS

Integrals in several variables are limits in exactly the same sense as in one variable, and thinking of approximating sums helps explain many properties of such integrals.

The last two sections introduced *derivatives* of functions of several variables and a few of their most basic properties. The next few sections, on *integrals*, continue our flying tour of the basic calculus of functions of two or three variables. This section concerns mainly what multiple integrals are and what they mean. In the following two sections we'll consider more systematically how to calculate multiple integrals.

Integrals and sums

Here we review quickly the idea of integrals as sums; many students will have forgotten.

All integrals—single, double, triple, or whatever—are defined to be certain limits of approximating sums (sometimes known as Riemann sums). This important idea is always studied in single-variable calculus, but it may be quickly (and perhaps gratefully) forgotten. Readers whose memories are vague on this score have an excellent excuse: Although integrals are *defined* as limits of approximating sums, they are often *calculated* in an entirely

There's not a Riemann sum in sight.

different way, using antiderivatives. Here's a typical calculation: ◄

$$\int_0^1 x^2 \, dx = \left. \frac{x^3}{3} \right]_0^1 = \frac{1}{3}.$$

This method of evaluating an integral—find an antiderivative for the integrand and plug in the endpoints—works just fine, thanks to the fundamental theorem of calculus.

So why bother with approximating sums? Here are two good reasons:

- **Antiderivative trouble**   The antiderivative method depends on finding a convenient antiderivative of the integrand. Unfortunately, not every function, even in single-variable calculus, *has* an "elementary" antiderivative, that is, an antiderivative with a symbolic formula built from the usual ingredients. The simple-looking function $f(x) = \sin(x^2)$ is an example. ◄ The best we can do with the integral

Spend a moment looking for an antiderivative formula. Nothing works.

$$I = \int_0^1 \sin(x^2) \, dx,$$

therefore, is to approximate it with some sort of sum using, say, the left rule, the midpoint rule, or the trapezoid rule. (For the record, approximating I with a trapezoid-rule sum with 10 subdivisions gives $I \approx 0.311$.)

- **What integrals mean**   The fundamental theorem (when it works) makes *calculating* integrals easy, but approximating sums may illustrate more clearly what the answers mean. Figure 1, for instance, illustrates the sense in which a midpoint-rule sum with four subdivisions approximates the area bounded by the curve $y = x^2$ from $x = 0$ to $x = 1$.

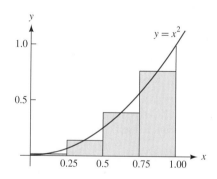

FIGURE 1

A midpoint estimate to $\int_0^1 x^2 \, dx$:
$M_4 = 63/192 \approx 0.328$

The basic idea of an integral as a limit of approximating sums is much the same for functions of two or more variables as for functions of one variable.

Integrals and approximating sums: A review   Let's review the main single-variable objects and notations that arise on the way to defining the integral of a function f over an interval $[a, b]$. The first step is to form Riemann sums.

> **DEFINITION** Let $[a, b]$ be partitioned into n subintervals by any $n + 1$ points
>
> $$a = x_0 < x_1 < x_2 < \cdots < x_{n-1} < x_n = b;$$
>
> let $\Delta x_i = x_i - x_{i-1}$ denote the width of the ith subinterval. Within each subinterval $[x_{i-1}, x_i]$, choose any point c_i. The sum
>
> $$\sum_{i=1}^{n} f(c_i) \, \Delta x_i = f(c_1) \, \Delta x_1 + f(c_2) \, \Delta x_2 + \cdots + f(c_n) \, \Delta x_n$$
>
> is a **Riemann sum** with n subdivisions for f on $[a, b]$.

Left-rule, right-rule, and midpoint-rule approximating sums all fit this definition. Each of these sums is built from a partition of $[a, b]$ into subintervals of equal length and some consistent scheme for choosing the sampling points c_i. (For left, right, and midpoint sums, respectively, we choose each c_i as the left endpoint, the right endpoint, or the midpoint of the ith subinterval.)

Graphical and numerical intuition suggest that all of these approximating sums (and others) should converge to some fixed number. Geometrically speaking, this number measures the signed area bounded by the f-graph from $x = a$ to $x = b$.

The limit definition of integral makes these ideas precise.

> **DEFINITION** Let the function f be defined on the interval $[a, b]$. The **integral** of f over $[a, b]$, denoted by $\int_a^b f(x) \, dx$, is the number to which all Riemann sums S_n tend as n tends to infinity and as the widths of all subdivisions tend to zero. In symbols,
>
> $$\int_a^b f(x) \, dx = \lim_{n \to \infty} S_n = \lim_{n \to \infty} \sum_{i=1}^{n} f(c_i) \, \Delta x_i$$
>
> if the limit exists.

Honesty dictates a brief admission: The limit in the definition, taken at face value, is a slippery customer. Understanding every ramification of permitting arbitrary partitions and sampling points, for example, can be tricky. Fortunately, these issues need not trouble us for the usual well-behaved functions (e.g., continuous functions) of single-variable and multivariable calculus. For such functions, almost any respectable sort of approximating sum does what we'd expect—approaches the true value of the integral as n tends to infinity.

We de-emphasize any possibility of pathological behavior, using regular partitions and well-behaved functions. For the moment the basic idea is the main point.

Two variables: Double integrals

Most of the differences between single-variable integrals and multivariable integrals are technical rather than theoretical. Indeed, the definitions of

$$\iint_R f(x, y) \, dA \quad \text{and} \quad \int_a^b f(x) \, dx$$

are almost identical. Now f is a function of two variables, and R is a region—a rectangle, in the simplest case—in the xy-plane. (The mechanics of evaluating these two types of integrals by antidifferentiation are quite different, on the other hand.)

First, let's list the ingredients that go into defining the **double integral** $\iint_R f(x, y) \, dA$. In each case, look for similarities to, and differences from, the one-variable situation.

- **R, the region of integration** In one variable, the region of integration is always an interval $[a, b]$ in the domain of f; this is implicit in the notation $\int_a^b f(x) \, dx$. In two variables, by contrast, the region of integration, denoted by R, may be almost *any* two-dimensional subset of the plane. In the simplest cases, R is a rectangle $[a, b] \times [c, d]$, and we sometimes write

$$\int_a^b \int_c^d f(x, y)\, dy\, dx, \qquad \text{not} \qquad \iint_R f(x, y)\, dA.$$

(The first notation suggests a fact we'll see in the next section—double integrals can sometimes be calculated by integrating "one variable at a time.")

- **Partitions**   In one variable, we partition an interval $[a, b]$ by cutting it, perhaps unevenly, into smaller intervals with endpoints $a = x_0 < x_1 < x_2 < \cdots < x_n = b$. The "size" of the ith subinterval is simply its length, Δx_i. In two variables, we do much the same thing: We chop the plane region R into m smaller regions $R_1, R_2, R_3, \ldots, R_m$, perhaps of different sizes and shapes. The "size" of a subregion R_i is now taken to be its *area*, denoted by ΔA_i.

  In practice—whatever the number of variables—it's usually convenient to choose the partition in some consistent way. In one variable, using equal-length subintervals is simplest. An analogous procedure in two variables, if R is a rectangle $[a, b] \times [c, d]$, is to cut R by an n-by-n grid in each direction, producing n^2 rectangular subregions in all. (This isn't the only possibility. Another alternative is to cut R into small squares.)

A key point is the close similarity between approximating sums in one and in several variables—a fact somewhat obscured by the multiple summation notation.

- **Approximating sums**   In one variable, an approximating sum has the form

$$f(c_1)\, \Delta x_1 + f(c_2)\, \Delta x_2 + \cdots + f(c_n)\, \Delta x_n = \sum_{i=1}^{n} f(c_i)\, \Delta x_i,$$

where each c_i is a sample point chosen from the ith subinterval. A two-variable approximating sum is similar. From each subregion R_i we choose a sampling point $P_i(x_i, y_i)$ and then form the approximating sum

$$S_m = f(P_1)\, \Delta A_1 + f(P_2)\, \Delta A_2 + \cdots + f(P_m)\, \Delta A_m = \sum_{i=1}^{m} f(P_i)\, \Delta A_i,$$

where ΔA_i is the area of R_i.

  Figure 2 illustrates the situation for the function $f(x, y) = x + y$ on the rectangle $R = [0, 4] \times [0, 4]$ with $n^2 = 4^2 = 16$ subdivisions. In each subinterval, sampling is done at the corner closest to the origin.

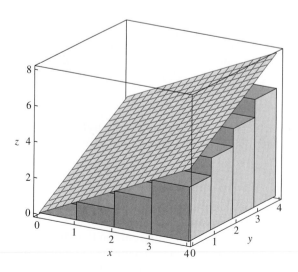

FIGURE 2
The surface $z = x + y$ and a Riemann approximation

The figure shows (among other things) that the approximating sum gives an estimate to the volume bounded above by the surface $z = f(x, y)$ and below by the rectangle $R = [0, 4] \times [0, 4]$. A close look and some back-of-the-envelope calculations show that the approximating sum shown adds up to 48.

It's reasonable to expect these estimates to converge to the "true" volume as n (the number of subdivisions in each direction) increases to infinity. A table of values supports this expectation.

Technology is almost essential to support such calculations. Simple programs using programs such as Maple and Mathematica do the job.

Approximating sums for various m	
Number of subdivisions (m)	Approximating sum (S_m)
2^2	32.00
4^2	48.00
8^2	56.00
12^2	58.67
16^2	60.00
20^2	60.80
24^2	61.33
28^2	61.71
32^2	62.00

Figure 3 shows another approximating sum for the same function over the same interval. This time, however, sampling is done at the *midpoint* of each subrectangle and the approximating sum adds up to 64.

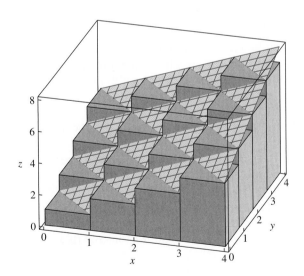

FIGURE 3
The surface $z = x + y$ and a midpoint approximation

- **What's dA?** The symbol "dA" in the double integral resembles the "dx" that appears in single integrals. The "A" reminds us of *area*.

EXAMPLE 1 Consider the double integral $I = \iint_R f(x, y)\, dA$, where $f(x, y) = x + y$ and $R = [0, 4] \times [0, 4]$. Calculate, by hand, an approximating sum S_4 with four equal subdivisions (two in each direction). In each square subregion, evaluate f at the corner nearest to the origin.

Solution   All four subregions are squares with edge length 2 and therefore area 4; all corners have integer coordinates. The sampling points just described are $P_1 = (0, 0)$, $P_2 = (2, 0)$, $P_3 = (0, 2)$, and $P_4 = (2, 2)$. The desired approximating sum is therefore

$$S_4 = \sum_{i=1}^{4} f(P_i) \, \Delta A_i = 0 \cdot 4 + 2 \cdot 4 + 2 \cdot 4 + 4 \cdot 4 = 32.$$ ■

Some additional subtleties—which we ignore—may arise for very ill-behaved functions.

The integral as a limit   We defined the one-variable integral $\int_a^b f(x) \, dx$ as a limit of approximating sums. The double integral $\iint_R f(x, y) \, dA$ can be defined in a similar way. The following definition is adequate for well-behaved functions $f(x, y)$. ◄

> **DEFINITION**   Let the function $f(x, y)$ be defined on the region R and let S_m be an approximating sum with m subdivisions. Let I be a number such that S_m tends to I whenever m tends to infinity and the diameter of all subdivisions tends to zero. Then I is the double integral of f over R, and we write
>
> $$I = \iint_R f(x, y) \, dA = \lim_{m \to \infty} \sum_{i=1}^{m} f(P_i) \, \Delta A_i.$$

As in the one-variable setting, the limit definition—although crucial to understanding integrals and often useful for approximating them—almost never lends itself to calculating integrals *exactly*. Fortunately, there are methods based on antidifferentiation for this purpose. We'll see some soon.

We mention the 3-d situation only briefly, for completeness. At this stage, 2-d integrals present sufficient challenges to intuition.

Triple sums and triple integrals

The idea of integral can be extended to dimension three (and even higher dimensions). We will consider only the simplest case: the **triple integral** of a function $g(x, y, z)$ over a rectangular parallelepiped (a "brick," to put it humbly) $R = [a, b] \times [c, d] \times [e, f]$, denoted by either

$$\iiint_R g(x, y, z) \, dV \qquad \text{or} \qquad \int_a^b \int_c^d \int_e^f g(x, y, z) \, dz \, dy \, dx.$$

As for double integrals, the second notation suggests, correctly, that such integrals can sometimes be calculated one variable at a time.

Triple integrals, just like single and double integrals, are defined formally as limits of approximating sums. An approximating sum in three dimensions is formed by subdividing a rectangular solid region R into m smaller rectangular subregions R_i, each with volume ΔV_i; choosing a sampling point P_i in each subregion; and then evaluating the sum

$$\sum_{i=1}^{m} f(P_i) \, \Delta V_i.$$

The triple integral is then defined as the limit of such sums as the diameter of all subregions tends to zero.

EXAMPLE 2   Consider the triple integral $I = \iiint_R g(x, y, z) \, dV$, where $g(x, y, z) = x + y + z$ and $R = [0, 2] \times [0, 2] \times [0, 2]$. Calculate an approximating sum S_8 with eight equal subdivisions (two in each direction). In each cubical subregion, evaluate g at the corner nearest to the origin.

Solution   All eight subregions are cubes with edge length 1 and (therefore) volume 1; all the corners have integer coordinates. The sampling points just described are $P_1 = (0, 0, 0)$, $P_2 = (1, 0, 0)$, $P_3 = (0, 1, 0)$, $P_4 = (1, 1, 0)$, $P_5 = (0, 0, 1)$, $P_6 = (1, 0, 1)$, $P_7 = (0, 1, 1)$, and $P_8 = (1, 1, 1)$. The approximating sum is therefore

$$S_8 = \sum_{i=1}^{8} g(P_i) \, \Delta V_i = 0 + 1 + 1 + 2 + 1 + 2 + 2 + 3 = 12.$$ ■

Calculating a very simple approximating sum like this one "by hand" (or "by head") could be a useful intuitive exercise.

Interpreting multiple integrals

Integrals can be interpreted geometrically, physically, or in other ways. A sampler of possibilities follows.

Thinking of integrals geometrically can be useful, but sometimes also limiting, especially in several variables. The notions of mass and density may offer a useful physical alternative to geometric views.

Double integrals and volume   The standard geometric interpretation of a single-variable integral $\int_a^b f(x) \, dx$ is in terms of *area*: If $f(x) \geq 0$, then $\int_a^b f(x) \, dx$ is the area of the region bounded above by the curve $y = f(x)$, bounded below by the interval $[a, b]$ in the x-axis, and having vertical sides. In a similar vein, as we've already seen from pictures, if $f(x, y) \geq 0$ for (x, y) in R, then the double integral $\iint_R f(x, y) \, dA$ measures the *volume* of the three-dimensional solid bounded above by the surface $z = f(x, y)$, bounded below by the region R in the xy-plane, and having sides perpendicular to the xy-plane.

Double integrals and area   If R is a region in the xy-plane and g is the constant function $g(x, y) = 1$, then (as the preceding paragraph says) the integral $\iint_R 1 \, dA$ represents the volume of the solid S bounded below by R and having vertical sides and *constant height* 1. Recall, however, that the volume of any such "cylindrical" solid S is the *area* of the base times the height. Therefore, in this special case the volume of S happens to be the same as its area. Thus, for any plane region R,

This idea is challenging for many students, for some reason, but students should understand that integrals have various interpretations.

$$\iint_R 1 \, dA = \text{area of } R.$$

Surprisingly, this fact is often of practical use in calculating areas of plane regions. The next section contains examples.

Triple integrals and volume   Triple integrals pose a special problem having to do with dimensions. There isn't "room" in three-dimensional space even to plot a function $w = g(x, y, z)$—*four* variables would be needed. For this reason, interpreting triple integrals geometrically is, as a rule, difficult or impossible.

There's one important exception to this rule. For reasons similar to those explained in the preceding paragraph, integrating the constant function $g(x, y, z) = 1$ over a solid region R in xyz-space gives the volume of the region R. In symbols:

$$\iiint_R 1 \, dV = \text{volume of } R.$$

Density, mass, and multiple integrals   Both double and triple integrals can often be interpreted physically in the language of density and mass. (This view has the special advantage of making sense for both double and triple integrals.)

For a double integral $\iint_R f(x, y) \, dA$, one thinks of the plane region R as a flat plate with variable density; at any point (x, y), $f(x, y)$ gives the density, measured in appropriate units (grams per square centimeter, say). From this viewpoint, the double integral $\iint_R f(x, y) \, dA$ is the total mass, in grams, of the plate R.

For a triple integral $\iiint_R g(x, y, z)\, dV$, one imagines a solid region R with variable density; at any point (x, y), $g(x, y, z)$ is the solid's density, measured in appropriate units (grams per cubic centimeter, say). From this viewpoint, the triple integral $\iiint_R g(x, y, z)\, dV$ is the total mass, in grams, of the solid R.

BASIC EXERCISES

1. Calculate by hand (without technology) the midpoint sum with four subdivisions for $\int_0^1 x^2\, dx$. Then check that *Maple* agrees. Finally, compare *Maple*'s answer for 100 subdivisions.

2. Calculate by hand (without technology) the double midpoint sum with $n = 3$ (i.e., nine subdivisions in all) for the integral $\iint_R \sin x \sin y\, dA$ over the rectangle $R = [0, 1] \times [0, 1]$. Check your answer using *Maple*. Finally, compare *Maple*'s answer for $n = 10$.

3. Calculate by hand (without technology) the triple midpoint sum with $n = 2$ (i.e., eight subdivisions in all) for the triple integral $\iiint_R xyz\, dV$ over the cube $R = [0, 4] \times [0, 4] \times [0, 4]$. Check your answer using *Maple*. Finally, compare *Maple*'s answer for $n = 4$.

4. Let $f(x, y) = x + y$, let $R = [0, 4] \times [0, 4]$, and let $I = \iint_R f(x, y)\, dA$. Here is a contour plot of f:

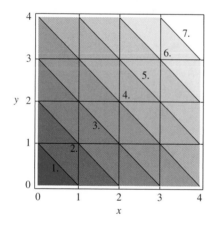

(a) Use the contour plot to evaluate a double midpoint sum for I with $n = 4$ (16 subdivisions in all).

(b) Use *Maple* to check your answer from part (a).

(c) Your answer in part (a) is, in fact, the exact value of the integral I. How does the symmetry of the contour map show this?

5. Let $f(x, y) = x^2 + y^2$, let $R = [0, 4] \times [0, 4]$, and let $I = \iint_R f(x, y)\, dA$. Here is a contour plot of f:

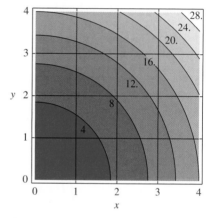

(a) Use the contour plot to evaluate a double midpoint sum for I with $n = 4$ (16 subdivisions in all).

(b) Use *Maple* to check your answer from part (a).

(c) Would you expect your answer from part (a) to overestimate or underestimate the true value of I? How can you tell?

Like ordinary integrals, double integrals can be evaluated by antidifferentiation — but with appropriate care.

It works thanks to the fundamental theorem of calculus.

M.6   CALCULATING INTEGRALS BY ITERATION

The preceding section was about *defining* multivariable integrals as limits of approximating sums. This section is about *calculating* multivariable integrals, using antidifferentiation. Approximating sums are conceptually simple and (with technology) easy to calculate. But approximating sums are only approximate; to evaluate integrals *exactly*, we'd like an appropriate multivariable version of the single-variable antiderivative method. ◄

How iteration works

The key idea is to integrate a multivariable function *one variable at a time*, treating other variables as constants. The process is called **iterated integration**. ➥ To start, here's an example to show *how* it works; we'll see *why* it works in a moment.

In mathspeak, "iterate" means "repeat."

EXAMPLE 1   Let $f(x, y) = x + y$, and let $R = [0, 4] \times [0, 4]$. Find $\iint_R f(x, y)\,dA$ by iterated integration. (We studied this integral in Section M.5; see the pictures and the table of values starting on page M-35.)

Solution   We integrate first in x, treating y as a constant. Watch each step carefully. ➥

Attaching variable names to the limits of integration is optional, but it can help remind us which variable is involved.

$$\iint_R f(x, y)\,dA = \int_{y=0}^{y=4} \left(\int_{x=0}^{x=4} (x + y)\,dx \right) dy$$

$$= \int_{y=0}^{y=4} \left(\frac{x^2}{2} + xy \Big]_{x=0}^{x=4} \right) dy$$

$$= \int_{y=0}^{y=4} (8 + 4y)\,dy = 64.$$

Observe:

- **The same answer**   The final answer, 64, should be familiar—it's what we estimated in Section M.5, using a midpoint approximation.

- **The answer as volume**   Interpreted as a volume, the answer says that the solid bounded below by $R = [0, 4] \times [0, 4]$, bounded above by the plane $z = x + y$, and having straight vertical walls has volume 64 cubic units. Figure 1 shows the solid in question.

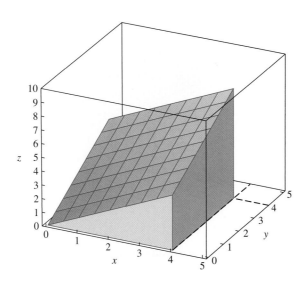

FIGURE 1
A solid bounded above by $z = x + y$

- **Checking answers with technology**   Is the answer 64 geometrically reasonable? Is it symbolically correct? Technology (e.g., *Maple*) can help with both questions. A plot

Similar commands work with Mathematica, the TI-89, or other technologies.

like the preceding one suggests that the answer 64 is at least in the ballpark. As a further check, here is *Maple*'s version of the *symbolic* calculation:

```
> int( int( x+y, x=0..4), y=0..4 );
                  64
```

- **Work from inside out**   Iterated integrals are calculated from the inside out. The "inner" integral (the x-integral in the preceding calculation) is found first.
- **Either order works**   There's nothing sacred about integrating first in x and then in y. For well-behaved functions we can integrate in either order, and both orders give the same answer. We'll return to this question.   ■

We discussed a cross-sectional area function earlier, in connection with finding volumes by single-variable integration.

Cross-sectional area: An intermediate function   In the preceding example, the inner integral was calculated with respect to x, with y treated as constant. The result was an intermediate function, g, of y alone; the formula is

$$g(y) = \int_0^4 (x+y)\, dx = 8 + 4y.$$

We integrated $g(y)$ with respect to y to get the final answer.

The function g has a nice geometric meaning: For any fixed y_0 in $[0, 4]$, $g(y_0)$ is the area under the curve $z = f(x, y_0)$ and above the xy-plane. In other words, $g(y)$ is the *area* of the cross section of the solid obtained by slicing with the plane $y = y_0$. Figure 2 shows the picture for $y = 2$.

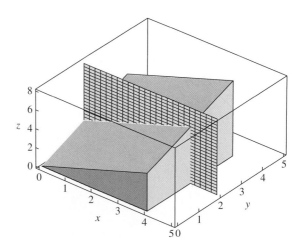

FIGURE 2
The cross section with the plane $y = 2$

Because $g(y) = 8 + 4y$, we get $g(2) = 16$; this is the area of the part of the plane inside the solid. As y runs from $y = 0$ to $y = 4$, $g(y)$ measures the area "swept out" by planes parallel to the one shown. ◄

This area increases with y, as the picture shows.

As a matter of fact, the idea of a cross-sectional-area function is not new; we used the same idea in Chapter 7 when we calculated volumes by integration. Back then, we put it like this:

> **FACT** Suppose that a solid lies with its base on the xy-plane between the vertical planes $x = a$ and $x = b$. For all x in $[a, b]$, let $A(x)$ denote the area of the cross section at x, perpendicular to the x-axis. If $A(x)$ is a continuous function, then
>
> $$\text{Volume} = \int_a^b A(x)\,dx.$$

Why iteration works

Why does the iteration method just demonstrated work? The preceding Fact gives some geometric feeling for the matter, at least when an integral can be thought of as the volume of a three-dimensional solid.

But not all integrals can or should be thought of in this way. A better reason why iteration works—a reason that makes sense in *any* dimension—is based on approximating sums. We describe the idea in two dimensions, but everything transfers readily to three (or even higher) dimensions. The main idea, in a nutshell, is that an approximating sum for a double integral can be grouped either along "rows" or along "columns." We first give an example and then a more general argument.

The reason iteration works boils down, roughly speaking, to the fact that summing function values at many points in a rectangle can be done in two steps—summing first along columns and then totalling column sums. (See the following table.)

EXAMPLE 2 Let $f(x, y) = 2 - x^2 y$, let $R = [0, 1] \times [0, 1]$, and let $I = \iint_R f(x, y)\,dA$. Figure 3 is a picture of the solid whose volume is given by I:

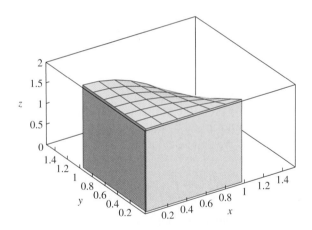

FIGURE 3
The solid under $z = 2 - x^2 y$ and over $[0, 1] \times [0, 1]$

Compute a midpoint approximating sum with 100 equal subdivisions (10 in each direction) for the integral $I = \iint_R f(x, y)\,dA$. Compare the result to the exact value of I found by iteration.

Solution It's easy to calculate I exactly by iteration. This time, for variety, we integrate first in y:

$$I = \int_0^1 \left(\int_0^1 (2 - x^2 y)\,dy \right) dx = \int_0^1 \left(2y - \frac{x^2 y^2}{2} \bigg]_0^1 \right) dx$$

$$= \int_0^1 \left(2 - \frac{x^2}{2} \right) dx = \frac{11}{6}.$$

To find an approximating sum, we first tabulate values (rounded to two decimals) of f at the midpoints of all 100 subrectangles of $[0, 1] \times [0, 1]$. For later use, column sums are at the bottom, rounded to one decimal place.

Values of $f(x, y) = 2 - x^2 y$										
y \ x	0.05	0.15	0.25	0.35	0.45	0.55	0.65	0.75	0.85	0.95
0.05	2.00	2.00	2.00	1.99	1.99	1.98	1.98	1.97	1.96	1.95
0.15	2.00	2.00	1.99	1.98	1.97	1.95	1.94	1.92	1.89	1.86
0.25	2.00	1.99	1.98	1.97	1.95	1.92	1.89	1.86	1.82	1.77
0.35	2.00	1.99	1.98	1.96	1.93	1.89	1.85	1.80	1.75	1.68
0.45	2.00	1.99	1.97	1.94	1.91	1.86	1.81	1.75	1.67	1.59
0.55	2.00	1.99	1.97	1.93	1.89	1.83	1.77	1.69	1.60	1.50
0.65	2.00	1.99	1.96	1.92	1.87	1.80	1.73	1.63	1.53	1.41
0.75	2.00	1.98	1.95	1.91	1.85	1.77	1.68	1.58	1.46	1.32
0.85	2.00	1.98	1.95	1.90	1.83	1.74	1.64	1.52	1.39	1.23
0.95	2.00	1.98	1.94	1.88	1.81	1.71	1.60	1.47	1.31	1.14
Sum	20.0	19.9	19.7	19.4	19.0	18.4	17.9	17.2	16.4	15.5

The approximating sum is found by totaling all the function values and multiplying by $1/100$, the area of each subrectangle. (In this case, therefore, the approximating sum is the average of the 100 table entries.) The result is 1.83; it compares nicely with the exact answer, $11/6 \approx 1.8333$.

A similar approach could be taken starting with row sums.

Now consider any *column* in the table. The last column, for instance, contains numbers of the form $f(0.95, y)$ for 10 equally spaced values of y, with $\Delta y = 0.1$. Therefore, the column sum multiplied by 0.1 (the answer is 1.55) is a Riemann sum for the integral $\int_0^1 f(0.95, y)\, dy$. We can calculate this last integral directly:

$$\int_0^1 f(0.95, y)\, dy = \int_0^1 (2 - 0.95^2 y)\, dy = 1.54875.$$

Integrals are rounded to two decimals.

That's not far from the Riemann sum. Tabulating results for the other columns produces the same pattern. The Riemann sum associated with each column closely approximates the corresponding y-integral. ◄

Column sums and y-integrals										
x	0.05	0.15	0.25	0.35	0.45	0.55	0.65	0.75	0.85	0.95
Column sum	20.0	19.9	19.7	19.4	19.0	18.4	17.9	17.2	16.4	15.5
$\int_0^1 f(x, y)\, dy$	2.00	1.99	1.97	1.94	1.90	1.85	1.79	1.72	1.64	1.55

The calculations are complicated, but the moral is simple: Whether adding up approximating sums or calculating integrals, it's OK to work with one variable at a time. ∎

A general argument Let's summarize the ideas of Example 2 in more general terms. To do so, suppose that we're given a rectangle $[a, b] \times [c, d]$ in the xy-plane and a function f defined on R. We'll see why the integral $I = \iint_R f(x, y)\, dA$ can reasonably be calculated by iteration.

To begin, let's write an approximating sum for I in the sense of the preceding section. First we subdivide both $[a, b]$ and $[c, d]$ into n equal subintervals. Their lengths are $\Delta x = (b - a)/n$ and $\Delta y = (d - c)/n$, respectively. This produces a grid of n^2 subrectangles R_{ij}, where $1 \le i, j \le n$; each rectangle has area $\Delta x\, \Delta y$. Let (x_i, y_j) be the midpoint of the (i, j)th rectangle; we'll use these midpoints as sampling points for an approximating sum S_{n^2} for I.

With all ingredients now in place, we can write the approximating sum:

$$S_{n^2} = \sum_{i,j=1}^{n} f(x_i, y_j)\, \Delta x\, \Delta y = f(x_1, y_1)\, \Delta x\, \Delta y + \cdots + f(x_n, y_n)\, \Delta x\, \Delta y.$$

(The subscript on the "Σ" means that we sum over all possible values of *both i* and *j* from 1 to *n*.) ➤

There are n^2 summands in all.

We can group and add the summands in any order or pattern we like. Here's one convenient pattern: ➤

It's OK to factor Δy out of each row because it's common to all summands.

$$S_{n^2} = \big(f(x_1, y_1)\, \Delta x + f(x_2, y_1)\, \Delta x + \cdots + f(x_n, y_1)\, \Delta x\big) \Delta y$$

$$+ \big(f(x_1, y_2)\, \Delta x + f(x_2, y_2)\, \Delta x + \cdots + f(x_n, y_2)\, \Delta x\big) \Delta y + \cdots$$

$$+ \big(f(x_1, y_j)\, \Delta x + f(x_2, y_j)\, \Delta x + \cdots + f(x_n, y_j)\, \Delta x\big) \Delta y + \cdots$$

$$+ \big(f(x_1, y_n)\, \Delta x + f(x_2, y_n)\, \Delta x + \cdots + f(x_n, y_n)\, \Delta x\big) \Delta y.$$

Here's the first of two key points:

> *The sum inside parentheses on each line above is a Riemann sum with n subdivisions for a* single-variable *integral in x.*

Specifically, the sum on the first line is a Riemann sum for the integral $\int_a^b f(x, y_1)\, dx$; the sum on the second line approximates $\int_a^b f(x, y_2)\, dx$, and so on. Now if n is large, then all of these sums are close to the integrals they approximate. Thus, for large n,

$$S_{n^2} \approx \int_a^b f(x, y_1)\, dx\ \Delta y + \int_a^b f(x, y_2)\, dx\ \Delta y + \cdots + \int_a^b f(x, y_n)\, dx\ \Delta y.$$

Here's the second key observation:

> *The sum on the right above is a Riemann sum with n subdivisions for the integral $\int_c^d g(y)\, dy$, where $g(y) = \int_a^b f(x, y)\, dx$.*

For large n this sum, too, is near the integral it approximates. ➤ In other words,

This should sound reasonable, and it is indeed true for the well-behaved functions in this chapter. But a rigorous proof is quite subtle; it depends on technical properties of the integrand function.

$$S_{n^2} \approx \sum_{j=1}^{n} g(y)\, \Delta y \approx \int_c^d g(y)\, dy = \int_c^d \left(\int_a^b f(x, y)\, dx \right) dy.$$

This shows (informally) what we hoped to show: For large n,

$$I \approx S_{n^2} \approx \int_c^d \left(\int_a^b f(x, y) \, dx \right) dy.$$

We conclude that we can indeed evaluate a double integral I over a rectangle R by integrating first in x and then in y. Nor does the order matter—we could just as well have reversed the roles of x and y throughout the preceding argument.

Iterated triple integrals   Iteration works exactly the same way for a triple integral defined on a cube in xyz-space.

EXAMPLE 3   Let $f(x, y, z) = x + y + z$, let $R = [0, 2] \times [0, 2] \times [0, 2]$, and let $I = \iiint_R f(x, y, z) \, dV$. Calculate I exactly, by iteration. (Compare Example 2, page M-36, where we calculated a crude approximating sum for I.) What could the answer *mean*?

Solution   We integrate in each of the three variables in turn:

$$\iiint_R f(x, y, z) \, dV = \int_0^2 \left(\int_0^2 \left(\int_0^2 (x + y + z) \, dx \right) dy \right) dz$$
$$\text{(integrate in } x)$$

$$= \int_0^2 \left(\int_0^2 \left(\frac{x^2}{2} + xy + xz \right]_0^2 \right) dy \right) dz$$

$$= \int_0^2 \left(\int_0^2 (2 + 2y + 2z) \, dy \right) dz$$

$$= \int_0^2 \left(2y + y^2 + 2yz \right]_0^2 \right) dz \qquad \text{(integrate in } y)$$

$$= \int_0^2 (8 + 4z) \, dz = 24 \qquad \text{(integrate in } z)$$

Maple does the same thing in one fell swoop:

```
> int( int( int( x+y+z, x=0..2), y=0..2), z=0..2);
                        24
```

What the answer means depends on our point of view. If we think of the integrand $f(x, y, z)$ as the density (in, say, grams per cubic centimeter) of the solid R at the point (x, y, z), then the integral tells the *mass* of the solid (in grams). ∎

The main difficulty here is often with setting up integrals rather than evaluating them. With technology, evaluation may be almost trivial.

Integrals over nonrectangular regions

Not every integral of interest is taken over a rectangular domain of integration. It's sometimes useful to integrate over regions with curved boundaries. Much the same process of iteration applies in this case as in that of integrals over rectangles and cubes, but some extra care is needed. We illustrate the process with an example.

EXAMPLE 4 Find $I = \iint_R (2-x)\,dA$, where R is the plane region between the curves $y = 0$ and $y = x$, and $x = 1$. ➡

It's essential to draw the domain; use an ordinary pair of xy-axes.

Solution The integral gives the volume of the solid figure shown in Figure 4.

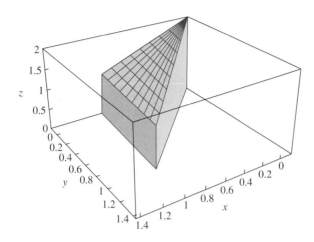

FIGURE 4
A surface with nonrectangular base

We can think of the domain R as bounded by the straight lines $x = 0$ and $x = 1$ on the left and right and by the curves $y = 0$ and $y = x$ on the bottom and top. As in earlier cases, we can integrate by iteration. The *outer* integral, in x, runs from $x = 0$ to $x = 1$. The upper and lower limits of the *inner* integral, however, depend on x, as the following computation shows:

$$I = \iint_R (2-x)\,dA = \int_{x=0}^{x=1} \left(\int_{y=0}^{y=x} (2-x)\,dy \right) dx$$

$$= \int_{x=0}^{x=1} \left(2y - xy \right]_{y=0}^{y=x} \right) dx$$

$$= \int_{x=0}^{x=1} \left(2x - x^2 \right) dx = \frac{2}{3}.$$

Again, *Maple* can do the whole thing at once:

```
> int( int( 2-x, y=0..x), x=0..1);
                    2/3
```

In fact, this integral is not much different from the preceding ones, which were over rectangular domains. The variable limits of integration in the inner integral simply reflect the fact that the domain of integration has varying "heights," depending on x. ■

Changing the order of integration For integrals over rectangles or cubes, we can integrate in any order we like. A similar result holds in the present case, too—as long as the region has an appropriate shape. We illustrate by redoing the preceding example but integrating the variables in the opposite order.

E X A M P L E 5   Redo the integral $I = \iint_R (2 - x)\, dA$ of Example 4, but now integrate first in x and then in y.

Solution   This time we think of R as lying between the lines $y = 0$ and $y = 1$. For given y, R starts at the line $x = y$ and ends at the line $x = 1$. Now the calculation is similar to the preceding one:

$$I = \iint_R (2 - x)\, dA = \int_{y=0}^{y=1} \left(\int_{x=y}^{x=1} (2 - x)\, dx \right) dy$$

$$= \int_{y=0}^{y=1} \left(2x - \frac{x^2}{2} \right]_{x=y}^{x=1} \right) dy$$

$$= \int_{y=0}^{y=1} \left(\frac{3}{2} - 2y + \frac{y^2}{2} \right) dy = \frac{2}{3}.$$

Here's *Maple*'s version:

```
> int( int( 2-x, x=y..1), y=0..1);
                    2/3
```

Not always so simple   Things aren't always quite so simple. Some domains of integration lend themselves more naturally to one order of integration than to another; the following exercises give examples.

BASIC EXERCISES

In Exercises 1–5, use iteration to calculate the integral by hand (without technology). Then, check your answer symbolically using Maple. *Finally, plot a 3-D surface over an appropriate domain and check that your answer is reasonable.*

1. $\iint_R \sin x \sin y\, dA$; $R = [0, 1] \times [0, 1]$

2. $\iint_R \sin(x + y)\, dA$; $R = [0, 1] \times [0, 1]$

3. $\iint_R (x^2 + y^2)\, dA$; $R = [0, 4] \times [0, 4]$

4. $\iiint_R x\, dV$; $V = [0, 1] \times [0, 2] \times [0, 3]$

5. $\iiint_R y\, dV$; $V = [0, 1] \times [0, 2] \times [0, 3]$

In Exercises 6–8, use iteration to calculate the integral by hand (without technology). In each case, the inner integral should be in y and the outer integral in x. Check your answer symbolically using Maple.

6. $\iint_R (x + y)\, dA$; R is the region bounded by the curves $y = x$ and $y = x^2$.

7. $\iint_R x\, dA$; R is the region bounded by the curves $y = x^2$ and $y = \sqrt{x}$.

8. $\iint_R 1\, dA$; R is the first quadrant part of the circle $x^2 + y^2 \le 1$.

9–11. Redo Exercises 6–8, but integrate first in x and then in y.

12. Consider the integral $I = \iint_R (x + y)\, dA$, where R is the region bounded by the curves $y = x^2$ and $y = 1$.

  (a) Calculate I by integrating first in y and then in x.

  (b) Calculate I by integrating first in x and then in y.

13. Let $f(x, y) = x$, and let R be the plane region bounded by the curves $y = e^x$, $y = 0$, $x = 0$, and $x = 1$.

  (a) Calculate $I = \iint_R f(x, y)\, dA$ by integrating first in y and then in x.

  (b) Calculate $I = \iint_R f(x, y)\, dA$ by integrating first in x and then in y. [HINT: First split the region R into two simpler pieces; each simpler piece should be bounded on the left by one curve and on the right by another.]

14. Let $y = f(x)$ be a function, with $f(x) \ge 0$ if $a \le x \le b$; let R be the plane region bounded by the curves $y = f(x)$, $y = 0$, $x = a$, and $x = b$.

  (a) What does single-variable calculus say about the area of R?

  (b) The double integral $I = \iint_R 1\, dA$ gives the area of R. Use an iterated integral to reconcile this formula with the one in part (a).

15. Let $x = g(y)$ be a function with $g(y) \geq 0$ if $c \leq y \leq d$; let R be the plane region bounded by the curves $x = g(y)$, $x = 0$, $y = c$, and $y = d$.

    (a) What does single-variable calculus say about the area of R?

    (b) The double integral $I = \iint_R 1 \, dA$ gives the area of R. Use an iterated integral to reconcile this formula with the one in part (a).

M.7 DOUBLE INTEGRALS IN POLAR COORDINATES

Changing coordinates in multiple integrals is treated in much more detail in multivariable calculus; here we take just a brief glance. Students need a good command of basic polar algebra, of course.

What makes a double integral $I = \iint_R f(x, y) \, dA$ hard to calculate? Both f and R can play a role: If either one is complicated or messy to describe, or both, then I may be correspondingly ugly. Let's see examples of both "good" and "bad" integrals.

EXAMPLE 1 Discuss $I_1 = \iint_{R_1} x^2 \, dA$ and $I_2 = \iint_{R_2} \sqrt{x^2 + y^2} \, dA$, where R_1 is the rectangle $[0, 1] \times [0, 2\pi]$, and R_2 is the region inside the unit circle $x^2 + y^2 = 1$. ➡

Draw R_1 and R_2 for yourself.

Solution The first integral is easy:

$$I_1 = \int_{x=0}^{x=1} \left(\int_{y=0}^{y=2\pi} x^2 \, dy \right) dx = \int_0^1 \left(x^2 y \right]_0^{2\pi} \right) dx = \int_0^1 2\pi x^2 \, dx = \frac{2\pi}{3}.$$

The ingredients of I_2 are more complicated to describe. ➡ The circular region R_2 can be thought of as bounded by the curves $y = \sqrt{1 - x^2}$ and $y = -\sqrt{1 - x^2}$ on the top and bottom, and by the lines $x = -1$ and $x = 1$ on the left and right. Now we can write I_2 in iterated form:

In xy-coordinates, at least. Polar coordinates will make things simpler.

$$I_2 = \int_{x=1}^{x=-1} \left(\int_{y=-\sqrt{1-x^2}}^{y=\sqrt{1-x^2}} \sqrt{x^2 + y^2} \, dy \right) dx.$$

The integral looks—and is—complicated. Just to get started on the inner integral, we'd need the ugly antiderivative formula

$$\int \sqrt{x^2 + p^2} \, dx = \frac{1}{2} \left(x\sqrt{x^2 + p^2} + p^2 \ln \left| x + \sqrt{x^2 + p^2} \right| \right).$$

Faced with this prospect, we retreat, but only temporarily—we shall return to I_2. ∎

What went wrong, and what to do The integral I_2 in Example 1 led to an unpleasant calculation in x and y for two reasons:

(i) The integrand, $\sqrt{x^2 + y^2}$, has a complicated antiderivative in x or y.

(ii) The domain of integration, although geometrically simple, is messy to describe in rectangular coordinates.

In polar coordinates, on the other hand, both the integrand and the domain have simple, uncluttered formulas. The integrand is

$$f(x, y) = \sqrt{x^2 + y^2} = r.$$

In polar language, the domain of integration is essentially a rectangle; it's defined by the inequalities

$$0 \le r \le 1 \quad \text{and} \quad 0 \le \theta \le 2\pi.$$

In this case, apparently, both the integrand f and the domain R "deserve" to be described in polar coordinates, not in rectangular coordinates. It seems reasonable, therefore, that the double integral I_2 should also be calculated using polar rather than rectangular coordinates.

That hunch is correct. We demonstrate in this section how to calculate double integrals in polar form, using r and θ, as opposed to Cartesian or rectangular form, using x and y. Integrals such as I_2, in which the integrand, the domain of integration, or both are simplest in polar form, are natural candidates for polar treatment.

Polar "rectangles"   A rectangle in Cartesian coordinates is defined by two inequalities of the form

$$a \le x \le b \quad \text{and} \quad c \le y \le d;$$

each of the coordinates x and y ranges through an interval. A **polar rectangle** is defined by two similar inequalities:

$$a \le r \le b; \qquad \alpha \le \theta \le \beta;$$

again, each of the coordinates r and θ ranges through an interval. Figure 1 shows generic pictures of both types of rectangles.

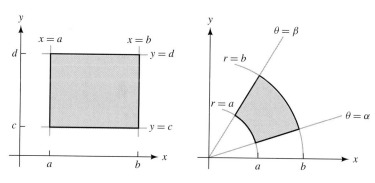

FIGURE 1
Cartesian and polar rectangles

For polar integrals, as for Cartesian ones, rectangles (in the appropriate sense) are the simplest regions over which to integrate.

Polar integration — How it works and what it means

We integrate first in y this time.

A double integral $I = \iint_R f(x, y)\, dA$ in rectangular coordinates, where $R = [a, b] \times [c, d]$ is an ordinary rectangle, is written in iterated form as follows:

$$\iint_R f(x, y)\, dA = \int_a^b \int_c^d f(x, y)\, dy\, dx.$$

(Here and later, we omit some parentheses. It's always understood that the inner integral is done first.)

Now suppose we're given a double integral $I = \iint_R g(r, \theta)\, dA$ in polar coordinates, where R is now a *polar* rectangle defined by inequalities

$$a \le r \le b \quad \text{and} \quad \alpha \le \theta \le \beta,$$

and $g(r, \theta)$ is a function defined on R. The following Fact gives the appropriate integral formula.

FACT (Double integrals in polar coordinates)   Let g and R be as before. Then

$$\iint_R g(r, \theta)\, dA = \int_{\theta=\alpha}^{\theta=\beta} \int_{r=a}^{r=b} g(r, \theta)\, r\, dr\, d\theta.$$

The "integrating factor" r on the right side is the mysterious ingredient for most students. We explain its presence below.

The formula prompts several important observations:

- **Trading x and y for r and θ**   Any function $f(x, y)$ can be "traded" for an equivalent function $g(r, \theta)$ by using the relations

  $$x = r \cos \theta \quad \text{and} \quad y = r \sin \theta.$$

  The same method works for *equations* in x and y. The equation $x = y$, for example, says in polar coordinates that $r \cos \theta = r \sin \theta$ or, equivalently, that $\tan \theta = 1$. This polar equation describes the same line as the original Cartesian equation. We'll use these principles when evaluating polar integrals.

- **A useful mnemonic**   Compare the preceding formulas for integrating in rectangular and polar coordinates. An important difference between the two has to do with the "dA" expression. The full mathematical story is much deeper. ➤ But as a quick aid to memory, the following formulas are very handy:

  $$dA = dx\, dy \quad \text{for Cartesian coordinates;}$$
  $$dA = r\, dr\, d\theta \quad \text{for polar coordinates.}$$

  We won't go into great depth, but we'll give some informal justification soon.

- **That extra factor of r**   What's that mysterious extra r doing in the polar formula $dA = r\, dr\, d\theta$? Why not just $dA = dr\, d\theta$? We certainly owe the reader an explanation. We'll honor that debt in a moment when we discuss *why* the formula works. First, however, let's see *that* it works.

EXAMPLE 2   Let R_2 be the region inside the unit circle. Use polar coordinates to calculate that troublesome integral $I_2 = \iint_{R_2} \sqrt{x^2 + y^2}\, dA$ from Example 1, page M-47.

Solution   First we write all the data in polar form. For the integrand, we have $f(x, y) = \sqrt{x^2 + y^2} = r = g(r, \theta)$. For the domain of integration, we translate the

Cartesian equation $x^2 + y^2 = 1$ into its (simpler!) polar form, $r = 1$. The rest is easy:

$$
\begin{aligned}
\iint_{R_2} \sqrt{x^2 + y^2}\, dA &= \int_{\theta=0}^{\theta=2\pi} \int_{r=0}^{r=1} r\, dA \\
&= \int_{\theta=0}^{\theta=2\pi} \int_{r=0}^{r=1} r^2\, dr\, d\theta && (da = r\, dr\, d\theta) \\
&= \int_{\theta=0}^{\theta=2\pi} \left. \frac{r^3}{3} \right]_0^1 d\theta && (\text{integrate in } r) \\
&= \int_{\theta=0}^{\theta=2\pi} \frac{1}{3}\, d\theta = \frac{2\pi}{3}. && (\text{integrate in } \theta)
\end{aligned}
$$

Notice especially the similarity to the integral I_1 of Example 1—I_1 and I_2 turned out to have the same value. This is no accident. After rewriting in polar coordinates, I_2 turned out to be the *same integral* in r and θ as I_1 is in x and y. ∎

We discussed some possible interpretations in Section M.5.

Polar integrals have exactly the same interpretations as any other double integrals. ◄ Depending on the situation and on our point of view, an integral might represent a volume, the area of a plane region, the mass of a thin plate, or many other things.

For example, both the integrals I_1 and I_2 of Example 1, page M-47, can be interpreted as volumes of solids. For I_2, the solid lies above the unit disk and below the surface $z = \sqrt{x^2 + y^2}$, as shown.

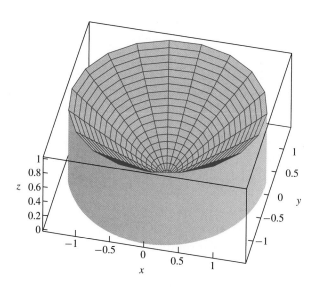

FIGURE 2
A polar solid

Does this seem reasonable from the picture, given the general size of units?

As we just calculated, the solid shown in Figure 2 has volume $2\pi/3 \approx 2.094$ cubic units. ◄

Polar integration — Why it works

Why does the polar integration formula work? Where, especially, does the r in $dA = r\, dr\, d\theta$ come from?

All properties of integrals—whether in Cartesian, polar, or any other form—stem ultimately from properties of the approximating sums that are used to define integrals. For any function f defined on a region R, we have

$$\iint_R f \, dA = \lim_{m \to \infty} \sum_{i=1}^{m} f(P_i) \Delta A_i,$$

where ΔA_i is the area of the ith subregion of R, and P_i is a sampling point chosen inside this subregion.

If $R = [a, b] \times [c, d]$ is a Cartesian rectangle, then it's natural to subdivide R into smaller rectangles, each with sides Δx and Δy. Any such rectangle has area $\Delta A_i = \Delta x \, \Delta y$. In the limit that defines the integral, therefore, $dA = dx \, dy$.

If R is a polar rectangle, the picture is a little different. In this case, a "polar grid" is the natural way to subdivide R. In Figure 3, each black dot represents a "centered" sampling point in its respective subdivision.

The picture links polar integrals to polar approximating sums and to the presence of the mysterious r in the area element.

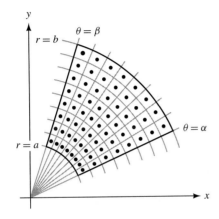

FIGURE 3
A polar grid on a polar rectangle

Notice the following features of the grid:

- **Similar subregions**   All subregions correspond to the same $\Delta\theta$ (the angle between any two adjacent dotted radial lines) and the same Δr (the radial distance from one arc to the next).

- **But not identical**   Similar as they are, the subregions shown are not identical. Here's the key point:

    In a polar grid, the subregions have different sizes. The area depends not only on $\Delta\theta$ and Δr but also on r: Larger values of r produce larger subregions.

    This fact explains the difference between polar and Cartesian integrals, and hints at why that extra r is needed.

- **The area of one subregion**   Each of the preceding subregions is a small polar rectangle with polar dimensions $\Delta\theta$ and Δr, inner radius r, and outer radius $r + \Delta r$. It's an important fact that, for such a polar rectangle,

$$\text{Area} = \Delta A_i = \frac{r + r + \Delta r}{2} \, \Delta r \, \Delta\theta.$$

(We'll leave verification of this straightforward fact to the exercises.) The first factor on the right is crucial—it represents the *average* radius of the given subregion, that is, the r-coordinate of the ith bulleted midpoint (r_i, θ_i) in the illustration. Therefore,

$$\Delta A_i = r_i \, \Delta r \, \Delta\theta.$$

This is just what we've been waiting for. It shows that, for a polar rectangular region, a midpoint approximating sum has the form

$$\sum_{i=1}^{m} f(r_i, \theta_i) \, \Delta A_i = \sum_{i=1}^{m} f(r_i, \theta_i) \, r_i \, \Delta r \, \Delta \theta.$$

The integral itself therefore has the limiting form $\iint_R f(r, \theta) \, r \, dr \, d\theta$.

Polar integrals over nonrectangular regions Polar integrals, like Cartesian integrals, can be taken over nonrectangular regions. The method is similar.

FACT Let R be the region bounded by the radial lines $\theta = \alpha$ and $\theta = \beta$, by an inner curve $r = r_1(\theta)$, and by an outer curve $r = r_2(\theta)$. ("Inner" and "outer" are understood relative to the origin.) Let $g(r, \theta)$ be a function defined on R. Then

$$\iint_R g \, dA = \int_{\theta=\alpha}^{\theta=\beta} \int_{r=r_1(\theta)}^{r=r_2(\theta)} g(r, \theta) \, r \, dr \, d\theta.$$

We illustrate with an example.

EXAMPLE 3 Use a polar integral to find the area of the region R inside the cardioid $r = 1 + \cos \theta$.

It applies equally well in polar coordinates!

Solution We use a familiar principle: ←

$$\text{Area of } R = \iint_R 1 \, dA,$$

but we calculate the integral in *polar* form, as follows:

$$\iint_R 1 \, dA = \int_{\theta=0}^{\theta=2\pi} \int_{r=0}^{r=1+\cos\theta} r \, dr \, d\theta$$

$$= \int_{\theta=0}^{\theta=2\pi} \frac{r^2}{2} \Big]_0^{1+\cos\theta} d\theta$$

$$= \int_{\theta=0}^{\theta=2\pi} \frac{(1 + \cos\theta)^2}{2} \, d\theta.$$

The last integral takes a little doing by hand. *Maple* has no trouble:

```
> int( (1+cos(t))^2, t=0 .. 2*Pi );
                3*Pi/2
```

■

BASIC EXERCISES

1. Let R be the polar rectangle defined by $a \leq r \leq b$ and $\alpha \leq \theta \leq \beta$.

    (a) Show that the area of R is $\dfrac{a+b}{2}(b-a)(\beta-\alpha)$.

    (b) Use part (a) to show that a polar rectangle with dimensions Δr and $\Delta \theta$ and inner radius r has area $\dfrac{r + r + \Delta r}{2} \Delta r \, \Delta \theta = \dfrac{2r + \Delta r}{2} \Delta r \, \Delta \theta$.

2. Let $f(x, y) = y$, let R be the upper half of the region inside the unit circle $x^2 + y^2 = 1$, and let $I = \iint_R f \, dA$.

    (a) Calculate I as an iterated integral in rectangular coordinates with the inner integral in y.

    (b) Calculate I as an iterated integral in rectangular coordinates with the inner integral in x.

    (c) Calculate I as an iterated integral in polar coordinates.

3. Let I_1 be the integral defined in Example 1.

    (a) Draw the solid whose volume is given by I_1.

    (b) Evaluate I_1 again but with the inner integral in x, not y.

In Exercises 4–6, use a polar double integral to evaluate the area of the region. (Draw each region first.)

4. Find the area of the region inside the cardioid $r = 1 + \sin \theta$.

5. Find the area of the region bounded by $y = x, y = 0$, and $x = 1$. Could you find the answer another way?
[HINT: First write the boundary equations in polar form.]

6. Find the area of the region bounded by the circle of radius 1/2 centered at $(0, 1/2)$. Could you find the answer another way?
[HINT: One approach is to write a Cartesian equation for the circle first and then change it to polar form.]

7. Use polar coordinates to find $\iint_R \dfrac{1}{\sqrt{x^2 + y^2}} \, dA$, where R is the region inside the cardioid $r = 1 + \sin \theta$ and above the x-axis.

8. Use polar coordinates to find the volume of the solid under the surface $z = 1 - x^2 - y^2$ and above the xy-plane. [HINT: First decide where the surface intersects the xy-plane.]

9. Use polar coordinates to find the volume of the conical solid under the surface $z = 1 - \sqrt{x^2 + y^2}$ and above the xy-plane. [HINT: First decide where the surface intersects the xy-plane.]

MACHINE GRAPHICS

Graphics—the ability to represent mathematical objects geometrically—is the most important advantage mathematical computing offers. Without computing, drawing graphs can be tedious, if not impossible. Computing makes graphs and the insights they offer easily accessible.

Graphical computing comes in many forms, from calculators to supercomputers. But all forms of graphical computing raise common questions; in this appendix we illustrate some of the power—and a few of the pitfalls—of computer graphics.

The *Maple* command

```
plot( sin(x), x=-5..5 );
```

produces a graph something like this:

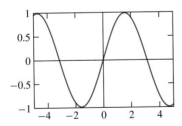

FIGURE 1
A machine graph

The *Mathematica* command

```
Plot[ Sin[x], {x,-5,5} ]
```

gives much the same result, as would a similar command on a graphing calculator. (Note that radian measure is the default in calculus.) What questions can such a graph raise?

The viewing window

The sine curve above is incomplete: the picture shows only what happens for $-5 \le x \le 5$, while the sine function itself vibrates on forever in both directions. Strictly speaking, we see only *part* of the graph. We won't always be that fastidious—we'll usually say "graph," not "piece of the graph." But the point remains: Because the full graph of a function may be infinitely long, a finite picture shows only part of it.

The term **viewing window** describes what *is* shown. In the preceding graph, for instance, the viewing window is the rectangle described by the inequalities

$$-5 \le x \le 5 \quad \text{and} \quad -1 \le y \le 1.$$

The square brackets in [−5, 5] indicate a closed interval—one that contains its endpoints. See Appendix B for more on intervals and interval notation.

The viewing window is the "product" of two intervals, one horizontal and one vertical. (It's sometimes convenient to use the "product notation" $[-5, 5] \times [-1, 1]$.) ◄ We'll call them, respectively, the **xrange** and the **yrange**. In computer jargon, xrange and yrange are **plotting parameters**.

No standard jargon. The names "xrange" and "yrange," although suggestive, aren't standard; there *is* no standard terminology. Other common names include "hrange," "vrange," "inputrange," and "outputrange."

Six views of the sine function The appearance of a graph depends (sometimes startlingly) on the viewing window. Figure 2 shows six views, in different windows, of the same function.

Graph 1:
Window = $[-30, 30] \times [-5, 5]$

Graph 2:
Window = $[-30, 30] \times [-1, 1]$

Graph 3:
Window = $[-1, 1] \times [-1, 1]$

Graph 4:
Window = $[-0.1, 0.1] \times [-0.1, 0.1]$

Graph 5:
Window = $[3.13, 3.15] \times [-0.1, 0.1]$

Graph 6:
Window = $[3.13, 3.15] \times [-0.01, 0.01]$

FIGURE 2
Six views of $y = \sin x$

Choosing a window A graph's shape depends—strongly—on the viewing window, and so every graphing device must somehow let the user choose the viewing window. Some devices try to guess what the user wants to see. For example, in the *Maple* and *Mathematica* commands

```
plot( sin(x), x=-5..5 );
Plot[ Sin[x], {x,-5,5} ]
```

only the xrange is specified explicitly; the programs somehow choose their own yrange. Leaving choices to the machine often works fine, but if something goes wrong, the user can and should intervene.

Plotting jargon

The six views of the sine function shown above reflect different choices of plotting parameters. A few technical words will be handy:

- **Scale**   The size of horizontal or vertical units on a graph. The horizontal and vertical scales on Graph 4 are ten times as large as those on Graph 3.
- **Zooming in**   The result of *enlarging* the scale, by a **zoom factor**, in one or both axis directions. Graph 4 results from zooming in on Graph 3 with zoom factor 10 on each axis. (Horizontal and vertical zoom factors may differ.)
- **Zooming out**   The result of *shrinking* the scale in one or both axis directions. Graph 3 comes from zooming out from Graph 4; both zoom factors are 10.
- **Aspect ratio**   Measures the relative sizes of horizontal and vertical units. The viewing window $[-1, 1] \times [-3, 3]$ has aspect ratio 3:1—horizontal units are three times as large as vertical units. Aspect ratios matter especially when we plot such objects as circles, for which the relative sizes of units matter.

Sample size; connecting dots   An unbroken curve has infinitely many points. Since plotting devices can handle only finite amounts of data, any machine-drawn graph can only approximate the "true" graph of a function. This limitation raises interesting metaphysical questions (for those who like that sort of thing), but it's seldom a problem for the everyday functions of elementary calculus. For most functions, 100 data points produce a passable graph. For the simplest functions, such as lines, even fewer data points suffice.

How to fool your machine

A good way to understand almost anything is to try to "break" it. It's fun and easy to fool even sophisticated plotting devices. Let's try.

Plotting devices use various strategies for drawing curves that look continuous. One simple strategy is to plot, say, 101 ➡ equally spaced points, join them with 100 line segments, and hope for the best. This often works fine, but not always. Observe what happens to the sine graph in a *huge* viewing window (Figure 3).

Why 101? Because 100 equal subintervals have 101 endpoints.

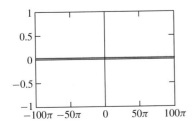

FIGURE 3

$y = \sin x$; **Sample size = 101 points**
Window $= [-100\pi, 100\pi] \times [-1, 1]$

The graph is just the x-axis.

The graph is obviously wrong. ← The sine curve actually oscillates *100 times* over the xrange shown. What went wrong?

Nothing—the plotter did as it was told. The xrange interval, $[-100\pi, 100\pi]$, was cut into 100 equal pieces, and the sine function was sampled at the end of each piece. By unlucky accident, each sample point fell at a multiple of 2π, where the sine function is zero. Our plotting sample was too small and too regularly spaced to capture the function's complicated behavior. Luckily, problems with sample size are uncommon in calculus applications. Many "smart" plotting devices recognize sticky situations and adjust sample sizes accordingly.

Cautions

Machine graphics should be viewed skeptically. Various surprises are possible; not all are the machine's fault. Here are some pitfalls to avoid.

- **Too few data**   Plotting functions with irregular or ragged graphs may require many, many data points. Using smaller windows (i.e., zooming in) sometimes helps.
- **Awkward windows**   If $f(x) = x^{10} - x$, then $f(0) = 0$ and $f(1) = 0$, and so the graph of f crosses the x-axis at $x = 0$ and at $x = 1$. Does a machine-drawn graph agree? Figure 4 provides a look (the machine chose its own yrange). ←

The notation 1e + 07 means 1×10^7, or 10 million.

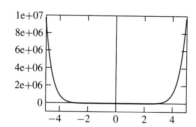

FIGURE 4
$y = x^{10} - x$
Window $= [-5, 5] \times [-10^6, 10^7]$

There is disappointingly little to see near $x = 0$. The tenth power is at fault: Even for modest values of x, $f(x)$ is gigantic. To show everything, yrange must be correspondingly huge. As a result, all but the grossest behavior disappears. Figure 5 shows the same function in a much smaller window.

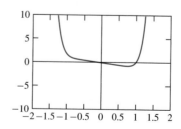

FIGURE 5
$y = x^{10} - x$
Window $= [-2, 2] \times [-10, 10]$

In this case, there is no really good choice of window.

Which graph is better? It depends (literally, in this case) on one's point of view. ←

- **Scale effects**   Different scales can give wildly different views of the same graph. Here are two views (Figure 6) of the function $y = x + \sin(200x)/200$, the second a tenfold magnification of the first.

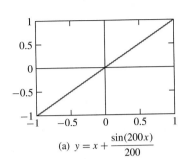

(a) $y = x + \dfrac{\sin(200x)}{200}$

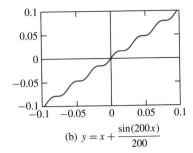

(b) $y = x + \dfrac{\sin(200x)}{200}$

FIGURE 6
Scale effects

Notice the differences: The first graph looks almost straight; it's a slightly wiggly version of the line $y = x$. ➡ In the second graph, with smaller values of x, the rapid oscillations of $\sin(200x)/200$ produce a wiggly result. The moral: Viewing the same graph from different scales can show different aspects of a function's behavior.

Compared to x, the second summand, $\sin(200x)/200$, is small, so it has little effect.

- **Slippery slopes**   Shouldn't the line $y = 10x$ look steeper than the line $y = x$? ➡ Yet the following graphs (Figure 7) look almost identical.

The lines have slopes 10 and 1, respectively.

(a) $y = 10x$

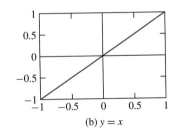

(b) $y = x$

FIGURE 7
Same appearance, different slopes

The apparent anomaly arises from different choices of yrange for the two graphs. The plotting device chose its yrange just large enough to fit the plotting data. (One curious effect of this policy is that all lines with positive slope "look the same"; all go from lower left to upper right.) Plotting both lines in the same window gives a very different view:

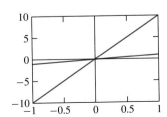

FIGURE 8
$y = x$ and $y = 10x$

Machine graphs in calculus

Graphs are crucial throughout this book. Some simple graphs are best drawn by hand, but we'll leave most of the plotting work to machines. More important than drawing graphs is learning to read them and understand what they say about functions.

EXAMPLE 1 Find the maximum value, and where it occurs, of the function $f(x) = x \sin x$ on the interval $[0, 4]$.

Solution A calculus concept, the derivative, will be useful later in solving such problems. Here, we'll just use graphs. The three that follow (Figures 9–11) are captioned with the *Maple* commands that produce them—note the different choices of xrange.

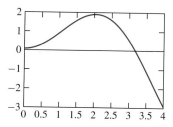

FIGURE 9

```
plot (x * sin(x), x = 0..4)
```

A maximum seems to occur around $x = 2$. Let's look more closely (Figure 10):

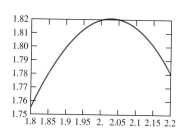

FIGURE 10

```
plot (x * sin(x), x = 1.8..2.2)
```

and still more closely (Figure 11):

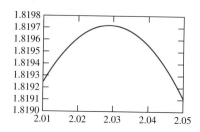

FIGURE 11

```
plot (x * sin(x), x = 2.01..2.05)
```

We conclude that the maximum value is about 1.8197; it occurs near $x = 2.03$. ∎

EXAMPLE 2 For x near 0, the function $p(x) = x - x^3/6$ is a good approximation to the sine function. ➡ *How well* does p approximate the sine function on $[-1, 1]$? On $[-2, 2]$?

Later we'll discuss how to find simple functions, such as p, that approximate more complicated functions such as the sine function.

Solution First we'll compare the graphs of $p(x)$ and $\sin x$ ➡ for x in the interval $[-2, 2]$.

Which is which?

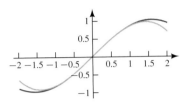

FIGURE 12
$y = \sin x$ and $y = x - \dfrac{x^3}{6}$

For $-1 \le x \le 1$ the approximation is good; there is little visible difference between the graphs. Things deteriorate when $|x| > 1$; by $x = \pm 2$, the graphs are far apart.

How might we *measure* how well one function approximates another on a given interval? One way is to find the largest difference, positive or negative, between the two functions on the given interval. On $[-1, 1]$, for example, we could plot the **error function** $p(x) - \sin x$:

FIGURE 13
$p(x) - \sin x$

The graph shows that, for x in $[-1, 1]$, the difference between the two functions is never more (in absolute value) than 0.009. In other words: *On $[-1, 1]$, $p(x)$ approximates $\sin x$ with error no worse than 0.009.* ∎

EXERCISES

NOTES: Most of the exercises in this section require some form of graphing technology. Almost any form will do; the main requirement is an ability to choose viewing windows (e.g., by zooming). When graphing trigonometric functions, be sure to use *radians* rather than degrees.

1. Example 2 discussed the fact that $\sin x \approx p(x) = x - x^3/6$ for x near 0. Another approximation of the sine function says that, for x near 0, $\sin x \approx \ell(x) = x$. This exercise pursues this approximation a bit further.

   (a) Complete the following tables, rounding your answers to five decimal places.

x	$\sin x$	$\lvert x - \sin x \rvert$
-1		
-0.5		
-0.1		
-0.01		

x	$\sin x$	$\lvert x - \sin x \rvert$
1		
0.5		
0.1		
0.01		

   (b) We said, "On $[-1, 1]$, $p(x)$ approximates $\sin x$ with error no worse than 0.009." Does the same statement apply if

$\ell(x)$ replaces $p(x)$? If not, what number could replace 0.009?

(c) Show that $p(x)$ approximates $\sin x$ with error less than 0.001 if $-0.65 \le x \le 0.65$.

(d) Find an interval $[-a, a]$ on which $\ell(x)$ approximates $\sin x$ with error less than 0.001.

2. Use the following sketch to answer each question.

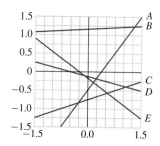

(a) Do any of the labeled lines have slope greater than 1? If so, which ones?

(b) Where do lines A and C intersect? Justify your answer.

3. Use the following sketch to answer each question. [NOTE: This is *not* the same graph as in Exercise 2.]

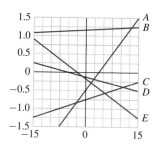

(a) Do any of the labeled lines have slope greater than 1? If so, which ones?

(b) Where do lines A and D intersect? Justify your answer.

4. Use the following sketch to answer each question. [NOTE: This is not the same graph as in Exercise 2.]

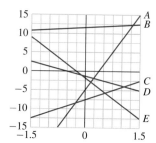

(a) Do any of the labeled lines have slope greater than 1? If so, which ones?

(b) Where do lines C and D intersect? Justify your answer.

5. In each of the following parts, experiment to find a viewing window in which the graph of $y = \sin x$ has (approximately!) the given shape or appearance. Express your answers in the form $[a, b] \times [c, d]$.

(a) A horizontal line.

(b) A diagonal line from lower left to upper right.

(c) A diagonal line from upper left to lower right.

(d) A vertical line.

(e) A rounded letter V.

6. Repeat Exercise 5, using the graph of $y = \cos x$.

7. Repeat Exercise 5, using the graph of $y = x^2$.

*A number r is a **root** of a function f if $f(r) = 0$. In Exercises 8–17, use a grapher to locate the roots of each function in the interval $[-5, 5]$. (Report answers to two decimal places.)*

8. $f(x) = x^2 - x$

9. $f(x) = 2^x - x^2$

10. $f(x) = x - \sin x$

11. $f(x) = x - \cos x$

12. $f(x) = x^3 - \sqrt{x^2 + 1}$

13. $f(x) = \sqrt{16 - 3x} - x^2 + 2$

14. $f(x) = x - 2 + 2\cos x$

15. $f(x) = (1 - x/6)^3 - \sin x$

16. $f(x) = (x^2 + 1)^{3/2} - 3x^2$

17. $f(x) = (x^2 - 1)^{2/3} + x$

18. For x near 0, the function $q(x) = 1 - x^2/2$ is a good approximation of the cosine function.

(a) How well does q approximate the cosine function on the interval $[-1, 1]$?

(b) Find an interval $[-a, a]$ on which $q(x)$ approximates $\cos x$ with error less than 0.001.

19. For x near 0, the function $r(x) = 1 - x^2 + x^4$ is a good approximation of the function $f(x) = 1/(1 + x^2)$.

(a) How well does the r approximate f over the interval $[-1, 1]$?

(b) Find an interval $[-a, a]$ on which $r(x)$ approximates $f(x)$ with error less than 0.001.

20. For x near 0, the function $s(x) = 1 + x + x^2$ is a good approximation of the function $g(x) = (1 - x)^{-1}$.

(a) How well does s approximate g over the interval $[-0.5, 0.5]$?

(b) Find an interval $[-a, a]$ on which $s(x)$ approximates $g(x)$ with error less than 0.001.

21. The function $f(x) = 1.08789 - 0.695660x + 0.121008x^2$ can be used to approximate the function $g(x) = (1 + x^2)^{-1}$ on the interval $[1, 3]$. How well does f approximate g over the interval $[1, 3]$?

22. For x near 0, the function $h(x) = x/(1 + x^2/6)$ can be used to approximate the sine function. Find an interval $[-a, a]$

on which h approximates the sine function with error less than 0.005.

Graphs of most calculus functions "look straight at small scale." (Graphs 4–6 on page A-2 illustrate what this means for the sine function.) In Exercises 23–34, find a window centered at the given point in which the graph of the function looks like a straight line.

23. $y = x^2$ at $(2, 4)$

24. $y = -x^3 + 3x^2 - 2$ at $(1, 0)$

25. $y = \cos x$ at $(0, 1)$

26. $y = \cos(x^2)$ at $(0, 1)$

27. $y = \cos(x^2)$ at $(5, \cos(25))$

28. $y = \cos(x^2)$ at $(10, \cos(100))$

29. $y = \dfrac{1}{1 + x^2}$ at $(0, 1)$

30. $y = \dfrac{1}{1 - x}$ at $(0, 1)$

31. $y = \dfrac{4 + x}{3x^2 + 2}$ at $(1, 1)$

32. $y = \sqrt{x}$ at $(4, 2)$.

33. $y = \sqrt{1 + x}$ at $(0, 1)$

34. $y = \dfrac{4x}{\sqrt{3 + x}}$ at $(1, 2)$

In Exercises 35–54, use graphics to estimate the maximum and minimum values of $f(x)$ when $-10 \le x \le 10$. (Round your answers to three decimal places.)

35. $f(x) = \sin x$

36. $f(x) = x + \sin x$

37. $f(x) = \dfrac{x}{x - 11}$

38. $f(x) = \dfrac{1}{x - 11}$

39. $f(x) = \dfrac{x^2}{x - 11}$

40. $f(x) = \dfrac{\sin x}{x - 11}$

41. $f(x) = x^2$

42. $f(x) = 2^x$

43. $f(x) = 2^x - x^2$

44. $f(x) = \dfrac{2x}{\sqrt{x^2 + 1}}$

45. $f(x) = \dfrac{3}{x^2 + 4}$

46. $f(x) = x^3 - 3x + 1$

47. $f(x) = (x + 1)^3$

48. $f(x) = (10 - x)^3$

49. $f(x) = x^4 + 5x^2 + 3$

50. $f(x) = \dfrac{x - 1}{x^2 + 3}$

51. $f(x) = x\sqrt{144 - x^2}$

52. $f(x) = \cos(x/5)$

53. $f(x) = \cos(\sin x)$

54. $f(x) = \sin(\cos x)$

Real Numbers and the Coordinate Plane

The real numbers might seem, at first glance, almost *too* familiar. What is there to say? Surprisingly, a great deal—far more than a calculus course could cover.

Here's just one hint at the subtleties: It's been known since Pythagoras (ca. 500 B.C.E.) that some numbers, such as $\sqrt{2}$, are **irrational**—that is, they can't be written as *ratios* of integers. But how thickly scattered are the irrationals among the reals? Are "most" real numbers rational or irrational? The answers are remarkable, even mysterious: "Most" real numbers are irrational; a dart thrown randomly at a number line will almost always hit an irrational. Yet plenty of rational numbers exist; in any interval, no matter how small, there are *infinitely many* rational numbers! Resolving these tantalizing mysteries must wait for a later mathematics course. For us, a brief, brisk, selective review of the properties of real numbers will suffice.

Newton managed.   Isaac Newton himself did quite well without a fully rigorous development of the real numbers. The first mathematically satisfactory definition of the real numbers was given by Richard Dedekind over 130 years after Newton's death.

The real number line

The real numbers are really no more *real*, in any deep philosophical sense, than the integers, the rationals, or even the complex numbers. The best reason for the adjective "real" may be that the set of real numbers can be thought of naturally as an unbroken, unending line. Once an origin and a unit of distance are fixed, every point has its own number and every number its own point. Figure 1 shows the usual picture with some famous numbers marked.

FIGURE 1

The real number line

Order   The line shows nicely how the real numbers are ordered: *As we move to the right on the line, real numbers increase.* This is important, and so we restate it as an inequality:

a > b if and only if a is to the right of b on the number line.

Thus, for example, $-3 > -4$, even though -4 has greater *magnitude* than -3.

Sets and subsets   The set of real numbers, like any infinite set, has infinitely many possible subsets. Some of them have fiendishly complicated structures. ("Fractals," for example, are sets that are irregular or ragged at *any* scale. The most spectacular fractal sets are usually shown in two dimensions, but many fractals have one-dimensional forms.) In calculus, luckily, most subsets of interest are easily understood.

Sets and subsets pop up often in mathematics. By using set notation efficiently, we can avoid tedious and sometimes confusing verbal descriptions. In calculus, for instance, we might ask:

Let $f(x) = x^3 - x$. For which real numbers x is $f(x) < 0$?

Plotting the curve $y = f(x)$ makes the answer—the **solution set**—apparent. ➤ The solution set, described in words, is

Plot the curve, say for $-2 \le x \le 2$, to see for yourself.

the set of real numbers x such that either x is less than -1 or x lies between 0 and 1.

That's a mouthful, even for this relatively simple problem. In set notation, the same answer is much more concise: $\{ x \mid x < -1 \text{ or } 0 < x < 1 \}$. (The vertical line | means "such that.") It's understood here that x represents a real number.

Intervals   Intervals are "pieces" chopped from the real line. They are the simplest and most useful subsets of the reals. Intervals come in various styles: They can be bounded or infinitely long, and they may or may not include their endpoints. (**Closed intervals** contain their endpoints; **open intervals** don't.) The following table of examples illustrates the full taxonomy. It illustrates, too, how intervals can be defined by one or more inequalities.

Taxonomy of intervals		
Interval	**Description**	**Inequality Form**
$(-2, 3)$	an *open* interval	$\{ x \mid -2 < x < 3 \}$
$[a, b]$	a *closed* interval	$\{ x \mid a \le x \le b \}$
$[2, b)$	a half-open interval	$\{ x \mid 2 \le x < b \}$
$(5, \infty)$	an infinite interval	$\{ x \mid x > 5 \}$
$(-\infty, \infty)$	another infinite interval	

Other subsets of the real numbers   Following are more examples of subsets of the reals. Notice carefully our use of various special notations, including $\mathbb{R}$, $\mathbb{Q}$, and $\mathbb{Z}$ for the sets of reals, rationals, and integers, and the $\cup$ (union) and $\cap$ (intersection) symbols for combining sets.

Subsets of the real numbers		
Set	**Explanation**	**Alternative notation(s)**
$\mathbb{R}$	the real numbers	$(-\infty, \infty)$
$\mathbb{N}$	the natural numbers	$\{1, 2, 3, \dots\}$
$\mathbb{Z}$	the integers	$\{0, \pm 1, \pm 2, \pm 3, \dots\}$
$\mathbb{Q}$	the rationals	
$\{0, 2, 5\}$	a finite set	$\{x \mid x = 0 \text{ or } x = 2 \text{ or } x = 5\}$ $\{x \mid x(x-2)(x-5) = 0\}$
$(1, 4) \cup (5, 6)$	union of two intervals	$\{x \mid 1 < x < 4 \text{ or } 5 < x < 6\}$
$(1, 6) \cap [4, 7]$	intersection of two intervals	$\{x \mid 1 < x < 6 \text{ and } 4 \le x \le 7\}$ or $\{x \mid 4 \le x < 6\}$ or $[4, 6)$

Drawing subsets   Simple subsets of the reals are easy to "draw" on the real line. Intervals are nicest of all: They appear as line segments, including some, all, or none of their endpoints. Errors of approximation can occur ◄ in *any* picture, but for most sets they do no harm. Several straightforward examples appear below; a *closed* dot indicates an *included* point; an *open* dot indicates an *excluded* point.

For example, because ideal "points" on a line, unlike pencil points, have zero thickness. Errors of omission are also inevitable; no picture can show everything.

Drawing subsets	
Set	**Picture**
$(-2, 3)$	
$[3, \infty)$	
$(-3, 2]$	
$\mathbb{Z}$	
$[-4, -2) \cup (1, 3)$	

The ∞ symbol: not a number   Every real number corresponds to a point on the real line. The symbol ∞ does not because ∞ *is not a real number.*

So what *is* ∞? That's a thorny question indeed. A fully rigorous answer is beyond the scope of this book. A "pretty good" answer is that the symbol ∞ represents the idea of unboundedness. When we say that the real line has *infinite* length, for instance, we mean that the line goes on forever.

The symbol ∞ is a useful shorthand, but it should be used sparingly, and with care; ∞ is not an ordinary number and seldom behaves like one. In particular, "algebra" with the infinity symbol takes special care. ◄

For more on "algebra with ∞," see Section 4.2.

Absolute value, distance, and inequalities

The idea of **absolute value** (or **magnitude**) should be familiar; its use in simple expressions such as

$$|-3| = 3, \qquad |\sin x| \le 1, \qquad \text{and} \qquad \sqrt{x^2} = |x|$$

will cause no trouble. Sometimes, however, a formal definition is helpful:

$$|x| = \begin{cases} x & \text{if } x \geq 0 \\ -x & \text{if } x < 0 \end{cases}$$

Familiar as all this is, absolute values can be sticky in practice—especially if inequalities are involved. The following two tricks of the trade may help:

- **Absolute value as distance**   For *any* numbers a and b, $|a - b|$ can (and should!) be thought of as the *distance between a and b*. Thinking of absolute value as distance helps us visualize algebraic expressions geometrically. For example, the absolute value equation $|x + 2| = 3$ can be solved algebraically, but the distance interpretation is more revealing. Because

$$|x + 2| = |x - (-2)| = \text{distance from } x \text{ to } -2,$$

  the equation $|x + 2| = 3$ says that x *lies 3 units away from* -2. Clearly, $x = -5$ and $x = 1$ are the only solutions of the equation.

- **Trading absolute values for inequalities: two for one**   Absolute values sometimes appear in inequalities, such as $|x + 2| < 3$. Solving such inequalities takes care. Here's the key idea:

  One absolute value inequality corresponds to two ordinary inequalities.

  The preceding inequality says that $x + 2$ lies between 3 and -3, that is that $-3 < x + 2 < 3$. Now, subtracting 2 from all parts of the inequality gives the solution set: $-5 < x < 1$.
  In general, for *any* quantities x and b (where $b > 0$):

  $$|x| < b \quad \text{if and only if} \quad -b < x < b$$
  $$|x| > b \quad \text{if and only if} \quad -b > x \quad \text{or} \quad x > b$$

  (Similar rules hold for $\leq$ and $\geq$ inequalities.)

EXAMPLE 1   Any open or closed finite interval can be described in terms of its **midpoint** and **radius**; absolute value inequalities help. The open interval $(-3, 5)$, for instance, has midpoint $x = 1$ and radius 4 because the distance from every point in the interval to 1 is less than 4. Therefore, the interval $(-3, 5)$ corresponds naturally to the inequality $|x - 1| < 4$. In formal language:

$$(-3, 5) = \{\, x \mid |x - 1| < 4 \,\}. \qquad \blacksquare$$

EXAMPLE 2   Solve the inequality $|2x + 3| \leq 5$.

Solution   By the first fact above, the inequality

$$|2x + 3| \leq 5$$

is equivalent to

$$-5 \leq 2x + 3 \leq 5.$$

Now the usual algebraic rules for inequalities apply:

$$-5 \leq 2x + 3 \leq 5 \iff -8 \leq 2x \leq 2 \iff -4 \leq x \leq 1.$$

(The symbol $\iff$ means "if and only if"; it indicates that each side implies the other.) We conclude that the inequality holds if and only if x lies in the interval $[-4, 1]$. $\blacksquare$

EXAMPLE 3   Solve $|x - 2| > |x + 3|$.

Solution   Having absolute values on *both sides* of the inequality complicates things. A workable—but tedious—strategy is to look separately at three cases: $x < -3$, $-3 \le x < 2$, and $x \ge 2$.

Convince yourself of this—it's easy but important.

An easier approach is to interpret both sides as *distance*. If we do, the inequality says that *x is farther from 2 than from* -3. ◄ Now the solution set is easy to visualize; it's everything to the *left* of $-1/2$, the point halfway between 2 and -3. In interval notation, the solution set is $(-\infty, -1/2)$. ∎

Absolute values in context   Absolute value inequalities are useful in measuring how closely one thing approximates another.

EXAMPLE 4   For which x does the inequality $|x - \sin x| < 0.1$ hold?

Solution   How might such an inequality arise? Why would we want to know? Consider the graphs of two functions in Figure 2.

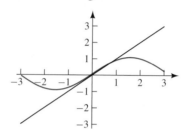

FIGURE 2
y = x and y = sin x

The picture illustrates an interesting approximation: $x \approx \sin x$ if $x \approx 0$. (The approximation is useful, too—it's used, for instance, in modeling the behavior of a pendulum.)

But *how* good is the approximation, and for which x is it useful? The inequality $|x - \sin x| < 0.1$ gets at just this question; it describes values of x for which x and $\sin x$ differ (in either direction) by less than 0.1.

In practice, it might take some trial and error to find a good plotting window.

We'll solve our inequality graphically. Figure 3 is a piece of the graph of $y = x - \sin x$. ◄

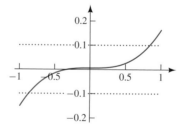

FIGURE 3
y = x − sin x

The graph shows (approximately, of course) that the inequality $-0.1 < x - \sin x < 0.1$ holds for $-0.8 < x < 0.8$. ∎

The coordinate plane

The real numbers correspond to points on a *line*. In much the same way, pairs of real numbers correspond to points in the **coordinate plane**.

The idea of attaching numerical coordinates to points in the plane is credited to the French philosopher René Descartes (1596–1650). It is no exaggeration to describe Descartes's idea, natural as it seems in hindsight, as one of the most important in mathematical history. Descartes's idea is powerful because it links geometry with algebra and analysis. Geometry is the study of figures—lines, curves, circles, and so forth—in the plane. Algebra and analysis study operations—such as addition and multiplication—on numbers and on functions.

Before Descartes, geometry was relatively isolated from other branches of mathematics; geometers used compasses and other drawing tools to construct and measure plane figures. Figures *not* based on circles and lines were harder to describe and manipulate. The parabola, for instance, was described geometrically as the set of points equidistant from a fixed point and a fixed line. Properties of the parabola (such as the **reflection property**: All rays parallel to the axis of symmetry "bounce" to the same point, the **focus**) were hard to understand and prove with purely geometric tools and ways of thinking.

The great advantage of Cartesian coordinates is that they allow *algebraic* descriptions of geometric figures in the plane. The algebraic equation $y = x^2$, for example, describes a parabola in a far simpler and more convenient fashion than its geometric definition.

When geometric figures are described algebraically, the powerful tools and ideas of algebra and analysis become available. The connection, moreover, goes both ways: Geometric intuition sheds light on algebraic and analytic problems.

This link is the essence of the field of mathematics known as **analytic geometry**. In its most familiar form, analytic geometry studies properties of lines, circles, ellipses, parabolas, and hyperbolas. Collectively, these figures are called **conic sections** because each can be thought of, geometrically, as a slice (i.e., "section") of a cone. (The cone in question is hollow and may be "double," as in the case of a hyperbola.)

The key idea for us is that the conic sections can be described *algebraically*, as graphs of quadratic equations. Thus, properties of quadratic equations are, from another point of view, properties of conic sections, and vice versa. Knowledge of either tells us something of the other.

Throughout calculus, linking geometric, algebraic, and analytic ideas is crucial to understanding; it is the most important theme of this book.

Coordinate systems   A **rectangular coordinate system** in the plane has three parts: two perpendicular axes, with scales, and an origin at the point where they intersect. By convention, the x-axis is horizontal and numbered from left to right; the y-axis is vertical and numbered from bottom to top. With a coordinate system in place, every point's coordinates are defined. Figure 4 presents the familiar picture; several points are shown with their coordinates labeled.

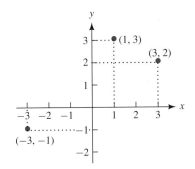

FIGURE 4
Rectangular coordinates

A coordinate system defines a one-to-one correspondence between points in the plane and pairs of real numbers: Each point corresponds to its two numerical coordinates.

Cartesian addresses.   The coordinates of a point are, in a sense, the point's "address"—they locate the point in the plane. A point's Cartesian address, moreover, gives explicit directions for getting there: To reach (a, b), from the origin, go a units "east" and b units "north." This is more than can be said for typical street addresses—123 Elm Street, for instance. (Some cities *do* use Cartesian-style addresses, such as 1234 56th Avenue.)

Calculating with coordinates: distance and midpoint

Cartesian coordinates help reduce many questions about points in the plane to straightforward calculations.

Midpoints   Recall the situation in *one* dimension. If x_1 and x_2 are points on the real *line*, their midpoint, m, is their numerical average: $m = (x_1 + x_2)/2$. A similar situation holds in the plane. To find the midpoint, M, of the segment joining points $P = (x_1, y_1)$ and $Q = (x_2, y_2)$, we average their x- and y-coordinates *separately*:

$$M = \left(\frac{x_1 + x_2}{2}, \frac{y_1 + y_2}{2} \right)$$

Figure 5 illustrates the situation.

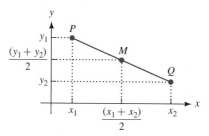

FIGURE 5
Finding a midpoint

Notice, in particular, that the two coordinates of M are midpoints of intervals on the two axes.

Distance   The distance between two points x_1 and x_2 on the real *line* is $|x_2 - x_1|$. The distance formula in the *plane* follows from the one-dimensional formula and from the Pythagorean theorem. What's the distance between the points $P = (x_1, y_1)$ and $Q = (x_2, y_2)$? Figure 6 illustrates this problem.

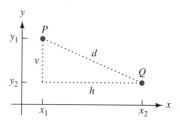

FIGURE 6
Distance between two points

As the picture shows, the distance d from P to Q is the hypotenuse of a right triangle with sides (labeled h and v) parallel to the axes. By the *one*-dimensional formula:

$$h = |x_2 - x_1| \qquad \text{and} \qquad v = |y_2 - y_1|.$$

From the Pythagorean theorem,

$$d = \sqrt{h^2 + v^2} = \sqrt{|x_2 - x_1|^2 + |y_2 - y_1|^2} = \sqrt{(x_2 - x_1)^2 + (y_2 - y_1)^2}$$

The last form is standard. To summarize:

> **FACT**   The distance from $P = (x_1, y_1)$ to $Q = (x_2, y_2)$ is given by $d(P, Q) = \sqrt{(x_2 - x_1)^2 + (y_2 - y_1)^2}$.

Elementary properties of distance in the plane follow from this formula:

- **Just as far either way**   Intuition says that the distance from P to Q should be equal to the distance from Q to P. The distance formula agrees:

$$d(P, Q) = \sqrt{(x_2 - x_1)^2 + (y_2 - y_1)^2} = \sqrt{(x_1 - x_2)^2 + (y_1 - y_2)^2} = d(Q, P).$$

- **Finding midpoints**   The midpoint M between points $P = (x_1, y_1)$ and $Q = (x_2, y_2)$ "should" lie equidistant from both. A computation bears this out:

$$d(P, M) = \sqrt{\left(\frac{x_1 + x_2}{2} - x_1\right)^2 + \left(\frac{y_1 + y_2}{2} - y_1\right)^2}$$

$$= \sqrt{\left(\frac{x_1 + x_2}{2} - x_2\right)^2 + \left(\frac{y_1 + y_2}{2} - y_2\right)^2}$$

$$= d(Q, M).$$

Using the distance and midpoint formulas

Simply finding distances and midpoints is not very edifying. Such calculations usually arise in more interesting contexts.

Circles   A circle is the set of points at some fixed distance, say r, from a center point, say $C = (a, b)$. The distance formula puts all this conveniently in algebraic form:

The point $P = (x, y)$ lies on the circle if and only if $d(P, C) = \sqrt{(x - a)^2 + (y - b)^2} = r$.

Squaring both sides gives the standard equation for a circle: $(x - a)^2 + (y - b)^2 = r^2$.

The ⟺ symbol means "if and only if."

E X A M P L E 5   Find an equation for the circle with radius 5 and center $C = (3, 2)$.

Solution   A point $P = (x, y)$ lies on the circle if and only if $d(P, C) = 5$, that is, if

$$\sqrt{(x-3)^2 + (y-2)^2} = 5.$$

If we're squeamish about square roots, there are other, equivalent, forms: ◄

$$\sqrt{(x-3)^2 + (y-2)^2} = 5 \iff (x-3)^2 + (y-2)^2 = 25$$
$$\iff (x^2 - 6x + 9) + (y^2 - 4y + 4) = 25$$
$$\iff x^2 + y^2 - 6x - 4y - 12 = 0$$
$$\iff x^2 + y^2 - 6x - 4y = 12$$ ∎

See Appendix D for more on this technique.

E X A M P L E 6   Is $x^2 + 4x + y^2 - 2y = 10$ the equation of a circle? If so, which one?

Solution   Let's **complete the square** in both x and y: ◄

$$x^2 + 4x + y^2 - 2y = 10 \iff (x^2 + 4x + 4) + (y^2 - 2y + 1) = 10 + 4 + 1$$
$$\iff (x+2)^2 + (y-1)^2 = 15$$

The answer can now be read off: The equation describes a circle of radius $\sqrt{15}$, centered at $(-2, 1)$. ∎

E X A M P L E 7   An ancient theorem in geometry asserts: *The segment joining the midpoints of two sides of a triangle is parallel to the third side, and half its length.* Classical geometers would have proved this "constructively" with drawing tools. With coordinates, the proof is an easy calculation.

Consider Figure 7 (we put one vertex at the origin for convenience):

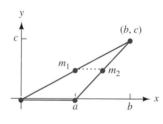

FIGURE 7
An ancient theorem

To prove our first claim—that the segment joining m_1 and m_2 is horizontal—it's enough to show that m_1 and m_2 have the same y-coordinate. By the midpoint formula,

$$m_1 = \left(\frac{b}{2}, \frac{c}{2}\right) \qquad \text{and} \qquad m_2 = \left(\frac{a+b}{2}, \frac{c}{2}\right);$$

this proves the result. We leave the claim about lengths as an exercise. ∎

EXERCISES

1. Draw each of the following intervals:

    (a) $[-3, 2)$

    (b) $(-3, 2)$

    (c) $[-3, 2]$

    (d) $(-3, 2]$

In Exercises 2–5, express the set as an interval.

2. $\{x \mid -10 < x \le 15\}$

3. $\{x \mid -6 \le x < 4\}$

4. $\{x \mid -13 < x < 17\}$

5. $\{x \mid 2 \le x \le 9\}$

6. Is ∞ a real number? Does ∞ correspond to a point on the real line? Explain.

7. (a) Write an absolute value inequality whose solution set is the interval $[-5, 3]$.

   (b) What is the midpoint of the interval $[-5, 3]$?

   (c) What is the radius of the interval $[-5, 3]$?

8. Consider the absolute value inequality $|x - 2| > 3$.

   (a) What is the distance interpretation of this inequality?

   (b) Write two ordinary inequalities that correspond to this inequality.

   (c) Draw a picture of the solution set of this inequality.

   (d) Write the solution set of this inequality using intervals.

9. Solve the inequality $|2x + 3| \geq 5$. Express your answer as an interval.

10. Solve the inequality $|3x - 2| < 5$. Express your answer as an interval.

11. Draw a picture of the solution set of the inequality $|x - 2| > |x + 3|$. [HINT: See Example 3.]

12. Consider the inequality $|x - 2| > |x + 3|$. Explain why the solution set can be obtained by the strategy of looking separately at each of the three cases $x < -3$, $-3 \leq x < 2$, and $x \geq 2$. [HINT: See Example 3.]

13. Solve the inequality $|x + 3| \geq |x - 2|$. Express the solution set as an interval.

14. Does the inequality $|x - \sin x| < 0.05$ hold in the interval $[-0.6, 0.6]$? Justify your answer.

15. Suppose that $|x - 11| \leq 0.02$. Find real numbers L and U such that $L \leq x \leq U$.

16. Suppose that $-5 < x < 7$. Explain why $|x| < 10$.

In Exercises 17–20, express the inequality in the form $|x - A| \leq B$, where A and B are real numbers.

17. $-3 \leq x \leq 9$

18. $2 \leq x \leq 10$

19. $-7 \leq x \leq -4$

20. $5.9999 \leq x \leq 6.0001$

In Exercises 21–26, express the interval using absolute value inequalities.

21. $(0, 10)$

22. $[-\pi, \pi]$

23. $(-2, 4)$

24. $(2, 8)$

25. $[-3, 7]$

26. $[-10, -2]$

27. Suppose that $L \leq x \leq U$. Let $C = \frac{1}{2}(L + U)$ and $R = \frac{1}{2}(U - L)$. Show that $|x - C| \leq R$. [HINT: Draw a picture of a number line with the points L, C, and U labeled.]

In Exercises 28–31, find the distance between the pair of points.

28. $(0, 0)$ and $(2, 3)$

29. $(1, 2)$ and $(3, 4)$

30. $(-4, 2)$ and $(-7, -4)$

31. $(-5, -2)$ and $(2, 5)$

32. Let $P = (x_1, y_1)$ and $Q = (x_2, y_2)$ be two points in the plane. Use the distance formula to show that $d(P, Q) = d(Q, P)$ (i.e., that the distance from P to Q is the same as the distance from Q to P).

33. Let $P = (x_1, y_1)$ and $Q = (x_2, y_2)$ be two points in the plane and M be the midpoint of the segment joining P and Q. Show that $d(M, P) = d(M, Q)$ (i.e., that M is equidistant from P and Q).

34. Does the point $(0, -2)$ lie on the circle with radius 5 and center $C = (3, 2)$? Justify your answer.

35. Find an equation for the circle with radius 3 and center $C = (1, -2)$.

36. Find an equation for the circle of radius 4 centered at $(-3, 7)$.

37. Show that $3x^2 + 3y^2 + 4y = 7$ is the equation of a circle. Find the radius and center of this circle. [HINT: Complete the square.]

38. Is $x^2 + y^2 - 6x - 8y = -9$ the equation of a circle? If so, which one?

39. Show that the line segment joining the midpoint of two sides of a triangle is half the length of the third side. [HINT: See Example 7.]

In Exercises 40–44, express the set as an interval.

40. $\{x \mid |x| \leq 3\}$

41. $\{x \mid |x - 2| \leq 5\}$

42. $\{x \mid |x + 3| \leq 4\}$

43. $\{x \mid |x - a| < b\}$

44. $\{x \mid |x - a| < a\}$

45. Find the points in the xy-plane that are at distance 13 from the point $(1, 2)$ and have y-coordinate equal to -3. [HINT: Draw a picture.]

In Exercises 46–49, write an absolute value inequality whose solution is the given set.

46. $\{x \mid x < -3 \quad \text{or} \quad x > 3\}$

47. $\{x \mid x < -5 \quad \text{or} \quad x > 3\}$

48. $\{x \mid -7 < x \quad \text{and} \quad x < 7\}$

49. $\{x \mid -7 < x \quad \text{and} \quad x < 5\}$

In Exercises 50–52, express the English sentence in mathematical notation using an absolute value inequality.

50. The temperature outside is within 5°F of freezing.

51. The temperature in that room is closer to 100°F than to freezing.

52. The high temperature today is closer to yesterday's high temperature than yesterday's high was to the high temperature 2 days ago.

In Exercises 53–56, explain why the statement is true if r is a real number such that $3 < r < 7$.

53. $|r| \geq -2$

54. $|r| < 7$

55. $|r| > 3$

56. $|r - 5| < 2$

In Exercises 57–66, suppose that x is a real number and that $-3 \leq x \leq 11$. Indicate whether the statement must *be true.*

57. $-3 \leq x \leq 9$

58. $2 \leq x \leq 10$

59. $-7 \leq x \leq -4$

60. $5.9999 \leq x \leq 6.0001$

61. $|x| < 12$

62. $|x| > -1$

63. $|x| \geq 2$

64. $|x| > 4$

65. $|x - 4| < 7$

66. $|x - 7| < 4$

Suppose that s is a real number and that $-2 \leq s \leq 1$. In Exercises 67–70, indicate whether the statement must *be true,* cannot *be true, or* may *be true, and justify your answer.*

67. $|s| \leq 1$

68. $|s| \leq 2$

69. $|s| \geq 0$

70. $|s| < 10$

71. Suppose that $|x - 3| \leq 0.005$ and $|y - 2| \leq 0.003$. Find real numbers A and B such that $|(x + y) - A| \leq B$.
[HINT: Draw a picture.]

LINES AND
LINEAR FUNCTIONS

Lines and linear functions are essential tools for calculus. Here we review some key definitions and techniques that we'll use often.

Slope Slope measures a line's *steepness*, the rate at which a line rises or falls. Before reviewing the familiar definition, study Figure 1, in which several lines are labeled with their slope. ➡

For some reason, the letter m almost always stands for slope; this may have to do with the French verb monter *(to climb).*

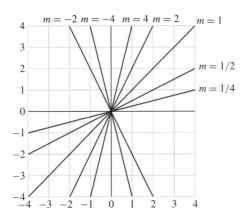

FIGURE 1
Lines with various slopes

The picture illustrates the general situation: Lines with *positive* slope rise (from left to right); lines with *negative* slope fall. The steeper the line, the larger the absolute value (i.e., the magnitude) of its slope.

DEFINITION The **slope** of a line is the ratio

$$\frac{y_2 - y_1}{x_2 - x_1} = \frac{\Delta y}{\Delta x} = \frac{\text{rise}}{\text{run}},$$

where (x_1, y_1) and (x_2, y_2) are any two points on the line.

Observe:

- **Same slope everywhere**   A line has the same slope everywhere: *any* two points can be used, in either order, to calculate the slope.
- **Parallel and perpendicular**   Lines with equal slope are *parallel*. The slopes m_1 and m_2 of *perpendicular* lines are negative reciprocals (i.e., $m_1 m_2 = -1$).
- **Horizontal and vertical**   Horizontal lines have slope 0; vertical lines have undefined slope. (The definition shows why.)
- **How steep? Scale effects**   It's easy to see that the line $y = x$ has slope 1. How steep the line *looks*, on the other hand, depends strongly on the size of units (i.e., the **scales**) on the x- and y-axes. The following graphs (Figure 2), all of which show the line $y = x$, show effects of scale.

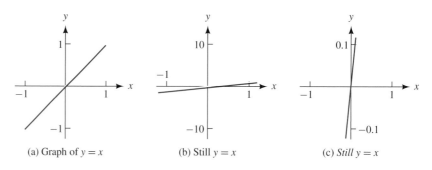

(a) Graph of $y = x$ (b) Still $y = x$ (c) *Still $y = x$*

FIGURE 2
Three views of the same line

If—but only if—identical scales are used on both axes, the line $y = x$ makes a 45° angle with the x-axis.

Convince yourself that these alternative versions really say the same thing.

- **Rise and run**   The formula for slope is sometimes written as $\Delta y / \Delta x$, or as *rise/run*. ◄ The Δ-notation is a convenient shorthand: Δ*anything* refers to a change in *anything*. It's usually calculated as the difference between a final value and an initial value. *Which* values these are must be made clear from context. For lines, things are simple: Δx is a *run*, or horizontal change; Δy is a *rise*, or vertical change. Either or both can be negative.
- **Slope as a rate**   Slope is defined as the *ratio* $\Delta y / \Delta x$. Slope is therefore a *rate*—the rate of change of y with respect to x. The straightness of a line means that this rate is constant.

Lines, equations, and functions

A line is completely determined by two bits of information: it's enough to know either (i) two points, or (ii) one point and the slope. In either case, several simple algebraic descriptions of a line are possible. Here are two:

> **DEFINITION   (Point–slope form)**   The line through (a, b) with slope m has equation $y = m(x - a) + b$.
>
> **(Slope–intercept form)**   The line with slope m and y-intercept b has equation $y = mx + b$.

EXAMPLE 1 Consider the lines

$$\ell_1 : \text{through } (0, 1) \text{ and } (2, 5); \qquad \ell_2 : \text{through } (-1, 3), \text{ with slope } -2.$$

Describe each in point–slope form and in slope–intercept form.

Solution Line ℓ_1 has slope $\Delta y / \Delta x = (5 - 1)/(2 - 0) = 2$. Now we know both the slope and (at least) one point on each line. Hence the point–slope equations are

$$\ell_1 : y = 2(x - 2) + 5; \qquad \ell_2 : y = -2(x + 1) + 3.$$

To find slope–intercept forms, we can just multiply out the right sides of the preceding equations to get

$$\ell_1 : y = 2x + 1; \qquad \ell_2 : y = -2x + 1. \qquad \blacksquare$$

Unique or not? There's only one way to write a line in slope–intercept form—in math-speak, the slope–intercept form is *unique*. The point–slope form, however, is not unique—*any* point on the line can appear in the point–slope equation. For example, $y = 2(x - 3) + 4$ and $y = 2(x - 5) + 8$ both describe the same line.

EXAMPLE 2 Write equations for the line ℓ through two points (a, b) and (c, d). Where does ℓ intersect each axis?

Solution If $a = c$, then ℓ is vertical; its equation is just $x = a$. ➡ If $a \neq c$, then ℓ has slope $\Delta y / \Delta x = (d - b)/(c - a)$ and the point–slope form applies:

This line has no point–slope equation.

$$y = \frac{d - b}{c - a}(x - a) + b.$$

Some algebra yields a (slightly clumsy) equation for ℓ in slope–intercept form:

$$y = \frac{d - b}{c - a}x + \left(b - a\frac{d - b}{c - a}\right).$$

The y-intercept can now be read off; it's the last summand. To find the x-intercept we set $y = 0$ and solve for x. The result:

$$x = a - b\frac{c - a}{d - b}. \qquad \blacksquare$$

EXAMPLE 3 How many lines do the equations

$$y + 2x = 6, \qquad y = -2(x + 2) + 6, \qquad y = -2(x - 5) - 8$$

represent? Why?

Solution Writing all three equations in slope–intercept form gives

$$y = -2x + 6, \qquad y = -2x + 2, \qquad y = -2x + 2.$$

Thus, the three equations represent two different lines. $\qquad \blacksquare$

EXAMPLE 4 An equation of the form $Ax + By = C$ (where A, B, and C are constants) describes a line. Which line? How do the values of A, B, and C affect the answer?

Solution The equation $Ax + By = C$ can be rewritten in various ways. For instance, if $B \neq 0$,

$$Ax + By = C \implies y = -\frac{A}{B}x + C;$$

thus, C is the y-intercept and $-A/B$ is the slope. If $B = 0$, the equation becomes $Ax = C$, which describes a vertical line. If $A = 0$, the equation becomes $By = C$, which describes a horizontal line. ∎

From the Latin, secare (to cut).

EXAMPLE 5 Find an equation in point–slope form for the line ℓ that meets the graph of $y = \sin x$ at $x = 1.3$ and at $x = 1.5$. (A line that "cuts" a graph at two prescribed points is called a **secant line**.) ◄ See Figure 3.

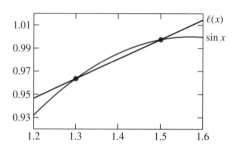

FIGURE 3
A secant line to the sine graph

Solution Any two points on ℓ can be used to find the slope. As the graph shows, ℓ passes through the points $\big(1.3, \sin(1.3)\big)$ and $\big(1.5, \sin(1.5)\big)$, and so the slope is

$$m = \frac{\Delta y}{\Delta x} = \frac{\sin 1.5 - \sin 1.3}{1.5 - 1.3} \approx \frac{0.9975 - 0.9636}{1.5 - 1.3} = 0.1695\,.$$

Hence, an equation for ℓ is

$$y = m(x - 1.3) + \sin(1.3) \approx 0.1695(x - 1.3) + 0.9636\,.$$ ∎

Linear functions

The line with equation $y = 5x + 2$ can be thought of in various ways: as a geometric figure, as an algebraic equation, or—more typically in calculus—as the *function* $f(x) = 5x + 2$. Functions whose graphs are lines are called, naturally enough, **linear functions**. ◄ They have an especially simple algebraic form:

Alas, the word "linear" has several meanings in mathematics.

> **DEFINITION** A linear function is one whose rule can be written in the form
> $$f(x) = Ax + B,$$
> where A and B are constants.

A crucial property of linear functions, for calculus purposes, is that they "grow" at *constant* rates. The next example explores what this means numerically.

EXAMPLE 6 The graph of the linear function $f(x) = 5x + 2$ has constant slope 5. Interpret this fact numerically.

Solution Here's a sampler of x- and y-values:

Sample values: $y = 5x + 2$										
x	-3.4	-3.3	-3.2	-3.1	-3.0	...	1.2	1.3	1.4	1.5	1.6
y	-15.0	-14.5	-14.0	-13.5	-13.0	...	8.0	8.5	9.0	9.5	10.0

Notice what the numbers say: Whenever x increases, y increases 5 times as much. In symbols: $\Delta y = 5\Delta x$. ■

EXAMPLE 7 The sine function has a curved graph, and so the function is *not* linear. How do numerical values reflect this?

Solution Here's a sampler of values of the sine function:

Sample values: $y = \sin x$										
x	-3.4	-3.3	-3.2	-3.1	$\ldots$	1.2	1.3	1.4	1.5	1.6
y	0.256	0.158	0.0584	-0.0416	$\ldots$	0.932	0.964	0.985	0.997	1.00

The nonlinearity of the sine function shows in the numbers: there's no regular "growth" pattern in the table. Increasing x by 0.1 produces varying increases (or even decreases) in y. ■

Lines and linear functions in calculus

Lines are important throughout calculus—perhaps surprisingly so, given that most functions of interest are not linear.

Local straightness A key idea of calculus is that a typical calculus function is "locally straight"—it "looks straight at small scale" near a point of its domain.

EXAMPLE 8 In what *graphical* sense is the sine function "locally straight" near $x = 1.4$? *Which* line does the sine graph resemble near $x = 1.4$? What does all this mean *numerically*?

Solution "Locally straight" means that the sine graph looks straight near the point $(1.4, \sin 1.4)$ if viewed in a small enough window—that is, after enough "zooming in." One view of the graph appears in Figure 3. Figure 4 shows two successively closer views: ➡

Zooming is easy with a graphing calculator. As always, a graph's appearance depends on the x- and y-scales.

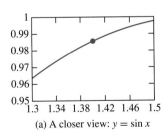
(a) A closer view: $y = \sin x$

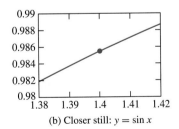
(b) Closer still: $y = \sin x$

FIGURE 4
Local "straightness"

The last view makes our point: the sine graph is all but indistinguishable from a straight line.

    Which straight line? Because our graph passes through $(1.4, \sin 1.4)$ with slope ≈ 0.17, ➡ the line we want has equation

To estimate the slope we used the values from the graph at $x = 1.38$ and $x = 1.42$.

$$y = \ell(x) \approx \sin 1.4 + 0.17(x - 1.4) \approx 0.17x + 0.7474.$$

What all this means is that $\sin x$, although *not* a linear function, behaves similarly to $\ell(x)$ for x near 1.4. Numerical data support this conclusion:

If $x \approx 1.4$, $\sin x \approx \ell(x)$								
x	1.380	1.385	1.390	1.395	1.400	1.405	1.410	1.415	1.420
$\sin x$	0.9819	0.9828	0.9837	0.9846	0.9854	0.9863	0.9871	0.9879	0.9887
$\ell(x)$	0.9820	0.9829	0.9837	0.9846	0.9854	0.9863	0.9871	0.9880	0.9888

EXERCISES

1. Use the definition of slope to explain why vertical lines have undefined slope.

2. Let ℓ be the line through the points $(1, -2)$ and $(1, 5)$.
  (a) Write an equation for ℓ.
  (b) Why can't ℓ be described by an equation in point–slope form?
  (c) Does ℓ have a y-intercept? If so, find it.
  (d) Does ℓ have an x-intercept? If so, find it.

3. Let ℓ be the line through the points $(-2, 3)$ and $(1, 3)$.
  (a) Write an equation for ℓ.
  (b) What is the slope of ℓ?
  (c) Does ℓ have a y-intercept? If so, find it.
  (d) Does ℓ have an x-intercept? If so, find it.

4. Let ℓ be the line through the points $(-2, 3)$ and $(1, 0)$.
  (a) What is the slope of ℓ?
  (b) Use Example 2 to find an equation for ℓ in slope–intercept form.
  (c) Where does ℓ intersect the y-axis?
  (d) Where does ℓ intersect the x-axis?

5. If A, B, and C are constants such that $|A| + |B| > 0$, the equation $Ax + By = C$ describes a line.
  (a) What can be said about the line if $A = 0$?
  (b) What can be said about the line if $B = 0$?
  (c) What can be said about the line if $A \neq 0$ and $B \neq 0$?

In Exercises 6–9, find the slope of the secant line that passes through the pair of points shown on the curve below and an equation of this line in point–slope form.

6. A, B   **7. A, C**

8. B, D   **9. C, D**

10. Find an equation in slope–intercept form for the secant line that meets the curve $y = x^2$ at $x = 2$ and at $x = 2.1$.

11. Find an equation in slope–intercept form for the secant line that meets the curve $y = \sqrt{x}$ at $x = 8.9$ and at $x = 9$.

12. Find an equation in slope–intercept form for the secant line that meets the curve $y = \sin x$ at $x = 1.3$ and at $x = 1.5$.

13. Find an equation for the secant line that meets the curve $y = \cos x$ at $x = 1.3$ and at $x = 1.5$.

14. Let $y = f(x) = 5x + 2$.
  (a) For each pair of adjacent entries in the table below, compute Δx, Δy, and $\Delta y / \Delta x$.

x	-10	-3	0	1	5	7
$f(x)$	-48	-13	2	7	27	37

  (b) Explain how your computations in part (a) show that f is a linear function.

15. Let $y = f(x) = \sin x$.
  (a) Fill in the second row of the table below.

x	-10	-3	0	1	5	7
$f(x)$						

  (b) Compute Δx, Δy, and $\Delta y / \Delta x$ for each pair of adjacent entries in the table in part (a).
  (c) Explain how your computations in part (b) show that f is *not* a linear function.
  (d) Fill in the second row of the table below.

x	1.35	1.37	1.40	1.41	1.43	1.47
$f(x)$						

  (e) Compute Δx, Δy, and $\Delta y / \Delta x$ for each pair of adjacent entries in the table in part (d).
  (f) Explain how your computations in part (c) show that f is a "locally straight" function near $x = 1.4$.

16. The cosine function is "locally straight" near $x = 1.4$.

    (a) Let ℓ be the line the cosine graph resembles near $x = 1.4$. Find an equation for ℓ.

    (b) Fill in the missing entries in the table below.

x	1.35	1.37	1.40	1.41	1.43	1.47
$\cos x$						
$\ell(x)$						

    (c) Explain how the table you completed in part (b) supports the assertion that the cosine function is locally straight near $x = 1.4$.

17. The graph of the cosine function is "locally straight" near $x = 1$. Which line does the cosine graph resemble near $x = 1$? (Express the equation of this line in point–slope form.)

18. The graph $y = \sqrt{x}$ is "locally straight" near $x = 4$. Which line does this graph resemble near $x = 4$?

19. The graph $y = x^3$ is "locally straight" near $x = 2$. Which line does this graph resemble near $x = 2$?

20. The graph $y = 1/x$ is "locally straight" near $x = 1$. Which line does this graph resemble near $x = 1$?

In Exercises 21–26, let L be the line that passes through the points $(1, 2)$ and $(-2, 0)$.

21. What is the slope of L?

22. Find an equation for L in slope–intercept form.

23. Using the point $(1, 2)$, find an equation for L in point–slope form.

24. Using the point $(-2, 0)$, find an equation for L in point–slope form.

25. Does L pass through the point $(\pi, 2\pi)$? Justify your answer.

26. Find an equation for the line that is perpendicular to L and passes through the point $(2, 1)$.

27. (a) Find an equation of the line through $(2, 1)$ that has slope $2/3$.

    (b) Find an equation of the line through $(2, 1)$ that is perpendicular to the line in part (a).

28. Find an equation for the line that is parallel to the x-axis and passes through the point $(-3, 2)$.

29. Find an equation for the line that is parallel to the y-axis and passes through the point $(2, 4)$.

30. Find an equation for the line that is parallel to the line $y = x$ and passes through the point $(-3, 1)$.

31. Find an equation for the line through $(-3, 1)$ that is perpendicular to the line $y = 5x + 7$.

32. Consider the line $3x + 4y = -12$.

    (a) What is the line's x-intercept?

    (b) What is the line's y-intercept?

    (c) Write an equation for the line in slope–intercept form.

    (d) Write the equation of a parallel line.

33. Consider the line $y = m(x - a) + b$.

    (a) What is the line's x-intercept?

    (b) What is the line's y-intercept?

    (c) Write an equation for the line in slope–intercept form.

In Exercises 34–38, find all values of k, if any, for which the line $2x + ky = -4k$ satisfies the condition.

34. The line has slope 3.

35. The line has slope $m \neq 0$.

36. The line passes through the point $(0, 4)$.

37. The line is horizontal.

38. The line is vertical.

POLYNOMIALS AND RATIONAL FUNCTIONS

Polynomials

Polynomials are among the simplest but most useful calculus functions. What follows is a brisk review of basics: ideas, terminology, techniques, and algebra.

> **DEFINITION** A **polynomial** in x is an expression of the form
> $$a_0 + a_1x + a_2x^2 + a_3x^3 + \cdots + a_nx^n,$$
> that is, a sum of *constant* multiples of *nonnegative integer* powers of x.

EXAMPLE 1 Which of the following expressions is a polynomial in x?
$$5x + 2, \qquad 3 - \frac{1}{x}, \qquad \sqrt{x}, \qquad -x + 5x^{17}, \qquad (x+3)(\pi x^{17} + 7), \qquad \frac{x+3}{\pi x^{17} + 7}.$$

Solution Each of the expressions
$$5x + 2, \qquad -x + 5x^{17}, \qquad \text{and} \qquad (x+3)(\pi x^{17} + 7)$$
is a polynomial in x. (*Linear* functions are among the simplest polynomials.) None of
$$3 - \frac{1}{x}, \qquad \sqrt{x}, \qquad \text{and} \qquad \frac{x+3}{\pi x^{17} + 7}$$
is a polynomial since all involve negative or fractional powers. ■

Here is a short glossary of polynomial language:

- **Degree** The **degree** of a polynomial is its largest power. (Constant polynomials have degree zero.) The polynomials $x^3 + 5x^2 + 1$, $-x + 5x^{17}$, and $(x+3)(\pi x^{17} + 7)$ have degree 3, 17, and 18, respectively.

  Polynomials of small degree have useful nicknames. Those of degree 1 through 5 are called, respectively, **linear**, **quadratic**, **cubic**, **quartic**, and **quintic**.

- **Factoring and expanding** To **factor** a polynomial is to write it as a product of lower-degree polynomials. To **expand** a polynomial is to multiply it out. Following are several polynomials in both factored and expanded forms:

Polynomials in two forms	
Expanded form	**Factored form**
$x^2 + 3x + 2$	$(x+1)(x+2)$
$x^4 - 1$	$(x+1)(x-1)(x^2+1)$
$x^4 + 6x^3 + 11x^2 + 6x$	$x(x+1)(x+2)(x+3)$
$x^2 + 2ax + a^2$	$(x+a)^2$
$x^3 + 3ax^2 + 3a^2x + a^3$	$(x+a)^3$
$x^3 - 3ax^2 + 3a^2x - a^3$	$(x-a)^3$
$x^3 - a^3$	$(x-a)(x^2+ax+a^2)$

- **Roots** A number r is a **root** of a polynomial ➜ p if $p(r) = 0$. Graphs show nicely the connections among real roots, intercepts, and factors. The following graph shows the polynomial function $y = x^5 - x = x(x+1)(x-1)(x^2+1)$.

The idea of root makes sense for any function f. The number r is a root of f if $f(r) = 0$.

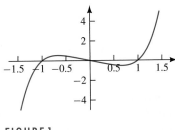

FIGURE 1
$y = x^5 - x$

Notice especially the *number* of roots. Each linear factor contributes one root in the "obvious" place. The remaining quadratic factor, $x^2 + 1$, is always positive, and so it contributes no roots. ➜

Polynomials may also have complex number roots, but that's another story.

- **Roots and factors** Roots and factors of polynomials have a close algebraic connection, which is sometimes known as the **factor theorem**:

  $(x - r)$ *is a* factor *of the polynomial* $p(x)$ *if and only if* r *is a* root.

This fact suggests a simple strategy for factoring polynomials: Somehow find (graphically, by guessing—whatever works) a root; then divide out the corresponding linear factor. It's easy to see, for instance, that $x = a$ is a root of the polynomial $p(x) = x^3 - a^3$. It follows that $(x - a)$ is a factor of $p(x)$.

- **How many roots?** A polynomial p of degree n can have at most n real roots. (Otherwise, p would have more than n linear factors, which is impossible.) This means that the graph of p can cross the x-axis no more than n times.

  As we've seen, some polynomials of degree n have fewer than n real roots; in fact, *any* number up to n is possible. Want a polynomial of degree 43 with 27 real roots? Here's one (of many):

  $$(x-1)(x-2)\cdots(x-27)(x^2+1)^8.$$

For a *quadratic* polynomial $ax^2 + bx + c$, the **quadratic formula**

$$r = \frac{-b \pm \sqrt{b^2 - 4ac}}{2a}$$

finds the roots—if any exist.

Completing the square It's often useful to rewrite a quadratic polynomial in the general form $a(x+b)^2 + c$; doing so is called **completing the square**. The following example illustrates the technique.

> **EXAMPLE 2** Let $p(x) = 2x^2 + 8x + 1$. Complete the square and use the result to find all roots of p.
>
> **Solution** We want to write $p(x)$ in the form $p(x) = 2(x+b)^2 + c$. Here goes:
>
> $$2x^2 + 8x + 1 = 2(x^2 + 4x) + 1 = 2(x^2 + 4x + 4) + 1 - 8 = 2(x+2)^2 - 7.$$
>
> The third expression above is key: Adding 4 to $x^2 + 4x$ "completed" the perfect square $(x+2)^2$. ◄ The roots of p can now be read off:
>
> $$p(x) = 0 \iff 2(x+2)^2 - 7 = 0 \iff (x+2)^2 = \frac{7}{2}$$
> $$\iff x + 2 = \pm\sqrt{7/2}$$
> $$\iff x = -2 \pm \sqrt{7/2}.$$
>
> (The quadratic formula gives the same roots—indeed, completing the square is the *idea* behind the quadratic formula.) ∎

We "paid" for doing so by subtracting 8 at the end.

Polynomial functions: domain and range A polynomial function is one whose rule is a polynomial expression. Because polynomials involve only multiplication and addition, every polynomial function has the same natural domain: all real numbers. By contrast, polynomials' ranges vary drastically. The range of $p(x) = 3$ is $\{3\}$, a set with just one member, while the range of $q(x) = x^2 + 3$ is $[3, \infty)$, an infinite interval. The range of $r(x) = x^3 - 7x^2$ is not obvious from the formula, but a graph (Figure 2) helps.

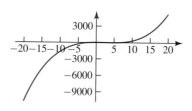

FIGURE 2
$y = x^3 - 7x^2$

The graph shows how r behaves in the long run. The function "blows up" (tends to ∞) for large positive x and "blows down" (tends to $-\infty$) for large negative x. Therefore, r "hits" all real values; its range is $(-\infty, \infty)$.

> **EXAMPLE 3** Find the roots of the polynomial $p(x) = x^4 + 6x^3 + 11x^2 + 6x$; interpret the results algebraically and graphically.
>
> **Solution** The given formula for $p(x)$ is not helpful. But the factored form reveals much more:
>
> $$p(x) = x^4 + 6x^3 + 11x^2 + 6x = x(x+1)(x+2)(x+3).$$
>
> Now it's clear from the formula that p has *four* roots—one where each of the four factors is zero. Figure 3 tells the same story:

FIGURE 3
$$y = x(x+1)(x+2)(x+3)$$ ∎

EXAMPLE 4   Consider the cubic polynomial $q(x) = x^3 - 2x^2 + x - 2$. Factor q as much as possible and find all of q's real roots.

Solution   Here (Figure 4) is a graph of q:

FIGURE 4
$$y = x^3 - 2x^2 + x - 2$$

The graph suggests that 2 is a root, and it's easy to check that, indeed, $q(2) = 0$. Therefore $(x-2)$ is a factor of q. Long dividing $(x-2)$ into $x^3 - 2x + x - 2$ shows that

$$q(x) = x^3 - 2x^2 + x - 2 = (x-2)(x^2+1).$$

No further factorization is possible, since additional factors would have to come from $x^2 + 1$. But $x^2 + 1$ has no real roots and hence no linear factors.

   Note that the factored form $q(x) = (x-2)(x^2+1)$ tells us something new: $q(x) = 0$ *only if* $x = 2$; that is, 2 is the *only* real root. ➔   ∎   *No (finite) graph could tell us this for sure.*

Rational functions

Adding or multiplying two polynomials creates a new polynomial. *Dividing* two polynomials doesn't (usually) give another polynomial; it gives a **rational function**.

> **DEFINITION**   A rational function is a function that can be written as the quotient, or "ratio," of two polynomials.

EXAMPLE 5   Explain why each of the following functions is rational:

$$f(x) = \frac{1}{x} \qquad\qquad g(x) = \frac{x^2}{x^2+3}$$

$$h(x) = \frac{x^7 + x^6 + x^5 - x^4}{x+1} \qquad k(x) = \frac{2}{x} + \frac{3}{x+1}$$

Solution The functions f, g, and h are already written as ratios of two polynomials. But the function k looks suspicious: It's certainly the *sum* of two rational functions, but is k itself rational? The answer is yes, because we can rewrite $k(x)$ in the form

$$k(x) = \frac{2}{x} + \frac{3}{x+1} = \frac{2(x+1)}{x(x+1)} + \frac{3x}{x(x+1)} = \frac{5x+2}{x(x+1)}.$$

■

This computation illustrates a more general fact:

> **FACT** Let r and s be rational functions. The sum, difference, product, and quotient of r and s are all rational functions.

Graphs of rational functions Rational functions can have an important feature that polynomials don't: **horizontal** and **vertical asymptotes**. Asymptotes are straight lines toward which a graph "tends" (in a sense we make more precise in Chapter 4).

EXAMPLE 6 Discuss the asymptotes of the rational function

$$r(x) = \frac{x^2}{x^2-1} = \frac{x^2}{(x-1)(x+1)}$$

and its graph (Figure 5).

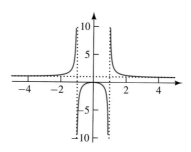

FIGURE 5
$$r(x) = \frac{x^2}{x^2-1}$$

Solution Technicalities aside, it's graphically evident that this function has two vertical asymptotes (the lines $x = -1$ and $x = 1$, which correspond to roots of the denominator) and one horizontal asymptote (the line $y = 1$).

Evident? Mathematicians use words like "evident," "clear," and "trivial" in peculiar ways. "Evident" does not mean "immediately obvious" or "This stuff is transparent to everyone with the slightest aptitude for mathematics; if it isn't clear to you, go away and never come back." "Evident" really means "not difficult to convince oneself of with sufficient time and effort."

It's natural to expect trouble where a denominator vanishes.

The *vertical* asymptotes correspond to real roots of the denominator. ← The *horizontal* asymptote (the line $y = 1$) reflects r's "long run" behavior: for large positive and large negative inputs, the numerator and denominator are large and nearly equal, and so $r(x) \approx 1$. The following table of numerical values gives the same message:

"Long-run" values of $r(x) = x^2/(x^2 - 1)$								
x	...	−1000	−100	−10	...	10	100	1000	...
$r(x)$	...	1.000001	1.001000	1.010101	...	1.010101	1.001000	1.000001	...

EXERCISES

1. Write the expression $(x+3)(\pi x^{17}+7)$ as a polynomial in standard form. [HINT: Multiply out the expression.]

2. Explain why the expression $2 + 5x^{1/3} + 4x^6$ is not a polynomial.

3. Is $4x^3 + 5x^2 - 6x + \sqrt{7}$ a polynomial? Justify your answer.

4. Is a linear function a polynomial? Justify your answer.

In Exercises 5–9, determine the degree of the polynomial.

5. $T(w) = 3 + 4w$

6. $p(x) = 2x^3 + 5x^2 - x$

7. $q(t) = 4t^5 - 6t^3$

8. $r(u) = 5u^{12} - 123u^8 + 47$

9. $s(z) = 17z^{123} - 26z^{19} + 71z^5$

10. Is $x - 3$ a factor of the polynomial $p(x) = 3x^3 - 11x^2 + 5x + 3$? Justify your answer.

11. Is $x + 2$ a factor of the polynomial $p(x) = 6x^4 - 13x^3 - 10x^2 + 19x + 10$? Justify your answer.

12. Let $p(x) = (x-1)(x-2)\cdots(x-27)(x^2+1)^8$.

  (a) Explain why p is a polynomial of degree 43.

  (b) Explain why p has exactly 27 real roots.

13. Let $p(x) = x(x-2)(x^2+4)(x-6)(x+8)(x^3-1)^9$.

  (a) What is the degree of p?

  (b) How many times does the graph of p cross the x-axis? Justify your answer.

  (c) Find all the real roots of p.

14. Find a polynomial of degree 5 with $x = -2$, $x = 1$, and $x = 3$ as its *only* real roots. Sketch its graph.

15. Write the equation of a polynomial that has roots at -16, 2, and 1/3.

16. Derive the quadratic formula by applying the technique of completing the square to the quadratic polynomial $ax^2 + bx + c$.

17. The graphs below show (i) a quadratic polynomial with two real roots, (ii) a quadratic polynomial with no real roots, (iii) a cubic polynomial with only one real root, and (iv) a cubic polynomial with three real roots.

Graph A

Graph B

Graph C

Graph D

  (a) Which graph is which? Match the graphs above to the polynomials (i)–(iv).

  (b) Find an equation for the quadratic polynomial with two real roots.

  (c) Find an equation for the cubic polynomial with three real roots.

  (d) The cubic polynomial with only one real root can be written in the form $p(x) = (x+r)(x^2+s)$. Find the values of r and s.

  (e) Find an equation for the quadratic polynomial with no real roots.

18. Let a be any constant. The table on page A-29 gives the formula $x^3 - a^3 = (x-a)(x^2+ax+a^2)$.

  (a) Verify the formula by multiplying out the right side.

  (b) If $a \neq 0$, then the second factor (i.e., $x^2 + ax + a^2$) cannot be factored any further. Show this by completing the square.

  (c) If $a \neq 0$, then the second factor (i.e., $x^2 + ax + a^2$) cannot be factored any further. Show this by using the quadratic formula.

  (d) Find a factored formula for $x^3 + b^3$. [HINT: Use the table on page A-29 and let $a = -b$.]

19. The table on page A-29 gives the formula $(x+a)^3 = x^3 + 3ax^2 + 3a^2x + a^3$.

(a) Verify the formula by multiplying out the left side.

(b) Let $p(x) = x^3 + 3x^2 + 3x + 1$. Show that $x = -1$ is a root of $p(x)$.

(c) Since $x = -1$ is a root of $p(x) = x^3 + 3x^2 + 3x + 1$, $(x + 1)$ must be a factor of $p(x)$. Divide $p(x)$ by $(x + 1)$ to get a quadratic polynomial.

(d) Write $p(x) = x^3 + 3x^2 + 3x + 1$ as a product of linear factors.

(e) Plot $p(x)$ and $q(x) = x^3$ on the same axes. How are the graphs related?

20. Match each of the functions (i)–(iii) to one of the graphs **A–C** shown below.

(i) $f(x) = (x - 1)(x + 2)$

(ii) $g(x) = \dfrac{x + 3}{(x - 1)^2}$

(iii) $h(x) = \dfrac{2x^2 + 3x - 1}{x^2 - 2x - 8}$

Graph A

Graph B

Graph C

In Exercises 21–26, determine all values of x for which the function is positive.

21. $f(x) = (x - 1)(x + 2)$

22. $k(x) = \dfrac{x + 1}{x - 2}$

23. $g(x) = \dfrac{x + 3}{(x - 1)^2}$

24. $j(x) = \dfrac{(x - 3)(x + 5)}{(x + 2)(x - 1)}$

25. $m(x) = \dfrac{x^2 - x - 4}{(x + 3)^2}$

26. $h(x) = \dfrac{2x^2 + 3x - 1}{x^2 - 2x - 8}$

In Exercises 27–31, factor the polynomial as much as possible and list all its roots.

27. $p(x) = x^3 - x^2 - 2x$

28. $q(x) = x^4 + x^2$

29. $r(x) = x^4 - x^2$

30. $s(x) = x^4 + 2x^2 + 1$

31. $t(x) = x^4 - 2x^2 + 1$

In Exercises 32–36, complete the square to find the roots of the polynomial or to show that it has none.

32. $x^2 + 2x$

33. $x^2 + 2x + 1$

34. $x^2 + 2x + 2$

35. $x^2 + x + 1$

36. $x^2 + bx + c$

37–41. Find the roots (if any) of the polynomials in Exercises 32–36 using the quadratic formula.

In Exercises 42–47, write the function as a ratio of two polynomials.

42. $\dfrac{1}{x} + \dfrac{1}{x + 1}$

43. $x + \dfrac{1}{x}$

44. $1 + \dfrac{x}{x^2 + 1}$

45. $3x \left(1 + \dfrac{5}{x} + \dfrac{2}{x^2} \right)$

46. $\dfrac{x + 1}{x - 2} - \dfrac{3 - x}{x + 4}$

47. $\dfrac{x - 3}{x + 5} + \dfrac{x + 6}{x - 1}$

48–53. Find the roots (if any) of each rational function in Exercises 42–47.

54. Is the function $\dfrac{1}{1 - 1/(1 + x)}$ a rational function? Justify your answer.

ALGEBRA OF EXPONENTIALS AND LOGARITHMS

Exponential functions

Exponential functions are among the most important in both the theory and the applications of calculus. To use such functions effectively requires a basic familiarity with exponential algebra.

An **exponential expression** is any symbolic expression that contains exponents. The following expressions are examples:

$$2^x, \quad 3^{x+h}, \quad b^3, \quad 2^{x^2}, \quad \frac{2^x}{3^x}, \quad \left(\frac{2}{3}\right)^x, \quad \left(1+\frac{1}{n}\right)^n.$$

In any expression of the form b^x, b is the **base**; x is the **exponent**.

The natural exponential function   The base-e exponential function, defined by $f(x) = e^x$, is called the **natural exponential function** or simply **the exponential function**. (The latter name can be a little confusing, since expressions with *other* bases, such as 2^x and 10^x, could also be called "exponential.") Several notations may be used for the natural exponential function, including

$$\exp(x), \quad \exp x, \quad \text{and} \quad e^x.$$

Exponential basics   The basic algebraic rules for exponential expressions are few and simple:

$$b^x b^y = b^{x+y} \tag{E.1}$$

$$\frac{b^x}{b^y} = b^{x-y} \tag{E.2}$$

$$(b^x)^y = b^{xy} \tag{E.3}$$

$$a^x b^x = (ab)^x \tag{E.4}$$

$$b^0 = 1 \tag{E.5}$$

$$b^{-x} = \frac{1}{b^x} \tag{E.6}$$

In each case, b can be any *positive* number; x and y can take any real values. ➡

We'll see below why b must be positive.

EXAMPLE 1   Explain Rule (E.1): $b^x b^y = b^{x+y}$, assuming that x and y are positive integers.

Solution   If x and y are positive integers, then

$$b^x = \overbrace{b \cdot b \cdot b \cdots b}^{x\text{-times}} \qquad \text{and} \qquad b^y = \overbrace{b \cdot b \cdot b \cdots b}^{y\text{-times}}.$$

Therefore,

$$b^x b^y = \overbrace{b \cdot b \cdot b \cdots b}^{x} \cdot \overbrace{b \cdot b \cdot b \cdots b}^{y} = \overbrace{b \cdot b \cdot b \cdots b}^{x+y} = b^{x+y}. \qquad \blacksquare$$

EXAMPLE 2   Make sense of the "zeroth power" rule: $b^0 = 1$.

Solution   Rule (E.5) follows directly from the addition rule: If b is any positive number, then

$$b \cdot b^0 = b^1 \cdot b^0 = b^{1+0} = b^1 = b.$$

Thus, $b \cdot b^0 = b$; dividing through by b gives $b^0 = 1$. $\qquad \blacksquare$

Rule (E.6) tells how to switch the *sign* of an exponent. It helps with calculations like this:

$$\left(\frac{1}{2}\right)^{-17} = \frac{1}{2^{-17}} = 2^{17}.$$

EXAMPLE 3   Derive Rule (E.6) from the other rules.

Solution   Using Rules (E.1) and (E.5), we get

$$b^{-x} \cdot b^x = b^{x-x} = b^0 = 1.$$

Dividing the first and last quantities by b^x gives Rule (E.6). $\qquad \blacksquare$

The next example involves some algebraic trickery, but it shows one way exponential algebra is really used in calculus.

EXAMPLE 4   Let k be any constant, and define the function f by $f(x) = 3^{kx}$. Show that

$$\frac{f(x+h) - f(x)}{h} = f(x) \cdot \frac{f(h) - f(0)}{h}.$$

Solution   Watch carefully—we'll use several of the rules (E.1) – (E.6).

$$\frac{f(x+h) - f(x)}{h} = \frac{3^{k(x+h)} - 3^{kx}}{h} = \frac{3^{kx+kh} - 3^{kx}}{h}$$

$$= \frac{3^{kx} \cdot 3^{kh} - 3^{kx}}{h} = 3^{kx} \cdot \frac{3^{kh} - 1}{h}$$

$$= 3^{kx} \cdot \frac{3^{kh} - 3^0}{h} = f(x) \cdot \frac{f(h) - f(0)}{h}. \qquad \blacksquare$$

Positive bases   Exponential expressions with negative bases can cause trouble. To see how, consider the expression $(-8)^x$ for several values of x:

$$(-8)^2 \qquad (-8)^{-2} \qquad (-8)^{1/2} \qquad (-8)^{1/3} \qquad (-8)^{3/2} \qquad (-8)^{4/3}$$

The first two make good sense: $(-8)^2 = 64$ and $(-8)^{-2} = 1/64$. The third, $\sqrt{-8}$, isn't a real number, while the fourth, $(-8)^{1/3}$, has the real value -2. The fifth expression also involves

$\sqrt{-8}$, and the sixth makes good sense:

$$(-8)^{4/3} = (-8) \cdot (-8)^{1/3} = (-8) \cdot (-2) = 16.$$

Faced with such difficulties, we retreat. We'll always require the base b in b^x to be positive.

Transcendental meditations The *exponential* function $f(x) = 2^x$ differs from the *power* function $g(x) = x^2$ far more than typography would suggest. One important difference is that the expression x^2 is an algebraic formula (i.e., an explicit recipe for computing output values). If, say, $x = 2.3$, it's easy, even without a calculator, to compute the output: $2.3^2 = 5.29$.

The expression 2^x, by contrast, is not algebraic. Finding the output value $2^{2.3}$ by hand is almost impossible. For this reason, exponential functions (and other "nonalgebraic" functions) are called **transcendental.** ➡

A curious word—it suggests that exponential functions somehow transcend the mundane realm of algebra.

Fractional and irrational exponents: abuse of powers? What does b^x mean if x isn't an integer? What if x is irrational?

> **EXAMPLE 5** Find (or estimate) decimal values for $2^{1/3}$, $1.6^{11/13}$, and $\pi^{-2/3}$.
>
> **Solution** $2^{1/3}$ is the *cube root* of 2. According to any scientific calculator, $\sqrt[3]{2} \approx 1.2599$. For any integer $n > 0$, $b^{1/n} = \sqrt[n]{b}$—the nth root is the $1/n$th power. This connection between roots and powers suggests how to estimate numbers like $1.6^{11/13}$ numerically:
>
> $$1.6^{11/13} = \left(1.6^{1/13}\right)^{11} \approx 1.0368^{11} \approx 1.4884.$$
>
> Similarly,
>
> $$\pi^{-2/3} = \frac{1}{\pi^{2/3}} = \frac{1}{\sqrt[3]{\pi^2}} \approx \frac{1}{\sqrt[3]{9.8696}} \approx \frac{1}{2.1450} \approx 0.4662.$$ ∎

So far so good: we can now handle *rational* exponents. For *irrational* exponents, as in the expression $\pi^{\sqrt{2}}$, the trick is to approximate everything in sight with decimal numbers:

$$\pi^{\sqrt{2}} \approx 3.1415^{1.4142} \approx 5.0472.$$

Logarithms

Logarithms, like exponentials, are key tools in calculus. To use them effectively requires a basic facility with the logarithmic algebra.

Relating logarithms and exponentials Logarithmic expressions like these—

$$\log_2 x, \qquad \log_{10} t, \qquad \log_e z, \qquad \ln w, \qquad \text{and} \qquad \log_b x$$

may be mystifying at first glance. What does "$\log_b$" *mean*? What is the role of b? What is "ln?" Some mystification is natural: Like "sin," "cos," and "exp," "$\log_b$" is the *name* of a function—not a recipe for computation. Demystifying logarithms means, above all, understanding how they're related to exponentials:

> **DEFINITION** For any suitable base b and positive number x, the expression $\log_b x$ is defined by the condition
>
> $$y = \log_b x \iff x = b^y.$$
>
> (NOTE: "Suitable" means $b > 0$ and $b \neq 1$.)

EXAMPLE 6   Use the definition to simplify the expressions

$$\log_2 8, \qquad \log_{10} 100, \qquad \log_e e^{25}, \qquad \text{and} \qquad \log_b \frac{1}{b^3}.$$

Solution   By definition, $y = \log_2 8 \iff 8 = 2^y$. It's clear from the second equation that y must be 3, and so $\log_2 8 = 3$. By similar reasoning,

$$y = \log_{10} 100 \iff 10^y = 100 \iff y = 2;$$
$$y = \log_e e^{25} \iff e^y = e^{25} \iff y = 25;$$
$$y = \log_b \frac{1}{b^3} \iff b^y = b^{-3} \iff y = -3. \qquad \blacksquare$$

Logarithmic basics   A few rules for logarithms go a long way. Here are four (as always, $b > 0$ and $b \neq 1$):

$$\log_b(xy) = \log_b x + \log_b y \qquad\qquad\qquad \text{(E.7)}$$
$$\log_b(x/y) = \log_b x - \log_b y \qquad\qquad\qquad \text{(E.8)}$$
$$\log_b x^r = r \log_b x \qquad\qquad\qquad\qquad\quad \text{(E.9)}$$
$$\log_b(1/x) = -\log_b x \qquad\qquad\qquad\qquad \text{(E.10)}$$

The rules simplify calculations that involve logarithms and exponentials—and even some that don't appear to.

EXAMPLE 7   Just before it died, your calculator said that $\log_{10} 2 \approx 0.301$ and $\log_{10} 3 \approx 0.477$. Now you *really* need to know

$$\log_{10} 6, \qquad \log_{10} 1/18, \qquad \log_{10} 2000, \qquad \text{and} \qquad \log_{10} 0.003.$$

What to do?

Check the results with your own (live) calculator.

Solution   With the rules, there's no problem: ←

$$\log_{10} 6 = \log(3 \cdot 2) = \log_{10} 3 + \log_{10} 2 \approx 0.301 + 0.477 = 0.778$$
$$\log_{10} 1/18 = -\log_{10}(2 \cdot 3^2) = -\log_{10} 2 - 2\log_{10} 3 \approx -1.255$$
$$\log_{10} 2000 = \log_{10} 1000 + \log_{10} 2 = 3 + \log_{10} 2 \approx 3.301$$
$$\log_{10} 0.003 = \log_{10} 0.001 + \log_{10} 3 = -3 + \log_{10} 3 \approx -2.523 \qquad \blacksquare$$

EXAMPLE 8   Solve (for x) each of the equations

$$200 \cdot 1.05^x = 375 \qquad \text{and} \qquad \ln x + \ln x^2 = 5.$$

Solution   For the first equation we'll take the natural logarithm of both sides and then use Rules (E.7) and (E.9):

$$200 \cdot 1.05^x = 375 \iff \ln 200 + \ln(1.05^x) = \ln 375$$
$$\iff x \ln 1.05 = \ln 375 - \ln 200$$
$$\iff x = \frac{\ln 375 - \ln 200}{\ln 1.05} \approx 12.8839.$$

To solve the second equation, we'll first use Rules (E.7) (in "reverse") and (E.9) and then apply an exponential to "undo" the logarithm. Notice first that

$$\ln x + \ln x^2 = \ln x^3 = 3 \ln x.$$

Therefore,

$$\ln x + \ln x^2 = 5 \iff 3 \ln x = 5 \iff \ln x = 5/3 \iff x = e^{5/3} \approx 5.2945. \qquad \blacksquare$$

Why the rules hold: trading logarithms and exponentials   The rules of logarithmic algebra are really just disguised versions of similar rules for exponentials. Rules of each type can be "translated" into the other form.

EXAMPLE 9   Use exponentials to explain Rule (E.7): $\log_b(xy) = \log_b x + \log_b y$.

Solution   The equation $\log_b(xy) = z$, for any real number z, means that $b^z = xy$. Thus Rule (E.7) really says

$$b^{\log_b x + \log_b y} = xy.$$

Now exponential algebra comes in:

$$b^{\log_b x + \log_b y} = b^{\log_b x} \cdot b^{\log_b y} = xy,$$

as claimed.   ∎

Which base?   The general ideas behind logarithms and exponentials are the same for *any* base b. In practice, though, $b = 10$, $b = e \approx 2.71828$, and $b = 2$ are the most common bases. The first two logarithms are known as the **common logarithm** and the **natural logarithm**, respectively. The natural logarithm function, usually written as $\ln x$, is, for several good reasons, the favorite in calculus; we'll use base e almost exclusively.

To exploit the advantages of base e—for both logarithmic and exponential functions— we'll need to move easily from *any* base b to the special base e. Two key identities tell how. For any base b and input x,

$$b^x = e^{x \cdot \ln b} \quad \text{and} \quad \log_b x = \frac{\ln x}{\ln b}.$$

Why do these rules hold? Both follow from rules mentioned earlier. For the first:

$$b^x = \left(e^{\ln b}\right)^x = e^{x \cdot \ln b}$$

for any x; taking $x = 1$ yields $b = e^{\ln b}$. The second identity is similar:

$$x = b^{\log_b x} \implies \ln x = \log_b x \, \ln b \implies \log_b x = \frac{\ln x}{\ln b}.$$

EXAMPLE 10   Rewrite 3^x and $\log_5 x$ in base e.

Solution   From the first rule above,

$$3^x = e^{x \ln(3)} \approx e^{1.0986 \, x}.$$

From the second rule above,

$$\log_5 x = \frac{\ln x}{\ln 5} \approx \frac{\ln x}{1.6094}.$$

∎

EXERCISES

In Exercises 1–6, evaluate 64^x exactly (i.e., as an integer or as a ratio of integers).

1. $x = 0$

2. $x = 1$

3. $x = 1/2$

4. $x = -1/2$

5. $x = 2/3$

6. $x = 5/6$

In Exercises 7–12, express the given number as 4^x for a suitable exponent x.

7. 16

8. 2

9. 8

10. $1/\sqrt{2}$

11. $4\sqrt{2}$

12. 16^{35}

In Exercises 13–20, rewrite the expression in the form a^x, where x is a number. (Assume a > 0.)

13. $(\sqrt{a})^2$

14. $1/a^2$

15. 1

16. a^3/a^4

17. $(a^3/a^5)^{10}$

18. $a/\sqrt[3]{a}$

19. $a^{-2}a$

20. $\sqrt[5]{a}/\sqrt{a}$

21. Here's further evidence for the fact that $b^0 = 1$:

$$b^0 \cdot b^0 = b^{0+0} = b^0.$$

Therefore, b^0 is its own square. Does it follow that b^0 must be 1? Justify your answer.

22. Let f be the function $f(x) = 5^{2x}$. Show that

$$\frac{f(x+h) - f(x)}{h} = f(x) \cdot \frac{f(h) - f(0)}{h} .$$

In Exercises 23–25, mimic the arguments given for the "addition" rule in Example 1 to show that the rule is "obvious" for positive integer powers.

23. Rule (E.2)

24. Rule (E.3)

25. Rule (E.4)

Let $g(x) = A e^{0.2x}$ where A is a real number. In Exercises 26–28, use the information given to find the value of A.

26. $g(0) = 5$

27. $g(1) = 5$

28. $g(-1) = 5$

In Exercises 29–32, translate the equation into the language of logarithms.

29. $8^{2/3} = 4$

30. $10^3 = 1000$

31. $10^{-4} = 0.0001$

32. $(1/2)^2 = 4$

In Exercises 33–38, translate the equation into the language of exponentials.

33. $\log_2 7 = x$

34. $\log_4 4 = 1$

35. $\log_5 1/25 = -2$

36. $\log_{10} 1000 = 3$

37. $\log_{64} 128 = 7/6$

38. $\log_{1/2} (1/4) = 2$

In Exercises 39–48, use properties of exponential and logarithmic functions to evaluate the expression exactly.

39. $2^{\log_2 16}$

40. $2^{\log_2 1/2}$

41. $10^{\log_{10} 7}$

42. $\log_6 \sqrt{6}$

43. $\log_5 5^3$

44. $\log_3 (1/27)$

45. $e^{2 \ln x}$

46. $\ln(e^2)$

47. $\ln(1/e)$

48. $\ln(\sqrt{e})$

Suppose that $\log_4 A = 2.1$. In Exercises 49–54, use properties of the exponential and logarithmic functions to evaluate the expression exactly.

49. $\log_4 A^2$

50. $\log_4(1/A)$

51. $\log_4 16A$

52. $\log_2 A$

53. $\log_{1/4} A^{-4}$

54. $\log_{16} A$

55. Interpret Rules (E.8) and (E.9) in exponential language.

Let $f(x) = 20e^{0.1x}$. In Exercises 56–59, find the value of x that solves the equation.

56. $f(x) = 20$

57. $f(x) = 40$

58. $f(x) = 80$

59. $f(x) = 10$

Let $h(x) = 20e^{kx}$ where k is a real number. In Exercises 60–62, use the information given to find the value of k.

60. $h(1) = 20$

61. $h(1) = 40$

62. $h(1) = 10$

Let $j(x) = Ae^{kx}$ where A and k are real numbers. In Exercises 63 and 64, use the information given to find the values of A and k.

63. $j(0) = 5$ and $j(3) = 10$

64. $j(1) = 5$ and $j(3) = 10$

In Exercises 65–67, find the value of x that solves the equation.

65. $\log_2(x+5) = 3$

66. $e^{x+3} = 7$

67. $5^{x-1} = e^{2x}$

68. **(a)** Explain why $\ln(x^2 - x - 2) = \ln(x-2) + \ln(x+1)$ if $x > 2$.

(b) Explain why $\ln(x^2 - x - 2) = \ln|x-2| + \ln|x+1|$ if $x < -1$.

(c) Is $\ln(x^2 - x - 2) = \ln|x-2| + \ln|x+1|$ if $-1 < x < 2$? Justify your answer.

69. Suppose that $a > 0, b > 0$ and $x > 0$ are real numbers. Show that $\log_b x = \dfrac{\log_a x}{\log_a b}$.

In Exercises 70–75, plot both graphs on the same axes. Explain what you see, referring to properties of exponential and logarithmic functions.

70. $y = 2^x$ and $y = 4^{x/2}$

71. $y = \ln(\exp(x^2))$ and $y = x^2$

72. $y = \ln((\exp x)^2)$ and $y = 2x$

73. $y = \exp(\ln x)$ and $y = x$

74. $y = \exp(2\ln x)$ and $y = x^2$

75. $y = \exp(\tfrac{1}{2}\ln x)$ and $y = \sqrt{x}$

TRIGONOMETRIC FUNCTIONS

The six trigonometric functions are defined in Chapter 1. Here we collect some more detailed information on trigonometric functions, their properties, and their graphs.

And a few others.

Trigonometric notation Trigonometric functions ← are usually typeset without the customary, $f(x)$-style parentheses. It's standard to write

$$\sin t, \quad \cos t, \quad \text{and} \quad \tan t, \quad \text{not} \quad \sin(t), \quad \cos(t), \quad \text{and} \quad \tan(t).$$

We'll usually follow the no-parentheses convention, although a bit reluctantly—parentheses remind us that *functions* are involved.

Another quirk of trigonometric notation involves *powers*. It's conventional, for instance, to write

$$\sin^2 t + \cos^2 t = 1, \quad \text{not} \quad \big(\sin(t)\big)^2 + \big(\cos(t)\big)^2 = 1,$$

Other powers are handled similarly: $\sin^n x$ means $(\sin x)^n$.

which means the same thing. ← Neither of these (true) equations should be confused with $\sin(t^2) + \cos(t^2) = 1$, which makes sense but happens to be false.

Sines, cosines, angles, and triangles

For calculus purposes, it's usually simplest to relate the trigonometric functions to the **unit circle** (the circle with equation $x^2 + y^2 = 1$): For any real number input t, the point at distance t units from $(1, 0)$, measured counterclockwise, has coordinates $(\cos t, \sin t)$. (If $t < 0$, move $|t|$ units *clockwise*.) ← For instance, $\cos 2 \approx -0.42$, because -0.42 is (approximately) the x-coordinate of the point 2 units of distance counterclockwise from $(1, 0)$ on the unit circle. Here's the picture—the dark arc has length 2. ←

For more on this interpretation, see the definitions on page 31.

Convince yourself that the estimate -0.42 is plausible.

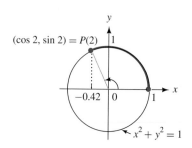

FIGURE 1
Why $\cos(2) \approx -0.42$

Sometimes we prefer to interpret inputs to the sine and cosine functions as *angles*, not arclengths. Any arc on the unit circle determines an obvious angle: the one between the two line segments joining the origin to the ends of the arc. In the picture above, $\cos 2$ is the cosine of the *angle* determined by an arc of length 2; this angle has radian measure 2.

Radians vs. degrees Two standard units (**radians** and **degrees**) are used to measure angles. Radian measure is much more convenient for calculus; we'll use it consistently. ➤ To convert between radians and degrees, use these formulas:

Lock your calculator in radian mode and throw away the key.

Radians $\rightleftarrows$ degrees
radian measure $= \dfrac{\pi}{180} \times$ degree measure
degree measure $= \dfrac{180}{\pi} \times$ radian measure

(Both formulas follow from the fact that 2π radians $= 360°$.) In particular, the angle in Figure 1 measures 2 radians, or $360/\pi \approx 114.6°$.

Right triangles "Trigonometry" comes from the Greek for *measuring triangles*. Our "circular" viewpoint on trigonometric functions is easily linked to right triangles; doing so sometimes aids intuition.

If a point $P(t)$ lies on the first quadrant part of the unit circle, t units from $(1, 0)$, then $P(t)$ naturally determines a right triangle with hypotenuse 1, and one angle of measure t radians, as shown in Figure 2.

It's easy to see that this triangle has the familiar ratios of sides that are sometimes used to define sines and cosines:

$$\sin t = \frac{\text{opposite}}{\text{hypotenuse}} = \frac{y}{1} = y; \qquad \cos t = \frac{\text{adjacent}}{\text{hypotenuse}} = \frac{x}{1} = x.$$

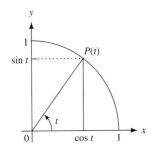

FIGURE 2
Triangles and trigonometric functions

Famous sines and cosines It's easy to see from the definitions of the sine and cosine functions that $\sin 0 = 0$ and $\cos(\pi/2) = 0$. Other important sines and cosines, such as $\sin(\pi/4) = \sqrt{2}/2$ and $\cos(\pi/3) = 1/2$, are also well known but a little less obvious. All the famous values can be computed as ratios of sides of 30–60–90 and 45–45–90 triangles. ➤ Know these important values:

We've already violated our prohibition against degree measure! Maybe we should have said $\pi/6$–$\pi/3$–$\pi/2$ and $\pi/4$–$\pi/4$–$\pi/2$ triangles.

Celebrated sines and cosines					
t	0	$\pi/6$	$\pi/4$	$\pi/3$	$\pi/2$
cos t	1	$\sqrt{3}/2$	$\sqrt{2}/2$	1/2	0
sin t	0	1/2	$\sqrt{2}/2$	$\sqrt{3}/2$	1

In daily practice one needs to know sines and cosines of *all* integer multiples of $\pi/4$ and $\pi/6$. This is easier than it seems. Combining the famous values tabulated above with the symmetry of the unit circle, we can find sines and cosines of many other angles.

EXAMPLE 1 Use symmetry to find $\sin(7\pi/6)$ and $\cos(7\pi/6)$.

Solution Figure 3 shows that $\sin\left(\dfrac{7\pi}{6}\right) = -\sin\left(\dfrac{\pi}{6}\right) = -\dfrac{1}{2}$ and $\cos\left(\dfrac{7\pi}{6}\right) = -\cos\left(\dfrac{\pi}{6}\right) = -\dfrac{\sqrt{3}}{2}$.

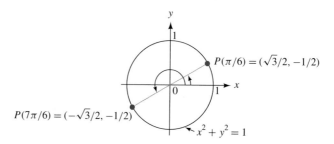

FIGURE 3
Exploiting symmetry

Not-famous values For most inputs, precise values of the trigonometric functions are far from obvious. For example, what are $\sin(1)$ and $\cos(13)$? We could estimate values graphically using a unit circle, but, as it turns out, there is no simple algebraic formula for computing *exact* values of trigonometric functions. Fortunately, calculus offers methods of *approximating* values of these functions.

Other trigonometric functions

Four more trigonometric functions are defined in terms of sines and cosines:

> **DEFINITION** For real numbers t,
>
> $$\tan t = \frac{\sin t}{\cos t} \qquad \cot t = \frac{\cos t}{\sin t}$$
>
> $$\sec t = \frac{1}{\cos t} \qquad \csc t = \frac{1}{\sin t}$$

Graphs of all these functions appear on page 32.

How many trigonometric functions? Cosine, sine, tangent, secant, cosecant, and cotangent make six. From another point of view, there are only two—sine and cosine—from which all the others are derived.

   If we were really determined, we could count at least *ten* trigonometric functions: the "usual" six and their (justifiably) obscure relatives *exsecant, versine, coversine,* and *haversine,* now seen chiefly in dusty old tomes. Taking the opposite tack, we might argue for only *one* trigonometric function, say cosine, from which sine, and hence all the others, spring.

Off on the tangent Among the "other" trigonometric functions, the tangent function is most important. Figure 4 gives a close look at its graph; notice the asymptotes, which are shown dotted.

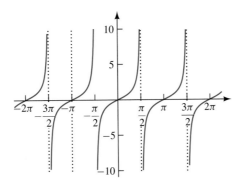

FIGURE 4
$y = \tan x$

Basic properties of the tangent function follow easily from its definition; most appear in the graph.

- **Domain and range** The tangent function accepts all real inputs t *except* those for which $\cos t = 0$ (i.e., $t = \pm\pi/2, \pm3\pi/2, \pm5\pi/2, \ldots$). Thus, the domain of the tangent function contains all real numbers *except* these obvious offenders (which generate the graph's asymptotes). The range is the full set of real numbers. ➦

  The graph shows this, too.

- **Periodicity—a small surprise** The tangent function (like the sine and cosine functions) repeats itself on intervals of length 2π. Here's why:

$$\tan(t + 2\pi) = \frac{\sin(t + 2\pi)}{\cos(t + 2\pi)} = \frac{\sin t}{\cos t} = \tan t.$$

This property can also be seen in the graph.

But look again. The tangent function's graph repeats its basic shape on intervals of length π—*twice as often* as the computation above suggests. Is something wrong? No. The tangent function repeats itself on intervals of length π because

$$\tan(t + \pi) = \frac{\sin(t + \pi)}{\cos(t + \pi)} = \frac{-\sin t}{-\cos t} = \tan t.$$

The second equality is the key. It holds because $\sin(t + \pi) = -\sin t$ and $\cos(t + \pi) = -\cos t$. ➦

These equalities follow from the relationship between the points $P(t)$ and $P(t + \pi)$ on the unit circle.

Trigonometric identities

Equations like

$$\sin^2 t + \cos^2 t = 1, \quad \sin(t + \pi/2) = \cos t, \quad \text{and} \quad \tan^2 t + 1 = \sec^2 t,$$

which relate various trigonometric functions to each other are known as **trigonometric identities**. Many such relations exist—not surprisingly because all six trigonometric functions come from the same unit circle idea.

Some trigonometric identities follow directly from the definitions; others are subtler. Memorizing every trigonometric identity is unnecessary, but a few ➦ are truly basic.

Like the three above.

Other—less obvious but still useful—trigonometric identities exist; one should know *that* they exist and where to find them. Following are several such examples:

FACT (Addition formulas)

$$\sin(s+t) = \sin s \cos t + \cos s \sin t$$
$$\cos(s+t) = \cos s \cos t - \sin s \sin t$$

(Double-angle formulas)

$$\sin(2t) = 2\sin t \cos t \qquad \cos(2t) = \cos^2 t - \sin^2 t$$
$$\sin^2 t = \tfrac{1}{2}\left(1 - \cos(2t)\right) \qquad \cos^2 t = \tfrac{1}{2}\left(1 + \cos(2t)\right)$$

The double-angle formulas are easily derived from the addition formulas.

E X A M P L E 2   Derive the formula for $\cos(2t)$.

Solution   Using the addition formula, we obtain

$$\cos(2t) = \cos(t+t) = \cos t \cos t - \sin t \sin t = \cos^2 t - \sin^2 t.$$ ∎

E X E R C I S E S

The angle drawn within the unit circle shown below measures 1.2 radians. The tick marks around the circumference of the circle indicate tenths of a radian.

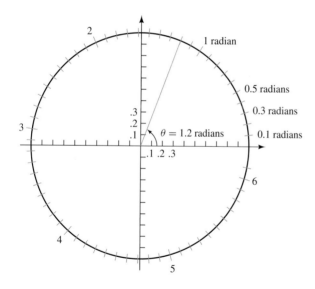

In Exercises 1–6, use the diagram above to estimate the value of the trignometric function.

1. $\cos(1.2)$

2. $\sin(0.5)$

3. $\tan(2.8)$

4. $\cos(0.2)$

5. $\sin(4.5)$

6. $\cos(13)$

7. Use the diagram above to estimate two values of x such that $\sin x = 1/2$. Check your answers with a calculator.

8. Use the diagram above to estimate two values of x such that $\tan x = 5$. Check your answers with a calculator.

In Exercises 9–12, let $P(t)$ be the point t units counterclockwise from $(1,0)$ on the unit circle.

9. Explain how $P(t)$ and $P(t+\pi)$ are related.

10. Explain why $\cos(t+\pi) = -\cos(t)$.

11. Explain why $\sin(t+\pi) = -\sin(t)$.

12. Explain why $\tan(t+\pi) = \tan(t)$.

Exercises 13–16 refer to the graphs of $y = \sin x$ and $y = \cos x$ shown below.

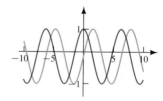

13. Which graph is which? Justify your answer.

14. It's a fact that $\cos x = \sin(x + \pi/2) \approx \sin(x + 1.57)$. How do the graphs reflect this fact?

15. For which values of x is $\tan x = 0$? How can you tell from the graphs above?

16. For which values of x is $\tan x = 1$? How can you tell from the graphs above?

In Exercises 17–22, suppose that a, b, and c are real numbers such that $\sin a = b$ and $\cos c = 0.3$. Evaluate the expression in terms of real numbers and the constant b.

17. $\sin(-a)$

18. $-\sin a$

19. $\cos(-c)$

20. $\sin c$

21. $\sin^2 a$

22. $\sin(2a)$

In Exercises 23–36, evaluate the expression exactly. (No decimal approximations allowed!)

23. $\sin(0)$

24. $\cos(0)$

25. $\tan(0)$

26. $\sin(3\pi/2)$

27. $\cos(3\pi/2)$

28. $\tan(\pi)$

29. $\cos(5\pi/6)$

30. $\sin(2\pi/3)$

31. $\tan(3\pi/4)$

32. $\cot(4\pi/3)$

33. $\sec(5\pi/3)$

34. $\csc(7\pi/4)$

35. $\sin(257\pi/3)$

36. $\tan(-2000\pi/3)$

In Exercises 37–40, use the addition formulas for sine and cosine to evaluate the expression exactly.

37. $\cos\left(\dfrac{5\pi}{12}\right) = \cos\left(\dfrac{\pi}{4} + \dfrac{\pi}{6}\right)$

38. $\sin\left(\dfrac{19\pi}{12}\right) = \sin\left(\dfrac{3\pi}{4} + \dfrac{5\pi}{6}\right)$

39. $\sin\left(\dfrac{\pi}{12}\right) = \sin\left(\dfrac{\pi}{4} - \dfrac{\pi}{6}\right)$

40. $\tan\left(\dfrac{7\pi}{12}\right) = \tan\left(\dfrac{5\pi}{4} - \dfrac{2\pi}{3}\right)$

In Exercises 41–46, determine whether the pair of expressions define the same function.

41. $\cos^2 x$ and $1 - \sin^2 x$

42. $\sin x$ and $\sqrt{1 - \cos^2 x}$

43. $\cos x$ and $\sin(x - \pi/2)$

44. $\sin x$ and $\cos(x + \pi/2)$

45. $\sec^2 x$ and $1 + \tan^2 x$

46. $\csc^2 x - 1$ and $\tan^2 x$

In Exercises 47 and 48, find a subtraction formula similar to the addition formulas given in the Fact on page A-46.

47. $\sin(s - t) = ???$

48. $\cos(s - t) = ???$

49. Derive the formula $\sin(2t) = 2\sin t \cos t$ using the trigonometric identities given in the Fact on page A-46.

50. Derive the formula $\cos^2 t = \dfrac{1}{2}(1 + \cos(2t))$.

Real-World Calculus: From Words to Mathematics

Translation

Calculus is more than a brilliant theoretical invention. It is also a practical tool—among the most powerful ever discovered—for posing and solving important real-world problems. Real-world problems seldom arrive as neat mathematical packages. More common are untidy bundles of questions, assumptions, information, and (sometimes) disinformation. Important parts may be missing; useless extras may be included.

The first (and sometimes hardest) step in tackling such problems is to translate them, as concisely as possible, into mathematical language. Because calculus operates mainly on functions, "translation" in calculus usually means interpreting a problem in *functional language.*

To understand real-world phenomena—the Consumer Price Index, gravitational forces, population growth, planetary motion, and others—we must be able to *predict* their behavior. Useful predictions, moreover, must be *quantitative*, not merely qualitative. Mathematics is the route to quantitative results.

Different areas of mathematics are best suited to describe and predict different sorts of phenomena. Describing phenomena of change is the special genius of calculus; calculus offers both language in which to describe changing quantities and rules with which to predict their behavior.

Story problems: you may feel a little discomfort ...

Mathematics has been compared (erroneously, of course) to dentistry. "Story problems," especially, sometimes elicit emotions normally associated with the approach of a high-speed drill. Such fear and loathing can be alleviated—and without pharmaceutical intervention. This is not to deny the difficulty. Translation of any sort is hard work.

Learn the words by heart Mastering basic mathematical vocabulary and "grammar" is the essential first step. Calculus has its own recurring key words and phrases—**proportional, parameter, domain, maximum, increasing**, and others. In this appendix we review some important mathematical terms and techniques and illustrate their use in calculus-style applications.

EXAMPLE 1 The force that Earth's gravity exerts on a rocket decreases as the rocket rises. This *qualitative* observation, although true, is useless in practice. It doesn't take a rocket scientist to see why. Without more information, we can't *compute* anything: how much fuel to load, how much thrust is needed, how long anything will take.

Newton's law of universal gravitation describes gravity's effect *quantitatively*. ➤ It says that for a 1000-kg rocket d kilometers from the center of the Earth, the force (in newtons) of Earth's gravity is given (approximately) by the function

$$F(d) = \frac{4.01 \times 10^{11}}{d^2}.$$

For more on Newton's law see page A-54.

The formula permits predictions. If, say, $d = 30{,}000$ km, ➤ then the force of gravity is only

A reasonable distance for a communications satellite.

$$F(30{,}000) = \frac{4.01 \times 10^{11}}{30{,}000^2} \approx 446 \text{ newtons.}$$ ■

Garden-variety optimization

Many real-life problems boil down to finding the largest or smallest value of some function. Finding the *right* function hidden in the verbiage may be the main challenge.

EXAMPLE 2 Gardener Alpha plans a rectangular lettuce patch; 100 feet of rabbit-proof fencing is available. What are the best dimensions for Alpha's lettuce patch? How much area can Alpha enclose?

Solution "Best" can mean different things; we'll take it to mean "largest in area." ➤ The problem, then, is to find the largest rectangle with perimeter 100 feet.

The answer is a square, 25 feet on a side. To see why, let x and y denote the lengths of the "vertical" and "horizontal" sides of the garden, as shown in Figure 1.

Could "best" mean anything else? Perhaps—for real lettuce patches, "best" might involve harvesting convenience, ease of watering, or other nongeometric factors.

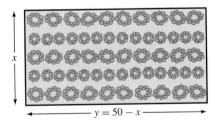

FIGURE 1
Alpha's garden

Because 100 feet of fence is available, we have $100 = 2x + 2y$, or $y = 50 - x$. Therefore, the area A is a function of x with formula

$$A = \text{length} \times \text{width} = xy = x(50 - x).$$

The rule $A(x) = x(50 - x)$ makes *algebraic sense* for *any* real number x. In the garden context, however, both x and $50 - x$ must be nonnegative because each represents a physical length. Thus, the "feasible" set of x-values is the interval $[0, 50]$. We've arrived at an optimization problem:

Find the maximum value, and where it occurs, of $A(x) = x(50 - x)$, *for x in* $[0, 50]$.

Since the area A is a *quadratic* function of x, its graph is (part of) a parabola, as shown in Figure 2.

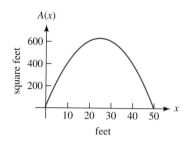

$A(x)$

square feet

600

400

200

10 20 30 40 50 x

feet

FIGURE 2

$A(x) = x(50 - x)$

The graph suggests that the maximum value of A occurs at $x = 25$, where the area is $A(25) = 625$ square feet. Graphical guesses are usually inexact, but this one is correct: The symmetry of parabolas guarantees that the vertex lies *exactly* midway between the two roots (at $x = 0$ and $x = 50$).

We've solved our problem: *Alpha's lettuce patch should be square, 25 feet on a side, with area 625 square feet.* ∎

Over 100 feet, say.

E X A M P L E 3   Beta, too, has 100 feet of fence, but a barn will form one side of a rectangular patch. (The barn is long enough ◀ so that its length isn't a constraint.) Which dimensions are best for Beta?

Solution   Figure 3 shows Beta's barnyard .

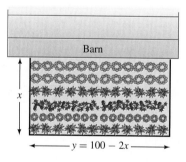

Barn

x

$y = 100 - 2x$

FIGURE 3

Beta's garden

Convince yourself that $y = 100 - 2x$.

Again, area is a function of the side we called x: ◀

$$A(x) = xy = x(100 - 2x) = 100x - 2x^2 = 2x(50 - x).$$

The feasible domain for x is (again) the interval $[0, 50]$; our problem is to *maximize the function A over this domain.*

Because the function A is (again) quadratic, ➡ its maximum value occurs at $x = 25$, midway between the two roots. The graph of A (Figure 4) agrees.

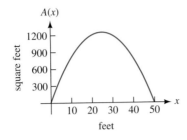

FIGURE 4

$$A(x) = 2x(50 - x)$$

Here is the result in barnyard language: *Beta's largest feasible garden has dimensions* $25' \times 50'$ *and area* $A(25) = 1250$ *square feet.* ∎

EXAMPLE 4   Gamma plans to fence exactly 1000 square feet of land—*any* rectangular shape will do. For convenient watering, one side lies along a (straight) river. How much fencing will Gamma need for the other three sides?

Notice the new twist: Alpha and Beta aimed to *maximize area, for a fixed perimeter.* Gamma wants to *minimize perimeter, for a fixed area.* Optimization problems often come in such pairs. ➡

Solution   A familiar picture (Figure 5) applies.

FIGURE 5

Gamma's garden

Let's find our function. Let x and y be the lengths shown, and let L denote the total length of the fence. By assumption, $xy = 1000$, and so our function is

$$L = 2x + y = 2x + \frac{1000}{x}.$$

What is L's "natural" domain? Technically, *any* positive number is a feasible input—a fence a mile long and 2.27 inches wide makes *mathematical* sense. Because no such ridiculously oblong design could possibly be most economical, we can safely ignore very large and very small positive inputs x. Given the general size of the numbers, the domain $5 \le x \le 50$ leaves plenty of room. Here, at last, is our problem:

Find the minimum value, and where it occurs, of the function $L(x) = 2x + 1000/x$ *on the interval* $[5, 50]$.

Notice that Beta's area function is simply twice Alpha's area function.

Paired optimization problems are known as "duals." This problem could be called a fencing dual.

Solving the problem without calculus is hard, and so we'll work, approximately, with the graph of L (Figure 6).

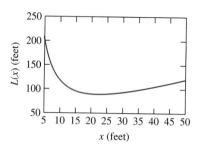

FIGURE 6

$L(x) = 2x + 1000/x$

With calculus techniques, we can find exact answers:
$x = \sqrt{500} \approx 22.3607$ *and*
$L(\sqrt{500}) \approx 89.4427.$

The graph shows that L attains its minimum value (about 90 feet) around $x = 22$. ◄ (We could zoom in on the graph to improve these estimates.) In agricultural terms: *Gamma needs 90 feet of fence; the garden should have approximate dimensions 22.5' × 45'.* ■

Parameters

We assumed earlier that Alpha and Beta each had 100 feet of fencing; our answers, naturally, reflected that assumption. But was the number 100 essential in either problem? Hardly. With 200 feet of fence, we'd *still* design a square garden for Alpha, and a rectangular one, with proportions 1:2, for Beta.

Such "accidental" aspects of a problem are conveniently handled using **parameters**—symbols that stand for *any* constant value. The next example illustrates one advantage of using parameters.

EXAMPLE 5 Delta and Epsilon, incompatible gardeners, agree to "divorce" their gardens, as shown in Figure 7.

FIGURE 7

Dividing the estate

They have L feet of fence. What shape is best?

Solution We'll solve the problem by treating the *perimeter L* as an unevaluated *parameter*. Let x and y be as shown. Then the area A satisfies the equation $A = xy$, while the garden's peculiar design dictates that the total length of fence needed is $L = 3x + 2y$, and so ◄

Solve this equation for y to get $y = (L - 3x)/2$.

$$A(x) = xy = \frac{x(L - 3x)}{2}.$$

In context, both x and $L - 3x$ must be nonnegative; thus, $0 \leq x \leq L/3$ must hold. Our problem, then, is to maximize A for x in the interval $[0, L/3]$.

The presence of the parameter L now complicates life slightly. We'll show two possible strategies.

- **Use algebra**   For *any* constant L the function

$$A(x) = \frac{x(L - 3x)}{2}$$

is *quadratic* in x; its graph is a parabola, opening downward. The parabola's vertex occurs midway between the two roots, one at $x = 0$ and the other at $x = L/3$. Thus, the largest value of A is $A(L/6) = L^2/24$.

- **Use graphics**   Another strategy is to plot $A(x)$ for *several* reasonable values of the parameter and look for a pattern; see Figure 8.

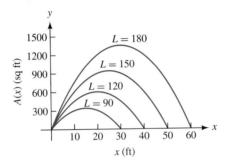

FIGURE 8
Graphs of A for various lengths L

The picture illustrates what we just saw algebraically: For each value of L, the maximum area occurs at $x = L/6$, the *midpoint* of the domain $[0, L/3]$.

We conclude that the most spacious double garden uses $L/6$ feet of fence for each of the three "vertical" runs. The remaining $L/2$ feet is divided equally for the two "horizontal" runs. Figure 9 shows the result, drawn proportionately to scale:

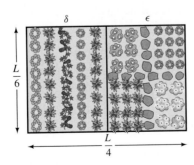

FIGURE 9
Biggest gardens with perimeter L

And so we take leave of our fences.

Proportionality

Proportionality and inverse proportionality are relationships between varying quantities:

> **DEFINITION** Let A and B be quantities that vary together. A is **proportional** to B if, for some nonzero constant k, the equation
>
> $$A = k\,B$$
>
> holds for *all* values of A and B. A and B are **inversely proportional** if
>
> $$A = \frac{k}{B}.$$

EXAMPLE 6 The formula $C = \pi\,d$ says that the circumference of a circle is proportional to the diameter, with **proportionality constant** π. The formula $A = \pi\,r^2$ says that the area of a circle is proportional to the *square* of the radius, but not to the radius itself. ◄   ■

Both formulas are familiar, but not trivial. That the same constant, π, appears in both formulas is a remarkable fact.

Gravity—applying proportionality It's well known that objects weigh less on the moon than on Earth. How much less? Why?

Newton's law of universal gravitation describes the relationships among quantities involved in gravitation:

> *The attractive force of gravity exerted on one object by another is proportional to the mass of each and inversely proportional to the square of the distance between them.* ◄

In each case, all other quantities are held constant.

In algebraic form, Newton's law says that

$$F = k\,\frac{M_1 M_2}{d^2},$$

where F represents gravitational *force*, M_1 and M_2 are the objects' masses, d is the distance between the objects' centers of gravity, ◄ and k is a constant of proportionality. The numerical value of k depends on the units chosen. In the metric system (using kilograms for mass, meters for distance, and newtons for force), $k \approx 6.7 \times 10^{-11}$.

For a sphere the center of gravity is the ordinary (geometric) center.

EXAMPLE 7 How much less does an object weigh on the moon than on Earth? What would the same object weigh on Jupiter?

Solution An object's weight is defined as the force gravity exerts on it. According to Newton's law, the "Earth-weight" F_e of an object with mass M, at the surface of the Earth, is

$$F_e = k\,\frac{M M_e}{R_e{}^2},$$

where M_e is Earth's *mass*, and R_e is Earth's *radius*. Similarly, the same object's "moon-weight" and "Jupiter-weight," are

$$F_m = k\,\frac{M M_m}{R_m{}^2} \qquad \text{and} \qquad F_j = k\,\frac{M M_j}{R_j{}^2}$$

respectively, where M_m and M_j are the masses and R_m and R_j are the radii of the moon and Jupiter, respectively.

Our problem is about the ratios F_m/F_e and F_j/F_e. By easy algebra,

$$\frac{F_m}{F_e} = \frac{M_m R_e^2}{M_e R_m^2} \quad \text{and} \quad \frac{F_j}{F_e} = \frac{M_j R_e^2}{M_e R_j^2}.$$

Remarkably enough, every constant above is known; physics and astronomy textbooks have tables like this one:

Celestial constants		
Object	**Mass (kg)**	**Radius (km)**
Moon	7.35×10^{22}	1740
Earth	5.98×10^{24}	6378
Jupiter	1.90×10^{27}	71,398

Now only simple arithmetic remains:

$$\frac{F_m}{F_e} = 0.165; \qquad \frac{F_j}{F_e} = 2.535.$$

In human terms, an astronaut weighing 75 kg (about 165 pounds) on Earth weighs only $0.165 \cdot 75 \approx 12.38$ kg (about 27 pounds) on the moon. On Jupiter, the same astronaut weighs a staggering 190.13 kg (over 418 pounds). ∎

Mass or weight? Physicists distinguish between an object's *mass* and its *weight*. An object's weight can vary (as our example shows), but its mass is the same everywhere. In the metric system, the standard unit of force (and therefore of weight) is the **newton**. At the surface of the Earth, an object with mass 1 kilogram has weight 9.8 newtons. (Actually, because the Earth is not perfectly spherical, an object's weight varies slightly as it moves about the Earth's surface.)

Functional language: uses and abuses

Everyday speech is a rich mixture of formal and informal language, names and nicknames, careful descriptions, and vague allusions. The common things of daily life—friends, places, e-mail addresses—are likeliest to attract nicknames, verbal shortcuts, and aliases.

In calculus, functions are the commonest objects of all. Mathematical language offers various ways of talking about functions, some clearer and more precise than others. Some linguistic tips follow.

Function vs. value It's sometimes important to distinguish between the name of a function, say f, and the value of a function, say $f(x)$. The statement

Consider the function $f(x) = x^2$

may be clear in context, but it blurs the distinction between f—a function—and $f(x)$—a value of f. It would be technically clearer (though less euphonious) to say ➤

We won't always be this fastidious.

Consider the function f defined by $f(x) = x^2$.

Functions vs. expressions The statement

The range of $x^2 - 6x$ is $[-9, \infty)$

is intelligible, but the *expression* $x^2 - 6x$ is used—not quite correctly—to describe a *function*. A scrupulously correct (if wordy) version of the statement preserves this distinction:

Let f be the function defined by $f(x) = x^2 - 6x$. The range of f is $[-9, \infty)$.

Here are two ways in which functions differ from symbolic expressions:

1. Not all functions are defined by symbolic expressions. Graphs, tables, and words are other possibilities.

2. Several different symbolic expressions may define the *same* function. For instance, the four expressions

$$x^2 - 6x, \quad t^2 - 6t, \quad \frac{x^2 - 6x}{\sin^2 x + \cos^2 x}, \quad \text{and} \quad \frac{x^4 - 6x^3 + x^2 - 6x}{x^2 + 1}.$$

look quite different, but all could define exactly the same function. In particular, functions don't care about variable names, while expressions do.

Computers know the difference.   Computer programs insist on the distinction between functions and expressions. In *Maple*, for example, the command

```
f := x^2 - 6*x ;
```

defines f only as an expression. To define f as a *function*, we could type

```
f := x -> x^2 - 6*x;
```

The latter form isn't pretty, but it's explicit: f is defined as an *operator* that assigns to any input x the output $x^2 - 6x$.

EXERCISES

1. Zeta plans to fence off a rectangular field along the bank of a river; no fence is needed along the river. Fencing costs $2 per foot for the ends and $3 per foot for the side parallel to the river. Zeta's budget is $900.

   (a) Let x be the length of the side of the field that lies along the river. Explain why the formula $A(x) = x(225 - 0.75x)$ describes the area of Zeta's field.

   (b) What is the domain of A? Why?

   (c) What are the dimensions of Zeta's *largest* field?

   (d) If given twice as much money, can Zeta enclose twice as much area? Why or why not?

2. Water is flowing into a cubical tank. Each side of the tank is 10 feet.

   (a) Write a formula for V, the volume of water in the tank, as a function of d, the depth of water in the tank.

   (b) What is the domain of V? What is the range of V?

   (c) Write a formula for d as a function of V.

3. Guido's pizza is delivered in boxes formed from 50 cm by 100 cm rectangular pieces of cardboard. The boxes are made by cutting out six squares of equal size, three from each of the 100-cm edges (one square at each corner, and one in the middle of the edge) and then folding in the obvious way. Find the volume of the box as a function of the length of the side of the square cutouts.

4. Coffee mugs can be manufactured for 60 cents each. At a price of 1 dollar each, 1000 mugs can be sold. For each penny by which the price is lowered, 50 more mugs can be sold. Let N be the number of coffee mugs manufactured (and sold!), and let x be the price reduction (in pennies).

   (a) Explain why $N(x) = 1000 + 50x$.

   (b) Explain why the profit on each mug sold is $(1 - 0.01x) - 0.60$ dollars.

   (c) Find a function that relates total profit and x.

   (d) What's the *best* price?
   [HINT: Graph the function from part (c).]

5. Suppose that A and B are *directly* proportional, but A and C are *inversely* proportional. Suppose, further, that if $A = 1$, then $B = 2$ and $C = 3$.

   (a) What are the values of B and C if $A = 10$?

   (b) Are B and C directly proportional? Inversely proportional? Explain.

   (c) Suppose that $B = 10$. Find values for A and C.

6. Is the circumference of a circle proportional to its radius? Justify your answer.

7. Is the area of a circle proportional to the square of its diameter? Justify your answer.

8. Is the volume of a sphere proportional to its radius? Justify your answer.

9. The weight of an object is inversely proportional to the square of its distance from the center of Earth. A satellite weighs 200 pounds when 10,000 miles from the center of Earth.

   (a) Express the weight of the satellite as a function of d, its distance from the center of Earth.

   (b) At what distance from the center of Earth does the satellite weigh 100 pounds?

10. An open box with a capacity of 36,000 cubic inches is needed. The box must be twice as long as it is wide. The material out of which the box is to be constructed costs $0.10 per square foot. Find the cost of the material for the box as a function of the width of the box.

11. It's 9:45 P.M. Your snowmobile is out of gas, and you are 3 miles due south of a major highway in a field. The nearest service station on the highway is 6 miles east of your position. You can walk 4 miles per hour on roads but only 3 miles per hour through snowy fields.

   Express the time to reach the service station as a function of the distance r you walk along the road.
   [HINT: You could walk straight through the fields, or partway through the fields and then on the road.]

12. A spherical iron ball 10 cm in diameter is coated with a layer of ice of uniform thickness.

   (a) Find an expression for the volume of the ice as a function of its thickness.

   (b) Find an expression for the surface area of the ice as a function of its thickness.

13. Digging in your backyard, you accidentally break a town water line. The water forms a circular pond of depth $\frac{1}{2}$ cm

in your backyard. Find an expression for the surface area of the pond as a function of the volume of water in the pond.

14. The sum of two positive numbers is 20. Find a formula for the product of the numbers as a function of one of the numbers.

15. The sum of two positive numbers is 45. Find a formula for the sum of the squares of the numbers as a function of one of the numbers.

16. The area of a sheet of paper for a poster is to be $18 \, \text{ft}^2$. The margins at the top and bottom are to be 9 in. wide; the margins at the sides are to be 6 in. wide. Find a formula for the area available for printing as a function of the width of the sheet of paper.

17. A day care center wants to fence in a rectangular play zone within a grassy plot that is in the shape of a right triangle with sides 4 m and 12 m. If two sides of the rectangle must parallel the sides of the triangle, find a formula for the area of the play zone as a function of one of its sides.

18. A long rectangular sheet of metal is to be made into a rain gutter with a rectangular cross section by turning up two sides at right angles. If the rectangular cross section of the rain gutter is to be $50 \, \text{in}^2$, find a formula for the width of the metal sheet as a function of the height of the two sides of the rain gutter.

19. The intensity of noise at a point away from its source is proportional to the noisiness of the source and inversely proportional to the square of the distance from the source. Suppose that two noisy machines, one four times as noisy as the other, are located 100 m apart. Find an expression for the intensity of the noise along the line between the machines as a function of the distance from the noisier machine.

20. Suppose that a limousine gets $(180 - 2v)/7$ miles per gallon when it is driven at a speed of v miles per hour. If the driver is paid $15 per hour and gas costs $1.50 per gallon, find a formula for the cost per mile driven as a function of speed.

SELECTED PROOFS

This appendix contains careful proofs of several results, more or less in order of subtlety. The proofs are intended to be read "as needed," although some readers may enjoy reading proofs for their own sake as an introduction to the formal ideas and methods of analytic mathematics.

A challenging limit

Many limits that arise in calculus courses can be evaluated either by "inspection" (i.e., at a glance) or with elementary algebra. All of the following limits are of these types:

$$\lim_{x \to \infty} \frac{1}{x} = 0; \qquad \lim_{x \to 3}(x+2) = 5; \qquad \lim_{x \to 2} \frac{x^2 - 4}{x - 2} = 4.$$

Only the last one requires any argument, and simple algebra is all that's needed:

$$\lim_{x \to 2} \frac{x^2 - 4}{x - 2} = \lim_{x \to 2} \frac{(x-2)(x+2)}{x - 2} = \lim_{x \to 2}(x+2) = 4.$$

One of the two or three most important in calculus.

The important limit ◄

$$\lim_{t \to 0} \frac{\sin t}{t} = 1$$

is different. Because $\sin t$ is *not* an algebraic expression, the usual proof tricks—factoring, expansion, and so on—are useless. A rigorous proof must take another tack.

Before beginning a rigorous proof, we remark that overwhelming circumstantial evidence—in graphical and numerical forms—is available. But pictures and numbers aren't proofs. On the contrary, what a computer or calculator "understands" about the sine function probably depends implicitly on some knowledge of the very limit in question.

Proof Because $\sin t$ and t are both *odd* functions of t, their ratio is *even*. Thus, it's enough to consider only positive values of t, that is, to show that

$$\lim_{t \to 0^+} \frac{\sin t}{t} = 1.$$

Figure 1, which involves the unit circle, describes the situation. The diagram illustrates three key claims:

(i) $\sin t \le t$; (the segment CP is shorter than the arc EP);

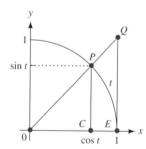

FIGURE 1

Why sin $t \approx t$

(ii) $t \leq \sin t + 1 - \cos t$; (the arc EP is shorter than EC + CP—the route traveling *west*, then *north*);

(iii) as $t \to 0^+$, $\dfrac{1 - \cos t}{t} \to 0$.

Claims (i) and (ii) are intuitively clear, but Claim (iii) requires some support. Here's an airtight proof:

$$\frac{1 - \cos t}{t} = \frac{1 - \cos t}{t} \cdot \frac{1 + \cos t}{1 + \cos t} = \frac{1 - \cos^2 t}{t(1 + \cos t)} = \frac{\sin^2 t}{t(1 + \cos t)}$$

$$= \frac{\sin t}{t} \cdot \frac{\sin t}{1 + \cos t} \leq \frac{\sin t}{1 + \cos t}.$$

(We used Claim (i) in the last step.) Now it follows that

$$0 \leq \frac{1 - \cos t}{t} \leq \frac{\sin t}{1 + \cos t}.$$

As $t \to 0^+$, the right side tends to 0. Since the left side *is* zero, the squeeze principle for limits implies that (iii) holds as claimed.

To finish our proof we'll use the squeeze principle again. Claims (i) and (ii) give

$$t - 1 + \cos t \leq \sin t \leq t.$$

Dividing through by t gives

$$\frac{t - 1 + \cos t}{t} = 1 - \frac{1 - \cos t}{t} \leq \frac{\sin t}{t} \leq 1,$$

and taking limits gives

$$1 - \lim_{t \to 0^+} \frac{1 - \cos t}{t} \leq \lim_{t \to 0^+} \frac{\sin t}{t} \leq 1.$$

From Claim (iii), the first limit is 1, and we're done.   □

Another proof   Another "squeeze" proof of the same limit can be based on *areas*. Figure 1 shows the following area relation:

$$\text{area(OCP)} \leq \text{area(OEP)} \leq \text{area(OEQ)}.$$

Here OCP and OEQ are triangles; OEP is a circular sector. Calculating these areas gives

$$\text{area(OCP)} = \frac{\text{base} \times \text{height}}{2} = \frac{\cos t \, \sin t}{2};$$

$$\text{area(OEP)} = \pi \times \text{fraction of circle} = \pi \times \frac{t}{2\pi} = \frac{t}{2};$$

$$\text{area(OEQ)} = \frac{\text{base} \times \text{height}}{2} = \frac{\tan t}{2}.$$

Thus,

$$\frac{\cos t \, \sin t}{2} \leq \frac{t}{2} \leq \frac{\tan t}{2}.$$

If $t > 0$, then $2/\sin t$ is positive, and so multiplying all three quantities by $2/\sin t$ gives

$$\cos t \leq \frac{t}{\sin t} \leq \frac{1}{\cos t}.$$

As $t \to 0^+$ the left- and right-hand quantities tend to 1; so, therefore, must the middle quantity.   □

Proving the product rule

> **FACT (The product rule)**   Suppose that functions u and v are differentiable at x. If $p(x) = u(x) \cdot v(x)$, then p is differentiable at x, and
>
> $$p'(x) = \big(u(x) \cdot v(x)\big)' = u'(x) \cdot v(x) + u(x) \cdot v'(x).$$

In Chapter 3 we argued the case for the product rule informally. A formal proof follows; notice that it also shows that if functions u and v are differentiable, so is their product uv.

Proof   Let u and v be differentiable functions. By definition,

$$(uv)'(x) = \lim_{h \to 0} \frac{u(x+h)v(x+h) - u(x)v(x)}{h}.$$

We need to show that this limit exists and that it equals $u'(x)v(x) + u(x)v'(x)$.

Check each step. ◄

An algebraic trick—subtracting and adding the same quantity in the numerator—does the job: ◄

$$
\begin{aligned}
(uv)' &= \lim_{h \to 0} \frac{u(x+h)v(x+h) - u(x)v(x)}{h} \\[4pt]
&= \lim_{h \to 0} \frac{u(x+h)v(x+h) - u(x)v(x+h) + u(x)v(x+h) - u(x)v(x)}{h} \\[4pt]
&= \lim_{h \to 0} \frac{u(x+h)v(x+h) - u(x)v(x+h)}{h} + \lim_{h \to 0} \frac{u(x)v(x+h) - u(x)v(x)}{h} \\[4pt]
&= \lim_{h \to 0} \frac{u(x+h) - u(x)}{h} \cdot \lim_{h \to 0} v(x+h) + u(x) \cdot \lim_{h \to 0} \frac{v(x+h) - v(x)}{h} \\[4pt]
&= u'(x)v(x) + u(x)v'(x).
\end{aligned}
$$

Notice especially the three limits in the last step. The first and third limits exist by definition of $u'(x)$ and $v'(x)$, which we assumed to exist. The remaining limit claim, $\lim_{h \to 0} v(x+h) = v(x)$, holds because v is *continuous* at x. (A differentiable function is automatically continuous—see Section 4.7 for details.)

The last equation is what we wanted to show. □

An ϵ–δ Limit Proof

Recall the ϵ–δ definition of limit:

> **DEFINITION**   Suppose that for every positive number ϵ, no matter how small, there is a positive number δ so that
>
> $$|f(x) - L| < \epsilon \qquad \text{whenever} \qquad 0 < |x - a| < \delta.$$
>
> Then
>
> $$\lim_{x \to a} f(x) = L.$$

Other limit properties, in the same spirit, appear in Theorem 5, page 107.

Recall, too, this plausible-seeming property: ◄

FACT   Suppose that

$$\lim_{x \to a} f(x) = L \qquad \text{and} \qquad \lim_{x \to a} g(x) = M,$$

where L and M are finite numbers. Then,

$$\lim_{x \to a} [f(x) + g(x)] = L + M.$$

A rigorous proof must use the rigorous definition. Here's how:

Proof   We need to show that for any number $\epsilon > 0$ there's a corresponding number $\delta > 0$ such that

$$0 < |x - a| < \delta \implies \left| (f(x) + g(x)) - (f(a) + g(a)) \right| < \epsilon.$$

Let $\epsilon > 0$ be given. To find the desired δ, we'll first set $\epsilon_1 = \epsilon_2 = \epsilon/2$. Since ϵ_1 and ϵ_2 are positive, there exist, by our assumption, other positive numbers δ_1 and δ_2 such that

$$0 < |x - a| < \delta_1 \implies \left| f(x) - f(a) \right| < \epsilon/2;$$
$$0 < |x - a| < \delta_2 \implies \left| g(x) - g(a) \right| < \epsilon/2.$$

If we now set δ to be the smaller of δ_1 and δ_2, then we have what we want:

$$0 < |x - a| < \delta \implies 0 < |x - a| < \delta_1 \qquad \text{and} \qquad 0 < |x - a| < \delta_2,$$

and so

$$\left| (f(x) + g(x)) - (f(a) + g(a)) \right| \leq \left| f(x) - f(a) \right| + \left| g(x) - g(a) \right|$$
$$< \epsilon/2 + \epsilon/2$$
$$= \epsilon. \qquad \square$$

A Graphical
Glossary of Functions

Graphical reasoning—representing functions and their derivatives graphically—is an invaluable skill in calculus. This appendix offers a brief "atlas" of representatives of the most important classes of calculus functions. Each function is shown together with its derivative.

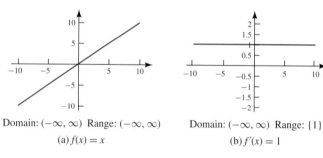

Domain: $(-\infty, \infty)$ Range: $(-\infty, \infty)$

(a) $f(x) = x$

Domain: $(-\infty, \infty)$ Range: $\{1\}$

(b) $f'(x) = 1$

FIGURE 1
A linear function and its derivative

Notes The derivative of a linear function is a constant function.

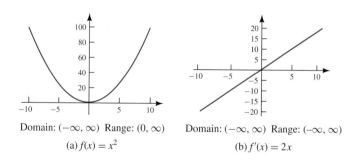

Domain: $(-\infty, \infty)$ Range: $(0, \infty)$

(a) $f(x) = x^2$

Domain: $(-\infty, \infty)$ Range: $(-\infty, \infty)$

(b) $f'(x) = 2x$

FIGURE 2
A quadratic function and its derivative

Notes The derivative of a quadratic function is a linear function. The quadratic function's vertex corresponds to a root of the derivative.

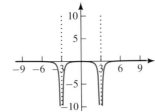

Domain: $\{x \mid x \neq \pm 3\}$ Range: $(-\infty, \infty)$ Domain: $\{x \mid x \neq \pm 3\}$ Range: $(-\infty, 0)$

$$(a)\, f(x) = \frac{x}{x^2 - 9}$$ $$(b)\, f'(x) = -\frac{x^2 - 9}{(x^2 - 9)^2}$$

FIGURE 3

A rational function and its derivative

Notes   The derivative of a rational function is another rational function. Notice the behavior of asymptotes: If f has a *vertical* asymptote at $x = a$, then so does f'. If f has a *horizontal* asymptote at $y = b$, then f' has a horizontal asymptote at $y = 0$.

Domain: $(-\infty, \infty)$ Range: $[-1, 1]$ Domain: $(-\infty, \infty)$ Range: $[-1, 1]$

(a) $f(x) = \sin x$ (b) $f'(x) = \cos x$

FIGURE 4

The sine function and its derivative

Notes   The sine function is 2π-periodic; so, therefore, is its derivative. Both the sine function and its derivative oscillate between -1 and 1. At the origin, the sine graph has slope 1.

Domain: $(-\infty, \infty)$ Range: $[-1, 1]$ Domain: $(-\infty, \infty)$ Range: $[-1, 1]$

(a) $f(x) = \cos x$ (b) $f'(x) = -\sin x$

FIGURE 5

The cosine function and its derivative

Notes   The cosine function is 2π-periodic; so, therefore, is its derivative. Both the sine function and its derivative oscillate between -1 and 1. At the origin, the cosine graph is horizontal.

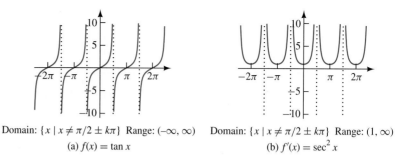

Domain: $\{x \mid x \neq \pi/2 \pm k\pi\}$ Range: $(-\infty, \infty)$ Domain: $\{x \mid x \neq \pi/2 \pm k\pi\}$ Range: $(1, \infty)$

(a) $f(x) = \tan x$ (b) $f'(x) = \sec^2 x$

FIGURE 6

The tangent function and its derivative

Notes The tangent function is π-periodic; so is its derivative. Unlike the sine and cosine functions, the tangent function and its derivative have vertical asymptotes. At the origin, the tangent graph has slope 1.

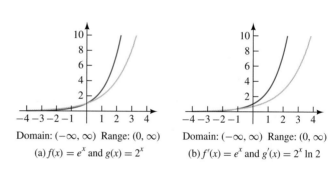

Domain: $(-\infty, \infty)$ Range: $(0, \infty)$ Domain: $(-\infty, \infty)$ Range: $(0, \infty)$

(a) $f(x) = e^x$ and $g(x) = 2^x$ (b) $f'(x) = e^x$ and $g'(x) = 2^x \ln 2$

FIGURE 7

Exponential functions and their derivatives

Notes The natural exponential function $y = e^x$ is its own derivative. Other exponential functions, such as $y = 2^x$, are *proportional* to their own derivatives. The $y = e^x$ graph has slope 1 at $x = 0$; the $y = 2^x$ graph has slope $\ln 2$ at $x = 0$. All exponential functions have horizontal asymptotes; so do their derivatives.

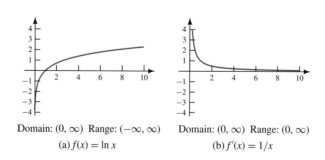

Domain: $(0, \infty)$ Range: $(-\infty, \infty)$ Domain: $(0, \infty)$ Range: $(0, \infty)$

(a) $f(x) = \ln x$ (b) $f'(x) = 1/x$

FIGURE 8

The natural logarithm function and its derivative

Notes The natural logarithm function $y = \ln x$ is the inverse function to $y = e^x$. It is defined only for positive inputs. The graph of $y = \ln x$ has slope 1 at $x = 1$.

ANSWERS TO SELECTED EXERCISES

Section 1.1

1. (a) 5700 feet   (b) 650 feet/minute

3. (a) yes; no

5. (a) ≈ 4.86 billion people   (b) ≈ 1.5 million people
     (c) ≈ 0.17 people

7. (a) $m(-4) = 3/2$ (b) $m(0) = -\sqrt{3}$
     (c) $m(2.3) = 1.3$ (d) $m(\pi) = 5 - \pi$

9. (a) $(x+1)^2 + y^2 = 4$

11. $f(x) = \begin{cases} 3 & \text{if } -5 \le x < -3 \\ -x - 2 & \text{if } -3 \le x \le 2 \\ 2x - 8 & \text{if } 2 < x \le 5 \end{cases}$

15. (a) $V(w) = w(24 - 2w)(32 - 2w)$.
     (b) $w \approx 4.5$

17. (a) $A(t) = 3t$ **19.** (a) $A(t) = t^2 + t$

21. (a) $[0, \infty)$ (b) yes

23. (a) 3 is in the domain of f.   (b) 7 is in the range of f.
     (c) yes   (d) yes
     (e) no

27. domain $= [0, \infty)$, range $= \{0, -2\} \cup [2, \infty)$

29. $(-\infty, -2] \cup [2, \infty)$

31. $(-2, 1)$

33. (a) $g(0) = 0, g(-1) = \sqrt{2}, g(1) = \sqrt{2}, g(2) = \sqrt{20}$,
     $g(500) = \sqrt{62,500,250,000}$
     (b) $g(x) = \sqrt{x^2 + x^4}$

35. (a) $j(2) = 3, \; j(1.1) = 2.1, \; j(1.01) = 2.01, \; j(0.99) = 1.99$,
     $j(0.9) = 1.9, \; j(0) = 1$
     (c) $j(x) = x + 1$ if $x \ne 1$

39. (a) $V(d) = 100d$ (b) $0 \le d \le 10$
     (c) $[0, 1000]$ (d) $d(V) = V/100$

41. (a) $(-\infty, \infty), [0, \infty)$
     (c) $(-\infty, 0) \cup (0, \infty), \{-1, 1\}$
     (d) $g(x) = \begin{cases} -1 & \text{if } x < 0 \\ 1 & \text{if } x > 0 \end{cases}$

Section 1.2

1. (a) $(-\infty, 0) \cup (0, \infty)$ (b) $(0, \infty)$
     (c) no   (d) yes
     (e) no

3. $x = -3$ **5.** $Y(\sqrt{2}) = 0$

7. neither   **9.** no

13. $t = 12$ **21.** $T(7) = 3$

25. (b) 7/5

27. $m_E < m_D < m_B < m_C < m_A$

29. $-1.8; -1.5$ **31.** no

33. yes   **41.** $(3, -5)$

43. (a) $g(x) = x^3 + 2$

45. (a) $g(x) = 2x^3$

47. odd   **49.** neither

51. $y = 2x - 1$ **53.** $L = 1, U = 7$

55. (a) $V(0) = 0$ (b) $V(10) = 2000\pi/3 \text{ ft}^3$
     (c) Graph C

59. $(4, 5)$

63. (a) yes   (b) yes
     (c) yes

65. $f(-1) = -3$ **69.** (b) $L = 5/2$

(e) yes, $y = 0$

(f) yes, $x = -3$

Section 1.3

5. yes

7. (a) $(-\infty, \infty)$ (b) 6

(c) 1   (d) yes

(e) yes   (f) no

9. $p(x) = 19x^2 + 18x + 4$, $q(x) = 5x^3 + 6x^2 + 5x + 6$

13. $(0, 1)$

15. (a) $(-\infty, \infty)$ (b) $(0, \infty)$

(c) $(-\infty, \infty)$ (d) no

(e) $(-\infty, \infty)$ (f) no

(g) no

17. (a) $(-\infty, \infty)$ (b) $[-1, 1]$

(c) yes   (d) yes, 4π

(e) nowhere   (f) no

(g) $(\pi, 2\pi)$ (h) yes, $x = \pi$

(i) yes, $x = \pi$

19. (a) $(-\infty, \infty)$ except $x = \pi/2 + k\pi$, where $k = 0, \pm 1, \pm 2, \ldots$

(b) $(-\infty, \infty)$

(d) yes; π

(e) $(0, \pi/2)$, $(\pi/2, 3\pi/2)$, $(3\pi/2, 2\pi)$

(f) no

(g) $(0, \pi/2)$, $(\pi, 3\pi/2)$

(h) yes, at $x = \pi/2, \pi$, and $3\pi/2$

(i) yes, at $x = \pi$

(j) $x = \pi/2$, $x = 3\pi/2$

21. (a) $(-\infty, \infty)$ (b) $(0, \infty)$

(c) nowhere   (d) no

(e) $(-\infty, \infty)$ (f) no

(g) no

23. (a) $(0, \infty)$ (b) $(-\infty, \infty)$

(c) nowhere   (d) no

(e) $(0, \infty)$ (f) no

(g) yes, at $x = 1$.

25. $(-\infty, \infty)$, $[-1, 1]$ **27.** $(-\infty, \infty)$, $(-\infty, -1)$

29. $(-\infty, \infty)$, $[e^{-1}, e]$ **31.** $(-1, \infty)$, $(-\infty, \infty)$

33. $(-\infty, \infty)$, $[3^{-1/3}, 1]$ **35.** 2π

37. 4π **39.** $2\pi^2$

41. (a) $(0, \infty)$ (b) $k = 1/\ln 10$

43. $e^B = A^2$

47. (b) $y = 2$ (c) $y = 7$

49. (b) $x \neq \pm 3$; $(-\infty, 0) \cup (0, 1/6) \cup (1/6, \infty)$

(c) $x \neq -3$; $(-\infty, 0) \cup (0, \infty)$

Section 1.4

7. kilometers per hour   **9.** 70

13. (a) $3\Delta x$ (b) $g'(x) = 3$

15. $f'(-2) \approx 10$

21. $h(t) = 5 + 30t - 16t^2$, $v(t) = 30 - 32t$

27. $f(1) \leq 6$, $f(-3) \geq -10$

29. (a) $g(x) \geq 3x + 1$ if $x \geq 0$, $g(x) \leq 3x + 1$ if $x \leq 0$

41. (b) $171 \leq t \leq 354$ **43.** yes

45. (a) $f'(11) = 0$ (b) $f'(x) = 0$

47. $y = 2x + 3$

49. (a) $g'(4) = -2$ (b) $y = -2x + 11$

53. (b) °C/minute   (c) yes

(d) no

55. $f(x) = x + 2$ **57.** $f(x) = -3x - 2$

59. $f(5) = 2$, $f'(5) = 1/5$ **61.** no

Section 1.5

1. $f'(1) = 2$ **3.** $y = 2x - 1$

9. (a) $f(0.8) = 0.64$, $f(0.9) = 0.81$, $f(1.1) = 1.21$,

$f(1.3) = 1.69$

(b) $f'(1) \approx 2.1$

11. $f'(-1) \approx -2$

15. (a) $f(1.38) \approx 0.98185$, $f(1.39) \approx 0.98370$,

$f(1.41) \approx 0.98710$, $f(1.43) \approx 0.99010$

(b) $f'(1.4) \approx 0.17$

17. (a) $f'(2) = 1$ (b) $f'(-3) = -1$

23. (a) $f'(3) = 6$ **25.** (a) $f'(0.5) \approx 1.65$

27. (a) $f'(-1) = 2.0$, $f'(0) = -2.0$, $f'(2) = 0.0$, $f'(3) = 2.0$

29. $f'(1/4) \approx 1.0$, $f'(1) \approx 0.5$, $f'(9/4) \approx 0.33$, $f'(4) \approx 0.25$,

$f'(25/4) \approx 0.20$, $f'(9) \approx 0.17$

31. (a) $f'(-1) \approx -2.72$, $f'(0) \approx 1.00$, $f'(1) \approx -0.368$,

$f'(1.5) \approx -0.223$, $f'(2) \approx -0.135$

33. yes; $y = 14x - 45$

35. (a) $f'(0) \approx 0$, $f'(1/2) \approx 0.75$, $f'(1) \approx 3.00$, $f'(3/2) \approx 6.75$,

$f'(2) = 12.00$

37. (a) $f'(1/4) \approx -16.00$, $f'(1/2) \approx -4.00$, $f'(1) \approx -1.00$,

$f'(2) \approx -0.25$, $f'(3) \approx -0.11$

39. (a) $f'(0) \approx 0$, $f'(\pi/6) \approx -0.5$, $f'(\pi/4) \approx -0.71$,

$f'(\pi/3) \approx -0.87$, $f'(\pi/2) \approx -1$, $f'(\pi) \approx 0$

41. (a) $m_a \approx 1$

(b) $m_b \approx 0.62$

(c) $m_c \approx 0.43$

(d) $m_a = \ln e$, $m_b \approx 1/\ln 5$, $m_c \approx 1/\ln 10$

43. (a) 0.693, 1.386, 2.773; 0.693

(b) $\ln 2 \approx 0.693$

45. (a) 2.30, 23.03, 230.26; 2.30

(b) $\ln 10 \approx 2.30$

47. (a) 2.89, 0.721, 0.144; 1.44

(b) $1/\ln 2 \approx 1.44$

49. (a) 0.869, 0.217, 0.0434; 0.434

(b) $1/\ln 10 \approx 0.434$

51. $h'(-3) \approx 0.141$, $h'(0) \approx 0$, $h'(1) \approx -0.841$, $h'(2) \approx -0.909$

53. $-3\Delta x$

55. $x = -1$

57. $x = 1$

59. $f'(\pi) = -1$

61. (a) $g'(9\pi/4) = -\sqrt{2}/2$ (b) $g'(-\pi/4) = \sqrt{2}/2$

(c) $g'(3\pi/4) = -\sqrt{2}/2$

Section 1.6

1. (a) slope ≈ 0

11. yes

17. $A–B$, $C–D$

19. $C–D$

21. (a) $(-5, -2), (2, 5)$

(b) $(0, 5)$

23. $x = 0$; $f'(0) \approx 1.4$

25. $(0, 5.5), (9, 10)$

27. $1, 5.5, 9$

29. $x = 9$

31. no

35. $y = -1$

37. $(-3, 4)$

39. $x = -3$, $x = 3$

41. $x = -3$

43. $x = -1$, $x = 3$

45. $y = 2x + 1$

47. (a) $1, x = 0$ (b) $(-\infty, 0)$

(c) yes

49. (a) none   (b) $(0, \infty)$

(c) no

51. (a) $(-\infty, -4), (2, \infty)$ (b) $x = -4$, $x = 2$

(c) $x = 2$ (d) $(-\infty, -1)$

53. (a) $(-\infty, \infty)$ (b) none

(c) none   (d) $(0, \infty)$

Section 1.7

3. (a) $h''(2) = 0$ **5.** yes

9. $f''(1) < f''(3) < f''(-2) < f''(-3)$

11. (c) no

13. (a) $-10 < x < 1$ (b) $1 < x < 10$

(c) $x = 1$

15. $(0, 3)$ **17.** no

19. $g'(0) < g'(1) < g'(2) < g'(3)$

21. yes

23. (a) $g''(0.5)=0.125$, $g''(1)= -1/2$, $g''(1.5)=1.125$, $g''(2)=2$

25. (a) (iv)   (b) (iii)

(c) (i)   (d) (ii)

27. $f \leftrightarrow$ **B**, $f' \leftrightarrow$ **A**, $f'' \leftrightarrow$ **C**

29. (a) $V''(t^*) = 0$ (b) $H''(t^*) < 0$

37. (a) at most one root; $-\infty < v < 2$

(b) $f(0) \geq 1$

39. (a) $f''(-1) = 0$, $f''(0) = 2$, $f''(2) = 4$

(b) 1

(c) $(-1, \infty)$

41. (a) $f''(-1) = -1/2$, $f''(0)$ does not exist, $f''(2) = 1/3$

(b) 0

(c) $(0, \infty)$

43. (a) $(2, \infty)$ (b) $(-\infty, 2)$

(c) 2, at $x = -1$ and $x = 2$ (d) yes, at $x = 2$

45. (a) $x > -1$ (b) $x < -1$

(c) 1, at $x = -1$ (d) 1, at $x = -1$

47. (a) yes   (b) no

49. (a) no   (b) yes

51. $f''(x) = 3 + 2x$

Section 1.8

1. $f(x) = 3x + C$

3. (b) $g'(x) = f'(x)$ (c) $g'(1) = 5$

5. $y = 3x - 3$ **7.** $g'(0) = 1/7$

11. $f'(-1) < f'(0) < f'(2) < f'(10)$

13. g, g, f, f **15.** $f \leftrightarrow$ **C**, $f' \leftrightarrow$ **A**, $g \leftrightarrow$ **B**

17. $x = 3$, $x = 6$ **19.** $(1, 2), (4.5, 7)$

21. $x = 0$

23. (a) $(-2, 1)$

(b) yes; local maximum point

25. (b) no   (c) no

(d) $(1, \infty)$ (e) $(-2, 0)$

(f) $x = -2$, $x = 0$

27. (a) $y = 3x - 2$ (b) yes

(c) $f(2.1) \approx 4.3$; no

31. yes   **33.** yes

35. $f \leftrightarrow$ **D**, $f' \leftrightarrow$ **C**, $f'' \leftrightarrow$ **A**, $g \leftrightarrow$ **B**

39. no   **41.** yes

43. no   **45.** yes

47. no   **51.** $x = -2$

53. (a) yes   (b) yes

55. $f(-2) = -5,\ f'(-2) = 4$ **57.** no

59. yes   **63.** no

65. no   **67.** $1, r = \sqrt{10\pi/3}$

69. $r = \sqrt{2\pi}$

73. (a) $h'(1) = 3$ (b) $h''(4) = 0$

77. $-2 < f'(1.5) < f'(3) < 0 < 0.5 < f'(4.5)$

79. no

83. (a) no   (b) yes
(c) local minimum point

85. $g(4) = -7$ **87.** must

89. might   **93.** (b) yes; $x = \sqrt{2\pi}$

95. $(\sqrt{\pi}, \sqrt{2\pi})$ **97.** $1; x = \sqrt{15\pi}/3$

CHAPTER 2

Section 2.1

1. 70 mph

3. (a) 5.005   (b) overestimates

7. $f'(-1) = -1$

11. (a) 0.96 dollars/hr   (b) 0 dollars/hr
(c) -4 dollars/hr

13. $f'(3) \approx 3.001$ **15.** $f'(0) \approx 0.999$

17. $f'(1.99) \approx 102.89$ **19.** $f'(2.01) \approx 108;$

21. $f'(1.9) \approx 4.357;$ **23.** $f'(2) \approx 2.95$

25. (a) -3.85 (b) 4.01
(c) 4.01

27. (a) $f'(1.9) \approx 6.86$ (b) $f'(2.0) \approx 7.43$
(c) $f'(2.01) \approx 7.43$

33. $f(x) = \sqrt{x}, a = 4, f'(a) = 0.25$

35. $f(x) = \cos x, a = 0, f'(a) = 0$

37. $f(5) = 14$

39. (b) $f'(1.999) \approx 0.3535974; f'(2) \approx 0.3535092;$
$f'(2.001) \approx 0.3534209$
(c) underestimates
(d) $f''(2) \approx -0.100$

41. $f'(4) = 2$ **43.** $f'(4) = 48$

45. (a) no   (b) no

47. no   **49.** 3

51. -1 **53.** 2

55. yes   **57.** $y = 5x - 7$

Section 2.2

3. $\dfrac{df}{dx} = \sin(2x)$ **5.** $f'(-1) = 3$

9. $l''(1) = 0, q''(2) = 2, c''(3) = 18$

11. $f'(9) = 1/6$

13. (a) $1, 2, 1/2, -1/2, 7/2, \pi$
(b) $1, 2x, \frac{1}{2}x^{-1/2}, -\frac{1}{2}x^{-3/2}, \frac{7}{2}x^{5/2}, \pi x^{\pi-1}$

15. $s''(x) = -\frac{1}{4}x^{-3/2}$ **17.** $f'(x) = 6x$

19. $f'(x) = 20x^4 + 6x - 1$ **21.** $f'(x) = 3x^2 - \frac{1}{3}x^{-2/3}$

23. $f'(x) = 6x^{1/2} + \frac{10}{3}x^{-5/3}$ **25.** $f''(x) = 6$

27. $f''(x) = 80x^3 + 6$ **29.** $f''(x) = 6x + \frac{2}{9}x^{-5/3}$

31. $f''(x) = 3x^{-1/2} - \frac{50}{9}x^{-8/3}$ **33.** $f'(x) = 3(x+2)^2$

35. $f'(x) = -(x+4)^{-2}$ **37.** $y = 8x - 16$

39. $y = 4x + 1$ **41.** $y = 4x + 3$

43. $y = 8x + 2$ **45.** $f'(x) = 6x + 2$

47. $f'(x) = \frac{5}{2}x^{3/2} - 2x^{-1/2} - \frac{1}{2}x^{-3/2}$

49. $y = -12x + 8$ **51.** $V' = 4\pi r^2$

53. (a) $\dfrac{dP}{dV} = -\dfrac{nRT}{(V-nb)^2} + \dfrac{2n^2a}{V^3}$
(b) yes

57. 10

59. $f^{(n)}(x) = (-1)^{n+1}\dfrac{(2n-3)(2n-5)\cdots(3)}{2^n}\,x^{-(2n-1)/2}$

61. two: at $x = -2$ and at $x = -1$

65. yes   **69.** $f'(x) = -(x+5)^{-2}$

71. $f'(x) = 3(x+2)^2$

Section 2.3

1. (a) 9   (b) no

3. (b) -6 (c) -6

7. (a) 1   (b) -1

9. (b) 2

11. $-\infty < a < \infty$ **13.** 2

15. does not exist   **17.** 1

19. 0   **21.** -2

23. -1 **25.** 1

27. 0   **29.** 3/2

31. does not exist   **33.** -2

35. 1

37. (a) $s(t) = t + 4$ (b) 7

39. 4   **41.** 1

43. 3   **45.** -10

49. 2

51. does not exist

53. does not exist

55. 4

57. 0

59. 1/2

61. yes

63. must be true

65. must be true

67. (a) $-1/2$ (b) no

Section 2.4

1. (a) no   (b) yes

3. 5

5. 1.14 and 8.19

7. -1.5

9. $y = 7x + 10$

11. no

13. $(3.2, 6) \cup (13.3, 15)$

15. $-2 < f(9) < f(3) < f(6) < f(14)$

17. $(0, 4.5) \cup (10.5, 15)$

19. (a) $(-\infty, 0)$ and $(2, \infty)$ (b) $(0, 2)$
     (c) $x = 0$ (d) $x = 2$

21. (a) $(-\infty, -\sqrt{2})$ and $(\sqrt{2}, \infty)$
     (b) $(-\sqrt{2}, \sqrt{2})$
     (c) $x = -\sqrt{2}$
     (d) $x = \sqrt{2}$

23. $7; 3$

25. $-2; -11.5$

29. $F'(x) = x \sin x$

31. no

33. $x \sin\left(e^x\right) - 1; x \sin\left(e^x\right); x \sin\left(e^x\right) + 2$

35. (b) $A = 1, B = 1$

37. (a) yes

     (b) $f'(x) = \begin{cases} -1 & -1 \le x \le 0 \\ 4x - 1 & 0 < x \le 1 \end{cases}$

41. $c(x) = 3x^2 - x^3$

43. $x = -4, x = 0, x = -A$, or $x = 3$.

47. no

49. (a) $a = -12, b = 7$

51. (a) $a = 4/125, b = -6/25, c = 0, d = 2$

53. none

55. 26/3

57. $2\sqrt{2}$

59. 20 km/hr

61. $30'' \times 60'' \times 20''$; $3.75

63. $a = 3, b = -1/9$

65. $c = 7$

67. $\ln(-x)$

Section 2.5

1. no

3. (a) $y(x) = 3x$ (b) infinitely many

5. yes

7. (a) $y' = y$ (b) $y'' = -32$

9. $y(x) = 3x^2 + 5x - 6$

11. $y(t) = -\sqrt{t + 3}$

15. (a) 493 meters   (b) ≈ 20.03 seconds

19. yes

21. no

25. no

29. object is falling at rate of 3 meters per second

33. $p'(t) = v(t) = 15$

35. $p'(t) = v(t) = k\sqrt{p}$

37. $h(10) = 70$

39. 6 meters

43. $T' = k(T - S)$

47. (a) remain constant   (b) decrease
     (c) increase   (d) 500

49. (b) $y' = k(y - 65)$

Section 2.6

3. yes

5. $y = 2e^x$

7. $h'(b) = 1/c$

9. $5^x / \ln 5, 5^x / \ln x + 1$

11. $y(x) = 2e^x - 2^x / \ln 2 + 2x$

13. (a) $y(x) = 37e^{3x}$ (b) one

15. $f'(x) = 2e^x$

17. $f'(x) = (\ln 2) 2^x + 2x$

19. $f'(x) = -2/x$

21. $f''(x) = 2e^x$

23. $f''(x) = (\ln 2)^2 2^x + 2$

25. $f''(x) = 2/x^2$

27. $F(x) = 2e^x + \pi x + C$

29. $F(x) = 2^x / \ln 2 + x^3/3 + 2x + C$

31. $y = x + 1$

33. $\ln 3$

35. (a) $P(40) \approx 22,285$
     (b) $P'(40) \approx -450$; decreasing

37. (a) $1/(e - 1)$ meters per second
     (b) $1/e$ meters per second.

43. $y(x) = 100e^{0.1x}$

45. $y(x) = 2^x$

47. $4451.08

49. (a) $a = 1, b = 1$ (b) $c = 1/2$
     (c) $d = 1/6$ (e) $[-0.48318, 0.41622]$
     (f) $[-0.90509, 0.78672]$ (g) $[-1.3225, 1.1683]$

51. $x = -1/\ln 2$

53. $a = e$

55. (b) $3,718.28

61. (b) ≈ 0.9095

63. ≈ 4.28 days

65. (a) at $t = 23$ hours   (b) ≈ 17.356 hours

67. 22,912 years ago

69. 1

Section 2.7

3. 1

7. $G(x) = -4\cos x + 3\sin x$

9. $F(x) = x^3/3 + \cos x$

11. $x = -\pi, x = 0, x = \pi$

13. no

17. $f'(x) = 2\cos x$

19. $f'(x) = 3\cos(3x)$

21. $f'(x) = 3\cos x + 2\sin x$

23. $f''(x) = -2\sin x$

25. $f''(x) = -9\sin(3x)$

27. $f''(x) = -3\sin x + 2\cos x$

29. $F(x) = -2\cos x + C$

31. $F(x) = -\frac{1}{3}\cos(3x)$

33. $F(x) = -3\cos x - 2\sin x + C$

35. (a) $x = 3\pi/2$ (b) $[0, 2\pi]$
(c) $\pi + 1; -1$ (d) $(\pi/2, 3\pi/2)$
(e) $f'(\pi/2) = 2$

43. (a) $x = \pi/4, x = \pi/2, x = 3\pi/4$
(b) $(\pi/4, \pi/2) \cup (3\pi/4, \pi)$
(c) $2\sqrt{2}/3; 0$

45. (a) $x = \pi; x = 2\pi/3, x = 4\pi/3$
(b) $x \approx 0.93593, x \approx 2.57376, x \approx 3.70942$

49. (a) $a = 0, b = 1$ (b) $c = 0$
(c) $d = -1/6$ (e) $[-0.85375, 0.85375]$
(f) $[-0.85375, 0.85375]$ (g) $[-1.6654, 1.6654]$

51. $\cos(x + k) = \cos x \cos k - \sin x \sin k$

53. $f(x) = \frac{1}{2}x^4 - \frac{1}{4}\cos(4x) + \frac{5}{4}$

55. $A = 2, B = 4$

59. (a) 2   (b) $-\sqrt{3}/2$

61. $4 + \pi$

63. (a) $y = x$
(b) $y = (x - \pi/3)/2 + \sqrt{3}/2$
(c) part (a)

65. -1

67. $\sqrt{2}$

Section 2.8

1. no

3. $f'(x) = 2x - 3e^x$

5. yes

7. $h(w) = 1 + 0.5w - \sin w$

9. yes

13. yes

15. 8

17. yes

19. $\frac{105}{6} + \frac{4}{3}(\ln 3 - \ln 2)$

21. 1.78 ppm per year

23. $f'(x) = \frac{3}{2}\sqrt{x}$

25. $f'(x) = 2x^{-1} - 3\sin x$

27. $\pi x + 2x^{-1/2}$

29. $z^6 - \frac{5}{9}z^{-9}$

31. no

33. $4 \cdot 2^{3/2}$

35. $1; 0$ or 10

37. yes

39. $F'(x) = x\sin(e^x)$

41. $g'(w) = 2\pi w + \frac{8}{3}w^{-1/3} + 1/w^2$

43. $P'(t) = 6t + 2t^{-1/2}$

45. $h'(w) = \cos w + \sin w$

47. no

49. no

51. (b) $h'(x) = k(x - c)^{k-1}$ (c) $k'(x) = -3(4 - x)^2$

53. $F''(\theta) = -\sin\theta$

55. $U''(r) = -r^{-2}$

57. 1000

61. $v(1/3) = \sqrt{3}\pi/4$ in./sec; $a(1/3) = \pi^2/4$ in./sec^2

63. $g'(0) = -\pi^2$

65. $j'(x) = 2x^2\cos x$

67. $F(x) + 3x$

69. $3F(x)$

CHAPTER 3

Section 3.1

3. $g'(t) = -\dfrac{t\sin t + 4\cos t}{t^5}$

5. $r'(x) = -2^{-x}\ln 2$

7. $g'(z) = e^z\tan z + e^z\sec^2 z$

9. $h'(x) = 0$

11. $h'(x) = \frac{5}{6}x^{-1/6}$

13. $h'(x) = 3e^{3x}$

15. $h'(x) = -x^{-2}$

17. $h'(x) = -2e^{-2x}$

19. $h'(x) = 1 + 2x$

21. $f'(x) = \sin x + x\cos x$

23. $f'(x) = \left(\frac{1}{2}\ln x + 1\right)/\sqrt{x}$

25. $f'(x) = (2\ln x + x^{-1})e^{2x}$

27. $f'(x) = (2x + x^2 + 3)e^x$

29. $f'(x) = \dfrac{x\cos x - 2\sin x}{x^3}$

31. $f'(x) = \dfrac{2(1 - x^2)}{(x^2 + 1)^2}$

33. $f'(x) = -3\csc^2(3x)$

35. $f'(x) = -6\csc(2x)\cot(2x)$

37. yes

39. yes

41. yes

43. $h'(2) = -16, h'(4) = 64$

45. yes

47. $m'(0) = -4, m'(2) = 0.64$

49. $g'(1) = 10$

51. $g''(1) = 34$

53. $g'(0) = 3$

55. yes

57. no

59. yes

61. $h''(0) \approx 7.5$

63. yes

65. yes

67. $k''(0) \approx 17$

69. (a) $a = 1, b = 0$ (b) $c = 1$
(d) $[-0.34375, 0.29334]$ (e) $[-0.62463, 0.54865]$

71. (a) $h''(x) = f''(x)g(x) + 2f'(x)g'(x) + fg''(x)$
(b) $h'''(x) = f'''(x)g(x) + 3f''(x)g'(x) + 3f'(x)g''(x) + f(x)g'''(x)$

73. $A = 3, B = 2$

75. $A = 1, B = -2, C = 2$

77. (a) $x = e; 1/e$ (b) $x = e^{3/2}$

79. (a) $x = \pi/4; x = \pi$ (b) $x = 0; x = \pi$

81. (b) $y(x) = (x + 7)e^{-2x}$

Section 3.2

1. (a) $h(x) = g(f(x))$ (b) $h'(x) = -2x\sin(x^2)$

3. $-2\sin(2x)$

5. $58x\left(x^2+3\right)^{28}$

7. $\dfrac{\cos x}{2\sqrt{2+\sin x}}$

9. $-3x^2\sin(x^3)$

11. $8x/(4x^2+3)$

13. $-\left(\frac{1}{2}x^{-1/2}-e^{-x}\right)\sin\left(\sqrt{x}+e^{-x}\right)$

15. $f'(x)=-6x^2\sin(x^3)\cos(x^3)$

17. $f'(x)=\dfrac{3x}{\sqrt{1+3x^2}}$

19. $\dfrac{2x+3\cos x}{x^2+3\sin x}$

21. $h(1)=3; h'(1)=12; h(2)=4; h'(2)=12; h(3)=1; h'(3)=4;$ $h(4)=2; h'(4)=1$

23. $x=2k\pi$, where $k=0,\pm1,\pm2,\dots$

25. $x=2\pi/3+2k\pi$ and $x=4\pi/3+2k\pi$, where $k=0,$ $\pm1,\pm2,\dots$

27. yes

29. (a) $h(-2)=1/2,\, h(1)=0,\, h(3)=1/4$
(b) $h'(-2)=-1/2,\, h'(1)=0,\, h'(3)=-1/8$

31. $x=-4,\, x=-3,\, x=-1.5,\, x=0,\, x=2.5,\, x=5$

33. yes

35. increasing; decreasing; decreasing

37. no

39. yes

41. $-\pi$

43. $j'(x)=2x^3\cos(x^2)+3$

45. (a) $y=2x+17-\pi$

(b) no

47. no

Section 3.3

1. (a) $(3/\sqrt{5},\sqrt{5});\,(-3/\sqrt{5},-\sqrt{5})$
(b) $(\sqrt{5},3/\sqrt{5});\,(-\sqrt{5},-3/\sqrt{5})$

3. $y=2-2x/3;\, dy/dx=-2/3$

5. $dy/dx=-x/y$

7. (a) $f_1(x)=\sqrt{1+2x^2};\, f_2(x)=-\sqrt{1+2x^2}$
(c) $dy/dx=2x/y$
(d) $(0,\pm1)$
(e) points: $(c,\pm\sqrt{1+2c^2})$; slopes: $\pm2c/\sqrt{1+2c^2}$

9. $\dfrac{dy}{dx}=-\dfrac{2x+y}{x+2y};\, \dfrac{dy}{dx}=\dfrac{-2x+y}{-x+2y}$

11. $\pm1/2,\pm2$

13. $(2/\sqrt{3},1/\sqrt{3}),\quad(2/\sqrt{3},-1/\sqrt{3}),\quad(-2/\sqrt{3},1/\sqrt{3}),$ and $(-2/\sqrt{3},-1/\sqrt{3})$

15. (b) $y'=-x/2y$

17. (b) $y'=(x+xy^2)/(y-x^2y)$

19. $y=4-x$

21. $y=(2x+20)/11$

23. $y=3(x-1)/2+1;\, y=-3(x-1)/2-1$

25. 1.025

Section 3.4

1. $\pi/2$

3. π

5. $\pi/4$

7. $\sqrt{1-x^2}$

9. $1/\sqrt{1+x^2}$

11. $\dfrac{1}{\sqrt{1+4x^2}}$

13. $\dfrac{2}{1+4x^2}$

15. $\frac{1}{2}\left((1-x^2)\arcsin x\right)^{-1/2}$

17. $\dfrac{e^x}{\sqrt{1-e^{2x}}}$

19. $\left(x\left(1+(\ln x)^2\right)\right)^{-1}$

21. $f'(x)=\dfrac{2}{\sqrt{x^4-4x^2}}$

23. $2x\arctan(\sqrt{x})+\dfrac{x^{3/2}}{2+2x}$

25. $x=\pm\pi/3,\, x=\pm7\pi/3$

27. $(5,-3)$

35. $g(x)=(x-a)/b$

41. $(-\infty,\infty)$, yes

43. (c) odd
(d) $f'(x)>0$
(e) $(-\infty,0);\,(0,\infty)$; yes, at $x=0$

45. (b) neither
(c) $f'(x)<0$
(d) $(-1,0);\,(0,1)$; yes, at $x=0$

47. (b) neither
(c) $f'(x)>0$
(d) $(-\infty,-1);\,(1,\infty)$; no

55. (a) $C=\pi/4$
(b) $\pi/2$
(c) $-\pi/2$

57. (b) $-\pi/2<\arctan x+\arctan y<\pi/2$

Section 3.5

1. $H'(z)=e^z(\cos z-\sin z)$

3. $r'(\theta)=3\sec^2(3\theta)$

5. $G'(w)=(2w+3w^2)e^{3w}$

7. $W'(u)=\left(2u\tan(\sqrt[3]{u})+\dfrac{1}{3}u^{-2/3}\sec^2(\sqrt[3]{u})\right)e^{u^2}$

9. $g'(z)=2ze^z+(z^2+3)e^z=(z^2+2z+3)e^z$

11. $f'(w)=-6w\sin(w^2)$

13. $R'(w)=3w^2\cos(4w)-4w^3\sin(4w)$

15. $f'(x)=\sin x+x\cos x$

17. $h'(r)=e^{r^2\sin r}(2r\sin r+r^2\cos r)$

19. $f'(x)=2x^{-2}e^{-2/x}=\dfrac{2}{x^2e^{2/x}}$

21. $f'(x)=\dfrac{\cos(\sqrt{x})}{2\sqrt{x}}$

23. $f'(x)=2\sec^2(2x+3)$

25. $f'(x)=4\left(e^{2x}-3\ln x\right)^3\left(2e^{2x}-3/x\right)$

27. $f'(x) = \dfrac{4 + 2\cos x + x\ln x\sin x}{2x(2 + \cos x)^{3/2}}$

29. $f'(x) = 6\cos\left(e^{3x}\right)e^{3x}$

31. $f'(x) = -12\sin^2\left(e^{-4x}\right)\cos\left(e^{-4x}\right)e^{-4x}$

33. $f'(x) = \dfrac{\cos(x+1)(e^x + e^{-x}) - \sin(x+1)(e^x - e^{-x})}{(e^x + e^{-x})^2}$

35. $f'(x) = e^{\pi+1}x^{e-1}$

37. $f'(x) = (\ln 2)2^x\ln x + 2^x/x$

39. $f'(x) = \dfrac{1}{3(\ln 2)x} + \dfrac{\log_2 e}{3} = \dfrac{1+x}{3(\ln 2)x}$

41. $f'(x) = \dfrac{(\ln 4)4^{\sqrt{\ln x}}}{2x\sqrt{\ln x}}$

43. $f'(x) = \dfrac{3e^{3x} + 2\sin x\cos x}{e^{3x} + \sin^2 x}$

45. $f'(x) = 2x\sec^2(x^2)e^{\tan(x^2)}$

47. $f'(x) = -3\cos(3x)\sin(3x)\left(4 + \cos^2(3x)\right)^{-1/2}$

49. $f'(x) = -6e^{3x}\cos\left(e^{3x}\right)\sin\left(e^{3x}\right)$

51. $f'(x) = \ln\left(2 + \sin(3x)\right) + 3x\cos(3x)\left(2 + \sin(3x)\right)^{-1}$

53. $f'(x) = 2\sin(x\cos x)\cos(x\cos x)(\cos x - x\sin x)$

55. $f'(x) = \dfrac{\sin x - x\cos x}{\sin^2 x}e^{x/\sin x}$

57. $f'(x) = -\dfrac{(10 + 8x)e^{2x}}{(3 + 4x)^2}\sin\left(\dfrac{e^{2x}}{3 + 4x}\right)$

59. $f'(x) = \dfrac{\frac{2x+x^3}{1+e^x} - (2 + 3x^2)\ln(1 + e^x)}{(2x + x^3)^2}$

61. $f'(x) = 2(\ln x)x^{\ln x - 1}$ **63.** $\ln\left(x^2 + 3x + 5\right) + C$

65. $\ln(2 + \sin x) + C$

67. $\arcsin x + C$

69. $\arctan(x/3) + C$

71. $\frac{1}{2}\arcsin(2x) + C$

73. $\frac{1}{2}\arcsin(x^2) + C$

75. $\arctan(\sin x) + C$

77. $\arctan(\ln x) + C$

Section 3.6

1. (b) $f(u) = -u;\ f(u) = u$ (c) no

3. (a) $(uv)'(3) \approx 1.5,\ (u/v)'(3) \approx 1.5,\ (u \circ v)'(3) \approx -1.8$,
(b) local minimum
(c) local minimum
(d) 0.02, 0.7, 1.7, 2.8, 3.7

9. $g'(-1) = 1/10;\ j'(-1) = 2.3;\ h(0) = 3;\ h'(0) = 2;\ f(1) = 0;$
$g'(1) = 4; h(1) = 3; j'(1) = 5$

11. $x\left(\log_b x - 1/\ln b\right)$ **13.** $y = -6(x - \ln 2) + 4$

15. no   **17.** no

19. no   **21.** $2xg(x^2)$

23. $f'(x) = n\left(g(x)\right)^{n-1}g'(x)$ **25.** $f'(x) = \dfrac{g'(x)}{g(x)}$

27. $f'(x) = g'(x)\sec^2\left(g(x)\right)$ **29.** $f'(x) = e^x g'(e^x)$

31. $f'(x) = \cos x\, g'(\sin x)$

33. (a) $t = 0$ (b) $t = 20$
(c) $t = 40$

35. (b) $h'(x) = 6f(x)\left(f'(x)\right)^2$ **37.** -1

41. $h'(\pi) = (1 + \ln \pi)\sqrt{1 + (\pi\ln\pi)^3}$

43. no   **45.** no

47. no   **49.** $-\pi/2 < \theta < \pi/2$

51. $-1 \le t \le 1$ **53.** (d) $k'(x) = 0$

CHAPTER 4

Section 4.1

1. (b) slope $= 3$ (c) slope $= -4$
(d) slope $= 0$

5. $y = 4(t + 2) + 1$ **7.** (vii)

9. (iii)   **11.** (viii)

13. (x)

23. (a) 4.46 minutes; 2.79 minutes; 68 °C; 57 °C
(b) 7.4 minutes; 4.6 minutes; 76 °C; 69 °C
(c) $k \ge -0.0446$

25. (c) $20\ln 9$ hours

27. (a) $v(t) = \dfrac{g}{k} - \left(\dfrac{g}{k} - v_0\right)e^{-kt}$

(b) $y(t) = \dfrac{g}{k}t + \left(\dfrac{g}{k^2} - \dfrac{v_0}{k}\right)e^{-kt} + \left(y_0 - \dfrac{g}{k^2} + \dfrac{v_0}{k}\right)$

29. (ii)   **33.** (b) $y(t) = (t + 2)e^{t+1}$

Section 4.2

1. (a) $-\infty$ (b) $-\infty$

3. does not exist   **5.** -1

7. does not exist   **9.** 0

11. $-\frac{1}{2}$ **13.** ∞

15. 0   **17.** ∞

19. 0   **21.** 0

23. $\cos 1$ **25.** -4

27. 0   **29.** ∞

31. 0.75   **33.** ∞

35. 0

37. no

39. no

45. (a) yes   (b) no

47. $p(x) = x^2 - 2x + 3, q(x) = x + 1$

49. $p(x) = x + 1, q(x) = x^2 + 2$

51. (a) $a = -21$ (b) $-\infty < a < \infty$

53. no

55. 0

57. 12

59. ∞

61. 1

63. 2

65. 1

67. 1

69. $-\pi/2$

71. 0

73. 0

75. 0

77. 0

79. 1

81. 0

83. 6

87. 1

89. e

91. 0

95. no

Section 4.3

1. $-5, 1, 5$

3. yes, at $x = 1$

5. (a) $g(4/5) = 4/5$ (b) yes

7. (a) $(0.7, 0.5)$ (b) $(\sqrt{2}/2, 1/2)$

9. $P(x) = 10x - x^2$ **11.** $4 - 2\sqrt{3}/9$

15. corners at $(\pm 1/2, 0), (\pm 1/2, \sqrt{3}/2)$; 50%

17. $8\sqrt{3}/9$

19. (a) $y_{max} \approx 22.96$; $x \approx 91.84$

21. (b) $m = 1$

23. (a) $b^2/(16hv)$ square feet; $x = b/4h, y = b/4v$
    (b) $\$4\sqrt{avh}$; $x = \sqrt{av/h}, y = \sqrt{ah/v}$
    (c) yes; $b/2; b/2$

27. (a) $b = 25/3, h = 25/3$ (b) $b = 25/3, h = 25/3$

29. (a) $0 \le x \le 6$
    (b) 6 miles; $W(6) = 100$ feet, $D(6) = 130$ feet
    (c) $W(0) = 220$ feet, $D(0) = 10$ feet
    (d) $W(4) = 60$ feet, $D(4) = 90$ feet
    (e) 0 miles downstream

31. use *all* of the wire for the circle

Section 4.4

7. No. 5

9. (a) $t = 3, t = 4, t = 9$, and $t = 10$; $t = 0, t = 1, t = 6$, and $t = 7$
    (b) ≈ 3 units per second
    (c) ≈ 1 unit per second

11. (a) circle of radius 2 with center at $(2, 1)$.
    (c) $x = 2 + \sqrt{13}\cos t, y = 3 + \sqrt{13}\sin t, 0 \le t \le 2\pi$
    (d) the point $(2, 3)$

13. (b) 3 times

15. (a) $(at_0 + b, ct_0 + d); (at_1 + b, ct_1 + d)$
    (b) $y = c(x - b)/a + d$
    (c) $x = a(y - d)/c + b$

17. (c) $s(t) = \sqrt{22,500 - 1024t^2}$

19. (b) at $t = 60.5/s_0$ seconds
    (c) Yes (if $s_0 > 0$)

21. (a) at $t = 4\left(e^{121/400} - 1\right)/3$
    (b) ≈ 3.4508 feet
    (c) ≈ 111.87 feet per second
    (d) $x \approx 80.569$ feet

Section 4.5

1. (b) $y' = -1/2$

3. (b) $y(0) = 0$; $x'(0) = 0$; at $(1, 0)$
    (c) $y(t_0) = \pm\sqrt{3}/2, y'(t_0) = \mp\sqrt{3}/3$

5. 30 feet, 7 feet/second

7. 22 cm^2/sec   **9.** -1.2 miles per hour

11. $-4\sqrt{5}$ ft/sec   **13.** increasing

15. (a) ≈ 0.702 nautical miles
    (b) ≈ 5.3 minutes

17. $A' \approx 78,040$ square feet/hr

19. (a) $T' = -10/144\pi$ in./min
    (b) $S' = -10/3$ square in./min

21. (a) ≈ 44.721 ft/sec   (b) ≈ 103 ft/sec

23. $8\sqrt{\pi/5}$ **25.** ≈ 0.39 ft/min

27. ≈ 83.8 m/sec   **29.** $5/6$ ft^3/min

Section 4.6

1. $x_1 = 9/4, x_2 = 161/72, x_3 = 51,841/23,184$

3. -1.88

5. (a) 0.706 (b) no

7. (a) $N(x) = \dfrac{x}{2} + \dfrac{a}{2x}$.
    (d) $1, 3/2, 17/12, 577/408, 665857/470832$

9. (a) $1.250000000, 1.025000000, 1.000304878, 1.000000046$;
    $0, 1, 3, 7$
    (b) $x_0 > 0; x_0 < 0; x_0 = 0$

15. (a) $-0.244817, 3.80675$, and 6.43807

17. 8.285 **19.** 7.91673

21. $\lim\limits_{n \to \infty} x_n = \infty$

Section 4.7

1. $f(0) = 1$, $f'(0) = 1$, $f''(0) = 2$, $f'''(0) = 6$, $f^{(4)}(0) = 24$, $f^{(5)}(0) = 120$, $f^{(6)}(0) = 0$, $f^{(131)}(1) = 0$

3. (a) $P_2(x) = 1 + 2(x - 1) + (x - 1)^2$
(b) $P_2(x) = x^2$

5. $P_2(x) = \dfrac{10}{9} + \dfrac{5}{36}x - \dfrac{1}{288}x^2$

9. $P_3(x) = 1 + x + x^2 + x^3$

11. $P_3(x) = (x - 1) - \dfrac{(x - 1)^2}{2} + \dfrac{(x - 1)^3}{3}$

13. $P_3(x) = 1 + \dfrac{x}{4} - \dfrac{(x - 4)^2}{64} + \dfrac{(x - 4)^3}{512}$

15. $\ell(x) = 1$; $[-0.1415, 0.1415]$
$q(x) = 1 - x^2/2$; $[-0.7028, 0.7028]$

17. $\ell(x) = 1 + x$; $[-0.14483, 0.13816]$
$q(x) = 1 + x + x^2/2$; $[-0.404503, 0.378969]$

19. $\ell(x) = q(x) = x$; $[-0.38249, 0.38249]$

21. (b) $P_2(x) = x$, $P_4(x) = x - x^3/6$, $P_6(x) = x - x^3/6 + x^5/120$,
$P_8(x) = x - x^3/6 + x^5/120 - x^7/5040$

23. (a) $f(0.5) \approx 0.42074$ (b) less than
(c) $f(0.5) \approx -0.28566$

25. 10.15 **27.** 0.84857

29. (a) $\ell_p(t) = 25t$; $\ell_p(1) = 25$; $\ell_p(1) = -25$
(b) $q_p(t) = 25t + t^2$; $q_p(1) = 26$; $q_p(-1) = -24$
(c) $\ell_v(t) = 25 + 2t$; $\ell_v(1) = 27$

31. (a) $\ell(t) = 100$ meters; $\ell(1) = 100$ meters
(b) $q(t) = 100 - 4.9t^2$ meters; $q(1) = 95.1$ meters

33. (a) $f(1) = 1$, $f'(1) = 0$ (b) no
(c) no (d) no

35. no

37. $f(0) = \sin 0 = p(0) = 0 - 0^3/6$; $f'(0) = p'(0)$; $f''(0) = p''(0)$;
$f'''(0) = p'''(0)$; $f^{(4)}(0) = p^{(4)}(0)$

43. (a) $q_{100}(x) = 1$ (b) $q_{010}(x) = x$
(c) $q_{001}(x) = x^2/2$

45. (a) yes
(b) $p_3(x) = 2 - 6(x - 1)^2 + 5(x - 1)^3$
(c) $x = 7/5$

Section 4.8

1. $[-4, -3)$, $(-3, -1)$, $[-1, 1]$, $(1, 2)$, $(2, 4)$

3. $[-4, -3)$, $(-3, -1)$, $(-1, 1)$, $(1, 2)$, $(2, 3)$, $(3, 4)$

5. $(-4, -3)$, $(-3, -1)$, $(-1, -1/3)$, $(-1/3, 1)$, $(1, 2)$, $(2, 3)$, $(3, 4)$

7. yes **9.** yes

19. $3/2, 7/4, 13/8, 27/16$

21. (a) 7 (b) 10
(c) 17 (d) 34

31. cannot **33.** must

35. might **37.** might

39. $[-1, 0]$

Section 4.9

1. If it's cloudy, then it's raining. true, false

3. If $x > 1$, then $x > 2$. true, false

5. If $f(x) = x^2$, then $f'(x) = 2x$. false, true

9. impossible **11.** $f(x) = \sin x$

13. impossible **15.** no

17. yes **21.** $c = 1.5$

29. (b) $3/2 \le f(3) \le 3$
(c) $-1 \le f(-1) \le -1/2$

31. (a) $f'(1) = 3$, $f'(3) = -1$
(b) $f(1) = 2$, $f(3) = 2$

33. (a) no (b) $125

CHAPTER 5

Section 5.1

1. 45 **3.** $A = 12$, $B = 20$

5. 4 **7.** $4 + 9\pi/4$

9. 0 **11.** $4 + 9\pi/4 + 4\pi + 12$

13. -3 **15.** 6

17. $21/2$ **19.** 9

21. 2π **23.** $-\pi^3/3$

25. 0 **27.** $\pi^3/3$

29. $A = 6$, $B = 8$ **31.** $A = 1/5$, $B = 1$

33. 74 **35.** -18

37. Joan **41.** 6

43. 3 **45.** 3

49. 0 **51.** 0

53. 0 **55.** $\pi + 2$

57. $\pi^2/8 + 1$ **59.** 200

67. 7

71. (b) $\displaystyle \int_0^2 \Big(f(x) - g(x) \Big)\, dx$

Section 5.2

3. $A_f(5)$ **7.** $A_f(-1)$

19. no

21. $F(x) = 3x^2/2 + 2x$, $G(x) = 3x^2/2 + 2x - 7/2$, $H(x) = 3x^2/2 + 2x - 2$

23. $F(x) - H(x) = 2$

25. $(-\infty, -2/3)$; $f(x) < 0$

27. no

29. $F(x) = 2x - 3x^2/2$, $G(x) = 2x - 3x^2/2 - 1/2$, $H(x) = 2x - 3x^2/2 + 10$

31. -10 **33.** $(2/3, \infty)$; $f(x) < 0$

35. yes; $(-\infty, \infty)$

37. (a) F is decreasing on $[a, b]$
    (b) F is concave up on $[a, b]$

39. (a) $A_f(x) = \begin{cases} 2x + x^2/2, & x \le 0 \\ 2x - x^2/2, & x > 0 \end{cases}$

41. $(-\infty, -2) \cup (2, \infty)$; $f(x) < 0$

43. $(0, \infty)$; f is decreasing

45. $A_f(x) = \begin{cases} 2x + x^2/2 - 3/2, & x \le 0 \\ 2x - x^2/2 - 3/2, & x > 0 \end{cases}$

47. $(-\infty, -2) \cup (2, \infty)$; $f(x) < 0$

49. $(0, \infty)$; f is decreasing

51. $G(x) = H(x) - 2\pi + 1/2$

55. $G(-5) = -3$; $G(-3) = 0$

57. 1   **59.** $1 + \sin(x^2)$

61. $F(4)$ **63.** $F(3) - F(-2)$

69. $\frac{1}{2}x\sqrt{a^2 - x^2} + \frac{a^2}{2}\arcsin(x/a)$

71. (a) $A_f(x) = x^3/3 + 9$ (b) yes

Section 5.3

1. yes   **3.** yes

5. yes   **7.** yes

9. $x = -3.5, x = -2, x = 2$

11. $[-5, -3.5) \cup (2, 5]$

13. $F(0) = 0$, $F'(0) = 2$, $F''(0) = 1$

15. $y = x - 0.5$

17. $x = -3, x = -2, x = 1, x = 3$

19. 4   **21.** $2/3$

23. $e^2 - e^{-1}$ **25.** 1

27. $499/10$ **29.** -1

31. (a) $y = 2x - 2$ (b) no

33. (b) $\frac{1}{2}\sin 9$

35. yes; at $x = 1$, $x = 5$, and $x = 9$

37. $x = 3$ **39.** yes

41. no   **43.** $f(2) = 12 + e^2 + \sin 2$

49. $2x\sqrt[3]{1 + x^4}$ **51.** $-2/3$

53. 2   **55.** $g'(4) = 2$

57. $(1, 4)$ **59.** $g'(4) = 4$

61. $x = 5$ **63.** $-4/3$

65. (a) $D(t) = 800 - 10t$; $P(t) = 900$
    (c) $I(t) = (5 - R/2)t^2 + 100t + 1680$
    (d) $R = 50$

Section 5.4

1. $-\frac{1}{8}(4x + 3)^{-2} + C$ **3.** $e^{\sin x} + C$

5. $\frac{1}{2}(\arctan x)^2 + C$ **7.** $-e^{1/x} + C$

9. $\arctan(e^x) + C$

11. $a = 4, b = 1$; $(\pi/4 - \arctan 4)/2$

13. $a = 1, b = 19$; $45/361$

17. $2(1 + \sqrt{x}) - 2\ln|1 + \sqrt{x}|$

19. $-\frac{1}{b}\ln\left|a + \frac{b}{x}\right| + C$

21. $\pi/3$

23. $\frac{1}{2}\sin(2x + 3) + C$

25. $\frac{1}{15}(3x - 2)^5 + C$

27. $\frac{1}{2}\ln(1 + x^4) + C$

29. $-\frac{1}{2}\ln|1 - 2x| + C$

31. $\frac{1}{10}(3 - 2x)^{5/2} - \frac{1}{2}(3 - 2x)^{3/2} + C$

33. $-\frac{2}{3}\left(1 + x^{-1}\right)^{3/2} + C$

35. $\frac{1}{12}\left(x^4 - 1\right)^3 + C$

37. $\frac{1}{3}\arctan\left(x^3\right) + C$

39. $\frac{1}{18}\left(4x^3 + 5\right)^{3/2} + C$

41. $\frac{1}{2}\ln\left(x^2 + 1\right) + 4\arctan x + C$

43. $-\frac{1}{3}\left(x^2 + 3x + 5\right)^{-3} + C$

45. $\frac{1}{4}\left(3x^2 + 6x + 5\right)^{2/3} + C$

47. $-\frac{1}{2}\left(2e^x + 3\right)^{-1} + C$

49. $2\ln|x + 1| - 1/(x + 1) + C$

51. $-\ln|\cos x| + C$

53. $\frac{1}{2}(\arcsin x)^2 + C$

55. $\frac{5}{6}\ln\left(3x^2 + 4\right) + C$ **57.** $\arcsin(\tan x) + C$

59. $-\frac{1}{2}\ln\left|\cos\left(x^2\right)\right| + C$ **61.** $-\frac{1}{3}\csc^3 x + C$

63. $\frac{1}{2}\left(1 + \sqrt{x}\right)^4 + C$

65. $\frac{1}{5}(x^2+2)^{5/2} - \frac{2}{3}(x^2+2)^{3/2} + C$

67. $-(e^x+1)^{-1} + C$ **69.** $6/25$

71. $1 - \cos 1$ **73.** 0

77. $2x^{1/2} - 3x^{1/3} + 6x^{1/6} - 6\ln\left(x^{1/6}+1\right) + C$

Section 5.5

1. $\frac{1}{3}x - \frac{1}{15}\ln\left(3+2e^{5x}\right) + C$

3. $\frac{1}{9}\ln\left|\frac{x}{3-x}\right| - \frac{1}{3x} + C$

5. $\ln\left|\frac{\sqrt{2x+1}-1}{\sqrt{2x+1}+1}\right|$

7. $\frac{1}{13}e^{2x}\left(2\cos(3x)+3\sin(3x)\right) + C$

9. $\frac{2}{\sqrt{2}}\arctan\sqrt{\frac{3x-2}{2}} + C$ **11.** $x - \arctan x + C$

13. $x - 2\ln|x+1| + C$ **15.** $\tan x - \sec x + C$

17. $\frac{1}{3}\arctan(3x) + C$

19. $\frac{1}{10}\tan^2(5x) + \frac{1}{5}\ln\left|\cos(5x)\right| + C$

21. $\frac{x}{2} + \frac{1}{8}\ln|4x+5| + C$

23. $\frac{1}{2(2x+3)} + \ln|2x+3| + C$

25. $\frac{1}{2}\ln\left(x^2+2\right) + \sqrt{2}\arctan\left(\frac{x\sqrt{2}}{2}\right) + C$

27. $\frac{5}{12}\ln\left|\frac{x+1}{x+4}\right| + C$

29. $\frac{1}{2}\left(x^2\sin(x^2)+\cos(x^2)\right) + C$

31. $-\frac{2x+3}{x^2+3x+2} - 2\ln\left|\frac{x+1}{x+2}\right| + C$

33. $\frac{1}{2}\arctan\left(\frac{e^x-1}{2}\right) + C$

35. $\frac{1}{2}\left((x+2)\sqrt{x^2+4x+1} - 3\ln\left|x+2+\sqrt{x^2+4x+1}\right|\right) + C$

37. $-\frac{4}{13}\ln|\cos x - 4| - \frac{1}{39}\ln\left|\cos x + \frac{1}{3}\right| + C$

39. $\frac{1}{9}\left(\sin(3x+4) - (3x+4)\cos(3x+4) + 4\cos(3x+4)\right) + C$

Section 5.6

1. (a) 4   **3.** (a) 7

5. (a) 3   **7.** 24

9. 28   **11.** 28

13. 34

15. $L_4 = 6, R_4 = 10, M_4 = 8, T_4 = 8, I = 8$

17. $L_4 = -8, R_4 = 8, M_4 = 0, T_4 = 0, I = 0$

19.

n	L_n	R_n	M_n	T_n
2	−0.75000	3.75000	1.5000	1.50000
4	0.37500	2.62500	1.5000	1.50000
8	0.93750	2.06250	1.5000	1.50000
16	1.21875	1.78125	1.5000	1.50000
32	1.35938	1.64063	1.5000	1.50000
64	1.42969	1.57031	1.5000	1.50000
128	1.46484	1.53516	1.5000	1.50000
256	1.48242	1.51758	1.5000	1.50000

$I = 1.5$

21.

n	L_n	R_n	M_n	T_n
2	0.06250	0.56250	0.21875	0.31250
4	0.14063	0.39063	0.24219	0.26563
8	0.19141	0.31641	0.24805	0.25391
16	0.21973	0.28222	0.24951	0.25098
32	0.23462	0.26587	0.24988	0.25024
64	0.24225	0.25787	0.24997	0.25006
128	0.24611	0.25392	0.24999	0.25002
256	0.24805	0.25196	0.25000	0.25000

$I = 0.25$

23.

n	L_n	R_n	M_n	T_n
2	1.57080	1.57080	2.22144	1.57080
4	1.89612	1.89612	2.05234	1.89612
8	1.97423	1.97423	2.01291	1.97423
16	1.99357	1.99357	2.00322	1.99357
32	1.99839	1.99839	2.00080	1.99838
64	1.99960	1.99960	2.00020	1.99960
128	1.99990	1.99990	2.00005	1.99990
256	1.99997	1.99997	2.00001	1.99998

$I = 2$

25. 0.85   **27.** 1.44

29. (a) $\int_5^{20} f(x)\,dx$ (b) $\int_0^{15} f(x)\,dx$

(c) $\int_{2.5}^{17.5} f(x)\,dx$

33. no

Section 5.7

1. $\displaystyle\sum_{k=1}^{50} k$

3. $\displaystyle\sum_{i=0}^{49}(2i+1)^2$

5. $137/60$

7. $\sqrt{2}/2$

9. 153

11. 385

13. (a) $\displaystyle\sum_{j=1}^{10} j^2$

(b) $\displaystyle 2\sum_{k=1}^{5}(2k)^2$

(c) $\displaystyle\frac{1}{2}\sum_{i=1}^{20}(i/2)^2$

(d) $\displaystyle\frac{1}{5}\sum_{n=1}^{50}(n/5)^2$

15. (a) $\displaystyle\sum_{i=1}^{10} i^2$

(b) $\displaystyle 2\sum_{j=0}^{4}(1+2j)^2$

(c) $\displaystyle\frac{1}{2}\sum_{k=0}^{19}(1+k/2)^2$

(d) $\displaystyle\frac{1}{5}\sum_{k=0}^{49}(1+k/5)^2$

17. (a) $\displaystyle\frac{1}{10}\sum_{i=0}^{9}\sqrt[3]{i/10}$

(b) $\displaystyle\frac{1}{5}\sum_{i=0}^{4}\sqrt[3]{i/5}$

(c) $\displaystyle\frac{1}{20}\sum_{i=0}^{19}\sqrt[3]{i/20}$

(d) $\displaystyle\frac{1}{50}\sum_{i=0}^{49}\sqrt[3]{i/50}$

19. (a) $\displaystyle\frac{1}{10}\sum_{i=1}^{10}\sqrt[3]{1+i/10}$

(b) $\displaystyle\frac{1}{5}\sum_{i=1}^{5}\sqrt[3]{1+i/5}$

(c) $\displaystyle\frac{1}{20}\sum_{i=1}^{20}\sqrt[3]{1+i/20}$

(d) $\displaystyle\frac{1}{50}\sum_{i=1}^{50}\sqrt[3]{1+i/50}$

21. (a) $\displaystyle\frac{2}{5}\sum_{i=1}^{10}\sin\!\big((3+2i/5)^2\big)$

(b) $\displaystyle\frac{4}{5}\sum_{j=1}^{5}\sin\!\big((3+4j/5)^2\big)$

(c) $\displaystyle\frac{1}{5}\sum_{k=1}^{20}\sin\!\big((3+k/5)^2\big)$

(d) $\displaystyle\frac{2}{25}\sum_{n=1}^{50}\sin\!\big((3+2n/25)^2\big)$

23. (a) $\displaystyle\frac{1}{2}\sum_{i=0}^{9}\sqrt{1/4+i/2}$

(b) $\displaystyle\sum_{j=0}^{4}\sqrt{1/2+j}$

(c) $\displaystyle\frac{1}{4}\sum_{k=0}^{19}\sqrt{1/8+k/4}$

(d) $\displaystyle\frac{1}{10}\sum_{n=0}^{49}\sqrt{1/20+n/10}$

25. $1/2$

39. $\displaystyle\int_{0}^{2}\sin x\,dx = -\cos 2 + \cos 0$

41. $\displaystyle\int_{0}^{1} x^3\,dx = 1/4$

45. (b) $T_6 = 38.75$; $L_6 = 38$; $M_3 = 50$

Section 5.8

1. (a) -65

7. (b) $y = x$

13. (a) no

(b) yes

27. $\frac{1}{3}\ln|x| + C$

29. $3\arctan x + C$

31. $-\frac{2}{3}\cos(3x) - \frac{4}{5}\sin(5x) + C$

33. $x + \frac{4}{3}x^{3/2} + \frac{1}{2}x^2 + C$

35. $9\ln|x| - 6x + \frac{1}{2}x^2 + C$

37. $e^x - \frac{1}{2}e^{2x} + C$

39. $-\frac{1}{2}\cos(x^2) + C$

41. $\frac{1}{4}e^{x^4} + C$

43. $\frac{1}{4}(\ln x)^4 + C$

45. $-\frac{1}{2}\Big(\ln|\cos x|\Big)^2 + C$

51. $\approx 74.5\,^\circ\mathrm{C}$

53. $\displaystyle\frac{5}{N}\sum_{j=0}^{N-1}\sqrt{3\cdot j\cdot\frac{5}{N}}$; $\displaystyle\frac{5}{N}\sum_{j=0}^{N-1}\sqrt{3\cdot(j+1)\cdot\frac{5}{N}}$; $\displaystyle\frac{5}{N}\sum_{j=0}^{N-1}\sqrt{3\cdot(j+0.5)\cdot\frac{5}{N}}$

55. $G(3)$

57. $G(2) - G(-2)$

59. (b) 0

61. $\int_5^3 g(t)\,dt < \int_0^2 g(u)\,du < -1 < h(1) < \int_1^1 g(x)\,dx < h(4) < 3 < 5$

63. no

65. 36

67. 2

69. -6

71. (a) $H(-3) > 0$

(b) $H(-2) = 0$

(c) $H(0) < 0$

(d) $H(2) > 0$

73. $H'(1) = e$

77. $G'(2) = 1$

79. yes

81. -19

83. $-0.5 < S(0) < S(1) < 0.5 < S(3) < S(2)$

85. no

87. 1

89. $z = \sqrt{2\pi}$

91. -3

93. cannot be determined

95. 4

97. 1.7

101. yes

103. yes

111. yes

113. no

115. yes

117. $4/3$

119. $5/2$

CHAPTER 6

Section 6.1

1. (a) $I = 2$

(c) $|I - L_3| = 0.28446$; $|I - R_3| = 0.21554$; $|I - T_3| = 0.034457$; $|I - M_3| = 0.016525$

(d) 0.00046875

5. (a) $L_{10} = 11.810$; $R_{10} = 22.530$; $T_{10} = 17.170$; $M_{10} = 16.098$; $S_{20} = 16.455$

(b) $|I - T_{10}| \le 10.72$

(c) $|I - S_{20}| \le 1.072$

7. (a) $L_4 = 1.1485$; $R_4 = 1.1805$; $T_4 = 1.1645$;
$M_2 = 1.1345$; $S_4 = 1.1545$

    (b) $1.1345 \leq I \leq 1.1645$

9. (a) $|I - L_{20}| \approx 0.02113$; $|I - R_{20}| \approx 0.02094$;
$|I - T_{20}| \approx 0.00010$; $|I - M_{20}| \approx 0.00005$;

11. $I - M_n < 0$ **13.** 0.31027

15. $f(x) = 1/x$; decreasing

17. $f(x) = 1 - x^2$; concave down

19. (b) yes

27. $L_{100} \leq T_{100} \leq S_{200} \leq M_{100} \leq R_{100}$

29. must   **31.** must

33. may   **35.** may

37. may   **39.** may

41. must   **43.** cannot

45. must   **47.** must

49. must   **57.** (b) $|I - M_n| \leq |I - R_n|$

59. no   **61.** $R_n \leq T_n \leq I \leq M_n \leq L_n$

63. yes

65. $R_n \leq M_n \leq S_{2n} \leq T_n \leq L_n$

67. $L_n \leq I \leq R_n$ **69.** must

71. may   **73.** may

Section 6.2

5. (a) $|I - R_8| \leq 10/n$ (b) $|I - T_8| = 0$

7. (b) no

9. (a) $I = 2$

    (b) $|I - L_3| = 0.28446$; $|I - R_3| = 0.21554$; yes

    (c) $|I - T_3| = 0.034457$; $|I - M_3| = 0.016525$; yes

    (d) $n \geq 13$

11. 772   **13.** 65

15. 22   **17.** 5

19. $f(x) = x$ **21.** $f(x) = x^2$

23. (a) 1/2

    (b) 1/4

25. no

27. (a) 8415   (b) 1683

    (c) 144

29. (b) 0.1629   **31.** 5

33. $n \geq 162$ **35.** cannot

37. cannot

Section 6.3

1. $167.20 - 9.72 \cdot 1 = 157.48$

5. (b) no

7. (a) $m_i = f\left(t_i, Y(t_i)\right)$ (b) nothing

9. (a) 2   (b) 2.4414

    (c) yes

11. (a) 2.0778   (b) 2.1074

13. (a) -0.59374 (b) -0.65330

15. (a) 2.6764   **17.** (b) 0.73092

CHAPTER 7

Section 7.1

1. (b) $L_5 = 4/25$ (c) underestimates

    (d) 1/6

3. (a) 1/3   (b) 1/3

    (c) 2   (d) 8/3

5. (a) 1.4793

7. $I = \int_0^{\pi} \sqrt{1 + \cos^2 x}\, dx$; $M_{20} \approx 3.820$

9. (a) 105 mi   (b) 105 ft   (c) 105 ft/min

11. (a)

t	1.0	1.1	1.2	1.3	1.4	1.5
$f'(t)$	-0.83	-1.17	-1.46	-1.70	-1.875	-1.965

t	1.6	1.7	1.8	1.9	2.0
$f'(t)$	-1.985	-1.925	-1.78	-1.57	-1.3

    (b) $M_5 = -1.666$; $f(2) - f(1) = -1.666$

    (c) 0.1194   (d) 1.9494

    (e) $-1.5983, 0.11875$

13. 8/5   **15.** 1/12

17. 16/3

19. $65/32 - 9\ln(9)/4 + 9\ln(4)/4$

21. $e - 1$ **23.** 125/6

25. 8/5   **27.** 1/12

29. 16/3

31. $65/32 - 9\ln(9)/4 + 9\ln(4)/4$

33. $e - 1$ **35.** 125/6

37. ratio $= 1.4271$ **39.** $\pi/2$

41. $\left(4\sqrt{17} + \ln\left(4 + \sqrt{17}\right) - 2\sqrt{5} - \ln\left(2 + \sqrt{5}\right)\right)/4$

43. $\left(80\sqrt{10} - 13\sqrt{13}\right)/27$

45. $40\sqrt{5}/3 - 8\sqrt{2}/15$

49. $53/6$

53. $\sinh(4) - \sinh(1)$

57. $\approx (4.3271, 31.4470)$

47. $36 + \ln(3)/4$

51. $49/9$

Section 7.2

1. ≈ 12.47 m^3

5. (a) $V = s^2h/3$

9. (b) yes

13. $1688\pi/21$

17. $\pi\left(16/\ln 2 - 8 - 6/(\ln 2)^2\right)$

19. $128/3$

23. $\pi r^2 h$

27. (a) $\approx 1.1514 \times 10^{10}$ mi^3
   (b) $\approx 1.1522 \times 10^{11}$ mi^3

29. $100\sqrt{3} + 800\pi/3$ ft^3

33. $45\sqrt{3} + 120\pi$ ft^3

35. (a) $(b-a)h$ (b) $\pi(b-a)h^2$
   (c) $\pi(b-a)\left((h+c)^2 - c^2\right)$
   (d) $\pi(b-a)\left(c^2 - (c-h)^2\right)$

37. $5\pi/6$

41. $\pi(\pi/2 - 1)$

45. $2\pi^2$

49. $\pi(e^2 + 1)/2$

51. $\pi h(r-a)(r^2 + ra - 2a^2)/3$

55. (b) $KR/2$

3. $140/3\pi$ m^3

7. $1 - 1/\sqrt[3]{2}$

11. $8^7\pi/7$

15. $128\pi/5$

21. $27\sqrt{3}/2$

25. $95\pi/12 \approx 24.87$ in.^{3}

31. $M_3 = 33.2$ in.^{3}

39. $625\pi/6$

43. $\pi h(b^2 - a^2)$

47. $4\pi/3$

Section 7.3

1. (a) $k = 5$

3. (a) $50k$ ft-lb

   (b) 80 in.-lb

   (b) $k(50 + 10a)$ ft-lb

5. $100{,}000$ ft-lb

9. $\pi\rho g r^4/4$

13. 12 ft-lb

17. (a) volume of the tank
   (b) $62.4 \displaystyle\int_0^h yA(y)\,dy$

7. The 50-lb bucket.

11. $171{,}360\pi$ ft-lb

Section 7.4

1. (a) $200\,^\circ$F; $160\,^\circ$F; $120\,^\circ$F; $70\,^\circ$F; $40\,^\circ$F

3. $y' = -0.1(y - 70)$, $y(0) = 70$

5. (a) $100\,^\circ$F; $70\,^\circ$F; $0\,^\circ$F

7. $y' = -0.1y$; $y(0) = 190$

11. $80 + 40e$

17. $y = -1/(x - 2)$

21. $y = 2/(3 - x^2)$

23. (a) $f(y) = 1/y$, $g(x) = x$
   (b) $F(y) = \ln y$, $G(x) = x^2/2$

25. (a) $2, 1.5, 1, 0.5$

27. $y = \tan(x + C)$

13. (a) $\displaystyle\lim_{t \to \infty} y(t) = T_r$

19. $y = -2e^{x^3/3}$

   (b) P_1; P_4

29. $y = \dfrac{2Ae^{4x} + 2}{Ae^{4x} - 1}$

31. $\ln\left(\sec y + \tan y\right) = x^3/3 + C$

Section 7.5

1. (a) $\approx \$251{,}579$
   (c) $\approx 10.011\%$

3. (a) $\approx \$631{,}284$
   (c) 7%

5. $\$53{,}317$; $\$36{,}120$

7. (b) 2π; 360; 360

9. yes

   (b) $\approx \$155{,}817$

   (b) $\approx \$398{,}519$

CHAPTER 8

Section 8.1

3. $-(1+x)e^{-x}$

5. (b) $x\arctan(2x) + \frac{1}{4}\ln(1 + 4x^2)$

7. (b) $(2\cos x - \sin x)e^{2x}$
   (c) $(2\sin x - \cos x)e^{2x}/5$

9. $\left(\sin(3x) - 3x\cos(3x)\right)/9$

11. $x\tan x + \ln|\cos x|$

13. $x(\ln x)^2 - 2x\ln x + 2x$

15. $1 - 2e^{-1}$; $M_{20} \approx 0.26435$

17. $(e^2 + 1)/4$; $M_{20} \approx 2.0970$

19. $\sqrt{2}\arctan(\sqrt{2}/2)/12 + 1/12 + \ln(3/4)/6 - \pi/12$;
   $M_{20} \approx -0.15361$

21. (b) $\sin x - x\cos x$

23. $x(\ln x)^3 - 3x(\ln x)^2 + 6x(\ln x - 1)$

29. (a) $x^3\left(\ln(x^3)-1\right)/3$

(b) $x^3\ln x - x^3/3$

31. $(x^2-1)e^{x^2}/2$

35. $\left(2x^2+2x\sin(2x)+\cos(2x)\right)/8$

37 $x^2\sin x - 2\sin x + 2x\cos x$

39. $\ln|\csc x - \cot x| - x\csc x$

41. $(6\ln x - 4)x^{3/2}/27$

43. $x\arctan(1/x)+\frac{1}{2}\ln(x^2+1)$

45. $2(\sqrt{x}-1)e^{\sqrt{x}}$

47. $x\left(\sin(\ln x)-\cos(\ln x)\right)/2$

49. $\sin(\sqrt{x})-\sqrt{x}\cos(\sqrt{x})$

51. $\frac{2}{3}x^{3/2}\arctan(\sqrt{x})-(1+x)/3+\frac{1}{3}\ln(1+x)$

53. $\sin x\left(\ln|\sin x|-1\right)$ **55.** $x\cosh x - \sinh x$

57. $x^2\cosh x - 2x\sinh x + 2\cosh x$

59. (d) $120-44e$ **61.** $f(x)=x^4/4$

63. -5

Section 8.2

3. $x - x/(1+x^2)$

5. (b) $2\ln|x+1|+3\ln|x+2|$

7. (c) $1+2x/(x-1)^2$

(d) $x+2\ln|x-1|-2/(x-1)$

9. yes   **11.** no

13. no

15. (d) $\frac{1}{2}\ln|x|-\ln|x+1|+\frac{3}{2}\ln|x-2|$

17. $\frac{4}{3}\ln|x-1|-2\ln|x+1|+\frac{5}{3}\ln|x+2|$

19. (e) $-\frac{1}{4}\ln|x|+\frac{5}{8}\ln\left|x^2+4\right|$

21. $q(x)=4x+17$

23. no

25. (e) $\ln|x+1|+(x+1)/2-1/\left(2(x+1)^2\right)$

27. (a) $1/\left(3(x-2)\right)-1/\left(3(x+1)\right)$

(b) $2/\left(3(x-2)\right)+1/\left(3(x+1)\right)$

(c) $-\left(2\ln|x-2|+7\ln|x+1|\right)/3$

29. (a) $1/\left(2(x-1)\right)-(x+1)/\left(2(x^2+1)\right)$

(b) $1/\left(2(x-1)\right)-(x-1)/\left(2(x^2+1)\right)$

(c) $1/\left(2(x-1)\right)+(x+1)/\left(2(x^2+1)\right)$

(d) $\frac{9}{2}\ln|x-1|-\frac{1}{4}\ln(x^2+1)+\frac{5}{2}\arctan x$

31. $-(3\ln 2+\pi)/10$

33. $\ln(x-2)+\ln(x+3)$

35. $x^{-1}+2\ln|x|+3\ln|x+2|$

37. $x+\frac{1}{4}\ln|x-1|-\frac{1}{4}\ln|x+1|-\frac{1}{2}\arctan x$

39. $x^2/2+\frac{1}{2}\ln|x-1|+\frac{1}{2}\ln|x+1|$

41. $\ln\left|\left(\sqrt{x+1}-1\right)/\left(\sqrt{x+1}+1\right)\right|$

Section 8.3

1. (a) $\sin x$ (b) $-\cos x$

(c) $\tan x$ (d) $\sec x$

3. no

5. (a) $\sin^5 x/5 - \sin^7 x/7$

(b) $\sin x(5\cos^6 x - 8\cos^4 x + \cos^2 x + 2)/35$

(c) yes

9. $\ln\left|x+1+\sqrt{x^2+2x+5}\right|$

11. $\left(6x-\sin(6x)\right)/12$

13. $\sin^3 x/3$

15. $-\cos^3 x/3+\cos^5 x/5$

17. $(x+\cos x\sin x - 2\cos^3 x\sin x)/8$

19. $\tan^3 x/3 - \tan x + x$

21. $\tan^3 x/3$

23. $\left(\tan x\sec x - \ln|\sec x + \tan x|\right)/2$

25. $\sec^3 x/3 - \sec x$

27. $-\left(\sqrt{4-x^2}\right)/4x$

29. $\left(x\sqrt{1-x^2}+\arcsin x\right)/2$

31. $\left(\arcsin x + x\sqrt{1-x^2}-2x\left(1-x^2\right)^{3/2}\right)/8$

35. $\sqrt{x^2-4}/4x$

37. $\sqrt{3}-\pi/3$

39. $\cos^2 x/2 - \ln|\cos x|$

41. $-2\left(\cos x\right)^{3/2}/3+4\left(\cos x\right)^{7/2}/7-2\left(\cos x\right)^{11/2}/11$

43. $\left(x\sqrt{1+x^2}+\ln\left|\sqrt{1+x^2}+x\right|\right)/2$

45. $\arctan x + 2\ln\left|x/\sqrt{1+x^2}\right|$

49. (b) $\left(ax+\cos(ax)\sin(ax)\right)/2a$

51. (b) $\sin^2(ax)/2a$

55. $\dfrac{(n-1)}{n}\cdot\dfrac{(n-3)}{n-2}\cdots\dfrac{3}{4}\cdot\dfrac{\pi}{4}$

61. $\tan(x/2)$ **63.** $\ln(4+\sqrt{2})-\ln(2)$

65. $I_n=\dfrac{x}{2(n-1)\left(1+x^2\right)^{n-1}}+\dfrac{2n-3}{2n-2}I_{n-1}$

Section 8.4

1. $1/(3+\cos x)$

3. $(3+4x^2)^6/48$

5. $3(x^2+4)^{2/3}/4$

7. $(\ln|x|)^3/3$

9. $(\ln|x|)^2/2$

11. $x/3-2\ln|3x+2|$

13. $\sin^3(3x)/9$

15. $e^{3x^2}/6$

17. $-(2-3x)^{11}/33$

19. $\ln|3+\tan x|$

21. $\ln|(x-1)/(x+2)|/3$

23. $x/2+\ln|4x+5|/8$

25. $\arcsin(e^x)$

27. $x(\ln|x|-1)$

29. $x\arcsin x+\sqrt{1-x^2}$

31. $\arctan((x+1)/\sqrt{2})/\sqrt{2}$

33. $\arcsin(2x)/2$

35. $-\ln|\cos x|$

37. $2(1+e^x)^{5/2}/5-2(1+e^x)^{3/2}/3$

39. $\arcsin((x+1)/2)$

41. $-1/\ln|x|+C$

43. $(\ln|3x-2|-\ln|3x+2|)/12$

45. $-4\sqrt{4-x^2}+(4-x^2)^{3/2}/3-x^2\sqrt{4-x^2}-2(4-x^2)^{3/2}/3$

47. $\ln|x^2-1|/2$

49. $\ln\left|x+\sqrt{9+x^2}\right|$

51. $-x^2/6-x/9-\ln|1-3x|/27+C$

53. $e^{3x}/3$

55. $x\ln(1+x^2)-2x+2\arctan x$

57. $(2x^2\arcsin x+x\sqrt{1-x^2}-\arcsin x)/4$

59. $\sqrt{2x+3}$

61. $-(2x+1)/(8(2x+3)^3)$

63. $-\cos^2 x/2$

65. $\ln|1-e^{-x}|$

67. $2\sqrt{x}-2\ln(1+\sqrt{x})$

69. $x^3\ln(3x)/3-x^3/9$

71. $2x^{3/2}\ln|x|/3-4x^{3/2}/9$

73. $\ln|x+3|+2\arctan x-\ln(x^2+1)/2$

75. $(3x\sin^3 x+\sin^2 x\cos x+2\cos x)/9$

77. $\ln|x|-\ln(x^2+1)/2$

79. $\Big((x+1)(x^2+2x+3)^{3/2}+3(x+1)\sqrt{x^2+2x+3}$
$+6\ln\left|\left(\sqrt{x^2+2x+3}+x+1\right)/\sqrt{2}\right|\Big)/4$

81. $2\sqrt{1+e^x}+\ln|1-\sqrt{1+e^x}|-\ln|1+\sqrt{1+e^x}|$

83. $\left(2\ln|x+1|-\ln|x^2-x+1|+2\sqrt{3}\arctan((2x-1)/\sqrt{3})\right)/6$

85. $x\tan x-x^2/2-\ln|\sec x|$

87. $\sin x/2-\sin(3x)/6$

CHAPTER 9

Section 9.1

1. (a) $1+2x+44x^2-12x^3+x^4$
   (b) $f(x)=160+50(x-3)-10(x-3)^2+(x-3)^4$

3. (a) 9   (b) 24/5

5. (a) 0   (b) $12!/13^4$

7. $1-x^2/2+x^4/24-x^6/720;\quad[-2.13,2.13]$

9. $x-x^2/2+x^3/3-x^4/4+x^5/5-x^6/6;\quad[-0.61,0.73]$

11. $x+x^3/6+x^5/120;\quad[-1.74,1.74]$

13. $\sqrt{2}\Big(1+(x-\pi/4)-(x-\pi/4)^2/2-(x-\pi/4)^3/6$
$+(x-\pi/4)^4/24+(x-\pi/4)^5/120\Big)/2;\quad[-0.76,2.22]$

15. $\Big(\sqrt{3}+(x-\pi/3)-\sqrt{3}(x-\pi/3)^2/2-(x-\pi/3)^3/6$
$+\sqrt{3}(x-\pi/3)^4/24+(x-\pi/3)^5/120\Big)/2;\quad[-0.41,2.45]$

17. $1-(x-1)+(x-1)^2-(x-1)^3+(x-1)^4-(x-1)^5;$
   $[0.58,1.49]$

19. $(x-1)-(x-1)^2/2+(x-1)^3/3-(x-1)^4/4+(x-1)^5/5;$
   $[0.45,1.67]$

21. $1+(x-1)/2-(x-1)^2/8+(x-1)^3/16-5(x-1)^4/128$
   $+7(x-1)^5/256;\quad[0.25,1.97]$

23. $1-(x-1)/2+3(x-1)^2/8-5(x-1)^3/16$
   $+35(x-1)^4/128-63(x-1)^5/256;\quad[0.47,1.64]$

25. no   **27.** $3-x/4-x^2/5$

31. $(x-1)-(x-1)^2/2+(x-1)^3/3-(x-1)^4/4$

33. $1-x/2+3x^2/8-5x^3/16+35x^4/128$

35. $x/2-x^3/48+x^5/3840$

37. $1-x+x^2/2-x^3/6+x^4/24-x^5/120$

39. $1+x^2+x^4/2+x^6/6$ **41.** $1-x^2+x^4-x^6$

49. $1-x^2+x^4/3-2x^6/45$

51. $2(x+x^3/3+x^5/5)$

53. $x-x^3/3+x^5/5$

Section 9.2

1. (a) 0.056   (b) yes

3. (a) $|\sin x-P_5(x)|\le 4/45$
   (b) $|\sin x-P_5(x)|\le 0.025$

5. (a) 0.35   (b) 0.015

9. (d) 0.00019

11. 0   **13.** 0

15. (a) $1 + x/2 - x^2/8$ (b) $2\pi\sigma\left(a^2/2r - a^4/8r^3\right)$

17. (a) 33/16   (b) 1/64

Section 9.3

1. (c) $\pi/2$

9. (a) $2/\pi$ (b) $2/\pi + 4\sin(3x)$
    (c) $2/\pi + 4\sin(3x)$

11. 3

15. (a) $a_0 = 1/2; a_k = 0$ for $k \geq 1; b_{2m} = 0$ and
$b_{2m+1} = 2/\left((2m+1)\pi\right)$ for $m = 1, 2, 3, \ldots$
(b) $q_1(x) = 1/2 + (2/\pi)\sin x$;
$q_3(x) = q_1(x) + (2/3\pi)\sin(3x)$;
$q_5(x) = q_3(x) + (2/5\pi)\sin(5x)$;
$q_7(x) = q_5(x) + (2/7\pi)\sin(7x)$

17. $\pi/2 - (4/\pi)\cos(x) - (4/9\pi)\cos(3x) - (4/25\pi)\cos(5x) - (4/49\pi)\cos(5x)$

19. $4 + \pi^2/3 - 4\cos x + \cos(2x) - (4/9)\cos(3x) + (1/4)\cos(4x) - (4/25)\cos(5x) + (1/9)\cos(6x) - (4/49)\cos(7x) + 6\sin(x) - 3\sin(2x) + 2\sin(3x) - (3/2)\sin(4x) + (6/5)\sin(5x) - \sin(6x) + (6/7)\sin(7x)$

CHAPTER 10

Section 10.1

3. $\lim\limits_{x \to 1^+} 1/(x^2 \ln x) = \infty$ **7.** 1/2

9. $2e^{-1}$ **11.** 1

13. e **15.** 4

17. 1/100   **19.** yes

23. 0   **25.** (b) no

27. (b) no   **29.** no

31. π **33.** diverges

35. $-3\sqrt[3]{2}$ **37.** $\sqrt{5} + \sqrt{7}$

39. 16/3   **41.** diverges

43. diverges   **45.** $\pi/2$

47. 2   **49.** $p > 1$

51. $p < 1$ **53.** none

55. (b) $\lim\limits_{x \to 0^+} \sin x/x = 1$ **57.** no

59. $C = 4$

61. $\displaystyle\int_0^1 \frac{du}{1 + u^3}$

63. $\displaystyle\int_0^1 \frac{u^2}{u^4 + 1}\,du$ **65.** $\displaystyle -\int_0^1 \frac{u\ln u}{u^4 + 1}\,du$

Section 10.2

1. (a) $1/g(x) < 1/f(x) < 1$
(b) $1/\left(g(x)\right)^r < 1/\left(f(x)\right)^r < 1$
(c) $1/\left(g(x)\right)^r < 1/\left(f(x)\right)^r < 1$

9. no   **11.** $a \geq 11.513$

13. $a \geq 100{,}000$

15. $\displaystyle\int_0^{12} \frac{dx}{x^2 + e^x}$

17. $\displaystyle\int_0^8 \frac{\arctan x}{(1 + x^2)^3}\,dx$ **25.** none

27. diverges   **29.** converges

31. yes   **35.** 1

Section 10.3

7. (a) 1   (b) -0.5

(c) $\displaystyle\frac{1}{\sqrt{2\pi}}\int_{-0.5}^{\infty} e^{-x^2/2}\,dx$ (d) $\displaystyle\frac{1}{\sqrt{2\pi}}\int_{-\infty}^{1} e^{-x^2/2}\,dx$

(e) $\displaystyle\frac{1}{\sqrt{2\pi}}\int_{-0.5}^{1} e^{-x^2/2}\,dx$

9. (b) ≈ 0.1151 **11.** ≈ 0.4333

13. ≈ 0.1151 **15.** ≈ 0.4

17. ≈ 0.15 **19.** ≈ 0.095581

21. $D \approx 2.987$ in.   **25.** $k = 1/\pi$

27. (b) $1/\lambda$ **29.** (a) 1

31. $\sqrt{\pi}$ **35.** $\pi/4$

37. 1/4

39. $(6 + \ln 2)/9$

CHAPTER 11

Section 11.1

1. no limit   **3.** ∞

5. 0   **7.** $\pi/2$

9. 0   **11.** 1

13. 0   **15.** 0

17. 1   **19.** $a_k = (-1)^k/k$

21. $a_k = k$

23. $a_k = e^{-k}$

27. 1

29. 1

31. 0

33. $x \leq 0$

35. $-\sin 1 < x \leq \sin 1$

39. $e^{-1/2}$

41. (c) converges

47. no

49. yes

53. yes

55. $x \geq 0$

Section 11.2

1. (a) 1/5; 1/25; 1/3125; 1/9765625; 6/5; 31/25; 3906/3125; 12,207,031/9,765,625

   (d) 5/4

   (e) 1/20; 1/100; 1/12,500; 1/39,062,500

   (g) 0

7. $\pi^4/90$

9. (a) $S_n = (n+1)a$

11. 1/8

13. $e/(e-1)$

15. $\pi^2/(16-4\pi)$

17. $-1/48$

21. $S_n = \arctan(n+1)$; $S = \pi/2$

23. $S_n = 1 + 1/\sqrt{2} - 1/\sqrt{n+1} - 1/\sqrt{n+2}$; $S = 1 + 1/\sqrt{2}$

25. (a) 4.97

            (b) 5

   (c) 0

27. $\pi^2/24$

29. $\pi^2/12$

31. $-1 < x < 1$; $1/(1-x)$

33. $-1 < x < 1$; $x^{10}/(1-x^2)$

35. $-2 < x < 0$; $-(1+x)^3/x$

37. 3/2

39. diverges

41. 3/2

43. diverges

45. 9/16

47. diverges

49. 1/5

51. diverges

53. 8 feet

59. (a) yes; $S = 3$

        (b) $\displaystyle\lim_{k \to \infty} a_k = 0$

61. (b) $a_k = (-1)^k$

Section 11.3

1. (c) $S_{10} \approx 1.6963$

        (d) no

3. $\displaystyle\sum_{k=2}^{n} a_k < \int_1^n a(x)\,dx < \sum_{k=1}^{n-1} a_k$

9. $1/2 < S < 3/2$

11. $2e^{-1} \leq S \leq 3e^{-1}$

13. (a) no

17. $1/2 < S < 2$

19. $1/\sqrt{2} < S < 2$

25. (c) no

27. (a) nothing

   (b) converges

31. converges; $N \geq 1000$

33. diverges; $N \geq 2999$

35. converges; $N \geq 4$

41. yes

45. converges; $\pi/8 < S < \pi/8 + 3\pi^2/32$

47. diverges

49. $1/3 < S < 1/2$

51. converges; $1/2 < S < 5/2$

55. $N \geq 6$

Section 11.4

1. conditionally

3. $14.902 < S < 14.918$

5. (a) $S_{50} \approx 0.23794$

   (c) $0.23774 < S < 0.23814$

7. no

9. $S \approx -0.94985$

11. $S \approx -1.625$

13. no

15. $p > 1$

17. $p > 1$

19. converges absolutely; $3/4 < S < 1$

21. diverges

23. diverges

25. converges absolutely; $0 < S < 1/12$

31. $a_k = (-1)^k/\sqrt{k}$

Section 11.5

3. 2

5. 1

7. 1; $(1, 3)$

9. 1; $[-6, -4)$

15. $\displaystyle\sum_{k=1}^{\infty} \frac{x^k}{k4^k}$

17. $\displaystyle\sum_{k=1}^{\infty} \frac{(x-2)^k}{3^k}$

19. $\displaystyle\sum_{k=1}^{\infty} \frac{(12-x)^k}{k4^k}$

25. (a) $R = 14$

          (b) $b = 3$

27. cannot

29. may

31. may

33. may

35. may

37. may

41. 0.820

43. $(-\infty, \infty)$

45. 0.581

47. $[-9, 1]$

49. 1.198

Section 11.6

1. 2

3. 2

5. $\displaystyle\sum_{k=0}^{\infty} (-1)^k x^{k+2}$

7. $\displaystyle\sum_{k=1}^{\infty} k(-x)^{k-1}$

9. $\displaystyle\sum_{k=0}^{\infty} (-1)^k \frac{(2x)^{2k+1}}{2k+1}$; $R = 1/2$

11. $\displaystyle\sum_{k=0}^{\infty}(-1)^k\frac{x^{2k+3}}{(2k+1)!}; R=\infty$

13. 29/48

17. $\displaystyle\frac{1}{2}\sum_{k=0}^{\infty}(-1)^k\left(\frac{1}{2}\right)^k; R=2$

19. $\displaystyle\sum_{k=0}^{\infty}(-1)^k\left(\frac{x^{2k}}{(2k)!}+\frac{x^{2k+1}}{(2k+1)!}\right); R=\infty$

21. $\displaystyle\sum_{k=0}^{\infty}(-1)^{k+1}\frac{(4k^2+2k+1)x^{2k+1}}{(2k+1)!}; R=\infty$

29. 1   **31.** 1/2

33. −1/2   **35.** 2

37. (b) $[-1,1)$

41. (a) $\displaystyle\sum_{k=0}^{\infty}\frac{(-1)^k}{(2k+1)\cdot k!}x^{2k+1}$ (b) 26/35

43. $2557/7020\approx 0.364$

45. $x^3+2x^4+2x^5+\frac{5}{6}x^6$

47. $1+2x+\frac{5}{2}x^2+\frac{8}{3}x^3$

49. $1+x+x^2/2-x^4/8$

51. $(1-x)^{-2}$ **53.** $x/(1+x)$

Section 11.7

1. (b) 9.1×10^{-5} **3.** $2^{100}/100!$

5. (a) $\displaystyle\sum_{k=0}^{\infty}\frac{(-1)^k x^k}{2^{k+1}}$ (b) $-259!/2^{260}$

9. (b) yes

11. (a) $\displaystyle\sum_{k=0}^{\infty}\frac{(-1)^k x^{2k}}{(2k+1)!}$ (b) $(-\infty,\infty)$

      (c) $f'''(1)\approx\dfrac{37}{210}$

Section 11.8

1. ∞ **3.** ∞

5. 0   **7.** 0

9. converges absolutely; $S<e$

11. diverges

13. converges absolutely; $S<1/3$

15. converges absolutely; $1<S<1+\sqrt{\pi}/2$

17. diverges

19. converges absolutely; $1/2<S<3$

21. converges absolutely; $3/4<S<1$

23. converges conditionally; $-1<S<-1/2$

25. diverges

27. converges absolutely; $S=583/120$

29. diverges   **31.** diverges

33. diverges

35. (a) $n^n e^{1-n}<n!$ (b) $N>be$

37. $[-1,1]$ **39.** $(-1/3,1/3)$

41. $[-1/3,1/3)$ **43.** $(1,5)$

45. $[-3,5)$ **47.** $[-6,-4]$

49. cannot   **51.** must

53. cannot   **55.** 0

57. 1/3

59. $\displaystyle\sum_{k=0}^{\infty}\frac{(x\ln 2)^k}{k!}; R=\infty$

61. $\displaystyle-\sum_{k=0}^{\infty}\left(\frac{2^{k+2}+(-1)^k}{2^{k+1}}\right)x^k; R=1$

63. $a_k=(-1)^{k+1}$

65. (a) no   (b) yes

69. $f(x)=1+3x^4+3x^8+x^{12}$

71. $g(x)\approx 1-3x^2/2+15x^4/8-35x^6/16$

73. 252/625

CHAPTER V

Section V.1

1. $(3,5)$ **3.** $(-4,-5)$

5. $\sqrt{5}$ **7.** $\sqrt{65}$

11. (a) $(3,4)$ (b) $w-v=(-1,2)$

      (c) $v-w=(1,-2)$

21. (a) $L(0)=(1,2); L(1)=(3,5); L(2)=(5,8);$
        $L(-1)=(-1,-1)$

(b) ray from $P(1,2)$ in same direction as the vector $(2,3)$

(c) line segment from $(-1,-1)$ to $(3,5)$

23. $\sqrt{65}$

25. (b) $y=-x$ (c) $5000\sqrt{2}$

27. (a) $p(t)=t(50,50\sqrt{3})+t^2(0,-g/2);$
        $v(t)=(50,50\sqrt{3})-t(0,g)$
      (b) $t=100\sqrt{3}/g$ seconds

(d) $t = 50\sqrt{3}/g$ seconds; $3750/g$ meters

(e) 50 meters per second, $\mathbf{v} = (50, 0)$

29. (a) $(13, -1)$ (b) $(-31/3, 1)$

(c) $\displaystyle\int_0^2 \sqrt{25t^4 + 30t^3 - 30t^2 - 26t + 17}\, dt$

31. (a) $\mathbf{v}(t) = (1, -t)$ (b) $\mathbf{p}(t) = (t, -t^2/2)$

(c) $\displaystyle\int_0^5 \sqrt{1 + t^2}\, dt$

33. 2π **35.** $M_{100} \approx 13.365$

37. $\sqrt{10}$

39. 3

41. $\sqrt{1 + t^2}$

43. $\sqrt{2}\,(e^\pi - 1)$

Section V.2

1. $(\pi, 0)$; $(-\pi, \pi)$; $(\pi, 2\pi)$

3. $(\sqrt{2}, \pi/4)$; $(\sqrt{2}, -7\pi/4)$; $(-\sqrt{2}, -3\pi/4)$; $(-\sqrt{2}, 5\pi/4)$

5. $(\sqrt{5}, 1.107)$; $(\sqrt{5}, -5.176)$; $(-\sqrt{5}, 4.249)$

7. $(\sqrt{17}, 1.326)$; $(\sqrt{17}, -4.957)$; $(-\sqrt{17}, 4.467)$

9. $(\sqrt{2}, \sqrt{2})$ **11.** $(\sqrt{3}/2, 1/2)$

13. $(0.5403, 0.8415)$ **15.** $(\sqrt{2}, \sqrt{2})$

17. $x = 2$ **19.** $y = \sqrt{3}x/2$

21. $r = 3$ **23.** $\tan\theta = 2$

27. (a) 2; 1.866; 1.5; 1; 0.5; 0.134; 0; 0.134; 0.5; 1; 1.5; 1.866; 2

(c) x-axis

(d) symmetric about $x = \pi$

49. center $= (a/2, b/2)$, radius $= \sqrt{a^2 + b^2}/2$

51. (b) $\left(x^2 + y^2\right)^3 = x^4$

53. $\sqrt{r_1^2 + r_2^2 - 2r_1 r_2 \cos(\theta_1 - \theta_2)}$

Section V.3

3. (b) $\theta = -\tan\theta$ (c) $\theta = \cot\theta$

(d) $y = \left(\dfrac{\sin 1 + \cos 1}{\cos 1 - \sin 1}\right)(x - \cos 1) + \sin 1$

5. $\pi/2$ **7.** $\pi a^2/2$

9. $2\pi + 3\sqrt{3}/2$ **11.** $3\pi/4 - 2$

13. $\pi + 1$ **15.** $m/2$

17. (a) $\pi/4n$ (b) $\pi/4$; $1/4$

19. $\left(e^{4\pi} - 1\right)/4$ **21.** $\pi/3 - \sqrt{3}/4$

23. $x = 2\cos t$, $y = 2\sin t$, $0 \le t \le 2\pi$

25. $x = 1$, $y = \tan t$, $-\pi/4 \le t \le \pi/4$

27. $x = t\cos t$, $y = t\sin t$, $0 \le t \le 2\pi$

29. $x = \cos(2t)\cos t$, $y = \cos(2t)\sin t$, $0 \le t \le 2\pi$

CHAPTER M

Section M.1

1. (a) x-direction   (b) y-direction

7. $x^2 + y^2 + z^2 = 4$ **9.** $x^2 + z^2 = 1$

11. $z = \sin x$

13. center $= (0, 3, 2)$; radius $= \sqrt{13}$

15. (b) $\sqrt{5}$ (c) $\sqrt{14}$

19. $(1, 1, 1)$, $(1, 1, -1)$, $(1, -1, 1)$, $(1, -1, -1)$, $(-1, 1, 1)$, $(-1, 1, -1)$, $(-1, -1, 1)$, $(-1, -1, -1)$

21. $-A/B$; $B = 0$

23. C/A; $A = 0$

25. $x = D/A$; $y + z = 1$

27. (a) $x + 3z = 3$; $(3, 0, 0)$; $(0, 0, 1)$

(b) $2y + 3z = 3$; $(0, 3/2, 0)$; $(0, 0, 1)$

(c) $2y + 3z = 2$

29. $x = 3$

31. $(1, 0, 0)$, $(0, 1/2, 0)$

Section M.2

1. $\mathbb{R}^2$; $[0, \infty)$

3. $\left\{(x, y) \mid (x, y) \ne (0, 0)\right\}$; $(0, \infty)$

5. $\left\{(x, y) \mid x^2 + y^2 \le 1\right\}$; $[0, 1]$

7. (a) circles with center $(0, 0)$

(b) circles with center $(0, 0)$

9. (a) vertical lines

(b) horizontal lines

11. east–west

15. (a) $f(x, y) = |x - 1|$

(d) lines parallel to the y-axis

Section M.3

1. $f_x(x, y) = 2x$; $f_y(x, y) = -2y$

3. $f_x(x, y) = \dfrac{2x}{y^2}$; $f_y(x, y) = \dfrac{-2x^2}{y^3}$

5. $f_x(x, y) = -\sin(x)\cos(y)$; $f_y(x, y) = -\cos(x)\sin(y)$

7. $f_x(x, y, z) = y^2 z^3$; $f_y(x, y, z) = 2xyz^3$; $f_z(x, y, z) = 3xy^2 z^2$

9. (c) $[2.9, 3.1]$

11. (c) $6.5, 6.1$ (d) 6

13. $g_x(1, 1) \approx -2.01$; $g_y(1, 1) \approx 3.01$;

15. (a)

x / y	−0.02	−0.01	0.00	0.01	0.02
0.02	0.02	0.02	0.02	0.02	0.02
0.01	0.01	0.01	0.01	0.01	0.01
0.00	0.00	0.00	0.00	0.00	0.00
−0.01	−0.01	−0.01	−0.01	−0.01	−0.01
−0.02	−0.02	−0.02	−0.02	−0.02	−0.02

17. (c) $L(x, y) = y + 2$

19. (b) $f_x(0, 0) \approx 1$; $f_y(0, 0) = 0$
(c) $f_x(\pi/2, 0) \approx 0$; $f_y(0, 0) = 0$

21. (b) $f_x(0, 0) = 2$, $f_y(0, 0) = 3$

23. (a) $L(x, y) = 1(x - 2) + 2(y - 1) + 2$

25. (b) $f_x(1, 2) = 2$; $f_y(1, 2) = 4$
(c) $L(x, y) = 2(x - 1) + 4(y - 2) + 5$

27. $L(x, y) = -5 + 4x + 2y$

29. $L(x, y) = x + y$

33. (a) $L(x, y) = 3x/5 + 4y/5$
(b) $g(2.9, 4.1) \approx 5.02$; $g(4, 5) \approx 6.4$
(c) no

35. (b) $f_x(x, 0) = 0$

Section M.4

1. (a) remains constant
(b) rises all the way; $(0.5, 1)$; 0.5

3. (a) $(1, \pi/2)$ is a local minimum; $(1, -\pi/2)$ is a local maximum
(b) $(0, 0), (2, 0), (1, \pi/2), (1, -\pi/2)$
(c) 15; -15

5. $(0, 0)$; saddle   **7.** $(1, 2)$; saddle

9. (b) $a = b = 0$ **11.** $g(x, y) = y^2$

13. $k(x, y) = (x - 3)^2 + (y - 4)^2$

Section M.5

1. $21/64$; $M_{100} \approx 0.333325$

3. 512; 512; 512

5. (a) ≈ 168
(b) $M_{16} = 168$
(c) underestimate

Section M.6

1. $(\cos(1))^2 - 2\cos(1) + 1$ **3.** $512/3$

5. 6 **7.** $3/20$

9. $3/20$ **11.** $\pi/4$

13. (a) 1 (b) 1

15. (a) area $= \displaystyle\int_c^d g(y)\, dy$

Section M.7

3. (b) $2\pi/3$ **5.** $1/2$

7. $\pi + 2$ **9.** $\pi/3$

APPENDIX A

1. (b) no; 0.16 (d) $0 < a < 0.18$

3. (a) no   (b) $(45/19, -7/38)$

5. (a) $[1.56, 1.58] \times [0, 2]$
(b) $[-0.1, 0.1] \times [-0.1, 0.1]$
(c) $[3.1, 3.2] \times [-0.05, 0.05]$
(d) $[1, 5] \times [-0.01, 0.01]$
(e) $[-\pi, 0] \times [-1, 0]$

7. (a) $[-0.1, 0.1] \times [-1, 1]$ works
(b) $[0.9, 1.1] \times [0.8, 1.2]$
(c) $[-1.1, -0.9] \times [0.8, 1.2]$
(d) $[0, 10] \times [24, 26]$
(e) $[-1, 1] \times [0, 1]$

9. $x \approx -0.767$, $x = 2$, $x = 4$

11. $x \approx 0.73$ **13.** $-2.62, 2.25$

15. $0.74, 3.02$ **17.** -1.91

19. (a) $|r(x) - f(x)| \leq 1/2$ (b) $a = 0.32$

21. $-0.033 \leq f(x) - g(x) \leq 0.018$

23. $[1.9, 2.1] \times [3.6, 4.4]$ **25.** $[-0.05, 0.05] \times [0.9, 1.1]$

27. $[4.995, 5.005] \times [0.9, 1.1]$ **29.** $[-0.01, 0.01] \times [0.9, 1.1]$

31. $[0.9, 1.1] \times [0.9, 1.1]$ **33.** $[-0.1, 0.1] \times [0.9, 1.1]$

35. $1, -1$ **37.** $0.476; -10$

39. $0, -100$ **41.** $100, 0$

43. $924, -99.999$ **45.** $0.750, 0.029$

47. $-729, 1331$ **49.** $3, 10503$

51. ± 72 **53.** $1, 0.540$

APPENDIX B

3. $[-6, 4)$

5. $[2, 9]$

7. (a) $|x+1| \le 4$
(c) 4

(b) -1

9. $(-\infty, -4] \cup [1, \infty)$

13. $[-1/2, \infty)$

15. $L = 10.98, U = 11.02$

17. $|x-3| \le 6$

19. $|x+5.5| \le 1.5$

21. $|x-5| < 5$

23. $|x-1| < 3$

25. $|x-2| \le 5$

29. $2\sqrt{2}$

31. $7\sqrt{2}$

35. $(x-1)^2 + (y+2)^2 = 9$

37. $5/3; (0, -2/3)$

41. $[-3, 7]$

43. $(a-b, a+b)$

45. $(13, -3), (-11, -3)$

47. $|x+1| > 4$

49. $|x+1| < 6$

51. $|T - 100| < |T - 32|$

57. no

59. no

61. yes

63. no

65. no

67. may

69. must

71. $A = 5, B = 0.008$

APPENDIX C

3. (a) $y = 3$
(c) $(0, 3)$

(b) 0
(d) no

5. (a) line is horizontal
(c) line has slope $-A/B$

(b) line is vertical

7. $-1/5, y = -x/5 + 16/5$

9. $1/3, y = x/3$

11. $y = 10(3 - \sqrt{8.9})x + (90\sqrt{8.9} - 267)$

13. $y = \dfrac{\cos(1.5) - \cos(1.3)}{0.2}(x - 1.5) + \cos(1.5)$

15 (a)

x	-10	-3	0	1	5	7
$f(x)$	0.544	-0.141	0	0.841	-0.959	0.657

(b)

Δx	7	3	1	4	2
Δy	-0.685	0.141	0.841	-1.80	1.62
$\Delta y / \Delta x$	0.098	0.047	0.841	-0.450	0.808

(d)

x	1.35	1.37	1.40	1.41	1.43	1.47
$f(x)$	0.976	0.980	0.985	0.987	0.990	0.995

(e)

Δx	0.02	0.03	0.01	0.02	0.04
Δy	0.00418	0.00554	0.00165	0.00300	0.00482
$\Delta y / \Delta x$	0.209	0.185	0.165	0.150	0.120

17. $y = -0.84147(x - 1) + 0.54030$

19. $y = 12(x - 2) + 8$

21. $2/3$

23. $y = \frac{2}{3}(x - 1) + 2$

25. no

27. (a) $y = \frac{2}{3}(x - 2) + 1$

(b) $y = -\frac{3}{2}(x - 2) + 1$

29. $x = 2$

31. $y = -x/5 + 2/5$

33. (a) $(a - b/m, 0)$
(c) $y = mx + (b - ma)$

(b) $(0, b - ma)$

35. $k = -2/m$

37. no such k exists

APPENDIX D

1. $\pi x^{18} + 3\pi x^{17} + 7x + 21$

3. yes

5. 1

7. 5

9. 123

11. no

13. (a) 33
(c) $-8, 0, 1, 2, 6$

(b) 5

15. $p(x) = (x + 16)(x - 1/3)(x - 2)$

17. (a) Graph C $\leftrightarrow$ (i);   Graph B $\leftrightarrow$ (ii);   Graph A $\leftrightarrow$ (iii);
Graph D $\leftrightarrow$ (iv);

(b) $q(x) = (x - 1)(x + 4)$
(c) $c(x) = (x + 1)(x - 1)(x - 2)$
(d) $q(x) = (x + 1)(x^2 + 1)$
(e) $q(x) = (x + 1)^2 + 1$

19. (c) $(x^2 + 2x + 1)$
(d) $(x + 1)(x + 1)(x + 1) = (x + 1)^3$

21. $(-\infty, -2) \cup (1, \infty)$

23. $(-3, 1) \cup (1, \infty)$

25. $(-\infty, -3) \cup \left(-3, \left(1 - \sqrt{17}\right)/2\right) \cup \left(\left(1 + \sqrt{17}\right)/2, \infty\right)$

27. $p(x) = x(x+1)(x-2); 0, -1, 2$

29. $r(x) = x^2(x-1)(x+1); -1, 0, 1$

31. $t(x) = (x^2-1)^2; -1, 1$

33. $(x+1)^2; -1$

35. $(x+1/2)^2 + 3/4$; no roots

37. $-2, 0$

39. no real roots

41. $\left(-b \pm \sqrt{b^2-4c}\right)/2$

43. $\dfrac{x^2+1}{x}$

45. $\dfrac{3x^2+15x+6}{x}$

47. $\dfrac{x^2+7x+33}{x^2+4x-5}$

49. no real roots

51. $\left(-5 \pm \sqrt{17}\right)/2$

53. no real roots

APPENDIX E

1. 1

3. 8

5. 16

7. 2

9. 3/2

11. 5/4

13. a^1

15. a^0

17. a^{-20}

19. a^{-1}

21. no

27. $A = 5e^{-0.2}$

29. $\log_8 4 = 2/3$

31. $\log_{10} 0.0001 = -4$

33. $2^x = 7$

35. $5^{-2} = 1/25$

37. $64^{7/6} = 128$

39. 16

41. 7

43. 3

45. x^2

47. -1

49. 4.2

51. 4.1

53. 8.4

55. $b^x/b^y = b^{x-y}; \left(b^x\right)^r = b^{xr}$

57. $10 \ln 2$

59. $-10 \ln 2$

61. $\ln 2$

63. $A = 5, k = (\ln 2)/3$

65. 3

67. $-\dfrac{\ln 5}{2 - \ln 5}$

APPENDIX F

1. ≈ 0.35

3. ≈ -0.35

5. ≈ -0.98

7. $x = 0.5, x = 2.6$

15. $k\pi, k = 0, \pm 1, \pm 2, \ldots$

17. $-b$

19. 0.3

21. b^2

23. 0

25. 0

27. 0

29. $-\sqrt{3}/2$

31. -1

33. 2

35. $-\sqrt{3}/2$

37. $\left(\sqrt{6} - \sqrt{2}\right)/4$

39. $\left(\sqrt{6} - \sqrt{2}\right)/4$

41. yes

43. no

45. yes

47. $\sin s \cos t - \cos s \sin t$

APPENDIX G

1. (b) $[0, 300]$

(d) yes

(c) $150' \times 112.5'$

3. $V(x) = x \cdot (100 - 3x) \cdot (50 - 2x)$

5. (a) $B = 20, C = 3/10$

(b) inversely proportional

(c) $A = 5, C = 3/5$

7. yes

9. (a) $w(d) = \dfrac{2 \times 10^{10}}{d^2}$

(b) $d = \sqrt{2} \times 10^4$ miles

11. $T(r) = r/4 + \sqrt{3^2 + (6-r)^2}/3, 0 \leq r \leq 6$

13. $S = 2V$

15. $s(x) = x^2 + (45 - x)^2$

17. $A(x) = 3x(4 - x), 0 < x < 4$

19. $I(x) = \dfrac{4}{x^2} + \dfrac{1}{(100 - x)^2}$

INDEX